2004

History of American Political Thought

APPLICATIONS OF POLITICAL THEORY

Series Editors: Harvey Mansfield, Harvard University, and Daniel J. Mahoney, Assumption College

This series encourages analysis of the applications of political theory to various domains of thought and action. Such analysis will include works on political thought and literature, statesmanship, American political thought, and contemporary political theory. The editors also anticipate and welcome examinations of the place of religion in public life and commentary on classic works of political philosophy.

Deadly Thought: "Hamlet" and the Human Soul, by Jan H. Blits

Reason, Revelation, and Human Affairs: Selected Writings of James V. Schall, edited and introduced by Marc D. Guerra

Faith, Reason, and Political Life Today, edited by Peter Augustine Lawler and Dale McConkey

Tyranny in Shakespeare, by Mary Ann McGrail

Sensual Philosophy: Toleration, Skepticism, and Montaigne's Politics of the Self, by Alan Levine

Gladly to Learn and Gladly to Teach: Essays on Religion and Political Philosophy in Honor of Ernest L. Fortin, A.A., edited and introduced by Michael P. Foley and Douglas Kries

Dissent and Philosophy in the Middle Ages: Dante and His Precursors, by Ernest L. Fortin; translated by Marc A. LePain

Behemoth *Teaches* Leviathan: *Thomas Hobbes on Political Education*, by Geoffrey M. Vaughan

The Dialogue in Hell between Machiavelli and Montesquieu, by Maurice Joly; edited and translated by John S. Waggoner

Cultivating Citizens: Soulcraft and Citizenship in Contemporary America, edited by Dwight D. Allman and Michael D. Beaty

Liberty, Wisdom, and Grace: Thomism and Democratic Political Theory, by John P. Hittinger

The Paradox of Philosophical Education: Nietzsche's New Nobility and the Eternal Recurrence in Beyond Good and Evil, by J. Harvey Lomax

Faith, Morality, and Civil Society, edited by Dale McConkey and Peter Augustine Lawler

History of American Political Thought, edited by Bryan-Paul Frost and Jeffrey Sikkenga

Totalitarianism and the Prospects for World Order: Closing the Door on the Twentieth Century, by Aleksandras Shtromas; and edited by Daniel J. Mahoney and Robert Faulkner

Liberalism under Siege: The Political Thought of the French Doctrinaires, by Aurelian Craiutu

History of American Political Thought

Edited by Bryan-Paul Frost and Jeffrey Sikkenga

LEXINGTON BOOKS
Lanham • Boulder • New York • Oxford

LEXINGTON BOOKS

Published in the United States of America
by Lexington Books
A Member of the Rowman & Littlefield Publishing Group
4501 Forbes Boulevard, Suite 200, Lanham, Maryland 20706

PO Box 317
Oxford
OX2 9RU, UK

British Library Cataloguing in Publication Information Available

Library of Congress Cataloging-in-Publication Data

History of American political thought / edited by Bryan-Paul Frost and Jeffrey Sikkenga.
     p. cm. (Applications of political theory series)
  Includes bibliographical references and index.
  ISBN 0-7391-0623-6 (alk. paper)—ISBN 0-7391-0624-4 (pbk. : alk. paper)
   1. Political science—United States—History. I. Frost, Bryan-Paul, 1961– II. Sikkenga, Jeffrey, 1967–
JA84.U5 H57 2003
320'.0973—dc21
                                               2003050127

Printed in the United States of America

♾™ The paper used in this publication meets the minimum requirements of American National Standard for Information Sciences—Permanence of Paper for Printed Library Materials, ANSI/NISO Z39.48–1992.

To our teachers,
and especially:

David Bolotin
James Ceaser
Clifford Orwin
Thomas L. Pangle

CONTENTS

PART THREE:
A DIVIDED NATION (1820–1865)

PART FOUR:
GROWTH OF AN EMPIRE (1865–1945)

Preface and Acknowledgments

Bryan-Paul Frost and Jeffrey Sikkenga

Unlike Western political philosophy, American political thought lacks a systematic, comprehensive volume of essays introducing its most important thinkers to students, professors, and the interested public. There are a number of good collections focusing on thinkers of particular historical periods or persuasions (e.g., seventeenth-century or New Deal political thought); and some collections even span the range of American history and politics. These latter collections, however, tend to be limited to either writers or statesmen, while in truth American political reflection has not been confined to one category of persons. For example, some of America's greatest thinkers (most notably the Founders) have been practicing politicians.

What is needed, therefore, is a comprehensive set of secondary essays that provides a solid introduction to the thought of the most important American statesmen, activists, and writers—whatever their historical age or political persuasion. This book hopes to be that collection—an introduction to what the most thoughtful Americans have said about the American regime, from the colonial period to the present.

Several criteria have been used to select the thinkers included herein. First is the depth and quality of their insight into the meaning of America. While some political commentators have offered trenchant insight into particular policies or controversies, not as many have done so as part of a systematic understanding of America and its political principles. We have sought such comprehensive thinkers. The second guiding principle is our desire for a broad historical representation. In order to illustrate both the change and continuity in the ideas of America, we tried to provide the most important thought from generally recognized periods in the nation's history. To that end, we have divided the book into five parts: From Colony to Nation (1608–1776); The New Republic (1776–1820); A Divided Nation (1820–1865); Growth of an Empire (1865–1945); and New Challenges at Home and Abroad (1945–present). With these divisions, however, some important thinkers from certain eras have been combined into one chapter or omitted altogether. This is simply a function of space considerations and a desire to give each historical period its due. The third criterion is the historical and political significance of a person's thought. Did he or she deeply influence how Americans (or others) think about America? This criterion explains in part why we have not included certain famous writers and statesmen who may have been important in their day but whose speeches, writings, and actions have not had a significant, lasting effect. The final criterion, with some important exceptions, is that the person no longer be living—or at least that their most important or mature thought has already been developed and expounded. The purpose is to capture a certain timelessness of thought that is hard to estimate in writers or statesmen whose thought is still evolving in significant ways.

With these four criteria, we have selected fifty-five thinkers, from the Puritans to contemporary feminists, as well as an introductory chapter on Alexis de Tocqueville. We believe that the field is broad but deep and that, combined, these people represent the best and most important political thought on America by Americans.

We conclude with one note. While we have selected which thinkers to include and have edited each of the chapters, the essays themselves are the product of the contributors themselves. The arguments and insights are theirs alone. We believe that the result speaks for itself about the seriousness of the subject and about the need for every generation of scholars and citizens to grapple anew with the meaning of the experiment known as America.

Acknowledgments

The editors would like to thank their respective institutions for the generous financial support given this project. In particular, Jeffrey Sikkenga would like to recognize Ashland University for its Faculty Publication Grant. He would also like to thank his department colleagues for their generous advice and, most importantly, his wife for her Job-like patience. Bryan-Paul Frost would like to thank A. David Barry, Dean of the College of Liberal Arts at the University of Louisiana at Lafayette, for his generous financial and moral support as well as James A. and Kaye L. Crocker, whose endowed professorship in political science contributed to a reduced teaching load during the last year of the project. He would also like to thank the entire Department of Political Science for their support, and in particular chairman Donn M. Kurtz II, who was exceedingly accommodating in terms of scheduling and the like. The editors gratefully acknowledge the assistance of Blaine Arnold for formatting and proofreading many of the chapters as well as Thomas Portteus and Corinne Sheppard in compiling the index. And lastly, the editors would like to thank Steve Wrinn, who first encouraged us to submit this proposal to Lexington Books, and especially Serena Krombach, who shepherded the project along from start to finish and whose patience and kindness was extraordinary: both are truly author's editors.

The editors gratefully acknowledge *Perspectives on Political Science* and Heldref Publications for allowing us to reprint material from David Fott's essay, "Dewey and the Threat of Tyranny of the Majority," *Perspectives on Political Science* 27 (Fall 1998): 206–11; *Polity* to reprint material from Eduardo A. Velásquez's essay, "Rethinking America's Modernity," *Polity* 29, no. 2 (1996); and the University of Chicago Press for permission to reprint a condensed version of the "Editors' Introduction" to Alexis de Tocqueville's *Democracy in America*, ed. and trans. Harvey C. Mansfield and Delba Winthrop (Chicago: University of Chicago Press, 2000).

Introduction

Alexis de Tocqueville's *Democracy in America*

Harvey C. Mansfield and Delba Winthrop

Alexis de Tocqueville was born on July 29, 1805, and died in his fifty-fourth year on April 16, 1859: not a long life, and one often afflicted with ill health.[1] He was born a French aristocrat and lived as one; he was also a liberal who both rejected the old regime of aristocracy and doubted the revolution that overturned it. An aristocratic liberal he was, and a Frenchman who knew America so well as to deserve a place in American political thought.

His *Democracy in America* is at once the best book ever written on democracy and the best book ever written on America. Tocqueville connects the two subjects in his "Introduction," and in his title, by observing that America is the land of democracy. It is the country where democracy is least hindered and most perfected—where democracy is at its most characteristic and at its best. Today that claim might be contested, but it is at least arguable. If the twentieth century was an American century, it is because the work of America—not altogether unsuccessful—has been to keep democracy strong where it is alive and to promote it where it is weak or nonexistent. Somehow, even into the twenty-first century, democracy is still in America.

Tocqueville's book has acquired the authority of a classic. It is cited with approval by politicians—by all American presidents since Eisenhower—as well as by professors in many fields. Universal accord in its praise suggests that it has something for everyone. But it also suggests that readers tolerate, or perhaps simply overlook, the less welcome passages that their political and scholarly opponents are citing. It is quite striking that both Left and Right appeal to *Democracy in America* for support of their contrary policies. Tocqueville seems to have achieved the goal, expressed at the end of his "Introduction," of standing above the parties of the day. Yet his widespread appeal should not mask the controversial and unsettling character of the work.

Tocqueville's Trip to America

Before writing *Democracy in America*, Tocqueville took a trip to America of a little more than nine months in the company of his friend Gustave de Beaumont (1802–1866).[2] Like Tocqueville, Beaumont was a magistrate; the two had studied law together and served on the same court at Versailles.[3] In 1830, they came to America as collaborators in a grand project to see "what a great republic is," as Tocqueville put it in a letter to another friend.[4]

Tocqueville was drawn to America to observe the future society of "almost complete equality of social conditions" toward which he believed Europe was moving inexorably. Although he said later that he did not go to America with the idea of writing a book, it seems clear that he and

Beaumont went with a large joint project in mind, for both refer to it in contemporaneous letters. They also had a definite smaller project to study penal reform in America, which Tocqueville described as a "pretext" for the voyage.[5] During the nine-month trip in America, Tocqueville and Beaumont followed an efficient itinerary. With time out for rest, research, and conversation with useful or important Americans, they still went almost everywhere. Starting from New York, they traveled upstate to Buffalo, proceeding through the Great Lakes to the frontier, as it was then, in Michigan and Wisconsin. There followed two weeks in Canada, from which they descended to Boston and Philadelphia and Baltimore. Next they went west to Pittsburgh and Cincinnati; then south to Nashville, Memphis, and New Orleans; then north through the southeastern states to Washington; and at last back to New York, from where they returned to France. Like tourists seeking characteristic experiences, they rode on steamboats (one of which sank) and stayed in a log cabin. They found it easy to gain access to prominent Americans, and they met with John Quincy Adams, Andrew Jackson, Albert Gallatin, James Kent, Francis Lieber, Daniel Webster, Sam Houston, Roger Taney, Charles Carroll, and many others less well known.[6] They both kept journals, and Tocqueville's has been published under the title *Journey to America*.[7] It contains notes for the two books he was to write and was not intended for publication. Though full of interest, the notes are mostly not composed or developed, and the result cannot be considered part of the abundant contemporary travel literature on America produced by English and French writers who came to have a look at the new democracy. Among those diaries, Tocqueville would have been especially mindful of Chateaubriand's *Voyage to America* (1827), with its brilliant reflections on democracy.

The two volumes of *Democracy in America* were published five years apart, in 1835 and 1840. They had different contents and different receptions. The first volume, with its lively picturing of America, was a sensation and made Tocqueville famous. The second volume, with its somber analysis of democracy, was received without enthusiasm, an event that somewhat disconcerted its author.[8] In a letter to John Stuart Mill (written in 1840 after the second volume came out), Tocqueville observed that Mill was the only one to have understood him. He went on to muse that there was something obscure and problematic in the second volume that "does not capture the mind of the crowd," and that he had wanted to portray the "general traits of democratic societies of which no complete model yet exists." In response, Mill assured him that the thoughts in the second volume were deeper and more recondite than those in the first.[9]

The polish, style, and insight of *Democracy in America* obscure the research that preceded it.[10] Footnotes that document his research can be found in some chapters of the first volume (*DA* I 1.1, 1.2, 1.5, 1.8, 2.10), and there are longer endnotes that both document and elaborate it. But there are long stretches of text, especially in the second volume, that seem to flow directly from his mind, unmediated by previous scholarship and unsubstantiated by reference to sources. The original working manuscript for the book tells a different story, however.[11] It shows how well he had studied; how far he had cast his net for fact and opinion; how ingeniously he had sought and produced the telling example; how surely he had reduced the manifold to the salient; how thoroughly he had prepared his generalizations; and how carefully he had formulated them.

Tocqueville's Liberalism

When Tocqueville wrote his book, it was to speak reprovingly, and sometimes severely, to the partisans of his day for and against democracy. Although the Old Regime has now faded into unremembered history and everyone has followed Tocqueville's advice to accept democracy, partisans remain within it, and they still divide over whether to restrain democracy or push it further. Tocqueville has something dismaying, but instructive, to say to both parties. He knows the extent of democracy in America because he sees better than we the resistances to it in America. He came to America to examine democracy up close and to be sure of what he thought he might find. Unlike other visitors, he knew that America was not merely derivative of Europe. It was not behind but ahead of Europe and in that sense exceptional. Tocqueville takes the measure of America's boast, repeated on the first page of *The Federalist*, to set an example for all mankind. He makes his ambition the study of America's ambition, in both cases an ambition that leaves others free. It is open to any country to surpass America if it can, and it is possible that some writer, some day, will write a better book on democracy in America than this one.

Today, Tocqueville seems readily accessible to us. His recognition of the democratic revolution and its problems appears right on the mark, and the success of most of his predictions seems uncanny. (He was, however, wrong about a coming war between the races: *DA* I 2.10.) On the Left in America, he is the philosopher of community and civic engagement who warns against the appearance of an industrial aristocracy and against the bourgeois or commercial passion for material well-being: in sum, he is for democratic citizenship. On the Right, he is quoted for his strictures on "Big Government" and his liking for decentralized administration as well as for celebrating individual energy and opposing egalitarian excess: he is a balanced liberal, defending both freedom and moderation. For both parties he is welcome in an era when democracy has defeated the totalitarians and is no longer under challenge to its existence, but faces new threats to its security from external enemies as well as challenges from those within who no longer take modern progress for granted as good.

In France, Tocqueville came into vogue in the 1970s and is now a strong presence. He benefits from national pride which, not only in France, has often been less than discerning. Although *Democracy in America* was a huge success when it first appeared, soon thereafter Tocqueville was allowed to fall into neglect. His books were not read and his style, his importance, and his insight were slighted. After World War II, Marxism, existentialism, and deconstructionism were on stage in France and liberalism was in hiding. Then French scholars and intellectuals were awakened to their heritage of nineteenth-century liberals, and above all to the discomfiting sagacity of Tocqueville, always more sensitive than reassuring. But after much false assurance from ready solutions, the wary observation and cool advice of liberalism can come as a relief.

Yet Tocqueville, a liberal, does not build his understanding of democracy on the liberal state of nature first conceived by Thomas Hobbes, Benedict Spinoza, and John Locke. He does not refer to that concept in *Democracy in America*.[12] His liberalism thus differs from that of James Madison. From his viewpoint, Madison's liberalism seemed lacking in concrete observation of America, above all of the democratic revolution there. In *The Federalist* no. 10, Madison's most famous statement of his liberalism, he distinguishes a democracy from a republic in which the people rule indirectly through their representatives. Representation works best, Madison says, in large, heterogeneous countries with many conflicting interests and sects that make it difficult to form a majority faction, the bane of popular government.

Tocqueville does not share Madison's confidence that the problem can be solved. He fears majority tyranny in America and actually sees it at work there in public opinion. For him, the danger is not so much factious interest or passion as the degradation of souls in democracy, a risk to which Madison does not directly refer but which Tocqueville states prominently in his "Introduction" to *Democracy in America*. As a sign of his fear, he habitually calls the American government a "democratic republic," thus spanning and overriding the distinction that Madison was at pains to establish. A modern republic, Tocqueville means to say, cannot help being a democracy, and a modern democracy necessarily has a hard task in getting equal citizens to accept authority without feeling they have been subjected and degraded. Madison's reliance on the state of nature was a way of avoiding examination of the human soul, for in that early liberal concept the soul disappears as a whole while being divided into disconnected passions such as fear, vanity, or pity. Tocqueville looks at the whole soul and at all of democracy. He considers individual, society, and government as involved with one another without the simplifying state-of-nature abstraction.

Tocqueville learned from fellow liberals, even as he departed from them. His work should be compared to that of two French contemporaries, Benjamin Constant (1767–1830) and François Guizot (1787–1874); to that of his friend in England, John Stuart Mill (1806–1873); and especially to those of three French philosophers—Pascal, Montesquieu, and Rousseau—who, he said, are "three men with whom I live a little every day." Of these only Montesquieu is a liberal, but Pascal and Rousseau helped to give Tocqueville's liberalism its particular cast.

Tocqueville's Political Science

We may preface our study of Tocqueville's text with remarks on his method—his political science. Hardly any statement of his is more prominent and provocative than the assertion in the "Introduction" to *Democracy in America* that "a new political science is needed for a world altogether new." What political science is that? Tocqueville does not tell us. Nowhere in the book does he elaborate this new political science; in fact, he does not refer to it again. "Political science" per se is spoken of four other times in the first volume and not at all in the second. After raising our expectations, Tocqueville disappoints them, or perhaps he returns them to us for elaboration. That he offers no methodology or compendium of axioms may be the first lesson of his new political science. It is neither to consist in abstraction nor is it to be made by or for disinterested observers. The new political science is for use in a new world.

The new world cannot be other than the world made by the democratic revolution—our world, the Western world, the modern world. The four references to "political science" following in the first volume cite inventions of modern political science already known and applied, such as the advantage of bicameralism, the novelty of American federalism, and the neutralizing of press bias (*DA* I 1.5, 1.8 [twice], 2.3). These institutional devices, though important, are not the "new political science" that Tocqueville calls for. They are items of the kind recommended in *The Federalist*, designed as brakes on the headlong rush of democracy toward its desires. A new political science, however, would need to explain democracy before it considered how to keep it in check. Without taking credit for his discoveries, Tocqueville gives political science three new features not seen before—the concept of the social state (*état social*), the notion of those like oneself (*semblables*), and the practice of making predictions.

What is the social state? The answer Tocqueville gives when introducing the concept is that it is both product and cause (*DA* I 1.3). It is the product of a fact or of laws or of both together which then becomes the "first cause" of most of the laws, customs, and ideas that regulate nations, modifying those it does not produce. Exceptions do occur; the social state is not historically determined of necessity. With this deliberate confusion of causality, Tocqueville refuses to go back to a prior event or condition that would establish the primacy of politics over society. There is no founding in the classical sense in Tocqueville, a planned beginning that gives a certain form and principle of rule to society. He speaks of the American Revolution and Constitution, but not as that sort of formative event. The Constitution is rather the work of a "great people, warned by its legislators" of a problem requiring a remedy (*DA* I 1.8).

More significant, apparently, than the Founding was the point of departure of the American people a century and a half earlier when the Puritans arrived. The American point of departure —not the later, more deliberate Founding—is the key, Tocqueville says, to almost the whole of his work. Americans did not make themselves democrats but came to America as democrats. America, to which the Puritans came for a reason, is the only nation whose point of departure is clear rather than shrouded in ignorance and fable.

If one puts together the democratic social state with the sovereignty of the people in a democracy, the result is the power of public opinion in democracies, of which Tocqueville makes so much. Public opinion is milder and less explicit than political authority, yet more confining than mere social agreement. It is the political and social combined, with a shift of weight from the former to the latter. "Public" opinion takes opinion out of private society and places it in broad daylight, to use one of Tocqueville's favorite phrases. Public and private are blurred together, and it becomes clear that democracy is government by public opinion. Private opinion—in the sense of what might be reserved to oneself against what most people think— tends to disappear; it proves to have required an aristocratic social state in which independent nobles had the standing to say what they pleased. This shows us why Tocqueville puts little trust in the power of representative institutions to hold out against the people's desires: public opinion makes the people's representatives conform to their desires regardless of the apparent latitude that representative offices with constitutional terms might seem to afford. He would have seen the public opinion polls of our day as vivid confirmation, with the aid of science, of the trend he saw already in his day.

The democratic social state comprises those like oneself (*semblables*). Tocqueville sees in democracy not only self and other but a third thing, those like oneself.[13] This notion may be taken as a second original feature of Tocqueville's new political science. Since all individuals in a democracy regard themselves and are accepted as equal, other individuals are not really different from oneself but similar. They are not really *other* in the deep sense implied by the dichotomy of self-other to be found in Hegel's theory or its variants. Here there is no real reconciliation between self and other in which one self finds itself in the other. Rather, that reconciliation is assumed from the beginning. The democrat considers others to be like himself, and if they are truly different, he *sees* them to be like himself regardless. He ignores or flattens out any differences that might call equality into question. Humanity consists of those like oneself: thus, compassion for those in distress is not demeaning and admiration for those who have done better is not humiliating. Envy is more likely, however. With the notion of *semblables*, humanity goes from biological or philosophical abstraction to political fact; for if one's countrymen are like oneself, so too are persons in all countries. Tocqueville speaks of appealing, in matters of justice, from the jury of one's fellow citizens to that of all humanity (*DA* I 2.7). It is not that democratic patriotism cannot exist; on the contrary, it can be more fervent than any previous patriotism. But it has to come to terms with humanity by claiming superior progress instead of insisting on excluding others by virtue of some permanent inequality such as race or nation.

Tocqueville's new political science makes predictions. These are not mere implicit predictions that we might infer; he repeatedly mentions trends or results that he "predicts," "augurs," or "foresees." He does not try to anticipate the scientific prediction of some political science in our day by seeking to establish exact or determinate outcomes. He says that it is imprudent "to want to limit the possible and to judge the future" (*DA* I 1.8); thus, prediction is not the object of his political science. His most famous particular prediction occurs at the end of the first volume. America and Russia, he says, stand for the democratic future, the one with freedom, the other with servitude. Each seems to have been called "by a secret design of Providence" to hold in its hands "the destinies of half the world" (*DA* I 2.10). During the Cold War, this picture seemed uncannily true to fact, but now we see that it was a representation. It represents an undetermined choice for us attributed by Tocqueville to Providence, not political science strictly. And his most general prediction, that of the democratic revolution, he calls a "providential fact" (*DA* Intro.).

Tocqueville's predictions and his mention of Providence belong together, however, because they are designed to remind us of a given fact: the democratic revolution. His political science is designed for this circumstance, and it does not attempt to rise above circumstance or to prescribe for a variety of circumstances. Tocqueville writes for a foreseeable epoch in history, the democratic era, and he does not try to see beyond the foreseeable as did the ancients. If he does not accept the democratic belief in indefinite progress, he does base his political science on linear history, from aristocracy to democracy, rather than on the nature of man as holding the potential for several regimes and several histories. In his prediction, he ministers to our human desire, common to both science and religion, to know what will befall us in the future. At the same time, forcing us to keep in mind the outstanding fact of our time, he requires us to make our choices without indulging our wishes. He reminds opponents of democracy that they must come to terms with democracy, and he tells proponents that democracy too can lead to despotism. By opening our mind to the new world of democracy and closing it to the old aristocratic world, he sharpens our choices. His political science has the focus of a statesman.

Although Tocqueville was a liberal (as we have said), he did not adhere to what might be called the formal liberalism of John Locke and his followers in Tocqueville's time and ours. He did not think it necessary or wise to lay down universal principles or rights to serve as the formal basis of politics, nor to leave the actual exercise of those rights unspecified, open to experience, and free to be applied as circumstances permit. His political science is concerned with the society actually inspired by liberal principles.

Tocqueville shows that equality in the state of nature of formal liberalism tends to become equality in society too. He does not speak of the state of nature, but he makes clear that the formal principle of equality has a constant democratizing effect. The fact that equality is not perfect, that all citizens are not equally secure, does not mean that equality does not exist; on the contrary, it creates pressure to perfect equality (*DA* II 4.3). It cannot be said too often that democracy, or modern democracy, is a democratic revolution. One could call it an institutionalized revolution if it were not apparent that the revolution operates against every institution so as to make it more democratic.

Tocqueville addresses a topic left undiscussed, for the most part, in formal liberalism—the actual capacity of individuals to exercise their rights and stand up in their defense. Liberalism assumes that by relying on the desire for self-preservation, supposed to be active in everyone, one need not enter into the question of capacity. Marxists and others who demand more democracy make the same assumption that everyone's capacity for exercising rights is or can be made adequate. But Tocqueville does not. He argues that modern democracy makes its people increasingly incapable as citizens as they become more isolated and weak.

The Democratic Revolution

"A great democratic revolution is taking place among us": that is the beginning and the guiding thought of *Democracy in America*. The democratic revolution is new and first seen to its astonishing extent in the United States. But it is also seven hundred years old, the time from which the aristocratic power of a few feudal families began to be challenged. A kind of democratic equality appeared in the clergy, which was open to all. Then it passed to lawyers, who checked the power of barons, and to merchants, whose wealth introduced a rival influence to that of arms. Competition between the king and the nobles led both, especially the former, to raise the condition of the people, and events from the Crusades to the discovery of America turned to the advantage of equality. Not least, the Enlightenment made intelligence a social force with which to be reckoned.

These groups—clergy, lawyers, merchants, and experts of all kinds—might seem to have brought only rival inequalities to that of the feudal lords who ruled aristocracies. But for Tocqueville, feudal lords are the essential inequality on which inequality as a principle depends. They hold landed property and they acquire it by inheritance. They sit on their lands; the other groups rise from social conditions that invite movement and offer opportunity. Opportunity makes for equality even though it leads to new inequalities because you feel that someone risen from your status is like yourself (*semblable*). The new elites (as we would call them) bring ever-increasing equality of conditions.

Tocqueville defines the democratic revolution historically and socially rather than politically. In the "Introduction" to *Democracy in America*, he does not speak of the French Revolution and only alludes to the conflict that the coming of democracy has brought in Europe by contrast to America. In the *Old Regime and the Revolution*, the burden of his argument is to show that the French Revolution was a long time in coming, that it merely culminated changes toward democracy initiated under the monarchy.[14] This "gradual development" makes it possible to call democracy "a providential fact" (*DA* Intro.). Although the changes Tocqueville mentions were made politically, they were not made intentionally to bring about democracy, and if they seem to have been coordinated, this could have happened only through a higher power than political choice.

Democracy in America contains a chapter on "Why great revolutions will become rare" (*DA* II 3.21). The reason given is that in democracies, interests take precedence over passions and beliefs are stubbornly held. The great majority are in the middle class, neither rich nor poor, very much attached to their property and consequently desirous of order. Democracies are stable—all too stable perhaps. They may have been introduced by a great revolution such as the French Revolution, but once made, democracies last. America, the model of democracy, did not reach that state by revolution: "The great advantage of the Americans is to have arrived at democracy without having to suffer democratic revolutions, and to be born equal instead of becoming so" (*DA* II 2.3).

Tyranny of the Majority

Tocqueville's theme in *Democracy in America* is what is to be hoped for and what to be feared from the democratic revolution (*DA* I Intro.; II 4.1, 4.5, 4.6). In the book, he describes two particular threats that democracy poses to independence and dignity: "tyranny of the majority" and "mild despotism," the latter of which he also calls "democratic" or "administrative" despotism. Although Tocqueville's name is associated with both terms, "tyranny of the majority" is discussed only in the first volume and "mild despotism" is found only in the second. He explains that a more detailed examination of the subject and "five years of new meditations" changed the object of his fears (*DA* II 4.6).[15] The phenomenon long conceived of as tyranny of the majority turns out to be more complex in the modern democratic world, and Tocqueville deepened his appreciation of its new character, even if his prescribed remedies for the two ills do not differ substantially.

For Tocqueville, the *foundation* of American democracy, as distinguished from its point of departure, is the principle or dogma of the sovereignty of the people, first announced in the fourth chapter of the book, and reiterated near the end of the first volume (*DA* I 2.10): "Providence has given to each individual, whoever he may be, the degree of reason necessary for him to be able to direct himself in things that interest him exclusively. Such is the great maxim on which civil and political society in the United States rests. . . . Extended to the entirety of the nation, it becomes the dogma of the sovereignty of the people." In politics, this means that each individual is supposed to be "as enlightened, as virtuous, as strong as any other of those like him," and he obeys society not because he is less capable than another man of governing himself but because union with those like him appears useful to him (*DA* I 1.5).

While even the most ardent democrat might well doubt that each individual is really as enlightened and as virtuous as every other, Tocqueville shows how the principle of popular sovereignty can work rather well in America, particularly in the New England township of which he paints a vivid, if idealized, picture (*DA* I 1.5). Here citizens take common decisions in frequent town meetings and then execute them through the numerous, short-term elective offices that many of them come to hold. When exercising sovereignty in this way, the people's reason is informed by firsthand knowledge and keen interest; they know how badly a road or a school is needed and how well its costs can be borne. And because the consequences of choices are readily visible, choosing well seems worth the time and effort; good results evoke personal pride (*DA* I 1.5, 2.6). Ambition is piqued, and it gravitates toward these offices, which afford independence and power. Yet since the objects of township concern remain modest, ambition stays within manageable bounds. Moreover, insofar as it personifies the sovereignty of the people, the township itself becomes an object of affection. In the township, the will of the majority may not always be prudent or just, but it is more or less well-informed, animated by interest and pride, relatively benign, and in any case, not always very effective (*DA* I 1.5, 2.8). Were tyranny to occur here, it would be petty and intrusive; but there is rarely cause or opportunity for such oppression, and occasional injustices are scarcely noticeable (*DA* I 1.5, 1.8). Here one finds democratic self-government at its best (*DA* I 1.8).

Beyond the township, however, the majority's willfulness has potential to do great harm, not only to minorities but also to itself (*DA* I 1.8), as Tocqueville shows in the second part of Volume One. It was the hope of America's Founders that republican forms, especially representative institutions and an "enlarged orbit" for the union of states, would remedy the defects of popular government by diminishing opportunities for demagogic manipulation of factious majorities; perhaps these forms would improve the quality of public deliberations (*The Federalist* nos. 9–10). Tocqueville gives little cause for optimism on these points (*DA* I 1.8, 2.5). He himself praises many of America's republican forms, notably the political practices of its Puritan settlers and the New England township, already in place when the federal constitution was drafted, and the Founders' specific constitutional provisions designed to curb majoritarian and legislative tyranny. Although the commendation is restated near the end of part two (*DA* I 2.9), the intervening lengthy discussion of how democracy tends to work in practice raises doubts about whether even these praiseworthy forms of democracy will be adequate to contain the matter of democracy—the people's actual sovereign will.

Earnest and able democratic citizens will often lack the time to choose representatives wisely. Others will be given to envy of those who they suspect really are their betters. And these better men will not be inclined to stand for election, preferring to make their fortunes by relying on themselves. Moreover, well-meaning but untutored, unsure, or merely busy, citizens can easily be led astray by political partisans; and in a democracy, they tend to be swayed by partisans who advocate the unlimited expansion of popular power (*DA* I 2.2). Democratic citizens will constantly be urged, and tempted, to press for increasing the power of the majority without being able to assure its wisdom or justice. Thus, contrary to widespread hopes, elections will not by themselves serve to bring "enlightened statesmen" to the helm.

Meanwhile, those who are elected will remain subject to envy and personal distrust. Every instance of petty corruption in which they might indulge will exacerbate ill will toward themselves and other elected officials, precisely because it is petty and therefore readily intelligible to ordinary citizens. Such distrust will, however, not prevent their being allowed considerable arbitrary authority to be used for good or ill; for the majority prizes arbitrariness to further its ends, and it knows well the punishment it can inflict at the next election on those who violate its sometimes misplaced trust or who merely displease it now. It will show itself quite tolerant of lawlessness when used in its name (*DA* I 2.5, 2.7).

For these reasons, the majority's government is as likely to be poorly administered as the majority is likely to be willful and undisciplined; it will often be lacking in apparent purpose and sustained effort, inexpert, and wasteful (*DA* I 2.5). One may suppose that democratic government will rarely be effective, efficient, or economical, even if it does not always produce tyranny. The majority itself will want to ignore its own laws and policies when inconvenienced by them or to change them hurriedly to suit its convenience and change them again according to newer convenience. This means that democracy's elected representatives, however feckless, will always find much to do. Democratic government will have an appearance of restive, almost anarchic, activity; one will easily remark a superficial legislative and administrative instability (*DA* I 1.8, 2.5, 2.7, 2.9, 2.10), which is especially worrisome because it reflects and aggravates democracy's tendency to regard the formalities of government as mere inconveniences (*DA* I 2.8, II 4.7). Beneath appearances, however, Tocqueville perceives a deeper and no less worrisome stability, or even immobility.

As Tocqueville describes the workings of America's majoritarian government and anticipates the future, he emphasizes not so much its incompetence as its omnipotence and its potential for tyranny or despotism.[16] In the modern world, the will of the majority comes to exercise a kind of "moral empire" previously unknown (*DA* I 2.7), a new authority that has two sources. Never before had the principle that everyone is as enlightened, as virtuous, and as strong as anyone else been accepted (*DA* II 1.3). Nor does Tocqueville himself accept it (*DA* I 1.3, II 2.13). In the ancient world, the special claims of the rich and well born, as well as those reputed for virtue or wisdom, were considered legitimate both in theory and fact. Tocqueville sees that in the politics of democracy, no minority whose opinions or interests are held to merit respect will stand ready to offer an obstacle to the majority's will. Once the dogma of equality is established, it becomes difficult to see why a greater number of supposedly equally enlightened and virtuous voters is not always more right than a lesser number. Indeed, it becomes all but impossible to see how wrong opinions could ever arise except from malicious intent. On what basis could some few correctly discern legitimate interests that differ from those of the majority?

The majority's moral authority will be further enhanced where no viable aristocracy has ever existed, as in the United States, by the notion that the *interests*, and not just the opinions, of the many should always prevail over those of the few. Where there is no aristocratic few long acknowledged to be distinctive, all are presumed to have the same interests, and all are therefore potential members of the majority. Though this situation might seem harmonious and beneficial, it worries Tocqueville. He sees that in the politics of democracy, no minority whose opinions or interests are held to merit respect will stand ready to offer an obstacle to the majority's will. Should someone nonetheless doubt the majority's wisdom or justice, and still feel the need to hear concerns that might once have been voiced by an aristocracy, these doubts can be expressed effectively only by objecting that a particular pronouncement of the majority has not been sufficiently inclusive (*DA* I 2.7). While such objections may suffice to improve the majority's judgment in any given instance, they may also serve to strengthen its authority in the long term. In a footnote to his discussion of majority tyranny, Tocqueville gives two examples of it: in Baltimore, two journalists who opposed the War of 1812 were killed by a mob of supporters of the war; and in Philadelphia, black freedmen were invariably too intimidated to exercise their right to vote (*DA* I 2.7).

Pride and Race in America

Tocqueville's second example of majority tyranny, racial discrimination, is one he returns to at length. Volume One of *Democracy in America* ends with a very long chapter ostensibly treating subjects that are American, in particular, rather than democratic, in general. More precisely, its theme is the races or peoples that inhabit the New World, or one might say, the modern world; thus, its theme is broader as well as narrower than democracy. In the narrower sense, Tocqueville looks at what the unfettered will of the American people—in effect, the white or "Anglo-American" majority—had thus far wrought, for good and ill, including the most egregious examples of its tyranny: virtual extermination of the Indians and enslavement of blacks. Tocqueville calls this tyranny, and he shows its effects on the tyrant as well as on its victims. In the broader sense, one can see more clearly how the seed of tyranny, "the right and the ability to do everything," germinates especially in modern peoples. Modern philosophy posits that there are in principle no limits on human will—for that is one meaning of the sovereignty of the people (*DA* I 1.4)— and the political forms of modern democracy are inadequate to contain a people's willfulness.

Tocqueville's account of the plight of the Indians chillingly brings to light the ease and hypocrisy with which majority tyranny comes to be exercised in the New World. Anglo-Americans, motivated not by ill will, much less by racial hatred or prejudice, but merely by greed and contempt, not only denied Native Americans their rights but were well on their way to exterminating them "with marvelous facility—tranquilly, legally, philanthropically, without spilling blood, without violating a single one of the great principles of morality in the eyes of the world" (*DA* I 2.10). How could this have happened? The Anglo-Americans, superior in modern learning and soon in strength as well, destroyed the wild game on which the Indians lived, thereby driving them from their traditional hunting grounds and leaving them to face death at nature's hand. They contemptuously dismissed the Indians' appeals to justice and common humanity. The Indian, for his part, was easily enough corrupted by modern man's luxuries; but at the same time, he was too proud of his traditional ways, too trusting in nature's goodness, to learn new arts to satisfy new desires or new arguments to counter new sophistries.

For his extermination of the Indian, the Anglo-American would pay little or no price. But in his enslavement of the black, Tocqueville saw the greatest threat to the United States. Here tyranny comes to follow a logic of its own when human will no longer sees any prohibitions arising from "nature and humanity." What Tocqueville saw occurring in the American South was, he says, "the most horrible and the most natural consequence of slavery" (*DA* I 2.10).

In *Democracy in America*, Tocqueville does not address the question of the natural inferiority of blacks; he attributes the character of the American black to the effects of tyranny.[17] As Tocqueville found him, the slave had neither the pride befitting a human being nor cause for such pride, having been deprived of almost all the "privileges of humanity"—family, homeland, language, religion, mores, even ownership of his person (*DA* I 2.10). Having lost virtually all pride in himself, he had lost the ambition to acquire the skills and habits that would enable him to set and accomplish goals and exhibit virtues in which he might reasonably take pride. "The very use of thought seem[ed] to him a useless gift of Providence" (*DA* I 2.10). His only experience of uncoerced behavior was servile imitation of his master, which was an expression of his shame, the last remnant of his human pride. Unaccustomed to hearing reason's voice, he would, if freed, likely give himself over entirely to his own needs or desires as to a new master. Thus, tyranny had denied the black not only responsibility for his actions but also a suitable model of responsible behavior; he effectively lacked the moral and intellectual faculties that justify human pride.

Once slavery had been reintroduced into the modern world and was now limited to blacks, it became all but impossible to dissociate the master's prejudice against his legal inferior from racial prejudice. The master deemed his black slave his moral and intellectual inferior, and the racial stigma could not then be overlooked. Moreover, these two prejudices were to be reinforced by what Tocqueville curiously refers to as "the prejudice of the white." What does Tocqueville mean by this? He remarks that democratic freedom gives rise to a certain individual haughtiness: "the white man in the United States is proud of his race and proud of himself" (*DA* I 2.10). The rest of the chapter on the New World treats the survival of the Union and of republican institutions, and the spirit of its commerce—all matters that concern the pride of white Americans. Above all, Tocqueville's Anglo-Americans are united among themselves and separated from all other peoples by a sentiment of pride in the success of their democracy, a success which they attribute to reason. They take pride in placing "moral authority in universal reason, as they do political power in the universality of citizens" (*DA* I 2.10).

From Tocqueville's contrast of the white man to the black and the Indian, we can infer that the distinctiveness of the white lies in the superiority not only of his way of life but also of the kind of pride he takes in it. His pride in reason, he believes, enables him to sustain his way of life. Yet in the account of the vitality of the American Union and republic, Tocqueville also suggests that in fact the (white) American *necessarily* misconceives both the source and extent of his pride. He puts his faith in universal reason, which in practice is the majority's reason. According to Tocqueville, this is at least in part a mistake. He is impressed with how well American democracy has prospered, but the explanation he leads his reader to supply is that in America, willfulness has been kept vigorous and informed by salutary mores and political institutions—not that the majority has always acted reasonably. The majority nonetheless believes it has acted reasonably, and there is some value in that misconception. Things are much worse when a majority loses sight of that desideratum and severs the connection between its will and reason.

When Tocqueville reviews the Union's prospects for the future, he notes that for good and ill, a willfulness or restiveness has animated Americans; they exhibit "*decentralizing* passions" (*DA* I 2.10). Their lives have been shaped not simply by needs but also informed by mores. Mores, one might say, "habits of the heart" (*DA* I 2.9), consist of certain distinct forms peculiar to a people of which they are proud: they are forms of pride.[18] They are at a distance from and sometimes at odds with needs, which as such are nothing to be proud of. Adhering to mores enables men to meet their needs as they wish; it allows them, to some extent, to dissociate themselves from their needs, to have an opportunity to take a critical look at them, and to form an opinion about them. The diversity of mores in America suggests a degree of freedom from needs, which are universal. The states and regions to which the hearts of Tocqueville's Americans were then still attached had served to preserve their distinctive forms of pride.

From the Proud Majority to a Herd

Tocqueville begins his second volume (*DA* II 1.1) by drawing a distinction between modern politics, which is suffused with, if not actually derived from, philosophic doctrine, and premodern politics, which was not. Americans practice the new politics, which takes as its foundation the principle that one should rely only on the effort of one's own reason, not on the opinions of others—whether fellow citizens or forebears. At the same time, Americans are unaware of their dependence on philosophic doctrine. Tocqueville now looks at this principle, the sovereignty of the people, under a different name—individualism—and comes to a different conclusion (*DA* II 2.2). He shows how the very principle that seems to support majority rule, and even majority tyranny, threatens eventually to transform a willful or restive and proud democratic majority into a "herd of timid and industrious animals" living under a new sort of despotism (*DA* II 4.6). The second volume is Tocqueville's reflection on the likely *practical* consequences of modern political theory—of its effects on the human soul, on reason and sentiment, and consequently on habits or mores, and thereby on politics.

In speaking of the modern principle as individualism, Tocqueville attributes it to an erroneous judgment (*DA* II 2.2). Although similar to the sentiment of self-love or self-preference, it is not so much a sentiment as a conviction that one should live one's life without paying serious attention to anyone but oneself, or at most to one's family and friends. How can this peculiarly modern sensibility sustain society and political life?

When modern political theory begins by positing autonomous individuals living in a state of nature, its purpose is to show us that it is reasonable even for those who most pride themselves on their power and capability to leave this natural state once and for all, to agree to live as members of some polity with laws, moral rules, customs, and authorities of various sorts, accepting these as legitimate and authoritative. But in the democratic practice Tocqueville describes, each individual insists, in effect, that his consent to depart from the state of nature be obtained in each instance and in each aspect of life. Forget the sovereign! Every act tends to be referred to the pretension of each to be capable of a rational determination of his own interests. Far from convincing the individual to leave the state of nature, modern political theory induces him to hold on to it.

What consequences might follow from this frame of mind? To say it more harshly than Tocqueville ever would have said it: the fundamental principle of modern democratic life is untenable; it is not true that each and every human being can judge everything for himself. What then can individuals do?

First, the weight of judging for oneself is eased somewhat by simplification. By making broad generalizations, relying on "general ideas" (*DA* II 1.3), one can bring oneself to believe that *similar* facts and beings are actually identical or equal. This makes thinking a bit easier. Since this manner of thinking permits the organization of a large number of facts, it may also facilitate the scientific progress on which the modern world prides itself. But excessive use of general ideas may also stem from haste or laziness, and so lead to intellectual sloppiness (see also *DA* II 3.15). And of course, generalizations, particularly about people, can sometimes be inaccurate.

Effective relief can also be found by seeking refuge in public opinion (*DA* II 1.2). An individual looks around and sees many other people holding more or less similar opinions, and their similarity makes them more credible. What everyone thinks must be so! At the same time, no particular person claims responsibility for these common opinions; thus, no one's pride is at risk in adopting them. Modern democracy, Tocqueville predicts, will be characterized by an unprecedented respect for public opinion. Already in the first volume, Tocqueville claimed to find less real freedom of thought in America than in any other time or place.

Yet the most problematic movements of the democratic intellect will start in philosophy and then eventually proceed to politics (*DA* II 1.7, 1.17, 1.20). We are told that democrats increasingly depend on an anonymous public opinion, that they rely excessively on general ideas; and then that they may succumb to a tendency Tocqueville calls "pantheism," in which the distinctiveness not merely of individual men, but of man, is lost to sight.

> As conditions become more equal and each man in particular becomes more like all the others, weaker and smaller, one gets used to no longer viewing citizens so as to consider only the people; one forgets individuals so as to think only of the species.
>
> In these times the human mind loves to embrace a host of diverse objects at once; . . . it willingly seeks to enlarge and simplify its thought by enclosing God and the universe within a single whole.

One must not be confused by the fact that Tocqueville's notion of "individualism" accuses democrats of living only for themselves and a close circle around them, while that of "pantheism" accuses them of forgetting the individual. The individual described under "individualism" has, in his weakness and vulnerability, lost his individuality. He seeks his identity in the very universal, mass forces to which he regards himself as subject. Democracy creates individuals, then leaves them unprotected so that, abetted by pantheism and "democratic historians," they easily fall into individualism.

Near the end of part one (*DA* II 1.20), Tocqueville makes clear the threat that pantheistic opinions pose to democratic politics. This he does in an uncharacteristically vigorous attack on "democratic historians"—who seem to include social and political scientists as well as those influenced by them.[19] Democratic historians trace all events to a few general causes or to historical systems rather than to influential individuals. By denying power to some individuals, they bring people to believe that no one acts voluntarily—that whole peoples, even the whole human race, are moved as if in obedience to a power above or below them. Worse, one attributes to that power an inexorable necessity that forecloses human choice. In this view, politics is meaningless and human freedom is impossible. It is a view of history that Tocqueville deems both inaccurate and harmful. But it could also be self-fulfilling, because people under its influence who *could* act decisively might abandon their attempts as futile.

Self-Interest Well Understood

Individualistic Americans bring themselves to cooperate with one another by means of a doctrine, made famous by this book, that Tocqueville calls "self-interest well understood." Tocqueville endorses the doctrine, but we should note first that it may easily worsen the evil he has termed "individualism." The purpose of the doctrine is to persuade democrats to sacrifice some of their private interests for the sake of preserving the rest of them, and in this it succeeds. Thus, it is an improvement on self-interest poorly understood, a strict utilitarianism which declares that "the useful is never dishonest." Self-interest well understood is "of all philosophic theories the most appropriate to the *needs* of men in our time," in part because it "marvelously accommodat[es] to the *weaknesses* of men" (*DA* II 2.8, emphasis added). Yet for this very reason, the theory risks making men even more aware of their needs and weaknesses and may appear to legitimate all means of alleviating them.

Mores, the habits of the heart of a people, the unreflective ways in which its citizens relate to one another, reveal the thoughts and sentiments of democratic individuals. Some of these manifestations are at first surprising. If in part two Tocqueville points out the dangers of excessive or wrong-headed democratic passions, in part three he shows how the excesses of individualism, egalitarianism, and materialism culminate, paradoxically, in democratic apathy.

Compassion, for example, forges a new sort of moral bond among democratic citizens, mitigating their individualism. But it does so in a way that is inseparable from egalitarianism and perfectly compatible, despite what one might think, with individualism. Compassion is literally an ability to feel what another human being is feeling, and it requires an act of imagination to put oneself in the place of another. This act is made possible, indeed effortless, by the equality and similarity that democracy brings, or more precisely by the dogmatic belief in equality on which it rests and by the customs and conventions of equality that it produces and maintains. For the same reasons, the fellow feeling it evokes is undiscriminating and shallow. Of Americans, Tocqueville says that "each of them can judge the sensations of all the others in a moment: he casts a rapid glance at himself; that is enough for him" (*DA* II 3.1).

As with individualism, democracy's facile compassion reveals the difference between the political principle of equality—which is strength—and the actual sense of weakness men feel when they are equal. In principle, the equality that Tocqueville's Americans recognize is an equal ability to reason about their own affairs. In fact, they are in the habit of acting on the neediness they feel. Since each person is all too aware of his own misery—that is, his needs and unsatisfied desires—he makes a "tacit and *almost involuntary* accord" with others to lend a support now that he hopes later to claim for himself in turn (*DA* II 3.4, emphasis added). Democracy's sense of justice and the explicit and intentional agreements that articulate it tend to be constituted with a view to "permanent and general needs" of the human race (*DA* II 3.18). However much claims of compassion and justice derive from needs, the surest bonds between democratic citizens apart from family relations are not these but fragile and narrow ones established by contracts (*DA* II 3.5) and cemented by money (*DA* II 3.7).

Thus, the daily life of a democratic society is, paradoxically, antithetical to the capability and strength of individuals that it presupposes. Tocqueville laments that moralists of our time constantly complain of pride. It is true enough that there is "no one who does not believe himself to be worth more than his neighbor," but this same man nonetheless diminishes both himself and his neighbor by "settl[ing] into mediocre desires." What democratic men most lack is pride. "I would willingly trade several of our small virtues for this vice" (*DA* II 3.19). What does remain of pride, having few reasonable expectations in politics, is mostly turned to business, where it may still be honored (*DA* II 3.18–20)—or in rare cases, pride becomes dangerously unruly, militaristic, and revolutionary (*DA* II 3.21, 3.26; Tocqueville's note XXVII, p. 704).

The citizen of democracies has contrary instincts, his sense of independence contending with his weakness. "In this extremity, he naturally turns his regard to the immense being that rises alone in the midst of universal debasement" (*DA* II 4.3). This immense being—replacing God—is the state.[20] The new mild despotism, as Tocqueville refers to it, will not be oppressive. It will care for citizens, ever attentive to the obvious needs of all and responsive to various pressures to satisfy unfulfilled desires. But by relieving individuals of the necessity of thinking and acting on their own, it gradually "rob[s] each of them of several of the principal attributes of humanity" and finally "reduces each nation to being nothing more than a herd of timid and industrious animals of which the government is the shepherd" (*DA* II 4.7).

Remedies for Majority Tyranny and Mild Despotism

Majority tyranny is the rule of a restive, prideful, often unreasonable people; mild despotism is efficient ministration by the "immense being" to the not unreasonable, though ultimately short-sighted, needs and desires of a tamed—nay, humbled—mass. Neither is to be desired. Yet if Tocqueville cannot approve of majority tyranny, he surely prefers the instinct animating it—

"intractability" (*DA* II 4.1)—to the apathy that sustains democratic despotism. In the first volume, Tocqueville elaborates several of the institutional means Americans employ to temper majority tyranny: what he calls "decentralized administration" in federalism, local self-government, judges and juries. He also speaks at length of the benefits of their mores, especially their religion, and of their habits of political activity. Near the end of the second volume, he specifies the means necessary to avert mild despotism: associations—among which he includes local government, a free press, an independent judiciary, respect for forms and formalities, in general, and for individual rights, in particular.

In the end, Tocqueville can praise the intractability to which democracy gives rise and on which it thrives, the same intractability that can animate majority tyranny, because he sees in it an untaught instinct for political freedom (*DA* II 4.1). He can, and does, praise American democracy for educating that instinct. Mild despotism is a "schoolmaster" (*DA* II 4.4, 4.6; see also Tocqueville's note I, p. 677) that all but suppresses political freedom; but townships, the judiciary, and associations are also said to be schools—schools of freedom (*DA* I 1.2, 1.5, 2.8; II 2.5). Moreover, the Americans have teachings, notably the idea of rights and the doctrine of self-interest well understood, that are put to work in these schools (*DA* I 2.6, II 2.8).

For Tocqueville, what we now refer to as "voluntary associations" are an indispensable supplement to government in a democracy, though not a substitute for it. On the contrary, he contends that "civil" associations could not easily be maintained without institutions of self-government (*DA* II 2.7). Tocqueville is a critic of big government, not of all government; he even grants that in democracies "the sovereign must be more uniform, more centralized, more extended, more penetrating, and more powerful" (*DA* II 4.7). What matters is how the sovereign's power is structured—how it is divided among secondary powers—to preserve some degree of individual independence. A democratic sovereign can enable and encourage citizens to do more for themselves, while for that reason doing what it must do more effectively.

In Tocqueville's judgment, dependence on a "general will" such as that proposed by Rousseau effectively vitiates each person's awareness of his or her particular interests and abilities, and thus increases the extent of everyone's dependence and degradation. He proposes instead mutual but partial dependence in the form of participation in associations of all sorts, from private contractual agreements to interest groups to political institutions and organizations.

Least obvious, most instructive, and potentially most valuable are the associations Tocqueville's Americans form for moral and intellectual ends. In bringing to the public eye new, uncommon sentiments and ideas, individuals influence one another, persuade others, perhaps even change mores and ultimately laws; thus, "the heart is enlarged, and the human mind is developed" (*DA* II 2.5). These associations can be understood as political in the sense that they are means of self-government which supplement or in fact replace, to some extent, government as ordinarily construed. When democratic citizens associate to make a display of their own abstinence from liquor in the hope of encouraging temperance in others, they behave, Tocqueville notes, as an aristocratic lord once might have done for those who looked up to him (*DA* II 2.5, 2.7, 4.6). In this example, both the association of ordinary, equal democratic citizens and the aristocratic lord rely on an informal mode of governing that is meant to work primarily by shaping mores. This tempers the democratic inclination to rely on more authoritarian methods of discouraging drunkenness found in early American Puritan legislation and in post-Revolutionary American and French bureaucratic regulation (*DA* I 1.2, 2.4, 2.5, 2.6; II 2.5). Finally, in uniting over a moral issue, they may also help to temper democracy's greater intoxications, individualism and materialism (see *DA* II 2.3, 2.10).

Among political associations proper, the township is a primary school in freedom; and citizens who attend it acquire the taste for freedom and its exercise (*DA* I 1.5). They come to appreciate how their choices might affect the world. The township is individual choice and responsibility, shared and writ large: A school, once built, stands.

Similarly, the jury is a free school, "the most energetic means of making the people reign, [and] the most efficacious means of teaching them to reign" (*DA* I 2.8). An independent judiciary gives even the weakest citizen an established weapon with which to fight the tyranny of either government or society. But the weapon will be powerful only as long as judicial niceties (i.e., formal rights and procedures) are respected. Fortunately, the American democracy Tocqueville saw had a distinct, and large, class of lawyers and judges, who by professional training and personal interest were encouraged to maintain this respect in society. It could also avail itself of county administrators called justices of the peace, who combine a respect for formalities, which poses an obstacle to despotism, with worldly common sense (*DA* I 1.5).

If townships and juries are schools of freedom, political associations like interest groups and parties, too, are "great schools, free of charge, where all citizens come to learn the general theory of association" (*DA* II 2.7). Political associations bring citizens together in a way that neither democratic compassion nor mild despotism's schoolmaster can do: "A political association draws a multitude of individuals outside themselves at the same time; however separated they are naturally by age, mind, fortune, it brings them together and puts them in contact. They meet each other once and learn to find each other always." Political associations energize citizens and then force them to reason about what is required to organize common efforts. This organization of efforts does not require a sacrifice of self-interest, nor is it begun by a facile identification of one's own interests with the interests of everyone. Otherwise different but similarly interested selves unite to advance one shared goal that is nonetheless recognized as partisan or partial. Thus, deliberation on how to link partial interests to what really might be general interests in a democracy is promoted over the unreflective and abstract identification of needs characteristic of democratic compassion. Political associations are free schools: they are free because they are inexpensive and relatively painless ways of exercising the habits of freedom; they are schools because they employ and instill reasonable expectations about what makes freedom possible for individuals and political communities.

Tocqueville is celebrated as the great advocate of civil associations and political participation, especially at the local level. But to cast him as a decentralizer and privatizer and nothing more is not enough. Even as he fears and denounces big government, Tocqueville insists on the value of great nations. This does not necessarily mean militarism, but it does mean "think[ing] a little more of making great men" (*DA* II 4.7). In France's case and, we can suppose, in America's as well, he understands that national greatness requires a vigorous defense of the principles of the Revolution in the world for the sake of the nation's soul.[21] Sustaining the independence and dignity of individuals must always be a matter for national attention, even when best accomplished by decentralized means.

The Virtue of Women

No survey of the schooling done by American associations would be complete without a peek inside the "conjugal association"; for, Tocqueville says, all that influences the condition of women has "great political interest in my eyes" (*DA* II 3.9, 3.12).

Not only does Tocqueville compare American attitudes about marriage and relations between men and women in society favorably with aristocratic patriarchalism, but he also presents a picture quite unlike the democratic egalitarianism of the late twentieth century. Within marriage as he portrays it, spouses are faithful to one another, with little or no public tolerance for infidelity. This he attributes partly to America's being religious, partly to its being commercial, but mostly to the fact that democrats marry by choice, not by parental arrangement, and that they choose with few if any arbitrary barriers—for example, between social or economic classes. American marriages join hearts, not bloodlines or bank accounts. And since the parties contract freely, it does not seem unreasonable for public opinion to hold them to their choices by frowning on adultery and divorce.

Americans hold that nature has made men and women so physically and morally different that one ought to put their different natural abilities to different uses. What are these natural physical and moral differences? Strikingly, Tocqueville says nothing of the most obvious physical difference, that women bear children; he merely suggests that women might be less suited for hard physical labor. And he is so far from finding moral differences that he speaks at length of women's courage and strength of will, of their *virile* habits and energy, of their *manly* reason; they show themselves to be *like*, not unlike, men in heart and mind (*DA* II 3.9–12). American men are nonetheless said to recognize their wives' intelligence and resolve, to esteem them, as well as to respect their freedom. Perhaps, then, they can seek from such women in private the kind of advice that democratic individualism and egalitarianism deny them in public.

Contrary to what his Americans claim, Tocqueville shows that American women are intellectually and morally *similar* to men, and arguably superior. He himself never says that it is natural for women as distinguished from men to live a private and subordinate life in the sense that their natures (as mothers) suit them to it. Insofar as Tocqueville approves of American attitudes toward women, he seems to approve of the assignment of "gender roles," as we would now say. What he shows is that in America, public policy first mistakes or at least greatly exaggerates the significance of natural differences and then goes on to make them the basis of a great conventional inequality. "The true notion of democratic progress" requiring different treatment for the sexes obviously violates the democratic dogma of the natural similarity of all human beings. At the same time, it inverts the notion of natural aristocracy, where the naturally, not conventionally, best rule. For the intellectual and moral superiority of women is, by convention, denied a title to political authority. Democratic progress seems to require that natural superiorities be fostered, yet in the case of women, be obscured from public view. How can this be justified?

Tocqueville's characterization of American men, especially in the chapters on women, is hardly flattering. These men exhaust themselves and their wives in a relentless, ever restive, unsatisfying, and ultimately petty pursuit of material well-being. They are decent, to be sure, if for no other reason than that they are too prosaic to imagine any really interesting indecencies in which to indulge; but they do not seem to be especially admirable or even happy human beings. Women, for their part, seem to spend their youths happily flirting and their married lives resolutely, even proudly, but sadly, packing and unpacking family copies of the Bible and Shakespeare as their husbands move on to the next business venture. What Tocqueville refers to as women's making "a sort of glory for themselves out of the voluntary abandonment of their wills" we might call inordinate passivity (*DA* II 3.12). It is difficult to imagine a vigorous society composed entirely of individuals resembling either American men or women as described.

For Tocqueville, democratic society is characterized by excessive individualism, egalitarianism, and materialism, and by an ever greater centralization of power. Each in its way contributes to the destruction of democratic freedom. If democratic society is to check its own excesses, it will do so in part by diffusing, or decentralizing, public power by employing associations, and in part by appreciating the limits on it that lie so to speak behind and above public life.

Behind public life lies the family. The nineteenth-century American marriage Tocqueville describes is one important aspect of modern democratic life that had not yet been thoroughly politicized. Here, one may hope to experience not an abstract compassion but "the sort of profound, regular, and peaceful affection that makes up the charm and security of life." Here, the frenetic activity of men may be restrained, ultimately for the sake of allowing them to focus and deploy their energies more effectively in places where social and political power can reach the goals set. This distinction between domains may be beneficial to all, even if a line drawn along gender seems arbitrary.

Above public life, so to speak, lies religion. Even in democracy, human beings may experience a dissatisfaction with existence that serves to remind them that there are yearnings that go beyond material well-being and even justice. To fulfill such yearnings the indefinite extension of public power would be useless. And where political power should not venture, religion is there to provide individuals with what guidance they might need.

The Superiority of Practice

Democracy in America shows the superiority of American practice to democratic theory, partly because some aspects of American practice had not yet been transformed by democratic theory, partly because practice tends to correct theory (*DA* II 2.4). Nonetheless, America's vocational schools of freedom do teach two doctrines: "self-interest well understood" and the idea of rights.

How can the doctrine of self-interest well understood be helpful? Tocqueville presents self-interest well understood as a moral doctrine universally accepted in America. It is meant to replace older moral teachings that urged almost divine selflessness or praised the beauty of virtue and the glory of sacrifice. The new moralists defend virtue as useful, and one learns to think not only that one always prefers oneself but also that it is part of one's interest to see that one's "particular interest is to do good" (*DA* II 2.8). Americans take to explaining everything they do by means of self-interest, even denying that they are ever given to the "disinterested and unreflective sparks that are natural to man." In so doing, "they would rather do honor to their philosophy than to themselves." This, Tocqueville says, is to do themselves an injustice. It is also to contradict their doctrine by honoring it above their interests, or to demonstrate that honoring something above oneself and one's interests is in one's interest.

Tocqueville contends that self-interest well understood is the moral doctrine best suited to modern democratic times, even though it is neither complete nor altogether self-evident. But it is "clear and sure"; and since it "marvelously accommodat[es] to the weaknesses of men, it obtains a great empire with ease" (*DA* II 2.8). It is unlikely to produce either true or lofty virtue, but it is nonetheless well suited to democracy because it is accessible to everyone and shows all how to behave well enough: "Consider some individuals, they are lowered. View the species, it is elevated" (*DA* II 2.8).

The doctrine of self-interest runs a risk in making citizens well aware of their needs and in appealing to them; they will very likely think too much about their needs. But it also urges on citizens the importance of attending to their needs in a responsible way. No less than older moral doctrines or democratic compassion, it is meant to prompt democrats to come to one another's aid. And it is more compatible than the alternatives with democratic self-government. Free political institutions and the habit of participating in them are still necessary to show democratic citizens what useful things they can do for themselves by combining their efforts. Self-interest *well understood* would keep citizens from being overwhelmed by their needs and succumbing to dependence on a schoolmaster government that might otherwise be understood as serving them.

How does the idea of rights support association and self-government? Near the end of *Democracy in America*, Tocqueville makes a remark that might strike Americans today as strange: "Another instinct very natural to democratic peoples and very dangerous is the one that brings them to scorn individual rights and hold them of little account. . . . [T]he very idea of these sorts of rights constantly tends to be distorted and lost among us" (*DA* II 4.7). Tocqueville insists that democracy is naturally hostile to individual rights, that rights are aristocratic in origin and character (*DA* II 4.4).

For Tocqueville, rights are essentially political, not social or economic, in content and in consequence. They make possible self-government and political responsibility, giving citizens more self-confidence and making them less cynical or resentful toward government. The newer, more cherished rights of late twentieth-century America—reproductive rights, the rights of various sorts of minorities, and increasingly, environmental and health-related rights—have, on the whole, the object of security, freedom from risk. Some are understood to be entitlements, rights whose existence depends on a governmental program and often a governmental expenditure. To rights of this sort American democracy seems far from hostile. The fact that Tocqueville seems to have been so wrong about how rights would come to be viewed suggests either that his predictions have gone awry or that they were all too accurate.

When Tocqueville elaborates at the end of the book on the means of forestalling the new despotism (*DA* II 4.7), he refers to his project as a "holy enterprise," although he does not speak of American religious mores. Insofar as Tocqueville has hopes for religion, they are of two sorts. Religion may diminish the threat of mild despotism by reminding citizens of the seriousness of life outside the busy search for material well-being in democracies. Belief in the soul and its afterlife may moderate materialism; and the sure answers any religion offers to the hardest questions can strengthen individual judgment in both private and public life (*DA* II 1.5). In these ways, religion may forestall democrats' psychological and intellectual susceptibility to mild despotism. But once again, Tocqueville's objective in strengthening the personal or nonpublic as against the public can only be one aspect of religion's potential benefit, since he also contemns those who neglect public concerns.[22] His second hope for religion is that it may serve as a reminder of what transcends the mediocrity of democratic public life, and thus of a greatness not usually within its scope.

In the second volume of *Democracy in America*, Tocqueville refers to religion as "the most precious inheritance from aristocratic centuries," as if it were foreign to democratic eras (*DA* II 2.15). And in the "Introduction" to the book, he makes it a question whether religion can be relied on to play an important role elsewhere in the modern world. He claims to have learned from American democracy that religion can remain vital in the new world if it is kept separate from politics. In America, clergy were precluded by custom, if not law, from holding political office; they entered into partisan political controversies no further than to support the general view that republicanism is a good thing. Later (*DA* II 1.2), Tocqueville clarifies his characterization of the separation of church and state, showing that it cannot be complete because at the base of politics and religion is one public opinion that sustains them both. He expects democracy to transform religion to make its form and content more consistent with democracy; and by 1830, American religion had made that accommodation. Religion, like family, may be separate from government, but both are parts of *self*-government; thus, the separation must itself be understood politically. This is how Tocqueville can say that religion ought to be considered as "the first of [America's] political institutions" (*DA* I 2.9).

When Tocqueville calls the reader's attention to Americans' insistence on separating church and state, he makes it clear that he thinks that the human power released by modern philosophy needs to impose some sense of limitation on itself. Yet the purpose of his recommendation of self-limitation is to keep democratic political power vigorous within its proper sphere (*DA* I 2.9). Modern political theory was meant to increase human power and give men better control of events; in practice, however, the instability of democracy may give greater scope to chance than was seen in political life when people did not believe everything was in their control, but was instead at the mercy of higher powers. From democratic instability arises the possibility of a majoritarian politics characterized by a continuous, meaningless flux. The flux may seem to justify an apathy that leaves the field to passionate, if fleetingly aroused, majorities; then, in the end, it subsides into mild despotism.

What is necessary, Tocqueville insists, is for democratic governments to set distant goals, goals to be achieved by moderate, yet steadfast, efforts. Surprisingly, however, Tocqueville specifies no great project. Instead, he suggests the seemingly limited, not to say modest, task of seeing to it that political office come only as a reward for skill and effort, for moderate ambition —and not for pleasing the people. But this modest goal is in truth an infinite one that calls forth continuous diligence. There will always be elections that can be won by pleasing the people; and winning the favor of the people, especially of a democratic people with unstable desires, will depend in large part on chance. It is beyond the capacity of a democracy to reward virtue regularly. Partial success is within reach to the extent that political institutions and mores can be well shaped; but without the support of a greater power, the goal will always remain elusive. Insofar as men do act confidently in the hope that virtue will be rewarded—accomplishing much along the way—they will, in effect, have returned to a kind of religious faith from which politics may benefit politically.

Tocqueville learned to admire democracy, sincerely, if not wholeheartedly: it would be different from aristocracy, with its own virtues and vices, its own good and bad penchants, its own ideas, its own sort of greatness and beauty, neither incontrovertibly superior nor inferior to what had preceded it (*DA* II 4.8). The fact that he criticizes democracy does not mean that he does not also speak ill of aristocracy or that he could not speak better of democracy, had he not deliberately left that to others (*DA* II Notice). In the end, Tocqueville was a democrat, and more of a democrat than many of his contemporaries. Because he insisted that only political freedom could remedy the ills to which equality of conditions gives rise (*DA* II 2.4), he hopefully accepted that equality and despite his fears, embraced the political freedom that democracy promised.

Notes

1. This chapter is condensed from the authors' "Introduction" to a translation of Tocqueville's *Democracy in America* (Chicago: University of Chicago Press, 2000). All references in the text are to this edition, hereafter cited as *DA*, followed by volume, part, and chapter number.

2. The following discussion is based on George W. Pierson, *Tocqueville in America* (Baltimore: Johns Hopkins University Press, [1938] 1996); James T. Schleifer, *The Making of Tocqueville's "Democracy in America"* (Chapel Hill: University of North Carolina Press, 1980); and André Jardin, *Tocqueville: A Biography*, trans. L. Davis (New York: Farrar Straus, 1988).

3. Jardin, *Tocqueville: A Biography*, 79–84.

4. Quoted in Jardin, *Tocqueville: A Biography*, 90.

5. Letter to Louis de Kergorlay of January 1835, Alexis de Tocqueville, *Selected Letters on Politics and Society*, ed. Roger Boesche (Berkeley: University of California Press, 1985), 93–96; Alexis de Tocqueville, *Oeuvres complètes*, 18 vols. (Paris: Gallimard, 1961–1998), 13.1:373–75, hereafter cited as *OC*. See also Jardin, *Tocqueville: A Biography*, 93.

6. Pierson, *Tocqueville in America*, 782–86.

7. Alexis de Tocqueville, *Journey to America*, ed. J. P. Mayer (London: Faber and Faber, 1959); also Alexis de Tocqueville, *Oeuvres*, 2 vols., ed. A. Jardin (Paris: Gallimard, éd. Pléiade, 1991–1992), 1:29–413, hereafter cited as *Oeuvres*.

8. In a deleted fragment, Tocqueville wrote of the two volumes: "The first book more American than democratic. This one more democratic than American." See Schleifer, *The Making of "Democracy in America,"* 29, and also Jardin, *Tocqueville: A Biography*, 271–76.

9. Letter to John Stuart Mill, October 10, 1840 (*OC* 6.1:329–31); in reply to Mill's letter of May 11, 1840, to Tocqueville, in which he says: "You have changed the face of political philosophy" (*OC* 6.1:328).

10. Jean-Claude Lamberti's *Notice* in *DA*, *Oeuvres*, 2:904; Jardin, *Tocqueville: A Biography*, 201.

11. The manuscript given to the printer has not survived, but Tocqueville's working manuscripts are preserved at the Beinecke Library at Yale. See *Oeuvres*, 2:934.

12. See *DA* II 2.1 for the closest approximation to the state of nature; in I 2.10, Tocqueville says that a republic is "the natural state of the Americans," and in that chapter he also gives an account of the origin of sovereignty without referring to the state of nature.

13. See Pierre Manent, *Tocqueville and the Nature of Democracy*, trans. J. Waggoner (Lanham, Md.: Rowman and Littlefield, 1996), 48.

14. Alexis de Tocqueville, *The Old Regime and the Revolution*, trans. A. Kahan (Chicago: University of Chicago Press, 1999), I 5, II 5, marvelously prefigured twenty years earlier in the essay Tocqueville had written for John Stuart Mill: "Social and Political Condition of France," in *OC* 2.1:65.

15. In the margin, Tocqueville notes: "New despotism. It is in the portrayal of this that resides all the originality and depth of my idea. What I wrote in my first work was hackneyed and superficial." Cited in Jean-Claude Lamberti, "Two Ways of Conceiving the Republic," in *Interpreting Tocqueville's "Democracy in America,"* ed. Ken Masugi (Lanham, Md.: Rowman and Littlefield, 1991), 18.

16. The term "tyranny of the majority" is used in I 2.4, 2.7 (four times), 2.8. "Despotism of the majority" is used in I 1.8, 2.7, 2.9. The "omnipotence" of the people or the majority is mentioned in I 1.8, 2 Intro., 2.4, 2.7 (eight times).

17. In a letter to his friend Arthur de Gobineau, November 17, 1853 (*Selected Letters*, 297–301; *OC* 9:201–4), Tocqueville criticizes the racialist theories of Gobineau's *Essai sur l'inégalité des races humaines* (1853) as "very probably false and very certainly pernicious."

18. Robert Bellah has made Tocqueville's phrase current; see Robert N. Bellah, Richard Madsen, William M. Sullivan, Ann Swidler, and Steven M. Tipton, *Habits of the Heart* (New York: Harper and Row, 1985).

19. For a similar attack on historians of the French Revolution of 1848, see *Recollections of Alexis de Tocqueville [Souvenirs]*, ed. J. P. Mayer (London: Harvill Press, 1948), 67–75.

20. Rousseau's Savoyard Vicar refers to God as the *Etre immense*; *Emile*, in Jean-Jacques Rousseau, *Oeuvres complètes*, 5 vols. (Paris: Gallimard, Pléiade ed., 1959–1995), 4:592. See also Descartes's description of God as "Immense, incomprehensible and infinite" in *Meditations* IV. Our thanks to Terence Marshall for these references. Tocqueville himself also uses the term in describing the pantheistic conception of the whole, which incorporates all of creation and the Creator himself (*DA* II 1.7).

21. While arguing in the Chamber of Deputies for the abolition of slavery in the French colonies, Tocqueville reminded his colleagues that the idea of freedom and therefore the "great idea [of abolition] is not only your property, it is not only among the mother ideas of your Revolution, but it lives or it dies in your hearts, depending on whether one sees living or reborn there all the elevated sentiments, all the noble instincts that your Revolution developed, those noble instincts by which you have done everything great that you have accomplished in the world and without which, I do not fear to say, you will do nothing and you will be nothing." "Intervention dans la discussion de la loi sur le régime des esclaves dans les colonies," in *OC* 3.1:125–26.

22. For an emphatic restatement of this point, see *The Old Regime*, 86–89.

PART ONE:

FROM COLONY TO NATION
(1608–1776)

》》➤ ◀《《

Chapter 1

John Winthrop, John Cotton, and Nathaniel Niles: The Basic Principles of Puritan Political Thought

Michael J. Rosano

With the words "We shall be as a Citty upon a Hill," John Winthrop established American political thought. They form the heart of Winthrop's sermon "Christian Charitie: A Modell Hereof," which he wrote in 1630 on board the *Arbella* in a company of Puritan pilgrims on the way to New England to found an unprecedented Christian political society. Winthrop's thought is distinctly Puritan, but it represents the essential and enduring spirit of American thought by combining a singularly idealistic sense of political destiny with a manifestly practical political program. From the beginning, words or ideas define and bind together American political society, and political deeds aim at amplifying and justifying those words. But ideas are open to debate, and practical actions can strain them to the breaking point. Debate implies the need to persuade Americans to reaffirm their principles on an ongoing basis, and thus the possibility of radical change, a possibility encouraged by the tension between their high ideals and sober pragmatism. We see this exemplified in Nathaniel Niles's sermon "A Discourse on Liberty," delivered on the eve of the Revolution (June 5, 1774) at the North Church in Newburyport, Massachusetts. In the spirit of his Puritan forefathers, he defended liberty as a blessing of heaven, and he depicted the increasingly violent relationship between Great Britain and the American colonies as a time the very prospect of which would have caused those forefathers to weep in bitterness of soul. But instead of placing the blame solely on British misgovernment, Niles called on Americans to recognize the part they played in fueling the crisis. Above all, Americans must put their own house in order; for although God bestowed the blessings of liberty upon them, they adopted a way of life that corrupts liberty, and aids and abets in their own oppression as well as the oppression of others. Niles urged Americans to return to their father's house by reaffirming the principles of Christian liberty that inspired the Puritan founders to build their "City upon a Hill." In short, it was high time to reform.[1] But Americans chose the path of revolution.

Niles's "Discourse on Liberty" may be regarded as at least equal to Thomas Paine's famous and influential *Common Sense* in its analytical and rhetorical power. Yet, in contrast to *Common Sense*, the "Discourse on Liberty" receives scant attention today. This disparity is due to the fact that Niles represents Puritanism while Paine represents liberalism. In order to understand the importance of that disparity, one must understand that both Puritanism and liberalism claim to have the true conception of liberty and good government, and both seek to form a distinct kind of human being and citizen. Puritanism represents traditional Christian political thought. It is based on the Bible as a sacred text revealed to human beings by God and regards the duty of charity or devotion to the community as the basis of liberty and good government. The tenants of Puritanism and related forms of Protestantism were so deeply rooted in the fabric of American life at the time of the Revolution as to represent traditional America. Liberalism, by contrast, originates in the work of such secular philosophers of the Enlightenment as John Locke; regards unaided human reason and the inalienable natural rights to life, liberty, and property as the basis of legitimate government; and constitutes a revolutionary break from that Christian tradition. Liberalism finds its primary and most powerful political expression in the American Revolution as defined by the Declaration of Independence and in the Constitution. Thus, at the time of the Revolution, Niles and Paine represent two alternatives on the path toward America's future as a free nation, and only one of those alternatives could prevail.

The victory of the liberal revolutionaries over the Puritan reformers makes it extremely difficult to understand Puritanism on its own terms today. Puritanism does not simply disappear from the scene, but it tends to be assimilated into liberalism or to be "liberalized"; in a sense, it is harmonized with the prevailing ideas and sentiments of liberal America. Those basic aspects of Puritanism that stand in stark contradiction to liberalism and cannot be assimilated tend to be castigated as "Puritanical." As such, they are dismissed out of hand as relics of a primitive period of American history that is defined by religious fanaticism and should be viewed with alarm as warnings against religious and political intolerance. But in order to understand American political thought as a whole, it is necessary to understand Puritan political thinkers on their own terms. First, as Alexis de Tocqueville observes in *Democracy in America*, a nation's moral and political origins, like the childhood education of an adult, often form the enduring foundation for its subsequent development, and that holds true especially for America and its Puritan heritage. For better or for worse, Protestant Christianity defined the moral substance of American culture before the Revolution, and most Americans of the revolutionary generation, including many of the revolutionaries, were nurtured on its principles. In key respects, Puritan principles may infuse the revolutionary spirit of 1776. Second, that infusion may obscure core principles of liberalism itself, and may obstruct or bolster the strengths and weaknesses of liberal political practice. Third, the need to accommodate the influence of Puritan principles at least conditioned the political practice of the liberal revolutionaries. Finally, the most important reason to understand Puritanism on its own terms is the possibility that Puritan principles—at least in certain decisive respects—may be more salutary and truer than the principles of liberalism. The fact that the Puritan reformers lost the political debate with the liberal revolutionaries does not mean that they deserved to lose that debate. Choosing liberalism over Puritanism might have been a mistake.

The possibility that Puritan principles are an ingredient of liberalism's political success and form a superior alternative to it requires a reevaluation of the original debate between the liberal revolutionaries and the Puritan reformers. Accordingly, this chapter begins by articulating the basic writings and analyzing the key principles of such Puritan forefathers as John Winthrop (1588–1649) and John Cotton (1584–1652), and it compares and contrasts Puritan principles with liberal principles throughout in order to define the relation between them. The chapter then proceeds to articulate Nathaniel Niles's (1741–1821) reaffirmation of Puritanism and to analyze his attempt to restore it to prominence in the hearts and minds of Americans. In sum, the chapter lays the groundwork for understanding Puritan political thought and the relation and dispute between Puritans and liberals that is at the heart of American political culture.

John Winthrop on the Model of Christian Charity

The analysis of Puritan political thought in America properly begins with an elaboration of John Winthrop's "Christian Charitie: A Modell Hereof." This sermon is not a work of systematic Puritan theology or political theory but an exhortation to it. As such, it is intended to remind his company of their purpose in undertaking their dangerous and unprecedented pilgrimage to the New World and to inspire them to live up to their high expectations. As the title indicates, Winthrop's sermon outlines the principles of Christian charity—the primary Christian virtue —and thereby constructs a model for them to live by. Its immediately practical purpose indicates the kind of human being they expect themselves to be and the way of life they expect to establish. Entrenched political and religious establishments and widespread moral corruption preclude the formation of such a Christian political society in Europe. Winthrop and his company believe that they are destined by divine Providence as well as their own determination to decide, by their conduct and faith, the question of whether Christians can establish a Christian political society. Winthrop thus exhorts his company to consider that the eyes of the world are on them, and they must strive to be models of Christian charity and to establish, as a shining example of Christian government, a "Citty upon a Hill."

Winthrop's opening statement sets the theoretical parameters and the moral tone for the whole exhortation. "God Almighty in his most holy and wise providence has so disposed of the condition of mankind, as in all times some must be rich some poor, some high and eminent in power and dignity; others mean and in subjection" (*CCM* 76). First and foremost, Winthrop appeals to God Almighty and divine Providence as the immediate cause of the basic social and political condition of mankind. Human beings can understand their essence and purpose on earth only in the light of faith in and devotion to the word of God as revealed in the Bible. But God gave man rationality, and with the aid of Scripture, human beings can also discern God's Providence in the order of nature and human affairs. The economic, social, and political inequality or hierarchy that is evident throughout the world is a purposeful and permanent condition. Winthrop's position contrasts with the Declaration of Independence's affirmation that the "Laws of Nature and of Nature's God" created all men equal by endowing them with inalienable natural rights that are "self-evident" or ascertainable by reason without the aid of revelation, and that securing those rights with the consent of the governed defines legitimate government. For Winthrop, by contrast, right begins and ends with God and obedience to divine ordinances, and nothing could be more evident than that all sorts of inequality and hierarchy characterize human affairs.[2]

Winthrop maintains that God establishes social stratification, economic inequality, and political hierarchy so as "to show forth the glory of his wisdom in the variety and difference of the Creatures and the glory of his power, in ordering all these differences for the preservation and good of the whole." God ordains that diversity in order to make the many parts of creation and conditions of human beings cohere into an organic whole that is greater than the sum of its parts. Human beings must find their place and play their part in that whole in order to become fulfilled as individuals. One's own life, liberty, and property are not properly understood as inalienable natural rights that are, in effect, claims made by individuals on their own behalf as against the political community but as gifts of God to be used to promote the common good. A Christian should act not as a possessor or owner of God's gifts but as a "steward" of God, who "counts himself more honored in dispensing his gifts to man by man, than if he did it by his own immediate hand." Hierarchy and inequality are a fact of life that should be used by one and all as an opportunity to serve others and the community as a whole (*CCM* 76).

Winthrop's position on this matter could be seen today as an ideological rationalization for oppression. But he is keenly aware that temptations to commit evil are a part of human affairs and often overwhelm them. The politically powerful can be corrupted by the temptation to oppress the community while those who are weaker can be tempted to shrink away from playing their part or to shirk their duty to the community. Indeed, Winthrop affirms that one of God's reasons for ordaining that human beings live in an interdependent community is to moderate and restrain the wicked "so that the rich and mighty should not eat up the poor, and despised rise up against their superiors, and shake off their yoke." The destruction of (well-ordered) hierarchy would exacerbate rather than solve the problem of corruption by fueling self-aggrandizement and undermining community (*CCM* 76).

To be sure, harmony, virtue, and public service do not characterize most political societies —but that is because most human beings behave badly. Winthrop makes a key distinction between those human beings who are "regenerate" and all others who are not, and he thereby distinguishes the political affairs of the "regenerate" from those of all others. In short, regenerate human beings are those who are born again by their faith in Jesus Christ and his Gospel of love and eternal salvation. Human beings can find the spiritual strength to resist temptations and stand up to evil on the basis of that faith alone; in that faith, Christians can exercise such virtues as love, mercy, temperance, patience, and obedience even in the face of danger. In sum, God ordains it that "every man might have need of other" so that "they might be all knit more nearly together in the Bond of brotherly affection." Community, then, is not an association for the satisfaction of need, and the political, social, and economic affairs of a community do not in themselves entail the end or purpose of community. The purpose of community is to attain that "bond of brotherly affection," for it is in that bond alone that human beings can best share the gifts of God's love. That bond, in turn, is the fruit of Christian faith (*CCM* 76–77).

Winthrop's position implies that all human beings are equal in the most important way. Human beings are equally subject to God's ordinances and in need of each other to attain God's love and graces. He repeatedly stresses that individuals are not given such gifts as wealth, honor, or authority over others for their personal benefit alone but for the "glory of his Creator and the Common good of the Creature, Man." Thus, "God still reserves the property of these gifts to himself." When God "is pleased to call for his right in any thing wee have, our own Interest we have must stand aside, till his turn be served." In these terms, no one can have an inalienable right to the benefits that God alone can give or take away. Indeed, to usurp such benefits in the name of one's own right is to alienate oneself from one's community and the true graces of God. The opportunity to know God's love and to love and obey God is true human equality (*CCM* 77, 80).

At this point, it is useful to remember that Winthrop is delivering his exhortation to the faithful. They must strive to accomplish that mission from the moment they set foot on the new land to their last moment on earth. Winthrop thus stresses that the "exhortacion must be generall and perpetuall" (*CCM* 80). But he thereby also stresses that even the faithful fall short and may even lose sight of those principles and stray from the path of righteousness. His exhortation must be applied generally and perpetually not only because it positively defines how they should live but also because it addresses the common vices and nearly constant temptations they must overcome. Those temptations will be all the more difficult to resist precisely because the standards are being set so high and because they are blazing a trail in a new country full of unique pitfalls, such as almost limitless opportunities to strike out on one's own and to strike it rich. Winthrop knows well that the pitfalls will be proportional to the opportunities and that he and his company must strive to remain faithful to the task of building a "Citty upon a Hill," lest they transform the new "promised land" into a paradise lost.

In this vein, Winthrop appeals to two closely related standards by which Christians can judge right from wrong: the law of nature or the moral law and the law of Grace or the Gospel (*CCM* 77). There is, however, a critical difference between them. God established the law of nature in man's original state of innocence. It applied immediately to Adam and Eve in the Garden of Eden, and it was intended to apply to their progeny as the family of man. The basic precept of the law of nature is that human beings should love their neighbors as themselves, and it is tantamount to the golden rule that you should do to others what you would have them do to you. This law of nature is, in a sense, self-evident in that it is expressed by a natural inclination that is immediately understandable and applicable to human beings in their original state of innocence. On this basis, human beings would thrive in a condition of mutual love and assistance focused on the love and benevolence of God. But paradise was lost along with innocence. Adam and Eve put other desires before God's commands, and following in the path of that original sin, human beings succumbed to selfishness or sin; the law of nature thus became obscure; and a state of enmity rather than mutual love prevailed. Cain's murder of his brother Abel shows that enmity infects even one's own home and carries the threat of violent death far beyond one's neighbors into the whole wide world (Genesis 1–4). The natural law cannot direct degenerate human beings who perceive that benevolence is practiced only at significant risk to oneself: in short, it cannot provide rules for dealing with enemies because in the state of innocence human beings were friends. Consequently, the law of nature needs to be bolstered and is superseded by the law of Grace or the Gospel. The Gospel is perhaps the least self-evident of all moral laws because it instructs human beings to love their enemies.

The law of Grace is based on the will of God to restore man to his original state of goodness. The Bible reveals how God works through His chosen people to redeem mankind as well as the law and moral precepts that are conditions of redemption. In Winthrop's view, the Bible is neither a work of human hands nor the product of human reason or imagination. Its primary occurrences and truths are not natural or self-evident or accessible to human beings by use of their reason or senses. Its authority over human beings, however, depends on their faith and obedience. The Bible testifies to the difficulty and rewards of being faithful and the dire consequences of committing evil. It reveals that God's Providence culminates in the advent of Jesus Christ and the law of Grace or the Gospel. Jesus spreads the word of love, as in the Sermon on the Mount, and ultimately makes manifest that love by allowing himself to be crucified as a criminal by his "enemies" and forgiving them of their sins. All who have faith in him and strive to follow his example of love, sacrifice, and forgiveness can be of good hope for eternal salvation. The Gospel restores the precept that one should love one's neighbor as oneself by going well beyond it, requiring that the faithful love even their enemies in order to love God and to save themselves. Degenerate human beings attain that kind of love only by being reborn in the spirit of God's grace and faith in Jesus Christ. Jesus is the perfect model of charity.

It is useful to contrast Winthrop's Puritan conception of the law of nature and the law of Grace or the Gospel with the liberal conception of the law (or laws) of nature as represented by John Locke and the Declaration of Independence. Liberal thought adopts the Christian terms "the law of nature" and "the state of nature" but gives those traditional terms new meaning. Locke refers to the "law of nature" as the "law of reason." It is thus a rule of conduct that reasonable people can apply in the "state of nature." The "state of nature" is the natural condition that all human beings are in whenever they "execute the law of nature" for themselves or are free to pursue their own good as reason dictates—that is, whenever their natural rights are not restricted by legitimate government or infringed upon by some form of unwarranted aggression. Reason can discover the self-evident truth that human beings are born with the equal capacity (and thus the right) to be free and independent. No divine authority is required to justify natural rights. The individual comes before and takes precedence over the political community. To be sure, Locke often appeals to God in one way or another as well as to the consideration that individuals should promote the public good and the good of mankind; but he shows that they should do so in order to secure their rights: self-preservation is the first principle of human nature. Needless to say, conflicts arise when individuals "execute the law of nature," especially if they are competing for scarce or valuable goods and defending their rights. Moreover, it is reasonable to assume that many people will be unreasonable when defining their interests or settling scores. Consequently, the "state of nature" slides into a "state of war" that poses such grave dangers that reasonable individuals consent to give up a part of their rights in order to institute a government that will secure the remainder of their rights. Government is legitimated by the consent of the governed. It has no divine basis or ends. The people, as a majority, have the right to choose, alter, or abolish their government. But liberal government should promote the right to pursue private property—especially money—in order to give individuals a greater stake in civil liberty and stable government. In Locke's view, securing natural rights is good for oneself, one's polity, and mankind (*Second Treatise of Government*, esp. chaps. 2, 3, 5, 8, 19).

The observation that human beings tend to be self-interested and belligerent would come as no surprise to Winthrop or any other Puritan. But Locke's scheme of government would seem like a futile attempt to make hay while the sun shines in the center of a storm. The teaching that self-interest properly understood is good for one and all is doomed to failure because it denies the wages of sin. To be sure, to improve the world one must deal effectively with the world as it stands; but true peace and prosperity can only be attained by understanding why the world is full of strife and by living as a Christian. Providence may separate political societies into classes, but only a deep dedication to the good of the community can harmonize its otherwise discordant parts. In this vein, Winthrop stresses that most people tend to seek wealth, even in a Christian community. The vices and temptations of the rich and the poor can fracture the community, and the religious and political authorities must establish strong inducements to virtue and restraints on self-aggrandizement. Accordingly, Winthrop focuses on such general and constant temptations as selfishness and greed, and he lays down strict guidelines for the proper relationship between the rich and the poor even before he and his pilgrims set foot on the new land.

Winthrop defines the rich rather modestly as "all such as are able to live comfortably by their own means duly improved; and all others are poor according to the former distribution." Insofar as a majority of the community can become rich in that sense, especially in the promising circumstances of America, he is not only reflecting on relationships between particular individuals who happen to be rich and poor but also on the proper way for the rich and the poor to regard wealth in terms of the common good. Christians should deal with one another according to two basic rules: "Justice and Mercy." Justice is defined by the political rules that regulate such ordinary actions as the making and keeping of contracts. Mercy defines the inner disposition with which Christians should treat others in need. Because justice involves rules of conduct that apply to particular cases in general circumstances, Winthrop sets aside the consideration of justice and focuses on mercy. The quality of mercy is constant and is the heart of justice. Doing one's duty as a member of the community; giving what is owed to others in the deepest sense; not claiming one's rights against one's debtors or, in a larger sense, against the community—together these bind individuals into a community. The quality of mercy puts the rich, who have received the gifts of God in abundance, at the service of the needy so as to share those gifts and thereby strengthen the community for the glory of God (*CCM* 77–79; cf. Locke, *First Treatise of Government*, par. 42).

The rich exercise the duty of mercy in three ways: giving, lending, and forgiving. There is no preset formula or regular procedure for exercising that duty, for the Gospel and reason indicate that mercy must be adapted to different social and political circumstances or spiritual seasons. In ordinary times, the rich give out of their abundance. But extraordinary times call for extraordinary measures. Christians stand ready to aid the community in peril or one's Christian brothers and sisters in distress even beyond one's means. The martyrs of the original communal church set the standard for all Christians. To be sure, in ordinary times, a Christian father must provide for his own family. Parental duty is a building block of a Christian community and warranted by the law of nature and Scripture. Nonetheless, even in ordinary times, he cannot do too much for the poor or the community. But times do change, and one should stand ready to forgive one's debtors, to sell one's goods and give the money to the needy, and, if called upon, to lay down one's life. A Christian should take his bearings not from the gifts God bestows on the faithful in good times but from the duty of mercy as performed in the most demanding circumstances of the most extraordinary times. The quality of mercy is defined by the life and sacrifice of Jesus Christ (*CCM* 79).

Winthrop's emphasis that the exhortation to use God's blessings in the service of God and the community must be "generall and perpetuall" implies the difficulty that even good Christians will have in living up to that standard. The love of wealth is a root of evil, and it steals the heart away from the love of God and the common good. Winthrop thus exhorts his company to remember the biblical injunction that "where your treasure is there will your heart be also." Lovers of wealth put life itself in its service at the expense of the true treasures that are gained by loving and obeying God. It is not only right but ultimately also in the service of one's own good to love and serve God; it is wrong and shortsighted to love wealth. Material goods are temporary and insubstantial; they are subject to rust, the thief, and the moth. The pleasures of the body are as ephemeral as the body itself, whereas the divine treasures of the heart are immediately fulfilling and as everlasting as the soul. Christians can hope that God will bless the righteous and merciful in this world, and that regardless of one's worldly circumstances—for God's ways are mysterious—God will reward the righteous and merciful when they stand before Him on the day of account (*CCM* 80).

Winthrop's conception of the "duty of mercy" goes beyond outlining the actions that Christians should perform in particular circumstances. Acts of mercy performed in obedience to the letter of God's law should be the outward expression of the spirit of the law. Duty requires right actions; but mercy arises from the proper state of affection in the soul. One should do one's duty like it or not, but in these terms one might shirk one's duty because it seems to require doing good to others at one's own expense. Scripture, however, enjoins that the duty of mercy is to be practiced "cheerfully." The cheerful doing of one's duty to serve others depends on love. The Gospel makes it plain that love is the fulfillment of God's law. Doing one's duty to be merciful in a properly loving manner constitutes Christian charity. Charity unites the right actions of the body with the proper condition of the soul. It is a full expression of one's love of God in this world. Winthrop therefore stresses that in promoting mercy one cannot rely on the reasonableness of doing one's duty, for reason may direct a rational mind to perform some present act of mercy, but it cannot form a habit in the soul that will prompt mercy on each and every occasion. It is only when Christians cultivate the love of God for all His children in their hearts that they perform their duty to be merciful reliably and with good cheer (*CCM* 81–84).

The problem of doing one's duty to be merciful involves original sin. God created Adam in His own image as a perfect model of mankind and he was perfect in his habit of love. But Adam's fall ensured that mankind would follow his bad example: "whence it comes that every man is borne with this principle in him, to love and seeke himselfe only and thus a man contunueth till Christ comes and takes possession of the soule, and infuseth another principle love to God and our brother." The seeds of spiritual rebirth and thus of Christian charity are sown in young souls in loving Christian families united together in a Christian community. Christian charity, in turn, is the ligament that binds the community together as one body. "Love," as the Scripture defines it, "is the bond of perfection." Only love can bond the members of the community together so closely that they can feel each other's pleasures and pains, and share in each other's infirmities and strengths. When bound together by love, if one member suffers all suffer; if one is honored, all rejoice. True community thus rests on neither common interests nor mutual obligations, for the quality of human life and community alike is strained without mercy. It is love in the spirit of Christ alone that makes the practice of mercy constant, easy, and the source of joy and fulfillment (*CCM* 84–86).

Winthrop freely acknowledges that someone might object that it is not possible to cultivate and uphold love without hope of requital. But Christian love does not require total self-abnegation. It is quite the opposite. Christian love is its own reward, and there is none greater. All of the blessings that God may bestow on a person in this world pale in comparison to the priceless treasures of love; indeed, the "soule covetts love more than all the wealthe in the world." When one gives to another in the spirit of Christian love, love is always returned to the advantage of the lover, and thus "love and affection among members of the same body are reciprocal in a most equal and sweet kind of commerce." Herein lies the heart of the truest kind of earthly equality within a political community. Subordinating oneself to the community and to the benefit of others is no real sacrifice inasmuch as "to love and live beloved is the soules paradise, both here and in heaven." To be sure, Winthrop's model of Christian charity acknowledges or justifies forms of political, social, and economic inequality. But, on its own terms, the real issue is whether or not Winthrop is correct when he avers that "to love and live beloved is the soules paradise" and that such a love is the fruit of Christian charity (*CCM* 88–89).

Winthrop reminds his company that their task of establishing a Christian community is being undertaken by their mutual consent in conformity with God's special Providence. They are to establish a due form of ecclesiastical and civil government. Thus, forms of government, like justice, are established with an eye to particular circumstances. Church and state are separate in structure and function but united in purpose. Christian government rests on the consent of the governed but is defined by its end: "The end is to improve our lives to do more service to the lord the comforte and encrease of the body of christe whereof we are members that our selves and posterity may be the better preserved from the Common corruptions of this evil world to serve the lord and work out our Salvacion under the power and purity of his holy Ordinances" (*CCM* 90). These are the ends that Winthrop and his company of Puritans have in mind as they approach the shores of the New World. They are consenting to be God's agents in the advancing of divine Providence. They are making a covenant with God. That covenant is made by each individual as a member of the corporate body of the community in the service of God. True consent entails a willingness to obey the ordinances of God, be subject to God's will, and do God's work. They are covenanting to be God's chosen people. By making that covenant, Winthrop and his company of Puritans are continuing the line of sacred covenants made between God and Noah, Abraham, Moses, and the nation of Israel. America is the new promised land. It can be a land of freedom, justice, and charity under God.

Winthrop therefore concludes by exhorting his companions that they must consider their political society "a Citty upon a Hill." Their safe passage to the shores of New England signifies God's ratification of their covenant. That covenant holds two possibilities. If they fail to observe its articles, God will bring down His wrath upon them. Failure will be evident by the prosecution of their "carnal intentions" or selfish worldly interests for themselves and their posterity: they shall be made "a story and a by-word" throughout the world and cause the enemies of God to speak evil of Him. But if they fulfill their covenant, the God of Israel will make them "a praise and a glory" so that all those who follow them will pray that their community will be like the one that the Puritan faithful established in the New World (*CCM* 91–93). They will be models of Christian charity.

Winthrop's conception of the Puritan founding as a "Citty upon a Hill" anticipates historically and stands in plain contrast philosophically and politically to America's revolutionary liberal founding. Paine's proclamation in *Common Sense* that Americans, by undertaking a liberal revolution, can enshrine freedom and "construct the noblest, purest constitution on the face of the earth" repudiates as well as parallels Winthrop's conception. Alexander Hamilton completes that proclamation in *The Federalist* no. 1 by stating that Americans, by adopting the Constitution, can settle the issue of whether "societies of men can establish good government by reflection and choice" or must continue to depend on "accident and force." Paine and Hamilton thereby imply that Winthrop's "Citty" belongs to a primitive period of history characterized by religious superstition, philosophical ignorance, and political oppression—the "dark and slavish times" of "accident and force"—that can be overcome by liberal enlightenment and revolution.[3]

The victory of liberalism tends to recast the Puritan founding so as to make it anticipate and thus to support the superiority of liberalism. In other words, oppressive Puritan politics seem to contradict the best of Puritan intentions in a way that points toward liberal ideals as the very fulfillment of the promise of Puritan society. In this light, the American Revolution and Founding seem to complete the "Citty upon a Hill." Liberty is the issue, and liberalism redefines Puritan liberty in liberal terms. As every schoolchild in America today knows, the Puritans came to America to escape from the rampant religious intolerance and political persecution that characterized illiberal Europe and sought to establish a political society in which one could practice religion freely. But preliberal Puritans carried the infection of religious intolerance and political persecution with them. Liberal liberty and toleration solve that problem inasmuch as citizens of a government that secures individual liberty and thus establishes a separation of church and state can worship freely. In this way, the aspirations of the Puritans are realized in the principles of the Revolution as defined by Jefferson in the Declaration and the "Act for Establishing Religious Freedom" as well as by the Constitution and its Bill of Rights.

It is this sort of recasting that makes it so difficult for Americans today to evaluate Puritanism on its own terms or to appreciate the possibility that Puritan principles infuse the virtues or alleviate the vices of liberal principles and politics. Needless to say, liberalism does not assimilate Puritanism all at once; and for a good while after the Revolution, some astute American patriots engaged in the attempt to bolster the virtues and remedy the vices of an ever more dominant liberalism by deliberately assimilating liberalism back into Puritanism. For example, George Bancroft portrays the fusion of America's dual founding in his "Oration Delivered to the Democracy of Springfield" of July 4, 1836. Like Tocqueville, Bancroft discerns that the principles embodied in the Declaration are the same as those interwoven in the fabric of the earliest settlements of New England and carried across the Atlantic in the *Mayflower* by the Pilgrims. In this view, liberty, democracy, and Christianity are essential dimensions of one and the same spirit, a spirit that brought into being "the golden age of New England," an age of grand accomplishment and progress that stands as the foundation and model for America. Bancroft believes that critical problems of America's liberal Founding can only be solved by reforming American liberalism in the light of the principles of the Puritan "Citty upon a Hill." The question is whether that accommodation of liberalism by Puritanism was ever even possible without undermining Puritan principles and inadvertently advancing the cause and historical course of liberalism.

John Cotton on the Principles of a Christian Calling

In "Christian Calling," John Cotton outlines the Puritan conception of vocation or work. Work is a necessary ingredient of any successful political society, and it plays an especially critical part in the personal and civic life of a Puritan in early America. The Puritan conception of work concerns a person's "calling" or particular vocation in the context of the religious and civic life of the community. It often focuses on one's task within the economy, and it includes the proper disposition of the individual and of the community toward material rewards or the acquisition of property. In short, Cotton defines what has come to be known as the Protestant work ethic. Winthrop's "Christian Charitie: A Model Hereof" outlines the general principles or attitudes with which Puritans should treat work and property once they arrive on the shores of New England; Cotton defines the requirements of work and property in an established and generally well-ordered Puritan community. Winthrop anticipates the most extraordinary and demanding circumstances while Cotton deals with the possibilities and problems of ordinary life. By defining what is and what is not a warranted Christian vocation, Cotton reflects Winthrop's concern that the exhortation to guard against "carnal" temptations and to foster Christian charity must be "generall and perpetuall."

Cotton introduces the topic of a Christian calling by stating that he will be speaking about how one should live by faith in one's outward and worldly affairs. He stresses that a true Christian practices his vocation in the light of faith in the teaching of Jesus Christ.[4] The first article of this faith is that it "drawes the heart of a Christian to live in some warrantable calling; as soon as ever a man begins to look toward God, and the ways of his grace, he will not rest till he find some warrantable Calling and employment." It is God who calls upon Christians to seek out some worldly vocation or work, and thus good Christians seek out and practice their vocations as a part of their covenant with God and a necessary path to their salvation both on earth and in heaven. Inasmuch as God assigns some sort of employment to every human being, to be unemployed is to fail to heed God's call or to refuse God's graces. In this sense, God is the great employer, and the primary duty or vocation of a Christian is to seek proper employment. It does not matter whether one becomes a farmer, a tailor, or a governor, and one must not rest until some warrantable calling is found. No one should work just to get by; no one should be seeking fortune and fame. Employment and its fruits are signs of God's grace and of one's good faith, and willful unemployment or improper employment is a vice and reflects a condition of sin. Needless to say, the performance of one's calling comprises a basic part of one's self-respect as well as of how one is regarded by the members of one's church or community (*CC* 319).

Cotton repeatedly emphasizes that a calling must be a "warrantable calling." Neither sheer faith, on the one hand, nor merely working hard, on the other hand, constitutes a warrantable calling. Faith and employment must be properly grounded, integrated, and directed. The touchstone of a warrantable calling that serves God is that it aims at the public good. A vocation is not a means to one's material self-interest but an opportunity and a vehicle to serve others. The core of the Protestant work ethic, then, is not hard work but good works. A calling strengthens one's faith as well as the Christian community inasmuch as all its members are working toward the same end. A calling, to use Winthrop's words, is a vehicle for God to spread his blessings to man by man, and thus it is a tangible expression of charity on the part of individuals and the community as a whole (*CC* 319).

Cotton defines several more specific conditions of a warrantable calling. God must give a person the gifts for a particular vocation. A person must have the intellectual capacity and emotional disposition to succeed or even to excel at one's vocation. Indeed, one must seek out that vocation that utilizes one's greatest gifts or capacities to the best advantage of the community. Insufficient ability indicates that God has not called one to practice that vocation. The hierarchy that Winthrop regards as God's vehicle for spreading his blessings to man by man reflects the natural distribution as well as the diversity of human talents. But individuals must always remember that they owe their talents and calling to God, and not to their own efforts, family background, or chance. Moreover, individuals can exercise their talents and practice their vocations only within the community as an interdependent whole. The distribution of talents and successful practicing of vocations thus entails duties or debts to the community and to God. In sum, a vocation is warranted when "one serves God by serving men, and serves men by serving God" (*CC* 320).

Searching for a warrantable vocation requires one to look for signs of God's Providence in one's own life or to follow where God is leading. One must gain employment by "warrantable means"—that is, directly and honestly and, in general, by being guided by the advice and approval of one's family, friends, neighbors, and community. Cotton also defines the proper attitude toward one's calling. One must humbly depend on God as the source of all benefits and for strength and the further development of one's abilities. Thus, however exalted one's position and successful one's endeavors, the credit goes to God and not oneself. Difficulties and dangers are confronted in the knowledge that the work of this world is performed in the spirit of God with an eye to heaven, and thus one can perform one's vocation with great peace of mind and comfortably, even in the face of grave dangers. One should work "cheerfully." If it seems warranted, one may even pursue a calling against opposition from the community. But one must not be proud, for pride springs from the overweening sense of one's worth and abilities. Indeed, faith encourages one to seek the most humble, homely, difficult, and dangerous of vocations, even or especially those that a "carnal and proud" heart would feel ashamed to perform. Finally, one must be ready to lay down one's vocation, however successful or exalted it seems, if Providence points in a new direction. In sum, a person of faith does not "pick and choose" among vocations as a worldly and proud person would but humbly seeks God's guidance in all ways, and he works comfortably and cheerfully in the knowledge that the fruits of one's labor belong to God (*CC* 321–26).

In this light, the Puritan concept of a calling may be compared to the liberal concept of the right to private property or to pursue happiness in one's own way. To a Puritan, obeying or refusing to obey God's ordinances is an act of free will. But one should answer God's call and choose that vocation for which one is suited according to talent and the common good. It is not a question of doing what one wants but knowing one's place. Once again, this view might seem like an excuse for inequality and oppression. As Winthrop argues, however, the diversity of abilities and unequal distribution of power and goods appears to be a fact of life. Liberalism itself observes that unequal talents and degrees of industry lead to political, social, and economic inequalities when individuals are free to pursue private property or happiness; but it protects the equal opportunity to that pursuit. The Puritan calling, however, also militates against a rigid class or caste system because talents and opportunities are considered on an individual basis and are not tied to considerations of family or class. In principle, every member of the community is open to God's call and respects the fruits of ability, virtue, and faith. Liberalism links the natural rights to life and liberty to private property, and promotes the rational and industrious acquisition of money or capitalism as a means to prosperity and peace, and thus to securing the rights to life, liberty, and the pursuit of happiness; it thereby promotes a way of life that is dedicated to rational industry in the name of one's own good and the public good. The Puritan calling, by contrast, attempts to shield one's own good and the common good from chance and the devices of self-aggrandizement; it is designed to be a vehicle of Christian charity that brings God's blessings directly to the community as a whole.

Puritanism and liberalism thus both stress an ethic of work but differ radically on its substance and goals. But the current doctrine, originally formulated by Max Weber in *The Protestant Ethic and the Spirit of Capitalism*, maintains that the Protestant work ethic itself gives rise to capitalism. In this view, the dedication to hard work and money making that animates capitalism is a psychological residue and historical consequence of a decayed and dying Puritan civilization; the Puritan devotion to work lives on in the spirit of capitalism after the influence of the Puritan religion has run its course. But that view may be a part of the recasting of Puritanism in the light of liberalism; if so, it fails to appreciate the core of a Christian calling and the irreconcilable differences between the Puritan work ethic and the spirit of liberal capitalism on their own terms.

Nathaniel Niles on Christian Liberty and Reform

In his "Discourse on Liberty," Nathaniel Niles appeals to Americans on the brink of revolution to reform their errant ways by reaffirming the principles of their Puritan forefathers. His immediate goal is to "awaken in his countrymen, proper sentiments and emotions, respecting both civil and spiritual liberty." He emphasizes the essential link between them by stressing that "the former, without the latter, is but a body without a soul." Niles thus implies that Americans, who are facing a grave crisis concerning civil liberty, have lost sight of that link by focusing on the concerns of the body while neglecting the critical concerns of the soul. The first step in awakening the proper sentiments toward liberty is to show that spiritual liberty is the essence of civil liberty. In sum, religion is the soul of the body politic. It is in this light that Niles seeks to inspire in his countrymen a "genuine spirit of true liberty" (*DL* 258).

Niles first presents this argument as a minister delivering a sermon to his congregation. He then publishes, in somewhat hasty fashion, the "Discourse on Liberty" in order to extend its reach to the general population as quickly as possible. That general population, in 1774, is uncertain and divided about how to regard the rapidly escalating dispute between American colonists and the British government. Are Americans defending their right to civil liberty as British subjects? Are they defending liberty in the name of natural rights as the birthright of all human beings? Are they defending the Christian liberty of their Puritan forefathers? Or is liberty somehow being viewed at once in all or some combination of these ways? General confusion about liberty among Americans points down the path of war with Britain and, what is worse, civil war. The contending conceptions of liberty, perhaps even more importantly, point toward radically different ways of life in the end. Niles, then, is addressing the practical question of what is to be done in the light of defining liberty in order to correct critical mistakes being made by his countrymen on both counts. His awareness of the profound and dangerous implications of the dispute as well as of the various political inclinations and capacities among the people leads him to write with circumspection and caution. Thus, Niles concedes that this is not the time or the place "for becoming entirely acquainted with civil liberty"; and, while he states that "the main ideas alone are attended to" in his "Discourse," he also indicates that the "inquisitive mind will be able to draw a number of important consequences." Niles implies that inspiring a "genuine spirit of true liberty" at this moment of decision depends on those Americans who can draw the right conclusions from his broad argument (*DL* 258).

Niles begins his "Discourse" by appealing to the Bible and quoting Paul in 1 Corinthians 7:21: "Art thou called being a servant? Care not for it; but if thou mayest be made free, use it rather." He admits that this passage, at first glance, seems to justify servitude. He thus raises the pressing issue of the Christian teaching on submission to political authority at its most critical point. To be sure, a good Christian acquiesces in servitude for God's sake to set an example of Christian virtue for one's masters (cf. 1 Peter 2:13). The state of the soul has absolute priority over the needs of one's body; and the love of God can free one's soul regardless of one's political position. Still, the Bible seems to tolerate if not to justify the prerogative of kings and other political authorities, and it does not condemn servitude or slavery as absolutely unjust. Niles thus strangely selects a biblical passage that seems to defend the prerogative of kings rather than the liberty of citizens. But that passage also provides a bridge between prerogative and liberty. As Niles avers, Paul clearly exhorts the servant to prefer liberty, and thus he must prefer liberty for himself and must also be teaching all others that liberty is preferable to servitude. Inasmuch as Christians regard Paul as an Apostle of Christ who is inspired directly by God, Niles indicates that God enjoins all human beings to regard their personal liberty as a great good and servitude as a great evil. Moreover, because Paul regards the personal liberty of an individual as a great good, he must also regard the liberty of a whole community as an even greater good; the slavery of a community is thus proportionately a greater evil than the slavery of an individual. Niles implies that the golden rule as well as Scripture requires Christians, whether kings or slaves, to promote the liberty of all human beings (*DL* 258).

Niles proceeds to define liberty by outlining the perfect standard of liberty and the general nature of civil liberty. He stresses that while no actual political constitution can ever reach the perfect standard of civil liberty, it is only in the light of the perfect standard that the degree to which any given constitution actually participates in civil liberty can be adequately evaluated. As a matter of course, Niles adopts the Christian and classical procedure of establishing the highest standard of how human beings should act or the best regime in principle as the basis for evaluating any given individual or constitution as it is. Niles's theoretical starting point stands in direct contrast to liberalism's defining of personal and civil liberty in terms of human nature as it is in the "state of nature." Niles, however, actually begins his analysis in a peculiar fashion that is explained by his awareness of the differences between his Puritan conception of liberty and the liberal conception of liberty that is now becoming entrenched throughout the land. Instead of proceeding directly to his analysis of the perfect standard of liberty, he finds it necessary to correct some basic mistakes that obscure or corrupt that perfect standard. This move certifies that Niles is directing his argument at two separate aspects of America's impending crisis. On the one hand, he is addressing the relation between liberty in America and the overbearing authority of Great Britain and its king; and on the other hand, he corrects mistaken conceptions of liberty that many Americans have used as the standard of judgment against that overbearing authority. In short, Niles singles out for criticism the poles of the liberal concept of liberty inasmuch as "liberty does not consist in persons thinking themselves free," and "though a certain constitution should be contended for and supported by a majority of voices; yet this would be no sure evidence that it is free." The unhindered pursuit of one's own desires should not be mistaken for freedom rather than license, and the consent of the majority, not to mention the rule of the majority, should not be mistaken for a necessary condition of civil liberty: the majority can be just as wrong, arbitrary, and tyrannical as a king. "Civil Liberty," as Niles defines it, "consists not in any inclinations of the members of a community; but in the being and due administration of such a system of laws, as effectually tends to the greatest good of a state." The nearer a constitution comes to that standard, the more civil liberty it embodies; and as a constitution moves further away from that standard, it must be viewed as a comparative evil (*DL* 259–60).

Perfect freedom requires that the rule of law extend equally to every member of the state and that every member, in turn, obeys the laws both in terms of what is required and what is proscribed. Following in the tradition of such forefathers as Winthrop and Cotton, Niles conceives of civil liberty as subjection to laws that promote the greatest good of the community. In principle, "every one must be required to do all he can that tends to the highest good of the state." Moreover, "every thing, however trifling, that tends, even in the lowest degree, to disserve the interest of the state must also be forbidden." This holds true for every member of the state: no one is above the laws, and good laws thus "render it as easy to bring a royal offender to trial . . . as . . . the meanest subject." The "full worth of a free constitution lies in the full and equal administration of its laws." Perfect freedom, then, entails the correspondence between personal liberty and civil liberty or the good of the individual and the common good, and it is made manifest by the constitution of the state and its laws (*DL* 260).

Niles thus outlines the Puritan principle of true liberty over and against the poles of the mistaken principles of liberal doctrine, and he proceeds to focus on the core issue that separates them: the relation of liberty to self-interest. He announces: "Originally, there were no private interests." That announcement introduces a long footnote that could not have been a part of the original sermon. It is intended to develop an issue that is pertinent to a broad constituency, but the density and theoretical cast of the argument must test the patience of many readers. In sum, that footnote offers a circumspect but critical analysis of the crux of the theoretical dispute between the long-standing and correct Christian doctrine on liberty and self-interest, and that of the newfangled and mistaken doctrine of liberalism. To be sure, it also clarifies the mistaken principles of those advocating the prerogatives of the king. But it scrutinizes the basically mistaken principles of liberty and government that many Tories and Whigs or liberals inadvertently share in common. Niles's chief concern is to put both liberals and Tories back on a proper Christian footing, and thus he emphasizes why threats to liberty in America from an intractable king of England cannot be adequately addressed on the basis of the essentially flawed principles of liberalism. Ultimately, Niles's footnote seems designed to dissuade influential American ministers, politicians, and educators from fomenting revolution instead of inspiring in their countrymen a "genuine spirit of true liberty" and dedicating themselves to Christian reform (*DL* 260).

Niles's announcement that originally there were no private interests is a point of departure for criticizing the liberal conception of the "state of nature." In sum, God alone is the original owner of all creation, and He graciously allows His creatures to participate in and enjoy possessions according to their capacities. Human beings, as rational creatures, are to manage God's blessings for the benefit of the whole of creation or the common good of mankind. Human beings, Niles implies, are not born free, equal, and independent of one another any more than they are born free, equal, and independent of God or of their parents. "Nor was there ever any thing in the world that anyone could call his own, to the exclusion of his fellow men, i.e., in a state of nature." Individuals remain "stewards" of God's blessings. Prior to compact or the agreement of the members of a community to order or distribute the use of the common goods to particular individuals for the advantage of the whole community, there is no such thing as private interest or private property, and "every appearance of private interest was the effect of violent seizure . . . and not of just distribution" (*DL* 260–64).

Niles's argument responds directly to the famous opening query of Locke in chapter 5 of his *Second Treatise of Government*, "Of Property": "how any one should ever come to have a *property* in any thing" if God gave the world to "Mankind in common," and "how Men might come to have a *property* . . . without any express Compact of all the Commoners"? Locke's answer begins with the claim that human beings have a property in their own bodies, and the natural right to self-preservation entails the right to acquire and possess the things that tend to secure and enhance one's life and liberty; investing one's labor in its acquisition makes property one's own and defines the right to private property. The hallmark of private property is that the possessor has the right to destroy it to satisfy himself. One great reason why people leave the state of nature and consent to government is to secure more effectively the right to private property. "*Political Power*," Locke avers, is "a *Right* of making Laws . . . for the Regulating and Preserving of Property, and of employing the force of the Community, in the Execution of such Laws, and in the defence of the Common-wealth from Foreign Injury, and all this only for the Public Good." The majority has the right to establish that form of government that seems most likely to secure their right to private property, and thus the securing of the right to private property is tantamount to the "public good." These Lockean principles, by and large, inspire the spirit of liberty of the American revolutionaries (*Second Treatise*, par. 3, 25; cf. *First Treatise*, par. 86, 92).

It is with this liberal conception of the relation between self-interest or private property and good government in mind that Niles stresses that there are two basic ways in which all earthly governments were originally founded. On the one hand, there is the overbearing and arbitrary exercise of power of individuals; and on the other hand, there "is a compact formed with a particular design to secure and advance the private interests of those by whom the compact was made." To be sure, all liberals would join Niles in condemning the tyrant as a usurper. But Niles maintains that both of these forms "had their rise in usurpation." In both cases, private interests override and undermine the common good. In principle, it makes no difference whether one, a few, or the many do the usurping. In this way, Niles is unmasking Locke's respectable appeal to the rule of law, the community, and the public good as a cover for well-organized selfishness. "Crowned heads," Niles announces, "have a prerogative of doing good, but no prerogative for any private emolument. . . . If he [the king] becomes an obstacle in the way of public good, he is to be removed like any other common nuisance." But that principle also holds true for all forms of government: an overbearing, self-interested majority operates according to "the maxim on which pirates and gangs of robbers live in a kind of unity." Conflicts between kings and majorities over interests should not be mistaken for justice and cannot secure the public good. "It matters not," Niles confirms, "whether men who build their notions of government of self-interest, call themselves whigs or tories, friends to prerogative, or to the liberties of the people." The Puritan forefathers built their "Citty upon a Hill" to replace both of those insupportable origins of government. Those forefathers may have erred in particular instances, but their scheme shows "on what principles we are to stand ready to lay down our lives in the cause of liberty, or which is the same thing, in vindication of good government" (*DL* 262–64).

Having thus outlined the principles of true liberty and carefully opposed them to the mistaken conceptions of liberty of Tories and Whigs alike, Niles proceeds to examine the actual condition of liberty in America in that light. He is no religious or political fanatic out to transform the world into a paradise by forcing others to conform to the perfect standard of liberty. Indeed, he shows the degree of political prudence and moderation implied by that standard by emphasizing that the "abstract notion of liberty" must be applied to political circumstances with all due caution. The complexities and uncertainties of politics, in combination with the partial views and limited capacities of human beings, render it difficult to pass judgment and improve conditions to the greatest advantage. "Some degree of partial oppression is, therefore, to be expected in every human state, even, under the wisest administration." Needless to say, this principle of prudence does not encourage submission to undue oppression; rather, it implies a modification of that perfect standard to allow it to be used as a rule of thumb to judge undue oppression and the means to deal with it. For example, Niles councils that whereas "liberty is not necessarily, nor invariably connected with the voice of a majority; yet, it is much more likely to be found in connection with such a voice, than with that of a minority." Indeed, he insists that "liberty is much rather to be expected in a state where a majority, first institutes, and then varies the constitution according as they apprehend circumstances require, than in any other." Niles's perfect standard of liberty in practice tends to support a government that has the consent of the people. It thus offers a parallel but qualified route to supporting the appeal of liberals to the consent of the governed as the principle of legitimate government. It is, however, only on the basis of true liberty that political opposition or military intervention against an oppressive government ever can be justified. Niles concludes, somewhat equivocally, that it is only "on these maxims that the present British monarch can be exculpated from the several charges of rebellion, treachery, and usurpation." But intelligent minds might conclude on that same basis that the king is dangerously close to proving that he is guilty as charged and that many of his opponents in America are not far behind (*DL* 265).

Niles judges the degree of liberty in any given state by its fruits. Liberty promotes individual virtue and public spirit. That includes promoting industry and producing wealth in a way that cultivates temperance by tying the prosperity of every individual to the prosperity of the community as a whole, and thereby prompts even the selfish passions of pride and avarice to imitate humanity and generosity. Liberty gives citizens the courage and capacity to defend their liberty, and it forms the community into a "bulwark against every assault of lawless power." "What is more than all," as Niles sees it, is that "liberty secures the rights of conscience, by protecting every member of the state in the free exercise of his religion" (but he qualifies that right on the basis of true liberty by adding that "unless it be such a religion as is inconsistent with the good of the state"). The religious education of a free spirit grounds civil liberty, and civil liberty must ensure the rights of conscience and make room for dissent. A broad degree of religious freedom itself nourishes religious devotion and is thus a vital aspect of liberty as well as its most precious fruit. In sum, liberty positively influences every aspect of one's personal and civic life: "every soft and pleasing affection of every soul, would be called forth into vigorous and harmonious exercise," and everyone would see how "*good* and how *pleasant* it is for brethren to dwell together in unity" (*DL* 267–70).

Niles reflects back on his analysis of the state of liberty in contemporary America and admits that he has continued to lead his countrymen to "imagine a state whose members are all of a free spirit." Once again, he seems to be outlining a model of liberty and good government instead of defining a useful course of action based on the actual condition of liberty. But because Americans have long been blessed with a great degree of liberty, and in that every actual bit of liberty reflects the essence of liberty, they can be led to see the form and substance of true liberty and thus the validity of the Christian model by reflecting on their own imperfect experience of it. Niles knows well that there are those who will stigmatize his scheme of liberty as "merely chimerical and romantic." But he insists, against all those who are blinded to the truth by their false realism, that the "reason why we do not experience all the pleasures of liberty . . . is, not any defect in liberty, but the perverseness of our selfish hearts." Niles cannot but confirm that human beings tend to act selfishly and thus that human nature places severe practical limits on the attainment of liberty; nonetheless, in the spirit of Winthrop and Cotton, he believes that he has shown that the very happiness that is coveted by human beings should lead a reasonable mind to recognize the necessity and possibility of Christian liberty (*DL* 270).

Niles presses home his point by offering a series of pithy formulations that recapitulate the key point that "good government is not inconsistent with liberty," for "perfect liberty and perfect government are perfectly harmonious, while tyranny and licentiousness are inconsistent with both" (*DL* 270). Thus, he anticipates and seeks to negate the attempt of such revolutionaries as Thomas Paine to transform such liberal principles as "government even in its best state is but a necessary evil" and its "design and end" is private "freedom and security" into a new "common sense" (*CS* 4–6). Indeed, Paine's liberal position that the end of government entails "securing freedom and property to all men, and above all things the free exercise of religion, according to the dictates of conscience" culminates in his unqualified position on the strict separation between religion and government (*CS* 32). "As to religion," Paine announces, "I hold it to be the indispensable duty of all government to protect all conscientious professors thereof, and I know of no other business which government has to do therewith" (*DL* 40). The difference between Paine and Niles on religious freedom is critical: Niles's qualification that religions inconsistent with the good of the state should not be tolerated is fully consistent with his principle that positive spiritual liberty is the soul of civil liberty; Paine's exhortation to Americans to dispel any lingering hopes of reconciliation with Britain by bringing "the doctrine of reconciliation to the touchstone of nature" implies a repudiation of Christianity and that religious freedom is a condition of freedom from religion itself (*CS* 24–25).

It may be that the likes of Niles, at least as of 1774, would have preferred reconciliation with the British Crown to the horrors of civil war—but not at any price, and surely not on the terms being set by the British. Niles thus continues to stress that anyone, regardless of one's political station, who infringes on liberty rebels against good government; and anyone who rises up against good government is an enemy to liberty. He continues to indicate that it is the king who must be treated as a rebel if he will not reconcile himself to liberty and good government. To be sure, lovers of liberty should encourage the king to reform, and they should not tolerate his usurpations and depredations. Precisely because liberty is a gift entrusted to human beings by "Heaven" or "the God of nature," and because citizens are "stewards" of that blessing, they have a sacred duty to defend liberty. Niles conspicuously appeals to "duty" and "stewardship" some six times in the course of a few sentences. On the one hand, he stresses the duty of citizens to participate actively in the defense of liberty; but, on the other hand, he underscores the differences between reform on the basis of Christian liberty and revolution in the name of alleged inalienable natural rights. Accordingly, Niles announces that "liberty is not an absolute right of our own, if it were, we might support, and guard, or neglect it at pleasure. It is a loan of heaven, for which we must account with the great God." The duty to defend liberty should not be placed in the hands of the few who govern while all others attend to their personal affairs; that common duty is urgent in the light of a "consideration of the avaricious, and aspiring disposition of mankind in general, and the peculiar opportunities and temptations that Governors have to indulge them." Indeed, the crisis in America makes it "the most simple common sense" that every man, woman, and child is called upon to "struggle for the preservation of those rights of mankind which are inexpressibly dear" (*DL* 271–72).

That last appeal to the "rights of mankind," especially in combination with the preceding appeal to the "God of Nature," raises a curious and even perplexing point of comparison between the principles that ground Niles's "common sense" and those that ground Paine's *Common Sense* and the Declaration. It seems that Niles in 1774 reaches a similar conclusion about the need to resist tyranny as the one reached by Paine and Jefferson in 1776. But Niles has thus far in his "Discourse" carefully pointed to the theoretical and moral differences between his path to that conclusion and the one taken by the liberal revolutionaries. And yet, at this high point in his argument, he also appeals to ideas that are characteristic of the liberal conception of liberty. Is he intentionally incorporating those appeals into his exhortation and harmonizing aspects of those discordant positions in order to reach out to as many of his countrymen as he possibly can so as to bring them back to "the most simple common sense"? Or is Niles inadvertently revealing that core liberal principles have penetrated so deeply into the fabric of his Christian culture that they have become "common sense" even to influential American Christians who are otherwise resisting the rising tide of liberalism?

This question becomes critical in the light of Niles's poignant conclusion. Americans must neither acquiesce in the king's usurpations nor resist them for the wrong reasons. Civil war between Americans making those opposite mistakes would most likely mean calamity for all Americans. Niles has indicated that self-interest conditions both of those positions, and he now pinpoints their common vices. The rampant growth of pride and luxury throughout America paradoxically installs the yoke of servitude while fanning the flames of revolution and war. Accordingly, Niles exhorts Americans to "encourage no practice, in ourselves or others, that tends to enslave our country." In that sense, it is all the same whether one supports the king's usurpations or rebels against him for the sake of one's material prosperity: both usurp liberty and promote slavery. The political conflict between them may be couched in terms of liberty and good government, but it is essentially over private goods. "Is it not to be feared," Niles queries, "that an appetite for the leeks and onions, is the source of our difficulty?" "But if we will risqué our country for the sake of a few superfluities, posterity may curse our pride and luxury, and the present generation may find that death and carnage will terminate their folly." Niles summarizes the goals of political opposition and also reiterates his own paradox by reconfirming that every individual should be "vigilant, zealous, and firm in pursuing any measures for the security of our rights" (*DL* 273).

Niles's culminating appeal to his countrymen to "encourage no practice, in ourselves or others, that tends to enslave our country" goes right to the heart of moral vice in America and returns to the theme of his opening quotation from Paul. He rivets attention on slavery in America: the swelling of pride and luxury comes to a head in this odious institution. It may be true, as Niles indicates, that the Bible acquiesces in slavery under certain circumstances, but the Bible never justifies slavery—indeed, it teaches that slavery is evil. American slavery is particularly heinous precisely because Americans have enjoyed the blessings of liberty to a great degree and for a long time. Indeed, Americans boast of their liberty and free spirit, but a truly free spirit would no more be inclined to subject others to slavery than to submit to it. A truly free spirit seeks neither license nor tyranny. The acquiescence of the majority in the existence of slavery reveals that license and tyranny hide in the facade of American liberty. Having succumbed to the "carnal" temptations that accompany liberty, Americans are usurping the "genuine spirit of true liberty." Slavery is only the most extreme and visible manifestation of that usurpation. The license and tyranny of the king parallels the license and tyranny of the majority. In this light, Americans have no moral basis on which to object when others subject them to an evil that they are themselves subjecting on others. In that case, liberty is already lost. The question is whether it can be regained. Niles advises: "Let us therefore choose the good and refuse the evil, that we may live and not die" (*DL* 274).

America can fulfill its promise as a "Citty upon a Hill" only insofar as a majority of Americans remain inspired by a "genuine spirit of true liberty." Americans can remain inspired only by remembering what it means to be free. The exhortation, as Winthrop knows from the beginning, must be "generall and perpetuall." Niles leaves little doubt that every American has a duty to resist the usurpations of the king. But he leaves no doubt that Christians have a duty to resist license as well as tyranny. Liberty, like charity, begins at home. Americans turn a blind eye to slavery because they privately covet luxury while boasting about liberty to indulge their pride. Niles reveals how liberty can be lost sight of even as the path of the Revolution becomes increasingly clear. At bottom, liberalism treats the body while corrupting the soul. At its best, liberalism inspires a dedication to the liberty and rights of mankind that brings citizens to rise above themselves in the spirit of patriotism and philanthropy. But it may be that Christian liberty and Christian charity infuse that noble liberal spirit, and thus the best as well as the worst of liberalism reveals the need for Americans to "return to their fathers house." "It is high time for us to reform."

Notes

1. John Winthrop, "Christian Charitie: A Modell Hereof," in *Puritan Political Ideas 1558–1794*, ed. Edmund S. Morgan (Indianapolis: Bobbs-Merrill Educational Publishing, 1965), 76–93, hereafter cited in the text as *CCM*; and Nathaniel Niles, "Two Discourses on Liberty," in *American Political Writings during the Founding Era 1760–1805*, ed. Charles S. Hyneman and Donald S. Lutz (Indianapolis: Liberty Press, 1983), 1:257–76, esp. 273, hereafter cited in the text as *DL*.

2. Winthrop may believe that divine will and Christian faith define the parameters of human affairs properly conducted, but he does not maintain that God or Christian faith (as will be made evident below in his reflections on the sinful nature of humanity) require human beings to abandon reason by accepting all of the ways that human beings tend to act for the way that they ought to act. Reason, properly understood, supports divine revelation and discerns divine Providence. Winthrop thus turns to a series of reasons that support his basic proposition about hierarchy and inequality, offers reasonable objections to those reasons, raises questions about the objections, and then provides answers to those questions. Of course, he ties his reasons to Scripture as the final proof, for he regards only instruction based on faith in the God of the Bible as perfectly reasonable. Ultimately, all attempts to understand human beings as they are and as they ought to be apart from revelation are bound to fail.

3. Thomas Paine, *Common Sense*, ed. Nelson F. Adkins (Indianapolis: Bobbes-Merrill Educational Publishing, 1953), 51 and 7, hereafter cited in the text as *CS*; and Alexander Hamilton, James Madison, and John Jay, *The Federalist Papers*, ed. Clinton Rossiter (New York: Mentor, 1961), 33.

4. John Cotton, "Christian Calling," in *The Puritans*, ed. Perry Miller and Thomas H. Johnson (New York: American Book Company, 1938), 319, hereafter cited in the text as *CC*.

Chapter 2

Thomas Hutchinson and James Otis on Sovereignty, Obedience, and Rebellion

Howard L. Lubert

By the 1760s and 1770s, no colonial figure was more reviled and subject to the wrath of the American colonists than Thomas Hutchinson (1711–1780). According to one colonist, he was "the first, the most malignant and *insatiable* enemy" of the colonies, having "committed greater public crimes, than his life can repair or death satisfy."[1] James Otis's (1725–1783) public reputation was less consistent. In the fall of 1765, however, when Hutchinson's infamy was settled and public fury over the Stamp Act was at its peak, no colonist was more revered than Otis.[2] And no colonial figure was more dedicated than Otis to soiling Hutchinson's reputation or more responsible for debasing it.[3]

Whatever the ultimate source of Otis's animosity, if the motivation was a belief that Hutchinson was a traitor to the colonial cause, then Otis's (and the public's) venom was misplaced. Hutchinson opposed the Stamp Act, lobbying the ministry privately against its passage. In fact, Otis and Hutchinson were in many respects political and philosophic kin. Both men were liberals who derived legitimate politics from the consent of the governed, linked liberty inexorably to the security of private property, and articulated a right to resist repressive rulers. Both men merit study because they were especially able and active political thinkers, standing at the cusp of an intellectual revolution in American political thought as the colonists replaced the common law tradition with a new constitutionalism.

In their writings, Hutchinson and Otis drew generously from liberal sources—in particular, John Locke's *Second Treatise of Government* (1690). Their indebtedness to Locke was typical among colonial thinkers of the period, who were drawn to Locke in part because the *Second Treatise* was a response to a seventeenth-century constitutional crisis not unlike the one emerging in the colonies. The former crisis involved a contest between the king and Parliament for possession of sovereignty. The 1688 Glorious Revolution resolved the conflict, locating sovereignty in Parliament (strictly speaking, in the King-in-Parliament). Three-quarters of a century later, parliamentary sovereignty was itself being challenged as the colonists vowed to prevent the Stamp Act's execution.

The colonists objected to the Stamp Act because, in their opinion, Parliament had levied a tax on them without their consent. Because they were legally denied the franchise in parliamentary elections, they were not represented at Westminster. Denied representation, Parliament could not lawfully tax them; otherwise, Parliament would possess arbitrary power over them, a power which, as Locke had shown, no government could rightfully wield. Of course, the colonists' argument could also justify noncompliance with all parliamentary law. At first, the colonists avoided this conclusion. Instead, they claimed that they had originally consented (through the colonial charters) to parliamentary rule over the general affairs of the empire, particularly in matters of trade and commerce. The colonial governments individually retained the power to tax and authority over their "internal police," that is, over matters wholly internal to a particular colony. In other words, the colonists presented a view of the empire in which sovereignty was divided among different legislatures, a direct challenge to the doctrine of parliamentary sovereignty.

Over the next decade, as the colonists questioned their relationship with England, they revolutionized the way people conceived of constitutional government. At the core of the new constitutionalism was the idea that a constitution is a fixed body of law, paramount to government and enforceable through the courts. Sovereignty resides with the people, who express their will and delegate authority through the constitution. Political authority might be embodied in a single, centralized government, or it might be divided federally among a central and local governments.

On the issue of sovereignty, Hutchinson and Otis actually maintained the traditional view, conceiving it as indivisible and locating it politically in Parliament. In order to justify parliamentary rule over the colonies, Otis and Hutchinson, while rejecting the typical argument for virtual representation, nonetheless discovered sources of colonial consent to parliamentary rule.[4] Both men thus conceived the empire as a decentralized rather than a federal state, acknowledging Parliament's plenary power over the colonies while counseling against its exercise of that authority. By conceding parliamentary sovereignty, and in presenting an equitable rather than a rights-based claim against parliamentary taxes, Otis and Hutchinson offered arguments concerning parliamentary rule far more conservative than those presented by the colonists generally.

In other important respects, however, Otis began to break away from both Hutchinson and from received constitutional thought. Hutchinson maintained the traditional, organic understanding of a constitution as an evolutionary body of laws and institutions that, while made venerable by time and custom, were nonetheless indistinguishable from statutory law. In contrast, Otis was a more original thinker, conceiving of a constitution as a body of fundamental law that limits governmental authority. Otis additionally suggested a role for the courts in upholding constitutional limits to legislative authority, and in doing so he seemed to advocate the doctrine of judicial review.

While Otis's writings today seem to resonate modern constitutional doctrine, Otis himself failed to discern the full import of his argument. Wedded to the idea of parliamentary sovereignty, faithful to the idea of a benevolent Parliament intent on acting in accordance with equity and law, and conceiving the courts as executive bodies, Otis ultimately failed to articulate and defend the claim for judicial review. All the same, Otis was the first colonial theorist to infuse these modern constitutional notions into the public discourse, and his writings are significant because they reflect—and indeed, helped to seed—the revolution in political and legal thought that was just starting to blossom in British America, as the colonists began to rethink the nature of constitutional government and their own constitutional relationship to Great Britain.

Otis as Constitutional Innovator

By 1765, when Parliament passed the Stamp Act, the doctrine of parliamentary sovereignty had become orthodoxy in English political thought. This doctrine held that sovereignty was by nature indivisible, illimitable, and resided in the King-in-Parliament. James Otis penned the first significant colonial response to the theory of parliamentary sovereignty. In his pamphlet *The*

Rights of the British Colonies Asserted and Proved (1764), Otis suggested that a constitution is a written form of fundamental law, created by the people (or their representatives) acting as a constituent sovereign and legally superior to ordinary legislative acts. He further suggested that the courts were empowered to enforce compliance with that fundamental law and could do so by refusing to execute statutory law that conflicted with it.

Otis's pamphlet in many ways was a restatement of an argument that he had made three years earlier while serving as counsel for Boston merchants in *Paxton's Case* (more famously known as the writs of assistance case [1761]). At the heart of that controversy lay a dispute over whether the Massachusetts Superior Court could issue writs of assistance to Crown officials in the colonies. The writs sought by the Crown officials were general search warrants that conferred broad police powers. A general writ empowered its holder, when accompanied by a

> Constable, Headborough, or other public officers . . . and in the day time to enter and go into any House, shop, Cellar, Warehouse or Room or other Place, and in Case of Resistance to break open Doors, Chests, Trunks and other Package, there to seize . . . any Kind of Goods, or Merchandize what soever prohibited and uncustomed and to put and secure the same in his Majesties store House.[5]

There were few significant restrictions on the use of these warrants. The holder of such a warrant decided which places to search, when to search them, and on what basis to conduct the search. He did not have to petition the court for a new warrant each time he wished to conduct a search, and thus he did not have to show a magistrate just cause for each search.

The controversy before the court stemmed from ambiguity in the statutes governing the use of writs of assistance. Through a number of seventeenth-century statutes, Parliament had extended to the Court of Exchequer the power to issue writs of assistance; however, it was unclear whether the legislation was intended to authorize the use of general warrants or, alternatively, special (i.e., limited) warrants. Jeremiah Gridley, the Crown attorney in the case, argued that precedent showed that in carrying out these parliamentary acts, the Exchequer had issued general writs. Moreover, under law, colonial customs officers enjoyed the same powers as their English counterparts. Finally, a provincial law had extended to the Massachusetts Superior Court the powers of the Exchequer. As a result, the court could issue the writ.

Otis challenged the reliability of the source of Gridley's precedent and further argued that the court was not required to follow a precedent that was inconsistent with fundamental principles of law. Otis then offered a far more sweeping and unconventional argument against the use of general writs. He told the court that an "Act [of Parliament] against the Constitution is void: an Act against natural equity is void: and if an Act of Parliament should be made, in the very Words of this Petition [i.e., the writ], it would be void. The executive Courts must pass such Acts into disuse." He then added a reference to Lord Coke's opinion in the celebrated *Bonham's Case* (1610), which he claimed supported his position.[6]

While rhetorically effective, Otis's claim here was not true to Coke's original meaning. Coke was not making a constitutional argument for limits to legislative authority, nor was he implying the power of judicial review. Instead, he was stating the common law doctrine regarding the judicial construction of statutes. Coke believed that statutes ought to and could be construed according to the common law because he believed that Parliament, in its capacity as the high court of England, was guided by the same principles of reason and justice that guided all judicial determinations. Through statutory interpretation, judges brought statutes into conformity with the principles of law inherent in the common law and which Parliament itself intended to promote. As Coke explained in *Bonham's Case*, "some statutes are made against law and right, which those who made them perceiving, would not put them into effect . . . and because it would be against common right and reason, the common law adjudged the said act of Parliament as to that point void."[7] Still, in construing a statute strictly or narrowly, a judge did not rule it unconstitutional in the modern sense. It was only through statutory construction that judges were able to control statutory effects in particular cases. Coke never directly challenged Parliament's legislative authority. As the high court, Parliament remained the final interpreter and expounder of the common law and ultimately of its own power. Where statutory intent was manifest, Parliament's word was final.

Otis, however, seemed to challenge Parliament's statutory authority directly. Otis told the court that if Parliament were to enact a statute manifestly allowing the use of general warrants, the statute would be against natural equity and the constitution—and hence void. Furthermore, he added that the courts would pass such a law "into disuse." The implication that the constitution forms a body of fixed law that the courts are charged to apply even in the face of contradictory parliamentary statutes reappeared three years later in an appendix to *The Rights of the British Colonies*. There Otis repeated almost verbatim the argument he had made to the superior court in *Paxton's Case*, and he cited and quoted a number of authorities to support his claim that Parliament could not enact a statute contrary to natural equity or the constitution.[8] Among the sources he quoted was a lengthy passage from Emmerich de Vattel's *Law of Nations* (bk. 1, chap. 1, § 34). The passage from Vattel, used in this context, is so suggestive of the new constitutionalism that it deserves to be quoted at length.

> A very important question here presents itself. It essentially belongs to the society to make laws both in relation to the manner in which it desires to be governed, and to the conduct of the citizens: this is called the *legislative power*. The nation may entrust the exercise of it to the prince or an assembly, or to the assembly and the prince jointly, who have then a right of making new and abrogating old laws. It is here demanded whether if their power extends so far as to the fundamental laws they may change the constitution of the state. The principles we have laid down lead us to decide this point with certainty that the authority of these legislators does not extend so far, and that they ought to consider the fundamental laws as sacred if the nation has not in very express terms given them the power to change them. For the constitution of the state ought to be fixed; and since that was first established by the nation, which afterwards trusted certain persons with the legislative power, the fundamental laws are excepted from their commission. (*RBC* 476)

Otis seemed to distinguish between a constitution and statutory law. Considered in the context of *Paxton's Case*, Otis seemed to argue that Parliament could not mandate the use of general search warrants without exceeding the powers conferred on it by the constitution.

Additionally, Otis again suggested that insofar as the constitution embodies the fundamental laws of the state, these constitutional limits could be enforced by ordinary courts of justice. "'Tis hoped," Otis wrote,

> it will not be considered as a new doctrine that even the authority of the Parliament of *Great Britain* is circumscribed by certain bounds which if exceeded their acts become those of mere *power* without *right*, and consequently void. The judges of England have declared in favor of these sentiments when they expressly declare that *acts of Parliament against natural equity are void*. That *acts against the fundamental principles of the British constitution are void*. . . . It is contrary to reason that the supreme power should have right to alter the constitution. This would imply that those who are entrusted with sovereignty by the people have a right to do as they please. . . . This is not very remote from a flat contradiction. (*RBC* 476–77)

As if to confirm the authority of the courts to pass laws "into disuse," he then cited numerous legal precedents on that point. Quoting the words of Sir Thomas Powys, who in the *Duchess of*

Hamilton's Case (1712) had cautioned that "[j]udges will strain rather hard than interpret an Act void *ab initio* [from the beginning]," Otis added: "This is granted, but still their [Parliament's] authority is not boundless if subject to the control of the judges in any case" (*RBC* 476).[9]

Where, exactly, did Otis purport to find this fixed body of law that circumscribed Parliament's authority? Otis maintained that British subjects had always lived under a compact. When King James II abdicated the throne in 1688, "the original compact was broken to pieces" (*RBC* 470). A new compact was needed and the Convention Parliament subsequently produced one. "[T]he form and mode of government is to be settled by *compact*, as it was rightfully done by the Convention after the abdication of *James* II" (*RBC* 429). For Otis, the Bill of Rights and the Act of Succession constituted a type of fixed, fundamental law which Parliament could not lawfully transgress. "The present establishment," he wrote, was "founded on the law of GOD and of nature [and] was begun by the Convention with a professed and real view in all parts of the *British* empire to put the liberties of the people out of the reach of arbitrary power in all times to come" (*RBC* 430). Otis then transcribed large portions of the Bill of Rights in order to "show the rights of all British subjects, both at home and abroad," which stand as "the first principles of law and justice, and the great barriers of a free state and of the British constitution in particular" (*RBC* 430).

Moreover, Otis anticipated the objection that the Bill of Rights was enacted by Parliament and thus was not a constitution in the modern sense of the term. He likewise anticipated the argument that King James had merely abandoned the throne and that, consequently, no dissolution of government had occurred. After stating that the "form and mode of government" were settled by the Convention Parliament, he explained that "[t]here was neither time for nor occasion to call the whole people together." Nevertheless, "[i]f they had not liked the proceedings [of the Parliament,] it was in their power to control them, as it would be should the supreme legislative or executive powers ever again attempt to enslave them" (*RBC* 429). In short, Otis implied that the Convention Parliament represented the people in their constituent capacity in a manner consistent with modern constitutional theory.

Otis's argument in the *Paxton's Case* and *The Rights of the British Colonies* is significant because it posits a rule of law superior to Parliament and further implies the doctrine of judicial review. Otis suggested that even an expressly stated statute which ran afoul of the constitution or natural equity would be passed "into disuse" by the courts. Moreover, his language implies that the court's invalidation of statutory law is decisive, and it is decisive precisely because Parliament's authority is not illimitable. Instead, its power is limited by a constitution derivative of the people. Paraphrasing Blackstone, Otis agreed that "an original supreme, sovereign, absolute, and uncontrollable *earthly* power *must* exist and preside over every society, from whose final decisions there can be no appeal but directly to Heaven." But this absolute power, he concluded, "is therefore *originally* and *ultimately* in the people" (*RBC* 424). In short, political authority was both limited and fiduciary, and it derived from the people acting in their capacity as the constituent sovereign.

Hutchinson the Constitutional Conservative

Hutchinson rejected the implication of judicial review in Otis's writings. According to Hutchinson, courts should not possess the power to declare statutes void; otherwise, it would give legislative power to an executive body—in his opinion, the very definition of tyranny. "If you once allow courts and juries to observe the laws or not according to their discretion, instead of being governed by known, established laws you are subjected to an arbitrary government by making the legislative and executive powers one and the same."[10] Consequently, in *Paxton's Case*, Hutchinson ignored Otis's more radical claim and instead focused on the question of precedent. Hutchinson investigated and found that general writs had been issued regularly by the Exchequer to the commissioners of the customs. Because customs officers in the colonies had the same powers as customs officials in England, and because the superior court had the powers of the Exchequer, the court ruled that it had the power to issue the writ.

By focusing on the issue of precedent, Hutchinson was operating within the common law tradition. Strictly speaking, the common law is not judge-made law. The common law emanates from established practice and custom, and through judicial determination, it is transcribed into law. Long established custom, codified through judicial rulings, is presumed to conform to reason. A judicial ruling that breaks with established precedent is presumptively unreasonable or unjust and cannot be considered law. When a judge disregards a bad precedent, he simply recovers an established custom from a judicial ruling that contravened it.

Although Hutchinson found the precedent for the issuing of general warrants to be well established, he could accept as a judicial principle Otis's charge that bad precedent could be overlooked by the court. He likewise believed that judges could construe statutes in order to reconcile them to fundamental constitutional principles "in all cases where there is room for doubt or uncertainty" about legislative intent (*DAE* 401). Where Parliament's intent was clear, however, judges were bound to apply its statutory word. As Hutchinson explained, judges could not "determine an act of Parliament to be void because it appears to them to be contrary to their rights. This would be *jus dare* instead of *jus dicere*"—that is, the power to make law rather than to discover and apply it (*DAE* 354). The power to make or annul law lay within the province of Parliament; the courts, which Hutchinson viewed as executive instruments, were charged only with interpreting and enforcing that law.

Legally, then, Parliament's authority was illimitable, and necessarily so, for if there existed another authority capable of overruling the legislature, law would grow arbitrary. For Hutchinson, government by definition assumes a lawmaking power whose decisions are binding and which can compel compliance. "By entering into [a] state of government," Hutchinson explained, "I subject myself to a power constituted over a society of which I become a member. It is immaterial in whom this power is lodged. Such power must be lodged somewhere or there is no government" (*DAE* 391). Yet, while the courts composed part of that governing power, no legislative power could be vested there. Specifically, if judges were allowed to annul statutes, they might rule differently in similar cases. Judicial discretion of this nature is objectionable precisely because it undermines the order and stability that civil society provides. To grant judges such power would be equivalent to conceding the notion that "every individual has a right to judge when the acts of government are just and unjust and to submit or not submit accordingly," a doctrine that Hutchinson proclaimed "repugnant to the very idea of government" (*DAE* 391). In short, to allow individuals (whether in their private or judicial capacities) to disregard legislative acts would return men to the state of nature. According to Hutchinson, this government-less state of nature was anarchic and insecure, a condition that easily explained why people voluntarily formed governments.

> The question now is not which is best, a state of nature or a state of government and civil society. Indeed nothing can make me doubt which is best. Such disorders and confusions as of late have prevailed not in the colonies only but in the kingdom from whence they sprange perhaps are necessary to convince men of the deplorable state they would be in without government and to reconcile them to the restraint of their natural liberties. (*DAE* 393)

Hutchinson's choice of words in this passage is revealing. The state of nature for Hutchinson is *deplorable*: it is literally a wretched state, a condition inferior to the state of government, for it is only in the civil state that personal security and the enjoyment of rights are ensured.

Men escape the insecurity inherent in the state of nature by freely entering into civil society. When they enter civil society, however, they relinquish their claims to natural rights. "[E]very change from a state of nature into government more or less deprive[s] us of the rights we enjoyed as men" (*DAE* 402). While there are principles of right associated with the state of nature, it is impossible for any particular government to incorporate all of these principles into its civil code. The civil law necessarily diminishes natural liberty while increasing civil liberty. Men willingly make this trade-off—giving up a claim to natural rights in return for the guarantee of some civil rights—precisely because the natural law remains a mere (and frequently violated) moral prescription until it is incorporated into and enforced through a community's legal code.

Since legal codes inevitably vary among societies, men in different countries enjoy varying degrees of rights. While the colonists claimed a natural right to dispose of their property by their own consent or that of their representatives, Hutchinson argued that they have "confounded the general principles of government with the principles of the particular constitution of the English government" (*DAE* 392). In other words, this principle of government that the colonists claim as a natural right and which they correctly perceive in the British constitution is not a principle that every government recognizes. "In Europe," Hutchinson explained,

> governments in general breathe more of the spirit of liberty. In Asia the climate or some other cause inclines to despotism. No prince in Asia has a right to deprive me of my natural liberty by compelling me to become his subject, but if for the sake of his protection I become or continue his subject, I have as much submitted my natural rights to his government there although I have parted with more of them as I should have done in Europe in what we call free governments. (*DAE* 402)

Moreover, the rights that a government accords its citizens might vary over time, and some citizens might not enjoy the same rights enjoyed by other members of their society. "What this writer means by the rights of citizens is very uncertain seeing you will scarce find any two cities where they are just the same, and the rights of British subjects vary in every age and perhaps every session of Parliament" (*DAE* 402). How can a government's recognition of rights vary over time and among citizens? More to the point, how could Parliament justify levying taxes on British subjects who lacked representation at Westminster? "The supreme authority acknowledge that it is a principle in the constitution that no man's property shall be taken from him without his consent in person or by his representative." Still, Hutchinson explained, "they say there is a higher principle than this— *Salus Populi*, the great end of all government" (*DAE* 398). Government's predominant obligation is to the public good, and the reasonableness of all legislation must be measured against that standard.

Hutchinson additionally argued that even those subjects denied the suffrage lived consensually under British law. British subjects were free to leave Great Britain and to become citizens of another country. Subjects who continued to live under British rule, even under conditions that they might deem inequitable, were nonetheless construed to consent to such rule. According to Hutchinson, though the American colonists were legally barred from voting in parliamentary elections and therefore not represented in Parliament, they were nonetheless subject to parliamentary rule.[11] The colonists certainly claimed a regular voice in parliamentary elections as their birthright. But "it is impossible the rights of English subjects should be the same," Hutchinson asserted, "in every respect, in all parts of the dominions." In fact, the parliamentary franchise was not even guaranteed to adults residing in England. In the colonists' case, they remove[d] from the kingdom, where, perhaps, they were in full exercise of this right, to the plantations, where it cannot be exercised, or where the exercise of it would be of no benefit to them. Does it follow that the government, by their removal from one part of the dominions to another, loses its authority over that part to which they remove, and that they are freed from the subjection they were under before. . . ? Will it not rather be said, that by this, their voluntary removal, they have relinquished for a time at least, one of the rights of an English subject?[12]

After all, Hutchinson observed, colonists could reclaim the franchise simply by moving to a part of the empire where the right could be exercised.

Hutchinson similarly rejected the colonial claim, more prevalent after passage of the 1768 Townshend Acts, that their charters gave them legislative independence from Parliament. According to this view of the empire, it had always been understood that the colonists could not be represented in Parliament. That is why when the colonies were established their charters empowered them to form their own legislatures. Properly speaking, the colonies were united with Britain not through a common legislature but rather through an allegiance to a common king. Hutchinson challenged this claim, pointing out that "allegiance is not local but perpetual . . . and as far as you owe allegiance to the King so far you owe it to the King in Parliament" (*DAE* 377). Why else, he asks, would the colonists seek charters from the Crown before departing England?

> Why did they not upon their arrival become subjects to the Indian princes? Instead of that, they took a formal possession for and in behalf of the government of England by virtue of charters and commissions from the crown, and this possession has been continued to this day, and the whole territory so possessed has been de facto for more than a century the dominions of England. (*DAE* 377–78)

Government policy, then, was geared toward the public good; and while Parliament ought not to tax those who were not represented at Westminster, it could legally do so when it determined that such policy was in the public interest. Likewise, while it might be unfair for Parliament to pass a law that affects "the property of particular subjects unequally," Hutchinson reasoned "that the property of these subjects from the very nature of government is at the disposal of the supreme authority for the good of the whole not in such easy and just proportions only as those subjects themselves shall judge necessary to promote his good but as the supreme authority shall judge it so" (*DAE* 396). For example, despite the constitutional maxim that no man's property shall be taken without his consent or that of his representative, Parliament had determined that it is "very agreeable to it and necessary to the ends of government that they [English Catholics] should be taxed and double taxed to the support of the nation" (*DAE* 398).[13] Were the colonial and Catholic cases not analogous? Catholics were denied the suffrage and thus were not represented in Parliament. Could they not also refuse to comply based on the claim that such laws violated the constitution and natural equity?

Effective government for Hutchinson requires that it possess complete authority to make laws for the public welfare, even when those laws arguably are inequitable or unjust. Indeed, Hutchinson claimed that when it came to their own exercise of legislative power, the colonists made the very same argument. As for the taxation of Catholics, Hutchinson was willing to grant "for argument sake" that Catholics hold religious principles "repugnant to government" and consequently "have no reason to complain" about inequities in the law (*DAE* 398). Even conceding the point, Hutchinson asked skeptically, what justified the colonial treatment of Quakers? Did the colonial legislatures not force Quakers to comply with laws they conceived to be contrary to natural justice? After all, the Quakers held all war to be morally abhorrent, yet the colonial legislatures compelled Quakers to help pay for the support of it. Hutchinson continued:

"Now I cannot see how you can justify exercising your authority to compel them to an act which they think contrary to natural justice, and at the same time urge an exemption from acts of a power you acknowledge to be the supreme authority over you because such acts are contrary to natural justice" (*DAE* 399). Furthermore, the colonists' justification for their treatment of Quakers was identical to the one used by Parliament to defend its taxes on the colonies. "You justify yourselves by saying the Quakers are people under your authority and your legislatures have a right to judge when to apply their property to answer the great end of government and when not" (*DAE* 399). This was precisely Hutchinson's point: allegiance is absolute, and once individuals have consented to live according to the laws of the land, they cannot pick and choose which laws to obey. Otherwise, Hutchinson cautions, the "compact [that] . . . you suppose [brought you out of the state of nature] would be a mere rope of sand" (*DAE* 399).

What Hutchinson described was a decentralized state, analogous to the relationship Rome had with her coloniae. The Roman coloniae, he explained, were "formed out of Roman Citizens or inhabitants of Latium and led forth to take possession of and inhabit Countries acquired by the Roman People." Many of these colonies, however, were too distant for their inhabitants to "exercise the Privileges of Citizens in Rome" (*ECR* 483–84). These colonies were therefore allowed to establish local governments and local self-rule, although they remained legally subordinate to Rome. Similarly, the American colonies were simply one among "a variety of corporations formed within the kingdom, with powers to make and execute such by-laws as are for their immediate use and benefit, the members of such corporations still remaining subject to the general laws of the kingdom." Parliament could still bind the colonists through its statutory authority. It could even revoke the colonial charters. The charters issued by the kings were "nothing more than a declaration and assurance on the part of the Crown, that . . . [the colonies] would be considered as part of the dominions of the Crown of England" and consequently "retain the liberties and immunities of free and natural subjects, their removal from, or not being born within the realm, notwithstanding" (*SGM* 337, 339). In other words, the charter did not grant or withhold any rights that the colonists would have enjoyed without a royal charter.

Instead, the colonists derived their rights from the British constitution. And while the constitution articulated certain fundamental principles that Parliament ought to hold dear, the colonists were misguided about the nature of these fundamentals. "[L]ook into the history of any government," Hutchinson wrote, and "you will find that in the course of years frequent material alterations have been made in fundamental points not by subsequent new agreements made by each individual but by acts of the supreme authority of such governments, and such alterations become to all intents and purposes parts of the constitution" (*DAE* 400). In theory, perhaps, the people, acting in a constituent capacity, might establish fundamental principles of law and government. In fact, however, "the [British] people [have never] assembled together in one body so as that we may suppose these fundamentals to have been settled by the majority of individuals" (*DAE* 403). Instead, it was their representatives in Parliament who had established and from time to time had altered and even repealed various fundamentals, including parts of Magna Charta. "The same power may just as well alter them and in fact from time to time have been making continual alterations ever since we have any knowledge of the history of the constitution" (*DAE* 403–4).[14] Parliamentary alterations of the fundamentals by which British freedom was defined was both historically precedented and constitutionally sound. And why not? If "[k]ing, nobles, and people agree to make an alteration in what were before fundamentals, who is there to complain" (*DAE* 403)? Hutchinson concludes: "Indeed, I know of no principle in the English constitution more fundamental and which is more certain always to remain than this, viz., that no act can be made or passed in any Parliament which it shall not be in the power of a subsequent Parliament to alter and repeal" (*DAE* 401). In short, Hutchinson held the traditional view of the British constitution. Through its statutory power, Parliament could alter the constitution, and it could (and did) periodically redefine the rights enjoyed by British subjects.

Nonetheless, in theory at least, it was conceivable that Parliament might abuse its fiduciary power and govern contrary to the public good. What recourse did the people have in the face of an irresponsible and unresponsive legislature? For Hutchinson, the people always retained a right to resist tyrannical government. The colonists, however, misconstrued the nature of that right. The right was neither an individual nor a legal right; rather, it was a communal and moral right. The right was communal in that only a majority of the community could refuse submission to government.

> You will say, perhaps the people never delegated the power of departing from fundamentals: admit it and see what will be the consequence. Not that every man or every part of the community may refuse obedience to such acts, for this, as I observed before, would be directly contrary to the fundamental principles in all government, but the body of the people may rise and change the rulers or change the very form of the government, and this they may do at all times and on all occasions, just when they please. (*DAE* 406)

Despite the contrary and popular view maintained in the colonies, Hutchinson wrote correctively, this communal understanding of the right was the proper interpretation of Locke's *Second Treatise*.

> I never can believe that [Locke] . . . could intend that it is a principle in government that any individual or any number of individuals short of the majority may refuse submission to every act of government which he or they determine in their own minds abridge them of more of their natural rights than the ends for which such government was instituted make necessary. (*DAE* 395)

Otherwise, government would fall prey to the innumerable grievances of individuals and minorities, and it would be incapable of fulfilling the primary function for which it was created. "Now if individuals or any particular parts of a government may resist whensoever they shall apprehend themselves aggrieved, instead of order, peace, and a state of general security—the great ends of government—we may well expect tumults, wars, and a state of general danger" (*DAE* 393).

Equally important, the right to resist government was a moral rather than a legal right. Again, the colonists misconstrued Locke's argument.

> [I]f you take the whole of Mr. Locke's work together you will find he intends no more by the passage you think so favorable to your cause than this, viz., that when the legislative and executive powers of government shall cease to make the ends for which government is instituted the rule of government, the people are under no moral obligation to continue subject to them but may revolt and remove their governors or mold themselves into any other form of government they think proper. (*DAE* 396–97)

Hutchinson's argument is carefully wrought here. While Parliament might govern in a manner seemingly inconsistent with the public interest, neither the people (nor again, the courts) have the constitutional power to overrule it. The colonists might satisfy themselves that morally they are not obligated to comply with a law they believe violates fundamental rights. Nevertheless, a duly enacted statute is by definition constitutional and binding on individuals and the courts. That is why subjects may pronounce a *bill* void while it is being considered, yet once it becomes law it is criminal to declare it so (*DAE* 404). Individuals who refuse to comply with a law, even out of a sense of obligation to a higher law, are necessarily subject to the "penal consequences of not conforming to the law" (*DAE* 405). Similarly, an individual who seeks to foment revolution "must take the consequence of a mistake if he attempts to stir up the body of a people to a revolt and should be disappointed." Hutchinson explains that "in a moral view he may perhaps be innocent (whether his attempt succeeds or not), but consider him as a member of the political body and he must be pronounced guilty by the judiciary powers of that society if he fails of success. This is a principle essential to the nature of government and to the English constitution as well as all others" (*DAE* 406). In short, there is no legal or individual right to revolution. To claim otherwise is to invite and justify the anarchy that government is instituted to overcome.

For Hutchinson, Parliament's statutory authority over the colonies was plenary. "I know of no line," Hutchinson wrote, expressing the orthodox view of sovereignty, "that can be drawn between the supreme authority of Parliament and the total independence of the colonies: it is impossible there should be two independent Legislatures in one and the same state" (*SGM* 340). Surely, Parliament ought to govern the colonies in accordance with long-established legal principles. It was nonetheless conceivable that in its pursuit of the public interest it might be necessary and reasonable for Parliament to "abridge British Subjects of what are generally called natural rights" (*ECR* 481). Only Parliament could make such determinations. And since "the Parliament must be the final Judges and it is possible that it may be determined that the natural right of a Colonist is not the same with the natural right of an Inhabitant of Britain and that the Colonists have no sufficient Plea from their Charters or Commissions for exemption from Parliamentary taxes," Parliament might well determine that taxes levied on the colonists are in fact reasonable and necessary for the public good (*ECR* 487).

What remains for the colonists is to seek a repeal based on a claim in equity, which Hutchinson was confident Parliament would receive sympathetically. "I would humbly hope notwithstanding [Parliament's authority to tax] that we shall be considered in equity and if we have not strictly a claim of right we have of favour" (*ECR* 487). Still, an equity plea is not equivalent to a claim for a legal exemption, and Parliament is not obligated to accept the plea. Nor, despite the colonists' baseless invocation of Locke, does Parliament's decision to tax them justify acts of resistance.

> Your quotation from Mr. Locke, detached as it is from the rest of the treatise, cannot be applied to your case. I know of no attempt to enslave or destroy you, and as you, very prudently, would not be understood to suggest that this people have occasion at present to proceed to such extremity as to appeal to heaven, I am at a loss to conceive for what good purpose you aduce it.[15]

The parliamentary measures that bind the colonies, particularly the tax measures, may be inequitable. They do not, however, constitute grave threats to the liberty of the colonists. Revolution—the extralegal "appeal to heaven"—is not warranted. Instead, the colonists must seek a repeal of the objectionable legislation by petitioning Parliament to repeal or alter the offending statute. Prudence dictates that such appeals should be made with due humility, for Parliament is less inclined to be sympathetic to an equity plea from the colonists that simultaneously appears to question Parliament's legal authority. Nevertheless, Hutchinson remains optimistic that Parliament will judge fairly. "When, upon the united representations and complaints of the American colonies, any acts have appeared to Parliament, to be unsalutary, have there not been repeated instances of the repeal of such acts?" (*SGM* 380).

Otis's Constitutional Argument Reconsidered

At this point, Otis and Hutchinson appear to occupy polar opposite positions. According to Hutchinson, Parliament was legally sovereign, and while it ought to honor the rights of British subjects "strengthened and confirmed by the most solemn sanctions and engagements," ultimately it defined those rights (*ECR* 481). Otis suggested the modern understanding of constitutional government in which political power is legally prescribed by a body of fundamental law that is judicially enforceable. In *The Rights of the British Colonies*, he argued that it is a natural right and a fundamental maxim of the British constitution for people to be free from taxation "*but by their consent in person or deputation*," and he seemed to maintain that the colonists were not represented in Parliament (*RBC* 446). From these premises one might expect Otis to call on the courts to pass the Stamp Act "into disuse." One might even expect Otis to conclude that Parliament did not possess any lawful authority over the colonies whatsoever.

In fact, however, Otis recognized Parliament's plenary authority in the colonies. "No less certain is it that the Parliament has a just and equitable right, power, and authority," he stated, "to *impose taxes on the colonies, internal and external, on lands as well as on trade*" (*VBC* 555). Like Hutchinson, Otis accepted the notion that Parliament was the sovereign or final legislative power in the empire. "In all states there is (and must be) an absolute supreme power, to which the right of *legislation* belongs: and which by the singular constitution of these kingdoms is vested in the King, Lords, and Commons" (*VBC* 560). Because final legislative authority was vested in the King-in-Parliament, Parliament necessarily possessed the authority to tax the colonists. Otis thus rejected the distinction between taxation and other forms of legislation. It was illogical to declare that Parliament was the supreme political authority in the empire and yet claim that it lacked the authority to tax the colonies. The power to tax, Otis explained simply, "is involved in the idea of a supreme legislative or sovereign power of a state" (*VBC* 555–56). If Parliament did not possess the authority to tax the colonists, it lacked any legitimate claim of authority over them whatsoever. "If the Parliament had not such authority," Otis reasoned, "the colonies would be independent, which none but rebels, fools, or madmen will contend for" (*VBC* 565).

For Otis, however, political authority—and particularly the power to tax—was grounded in representation. The colonists were not represented in Parliament; therefore, Parliament could not tax the colonies. Nevertheless, Parliament was the supreme authority in the empire and thus possessed plenary authority in the colonies. Otis reconciled these positions by conceding in principle the notion of virtual representation. Given his view that the legislative authority in a society must be indivisible; given his beliefs that political authority was fiduciary and that representation is a necessary precondition for the exercise of lawful authority; and given the fact that the colonists were denied the suffrage in parliamentary elections, the acceptance of virtual representation stood perhaps as the only path by which Otis could defend parliamentary rule. This concession was rather expedient, a necessary step given his belief that Parliament's authority over the colonies was either complete or nugatory. Moreover, it was a concession with which he was never fully comfortable, as evidenced by the occasional lack of clarity in his remarks on the issue and by his consistent plea for extending the suffrage to the colonists.

Yet while Otis accepted the notion of virtual representation, he did not simply echo the argument for virtual representation offered by leaders in England. Like Hutchinson, Otis rejected the claim that the colonists were virtually represented in the House of Commons. Lack of representation in the House of Commons, however, did not imply a similar denial "of the authority of that august and transcendent body the Parliament, which is composed of the three branches of the grand legislature of the nation considered as united" (*VBC* 556). The "king, lords and commons, conjointly, as the supreme legislature, in *fact* as well as in *law*," Otis emphasized, "represent and act for the realm, and all the dominions, if they please" (*CBC* 125). What explained the distinction between a lack of virtual representation in the House of Commons and the actual (as well as virtual) representation in Parliament? Since in "truth . . . the colonists are no more represented in the [H]ouse of Commons than in the [H]ouse of Lords," the answer must reside with the king (*CBC* 125).

Otis ultimately argued that it was the king and not members in Commons who represented British subjects throughout the empire (and in particular, in the dominions). The king served this representative function in two capacities. First, the king represented the colonies in the administration of the laws. "The king in his executive capacity, in *fact* as well as *law*, represents all his kingdoms and dominions" (*CBC* 125). For example, it was the king (and not the Lords or Commons) who enforced the laws through his various colonial officers, and colonial interests and grievances were heard in the king's privy council and other royal boards such as the Board of Trade. Second, the king represented the colonists as a participant in the supreme legislature. The king could serve in this second, representative capacity because he saw in the welfare of the empire the legacy of both his person and the Crown. A genuine love for his subjects and a desire to achieve glory led the king to pursue the common good for all his subjects. "We are blessed," Otis declared, "with a prince who has given abundant demonstrations that in all his actions he studies the good of his people and the true glory of his crown, which are inseparable" (*RBC* 448).

Otis's argument about representation is important to understanding his response to the Stamp Act; once Otis found that the colonists were represented in Parliament, it followed that Parliament's plenary power rightfully extended to the colonies. And if Parliament was the supreme legislative power for the colonies, it followed that the Stamp Act did not raise a constitutional issue regarding Parliament's legal authority. Rather, for Otis—as for Hutchinson—the issue of parliamentary taxation raised the issue of equity. "The right of a supreme power in a state to tax its colonies is a thing that is clear and evident; and yet the mode of exercising that right may be questionable in point of reason and equity" (*VBC* 564). According to Otis, Parliament possessed the legal authority to tax the colonists; however, long-standing custom showed that the colonies had always been exempt from parliamentary taxation—a point with which Hutchinson largely concurred. More important, "the rules of equity and the principles of the constitution seem to require this [exemption]" (*RBC* 468). Since the colonists did not participate in parliamentary elections and thus did not return members to Commons, Parliament ought not to levy taxes on them. Still, because the colonists were ultimately represented in Parliament by the king, the British legislature possessed the legal authority to tax them.

> [I]n special cases the British Parliament has an undoubted right as well as power to bind both [Ireland and the American colonies] by their acts. But whether this can be extended to an indefinite taxation of both is the great question. I conceive the spirit of the British constitution must make an exception of all taxes, until it is thought fit to unite a dominion to the realm. Such taxation must be considered either as uniting the dominions to the realm or disenfranchising them. If they are united they will be entitled to a representation as well as Wales; if they are so taxed without a union or representation, they are so far disenfranchised. (*RBC* 467)

For Parliament to tax the colonists while they were denied an actual representation in Commons violated fundamental principles of equity and the spirit of the constitution. The politically just thing to do, Otis insisted, was for Parliament to allow an American representation at Westminster. "When the Parliament shall think fit to allow the colonists a representation in the House of Commons, the equity of their taxing the colonies will be as clear as their power is at present of doing it without, if they please" (*RBC* 465). Equity demanded that taxation and the franchise coincide. Until the colonists returned members to Commons, justice demanded that they remain exempt from parliamentary taxation.

Furthermore, because for Otis the Stamp Act raised issues pertaining to equity and not legal authority, Otis did not call upon the courts to judge the Stamp Act void. It was evident to Otis that in equity cases judges could not disregard the manifest intent of Parliament. "The *equity* and *justice* of a bill may be questioned with perfect submission to the legislature," Otis explained. "Reasons may be given why an act ought to be repealed, and yet obedience must be yielded to it till that repeal takes place" (*RBC* 449). Why were the courts powerless in the face of legislative statutes that seemed to violate natural equity? "There would be an end of all government if one or a number of subjects or subordinate provinces should take upon them so far to judge of the justice of an act of Parliament as to refuse obedience to it" (*RBC* 448). Otis was sensitive to the same objections Hutchinson raised regarding the judicial authority. If the courts could rule authoritatively in equity cases, political stability would suffer. Upset over the effects of legislation, subjects might appeal to judges to have the laws annulled. Judges exercising such discretionary power might act more as legislators than as judges, and if subjects could appeal to judges to have statutory laws vacated, they might always look for a judge sympathetic to their plea.

Once Otis's concerns regarding the courts' equity jurisdiction are understood, his remarks about the Stamp Act grow clear. Judges could pass judgment on legislation they conceived to be inconsistent with equity, but when the legislature spoke declaratively, judges were bound to apply the statute. Judicial opinions against an inequitable law were just that: opinions. They were dicta and carried no legal weight. When the legislature spoke decisively, judicial opinions against a statute were akin to private judgments. "If there is not a right of private judgment to be exercised," Otis explained in a passage that captures his constitutional argument,

> so far at least as to petition for a repeal or to determine the expediency of risking a trial at law, the Parliament might make itself arbitrary, which it is conceived it cannot be by the constitution. I think every man has a right to examine as freely into the origin, spring, and foundation of every power and measure in a commonwealth as into a piece of curious machinery or a remarkable phenomenon in nature, and that it ought to give no more offense to say the Parliament have erred or are mistaken in a matter of fact or of right than to say it of a private man, if it is true of both. If the assertion can be proved with regard to either, it is a kindness done them to show them the truth. With regard to the public, it is the duty of every good citizen to point out what he thinks erroneous in the commonwealth. (*RBC* 449–50)

Like private individuals, judges could voice their opinions on the inequity of a law. When judges declared that a law violates natural equity, they merely exercised the right that "every subject has ... to give his sentiments to the public, of the utility or inutility of any act whatsoever, even after it has passed, as well as while it is pending" (*RBC* 449).[16] This right was consistent with parliamentary supremacy. Voicing objections to a statute was not in itself a sign of disloyalty. It was a sign of fidelity, an act of "kindness" which reconfirmed the public's faith in Parliament's benevolence. Only acts of disobedience could be construed as a sign of faithlessness.

Otis went further. It was not merely a right but a public obligation for subjects to express their opinions on parliamentary measures. For judges, it was a constitutional obligation. "If the reasons that can be given against an act are such as plainly demonstrate that it is against *natural* equity, the executive courts will adjudge such acts void. It may be questioned by some, though I make no doubt of it, whether they are not obliged by their oaths to adjudge such act void" (*RBC* 449). Only by expressing their legal objections to a parliamentary statute could judges, as representatives of the king, exercise their constitutional function to check and balance the legislature. In the British constitution, he maintained, "[t]he supreme *legislative* and the supreme *executive* are a perpetual check and balance to each other. If the supreme executive errs it is informed by the supreme legislative in Parliament. If the supreme legislative errs it is informed by the supreme executive in the King's courts of law" (*RBC* 455). Judges thus played an important role in maintaining the constitution and in restraining Parliament from exercising its power in an inequitable manner. Judges performed this role in part through their power of statutory interpretation. But Otis stops short of arguing that judges could check legislative action by refusing to enforce a statute in cases where Parliament's intent was clear. "There is nothing in all this [the judicial construction of statutes] that can in the least impeach their power, right and authority to make laws" (*DHL* 169). Where Parliament sought to govern, the courts could merely "inform" Parliament of its error. In sum, while judges could not disregard a clear statutory mandate that contradicted natural equity, they could rule in a way that would alert Parliament to its error, confident that the legislature, which sought to govern in accordance with equity and the constitution, would alter or rescind the law once it became aware of the statute's flaw.

But what if Parliament deliberately enacted a law patently offensive to reason and justice? It was impossible to conceive. It would "be the highest degree of imprudence and disloyalty to imagine that the King, at the head of his Parliament, could have any but the most pure and perfect intentions of justice, goodness, and truth that human nature is capable of " (*RBC* 448). Because one might presume that Parliament intended to govern according to law and equity, one could trust that judicial determinations would bring relief. Meanwhile, people must obey the law while it was in place, confident that Parliament would remedy the mistake. The point was that Parliament sought to govern for the common good. Statutes which were not in the common interest or which violated principles of equity were either the result of inadvertent error or, as was unfortunately the case with the colonies, the result of erroneous information given to Parliament by "vile informers" who deliberately misled Parliament in an effort to promote their own fortunes (*CBC* 119).

What Otis's *Rights of the British Colonies* was designed to do, then, was to persuade Parliament of the inequitable nature of the Stamp Act and to secure its repeal in a manner consistent with respectful, private judgment. In fact, Otis's pamphlet can be read as a type of legal brief, a complaint in equity typically reserved for pleas in private cases. Otis's pamphlet sought to demonstrate that the colonists had standing to bring the suit and that the statute effected particular, that is, unequal injustice in the colonies. Still, the pamphlet was directed at Parliament, since equitable relief from an onerous statute was available only from Parliament itself.

Conclusion

In the end, Otis offered an argument that was nearly identical to Hutchinson's in its conclusions and in significant ways similar in its presuppositions. Sovereignty was by nature indivisible, and in the wake of the Glorious Revolution it was placed in the King-in-Parliament. By discovering sources of colonial representation or consent, Otis and Hutchinson reconciled the fact of parliamentary rule with their beliefs about the consensual basis to legitimate politics. At the same time, both men urged that the colonial charters ought to be considered "as a perpetual rule of Government for the respective Colo[nies] that they should have Assemblies of their own chusing to ma[ke] laws for their government [and] to raise moneys by taxes &c." (*ECR* 481–82). As long as the colonies were denied representation in the House of Commons, adherence to equity and constitutional principles required that they remain exempt from parliamentary taxation.

Otis further held that even if Parliament invited the colonists to return members to Parliament, there remained compelling reasons why the colonial legislatures, rather than Parliament, ought to exercise the taxing power in the colonies. "No representation of the colonies in Parliament alone would . . . be equivalent to a subordinate legislative among themselves," he concluded, "nor so well answer the ends of increasing the prosperity and the commerce of Great Britain. It would be impossible for the Parliament to judge so well of their abilities to bear taxes, impositions on trade, and other duties and burdens, or of the local laws that might be really needful, as a legislative here" (*RBC* 445–46). Prudence, if not equity, directed that the colonial governments continue to enjoy the privileges they historically had been granted. There was no compelling need for the introduction of parliamentary taxes. After all, Parliament had regularly exercised its authority over colonial trade—even to the point of prohibiting certain commercial endeavors in the colonies—for the benefit of the mother country. It was for the very purpose of protecting and expanding the "advantageous trade she had so long carried on with her Colonies," Hutchinson observed, and not to "save them from french Vassalage," that Great Britain waged the Seven Years' War (*ECR* 489). Nevertheless, the colonies contributed generously to the war, despite the fact that England was the prime beneficiary and despite the fact that historically the colonies had not received any assistance from England to defend themselves from the French.

One could understand, then, why Otis chafed at the notion held by members of Parliament, as well as by Hutchinson, that the colonies were equivalent to corporations (i.e., subordinate governments) in England. Unlike the colonies, Otis pointed out, such corporations were in fact represented in Parliament, and they were not burdened with the "great expense [of] raising men, building forts, and supporting the King's civil government here [in the colonies]" (*RBC* 468). For Parliament to tax the colonies while they were denied the franchise "would seem to be a contradiction in practice to the theory of the constitution" (*RBC* 470). Still, Otis ultimately presumed that parliamentary law was legally binding until Parliament, "convinced that their proceedings are not constitutional or not for the common good," amended or rescinded the offending statute (*RBC* 448). Like Hutchinson, Otis perceived the courts to be a component of the executive. Lacking coequal constitutional status with the legislature, the courts could not compel Parliament to comply with the constitution. Certainly, there were limits to Parliament's authority.

> To say the Parliament is absolute and arbitrary is a contradiction. The Parliament cannot make 2 and 2, 5: omnipotency cannot do it. The supreme power in a state is *jus dicere* only: *jus dare*, strictly speaking, belongs alone to GOD. . . . Should an act of Parliament be against any of *his* natural laws, which are *immutably* true, *their* declaration would be contrary to eternal truth, equity, and justice, and consequently void. (*RBC* 454)

The point was that Parliament itself would adjudge it void once it recognized its error. "Upon this great principle Parliaments repeal[ed] such acts as soon as they find they have been mistaken in having declared them to be for the public good when in fact they were not so" (*RBC* 454–55).

To say that *strictly speaking* Parliament could do no wrong, however, did not preclude Otis and Hutchinson from looking to extralegal measures as the ultimate check on government's exercise of power. Here, finally, we begin to discern important (if subtle) differences between them. Otis was much more aggressive than Hutchinson in his assertion of the right to revolution. Whereas Hutchinson seemed far more concerned about the potential abuse of the right, Otis emphasized its obligatory nature. For Otis, the law of nature requires that "they [who] verge towards tyranny . . . are to be opposed" (*RBC* 427). While Otis never directly explains the nature of this obligation—when analyzing the right, he instead appears content to quote at length from Locke—his suggestion that the duty stems from a source of binding law independent of government is an important indication of the novel constitutional framework he was attempting to erect.

It is in his characterization of the British constitution as a rule of law that Parliament is bound to respect that Otis's argument takes on special significance. For Otis, the British constitution establishes "first principles of law and justice" that limit Parliament as well as the king. Indeed, for Otis the constitution was "re-established at the Revolution" with the intent of securing in perpetuity the rights of British subjects (*RBC* 446). These rights are "part of a British subject's birthright, and as inherent and perpetual as the duty of allegiance" and therefore are to be "held sacred and inviolable" (*RBC* 466). Moreover, Otis suggested that these limits are fixed and known at law. It is here in particular that Otis's writings reveal the efforts of an innovative thinker grappling with new ideas and their implications. In suggesting that the British constitution was a fundamental body of law paramount to Parliament, Otis's argument diverged from Hutchinson's and challenged a prevailing norm. For Otis, unlike Hutchinson, it was possible for Parliament to enact a law that was unconstitutional. The constitution was in this sense fixed. That is why citizens could pronounce their opinions about legislation even after it became law. Judges in particular were obligated to declare their opinions on parliamentary statutes. Passing judgment on legislation—even nonbinding judgment—was for Otis not merely an abstract moral duty but a constitutional obligation, for it was through this process that Parliament was led to correct its errors and govern in accordance with the constitution. While ultimately he did not articulate the power of judicial review, he nonetheless perceived a constitutional role for the courts in controlling Parliament and, therefore, in maintaining the constitution.

Finally, while Otis did not recognize the full implications of his argument, and while in his various essays he failed to articulate his ideas clearly and thus left himself open to charges of inconsistency, he was the first colonial thinker to inject these ideas into the political discourse. Other thinkers would build on them. Within a decade, clear expressions of modern constitutional doctrine were available in the colonies. Years later, John Adams would reflect on Otis's influence on colonial thinkers. "Otis was a flame of Fire," Adams would write, reminiscing on Otis's performance before the bench in *Paxton's Case*. "With the promptitude of Classical Allusions, a depth of Research, a rapid Summary of Historical Events and dates, a profusion of legal Authorities, a prophetic glare of his eyes into futurity, and a rapid Torrent of impetuous Eloquence, he hurried away all before him; American Independence was then and there born."[17]

Notes

1. Leonard Levy, *Emergence of a Free Press* (New York: Oxford University Press, 1985), 63, quoting Joseph T. Buckingham, *Specimens of Newspaper Literature* (Boston: Little and Brown, 1852), 1:191.
2. According to the American colonists, the Stamp Act (1765), along with the Sugar Act (1764), represented a major change—and a dangerous precedent—in British policy toward the colonies. Both laws levied taxes on the colonists. The Stamp Act was viewed by the colonists as especially objectionable, requiring the use of specially stamped paper (shipped from London and for which the colonists would pay a tax) for legal documents, diplomas, property deeds, newspapers, advertisements, and more.
3. There is no single cause for Hutchinson's public disaffection. Even before the Stamp Act crisis, Hutchinson had a reputation—not wholly unearned—for being covetous of appointed office. At the time of the Stamp Act, he held four posts in the Massachusetts colony: lieutenant governor, president of the council, chief justice, and judge of probate. Hutchinson himself believed that his role in the writs of assistance case in 1761 (discussed below) had helped to make him an unpopular figure. Moreover, by 1761 Hutchinson and Otis were feuding, the result of Hutchinson's appointment in 1760 as chief justice of the superior court. Otis's father believed that he had a claim to a position on the bench, and when Governor Bernard instead tapped Hutchinson, Otis concluded that Hutchinson had cheated his father out of the office. From that moment, Otis and Hutchinson continually feuded. As leaders in their respective legislative

chambers, Otis and Hutchinson often clashed, with Otis's public declamations against Hutchinson intensifying in the months following passage of the Stamp Act. On Hutchinson's political career and his relationship with Otis and Bostonians generally, see Bernard Bailyn, *The Ordeal of Thomas Hutchinson* (Cambridge, Mass.: Harvard University Press, 1974).

4. The idea of virtual representation was a response to the claim that people denied the suffrage were not represented in Parliament. Essentially, virtual representation assumed a compatibility of interests between voters and nonvoters. Nonvoters were represented because they shared common interests with citizens who possessed the franchise: while representing the interests of voters, members of Parliament would simultaneously pursue the interests of nonvoters. During the Stamp Act crisis, members of Parliament argued that the colonists were virtually represented. The colonists rejected this claim.

5. This statute was enacted in 1662 and is quoted in *Legal Papers of John Adams*, ed. L. Kinvin Wroth and Hiller B. Zobel, 3 vols. (Boston: Harvard University Press, 1965), 2:131. The editors provide a fine summary of the controversy, to which I am indebted.

6. *Papers of John Adams*, 2:127–28. In *Bonham's Case*, Thomas Bonham was fined by the president and censors of the Royal College of Physicians for practicing medicine in the city of London without a certificate from the college. The president and censors also forbade him, under pain of imprisonment, from practicing medicine until he had been admitted by them. Bonham continued to practice, however, and when he was imprisoned, he brought an action of false imprisonment against the leading members of the college. Chief Justice Sir Edward Coke ruled that the college did not possess the authority to fine and imprison unlicensed physicians. Because the censors were to receive one-half of the fines, they would be judge and party to any case that came before them. The statute in question thus contradicted a maxim of the common law that no man can be a judge in his own case. Coke wrote: "And it appears in our books that in many cases the common law will controul acts of parliament and sometimes adjudge them to be utterly void: for when an act of parliament is against common right or reason, or repugnant, or impossible to be performed, the common law will controul it and adjudge such act to be void." The reference to *Bonham's Case* is in Coke, *The reports of Sir Edward Coke* . . . , Bk. 8:118a, cited by Otis from an extract provided in Charles Viner, *A General Abridgment of Law and Equity, Alphabetically Digested under Proper Titles* . . . (Aldershot, 1741–1751), 19:512–13.

7. *Bonham's Case*, in Coke, *The reports of Sir Edward Coke* . . . , Bk. 8:118a.

8. James Otis, *The Rights of the British Colonies Asserted and Proved*, in *Pamphlets of the American Revolution, 1750–1776*, ed. Bernard Bailyn (Cambridge, Mass.: Harvard University Press, 1965), 476, hereafter cited in the text as *RBC*. References to three other Otis pamphlets, all published in 1765, will also appear parenthetically in the text: *A Vindication of the British Colonies, against the Aspersions of the Halifax Gentleman*, in *Pamphlets of the Revolution*, as *VBC*; *Considerations on Behalf of the Colonists, in a Letter to a Noble Lord*, in "Some Political Writings of James Otis (Part II)," ed. Charles F. Mullett, *The University of Missouri Studies: A Quarterly of Research* 4, no. 4 (October 1929): 109–25, as *CBC*; and *Brief Remarks on the Defence of the Halifax Libel on the British-American Colonies*, in "Some Political Writings," 157–76, as *DHL*.

9. Otis cites three cases which purport to buttress Coke's argument in *Dr. Bonham's Case*. The cases are: Hobart's judgment in *Day v. Savadge* (1614), *Duchess of Hamilton v. Fleetwood*, and Holt's decision in *City of London v. Wood* (1701). According to John Adams, who was present during oral argument in *Paxton's Case* and whose notes provide the only documentary record of those arguments, Otis used the same references (including the reference to Vattel) in his argument before the bench. See John Adams to William Tudor, August 21, 1818, in *Works of John Adams*, ed. Charles Francis Adams, 10 vols. (Boston: Little and Brown, 1850–1856), 10:351.

10. "A Dialogue between an American and a European Englishman by Thomas Hutchinson (1768)," ed. Bernard Bailyn, *Perspectives in American History* 9 (1975): 396, hereafter cited in the text as *DAE*.

11. Hutchinson apparently accepted the idea of virtual representation in Parliament, but he denied that the colonists were virtually represented there. See Thomas Hutchinson, "Essay on Colonial Rights (1764)," in Edmund S. Morgan, "Thomas Hutchinson and the Stamp Act," *New England Quarterly* 21 (1948): 486, hereafter cited in the text as *ECR*.

12. Thomas Hutchinson, "Speech of the Governor to the Two Houses," January 6, 1773, in *Speeches of the Governors of Massachusetts, 1765–1775*, ed. Alden Bradford (New York: Da Capo Press, 1971), 339–40, hereafter cited in the text as *SGM*.

13. Under English law at the time, Roman Catholics were subject to double taxation on land.

14. Hutchinson adopts the interpretation of the 1688 Revolution put forth by the Convention Parliament, namely, that no dissolution had occurred and that Parliament, acting in accordance with precedent and the constitution, had merely filled a vacancy of the throne. He writes: "There was no new constitution settled at the [Glorious] Revolution. The Bill of Rights was declaratory. In former reigns there had been a deviation" (*DAE* 376).

15. Thomas Hutchinson, "The Lieutenant-Governor's Answer to . . . both Houses at the opening of the Session," in Thomas Hutchinson, *The History of the Colony and Province of Massachusetts-Bay*, ed. Lawrence Shaw Mayo (Cambridge, Mass.: Harvard University Press, 1936), appendix S, 395.

16. One might read Otis narrowly here to mean only that subjects could question the wisdom—and not the legality—of legislation once it had passed. I think he intends otherwise. Recall that he states that subjects may properly question a law's compatibility with the constitution: "I think every man has a right to examine as freely into the origin, spring, and foundation of every power and measure in a commonwealth as into a piece of curious machinery or a remarkable phenomenon in nature, and that it ought to give no more offense to say the Parliament have erred or are mistaken in a matter of fact or of right than to say it of a private man" (*RBC* 450). Moreover, even if one read's Otis's statement as a prohibition of sorts against private individuals "declaring" a law to be contrary to the constitution and hence void, it does not follow that judges, acting in their legal capacity, are similarly bound.

17. John Adams to William Tudor, March 29, 1817, in *Works of John Adams*, 10:248.

Chapter 3

Thomas Paine: The American Radical

John Koritansky

The importance of Thomas Paine's (1737–1809) writings for us today could be indicated with reasonable precision by describing him as the American radical. In other words, it is as if Paine is attempting to demonstrate what sort of radicalism is consistent with American principles and even why what is really fundamental about America is radical.

One may, of course, object that each element of this description is so vague, and politically loaded, as to be useless. It must be granted that the term "radical" has been applied by or appropriated to all sorts of stances—sometimes to embarrass one's opponents, sometimes to insist on the integrity or uncompromisability of one's own views. Still, the term is owned most comfortably, and with the least element of contentiousness, by those who are also spoken of, again with some irremovable latitude, as being on the Left. The radicals of the 1960s were those who sought to axe the root of the contemporary American capitalist establishment as a necessary first step toward bringing about a more just—by which they meant a more egalitarian and democratic—society. Paine held a high status within this movement, and it remains the case that he is held in highest regard by those whose politics are of the Left.[1] As for "American," Paine stipulates for himself the meaning of the term. It means the principles articulated in the Declaration of Independence: that all human beings are created equal; that they are endowed by their creator with inalienable rights which include the right to life, liberty, and the pursuit of happiness; and that to secure these rights human beings create government through their consent. Among the Founders, Paine is the one who attempts to derive from the basic principles of the Declaration of Independence the most democratic and egalitarian consequences. It is on this point, though, that the real question lies. Are Paine's derivations from the principles of the Declaration sound? The answer is, probably not; almost certainly they are not accepted as sound by anyone today—neither Paine's opponents nor his would-be friends or allies. Because of this, contemporary radicals are more inclined either to hold back from adulation of Americanism or purport to use the term as meaning something more, or quite different from, the Declaration.

Paine's American radicalism appears archaic today because contemporary radical thought derives from an original critique of Paine's, and the Declaration's, principles. The problem is that, read very strictly, the terms of the Declaration give no endorsement to any particular form of government or society. Consent is the complete ground of the legitimacy of all forms of authority, and legitimacy is the whole standard. Therefore, whatever constitutional arrangements people consent to are legitimate and proper—for them. A monarchy, or even what some might call a tyranny, can be legitimate by this criterion. The original progenitors of the principles articulated in the Declaration understood its neutralism and were quite explicit about it. John Locke asserts in his *Second Treatise of Government* that monarchy and oligarchy are among the possible legitimate forms of government.[2] He also says, with equal explicitness, that very great differences in material well-being are sanctioned by an implicit consent that may be inferred just from the fact that people employ the convention of monetary currency.[3] Additionally, the doctrine of legitimation by consent has the consequence of obliterating distinctions among the manner or motive from which one gives consent. A consent to someone's authority that is extracted by threat would have to be said to be as legitimating as consent given in a mood of cool deliberation, balancing less pressing good and evils. In other words, knuckling under to superior force would count as a mode of giving consent. Locke's *Second Treatise* is considerably subtler in its treatment of this latter point than it is of the former one; it is nevertheless clear enough if one considers carefully his discussion of "conquest" in chapter 16. The upshot of his argument is practically indistinguishable from what had been said earlier, more candidly, by Thomas Hobbes in connection with his doctrine of "government by acquisition."[4]

The starkness of Locke's and Hobbes's political teaching was perceived and exposed clearly in the eighteenth century by Jean-Jacques Rousseau, who responds by altering their fundamental premises and thus sets modern political thought in a new direction. For Rousseau, the consent that legitimates government cannot be something that exists only "tacitly," or pro forma, so to speak. If government is to be legitimate, human beings must remain "as free as before" they submitted themselves. There must be no contradiction between their duty to society under law and their will and happiness. This situation is possible only where human beings abandon every last one of their natural rights as the condition of their membership in civil society.[5] Only in this way do they each hold membership on equal terms with each of the others, and only in this way can each and all be free—to do their duty. Directly or indirectly, all later modern political thought derives from Rousseau's critique and fundamental reformulation of his predecessors. His influence is most direct among radicals of the Left. Rousseau's new understanding of liberty has equality as a necessary corollary, and equality here means not merely equal formal standing before the law, as Hobbes and Locke had required, but equal participation in social and political life. Liberty and equality in this sense obviously also involve a notion of fraternity—that third element of the slogan of the French Revolution which most sharply distinguishes its spirit and aim from, for example, England's Glorious Revolution or the American War of Independence.

Paine's radicalism owes nothing to Rousseau. He had read some of Rousseau's writings, but his references to him are few and spare. They show no indication of recognizing the fundamental importance of Rousseau's new teaching. Still, for that very reason, Paine bears a reexamination today. For one thing, there is always the possibility that Paine's radical thought might prove ultimately more acceptable than the latter-day, postmodern version of Rousseau's thought which is so dominant among us. A more modest but more likely effect of such a reexamination is that we would be helped to understand what it is about America and American thought that conditions our receptivity to the transformed version of modern thought. One may provide a useful outline of Paine's thinking in connection with three headings: his constitutional thought, his discussions of political economy, and his arguments concerning religion.

Constitutional Thought

Paine sets out his basic philosophy of nature and human society in the clearest and most forceful way in his 1776 pamphlet, *Common Sense*.[6] This pamphlet was critically important in galvanizing the passion and sentiment of the American colonists toward war with England. There was, however, much more to it than enthusiastic rhetoric. Until Paine's statement, the colonists were all foundering in an attempt to argue that Parliament had exceeded implicit limits on its authority over the colonies, limits that derived both from precedent and from the fundamental principle that the colonists' consent was necessary to legitimate Parliament's legislation over them. How far this principle applied (for example, whether only to tax legislation or to all legislation) and what sort of consent was required had been, though, a matter of dispute among the colonists themselves, at least since the Sugar and Stamp Acts of 1763 and 1764. The basic difficulty was that every attempt to qualify or limit Parliament's authority ran up against the consequences of Parliament's sovereignty as holding the legislative power in and for the empire. It was, therefore, ultimately a matter of parliamentary discretion whether certain powers of taxation and other legislation might be allowed the colonial governments, and it was up to Parliament to decide how far precedent was to be followed in any given instance. Paine cut through this heated and yet plodding debate by ignoring the whole issue of the limits of Parliament's traditional constitutional authority. Rather, for him, what was of decisive importance was the rottenness of the whole, much vaunted, English system of government. England was evil and America was good; but her goodness would not persist long if she remained united to the empire. The time for separation was at hand. A generation earlier America was still too young and too weak economically and militarily to challenge England. Perhaps no more than a generation hence, and America would no longer be staunch enough to fight or pure enough for a war of independence to be worthwhile. The rot would have spread. Much of *Common Sense*, then, was a comparative assessment of America's and England's moral and physical resources, intended to convince Paine's trepidatious countrymen that America could win the war. England was not as fearsome as she seemed; America would be more so. The moment was at hand for a new birth for human freedom on the American continent; and it was either now or perhaps never.

What made America good was that here the true and proper status of government as the servile instrument of naturally free human beings was widely understood and maintained with practical effect. In England this principle was given lip service at best and in many quarters denied. In his first few pages, Paine explains the origin and nature of civil society, which is implicit in the American common sense. Nature as such is good. It is the standard for whatever may be spoken of as good or right. All too often men lose their way at the outset by forgetting this simple point and thinking that government corrects against evils that are *natural*. Although Paine does not mention specifically in this connection Locke or Hobbes, one may observe that he is attempting to avoid a difficulty that does trouble Hobbes's and Locke's assertion that human beings were originally in a presocietal state of nature. Most succinctly put, Hobbes's and Locke's account of human nature is such that human beings cannot be at home in their state of nature; or that for human beings the state of nature is unnatural. Paine parts company with Hobbes and Locke by asserting that society *is* human beings' natural condition. Human society may not be coterminous with human being, but it is the case that human beings come into their own, so to speak, in society. The somewhat subtle but key distinctive point is that for Paine human beings do not form or enter civil society in order to protect their lives and their acquisitions from each other's assaults. Rather, they *do* form or enter civil society in order to attain, through cooperative effort, things that they could not attain through their individual effort. Human beings are naturally cooperative. They imagine satisfactions that require cooperation; they imagine employing their own resources in cooperation; and they can, by nature, communicate what they imagine to each other so as to bring about the result.

In saying this, Paine does not go so far as to assert a premodern, Aristotelian notion of a common good. The aims for the sake of which human beings cooperate are, still, individual ones. Thus, for example, Paine does not say that cooperation, or society, are in themselves goods. Were he to move all the way over to the Aristotelian way of thinking about this matter, Paine would also have to say, as does Aristotle, that human beings are political as well as social beings.

That is because if many were to share a genuine common good it would have to be as partici-pants; and there would have to be some organiclike structure to that participation for the good to be one, common good. Then, as Aristotle points out, there would be an element that ruled—that is, that defined the good and established the terms whereby others could participate. Paine rejects such a notion of a common good no less than any other modern thinker. Nevertheless, within the modern tradition, Paine, along with some others, had reached a point where it seemed necessary to qualify the natural individualism asserted by the progenitors of modern thought, Hobbes and Locke. Adam Smith, for example, with his famous observation of human beings' natural disposition to "truck, barter, and exchange," and in a similar way David Hume had either amended or abandoned the original idea of a social contract through which human beings launched civil society.[7] Paine does think that human society begins with the expression of agreements—contracts, if you will. The key distinctive point is that, for him, these agreements do not originally require a trustee to enforce them. Instead, they derive their strength from our own natural goodness.

While human goodness is adequate to support cooperation for the most part, still Paine does admit that it is not completely adequate. Occasionally, someone might try to get more than his share; and in such cases something like government is useful to bring the miscreant back into line. "Nothing but heaven is impregnable to vice," he acknowledges (*CS* 5). Therefore, although society results directly from the expression of our natural capacities, or virtues, "government, like a dress, is the badge of lost innocence" (*CS* 4). Government thus understood is decidedly arti-ficial; Paine is insistent about that. It is best if government be kept small and simple. Under all circumstances government ought to be limited as to scope and power. This is because it operates according to a charge, given by human beings already in society for the sake of maintaining civil society. Government ought to remain responsible to the human beings who created it by re-maining within the limits of its charge, and its creators ought to remain mindful of that relation-ship. As for sovereignty, it resides with the human beings in society and, although it may be forgotten or confused, it cannot be transferred.

Much of the appeal of Paine's thinking can be appreciated by drawing a comparison and also a distinction between him and Henry David Thoreau. Both exhibit a sort of hyper-Americanism insofar as they both want to find in the Declaration a fundamental, morally substantive principle of right human life and right social order. Both make the primacy of the autonomous individual over government not only grounds for the legitimate assertion of political authority but also the aim that distinguishes good government and good society. Thoreau goes further in this direction than Paine, reaching an apotheosis of sorts, when he asserts that the truest and most mature meaning for American freedom would be achieved when government is seen to have no authority to command any individual to compromise the dictate of the individual's conscience. In other words, Thoreau recommends anarchy, but which he believes will be a civilized anarchy once the full implication of the American idea of freedom is reached.[8] Thoreau goes further than Paine in this way because he has a different diagnosis of what stands in the way of human beings' recognition of themselves as autonomously free. Thoreau thinks that the problem is that in our immaturity as a human race, we have been all too easily beguiled into a false assessment of what we really need in order to be happy. We are all caught up in a false economics, wearing ourselves out in the pursuit of the means for happiness and never allowing ourselves the ease of its attainment. The solution requires more than merely being admonished to wake up and get hold of ourselves. What is needed is an experience of transcendence, attained through the sort of poetry of *Walden*. We need to be brought to understand that we do *not* belong to the natural realm, not entirely. We are but sojourners here. We may take from the earth a bounty such as is offered by a hospitable host but we should be liberated from the foolish, desperate hope to find the full satisfaction of our soul's longing in the acquisition of the earth's treasures. The mature soul's transcendence of the world allows it to live easy in the world—and in that way allows it to be free.

The contrast between Paine and Thoreau is indicated by the fact that poetry is not so critically important for Paine. The reason for this is that Paine does not think that human beings are cut off from a sense of their true selves and their true needs because they are too much in and of the world. For the same reason, Paine is not at all an opponent of industrial capitalism. Paine thinks that we do know ourselves and what we truly want and need pretty well, as a matter of common sense. The root evil by his account is, rather, the fantastic, nonsensical notion associated with monarchical systems that some human beings are more exalted than others—that according to some natural or divine ordinance some are born to command others for their own purposes. In fact, poetry, a certain form of poetry, has been part of the problem, obscuring the prosaic sense of the freedom that we are all entitled to by nature.

Paine would agree with the ancient proverb that men do not become tyrants for want of bread. There can be, of course, competition for material wherewithal, but this is not what tends to make human beings enemies of each other. Instead we are usually quite able and willing to calculate our gains and losses and cut a deal. It is true that one may be tempted to cheat, but this is not a crippling problem. The natural direction of our thinking, which first conceives the prospect of a deal, is to imagine and expect that the deal be kept by all parties. And we tend, again just naturally, to be impressed with the loss we would experience personally if, when someone entered an agreement, it was with the reservation that it might be broken unilaterally. Crimes committed for the sake of material gain are an abnormality which can be corrected by way of restoring nature's norm. If that were not so—if human beings were congenitally wicked—then all political theorists, all self-styled friends of humanity, might cease their labors. There could be no genuinely effective mitigation of evil. And yet no one, almost no one, is prepared to concede that. The really great evils from which we suffer, then, are rooted in something unnatural or monstrous, and that something is monarchy. The rewards that humans hope to enjoy from being the monarch, or even from being associated with the Crown and basking in its glow, are not such as can enter into a rational calculation of gain and loss. Relatedly, its advantages cannot be mutual. One is exalted in contrast to the others; one commands insofar as the others obey. The competition for that cannot be other than invidious. Whatever cooperation might exist among competitors for monarchical rule would be like that among petty thieves. It would be suspicious and destined to be violated at some point. In *Common Sense*, Paine drives this thought home by representing the history of the Jews from the Old Testament. The institution of monarchy was the true fall of man. The corruption of our minds and souls that followed from that are the wages of our original sin.

Given his hatred of monarchy, it follows that Paine is decidedly unimpressed with the defense of the peculiar features of the British monarchical system. The received opinion, associated with Montesquieu, was that the British system offered the greatest security to human liberty that ever existed in the world because of the way that it institutionalized the old conflict between the two great social classes. Lords and commons were each given a share of the fundamental power of legislation; neither could act alone, and a balance of power was continually being restored between them by the Crown. By creating new peerages, and through a myriad of lesser devices, the Crown could augment the power of the landed aristocracy vis-à-vis the common folk. The Crown might do this because, being hereditary, it was not responsible to or controlled by either class. Most Americans were deeply impressed with this argument and accorded "the celebrated Montesquieu" a rank among the greatest political theorists. They tended to view with regret that they lacked the materials, especially landed aristocracy, that might have enabled them to attain the advantages of the British model through direct imitation. If they accused Parliament of corruption, it was despite the features of the system of government, not because of them. In this respect, Paine parted company with the preponderant view of his countrymen. His hostility toward *any* form of monarchy displaced the favor in which Americans held the British system until practically the eve of the Revolution.

While holding back mention of his name, Paine responds in *Common Sense* to the thought of Montesquieu with arguments that are simple and quite forceful. The British system simply cannot work in the way its defenders say that it does, for by their account the British system amounts to "a house divided against itself" (*CS* 8). However complex the arrangements, there simply must be one agency that ultimately drives the whole.

> [A]s all the wheels of a machine are put into motion by one, it remains to know which power in the constitution has the most weight, for that will govern; and though others, or a part of them, may clog or, as the phrase is, check the rapidity of its motion, yet so long as they cannot stop it, their endeavors will be ineffectual. The first moving power will at last have its way, and what it wants in speed is supplied by time. (*CS* 8)

In England, that one agency is the Crown. No one is so truly blind as not to see that. The vaunted system of checks and balances is but a set of semitransparent cloaks. In tearing away those cloaks, Paine intends to show that the Crown is in fact responsible for the existence of all the evils that the system's defenders think make it necessary. The corrupt ambition of her kings has embroiled England in foreign contests and war. The unjust force by which the royal house was established, as with all royalty, makes for a continued excuse for foreign powers to threaten. As for the most seemingly plausible argument that kings protect against civil war, England's whole bloody history of rivalry between the houses of Lancaster and York "disowns the fact" (*CS* 15). Indeed, the defense of the complex monarchical system of eighteenth-century England did entail a recognition that simple, untrammeled monarchy was bad. Paine thought the time had finally come to draw the bold, clear conclusion from that recognition. Let monarchy be repudiated and swept away.

What frame of government, then, would meet with Paine's approval? Paine does address himself to this question but with a certain reluctance and disinterest. It is as if the issue would just take care of itself, so to speak, so long as it were approached in the right way—that is, so long as we understand that government is our servant rather than our master. Still, there have to be some positive indications. We have to be able to imagine, at least, a form of government that would not exhibit monarchy. So, toward the latter part of *Common Sense*, Paine does allow himself some rather truncated suggestions, "hints," regarding a constitutional frame that would be suitable for a new American nation. Let each new state be divided into some six to ten districts, each sending "a proper number of delegates to Congress" (*CS* 28). The size of Congress would be about 390 persons. Congress would elect its own president, first from all the delegations at large and then, sequentially, from all of the delegations excepting the ones from which an earlier selection had been made. There would be no separate or independent executive. For any legislation to be enacted it would have to be passed by a three-fifths majority of the Congress. Paine spends no time in regards to the delineation of the government's powers; and there is nothing on the judiciary.[9] Rather, having settled to his own satisfaction what he thinks are the fundamental issues of constitutional form, Paine asserts that "[h]e will promote discord under a government so equally formed as this would have joined Lucifer in revolt" (*CS* 28).

There is an obvious parallel between Paine's recommendations for an American constitution in *Common Sense* and what would actually emerge as America's first constitution under the Articles of Confederation. The parallel extends, though not so exactly, to the new state constitutions that replaced the royal charters and compacts that had been held by the colonies. All of this new American exercise in constitution making was affected by the thought that republican government should be simple and representative, structured so as to reflect directly the people's own ready understanding of the limited practical requirements of their common good. Political union and strength would simply follow from the natural, social harmony among human beings once the sources of corruption had been cleared away. One overstates things only slightly in saying that American government under the Articles was an experiment in Paine's philosophy of nature and human nature. What, then, might Paine say of the evidence that this experiment was a profound failure? How might he have responded to the powerful divisive forces: sectional rivalries and, more important, the elusiveness of a practical notion of a common good among opposing economic interests such as debtors and creditors? When Alexander Hamilton attacks the presumptions of the supporters of loose confederation in *The Federalist Papers*, his remarks apply so precisely to Paine that it is as if he had Paine in mind. "Is it not time to awake from a deceitful dream of a golden age and to adopt as a practical maxim for the direction of our political conduct that we, as well as the other inhabitants of the globe, are yet remote from the empire of perfect wisdom and perfect virtue?"[10] We have learned our lesson, in other words. Even though we have thrown off monarchy, we remain just as much in need of a government that is aggressive and one that guards against tyranny—popular tyranny—by a complex scheme of checks and balances among separate branches. For his part, Paine does not enter the debate over the ratification of America's second, more Montesquieuian, Constitution. Instead, during this period his attentions were drawn toward Europe. In 1787, Paine returned to his native England and then, in 1790, accepted an invitation from Marquis de Lafayette and Condorcet to come to France. For the next few years he would be occupied with French politics, defining and defending the aims of the French Revolution in his book *The Rights of Man* (1791–1792).

Paine's aim in *The Rights of Man* is to defend the French Revolution against the calumnies that had been published by Edmund Burke in his *Reflections on the French Revolution*. Burke's central point had been that civilized society requires a respect for traditional structures and norms. Without a deference to authority that has become habitual, human life will be raw and savage. Burke pans the French revolutionaries as failing to appreciate civilization's fundamental requirement. Paine responds to this with a disappointment that appears quite genuine. He is sorry to see that the old friend of liberty, when the American colonies were struggling to express their opposition to Parliament, should now place himself in the antirevolutionary camp. How could anyone not see that the cause of American freedom and the aim of the French Revolution are but one? Paine was sure that, to their credit, the people of England were not the enemies of France. Their instinct was already republican, and they might attain legitimate institutions without violence if people like Burke would employ his genius in their assistance rather than to persist in his vain attempt to support the unsupportable.

The Rights of Man contains no new teaching from Paine, nothing that should be surprising to any reasonably careful reader of *Common Sense*. Some of the problems that have already been indicated, though, become somewhat more obvious in the later book. His main burden is to defend the French Declaration of Rights. More particularly, the first three articles of the Declaration are defended as containing a full statement of the founding principles of a legitimate, constitutional order, and they entail all of what follows.

> I. *Men are born, and always continue, free, and equal in respect of their rights. Civil distinctions, therefore, can be founded only on public utility.*
> II. *The end of all political associations, is, the preservation of the natural and imprescriptible rights of man; and these rights are liberty, property, security, and resistance of oppression.*

III. The nation is essentially the source of all sovereignty; nor can any INDIVIDUAL, or ANY BODY OF MEN, be entitled to any authority which is not expressly derived from it.

These principles are the basis of true constitutionalism (*RM* 314). That is, Paine explicates, they reflect what a constitution properly speaking *is*. The principles contain the recognition that the fundamental social contract that is at the root of all our obligations cannot be between individuals and their government. Rather, that contract is among individuals, arrived at deliberately and for the sake of their mutual advantage. It forms a social body. Government owes its legitimate existence to a second, subordinate act, performed by the social body. This is the enactment of a constitution, a sort of charter that arranges and defines government's powers. Specific limitations on government's powers are entirely in keeping with the nature of the constituting act.

The basic kinds of constitution are democracy, aristocracy, and monarchy. Originally, Paine speculates, all governments consisted of one of these basic forms. Beyond this categorization, however, it is necessary to distinguish governments that are *republican*. This word refers not to a form, but rather to a still more fundamental character. Government is republican when it aims at the *res publica*, the public things, as versus the things that belong distinctively to those who rule. In this attempt at careful language, Paine comes close to what had been said already by Aristotle, namely, that we may properly speak of a *politeia* (constitution) only where government serves the common good. For where the rulers serve their own good at the expense of those they rule, there exists only a deceitful imitation of a constitution. The difference between Aristotle and Paine, though, is that Paine could never accept Aristotle's idea that some few or even a single person might represent or even embody the common good to a greater degree of actuality than the aggregate whole.

All constitutional government, properly speaking, is republican. Democratic governments are republican automatically, insofar as the people rule themselves directly. This, Paine holds, is how governments actually began. However, as civil societies grew in size and population, direct popular government became impossibly inconvenient. Governments became more aristocratical and then monarchical, and because there were insufficient guarantees that the rulers would continue to serve the common good, they ceased to be republican. Only in comparatively recent times have human beings discovered an antidote to this process, that being formal representative institutions. To this limited extent Paine does agree with Montesquieu and with the authors of *The Federalist Papers* that representative institutions are the great political invention of modern times.

With this as his foundation, Paine proceeds to turn the tables on Burke. The British system of government is, in reality, not a constitutional system at all. Its delicate complexities, which Burke defends, only obscure this fact. Two specific points are especially revealing in this connection. First, in England, the government permits itself the authority to alter its own structure and powers. What Paine has in mind are the important acts of Parliament and even courts that are said to amend by reinterpreting England's unwritten constitution. Paine insists that when government alters itself in this way it means that government is obscuring or ignoring the crucial fact that government is the creature of the people and, as such, can only be altered by them. Second, and relatedly, Paine objects that the people of England are denied the right of altering their mode of government. This, of course, is a point that Burke insists on as a necessary advantage. Burke fears that if a people may be presumed to be able to alter their system of government it would mean that the whole set of fundamental institutions and norms are put into suspension. And then, how could they *act* at all?[11] Therefore, we must conclude that a people are not free in this way. They are rather bound by the terms of a previous agreement of long standing—of a previous generation!

This is for Paine anathema. He insists it is inappropriate, indeed impossible, for one generation to bind another. The same authority one generation has to make or unmake an agreement must belong to any other. The deference to the tradition that Burke recommends and apologizes for involves selling out our *natural* liberty. Burke's argument is a sophistry that underlies monarchy, at least where monarchy is not so openly brutal as to be able to rely on open force rather than sophistry.

It might occur to some of Paine's readers to ask at this point whether such traditionary sophistries as Burke's are bad insofar as they are in the service of monarchy or whether English monarchy is bad insofar as it is based on sophistry. Doubtless Paine would have little patience with such a question. For him, these are but two sides of the same bad coin.

In the 1790s, and for some time thereafter, it seemed to many that Paine's *The Rights of Man* was a dangerously incendiary book. Paine expected that the American and the French Revolutions would prove to be the first two steps toward a worldwide movement; and there were many who feared that he might be right. One must question, though, whether Paine's basic thought is in truth as incendiary as both he and so many of his opponents took it to be. Has it not become obvious now, if it was not in Paine's time, that government of all sorts might deftly incorporate a reference to the notion of the legitimating consent of the governed while preserving, or re-constituting, forms and prerogatives that Paine opposed? Is this not precisely what has happened? The excuse for such a development is the doctrine of *tacit* consent. This, of course, is by no means a novelty. In his *Second Treatise of Government*, Locke had already asserted that what a people do not actively oppose they might be presumed to consent to tacitly and that such consent is legitimating. For his part, Paine cannot deny that; and from time to time he even recognizes that a presumption of a people's tacit consent is necessary to the legitimacy of any stable system of law. Thus, for example, in elaborating his quarrel with Burke, Paine prudently acknowledges:

> It requires but a very small glance of thought to perceive, that although laws made in one generation often continue in force through succeeding generations, yet they continue to derive their force from the consent of the living. A law not repealed continues in force, not because it *cannot* be repealed; and the non-repealing passes for consent.

Still maintaining his argument against Burke, though, Paine goes on to insist:

> But Mr. Burke's clauses have not even this qualification in their favor. They become null, by attempting to become immortal. The nature of them precludes consent. They destroy the right which they *might* have, by grounding it in a right which they *cannot* have. Immortal power is not a human right, and therefore cannot be a right of Parliament. (*RM* 254)

So Burke has made a mistake if he thinks that tradition can be somehow put beyond repeal. But what Paine concedes in this very context is the weightier point. Popular consent may be presumed to legitimate pretty much anything, even, for example, government's altering itself, so long as its actions are not actively repealed.

Even concerning the question of the form of government, Paine cannot consistently avoid an ambivalence that stems from his concession to the doctrine of tacit consent. This is apparent in the manner in which he defends various features of the constitution of the French Republic. For example, Paine supports the unicameral legislature. He obviously has no truck with the Montesquieuian idea that there ought to be a second legislative chamber in which only a privileged class or nobility is represented. As for the arguments in behalf of an upper house providing some sober second thought in the legislative process, Paine rejoins with suggestions whereby a single chamber might employ procedures that would accomplish the same result. Still, Paine does not and cannot say that a bicameral legislature is necessarily illegitimate. He would not raise such a charge against the American bicameral legislature, for instance. If the people consent, that is the whole answer to the question of legitimacy, and, as with any other form of law, their consent may be presumed as given tacitly. What is true of the issue of the structure of the legislature, however, must ultimately be true for the issue of the structure of all the branches of government, and therefore even monarchy must be allowed a possible legitimacy. Considered carefully, Paine's brief remarks on the meaning of the basic forms of government and on the term "republic," mentioned above, imply this admission.

> The only forms of government are, the democratical, the aristocratical, the monarchical, and what is called the representative. What is called a *republic,* is not any *particular form* of government. It is wholly characteristical of the purport, matter, or object for which government ought to be instituted, and on which it is to be employed, *res-publica* the public affairs, or the public good; or, literally translated, the *public thing.* (*RM* 369)

A republic is not any particular form of government; that also means that it is not necessarily exclusive of any particular form—not according to their definitions. There might be a republican monarchy. Monarchy, the evil that is the source of all evil, *might* not be evil.

Political Economy

When it comes to social legislation, Paine has considerably more substantive and detailed proposals to recommend than he has respecting constitutional matters. His proposals exhibit what in more contemporary language might be termed his "social conscience." Especially in this connection one sees that Paine's hostility toward monarchy is not only an expression of ideological ardor or jealousy. He thinks that monarchy's evils bear most painfully on the poor, and he has unmistakable compassion for them. At the same time, however, Paine tries to prevent his reader from thinking that his redistributive measures are recommended out of compassion per se. What the poor would get from Paine's legislative proposals is due them *by right*. What is owed is not charity but justice (*AJ* 612). Surely it is this bold claim that fixes our interest. Wherein lies the justice of improving the condition of the poor? Can Paine show this while at the same time resting squarely and exclusively on his fundamentally liberal, individualistic principles?

Paine's recommendations for social legislation are made in two places. A major section of *The Rights of Man* (Part II, section 5) is devoted to the subject, and there is also a briefer work, *Agrarian Justice,* published in 1796. This was Paine's last published book. The proposals in these two works are similar but not identical. In *The Rights of Man*, most of what Paine has to say concerns the excessive burden of taxes, made necessary by monarchy. Paine is almost convinced that it is that burden that causes poverty (*RM* 424). He is certain that the huge tax reductions that will be affordable when monarchy is eliminated will more than any other measure improve the lot of the poor. In particular, if the English people follow the example of the French and throw off their king, they will enjoy a tax savings that Paine tries to gauge by way of an ingenious and very interesting argument. From 1066 until 1466, Paine shows that the revenues drawn by taxes fell by a factor of four. Then, from 1466 until Paine's own time, there was a precipitous rise, from 100,000 to 17 million pounds. This is attributable entirely to "the destructive system of continental intrigues, and the rage of foreign wars and foreign dominion" in which the monarchy has engulfed the nation, especially since the Hanover Succession (*RM* 417). Paine concludes from these figures that if that whole rotten system were shucked off, the actual revenue requirements of a republican government for England would be not more than 1.5 million pounds, leaving a savings of 15.5 million to be enjoyed by the general population, which at the time numbered approximately 7 million persons (*RM* 424).

Paine's projected lowering of taxes, taken by itself, almost suffices to sustain his confidence that the condition of the poor would be vastly improved under republican government. Still, he does go somewhat further, recommending that out of the dividend a program of what we now call "transfer payments" be made to those most in need. Again with respect to England, he proposes that taxes on the poor, the so-called poor rates, be abolished altogether and that in their place a remission be paid to the poor double the current rate. This remission would finance public assistance for some 252,000 poor families, and support for the education of more than 1 million children whose families cannot bear the cost. He recommends provision for an estimated 140,000 aged persons. Government would make a donation of 20 shillings to each of 20,000 marriages and each of 50,000 births. Funeral expenses would be provided to the poor. The total cost of these programs Paine estimates at roughly 4 million pounds, expended in the various ways over 1.4 million persons, or about one-fifth the total population of the nation. With respect to those he calls the "casual poor," Paine would have government guarantee "employment at all times" in the great cities of Westminster and London. Finally, he recommends some compensation to assist soldiers and sailors, who will of course not be needed in the new era.[12]

Equally important, Paine proposes alterations in the structure of English taxes. He outlines a program of progressive tax rates on the value of landed estates (*RM* 434–39). The rates are moderately steep, though not so much that there would not remain very considerable disparities among the population. It is his assertion of the justice of this measure in particular that gives most pause.

> Admitting that any annual sum, say for instance, one-hundred thousand pounds, is necessary or sufficient for the support of a family, consequently the second thousand is of the nature of a luxury, the third still more so, and by proceeding on, we shall at last arrive at a sum that may not improperly be called a prohibitable luxury. It would be impolitic to set bounds to property acquired by industry, and therefore it is right to place the prohibition beyond the probable acquisition to which industry can extend; but there ought to be a limit to property, or the accumulation of it, by bequest. (*RM* 434)

In other words, the rich do not need it and are unlikely to have earned it.

It is obvious that Paine cannot hold these assumptions without going beyond, that is violating, his fundamentally individualistic, liberal principles. If, as the Declaration of Independence says, all men have a right to the pursuit of their own happiness, it follows that no one may rightfully impose a sacrifice on another's pursuit of the other's happiness for the sake of his own. In the language of contemporary economists, there is no "interpersonal comparison of utility"; that is, I cannot rightfully compare the value of another's happiness with my own. This, however, is precisely the consequence of individualistic liberalism that so frustrates contemporary egalitarians, for it undermines the case for any sort of enforced transfer of "utility" from one person to another, irrespective of their condition. One, then, might take an expression like "prohibitable luxury" to be a clear indication of Paine's partial abandonment of his liberalism; and reflection shows that the same is true for all of his positive social legislation prescribed in *The Rights of Man*. However, since there is nowhere to be found in Paine's writing any general theory of justice that contrasts with strict liberalism, it would seem that contradiction is inadvertent.

In *Agrarian Justice,* Paine offers a somewhat different plan for poor relief than he had in *The Rights of Man* and, more to our interest, a more elaborate and ingenious defense of its justice. It seems likely that in the interim since he published *The Rights of Man*, he realized that a justification for poor relief was still needed. In the main, Paine's new proposal is to create a national fund, from which every person would be paid 15 pounds upon attaining twenty-one years of age. Beyond that, every person would be paid 10 pounds annual subsidy beginning at age sixty and continuing for life (*AJ* 612–13). It is the poor who would mostly be benefited by this plan but, as Paine is careful to note, the entitlement is universal. From what does this entitlement derive? Here is his thought. "Nothing," Paine acknowledges, "could be more unjust than agrarian law in a country improved by cultivation; for though every man, as an inhabitant of the earth, is a joint proprietor of it in its natural state, it does not follow that he is a joint proprietor of cultivated earth" (*AJ* 612). On the other hand, of the earth in its "natural"— uncultivated—state mankind *were* the joint proprietors. In civil society, where land is owned and cultivated, it is of course the case that the original joint proprietorship of the land in its natural condition has been obliterated. Nevertheless, our right to the value of our original share has not been, nor could it be, repealed. It remains as something owed to us as a sort of "*ground rent . . .* for the land which [the legal proprietor] holds" (*AJ* 611). This much of the argument is tempting; but the difficulty comes with setting the economic value in a contemporary society of each of our share of land in its uncultivated state. To put the question in John Locke's language, who in his *Second Treatise* considers the very same subject, "if we will rightly estimate things as they come to our use and cast up the several expenses about them, what [we may ask] in them is purely owing to nature, and what to labor[?]"[13] Paine ventures as his answer to this question that human cultivation "has given to the earth a tenfold value," so that the ground rent due all of us would equal one-tenth of the total value of the real property in society (*AJ* 612). It is here, obviously, where lies the heroic assumption. Why one-tenth? Paine offers not a word of explanation— because there could be none to give. Had he been reading his John Locke, he might have found that the ratio of one to ten is what Locke proposes in his first word describing the comparison of the value of uncultivated to cultivated land. But had Paine in fact been reading Locke with any care, he would have also seen that Locke later revises his estimate in favor of a much more disparate ratio.[14]

Paine's attempt to estimate the value of mankind's natural proprietorship of the earth as the basis for his basic entitlement program is too speculative to settle anything, indeed too fantastic to be taken seriously. Perhaps the most charitable attitude toward that attempt would derive from observing what he says on this point and his thoughts about the natural sociality of human beings, described earlier. Paine's general sense of "the state of nature" is that it is, so to speak, more natural than it had been said to be by Thomas Hobbes or John Locke. We might have lived comfortably there.

Religion

As we have seen, Paine thinks that monarchy institutionalizes something unnatural—that is, a perverse desire for an exaltedness over others that contradicts the natural equality among human beings. This thought invites the following question: how came there to be such a thing as monarchy originally? Part of the answer that Paine advances is sheer brute force. All monarchies trace their origins to some act of force. The English monarchy, for example, was established by "[a] French bastard landing with an armed banditti and establishing himself king of England against the consent of the natives . . . [which is] plainly a very paltry, rascally origin" (*CS* 14). And yet, this answer, Paine knows, cannot be fully satisfactory. It runs afoul of what Paine has also said about the goodness of human nature and the naturalness of our sociality. Even if we might hold, without contradiction, that one or a very small number of people might be animated by a passion for dominion that could not be natural or normal, there remains the question of how such a one could induce anyone to take him seriously. To exercise force, he would have to have an army; and who would commit himself to his service? Granting that he might, somehow, command a few swords, why would not most people simply ignore his claims as soon as the sword point was withdrawn? Paine's fuller, but more implicit, answer to this question, then, is that men are not just brutally compelled to accept a king but also seduced into believing his claims. Despite their natural healthy goodness, human beings must be susceptible to the fantastic notion of an exaltation of some over others. The direct expression of this susceptibility is their religion. A belief in God appears to be a necessary corollary of monarchy. It is also clear that the sort of God who serves this purpose must be one who exercises monarchical prerogatives: favor and disfavor, reward and punishment.

Human beings' original vulnerability to monarchy and their vulnerability to religion are really the same. It is also quite understandable that we should have suffered this in the world's early stages, when human beings understood nothing of the natural causes of the beneficent or calamitous forces to which they were subject. We were corrupted, then, before we had the intellectual strength to resist. In his *Common Sense*, Paine leads us quite cleverly from this sense of despair to hope. In America, the life of the human race might begin anew. It is—not literally so—but as if part of the planet were held in reserve for human nature and human society to reestablish itself—this time among mature human beings, in command of their faculties, with no demons or tyrant Gods to plague them.

Does Paine think that anything of religion will remain in the future ages of enlightenment? Or should it? The answer is yes, but it is a complicated yes. For one thing, belief in the Bible as the source of divine revelation is still very strong, and the sects that stem from that will be around for an indefinite future. For this reason, Paine has to at least make his peace with biblical religion. In *Common Sense*, he tries even to avail himself of biblical authority by showing that monarchy is in truth devoid of biblical support. A considerable section of the book is devoted to retelling Old Testament history. In Paine's hands, it appears that man's original bliss extended far past the Garden of Eden. He makes it seem that our true fall came with the coronation of Saul.

Paine concedes by his own practice that human beings will still have religious beliefs in the future. This means too, he knows, that we will be divided by our different beliefs. Paine does not think, however, that there is any necessity or likelihood that these differences will makes us enemies. Part of the reason for this is that Paine is confident that religions in general, the *genus* religion, is benign (*RM* 292). It is only insofar as religions have been appropriated by political authorities that they have appeared to be divisive. This connection will be broken. In this respect, Paine defends as an especially key point the provision of the French Declaration of Rights that guarantees the universal right of conscience. He is very explicit that this right goes beyond the recognition of the value of religious "tolerance" that is sometimes defended in England, for example. We may be tolerant of what we recognize to be an evil, so long as it is not too threatening. Tolerance may be the better part of prudence, so to speak. The universal right of conscience, however, implies that all contents of religious conscience are equal—equal in substantive truth. "But with respect to religion itself, without regard to names, and as directing itself from the universal family of mankind to the divine object of all adoration, *it is Man bringing to his maker the fruits of his heart*; and though these fruits may differ from each other like the fruits of the earth, the grateful tribute of everyone is accepted" (*RM* 292). Paine caps this sweet thought by saying that God himself must intend there to be a variety of religions. And yet, is there not an all too obvious contradiction in these very words? The universal right of conscience is grounded in his argument for the equal truth value of all religions; but that in turn appears to be grounded in his own distinctive theological assertions.

This sort of question cannot help but cause us to be suspicious regarding everything that Paine says about religion. It is obvious that what he says in *Common Sense* about the status of kingship according to the Bible is addressed to people whose faith is other than his own. Might not the same thing be true of all his religious statements? For most religious Americans during the eighteenth century, it was largely a commonplace that Paine was an atheist. Such a view is understandable, and *may* be correct. It is tempting to think that an absolute right of conscience entails a profound indifference to the truth claims of different religions and that that in turn entails a dismissal of all of them as bunk. Religions are not all equally true because God loves them all; rather, they are equally false. It is not that God has no preference, but that there is no God to have a preference.

Despite the widespread view of Paine as an atheist, though, his book *The Age of Reason*, published in 1794 and 1795, belies it. In it he sets forth his own "conscientious belief" in a religion that he terms "Deism." It is a simple religion, to which one may be guided speculatively by one's own rational powers, and which gratifies and sustains those powers as well as other virtues that make us good neighbors and good citizens. Assuming a more candidly personal stance than he had in earlier books, his case for his deistic religion is put together with a polemic against the religions of the Bible; and that polemic forms the bulk of the book. Paine intends that Deism emerge from the rubble to which he attempts to reduce the Bible. To weigh the full force of Paine's polemic, it is necessary to read the book in its entirety and to engage the arguments at close quarters. Here it is possible only to give a brief outline.

Paine does not quarrel with the possibility of divine revelation. However, since for him and the rest of us biblical revelation is mediated by the human authors of the Bible, who, as prophets, claim to have received the revelation, Paine sets out to examine whether that human claim is credible. He finds it not so. In the first place, the Bible itself hints that the ancient Hebrews did not understand the term "prophecy" in this way. Rather, when King Saul, for example, speaks of his own prophetic powers it is in a way that suggests something more like what others call poetry. It is a sort of hyperactivity of the imagination that does not presume to be literal. As for the content of prophecy, Paine says that for his own part it is sufficient to observe that both the Old and the New Testaments are childish, brutal, and immoral in order to be certain of their falsehood. He acknowledges that others, however, might not be convinced by that sort of evidence, and so he enters into a form of exegesis to show that the Bible is inconsistent on its own terms and that it could not have been written by those whose authority it claims.

As for the Old Testament, Paine is especially horrified with the account that God should have commanded the wholesale slaughter of an innocent people in order that His chosen people might make way for themselves in their promised land. Surely this is the morality of a crude, barbaric people who have not yet learned the virtue of humanity. Next, the Old Testament history is said to depend on the authority of the prophets, mainly Moses, Joshua, and Samuel. What evidence, though, is there that these prophets actually wrote the Bible? Nowhere does the Bible contain any direct claim by these persons, in their own name, that what we read is their word. The presumption that it is theirs might be charitable but it is impossible. This Paine attempts to demonstrate by drawing out many anachronisms that would follow from an original prophetic authorship. To cite just one example, Exodus is presumed to be a book of Moses; but the book not only speaks of him in the past tense but also contains an account of things that occurred after Moses' death—in a few cases well after. Paine also cites many conflicting accounts of what appear to be the same events given in different books of the Old Testament. Sometimes sequences differ; sometimes important details are altered or omitted from one book to another. The largest scale example of this sort of thing is that many, or most, of the prophets who have books that bear their names as titles, such as Ezekiel or Daniel or Amos, do not even appear in the books of Kings or Chronicles, even though they are said to have lived during the period for which Kings and Chronicles claim to give the comprehensive historical record. In sum, this part of the Bible gives every evidence of having been compiled much later than the events of which it gives account, compiled somewhat clumsily and not too faithfully out of an earlier tradition that was incomplete, self-contradictory, and full of confusion.

Turning to the New Testament, it fares little better than the Old. It too is fundamentally immoral, although not in quite the same way. Paine does acknowledge that Jesus himself exemplified and taught genuine human virtues, of brotherly love and the like. The attitude that emerges from *The Age of Reason* toward Christianity is very similar to today's Christian humanism, but with a sharper edge of hostility toward the more literalist tradition. The New Testament's one great drama implies a horrid God. For Paine, it is a blasphemous obscenity. In the first place, there is no way that an innocent person can expiate someone else's guilt merely by accepting the punishment due the guilty. In the administration of justice among human beings, such a thing is unthinkable; and it does not become thinkable by virtue of the mind numbing, cosmic magnitude of the sacrifice. Also, the specific character of that sacrifice bears no relation to its avowed meaning. That is, even if Jesus' death was intended, somehow, to be the basis of our atonement, there is no necessity for that death to result from his having been falsely convicted and executed on a cross. Why would not death from sickness or accident, or just old age, serve as well? Most important, the whole notion that Jesus' suffering and death might stand instead of our own implies that God has a desire for suffering and death. He enjoys the spectacle! To attribute such a character to the King of the Universe, Paine is sure, would be possible only for someone whose ideas about kingship are formed out of experience with those most perversely wicked prerogatives of kingship that the ancient world exhibited. Paine then adds to this criticism the evidence that the books of the New Testament were all written many years after the events; and that they contain several embarrassments of direct contradiction or suspicious omissions.

In what way, then, is the positive case for Paine's own deistic religion connected to the foregoing polemic? Paine's answer appears to be that if he can show that the whole Bible is not only an unlikely tale but also that its teaching is in fact ugly and despicable, he will deprive it of the awe in which it is held by the believers. In so doing, he thinks he will confirm our confidence in our own powers of reason and judgment, whereby the fact that the universe is divinely ordered will be self-evident. It appears that a thoroughgoing reductionism holds so little plausibility for him as to require no response. His discursive argument proceeds from his observation that the world is in general a hospitable realm for human beings. The degree and varied manner of that hospitality is continually surprising to whoever opens his eyes and reflects. For one thing, the fruits of the earth are in fact abundant. This means that it is possible for human beings to acquire the wherewithal to satisfy their needs comfortably without spending all of their energies. The world makes it possible for us to attain some leisure, so that we might afford the exercise of our higher faculties. Not only that, but Paine also finds especially worth mentioning that the world appears to contain hints to human beings to help them figure out its true structure. For example, if there were no planets, whose wandering motions contrast with the revolution of the stars, it would have been much more difficult for Copernicus to have finally discovered the untruth of the Aristotelian/Ptolemaic cosmology. Such phenomena are like pointers that seem to have been put there by a God who wishes His order to become known. In this way, we may say that speculative reason supplies to itself a grounding in an idea of God's Providence. God has the virtue of humanity. He wishes us to see by our own lights and helps us to do so. If we are aware of this true character of God, we cannot help but be soothed and moved to imitate him. Our natural sociality and cooperative instincts, mentioned above, are in this way confirmed by what speculative reason concludes is right with God. It by no means follows from this that God punishes our sins or shortcomings, nor does he reward us. What could God gain from retribution? Our virtues, being natural, are their own reward, and our attainment of them must cause the Author of Nature to smile. Here, then, is a religion worthy of what Americans are and what the French aspire to be: equal, free and independent of mind and heart, and naturally good.

To conclude the account and assessment of Paine's thought, it is necessary to return to the question of the relationship between the arguments of *The Age of Reason* and his intense, radical endorsement of the "universal right of conscience." Is there not a problem? Those who are entirely satisfied by slogans such as "I hate your faith but would defend to the death your right to hold it" will of course deny that there could be a problem. But that is obtuse. Paine's partisanship, especially his attachment to the universal right of conscience is, in his mind, connected at a fundamental level with the "conscientious belief" that Deism is the truth. The alternative to the universal right of conscience is enforced hypocrisy; but God Himself prefers the doubter and the denier to the hypocrite. Paine can be generous toward unbelief because his heart is steeped in the belief in a humane God and he knows that. His hostility to the Bible also involves hostility to belief in the Bible. It is corrupting. He hopes it will disappear. For the time being, it might be well to give it official "tolerance," but this is to temporize with the evil. Freedom will not be secure in the world until Paine's religion conquers the field. Paine's Deism is such that it precludes the possibility of proscribable heresy. Still, if it is contentful at all, it is a basis from which error can and must be identified as such. If the error is necessarily corrupting, as Paine is certain it is, neither he nor God can be indifferent.

Finally, how compelling *is* the argument in *The Age of Reason*? Let us try to compress it to the briefest formula: the only God that could exist is not the biblical God but rather Paine's gently provident, humane God. But is this not arrogant presumption? Who are we, mortals, to set limits on the character of God? Why might God not be jealous and fearsome? Why might He not have a chosen people whose special mission could entail extraordinary and even inhumane deeds? Or why might not the peculiar character of divine justice somehow involve God's experiencing for Himself the penalty He imposes for human sin? As for the anachronism and contradictions within the text, should it be surprising that human language should founder among contradictions when it seeks to speak of God? Such questions, doubtless, could not trouble a person like Thomas Paine. But they are forceful for a soul deepened by loving submission and obedience to biblical authority. Paine does not plumb these depths. He cuts with brave and unrelenting energy—but not to the root.

Notes

1. For example, Staughton Lynd, *Intellectual Origins of American Radicalism* (Cambridge, Mass.: Harvard University Press, 1982), in which references to Paine abound. Cf. especially 74–77.

2. John Locke, *The Second Treatise of Government,* ed. Thomas P. Peardon (Indianapolis: Bobbs-Merrill Company, 1952), chap. 10.

3. Locke, *Second Treatise*, 29.

4. Thomas Hobbes, *Leviathan*, ed. Michael Oakshott (New York: Crowell-Collier, 1962), pt. II, chap. 20. As for Locke, this is one of the instances of his notorious wiliness. Section 186 of *The Second Treatise* does deny that promises extorted by force are binding and thus denies the legitimacy of sovereignty established by conquest. Nevertheless, in section 193, Locke bows to practical necessity and grants that a conqueror, at least a just conqueror, has a right to the estates as well as power over the persons conquered. The ongoing consent of the conquered is then necessary and sufficient to legitimate the sovereign's authority. Later, in chapter 19 (sections 235–43), Locke undermines the grounds of his own distinction

between just and unjust conquest so that his ultimate position is fully reconciled with that posited by Hobbes.

5. Jean-Jacques Rousseau, *The Social Contract*, trans. Maurice Cranston (London: Viking-Penguin, 1968), 60.

6. Quotations from and references to Paine's works will be from volume one of *The Complete Writings of Thomas Paine*, ed. Philip S. Foner, 2 vols. (New York: Citadel Press, 1945). Quotations and references will be cited in the text according to the following abbreviations: *AJ = Agrarian Justice*; *CS = Common Sense*; and *RM = The Rights of Man*.

7. See Adam Smith, *The Wealth of Nations* (New York: E. P. Dutton and Co., 1937), vol. I, bk. 1, chap. 2, 14, and David Hume *A Treatise of Human Nature*, ed. L. A. Selby-Brigge (London: Oxford University Press, 1965), bk. III, pt. 2, sec. 2, esp. 493. Rousseau's response to the problem referred to in this paragraph might be said to be the most extreme. He too begins by observing that man is cooperative by nature. As noted though, he goes so far as to hold that the societies men form can be good only if we abandon reference to our natural rights and needs. In other words, there *is* a common good; but, in contrast with Aristotle, it is not natural! We participate in the artificial good, society itself, since we have become, largely, artificial beings.

8. As an illustration, for example, consider how different is Thoreau's case for civil disobedience from that of Martin Luther King, Jr. In his "Letter from a Birmingham Jail," King insists that the practice of civil disobedience will tend to purify and hence strengthen the rule of law. Thoreau, in contrast, recommends civil disobedience as a principled tactic which, when it becomes widespread, will bring about the civilized anarchy toward which America is pointing. Cf. Thoreau, *Resistance to Civil Government*, in *Walden and Resistance to Civil Government*, ed. William Rossi, 2nd ed. (New York: W. W. Norton and Co., 1992), as well as the the second and tenth chapters of *Walden*.

9. Paine's silence as to the constitutional status of the judiciary in *Common Sense* is consonant with his argument in the later book, *The Rights of Man*, wherein he explains that the judiciary is not a separate branch but rather one department of all that should be called "administration" (*RM* 388). His view, in fact, anticipates that of Frank J. Goodnow, pioneer in the emerging study of public administration with his book *Politics and Administration: A Study in Government* (New York: Macmillan Company, 1914), with whom there exist many parallels.

10. *The Federalist Papers*, ed. Clinton Rossiter (New York: New American Library of World Literature, 1961), no. 6, 59.

11. Paine approves of the mode whereby the American Constitution was ratified as conforming to his notion that it was an extralegal, directly popular act. Surely, though, he finesses this matter and overlooks difficulties. The American Constitution was ratified in extraordinary conventions, to be sure, but these conventions were established in the states, by the legislatures of the states. When nine states had acted in this way, the Constitution became effective. One should also consider the role that governmental institutions exercise under the Constitution in amending the Constitution. Rousseau speaks directly to this question, which is merely begged by Paine, as to how a people can act beyond the institutions of government. The amusing ingenuity of his solution in fact illustrates the impossibility of any genuine solution. Cf. chapter 17 of *The Social Contract*, 145–46.

12. *RM* 431 for the summary of these measures. The foregoing several pages explain them in more detail.

13. Locke, *Second Treatise*, 25.

14. Locke, *Second Treatise*, 23–25.

Chapter 4

Benjamin Franklin: A Model American and an American Model

Steven Forde

Though he was one of the most renowned and influential of the American Founders, Benjamin Franklin (1706–1790) never produced a systematic work of political philosophy. He tended to think of such exercises in "metaphysical Reasonings" as futile and unreliable guides to political and moral life. Yet he was not a man of uncertain conviction. To the contrary, he was quite outspoken in his political views, and all his public writings are devoted in one way or another to spreading a certain set of principles and ideas. These ideas and principles constitute a well-considered and coherent body of thought, but one whose contours must be inferred from writings whose focus is hardly ever theoretical. In all important respects, Franklin's ideas are in accord with those of his fellow Founders. Intellectually, Franklin is firmly within the horizon of modernity laid out by the likes of John Locke and David Hume. Due to his distinctive intellectual concerns, Franklin's thought makes some novel contributions to the modern intellectual project as a whole.

Franklin's career took him down a very different path from that of the other American Founders. Born in very humble circumstances in Boston in 1706, he made his way to Philadelphia at age seventeen, where he set up as a printer. This trade kept him in constant contact with the intellectual productions of Britain, and it helped him become an accomplished essayist (and propagandist) himself. His researches in electricity, which made real contributions to scientific understanding, gained him notice on both sides of the Atlantic. He had a long-standing interest in politics and served in many official and unofficial capacities in Philadelphia. In 1757, he was sent to London to represent the interests of colonial Pennsylvania. He stayed there, representing one or more of the colonies, for all but two of the years from 1757 to 1775. In 1776, after a brief return to America, he was sent to Paris as diplomat from the fledgling United States to the French court. He returned to Philadelphia in 1785 and participated in the Federal Convention of 1787 before his death in 1790. By the end of his life, Franklin's reputation in America was such that some thought the Constitution was ratified only due to widespread knowledge that he and George Washington supported it. Franklin was the only American whose name was widely known outside America before 1776, based on his researches into electricity and his diplomacy on behalf of the American colonies. Jacques Turgot's famous eulogy, *Eripuit caelo fulmen sceptrumque tyrannis*—"he seized lightning from the heavens and the scepter from tyrants"—encapsulated Franklin's international renown. These two things—the advancement of science and the struggle for political freedom—epitomize not only Franklin's career but also the aspirations of modern philosophy as such.

I

His *Autobiography* (written in three parts, in 1771, 1784, and 1788, but published posthumously) is the most extensive piece of writing Franklin produced. Though it is unfinished, it was written deliberately for educational purposes, and it represents the most complete statement of the teaching Franklin wanted to bequeath to his posterity. The *Autobiography* shows Franklin rising from low origins to a position of prosperity and influence, all the while living a life of the greatest contentment. It shows Franklin learning some hard lessons, curing himself of some vices, and discovering the virtues that lead to success and happiness both. The *Autobiography* presents Franklin self-consciously as a model citizen for the democratic and commercial societies that were then taking shape. It reflects Franklin's considered teaching regarding the requirements of such societies and of the happiness of the individuals in them.

The early pages of the *Autobiography* show us an unusually bookish young man, initially destined for the clergy, who devoured the volumes he found in his father's library in Boston. Among these were Plutarch, Daniel Defoe's *Essay on Projects*, and Cotton Mather's *Essays to Do Good*, all of which, Franklin tells us, had a profound, positive effect on him. He also found many books of "polemic Divinity," whose influence was less salutary. They helped give his thinking and his speech a disputatious turn, a vice into which "Persons of good Sense" seldom fall.[1] As to the substance of these books, the precocious Franklin found the Deist positions being attacked more persuasive than the polemics against them, making him a "thorough Deist" by age fifteen. He soon fell upon a copy of Xenophon's *Memorabilia* and adopted an eristic style of questioning patterned on the Socrates he found there. Putting these two things together, he took to questioning his fellow Bostonians on their religious beliefs. In short order, he came to be regarded by them with "Horror," as an "Infidel or Atheist" (1321, 1325). For this and other reasons, he shortly felt compelled to leave Boston.

This series of events, Franklin tells us, taught him something about civility and social order: an affirmative and dogmatic conversation is liable to make enemies rather than friends, make social relations unpleasant, and limit one's influence by limiting one's ability to persuade (1321–22). Hence, he abandoned his dogmatism and his eristic style and developed the habit of almost never expressing himself in terms of affirmative certitude. He did not, however, lose his fascination with abstract reasoning upon religious and philosophical subjects, at least not immediately. To the contrary, he was so enamored with this type of thought that, at different moments during his early life, he composed two separate essays arguing opposite and incompatible positions on free will, virtue, and Providence. Yet the two arguments were equally unimpeachable, so far as he could tell. This experience led him to the momentous conclusion that such questions could not be resolved by human reason. "The great uncertainty I found in metaphysical reasonings disgusted me," he later told a correspondent, "and I quitted that kind of reading and study for others more satisfactory" (1016; cf. 1359).

The new studies to which Franklin turned embraced the subjects of politics, morality, and even religion. What he renounced were attempts to ground his understanding of these matters in "metaphysics." The *Autobiography* relates a pivotal series of episodes in which the young Franklin discovered that his metaphysically anchored Deism corrupted some of his companions. His demonstrations convinced them that there could be no particular Providence; but, without the prospect of divine rewards and punishments, their morality proved evanescent. These friends subsequently "wronged me greatly without the least Compunction," Franklin complains, leading him to an epiphany of sorts. "I began to suspect that this Doctrine tho' it might be true, was not very useful," and he replaced it with a moral outlook based on the premise that "*Truth, Sincerity*

& Integrity in Dealings between Man & Man, were of the utmost Importance to the Felicity of Life" (1359).

We must be careful to understand correctly this intellectual and moral turn in Franklin's life, for it forms the foundation of all his subsequent thinking. It is not that Franklin rejects "truth" in favor of what is "useful"; rather, he is careful to clarify, the harmful consequences of his Deism led him to suspect that the logic behind it had been defective, since error is liable to creep into all speculative "metaphysical Reasonings" (1359). It is their uncertainty that leads Franklin to leave such reasonings behind in favor of the conviction that *"Truth, Sincerity & Integrity* in Dealings between Man & Man" is the touchstone of morality. Henceforth, this principle and its derivatives become the poles of Franklin's moral compass.

In doubting metaphysics, however, Franklin does little more than some of his predecessors in modern moral philosophy. Locke's *Essay Concerning Human Understanding*, a work with which Franklin was familiar, begins with a declaration that human reason is incapable of resolving many of the metaphysical disputes in which earlier philosophy (and theology) became embroiled. Locke nonetheless says that reason is capable of putting morality on a new and more solid foundation, rooted in an empirical assessment of what is good for man's life. David Hume, a man personally known to Franklin, says that our social and political duties have two sources, neither of which is "metaphysical": the first is humane moral sentiments; the second is the benefits that moral action brings to society. It is essentially an empirical question what rules of justice and decorum benefit society. Hume's well-known denial of the social contract reflects this outlook: our obligations stem not from some hypothetical original agreement but from the goods that society confers on us. The obligation is based not on a priori speculation but on a posteriori discovery of social utility.

Franklin is not simply a disciple of Locke or Hume, but these examples show the type of reasoning that lies behind his political and moral thought. When he renounces "metaphysical Reasonings" about morality in favor of the principle of *"Truth, Sincerity & Integrity* in Dealings between Man & Man," he is not outside the fold of modern philosophy. His moral lodestar is not metaphysically, but empirically derived. Morality is that which experience shows to be most conducive to human happiness—"the Felicity of Life," as he put it. That this type of utility is the cornerstone of morality is a theme Franklin returned to again and again in his writings. In part II of the *Autobiography*, where he gives the most systematic account of his moral teaching, he states his position this way: "vicious Actions are not hurtful because they are forbidden, but forbidden because they are hurtful, the Nature of Man alone consider'd" (1392). Morality is (or should be) nothing but the sum of rules that serve our happiness, according to a proper under-standing of our nature. Virtue is not in its essence self-suppression or self-sacrifice; rather, it is almost the reverse. Virtue might require the regular denial of certain appetites and pleasures but only in the name of greater overall happiness.

Armed with this view of things, Franklin (like Locke, Hume, and others) sifted the morality that had been bequeathed to him, rejecting some rules and accepting others based on his candid assessment of human nature and the happiness of which it is susceptible. This is what allows Franklin, despite his metaphysical skepticism, to make such sweeping statements as: "the chief Ends of Conversation are to *inform*, or to be *informed*, to *please* or to *persuade*" (1322). This statement is the culmination of Franklin's critique of disputatiousness and dogmatism in speech: these become vices because they undermine the prospects of pleasant and mutually beneficial social relations, and thereby the happiness of the speaker and those with whom he has to deal. The same principle is at work in the remarkable "Speech of Miss Polly Baker" (1747), a fictional piece in which the heroine is hailed before a court "for having a Bastard Child"—for the fifth time (305–8). In her defense, she appeals to nature, whose purposes include the propagation of the race. Though a perfectly upstanding citizen in every other respect, she says, she has been repeatedly abandoned by scurrilous men, including some prominent in the community. In fine, not her behavior but the law needs adjustment, in order to bring it into line with nature and with human well-being. In typical fashion, Franklin adds that this speech induced the court to pardon her—and one of the judges to marry her.

It is easy to see, on the basis of vignettes like this, why John and Abigail Adams regarded Franklin as a libertine. Yet this is only a consequence of Franklin's principle that every moral stricture that cannot be justified by social utility and personal happiness is to be rejected, no matter how apparently sacrosanct. A large part of Franklin's motivation as a thinker and essayist is the humane one of liberating mankind from needless restrictions on their appetites, clearing the way for the pursuit of happiness rationally understood. In this fundamental undertaking, he treads solidly in the footsteps of his philosophical forebears.

II

This background is necessary in part because Franklin is so often viewed as the apostle of a dreary bourgeois morality, a bloodless and repressive "Protestant Ethic." This impression stems from Franklin's emphasis on industry, frugality, and the other virtues of economic gain, and from the relentless moralizing of Poor Richard in largely the same vein.[2] A compendium of Poor Richard's sayings that Franklin composed in 1757 became widely known as "The Way to Wealth"—and for good reason. There is no denying that this is the part of Franklin's moral teaching that he took most care to spread far and wide. He tells us that he inserted the sayings of Poor Richard in his almanac "as a proper Vehicle for conveying Instruction among the common People, who bought scarce any other Books" (1397). He also proposed putting such sayings on coins, fireplace tiles, and other places where they might be constantly seen (888, 1011). He wished no opportunity for instruction in these simple virtues to go unused.

The *Autobiography* explains Franklin's reasoning. He advertised industry and frugality "as the Means of procuring Wealth and thereby securing Virtue, it being more difficult for a Man in Want to act always honestly, as . . . *it is hard for an empty sack to stand upright*" (1397). The emphasis on these two virtues is appropriate because they form a bulwark against poverty and the temptations to dishonest gain that it brings. A certain level of economic prosperity is necessary to "secure" virtue. Industry and frugality are vital precisely *because* they are linked to economic gain; gain to prosperity; and prosperity ultimately to virtue. Franklin's procedure presumes that it is futile to expect virtue from destitution—that human nature will not reliably hew to the path of virtue without a certain level of comfort. Besides, if virtue in its essence is the servant of human happiness, it cannot be estranged from economic gain. It is important to recognize, though, that economic gain is not for Franklin an end in itself. The virtues of economic gain are the beginning, not the end, of his moral teaching. The point is not to fill the sack but to allow it to stand upright.

In part II of the *Autobiography*, Franklin outlines a project that he once conceived to develop an "Art of Virtue." Originally intended to be the subject of a separate publication, its purpose is to allow anyone to cultivate virtue—indeed, to achieve "moral Perfection" (1383). Its centerpiece is a list of thirteen virtues, with a brief gloss on each:

1. TEMPERANCE (Eat not to Dulness. Drink not to Elevation).
2. SILENCE (Speak not but what may benefit others or your self. Avoid trifling conversation).
3. ORDER (Let all your Things have their Places. Let each Part of your Business have its Time).

4. RESOLUTION (Resolve to perform what you ought. Perform without fail what you resolve).
5. FRUGALITY (Make no Expence but to do good to others or yourself: i.e. Waste nothing).
6. INDUSTRY (Lose no Time—Be always employ'd in something useful—Cut off all unnecessary Actions).
7. SINCERITY (Use no hurtful Deceit. Think innocently and justly; and, if you speak, speak accordingly).
8. JUSTICE (Wrong none, by doing Injuries or omitting the Benefits that are your Duty).
9. MODERATION (Avoid Extreams. Forbear resenting Injuries so much as you think they deserve).
10. CLEANLINESS (Tolerate no Uncleanness in Body, Cloaths or Habitation).
11. TRANQUILITY (Be not disturbed at Trifles, or at Accidents common or unavoidable).
12. CHASTITY (Rarely use Venery but for Health or Offspring; Never to Dulness, Weakness, or the Injury of your own or another's Peace or Reputation).
13. HUMILITY (Imitate Jesus and Socrates).

These are very basic virtues—the classical philosophers Aristotle and Cicero would scarcely acknowledge some of them as virtues—but they are the virtues that humble folk need to cultivate in order to gain a solid footing in life. They involve considerable discipline, which is why Poor Richard must harp on them constantly. But they impose no needless restraint on our actions or appetites (consider but the loopholes in the virtue of "Chastity"). The first step to a life of happiness involves the development of habits of self-control outlined in these virtues.

It is always necessary to bear in mind Franklin's audience when considering his moral teaching. Unlike most of his fellow Founders, and unlike most of his comrades in the modern philosophical movement, Franklin addressed himself forthrightly and deliberately to the common people. If Franklin has a distinctive contribution to make to the development of modern political thought, it is his reflections on the virtues that these people would need in the emerging liberal and egalitarian order of things. These virtues of self-reliance and self-advancement are as different from the old virtues as is the new order itself from its predecessors. We might even say that Franklin's homely virtues represent the true face of modern moral philosophy (or at least a part of it, for industry, frugality, and the other virtues listed above are not the whole of Franklin's moral teaching).

The primary difference between Franklin and other modern thinkers might therefore be said to be rhetorical. From the very beginning of his intellectual career, as a printer's apprentice to his brother in Boston, Franklin was writing essays aimed at shaping public morality—above all, the morality of common folk. The *noms de plume* alone convey his message. Silence Dogood, who appeared in 1722, was a Boston widow—"an Enemy to Vice, and a Friend to Vertue"— endowed with "a natural Inclination to observe and reprove the Faults of others" (8). Some years later, the "Busy-Body" debuted in Philadelphia, a self-proclaimed *Censor Morum* for the public good. Since *"what is every Body's Business is no Body's Business,"* this public servant proposed to make use of the delight people take in the censure of others to expose those vices and delicts that lie beneath the notice of law, yet which are harmful to society (92, 104). While the modern understanding of liberty prevents government from policing morality per se, good mores are nonetheless vital to the health of society. As Tocqueville was later to argue at length, this means that modern democratic societies must police themselves. This is the task that Franklin took up with wit and gusto, using his bully pulpit to chide his fellow Americans into virtue.

Franklin was significantly older than most of the other American Founders, and he lived during a time when the liberal and egalitarian political dispensation was still gestating. Beginning with Silence Dogood, Franklin's writings evince a distinctive view of the requirements of social health within the parameters of the coming order. For the first time, human beings—particularly the common people—were free to govern themselves, both politically and privately. Colonial

America was the first real laboratory for this experiment. Though inheriting the culture of aristocratic and monarchical Europe, it was de facto an egalitarian society. Nominally ruled from abroad, it was allowed to rely largely on local self-government from the beginning. In a sense, it had to develop on its own the culture that would make the new order viable. Franklin's essays—indeed, his oeuvre as a whole—reveal his intention to be the midwife of this emerging culture.

The new order, to a much greater extent than the old, would stand or fall by the virtues of the common man. While the common man now had unprecedented freedom, he would have to make proper use of it. The first virtues for free people who begin life with little are necessarily the virtues of economic self-reliance. As Franklin's parable of the empty sack indicates, a measure of prosperity must be earned by such people before they can concern themselves with anything else. The situation in America was unusually hospitable to this project, as opportunity abounded, and industry and frugality were virtually certain to be rewarded. Even so (as numerous emerging nations have since learned), opportunity, even with the incentive of material advancement, is not enough in itself to guarantee individual or social prosperity. The virtues of honest gain are required as well, and these are the virtues that Franklin, and Poor Richard, concern themselves with first. They know that illicit or unearned gain, or even slothful poverty, are standing temptations. In some writings on the unintended consequences of poor laws, Franklin is remarkably harsh toward those who take advantage of the dole to cease working: "[I]f we provide encouragements for Laziness, and supports for Folly, may it not be found fighting against the order of God and Nature, which perhaps has appointed Want and Misery as the proper Punishments for, and Cautions against as well as necessary consequences of Idleness and Extravagancy" (469). Franklin was a great friend to the common man, but he had little patience for the vices into which he might fall, vices that needed constantly to be guarded against. As Poor Richard notes at the conclusion of "The Way to Wealth," where his sayings on industry, frugality, and honest gain are strung into a single harangue: "the People heard it, and approved the Doctrine, and immediately practiced the contrary" (1302). Humble as they may be, virtues such as industry and frugality are not to be taken for granted. They are, in some sense, the founding virtues of the new social order.

III

To say that they are the founding virtues, however, is not to say they are the only virtues, and Franklin's emphasis on them should not blind us to the rest of his moral teaching, nor to his fully developed view of a healthy social order. Economic self-reliance may be the indispensable first step toward a successful regime of individual freedom, but it is only a first step. There is a report that Franklin was asked as he departed the Constitutional Convention what form of government the Framers had devised for the nation. His reply: "A Republic, if you can keep it." Free government can only be sustained by a people who have the habits and virtues appropriate to it—the mores of freedom, we might say—and the development of these was as a rule of greater concern to Franklin than institutions or laws. He aims to cultivate in Americans forms of self-reliance that go beyond the economic—forms of social if not political activism that make up good citizenship. In Franklin's list of thirteen virtues, this is visible only as a muted emphasis on doing good to others. The lessons in citizenship become much more visible as we turn our attention to the *Autobiography* as a whole.

When we read the *Autobiography* with this concern in mind, we see that it is permeated with the spirit of public service. One of the principal reasons Franklin tells us he turned away from the disputatiousness of his early youth was that it limits one's power of doing good (1322). Among the readings of his youth that he did not regret, we recall, were Defoe's *Essay on Projects* and Mather's *Essays to Do Good*. These are works whose impress remained on Franklin throughout his life. The Franklin of the *Autobiography* is nothing if not a projector—rich in ideas for the improvement of the life of the community and tireless in the promotion of them. We see him organizing night watches, acting to improve street lights and street cleaning, putting together fire and civil defense brigades, and mustering support for the first public library, hospital, and school in Philadelphia. His purpose in narrating these undertakings is neither to glorify himself nor to promote any particular agenda of public improvement, but to insinuate a spirit of civic activism into his readers. Again anticipating Tocqueville, Franklin believes that the spirit of citizen initiative is essential to the success of the modern democratic polity. Franklin is not in principle against government taking over many of the functions just described, but like Tocqueville he sees a healthy egalitarian and democratic polity as one whose citizens are accustomed to taking thought for the common good and acting upon it. Having become self-reliant in economic matters, the citizens of such a polity must also become collectively self-reliant in tending to their common good.

It was always Franklin's conviction that "one Man of tolerable Abilities may work great Changes, & accomplish great Affairs among Mankind" if he will simply form a plan and pursue it diligently (1397). The emphasis is not on exceptional talent but on devotion to the public good and diligence in pursuing it. These are qualities in which many might share, and Franklin desires to spread them as widely as possible. Still, there is a type of leadership involved here. To some degree, citizen initiative must take the place of traditional leadership if a democratic, egalitarian society is to remain healthy; but good citizenship in Franklin's view includes an element of leadership. Projects of the type he undertakes in the *Autobiography* require the cooperation of many, and the public-spirited citizen must learn how to enlist such cooperation. Tocqueville later found in Americans a great talent for forming such cooperatives, which he called civil associations, but this talent does not arise spontaneously any more than does civic-mindedness itself. Franklin learned to become a master at this type of social organization—an impresario of public service, we might almost say—and the *Autobiography* shows us how to do the same. The first thing we must recognize, however, is that the egalitarian social milieu poses special challenges to leadership. Leadership is not a particular problem in aristocracies, where it is built into the regime, so to speak. In contrast, egalitarian culture creates a presumption against leadership, an obstacle that is inseparable from the very virtues of egalitarianism. Pride is no longer confined to the elite and in a sense forms the backbone of egalitarian society. This pride is jealous of its privileges and ever-vigilant against threats to liberty. As midwife to the new social order, Franklin is committed not only to accommodating this prickly republican pride but even to fostering it. It does, however, require him to find novel ways to exercise leadership.

Perhaps the principal obstacle to this type of leadership is the resentment it can create. Since Franklin was such an indefatigable projector, he was in danger of running up against this almost constantly. He tells us that he early became sensible of the resistance met by any proposer of a "useful Project that might be suppos'd to raise one's Reputation in the smallest degree above that of one's Neighbors" (1380). The problem is not only suspicion of "elitism" in the proposer but jealousy of any degree of prestige above the common. Egalitarians, it turns out, are exceedingly sensitive to differences in reputation, and anyone who would succeed even in doing them good must gracefully accept this fact. Franklin discovered that the most effective way around this was to propose each of his projects as "a Scheme of *a Number of Friends*," even if the idea was wholly his (1381; cf. 1418). The appearance of collective initiative effectively disarmed jealousy. The similarity is evident with Franklin's discovery that an affirmative and disputatious air raises unnecessary obstacles to persuasion and to doing good. In this case, a beneficent deceit (cf. Franklin's gloss on the virtue of "Sincerity") disguised Franklin's leadership and allowed him more effectively to serve the public good. He recommends the same expedient to us, and reassures us that our pride too will be satisfied by it in the long run, because such leadership does not remain truly unknown. If someone else claims the authorship of a project, he says, resentment itself will wrest from him the reputation and return it to its rightful recipient (1381). Indeed, despite the ruses he used to disguise his leadership, Franklin became so well known as a projector for the public good that the people of Philadelphia in time became reluctant to support any proposal unless it was known that Franklin too supported it.

Obviously, Franklin exercised leadership going well beyond the average; his self-conceal-ment was to some degree disingenuous, as is his claim in the *Autobiography* to be nothing more than a model for everyman. Franklin's teaching on citizenship and leadership might be said to be twofold. He desires to create a citizenry that is as public-spirited and activist as possible, providing a model for widespread imitation. But he is also aware that leadership of a more exalted character is necessary, and he provides a model for this as well, though in a more muted way. In effect, he simultaneously teaches the common man the need for active citizenship and its small exertions of leadership, while showing the uncommon man the way to more ambitious public service.

At the beginning of part III of the *Autobiography*, Franklin outlines a plan he once formed to organize a "Party for Virtue" (1395). This party, whose very existence would be secret at least to begin with, would include well-meaning men of all nations. By their collective exertions, Franklin argues, much good could be done that is presently thwarted. The party is conceived essentially as a conspiracy on behalf of the public good—indeed, the good of mankind as a whole. In Franklin's plan, the members of this party would all subscribe to a religious creed of his devising and would all have undergone training in the thirteen virtues as outlined in his "Art of Virtue" (1396). In short, Franklin places himself in the central, if not ruling, position in this conspiracy for the public good. This plan was never executed, but one society Franklin actually did organize, the "Junto," was remarkably similar. A society formed for "mutual Improvement," the Junto debated issues of private and public concern, but it also became a way to exert the influence of its members for the public good (1361; 205–12). Proposals adopted by the Junto could be advanced by the exertion of the various members, magnifying the influence of each. Eventually, cognate groups were to be formed by each of the members, and proposals adopted by the Junto were on at least one occasion spread abroad through these groups, without anyone knowing their true source (1405). The conspiratorial nature of this undertaking is clear, but it takes this shape largely in response to democratic social conditions. Where egalitarianism creates resentment against extraordinary exercises of leadership, that leadership must to some extent go underground.

This does not mean that Franklin chafed at the limits imposed by egalitarianism. Despite his own exceptional character and the position he attained, Franklin remained a wholehearted believer in natural and political equality. He gracefully accepted the obstacles it placed before his, and others', schemes for the public good. From the time of his first Silence Dogood essays, he displayed unwavering animosity toward pretensions to superiority and toward aristocracies of the type found in the Old World (cf. 12, 874, 977). When the Society of the Cincinnati was proposed as a quasi-aristocratic organization for America, Franklin had nothing but scorn (1084, 1108; cf. 49–50). In his view, uncommon men such as he do not and should not form an elite social class, much less a hereditary caste. Their hearts are to remain popular just as the goal of their action is to remain the common benefit, understood in a fundamentally democratic way. There is no hint in Franklin that men of talent, or lovers of honor or fame, constitute a separate breed, as John Adams or Alexander Hamilton believed. In fact, he was more likely to regard the love of fame as a supremely dangerous thing. In *Poor Richard's Almanack* for 1748, he inserted these lines:

> Alas! that Heroes ever were made!
> The *Plague*, and the *Hero,* are both of a Trade!
> Yet the Plague spares our Goods which the Heroe does not;
> So a Plague take such Heroes and let their Fames rot. (1248)

We might even say that one goal of Franklin's writing is to lead uncommon men to a more egalitarian view of themselves and their role in society. Above all, they are not to regard themselves as aristocrats, and they are to accommodate the republican pride of their fellow-citizens. It is not that leading men should not be permitted to have their "vanity" flattered in ways appropriate to their services and their position. Franklin clearly relished the reputation he gained from his achievements, even announcing at the beginning of the *Autobiography* that vanity (including the vanity of writing an autobiography) is productive of some social good (1308). But this is a lesson he applies to the humble as well as the great. In the economy of egalitarian culture, reputation may be distributed differentially, but none are a breed apart, and pride is the province of all.

IV

Though Franklin was in general more concerned with the moral and cultural underpinnings of the Republic than with its political institutions, he was not completely silent on the institutional concerns that so preoccupied most of his fellow Founders. He had definite opinions on the best political arrangements, and he was a participant in the Constitutional Convention of 1787, though his contributions to it, as recorded by James Madison, were few.

When it came to fundamental political arrangements, Franklin was essentially in accord with his colleagues. He agreed that a constitution needed to support the rights and liberties that the English had originally developed and bequeathed to America. Franklin, whose political career began well before the breach between England and America, defended those rights originally as positive rights—the rights of Englishmen rather than natural rights. This was common for Americans of that period, but Franklin displayed a marked reluctance (though not refusal) to use the language of natural rights and de novo social contracts throughout his life. Such arguments might well have fallen under the ban against "metaphysical Reasonings" that he imposed upon himself early in life. If Franklin was not in accord with the most prominent of the Founders on this score, he was in accord with the antimetaphysical strain of modern philosophy. David Hume was a prominent critic of the philosophy of natural rights and the social contract, seeing them as needless abstractions. Hume thought that government could as effectively be brought into line with liberty and justice, and the obligations of citizens as effectively established, by tying them more simply to social utility in the way described earlier. Franklin's political outlook may be described in similar terms. If *"Truth, Sincerity & Integrity* in Dealings between Man & Man" are the goals that determine what is moral and immoral in personal life, a similar set of goals can determine right and wrong in politics, without recourse to "metaphysical" abstractions.

As we have already seen, such a standard is empirical rather than metaphysical, a posteriori rather than a priori. It is teleological in the sense that it takes its bearings by the ends of political life rather than its beginnings. The argument can certainly be made that experience is the best guide in determining what political arrangements most effectively secure the political goods on which Franklin and his more metaphysically minded colleagues agree. This is the thinking that underlies the one extended foray into political education proper to be found in Franklin's writings. In 1749, he advanced a proposal for an English school in Philadelphia (on behalf of "some publick-spirited Gentlemen," he says [323; cf. 1418]). This proposal included a detailed outline for the school's curriculum, one explicit purpose of which is to produce citizens who understand the preconditions of liberty and who will be vigilant in its defense. History is almost exclusively the subject that Franklin uses to convey these lessons:

> *History* will also give Occasion to expatiate on the Advantage of Civil Orders and Constitutions, how Men and their Properties are protected by joining in Societies and establishing Government; their Industry encouraged and rewarded, Arts invented, and Life made more comfortable: the Advantages of *Liberty*, Mischiefs of *Licentiousness*, Benefits arising from good Laws and a due Execution of Justice, &c. Thus may the first Principles of sound *Politicks* be fix'd in the Minds of Youth. (337)

Franklin is in accord with thinkers such as Locke and Hume, as well as his fellow Founders, regarding the goods of political life and how they are to be secured. But he does not rely on natural rights and contract theory to ground them or to fix them in the minds of youth. He does refer obliquely to a social contract (men join in society and establish government), but the focus is on the ends of society rather than on its origins. Indeed, the original contract cannot be a subject of "history"; rather, history is appropriate to an empirical or experiential investigation of the most effective means of attaining the goods of society. It is striking that, in this curriculum, Franklin never has his pupils study contract theory or the contract theorists. He assigns Grotius and Pufendorf, both of whom discuss original contracts, but only to teach his pupils moral logic (337–38).

In the Constitutional Convention of 1787, Franklin's limited participation revealed a similar preference for the lessons of experience over those of theory. He spoke on such issues as salaries for public officials (adding material incentives to those of ambition is dangerous, as the experience of England demonstrates), and the allotment of representatives (it should be done by population, though he was instrumental in fashioning the Great Compromise on the issue). Overall, his contributions reflect a somewhat more populist or egalitarian outlook than that of other participants. In fact, many proposals that he supported were rejected by the Convention. Though the Convention agreed with him in removing all restrictions on suffrage and property qualifications for office, proposals he supported for a multiple executive and (apparently) a single legislative house were rejected.

Given the views he expressed that summer, it almost seems that Franklin should have found the Anti-Federalist camp more hospitable than the Federalist. Yet, when the Convention's work was done, it was Franklin who called for the delegates to support the final document unanimously, despite any flaws they found in it. Unanimity would enhance the prospects of adoption, he pointed out; and besides, all should reflect that human reason is fallible in such matters and that the precise form of government is less important than popular acceptance of it or how it is ultimately administered (1140–41). This reasoning is a perfect example of Franklin's approach to politics. A priori reasoning is not capable of pronouncing definitively on the virtues or vices of a constitution; experience alone will tell. Or even more strongly, forms of government are less significant than how they are implemented in practice. Here, Franklin may have had in mind a favorite couplet from Alexander Pope's *Essay on Man*: "For forms of government let fools contest;/ Whate'er is best administer'd is best" (III.303–4).

V

The succeeding couplet from Pope's *Essay on Man* could serve as an epitome of Franklin's religious thought: "For modes of faith let graceless zealots fight;/ His can't be wrong whose life is in the right" (III.304–5). Franklin follows his forbears in the modern philosophical movement in devoting serious attention to questions of religion and religious toleration. This concern is reflected in the *Autobiography*. We recall the blame Franklin there placed on the dogmatic tracts of "polemic Divinity" for nurturing his unfortunate youthful taste for disputatiousness. We recall also that his own religious polemics led Bostonians to shun him and that his early Deism corrupted some of his own friends. Franklin knew from direct experience of the dangers of religion with which modern political philosophy was so preoccupied. Yet the religious creed that the mature Franklin ultimately endorsed was a form of Deism, and he went to some lengths to broadcast this creed among his fellow Americans. Indeed, there is probably no subject on which Franklin risks alienating his intended audience so much as religion. He does this in order to advance the cause of toleration.

The *Autobiography* pairs Franklin's discovery of the true foundation of morality in truth, sincerity, and integrity, with a new attitude toward revelation:

> Revelation had indeed no weight with me as such; but I entertain'd an Opinion, that tho' certain Actions might not be bad *because* they were forbidden by it, or good *because* it commanded them, yet probably those Actions might be forbidden *because* they were bad for us, or commanded *because* they were beneficial to us, in their own Natures, all the Circumstances of things considered. (1359–60)

This amounts to a qualified endorsement of Scripture—at least a part of its moral teaching is valid—but on the grounds of a kind of natural theology. Its teaching is valid because, and to the extent that, it serves the human good and not because it is the word of God. Franklin is careful to insist that the actions in question must be harmful or beneficial in themselves, for our lives (that is, without reference to an afterlife). This theology is very much in the spirit of John Locke and other modern thinkers. Like Franklin's moral teaching in general, its beginning and end is a particular analysis of the human good—truth, sincerity, and integrity between man and man. It must also be noted that this theology, like Locke's, supposes that man's nature is not fallen and that his natural impulses are not intrinsically evil. A fair encapsulation of this view was seen in the speech of Miss Polly Baker, whose appeal to nature's intent of procreation involved an appeal to divine will as well (307). As with Locke, nature, including our (rationally supervised) appetites, is the true guide to divine will. Franklin's morality indulges every appetite not harmful to personal and social happiness; his God does the same.

Franklin's mature theology is a form of Deism that includes particular Providence—individual rewards and punishments to support morality. He provides us with a list of its tenets in the *Autobiography*:

> That there is one God who made all things
> That he governs the World by his Providence.—
> That he ought to be worshipped by Adoration, Prayer & Thanksgiving.
> But that the most acceptable Service of God is doing Good to Man.
> That the Soul is immortal.
> And that God will certainly reward Virtue and punish Vice either here or hereafter. (1396)

Whether Franklin believed his creed to embody indubitable truth is questionable on the basis of his other public and private writings, but what cannot in his mind be doubted is the salutary effect this belief would have on human affairs. Franklin claims that when he formulated this creed he took it to contain "the Essentials of every known Religion, and [to be] free of every thing that might shock the Professors of any Religion." Whether a creed that regards such principles as the divinity of Jesus to be "non-essential" would be viewed so benignly by his fellow Americans is open to question. He did write to Ezra Stiles near the end of his life that he had doubts as to Jesus' divinity, "though' it is a question I do not dogmatize upon" (1179). What Franklin hopes to accomplish by promulgating his own creed so publicly, as part of his *Autobiography*, is to bring his readers to regard the controversial points of theology, over which Christians had shown an alarming willingness to kill each other, as nonessential, and to regard good works to our fellow man as the true core of religion. This is certainly Franklin's view. In his mind, charity ranks above faith and hope in the hierarchy of religious virtue (756).

Though Franklin professes respect for virtually all sects, he judges their merits based on his own creed. He forswore attending the services of one minister when he concluded that the aim of his sermons was "rather to make us Presbyterians than good Citizens" (1383)—a reversal of the proper priority, in Franklin's mind. He singles out the Dunkers for praise, a sect that declined to put its doctrines into writing since it was not sure that it was in possession of the final truth. "This Modesty in a Sect is perhaps a singular Instance in the History of Mankind," he comments, contrasting them to the Quakers in particular, whose pacifism rendered them unable to cope with the legitimate requirements of defense (1417). Still, he not only tolerated all the sects that he found in his native land but also generally supported them when they applied to him for it. He did not try to shake anyone's religious beliefs and looked with disfavor on anyone who did so. After all, it is his claim that all sects incorporate his "essentials," though they typically add extraneous principles. They all perform the basic service of supporting morality. Franklin ranked religious sects depending upon the extent to which their doctrines placed the essentials at the center or distracted from them, but there were none that strayed completely from the proper office of religion.

VI

Despite his failure, or rather refusal, to write systematically on political philosophy, Benjamin Franklin had a firm set of political convictions grounded in serious reflection on the human condition and especially on the needs of the newly emerging liberal and democratic age. Given his supremely practical or empirical bent, Franklin's reflections on the virtues that the new dispensation would require and the mores it would need to develop were unsurpassed. His oeuvre as a whole represents a carefully contrived attempt to cultivate those virtues and those mores in his readers.

Franklin's thought and action in a way gather together all the strands of modernity. He reflected on the political institutions appropriate to modern liberty, and he had a hand in shaping those institutions for the United States. But he saw the mores that would underlie the institutions as even more important to their ultimate success and devoted himself primarily to cultivating those mores. He was keenly aware of the role of economic activity in the new order and the consequent need to cultivate virtues of honest acquisition among its citizens. He knew that religious doctrine had an important if somewhat concealed role to play in the unfolding of the new dispensation and that a refashioning of theology was required to bring it into line with the regime of liberty and prosperity. And the foundation of all was a new understanding of man's nature, his condition, and the morality appropriate to these. Rather than aspiring to a perfection beyond human nature, this morality took its bearings by man as he is and the happiness that is accessible to many in this life.

The result is a morality much less demanding than its predecessors, though requiring its own type of discipline. Self-reliance in the pursuit of one's own good is the beginning of this ethic, to which Franklin strives to add service to the interests of mankind at large. His own scientific work, in the spirit of modern science in general, is conceived of as a kind of service to humankind. Franklin's researches into electricity were doubtless motivated by the simple desire to know, but those researches—and numerous other scientific inquiries that his restless curiosity suggested to him—were always tied closely to useful applications, from his Pennsylvania Fireplace to the lightning rod. He founded the American Philosophical Society as a way of "promoting useful Knowledge" in the Americas. In reality, Franklin's scientific activity was but another expression of the principle that service to the interests of mankind is the essence of the moral good.

The modern project at large is open to the objection that by grounding morality in material comfort and self-interest, it leaves service to the common good insufficiently supported. As a result, goes the objection, people raised under the liberal regime will not be willing to serve society when it does not serve their interests as well, placing society itself in jeopardy. Liberal morality may diminish the conflict between the public and private good by defining the common good as a mere aggregate of individual interests, but it by no means eliminates the conflict altogether. Franklin often proclaims, in response to this difficulty, some version of the precept that the individual's true or long-term utility is always in accord with the general good. But this is true only if virtue, and in particular service to others, brings a measure of happiness to the individual of its own right. In the spirit of Franklin himself, we might say that this is an empirical as much as a theoretical question. Certain it is that example will be more effective than any theoretical discourse for the purposes of persuading people of the truth of the proposition. A document like Franklin's *Autobiography* is better suited than any other to bear the burden of this persuasion. More effectively than any discourse, it shows us how a life lived in accordance with simple virtues of industry and frugality, as well as the more elevated virtues of public service, is also a supremely happy life. Franklin says at the beginning of the *Autobiography* that his purpose is to show the means by which he, starting from so humble a station, was able not only to rise so far but to enjoy such a "considerable Share of Felicity" in life. He also says that he would have no hesitation about living the same life over again (1307). After reading the work, few would deny that his was indeed an enviable life. And once we have seen that, we have seen how even the other-regarding virtues of modernity can amply repay their possessor.

Notes

1. Franklin, *Writings* (New York: Library of America, 1987), 1318–19. Citations from this volume will henceforth be inserted in the text.
2. From 1732 to 1757, Franklin published *Poor Richard's Almanack*, featuring the fictional character Richard Saunders. The almanac contained moral sayings, such as "early to bed and early to rise, makes a man healthy wealthy and wise" (from the 1735 *Almanack* [1198]).

PART TWO:

THE NEW REPUBLIC
(1776–1820)

≫➤ ⬅≪

Chapter 5

Liberty, Constitutionalism, and Moderation: The Political Thought of George Washington

Paul O. Carrese

George Washington (1732–1799) is less appreciated by his countrymen in the twenty-first century than during the first two centuries after his singular role in America's Founding. The declining status of a man hailed in his lifetime as the Father of his country stems in part from our admiration in modernity for theoretical innovation and abstract concepts over practical judgment, despite the latter's obvious importance for political action. Simply put, few of the teachers of his countrymen today—professors, writers, and other opinion shapers—find him an exemplar of American political thought worthy of serious study. Washington's best known writing is his Farewell Address (1796), declaring to "Friends, and Fellow-Citizens" his retirement from public life. For the second time in a long career, he relinquished near-absolute power when equally ambitious yet less principled men usually have grasped for more. Such deeds, and his statements of principle about them, led his countrymen to rank him with an ancient Roman renowned for twice relinquishing absolute power once the threat to his country passed: he was the American Cincinnatus. Washington used his Farewell not only to offer prayers to Heaven for continued blessings upon his country but also to "offer to your solemn contemplation, and to recommend to your frequent review" advice on union, constitution, republican government, and foreign policy.[1] He sought a legacy in thoughts as well as deeds, so that "these counsels of an old and affectionate friend" would make a "strong and lasting impression" and yield "a wise People" (*W* 976, 970).

Subsequent ideas about politics now block this message, for after centuries of Machiavellian reason working its way in the world we deem it softheaded to think that anyone places principle or duty above interest. We also tend to dismiss Washington's political testament because, as everyone knows, James Madison and Alexander Hamilton really wrote it. Confident in our rational analyses of power and interest, we miss the central lesson of the Address about subordinating these drives to principles. Convinced that Washington cannot be genuine, we overlook his careful use of his bright advisers, managing them so as to always maintain his independent judgment. In the third century after Washington's principled deeds and practically wise thoughts, we review his advice less frequently than he, or the first several generations of his political children, would have hoped. Few anthologies of American political writings include even excerpts of the Farewell Address anymore.[2] We associate Washington with deeds, not thoughts; many now discount even his deeds simply for their distance from our present concerns—and because he was a slave owner. It is not just that we overlook his eventual repudiation of slavery and emancipation of his slaves; more generally, our democratic, modern temperament has

95

difficulty appreciating this remote father-figure and martial hero, the embodiment of gravity and propriety.[3]

We should rediscover the serious political thought in Washington's writings from three decades as the leading citizen in a republic, stating his basic principles of liberty, constitutional order, and moderation. This last is the most difficult for modern and democratic minds to grasp. Contrary to the Enlightenment doctrines of mathematical clarity in all areas of thought and absolute equality of all rights-bearing individuals, moderation counsels that awareness of the complexity of reality must guide our theorizing and acting. Regarding practice, institutional complexity and space for prudent judgment in specific offices should balance the democratic principle. As to theory, it suggests that we best understand humans and politics by dialectically weighing the merits of not just one principle but several, seeking a sound balance among them to avoid extremes. This principle of moderation is most evident in the complexity and balance characteristic of both separation of powers and federalism.[4] It also explains the alloy of views the American Framers achieved—drawing on Lockean liberalism and classical republicanism but also Whig opposition thought, English common law, and Protestant Christianity. Washington's political thought exemplifies, in fact, the distinctively American synthesis of schools that seem incompatible or contradictory to some theorists. He concluded his First Inaugural Address in 1789 on this note of moderation and balance, urging America's new representatives to strive for "the enlarged views" and "temperate consultations" indispensable for "the success of the Government" (*W* 734). Concern for liberty and individual rights must be balanced by commitment to the complex rule of law entrenched in the Constitution in order to distinguish liberty from license in domestic or foreign policy. Provision for special offices and talents in government must balance the commitment to equality and popular representation in order to keep the Republic on an even keel and steady course.

Washington saw these fundamental tenets of liberty, constitutionalism, and moderation as drawing upon and reinforcing his more specific principles, including the subordination of military to civil authority; a complex, federal Union; the need in republics for statesmanship, especially executive power; and realistic but just foreign policies. Less obvious to us today is his emphasis upon religious faith in republics, and upon civility and honor. Beyond his unrivaled deeds for America, his importance for shaping American political thought was as great as that of more recognized thinkers of the Founding era. This is not to deny his own concerns, as a surveyor, soldier, and farmer, that he was less educated than such advisers as George Mason, Thomas Jefferson, Madison, Hamilton, and John Jay. Nonetheless, he sought to refine his thoughts, not replace them, by consulting these minds; in the process, he often refined or moderated theirs. His earliest writings, from letters and journals to his copying of "Rules of Civility and Decent Behavior in Company and in Conversation," do not reveal theoretical genius. By the time, however, he was a colonial officer in the British army during the French and Indian War from 1752–1758, he wrote copiously and carefully copied each item. By the late 1760s, after serving several terms in the Virginia House of Burgesses, even his private letters suggest concern with a public audience and posterity; his ambition extends beyond fame and honor to justifying his opinions and deeds. Copying those 110 rules of civility, penned by French Jesuits in the sixteenth century to educate for private and political life, instilled both ethical principles and an intellectual trait of clarifying the ultimate principles to guide one in any stage of life (*W* 3–10). This explains why his library at Mount Vernon held over 900 books by his death, a collection that extends beyond military and agricultural topics. During the last decades of his life, at the peak of his authority, he advocated founding a national university and national military academy, and when thwarted he privately endowed schools and educational funds—Washington and Lee University is one instance of this commitment to learning. The intellectual confidence he had developed allowed him to consult with a range of learned advisers and to rely upon one over another according to his own judgment. As study of the Farewell Address shows, he revised every argument or draft provided to him and made it his own.[5] Moreover, he never shifted his principles with the winds of public opinion. A perceptive analysis concludes that Washington was "a leader who sought explanations and explainers all his life, and who mastered both what he was told and those who told him."[6]

Washington's public statements of his principles are brief enough to be accessible to nearly any citizen or student, and the coherence of his thought easily permits supplementation with important letters. The scope and balance of his thinking reveal a mind not easily reduced to the Federalist, Anti-Federalist, or Democratic-Republican camp; he effectively was a moderate Federalist, but he deplored the partisanship that undermined sobriety and civility at the end of the Founding era. Hamilton was an important influence on him; but beyond the fact of his consultations with others is his emphasis upon moderation and compromise, principles not easily attributed to his brilliant but immoderate protégé.[7] That said, while Jefferson echoed Washington's spirit in stating "[w]e are all Republicans, we are all Federalists" after his election in 1800, neither his zealous democratic theory nor his partisan practices really adhered to that standard.[8] A just assessment concludes that "General and President Washington, all hagiography aside, was the linchpin that—to the extent one man could do so—held together a fragile Revolution and afterward a federal Union torn by domestic and foreign controversies in the 1790s."[9] Upon his death, the resolutions in the House of Representatives declaring him "first in war, first in peace, first in the hearts of his countrymen" were moved by a Federalist, John Marshall, but drafted by a Federalist and a Democratic-Republican, Henry Lee and James Madison.[10]

The Farewell Address is Washington's summation of his thoughts on liberty, constitutionalism, and moderation, drawing upon writings throughout his career. The most important of these include his 1783 speech at Newburgh, New York, to quell an officer rebellion against civil authority and his 1783 Circular to the States endorsing four "Pillars" for America's security and happiness—a strong union, strong national finances, a sound defense, and a "national Character" unifying all states and regions (*W* 516–19). After resigning in 1783 with an address affirming military obedience to civil authority, he supported Madison, Hamilton, and others trying to reform the weak federal government of the Articles of Confederation. Both sides in the ensuing debates thought his support for the new Constitution was essential to its eventual ratification. He further enunciated principles in two Inaugural Addresses and in Annual Messages (the name used for State of the Union Addresses). The lessons he bequeathed in his Farewell cap a career of pairing actions with reflection and justification; two decades earlier, his General Orders of July 9, 1776, ordered the Declaration of Independence read to the troops, so that they might understand "the grounds & reasons" of the war (*W* 228). Nonetheless, some find a Machiavellian cunning in the Farewell Address and his entire career—that Washington saw the need, in a democratic republic, to resign power or pretend not to want it so as to gain greater power or glory. However satisfying this view is to some, in reality each principle in the Address affirms earlier deeds and statements on the same point. Such consistent dedication to liberty, constitutionalism, and moderation bespeaks a practical wisdom serving higher principles in particular circumstances. Indeed, study of Washington challenges the Machiavellianism pervading much political analysis now, for his moderation and commitment to principle made him an extraordinarily effective statesman. Such study is also indispensable for educated citizens concerned with the statesmanship that translates constitutional principles into sound policies, both domestic and foreign.

The "liberty and justice for which we contend": Civil-Military Relations and Character

Washington served in Virginia's legislature from 1758, and after the tumultuous British-American politics of the 1760s, he chose to defend liberty and natural rights. Since "our lordly Masters in Great Britain will be satisfied with nothing less than the deprivation of American freedom, it seems highly necessary that something shou'd be done to avert the stroke and maintain that liberty which we have derived from our Ancestors." Indeed, "no man shou'd scruple, or hesitate a moment to use a--ms in defense of so valuable a blessing, on which all the good and evil of life depends." Still, he tempered his zeal for liberty; if petitions about American "rights & priviledges" failed, then a trade embargo should be tried before resorting to arms (*W* 130). Washington has been called a constitutional or conservative revolutionary for such moderation; however, he grounded the American cause not only in abstract rights but also in the tradition of Anglo-American common law. As early as 1765, he argued that laws enacted without the consent of the colonists' elected representatives were an "unconstitutional method of Taxation" and "a direful attack upon their Liberties."[11]

By 1774, Washington put his prestige behind the cause of liberty; as the former commander of all Virginian colonial forces in the French and Indian War, he already was known throughout the colonies. He voted for a congress of all the colonies; he presided over the drafting of the Fairfax County resolutions advocating the right to colonial self-government and a trade boycott against Britain; and he was a delegate to the First Continental Congress. He justified these actions by reflecting that "an Innate Spirit of freedom first told me" that the acts of the British administration "are repugnant to every principle of natural justice." Indeed, they are "not only repugnant to natural Right, but Subversive of the Laws & Constitution of Great Britain itself"; the king's ministers were "trampling upon the Valuable Rights of American's, confirmed to them by Charter, & the Constitution they themselves boast of" (*W* 157). When the Second Continental Congress appointed him general and commander in chief of the Continental army, his address balanced humility and pride: he was grateful for the "high Honour" being done him yet fearful for his "reputation," since his abilities and experience "may not be equal to the extensive & important Trust"; he also refused any pay, asking only reimbursement for official expenses (*W* 167). He already had linked sacrifice and virtue in justifying America's actions: "the once happy and peaceful plains of America are either to be drenched with Blood, or Inhabited by Slaves. Sad alternative! But can a virtuous Man hesitate in his choice?" (*W* 164).

General Washington's military tactics and grand strategy of matching geopolitical alliances and tactics deserve study, but two of his political-military principles overlooked today are civil-military relations and virtuous character.[12] Around the world, liberty mostly either never arises or is short-lived because military despots squash any genuine politics or rule of law. America and the world owe to Washington the principle that a professional military is necessary to protect liberty and can be safe for it through subordination to laws and civil authority. This accorded with his political moderation: real liberty is ordered liberty, securing self-government and political decency under law. John Marshall, the great chief justice of the United States who was a young officer under Washington, further concluded that without his distinctive character, formed in part through earlier military experience, the American cause likely would have failed. He marveled at the moral toughness of a commander who kept his outmanned, undersupplied, ill-equipped army in the war until victorious. In one dark hour, the winter of 1776–1777, this character permitted Washington to conceive counterattacks at Trenton and Princeton: "Among the many valuable traits in the character of Washington, was that unyielding firmness which supported him under these accumulated circumstances of depression.... To this unconquerable firmness—to this perfect self-possession under the most desperate of circumstances, is America, in a great degree, indebted for her independence" (*LGW* 75). A larger lesson here is that the American judiciary and rule of law are indebted to Washington for instilling such character in one who became a chief justice: in the early 1800s, the Supreme Court was nearly irrelevant and would have been fully so if not for Marshall's perseverance amid adversity. Today, one wonders how the American republic, which no longer requires service in organizations that instill these traits, thinks it nonetheless provides for such experiences, principles, and character—or, whether it considers these unnecessary, even backward.

America and the cause of liberty in the world are also fortunate that Washington was not tempted by absolute power when the war prospects brightened. After the victory at Yorktown, an American colonel suggested that he should be king, an offer that might tempt a general deeply admired by his army and—like a Caesar, Cromwell, Napoleon, or Benedict Arnold—also ambitious himself. The temptation might strengthen given how disorganized Congress was during the war, how often Washington had proposed executive offices to remedy this, and how he witnessed the daily wants in supplies, equipment, and pay for the men to whom he was devoted. Colonel Lewis Nicola exploited these points, proposing that disorganization in Congress and suffering in the army proved to all "the weakness of republicks, & the exertions the army has been able to make by being under a proper head"; hence, many in the army would support him if he chose to be king (*W* 1106 at note 468.31). Washington replied immediately, expressing "abhorrence," "astonishment," and "painful sensations" upon learning of "such ideas existing in the Army." To be sure, "no Man possesses a more sincere wish to see ample justice done to the Army," but he would pursue this only "as far as my powers and influence, in a constitutional way extend." He used Nicola's regard for him against such a plan, again connecting principles to the character needed to animate them: "Let me conjure you then, if you have any regard for your Country, concern for yourself or posterity, or respect for me, to banish these thoughts from your Mind" (*W* 468–69).

Washington already had supported military discipline and civil authority during two troop mutinies early in 1781 over lack of pay and supplies. He dealt moderately with the first but severely with the second. To Marshall, these events "threatened the American cause with total ruin," and he contrasts the "miserably defective" organization of Congress that caused such problems with the good fortune that America's one effective executive restored order and then pressed, yet again, for reform measures (*LGW* 245–48). Trouble arose again in 1783, with a peace process under way that might disband the army before being paid its due. Officers at Washington's headquarters in Newburgh, New York, thought he might finally support a threat of mutiny against Congress; the states would not pay their requisitioned funds, Congress could not compel them, and the army suffered. An anonymous letter summoned all the officers to a meeting and suggested they seek the support of their "Illustrious Leader" for this plot (*W* 1107–9 at note 490.13–14). Washington denounced that meeting but called for an official one at which "mature deliberation" should develop "rational measures" for Congress to consider (*W* 490). He implied he would not attend; the element of surprise was his when, in the officers' meeting house—called the Temple of Virtue—he strode in. His speech contrasted the "unmilitary" character and "blackest designs" of the plot with the "rules of propriety" and "order and discipline" more fitting to "your own honor, and the dignity of the Army." Ultimately, "the calm light of reason" and "moderation" must control "feelings and passions," for "sowing the seeds of discord and seperation between the Civil and Military powers" would undermine "that liberty, and . . . that justice for which we contend." To support these principles, he invoked their long-standing affection for him, since no one had been more "a faithful friend to the Army" (*W* 495–500).

Washington also defended Congress as an "Hon[ora]ble Body" that should not be distrusted just because "like all other Bodies, where there is a variety of different Interests to reconcile, their deliberations are slow." His final appeal was to both reason and emotion: "let me conjure you, in the name of our common Country, as you value your own sacred honor, as you respect the rights of humanity, and as you regard the Military and National character of America," to reject this plot to "overturn the liberties of our Country" through civil war. This would prove them models of "unexampled patriotism and patient virtue" and "afford occasion for Posterity to say . . . 'had this day been wanting, the World had never seen the last stage of perfection to which human nature is capable of attaining'" (*W* 498–500). Washington sealed his efforts with another dramatic gesture, again using the army's devotion to him not for his own advantage but for law and liberty. He began to read a letter from a congressman and then stopped: "Gentlemen, you will permit me to put on my spectacles, for I have not only grown gray, but almost blind, in the service of my country" (*W* 1109 at note 496.12). Some of the officers, no longer rebellious, were in tears. After he left, they unanimously repudiated the plot and reaffirmed their allegiance to civil authority.

Washington's influence was not only immediate but lasting. Indeed, the main doctrinal statement of the U.S. Army today opens by recounting "Washington at Newburgh: Establishing the Role of the Military in a Democracy," finding in these deeds and words "the fundamental tenet of our professional ethos."[13] Principled to the end, Washington disbanded the army once the peace treaty was official. After a last Circular Address to the states recommending policies for the future, and final orders to the army giving further political advice, he resigned his commission before Congress in December 1783. He professed "honor" at being present to "surrender into their hands the trust committed to me" and asked "the indulgence of retiring from the Service of my Country." With repeated recognition of "the interposition of Providence" which had secured America's independence, and gratitude for the support of his countrymen and trusted aides, he bade farewell: "Having now finished the work assigned me, I retire from the great theatre of Action; and bidding an Affectionate farewell to this August body under whose orders I have so long acted, I here offer my Commission, and take my leave of all the employments of public life" (*W* 547–48). Jefferson soon wrote to him: "the moderation & virtue of a single character has probably prevented this revolution from being closed as most others have been, by a subversion of that liberty it was intended to establish."[14]

The "Great Constitutional Charter": Constitutionalism, Union, and the Aims of Republicanism

Washington's judgment that liberty and constitutionalism require a principle of civil-military relations fits well with other principles central to America's political tradition that he was among the first to enunciate. He stated ideas about union, constitutionalism, and statesmanship years before Madison, Hamilton, or others elaborated them. Indeed, more scholarly minds could expound notions of constitutional reform in part because his statements paved the way; Hamilton is not the only leading mind at the Founding who could have said that Washington had been an "Aegis," a shield, "very essential" to him.[15] Washington was a leader in the constitutional reform movement from 1783 to 1789, both in his own voice and by quietly encouraging others. Many who became Federalists, arguing for balance between union and states, looked to him as a defender of liberty and the Revolution who also had published a plea for rescuing liberty from anarchy. His 1783 Circular to the States proposes a more perfect union by rebalancing state sovereignty with the common good and America's "National Character." He then risked his reputation on a program of constitutional reform, ending his retirement to support it. Indeed, the reflection on ultimate principles in the Circular, combined with advocacy of specific policies, informs the two major statements of his later career, the First Inaugural and Farewell Address.

By 1783, Washington had supported efforts by Hamilton, Madison, and others in Congress to augment national powers on taxation, finances, and trade. Having nearly lost the prize of liberty due to excessive fear of governmental authority, he feared America might squander the peace in economic and political chaos. In early 1783, Congress proposed to the states that it assume all the state war debts and enact a national tax to pay for this; it also finally resolved to pay the officers. Throughout the war, Washington used circular addresses to send a uniform message to the state governors and legislatures, since he was often the only executive coordinating America's military, diplomatic, and financial policies. He used his final Circular not only to congratulate the states on the success of the war and to announce his retirement from public life but also to urge support for the recent congressional measures; indeed, he proposed the constitutionalist principles America must develop to secure and perpetuate liberty. He noted that a general should refrain from political activity, but he knew of his extraordinary stature in America and decided to use it a final time for the common good. Indeed, it was "a duty incumbent upon me" to address these issues since, in "the present Crisis" of affairs, "silence in me would be a crime" (*W* 516–18).

The Circular opens and closes with gratitude for Providence, given the great "prize" at issue in the war, success despite long odds, and the "natural," "political," and "moral" blessings Americans now enjoy (*W* 516–17). The "Citizens of America" should note the providential fact that "our Republic" came to freedom in an era of history providing "a fairer opportunity for political happiness" than any other: "The foundation of our Empire was not laid in the gloomy age of Ignorance and Superstition, but at an Epocha when the rights of mankind were better understood and more clearly defined, than at any former period." However, America must work to secure these achievements of the Western tradition:

> the researches of the human mind, after social happiness, have been carried to a great extent[;] the Treasures of knowledge, acquired by the labours of Philosophers, Sages, and Legislatures, through a long succession of years, are laid open for our use, and their collected wisdom may be happily applied in the Establishment of our forms of Government; the free cultivation of letters, the unbounded extension of Commerce, the progressive refinement of Manners, the growing liberality of sentiment, and above all, the pure and benign light of Revelation, have had a meliorating influence on mankind and increased the blessings of Society. (*W* 517)

This might seem to resemble the liberal doctrine of a Locke or Voltaire, but the emphases on duty, decency, and Providence suggest otherwise. Indeed, the Circular evokes an Aristotelian and Tocquevillean blend of virtue and interest, warning that without prudent judgment and virtuous effort Americans will squander their blessings: if the "Citizens should not be completely free and happy, the fault will be intirely their own" (*W* 517).

The current crisis in domestic and foreign affairs was America's "political probation"; it will be either "respectable and prosperous, or contemptuous and miserable as a Nation." Only if it established a "national Character" and stopped "relaxing the powers of the Union, annihilating the cement of the Confederation," could America be independent; separate states would be "the sport of European politics," manipulated by great powers. Now is "the favorable moment to give such a tone to our Federal Government, as will enable it to answer the ends of its institution": at stake was not only whether "the Revolution" was "a blessing or a curse" for Americans and "the present age" but more—"for with our fate will the destiny of unborn Millions be involved" (*W* 517–18). To establish a "wise and liberal government," Washington proposed four "Pillars" to support "the glorious Fabrick of our Independency and National Character"; while "Liberty is the Basis," these would protect that foundation from disintegrating. The principles necessary for "the well being" and even "the existence of the United States" were:

> 1st. An indissoluble Union of the States under one Federal Head. 2dly. A Sacred regard to Public Justice. 3dly. The adoption of a proper Peace Establishment, and 4thly. The prevalence of that pacific and friendly Disposition, among the People of the United States, which will induce them to forget their local prejudices and policies, to make those mutual concessions which are requisite to the general prosperity, and in some instances, to sacrifice their individual advantages to the interest of the Community. (*W* 518–19)

Washington claims to leave national comity to "the good sense and serious consideration of those immediately concerned," but his arguments for the first three pillars in fact promote American fraternity and national spirit as the fitting fruit of the Revolution. This echoes the Aristotelian and Christian view that friendship, both utilitarian and charitable, is as important to humane politics as the right institutions.[16] As to the first pillar, it was his "duty" and that of "every true Patriot" to observe that, beyond the "great question" of whether the states should "delegate a larger portion of Power to Congress or not," Congress must be allowed to exercise powers it is "undoubtedly invested with by the Constitution." Every state thus should support "the late proposals and demands of Congress." Beyond specific policies, Washington's prescient concern was "the Constitution" and new ideas of constitutionalism and federalism. Knowing that fixed battle with a powerful opponent is not always wise, he obliquely undermined state-centered republicanism to bolster America's fundamental law and federal structure. At stake were "the fruits of the Revolution," "our Independence," "our Credit" among nations; without a constitutionalism informed by "entire conformity to the Spirit of the Union," America would descend to "a state of Nature," left with "the ruins of Liberty abused to licentiousness" (*W* 518–20).

Washington's description of financial obligations as "Public Justice" might suggest a fixation with property and prosperity; in fact, his complex thought echoes Montesquieu's tempering of Lockean individualism and materialism. He was indeed concerned with his success as a farmer and landowner and with America's prosperity. Still, he tempered these interests with devotion to honorable and just conduct, charitable and Christian aims, and political fraternity; his broader motives for promoting internal navigation and commerce—and for emancipating his slaves— exemplify this complexity. He invokes the "honor," "honesty," "justice," and "feelings of humanity" that require repayment of both creditors and of "the bravery, and the blood" of soldiers (*W* 520–24). This moderation informs his third pillar, "placing the Militia of the Union upon a regular and respectable footing." Experience and the common good counsel sacrifices of money and local autonomy; state militias at least must have "absolutely uniform" organization, equipment, and training (*W* 524). The Circular closes by invoking "the immutable rules of Justice" and the civic duty to leave a "Legacy" that will be "useful to his Country." As with his later addresses, the Circular balances liberalism and republicanism, liberty and fraternity, human agency and belief in the transcendent. Washington bids "adieu" to "public life"; the soldier-statesman's last act is to elevate the gaze of his fellow citizens:

> I now make it my earnest prayer, that God would have you and the State over which you preside, in his holy protection, that he would incline the hearts of the Citizens to cultivate a spirit of subordination and obedience to Government, to entertain a brotherly affection and love for one another, for their fellow Citizens of the United States at large, and particularly for their brethren who have served in the Field, and finally, that he would most graciously be pleased to dispose us all, to do Justice, to love mercy, and to demean ourselves with that Charity, humility and

pacific temper of mind, which were the Characteristicks of the Divine Author of our blessed Religion, and without an humble imitation of whose example in these things, we can never hope to be a happy Nation. (*W* 524–26)[17]

Washington's deeds and thoughts during the last phases of his career, as Constitution-maker and Constitution-enactor, flow from the character he established by 1783. The principles of his Circular guide his efforts to reform and then replace the Articles for the sake of ordered liberty and an American character. Indeed, his first reentry into public affairs led directly to his work for constitutional reform. By 1784, he advocated public development of a waterway linking the Potomac River and the West, a project he had promoted as a colonial legislator. As owner of many thousands of acres in the Ohio Territory, he would benefit from its economic development; but even concern about accusations of seeking public funding for private gain did not deter him. Washington had long argued that virtue and interest must be joined if human nature could be expected to pursue just conduct. He had used this rationale in pressing Congress on pay and terms of enlistment, and in refusing to seize supplies from civilians outside a governmental system; a war effort needed practical motivations for its supporters and as few disgruntled opponents as possible. Such moderate realism did not make him a strictly modern thinker beholden to Machiavelli or Locke, for Aristotle recognized the necessity of co-opting interest to achieve higher aims.[18] Thus, his proposal to the governor of Virginia for a waterway emphasized national political development. It would bolster American independence, since a people "possessed of the spirit of Commerce" will "pursue their advantages" and "may atchieve almost anything." Moreover, such commerce would strengthen the Union, a good and necessary thing: "the flanks & rear of the United States are possessed by other powers—& formidable ones, too . . . how necessary it is to apply the cement of interest to bind all parts of the Union together by indissoluble bonds" (*W* 561–62).

Washington's leadership on commercial cooperation led to the 1785 Alexandria Conference between Virginia and Maryland on trade and tax policies; indeed, the delegates began their meetings in Alexandria but concluded them at Mount Vernon. The Virginians then proposed that all the states send representatives to a national convention on commerce the next year. Only five states attended the 1786 Annapolis Convention, but they proposed to Congress and the states that a national convention be held in 1787 to discuss all the defects of the Articles. Madison pushed the convention in the Virginia legislature and nominated Washington as a delegate; after lobbying by Madison, Governor Edmund Randolph, and others across the nation, he reluctantly accepted. He then expended his unrivaled national prestige for the Convention's success. Recognizing Madison's ability to conceptualize reforms he had long promoted, Washington endorsed bold measures to the man whose efforts would earn him the title Father of the Constitution: "a thorough reform of the present system is indispensable"; the government "wants energy and that secrecy and dispatch . . . which is characteristick of good Government." The precise measures for a new federalism "indeed will require thought," but he gave Madison his aegis: "my wish is, that the Convention may adopt no temporising expedient, but probe the defects of the Constitution to the bottom, and provide radical cures; whether they are agreed to or not. A conduct like this, will stamp wisdom and dignity on the proceedings, and be looked to as a luminary, which sooner or later will shed its influence" (*W* 647–48). In fact, Madison had been studying republican forms and already had proposed the outlines of a new constitution to Jefferson. Still, a comparison of Washington and Madison as constitutionalists and chief executives would find Madison the more learned and the more timid. Washington's endorsement of Madison's nascent plans must have emboldened him to further develop a specific strategy for achieving reform in Philadelphia.

Washington sustained this drive for a newly ordered liberty in the crucial years ahead. His public statements or speeches at the Convention do not reveal his full role in the birthing of a new order. His prudent use of overt and subtle support for a constitutional revolution was indispensable, such that Madison might be asked to share the honor of fathering the Constitution. Tocqueville's analysis of the Convention praises the delegates as including "the finest minds and noblest characters that had ever appeared in the New World," and he lists "Washington, Madison, Hamilton, the two Morrises" as attending; still, he emphasizes one above all: "George Washington presided over it."[19] The larger political context reveals the importance of this largely hidden hand guiding the Constitution to life. By 1786, discontent with America's affairs was growing, and the armed conflict in Massachusetts called Shays's Rebellion had sparked momentum for reform. Congress was helpless in restoring order or redressing the financial and commercial policies, or lack thereof, which led to such crises. Still, even after these events, Washington faced the view that the Philadelphia Convention was illegal without approval by Congress. Once that was gained, Rhode Island's refusal to participate meant that the amendment provision of the Articles, requiring approval of all the states, would not sanction any product of the Convention. Washington's imprimatur was crucial, and he let it be known that he would attend nonetheless. He arrived weeks before a quorum formed and worked with his delegation to refine the opening salvo for reform, the Virginia Plan. Only one other delegate could legitimize the Convention so much; yet, it was Benjamin Franklin who spoke of the propriety and necessity of electing Washington to preside. Both in symbolic and practical ways, he then kept the Convention and reform on track by attending every session for four months and voting on all motions, by enforcing the secrecy rule that permitted—as Madison's notes reveal—extraordinarily candid deliberations, and, finally, by signing the Constitution and the letter transmitting it to Congress.

Washington also must be credited for restraint at the Convention, since refraining from certain actions bolstered the viability of its product. He occasionally voted against Madison's political science of efficient national sovereignty in the Virginia Plan to accommodate concerns of nascent Anti-Federalists. He could have used his prestige to enact his pet ideas, especially on the single executive for which, it is widely recognized, he was the delegates' model; instead, he moderated his role so as not to abuse his authority. When he rose on the last day for a rare intervention, Madison notes that he addressed this first: "his situation" as presiding officer "had hitherto restrained him from offering his sentiments on questions depending in the House, and it might be thought, ought now to impose silence on him." Nonetheless, in a spirit of compromise, he backed a motion to enlarge the House of Representatives: "it was much to be desired that the objections to the plan recommended might be made as few as possible," and this motion was "of so much consequence that it would give him much satisfaction to see it adopted." This idea had been debated and defeated regularly in the final weeks; now it was approved unanimously, without debate.[20] A less principled man might have used such influence quite differently.

In the ratification debates as well Washington told associates to use his name; yet, knowing that he might be the first president, he did not campaign himself. He did arrange publication in Virginia of *The Federalist*, the New York essays of his associates Hamilton, Jay, and Madison. He wrote to Hamilton that, having read many Federalist and Anti-Federalist efforts, none was better designed to "produce conviction." Indeed, his verdict on *The Federalist* is remarkably perceptive: "When the transient circumstances & fugitive performances which attended this *crisis* shall have disappeared, that work will merit the notice of Posterity; because in it are candidly and ably discussed the principles of freedom & the topics of government, which will always be interesting to mankind so long as they shall be connected in Civil Society" (*W* 691–92). Both sides thought his public support tipped the scales toward the Constitution's narrow victory; for Marshall, "had the influence of character been removed, the intrinsic merits of the instrument would not have secured its adoption" (*LGW* 325). James Monroe wrote to Jefferson that "his influence carried this government."[21]

Although pledged to perfecting the Union through constitutional reform, Washington reluctantly assumed the office of president. His First Inaugural Address, to "Fellow Citizens" of the Senate and House, opens by noting his "anxieties." Having been "summoned by my Country," he surrendered what had been an "immutable decision" to retire (*W* 730).[22] He expressed concern, as he had twice before, that his countrymen overestimated him, and he asked forgiveness for any errors arising from his "deficiencies" as to "civil administration." Given his still more reluctant acceptance of a second term in 1792, his decisions to serve stem not only from civic duty but also from two principles he had long advocated: the executive statesmanship needed in republics and deference to popular consent. Washington knew from the war that effective statesmanship and popular opinion did not always harmonize; during his presidency he would hazard his happiness and reputation in balancing them as he judged best for American constitutionalism. He was a strong but moderate and faithfully constitutional executive, justifying decisions with stated principles. He sought to quell the partisanship gripping America by calling his countrymen to the enduring interests and higher ends that united them. His letters before his inauguration predict how difficult the unprecedented task of chief executive would be and how contentious the politics might become.

His Inaugural Address dropped the constitutional and policy discourses he had drafted in order to emphasize instead the principles of American republicanism. It was fitting to offer "fervent supplications to that Almighty Being who rules over the Universe" that "his benediction may consecrate to the liberties and happiness of the People of the United States, a Government instituted by themselves for these essential purposes" (*W* 731). "No People can be bound to acknowledge and adore the invisible hand, which conducts the Affairs of men" more than Americans; in the recent "revolution," the "tranquil deliberations, and voluntary consent of so many distinct communities" contrasted with the way "most Governments have been established," suggesting a "providential agency." He quoted "the Great Constitutional Charter" for the terms by which he should relate to Congress, and he urged Congress, too, to consult the Constitution for its powers and agenda. He praised the "talents, the rectitude, and the patriotism which adorn the characters" of those elected, since such "honorable qualifications" should ensure that "no local prejudices" or "party animosities, will misdirect the comprehensive and equal eye which ought to watch over this great Assemblage of communities and interests." Thus, "the foundations of our national policy, will be laid in the pure and immutable principles of private morality," and such "pre-eminence" would win for free government "the respect of the world." Since "the preservation of the sacred fire of liberty, and the destiny of the Republican model of Government, are justly considered as *deeply*, perhaps as *finally* staked, on the experiment entrusted" to America, the government must abide by "the eternal rules of order and right, which Heaven itself has ordained." For "there is no truth more thoroughly established, than that there exists in the œconomy and course of nature, an indissoluble union between virtue and happiness, between duty and advantage, between the genuine maxims of an honest and magnanimous policy, and the solid rewards of public prosperity and felicity" (*W* 731–33).

After endorsing the moderate, Madisonian strategy for constitutional amendments only regarding "the characteristic rights of freemen," and again requesting reimbursement for expenses in lieu of any salary, Washington closed by reiterating the humility, civility, and moderation fitting for American politics. Just as "the benign Parent of the human race" had again favored America's "happiness" by promoting tranquil deliberations and reform toward greater security for the Union, so Washington hoped "this divine blessing may be equally *conspicuous* in the enlarged views—the temperate consultations, and the wise measures on which the success of this Government must depend" (*W* 732–34). He abided by this principled moderation during the tumultuous years ahead, even though he may have been tempted to drop it in self-defense amid ferocious partisanship and popular outrage. His deeds proved his view that liberty and constitutionalism require a balanced, complex kind of prudential judgment that avoids the theoretical and practical extremes to which human politics can tend; the American experiment might not have survived if not for his moderation.

"As our interest guided by our justice shall Counsel": Statesmanship and Moderation in Domestic and Foreign Affairs

Washington's Farewell Address, announcing his withdrawal from consideration for a third term and his retirement from public life, offers parting advice to his country while affirming the principles that guided him in office. It is indispensable reading for studies of American politics and history, and of republicanism and statesmanship more broadly. The issue of how much the ideas are Washington's, or Madison's or Hamilton's, evaporates upon examining his control throughout the drafting process and the clear lineage of ideas and phrases from his earlier writings.[23] More important is his direction to Hamilton that the address retain Madison's 1792 draft of a farewell; he had wanted to retire then, but pleas from all sides persuaded him to remain as the obvious choice for president again. Washington wanted these rival figures involved with his final statement to symbolize the balanced views and shared principles overlooked by the partisanship of the 1790s. This in itself confirmed a practical wisdom and moderate sense of justice surpassing that of any of his protégés, amid dilemmas dwarfing those faced by any successor save Lincoln. Indeed, Jefferson and Madison deemed the Farewell Address so important for American political thought that they placed it and his First Inaugural on the reading list for the University of Virginia, with the Declaration of Independence and *The Federalist*.[24] Also included was the 1799 Virginia Resolution against the Alien and Sedition Acts, perhaps to meet Democratic-Republican concerns about the views of executive power and foreign policy in the Address. Tocqueville was warmer to Washington's principles, describing this "admirable letter addressed to his fellow citizens, which forms the political testament of that great man," as the basic charter of American foreign policy.[25]

The great, related themes of Washington's presidency were that executive power was safe for republicanism, and that constitutional government, not populism or parties, should guide the way through domestic and foreign trials. These principles animated his speeches and deeds, including his statement that a republic's chief executive should not hold office for life. The Constitution provided a strong keel and rudder, but the final phase of his career proves how crucial his practical wisdom and adherence to constitutionalism was in guiding the ship of state past storms and siren songs. His commitment to making the Constitution work by fleshing out the powers sketched in Article II and throughout still shapes our politics today, beyond his efforts to protect the Republic from European powers and visionary creeds. Ideas of presidential power and of statesmanship or leadership have changed in two centuries, but Washington's principles remain a benchmark for evaluating whether these are improvements. To him we owe not only the republican principle limiting a president to two terms, deviated from only by Franklin Roosevelt and then entrenched in constitutional amendment. He also established that presidents should recruit the best talents and characters for offices, from a range of political and regional viewpoints, unaffected by patronage: his cabinet included Hamilton and Jefferson, and he nominated to the Supreme Court such leading jurists as John Jay and James Wilson. His adherence to separation of powers dictated respect for the legislative dominance of Congress;

instead of pushing an extensive program, the president should recommend a few measures, mostly concerning core Article II powers of foreign and security policy. Similarly, the executive should use the veto power with care, on constitutional and not policy grounds; his qualification to this was a veto over a core presidential power, the size of the army. The executive and Senate should collaborate on treaties while maintaining separate roles and judgments; however, he insisted that the House play no role, given "the plain letter of the Constitution" and his direct knowledge from the 1787 Convention of "the principles on which the Constitution was formed" (*W* 930–32). The executive and legislature, not just the courts, should weigh the constitutional merits of controversial measures, as he did in canvassing Hamilton and Jefferson on the National Bank. Perhaps dearest to him was the principle that the president represents all the American citizenry, its various regions and states, its common principles and highest ideals, and not merely one party or set of policies. Similarly, he balanced republican dignity and republican simplicity in the presidency, as exemplified in the simple but formal ceremony of his inaugurations—to include supplementing the constitutional oath of office with "so help me God," sworn upon the Bible.

Washington's conduct amid the partisanship that rocked his presidency offers lessons of prudence and moderation worth pondering. The two great domestic disputes concerned national finances: first, opposition to the National Bank and other parts of the economic plan devised by Treasury Secretary Hamilton; second, the protest in western Pennsylvania against the tax on distilled spirits. The two great foreign policy disputes involved the upheaval of the French Revolution and the radically egalitarian, antimonarchical theory France sought to impress upon the world, and especially America. Washington's two measures to protect America from such turbulence—his 1793 Neutrality Proclamation and 1795 treaty with Britain (the Jay Treaty)—occasioned bitter partisan attacks. His policies on this range of domestic and foreign issues were remarkably consistent, informed by his view that liberty is best secured by a complex constitutionalism balancing popular consent with competent offices, and by moderation regarding the theoretical and practical temptations always haunting politics. In domestic policy, his annual messages praise Congress for enacting his administration's funding and financial plans, and he reports their evident benefits for America's public credit, private commercial activity, and prosperity. He commends sober deliberation among separated powers for discerning sound policies for the Republic, unaffected by short-term concerns over creeds, personalities, class conflict, or reelection. The basic outlines of Washington's financial system remain today, grounded in the principles he directed Hamilton to develop into a detailed plan. Without dismissing criticisms raised concerning national administrative power, commercialism, and inequality, it has helped to produce more liberty, prosperity, and equality than perhaps any regime in history can boast.[26]

The same complex, Montesquieuian conception of liberty informed Washington's response to protests against federal taxation and his policy of neutrality toward France and Britain. In Pennsylvania, opposition to the so-called whiskey tax exploded from 1791 to 1794 into a grassroots movement against the authority of the national government, peaking in armed resistance to collecting the tax or enforcing any federal laws. From his Third Annual Message in 1791, he proposed "wise moderation" in addressing the reasonable concerns of the Pennsylvanians; but as the revolutionary fervor and violence of the opposition grew, so did his determination that the rule of law must not yield to popular sentiments or partisan creeds. He issued proclamations in 1792 and 1794 on his constitutional duty to enforce duly enacted laws and the duty of citizens to comply with them, and he explained his policy in his Fourth, Sixth, and Seventh Annual Message. He ultimately readied militias from four states to suppress an armed resistance that was "subversive equally of the just authority of Government and of the rights of individuals"; when this mobilization and final efforts at conciliation failed to persuade the "insurgents," he sent an overwhelming force of 15,000 troops—an "army of the constitution"—to restore order. The Whiskey Rebellion was dispersed, and the leaders arrested and tried in the courts; Washington ultimately pardoned, however, those convicted of treason and sentenced to death. At stake had been "the fundamental principle of our constitution, which enjoins that the will of the majority should prevail." The lesson for citizens was to "persevere in their affectionate vigilance over that precious depository of American happiness, the constitution of the United States," and to ask continued protection from "the Supreme Ruler of nations" over a government dedicated to securing "human rights" (*W* 789, 829, 870–73, 882–84, 887–93, 922).

A similarly partisan, popular resistance arose to Washington's neutrality policy and to the treaty with Britain that prevented war with that great power—at the risk of offending the revolutionary French republic and its zealous supporters in America. He withstood charges of monarchism and of groveling to Britain, defending the policy as the best way to maintain both America's true independence and a just peace. In his Seventh Annual Message and his letter to the House rejecting their request for the Jay Treaty documents, he defended the Framers' principle that foreign policy should not bow to current popular sentiments or abstract creeds but should be debated and formulated by the branches somewhat insulated from popular opinion, the indirectly elected Senate and indirectly elected executive. Indeed, despite his reservations about the treaty, he pressed to ratify it in part to quell partisan and popular disorder from the same sorts of local clubs that had stoked the violence of the French Revolution and the Whiskey Rebellion. The "prudence and moderation" which had obtained and ratified the treaty sought an honorable peace as the foundation for America's future prosperity and strength. These "genuine principles of rational liberty" would prove essential to "national happiness"; having been "[f]aithful to ourselves, we have violated no obligation to others" (*W* 920–22, 930–32). Tocqueville extolled this achievement in 1835:

> The sympathies of the people in favor of France were . . . declared with so much violence that nothing less than the inflexible character of Washington and the immense popularity that he enjoyed were needed to prevent war from being declared on England. And still, the efforts that the austere reason of this great man made to struggle against the generous but unreflective passions of his fellow citizens almost took from him the sole recompense that he had ever reserved for himself, the love of his country. The majority pronounced against his policy; now the entire people approves it. If the Constitution and public favor had not given the direction of the external affairs of the state to Washington, it is certain that the nation would have done then precisely what it condemns today.[27]

The Farewell Address encapsulates and elevates the principles Washington had stood for during his presidency and entire career. True to his concern about demagoguery, he published the text in a newspaper, foregoing a ceremonial speech. True to his republicanism, it had no grand title, only "United States, September 19, 1796," to "Friends, and Fellow-Citizens"; another newspaper later termed it his Farewell Address. The harmony with earlier writings is striking: the Address opens by invoking republican virtue and civic duty; patriotic devotion to the common good; gratitude to Heaven for the country's blessings and prayers for continued Providence; and the need for prudence and moderation to sustain such goods. He pledged "unceasing vows" that America and the world would enjoy five further blessings:

> that Heaven may continue to you the choicest tokens of its beneficence; that your Union and brotherly affection may be perpetual; that the free constitution, which is the work of your hands, may be sacredly maintained; that its Administration in every department may be stamped with

wisdom and Virtue; that, in fine, the happiness of the people of these States, under the auspices of liberty, may be made complete, by so careful a preservation and so prudent a use of this blessing as will acquire to them the glory of recommending it to the applause, the affection, and adoption of every nation which is yet a stranger to it. (*W* 963–64)

He then cites his 1783 Circular as a precedent for offering advice as well as prayers, and he proceeds to propound several lessons for the "solemn contemplation" and "frequent review" of the citizenry. The first lesson concerns liberty: that Americans are so deeply attached to it he need say no more. This subtly implies an imbalance needing redress; the advice to follow concerns ordering and sustaining liberty. Indeed, the next two lessons reinforce two of his prayers: America must strengthen the Union and cherish the Constitution if it truly prizes liberty. These two aims were the central concerns of Washington's public service and writings from 1783, and they garner the bulk of the Address. Brief advice follows on three principles supporting these ends: adherence to separation of powers and the rule of law over populism and passion; the need for religion, morality, and education in republics; and responsible public finances. The final counsel, nearly as long as those on union and constitution, concerns America's independence and capacity for justice in foreign affairs (*W* 964–72).

Washington's maxim "to steer clear of permanent Alliances" is among the best-known points of the Address, along with his call to inculcate religion and morality in a self-governing citizenry (*W* 975). That said, many accounts of his foreign policy mistakenly cite Jefferson's later maxim about "entangling alliances," and they mischaracterize the Address as launching a doctrine of isolationism. In fact, Washington criticized the French Revolution and its effects in America for imposing visions and doctrines when knowledge of human nature and practical realities supported more moderate views. Such prudence also suggests, however, that he would question any use of his advice today as an abstract rule book for the problems of our very different context. This is not to say that he defined prudence merely as self-interested calculation to rationalize expedient deeds. His main principle was that a secure, independent nation must surrender to neither low interest nor abstract justice, but must balance the two. In this prudential spirit, he cites the specific circumstance of the 1790s that suggests America should be a "slave" neither to hatred of Britain nor to adoration of France: "a predominant motive has been to endeavor to gain time to our country to settle and mature its yet recent institutions, and to progress without interruption, to that degree of strength and consistency, which is necessary to give it, humanly speaking, command of its own fortunes" (*W* 973, 977).

America now is a lone superpower. Washington's prudential counsels still are relevant, but they do not fit our international relations doctrines, whether isolationism or internationalism, unilateralism or multilateralism, realism or liberal idealism. His main concern was that a nation be independent enough to act wisely and justly; the fundamental principle was to be able to "choose peace or war, as our interest guided by our justice shall Counsel" (*W* 975). He had long argued that interest requires provision for "the national security"; Theodore Roosevelt praised his maxim that "[t]o be prepared for war is one of the most effectual means of preserving peace" (*W* 749, 791–92, 848).[28] However, the Address also called America to "[o]bserve good faith and justice towds. all Nations. Cultivate peace and harmony with all. Religion and morality enjoin this conduct; and can it be that good policy does not equally enjoin it?" He cited the utilitarian maxim that "honesty is always the best policy," but he exhorted America to "give to mankind the magnanimous and too novel example of a People always guided by an exalted justice and benevolence" (*W* 972, 975). These balanced principles lie within the just war tradition of classical philosophy, Christianity, and modern natural law and international law, which developed guidelines for informing, not replacing, the prudence of statesmen. Our challenges may be different given our immense power, but the aim is still Washington's, to benefit both mankind and ourselves by respecting "the obligation[s] which justice and humanity impose on every Nation." America seeks justice, and government by and for the citizenry, while being a global hegemon. The ancient Romans, of course, lost their republic to empire; the modern British gave up their empire to preserve the republicanism of a constitutional monarchy. Such challenges, on top of the more particular ones of the twenty-first century world, call out for recurrence to Washington's counsels and principled prudence (*W* 977).

The exhortations in the Address to instill religious faith as well as moral and intellectual virtue also defy today's doctrinal categories. Washington endorses neither a secularist wall of separation between religion and government nor a sectarian view that America is a Christian nation; similarly, a republic should neither ignore the mutual influence between governmental and private morality nor use nocturnal tribunals to review the morals of citizens. Throughout his career, he balanced respect for Christian churches with liberal, enlightened forbearance from any coercion of belief. His Thanksgiving Proclamation of 1789 is an extraordinary exhortation to the citizenry, invoking piety, republicanism, religious liberty, and liberal enlightenment.[29] His letters to two minority religions in America, Jews and Roman Catholics, are meditations on the harmony between biblical faith and the "natural rights" of peaceful citizens to pursue their own piety. A just government "gives to bigotry no sanction, to persecution no assistance" and thus transcends mere "toleration," but it should exhort citizens to "the cultivation of manners, morals, and piety."[30] As with all his major addresses, his Farewell opens and closes by invoking Providence in a manner inclusive of all believers in a transcendent deity without threatening those of other views. He balances the utility of piety and morals with genuine appreciation for them: "Of all the dispositions and habits which lead to political prosperity, Religion and morality are indispensable supports"; "A volume could not trace all their connections with private and public felicity"; just policies are "recommended by every sentiment which ennobles human Nature" (*W* 971, 972–73). Indeed, as he had done since his First Annual Message, he endorsed liberal learning and institutions "for the general diffusion of knowledge," it being "essential that public opinion should be enlightened" (*W* 972, 750). The guiding spirit of the Address is moderation, that prudence should guide domestic and foreign affairs, private and public life; he hoped these "counsels of an old and affectionate friend" would "controul the usual current of the passions" and "moderate the fury of party spirit" (*W* 976; see also 832, 851, 924). An element of Christian Aristotelianism tempers his enlightened liberalism and classical republicanism, the mark of the "Rules of Civility" he imbibed as a youth—the last of which states: "Labour to keep alive in your Breast that Little Spark of Celestial fire Called Conscience" (*W* 10).[31]

Well-intentioned judgments about Washington's complicity in slavery often prevent us from appreciating his thought and character today. In fact, his thoughts and deeds on slavery are a model for any struggle to rise above historical circumstance and self-interest to do the right thing, a model always needed in politics. For the last three decades of his life, he stated that slavery was unjust—at first ambiguously, complaining that the British sought to "make us as tame, & abject Slaves, as the Blacks we Rule over with such arbitrary Sway," but then with moral clarity, expressing "regret" at being a slave master and hoping it would not be "displeasing to the justice of the Creator" if he made his adult slaves "comfortable" while laying "a foundation to prepare the rising generation for a destiny different from that in which they were born" (*W* 158, 701–2). From the early 1770s he never sold slaves, a costly policy: their number at Mount Vernon doubled, and while he shifted from tobacco to wheat and other crops to escape a slavery plantation economy, he had more slaves than was profitable. After decades of deliberation with Lafayette and others, and various proposed schemes for emancipation, and even discretely freeing some, he finally resolved in his Last Will and Testament to emancipate all of them upon Martha's death. Legal protections for widows prevented him from freeing those she brought to the marriage, and since he had encouraged marriage and families on the plantation he could not free his slaves but not hers without causing "insuperable difficulties" and "painful sensations" for them. He also wanted to complete the preparations he had made for the slaves' education and skills so as to give them some reasonable chance in the world. The aged and orphans among them not wishing or able to be freed were to be cared for, educated, and trained in skills by his estate. He emphasized that these directions be "religious fulfilled" by his heirs "without evasion, neglect or delay"; the estate spent money on pensioners until 1833 (*W* 1023–24).[32] Like Lincoln, he was neither slavery apologist nor abolitionist, judging this moderate plan more humane and also a model to fellow gentry that an estate need not be destroyed by emancipation. He may also have feared that more conspicuous statements or actions on his part would fan civil discord between North and South more than it would have helped the slaves. He admitted that he had redressed the evil later than he should have, but we should consider that no other slaveholding president freed all his slaves. We should also reflect upon the more lax, comfortable moral state of America today before condemning a man who inherited an evil practice and strove to help eradicate it through his example of prudence and principle.

Marshall's biography concludes by emphasizing the bond between a statesman's moral and intellectual virtue, and that all "candidates for political fame" should study Washington's "sound judgment," his "incorruptible" integrity, and "the texture" of a mind that balanced "modesty" with "dignity" and "an unvarying sense of moral right" with prudence about the possible (*LGW* 465–69). Democratic republics always will look for leaders to ascend from campaigning to governing, from popularity to statesmanship. In domestic and foreign affairs, we would do well to study Washington's thought and example. As a political father, he committed himself to freedom for his children; we would not use it wisely if we ignored him now.

Notes

This chapter does not represent the views of the U.S. Air Force Academy or the U.S. government. I am grateful to my colleagues Jeff Anderson and Lance Robinson for comments on earlier drafts of this chapter.

1. Farewell Address, in *George Washington: Writings*, ed. John Rhodehamel (New York: Literary Classics of the United States, 1997), 962, 964, hereafter cited in the text as *W*. See "Note on the Texts" (*W* 1076–81) about this one-volume selection and various multivolume collections. Washington's writings are quoted as in the originals, with spelling and emphases retained. Another useful one-volume edition is *George Washington: A Collection*, ed. William B. Allen (Indianapolis: Liberty Fund, 1988).

2. A welcome exception is *Leading and Leadership*, ed. Timothy Fuller, *Ethics of Everyday Life* series (Notre Dame, Ind.: University of Notre Dame Press, 2000), 135–36, 140–47.

3. See Alexis de Tocqueville, *Democracy in America*, ed. and trans. Harvey Mansfield and Delba Winthrop (Chicago: University of Chicago Press, 2000), "Social State of the Anglo- Americans" (vol. 1, pt. 1, chap. 3), "On Some Tendencies Particular to Historians in Democratic Centuries" (vol. 2, pt. 1, chap. 20), and "Why Democratic Peoples Show a More Ardent and More Lasting Love for Equality than for Freedom" (vol. 2, pt. 2, chap. 1).

4. For the conception of moderation that most influenced the American Founders, see Montesquieu, *The Spirit of the Laws*, trans. Anne Cohler, Basia Miller, and Harold Stone (Cambridge: Cambridge University Press, [1748] 1989), preface and bk. 29, chap. 1; see also bk. 9, chaps. 1–3, and bk. 11, chaps. 5, 6, 8, 20.

5. See Matthew Spalding and Patrick Garrity, *A Sacred Union of Citizens: George Washington's Farewell Address and the American Character* (Lanham, Md.: Rowman and Littlefield, 1996).

6. Richard Brookhiser, *Founding Father: Rediscovering George Washington* (New York: Free Press, 1996), 139; see his chapters on "Morals" and "Ideas," 121–56. Throughout this chapter, I freely draw upon Brookhiser's study and these other indispensable works: John Marshall, *The Life of George Washington: Special Edition for Schools*, ed. Robert Faulkner and Paul Carrese (Indianapolis: Liberty Fund, [1838] 2000); Glenn Phelps, *George Washington and American Constitutionalism* (Lawrence: University Press of Kansas, 1993); Spalding and Garrity, *A Sacred Union of Citizens*; and Robert Faulkner, "Foreword," in Marshall's *Life of Washington*, and "Washington and the Founding of Constitutional Democracy," in *Gladly to Learn and Gladly to Teach: Essays on Religion and Political Philosophy in Honor of Ernest L. Fortin, A. A.*, ed. Michael P. Foley and Douglas Kries (Lanham, Md.: Lexington Books, 2002).

7. On the complexity of influences and advisers surrounding Washington, see Stuart Leibiger, *Founding Friendship: George Washington, James Madison, and the Creation of the American Republic* (Charlottesville: University Press of Virginia, 1999). After his retirement, Washington severely criticized Democratic-Republican partisanship, but he also chastised Federalists for emphasizing personalities and partisanship over principles; see letters to Patrick Henry, January 15, 1799, and to Jonathan Trumbull, Jr., August 30, 1799 (*W* 1016–18, 1048–50).

8. First Inaugural Address, March 4, 1801, in *Thomas Jefferson: Writings*, ed. Merrill D. Peterson (New York: Literary Classics of the United States, 1984), 493.

9. Don Higginbotham, "Introduction," in *George Washington Reconsidered*, ed. Don Higginbotham (Charlottesville: University Press of Virginia, 2001), 6; in the same volume, see also W. W. Abbot, "An Uncommon Awareness of Self: The Papers of George Washington," and Gordon Wood, "The Greatness of George Washington."

10. Marshall, *Life of Washington: Special Edition*, 463. Subsequent references to this one-volume edition of his larger work, completed by Marshall just before his death, are cited in the text as *LGW*.

11. To Francis Dandridge, September 20, 1765, in *Washington: A Collection*, 22.

12. Regarding military strategy and military affairs generally, see Don Higginbotham, *George Washington and the American Military Tradition* (Athens: University of Georgia Press, 1985).

13. Department of the Army, *The Army*, Field Manual 100–1 (Washington, D.C.: Department of the Army, 2001). See also Douglas V. Johnson and Steven Metz, "Civil-Military Relations in the United States," in *American Defense Policy*, ed. Peter Hays, Brenda Vallance, and Alan Van Tassel, 7th ed. (Baltimore: Johns Hopkins University Press, 1997), 495–96.

14. Jefferson to Washington, April 16, 1784, in Jefferson, *Writings*, 791. Compare Marshall's extraordinary tribute in *LGW* 301.

15. Hamilton to Tobias Lear, January 2, 1800, in *Selected Writings and Speeches of Alexander Hamilton*, ed. Morton J. Frisch (Washington, D.C.: AEI Press, 1985), 456.

16. See Aristotle, *Nicomachean Ethics*, 8.1, 8.9–11 (1155a22–28, 1159b25–1161b10); Thomas Aquinas, *Summa Theologiae*, I–II, q. 105, a. 5; II–II, q. 23, aa. 7, 8; q. 25, aa. 8, 9; q. 26, a. 8.

17. Compare the Book of Micah 6:8, and the Gospel of Matthew 23:23.

18. Aristotle, *Politics*, 3.11 (1281b21–30), teaches superior statesmen to incorporate the masses into governance to some degree in order to avoid having a city "full of enemies"; see also 2.2 (1261a22–31), 2.9 (1270b17–27), 3.4 (1276b35–1277a11), and 7.14 (1332b16–31).

19. Tocqueville, "History of the Federal Constitution," in *Democracy in America*, vol. 1, pt. 1, chap. 8, 107.

20. James Madison, *Notes of Debates in the Federal Convention of 1787*, ed. Adrienne Koch (New York: W. W. Norton, 1987), 655.

21. Monroe to Jefferson, July 12, 1788, in *The Papers of Thomas Jefferson*, ed. Julian Boyd et al. (Princeton, N.J.: Princeton University Press, 1950–), 13:352.

22. This is not the discarded First Inaugural, a longer address he prepared with his secretary David Humphreys but then decided not to use. On this interesting text and surviving fragments, see *Washington: A Collection*, 440–42, 445–59, and *W* 702–16, 1116–17.

23. For some of the correspondence and drafts, see *W* 804–6, 938–48, 950–51, 954–56, 960–61. Spalding and Garrity, *A Sacred Union of Citizens*, 46–57, defend in great detail Washington's authorship; see also *Washington's Farewell Address*, ed. Victor H. Paltsits (New York: New York Public Library, 1935).

24. Madison to Jefferson, February 8, 1825, in *The Mind of the Founder: Sources of the Political Thought of James Madison*, ed. Marvin Myers, rev. ed. (Hanover, N.H.: University Press of New England, 1981), 350.

25. Tocqueville, "The Manner in Which American Democracy Conducts External Affairs of State," in *Democracy in America*, vol. 1, pt. 1, chap. 5, 217.

26. See Sketch of a Plan of American Finance, October 1789, in *Washington: A Collection*, 535–37; and economic and financial issues in the discarded First Inaugural in *W* 713–15.

27. *Democracy in America*, vol. 1, pt. 2, chap. 6, 220. Tocqueville cites Marshall's *Life of Washington* as his authority on this, quoting it at length.

28. See Theodore Roosevelt, "Washington's Forgotten Maxim" (address as assistant secretary of the navy, Naval War College, 1897), in *The Works of Theodore Roosevelt*, national edition (New York: Charles Scribner's Sons, 1926), 13:182–99.

29. Thanksgiving Proclamation, October 3, 1789, in *Washington: A Collection*, 534–35.

30. To Hebrew Congregation, August 18, 1790 (*W* 766–67); to Roman Catholics, March 15, 1790, in *Washington: A Collection*, 546–47.

31. See *George Washington's Rules of Civility: Complete with the Original French Text and New French-to-English Translations*, ed. John T. Phillips II, 2nd ed. (Leesburg, Va.: Goose Creek Productions, 2000), 7–14.

32. See Brookhiser, *Founding Father*, 177–85, and James T. Flexner, "George Washington and Slavery," in *George Washington, Anguish and Farewell* (Boston: Little, Brown, 1972), 112–25.

Chapter 6

John Adams and the Republic of Laws

Richard Samuelson

John Adams (1735–1826) was born in Braintree, Massachusetts. Though his parents were not wealthy, they saved enough money to send John, their eldest son, to Harvard College, from which he graduated in 1755. After some hesitation, Adams chose law as his profession, and he rose rapidly though the colony's legal ranks. By the late 1760s, he was among the top lawyers in the colony. As the imperial crisis waxed, Adams took up his pen to help make the colonial case against British taxation, and he helped organize the colonial resistence. In 1774 and 1775, Massachusetts put Adams in its delegation to the Continental Congress. By the late spring and early summer of 1776, Adams was the leader of the proindependence forces in Congress. The fledgling Union sent Adams to Europe, first to help Benjamin Franklin and others negotiate a treaty of alliance with the French, and then to lead the American negotiations with Britain to end the war. After the Peace of Paris of 1783, Adams remained in Europe as a diplomat. Returning from Europe not long before the federal Constitution came into effect, Adams was elected vice president in 1788 and was returned to that office in 1792. In 1796, Adams defeated Jefferson in the race to succeed George Washington; in 1800, Jefferson turned Adams out of office. Adams retired from politics in 1801 and spent the rest of his life on and around his farm, reading his books and writing letters to friends. He died on July 4, 1826.[1]

The rule of law was the main focus of Adams's political thought. In the influential pamphlet of the spring of 1776, "Thoughts on Government," Adams wrote that "there is no good government but what is republican" and that "the very definition of a republic is 'an empire of laws and not of men'" (*WJA* 4:194).[2] An understanding of the law and the nature of its rule is therefore fundamental to understanding his thought. Adams highlighted two means of securing the rule of law: consent, and checks and balances. As we discuss his thoughts about the rule of law, we should keep in mind that Adams denied that theory was separable from practice. Hence, we will at times find it necessary to discuss concrete examples to elaborate upon his political thought.

I

Adams held that having known and fixed laws was a necessary but not sufficient condition of good government. "No man will contend that a nation can be free that is not governed by fixed laws. All other government than that of permanent known laws, is the government of mere will and pleasure, whether it be exercised by one, a few, or many" (*WJA* 4:403; cf. 4:401, 526). At the same time, Adams did not think all laws were created equal. Rightly understood, law was more than force backed by authority. In an 1811 essay on "A Government of Laws and Not of

Men," Adams commented that "it is very true there can be no good government, without laws: but," he added, "those laws must be good, must be equal, must be wisely made."[3]

How could some laws be contrary to rule of law? During the imperial crisis of the 1760s and 1770s, Adams found that most of the lawyers who had taken up their pens in the dispute had missed that paradoxical truth.

> Some have defined it [the British Constitution] to [be] the practice of parliament; others, the judgements and precedents of the King's courts; but either of these definitions would make it a constitution of wind and weather, because the parliaments have sometimes voted the King absolute and the judges have sometimes adjudg'd him to be so. Some have call'd it custom, but this is as fluxuating and variable as the other. (*PJA* 1:165)

Truly to be fixed, the law had to be above the control of the men who held offices under it. The law could not render the king or Parliament absolute without contradicting its very nature. Similarly, custom was not an adequate anchor for the law because customs change. All efforts to reason exclusively with human precedents contained all the inconsistency and mutability of the human race. Law had to be tethered to something beyond the inventions of the human mind. While arguing against Parliament's right to legislate for the colonies without their consent, Adams quoted Hugo Grotius, the seventeenth-century Dutch authority on law: *"Whatever is originally in its Nature wrong, can never be sanctified or made right by Repetition and Use"* (*BAR* 61). In its profound sense, law had to do with right and justice. Adams quoted one of his favorite authors, Cicero, who wrote that laws, "as they are founded on eternal morals, are emanations of the Divine mind" (*WJA* 6:56). The laws could be said to govern when a people submitted to the authority not of some imperfect human legislator but of the eternal Legislator of the universe.

Adams chose a seemingly impossible standard for the rule of law, but he also thought it was the only reasonable one. If the rule of law entailed only the submission to the commands of some authority, then all men except the commanders would be slaves, submitting to the will of the rulers rather than to a law which bound all equally. Moreover, unless the sovereign was wise and virtuous, that would mean submission to the passions and errors of one, few, or many. The laws could be said to govern only where the laws were organized around some principle of justice. Adams believed that the law of justice was the law of liberty. God did not make men to be slaves, for "man has certainly an exalted soul" (*PJA* 1:111). Adams realized that man had passions and instincts, but he did not conclude from that reality that man was a beast who followed them blindly. Man had reason, which allowed him to contemplate means and ends, including ends beyond himself. Man could pursue justice. In 1811, Adams grew frustrated with the abuse to which the idea of the rule of law had been put. "Suppose we should say, a government of the Virtues and not of Men: a government of Wisdom and not of Men: a government of Religion natural or revealed, and not of Men: a government of Morality and not of Men: a government of policy and not of Men: would not any of these propositions be as intelligible, as true, and as important, as our motto?"[4] Properly understood, law was bound up with the virtues, wisdom, religion, morality, and policy. Law was right reason in practice.

Adams believed God had made men for liberty. God was not cruel, creating man with free will but leaving him helpless to determine what he should do with that freedom. Rather, God gave man reason:

> Philosophy which is the result of Reason, is the first, the original Revelation of The Creator to his Creature, Man. When this Revelation is clear and certain, by Intuition or necessary Induction, no subsequent Revelation supported by Prophecies or Miracles can supercede it. Phylosophy is

not only the love of Wisdom, but the Science of the Universe and its Cause. There is, there was and there will be but one Master of Phylosophy in the Universe. Portions of it, in different degrees are revealed to Creatures. (*AJL* 412)

Men were born ignorant and in need of education to determine what they were to do with themselves in life. That was why God had given man reason. By discovering itself, reason discovered free will. Man had the ability to choose his course in life (within certain limits of circumstance). At the same time, human reason was neither all-powerful nor all-knowing. Rather than finding that reality disappointing, Adams found it another cause for wonder at God's gift of freedom to man. Were human reason always able to determine with ease and with certainty what man should do, man would hardly be free; God would dictate to man through the instrument of reason.[5] The limits of reason were reflected in the limits of legitimate government. The diversity of human life and circumstances guaranteed that the law could not accommodate every case. "Society can be governed only by general rules. Government cannot accommodate itself to every particular case as it happens, nor the circumstances of particular persons" (*WJA* 9:378). Those who wrote the laws should have a certain humility about their work.

Adams was of that ancient school which held that human knowledge was possible only after one accepted certain things on faith. As he told Jefferson, "I hold there can be no Phylosophy without Religion" (*AJL* 358). All study of the empirical world accepted that the data gathered by the senses were accurate. Yet the order which is apparent to the sense may or may not be real, and the way one chooses to think about the sensible world is itself a moral choice. From his reflection upon that problem, and upon the moral universe more generally, Adams concluded that ethical monotheism was the best faith.

The Hebrew unity of Jehovah, the prohibition of all similitude, appears to me the greatest wonder of antiquity. How could that nation preserve its creed among the monstrous theologies of all the other nations of the earth? Revelation, you will say, and especial Providence; and I will not contradict you, for I cannot say . . . that a revelation is impossible or improbable. (*WJA* 10:235)[6]

Human knowledge did not penetrate far enough into the mysteries of the universe to reject the possibility of direct revelation outright, even though the first revelation of God to man was reason. By accepting on faith that there was one God who created and ordered the world, and by admitting that he was doing so, Adams brought a certain humility to his thought. Humans used words like "matter" and "spirit" and had some sense of what they meant by them, but men did not really know whether the meaning reflected anything final because "we know nothing of Essences." Adams was emphatic on the point: "I insist upon it that the Saint has as good a right to groan at the Philosopher for asserting that there is nothing but matter in the Universe, As the Philosopher has to laugh at the Saint for saying that there are both Matter and Spirit" (*AJL* 564). Ultimately, Adams's beliefs that men were free and had reason were inextricably linked to ethical monotheism. Adams was convinced that "some Essence does exist, which causes our minds with all their ideas, and this visible World with all its wonders. I am certain that this Cause is Wise, Benevolent and powerful, beyond all conception; I cannot doubt, but what it is, I cannot conjecture" (*AJL* 563–64). The order men perceive in the universe allowed men to function and to enjoy liberty so long as men did not claim to know too much about that order.

By observing nature with the instrument of reason, man learned about his obligations. Finding himself sharing the world with other people, each individual had to determine what, if anything, he owed himself and others. "I must judge for myself," Adams wrote, "but how can I judge, how can any man judge, unless his mind has been opened and enlarged by reading."[7]

Education was a duty. At the same time, possession of that duty implied the right to pursue it. Duty and right were linked symbiotically.

Man's duty to judge for himself the proper course in life was not absolute but rather was limited by the principle itself. These limits involved oneself and others. Regarding oneself, one did not have the right to chose to be a slave, blindly and unreflectingly submitting to the will or thoughts of another. On the other side, one did not have the right to treat others as instruments of one's own will. Adams upheld the golden rule, one of the ethical commands in both Testaments, as the model: "I would define liberty as the power to do as we would be done by. The definition of liberty to be the power of doing whatever the laws permit, meaning the civil laws, does not appear to be satisfactory" (*WJA* 10:377).[8] Understood in its most profound sense, liberty was the ability to choose to treat others justly. It was the ability to educate oneself in one's duties and obligations to oneself and others, coupled with the ability to act on the conclusions one reached. At the same time, one's rights extended so far, and no further, than the rights of others to educate themselves and to act upon their informed judgment. The golden rule itself grew from the obligation to pursue justice. Submission to the law of justice was the rule of law. In this sense, law was not the antithesis of freedom. Law was liberty.

What did all that reasoning have to do with the law as most people knew it? How did it help one judge any specific law or system of laws? Adams wrestled with this problem throughout his life. Given the limits of human reason, the best that men could do was to think seriously about the laws of their society and seek to keep them tethered to the golden rule of liberty. Adams found two means to that end: consent, and checks and balances. Governments gained the right to coerce men because men gave governments the right to use force to enforce the laws. It was "*consent alone* that makes any human Laws binding" (*BAR* 140). While consent was necessary, it was not sufficient. The right to consent to laws did not make whatever laws they consented to right. Adams was particularly worried that voters would abdicate their duties. From his observation of political man, Adams concluded that "human nature itself from indolence, modesty, humanity or fear, has always too much reluctance to a manly assertion of rights" (*PJA* 1:123). By itself, consent was inadequate to secure liberty because most men were too lazy to pay close attention to the management of their affairs. Self-government required a commitment of time and energy. The solution to that problem was checks and balances. To ensure liberty in a large democratic republic, "orders of men, watching and balancing each other, are the only security; power must be opposed to power, and interest to interest" (*WJA* 4:557). A well-ordered constitution would check the ambitious few to serve the public good and cajole the lazy many to remain vigilant in defending their liberty.[9]

II

Before the modern era, men had given more thought to the quality of the laws than to who made them. Why did Adams think differently? Why did he think that consent was essential to the creation of good laws? Adams reasoned that because each man had the duty to judge for himself, properly constructed societies respected the right of individuals to think, speak, and act. Men with a just appreciation for their obligations to themselves and to others would only submit to laws by mutual agreement. No man had the right to rule another without his consent. "The idea of a man born a magistrate, law-giver, or judge, is absurd and unnatural" (*PJA* 8:239). Men should participate not only in the process whereby governments were created but they should also consent to new laws as they are made.

The question of taxation without representation, which was of critical importance before 1776, was the principle of consent applied to a particularly important case. Taking it for granted that men could not live together without private property, Adams held that no one had the right, in ordinary circumstances, to appropriate another's property for his own ends.

> Property is surely a right of mankind as really as liberty. The moment the idea is admitted into society, that property is not as sacred as the laws of God, and that there is not a force of law and public justice to protect it, anarchy and tyranny commence. If "THOU SHALT NOT COVET," and "THOU SHALT NOT STEAL," were not commandments of Heaven, they must be made inviolable precepts in every society, before it can be civilized or made free. (*WJA* 6:8–9)

The right of property included the right to the fruits of one's labor. As Adams wrote in the controversy over the Stamp Act, "a great Part of the Public Money is Toil and labour of the People" (*PJA* 1:135). All members of a society had an obligation to consider the common goods to which their property would be put, and, outside the narrow confines of a town, representation was the best means of obtaining such consent.

For both principled and practical reasons, Adams and the other men of 1776 believed that the right to alter or abolish the government was fundamental to the idea of consent. In principle, the people had the right to change their government if they wanted; in practice, consent helped to keep the government in line. If one lost the right to resist authority after assenting to a government, what was one to do if that government acted contrary to its mandate? One of Adams's opponents in the 1770s complained that it was a recipe for anarchy to say "that all men are by nature equal; that kings are but the ministers of the people; that their authority is delegated to them by the people for their good, and they have a right to resume it . . . whenever it is made use of to oppress them." Adams found this argument laughable. At least since the Revolution of 1688, the English constitution itself was established on the idea of consent. "These are what are called revolution-principles. . . . The principles of nature and eternal reason. The principles on which the whole government over us, now stands." No British subject could defend the constitution without defending the principles which justified the Glorious Revolution. Adams's opponent claimed that Adams's principles, "adopted in private life . . . would introduce perpetual discord." Adams disagreed. "I think it plain, that there never was an happy private family where they were not adopted" (*PJA* 2:230).[10] All principles had limits. The duty of children to honor and obey their parents was limited by the duty of parents to look after the good of their children. Mutual obligations, managed by reason, were the essence of good society and hence the essence of good law. To think properly about constitutions, Adams found, men had to think about why they had governments in the first place (cf. *WJA* 4:554).

That men had the right to resist unjust or illegitimate authority did not mean it was always wise and proper to do so. The challenge in the years before 1776 was to determine when the violations by the government became both fundamental and irrevocable. Adams found that the analogy to marriage was apt. No marriage was without tensions and strife; only when the violations of the marriage were fundamental to the nature of marriage itself was divorce called for—so too with the divorce of Anglo-America from Britain (*PJA* 2:230). When the argument between America and Britain reached a fundamental and unnegotiable impasse, Adams concluded that independence was the prudent course. The Declaratory Act of 1766 (6, George III, cap. 12) claimed for Parliament the right to legislate for the colonies in "all cases whatsoever." As the years passed, Parliament began to show that it actually believed it could dictate law to the colonies, and it was determined to force the Americans to submit to its will. Hence, it was necessary to quit the empire.

In the decision for independence, thought and action were unified in the exercise of prudence. Adams gave prudence a central place in politics. In a letter to Adams, Benjamin Rush quoted Charles Lee's dismissal of prudence as a "rascally virtue." Adams replied that "his meaning was good. He meant the spirit which evades danger when duty requires us to face it. This is cowardice, not prudence." That, however, what not what Adams meant by prudence.

> By prudence I mean that deliberation and caution which aims at no ends but good ones, and good ones by none but fair means, and then carefully adjusts and proportions its good means to its good ends. Without this virtue there can be no other. Justice itself cannot exist without it. A disposition to render to everyone his right is of no use without prudence to judge of what is his right and skill to perform it. (*SF* 99)

Political decisions could not be made with mathematical certainty, but they had to be made. A prudent man proceeded responsibly—reading, thinking, talking, and reflecting at the level of attention the seriousness of the question merited. That was how Adams made the decision for independence in 1775 and 1776, and why some of his contemporaries called him the "Atlas of American Independence" (*WJA* 3:56n).

III

The "principles of liberty" and law were much easier to put into practice when breaking away from an established authority than they were in establishing a new one (*WJA* 6:412).[11] This work was of fundamental importance, for "there is nothing on this side of Jerusalem of equal importance to mankind" as "a free constitution of civil government."[12] "Revolution principles" could lead to anarchy were they improperly understood or applied, and Adams feared that could happen. After reading Thomas Paine's *Common Sense*, the sensation of 1776, Adams wrote that the English firebrand "has a better hand in pulling down than in building [up]."[13] To embolden Americans to support independence in 1776, polemics were necessary. Yet polemical discourse was far more effective against than in support of authority.

However risky, independence was also an opportunity. Men seldom had the chance to create free governments. "You and I, my dear friend," Adams wrote in the spring of 1776, "have been sent into life at a time when the greatest lawgivers of antiquity would have wished to live. How few of the human race have ever enjoyed an opportunity of making an election of government, more than of air, soil, or climate, for themselves or their children!" (*WJA* 4:200). By beginning well, America could demonstrate how to create legitimate governments based upon the consent of the governed and that such governments could work in practice. Throughout history, every republic had failed. It was surely folly for America's Founders to think they could create a republic that remained free when Solon, Plato, Lycurgus, and others had failed. By making a new experiment in republican self-government, Adams and his peers took a great responsibility upon themselves. If the American republic collapsed or grew tyrannical, it would only strengthen that conventional wisdom, rendering it that much harder to defend the holy causes of liberty and self-government in the future. "The people of America have now the best opportunity and the greatest trust in their hands, that Providence ever committed to so small a number, since the transgression of the first pair; if they betray their trust, their guilt will merit even greater punishment than other nations have suffered, and the indignation of heaven" (*WJA* 4:290). Should the Americans succeed, they would vindicate the honor of man before the court of history.

In 1776, Americans transformed their constitution. However liberal it was, the British constitution retained feudal elements (cf. *BAR* 127). In practice, the feudal remnant did not survive the voyage across the Atlantic, for "the truth is, that the people have ever governed in America" (*WJA* 4:360). With independence, the Americans made their political principles explicitly reflect that reality. Many years after the Revolution, Adams reflected, "the revolution was effected before the war commenced. The Revolution was in the minds and hearts of the people; a change in their religious sentiments of their duties and obligations." Adams indicated what he meant by this strange phrase in his next few sentences:

> While the king, and all in authority under him, were believed to govern in justice and mercy, according to the laws and constitution derived to them from the God of nature and transmitted to them by their ancestors, they thought themselves bound to pray for the king and queen and all the royal family, and all in authority under them, as ministers ordained of God for their good; but when they saw those powers renouncing all the principles of authority, and bent upon the destruction of all the securities of their lives, liberties, and properties, they thought it their duty to pray for the continental congress and all the thirteen State congresses, &c. (*WJA* 10:282)

All governments had a certain principle at their core from which all else emanated. In the American Revolution, the people of the thirteen colonies not only resisted the efforts of foreigners to govern them but they also emphatically endorsed the notion that men were citizens, not subjects. The Americans chose liberty rather than accepting it as a heritage. In so doing, they embraced the notion that all legitimate governments were based on compacts which had great ends. The principle of self-government, which made 1776 both necessary and possible, reminded men of their duties to themselves, to others, and to God. Good government helped them to practice the virtues because it was not "possible, humanly speaking, that men should ever be greatly improved in knowledge or benevolence, without assistance from the principles and system of government" (*WJA* 6:415). By making liberty the foundational principle of American government, both as the necessary premise of declaring independence from Britain and as the explicit object of the new constitutions, the Americans made a good start in that direction. Their government would help them to pursue happiness. Adams held that:

> Upon this point all speculative politicians will agree, that the happiness of society is the end of government, as all divines and moral philosophers will agree that the happiness of the individual is the end of man. . . . All sober inquirers after truth, ancient and modern, pagan and Christian, have declared that the happiness of man, as well as his dignity, consists in virtue. (*WJA* 4:193)

Having declared independence, the men of 1776 faced two great problems: to discover a means of establishing (or reestablishing) governments and to determine the proper form those governments should take. Adams spent more time and energy on the latter than the former problem, but we should consider both cases. Adams held that the proper means of establishing new governments grew from the principles which justified the Revolution. The principles involved in declaring independence were not particularly original. With the rest of the committee charged with drafting the Declaration of Independence, and the other men of 1776, Adams held that all men are created equal, with the rights to life, liberty, and the pursuit of happiness, and that men created governments to secure those rights. The task was to create a process based on that principle.

Massachusetts deserves much of the credit for discovering the process by which American constitutions are created and ratified. When Congress met after the battles of Lexington and Concord in the spring of 1775, Massachusetts was effectively without a legitimate government. Adams advised his fellow congressmen that:

We must realize the Theories of the Wisest Writers and invite the People, to erect the whole Building with their own hands upon the broadest foundation. That this could be done only by Conventions of Representatives chosen by the People. . . . Congress ought now to recommend to the People of every Colony to call such Conventions immediately and set up Governments of their own, under their own Authority: for the People were the Source of all Authority and the Original of all Power.[14]

In 1776, an unknown citizen of Concord improved upon Adams's idea by suggesting that a constitution is not legitimate until the people vote on it. When Massachusetts finally wrote and ratified its constitution in 1779 and 1780, it established the norm that we now take as a given: it called a constitutional convention, the convention drafted a constitution, and the people ratified it (cf. *PJA* 8:237).

If the people had the right to approve their governments, the question arose of whether there were limits to that principle. Could a people choose to submit to a dictator? Either response yielded a contradiction. If yes, the people may choose slavery; if no, then the people would have laws forced upon them. In short, "there can be no way of compelling nations to be more free than they choose to be" (*WJA* 4:402).[15] As a practical matter, Adams yielded to the wishes of the people. "The right of the people to establish such a government as they please, will ever be defended by me, whether they choose wisely or foolishly" (*WJA* 9:430). Explicitly to limit the right of the people to chose their form of government threatened liberty.

Adams confronted the question of the limits of original authority in the context of religious liberty. Adams was a firm believer in the liberty of conscience and opposed the establishment of religion. The individual's right to believe and practice as he chose so long as it did not harm another was of a piece with the individual's right to choose the government under which he would live. When he drafted the Massachusetts Constitution in 1779, these beliefs presented Adams with a problem. The people expected the state to require public support for churches, yet Adams thought such an establishment was wrong in principle. Faced with the issue, Adams finessed it. He wrote Article II of the State Declaration of Rights, which guaranteed to all people the right to worship God after their own fashion and to discuss their religious opinions in public, so long as it did not impinge upon the same in others. He let others write the guarantee of public support for religion.[16] As Adams believed that it was of fundamental importance to allow the people to create a government of their own choosing, to have forced disestablishment on the people would have taught them to obey leaders rather than to think through issues for themselves. It was far better to have a state, for the first time in history, formally approve its constitution through a regular process than it was to make sure all the details were right. Over time, the system itself would teach the citizens of Massachusetts the injustice of a religious establishment. To Adams's chagrin, it did not occur within his lifetime. When Massachusetts rewrote its constitution in 1820, Adams gave the convention a lecture on religious liberty. Again, he failed to bring a majority to his opinion. In 1832, the people of Massachusetts finally consented.

IV

After the principle of consent, the most important element of Adams's constitutional thought and practice had to do with checks and balances. From well before 1776 through the end of his life, Adams upheld a constitution with two sets of checks and balances as the only kind for a free nation because they were the only means of securing the rule of law. The first set of checks is more conventionally labeled the separation of powers among the legislative, executive, and judicial branches. The second is within the legislative power, divided between two houses and coupled with an executive with a veto. Adams made this model of constitution popular in Massachusetts, and the U.S. Constitution followed that model. Americans sometimes forget that a great debate raged in America and Europe in the late eighteenth and early nineteenth centuries over how to construct a government. Adams was the preeminent defender of bicameralism and the executive veto in his day. As we consider Adams's political thought, we should remember that he believed that no two societies were alike in all particulars, and for that reason no single form of constitution was suited to all societies. The challenge a constitution writer faced was to reconcile such general principles as existed with each particular case. The best constitution writers

> adopted the method of a wise architect. . . . They determined to consult Vitruvius, Palladio, and all other writers of reputation in the art; to examine the most celebrated buildings . . . to compare these with the principles of writers; and to inquire how far both the theories and models were founded in nature, or created by fancy; and when this was done, so far as circumstances would allow, to adopt the advantages and reject the inconveniences of all. (*WJA* 4:293)

To say that Adams was a student and practitioner of constitutional architecture was to say that he was a political scientist (cf. *WJA* 4:483–84). Adams feared that few of his contemporaries truly understood what political science was. It was an ancient science. Conceptually, Adams's political science was poised between the medieval sciences, of which theology was the queen, and the modern sciences that we have today, in which chemistry is paradigmatic. In other words, it would sit between art and science, as we now use these terms. Adams was surprised to find that in the centuries before his own, man had made great advances in astronomy, chemistry, and other sciences, but not in politics. "Is it not unaccountable that the knowledge of the principles and construction of free governments, in which the happiness of life, and even the further progress and improvement in education and society, in knowledge and virtue, are so deeply interested, should have remained at a full stand for two or three thousand years?" (*WJA* 4:283–84). His work was an effort to remedy that situation. Adams understood political science to be empirical, in that it involved studying political phenomenon and drawing rules and conclusions from that study, and he praised Francis Bacon for lighting the way of science. At the same time, Adams denounced "political empiricism," by which he meant the manipulation of political facts without any consideration of greater or lesser goods (*WJA* 6:159). All science, Adams held, had moral implications. The decision of what to study and how to study it could not be morally neutral. Perhaps for that reason he took morals to be the supreme science.[17] The trouble was that there could never be a true and certain science of morals. Politics would always involve prudential judgments on questions of consequence, and such judgments could be made only with great difficulty. This difficulty led him to focus on checks and balances.

The principle of checks and balances grew from the rule that no one should be both judge and party to the same case. This principle was most obvious regarding the separation of powers: the legislature wrote laws, the executive enacted them, and the courts judged under them. Were the legislative and executive power combined, there would be little incentive to make fixed and known laws; in such a case, the legislative/executive would give itself power en masse to achieve whatever ends suited it on any given day. Were the executive power combined with the judicial, the executive/judicial would have no incentive to carry out the laws as they were written. Were the legislative and judicial powers combined, the legislature would hardly have any reason to write laws or to follow those it did write. To describe checks and balances in action, Adams turned to a metaphor that the seventeenth-century English political thinker James Harrington made famous, describing two young girls with a cake that they were to share: one cut it and the other chose which half she would eat, ensuring that each had an interest in a fair division (*WJA*

4:390). By forcing men to keep vigilant watch over each other's actions, a good constitution would compel them to find mutual interests. The separations of power Adams created in the Massachusetts Constitution were not absolute: by giving all three branches overlapping powers, each branch had the ability to defend its prerogatives.

By the 1780s, few of Adams's contemporaries criticized the separation of power among the branches, but many supported unicameral government. Why did Adams disagree? If consent made laws binding, why limit and restrain consent with checks and balances? The French minister and philosophe Jacques Turgot spoke for many of Adams's contemporaries in Europe and America when he complained that:

> I observe that by most of them [American state constitutions] the customs of England are imitated, without any particular motive. Instead of collecting all authority into one center, that of the nation, they have established different bodies; a body of representatives, a council, and a Governour, because there is in England a House of Commons, a House of Lords, and a King.[18]

Adams disagreed. While all good government consulted the people through their representatives, the ritual of democracy could not sustain liberty under law on its own. A unicameral government would not remain a free government for long.

Adams found three defects in unicameral government: the majority would make unreasonable and oppressive demands of the minority, nothing would restrain the people's chosen representatives from usurping power, and the people would abdicate their rights. The first problem usually goes by the name of majority tyranny. There was no guarantee that 50 percent plus one would do right by the rest of society, nor was there any guarantee that they would not ignore the limits upon their own power enshrined in the constitutional compact. The need for restraints on the democratic power grew from the reality that the will of the majority at any moment in time (or even of the people in general) was not necessarily the true interest of the society or even of the majority (see *WJA* 4:402, 585). Second, beyond majority tyranny, Adams worried about the people's representatives. What was to keep them within the constitutionally prescribed limits on power? The people elected to office men they trusted to represent them; but, what guarantee would there be that they would not betray that trust (*WJA* 4:400)? Third, the people could turn against liberty and demand that the government take care of them. A majority

> may establish uniformity in religion; it may restrain trade; it may confine the personal liberty of all equally, and against the judgment of many, even of the best and wisest, without reasonable motives, use, or benefit. We may go farther, and say that a nation may be unanimous in consenting to a law restraining its natural liberty, property, and commerce, and its moral and religious liberties too, to a degree that may be prejudicial to the nation and to every individual in it. (*WJA* 4:402)

In sum, a single group of men acting in concert resembled an individual. Any given assembly could act reasonably and responsibly some of the time, but only a fool would expect it to do so enough of the time. "A single assembly is liable to all the vices, follies, and frailties of an individual; subject to fits of humor, starts of passion, flights of enthusiasm, partialities, or prejudice, and consequently productive of hasty results and absurd judgments" (*WJA* 4:195). Unicameral government could hardly be reconciled with the rule of law.

V

To help him think through and find a solution for the defects in unicameral government and unrestrained democracy, Adams studied human nature. A well-formed government worked with human nature and not against it, accepting man as he is, in order to move men in the direction of what they ought to be. To that end, Adams reflected upon his own firsthand experience and upon the past experience recorded in history. This observed nature was not essential and absolute; human knowledge did not go so far. Rather, it was merely a description of patterns which Adams found in all societies in all places at all times.[19]

From his observation, Adams discovered the inevitability of human contention. This contention would sometimes be over grand objects and sometimes over petty objects, but it would endure. Because men could only aspire to imperfect knowledge, and because all men tended to exaggerate their own claims, they inevitably would clash as each individual tried to live according to his imperfect notion of the good life. Adams learned the political implications of this reality in his youth. He had grown up observing a New England town meeting, the most democratic government anywhere in the world at the time. In the towns, people struggled with each other for power and place, gathered parties to help them gain power, and sought to use the laws to further their narrow ends, just as they did in the courts of Europe. Not only would men always contend for power, but they would always do so unequally. Certain men had more true, more useful, or more persuasive ideas than others. Perhaps more important, certain men always would be more able to assert power than others. In any given society, some led and others followed (*WJA* 4:427). Adams advised Jefferson: "Pick up, the first 100 men you meet, and make a Republick. Every Man will have an equal Vote. But when deliberations and discussions are opened it will be found that 25, by their Talents, Virtues being equal, will be able to carry 50 Votes" (*AJL* 398). And those twenty-five would divide into parties and struggle for preeminence.

Inequalities existed in society because of human diversity and human passions. Because all men were made in God's image, all men enjoyed equal rights (*AJL* 382, quoting Genesis 1:27). But Adams also asked:

> [W]hat are we to understand here by equality? Are the citizens to be all of the same age, sex, size, strength, stature, activity, courage, hardiness, industry, patience, ingenuity, wealth, knowledge, fame, wit, temperance, constancy, and wisdom? Was there, or will there ever be, a nation, whose individuals were all equal, in natural and acquired qualities, in virtues, talents, and riches? (*WJA* 4:391–92)

Because each individual was unique, each individual had different abilities to rise in any given society. Those things which helped men rise were "talents." "Education, Wealth, Strength, Beauty, Stature, Birth, Marriage, graceful Attitudes and Motions, Gait, Air, Complexion, Physiognomy, are Talents, as well as Genius and Science and Learning" (*AJL* 398). According to Adams's scientific definition, a talent was that which helped one man advance over another. It did not make one man better than another in any absolute sense. "The equality of nature is moral and political only, and means that all men are independent."[20]

While Adams's observation of human diversity led him to conclude that men were not, for practical purposes, equal, his study of the passions led him to conclude that men do not want to be equal. "Why . . . should any man be ashamed to make known his own poverty," Adams asked. "What glory in a coach? What shame in a wagon?" (*WJA* 6:238). Material possessions were not the true measure of value, but most men, most of the time, valued them nonetheless; they allowed men to compare themselves to their neighbors. "Every man hates to have a superior, but no man is willing to have an equal" (*WJA* 6:209). No one wants his neighbor to have a nicer house than his own, but every man wants his own house to be nicer than that of his neighbor. While some of Adams's contemporaries thought that these passions grew from accidents of history, and that politicians and philosophers could recast them, Adams held that they were fundamental to human nature. "It is weakness rather than wickedness, which renders men unfit to be trusted with unlimited power. The passions are all unlimited; nature has left them so; if they could be bounded, they would be extinct; and there is no doubt they are of indispensable importance" (*WJA* 4:406). Just as God gave men reason, so too did He give men passions. These passions, which made men want to live together, made society necessary and possible, and "millions in a state of society are supported with less difficulty than dozens in a state of nature."[21]

Other thinkers of the day, particularly the supporters of the French Revolution, thought that because men were naturally sociable, they would get along harmoniously once government got out of the way. Adams thought otherwise. Human sympathy led men to want to be loved by their fellow men. "'Who will love me then?' was the pathetic reply of one, who starved himself to feed his mastiff, to a charitable passenger, who advised him to kill or sell the animal," Adams commented. "In this *'who will love me then?'* there is a key to the human heart; to the history of human life and manners; and to the rise and fall of empires" (*WJA* 6:239). This desire to be loved made men political creatures; it yielded the "passion for distinction" or "*spectemer agendo*" (the desire to be seen in action, or to be conspicuous) which was elemental to political man (*WJA* 6:232, 234). By placing himself on stage and outshining his neighbors, men hoped to gain the notice of others. Once they had their neighbors' attention, they hoped to draw their affection. In government, men would use their position to make their neighbors—many of whom would be pleased to shed the burden of self-government—dependent. Unless it was checked, the narrow self-interest of the few and the lassitude of the many conspired against liberty. Adams took issue with those thinkers who thought that men were by nature good and peaceable, and who held that once the artificial aristocratic and priestly orders were removed, politics could be left behind. Instead, Adams found that man's sociability and desire to be loved caused political strife.

Adams designed the bicameral legislature to keep the "natural aristocracy" in line.[22] The unequal distribution of talents made certain men more useful in society than others, but when combined with the passion for distinction, it made the same men the most dangerous to liberty (*WJA* 4:397). The challenge a constitutional architect faced was to create a regime that made use of the talents of the natural aristocracy but kept them from transgressing the boundaries of law.[23] That was the purpose of the Senate. "The rich, the well-born, and the able, acquire an influence among the people that will soon be too much for simple honesty and plain sense, in a house of representatives. The most illustrious of them must, therefore, be separated from the mass, and placed by themselves in a senate; this is, to all honest and useful intents, an ostracism" (*WJA* 4:290).[24] The ambition of the talented would naturally drive them to seek a seat in the more exclusive house of the legislature. Once there, their talents could be put to use. By creating a legislature with a lower and upper house, each with an equal vote, a society balanced the many against the few.

Beyond bicameralism, Adams's most innovative contribution to constitutional construction had to do with the executive veto. Adams found that in all societies there was an individual who stood above the rest, and he concluded that "if there is no example, then, in any free government, any more than in those which are not free, of a society without a principle personage, we may fairly conclude that the body politic cannot subsist, any more than the animal body, without a head" (*WJA* 4:379). Nature decreed that all societies would have a first man. That occurred because the most powerful men always contended among themselves for preeminence, and at any given time one man would inevitably be on top. A wise constitution writer accommodated that reality in the forms of government. Formal (or institutionalized) power was better than informal power. Formal power could be discussed and checked; by its nature, informal power was harder to tame. A distinct executive also allowed the many to turn to a single champion to help them against the senators. The executive teamed up with the people at large to keep the rich and powerful in line.

In effect, Adams believed in a tricameral legislature. A good constitution set up a "triple-equipoise," with three equal powers in the legislature, each with a veto on the other two.[25] When all three powers in the legislature were equal, and each had an independent power base, they each could defend their place effectively. When any one house grew powerful through institutional slippage, popular acclaim, or some other reason, the other two could combine to tame it. Were there only two houses, the victory of one over the other was more likely to be final. "Without three divisions of power, stationed to watch each other, and compare each other's conduct with the laws, it will be impossible that the laws should at all times preserve their authority and govern all men" (*WJA* 4:462).

A properly mixed and balanced constitution was essential to the establishment of the rule of law. Such a constitution would ensure the stability of the laws, and it would also contribute to their quality. Whether politicians, statesmen, and constitution writers acknowledged the fact, government was by nature a moral affair. The challenge was to draw men toward the good in their natures, helping reason to guide the passions, rather than allowing the opposite to be the case. That was the end of a well-ordered constitution. Near the end of the *Defence*, Adams wrote:

> Happiness, whether in despotisms or democracy, whether in slavery or liberty, can never be found without virtue. The best republics will be virtuous, and have been so; but we may hazard a conjecture, that the virtues have been the effect of the well ordered constitution, rather than the cause. And, perhaps, it would be impossible to prove that a republic cannot exist even among highwaymen, by setting one rogue to watch another; and the knaves themselves may in time be made honest men by the struggle. (*WJA* 6:219)

Under a good constitution, mutual checks and mutual vigilance would force each individual to do right by his neighbor. Once they started to do right because of the necessity of the case, perhaps they would internalize the principle.

Checks and balances were only part of the story in America. Adams was pleased that the United States lacked an artificial, or titled, aristocracy. Yet he thought of the House, Senate, and president as the equivalent of the classical mixed regime of the many, the few, and the one all balanced together. "In America," he wrote, "there are different orders of *offices*, but not of *men*" (*WJA* 4:381). By replacing established orders with elected orders, the people of America set the moral tone for their society. Even as the citizens struggled for status, and as the politicians competed for rank, all did so beneath the grand principle of the right of all men to self-government: the greatest man in America would be the greatest servant of that principle. That benevolent ambition pervaded society. "That elevation of sentiment inspired by such a government, makes the common people brave and enterprising. That ambition which is inspired by it makes them sober, industrious, and frugal" (*WJA* 4:199). In sum, as one student of Adams's political thought put it, "Adams' political thought represents a unique and powerful attempt to synthesize the classical notion of mixed government with the modern teaching of separation of powers."[26] Such a regime was most likely to ensure the rule of law.

VII

From July 2, 1776, the day Congress declared that "these colonies are and of right ought to be free and independent states," Adams realized that the Americans had done something of world-historic importance.[27] By asserting the principles of liberty, Americans had taken a great responsibility upon themselves. Men could use political liberty for good or for ill. For that reason, it would be difficult to ensure that American liberty would be a blessing rather than a curse (*WJA* 6:448).

Adams's worries about the future of liberty took shape in his reaction to the French Revolution. Reflecting upon the effects that the American Revolution had upon Europe, he wrote Benjamin Rush in 1811: "Have I not been employed in mischief all my days? Did not the American revolution produce the French revolution? And did not the French revolution produce all the calamities and desolations to the human race and the whole globe ever since?" (*WJA* 9:635). Adams knew many of the men who would lead the French Revolution (at least its early stages), and he had tried to teach them. To his eternal regret, too few listened. When the French Revolution broke out, Adams sensed what would happen: "poor France I fear will bleed" for its political sins.[28] Adams did not want informed opinion throughout the world to conclude that the principles of liberty led inevitably to violence, terror, bloodshed, and, ultimately, dictatorship. Hence, he did his best to disassociate the French Revolution from the American. Denouncing the French Revolution was not a popular thing to do in America in 1789 and 1790, and Adams's reputation has never recovered from the blow. Jefferson railed against Adams's "heresies."[29] Yet Adams pressed on, consoling himself with the knowledge that "virtue is not always amiable."[30]

Adams concluded that what the country most needed was candor. The sloganeering of the American Revolution had become the professed political gospel to many political men and their followers in America and Europe. They taught that the light of reason was leading men forward to a better and brighter future. In the future, the people would enjoy equal power and men would create a world of perpetual peace. Adams disagreed, and he sought to undeceive the nation. There was a school of political thought in Adams's day which taught that "if the good people wish to be deceived, deceive them" (*SF* 106).[31] The chief modern deception was that the chaos of life could be turned into a universal order of peace, justice, and brotherhood. That myth made people reluctant to admit such ageless truths as "if you wish peace, prepare for war" (*SF* 134). It made them blind to the inequalities that exist in every society, and hence less able to manage them. Most seriously, it made them think that the good life was easy. Adams held all that to be false, and he wrote as much: "the perfectability of man is only human and terrestrial perfectibility. Cold will still freeze, and fire will never cease to burn; disease and vice will continue to disorder, and death to terrify mankind" (*WJA* 6:279). There was a human condition that people could ignore but not overcome. Men had to plot their course in a world which they would only understand imperfectly.

The great deception Adams perceived in the philosophes and their disciples was the claim to clear, certain, and communicable knowledge. They claimed that reason could lead men to certainty about their rights and duties in the world, and that the great political problems could be solved. Adams found that belief not only incorrect but also dangerous. To defend the proposition that reason could provide sure guidance, the proponents of reason needed to explain why it had failed to do so in the past. Their answer was that priests, kings, and prophets had deceived and manipulated men, leading them to believe in absurd things. These bad men had established systems of laws and religion which allowed them to control information and continue their power thereby. But, the enlightened defenders of reason contended, over time reason had been freed from her fetters and would lead the people forward, away from the vices, follies, and crimes of the past and toward a happy, healthy, and peaceful future. Adams was much less sanguine about the capacities of reason. He held that the evils of the past grew from man's basic ignorance, coupled with his passions. As he saw it, independence presented Americans with an opportunity to find a new way to manage passions and ignorance, not to overcome them. The prophets of reason and of progress built up a false hope which Adams feared would lead men to repeat the crimes of the past. Adams saw no other solution than checks and balances. As he told Jefferson:

> Checks and balances, Jefferson, however much you and your Party may have ridiculed them, are our only Security, for the progress of the Mind, as well as the Security of the Body. Every Species of these Christians would persecute Deists, as soon as either Sect would persecute another, if it had unchecked and unbalanced Power. Nay, the Deists would persecute Christians, and Atheists would persecute Deists, with as unrelenting Cruelty, as any Christians would persecute them or one another.

To emphasize his point he concluded with a Socratic flourish: "Know thyself, human Nature!" (*AJL* 334).[32]

Beneath the popular claim to certainty, Adams saw a pernicious philosophy. The supporters of the French Revolution rested their hopes for progress on certain philosophic premises. Jefferson was sympathetic to that camp. As he wrote Adams, "on the basis of sensation, of matter and motion, we may erect the fabric of all the certainties we can have or need" (*AJL* 567). Adams found that doctrine to be both false and insidious. It was false because the knowledge which men derive from their senses is by no means certain; it was insidious because it meant that men were nothing more than common clay. As he wrote in his reaction to the French Revolution, rather than allow that the "government of nations may fall into the hands of men who teach the most disconsolate of all creeds, that men are but fireflies, and that this *all* is without a father[,] . . . *give us again our popes and hierarchies, Benedictines and Jesuits, with all their superstition and fanaticism, impostures and tyranny*" (*WJA* 6:281). There were two ways to think about human equality. Many philosophes discovered human equality by reducing everyone to the same material parts. Adams believed that doctrine to be false, and he feared that it would lead men to behave as beasts, for it gave them no reason to think men were superior to animals. Adams, by contrast, held that men were equal because they were all made with an exalted soul. The task after 1776 was to remind Americans of that fact and of its implications.

Adams had great ambitions for America. Adams knew that Americans would always have to struggle to uphold what was best in their heritage. On June 7, 1826, less than a month before his death on July 4, 1826, Adams gave a final lesson. American independence would be "a memorable epoch in the annals of the human race; destined in future history to form the brightest or the blackest page, according to the use or the abuse of those political institutions by which they shall in time to come be shaped by the *human mind*" (*WJA* 10:417). The future would be what Americans chose to make it. Adams hoped that Americans would do the great work of liberty.

Ultimately, Adams tried to bring some moral gravity to his countrymen. To preserve the spirit of liberty in America would be no mean feat. It would require that the children of the Founders and their children's children not cower before their ancestors. It would require that a certain number of them treat the Founders as peers in a conversation about constitutions and politics, not as demi-gods whose work ought never to be questioned or changed. As he aged, Adams worried that too few Americans were up to that task. They thought too highly of the Founders and not highly enough of themselves to do the hard work of liberty. "I would to God there were more ambition in the country," Adams wrote, "ambition of that laudable kind, to excel."[33] Only when a certain number of men in every generation shared the Founders' profound ambition would it be possible to keep liberty secure. More generally, Adams tried to teach his countrymen that the life of liberty was never easy. Men always chafed, politically and intellectually, at the restraints of the law. The best that men could do was to reconcile themselves to the struggle. That was what Adams's designed his constitution to do. A well-checked and balanced constitution would moderate the conflicts that inevitably arose in American political life. For an epigraph to the *Defence*, Adams turned to Alexander Pope: "All Nature's difference keeps all Nature's peace" (*WJA* 4:271). For long years he had puzzled over that problem. How could a nation reconcile liberty, order, and conflict? That the American Constitution had endured so long is partly a tribute to the wisdom with which Adams answered that question.

Notes

1. The best biographical treatment of Adams is still Page Smith, *John Adams* (Garden City, N.Y.: Doubleday, 1962). David McCullough, *John Adams* (New York: Simon and Schuster, 2001) is also good as are the shorter treatments by Gilbert Chinard, *Honest John Adams* (Boston: Little, Brown, 1933) and Peter Shaw, *The Character of John Adams* (Chapel Hill: University of North Carolina Press, 1976). C. Bradley Thompson, *John Adams and the Spirit of Liberty* (Lawrence: University Press of Kansas, 1998) is the best treatment of Adams's political thought. John P. Diggins also has a fine discussion of Adams's political thought in *The Lost Soul of American Politics: Virtue, Self-Interest and the Foundations of Liberalism* (New York: Basic Books, 1984), while John Howe gives an ideological interpretation in *The Changing Political Thought of John Adams* (Princeton, N.J.: Princeton University Press, 1966).

2. Quotations from and references to Adams's works are cited in the text using the following abbreviations:

> *AJL:*   *The Adams-Jefferson Letters: The Complete Correspondence Between Thomas Jefferson and Abigail and John Adams*, ed. Lester J. Cappon (Chapel Hill: University of North Carolina Press, 1959).
>
> *BAR:*   *The Briefs of the American Revolution: Constitutional Arguments between Thomas Hutchinson, Governor of Massachusetts Bay, and James Bowdoin for the Council and John Adams for the House of Representatives*, ed John Philip Reid (New York: New York University Press, 1981).
>
> *PJA:*   *Papers of John Adams*, ed. Gregg Lint, Robert Taylor, et al., 10 vols. to date (Cambridge, Mass.: Belknap Press, 1989–). "The Dissertation on the Canon and Feudal Law" appears in volume 1 and the *Letters of Novanglus* in volume 2.
>
> *SF:*   *Spur of Fame: Dialogues of John Adams and Benjamin Rush, 1805–1813*, ed. John A. Schutz and Douglas Adair (Indianapolis: Liberty Fund, 2001).
>
> *WJA:*   *The Works of John Adams*, ed. Charles Francis Adams, 10 vols. (Boston: Little and Brown, 1850–56). "Thoughts on Government" appears in volume 4; *Defence of the Constitutions of Government of the United States of America* in volumes 4–6; and the "Discourses on Davila" appears in volume 6.

(As much as possible, we have maintained Adams's original spelling, punctuation, and capitalization as it is presented in each edition of his works, some of which regularize his style and some of which do not.) Adams also wrote that "a free republic is the best of governments. . . . An empire of laws is a characteristic of a free republic only" (*WJA* 4:370–71; cf. 4:283, 404–5; 5:453).

3. "A Government of Laws and Not of Men," *Monthly Anthology* X (1811): 243.

4. "A Government of Laws and Not of Men," 243.

5. "If there were no ignorance, error, or vice, there would be neither principles nor systems of civil or political government" (*WJA* 6:415).

6. In a striking passage, Adams declared that "I will insist that the Hebrews have done more to civilize men than any other nation. If I were an atheist, and believed in blind eternal fate, I should still believe that fate had ordained the Jews to be the most essential instrument for civilizing the nations. If I were an atheist

of the other sect, who believed or pretend to believe that all is ordered by chance, I should believe that chance had ordered the Jews to preserve and to propagate to all mankind the doctrine of a supreme intelligent, wise, almighty sovereign of the universe, which I believe to be the great essential principle of all morality, and consequently of all civilization" (*WJA* 9:609).

7. McCullough, *John Adams*, 223.

8. "Being men, they have all what Dr. Rush calls a *moral faculty*; Dr. Hutchinson, a *moral sense*; and the Bible and the generality of the world, *a conscience*. They are all, therefore, under moral obligations to do to others as they would have others *do to them*" (*WJA* 6:449).

9. "The multitude have always been credulous, and the few artful" (*WJA* 4:292).

10. "Every citizen must look up to the laws, as his master, his guardian, and his friend; and whenever any of his fellow-citizens, whether magistrates or subjects, attempt to deprive him of his right, he must appeal to the laws" (*WJA* 4:462). When the laws themselves fail that task, the situation grows revolutionary.

11. Thompson, *John Adams*, considers the "Principles of Liberty" and the "Principles of Political Architecture" to be the main parts of Adams's thought, and he makes them the titles of the two parts of his book.

12. McCullough, *John Adams*, 125–26.

13. *Adams Family Correspondence*, ed. L. H. Butterfield et al. (Cambridge, Mass.: Belknap Press, 1963), 1:363. Adams used the same language elsewhere (*WJA* 6:422).

14. *Diary and Autobiography of John Adams*, ed. L. H. Butterfield (Cambridge, Mass.: Belknap Press, 1961*)*, 3:352. See also *WJA* 5:226.

15. Immediately preceding this statement, Adams wrote: "To take in M. Turgot's idea [that being subject to law is not a sufficient definition of liberty] we must add to Dr. Price's ideas of *equal laws* by *common consent*, this other—for the *general interest* or the *public good*. But it is generally supposed that nations understand their own interest better than another; and, therefore, they may be trusted to judge of the public good."

16. Massachusetts's establishment required citizens to support the church that they attended. Officially, it did not favor any denomination. Article II of the Declaration of Rights proclaimed "the duty of all men in society, publicly and at stated seasons to worship the Supreme Being. . . . And no subject shall be hurt, molested or restrained, in his person, liberty, or estate, for worshiping God in the manner most agreeable to the dictates of his own conscience" (*PJA* 8:238).

17. "I have ever considered all arts, sciences, and literature as of small importance in comparison of morals" (*SF* 73).

18. Jacques Turgot, in *The Correspondence of Richard Price: Vol II, March 1778–February 1786*, ed. D. O. Thomas (Durham, N.C.: Duke University Press, 1991), 13.

19. Responding to John Taylor of Caroline's complaint that there is no such thing as human nature, Adams stated: "It is unnecessary to discuss the nice distinctions, which follow in the first page of your respectable volume, between mind, body, and morals. The essence and substance of mind and body, of soul and body, of spirit and matter, are wholly withheld as yet from our knowledge" (*WJA* 6:450).

20. Adams, in Clinton Rossiter, "The Legacy of John Adams," *Yale Review* 46 (1956–57): 536.

21. Zoltan Haraszti, *John Adams and the Prophets of Progress* (Cambridge, Mass.: Harvard University Press, 1952), 85. Adams penned this comment in the margin of Rousseau's "Discourse," next to the statement, "He had in his instinct alone everything he needed to live in a state of nature; his cultivated reason barely provides him with what is necessary to live in society."

22. Having concluded that there would be some with more and some with less power in every society, Adams defined an aristocrat at someone with more than the average of power. An aristocrat could control more than one vote (*WJA* 6:451). For Adams's discussion of "natural aristocracy" with Jefferson, see *AJL* 365–402.

23. "I can never too often repeat that aristocracy is a monster to be chained; yet so chained as not to be hurt, for he is a most useful and necessary animal in his place. Nothing can be done without him" (*SF* 189).

24. "The only remedy is to throw the rich and proud into one group, in a separate assembly, and there tie their hands; if you give them scope with the people at large or their representatives, they will destroy *all equality and liberty, with the consent and acclamations of the people themselves*" (*WJA* 4:444–45).

25. The phrase belongs to C. Bradley Thompson, "John Adams and the Science of Politics," in *John Adams and the Founding of the Republic*, ed. Richard Ryerson (Boston: Massachusetts Historical Society, 2001), 249. See *WJA* 4:585.

26. Thompson, "John Adams and the Science of Politics," 246.

27. As Adams wrote in a letter to Abigail Adams on July 3, 1776: "Yesterday the greatest question was decided, which ever was debated in America, and a greater perhaps, never was or will be decided among men." See *Adams Family Correspondence*, 2:27–30.

28. Haraszti, *John Adams*, 20.

29. Jefferson to J. B. Smith, April 26, 1791, in *Papers of Thomas Jefferson*, ed. Julian P. Boyd (Princeton, N.J.: Princeton University Press, 1982), 20:290.

30. McCullough, *John Adams*, 207.

31. Adams held that some were "honest enthusiasts carried away . . . but the greater part of politicians and philosophers who prated about the perfectibility of man mean nothing but to seize, occupy, and confound the attention of the public" (*SF* 74).

32. Russell Kirk's discussion of Adams's argument with the philosophes is still worth reading. *The Conservative Mind: From Burke to Eliot* (Washington, D.C.: Regnery, 1986), chap. 3.

33. McCullough, *John Adams*, 640.

Chapter 7

Legitimate Government, Religion, and Education: The Political Philosophy of Thomas Jefferson

Aristide Tessitore

Of all the members of the Founding generation, Thomas Jefferson (1743–1826) has the most direct claim to status as a philosophic thinker. Notwithstanding this fact, anthologies of political philosophy typically exclude the "sage of Monticello" (and the Founders generally), perhaps in large part because he never elaborated a complete political theory. Indeed, Jefferson is the author of a single book, *Notes on the State of Virginia* (1787), and one is compelled to turn to a handful of important public documents and especially his voluminous private correspondence to encounter the vast majority of his written ideas. A second and related reason for Jefferson's exclusion from the canon of political philosophers is that his general views about politics emerge from direct engagement in a particular political project: namely, the Founding and shaping of the American experiment. If this second source of neglect points to a limit in Jefferson's status as a philosophic thinker, it simultaneously emphasizes his importance for understanding the intersection between political philosophy and actual political practice. While it is true that Jefferson's deep involvement in politics inhibited his development as a philosopher and that his susceptibility to philosophic ideas at times clouded his judgments about politics, it is also true that Jefferson's enduring legacy lies precisely in his ability to infuse the daily business of political life with philosophic principles.

Assessing Jefferson is complicated not only by the absence of any fully elaborated political theory but also by controversy both during his lifetime and at present, by discrepancies between espoused principle and tangible practice, and by the changes that characterized his thinking over a long life of reflection and active political involvement. Notwithstanding these complications, the best way to bring to light the guiding principles of Jefferson's political philosophy comes from the epitaph he designed for himself. He recorded there what he considered to be his three greatest accomplishments: the Declaration of Independence, the Bill for Establishing Religious Freedom, and the founding of the University of Virginia (epitaph, 1826).[1] All three point to Jefferson's legacy as a Founder and involve him in the work of human liberation—political, religious, and intellectual. Moreover, each of these accomplishments is related to profound themes in the tradition of political philosophy: the nature and purpose of legitimate government, the relationship between religion and politics, and the long-standing preoccupation of philosophers with political education. Sustained consideration of each of these related themes constitutes the core of Jefferson's political philosophy and animates the legacy he has bequeathed to the American republic, one that, despite current controversies, deserves to endure.

The Nature and Purpose of Legitimate Government

Jefferson placed the Declaration of Independence at the head of his list of accomplishments, the act for which he most wanted to be remembered. As chief draftsman of the Declaration, Jefferson enjoyed growing renown and endured as well the inevitable jealousies that accompany fame. Against those who accused him of having essentially stolen the text from other sources, Jefferson maintained that such criticism was entirely off-point.

> [T]he object of the Declaration was . . . [n]ot to find out new principles, or new arguments, never before thought of, not merely to say things that had never been said before; but to place before mankind the common sense of the subject. . . . Neither aiming at originality of principle or sentiment, nor yet copied from any particular and previous writing, it was intended to be an expression of the American mind. (to Henry Lee, May 8, 1825)

By his own reckoning, Jefferson's greatest accomplishment was devoid of originality; rather, its importance rests upon the extent to which he succeeded in capturing "the harmonizing sentiments of the day" (to Lee, May 8, 1825). From the outset, the Declaration was intended to be what in fact it became—an authoritative statement of the American political creed. (There is, as we shall see, a certain symmetry in Jefferson's desire to be most remembered for a document that best articulates the prevailing views of the American people as a whole.) Notwithstanding Jefferson's modesty, the ability to put into words the political creed of a fledgling nation, and to do so with an unrivaled degree of concision, eloquence, and dramatic power is no small accomplishment. Still, it should be kept in mind that the Declaration does not attempt to present Jefferson's own personal views so much as a consensus that could command widespread assent. This is in no way to suggest that the Declaration fails to reflect Jefferson's own views (in the 1790s, Jefferson formed the Republican party to recover the principles expressed in the Declaration), but it is to caution against an overly facile identification of Jefferson's attempt to speak on behalf of a nation with a fuller understanding of his own political and philosophic principles.

The Declaration proceeds with admirable cogency to establish its claim that the political bonds connecting the American colonies to Great Britain are and ought to be totally dissolved. The principled basis for this argument is contained in the rightly famous second paragraph, which provides a remarkably succinct teaching on the nature and purpose of legitimate government. Lincoln aptly captures Jefferson's accomplishment when he praises him for having "the coolness, forecast and capacity to introduce into a merely revolutionary document, an abstract truth, applicable to all men and all times" (to H. L. Pierce and others, April 6, 1859). On the basis of this "abstract truth," the Declaration submits facts in the form of grievances to a candid world, all driving inexorably toward the conclusion that "these United Colonies are, and of Right ought to be, Free and Independent States."

Nothing is more familiar or more controversial than the first "self-evident truth" of the Declaration: "all men are created equal." To claim that something is self-evident does not mean that it is apparent to all. Rather, a self-evident truth is one that follows necessarily from its subject. As in geometry, a proper understanding of the nature of the subject under investigation enables one to move through a series of logical steps to a conclusion that follows of necessity from the thing itself. The key notion here is "nature," something that points to a first difference between the writer of the Declaration and the views of those it purports to harmonize. The self-evident truth of equality presupposes a proper understanding of human nature, one from which the "evidentness" of human equality immediately follows. This truth is so far from obvious that most people at most times have believed the opposite, basing their regimes on the rule of the "better sort" of persons—that is, on a principle of *in*equality. Indeed, as is all too apparent, even the nation espousing the claim of equality was marred by the searing inequality of slavery. The self-evident truth of equality was at odds with the obvious facts of human inequality.

Drawing especially but not exclusively on the political thought of John Locke—one of "the three greatest men that have ever lived, without any exception" (to John Trumbull, February 15, 1789)—the Declaration offers a summary account of the natural state of human beings and then goes on to draw the relevant consequences for understanding the purpose and limits of government. The natural state for human beings is one bereft of rightful authority, a negative truth that simultaneously provides the basis for a positive affirmation of equality. Prior to the institution of legitimate authority, all men are equal in the sense that they are not subject to the authority of any other human being. Although Jefferson affirmed that human beings are by nature social animals (to Thomas Law, June 13, 1814), he effectively rejected the Aristotelian doctrine that man is by nature a *zoon politikon*; for Jefferson, the natural state of human beings preceded government. The Declaration teaches that government is an artifice, a product of human making. Since government arises neither from nature nor God, it is not sacrosanct and can be changed, indeed improved, in the measure that the science of politics is improved. Not only does the Declaration fail to specify any particular form of government, but its explicit and unprecedented affirmation of the right to revolution—"the right of the people to alter and to abolish" government—is at odds with the kind of reverence that time and prejudice typically bestow upon political institutions. Jefferson was willing to go much further than his contemporaries in drawing out the radical implications of this doctrine. He maintained that no society could justly make a perpetual constitution; each generation should decide this anew for themselves. James Madison firmly rejected this implication. In his view, a government frequently revised would "become too mutable to retain those prejudices in its favor which antiquity inspires," prejudices that furnish "a salutary aid" to even the most rational and enlightened of governments (to Madison, September 6, 1789, and from Madison, February 4, 1790).

Neither Jefferson nor the Declaration maintained that human beings were equal in every respect. Jefferson here followed Locke, who wrote: "Though I have said that all men by nature are equal, I cannot be supposed to understand all sorts of equality." He went on to cite age, virtue, merit, high birth, and benefits given or received as qualities that may distinguish one person from another. "Yet all this consists with the equality which all men are in, in respect of jurisdiction or dominion one over another, which was the equality I there spoke of" (*Second Treatise of Government*, sec. 54). Jefferson's affirmation of natural equality in the Declaration was perfectly consistent with his recognition of a "natural aristocracy of virtue and talent" to which he assigned a privileged political role. "[T]here is a natural aristocracy among men. The grounds of this are virtue and talents. . . . The natural aristocracy I consider as the most precious gift of nature for the instruction, the trusts, and government of society" (to John Adams, October 28, 1813). While recognizing the existence of natural inequalities, Jefferson insisted that such differences did not convey either a natural or God-given right to rule. The lack of rightful authority in our natural state and resulting condition of equality was the relevant truth upon which legitimate government should be erected. Something of the complexity of Jefferson's thought can be suggested in this way: The self-evident equality of the Declaration means that legitimate government is based on the consent of the governed and the will of the majority, even while it requires the talent and virtues of the "natural *aristoi*" to found and sustain itself.

The Declaration is unequivocal in its teaching about the purpose of government. Governments are instituted by human beings to secure their otherwise vulnerable natural rights and, in the absence of any natural standard of authority, legitimate government can only derive its powers from the consent of the governed. The source of these rights is said to be the "Creator," a being who is in other respects deliberately left unidentified. Jefferson drew upon the tradition of natural as opposed to revealed theology in the Declaration, referring in the introduction to "the laws of nature and of nature's God." The giver of natural rights is the God who can be known through a rational investigation of nature. Whereas governments are the work of human artifice, the Declaration simultaneously invokes a standard not of human making by which the variety of political artifices can be evaluated. Although he believed, at least in theory, that each generation had the right to change the laws and institutions of government to suit themselves, this belief derived from the one fixed point in Jefferson's political philosophy: "Nothing is unchangeable but the inherent and unalienable rights of man" (to Major John Cartwright, June 5, 1824).

We should note that the self-evidence of the inalienable rights to life, liberty, and pursuit of happiness affirmed in the Declaration would be apparent only to those who take their bearings from science or, more specifically, the moral and political principles uncovered by political philosophy. Commenting on the Declaration at the end of his life, Jefferson wrote that "[t]he general spread of the light of science" is responsible for the growing recognition of "the rights of man" (to Roger Weightman, June 24, 1826). For a majority lacking leisure, ability, or education to pursue such inquiries, the evidence for these rights is replaced with a kind of faith or belief; they are *held* to be "self-evident" within the political community dedicated to making them effective. Whereas the self-evident truths of equality and natural rights were the product of a long and controversial chain of philosophic reasoning, they were harmonized in the Declaration as the creedal starting point for political action and reasoning.

The continued viability of Jefferson's teaching on equality turns on whether "all men" includes both males and females as well as persons of all races. However one might assess Jefferson's compromises with respect to slavery, from the beginning to the end of his public life, Jefferson maintained its injustice on the basis of the natural rights doctrine expressed in the Declaration.[2] Although he hazarded some "conjectures" "with great diffidence" about the intellectual inferiority of the Negro race (*Notes* 191–93)—conjectures he tepidly claimed to withdraw later in life (to Benjamin Banneker, August 30, 1791; to Henri Grégoire, February 25, 1809)—Jefferson consistently maintained that intellectual superiority confers no right for one human being to rule another: "Because Sir Isaac Newton was superior to others in understanding, he was not therefore lord of the person or property of others" (to Grégoire, February 25, 1809). Although Jefferson tentatively suggested that nature may have been less bountiful to blacks "in the endowments of the head," he simultaneously asserted that "in those of the heart she will be found to have done them justice." He continued his reflection by taking issue with a pervasive stereotype: the disposition of slaves to theft "must be ascribed to their situation, and not to any depravity of the moral sense" (*Notes* 191).

For Jefferson, the heart was the locus of morality and seat of the natural moral sense (cf. to Maria Cosway, October 12, 1786). This doctrine was something he seems to have learned from his reading of the Scottish moral sense philosophers, especially Francis Hutcheson, Lord Kames, David Hume, and Adam Smith. The equality asserted in the Declaration is at root a moral quality grounded in the natural sociability of human beings. "[N]ature hath implanted in our breasts a love of others, a sense of duty to them, a moral instinct, in short, which prompts us irresistibly to feel and to succor their distresses. . . . The Creator would indeed have been a bungling artist, had he intended man for a social animal, without planting in him social dispositions" (to Thomas Law, June 13, 1814). This does not mean that the moral capacities of human beings are equal in every respect, any more than are their intellectual capacities. Indeed, Jefferson acknowledged that only some of those who are deficient in moral sensibility can be improved through education. Still, he maintained that it would be wrong to mistake the exceptional case of someone completely lacking in benevolence for a general rule. The moral sense is a defining attribute of the human species in the same way that two hands are descriptive of the human body despite the existence of one-handed persons. For Jefferson, both an innate sense of duty toward others and the radically selfish concern for self-preservation are natural to the human heart. Indeed, it was the collision of these two natural sentiments that fueled America's traumatic attempts to deal with the juggernaut of slavery. As Jefferson famously writes: "[W]e have the wolf by the ears, and we can neither hold him, nor safely let him go. Justice is on one scale, and self-preservation in the other" (to John Holmes, April 22, 1820).

In Jefferson's estimation, the practice of slavery was inimical to a government based on the truth about human nature; slavery eroded in *both* blacks *and* whites the very qualities most needed to sustain the natural liberty and equality upon which the American experiment purported to rest (*Notes* 214–15). Early in his career, Jefferson presented a plan for the emancipation and colonization of slaves, one that he continued to favor throughout his life. As a young man, Jefferson quickly learned that nothing was to be expected from the former generation, and he vested his hopes in the young, who would receive "their early impressions after the flame of liberty had been kindled in every breast, and had become as it were the vital spirit of every American." These early hopes were, however, eventually engulfed by "the general silence that prevails on this subject." Yet, notwithstanding "an apathy unfavorable to every hope" and Jefferson's own backward evolution on emancipation, he could still affirm—with a kind of inevitability he had in part engineered—that "the hour of emancipation is advancing, in the march of time" (to Edward Coles, August 25, 1814). Jefferson regarded the conflict between the theory of justice inserted into the Declaration and the practice of slavery to be unsustainable; the tension demanded resolution, and he feared it would be a violent one. In his only published book, he writes: "I tremble for my country when I reflect that God is just: that his justice cannot sleep forever. . . . The Almighty has no attribute which can take side with us in such a contest." Jefferson looked to a total emancipation of the slaves and hoped it would take place "with the consent of the masters, rather than by their extirpation" (*Notes* 215; cf. to Coles, August 25, 1814). Still, Jefferson seems never to have realized the extent to which his own involvement in scientific theories of race weakened the power of his principled argument regarding the injustice of slavery—a case in which his intermittent forays into the realm of natural philosophy may well have impinged upon the prudence requisite for statesmanship.[3]

Jefferson's own understanding of the Declaration's principled condemnation of slavery was clearly at odds with the views of many of those whose sentiments he sought to harmonize. It was, however, especially in matters of religion that the sharpest disparity between Jefferson's own philosophically informed understanding and the "American mind," whose creedal statement he authored, comes most into view. In his final letter, Jefferson described the Declaration as "an instrument pregnant with our own, and the fate of the world," and he expected that it would in time become to all peoples "a signal arousing men to burst the chains under which monkish ignorance and superstition had persuaded them to bind themselves" (to Weightman, June 24, 1826). In Jefferson's final and most mature assessment of the significance of the Declaration, he maintained that a certain understanding of revealed religion—not King George—constitutes the persistent obstacle to governments based on political equality. For Jefferson, the revolutionary character of political equality was inseparable from issues of religion; indeed, the radical character of rights grounded in "nature" and "nature's God" becomes most apparent when contrasted with those who claimed privileged rights on the authority of revelation—the "favored few booted and spurred, ready to ride them [the mass of mankind] legitimately, *by the grace of God*" (emphasis added). Jefferson's grand expectations were based on his belief that the teaching on "the rights of man" encapsulated in the Declaration derived from the authority of science and, as such, was accessible not merely to a chosen few but to all human beings at all times (at least in principle). For Jefferson, the Declaration's enduring significance lay in the fact that it articulated the principled basis for legitimate government. Legitimate government does not result from the arbitrary forces of geography, history, or religion; it is based on a true understanding of nature—an understanding discovered by the architects of modern political philosophy and now revealed for all to see in the "abstract truths" of America's Declaration of Independence.

Religion and Politics

Although the relationship between religion and politics had become thematic for political philosophy since the execution of Socrates for impiety, it became absolutely central in the early modern period. The cultural triumph of Christianity brought with it a political problem that became particularly acute with the subsequent fragmentation of Christianity in the sixteenth century. Rousseau stated the underlying issue with admirable brevity: "[T]his double power [church and prince] has given rise to a perpetual jurisdictional conflict . . . and no one has ever been able to know whether it is the priest or the master whom one is obliged to obey" (*Social Contract* IV 8). It was especially the problem of competing authorities and the wars to which they had given rise that engaged the efforts of Hobbes, Locke, and Spinoza. If they can be said to have groped their way toward a solution on the level of principle, it fell to the American Founders to find a way to inject their ideas into the always-constrained possibilities of actual political practice. Jefferson is often regarded as uniquely authoritative—albeit controversial—in fashioning the American response to this issue. Drawing deeply from Enlightenment thinkers for his understanding of the religious problem, Jefferson was pivotal in shaping three related areas of this relationship as it developed in America: the disestablishment of religion, the effort to maintain the reasonableness of Christianity, and the separation of church and state.

Disestablishment and the Primacy of Religious Freedom

Whereas it was necessary to accommodate established religions in the states, Jefferson (and Madison) worked to bring this vestige of the old regime into line with the principled basis of American government articulated in the Declaration. For ten years (1776–1786) Jefferson fought to disestablish the Anglican Church in Virginia—a series of battles he later described as the "severest contests" in which he was ever involved. His efforts culminated in the passage of a modified version of his Bill for Establishing Religious Freedom, a celebrated manifesto of Enlightenment religion that made generous use of the ideas and arguments of Locke's *A Letter Concerning Toleration.*

Notwithstanding the fact that the revised statute began with the words "Whereas Almighty God hath created the mind free," the disestablishment of religion did not and could not rest on the foundation of religious authority. Since the meaning of Scripture was itself contested, disestablishment required a nonreligious source that could be considered authoritative by members of different and sometimes warring religious traditions. As we have seen, Jefferson's uniquely authoritative expression of the American mind—resting, as it did, on the scientific illumination of natural rights—provided precisely those principles by which to mount an assault. The natural rights teaching of the Declaration did not derive from revelation but from the discovery of the "state of nature" by Hobbes and Locke—a state deeply at odds with both the biblical account of human origins and the fundamental law of the New Testament.[4]

Precisely because the political institutions of America were not built upon the revealed truths of religion, Jefferson could consistently claim that Americans cannot regard the profession of "twenty gods or no god" as an injury for which law is the proper remedy, since such a profession "neither picks my pocket nor breaks my leg" (*Notes* 210). The priority of free and equal individuals in the state of nature requires that individual freedom—not any form of organized religion —stand as the fundamental ground for religion in America. Indeed, the Bill for Establishing Religious Freedom asserted that religious liberty was one of the "natural rights" that governments are mandated to secure. Religious freedom necessarily includes the freedom to criticize and evaluate particular religious views according to the perceptions of individual opinion; each individual is not only free but is in some sense required to navigate among competing traditions with their rival claims to authority. Jefferson's bill effectively displaced the authority of religious orthodoxy with the authority of private conscience. The ultimate authority of private conscience in religious matters with which Locke's lengthy and carefully written *A Letter Concerning Toleration* concluded furnished the self-evident starting point for Jefferson's argument in the Virginia statute.

Jefferson's bill, however, stopped short of contemporary notions of freedom that affirm belief in an autonomous human will. To the contrary, Jefferson understood the will itself to be constrained by what it perceives. The unedited version of the Bill for Establishing Religious Freedom began: "Well aware that the opinions and belief of men depend *not* on their own will, but follow involuntarily the evidence proposed to their minds . . . " (emphasis added). Differences in ability and education lead different individuals to adhere to different beliefs, and they are not free to do otherwise. For Jefferson, it was precisely the *absence* of individual choice in matters of religion that brought to light the most compelling moral argument for establishing the priority of freedom; religious freedom becomes a fundamental moral necessity in a society where individuals are compelled by the internal evidence of their own minds to affirm different religious opinions. Freedom of religion is not grounded on an authoritative claim about religious truth but arises necessarily for a society uncertain of that truth and so committed to a plurality of religious traditions.

The Reasonableness of Christianity

More deeply and personally, Jefferson believed that the constraints imposed upon individual conscience arose not from the authority of religious tradition but from that of nature. In another section of the long introductory sentence that was edited out of the final version of the Virginia statute, Jefferson referred to "the plan of the holy author of our religion, who . . . chose . . . to extend [religion] . . . by its influence on reason alone." As a student of political philosophy, Jefferson sought to discover the natural ground for religion or, in language alluded to in the Declaration, the god of nature. Keenly aware of the differences separating his own views concerning religion from those of the majority of his countrymen, Jefferson reserved the candid expression of his ideas to private conversation and correspondence. In a famous letter to Benjamin Rush, he wrote: "To the corruptions of Christianity I am, indeed, opposed; but not to the genuine precepts of Jesus himself. I am a Christian, in the only sense in which he wished any one to be; sincerely attached to his doctrines, in preference to all others; ascribing to himself every *human* excellence; and believing he never claimed any other" (April 21, 1803, emphasis in original). Whereas Jefferson maintained that his views on Christianity were "the result of a lifetime of inquiry and reflection," he believed most of his countrymen to have been corrupted by the distorted version of Jesus' teaching preserved in the Bible. The core problem stems from the fact that, like Socrates, Jesus wrote nothing himself. Since he was rejected by the most enlightened citizens of his country, it fell to "unlettered and ignorant men" to record his life and doctrine, and to do so from memory long after the fact. The result of Jesus' premature death, before his reason had "attained the *maximum* of its energy," is that he bequeathed to posterity only a work in progress. Worse, his fragmentary teachings were further "disfigured by the corruptions of schismatizing followers" who perverted and mutilated his "simple doctrines" with "the mysticisms of a Grecian sophist" (namely, Plato). Notwithstanding these limitations, Jefferson considered Jesus' moral teachings, particularly with respect to universal philanthropy, to be "the most perfect and sublime that has ever been taught by man" ("Syllabus of an Estimate of the Merit of the Doctrines of Jesus, compared with those of others," III 1–5, addendum to Benjamin Rush, April 21, 1803).

Jefferson's rational approach to the moral truth of the Gospels also characterized his approach to the miraculous claims of the Bible. When he informed his seventeen-year-old nephew, Peter Carr, that he now possessed the requisite maturity to undertake such a study, Jefferson advised Carr to read the Bible as he would Livy or Tacitus.

> The facts which are within the ordinary course of nature you will believe on the authority of the writer, as you do those of the same kind in Livy and Tacitus. The testimony of the writer weighs in their favor in one scale, and their not being against the laws of nature does not weigh against them. But those facts in the bible which contradict the laws of nature, must be examined with more care, and under a variety of faces. (August 10, 1787)

Jefferson explained that the pretension to divine inspiration deserves serious consideration because it is believed by so many. Yet this should be weighed against what science has revealed about the laws of nature, something that in turn compels one to examine evidence for the claim to divine inspiration itself. Jefferson exhorted his nephew to shake off both fears and prejudices and to "fix reason firmly in her seat, and call to her tribunal every fact, every opinion." With respect to the New Testament, Jefferson invited his nephew to consider the opposing claims of those who allege that Jesus' divine status enabled him to suspend and reverse the laws of nature at will and those who maintain that he was a man "of illegitimate birth, of a benevolent heart, enthusiastic mind, who set out without pretensions to divinity, ended in believing them, and was punished capitally for sedition." He concluded by reaffirming his central counsel: "[L]ay aside all prejudice on both sides, and neither believe nor reject any thing because any other person, or description of persons have rejected or believed it. Your own reason is the only oracle given you by heaven, and you are answerable not for the rightness but the uprightness of the decision."

Jefferson's advice to his nephew is revealing not only for the priority it assigns to religious freedom, but also for the light it sheds on his own approach to the miraculous claims of the Bible. The underlying issue is nothing less than the authority of revelation itself. As Locke had explained, miracles furnish "the basis on which divine mission is always established, and consequently that foundation on which the believers of any divine revelation must ultimately bottom their faith."[5] To investigate as an open question the veracity of miraculous claims is to call into question both the privileged status of the Bible as an inspired text as well as the divine mission and status of Jesus himself. In political terms, both freedom of religious expression and the elevation of the authority of reason in religious matters effectively weaken the secular authority of the clergy—an authority that Jefferson believed posed the gravest and most enduring threat to the Declaration's teaching on natural equality.

Jefferson's candor on these questions was, however, limited to private conversation and correspondence; his temperamental distaste for controversy led him to take a very different tack in public. Jefferson's more politic public expressions of his ideas on religion aimed at a dual goal that stands in some tension to itself—he sought to perpetuate religion as a useful ground for moral convictions while simultaneously weakening its capacity to elicit an attachment that might rival that of citizens to the natural rights philosophy of the Declaration.

Separation: Perpetuating and Transforming Religion in America

To return to the celebrated Bill for Establishing Religious Freedom, Jefferson anticipated that practical effects would follow from an increasingly pervasive acceptance of religious freedom as the philosophic point of departure for religious matters in America. Following Locke, he maintained that "our civil rights have no dependence on our religious opinions, any more than our opinions in physics or geometry." Not only is there a "natural right" to freedom of religious expression, but the use of civic authority in religious matters tends "to corrupt the principles of that very religion it is meant to encourage." By providing political incentives for outward conformity to a religion in which one does not believe, established religions inadvertently foster a kind of hypocrisy and mean-spiritedness diametrically opposed to the teachings of the Gospel. Jefferson concluded that truth in religious matters would prevail only if religion was left to itself, free from all governmental coercion. In short, Jefferson's Bill for Establishing Religious Freedom as well as his famous letter referring to a "wall of separation" between church and state (to the Danbury Baptist Association, January 1, 1802) emphasized the ways in which the disengagement of religion from the powers of government was something emphatically good for religion. Religion ought to be consigned to the private sphere of individual conscience not because it was unimportant, but precisely because it was too important to entrust to any authority, no matter how seemingly benign.

It was also the case, however, that Jefferson's efforts to erect a wall of separation between church and state was part of a strategy to transform religion by encouraging a multiplicity of sects that would check and balance the excessive enthusiasms to which religion is prone. As he wrote in *Notes on the State of Virginia*: "Difference of opinion is advantageous in religion. The several sects perform the office of a Censor morum over each other" (212). Jefferson did not wish to encourage the sort of freedom that would enable a particular religious tradition to flourish but rather the kind of freedom that brought a multiplicity of religions under the same political roof. Referring to the then-novel experiments with disestablishment in Pennsylvania and New York, Jefferson wrote: "They flourish infinitely. Religion is well supported; of various kinds, indeed, but all good enough; all sufficient to preserve peace and order" (*Notes* 212). Jefferson was not primarily concerned that religion be "good enough" to attain salvation (something about which he appeared to entertain doubts) but that it should contribute to the political goods of "peace and order." Pennsylvania and New York had found a way to replace religious enthusiasm with "unbounded tolerance" and religious dissension with "unparalleled" harmony: "They have made the happy discovery, that the way to silence religious disputes, is to take no notice of them" (*Notes* 213).

By endorsing no religion in particular, all religions are placed on an equal footing. In a way analogous to the situation of individuals in the "state of nature," the establishment of a fundamental equality among religions under the state precludes the possibility of dominance by any one; rather, it is in the interest of each to secure the conditions of its own liberty. The artifice of a "wall of separation" effectively transforms religion by directing those citizens who are religiously minded to embrace freedom of religion—not religion itself—as the primary condition for authentic religious practice. The elevation of individual conscience in religious matters to the status of a "natural right" helps to secure the attachment of citizens to a philosophy of natural rights as the almost invisible optic through which they view and scrutinize the claims of any particular religious tradition.

The desired result of diversity in religion was not only that a plurality of sects would check the eccentricities to which religious passion gives rise but also that a multiplicity of religions would throw into relief basic moral teachings held in common. For Jefferson, separation of church and state aimed primarily at the political goal of preserving peace and order. If religion was not philosophically necessary to institute a government based on nature and the sovereignty of the people, it would prove crucial—at least for the great majority of Americans—for its future preservation. It was for this reason that Jefferson publicly favored religion over irreligion, maintaining that the only secure basis for preserving liberty was "a conviction in the minds of the people that these liberties are of the gift of God" (*Notes* 215). Religion rendered harmless to liberty by the very fact of its diversity was, for Jefferson, in the best interest of free government. By marshaling its considerable moral authority to extend natural rights to others even when not in the economic interest of its adherents to do so, religion fosters habits of mind and heart conducive to the "blessings and security of self-government."

It is important to note that Jefferson's assertion that religious conviction provides the "only firm basis" for preserving "the liberties of a nation" occurs within the context of his discussion of slavery. Although slavery was contrary to natural justice, Jefferson also explained that it was held in place by the powerful passions of greed and sloth: "For in a warm climate, no man will labor for himself who can make another labor for him" (*Notes* 215). The natural liberty affirmed in the Declaration was at odds with the powerful passions supporting economic self-interest. It was a contest that liberty could not win without the support of religious conviction—specifically, belief by a majority of the people that all liberties are a gift from God. Although Jefferson did not live to see it, it was precisely in this way that the glaring contradiction of slavery was eventually eradicated. It was through the activity of churches—not official channels of government—that the majority of Americans eventually came to put the natural rights of slaves over economic self-interest. If religion had done much to convict the institution of slavery, it also required the prudential statesmanship of Abraham Lincoln to press the "abstract truth" of the Declaration and, in so doing, enable Americans to draw "a new birth of freedom" from the ruins of civil war.

Religious Tolerance and Political Orthodoxy: Jeffersonian Political Religion

Jefferson's opposition to organized religion shares something in common with his anonymous authorship of the Kentucky Resolutions and inadvertent introduction of a system of parties into American politics. Both his volatile assertion that the Constitution should be understood as a "compact of states" in the Kentucky Resolutions and his passionate resistance to the Federalists (described as the "Anglican, monarchical, aristocratical party" in his letter to Phillip Mazzei, April 24, 1796) were directed against the consolidating tendencies of political power. For Jefferson, the universal cause of the loss of liberty and the rights of man was to be found in "generalizing and concentrating all cares and powers into one body." As a result, "the way to have good and safe government, is not to trust it all to one, but to divide it among the many" (to Joseph Cabell, February 2, 1816). These remarks about government can also be applied to religion. Dividing and subdividing power—whether in national government or in organized religion—was Jefferson's consistent strategy for dealing with the corrupting tendencies of unchecked power in all its forms.

For Jefferson, party (and, more generally, partisanship) arose from two kinds of sentiment that he believed to be rooted in nature: "The same political parties which now agitate the U.S. have existed thro' all time. . . . And in fact the terms of whig and tory belong to natural, as well as to civil history." The decisive difference between these natural parties was whether "the power of the people, or that of the *aristoi* should prevail" (to John Adams, June 27, 1813). Like Machiavelli, Jefferson considered the opposition between "the people" and "the great" (to use Machiavelli's terms) a permanent and ineradicable source of conflict in politics. Although Jefferson most often spoke of party conflict in terms of politics, his distinction extended to religion as well. Writing again to John Adams, Jefferson referred to the Virginia Bill for Establishing Religious Freedom as the "law for religious freedom" which "put down the aristocracy of the clergy" and "restored to the citizen the freedom of the mind" (October 28, 1813). Adams fully agreed with Jefferson that parties—a term he applied to governments, religions, and even revolutionaries —have existed throughout all time, although he was more inclined to attribute this to the corrupting influence of power than to what Jefferson called "the temper and constitution of mind of different individuals": "Democrats, Rebells and Jacobins, when they possessed a momentary power, have shewn a disposition, both to destroy and to forge Records, as vandalical, as Priests and Despots. Such has been and such is the World We live in" (cf. to Jefferson, July 9, 1813, and to Adams, June 27, 1813). Despite their disagreements, both Jefferson and Adams regarded the deepest obstacles to scientific progress in both government and religion to be rooted in the natural disposition to partisanship. But for Jefferson, religious and political partisanship had come together in the Federalist party. In a letter that would subsequently strain his relationship with Adams, Jefferson intemperately described to Joseph Priestley the party strife leading up to his successful presidential election in 1800:

> What an effort . . . of bigotry in Politics and Religion have we gone through! The barbarians really flattered themselves they should be able to bring back the time of vandalism, when ignorance put everything into the hands of power and priestcraft. All advances in science were proscribed as innovations. . . . We were to look backwards, not forwards, for improvement. (March 21, 1801)

The degree of passion expressed in this letter points to the most profound difference distinguishing Jefferson's approach to politics from his approach to religion. Whereas he looked upon differences in religious opinion with serene disinterestedness, this was not true when it came to politics. The disengagement of religion from politics seems to have led Jefferson to embrace political orthodoxy with an almost religious zeal. Indeed, Tocqueville described Jefferson as "the most powerful *apostle* that democracy has ever had," and there was in fact an almost religious enthusiasm in Jefferson's attachment to the principles of republican government.[6] Jefferson's defense of the French Revolution at times assumed the proportions of a true believer, something that finally led the sober John Adams to criticize his erstwhile friend as a dangerous dreamer. In a moment of revolutionary fervor, Jefferson dismissed critics of the mass executions in France: "My own affections have been deeply wounded by some of the martyrs to this cause, but rather than it should have failed, I would have seen half the earth desolated. Were there but an Adam and an Eve left in every country, and left free, it would be better than as it is now" (to William Short, January 3, 1793).[7] As Tocqueville explained and Jefferson in some measure corroborated, the French Revolution aimed more at "the regeneration of the human race" than "the reform of France." As a result, it ignited passions more akin to a religious revolution than a political one; indeed, "it itself became a new kind of religion."[8] If Jefferson believed that differences in religious opinion were advantageous for religion, this was emphatically not the case when it came to political opinions concerning the rights of man.

Although Jefferson regarded the self-evidence of the "rights of man" to have been disseminated by the "light of science" (to Weightman, June 24, 1826), he also knew that most citizens were not scientists. Given the almost irresistible tendency of those in power to consolidate it to their own advantage, Jefferson was keenly aware of the need to inculcate in citizens an attachment to the principles and practices of republican liberty. Orthodox attachment of citizens to the creedal truths of the Declaration was the aim not only of Jefferson's Republican party but also and especially of his thoughts on education.

Education and Politics

Like his lifelong friend and collaborator, James Madison, Jefferson found some initial security for republican government in the new institutional arrangements arising from recent improvements in the science of politics, most notably the separation of powers and pervasive system of checks and balances. Jefferson, however, was cooler to the constitutional arrangement than Madison (who, at the Virginia Ratifying Convention, had to employ his considerable diplomatic skills to suppress rumors of Jefferson's lukewarm support). In his *Notes on Virginia*, Jefferson had already expressed the fundamental reason why institutional provisions, however ingenious, would necessarily prove insufficient. "In every government on earth is some trace of human weakness, some germ of corruption and degeneracy, which cunning will discover, and wickedness insensibly open, cultivate, and improve. Every government degenerates when trusted to the rulers of the people alone" (*Notes* 198). The best surety and, in Jefferson's mind, only effective safeguard against the universal tendency of government to slide toward tyranny was to be found in the people. Jefferson's belief in the necessity of a vigilant citizen body led him to think deeply and persistently about the relationship between education and politics and, more specifically, about the need for general education in order to sustain republican liberty. For Jefferson, the preservation of freedom would require a diffusion of knowledge among the people.

Whereas Jefferson's founding of the University of Virginia is well known, it is sometimes overlooked that this was only one part (albeit the crowning achievement) of a comprehensive vision for education in America. Notwithstanding the attention he lavished upon this project, Jefferson considered the primary stages of education to be more important than the development of a university. As he wrote to Joseph Cabell, "it is safer to have a whole people respectably enlightened, than a few in a high state of science, and the many in ignorance" (January 13, 1823). Although Jefferson was never successful in bringing the rest of his plan to fruition, his vision for education derived from the ideas about equality and inequality expressed and implied in the Declaration of Independence. His comprehensive vision for a system of public education aimed at discovering and cultivating a natural aristocracy of talent and virtue for positions of public leadership and, at the same time, at arming the general public with the intellectual and experiential resources necessary to keep their representatives responsive to the best interests of the people as a whole.

During the summer of 1776, in the full flush of revolutionary fervor, Jefferson headed a three-person committee charged with proposing revisions that would bring the laws and statutes of Virginia into line with the principles of the Declaration. Of the 126 bills reported for legislative consideration, Jefferson considered the most important to be a comprehensive three-stage scheme to reform state education (to George Wythe, August 13, 1786). This proposal eventually reached the floor as the 1779 Bill for the More General Diffusion of Knowledge. Although this reform was intended for Virginia, Jefferson hoped that Virginia would in this, as in much else, prove a model for the newly emerging nation.

The bill called for a division of each county into smaller units called "hundreds" and later called "wards." The size of each hundred was to be large enough to include a sufficient number of children to comprise a school and small enough to allow each child to attend on a daily basis. All free children, male and female, would have access to three years of education gratis and could continue thereafter as long as they wished at private expense. This first tier of Jefferson's educational system focused on reading, writing, and common arithmetic. Jefferson was so convinced of the crucial importance of literacy—not only for economic independence but especially for political participation—that his 1817 Act for Establishing Elementary Schools contained a provision disenfranchising future citizens who, after the age of fifteen, "cannot read readily in some tongue, native or acquired." He would have preferred a system of compulsory elementary education but thought it would pose too great a shock to prevailing sentiments. Consequently, he directed his energies to removing the most common barrier to procuring an education by proposing that it be made available to all free of charge.

Jefferson was, however, willing to break with the traditional practice of using the Bible to teach children to read. Instead of putting the Bible into the hands of children "at an age when their judgments are not sufficiently matured for religious inquiries," Jefferson proposed a curriculum that was centered on "the most useful facts from Grecian, Roman, European and American history" together with a cultivation of "the first elements of morality" (*Notes* 197). Jefferson thought it important for young people to become acquainted with history and science before attempting to evaluate the miraculous claims of the Bible. The skills necessary to sift the authentic teachings of Jesus from the vehicle through which they have been transmitted far exceeded the capacity of a child and should, as a consequence, be postponed until a student was mentally and morally prepared for such an undertaking. But in the schools (and especially the primary schools) Jefferson considered it far more important that future citizens know the facts of political history: "[P]ossessed thereby of the experience of other ages and countries, they may be enabled to know ambition under all its shapes, and prompt[ed] to exert their natural powers to defeat its purposes" (preamble to 1779 Bill for the More General Diffusion of Knowledge). For Jefferson, public education should have an explicitly political aim; it was not to be directed to salvation but to freedom and happiness in this world.

The intermediate stage of education would be furnished by regional grammar schools or, as they were sometimes called, "academies." Two or more of the most promising students from the primary schools would be subsidized, while the rest of the student body would be drawn from those who could afford to pay. The primary focus for this level of study was language, especially Greek and Latin. Despite the fact that the study of classics was going out of vogue in Europe, Jefferson believed that the study of classical languages was both developmentally appropriate (given the dependence of language on memory) and good preparation for the study of science. Jefferson's concern with useful knowledge led him to add several modern subjects to his initial proposal for the grammar schools. His 1779 bill included English grammar and his proposals of 1817 and 1818 added other modern languages as well as geography, surveying, and navigation.

The final stage in this scheme was the university, the only part of the plan that Jefferson was able to realize during his lifetime. Jefferson viewed the university as a training ground for future leaders; his recommendation to subsidize tuition for the most gifted was intended "to avail the state of those talents which nature has sown as liberally among the poor as the rich, but which perish without use, if not sought for and cultivated" (*Notes* 198). Here students were to apply themselves especially to the study of science, particularly those sciences most likely to prove useful to their fellowmen. Noticeably absent from the curriculum were the "foggy" disciplines of metaphysics and theology (Report to the Commissioners for the University of Virginia, August 4, 1818; cf. to Adams, July 5, 1814, and March 14, 1820). Jefferson maintained that the absence of a professor of divinity at the University of Virginia was called for by "the principles of our Constitution which placed all sects of religion on an equal footing." Moreover, he expected that the general principles common to all religious traditions would properly fall within the purview of the professor of ethics (Report of the Commissioners for the University of Virginia, August 4, 1818). When the university came under fire as an antireligious institution, it was decided that different religious denominations should be encouraged to establish their own professorships as long as they preserved their independence both from each other and the university. The anticipated result, Jefferson wrote to Dr. Thomas Cooper, was that "by bringing the sects together, and mixing them with the mass of other students, we shall soften their asperities, liberalize and neutralize their prejudices, and make the general religion a religion of peace, reason, and morality" (August 4, 1822).

One of the ironies of Jefferson's educational legacy is that his war against religious intolerance was accompanied by an attempt to impose a rigid political orthodoxy. This extended not only to the omission of metaphysics and theology but also included many authors within the camp of modern liberal democracy itself. For example, Jefferson considered Locke and Sydney well suited to impress upon the young the right to self-government and to inspire them with a love of free governments; but Hume and Montesquieu were deeply problematic as was "the honied Mansfieldism of Blackstone" (to William Duane, August 12, 1810; to Madison, February 17, 1826; to John Tyler, May 26, 1810). Students were of course free to read these and other excluded authors in private, but Jefferson insisted that if the "vestal flame" of republicanism were to be kept alive, it was necessary to be "rigorously attentive to . . . [the] political principles" of teachers, or, in the case of courses on government, to lay down the principles which are to be taught "by a previous prescription of the texts to be adopted" (to Madison, February 17, 1826, and February 1, 1825). Jefferson's thinking about university education was characterized by a deep tension between his long-standing philosophic attachment to freedom of inquiry and expression and an urgent political concern to imbue future leaders with sound principles, which they in turn could go on to "spread anew over our own and the sister states" (to Madison, February 17, 1826).

It was especially after Jefferson left the presidency that his idea to divide counties into "hundreds" was gradually superseded by the notion of "wards." To his proposal for universal public education, he now added an ongoing civic education that would take place outside the classroom. The ward system of "little republics" was intentionally modeled on the New England townships which—notwithstanding and in part because of their effective resistance to his policies as president—Jefferson considered "the wisest invention ever devised by the wit of man for the perfect exercise of self-government, and for its preservation" (to Samuel Kercheval, July 12, 1816). By taking charge of those matters on which they were competent (for example, caring for the poor, building roads, running elections, selecting jurors, raising a militia, and attending to small cases of justice), the wards would become schools for the practice of self-government. Jefferson wrote to John Tyler that two great and related measures are necessary to sustain republican principles—general education and the establishment of "these little republics" (May 26, 1810).

The idea of wards became increasingly important for Jefferson as a means of bringing public affairs within the grasp of ordinary citizens and thus keeping alive the kind of civic spirit essential for republican government. In a letter to Samuel Kercheval, Jefferson asked where, in the American political system of government, the principle of republicanism was to be found. His answer made explicit the inchoate reservations about constitutional safeguards expressed thirty years earlier: "Not in our constitution certainly, but merely in the spirit of our people" (to Kercheval, July 12, 1816; cf. *Notes* 198). As he had explained a couple of years earlier with respect to the state of Virginia, "I have long contemplated a division of it into hundreds or wards, as the most fundamental measure for securing good government, and for instilling the principles and exercise of self-government into every fibre of every member of our commonwealth" (to Joseph Cabell, January 17, 1814). Jefferson's continuing reflection on the relationship between education and politics sharpened and, in some sense, radicalized his understanding of the nature and requirements of republican government itself.

Jefferson's postpresidential years were largely given over to the development and promulgation of that version of republicanism with which he has become most closely associated, namely, the direct political participation of the people in those decisions that fall within their competence. Criticizing his own earlier attempt to draft a republican constitution for Virginia, Jefferson attributed its inadequacy to a lack of experience. "In truth, the abuses of monarchy had so much filled all the space of political contemplation, that we imagined everything republican which was not monarchy. We had not yet penetrated to the mother principle, that governments are republican only in proportion as they embody the will of their people, and execute it" (to Kercheval, July 12, 1816). In an attempt to dispel misunderstandings attached to the notion of a republic, Jefferson offered his most radical and succinct definition of republicanism.

> Were I to assign to this term a precise and definite idea, I would say, purely and simply, it means a government by its citizens in mass, acting directly and personally, according to rules established by the majority; and that every other government is more or less republican, in proportion as it has in its composition more or less of this ingredient of the direct action of the citizens. (to John Taylor, May 28, 1816; cf. to Dupont de Nemours, April 24, 1816)

Jefferson recognized that this standard would not be practicable beyond the extent of a New England township or his proposed division of counties into wards. Nevertheless, he recommended it as a useful measure against which earlier constitutional arrangements could be judged and amended. It was on this basis that he criticized the initial arrangements of the Constitution, especially the Senate and judiciary, as being too far removed from the people.

> The Constitution . . . is a mere thing of wax in the hands of the judiciary, which they may twist and shape into any form they please. It should be remembered, as an axiom of eternal truth in politics, that whatever power in any government is independent, is absolute also; in theory only, at first, while the spirit of the people is up, but in practice, as fast as that relaxes. Independence can be trusted nowhere but with the people in mass. They are inherently independent of all but moral law. (to Judge Spencer Roane, September 6, 1819)

Although willing to tolerate moderate imperfections, Jefferson insisted that "laws and institutions must go hand in hand with the progress of the human mind." Indeed, late in life he returned to the utopian maxim he had first floated with Madison in 1789 regarding the sovereignty of each generation, and he argued for an amendment to the Virginia Constitution that would require its revision every nineteen to twenty years as each new generation reached maturity (to Kercheval, July 12, 1816, and to Madison, September 6, 1789). Although the radical implications of Jefferson's views on republicanism were rejected by Madison for the opening they afforded to tyranny of the majority (consider Madison's famous argument in *The Federalist* no. 10) and for disregarding the anarchic consequences arising from frequent changes in the laws (Madison to Jefferson, February 4, 1790; cf. Adams to Jefferson, May 11, 1794), Jefferson's most extreme version of republican principles derived from long-standing fears about the dangers of consolidation. If the initial experience of a distant and unresponsive British government had precipitated a revolutionary war for independence in 1776, more recent experience with the growing powers of national government under the Federalist party had given rise to "the revolution of 1800." In his mind, the principles of the Declaration had been eclipsed during the Federalist administration by a consolidation of power—despite the institutional protections of the Constitution. In contrast to those who looked upon constitutions with "sanctimonious reverence," Jefferson's continuing attraction to Enlightenment ideas of progress and his forty years of experience had taught him that the "secret" of republican liberty "will be found to be in the making . . . [of each citizen] the depository of the powers respecting himself, so far as he is competent to them, and delegating only what is beyond his competence" (to Cabell, February 2, 1816; cf. to Kercheval, July 12, 1816).

If Jefferson's views on republican government and education evolved over time, there was nevertheless an underlying consistency that characterized his thoughts about education from beginning to end. Like Aristotle (although in a way different from him), Jefferson insisted not only on the importance of education but also that it be "education relative to the regime" (*Politics* 1310a12–14).[9] Jefferson was especially concerned to inculcate an orthodox attachment to the principles of the Declaration as the surest guarantor for the continuing success of the American experiment in self-government. Moreover, he anticipated Tocqueville with his insistence that institutional arrangements, however ingenious, were not by themselves sufficient to sustain self-government and that what was needed were habits and sentiments inspired by direct participation in local affairs. Jefferson's most mature thinking on education attempted to shape the mores of the American people so as to awaken and sustain the spirit of vigilance most apt to secure the blessings of liberty. His constant aim in proposing a combination of academic and practical education for the general public was that of "rendering the people safe" by giving them the wherewithal to become "guardians of their own liberty" (*Notes* 198). The success of liberal democracy could not be safe even in the hands of the "natural aristocracy of virtue and talent" with which Jefferson's scheme of education sought to displace the "pseudo-aristocracy of wealth and birth."

> If once . . . [the people] become inattentive to the public affairs, you and I, and Congress, and Assemblies, judges and governors shall all become wolves. It seems to be the law of our general nature, in spite of individual exceptions; and experience declares that man is the only animal which devours his own kind. (to Edward Carrington, January 16, 1787)

Notwithstanding his awareness of the tendency of the people to be led astray, Jefferson consistently maintained that a sustained program of general education must, before all else, cultivate the good sense of the people as they alone constitute the "only safe depositories" of government (cf. to George Wythe, August 13, 1786, and *Notes* 198).

As noted at the beginning of this essay, Jefferson's status as a political philosopher is inextricably bound up with his stature as one of the Founders of the American experiment. Although he thought deeply about the nature and purpose of legitimate government, the relationship between religion and politics, and the importance of an educated and vigilant citizenry, the translation of his ideas into actual political practice was necessarily constrained by the fortuitous configurations of political circumstance. Moreover, in none of the three enterprises he considered most significant—the Declaration of Independence, the Bill for Establishing Religious Freedom, and the University of Virginia—was he acting on his own. In each case, Jefferson worked through the medium of a committee and was, as a consequence, dependent upon the skills and consent of others to bring his vision into effect. If the unavoidable compromises that accompany political success to some extent clouded the original vision that inspired it, the necessity of compromise should itself be understood as part of Jefferson's legacy. Jefferson's overriding political vision was directed to the possibility of self-government, and his work as a Founding legislator in politics, religion, and education consistently aimed at establishing conditions that would best enable a people to legislate for themselves.

Notes

I wish to thank the Earhart Foundation for their generous support in the summer of 2001, during which time I was able to write this chapter.

1. There is no satisfactory and complete critical edition of Jefferson's writings at present. The collection edited by Julian P. Boyd et al. will fill this lacunae should it ever be finished: *The Papers of Thomas Jefferson,* 28 vols. to date (Princeton, N.J.: Princeton University Press, 1950–). I have simply identified references to Jefferson's short documents and letters by name and date so they might be readily found in any number of collections. Citations from Jefferson's lengthy *Notes on the State of Virginia* (*Notes*) include page references to the edition most commonly used for classroom instruction, *The Portable Thomas Jefferson,* ed. Merrill D. Peterson (New York: Penguin Books, 1977).

2. Cf. Jefferson's expunged remarks on the slave trade in his final draft of the Declaration; *Notes* 215; to Edward Coles, August 25, 1814; and to John Holmes, April 22, 1820.

3. Jefferson's political condemnation of slavery was undercut by his philosophic speculations on "varieties in the race of man." On the one hand, Jefferson's statesmanlike opposition to slavery and outline of a plan for its eventual abolition was widely disseminated through the publication of *Notes on the State of Virginia* (esp. 214–15 and 185–86). On the other hand, these very arguments were embedded in disputations about natural philosophy that entailed Jefferson's philosophic speculations about the racial inferiority of blacks (esp. 78–79, 93–103, 186–93), speculations that could only work against the cause of emancipation.

4. Compare, for example, the fundamental natural law of self-preservation in the accounts of both Hobbes and Locke with Jesus' only commandments in the New Testament—to love God before all else and one's neighbor as oneself. As starting points for understanding how to live, these principles point to profoundly different ways of life.

5. John Locke, *The Reasonableness of Christianity with A Discourse of Miracles*, ed. I. T. Ramsey (Stanford, Calif.: Stanford University Press, 1958), 86; cf. 82.

6. Alexis de Tocqueville, *Democracy in America*, trans. and ed. Harvey Mansfield and Delba Winthrop (Chicago: University of Chicago Press, 2000), 249, emphasis added.

7. In fairness to Jefferson, it should be noted that these remarks were made six months before the onset of the "reign of terror." Looking back upon these events in 1816, the original fervor expressed in Jefferson's 1793 letter to William Short is considerably muted, but not his hopes for the cause itself. In a series of exchanges with John Adams evaluating the eighteenth century as a whole, Jefferson observed that the moral world of Europe had been "thrown back again to the age of the Borgias, to the point from which it had departed 300 years before." He added, "I did not, in 89, believe . . . [the convulsions] would last so long, nor have cost so much blood. But altho' your prophecy has proved true so far, I hope it does not preclude a better final result" (to Adams, January 11, 1816).

8. Tocqueville, *The Old Regime and the Revolution*, ed. François Furet and Françoise Mélonio, trans. Alan Kahan (Chicago: University of Chicago Press, 1998), 101.

9. The difference between Aristotle and Jefferson on this point is also instructive. Whereas Aristotle considered education of citizens in the spirit of the regime to be the best guarantor of stability, he also explained that this entails an education that fosters in citizens a capacity to *resist* the subtle but powerful pressure of regimes to imbue them with an uncritical and excessive attachment to its dominant principles. See *Politics* 1310a12–38.

Chapter 8

The Political Science of James Madison

Michael P. Zuckert

eorge Washington has his monument and Thomas Jefferson has his memorial, but James Madison (1751–1836), the reputed "father of the Constitution," has no such edifice in the nation's capital. Instead, the Washington, D.C.-based American Political Science Association gives an award in his name to the outstanding political scientist of the day. The political scientists recognize Madison as a fellow political scientist—as their patron saint, one might say. Indeed, although he accomplished great things as a political actor, his greatest distinction was as a political scientist. To single out those accomplishments is to contrast political science not only with political practice but with political philosophy as well. John Locke, an important philosophic source for Founding generation Americans, had said of the study of politics that it "contains parts very different the one from the other, the one containing the original of societies and the rise and extent of political power, the other, the art of governing men in society." He placed his own *Two Treatises of Government* in the first rather than the second category.[1] A century later, Thomas Jefferson restated and somewhat modified Locke's distinction. He identified two classes of political writing: "theory" and "practice." The first promulgates "the general principles of liberty and the rights of man, in nature and in society." He neglected to provide a general description of the second kind, but he supplied examples of each—Locke's *Treatises* in the first class, and a text in which Madison had a great hand, *The Federalist*, in the second.[2] It is not that Madison had no thoughts at the level of "theory" or political philosophy; but his originality and unique contributions lay in the sphere of practice, or political science.

Like most of the Founders, Madison left his thoughts scattered in various places, often in texts written for one or another immediate political occasion. Even *The Federalist*, the closest thing to a book that Madison produced, is no exception. The text was prepared with an immediate political purpose in mind: to help secure ratification of the Constitution. The project was led by Alexander Hamilton, who wrote a much larger share of the essays than did Madison. Moreover, *The Federalist* was a series of essays in defense of the Constitution; but in a letter written at the close of the Constitutional Convention, Madison expressed very grave reservations about the document he allegedly fathered: as it came from the hands of the Convention, it did not embody the principles of Madisonian political science to a sufficient degree to please him or to make him confident of the government's prospects under it.[3] Nonetheless, Madison believed the proposed Constitution superior to the old Articles of Confederation; and so, biting his tongue but acting in perfectly good conscience, he fought hard to secure adoption of the Convention's product, suppressing, as a good advocate must, his substantial reservations. One important implication of these various facts is that *The Federalist* is at best an imperfect source for gleaning Madison's political thought. I propose, therefore, to look elsewhere for the most part. The political analysis in terms of which he both proposed or "fathered" the Constitution and came to hold such important reservations about his own child emerged in the years immediately preceding the Constitutional Convention and found expression in memoranda, letters, and speeches prepared before and during the Convention.

Looking at these sources, we see that Madison's claim to greatness as a political scientist is twofold: he developed a revolutionary theory of federalism, which made possible an altogether new kind of union; and he developed a revolutionary theory of republicanism, which made possible an altogether new kind of republican government. These were inventions or discoveries that made possible the transformations of political life that we have come to think of as modern politics. Considerations of space demand a focus only on the second, more fundamental, of Madison's two great political innovations.[4]

I. Political Philosophy

We cannot understand Madison's contribution without considering his thinking about the issues of political philosophy. He understood that a science of practice must be guided by knowledge of the ends and grounds of practice. Like other leading Founders, he thought of the grounds, foundations, and ends of politics in the terms captured in the Declaration of Independence, a document (its author Thomas Jefferson tells us) meant "to place before mankind the common sense of the subject. . . . Neither aiming at originality of principle or sentiment, . . . it was intended to be an expression of the American mind."[5]

Probably the most concentrated and visible opportunity Madison had to express himself on the themes of political philosophy came in his role as "father of the Bill of Rights." The original Constitution's lack of a bill of rights was held to be a major defect by those who feared the power and centralization they saw in the new Constitution. Bills of rights normally came at the beginning of state constitutions and resembled the theoretical sections of the Declaration of Independence more than the Bill of Rights that eventually was adopted. When he introduced a draft bill of rights in Congress in 1789, Madison had in mind a bill of rights of this character. Thus, he proposed as a first amendment to the Constitution:

> That there be prefixed to the Constitution a declaration, that all power is originally vested in, and consequently derived from, the people. That Government is instituted and ought to be exercised for the benefit of the people; which consists in the enjoyment of life and liberty, with the right of acquiring and using property, and generally of pursuing and obtaining happiness and safety. That the people have an indubitable, unalienable, and indefeasible right to reform or change their Government, whenever it be found adverse or inadequate to the purposes of its institution.[6]

Madison invokes the social contract theory of politics most often associated with Locke. According to this theory, political power traces back to the people and nowhere else. Thus, the people are sovereign. Rulers possess what are, in effect, delegated powers. The people empower government for the sake of their own good and not the good of the rulers. Consequently, the exercise of political power is to be judged according to whether it serves that good. Like Locke, Madison understands the good for the sake of which government is created as the security of preexisting (i.e., natural) rights or the objects of preexisting rights—"the enjoyment of life and liberty, with the right of acquiring and using property; and generally of pursuing and obtaining happiness and safety." Madison gives a version of natural rights closer to the original Lockean formulation of "life, liberty, and estate" than to Jefferson's triad of "life, liberty, and the pursuit of happiness." Finally, Madison caps his list of first principles with the "indubitable, unalienable, and indefeasible right to reform or change their Government, whenever it be found adverse or inadequate to the purposes of its institution." Again, Madison closely echoes Jefferson's parallel "right to alter or abolish" governments that fail to secure the end for which they exist (to secure rights).

Madison's sketch of "the original of societies and the rise and extent of political power" as prepared for inclusion in his proposed bill of rights needs to be supplemented by two other important Madisonian statements of political philosophy. In the one, Madison draws some of the implications of the social contract philosophy for the proper or legitimate form of government. By 1792, Madison was forced to recognize and to defend the existence of political parties (or at least of the party of which he was one of the chief organizers). His party "consists of those who, [believe] in the doctrine that mankind are capable of governing themselves and [hate] hereditary power as an insult to the reason and an outrage to the rights of man" (*MF* 247). The "rights of man" imply that only "republican government" is legitimate. If, as the social contract theory says, political authority derives exclusively from the people, then no set of rulers can claim any share or piece of it that does not derive from the people. That principle disqualifies all hereditary and other forms of self-appointed political authority. It is from this understanding of the sole legitimacy of republicanism that Madison derives his famous definition of that form of government in *The Federalist* no. 39 as:

> a government which derives all its powers directly or indirectly from the great body of the people; and is administered by persons holding their offices during pleasure, for a limited period, or during good behavior. It is *essential* to such a government, that it be derived from the great body of the society, not from an inconsiderable proportion, or a favored class of it. . . . It is *sufficient* for such a government, that the persons administering it be appointed, either directly or indirectly, by the people; and that they hold their appointments by either of the tenures just specified.[7]

Earlier followers of the social contract philosophy did not draw this same conclusion: thinkers like Locke, Montesquieu, and Blackstone accepted as legitimate that part of government be in the hands of hereditary ruling groups.[8] When Madison and the other Americans rejected that part of earlier political philosophy, they set the terms for the task to which Madison's political science was most emphatically directed: to build a wholly republican system (what we would today call a democracy) that successfully achieves the task for which all governments rightly exist—to secure all in their rights. With that the Americans introduced into the world a thought that became one of the master ideas of modern politics—that only democratic government is supportable, and that such government must govern with respect for the human rights of its citizens. In other words, the Americans are the first to commit themselves to liberal (rights-respecting and rights-securing) democracy as solely legitimate.

Legitimate government must be republican, and it must be rights-securing. Madison has a good deal more to say about rights in a remarkable essay he wrote at about the same time as his defense of his political party. Entitled "Property," this essay follows the curious usage of Locke, who had spoken of all rights, or the objects of all rights, as property. Madison helps explain Locke's usage when he identifies property as a "dominion which one man claims . . . in exclusion of every other individual" (*MF* 243). There are two elements to rights: dominion and exclusivity. The first means that the right-holder has a kind of control over that to which he has a right; the second means that he has a kind of immunity from the intrusions of others on that to which he has a right. Like Locke, Madison recognizes that the more usual meaning or "particular application" of the term property involves "the external things of the world." But also like Locke, Madison identifies a broader meaning: "In its larger and juster meaning, [property] embraces everything to which a man may attach a value and have a right, and *which leaves to everyone else the like advantage*" (*MF* 243, emphasis in original). Madison includes in property in this broad and more proper sense "safety and liberty of . . . person, . . . the free use of . . . faculties, and free choice of the objects on which to employ them"—the rights that Locke (and then Jefferson) included in the catalog of rights as "life" and "liberty." Madison emphasizes more strongly even than Locke had done "a property in opinions and the free communication of them," especially religious opinions and practices. "Conscience is the most sacred of all property." In sum, Madison says, "as a man is said to have a right to his property, he may be equally said to have a property in his rights" (*MF* 243–44).

Madison (again following Locke) asserts that "government is instituted to protect" this very broad kind of property. Some scholars see Madison as obsessed with property in the narrow sense, others with republicanism and personal rights. Neither side captures the real Madison: "that alone is a *just* government which *impartially* secures to every man whatever is his *own*" (*MF* 244). In order to secure property in external goods, just government must not invade property in personal rights; must not seize the property which a man has in "his personal safety and personal liberty"; nor must men be denied "the free use of their faculties and free choice of their occupations" because of "arbitrary restrictions, exemptions, and monopolies." Just governments neither "invade the domestic sanctuaries of the rich" nor "grind the faces of the poor" (*MF* 245). All equally have rights, and all have an equal right to have their property secured; but the task of just governance is rendered difficult by the fact that some have more (sometimes much more) of the external things of the world than others.

Madison understands the fundamentals of political philosophy in such a way as to point to a series of tensions in the tasks set for political science. Three such tensions are especially central. First, the principles of political right require that government be "wholly republican" (i.e., rule by the majority) but that it also impartially respect the property or rights of all. Second, although all have equal rights (and therefore equal property in one sense), all do not have equal property in the other sense. In one form or another, property tends to translate into political power, and the holders of political power are seldom neutral or fair-minded in the way they wield political power. Third, government exists to secure property in the extended sense; therefore, it must be strong enough to do that but not too strong to do more than that. "Where an excess of power prevails, property of no sort is duly respected. No man is safe in his opinions, his person, his faculties, or his possessions." The answer, however, cannot be merely to control or check power: "where there is an excess of liberty, the effect is the same, though from an opposite cause" (*MF* 244).

Madison's political philosophy thus poses three especially difficult problems for his political science to solve. First, how can one combine securing rights with republican government? Second, how can one impartially secure property in both the narrow and the extended senses of the term? Third, how can one navigate the narrow passage between too strong government and too much liberty? Madison's greatness as a political scientist lies first in his clear recognition that *these* are the problems that political design must solve; and second, in his recognition that all previous models, including those most widely accepted in the America of his day, were inadequate to the challenge posed by these three problems. Finally, he invented or discovered almost entirely new solutions to these three problems.

II. Political Science

The requirements of legitimate politics had the unanticipated effect of disqualifying the two main models of political regime prevalent in eighteenth-century America. As much as anything, this fact forced Madison onto his paths of innovation. The leading political authority in America was the French philosopher Baron de Montesquieu. His *Spirit of the Laws* was probably the greatest achievement of modern political philosophy to that day, and it deservedly stood high in the eyes of the world. Part of the basis for his very wide appeal was the great range of topics he covered, together with sufficient ambiguity in his presentation so as to allow different readers to find in him authority for quite different positions. Strange to say, the two dominant models Madison had to break from both traced in large part to Montesquieu. The first model is what Montesquieu put forward as a rationalized version of the English constitution of the eighteenth century, a complex affair which uniquely aimed at liberty as its object—what we might call the Montesquieuean "free constitution" (*SL* XI:5). The other model to which many Americans looked was Montesquieu's rendition of the classical republic (*SL* III–VII). The first was most attractive to Madison himself and others who went on to become Federalists in the battle over ratification of the Constitution. The other proved most attractive to those who went on to become Anti-Federalists.

Montesquieu's free constitution was an obvious influence on Madison and the other American Founders, for it is the model that introduced the modern theory of separation of powers to the world. That apparent familiarity conceals from us the great complexity and marvelous richness of the Montesquieuean theory, however, for that theory combines at least the four following elements: the discrimination of separate functions of governance, the articulation of the need for separateness of personnel to carry on the different functions, the mixed regime as the only means by which to achieve the needed separation, and checks and balances as the necessary means by which to maintain the separation (see *SL* XI:6).

The classification of governmental powers into the categories of legislative, executive, and judicial is largely the accomplishment of Montesquieu. He takes his bearings in doing so from thinking through the nature of the rule of law. The three functions are stages in the process of governance by law. The regime that explicitly aims at liberty is the regime that best articulates the requisites of the rule of law. Legislation involves the making of laws, that is, of general rules that apply impartially across the society; when law rules, the rulers are subject to the law also, and so proper laws apply to legislators as well as to everyone else. The executive is that part of government explicitly possessing that property that distinguishes government from all other social organizations—coercive authority. The executive uses coercion to apply the rules made by the legislature. The judiciary shares with the executive the task of applying the law, but it does not possess the tools of coercion itself. Nonetheless, its authorization is necessary before the executive may apply coercion to individuals. The judiciary, in a way the weakest part of government, stands between the coercive authority of government and individuals. It guarantees that coercion is applied in accord with law and not arbitrarily. Montesquieu thus assigns a particularly high ranking to the judicial function.

These three governmental functions are not only conceptually distinguishable, but, Montesquieu says, they must be institutionally separate as well in order for the rule of law to prevail.[9] Montesquieu has in mind with his theory of *separation* of powers something like a relay race: each of the powers must be located in a separate and independent body, each of which acts in turn and passes on to the next body the baton of the law. The laws must be made by one body (composed according to certain specifications that Montesquieu lays down); they must be coercively applied by another body; and they must be adjudicated (i.e., tested to see whether they rightly apply to specific individuals) by yet a third. The combination of all three, or even of any two powers in the same set of hands, endangers the rule of law and thus liberty. The central idea here is to have, as the ruling element of society, general rules that are formulated in a body constructed so as to increase the likelihood of the justice and wisdom of the rules. Those who control the means of coercion, always so terrible and always such a temptation to misuse, must be prevented from using their coercive authority to further their own interests or passions. Thus, they must apply a rule taken from elsewhere and have authorization from the judiciary before they can apply it.[10]

Montesquieu's constitutional theory takes its bearings from the principles of modern political philosophy in that he sets as the chief and proper aim of political life the security of rights, best achieved through guaranteeing the rule of law. Nonetheless, he frequently confuses readers because he combined the theory of separation of powers with the much older idea of the mixed regime, a theory with its roots in the classical political philosophy of Plato and Aristotle, and its peak expression in the writings of Polybius. This theory did not begin where Montesquieu did—with the goal of rights-securing, the means of rule of law, and conceptual tools taken from the stages of law. Rather, it began with the classical theory of regimes—rule by one, by the few, or the many—with each type of rule subject to good and bad forms. In its mature Polybian form, this theory contained the notion of a cycle of regimes—each good form tends to degenerate into its opposite bad form, which then tends to set in motion a corrective so that the bad form is in turn replaced by the next good form. The cycle had certain disadvantages, including great instability and bad rule half the time. Polybius claimed that the cycle could be arrested and good rule secured through a mixed regime—that is, a sharing of power among the three ruling elements of the pure regimes. This theory was extremely influential all through antiquity and the Middle Ages, and indeed into modern times.

Montesquieu argued that the free constitution required something like a superimposition of the mixed regime onto the separation of powers scheme. It was particularly important that the legislature contained the three elements of the pure regimes. Montesquieu thought the British constitution, with its democratic lower house, its aristocratic upper house, and its monarchical executive who was also part of the legislature, was the model regime. The legislature contained all elements of society and gave each in effect a veto power. It would necessarily take account of the rights of all. The democratic lower house guaranteed that the personal rights of the many would not be sacrificed to the property rights of the few. The aristocratic upper house guaranteed the reverse. The monarchic executive—the scion of a long-established hereditary line with deep common interests with the good of the whole community—was partly above the fray of the two houses of the legislature and independent, and it could therefore hold the balance between the two houses and provide leadership when stalemate threatened. Likewise, the hereditary monarch was the ideal possessor of the executive authority (so long as he was surrounded by the legislature and judiciary), for as a unitary force he could supply the energy and decisiveness needed to act in both the domestic and foreign arenas. Finally, Montesquieu understood the judiciary essentially as the "jury of one's peers." Like the legislature, then, it would embody the elements of the community and contribute to the sense of security in rights that citizens would feel, for they would know that the state could not apply the law to them except with the acquiescence of members of society like themselves.

Finally, Montesquieu added to the cauldron the notion of checks and balances. This was not, as is usually said in textbooks, the primary feature of the theory of separated powers. Checks and balances were needed in order to maintain the separation of powers, not to produce a government of stalemate or gridlock. The chief point of checks and balances is to check the legislature: "If the executive power does not have the right to check enterprises of the legislative body, the latter will be despotic, for it will wipe out all the other powers, since it will be able to give itself all the power it can imagine." The judiciary is no part of the system of checks (neither checker nor checkee) and the legislature is a part only as the body to be checked. "But the legislative power must not have the reciprocal faculty of checking the executive power." Checks and balances are thus a much smaller and different part of the free constitution than we are accustomed to conceive them (*SL* XI:6).

Although there were many political leaders in America in 1787 ready to pronounce the British constitution the best in the world and the model that all free nations should follow, it can easily be imagined that immediately after the Revolution this viewpoint would also have its detractors. Like Madison himself, most Americans came out of the agitation leading up to the Revolution firmly committed to republicanism, understood (at least) as the absence of all hereditary authority. The Montesquieuean free constitution did not qualify as republican under this standard because hereditary institutions played so large a role in it. Moreover, the conflict leading up to the Revolution led most Americans to focus on the dangers of overbearing governments, and especially the dangers posed by nonelected political authorities like kings. These concerns found echo in another part of Montesquieu: in his presentation of the classical republic. The second model constitution that had great favor in America in the mid-1780s was a blend of theories from Montesquieu's republics and from inferences the Americans drew from their own experience and their prior commitments to Lockean politics.

Two themes from Montesquieu's republicanism particularly resonated for the Americans. One was his theory of size: republics had to be (relatively) small. Large political societies could not sustain the republican form but had to be either monarchies or despotisms (*SL* VIII:15–20). The Americans, of course, wished to be neither of the two last. Montesquieu had also identified as the "spring" of republics a quality he called "virtue," by which he meant a willingness to subordinate one's private good to the public good, or rather a dominant identification of one's own good with the public good (*SL* III:2; IV:5–8; V:1–7). The good republican citizen had no good other than the public good—that at least was the heroic ideal of republicanism, an ideal to which the ordeal of the revolutionary struggle gave life and meaning.

Fused with these themes from Montesquieu were some others the French thinker had not emphasized. The Americans came to see the chief political problem as the potential oppressiveness of government. They came to see the chief solution to that problem in a robust kind of political responsibility.[11] Rulers needed to be controlled, and this meant they were to be subjected to electoral control through frequent elections and short terms of office. They were not to be trusted with large powers and independent range of action. They were to be kept as much like the citizenry as a whole as possible. They were not to make political service into careers—they were to "rotate" in office through term limits, and they were to return to the population at large before they developed an attachment to their authority and a sense of themselves as somehow different. Men love power and are too easily corrupted by it. The Americans recognized that direct democracy was impossible in the states that they had, but they accepted representation as a necessary evil at best. This meant, among other things, large governing bodies, so that the differences in the community could be readily contained in the government; but even more, it meant commitment to social homogeneity so that all the people had roughly the same interests and that the convergence between private and public interest could be easy to effectuate. This desire for homogeneity reinforced the commitment to small size.

This second model can fruitfully be conceived of as "short-leash republicanism": the main theme in constitution making was devising multiple and redundant ways of keeping governors on a short leash. It can also be thought of as a "no-gap polity." The central idea was not to have gaps, either within the society (i.e., all were to have the same interests so far as possible) or between government and society. The development of an identity and interests separate from the people—that is, gaps—appeared to be the source of all political evil.

Madison's understanding of the requirements posed by the truths of political philosophy led him to see that both models, the Montesquieuean free constitution and the short-leash republic, were unacceptable. He found the Montesquieuean free constitution impossible for America, not only because America lacked the raw materials for it (having no hereditary aristocracy and no royal line) but even more decisively because hereditary power of any sort was inherently illegitimate. The free constitution did not satisfy the requirement that government be wholly republican through drawing all its power directly or indirectly from the people. The short-leash model failed as well. It could not satisfy two other of the principled requirements Madison accepted. For one, Madison understood that government had to be strong enough and effective enough to protect rights, although not so strong and uncontrolled as to endanger rights itself. The short-leash model took one-half of this task seriously—attempting to protect the populace from government—but it failed to take seriously the other and primary task—the construction of government able to do what governments existed to do. Madison also recognized the complexity of the task of rights-securing deriving from the dual character of rights and the unequal distribution of one kind of property (material) coupled with the equal distribution of the other kind (rights). The no-gap theory failed to recognize the complexity of rights or the two sorts of property, and it therefore failed to build in proper devices for safeguarding the rights of all. As Madison famously argued in *The Federalist* no. 10, the small republics the short-leashers had established in the states tended to degenerate into tyrannies by the majorities that controlled them. Montesquieu's free constitution did a far better job of protecting the full range of rights, for it built in a separate part of the legislature for the holders of each type of property. In general, the Montesquieuean free constitution was superior to the short-leash model on all grounds except the fundamental criterion that legitimacy required republicanism.

Madison's political science, then, attempts to find a way to achieve all that Montesquieu's free constitution achieves on the sole basis of republican or popular government. This effort led him to reject nearly everything in the short-leash model except the very commitment to republicanism itself. It led him to reject nearly everything about the workings, although not the aims, of the free constitution as well. This last is crucial to understanding Madison, for at least since Charles Beard the claim has been raised that Madison sought to evade or overcome democracy.[12] It is true that Madison sought to evade or overcome some of the potential ill-effects of democracy, not because he was an antidemocrat but because he was so thoroughly committed to democracy (or republicanism).

We have already noticed Madison's definition of republicanism. His is a much more popular or democratic definition than was current in his day. Montesquieu, for example, considered hereditary aristocratic regimes to be republics, and it was common usage to call all nonmonarchical regimes republics. Madison denies the label "republic" to regimes with any element of hereditary authority; and he moves even further in the popular direction by insisting that all governing powers must be derived directly or indirectly from the great body of the people and that all must serve either for a set term or be removable for misbehavior in office. According to Madison's definition of republic, political authority is thoroughly *public* in character—no one has any private or personal claim of any sort to it, and the people must ultimately appoint and be able to remove all their governors.

Madison's definition of republic is much less democratic, however, than the definition later proffered by his friend and colleague, Jefferson. "Were I to assign to this term republicanism a precise and definite idea, I would say, purely and simply, it means a government by its citizens, acting directly and personally; . . . the further the departure from direct and constant control by the citizens, the less has the government of the ingredient of republicanism."[13] Jefferson insists on direct and immediate involvement of the people, while Madison accepts indirect and ultimate derivation from the people. The two friends and political allies split over whether the substantive end of politics ("to secure these rights") or the processual means ("consent of the governed") had primacy. Madison was also more alive to the array of purposes a properly constructed political system must fulfill, and he saw that republican government could be constructed in such a way as to fulfill successfully that broad array of ends only on the basis of his somewhat laxer definition of republic. Jefferson's more strenuous definition would make impossible many of the devices Madison thought essential to constructing a free constitution on a republican basis. Jefferson was more like the Anti-Federalists: he feared the oppressive potentiality of power, and he sought to keep it tightly checked by the people, whose original rights were both the source and the purpose of government.

Even with his relatively laxer definition of republic, Madison well understood that his project of a free constitution on wholly republican grounds would be extremely difficult to achieve. As he thought about this problem, he was led to formulate with greater comprehensiveness than the short-leash republicans ever did and with greater explicitness than Montesquieu what the operational qualities of an effective and legitimate political system must be. His best formulation of these qualities occurred in the extraordinary *The Federalist* no. 37. In that essay, Madison speaks of the difficulties the Constitutional Convention faced in trying to draft a constitution. The most fundamental of those difficulties stemmed from the facts that the qualities good governments must have are multiple and complex and, he showed clearly, the arrangements which produce one quality tend to undermine the others. The requirements are not only complex, but somehow incompatible, or at least in tension with one another and with republicanism. In *The Federalist* no. 37, Madison identifies three different requirements of good government—energy, stability, and republican liberty. These are among the requisites of any government that can fulfill the tasks posed by political philosophy.

Madison is quite insistent that energy is "essential" to government. It is the capacity to act with decision and effectiveness. Having laws is not enough—the laws must be executed, and energy is the quality that facilitates "prompt and salutary execution of the laws." Without government, political philosophy says, rights are insecure. Government supplies not only the standing rules around which individuals structure their behavior but the "teeth" that get people to follow those rules. If voluntary compliance were sufficient, as short-leash republicans sometimes seemed to believe, then government itself would not be necessary. In emphasizing energy as a requisite of government, Madison was recognizing and carrying to a higher degree of explicitness an insight present in Montesquieu's treatment of the executive as a separate "power," deriving its legitimacy and strength from its royal character (*FP* 37:233).

Madison also identifies stability as a requisite of good government. By stability, Madison means a high degree of continuity of the laws governing behavior. People do not respect laws that constantly change, and they cannot lead successful lives for themselves in an environment in which the legal structure is unstable (see *FP* 49; *PJM* 13:18–21). Instability of law prevents people from planning for the future, and in the middle run stultifies liberty and initiative: people will not undertake long-term projects if there is no reasonable prospect that the environment will remain stable enough for them to see those projects through to reap their fruits.

The final criterion Madison identifies in *The Federalist* no. 37 is republican liberty. Madison here refers to the ability of the people to keep government under control and checked—to prevent it from being dangerous to them. Madison also referred to this requirement as "safety." This criterion is clearly a direct implicate of the three tasks political philosophy sets for political science, and the one that short-leash republicans most clearly appreciated.

These requirements of good governments are not only multiple and therefore complex, but they appear to be conflicting. Safety, Madison says, seems to require weak government—with weak powers, with many governors, with short terms of office, term limits, and other such devices to facilitate popular control and to hinder the opening of gaps between rulers and ruled.

Energy, on the other hand, requires strong powers with few officers wielding power, while stability requires consistency of policy and therefore long terms of office, and perhaps an intermediate number of officeholders, since both large and very small bodies tend to be quite changeable.

The short-leash republicans focused more or less exclusively on only one of these requirements (safety), and in their proposals for political institutions, they built exclusively with that requirement in mind. They were too simplistic, and Madison thought it no wonder that the political systems they had designed—the Articles of Confederation and the state governments —were not working well. Madison thus revised the accepted political science of the day by calling attention to the much greater range of qualities that governments must possess and, perhaps even more important, by showing the conflicting character of those requirements. The incompatibilities among the various requirements were so severe as to raise questions about whether any government could possibly satisfy all the criteria posed by political philosophy; the Montesquieuean free constitution came the closest, but it did so only on the basis of mixing in nonrepublican elements. The hereditary monarch and the hereditary upper legislative house were essential to the achievement of two of the goals Madison emphasizes in *The Federalist* no. 37, energy and stability. Without those nonrepublican elements, Madison had to wonder how a political structure could manage to combine the various qualities needed to achieve adequately strong and competent government.

The commitment to wholly republican systems also rendered questionable the ability of government to achieve the other tasks set by the principles of political philosophy. The difficulty can be stated in a number of different ways. On the one hand, there were the two sides of property—property as personal rights and property as external goods. To place political power in the hands of the "great body of the people" might seem a fairly reliable way to produce at least the political will to support and protect the personal rights that were universally shared by all. But it was not as likely to produce a will seeking to protect property in external goods, rights equally requiring respect and protection. Madison believed that the history of America in the short time since independence illustrated what the entire history of popular republics showed: that the rights of property were ill-served, with the result not only of the direct commission of injustices but also the production of intense struggle and factional disorder. The ultimate result in the course of history was frequently the loss of republican liberty and the discouragement of the exercise of the unequal faculties of individuals on which the flourishing of human communities ultimately depends (see *FP* 10). In Montesquieu's model of a free constitution, the complex task of securing property (in the extended sense) was achieved via the admixture of nonpopular, hereditary or self-selecting elements. The aristocratic upper house could be counted on to protect rights to property (in the narrow sense) as a complement to the democratic lower house, which would be solicitous of personal rights (property in the extended sense).

Madison's problem could be stated more generally as well. He was not concerned solely about the propertied but about any minority in a majority rule system. As he insisted at the Constitutional Convention, divisions can occur on many grounds other than wealth and property interests. Regionalism and religion, for instance, are two such bases of division. "In all cases where a majority are united by a common interest or passion, the rights of the minority are in danger" (*MF* 101). Montesquieu's free constitution does not have entirely reliable means of securing the rights of minorities of these sorts, but the role of the monarch offers some promise of doing so. The monarch stands above the factional elements in society and therefore has a certain independence from them. The monarch has, moreover, an incentive to look with an impartial eye over the various interests and factions in the community and has some incentive to consider himself the neutral protector of the rights of all. The monarch, possessing a veto power in the legislature, has the capacity, both in terms of power and position, and some incentive to act the part of protector of the rights of minorities generally. The wholly republican system lacks any such "will independent of society" (see *FP* 51).

The short-leash republicans had no solution to this problem—indeed, they were not really aware of it as a problem. The division they were most concerned about was between government and society, or between rulers and ruled. The danger they focused on was oppression of the latter by the former. The solution they favored was to keep rulers like the ruled and controlled by the ruled. Two of Madison's most characteristic insights challenged the main elements of this short-leash approach. Madison insisted that their analysis of society and social dynamics was naively inadequate and ultimately dangerous. As he said at the Convention in an analysis he would expand into his famous argument in *The Federalist* no. 10: "All civilized societies would be divided into different sects, factions, and interests, as they happened to consist of rich and poor, debtors and creditors, the landed, the manufacturing, the commercial interests, the inhabitants of this district, or that district, the followers of this political leader or that political leader, the disciples of this religious sect or that religious sect" (*MF* 101; cf. 89). In all his formulations of this point, Madison emphasized its applicability to "civilized societies"; these are societies marked by (relatively) secure property holdings, the progressive development of arts and sciences, increase of population, and a general increase in the degree of division of labor and specialization present in the society. Civilized societies are anything but homogeneous in composition and interest. The short-leash theory ignored this aspect of civilization and divided-ness within society to concentrate on the dividedness between society and governing authorities, proceeding as though society could be taken as one undifferentiated and homogenous mass over and against government. So far as they were aware of the possibilities of differentiation within society, they sought to keep society small and relatively simple in order to minimize those divisions.

Madison considered the typical short-leash institutional responses to be wholly inadequate. The effort to prevent the emergence of social differentiation through engineered homogeneity would not work, and in any case it would require a suppression of the forces that produced differentiation—the free use of human faculties. Moreover, the typical short-leash republican prescription for the tight control of government by society exacerbates the problem; the ideal short-leash outcome has government reflecting and embodying exactly the array of forces in society, with the result that if there is a majority with an interest in oppressing some minority, that majority will face no barriers whatever to its enterprises. In his memorandum on "Vices of the Political System of the U.S.," Madison pointed out that in "republican government the majority, however composed, ultimately give the law. Whenever . . . an apparent interest or common passion unites a majority," he asks, "what is to restrain therefore unjust violations of the rights and interests of the minority, of individuals?" (*MF* 89). He has little confidence in moral and religious self-restraint to inhibit the self-interested action of ruling majorities (*MF* 89–91). The short-leash approach can at best solve one part of the problem of oppression: majorities can protect themselves against minorities. But the short-leash approach could not alleviate the dangers of majority tyranny, which, it should be clear, is the chief danger in Madison's eyes precisely because this is a republican (that is, majority rule) system. As Madison once wrote to Jefferson:

> Wherever the real power in a Government lies, there is the danger of oppression. In our Govern-ments the real power lies in the majority of the community, and the invasion of private rights is *chiefly* to be apprehended, not from acts of Government contrary to the sense of its constituents, but from acts in which the Government is the mere instrument of the major number of the Constituents.

Madison understood how much he was overturning reigning opinion in America with this view. "This is a truth of great importance, but not yet sufficiently attended to. . . . Wherever there is an interest and power to do wrong, wrong will generally be done, and not less readily by a powerful and interested party than by a powerful and interested prince" (*MF* 206–7).

The tasks imposed by the principles of political philosophy would be very difficult to accomplish on a wholly republican basis, and the approaches prevalent in eighteenth-century America could not possibly succeed. Madison's greatness as a political scientist lay in his success at figuring out a solution to this set of apparently insoluble conundrums. The general line of his solution was the exact opposite of the short-leash republicans: he sought to construct what we might call a "gappy republic"—that is, a structure embodying, encouraging, and exploiting the very distancing of governors from governed that the short-leash model strove to avoid.

The role of gaps and of Madison's less stringent definition of republicanism are visible in his proposals for satisfying the first requisite of building a free constitution: a free constitution requires separate powers. Montesquieu had argued that it is not sufficient merely to have separate governing institutions: these must also derive from different constituencies or else they will not be truly independent. He gave the example of the republic of Venice, which had separate institutions, but where all officeholders were selected by the same body and responsible to it. The selecting body was able to exercise great control over the allegedly separate and independent institutions, thus overcoming informally but effectively the official or formal separation. Montesquieu had, of course, solved this problem via his recourse to the "mixed regime" model overlaid on the separation of powers.

The Montesquieuean solution was foreclosed to Madison, but he began his constitutional thinking in a very orthodoxly Montesquieuean manner: a free constitution requires separation of powers, and thus one of the unshakeable pillars of Madison's political science was the need, even in a republic, to have separate legislative, executive, and judicial branches. This was a major break with the structure prevalent theretofore in the government of the Union under the Articles of Confederation, which had but one branch, a legislature. To decree separate powers was easy enough, but to make them genuinely separate was much more difficult under the constraint imposed by the all-republican rule. Madison's first answer was to attempt to derive the different powers so far as possible from different constituencies, or to make them responsible in different ways to the same constituency. Thus, in his original planning for a new constitution, he would have the lower house of the legislature elected directly by the people, as the House of Commons was. As he said at the Constitutional Convention, he "considered the popular election of one branch of the national legislature as essential to every plan of free government."[14]

The way in which Madison's political science modified both the chief models of his day is visible in such a small detail as the composition of the lower house. In Britain the members of the Commons sat for no set term; parliamentary elections were called instead by the king. This royal power, of course, was a tool the king used to extend his influence into the legislature and thus was a weapon in overcoming the separation of powers. Madison instead projected a set term of office for representatives far more in line with the prevalent arrangement in the short-leash model. Madison further republicanized the lower house by seeking a much shorter term of office than the maximum possible under the British system.

Relative to the Montesquieuean model, Madison's plan was more republican. Relative to the short-leash model, however, it was much "gappier." Where he favored three-year terms, the short-leash preference was for substantially shorter terms, in part to facilitate popular control over the legislature and, even more important, to prevent legislators from coming to think of themselves as different and separate from their constituents. Thus, the short-leash model favored one year or in some cases even six-month terms of office. A favorite motto of the day was:

"Where annual elections end, there tyranny begins." To this short term was frequently added rotation. The purpose of this was much the same as the short terms—to prevent the emergence of gaps.

Where the short-leash model sought to foreclose gaps, Madison attempted to build them in. The three-year term he sought would indeed make the representatives different from the ordinary citizen in many ways, but these differences would be all to the good. "Instability, is one of the great vices of our republics, to be remedied. Three years will be necessary, in a government so extensive, for members to form any knowledge of the various interests of the states to which they do not belong. . . . One year will be almost consumed in preparing for and traveling to and from the seat of national business."[15] Madison hoped, furthermore, that the longer term and the possibility of indefinite reelectability would work a change in the psychological identifications and aims of representatives. One need, relating to the federal more than the republican character of the new constitution, was for representatives to identify with the government of the Union rather than with that of the states from which they hailed. The fact that they could make careers in the Union government could attach them to it and to the enterprise of making that government strong, effective, and able to resist the centrifugal forces applied constantly by the states. Madison, moreover, tried to show the short-leash republicans that their goal of maintaining popular (republican) control over government was facilitated, not opposed, by the judicious use of gaps. For example, he favored the indefinite reeligibility of representatives, which would indeed allow those who stood for office to think of themselves as professional politicians seeking a career in public office. That would work beneficially, however, for it would give them both an opportunity and an incentive to attend to the views and the good of their constituents. The possibility of a career in Congress would make them more, not less, responsive to the people in whose hands their future prospects lay.[16]

The other essential part of a free constitution, the upper house, must also be republican; but it cannot be drawn from or be responsible to the same constituency as the lower house or else it will not be sufficiently independent in its action and operation. The original Madisonian solution, as embodied in the Virginia Plan, provided for election by the lower house, but the candidates for election would be nominated by the state legislatures and could not be members of the lower house, nor for that matter hold any other office in either the state or the Union governments. These provisions are attempts to make the upper house separate and independent of the lower house, but the election by the lower house itself shows how much the requirement of a completely republican system limits the options. Madison believed that the indirect election of the upper house was conformable to republican principle and that, strange to say, election by the lower house under the terms proposed would produce an upper house more independent of the lower house than would popular election. That independence could accrue only if the term of office were very long. Madison favored seven years: by the time a member of the upper house came up for reelection, he would have been in office a long time without having to answer directly to his constituents (the lower house and the state legislators), and, in that time, there would have been two elections to the lower house (under the three-year term contemplated at the time), making likely a turnover in personnel such that the lower house would not well be able to impose any close control over members of the upper house. In some respects, selection by the states, as was ultimately provided for by the Constitution, was better at making the upper house independent of the lower; but for reasons having to do with his attempts to curb the ability of the states to interfere with the general government, Madison did not at first favor this expedient. In any case, it is clear that Madison is relying here on gappiness to achieve separate and independent powers.

The free constitution must also conduce to competent governance. Madison stressed how multifarious and problematic the combination of qualities was that together added up to competence. Montesquieu had solved the problem, so far as it could be solved, with his overlay of a mixed regime model on the separation of powers. Madison attempted to mimic the effect of the mixed regime model by designing into the separation of powers scheme institutional features that would encourage the behavior the mixed regime model produced in its very different manner. The mixed regime model was, in its own way, a no-gap system, for it attempted to bring into government different elements of society that would operate in the government as they would on the basis of their pregovernmental social and personal qualities. Thus, the upper house would be composed of aristocratic and wealthy men, members of old families of great standing in the community. The monarchy would be held by a member of the royal family, in the best case well established, with a long history and the prospect of a long future. The king and his family would stand so far above the rest of society as to supply a certain neutrality and legitimacy to its actions.

Madison could rely on none of this. There could be no governance by "estates" and select families. The institutions themselves had to produce the behaviors required by the system. The ways in which this happens was the chief subject of the extensive discussions of each branch in *The Federalist*, which can only be briefly discussed here. One of the greatest needs for competent governance, as Madison described those needs in *The Federalist* no. 37, was for energy, coupled with stability and republican responsibility. Madison's first insight (probably taken from Montesquieu) was that the different institutions of the separation of powers scheme could be differently constructed to produce different institutional competencies. Energy requires unity and a top-down mode of authority. The executive can be constructed in this way, although in the American context there were great barriers to doing so, the chief being the fear of monarchy and the suspicion that a unitary executive could be "the fetus of monarchy," as was often said at the Constitutional Convention. Stability has other requirements, which came to be met through the structure of the Senate, while the chief seat for meeting the requirement of republican liberty would be the House of Representatives. All of these efforts to construct institutions with differential modes of operation and specialized competencies depended on deploying the kind of gappiness the short-leash republicans abhorred. They distrusted concentrated power and they disliked long terms of office, so they debarred themselves at the outset from constructing institutions with the necessary qualities.

The free constitution required a way of keeping the powers separate. Officeholders needed both the ability (sufficient powers) and the motives to resist encroachments by other branches. The former required defensive powers the branches could use to check encroachments by the others. Madison believed the greatest danger of encroachment derived from the legislature, a conclusion Montesquieu shared, but one which Madison saw to be much greater in a republic where the legislature had the deepest and most immediate ties to the people. Madison then saw that the integrity of the free constitution depended on building in checks against the legislature above all. His preferred check was a Council of Revision, a body composed of the executive and some of the judges which could exercise a veto power over the legislature. The two together would have both the strength and the separate competencies to exercise well the veto power. The Council of Revision violated several principles of short-leash republicanism. Most important, it gave this very potent power to the two institutions of government most distant from the community, because of the indirect appointment of both and their long tenure in office, especially of the judges. It also violated the doctrinaire (and erroneous) interpretation of the doctrine of separation of powers held by many devotees of short-leash republicanism, for here was a clear case where the powers were being mixed in what appears anomalous ways—the executive and judiciary sharing in the legislative power. Of course, that had already been the case in Montesquieu's classic formulation of separation of powers theory.

Madison also had to oppose the no-gap principles of short-leash republicanism in developing a way to supply the motives for maintaining the separation of powers. In direct opposition to the no-gap principles, Madison famously said:

> [T]he great security against a gradual concentration of the several powers in the same department, consists in giving to those who administer each department, the necessary constitutional means, and personal motives, to resist encroachments. . . . Ambition must be made to counteract ambition. The interest of the man must be connected to the constitutional rights of the place. (*FP* 51:349)

Rather than countering personal ambition and separate interest, Madison would indulge it and then use it to good effect. If the officeholders value their offices and find in them avenues for the satisfaction of their own ambitions and interests they will act to protect their offices against those who would diminish them. Officers of the general government will defend the Union from encroachments by the states; senators will defend against encroachments by the representatives; and the executive and judiciary will defend against encroachments by the legislature. This self-interested behavior, on its face so contrary to the short-leash demand for virtuous or purely public interested behavior, actually conduces more to the public benefit than cooler, less self-interested behavior would. Madison, in this regard like Machiavelli, shows that the less elevated but more reliable self-interested passions, if properly channeled, produce not only more reliable but on the whole better results than behavior better motivated.

The most difficult problem Madison thought he faced was one that short-leash republicans thought they had most completely solved. If government operates in the no-gap manner, they thought, it might possibly not work wisely, but it would operate with a good will—that is, it would will the public good, for the will of the whole society would be expressed in it. Madison, to the contrary, saw here the danger of injustice in addition to incompetence. He recognized that all societies—and especially modern "civilized," commercial societies—are internally heterogeneous, with different interests marking different groups in society. Following Montesquieu again, he appreciated the paradox of political life: politics may benefit all, but it benefits some more than others, and much of politics involves a struggle among competing groups for the differential benefits of social and political life (*SL* I:3; *FP* 10). So fierce can this struggle become that the genuine common good is frequently lost sight of and endangered because of it. Majorities, Madison insisted, can be equally as bent on unjustly taking advantage of others as any minority in society. Republican government arms majorities—whether just or unjust—with power to transform their unbridled aims into law.

In a letter to George Washington on the eve of the Constitutional Convention, Madison laid out the issue with his usual perspicacity and concision. "The great desideratum, which has not yet been found for Republican Governments, seems to be some disinterested and dispassionate umpire in disputes between different passions and interests in the State. The majority who alone have the right of decision, have frequently an interest, real or supposed, in abusing it" (*MF* 96). The degree to which Madison's thinking on this was shaped by Montesquieu's earlier efforts to grapple with it is visible in his grasp of how the problem is soluble in nonrepublican regimes: "In absolute monarchies the prince is sufficiently neutral toward his subjects, but frequently sacrifices their happiness to his ambition or his avarice. In small republics, the sovereign will is sufficiently controuled from such a sacrifice of the entire society, but is not sufficiently neutral towards the parts composing it" (*MF* 91). The Montesquieuean solution Madison sees is the combination of the two pure forms—"a limited monarchy tempers the evils of an absolute one."

The "limited monarchy," constructed like England, combines the kingly and the popular forms so that the king's neutrality counters the popular partiality, and popular control counters royal irresponsibility. The Montesquieuean mixed regime can succeed as the republic by itself cannot.

Madison's most famous innovation—the idea of the extended republic—is his attempt to supply a wholly republican solution to this problem hitherto soluble only on nonrepublican grounds. The theory of the extended republic is not only the most famous but the most misunderstood of all the elements of Madison's political science, as is visible in how he describes it in his memorandum on the "Vices" of politics in America: "As a limited monarchy tempers the evils of an absolute one; so an extensive Republic meliorates the administration of a small Republic." Just as the "limited monarchy" combines the absolute monarchy and the republic, so Madison seeks to combine the extended and the small republic.

Appreciating his analysis here requires familiarity with a proposal he was promoting assiduously before and at the Convention. He sought to arm the general government with certain positive powers to carry out the rather limited but very important business entrusted to that government; he sought to include "over and above this positive power, a negative *in all cases whatsoever* on the legislative acts of the states, as heretofore exercised by the kingly prerogative." He considered this extraordinary power to be "absolutely necessary" not only to protect the government of the Union from state encroachments but even more importantly to put some "controul on the internal vicissitudes of state policy, and the aggressions of interested majorities on the rights of minorities and of individuals" (*MF* 96). The constitutional scheme Madison projects mimics the Montesquieuean model by combining the Congress of the government of the Union, playing the part of the monarch, but being itself a republican body, with the small republics of the states, playing the part of Parliament.

This proposal is premised on the assumption that most of the significant governance that concerns the rights and interests of individuals and groups will be conducted in the states. The congressional involvement is to embody monarchical neutrality and to exercise the monarchical veto. The goal is neutrality or fair "umpiring," namely, umpiring that pays attention to the true rights and interests of the parties involved, a practice not to be relied on from the partisans directly involved in the conflicts.

The obvious question, however, is why should Madison expect Congress, an elected majoritarian body, to be more neutral and fairer than the state legislatures? Madison has two answers: one simpler, the other a bit more complex. The simpler answer is this: the larger the unit, the more different interests are likely to exist within it and thus to find representation in a republican legislature. Relative to the interests present in any given state legislature, the number of interests present in Congress is likely to be much greater. An interest that makes up a majority faction within a state is unlikely to do so within Congress. The parties most present in any given state are likely to be a small part of Congress and therefore likely to be greatly outnumbered by congressmen more or less neutral and uninvolved in the division of interests within the state. Thus, the large republic of the Union can reproduce the neutrality of the monarch and can (under Madison's proposed veto power) intervene in the states to prevent the dominance there of unjust and overbearing majorities.

The more complex mechanism involves the replacement of natural majorities by artificial or constructed majorities. In a small, relatively undifferentiated society, there is a greater likelihood that there will exist a "natural majority"—that is, a set (or sets) of interests that naturally amount to a majority of the politically empowered population and thus of the republican legislature. In a larger, more heterogeneous society, it is much less likely that majorities will exist naturally; most interests will be distinct minorities. But governance requires majorities in the large as much as in the small republic; majorities will now have to be constructed or put together from the smaller packets of interested minorities.

In *The Federalist* no. 51, Madison makes one of his most telling but also important claims: "In the extended republic of the United States, and among the great variety of interests, parties and sects which it embraces, a coalition of a majority of the whole society could seldom take place upon any other principles than those of justice and the general good" (353). Madison is not looking to a stalemate system where no majorities can form, or to rule by minorities, as many of his interpreters believe, but rather to a process that almost by magic allows only good majorities to form. How can that be? Madison has in mind here the difference in character between natural and constructed majorities. Natural majorities have an immediate interest in common and are able to translate it, more or less unmodified, into law. Where there is no natural majority, however, the preexisting interests must undergo a process of transformation before they can become a majority. Common ground must be found on which the different interests can coalesce. That requires transformation and modification of the original interests in the direction of finding broader kinds of commonality. The process of majority construction leads to a search for common ground that approaches something like a common good and a more neutral stance than any of the parties began with. There are, moreover, moderating effects imposed by the process of coalition formation in a system of fragmented interests. Coalition forming is not likely to be a once and for all matter; majorities are likely to be fluid and changing. Today's coalition partner is very possibly tomorrow's coalition opposition—and vice versa. Parties and interests come to view each other as long-run potential majority partners and recognize their mutual interest in treating each other moderately and fairly. Madison recognized that he overstated the case when he said that the majorities would seek only justice and the common good, but he had a serious point beneath his hyperbole. The process pushes parties toward justice and the common good in a way that majority rule in small republics does not. The large republic is thus likely to have better majorities, and the congressional power to negate state laws provides a rough equivalent to the monarch's neutrality and fairness on a completely republican basis. All this is possible only on the basis of the "gappiness" Madison builds into his institutional science.

Madison was not able to convince his fellow convention delegates to adopt several of the most central parts of his plan; the Council of Revision and the congressional negative over state laws were particularly irksome losses and led to his skepticism over the likely longevity of the Constitution the Convention proposed. The loss of these features, together with an overemphasis on *The Federalist*, has, for the most part, prevented us from grasping the full scope or character of the Madisonian political science.

Notes

1. John Locke, "Some Thoughts Concerning Reading and Study for a Gentleman," in *Political Essays*, ed. Mark Goldie (Cambridge: Cambridge University Press, 1997), 351–52.

2. Thomas Jefferson to Thomas Mann Randolph, May 30, 1790, in *Life and Selected Writings*, ed. Adrienne Koch and William Peden (New York: Modern Library, 1944), 496–97.

3. James Madison to Thomas Jefferson, September 6, 1787, in *The Papers of James Madison*, ed. Robert A. Rutland et al. (Charlottesville: University Press of Virginia, 1984), 9:162–64, hereafter cited in the text as *PJM*.

4. On Madison's new federalism, see Michael P. Zuckert, "A System without Precedent," in *The Framing and Ratification of the Constitution*, ed. Leonard Levy and Dennis Mahoney (New York: MacMillan, 1988).

5. Jefferson to Henry Lee, May 8, 1825, in *Writings*, ed. Merrill Peterson (New York: Library of America, 1984), 1501.

6. *The Mind of the Founder: Sources of the Political Thought of James Madison*, ed. Marvin Meyers (Indianapolis: Bobbs-Merrill Co., 1973), 215, hereafter cited in the text as *MF*. Much of the actual language Madison uses here comes from the Virginia Constitution and Bill of Rights, a document from which Jefferson also borrowed heavily when he wrote the Declaration. See Pauline Maier, *American Scripture: Making the Declaration of Independence* (New York: Alfred A. Knopf, 1997), 125–28.

7. Alexander Hamilton, James Madison, and John Jay, *The Federalist*, ed. Jacob E. Cooke (Middletown, Conn.: Wesleyan University Press, 1961), no. 39, 251, hereafter cited in the text as *FP* (e.g., *FP* 39:251).

8. See Locke, *Second Treatise*, chap. 10, sec. 132; William Blackstone, *Commentary on the Laws of England* (Chicago: University of Chicago Press, 1979), bk. I, chap. 3; and Montesquieu, *The Spirit of the Laws*, trans. Anne Cohler, Basia Miller, and Harold Stone (Cambridge: Cambridge University Press, 1989), bk. XI, chap. 6, hereafter cited in the text as *SL*.

9. In *The Federalist* no. 47, 324, Madison expresses the Montesquieuean idea very clearly: "The accumulation of all powers legislative, executive and judiciary in the same hands, whether of one, a few or many, and whether hereditary, self appointed, or elective, may justly be pronounced the very definition of tyranny."

10. The Montesquieuean separation is thus particularly aimed at taming the executive. See Harvey C. Mansfield, *Taming the Prince* (New York: The Free Press, 1989), 213–46.

11. These themes are best developed in the writings of the Anti-Federalists. For a representative sampling, see *The Anti-Federalist: Writings by the Opponents of the Constitution*, ed. Herbert J. Storing and Murray Dry (Chicago: University of Chicago Press, 1985).

12. Charles Beard, *An Economic Interpretations of the Constitution* (New York: Macmillan and Co., 1935); Richard K. Matthews, *If Men Were Angels* (Lawrence: University Press of Kansas, 1995).

13. Jefferson to John Taylor, May 28, 1816, in *Writings*, 1392–93.

14. Madison, Speech in the Constitutional Convention, May 31, 1787, in *The Records of the Federal Convention of 1787*, ed. Max Farrand (New Haven, Conn.: Yale University Press, 1937), I:49.

15. Farrand, *Records*, I:214.

16. Cf. Resolution 4 of the Virginia Plan with the action of the Convention on June 12 (Farrand, *Records*, I:20, 217).

Chapter 9

Alexander Hamilton on the Strategy of American Free Government

Karl-Friedrich Walling

Alexander Hamilton (1757–1804) appears in many extreme guises in the history of American political thought. In the various records of the Federal Convention of 1787, he sometimes comes off as both a critic of republics who leaned in the direction of monarchy and as a governmental centralizer willing even to abolish the states, if such measures had been politically feasible at the time.[1] For egalitarian liberals of the twentieth century, he seemed to be the arrogant defender of privilege and the first great champion of unbridled capitalism. For contemporary conservatives with a libertarian streak, however, he looks like an advocate of economic planning. For strict constructionists of all stripes, his broad reading of the Constitution appears to lead directly to unlimited government, backed by an unaccountable judiciary and headed by an uncontrollable executive. Paradoxically, Hamilton often seemed to advocate both an ultramodern ethic of self-interest and an old-fashioned aristocratic vision of the life of honor. Hence, in recent times, he has become something of a bogeyman in the eyes of liberals and conservatives alike as they have become increasingly concerned with an alternative ethic of self-sacrificing civic virtue that they hope to find in the thought of other Founders.[2] To both Thomas Jefferson and John Adams, Hamilton looked like an American Caesar, Cromwell, and Napoleon all rolled into one. Not surprisingly, then, at the height of the Vietnam War, when some blamed that tragedy on what they called "militarism," Hamilton was even considered the "most dangerous man" of America's Founding era because of his supposed eagerness to use force to settle disputes with opponents at home and abroad.[3] For all these reasons, Hamilton has had few champions in his country. Even on Wall Street, the financial dynamo for which Hamilton perhaps deserves most credit, his name is rarely heard.

What accounts for the almost universal distrust—if not even loathing—of Hamilton by both the Right and the Left in America? Hamilton was no saint, especially within his marriage. Sometimes, too, he displayed a glaring lack of political judgment and self-mastery. By proposing energetic institutions at the Federal Convention of 1787 far beyond what Americans could tolerate, he did little but ensure that his political opponents would have a ready weapon with which to vilify him as a closet monarchist—or still worse, as an advocate of despotism. By attacking the president, John Adams, a leader of his own party, in print shortly before the critical election of 1800, he made public fissures within the Federalist party that may well have contributed to its defeat by Thomas Jefferson and the Republicans. Perhaps the primary reason for Hamilton's enduring unpopularity, however, is his moderation—not about everything, but about one big thing: the problem of waging war effectively and remaining free at the same time. His understanding of that problem and the range of solutions for addressing it have been vindicated so often in the course of his nation's history that his critics have been forced to eat their words and embrace Hamiltonian institutions. Thus, for example, in the aftermath of humiliating American defeats during the War of 1812, both Thomas Jefferson and James Madison reluctantly came to support a national bank, a professional army, an oceangoing navy, and an energetic executive (all of which they once decried as dangerous to liberty) as the best means for Americans to provide for their defense and freedom. Thus, Hamilton's program to build a mighty but free nation survived his departure from political power and influence—although ironically, the program was implemented by his greatest political adversaries.

Hamilton's greatest priority was to enable his adopted country to defend itself against all enemies, foreign and domestic, while retaining the freedoms he had fought for as a soldier of the American Revolution. This moderation arose from Hamilton's realism about both the value and limits of political theories in a warlike world. He distrusted both those he regarded as overly theoretical in their approach to practical politics (like John Adams and Thomas Jefferson) and those who seemed to make a virtue out of having no theoretical principles at all (like Aaron Burr). By situating himself between what he regarded as impractical ideologues and unprincipled pragmatists, he sought to reconcile the new American principles of universal liberty with the older practice of statecraft, especially as that craft pertained to war. From the beginning of the American Revolution until the little known Quasi-War with France in 1798, he believed his countrymen had erred so much in the direction of suspicion of power that they forgot the necessity of establishing formidable military power to win and preserve their independence. If there is such a thing as an American way of war, in which Americans mobilize seemingly unlimited resources to overwhelm their adversaries, that strategic bent originates in the mind of Hamilton more than anyone else. Not surprisingly, then, he is one of the few Americans, and the only American Founder, commonly studied in histories of strategic thought.[4] During the Quasi-War, however, he began to fear that his own party, the Federalists, had confused the energy necessary to any effective government with suppression of political opposition. After the election of 1800, he also began to fear similar extremism from Jefferson's party. Thus, in the first, longest, and most innovative part of his career, he advocated an ethic of responsibility in government to curb the excesses of revolutionary vigilance, or jealousy of power. In the last years of his career, however, he called for greater vigilance to check those in Jefferson's administration whom he believed were using power irresponsibly.

A case could be made that this change of tack resulted more from necessity than principle. Nonetheless, Hamilton in his youth, before he became a soldier, often sounded like his ever-vigilant political opponents in their maturity. It could be that his opponents were right, that Hamilton became an apostate to the American Revolution. It might also be the case that Hamilton innovated within the American political tradition by finding new, better, and extremely durable means to combine the blessings of liberty with the common defense. Careful attention to what Hamilton said about war and freedom as a sixteen-year-old revolutionary may therefore help us understand what he was trying to say later in his career as the mature statesman who defended the Constitution of 1787; still later as the prime mover of the Washington administration in the early 1790s; and finally, as a Federalist party leader in the administrations of John Adams and Thomas Jefferson.

Revolutionary Constitutionalist

Hamilton's first political tracts, "A Full Vindication" (December 1774) and "The Farmer Refuted" (February 1775) were directed against a Tory minister in New York City, Samuel Seabury, who protested that recent measures by the Continental Congress calling for a boycott and embargo of British goods were both unjust toward England and imprudent for the Americans. Seabury thus compelled Hamilton to do what he did best: to argue at both the level of high principle and political prudence. Hamilton justified the boycott and embargo by arguing that British efforts to tax Americans without their consent violated the British constitution, New York's compact with the Crown, and the "natural rights of mankind," which he insisted, "are written, as with a sun beam, in the whole *volume* of human nature." In other words, though he made use of historical and legal authority to justify resistance to Parliament, he did not rest his argument ultimately on authority, but rather on nature. From the very beginning of his career, he insisted that power must be regulated by some form of higher law. He also insisted that no authority was legitimate unless it was rooted, directly or indirectly, in popular consent. Indeed, for Hamilton, it was the ability to consent to laws applying equally to every citizen that defined the difference between free and tyrannical governments, "for what original title can any man, or set of men have, to govern others, except their consent?" A free people, he warned, had to be ever vigilant against efforts to deny them of this most precious right, lest they lose their chief security against despotism. "Tell me not of the British Commons, Lords, ministry, ministerial tools, placemen, pensioners, parasites. I scorn to let my life depend on the pleasure of any of them." Instead, Hamilton wanted what virtually every other supporter of American rights demanded. "Give me the steady, uniform, unshaken security of constitutional freedom, give me a right to be tried by a jury of my own neighbors, and to be taxed by my representatives only."[5]

Hamilton had more difficulty proving that Congress's boycott and embargo were also prudent. To be good policy, Hamilton argued, the economic sanctions had to be clearly necessary; the good they sought to achieve had to outweigh the evils they might cause; and there had to be a probability of success. He believed the sanctions were clearly necessary because talk had proved cheap. Americans had been protesting to king and Parliament for over ten years with no result. Instead, each new effort to tax Americans without their consent, enforced by troops from England, the military occupation and government of Boston, and other outrages, seemed to evidence a "design" in England to deprive Americans of both their natural rights and their traditional rights as Englishmen. Hamilton believed that the good of the sanctions would outweigh the evil because liberty had an "infinite" value. It was both the necessary precondition of all other goods achievable for human beings and the property that most distinguished a human being from an animal. To lose this property, then, would be for Americans to sacrifice their very humanity. Hamilton was least convincing in shouldering his last burden of proof, that the sanctions were likely to succeed. Try as he might, he could not make a convincing argument that sanctions alone would hit the British hard enough in their pocketbooks to overcome the combination of pride and self-interest that seemed to be driving the mother country to rule its colonies despotically. One result of this difficulty was that, in contrast to Jefferson and Madison, who relied on sanctions as an alternative to developing military power during their presidencies, Hamilton never again argued that sanctions alone would suffice to secure American rights in competitions with other nations. He usually argued for using sanctions to signal American preparations for war, while also demanding that Americans build up the military so that they could negotiate from strength. Whether this change of approach arose from the failure of sanctions to influence England in 1775 is hard to say. It might well be the case that Hamilton, who is not usually said to have had a keen sense of public opinion, knew quite well that Americans could not secure their rights without gaining their independence, which would require a war; but he also knew that Americans would not go to war willingly until they had given all peaceful means, including sanctions, a chance to settle the dispute without violence. In other words, his political tracts may well have been less a defense of peaceful means of coercion than an effort to prepare public opinion for the very real possibility that once sanctions failed, they would have no alternative left but to go to war (*P* 1:51–58).

Shortly after writing these last ditch appeals for a peaceful settlement of America's quarrel with England, Hamilton joined the New York Artillery, in which he served as a captain. He soon attracted General Washington's attention for covering his retreat during the Continental army's humiliating defeat in New York in 1776, and he was invited to join Washington's staff. He rose rapidly to become a lieutenant colonel and a principal military and political adviser to Washington at the age of twenty-three, when he began to display an understanding of the relation between politics and strategy far beyond his years. Prior to the outbreak of the war, Hamilton seemed to believe that American victory would be easy, given American superiority in manpower in the theater and the ardor of Americans for liberty; but Washington's defeat in New York and many other defeats soon to follow led Hamilton to a fundamental change of mind. Superior resources and spirit mean little in war without effective means of mobilizing and employing them. Although the Americans had plenty of resources, Hamilton saw their soldiers die of hunger, cold, and sickness, and the army dwindle through desertion year after year while poorly trained and equipped militia fled at almost the first shot in major battles. Something was wrong with the way Americans had mobilized themselves for war.

In a famous letter from Washington's headquarters to his friend James Duane in 1780, Hamilton penned one of the first American calls for a new constitution to replace the wartime Articles of Confederation, which Hamilton considered "fit neither for war nor peace." Its most important flaw was that it did not give Congress sufficient power to raise troops and revenue to support the army in the field. Nor did the Articles establish executive departments to encourage members of Congress to take responsibility for logistics, finance, and foreign affairs. All of this, Hamilton believed, had led to a crisis of "confidence" in the army, in Congress, and among the people at large. The problem was not lack of popular affection for the patriot cause; instead, it was extreme doubt that the army could win victory on the field of battle, based on even graver doubts about the capacity of the government to support the army. A case in point was the continental currency, which became almost worthless by the end of the war because Congress, lacking power to raise funds on its own authority, had resorted to inflating the currency by printing ever more dollars. As Hamilton well knew, in the last years of war, when the continental currency could buy practically nothing, the army was compelled to meet most of its needs through impressments—that is, by confiscating private property while issuing chits on which Congress promised to pay citizens back once independence was achieved. Together with loans from France and the Netherlands, these measures proved barely sufficient to sustain the army to the end of the war, but Hamilton worried that the necessity of stealing to support the army would deprive both the government and the army of popular legitimacy and popular support. As a result of these concerns, Hamilton proposed a bold plan to restore public confidence through radical political and economic reform, including a new constitution granting Congress complete sovereignty over any task of government relevant to the war; executive departments to supply system, method, energy, and responsibility to the administration of the government; an impost to raise taxes and a national bank, to restore confidence in the currency and secure funds for the war effort; and a draft to raise troops serving long enough to defeat the greatest military power of the eighteenth century in a long war of attrition. These radical proposals went nowhere until other concerns (Shays's Rebellion, faction within the states, and so on) led others to think about a new constitution, but they were the foundation for Hamilton's future work as a constitutional, economic, and military reformer (*P* 2:401–16).

Surprisingly, given his early support for constitutional reform, Hamilton does not appear to have had great influence at the Federal Convention of 1787. His six-hour-long speech of June 18, 1787, was apparently applauded by all but supported by none. This blunt speech points to an aspect of Hamilton's character that is arguably both a virtue and a vice. On the one hand, he almost seemed to go out of his way to shock the republican sensibilities of his fellow delegates with his unsentimental appraisal of the defects of both the confederation and the plans proposed by New Jersey and Virginia to remedy them. His overly ambitious alternatives included an elected senate and executive serving during good behavior (and thus, in many cases, for life) and either abolishing the state governments or allowing the executive to appoint governors for each state with an absolute veto over their legislatures. In light of Hamilton's understanding of republicanism, based on popular consent, the rule of law, and government serving the public good, these proposals or something approximating them were not only compatible with republican government but also necessary to give it the stability and energy required for it to endure. Given the republican (and increasingly democratic) character of the American people, and of the delegates themselves, however, these proposals were bound to fail to acquire support. They point to an almost quixotic streak in the most famous political realist among the Founders. On the other hand, Hamilton had a clear sense of the necessary relation between ends and means. Quoting the famous French finance minister, Jacques Necker, Hamilton praised the British constitution as a model for Americans because of its unrivaled combination of "'public strength and private security'" (*P* 4:193). Whereas other governments built public strength on the ashes of private liberty, or sapped public strength to protect liberty, the British had found a way to generate sufficient power to protect their people from war, largely through the wealth arising from securing private property. Hamilton did not say that Americans needed to import a king, establish an aristocratic upper house, or rely on ministerial corruption to manage Congress; but, he did believe Americans would not be able to preserve their liberty without the union of public strength and private security he found in the British constitution.

In Hamilton's case, the most important task of the Constitution was to secure liberty. For this end, a variety of means were requisite in the following order of priority: independence, not merely from England, but from all foreign powers; union, both as a means to independence and as a way to avoid civil war; institutions of government capable of making the nation's potential energy kinetic, especially in time of foreign and civil war; and finally, procedures to ensure that those entrusted with using the nation's power neither abused their powers nor lost their sense of accountability to the electorate.[6]

Already, one can see why many of Hamilton's contemporaries were increasingly suspicious of him. The means he ranked least important, such as a bill of rights or state and local government, were frequently what they ranked most important. This does not necessarily mean that what others valued most was unimportant to Hamilton. Yet if compromises and trade-offs had to be made, he was clear in his mind what counted most and why. Before Americans could talk about security from abuse of power by the national government, they had to have an effective national government. Moreover, Americans already had strong institutions of local government and an instinctive mistrust of any power not directly subject to their control, even if that power was absolutely necessary for their liberty. Since it was unlikely that either those local institutions or that suspicious instinct would wither away in the near or probable future, Hamilton believed that the greatest dangers to American liberty would arise from the weakness rather than the strength of the national government.

Strategy, whether military or political, is not geometry or algebra. It admits of no certain answers. Hamilton took a calculated risk that American liberty would survive and prosper more if Americans strengthened their national government than if they allowed it to atrophy to the highly probable point of disintegration. At great risk both to his reputation and political career, he swam against the current of popular prejudice in an effort to convince Americans to want the kind of government he believed would be necessary to secure their liberty, especially in time of war. Hence, it is a mistake to cast the debate over the Constitution of 1787 and how to interpret it as one between partisans of liberty, on the one hand, and partisans of order, on the other hand. That prejudices our view of the parties from the beginning and thereby obstructs a judicious estimation of the merits of their arguments. In truth, both sides, whether called Anti-Federalists and Federalists, or Federalists and Republicans, were partisans of liberty first and foremost. They disagreed, however, on the kind of political order best suited to secure liberty (*F* 1:4–6).

Independence

Why would Hamilton treat independence as the most important means to secure American freedom? To begin with, he was not alone in thinking that way. Indeed, at the beginning of the Revolution, virtually everyone who called himself a Patriot agreed with him. Prior to 1776, Americans protested to king and Parliament demanding that their liberties be secured. If possible, they meant to have those liberties while remaining members of the British empire; but if that were not possible, they would fight for independence so that they could secure their liberties on their own. This move led them, first, toward becoming republicans rather than monarchists, and second, toward establishing their own empire in North America. The Treaty of Paris granted Americans their formal independence in 1783, but real independence required much more than diplomatic recognition from England.

Consider the strategic situation of the United States in 1787, just four years after the end of the War for Independence. Contrary to the Treaty of Paris settling the war between England and the United States, England continued to occupy its forts in the Northwest Territories, in large part because Americans had failed to comply with provisions of that treaty requiring them to pay their prewar debts to British creditors, restore property confiscated from Loyalists during the Revolution, and otherwise treat former Loyalists as full citizens of the United States. Spain controlled the Gulf of Mexico, including the Floridas and the port of New Orleans, so it was able to block American foreign trade west of the Appalachians at will. Congress had no independent means to raise revenue, and the United States was in enormous debt not merely to creditors at home but also to France and the Netherlands. Americans had no navy. The army consisted of fewer than 700 men stationed at West Point and scattered forts across the West. In other words, if a struggle came with England, Spain, or some other foreign power, the government had neither the troops nor the money to vindicate its independence by force of arms.[7]

American failure to comply with the Treaty of Paris gave England legitimate cause to renew the recent war at a time and place of its own choosing. Competition with England over fishing rights and with both England and France over the right to trade with their empires was a likely source of quarrel with either or both of them. Sometimes, impatient of waiting for Congress to help them, Americans were more than willing to settle quarrels with foreign powers on their own. Georgia had waged war against Indian tribes in direct violation of treaties made by Congress. Frontiersmen even tried to organize filibustering expeditions to seize the Floridas and New Orleans, though at grave risk that Spain would blame the United States as a whole for these outrages. Some even talked of leaving the Union and joining Spain if Congress could not find a way to give their exports secure access to the Gulf of Mexico. Indeed, there was some talk that the best strategic solution for the problems of the United States was to disunite them into two or three regional confederacies. In Hamilton's view, however, this would create the risk that the different confederations might become rivals of each other, seek the aid of European powers against each other, and become satellites of the Europeans. This scenario had played itself out in most confederations from the Achaean League of ancient Greece to the Tuscan League of Renaissance Italy to the Holy Roman Empire of early modern Europe. A statesman with a sense of history could not help fearing that a collapse of the confederation in America would produce similar effects, with the result that all that he had fought for during the Revolution would come to nothing (*F* 1:7, 3–5:13–27).

Because the Union was beginning to recover economically from the war in the mid-1780s, a case could be made that Hamilton's sense that Americans were in a strategic crisis was too rhetorical and highly overblown. Hamilton's point, however, was not merely that history was on his side. It was also and, more important, that the Union was bound to collapse because it was little more than an alliance, relying for its existence and effectiveness on the good faith of the states. It is in the nature of alliances to endure only so long as they serve the immediate interests of their members. In that respect, the Union under the Articles did not establish a social compact but a mere treaty among independent states. Hamilton would no doubt have given his full support to those who argued that Union preceded the confederation, and thus, that Americans became a nation independent of England but not of each other when Congress signed the Declaration of Independence. Yet such words, however edifying and perhaps even true, would have been irrelevant to the political reality of 1787, when the states, not Congress, had the most political power. So long as the charter of American liberty was construed as a mere alliance of states rather than a genuine social compact formally binding Americans as one nation under one national government, the nature of the Union would tend toward disintegration, with the almost inevitable risk of wars among the states, between Congress and the states, and between the states and foreign powers (*F* 15–16:89–105, 22:144–46).

For Hamilton, the desideratum of American independence was the ability to abide by the law of nations, which in turn implied establishing the rule of law throughout the United States. Indeed, in the case of *Rutgers v. Waddington* (1784), he used his growing law practice in the service of his constitutional statesmanship. Some major constitutional issues hinged on a seemingly mundane case. During the war, a Loyalist had occupied a brewery in New York City, which was owned by a Patriot widow, who had fled the city. After the war, New York passed laws allowing Americans to sue for trespass when their property had been occupied by Loyalists. Hamilton defended the Loyalist on two separate grounds. First, occupation was allowed under the laws of war, which were part of the common law that had been incorporated in New York's constitution. Second, the Treaty of Paris forbade prosecution of Loyalists for such offenses, so both New York's constitution and the treaty, enacted under the Articles of Confederation, superceded New York's civil law. Thus, in Hamilton's view, the judges were bound to declare that law "null and void."[8] In other words, he made perhaps the first American arguments in favor of the supremacy of a written constitution and judicial review precisely because he feared that failure to enforce the Treaty of Paris against the states would result in thirteen independent states with thirteen different foreign and defense policies. Largely because our courts tend to shy away from engaging in what they call political questions, we do not usually think of the federal courts, especially the Supreme Court, as important players in American national security policy. For Hamilton, however, federal courts were essential to ensure that treaties were regarded as part of the "Supreme Law of the Land." If federal courts were established, if they came to consider themselves guardians of a written constitution, and if they applied the treaty power against the states, then the United States could have a united foreign and defense policy. As Adam Smith observed, the invisible hand is not simply natural: it requires the rule of law and thus statesmanship to establish that rule in order to become second nature for modern commercial peoples (*The Wealth of Nations*, bk. 5, chap. 2). Likewise, what we take for granted—that the states will uphold rather than sabotage our foreign and defense policies—did not arise from an invisible hand. The federal courts are the almost invisible hand that makes it possible for us to speak and act as one nation in our relations with foreign nations. On the one hand, they deter the states from violating international law and our treaties with foreign nations. This minimizes the possibility that an errant state, pursuing its own foreign and security policy, might provoke a war with a foreign power that would drag the entire nation, against both its interests and its inclinations, into war on that state's behalf. On the other hand, the courts enable us to speak with authority to other nations because we can speak as one people. The mere thought of tangling against a united America might then suffice to deter other nations from doing so (*F* 3–4:13–27, 22:143–44, 80:534–41).

Deterrence, however, works best when coupled with a demonstrated capacity for self-defense, which often requires the ability to take the offensive against a nation's rivals and enemies. In theory, under the Articles of Confederation, Congress had the authority to build a navy and raise as large an army as necessary to secure American independence. In practice, said Hamilton, the states had a de facto veto over American national security policy because it was left to them to execute congressional requisitions for men and money in both war and peace (*F* 15:93). The result was that the states most in danger from the enemy during the Revolution contributed the most to the common cause. Those isolated from British attack contributed little, or even obstructed efforts to supply the means necessary to win the war. With enormous amounts of French aid, Washington was just barely able to keep an army in the field long enough to win the decisive battle against General Cornwallis at Yorktown—but the next war might be different. The French might become America's enemies rather than its allies. Americans would therefore have to rely on their own resources—but how?

For Hamilton, constitutional reform was partly a means for military reform. He had been advocating a rapidly expandable professional army since 1783, when he chaired a postwar congressional committee responsible for establishing the "military-peace establishment" of the United States. He tinkered with the plan for seventeen years, but its essential rationale and outlines remained the same. Sooner or later, Americans would find themselves at war again, perhaps even on their own territory, with a major European power, the kind most capable of inflicting serious damage on them. The militia had proved essential to American victory over the British during the Revolution, but they were not sufficient. They lacked the discipline, equipment, and training to stand up to a modern European army on their own. Yet the cost of the large armies of continental European powers was far beyond the meager means of Congress for as far into the future as most Americans could see. Moreover, American distrust of standing armies was so strong that it was unlikely there would be a constituency for a sizable army, and certainly not for long (*P* 3:381–83).

Compared to the rest of Europe, however, England had managed to avoid a large standing army while still providing for its security. The union of England, Scotland, and Wales had enabled the British to take advantage of their insular situation. Since they had relatively little fear of war at home, they could concentrate for defense on their navy, while keeping a small army for both internal security and foreign expeditions. Likewise, Hamilton thought, Americans might get by with an extremely small professional army of 3,000 officers and men, but only if they developed a substantial navy capable of tilting the balance of power in competitions among European powers in the New World. The army, however, was to be constituted so that it would be capable of almost infinite expansion (according to the nature of the threat) because the fundamental job of the professionals would not be to fight wars themselves but to teach reservists and raw recruits called up in crises how to be soldiers. As crises faded, the army would then demobilize, thus saving Americans much money and many worries about the dangers standing armies might pose to liberty. This plan to mobilize and demobilize quickly has been the corner-stone of American national security policy ever since Hamilton first devised it. Partisans could dispute whether Americans were mobilizing or demobilizing the army quickly enough, according to their perception of the crisis at hand; but the capacity to do so, rooted in the semi-insular situation created by the Union, is the product of Hamilton and the Constitution of 1787 (*F* 8:47–50).

Under most circumstances, however, a powerful navy would make it unnecessary to mobilize a substantial land force. By projecting their power at sea, which would be essential if Americans meant to be a commercial nation, Americans could keep war far from their shores and, no less important, carry war to their enemies. Not coincidentally, then, Hamilton believed a maritime strategy would have substantial collateral benefits for liberty at home. Unlike many of his contemporaries, he never confused a free government with a republican one. When he looked abroad for the most durable free government in the world, he saw England, which had a king and hereditary aristocracy to be sure, but also a rule of law rooted in the consent of the commons, a free press, competitive elections, and most of the institutions we associate with free government today. Liberty fared much worse among the continental powers of Europe, which lived in such fear of attack by land that they were compelled to maintain large, expensive armies in time of peace. Frequent wars with each other led not merely to arms races, but a virtual race toward despotism, as each of the continental powers found it necessary to concentrate ever more power in the hands of their executives. Their peoples, terrified by war, willingly acquiesced. By means of its navy and union, however, England had not only avoided that problem but also shifted power toward the legislature, in large part because it had little fear of invasion (*F* 8:49, 11:68–73).

Union

England's favorable insular situation, both for defense and for liberty, suggests why union was the second most important means in Hamilton's grand strategy for American liberty. Union could transform the United States into a de facto island, especially if the other European powers were gradually expelled from the Western Hemisphere. A maritime strategy would be essential for that end; but it would also make it much less likely that the Americans would follow in the dangerous footsteps of continental European powers. If Americans did not have a firm union, they might well re-create the conditions of continental Europe in North America and suffer exactly the same consequences. What worried Hamilton most was the impact of frequent land wars on the American spirit of liberty. As he said:

> Safety from external danger is the most powerful director of national conduct. Even the ardent love of liberty will, after a time, give way to its dictates. The violent destruction of life and property incident to war—the continual effort and alarm attendant on a state of continual danger, will compel nations the most attached to liberty, to resort for repose and security, to institutions, which have a tendency to destroy their civil and political rights. To be more safe they, at length, become willing to run the risk of being less free. (*F* 8:45)

This passage from *The Federalist* no. 8 is sometimes construed to show that Hamilton, and perhaps even his other collaborators in *The Federalist*, were crude Hobbeseans, willing to sacrifice everything—even liberty itself—for the sake of repose and security. A closer reading, however, suggests Hamilton meant something different. If the spirit of liberty—one of the finest fruits of civilization and the one that made it possible for Americans to undertake their Revolution—were to endure, then it was absolutely essential to ensure that Americans felt safe from the dangers of war, lest the desire for self-preservation (and even far uglier passions) trump their love of freedom. To be sure, the spirit of liberty has many roots, some of which Hamilton, perhaps to his discredit, rarely discussed, such as local government or a sense of principles written in the hearts of Americans that might come through or be reinforced by a bill of rights as a kind of secular Ten Commandments. Correctly, however, Hamilton believed these schools of freedom were not likely to match the terrifying—indeed brutalizing—school of war if it occurred on American soil. As valuable as these other schools may be for nurturing the spirit of liberty, it was radically more important to prevent Americans from learning the wrong lessons from war, which crushes the spirit of liberty by teaching human beings to accept any authority, so long as it can make them feel safe. In that respect, nothing was more important for preserving the spirit of liberty than a durable Union.

So what could make the Union endure? Hamilton supplied an answer on June 18, 1787, at the Federal Convention. He believed that the Union at the time was weak because the balance of power between Congress and the states was overwhelmingly in favor of the states. Not only did they have a de facto veto over acts of Congress, but they also had much stronger popular support. There are five main props of government, Hamilton said: interest, ambition, fear, custom, and honors. Custom was on the side of the states, which had existed as colonies long before they joined the Union. Because Congress had little power, men of ambition would serve themselves best by serving in the state governments. Since Congress had no money, it had few offices to bestow, so it had little attraction for those moved by interest and a desire to look important. Congress had no authority to enforce its laws against individuals, but the states had the last resort of the rule of law: sanctions, including the ultimate punishment—legal execution—to instill fear in the lawless. If the balance of power in the Union favored the states too much, then the only practicable solution was to shift the balance of loyalties on which that power was based. The national government would have to have the ability to instill fear in the lawless by applying laws directly to individuals through the medium of the courts. The Union would also have to acquire real power over the most important national functions of government (war, foreign policy, commerce, and finance) or the ambitious would refuse to serve in it. If it had such power, it could then bestow offices and honors. Most important, if the national government proved itself capable of administrating its delegated responsibilities more effectively and responsibly than the states, which Hamilton believed it could (especially if he set the tone of Washington's first administration), then over time it would enjoy the enormous advantage of custom. This, in turn, would make Americans accept its authority out of habit and the well-grounded conviction that it was a necessary guardian of their freedom. If the national government had all five of these props on its side, then the Union would endure, or endure longer, because the balance of loyalties among Americans would have changed from favoring their own states toward favoring the Union (which, of course, was not incompatible with preserving their states as well). Indeed, said Hamilton, speaking the language of realpolitik, if either the national or the state governments seemed to be acquiring too much power, the people had the option, through elections, of choosing representatives who could adjust the balance as seemed most likely to secure their liberties (*P* 4:207; *F* 17:107, 27:174, 28:179–80, 85:594–95).

Since we Americans consistently look to the Founders to learn how to establish and preserve liberty, it deserves special notice that Hamilton thought carefully about how to establish and preserve authority—not for the sake of authority itself, but for the sake of making authority compatible with liberty in the hearts and minds of his people. His five key props of government in his speech of June 18 are only the beginning of the story, which is about free allegiance. Men are born free, said Rousseau, but live their lives in chains. Since the bonds of authority were unlikely to wither away, the most important question was what could make authority legitimate —that is, what could make it compatible with freedom. Hamilton usually had little in common with Rousseau, but he understood that the French philosopher's theoretical question had enormous practical significance. As Edmund Burke suggested, Americans characteristically "snuffed tyranny in every tainted breeze." They would not accept any authority, however necessary, unless it was seen as a product of and safe for their freedom.[9]

This enduring American disposition suggests that making the Union durable was as much a problem of political psychology as anything else for Hamilton. An important part of his strategy was to cast the ratification of the Constitution as the collective act of the American people as a whole: as a national social compact rather than one between the states. That, he suggested, is what most distinguishes a political constitution from a mere alliance. Indeed, for Hamilton, establishing such a compact, by reflection and choice rather than the customary means of force, fraud, and accident, was a collective challenge that entitled each American of 1787, and especially the Founders themselves, to claim some share of glory as pioneers of a *novus ordo seclorum*—a new political order for the ages. They might demonstrate that modern social compact theory was not the mere product of philosophers in their caves but a practicable possibility in America, and by implication, for mankind itself. In that respect, what is often called American exceptionalism ought not to be treated merely as a religious phenomenon among those who cherish the vision of their country as a shining city upon a hill. Within that vision is a sense that Americans would perform a service for mankind not by crusading but by setting an example for others to follow. Quite subtly, Hamilton made an indirect appeal to the passionate conviction among his highly religious people that their country was some kind of Promised Land. Yet his memorable rhetoric did not rest on faith alone. The Founding of the United States appeared to be the first great test of the enlightened theory that human beings are rational enough to establish good government through popular consent. Demonstrating the truth of that proposition, in the conduct and example of the Americans, thus offered those who supported it an opportunity to go boldly where few peoples had gone before, and none on such an extensive scale. Indeed, the combination of religious passion and enlightenment zeal might also make it a test of honor, and promise of glory, for future generations to perpetuate what had been bequeathed to them in 1787. In that sense, Hamilton developed a sixth prop of government, and it was probably the most important of all, because it became second nature to Americans. His personal sense of mission led him to found Americans' unique sense of national identity on the popular sense that the United States was a country with a universal purpose. To be sure, other Founders made similar claims, and later Lincoln's poetry made this appeal a kind of political religion. Still, perhaps no Founder made this appeal more self-consciously, with the dual intention of using the nation's sense of mission to support the Union, and vice versa (*F* 1:3, 11:72–73, 22:145–46, 85:594–95).

Of course, not everyone agreed with Hamilton on the need for stronger government, or even on the need for a consolidation of interests and affections to make Americans a people rather than temporary allies. It was common to say that Americans were not only republicans but a commercial people as well. Whereas the weight of tradition suggested that no large republic could be durably free, enlightened theory suggested that small states do not have to become members of vast empires to provide for their security. Commerce, so the argument goes, unites trading nations by their pocketbooks. Moreover, though kings and other unaccountable leaders may wage war merely for glory or personal interest, republics are compelled by their very nature to look out for the common interests of their peoples, who (in commercial ages) want peace for the sake of trade, and trade for the sake of peace. To some, this suggested that commerce alone would be a sufficient bond of American union, because, after all, Americans were rational calculators of their best interests. Since a commercial union did not involve the danger of a runaway national government—that is, of a monstrous Leviathan state—it also seemed safer for liberty to rely on trade rather than a strong national government to establish the American Union.[10]

Since this enlightened theory is the foundation of many contemporary hopes for an end of war through the "end of history," in which all countries will become commercial republics like the United States, Hamilton's response merits careful consideration. In the first place, commerce can divide nations as well as unite them. Interdependence is often as much a source of competition as cooperation among nations. Moreover, commerce does not necessarily replace traditional competitions for power and glory. Indeed, in modern times, commercial rivalries have been among the most common means by which such competitions take place. Early modern commercial societies did in fact breed imperialism, which led to war both among imperial powers, and between them and the colonial peoples they sought to subjugate. Moreover, though republican government rests on the premise that the people can be rational, only a fool or a flatterer would assert that they are simply rational. They too are capable of longing for power and glory. Overweening national pride affects them as much as their leaders. Sometimes their leaders have been pushed into war against their best judgment by the fear, pride, and hatred animating their peoples. So under no circumstances can commerce or republican government, or both, be considered a guarantee of peace among states. To assume that is to risk civil war at home and court war abroad with those who would rather fight than trade. Certainly this much is true: in Hamilton's time, neither commerce nor republicanism had generated peace, not even among commercial republics. Far from it: the history of commerce and republican government constituted much of the history of ancient and modern warfare in Athens, Rome, Carthage, Venice, Holland, England, Spain, France, and so on. Since there was no empirical evidence to support this theory, Hamilton believed it would have been irresponsible to rest the security and freedom of Americans on the mere hope that the theory might someday be proved true (*F* 6:28–36).

Yet Hamilton's critique of this theory ought not to be construed as a simple rejection of its promise. The theory presumed that trade among the states would be free, lest trade wars lead to shooting wars. Not only would common republican principles provide the basic cultural bond of union but also free trade among the states would help remove an aspect of early modern commercial societies (exclusive trading spheres) that had made them tools of imperialists and a frequent cause of war. In that respect, commercial republicanism, grounded in free trade, was a necessary, though not sufficient, fabric of peace among the states and potentially between the United States and other nations. Among nations trade is made free through treaties and international agreements; within the United States, the most effectual way to make trade free was to give the national government power to regulate commerce for the sake of promoting as much commerce as possible among the states, lest trade wars among the states issue in shooting wars as well (*F* 7:39–40, 22:135–37). In that crucial respect, Hamilton's famous argument in *The Federalist* no. 6 is less a critique of enlightened theory than a prudent adjustment necessary to make it effective within the Union.

If Hamilton's strategy for durable union depended on free trade, at least among the states, and if he had some (though not high) hope that free trade might also contribute to peace among nations, one must wonder how he could reconcile that strategy with his famous *Report on the Subject of Manufactures* (1791), which called for tariffs. The simplest answer is that Hamilton would not have written his report if trade among the commercial nations of his time had actually been free. To practice free trade when no one else does is not prudent statesmanship but instead martyrs one's country for an economic ideology, which, in Hamilton's time, was yet unproved. In the 1790s, unilateral free trade risked making the United States a "victim" of the international trading system, in which much American trade was excluded from European markets. Until the Europeans opened their markets, Americans would need to develop their own. In the next place, Hamilton called for both tariffs and bounties in his report. The tariffs were nondiscriminatory and designed primarily to raise revenue for his funding system, the scheme he devised to restore national credit—and one that proved enormously successful in his time. The bounties were to have short terms, like patents, and thus were not meant to reward any special economic interest. Indeed, they were less for the sake of encouraging infant industries in general than particular infant strategic industries, such as mining coal and saltpeter, forging iron, and so on. In other words, they were designed to render the United States as independent as possible for the industrial foundations of modern warfare.

In this regard, it deserves notice that war, like politics, science, and technology, goes through periods of revolutionary change. The most significant revolution in military affairs in Hamilton's times was England's financial revolution, on which he modeled his funding system, and its embryonic industrial revolution, which he meant to match head-on. Indeed, the prologue to the *Report on the Subject of Manufactures* states what is commonly forgotten: that Hamilton's purpose was less economic than military—to render the nation self-sufficient in the manufactures required for war (though he recognized that by encouraging the spirit of industry and self-reliance, manufacturing would eventually strengthen the spirit of individual liberty as well). He also reflected that by multiplying the division of labor exponentially, an American industrial revolution would increase Americans' dependence on each other. Thus, this revolution could reinforce the bonds of union he hoped for from free trade among the states. True, he was myopic about the impact of this revolution on women and children, whom he thought might benefit from employment in factories, but most strategic plans have unintended consequences. He was not encouraging exploitive labor practices. Instead, he was trying to make Americans united and self-reliant, both in their conflicts with other nations and in their mode of making a living, and he largely succeeded, though less through his *Report on the Subject of Manufactures*, which Congress failed to pass, than through his funding system, which created the capital required to produce Hamilton's industrial revolution (*P* 10:231–35, 261–65, 266, 291, 299–301, 313–17, 334).

Much is often made of Hamilton's funding system as well as his proposal for a national bank in the 1790s as none too subtle means to tie the interests of the wealthy to the survival of the Union. The more they invested in government securities, the greater the stake they would have in the perpetuation of the Union. Since their influence was disproportionate to their numbers, it was essential to turn these men's interests to the side of the national government as quickly as possible. Yet there was much more to Hamilton's funding system than that, and much more to his political psychology of free allegiance as well. Another revolution in military affairs was just beginning to happen. It is most commonly ascribed to the French Revolution, which produced a nation in arms—that is, mobilized an entire people for war against more traditional continental powers fighting with small professional forces. The American Revolution anticipated not only the French political revolution but also their military revolution, because it gradually mobilized a people, both numerous and armed, to defeat the professional forces sent from England. The problem was that the means used to feed, arm, and clothe the army during the last years of the Revolution (impressments) had also cost both the army and Congress much popular support. Impressments violated one of the fundamental rights for which Americans fought: the right to private property. Impressments were a temporary expedient to support public strength at the expense of private security that, in the long run, seemed likely to undermine public confidence in both the legitimacy and the competence of the government.

On the one hand, Hamilton worried about how the army would be funded in the next war. If it resorted to impressments again, might not many Americans come to consider the army as much a threat to their rights as the enemy? How could a republican army wage a war effectively without popular support? Would it even deserve popular support if its necessities proved as dangerous to American rights as enemy offensives? On the other hand, Hamilton understood the direct link between credit and public confidence. Credit comes from the Latin word, *credere*, for faith. When citizens lend money to government, as they usually must in time of war, they lend not only money but also faith that they will be paid back. Their faith in the government, which is a tangible form of civic virtue, even has an index: the securities market. When government securities rise in value, this shows that citizens' trust in and willingness to take risks in support of the government has increased; when government securities decrease in value, this shows that citizens have lost faith in their government. Since the securities issued by Congress during the war had lost almost all their value, this meant that few had much faith left in Congress. Because they had little faith, their loyalty to the national government was uncertain. To change the balance of loyalties not merely among the wealthy but also among ordinary citizens, it was essential to give them reason to believe that continental securities were as good as gold so that those securities could be traded easily and quickly, as if they were money. Partly by funding and monetizing the national debt, and partly by establishing a national bank to facilitate trading in both bank stock and government securities, Hamilton both stabilized the value and increased the quantity of money in America. In turn, this fueled investment and led to the first great economic expansion under the Constitution in American history. Valuable as Hamilton's system proved to be for its tangible economic results in goods and services, the primary value of the program was intangible. It made Americans willing to trust the government with their most precious assets, and thus, increasingly loyal to the Union (*P* 2:401–17, 19:52–53).

Energetic Yet Stable and Deliberative Political Institutions

The need to inspire public confidence explains a great deal about the third most important component in Hamilton's strategy for durable American liberty: stable, energetic, and highly deliberative political institutions as they manifest themselves in one of the Constitution's most celebrated devices, the separation of powers. In addressing those institutions, however, we must face another revolution in military affairs beginning in Hamilton's time. It was not about manpower, finance, or industry, but rather about how to understand the nature of war itself. In other words, it was a theoretical revolution with enormous practical consequences for how modern nations have waged war ever since. It was pioneered by one of Hamilton's contemporaries, the German strategist Carl von Clausewitz, who suggested that war always consists of a paradoxical trinity. The first part of the trinity is policy, which supplies a rationale for beginning, prosecuting, and ending a war; the second is creativity, where chance and probability have the greatest effect; and the third is primordial passion, which leads us to hate an enemy badly enough to be willing to kill him. Partly as a result of Clausewitz's influence, in nineteenth-century European states it was common to assume that the government supplied not only political direction to a war but the reasons to justify the violence war entails; that the role of the military was to find creative ways to use violence in the service of the political authorities; and that the function of the people was to hate the enemy badly enough and long enough to bear the costs of a war in lives and treasure.[11]

As both Hamilton and Clausewitz were well aware, however, this theoretical division of labor does not always work in practice. If war is to be rational, it must serve some political objective; but, what if the political objective is irrational? Then strategy must often be irrational as well. Or what if the political objective changes over time, often as the result of competition among political leaders and parties for influence and power? Then the strategy must change too, and not necessarily for the better. Representative democracies, like the United States, were new in Clausewitz's time, and they introduced new problems for rationalizing a wartime trinity. When government is held accountable to the reason of the public, it also becomes more likely to be influenced by the public's passions. Sometimes, too, governments are more creative than their militaries. Indeed, when the military is stuck in a rut and wasting lives as a result, it is a funda-mental responsibility of governments to find more creative ways to use violence (lest the costs of the war outweigh its benefits) or sue for peace because both the government and the military cannot find a way to win at an acceptable cost. If a government fails to find creative ways to minimize friendly casualties and defeat an adversary, usually by inflicting heavy casualties on him, then it will usually, and quite justifiably, forfeit the confidence of its people.

If the people are lucky, they may find peaceful ways to change their political leadership (for example, through elections or votes of no confidence) so that they can prosecute the war more effectively or end it on the least costly terms. If they are unlucky, however, they may have to rise up and overthrow their government, though at the risk of being caught in a civil war while engaged militarily with a foreign adversary. In that respect, free elections, though most valuable for preserving consent as the foundation of government, are also extremely helpful for ensuring that necessary changes in political and military leadership occur by peaceful means and in a manner that can deny an adversary a way to exploit internal divisions for its own advantage. Yet there is also a grave weakness: the vulnerability of policy and therefore strategy to party politics, or what Madison and Hamilton called faction: the self-interested, ambitious, and even ideological kind of partisanship that can blind free peoples and their leaders to their country's best interests.

With respect to waging war effectively and preserving liberty at the same time, a constitution meant to endure for ages must attempt something that seems impossible. It must find a rational way for political leaders to change and adapt policy and strategy while remaining essentially the same in its political structure and principles. It must enable change and adaptation because, says Clausewitz, war is more than a true chameleon (*On War*, bk. 1, chap. 1). It changes not merely its colors, but its character. Yet the kind of change demanded by war is frequently destabilizing politically, and perhaps no more so than for free peoples. While they want minimum authority, war sometimes demands the maximum. They want a rule of law, but war may well know no laws. They want a government responsive to their immediate interests and sentiments, but sometimes nothing is more irresponsible or self-destructive than to allow their passions to usurp the place of reason in establishing and executing policy within the well-balanced trinity that Americans too must bring to war, if they are to be successful.

Consider now how the separation of powers can be interpreted to serve the purpose of giving Americans a Clausewitzian trinity capable of providing for the common defense, on the one hand, and preserving their constitutional balance, on the other hand. Long ago, Montesquieu (who was something of a model for Clausewitz) observed that the point of separating powers of government is not to prevent governmental action, for that would prevent effective government (and effective strategy too). Instead, said Montesquieu, the purpose was to ensure that when the government acted, all of its components acted more or less together, without sacrificing the responsibilities and powers that produce a semblance of balance among the parts and an opinion of security from abuses of power among the people (*The Spirit of the Laws*, bk. 11, chap. 6). In other words, the point was to enable a government to adapt to a changing world without a de facto coup or revolution that changed the form of the government from a free to a less free one. This Montesquieuean strategy to combine strategic adaptability with constitutional stability permeates everything Hamilton wrote about Congress, the executive, and the judiciary.

In the case of Congress, for example, some Anti-Federalists at the New York Ratifying Convention objected strongly to the powers granted Congress to tax, borrow, and spend for war by simple majority votes. This, they feared, could perhaps allow members of Congress to drag the nation into unjust wars of ambition and national aggrandizement, which sometimes happen in the life spans of all nations, including republics. To this sort of objection, Hamilton responded with several rhetorical questions. Is it better to risk that, occasionally, the nation might wage unjust or imprudent wars, or to deny a simple majority the means to provide for the common defense against the injustice or ambition of other nations? If, as some suggested, the required constitutional majority to declare and fund a war were raised to two-thirds or three-fourths, would Americans observe that parchment barrier in time of danger?

Likewise, some suggested that a bill of rights, which the Constitution sorely needed, ought to include a ban on standing armies in time of peace; but the business of soldiering cannot be learned in a day. Out of fear of military despotism, would opponents of the new Constitution deny the nation the means to train, plan, and organize its military long before the winds of war became a tempest? Would such constitutional limits even be heeded in time of danger that was not quite yet war? All political powers, most especially those related to the military, are dangerous and liable to abuse; but would Americans fear each other more than their potential and actual enemies abroad? The harsh truth was that the powers required for the support and direction of the armed forces had to exist

> without limitation: *Because it is impossible to foresee or define the extent and variety of national exigencies, or the corresponding extent and variety of the means which may be necessary to satisfy them.* The circumstances that may endanger the safety of nations are infinite; and for this reason, no constitutional shackles can wisely be imposed on the power to which the care of it is committed. (*F* 23:147)

Either such shackles would be effective or not. If effective, they would cripple the government in its efforts to secure American liberty by securing American independence, as Hamilton believed the Articles of Confederation had done during the Revolution. If fear trumped constitutional scruples, however, the shackles would be ineffective and produce the opposite of their intended result by teaching political leaders to disregard the Constitution in time of crisis and the people to put up with such behavior as a necessary prerogative of statesmanship. Sometimes such prerogative may be unavoidable, but it was not safe for durable liberty to build the temptation to exercise it into the Constitution itself.

It mattered greatly to Hamilton that Congress was a bicameral institution that might combine responsiveness to the people in the House with a sense of responsibility for their long-term interests in the Senate. For strategy to be rational, policy must be rational first. Sympathy with the people in the House was a reasonable security that in supporting a war, that branch would usually have no desire to abuse its powers. In most circumstances, it was also unlikely to tolerate such abuse from others. In contrast, the Senate, with its experience, greater independence, and deliberative character, had the potential to moderate the passionate element of Clausewitz's trinity so that it would not prevent a rational calculation of the demands of American principles and political prudence in the initiation, conduct, and termination of a war (*F* 23:150; *P* 5:68–69). This division of constitutional functions in time of war applied in Hamilton's mind to the executive perhaps most of all, because, as commander in chief, the president was most responsible for articulating American defense policy, on the one hand, and ensuring that the military devised creative strategies to serve it, on the other hand.

To play that role in America's wartime trinity, Hamilton argued that the defining character of the American executive had to be energy, which has several different forms. The first is speed, understood as the ability to act decisively, for which nothing was more important than unity, defined as one person (the president) having the authority to direct the armed forces amidst the constant flux and seemingly impenetrable fog of war. Energy is not the same thing as wisdom, but sometimes the wisest thing to do is to act energetically, either by exploiting an unexpected opportunity or by getting out of the way of unanticipated danger. Indeed, in Hamilton's first wartime proposal for a new constitution in 1780, when army morale was low and public confidence in the government had reached its nadir, Hamilton suggested that such energy was no less important for arousing and sustaining the passion of the people and the army to persevere despite their suffering than it was to direct the armed forces effectively. Thus, the executive was responsible for holding the American trinity together in a manner that generated a sustained will to fight without being overwhelmed by the primordial passions that fighting inevitably produces. An equally important form of energy is stamina, or the personal firmness of the executive, which Hamilton argued would result primarily from his term of office and the opportunity for reelection (*P* 2:401–17; *F* 71–73:471–92). Because Hamilton knew war personally, he had no desire to wage it unless it was the last practicable resort for securing American rights and independence. Yet, because war is at least as common as peace in the ordinary course of nations, he understood that Americans had to become ready for war rapidly, in the 1790s, before war came to them. For that end, Americans needed an executive steady as a rock, the sort who could listen to good strategic advice and stick to his decisions, even though they aroused ever growing popular opposition. He found that man in George Washington, who needed Hamilton's pen as much as Hamilton needed his stature with the American people.

Unfortunately for Hamilton, Washington, and the new American republic, the French Revolution of 1789 initiated the first modern world war. Fearing attack from Austria and Prussia, which meant to restore the French monarchy, the new French republic declared war on them in 1793. That war, which soon involved all the major powers of Europe, did not truly end until the defeat of Napoleon and the Congress of Vienna in 1815. Though many Americans, including the Republican opposition and its leaders, Thomas Jefferson and James Madison, as well as Hamilton himself, were initially sympathetic with revolutionary France, none wished to become involved in this war, which might well strain the limited resources and fragile institutions of the American republic beyond endurance. Hamilton was perhaps most concerned to keep Americans out of the war, because if Americans sided with France, England would become America's adversary again at a time when his entire funding system depended on revenue generated by tariffs on imports that came primarily from England. Unfortunately again, Americans had a defensive alliance with France left over from their own Revolution. The task of statesmanship in the face of America's limited treaty obligations to France was to honor the alliance, act decisively and firmly to keep the United States out of the growing world war, and augment the army and navy rapidly so Americans could defend themselves if they were compelled to go to war.

Hamilton did this, in part, by encouraging Washington to declare American neutrality, an act that Madison and Jefferson considered blatantly unconstitutional and biased toward England. If it belonged to Congress to declare war, then in principle it belonged to Congress to say that America was not at war, or so it seemed to Madison and Jefferson. In defense of Washington's Neutrality Proclamation (one of the first examples of what Hamilton meant by executive energy),

Hamilton wrote his *Pacificus* essays, which he considered his finest written work. His long-term goal remained the same: to preserve American liberty by preserving American independence and Union. In the short term, however, his goal shifted toward construing the Constitution broadly, both to defend Washington's Neutrality Proclamation and to make similar acts of executive energy defensible in the future. One part of his argument was that Washington was charged with upholding the laws of the nation. Until Congress declared war, the law of the land was peace and the international laws necessary to uphold it. So in proclaiming neutrality, Washington merely stated his opinion, that under international and American law, America was now at peace, and the executive had a constitutional duty to uphold the laws of peace. Since France initiated the war, the mutual defense clause of the treaty was not in operation. Americans were thus free, legally and honorably, to follow their best interests, which were to keep out of this war as long as possible (*P* 15:40–41).

Another part of Hamilton's defense, however, is almost always misunderstood. Hamilton argued, first, that the executive power as such was vested in the president under Article II of the Constitution; and second, that the right to proclaim neutrality was by its very nature an executive power. This was only true, said Madison in his response, the *Helvidius* essays, in monarchies, where decisions on war and peace are traditional executive prerogatives. Since the United States is not a monarchy, but a republic, based on the rule of law and popular consent, Madison asserted that the law-making branch should make these sorts of decisions. The text of the Constitution seemed to reinforce this theoretical argument by specifically placing the power to declare war in Congress. While making this argument, Madison quoted extensively from Hamilton's *Pacificus* essays but in a manner that has distorted Hamilton's argument ever since. Apparently, Madison was so sure that Hamilton meant to defend prerogative that he unconsciously inserted that term into Hamilton's own words, though Hamilton never used the term itself, in large part because it implied a right in the executive to disregard the Constitution.[12]

For almost two hundred years now, scholars have assumed this was a debate between Madison and Hamilton over whether there is such a thing as executive prerogative under the Constitution and what scope it may have. In hindsight, the debate looks absurd because both Hamilton and Madison stood for the rule of law, and both understood that prerogative, in the Lockean sense of acting without or against law in extraordinary emergencies, was (by definition) not a constitutional, but a natural, occasionally necessary, yet highly dangerous power. Granted, extraordinary circumstances might justify asserting prerogative, and then, as Locke said, the people must judge whether it is defensible; but Hamilton was actually trying to translate a different theme of Lockean social compact theory into American practice. For Locke, there are not three, but five powers of government: executive, judicial (which he sometimes included under the executive), legislative, federative, and prerogative. The federative power is different from prerogative, because it is not about acting without or against the law but rather applies to how one nation conducts its relations with others. In theory, Locke suggested, the federative power to make war and peace, form alliances, and otherwise handle a nation's relations with other nations could be placed in the legislature, but it is commonly placed in the executive because in the constant flux of changing foreign relations, shifting alliances, offense and defense, and so on, it is more prudent to place the federative power in the executive, who is most capable of acting decisively to meet emergencies and opportunities as they occur. The other great theorist of the separation of powers, Montesquieu, recognized this necessity of executive energy in foreign affairs too, though he added a good deal of confusion to the Founders' and subsequent American understandings of the executive power by using the term "executive power" to cover *both* Locke's executive power to enforce laws at home *and* Locke's federative power to direct foreign and defense policy. Hamilton appears to have used Montesquieu's overly vague theoretical language in order to make Locke's highly practical point, that all things considered, it was safer to leave the federative power in the hands of the executive than anyone else. When Hamilton said that the power to declare neutrality belonged to the executive, he meant that unless the Constitution specifically stated otherwise, the federative power was essentially the property of the executive. In other words, he was construing the executive power broadly so that the American executive could meet the demands of statesmanship in foreign affairs without having to resort to prerogative, which might well undermine the rule of law at home. It is perhaps in the nature of republicans to wish to subject everything to the rule of law, but it is in the nature of foreign relations for the rule of law to stop at each nation's own borders. Outside those borders, practicality required enabling the executive to adapt to a continually changing world.[13]

Indeed, for Hamilton, this adaptability, or energy as he called it, was the quasi-Aristotelian golden mean between unconstitutional acts of prerogative that might undermine the republican rule of law, on the one hand, and constitutional weakness that might make it impossible to provide effectively for the common defense, on the other hand. If the executive were constitutionally incapable of proclaiming neutrality or otherwise leading in time of crisis—if Americans had to wait for Congress to do so—then in some cases the danger of war might be so great that the executive might have to choose between his duty to uphold a strict construction of the Constitution and his responsibility to protect Americans, their independence, and their Union. Since independence and Union are vital to American liberty, the purpose of the Constitution might therefore be undermined by a strict construction of its meaning. The executive's higher duty might therefore be to sacrifice the letter to the spirit of the Constitution. Contrariwise, an executive whose powers included every federative power not specifically delegated to Congress would be much less likely to have to face the dilemma. Energy in the executive was both safer for liberty and the common defense because it supplied a means of preserving constitutional forms while adapting to the necessities and accidents of war.[14]

Now we come back to the judiciary, which Hamilton hoped would uphold his philosophy of broad construction. In all reason, he could not have anticipated that the first great chief justice, John Marshall, would be a younger and, if only because he avoided duels and other unnecessary quarrels, more prudent version of himself. Despite the darkest hours of the Federalist defeat in 1800, Marshall proved exceedingly skillful, in such cases as *McCulloch v. Maryland* (1819), at providing legitimacy to the kind of energy Hamilton expected from Congress and the president. By making energy constitutional, one might say that Marshall and Hamilton together made prerogative much less necessary, and thus, the rule of law much more durable. In response, one might also say, as Jefferson, Madison, and the Republicans did frequently, that in reality Hamilton and, later, Marshall disguised fundamental changes in the constitutional balance in the garb of broad construction. This, of course, is the fundamental danger latent in broad construction, but Hamilton's fourth priority (procedures to guard against abuse of power and to hold government accountable to constituents) in his list of means to secure American liberty provides substantial (though never complete) security against that danger arising frequently. The "internal structure" of the Union (federalism, representation, separation of powers, impeachment, judicial review, and so on) is the primary subject of over half of *The Federalist* (essays 37–85) and is anticipated in earlier essays as well. The important point is that even a free government must in fact be a government. It must have all powers necessary to govern effectively; then one must turn to devices to prevent such powers from being abused. Otherwise, in Hamilton's view, one puts the cart before the horse (*F* 23:150–51). Since no system is perfect, and every power is liable to abuse on some occasion, relying on the internal structure of the government seemed to be the most Hamilton (and his collaborators, Madison and Jay) thought any constitution could do to make sure that necessary powers were used in proper ways. More they could not promise; to ask for more was to demand more than any constitution could deliver.

Elder Statesman and Party Leader

Debate over Hamilton's funding system as well as Washington's response to the revolution in France helped give birth to the American party system, with Hamilton leading his informal governing party (the Federalists) in Washington's administration, and Jefferson and Madison forming their own informal opposition party (the Republicans) in response. The names of the parties reveal not only what they stood for but also what they stood against and what they feared from their opponents. The Federalists stood for a firm union, under the Constitution read broadly, as the foundation of American independence and liberty; the Republicans stood for popular government, under the Constitution read strictly, as the chief security against abuses of power. For most of Washington's administration, the quarrel between these parties was heated, but if only through respect for Washington, generally under control. Indeed, with Hamilton as his chief speechwriter, Washington gave his famous Farewell Address in a last effort to keep the increasing partisanship of Republicans and Federalists from leading to disunion and even civil war.[15] The outbreak of a little known undeclared war with France, the Quasi-War, which was part of the larger world war between revolutionary France and the rest of Europe, however, unleashed a storm of partisan conflict that threatened to destroy the Union. Perhaps more by luck than moderation among Americans, that partisan conflict destroyed the careers of both Hamilton (who was eventually appointed inspector general of the army and responsible for American planning vis-à-vis France) and President John Adams, instead of the Union itself.

Until the famous XYZ affair in 1798, virtually all Americans, including and especially Hamilton, wanted to stay out of this war, but when the French foreign minister Tallyrand secretly demanded bribes even to speak to American negotiators, a torrent of angry public opinion led to demands to build a much stronger army and navy. It also led to efforts to prevent French agents and sympathizers from attempting to manipulate public opinion against the government, as they had tried to do on several occasions, most notoriously through their envoy Citizen Genet. For Hamilton, the crisis of 1798 was both the best of times and the worst of times. Having labored mightily to establish the durable foundations of the power of the purse in Washington's administration, he was determined to use this crisis to establish equally durable foundations of the power of the sword under Adams. In particular, he worked night and day to accomplish his career-long plan for a small but rapidly expandable professional army and an oceangoing navy. Nonetheless, he was disturbed that members of his party might seek to establish public strength on the ashes of private security. Upon first hearing of bills that later became the notorious Alien and Sedition Acts, the elder statesman wrote to members of his party: "Let us not establish tyranny. Energy is a very different thing from violence" (*P* 21:522–23). He consistently opposed the Alien Acts for denying due process to foreigners. He eventually came to support what became the Sedition Act because it contained two securities to liberty that made it a significant advance in libel law. First, citizens accused of seditious libel could introduce truth as a defense. If they could prove what they said was true, they would be acquitted. Second, juries would be allowed to judge the law as well as the facts in libel cases: if they believed both judges and prosecutors were colluding to get party enemies locked up in jail, they could interpret the law to allow the accused to go free. Largely because members of Hamilton's party (though not Hamilton himself) did use these laws to harass their political opponents, these acts have become a stain on his party's reputation in both the popular and scholarly mind, but the securities to the accused led Hamilton to support them at a time that the country seemed to him and many others on the brink of a civil war in which the North and the Federalists would side with England, while the South and the Republicans would side with France. This was his worst nightmare—the disintegration of the Union he had labored most of his life to build.

A major cause of this bitter partisanship was divergent views of the French Revolution. Generally, Jefferson, Madison, and other Republicans believed the French were fighting for the same cause (liberty) for which Americans had fought their own Revolution. From the beginning, neither Hamilton nor John Adams was quite so sure. This was partly because the unicameral legislature of the French government lacked checks and balances to secure individual liberty. It was also because the Terror in France confirmed their worst suspicions that the French philosophes were bent more on tyranny than liberty. Not least of all, it was because the French began to conquer most of Europe and treat the vanquished as subjects to be exploited for French interests. With a perspicacity rivaled perhaps only by Edmund Burke, Hamilton believed the French Revolution had inaugurated not merely a new age of warfare but also a new age of despotism. He did not have a term to describe such an unprecedented event, but he frequently compared the fanaticism of French revolutionaries to that of earlier ages of religious enthusiasm, in which belief in the justice and ultimate victory of one's faith seemed to justify any form of violence and cruelty. Correctly, he predicted that the violence within France could only end when a strong man established a military dictatorship, but if that happened, France's threat to its neighbors, and potentially, to even the United States, was bound to increase. So while Republicans tended to regard revolutionary France with the same admiration and sympathy that many on the Left had toward revolutionary Russia in the 1930s or China and Vietnam in the 1960s, Hamilton tended to treat the rise of Jacobinism in France with the same fear and loathing displayed by Winston Churchill toward the rise of Nazi Germany in the 1930s and the Soviet Union at the beginning of the Cold War (cf. *P* 17:585–88, 20:339–40, 494–95, 21:382–87, 396–97, 402–8).

With such radically different views of whether the French Revolution served universal liberty or constituted an unprecedented threat to freedom, it was inevitable that the parties would have equally divergent views about American policy toward revolutionary France. Although French attacks on American commerce gave rise to the Quasi-War, Republicans did not believe the French had any intention of attacking North America, and doubted that with the Royal Navy ruling the waves, the French could even get a significant force to the United States. Although Adams's view of the French Revolution was at least as bleak as Hamilton's, he shared not only Republican skepticism about French capabilities to attack North America but also their fears of standing armies, which they worried might become a tool by which Hamilton himself would seize power by unlawful means. In contrast, although he did not believe the French had the will or the means to attack the United States directly, Hamilton worried that they might try to reacquire New Orleans, which they had surrendered to Spain at the end of the Seven Years' War, as a prelude to efforts to rebuild their empire in North America and to dominate the Gulf of Mexico. Thus, for both Adams and the Republicans there was no logical necessity to establishing a significant army, whereas for Hamilton a larger force was necessary in case the French did try to attack New Orleans. If the French threatened that vital geopolitical point, Hamilton meant to send the army down the Mississippi "like lightning." Washington, who had been recalled from retirement to serve once more as his country's commanding general, agreed completely with this strategy (*P* 21:345, 462, 22:342–52, 23:227, 407, 417–28).

In general, scholars of this period have sided with Adams, who directed a successful naval war against France in the West Indies and eventually negotiated peace with France, thereby making Hamilton's army seem unnecessary, if not even an illegitimate effort to establish authority through force against his opponents. This is the source of Hamilton's reputation as a "militarist" among the Founders. It matters, however, that on the same day that American negotiators signed a treaty of peace with France at the end of Adams's term in 1801, Napoleon secretly negotiated a treaty with Spain for the retrocession of all of Louisiana to France. Had Adams known of Napoleon's duplicity, he might well have unleashed Hamilton's dogs of war to seize New Orleans, through which most American trade in the West had to exit. But it was too late; there were no dogs left to unleash. Adams had led the effort to demobilize Hamilton's army, so Napoleon won at the bargaining table what France failed to win in battle. Shortly after signing this secret treaty, Napoleon sent two armies to New Orleans to begin the reoccupation of France's North American empire. However, one wound up frozen in port in Holland and never made it to the North America, and the other was rerouted to Haiti, where black slaves raised the American cry of liberty against their French colonial masters.[16] In the meantime, the high taxes required to support the army and the Alien and Sedition Acts had made the Federalists increasingly unpopular. They were swept away in the critical election of 1800, when Jefferson and his party came to power, completed the demobilization of the army, and sent Hamilton and Adams into a political wilderness from which they never returned.

At first, Hamilton was despondent in his wilderness years, complaining that this American world, which he had done so much to create, was not meant for him. Before he was gunned down by Vice President Burr in 1804, however, he made one last innovation in American political thought. Federalist defeat in 1800 arose from many causes, but one of them was rank disorganization. He therefore proposed a new political party, the Christian Constitutional Society, which would use the Constitution to support religious freedom (against the alleged Jacobinism of the Republicans) and religious sentiment to establish the American political religion of veneration for the Constitution. The new party would have its own party newspapers, chapters in every state, and a national committee to be led by Hamilton himself. The state chapters would go after an increasing portion of the Republicans' constituency, the immigrant vote, by establishing charities for their improvement—that is, political machines to get out their vote.

To lift the morale of defeated Federalists, Hamilton even tried to put a sitting president, Thomas Jefferson, on trial in the court of public opinion. Under Jefferson's encouragement, the state of New York prosecuted a Federalist newspaper editor, Harry Croswell, for libel, for asserting that Jefferson had encouraged Republican newspaper editors to libel John Adams, Washington, and other Federalist leaders, as in fact Jefferson had done. As the leading lawyer in New York, Hamilton was called to defend Croswell. He turned the tables on Jefferson by defending free speech, based on the Sedition Act's standard of truth as a defense, as the foundation of effective opposition to tyranny. Sounding like a vigilant Republican in 1798 (and himself in 1774), Hamilton argued that to "watch the progress" of efforts to enslave the people "is the office of a free press. To give us alarm and put us on guard against the encroachments of power. This, then, is a right of the utmost importance, one for which, instead of yielding it up, we ought rather to spill our blood." Without truth as a defense in libel suits, Hamilton told the court, "you must forever remain ignorant of what your rulers do. I never can think this ought to be; I never did think truth was a crime. . . . My soul has ever abhorred the thought that a free man may not speak the truth." "Never," said the former general whom Adams and Jefferson accused of Caesarism, "can tyranny be introduced into this country by force of arms . . . it is only by the abuse of the forms of justice that we can be enslaved." Not the "few thousand of miserable, pitiful" soldiers he had once commanded, but the "pretense of adhering to all the forms of law" while "breaking down the substance of our liberties" was the great danger to public and private liberty in America.[17]

When dealing with a statesman gifted at translating theory into practice, facts are as relevant as principles. From 1798 to 1800, many feared that Hamilton would use the army for Napoleonic exploits of his own; but against his better judgment, he obeyed every order from Adams, whom he considered strategically naive, to demobilize the army. Had just one of Napoleon's armies reached New Orleans, our opinion of this dramatic period in American history would likely be very different, with Hamilton appearing as something like an American Churchill. The difference between them is that Hamilton not only assessed the threat to his country correctly in his own time, but also supplied Americans with the economic, military, and political institutions to adapt strategically while remaining essentially the same in their political constitution. It is inconceivable that Americans could have survived the great wars of their history with their liberties not only substantially intact, but frequently enhanced, without the national independence, the union, and the stable yet energetic institutions that Hamilton sought to build. Reminding Americans that their freedom depended not merely on security against abuse of power, but public strength as well, was Hamilton's major contribution to American political thought.

Notes

1. See, for example, Hamilton's Speech of June 18, 1787, in James Madison's *Notes of the Debates of the Federal Convention of 1787*, ed. Adrienne Koch (Athens: Ohio University Press, 1966), 129–39.

2. See Gordon S. Wood, *The Creation of the American Republic* (New York: W. W. Norton, 1969), 610n3.

3. See Richard H. Kohn, *The Eagle and the Sword: The Federalists and the Origins of the American Military Establishment, 1783–1802* (New York: The Free Press, 1975).

4. See Edward Meade Earle, "Adam Smith, Alexander Hamilton, and Friedrich List: The Economic Foundations of Military Power," in *Makers of Modern Strategy, from Machiavelli to the Nuclear Age*, ed. Peter Paret, rev. ed. (Princeton, N.J.: University Press, 1986), 217–61.

5. "A Full Vindication" and "The Farmer Refuted," in *The Papers of Alexander Hamilton*, ed. Harold G. Syrett and Jacob E. Cooke, 26 vols. (New York: Columbia University Press, 1961), 1:75–76, 94, 122, 141. Hereafter citations from Hamilton's *Papers* will be cited in the text of this chapter and listed as *P* 1:122, and so on, where the first number refers to the volume and the second to the page.

6. This sense of priorities is reflected in the very structure of *The Federalist*, a more politic work than his imprudent speech of June 18, 1787. Hamilton organized the project on his own before finding the other contributors to complete it, James Madison and John Jay. Indeed, Hamilton wrote most of the essays, including all of the essays on the executive and judiciary. The first section (essays 1–14) on the utility of a well-constructed Union is devoted primarily to the dangers of foreign and civil war to American independence and liberty. The second and third sections (essays 15–36) cover the insufficiency of the Articles to preserve the Union and the necessity of a government at least as energetic as the one proposed in the Constitution to do so. The fourth section (essays 37–85) addresses the conformity of the Constitution to the true principles of republican government (as well as many other subjects) but with enormous emphasis on showing why the powers necessary to the new government were not likely to be abused frequently. See Alexander Hamilton, James Madison, and John Jay, *The Federalist*, ed. Jacob E. Cooke (Middletown, Conn.: Wesleyan University Press, 1961), nos. 1:6–7, 15:90, 23:146, and 37:231. Hereafter, *The Federalist* will be cited in the body of this chapter and listed as *F* 15:91, and so on, with the first number citing the essay and the second the page.

7. For a useful appreciation of the strategic and diplomatic position of the United States during the framing of the Constitution, see Frederick W. Marks III, *Independence on Trial: Foreign Policy and the Making of the Constitution* (Wilmington, Del.: Scholarly Resources, 1973). Hamilton also argued that the inability of Congress both to uphold its obligations under the Treaty of Paris and to punish violations of that treaty by England had brought the United States to "the last stage of national humiliation" (*F* 15:91).

8. Hamilton's brief for *Rutgers v. Waddington*, in *The Law Practice of Alexander Hamilton*, ed. Julius Geobel (New York: Columbia University Press, 1964), 1:296–97.

9. Jean-Jacques Rousseau, *On the Social Contract*, ed. Roger D. Masters, trans. Judith R. Masters (New York: St. Martin's Press, 1978), 46; Edmund Burke, "Speech on Moving Resolution for Conciliation with the Colonies" (1775), in *Select Works of Edmund Burke*, ed. Francis Canavan (Indianapolis: Liberty Press, 1999), 237–43.

10. See, for example, the First and Seventh Letters of Agrippa, November 23 and December 25, 1787, in *The Anti-Federalist: Writings by Opponents of the Constitution*, ed. Herbert J. Storing (Chicago: University Press, 1981), 230–43, and Montesquieu, *The Spirit of the Laws*, trans. Thomas Nugent (New York: Hafner, 1949), bk. 9, chap. 2 (127–28); bk. 11, chap. 3 (150–51); bk. 20, chaps. 1–2 (316–17); bk. 21, chap. 14 (358–59).

11. Carl von Clausewitz, *On War*, ed. Michael Howard (Princeton, N.J.: University Press, 1976), bk. 1, chap. 1 (89). The point is not that Hamilton read Clausewitz, who wrote *On War* after Hamilton's death, but rather that Hamilton employed the separation of powers to address the enduring strategic problems exposed by Clausewitz's trinitarian analysis, especially the problem of subordinating both the military and popular passion to rational policy.

12. Madison made several errors while transcribing from *Pacificus*. He wrote: "In support of this conclusion [that Hamilton was supporting prerogative] it would be enough to echo, 'that the prerogative, in this active sense, is connected with the executive in various capacities—as the organ of intercourse between the nation and foreign nations—as the interpreter of treaties . . . as the power which is charged with the execution of the law—as the power which is charged *with the command and execution of the public force*'" (*Helvidius* 4, in *The Mind of the Founder: Sources of the Political Thought of James Madison*, ed. Marvin Meyers [Hanover, N.H.: University Press of New England, 1981], 210). Hamilton's actual words never included the term "prerogative." He stated that the power to declare neutrality "appears to be connected with the executive in various capacities, as the *organ* of intercourse between the nation and foreign nations—as the interpreter of treaties when the judiciary is not competent, that is the cases between Government and Government—as that Power which is charged with the Execution of the Laws, of which treaties form a part,—as that power which is charged with the command and application of the Public Force" (*P* 15:38). Although Hamilton did not use the term, prerogative, in this passage or anywhere else in *Pacificus*, Madison used the term three times in the passage preceding his misquotation from Hamilton, thus creating the illusion that Hamilton's own words supported his conclusion. Madison also left out Hamilton's qualifying phrase, "where the judiciary is not competent," thus ignoring the role Hamilton advocated for the courts as interpreters of treaties. Failure to compare what Hamilton actually said with what Madison attributed to Hamilton has thus led scholars to adopt Madison's version of the debate, in which he crusades for the rule of law against a straw man bent on monarchizing the executive with prerogative. In truth, Hamilton was advocating energy in the executive, based on its retention of every federative power not explicitly transferred to Congress in the text of the Constitution, in order to avoid the twin dangers of constitutional weakness and unlawful prerogative. The term "prerogative" occurs eighteen times in *The Federalist*, with Hamilton using it ten times and Madison using it on eight occasions. In no case, however, do they use it in its Lockean sense. Instead, they use it in a more traditional sense of an act of judgment belonging to one part of a government or another. Why do they not invoke Locke? Because they were not fools! You cannot sell a constitution to the American people while speaking the harsh truth that sometimes, and quite regrettably, even the freest governments must act without or against law. Precisely because Hamilton understood this fact in *The Federalist*, he did not resort to prerogative in *Pacificus*. Instead, he innovated by incorporating federative under executive power, thus making prerogative less necessary and less likely in the executive. See *The Federalist Concordance*, ed. Thomas S. Engeman, Edward J. Erler, and Thomas B. Hofeller (Chicago: University of Chicago Press, 1988), 420.

13. John Locke, *Second Treatise of Government*, in *Two Treatises of Government*, ed. Peter J. Laslett (Cambridge: University Press, 1991), secs. 364–66 (143–48) and secs. 374–80 (159–68); Montesquieu, *Spirit of the Laws*, bk. 11, chap. 6 (151); *Pacificus* 1, *P* 15:39–42. Hamilton actually invoked the term "federative power" in his defense of the Jay Treaty. See *P* 20:9–10, 16, 20.

14. In considering the wartime merits and demerits of Hamilton's broad construction, compare, for example, the Constitution of the United States with the Constitution of the Southern Confederacy during the American Civil War. A broad construction of the former supplies the means for Congress and the executive to act with energy in time of both foreign and civil war. The latter was not only informed by strict-constructionist principles but was something of a throwback to the Articles of Confederation because it was a compact between independent states rather than among the people as a whole. The former enabled the government to prosecute a long and bloody war to preserve the Union while, for the most part, remaining within its traditional constitutional forms. The latter was so dependent on the states that it was crippled, by its very constitutional forms, from generating sufficient arms and wealth to defend itself. Perhaps the Confederacy would have been defeated even if it had possessed a better constitution, but this contest was closer than many think, and one cannot simply assume that victory of the Unionist side was inevitable. Hence, one cannot help wondering whether the South died of a cause: states' rights and the strict construction of legislative and executive powers it produced.

15. Shortly before the end of his first term, when he hoped to retire, Washington invited James Madison to draft his Farewell Address, but Hamilton and others prevailed on Washington to serve a second term. Near the end of his second term, Washington gave Hamilton Madison's draft and asked him to revise it. Hamilton deleted all but Madison's introduction and, under Washington's direction, wrote the bulk of the Address, including its warnings against the spirit of party, its admonition to preserve the Union and the Constitution at all cost, and its advice to remain generally aloof from foreign quarrels. In that respect, this state paper is as much Hamilton's Farewell Address as Washington's. See Felix Gilbert, *To the Farewell Address: Ideas of Early American Foreign Policy* (Princeton, N.J.: Princeton University Press, 1961).

16. See Forrest McDonald, *Alexander Hamilton: A Biography* (New York: Norton, 1979), 347–48, 357.

17. "Speech in the Case of Harry Croswell [Waite's version]," in Goebel, *Law Practice of Alexander Hamilton*, 1:809, 813, 820, 831.

Chapter 10

America's Modernity: James Wilson on Natural Law and Natural Rights

Eduardo A. Velásquez

There are at least two compelling reasons students of American political thought ought to consider the writings of America's Scottish Founding Father James Wilson (1742–1798). It is arguable that Wilson provides the most systematic and sustained examination by an American Founder of the natural law and natural rights theories that inform the American republic. To see Wilson is to see something of ourselves. Moreover, unlike contemporary critics of modern, liberal, Enlightenment thought and practice, Wilson does not think that such theories inevitably give sway to unabated selfishness if properly qualified. Wilson provides a curious synthesis of the admittedly "individualistic" natural rights theories of Thomas Hobbes and John Locke with the philosophy of moral sensibility taken from the Scottish Enlightenment thinkers. The result is a natural rights theory that charts a course between unabated selfishness and the austere demands of selflessness. In doing so, however, Wilson does not resort to a classical or medieval understanding of selfless duty to God and others as a means to repair the potential excesses of self-love. The classical understanding is hard to square with a modern, liberal republic that extols the virtues of private property, acquisition, and religious liberty. Wilson's appropriation of the Scots should not be understood as a revival of classical concerns but as hospitable with a modern teaching on rights.

I begin an analysis of Wilson's synthesis of English and Scottish moral philosophy by turning to his natural law teaching.[1] A detailed examination of the law of nature is necessary for two reasons. First, Wilson claims that his political philosophy opens "to view, the very close and interesting connection, which subsists between the law of nature and the municipal law" (2:587).[2] The American practice supposedly "imitate(s) . . . the operations of nature" (2:583). Second, the failure of scholars to understand Wilson's natural law teaching has led to a pervasive misunderstanding of the character of America's Founding. The prevailing view is that Wilson's natural law is of Thomistic origin.[3] Against this view, I show that Wilson's natural law does not amount to a human being's participation in the higher law of reason or logos. A human being's natural understanding may be supplemented but is not necessarily perfected by Grace or the Bible.[4] Rather, the law of nature is for Wilson as for Hobbes firmly rooted in the passions, not least of which is the ubiquitous desire for self-preservation. Reason is an instrument in the service of fundamental feelings. Examining the character of Wilson's natural law shows the extent of his indebtedness to the modernity of Hobbes and Locke.[5]

Although affirming his preference for "moderns" over "ancients" (1:107, 123, 139), Wilson also speaks of the "social" principles of human nature such as sympathy, gratitude, and love. He argues that liberal republicanism requires for its success civic virtues such as "conscious rectitude" (1:234–37). I show that Wilson's account of human sociability supplements the modern understanding of natural law and draws extensively from the Scottish philosophers, especially Francis Hutcheson, David Hume, Adam Smith, and Thomas Reid.[6] Wilson views the Scottish philosophy of moral sensibility as compatible with the modern emphasis on the primacy of the passions, and as friendly to Locke's modern liberal teaching on toleration (or rights), consent, and social contract (1:71, 239). Wilson squares his *modern* natural law teaching with his *modern* natural rights teaching. To the extent that Scottish philosophy makes its way into Wilson's political thought, this chapter demonstrates that it does so as a supplement to and not as a hostile competitor with the modern liberal principles enunciated by Hobbes and developed by Locke.[7]

I grant at the outset that students of the Scots are bound to find Wilson's appropriation of the Scottish Enlightenment thinkers dissatisfying. Wilson makes no distinctions among the various Scottish philosophers and thus ignores the important differences regarding the content of the moral sense. Neither does Wilson note the important differences between the distinct faculty of the "moral sense" (Hutcheson) and the "moral sentiments" (Smith), the former understood as a means of adjudicating between selfish and benevolent "instincts," the latter understood as an array of feelings both self-regarding and benevolent. He does not pause to consider the differences between the "moral sense" (Hutcheson and Hume) and "common sense" (Reid). Readers interested in a clear statement regarding (1) the disputes among the Scots regarding the "moral sense," "common sense," and "moral sentiments," and (2) the epistemological status of the moral sense itself, will unfortunately find no satisfying answers in Wilson's writings. Wilson appropriates freely from his Scottish mentors in order to advance one point, namely, that the law of nature is rooted in common *feelings* of pleasure and pain. Wilson sometimes calls this mass of feelings a "moral sense," at others a "common sense," at others a "conscience." As will become clear in this chapter, these feelings are for Wilson the "first principles" of political life. Reason is for Wilson what it is for Hobbes and the Scots generally—an instrument of the passions, not the source of first principles. On this point the Scottish Enlightenment thinkers are in agreement with their English predecessors and thus with the modern understanding of natural law and natural rights.

From Scotland to America

A preliminary detour to examine Wilson the man and his background is a useful way of illustrating the connections between Scotland and America. James Wilson was born in the shire of Fife in the Scottish lowlands on September 14, 1742.[8] His Scottish origin suggests more than is readily apparent. The lowlands where Wilson was born "contained much of the best spirit of eighteenth-century Scotland," according to his biographer Charles Page Smith. The intellectual center of this spirit was the University of Edinburgh, "the heart of the unfolding glory of the Scottish Renaissance . . . [and] for a generation or more, the greatest university in Christendom."[9] The fertile intellectual climate of his times had a significant impact on the young Wilson.

Pledged to the ministry by humble and pious parents at an early age, Wilson was "kept constantly in school from the time he was capable of receiving instruction." As a grammar school student, Wilson "studied the standard subjects—Sallust and Virgil, Euclid's Geometry, Penmanship and Rhetoric, . . . Latin and Greek." Enrolled at St. Andrews in November 1757, Wilson continued this scholarly diet with "more Latin, Greek, and mathematics," to which "in successive terms were added courses in logic, moral philosophy, ethics, and natural and political philosophy."[10] At St. Andrews Wilson was formally introduced to the new thinking of his age. "Newton's revolutionary physics had been embraced at St. Andrews and the new natural philosophy based on it had been taught by James Gregory before 1691. What was true of the new physics was also true of the new Lockean psychology and the new philosophies of Hutcheson, Hume, Berkeley, and Shaftesbury."[11]

There is apparently no record of the books Wilson read at St. Andrews, but his biographer Smith speculates that "he must have been much influenced by the fresh and exciting forces of the Scottish and English Enlightenment." It is difficult to say exactly how the new teachings affected Wilson's path toward the ministry, although he seems not to have wavered. After four years at St. Salvator's College in St. Andrews, he "moved on to the school of divinity at St. Mary's College and spent a year studying under Dr. Andrew Shaw."[12] According to Smith, Wilson did not see his divinity studies through to the end. After his father's death, Wilson supposedly withdrew from St. Mary's in order to help support his three younger brothers, three elder sisters, and mother. But there is ambiguity in the historical record. Konkle and Waln argue that Wilson, after leaving St. Andrews, continued his studies at Edinburgh and Glasgow, an event curiously missing from Smith's biography.[13] If Konkle and Waln are correct, then it cannot escape our attention that these great universities were the home of none other than Hume, Ferguson, Smith, Hugh Blair, and William Robertson. According to Konkle, "[j]ust how long Wilson studied at Edinburgh is not known, although its records show that he entered upon Blair's studies in Rhetoric in 1763 and began logic and ethics under Stevenson and Ferguson, respectively, in early 1765."[14] It was about this time that Wilson decided to emigrate to America.

Wilson arrived in New York in the fall of 1765 with little money and few belongings. Wilson eventually made his way to Philadelphia to meet with friends and relatives "who might find it in their power to help a young adventurer from the homeland."[15] With his solid learning, Wilson had no difficulty securing an appointment as a tutor in the College of Philadelphia, then under the guidance of Benjamin Franklin and the Reverend William Smith. According to Waln, "Mr. Wilson was considered by the trustee, before whom he was examined, as the best classical scholar" to tutor in the Latin department of the college.[16] Tutoring classical languages, however, was apparently not the career for which Wilson was most suited. After a few months teaching at the College of Philadelphia, Wilson applied to study law under perhaps the most "outstanding lawyer in the colonies and an eloquent champion of colonial liberties," John Dickinson.[17]

Wilson's encounter with Dickinson had a decisive influence on the young Scot's political maturation. Seeking to ameliorate the burdens of the Seven Years' War with France that doubled its national debt, in addition to the costs of administering its new territories in Canada and the Mississippi Valley, the English Parliament saddled the colonies with the Sugar and Stamp Acts. The storm over the passage of these acts had hardly passed before the Townsend Duties were levied on goods from Britain imported into the colonies, including, as we know so well, tea. Soon after these duties were imposed, John Dickinson, under the pen name "Pennsylvania Farmer," began to attack the parliamentary authority to tax the colonies. As an apprentice, and, later, as a young lawyer, Wilson found himself in the midst of a burgeoning revolution. Smith argues that the "intense drama of the times gave Wilson's study of the law a new perspective and raised it to a higher plane." To the study of "pleadings, forms, terms of contract, replevins, and torts," Blackstone, and the common law, Wilson added "constitutions and frames of government —Hume and Montesquieu, Adam Ferguson, . . . Algernon Sidney, Locke, Richard Hooker, Lord Bacon, Bolingbroke, . . . and dozens of others, combing them for arguments that might go into the colonial armory."[18] "Mr. Wilson would not remain an idle spectator of passing events," argues Waln.[19] It did not take long for Wilson to bring his astonishing eclecticism to bear on the colonial struggle against Britain.

With his good friend William White, Wilson had already published a series of essays under the pseudonym "The Visitant" before he penned the "Considerations on the Nature and Extent of the Legislative Authority of the British Parliament."[20] First conceived in 1768—but not published until 1774 because some of his friends and advisors thought it was perhaps a bit too inflammatory—one commentator argues that the "Considerations" is "perhaps the most far-sighted, coherent, and logical [revolutionary pamphlet] that came from the pen of any colonial disputant in the years prior to the American Revolution."[21] If viewed in the light of John Adams's "Novanglus" or Thomas Jefferson's "Summary View of the Rights of British America," Smith's claim may be a bit far-fetched. Be that as it may, there is no denying the logic and elegance of the essay, and the persuasive evidence marshaled by Wilson against the British Parliament. This early revolutionary pamphlet provides the optimal starting point from which to begin assessing the character and content of Wilson's political thought.

Wilson begins the "Considerations" (as he will later begin the *Lectures on Law*) by identifying Sir William Blackstone as the principal and authoritative exponent of the view that "the parliament of Great Britain have power to make laws binding the American colonies" (2:723). Quoting from the *Commentaries*, Wilson writes that Blackstone is of the opinion

> "That there is and must be in every state a supreme, irresistible, absolute, uncontrolled authority, in which the *jura summi imperii*, in the rights of sovereignty, reside." "That this supreme power is, by the Constitution of Great Britain, vested in the kings, lords, and commons." "That, therefore, the acts of the king, lords, commons, or, in other words, acts of parliament, have, by the British constitution, a binding force on the American colonies, they composing a part of the British empire." (2:723)[22]

Of note is one passage of the "Considerations" that illumines some of the most important themes of Wilson's political philosophy. In response to Blackstone, Wilson writes:

> All men are, by nature, equal and free: no one has a right to any authority over another without his consent: all lawful government is founded on the consent of those who are subject to it: such consent was given with a view to ensure and to increase the happiness of the governed, above what they could enjoy in an independent and unconnected state of nature. The consequence is, that the happiness of society is the *first* law of every government.
>
> This rule is founded on the law of nature: it must control every political maxim: it must regulate the legislature itself. The people have a right to insist that this rule be observed; and are entitled to demand a moral security that the legislature will observe it. If they have not the first, they are slaves. If they have not the second, they are, every moment, exposed to slavery. (2:723)[23]

We will see later how each of these important claims is fully developed in the *Lectures*.

The "Considerations" established Wilson as one of the most eloquent champions of colonial rights. The honor bestowed on him of addressing the delegates of the Continental Congress on the justice of the colonial cause in January 1775 testifies to the esteem in which Wilson was held by his country. Wilson's membership in the Congress was erratic—serving three periods between 1775 and 1777, 1782 and 1783, 1785 and 1787—but his contributions were nonetheless significant.[24] Waln so concisely summarizes Wilson's accomplishments there that he is worth quoting at length.

> In June, 1775, [Wilson] was of the committee which prepared an eloquent and nervous appeal to the assembly of Jamaica; and in July of the same year, when the Indians were divided into three departments, the northern, middle, and southern, and commissioners appointed by congress to superintend Indian affairs in behalf of the colonies, [Wilson] was elected a commissioner for the middle department. He was also a member of the several committees, to take into consideration the state of the colonies, and report what number of forces would be necessary for their

defense: To prepare a letter to the inhabitants of Canada; to prepare an address to the united colonies; . . . to confer with General Washington, and concert a plan of military operations; to devise ways and means for supplying the treasury; to form an effectual plan for surpressing the internal enemies of America; . . . to explain to the several states, the reasons which induced congress to enlarge the powers of general Washington; . . . He was a member of the standing committee appointed to hear and determine upon appeals brought against sentences passed on libels, in the courts of admiralty in their respective states. He was also attached to the first board of war. In fact, no member was more frequently called upon to exert his talents, and no member exhibited more industry, capacity, and perseverance, in obeying the calls of duty, than James Wilson.[25]

By the time Wilson was elected to the Constitutional Convention of 1787, he was an established national statesman of long and distinguished service to his country. Wilson's contributions to the Constitutional Convention are often the point of departure for most Wilson commentators. Familiarity precludes my pausing to consider them here.[26]

Following the Constitutional Convention, a young Philadelphia lawyer named Charles Smith placed, through his father, the Reverend William Smith, a recommendation before the trustees of the College of Philadelphia for "'a law Lecture or Lectures' [to] be included 'among the many other improvements of the plan of a liberal education in this college.'"[27] Wilson, a trustee of the College, wasted no time in submitting his own proposal for such lectures, which he hoped would "'furnish a rational and useful entertainment to gentlemen of all professions; and in particular to assist in forming the Legislator, the Magistrate and the Lawyer.'" The trustees nominated Wilson. Wilson's lectures would mark "the first important law course to be established since the inception of the Federal Government, and thus, with its distinguished lecturer, it attracted special attention as the potential incubator of a new *American system* of jurisprudence." That the new government was making its home in Philadelphia, at least for the time being, provided Wilson the opportunity to deliver the introductory lecture to a most distinguished audience. In attendance were President George Washington, Vice President John Adams, members of Congress, the officers of the new government—perhaps Alexander Hamilton and Thomas Jefferson, both of whom had recently moved to Philadelphia—the wives of some of these dignitaries, and members of the state senate and house. The introductory lecture was delivered in the college's main building the evening of December 15, 1790. On the heels of Wilson's long and distinguished service on behalf of the new Republic, the "moment was, in a sense, the climax of his career."[28]

Discovering the Law of Nature

We noted at the outset that the law of nature is at the heart of Wilson's political teaching as it is at the heart of political life itself. On this latter point Wilson stands with John Locke, who argues that "a great part of the *Municipal Laws* of Countries, which are only so far right, as they are founded on the Law of Nature, by which they are to be regulated and interpreted."[29] No understanding of Wilson's comprehensive political teaching is possible without a detailed examination of the law of nature.

Wilson begins the chapter "Of the Law of Nature" by arguing that "all that is to be known, all that is to be done, all that is to be enjoyed depends upon the proper exertion and direction of our numerous powers." In a passing reflection on those powers, Wilson provisionally concludes that it is inconceivable that the "all-gracious and all-wise Author of our existence," who has "formed us for such great and such good ends," has "left us without a conductor to lead us in the way, by which those ends may be attained." In the course of his investigations, Wilson anticipates that "[w]e shall probably find that, to direct the more important parts of our conduct, the bountiful Governour of the universe has been graciously pleased to provide us a law; and that, to direct the less important parts of it, he has made us capable of providing a law for ourselves" (1:126). Wilson is referring to the law of nature and to the municipal law. We are now concerned with the former, which, according to Wilson, "we shall find to be reduced to this one paternal command—Let man pursue his own perfection and happiness" (1:129).

To discover the meaning of the law of nature, Wilson argues that we must turn to an important and related question: What is the "nature and cause of obligation" (1:130)? Wilson does not say why it is necessary to address this query, although one may suppose that the questions "What is the law of nature?" and "What is the nature and cause of obligation?" are in some manner inseparable. According to Wilson, nature dictates a particular course of action for human beings, and we are "obliged" to heed the dictates of the natural law. In doing so, however, "it will be proper to ascertain the precise state of the question before us." That question "is this—what is the efficient cause of moral obligation—of the eminent distinction between right and wrong?" The investigation of this question, Wilson argues, "has been often and injudiciously blended with another question, connected with it, but from which it ought to be preserved separate and distinct. That other question is—how shall we, in particular instances, learn the dictates of our duty, and make, with accuracy, the eminent distinction, which we have just now mentioned?" According to Wilson, the "first question points to the *principle* of obligation." The "second points to the *means* by which our obligation to perform a specified action, or a series of specified actions, may be deduced" (1:132). Wilson examines each in turn.

In regard to efficient cause of moral obligation, Wilson says it is "the will of God. This is the supreme law. His just and full right of imposing laws, and our duty of obeying them, are the sources of our moral obligations" (1:132). Having asserted that the efficient cause of moral obligation is the will of God, some of his readers may wonder why this is to be believed. On this point Wilson deserves to be quoted at length:

> If I am asked—why do you obey the will of God? I answer—because it is my duty so to do. If I am asked again—how do you know it is your duty? I answer again—because I am told by my moral sense or conscience. If I am asked a third time—how do you know that you ought to do that, of which your conscience enjoins the performance? I can only say, I *feel* that such is my duty. Here my investigation must stop, reasoning cannot go farther. The science of morals, as well as other sciences, is founded on truths, that cannot be discovered or proved by reasoning. Reason is confined to the investigation of unknown truths by means of such as are known. We cannot, therefore, begin to reason, till we are furnished, otherwise than by reason, with some truths, on which we can found our arguments. Even in mathematicks, we must be provided with axioms perceived intuitively to be true, before our demonstrations can commence. Morality, like mathematicks, has its intuitive truths, without which we cannot make a single step in our reasonings on the subject. . . . If a person was not possessed of the feeling before mentioned; it would not be in the power of arguments, to give him any conception of the distinction between right or wrong. These would be to him equally unintelligible, as the term *colour* to one who was born and has continued blind. But that there is, in human nature, such a moral principle, has been felt and acknowledged in all ages and nations. (1:132–33)[30]

Note the descent. Wilson begins by invoking God, our Creator, whose "will" we are bound to obey. When pushed, however, Wilson reduces God's will and its dictates, first, to the moral sense and conscience, and then to "feeling." The principle, or what Wilson terms the *cause*, of our duty is a feeling.

From the viewpoint of medieval Christianity, some might argue this is unproblematic. Thomas Aquinas, for example, is of the view that "the order of the precepts of natural law is according to the order of natural inclinations." But there is also for Thomas a natural hierarchy of inclinations culminating in the sovereignty of reason. First, Aquinas argues that "inasmuch as every substance seeks the preservation of its own being according to nature, and by reason of this inclination, whatever is a means of preserving life and of warding off its obstacles belongs to the natural law." Second, "there is in man an inclination to things that pertain to him more especially according to that nature which he has in common with other animals, and in virtue of this inclination, those things are said to belong to the natural law 'which nature has taught all animals,' such as sexual intercourse, education of offspring, and so forth." Third, and most important, "there is reason, which nature is proper to him; thus man has a natural inclination to know the truth about God and to live in society, and in this respect, whatever pertains to this inclination belongs to the natural law, for instance, to shun ignorance, to avoid offending those among whom one has to live, and other things regarding this inclination."[31] The question before us is whether Wilson accepts Thomas's hierarchy culminating in the rule of reason. Wilson does not, and this can be demonstrated by examining the *means* by which the law of nature is known. According to Wilson, the law of nature is known "by our conscience, by our reason, and by the Holy Scriptures" (1: 133). Wilson begins with conscience.

Conscience and the Instrumental Character of Natural Reason

"The power of moral perception" or conscience, Wilson writes, is "an original power—a power of its own kind; and totally distinct from the ideas of utility and agreeableness" (1:133). "By that power," he continues, "we have conceptions of merit and demerit, or duty and moral obligation. By that power, we perceive some things in human conduct to be right, and others to be wrong." Wilson argues that it is possible to "rely on the dictates of this faculty" as we would "upon the determination of our senses" (1:133). "Never was there any of the human species above the condition of an idiot, to whom all actions appeared indifferent" (1:136). Accordingly, there "must . . . be in morals, as in other sciences, first principles, which derive not their evidence from any antecedent principles, but which may be said to be intuitively discerned" (1:136). These principles Wilson calls "self-evident truths." They constitute the first principles of human action. These "truths" or "feelings" are discovered by intuition and introspection. They are not posited by reason (1:136–37).[32]

Although human beings do not ascend by rational deliberation to Platonic forms or to an architectonic logos in search for eternal truths, reason is nonetheless "usefully introduced, and performs many services." Reason sometimes "regulates our belief; and in many instances she regulates our conduct. She determines the proper means to any end; and she decides the preference of one end over another." The ends to which Wilson here refers are not fundamental ends, the apprehension of which he has left to the conscience or the moral sense. Reason "judges concerning subordinate ends; but concerning ultimate ends she is not employed" (1:137). A "very accurate reason or judgment is . . . requisite, to give the true determination amidst intricate doubts, arising from obscure or opposite utilities" (1:138). The means to particular ends are generally open to variance and thus to deliberation.[33]

Wilson extends the province of reason by arguing that it also "serves to illustrate, to prove, to extend, to apply what our moral sense has already suggested to us, concerning just and unjust, proper and improper, right and wrong" (1:138). Reason "considers the relations of actions, and traces them to the remotest consequences." Often we "see men, with the most honest hearts and most pure intentions, embarrassed and puzzled, when a case, delicate and complicated, comes before them." Although they "feel what is right" and "are unshaken in their general principles

. . . they are unaccustomed to pursue [principles] through their different ramifications; to make the necessary discrimination and exceptions, or to modify them according to the circumstances of time and place" (1:138). Clearly, Wilson is no misologist. Reason is a "noble faculty" that when "kept within its proper sphere, and applied to its proper uses, exalts human creatures *almost* to the rank of superior beings" (1:212, my emphasis). But "reason has no other root than the principles of common sense: it grows out of them: and from them it draws its nourishment" (1:223). Wilson collapses any distinction we might be tempted to draw among conscience, moral sense, and common sense. The language of "feeling" or "sense" gradually replaces that of conscience. At this point it is useful to recall that for Thomas "conscience is nothing else than the application of knowledge to some action," where "knowledge is in reason."[34]

Having demonstrated his allegiance to the modern principle that the root of moral action is feeling, Wilson turns to the content of the moral sense. Following the lead provided by Hume, Wilson writes:

> The *ultimate* ends of human actions, can never, in any case, be accounted for by reason. They recommend themselves entirely to the sentiments and affections of men, without dependence on the intellectual faculties. Why do you desire exercise? Because you desire health. Why do you desire health? Because sickness is painful. Why do you hate pain? No answer is heard. Can one be given? No. (1:142)[35]

According to Wilson, then, sensible human beings can agree that pain is bad and that pleasure is good. When coming to that crucial point in his analysis, Wilson equates the moral sense or conscience to feelings of pleasure and pain common to most, if not all, human beings. Wilson then proceeds to equate pleasure and pain with "virtue and vice" (1:142). It "were well for us," Wilson concludes, if "on many occasions . . . we laid our reasoning systems aside, and were more attentive in observing the genuine impulses of nature" (1:141). Indeed, "without the moral sense, a man may be prudent, but he cannot be virtuous" (1:143).

Scripture

The role of reason and sentiment ascertained, Wilson then turns to Scripture. The turn to Scripture is necessary, for according to the medieval philosophers our human or natural understanding is imperfect and must be supplemented by supernatural truths. Wilson discredits this view in the service of religious liberty, but not without first engaging in an elaborate circumlocution. Toward the end of the chapter "Of the Law of Nature," Wilson writes that "[r]eason and conscience can do much; but they stand in need of support and assistance" (1:143). While conscience and reason are "useful and excellent monitors," their "admonitions are not sufficiently clear; at other times, they are not sufficiently powerful; at all times, their influence is not sufficiently extensive." Thus, in "compassion to the imperfection of our internal powers, our all-gracious Creator, Preserver, and Ruler has been pleased to discover and enforce his laws, by a revelation given to us immediately and directly from himself. This revelation is contained in the holy scriptures" (1:143).

At first glance, then, Wilson argues that Revelation is handed down to human beings in order to correct the deficiencies of natural knowledge. These initial observations aside, Wilson then writes that the "moral precepts delivered in the sacred oracles form part of the law of nature, are of the same origin, and of the same obligation, operating universally and perpetually." In other words, the sacred oracles form part of that law of nature which Wilson went to lengths to secure in common "feelings" of pleasure and pain. While Wilson began the discussion with Scripture reigning supreme, he has in a few sentences collapsed Revelation into the law of nature. Wilson then offers this startling conclusion: "On some subjects, those in particular, which related to the Deity, to Providence, and to a future state, our natural knowledge is greatly improved, refined, and exalted by that which is revealed" (1:143–44). We wonder what guidance is provided for our *present* state. Wilson then argues that whoever expects to find in the Scriptures "particular directions for every moral doubt which arises, expects more than he will find." The Scriptures "generally *presuppose* knowledge of those principles of morality; and they are employed not so much in teaching new rules on this subject, as in enforcing the practice of those already known, by greater certainty, and by new sanctions." We wonder whether the "new sanctions" may not be a reference to the civil magistrate. Though the Scriptures "present the warmest recommendations and the strongest inducements in favor of virtue," and though "they exhibit the most powerful dissuasives from vice," they do not explain the "origin, the nature, and the extent of the several rights and duties." Nor "do they specify in what instances one right or duty is entitled to preference over another." The Scriptures can only support what we already know by means of feeling and what reason teaches us about those feelings. The Scriptures "are addressed to rational and moral agents, capable of *previously knowing the rights of men,* and the tendencies of actions; of approving what is good, and of disapproving what is evil" (1:144, my emphasis). Following Francis Hutcheson, Wilson concludes:

> [T]he scriptures support, confirm, and corroborate, but do not supersede the operations of reason and the moral sense. The information with regard to our duties and obligations, drawn from these various sources, ought not to run in unconnected and diminished channels: it should flow from one united stream, which, by its combined force and just direction, will impel us uniformly and effectually towards our greatest good. (1:144)[36]

Wilson brings the chapter on the law of nature to a close by arguing that "[t]he law of nature is immutable, not by the effect of an arbitrary disposition, but because it has its foundations in the nature, constitution, and mutual relations of men and things" (1:145). We are constituted with a God-given sentiment, a moral sense, by virtue of which we can "know," "prove," or "perceive" happiness and misery, pleasure and pain. This is the foundation of the law of nature. "This immutability of nature's laws has nothing in it repugnant to the supreme power of an all-perfect Being." Indeed, because the Creator is the author of our constitution, "he cannot but command or forbid such things as are *necessarily* agreeable or disagreeable to this very constitution. He is under the glorious *necessity* of not contradicting himself" (1:145, my emphases). The law of nature and necessity coincide. To heed the dictates of necessity is coeval with obedience to God's will. Reason is called upon to service the pleasures and avoid the pains. Wilson does equate the law of nature with "right reason" and appeals to antiquity by quoting Cicero.[37] But this law is "an inference from the passions," if you will, for the sake of peace, order, and sociability.

> Whatever promotes the greatest happiness of the whole, is congenial to the principles of utility and sociability: and whatever unites in it all the foregoing properties, must be agreeable to the will of God: for, as has been said once, and as ought to be said again, his will is graciously comprised in this one paternal precept—*Let man pursue his happiness and perfection.* (1:145, my emphasis)

The reader should note that the paternal precept at the beginning of the chapter is: "Let man pursue his own perfection and happiness" (1:129). I do not think that the replacement of "perfection and happiness" for "happiness and perfection" is by any means fortuitous. As soon as Wilson reverses the order of the paternal precept, he writes that "the poet" (referring perhaps to

Alexander Pope) says that "'Man never *is* . . . but always *to be* blest'" (1:146). Wilson then argues that this "sentiment would certainly be more consolatory, and, I think, it would be likewise more just, if we were to say—man ever *is*; *for* always to be blest" (1:146). Though subtle, Wilson's editing is revealing. The "poet" would have human beings depend on the grace of God for their good fortune. The statement that man "never is" until "blest" harmonizes with the religious teaching according to which human beings are worthy only insofar as the Grace of God is extended to them. Wilson would elevate human nature above a threshold acceptable to the religious teachings he sets out to reform, and says that "man ever is." Humans need not wait for the beneficence from above, but instead ought to labor and thus to provide for themselves (1:392).

> That we should have more and better things before us, than all that we have yet acquired or enjoyed, is unquestionably a most desirable state. The reflection on this circumstance, far from diminishing our sense or importance of our present attainments and advantages, produces the contrary effects. The present is gilded by the prospect of the future. . . . It is the glorious destiny of man to be always progressive. Forgetting those things that are left behind, it is his duty, and it is his happiness, to press on towards those that are before. In the order of Providence . . . the progress of societies towards perfection resembles that of an individual. (1:146)

While Wilson began the chapter by arguing that the natural law has to do first with human perfection, and then with human happiness, the development or unfolding of the argument makes clear that human happiness or pleasure is the foundation of the natural law. Human beings necessarily have their own pleasure first in mind—hence the need to reverse the paternal precept so that happiness is first and perfection second. While the word "perfection" would seem to indicate that he speaks of a perfection to which ancients or perhaps Christians may subscribe, perfection turns out to be a rational process by means of which human beings satisfy and secure what is most decisive or necessary. Accordingly, Wilson refers to the law of nature as "progressive" (1:147). Once we recognize that we are emancipated from the constraints placed on what was once deemed base, reason can then operate to service emancipated desire.

The Law of Nature as the Law of Nations

We learned from a close reading "Of the Law of Nature" that Wilson quietly but explicitly distances himself from a dependence on Aquinas's natural law teaching. The natural law is, in Wilson's words, "known," "perceived," or "proved" by the feelings of pleasure and pain present in human beings qua human beings. While Wilson's discussion of the law of nature thus far would seem to point to his disagreement with Aristotelian scholasticism and his agreement with the modern transformation of natural law initiated by Hobbes, I do not think that the evidence in "Of the Law of Nature" alone suffices to support this conclusion. There is, for example, no mention of natural rights in the chapter "Of the Law of Nature." Wilson has spoken of pleasure and pain in a most general sense, but not specifically of the desire for self-preservation that is central to Hobbes and Locke's natural law. Wilson has yet to mention the state of nature. Wilson's analysis tempts but it does not persuade. No doubt, it is a question of no small importance why much of what the reader might think is properly the subject of the chapter "Of the Law of Nature" occurs in "Of the Law of Nations." This section will show that the most important characteristics of the natural law make their appearance in the section "Of the Law of Nations" for the following reasons. The "international system"—whose salient feature is the absence of a sovereign—is used by Wilson as a metaphor for the state of nature. The return to a prepolitical state of nature uncovers a human being's "natural state," where his or her natural inclinations,

obligations, and *rights* are revealed. Political life must be understood in terms of its beginnings
—the human passions—not its rational "ends" perfected in the polis, as both Aristotle and
Aquinas would have us believe. It is in the analysis of the state of nature or the law of nations
that Wilson's political first principles come to light.

Wilson argues that "[t]he opinions of many concerning the law of nations have been very
vague and unsatisfactory," not least of which are those of the so-called father of international
law, Hugo Grotius (1:149). Although "[i]n this science Grotius did much," Wilson claims that
Grotius was "unfortunate in not setting out on the right and solid principles. His celebrated book
of the *Rights of War and Peace* is indeed useful; but it ought not to be read without a due degree
of caution" (1:150). Grotius's error consists in having separated the law of nations "from the law
of nature"—in having assigned "to it a different origin." According to Wilson, Grotius traces the
law of nations "from the principle of universal consent."[38] As a consequence, "the law of nations
would be only obligatory upon those by whom the consent was given, and only by reason of that
consent. The further consequence would be, that the law of nations would lose a part, and the
greatest part, of its obligatory force, and would also be restrained to the sphere of its operations"
(1:150). Wilson will "freely admit that there are *laws* of nations, which are founded altogether
upon consent" (my emphasis). For example, "[n]ational treaties are laws of nations, obligatory
solely by consent," as are the "customs of nations." But Wilson separates himself from Grotius
in thinking that "[t]he law of nations, properly so called, is the law of nature applied to states and
sovereigns, obligatory upon them in the same manner, and for the same reasons, as the law of
nature is obligatory upon individuals. Universal, indispensable, and unchangeable is the obligation of both" (1:150–51). The law of nations then is not the *consensus gentium*, but rather a set
of theoretical principles regarding the rights and the duties of sovereigns, just as the law of nature
is the same set of theoretical principles with respect to individuals (1:148–49). A study "Of the
Law of Nations" brings to light those principles which Wilson chose not to reveal in the chapter
"Of the Law of Nature."[39]

Wilson proceeds to illumine the principles of the natural law by first chiding Burlamaqui and
others who claim that the law of nations is "'nothing more than the general law of sociability'"
or the "'the law of beneficence'" (1:154). To correct the "imperfect conceptions" of this and
other authors, Wilson would have us "recur to what the law of nature dictates to the individual."
Wilson asks: "Are there not duties which he owes to himself? Is he not obliged to consult and
promote his preservation, his freedom, his reputation, his improvement, his perfection, his
happiness?" (1:154). In other words, Wilson questions those who would interpret the law of
nature as dictating an obligation to others *over and above oneself*. We need not interpret this as
an assault on natural duties of all kinds. The question before us concerns the *primary* dictum of
the law of nature.

Wilson argues that the "first and most necessary duty of nations, as well as men, is to do no
wrong" (1:160). Note Wilson's modification of the Golden Rule: "If the law of the great society
of nations requires, as we have seen it to require, that each should contribute to the happiness of
others; the first degree of this duty surely is, that each should abstain from every thing, which
would positively impair that perfection and happiness." Granted, the statement is conditional, and
it suggests that human beings ought to contribute to the happiness of others; but, the conditional-
ity of the statement should not eclipse from view the primary dictum of the law of nature. Wilson
argues:

> If . . . a nation, in the necessary prosecution of its own duties and rights, does what is disagreeable
> or even inconvenient to another, this is not to be considered as an injury; it ought to be viewed
> as the unavoidable result, and not as the *governing principle* of its conduct. If, at such conduct,

offense is taken, it is the fault of that nation, which takes, not of that nation, which occasions it. (1:160, my emphasis)

The law of nature teaches: Do no harm. It counsels preemptive measures if and only if necessary.

Wilson seems to retreat from the primary dictum of the law of nature by arguing that "nations are not only forbidden to do evil; they are also commanded to do good to one another" (1:160). We must look very closely at what Wilson means by doing "good to one another," or what he refers to as "humanity." Wilson argues:

> The duties of humanity are incumbent upon nations as well as upon individuals. An individual cannot subsist, at least he cannot subsist comfortably, by himself. What is true concerning one, is true concerning all. Without mutual good offices and assistance, therefore, happiness could not be procured, perhaps existence could not be preserved. Hence the *necessity* of the duties of humanity among individuals. Every one is obliged, in the first place, to do what he can for himself; in the next, to do what he can for others; beginning with those with whom he is most connected. The consequence is, that each man is obliged to give to others assistance, for which they have real occasion, and which he can give without being wanting to himself. What each is obliged to perform for others, from others he is entitled to receive. Hence the advantage as well as the duty of humanity. These principles receive an application to states as well as to men. (1:160–61, my emphasis)

It is arguable that the foregoing account of "humanity" and "doing good" provides evidence of Wilson's reliance on Hobbes, Locke, and the Scots, not on Christian Aristotelians. "Doing good" does not amount to saintly self-abnegation. According to the Bible, the Golden Rule amounts to this: "whatsoever you wish that men would so to you, do so to them" (Matt. 7:12). This could be read as an exhortation to the duty of charity. Hobbes makes a slight alteration to the Bible that is of enormous consequence for liberal political practice. At first, Hobbes seems to concur: "This is the law of the Gospell; *Whatsoever you require that others would do to you, that do ye to them*." However, the author of the *Leviathan* prefers the so-called "law of men, *Quod tibi fieri non vis, alteri ne feceris*," or as Hobbes translates with further modifications later, "*Do not that to another, which thou thinkest unreasonable to be done by another to thy self.*"[40] Now, it is clear that the duty to do good and the duty to avoid inflicting harm are not incompatible. But they are not identical. In constituting modern liberal principles, Hobbes took note of the horrendous examples of "doing good" that involved war against infidels and heretics. We need not speak of sectarian zealotry or bigotry. An excessive and cruel concern for the "purity" of my neighbor's conscience is avoided by adopting Hobbes's Golden Rule. The law of the Gospel is potentially illiberal; Hobbes's is not. Hobbes's rule is entirely consistent with toleration, the liberal principle par excellence. It is consistent with a political doctrine based on natural rights.[41]

At first glance, it would seem that "doing good" amounts to leaving others alone. According to Wilson, however, this is an inadequate or insufficient reading of toleration. For Wilson as well as for his modern predecessors, toleration implies an other-regarding sense, often ignored by the contemporary critics of liberalism. The author of the *Second Treatise*, for example, argues that the law of nature dictates that "[e]veryone is *bound to preserve himself*, and not to quit his station wilfully." But Locke also argues that when our own preservation comes not into competition, we ought as much as we can "*to preserve the rest of Mankind*, and may not unless it be to do Justice to an Offender, take away, or impair the life, or what tends to the Preservation of the Life, the Liberty, the Health, Limb or Goods of Another."[42] In Locke we thus find an explicit duty to respect the rights of our fellow human beings to life, liberty, and estate. We are also called upon to "preserve Mankind" by punishing offenders of the law of nature.[43]

In a similar vein, Adam Smith argues "that to feel much for others, and little for ourselves, that to restrain our selfish, and to indulge our benevolent affections, constitutes the perfection of human nature." Smith, however, aims at something less than perfect, less demanding, and thus attainable. "As to love our neighbour as our selves is the great law of Christianity," Smith writes, "so it is the *great precept of nature* to love ourselves only as we love our neighbour, or what comes to the same thing, as our neighbour is capable of loving us."[44] Wilson situates himself between the early moderns and the Bible by arguing that doing good amounts to reciprocal assistance. Our neighbor is indeed capable of loving us as we are of loving him or her. There are numerous instances when "doing good" is called for. But according to the liberal thinkers, we must understand each others' limitations in this regard. An excessive expectation of others—that they love us as we love ourselves—may sometimes cloud from view our responsibilities to ourselves and to others. It may cloud from view a passion that is especially pernicious to political life and that often parades in the guise of "justice"—that is, the desire for mastery. We love to have it our way and often insist that others act as we demand. In response to the tyrannical impulses of human nature, Wilson and the Enlighteners from whom he draws inspiration make the law of nature a restraint upon pernicious passions and a respect for the rights or freedoms of my fellow human beings, not the means to the perfection or salvation of our souls and of society.

Only in the light of the foregoing considerations can we properly understand why Wilson's natural *law* teaching is not at odds with his natural *rights* teaching. In the chapter "Of Natural Rights of Individuals," Wilson argues that the "defense of one's self, [is] justly called the primary law of nature" (2:609). This is a law that should not "be abrogated by any regulation of municipal law. This principle of defense is not confined merely to the person; it extends to the liberty and property of man: it is not confined merely to his own person; it extends to the persons of all those, to whom he bears a peculiar relation—of his wife, of his parent, of his child, of his master, and of his servant" (2:609). This law extends to the "person of every one . . . whose liberty is unjustly and forcibly attacked. *It becomes humanity as well as justice*" (2:609, my emphasis). According to Wilson, "liberty is frequently used to denote all the absolute rights of men" (2:586). "Rights" are the primary fact from which Wilson reasons toward civil society and government. Our natural "rights result from the natural state of man; from that situation, in which he would find himself, if no civil government was instituted." Wilson takes his bearing from natural liberty in the state of nature. It is for this reason that his most explicit pronouncements about the natural law take place in the chapter "Of the Law of Nations." The "international system" is characterized precisely by the absence of a sovereign. It is the clearest example of the state of nature. "In his unrelated state," Wilson argues, "man has a natural right to his property, to his character, to liberty, and to safety." In other words, human beings have a right to life, to the means of securing life, to a modicum of dignity and respect, and the law of nature dictates that each should do what is necessary to secure those fundamental rights: "I shall certainly be excused from adducing any formal arguments to evince, that life, and whatever is necessary for the safety of life, are the natural rights of man" (2:596). "Government," Wilson continues, "should be formed to secure and to enlarge the exercise of the natural rights of its members; and every government, which has not this in view, as its principal object, is not government of the legitimate kind" (2:592).

Sociability

Following Hobbes and Locke, then, Wilson argues that the "primary law of nature" is the "defense of oneself" (2:609). Man is not only "justified in defending" but also "justified in re-taking, his property, or his peculiar relations, when from him they are unjustly taken and detained." And "this redress," Wilson concludes, is "dictated by nature" (2:610). Now, if this is the truth about human nature and the human condition, then we are compelled to wonder to what extent the "self" Wilson describes is compatible with "society." We wonder how civil society can be born from a condition where human beings are judges of what constitutes a threat to their natural rights. We wonder how civil society is possible among human beings who are impelled by nature and are dictated by necessity to care for themselves first. For our present purposes, the problem concerning the relationship between the self-regarding "individual" and civil society is compounded by the fact that Wilson refers to human beings as "social beings" (1:230). Commentators consider these references as evidence of Wilson's debt to Thomas, classical republicanism, or civic humanism. We turn to Wilson's discussion of the constitution of civil society and government to explain the relation between the self-regarding and other-regarding passions, and the relation between these and the liberal principle of consent.

That we are indeed "fitted and intended for society, and that society is fitted and intended for us," will become "evident by considering our passions and affections, as well as by considering our moral perceptions, and the operations of our understandings" (1:233). Wilson returns to the discussion of the passions. Our moral perceptions show that "we have all the emotions, which are necessary in order that society may be formed and maintained."

> We have tenderness for the fair sex: we have affection for our children, for our parents, and for our other relations: we have attachment to our friends: we have a regard for reputation and esteem: we possess gratitude and compassion: we enjoy pleasure in the happiness of others, especially when we have been instrumental in procuring it: we entertain for our country an animated and vigorous zeal; we feel delight in the agreeable conception of the improvement and happiness of mankind. (1:233)[45]

It should not escape notice that there is a "progression" or an ordering here. First, Wilson claims that we have "tenderness for the fair sex." Society is thus rooted in the sexual and tender pleasures for the opposite sex.[46] Beyond the immediate attachments between parents and children, human beings have a high regard for reputation and esteem. Humans delight in the praise given to them by other human beings. Only after considering the strongest passions does Wilson speak of gratitude and compassion, of the pleasure of enjoying the happiness of others—especially when we have been instrumental in procuring it—and then of patriotism and of philanthropy.

In explaining the progression of sentiments described at the outset, Wilson turns first to one he considers basic: sympathy. He argues that "sympathy is an important quality of many of our passions: in particular, it invites and produces a communication of joys and sorrows, hopes and fears." He provides an example:

> So soon as a child can speak, he can ask, and he can have an answer: before he can speak, he shows signs of love, of resentment, and of other affections necessarily pointed to society. He is capable of social intercourse long before he is capable of reasoning. We behold the charming intercourse between his mother and him, before he is one year old. He can, by signs, ask and refuse, threaten and supplicate. In danger, he clings to his mother—for I will not, on this occasion, distinguish between mother and nurse—he enters into her joy and grief, is happy in her caresses, and is unhappy in her displeasure. (1:234)

This example paints images of love, tenderness, and affection, but also of dependence, need, even resentment and threat. The social operations are as much instruments by which humans are drawn together in love and in need as they are operations by which we push each other apart.

Wilson speaks of sympathy as if it were a mechanism capable of identifying emotions that are both self-regarding and other-regarding.[47]

Not only does Wilson view the social sentiments in this complex manner, but in a separate discussion, "Of Man, as a Member of a Confederation" (1:247–69), he goes on to explain why other-regarding sentiments *alone* are not the basis by which a well-regulated, viable political life is erected and maintained.[48] Wilson grants that "[a] union of hearts and affections, as well as a union of counsels and interests, is the very life and soul of a confederated republick." Indeed, "[t]he operations and aims of our social powers" are "capable of being raised to the greatest height." But, Wilson warns, the social passions "partake of human imperfection." Even "in their most useful and amiable forms, they sometimes degenerate into irregularity, abuse, and what I may call an excess concentricity: by this I mean, overstrained exertions within a narrow and contracted sphere. Faction itself is frequently nothing less than a warm but inconsiderate ebullition of our social propensities" (1:266).[49] A human being's social propensities are as problematic as they are necessary to political life. The social operations "will be beneficial or pernicious, according to the direction, which [they] first receive, and the objects to which [they] ultimately tend" (1:266). The extended republic will ensure that the passions will not become too narrow and mean spirited.[50]

After providing an example of the complex bond between mother and child, Wilson proceeds to show that "[s]ociety is necessary . . . to us" (1:234). The shift from the so-called "natural" origins of society to "necessity" opens to view the manner in which necessity—that is, the condition of danger and scarcity in the state of nature—is as binding a force of society as the social passions. Wilson argues:

> To support life, to satisfy our natural appetites, to obtain those agreeable enjoyments of which our nature is susceptible, many things are indispensable. In order to live with any degree of comfort, we must have food, clothing, habitations, furniture, and utensils of some sort. These cannot be procured without much art and labour; nor without the friendly assistance of our fellows in society. (1:234–35)

The "needs" that give rise to society are basic: natural appetites, enjoyment, and those things which are indispensable or necessary. But given that nature does not furnish us immediately or directly with what is most necessary for life, the human being must resort to art and labor. Drawing upon Thomas Reid, Wilson writes:

> Let us suppose a man of full strength, and well instructed in all our arts of life, to be reduced suddenly to solitude, even in one of the best soils and climates: could he procure the grateful conveniences of life? It will not be pretended. Could he procure even its simple necessities? In an ingenious and excellent romance, we are told this has been done. But it will be remembered, that the foundation of Robinson Crusoe's future subsistence, and of all the comforts which he afterwards provided and collected, was laid in the useful instruments and machines, which he saved from his shipwreck. These are the productions of society. (1:235)[51]

A human being cannot survive alone. "The reciprocal assistance of those, who compose a single family, may procure many of the necessities of life; and may diminish its dangers" (1:235).[52]

Wilson's purpose in alerting us to the role necessity plays in bringing us together is not to deny the spontaneous and genuinely other-directed passions by which human society is bonded. He intends, rather, to alert us to the fact that without the conquest of necessity, the higher pleasures of life cannot be properly cultivated and enjoyed. When the immediate and necessary requirements of life are secured, "room will be afforded for social enjoyments, and for the finer operations of the mind." And, then, "[s]till greater pleasures and advantages would be obtained by the union of a few families in the same neighborhood." Once these families "undertake and execute laborious works for the common good of all," the "social operations" are afforded new opportunities and thus "would operate in a less contracted circuit" (1:235). While society seems to be partly based on sympathy, the inconveniences of the state of nature persist. A human being's volatile condition in the state of nature draws him toward other human beings with whom he is capable of satisfying basic needs. According to Wilson, then, society and the primary law of nature, sociability and self-love, are not necessarily incompatible.

> The wisest and most benign constitution of a rational and moral system is that, in which the degree of private affection, most useful to the individual, is, at the same time, consistent with the greatest interest of the system; and in which the degree of social affection, most useful to the system, is, at the same time, productive of the greatest happiness to the individual. Thus it is in the system of society. In that system, he who acts on such principles, and is governed by such affections, as sever him from the common good and publick interest, works, in reality, towards his own misery: while he, on the other hand, who operates for the good of the whole, as is by nature and nature's God appointed him, pursues, in truth, and at the same time, his own felicity.... Regulated by this standard, extensive, unerring, and sublime, *self-love and social are the same.* (1:238, my emphasis)

Consent

On the basis of the foregoing, we can say Wilson's "social" animal is more "gregarious" than "political." He or she bears little resemblance to the Aristotelian or Thomistic "political" animal who is sternly ruled by the dictates of an architectonic Reason. Sociability is constituted out of basic human passions and by no means comes at the expense of the "individual's" concern for him- or herself. Contrary to Aristotle's doctrine, the individual in Wilson's and Scottish thought remains *prior* to the political community.[53] For this very reason, the discussion of human sociability is not at odds with Wilson's view that civil and political society is a social contract constituted by the consent of the governed.

Following the lead provided by Hobbes, Locke, and the social contract tradition of the seventeenth and eighteenth centuries, Wilson argues: "The only rational and natural method . . . of constituting civil society, is by the convention or consent of the members, who compose it. For by civil society we properly understand, the voluntary union of persons in the same end, and in the same means requisite to obtain that end. This union is a benefit, not a sacrifice: civil is an addition to natural order" (1:239).[54] We should not be misled by the play upon words. Wilson indeed refers to the "natural method" by which civil society is constituted. He refers to civil society as an "addition to natural order." But the "addition" is a product of the "convention or consent of its members." Civil society may be said to be "by nature" only if one is clear about what Wilson means "by nature." Nature inclines us toward self-preservation; it provides us with a moral sense and with fellow-feelings. Society is rooted in those passions and its "end" is their satisfaction. But though rooted in a particular understanding of human nature, civil society is a "social compact" in which "each individual engages with the whole collectivity, and the whole collectivity engages with each individual." "These engagements," Wilson argues, "are obligatory, because they are mutual." Human beings, naturally free and endowed with equal rights, oblige themselves to the rules and regulations of the social compact by freely consenting to membership. "The individuals who are not parties to" these engagements "are not members of the society" (1:239). Obligation follows from consent—from the promise each individual freely makes to be part of the social compact. "The foregoing account of the formation of civil society, which refers to its initial engagements . . . resolves the duty of submission to the laws of society, into the universal obligation of fidelity in the performance of promises" (1:240).

Wilson arrives at the principle of consent by means of an understanding of human beings whose nature is discerned by reference to a prepolitical condition. In the state of nature, "previous to civil government, all men are equal; so, in the same state, all men are free. In such a state, no one can claim, in preference to another, superior right: in the same state, no one can claim over another superior duty" (1:241).[55] Succinctly put, our "duties are, to do no injury, and to fulfil the engagements, which [we] have made. On these two pillars principally and respectively rest the criminal and the civil codes of the municipal law. These are the pillars of justice." Regarding the "municipal law, the rights and duties of benevolence are sometimes, though rarely, the objects" (2:592–93). The law of nature and political life coincide.

It should be clear by now that Wilson's appeal to the Scots is properly understood as a means of expanding and refining a modern teaching about the passions, not as a repudiation of Hobbes and Locke. For Wilson, as for Hobbes and Locke, politics is an artifice in the service of fundamental passions. We should note that no less vigorous an advocate of the moral sense than Wilson, David Hume nonetheless argues that justice is an "artificial virtue."[56] Of course, one must be very careful with Hume's formulation. Hume is not saying that justice has simply no foundation in human nature. Hume is arguing that the sympathetic and benevolent passions alone do not suffice, and that politics depends in great measure on artifice or conventions.[57] For all of his important elaborations on the moral sentiments, Thomas Reid does not deny the existence of the state of nature, nor does Francis Hutcheson.[58] Were the reader to point out that Hume takes issue with Locke on the centrality of consent in the constitution of government, it must be noted that both Wilson and Reid side with Locke against Hume on this issue.[59] Properly understood, Wilson's turn to the Scots is neither intended to support a Thomistic, classical republican, or civic humanist understanding of human nature, and civil and political society; nor is it meant as a repudiation of modern, liberal social contract theory.

Conclusion: The Character of Liberal Republicanism

The poverty of our modern, liberal political arrangements is generally understood in contradistinction to the supposedly noble, public spirited, and mutually binding principles of antiquity —both classical and medieval. In the past there were "citizens"; now there are only "individuals." Lost in this understanding of liberalism is the awareness of how seriously liberals were themselves concerned with the limited understanding of human nature and civil society articulated by Hobbes and Locke. But rather than return to the ancient polis, the Scots—and Wilson following the Scots—sought to supplement and thus rehabilitate liberalism on modern principles: that is, on a more comprehensive teaching of the human passions. They sought to vindicate the human capacity for self-government, and in so doing to realize on the plane of politics the universal aspiration for freedom and equality properly understood. Wilson and the Scots found in our passionately "social" rather than in our rationally "political" nature an understanding of our shared humanity that would preserve a space for human autonomy and a measured dependence on our fellow human beings.

In bringing politics down from the heights proposed by classical antiquity and medieval Christianity and to have it rest on a proper understanding of self-love, the Enlighteners deny neither the genuinely other-directed passions of our nature nor condone unabated egoism. In fact, the meaning given to self-love by Wilson and the Enlighteners is something significantly different from the meaning given to it by the contemporary critics of liberalism. Francis Hutcheson, for example, argues that a "moderate desire of self-preservation is both necessary and easy." Were human beings wanting in such proper regard for themselves, we would "shew a desperate audacious disposition without any caution." It is true that the desire for self-preservation is often "restless, turbulent, and destructive both to the person himself and to the society in which he lives." Where the care for oneself is excessive, "it appears in timidity and cowardice; dispositions quite useless to the publick, and tormenting to their person."[60] In spite of its excesses, the desire for self-preservation is necessary to private and public life. To deprecate this useful passion is to strip society of its necessary foundation.

Hutcheson also argues that "[a] moderate relish for sensual pleasures is useful, nay necessary." To be somehow destitute of "sensibility" would deprive human beings of "innocent pleasures." Among these one could include affections for others as well as for material goods. As in the case of the desire for self-preservation, sensuality is liable to excess. For example, "where the taste is too high, which we call luxury or intemperance, it generally excludes all the more manly enjoyments, neither consulting reputation nor honour; nor even health and fortune, or the preservation of life." But kept within bounds, the love of sensual pleasures is a spur to industry and thus to liberality and magnificence. These virtues in turn activate one of the most useful passions in humans, the love of fame.[61]

According to the Enlighteners, the concern for one's character or reputation is thus rooted in a proper understanding of self-love. Wilson argues that "[t]he love of reputation and the fear of dishonour are, by the all-gracious Author of our existence, implanted in our breasts, for purposes the most beneficent and wise." The love of fame, to use Hume's words, "well may it be classed among those rights, the enjoyment of which it is the design of good government and laws to secure and enlarge" (2:593–94).[62] Wilson calls honor a species of "property" because it is acquired or "purchased" through honest labor (2:595). Human beings work to secure a good name because this is pleasing to us. Though rooted in a love of self, Wilson's appeal to honor is not a sanction for unbridled egoism. "I will not appeal to vanity, and ask, if any thing can be more flattering, than to *obtain* the praises and acclamations of others. But I will appeal to conscious rectitude, and ask, whether any thing can be more satisfactory, than to *deserve* their regard and esteem" (1:237).

From the point of view of classical antiquity or medieval Christianity, the love of honor, reputation, or fame—what Wilson refers to as "conscious rectitude"—is not the highest virtue. But for Wilson as well as for his Scottish mentors, care for one's character is of public utility and at least points in the direction of virtue (1:238, 405). Thomas Reid, for example, argues that if "perfect virtue" were "joined with perfect knowledge," this "would make our appetites and desires unnecessary incumbrances of our nature." But "as human knowledge and human virtue are both imperfect," our "appetites and desires are necessary supplements to our imperfections." Indeed, human beings who "have no virtue are induced by a regard for character."[63] The regard for character is often "very friendly to real virtue."

> A man that is not quite abandoned must behave so in society as to preserve some degree of reputation. This every man desires to do, and the greater part actually do it. In order to do this, he must acquire the habit of restraining his appetites and passions within the bounds which common decency requires, and so as to make himself a tolerable member of society, if not an useful and agreeable one.[64]

Human beings are thus socialized by their concern for character and are "tamed and civilized by the principles *that are common to good and bad men*." This concern teaches human beings "to bring their appetites and passions under due restraint before the eyes of men, which makes it more easy to bring them under the rein of virtue."[65]

The approach taken by Hutcheson, Reid, and Wilson—particularly as it concerns a certain "lowering" of the demands of virtue—is perhaps better illumined in the light of Adam Smith's "impartial spectator." According to Smith, when a person

> views himself in the light in which he is conscious that others will view him, he sees that to them he is but one of the multitude in no respect better than any other in it. If he would act so as that the impartial spectator may enter into the principles of his own conduct, which is what of all things he has the greatest desire to do, he must, upon this, as upon all other occasions, humble the arrogance of self-love, and bring it down to something which other men can go along with.[66]

The impartial spectator takes his or her bearings from what humankind as a whole "may enter into" and not from the superior excellence of one human being, philosophic or religious.[67] The liberal virtues are democratic, not aristocratic. They are based on a mutual recognition of rights, on the duty required by *all* to respect the rights of *all* human beings to life, liberty, and estate. This duty flows from the dictates of the moral sense and the natural law.

For Wilson, the liberal republic constituted by the American Founders is the arena for the activation of the moral sentiments. In "a free country," Wilson writes, "every citizen forms part of the sovereign power." The citizen "possesses a vote, or takes a still more active part in the business of the commonwealth." In a free country such as the "United States, every citizen is frequently called upon to act in this great publick character." As sovereign, the people perform the "rights and the duties of jurors" (1:74). In America, where "the doors of publick honours and publick offices are, on the broad principles of equal liberty, thrown open to all," the people will "legislate, not merely for a single state, but for the most august Union that has been formed on the face of the globe" (1:75). The liberal republic is constituted out of the needs and the sentiments of a people. It is administered by them who are the legitimate sources of political power. Civic engagement is expected because the citizenry have a greater stake in the republic.

When responsibly engaged in the administration of their own affairs, citizens will discover that the liberal republic will in turn have an effect on their sentiments. Echoing Publius, Wilson considers how in a well-administered liberal republic the citizen's

> mind is roused and elevated: his heart is rectified and enlarged: dignity appears in his countenance, and animation in his every gesture and word. He knows that if he is innocent and upright, the laws and constitution of his country will ensure him protection. He trusts, that, if to innocence and integrity he adds faithful and meritorious services, his country, in addition to protection, will confer upon him honourable testimonies of esteem. Hence he derives a cheerful and habitual confidence, this pervades and invigorates his conduct, and spreads a noble air over every part of his character. (1:307)[68]

The law of nature, which is understood by reference to the fundamental human passions, is thus brought close to and informs political life. To repeat: America opens "to view, the very close and interesting connection, which subsists between the law of nature and the municipal law" (2:587). America "imitate[s] . . . the operations of nature" (2:583).

Not only is the liberal republic meant to satisfy the basic sentiments and needs of the citizenry; it also is an edifice intended to enlarge them. We noted earlier that in Wilson's view the problem of faction is often the result of excessive concentricity. An extended republic compels citizens who too often have limited and illiberal opinions to seek the assistance of a wider and thus a more diverse audience. The extended republic fosters accommodation at the same time that it softens manners. This is an important addendum to Madison's solution to the problem of faction in *The Federalist* no. 10. According to Madison, one of the gravest threats to liberty comes from majoritarian tyranny. This is avoided by rendering the majority "by their number and local situation, unable to concert and carry into effect schemes of oppression." Extend the sphere and the impulse and opportunity to oppress is less likely to coincide.[69] Wilson concurs. But "liberal" means more than "free." Liberal is also at the heart of the word liberality, and hence of generosity. As one takes in more views, the human heart is expanded.

The study of American politics and America's modern philosophical roots are replete with discussions about the primacy of institutional arrangements, balances of power, and the like—all of which are important. But their importance should not conceal from us the extent to which the edifice was understood by the Founders as relying upon a rightly exercised moral sense. We should recall that even Publius was of the view that liberal republican government rests on the American people's "conduct and example," on their capacity to establish good government by "reflection and choice," rather than to remain "destined to depend, for their political constitutions, on accident and force." By taking it upon themselves to vindicate on the plane of politics the capacity of human beings to govern themselves properly, Publius argued that "the inducements of philanthropy" will be added to those of "patriotism," and thus "heighten the solicitude, which all considerate and good men must *feel* for the event."[70] Madison appeals as strongly as Wilson to the conscious rectitude of the American people by arguing that republican government depends on "that honorable determination, which animates every votary of freedom, to rest all our political experiments on the capacity of mankind for self government."[71] Wilson echoes these sentiments and reminds us that "[f]or a people wanting to themselves, there is indeed no remedy in the political dispensary" (1:296). Although turning away from the aristocratic grandeur of ancient politics to the egalitarian principles of modernity, Wilson and the liberal republicanism he helped to conceive, defend, and secure for posterity seems to demand something less from politics. At the same time, it demands something more from each and every one of us.

Notes

1. There are, of course, important differences between the terms "law of nature" and "natural law." As F. C. Coppleston argues, the "term 'natural law' does not bear the same sense . . . that is borne by the term 'law of nature' when the law of gravitation, for example, is spoken of as a law of nature or as a natural law. Irrational things do indeed reflect the eternal law in their activities and behaviors; but if we talk about them obeying a natural law the word 'law,' insists Aquinas, is used analogically. For law is defined as an ordinance of reason, and irrational creatures, being irrational, cannot recognize and promulgate to themselves any natural law. Human beings, however, can do so. And the term 'natural law' is applicable in the strict sense, not to the natural tendencies and inclinations of man on which his reason reflects, but to the precepts which his reason enunciates as the result of this reflection." See F. C. Coppleston, *Aquinas* (New York: Penguin Books, 1986), 221–22. Wilson, however, uses the terms interchangeably, for reasons which will become clear as we proceed.

2. All references to Wilson's writings are taken from Robert G. McClosky, *The Works of James Wilson*, 2 vols. (Cambridge, Mass.: Harvard University Press, 1967), cited by volume and page number. Wilson's spelling is not modernized.

3. Among the most notable Thomistic interpreters of Wilson are: Charles Page Smith, *James Wilson: Founding Father, 1742–1798* (Chapel Hill: University of North Carolina Press, 1956), 319; William F. Obering, *The Philosophy of Law of James Wilson: A Study in Comparative Jurisprudence* (Washington, D.C.: Issued by the Office of the Secretary of the American Catholic Philosophical Association, 1936), 6, 49, and 62; Homer T. Rosenberg, "James Wilson's Theories of Punishment," *Pennsylvania Magazine of*

History and Biography 73 (1949): 47; Randolph G. Adams, *Selected Political Essays of James Wilson* (New York: Alfred A. Knopf, 1930), 7; and Arnaud B. Leavelle, "James Wilson and the Relation of Scottish Metaphysics to American Political Thought," *Political Science Quarterly* 57 (1947): 402. The most recent and comprehensive statement of Wilson's Thomism is Mark David Hall, *The Political and Legal Philosophy of James Wilson 1742–1798* (Columbia: University of Missouri Press, 1997). For my review of Hall, see *Law and History Review* 17 (Spring 1999): 184–87.

4. My claim is not that Wilson rules Scripture out as a moral guide altogether. The argument here is about emphasis, and on the primacy of the law of nature. For a reading that shifts that emphasis, see George W. Carey, "James Wilson's Political Thought and the Constitutional Convention," *Political Science Reviewer* 17 (Fall 1987): 57, and Jean-Marc Pascal, *The Political Ideas of James Wilson: 1742–1798* (New York: Garland Publishing, 1991), 54. Thomas L. Pangle, *The Spirit of Modern Republicanism: The Moral Vision of the American Founders and the Philosophy of Locke* (Chicago: University of Chicago Press, 1988), 122–25, initially shares my reading, but then backtracks in *The Ennobling of Democracy: The Challenge of the Postmodern Age* (Baltimore: Johns Hopkins University Press, 1992), 115–17.

5. Although Hobbes argues that "A LAW OF NATURE, (*lex naturalis*), is a Precept, or generall Rule, found out by reason," there is no doubt that this construct of reason which is the law of nature is founded in the passions. According to Hobbes, "[t]he passions that encline men to Peace, are Feare of Death; Desire of such things as are necessary to commodius living; and a Hope by their Industry to obtain them. And Reason suggesteth convenient Articles of Peace, upon which men may be drawn to agreement. These Articles, are they, which otherwise are called the Lawes of Nature." See Thomas Hobbes, *Leviathan*, ed. Richard Tuck (New York: Cambridge University Press, 1991), 90–91 (chaps. 13–14). Elsewhere, Hobbes argues that "[t]hese dictates of Reason, men use to call by the name of Lawes, but improperly: for they are but Conclusions, or Theorems concerning what conduceth to the conservation and defence of themselves; whereas law, properly is the word of him, that by right hath command over others." A law of nature is an "Inference, made from the passions." *Leviathan*, 89 (chap. 13) and 111 (chap. 15).

6. The most notable attempt to link Wilson to the Scottish Enlightenment is the work of Stephen A. Conrad. See his "Polite Foundation: Citizenship and Common Sense in James Wilson's Republican Theory," *Supreme Court Review* (1984): 359–88; "Metaphor and Imagination in Wilson's Theory of Federal Union," *Law and Social Inquiry* 13 (1988): 1–70; and "James Wilson's 'Assimilation of the Common Law Mind,'" *Northwestern University Law Review* 84 (1990): 186–219. Conrad argues that Wilson appealed to the Scottish moral sense philosophy because it "was characterized by its tendency to portray as an empirically verifiable proposition the rosate view that man is by nature predominantly sociable and this in fact governs much of everyday life and historical development. . . . 'Sociability' was thus thought to be a dependable and salutary wellspring in human nature, from which countless social virtues emerged, 'decency' and 'complaisance' certainly to be counted among them." Politically this means, Conrad continues, that "Wilson sought to expound a consent theory of liberal republicanism that was in no way tied to the profound but constraining myth of a social contract, or to any legal or quasi-legal form whatsoever. Indeed, nothing about Wilson's republican vision is more significant than the irony that one of the preeminent lawyers of the Founding generation sought to locate the Founding not in the events that erected a 'superstructure' of law and government but in the evidence of and prospects for a 'polite' foundation." See Conrad, "Polite Foundation," 364, 387–88. This reading of "sociability" as explicitly antiliberal is shared by Carl J. Richard, *The Founders and the Classics: Greece, Rome, and the American Enlightenment* (Cambridge, Mass.: Harvard University Press, 1994), 176–77, who would classify Wilson within a classical republican tradition. See also Mary T. Delahanty, *The Integralist Philosophy of James Wilson* (New York: Pageant Press, 1969), 4.

7. Garry Wills advances the argument according to which the Scots and the American Founders appropriation of the Scots are to be understood *contra* Lockean liberalism. See his *Inventing America: Jefferson's Declaration of Independence* (New York: Double Day and Company, 1978), 168–80. For a corrective to Wills's thesis upon which this article builds, see Frank D. Balog, "The Scottish Enlightenment and the Liberal Political Tradition," in *Confronting the Constitution: The Challenge to Locke, Montesquieu, Jefferson, and the Federalists from Utilitarianism, Historicism, Marxism, Freudianism, Pragmatism, Existentialism. . .*, ed. Allan Bloom (Washington D.C.: The American Enterprise Institute, 1990), 191–208; Ronald Hamowy, "Jefferson and the Scottish Enlightenment: A Critique of Garry Wills' *Inventing*

America: Jefferson's Declaration of Independence," *William and Mary Quarterly*, 3rd. ser., 36 (October 1979): 503–23; and Richard C. Sinopoli, *The Foundations of American Citizenship: Liberalism, the Constitution, and Civic Virtue* (New York: Oxford University Press, 1992), 70–71.

8. Burton A. Konkle, "James Wilson and the Constitution," The Opening Address in the Official Series of Events Known as the James Wilson Memorial, delivered before the Law Academy of Pennsylvania, November 14, 1906, published by order of the Law Academy, Philadelphia, Pennsylvania, 1907. Konkle's monograph proves a useful guide to the details of Wilson's life, although the most thorough and comprehensive study is the only full-length biography of Wilson by Charles Page Smith, *James Wilson: Founding Father, 1742–1798* (Chapel Hill: University of North Carolina Press, 1956). One of the first biographical sketches of Wilson is Richard Waln, "James Wilson," in *Biography of the Signers of the Declaration of Independence*, ed. John Sanderson, 2nd ed. (Philadelphia: William Brown and Charles Peters, 1828), 3:259–301. The reader may also find useful Lucien H. Alexander, "James Wilson: Nation Builder," *Green Bag* 19 (1907): 1–9, 98–109, 137–46, 265, 76. This chapter draws heavily on these sources for the details of Wilson's life.

9. Smith, *James Wilson*, 4–5.

10. Smith, *James Wilson*, 8, 9, and 15.

11. Smith, *James Wilson*, 16.

12. Smith, *James Wilson*, 16.

13. See Konkle, "James Wilson and the Constitution," 7, and Waln, "James Wilson," 259.

14. Konkle, "James Wilson and the Constitution," 8.

15. Konkle, "James Wilson and the Constitution," 19.

16. Waln, "James Wilson," 260.

17. Smith, *James Wilson*, 23.

18. Smith, *James Wilson*, 27 and 24–26.

19. Waln, "James Wilson," 262.

20. See the *Pennsylvania Chronicle and Universal Advertiser*, February 1–May 16, 1768.

21. Smith, *James Wilson*, 58. See also McCloskey's assessment of the "Considerations" in his "Introduction," *The Works of James Wilson*, 9–11.

22. Sir William Blackstone, *Commentaries on the Laws of England* (Chicago: University of Chicago Press, 1979), 1:48–51.

23. John Locke, *Two Treatises of Government*, ed. Peter Laslett (New York: Cambridge University Press, 1988), 275 (sec. 12).

24. Geoffrey Seed, *James Wilson* (Milwood, N.Y.: KTO Press, 1978).

25. Waln, "James Wilson," 269–70.

26. One of the most noted scholars of the Constitutional Convention argues that Wilson was "almost on par with Madison" in pushing for and ultimately securing the Federalist cause. For the details of Wilson's contributions at the 1787 Convention, see Max Farrand, *The Framing of the Constitution of the United States* (New Haven, Conn.: Yale University Press, 1913), 197, passim.

27. Quoted in Smith, *James Wilson*, 308.

28. Smith, *James Wilson*, 308, 309, and 310–11.

29. John Locke, *Second Treatise*, 275 (sec. 12).

30. Cf. David Hume, *A Treatise on Human Nature*, 2nd ed., with text revised and notes by P. H. Nidditch (New York: Oxford University Press, 1990), 471 (bk. III, pt. I, sec. II), and *Enquiries Concerning Human Understanding and Concerning the Principles of Morals*, 3rd ed., with text revised and notes by P. H. Nidditch (New York: Oxford University Press, 1975), 293 ("Appendix I," sec. 244); and Pascal, *The Political Ideas of James Wilson*, 48–111.

31. St. Thomas Aquinas, *On Law, Morality, and Politics*, ed. William P. Baumgrath and Richard J. Regan, S.J. (Indianapolis: Hackett Publishing Company, 1988), 48 (ST. I–II, Q. 94, A. 2).

32. Cf. Hume, *Treatise*, 455–70 (bk. III, pt. I, sec. I), and Thomas Reid, *Inquiry into the Human Mind and the Principles of Common Sense*, in Reid, *Inquiry and Essays*, ed. E. Beanblossom and Keith Lehrer (Indianapolis: Hackett Publishing Company, 1983), 57–58 (chap. V, sec. VII). See also Pascal, *The Political Ideas of James Wilson*, 62–64.

33. Cf. Francis Hutcheson, *A System of Moral Philosophy* (New York: Augustus M. Kelly, Publishers, 1968), 38 (bk. I, chap. 3, sec. 1).

34. Aquinas, *On Law, Morality, and Politics*, 5 (ST. I–II, Q. 19, AA. 5–6).

35. Cf. Hume, *Enquiries*, 293 ("Appendix I," sec. 244).

36. Cf. Hutcheson, *System*, 129 (bk. II, chap. 17, sec. 7). See also Pascal, *The Political Ideas of James Wilson*, 76–78.

37. See Richard, *The Founders and the Classics*, 176–77.

38. See Hugo Grotius, *The Rights of War and Peace*, trans. A. C. Campbell (Westport, Conn.: Hyperion Press, n.d.), 25 (bk. 1, sec. 14).

39. Of the Lockean law of nations, Cox writes that "it is a doctrine which necessarily partakes of all the singular characteristics of his general theory of natural law: his law of nature, viewed as a law of nations, is not a body of law strictly speaking, but rather a body of theoretical principles regarding the abstract rights and duties of sovereign bodies, just as the law of nature is such a body of principles with respect to individual men living in a state of nature." See Richard H. Cox, *Locke on War and Peace* (Oxford: Oxford University Press, 1960), 138. The same may be said of Wilson.

40. Hobbes, *Leviathan*, 92 (chap. 14) and 188 (chap. 26).

41. I owe this insight concerning the modern transformation of the biblical Golden Rule to Joseph Cropsey, *Polity and Economy: An Interpretation of the Principles of Adam Smith* (Westport, Conn.: Greenwood Press, 1977), 1–55.

42. Locke, *Second Treatise*, 270–71 (sec. 6).

43. Locke, *Second Treatise*, 272 (sec. 8).

44. Smith, *The Theory of Moral Sentiments*, ed. D. D. Raphael and A. L. Macfie (Indianapolis: Liberty Fund, 1982), 25 (pt. I, chap. V, sec. 5, my emphasis).

45. Cf. Locke, *Second Treatise*, 320 (sec. 80).

46. Locke, *Second Treatise*, 319–20 (secs. 78–79). See also Reid, *Essays on the Active Powers of the Human Mind* (Boston: Massachusetts Institute of Technology Press, 1969), 145–48 (essay III, chap. IV).

47. Cf. *The Theory of Moral Sentiments*, 10 (pt. I, chap. I, sec. 5). Smith writes: "Pity and compassion are words appropriated to signify our fellow-feeling with the sorrow of others. Sympathy, though its meaning was, perhaps, originally the same, may now, without much impropriety, be made use of to denote our fellow-feeling with any passion whatever." Sympathy is not benevolence.

48. Cf. Hume, *Treatise*, 498–501 (bk. III, pt. II, sec. II).

49. Cf. David Hume, "Of Parties in General," in David Hume, *Essays Moral, Political, and Literary*, ed. Eugene F. Miller (Indianapolis: Liberty Press, 1987), 54–63.

50. Cf. "Idea of a Perfect Commonwealth," in Hume, *Essays Moral, Political, and Literary*, 512–29. A useful examination of the relation between the social passions and Wilson's federalism is Samuel H. Beer, *To Make a Nation: The Rediscovery of American Federalism* (Cambridge, Mass.: Harvard University Press, 1993), 341–77.

51. Cf. Thomas Reid, *Practical Ethics Being Lectures and Papers on Natural Religion, Self-Government, Natural Jurisprudence, and the Law of Nations*, ed. Knud Haakonssen (Princeton, N.J.: Princeton University Press, 1990), 249 (lecture XVI).

52. Cf. Locke, *Second Treatise*, 320–21 (sec. 80).

53. Cf. Aristotle, *Politics*, trans. Carnes Lord (Chicago: University of Chicago Press, 1984), 37 (1253a19–29).

54. Cf. Locke, *Second Treatise*, 330–31 (sec. 95), and Hobbes, *Leviathan*, 120 (chap. XVII).

55. Cf. Locke, *Second Treatise*, 269 (sec. 4).

56. Hume, *Treatise*, 477–84 (bk. III, pt. II, sec. I).

57. Hume, *Treatise*, 484 (bk. III, pt. II, sec. I) and 499–500 (bk. III, pt. II, sec. II).

58. Reid, *Practical Ethics*, 190–91 (lecture X), and Hutcheson, *System*, 281–99 (bk. II, chap. IV).

59. See "Of the Original Compact," in Hume, *Essays Moral, Political, and Literary*, 465–87, and Reid, *Practical Ethics*, 269 (lecture XVII).

60. Francis Hutcheson, *A Short Introduction to Moral Philosophy* in *The Collected Works of Francis Hutcheson*, facsimile editions by Bernhard Fabian, vol. 4 (Hildesheim: Georg Olms Verlagsbuchhandlung, 1969), 93 (bk. I, chap. 6).

61. Hutcheson, *Short Introduction*, 93–95.

62. Hume, *Treatise*, 316–24 (bk. II, sec. XI) and 592–602 (bk. III, sec. II).

63. Reid, *Essays on the Active Powers of the Human Mind*, 132–33 (essay III, chap. II).

64. Reid, *Essays*, 134.

65. Reid, *Essays*, 134–35, my emphasis.

66. Smith, *Theory of Moral Sentiments*, 83 (pt. II, chap. II, sec. 1).

67. See Cropsey, *Polity and Economy*, 1–55.

68. Cf. Hamilton, *The Federalist*, no. 27, in *The Federalist*, ed. Jacob E. Cooke (Middletown, Conn.: Wesleyan University Press, 1961), 173–74.

69. Madison, *The Federalist*, 61 (no. 10).

70. Hamilton, *The Federalist*, 3 (no. 1, my emphasis).

71. Madison, *The Federalist*, 250 (no. 39).

Chapter 11

Anti-Federalist Political Thought: Brutus and The Federal Farmer

Murray Dry

The Essays of Brutus and Letters of The Federal Farmer constitute the Anti-Federalist counterpart to the writings of Publius, widely known as *The Federalist Papers*. As was common at the time, each author wrote under a pseudonym in order to emphasize the argument and play down the authority of the individual. While the authors of *The Federalist Papers* (James Madison, Alexander Hamilton, and John Jay) were soon known, authorship of the most extensive and thoughtful Anti-Federalist writings remains uncertain. The Federal Farmer was generally thought to have been Richard Henry Lee (1733–1794) of Virginia, and the Essays of Brutus have been attributed to Robert Yates (1738–1801) of New York; but doubt surrounds each attribution.[1]

Since Brutus and The Federal Farmer did not collaborate as Hamilton, Madison, and Jay did, their writings lack the coherence of *The Federalist Papers*. I have chosen to present the political thought of both writers, however, because together they offer the most extensive Anti-Federalist commentary on the proposed Constitution as well as the clearest alternative to Publius' conception of republican government.[2] For example, while both writers discuss federalism, representation, and a bill of rights, Brutus provides a comprehensive discussion of the judiciary but does not mention the executive; by contrast, The Federal Farmer discusses the executive and provides rich discussions of the Senate and of federalism. And both writers discuss republican government, with Brutus quoting and applying Montesquieu and The Federal Farmer providing a full account of democracy and aristocracy.

The importance of the proposed Constitution for the happiness and well-being of the country generated extensive written commentary, directed both to American citizens at large and to those who would vote in state ratifying conventions. The question was whether the proposed Constitution should be ratified as is, rejected, or amended in any significant respect by the state conventions. Perhaps because the burden was on the Anti-Federalists to say what was wrong with the Constitution, they said more about the form and character of free government than the Federalists did. The Federalists, and especially the authors of *The Federalist Papers*, focused on the requirements of union, the deficiencies of the Articles of Confederation, and the provisions of the proposed Constitution.

The political thought of both sides takes for granted the principles of government expressed in the Declaration of Independence, along with the conviction that only a republican form of government will suit America. In that sense, neither side presents a full-fledged political philosophy, and each side agrees on the fundamental principles of government, both in themselves and for America. The ratification debate still provides extensive discussion and significant disagreement. The most obvious disagreements concern the importance of a bill of rights and the nature of federalism. The Anti-Federalists assert the necessity of a bill of rights, and they regard the structure of the proposed government as incompletely federal—indeed, as bordering on consolidation. Of course, they dispute the name Anti-Federalist, hoisted upon them by the advocates of ratification, who claimed the name Federalist.

Brutus and The Federal Farmer were moderate critics of the proposed Constitution; they preferred to work from it rather than from the Articles of Confederation. At the same time, they feared for republican government in America if the Constitution was ratified without amendments. They were convinced that the government under the proposed Constitution would consolidate all political power; such an appropriation would put an end to federalism, and thus to republican government and political freedom.

The first part of this chapter will therefore discuss the views of Brutus and The Federal Farmer on federalism and republican government. In each case, the views differ significantly from those of Publius. The second part will turn to their detailed, critical examination of the proposed Constitution. The third part of the chapter will examine their arguments in favor of a bill of rights. A brief conclusion will examine the Anti-Federalist legacy, using Brutus and The Federal Farmer as the major spokesmen for that legacy.

I. Federalism and Republican Government

A. Federalism

Montesquieu's *Spirit of the Laws* (1748) was the authority for the American Founders on both federalism and the separation of powers. Both topics bear on the more fundamental question concerning the nature of republican government. Brutus and The Federal Farmer considered the Constitution as more flawed in terms of the requirements of federalism than with regard to the separation of powers. Their first general observations on the Constitution make that clear:

> It appears to be a plan retaining some federal features; but to be the first important step, and to aim strongly to one consolidated government of the United States. (*FF* I, 2.8.1)

> The plan of government now proposed is evidently calculated totally to change, in time, our condition as a people. Instead of being thirteen republics, under a federal head, it is clearly designed to make us one consolidated government. (*FF* I, 2.8.4; cf. I, 2.8.9)

> The first question that presents itself on the subject is, whether a confederated government be the best for the United States or not? Or in other words, whether the thirteen United States should be reduced to one great republic, governed by one legislature, and under the direction of one executive and judicial; or whether they should continue thirteen confederated republics, under the direction and controul of a supreme federal head for certain defined national purposes only? (*B* I, 2.9.4)

> So far therefore as its powers reach, all ideas of confederation are given up and lost. (*B* I, 2.9.5)

These quotations raise two questions. First, were The Federal Farmer and Brutus right in their charge that the proposed Constitution violated the requirements of federalism?; and second, if so, how did the Constitution's critics get stuck with the label "Anti-Federalist"? To answer these questions, we need to consider the Articles of Confederation, and the deliberations and work of the Federal Convention of 1787.

During the confederation period, the terms "Federal" and "Anti-Federal" referred to a willingness or unwillingness to support the institution of the federation: the United States in Congress assembled. The essential elements of that federal form were: (1) state equality in voting as well as active state control of Congress via financial support, annual elections, and rotation and recall of its congressional delegation; (2) strict construction of the powers granted to the Congress, with a nine state requirement for approval of major matters; and (3) reliance on state requisitions for the raising of armies and money. The states were clearly the primary political units, and the government under the Articles was considered a strong federal system.

To understand the effect of the newly proposed Constitution on the federalism issue, we need to consider certain proposals and speeches that took place during the Federal Convention and others that took place during the debate over congressional apportionment (i.e., representation). The Virginia Plan, written by Madison, proposed direct popular election to the lower house, proportional representation in both houses of Congress, separate executive and judicial branches, a general grant of legislative power in Congress, and a national negative (i.e., veto) on state laws. Both Gouverneur Morris and George Mason thought such a proposal reflected the national principle of union in contrast to the federal principle of the Articles. William Paterson's New Jersey Plan offered the Convention an alternative that modified the Articles of Confederation: it contained a limited tax power on imported goods and a federal power to coerce the states into making good on their requisitions when necessary; it also proposed a separate executive and a limited judicial power. The Convention voted 7–3–1 to work from the Virginia Plan and then proceeded to change some of its key provisions: the state legislatures would elect the federal Senate and, as a result of what is called the Great Compromise, each state would have two senators regardless of population; the general grant of legislative powers was replaced with a specific enumeration of powers (including a final "necessary and proper" clause); and the national negative was dropped.[3] Supporters of the Great Compromise over apportionment claimed that "we were partly national; partly federal."[4] In his last attempt to defeat state equality in the Senate, Madison contested that claim by asserting that the mode of operation of the government—that the legislative power acted directly on the individuals, not on the states as corporate bodies—made the government entirely national.

Later, in *The Federalist* no. 39, Madison defended the Constitution in two ways against the charge that it was not federal. First, he introduced four other criteria, in addition to mode of operation, to determine federal or national features: mode of ratification, source of authority (as denoted by mode of election), extent of powers, and mode of amendment. Second, he interpreted any recognition of the states in the constitutional structure as a reflection of the federal rather than the national principle. For example, the Senate clearly reflected the states and hence federalism, even though the voting was by individual senator (and not by state delegation), and even though there was no rotation or recall; the powers were enumerated, which presupposed the existence of state governments; and the adoption of the Constitution as well as the mode of its amendment included ratification by states. Likewise, in *The Federalist* no. 9, Hamilton played down the significance of the difference between reliance on requisitions and the direct coercive power of law, even though in *The Federalist* no. 15 he attacked requisitions as the chief vice of the Articles of Confederation.

Thus, the meaning of "federal" underwent a transformation, partly because the supporters of the Constitution could not afford to concede the "Federalist" title to their opponents. Herbert Storing has pointed out, however, that the larceny charge against the Federalists (i.e., that they stole the term "federal") is overstated, since during the confederation period "federal" referred to men and measures supportive of the government of that union.[5] This usage occurred once in the Federal Convention, when Oliver Ellsworth responded to Madison's criticism of Connecticut for refusing to pass a law to comply with its requisitions by retorting that "the State was entirely federal in her disposition."[6] Nevertheless, Storing indicates that the federal authority could be strengthened in such a way that the federal principle—requisitions—was discarded.[7] The Framers of the Constitution did this, and when the supporters of the Constitution succeeded, a new form of federalism arose.

The Anti-Federalist position was further complicated by their conceding the necessity of strengthening the Articles of Confederation. This concession meant that the Anti-Federalists also moved away from a strict view of federalism. The fullest example of this comes from The Federal Farmer. In his first Letter, The Federal Farmer describes three plans, which he calls federal, consolidation, and partial consolidation. The first involved "distinct republics connected under a federal head," or a system similar to the Articles. The second involved a consolidation of the states into "one entire government." The third involved a partial consolidation of the states "as to certain national objects, . . . leav[ing] them severally distinct independent republics, as to internal police generally." "Touching the first, or federal plan," The Federal Farmer says, "I do not think much can be said in its favor" (I, 2.8.10–11). He supports the third plan and claims that the Constitution will eventually produce a complete consolidation. But when he describes the parties to the contest over the Constitution in the first of his Additional Letters, he calls the third or middle-ground position federalism:

> Some of the advocates are only pretended Federalists; in fact they wish for an abolition of the state governments. Some of them I believe to be honest Federalists, who wish to preserve *substantially* the state governments united under an efficient federal head; and many of them are blind tools without any object. Some of the opposers also are only pretended Federalists, who want no federal government, or one merely advisory. Some of them are the true Federalists, their object, perhaps more clearly seen, is the same with that of the honest Federalists; and some of them, probably, have no distinct object. We might as well call the advocates and opposers tories and whigs, or any thing else, as Federalists and Anti-Federalists. To be for or against the constitution, as it stands, is not much evidence of a federal disposition; if any names are applicable to the parties, on account of their general politics, they are those of republicans and anti-republicans. (VI, 2.8.72; emphasis in original)

The Federal Farmer thus appropriated the term federalism for what he first called the partly federal, partly consolidated position; he also identified those who wanted a merely advisory government, which resembles reliance on state requisitions, with those who wanted no federal government.

In his last discussion of federalism, The Federal Farmer returns to the distinction between consolidated and federal government. In a federal government, "the state governments are the basis, the pillar on which the federal head is based" (XVII, 2.8.205). We shall see what this means in constitutional terms in the next part. Now it is time to follow The Federal Farmer's suggestion and consider what he and Brutus understand by republican government; for this subject contains the deepest ground of disagreement between the two parties.

B. Republican Government

Brutus and The Federal Farmer present a view of free government that emphasizes popular control lest the government fall into the hands of the few, who are naturally inclined to oppress the many. Brutus regards it "as an axiom in politic, that people should never authorize their rulers to do any thing, which if done, would operate to their injury" (VIII, 2.9.98). And The Federal

Farmer describes various governments as "reducible to two principles—the important springs which alone move the machines, and give them their intended influence and controul, are force and persuasion: by the former men are compelled, by the latter they are drawn" (VII, 2.8.93). "Our true object," The Federal Farmer continues, "is to give full efficacy to one principle, to arm persuasion on every side, and to render force as little necessary as possible." The Federal Farmer spelled this out earlier:

> The essential parts of a free and good government are a full and equal representation of the people in the legislature, and the jury trial of the vicinage in the administration of justice—a full and equal representation, is that which possesses the same interests, feelings, opinions, and views the people themselves would were they all assembled—a fair representation therefore should be so regulated, that every order of men in the community, according to the common course of elections, can have a share in it—in order to allow professional men, merchants, traders, farmers, mechanics, etc. to bring a just proportion of their best informed men respectively into the legislature, the representation must be considerably numerous. (II, 2.8.15)

The Anti-Federalist reliance on representation and jury trial to define republican government reflects an American application of Montesquieu's account of republican government. Brutus even quotes Montesquieu at length on the nature of republican government after asking whether the United States "should be reduced to one great republic or not?" (I, 2.9.10).

> "It is natural to a republic to have only a small territory, otherwise it cannot long subsist. In a large republic there are men of large fortunes, and consequently of less moderation; there are trusts too great to be placed in any single subject; he has interest of his own; he soon begins to think that he may be happy, great, and glorious, by oppressing his fellow citizens; and that he may raise himself to grandeur on the ruins of his country. In a large republic, the public good is sacrificed to a thousand views; it is subordinate to exceptions, and depends on accidents. In a small one, the interest of the public is easier perceived, better understood, and more within the reach of every citizen; abuses are of less extent, and of course are less protected." (I, 2.9.11, quoting *The Spirit of the Laws*, bk. VIII, chap. 16)

Brutus's as well as The Federal Farmer's conception of republican government departs from Montesquieu's in not requiring as complete a dedication of the individual to the community. This is evident from Brutus's omissions of, and additions to, Montesquieu's description of the ancient republic. Brutus understands that the consent of the governed will be given through representatives, whereas Montesquieu does not introduce the concept of representation until he discusses England—a republic in the guise of a monarchy and a very different kind of republic from that which Montesquieu had previously described under that head. The principle of Montesquieu's republic was virtue, understood as love of equality and love of country. He described this political virtue as "a renunciation of oneself, which is always a very painful thing. One can define this virtue as love of the laws and the homeland. This love, requiring a continuous preference of the public interest over one's own, produces all the individual virtues; they are only that preference."[8]

Brutus and The Federal Farmer express more concern about maintaining a republican character in the people than Publius does, but they do not go so far as to advocate restrictions on the individual right to acquire wealth, as Montesquieu suggests when he writes about the propriety of sumptuary laws for republics.[9] Likewise, Brutus's discussion of representation indicates that he does not insist on direct popular government or the random selection of magistrates, apart from juries; and his discussion of natural rights indicates that he agrees with Publius on the purpose of government.

In a state of nature every individual pursues his own interest; in this pursuit it frequently happened, that the possessions or enjoyments of one were sacrificed to the views and designs of another; thus the weak were a prey to the strong, the simple and unwary were subject to impositions from those who were more crafty and designing. In this state of things, every individual was insecure; common interest therefore directed, that government should be established. . . . The common good therefore is the end of civil government. (II, 2.9.24)

The end of government for Brutus and The Federal Farmer is not so hostile to the individualism of the "pursuit of happiness" as was Montesquieu's small, and morally severe, republic. The Federalists (and especially Publius) agreed with Montesquieu about the benefits of a refined representation and a separation of powers that included a monarchical executive. They could not come right out and say so, however, without appearing to support an elective monarchy. As a result, Publius essentially defined republican government by the elective principle, regardless of the level of inequality between the few and the many (cf. *The Federalist* no. 39). Brutus and The Federal Farmer sought a compromise between England and Montesquieu's republic, one that restrained inequality as well as ethnic or religious diversity in the name of a healthy moral tone. Sometimes this position manifested itself in illiberal ways. The Federal Farmer, for example, objected to the limited qualifications for the office of representative—age, citizenship, and residency—by warning that under the proposed Constitution there can be "no objection to the elected, that they are Christians, Pagans, Mahometans, or Jews; that they are of any colour, rich or poor, convict or not: Hence many men can be elected, who cannot be electors" (XII, 2.8.150).

The concern here, as with the larger issues of representation and governmental power, is that the people's confidence in its government, so essential for it be do its job without reliance on excessive force, depends upon a cohesive community that is substantially related to their government. The people do not have to give up their individual interests, but the government must remain close enough to them that the rich and talented do not subvert the government for their own interest. Both Brutus and The Federal Farmer share this view, but The Federal Farmer's discussion of representation and classes is the fuller of the two accounts.[10]

The famous argument of *The Federalist* no. 10 celebrated representation and the extended sphere for their meliorating effects on faction—the concerted interests of some, whether a majority or a minority, "adverse to the rights of other citizens, or to the permanent and aggregate interests of the community." In that argument, Madison tacitly equated representation with election, and then suggested that a larger sphere meant greater electoral competition, and that the result was likely to improve the quality of representation. The Federal Farmer offered his fullest argument that the federal representation was inadequate in his Additional Letters, published a month after *The Federalist* no. 10. Shortly thereafter Publius replied, in *The Federalist* no. 35, asserting that a representation of all classes in an elective system was "altogether visionary" and that the learned professions (lawyers especially) would mediate between the landowners and the merchants, and that the large landowners would represent the interests of the small landowners just as the merchants would represent the interests of the manufacturers.

The Federal Farmer refuses to accept this form of "virtual representation" of the poor or middling classes by the rich. After distinguishing a constitutional from a natural aristocracy, and remarking that a constitutional aristocracy does not exist "in our common acceptation of the term," The Federal Farmer presents this account of natural aristocracy and natural democracy.

In my idea of our natural aristocracy in the United States, I include about four or five thousand men; and among these I reckon those who have been placed in the offices of governors, of members of Congress, and state senators generally, in the principal officers of Congress, of the army and militia, the superior judges, the most eminent professional men & men of large property.—the other persons and orders in the community form the natural democracy; this includes in general the yeomanry, the subordinate officers, civil and military, the fishermen, mechanics, and traders, many of the merchants and professional men. (VII, 2.8.97)

The men in the first class "associate more extensively, have a high sense of honor, possess abilities, ambition, and general knowledge." The men in the second class "are not so much used to combining great objects . . . possess less ambition, and a larger share of honesty: their dependence is principally on middling and small estates, industrious pursuits, and hard labour, while that of the former is principally on the emoluments of large estates, and of the chief offices of government" (VII, 2.8.97).

The Federal Farmer wanted "the two great parties" to be "balanced," and the only way to do that was to balance the powers of the state and federal governments. This is based on the obverse argument of *The Federalist* no. 10: the larger constituencies will result in a more "refined" selection of representatives, and the resulting government will not represent the sentiments, feelings, and interests of the middle class nor maintain the confidence of the people. This is what Brutus and The Federal Farmer mean when they argue that the Constitution poses an aristocratic threat to republican government.

The Anti-Federalist argument about republican government, with its emphasis on a substantial representation of the middling class, stands between the *Federalist* position—which requires no more than the elective principle and favors a separation of the people from the administration of government—and Montesquieu's definition of the republic of virtue—which emphasizes the love of country and the priority of obligations of citizenship over individual rights.

II. The Constitution's Structure of Government

A. The Legislature and Legislative Power

Most of The Federal Farmer's Letters and Brutus's Essays examine specific provisions of the proposed Constitution. After two introductory Essays on the federal republic and a bill of rights, Brutus devotes eight Essays to the legislative article, including six on the enumeration of powers. While he does not discuss the executive, Brutus devotes five Essays to the judiciary. The Federal Farmer's account follows Brutus in part, but he includes a fuller discussion of the Senate and he also provides commentary on the executive.

To begin with the legislative article, the Great Compromise and the related sectional compromise over the apportionment principle in the House (number of free inhabitants, plus "three-fifths others," excluding Indians not taxed) made the Constitution's ratification possible. The Federal Farmer and Brutus barely take note of either of these topics. Brutus (perhaps Robert Yates from New York) did express his opposition to counting slaves in the apportionment but did not make much of it; in contrast, The Federal Farmer (perhaps Richard Henry Lee from Virginia) never mentioned it. The Federal Farmer did, "on reflection, . . . acquiesce in making [the states] the basis of the senate" (XI, 2.8.143), while Brutus opposed state equality in the Senate: "On every principle of equity, and propriety, representation in a government should be in exact proportion to the numbers, or the aids afforded by the persons represented" (III, 2.9.40).

It might appear that The Federal Farmer contradicted his position on representation in supporting the Great Compromise, but that is not the case. The Anti-Federalist representation argument, as we have seen, is connected to their republican government argument. The state governments, by virtue of their smaller size, will be more republican than the government for the

Union since they will have fewer constituents for each representative. This applies even to the larger states, although to a proportionally smaller degree. The Federal Farmer acknowledges that in the Federal Convention Madison attempted to double the initial number of representatives, from 65 to 130, but failed. But he points out that the federal representation was bound to be inferior to the popular representation in the states, since all legislative bodies have an upper limit of membership for the sake of efficiency. The federal representatives would have to number 1,500 to equal the representation in the several states (IX, 2.8.116).

While not nearly as controversial, the Convention's decision to replace a general grant of legislative power with an enumeration and to drop the national negative on state legislation also made ratification possible. But the enumeration, with its concluding "necessary and proper" clause, did not evince a determination to restrict powers strictly. Brutus and The Federal Farmer focus on the enumeration of powers, claiming that they are extensive and out of proportion to the scant representation. As The Federal Farmer put it, "there is no substantial representation of the people provided for in a government in which the most essential powers, even as to the internal police of the country, is proposed to be lodged" (V, 2.8.65).

Brutus starts by highlighting the preamble ("provide for the common defense, promote the general welfare . . . ") and the supremacy clause, which, taken together, assert the supremacy of the government of a single people. He then quotes the "necessary and proper" clause and construes it in terms of the preamble. "The inference is natural that the legislature will have an authority to make all laws which they shall judge necessary for the common safety, and to promote the general welfare" (V, 2.9.57). Brutus knows that the taxing power is for the purpose of providing for the common defense and general welfare, but he still claims that his construction of necessary and proper (that it can justify anything that is done for the common defense and the general welfare) is the "most natural and easy." He was wrong about this but he was on the right track. Later on, in discussing the judiciary, Brutus writes: "Every adjudication of the supreme court, on any question that may arise upon the nature and extent of the general government, will affect the limits of the state jurisdiction" (XI, 2.9.139). Brutus then discusses the necessary and proper clause in relation to the tax power and the power to raise troops. Noting the Federalist position (in *The Federalist* nos. 33 and 44) that the clause adds no power not already conferred, Brutus writes: "though I believe this is not the fact, yet, admitting it to be, it implies that the constitution is not to receive an explanation strictly, according to its letter; but more power is implied than is expressed" (XI, 2.9.41).

The issue of the extent of "implied powers" was confronted in the First Congress at two different times. First, during its 1789 deliberations on a bill of rights, the House decisively (17–32) rejected an attempt to include "expressly" in what became the Tenth Amendment. Second, when Congress established a national bank in 1791, Madison, who spoke against the motion to add "expressly" in the prior debate, argued against the authority to establish a bank; but the measure passed by a vote of 39–20.[11]

The more detailed discussion of the powers of government involved an attempt at making fine distinctions and, as a result, several important proposals for amendment. Both The Federal Farmer and Brutus try to apply the distinction between internal and external powers as they draw the boundary between state and federal government powers. The Federal Farmer's delineation recognizes that some powers—such as commerce among the states, weights and measures and currency, post offices, and naturalization—"respect internal objects" and yet belong with the federal government. His chief concern is to protect the "internal police" of the states; this includes the powers "to lay and collect internal taxes, to form the militia, to make bankruptcy laws, and to decide on appeals, questions arising on the internal laws of the respective states" (III, 2.8.35).

In Essays V–X, Brutus provides an extensive discussion of the most important powers—the powers to raise money and armies. These Essays were published at the same time as Publius' essays on the legislative powers, and they respond to some of the key arguments in favor of these constitutional provisions.

Concerning taxes, Brutus argues that the preservation of the state governments requires that the distinction between external and internal taxes be maintained. The federal government should only have the power to tax imports; if more revenue is needed, he is prepared to allow a limited tax on exports (V, 2.9.63). Both governments have a concurrent power to tax objects of trade. Brutus hypothesizes that if the taxes exceed the ability or willingness of the people to pay, Congress would, under the necessary and proper clause, be able to suspend the state's tax law (VI, 2.9.67). Again, Brutus may be wrong in the particulars, but it is reasonable to observe that a full federal tax power may well limit a state's ability to raise its own revenues.

As for the power to raise money for armies, Brutus begins by quoting Publius (*The Federalist* no. 23) to the effect that the power to raise armies must be without limit "'because it is impossible to foresee, or to define, the extent and variety of national exigencies, or the correspondent extent and variety of the means which may be necessary to satisfy them'" (VI, 2.9.79). This is the strongest argument in support of giving the federal government tax and war powers without limit; one depends on the other and the extent of the need depends on the threat. Brutus replies by reminding his readers that even Publius concedes "'the circumstances of our country are such, as to demand a compound, instead of a simple, a confederate, instead of a sole government.'" Brutus claims, however, that the end of government in America is complex: "it is as necessary, that the state governments should possess the means to attain the ends expected from them as for the general government" (VI, 2.9.80). This means that the states should have their own source of revenue, not subject to congressional use. Aware of the possible shortfall, Brutus is willing to allow Congress to tax exports at a specified rate (VII, 2.9.92, and V, 2.9.63).

In his next Essay, Brutus quotes another passage from *The Federalist* no. 23 that makes the same point about the unlimited needs for common defense. His reply this time draws on his conception of republican government. First, "a defensive war is the only one I think justifiable"; and second, America, unlike European nations, will not engage in war for the sake of glory. "We ought to furnish the world with an example of a great people, who in their civil institutions hold chiefly in view, the attainment of virtue, and happiness among ourselves." The most important end of government in America is "the proper direction of its internal policy, and oeconomy," and "this is the province of the state governments" (VII, 2.9.86–87) This position differs significantly from Publius. It was presented in the Federal Convention, most notably by Charles Pinckney, but it did not appear to affect any key decisions.[12]

After a brief discussion of the power to borrow money, which he thinks should require a two-thirds vote in both houses, Brutus turns to the power to keep standing armies in time of peace (cf. *FF* III, 2.8.39 and XIII, 2.8.168). His position is that standing armies in peacetime are dangerous and not necessary; they should have been treated as the Framers treated the suspension of the privilege of the writ of habeas corpus (IX, 2.9.104). Brutus eventually comes up with such a proposal, and he then recites the limited exceptions, which include guards to arsenals or garrisons for frontier posts or to facilitate trade with the Indians. He also takes note of another special case: "when the United States are threatened with an attack or invasion from some foreign power." Brutus concludes by stating that in all such cases, the assent of two-thirds of each house of the legislature should be required (X, 2.9.126).

Brutus and The Federal Farmer thus want to protect the people against any possible misuse of power, and they trust to the efficacy of qualified limitations on legislative powers rather than, as Publius does, to the responsibility of the governors to periodic elections. This distrust manifested itself in a fear that under the "Times, Places and Manner" clause, Congress might insist on "at-large" elections (rather than elections in single member districts) for the House, or it might allow elections by pluralities, not majorities.[13] And The Federal Farmer thought that members of Congress should be disqualified from appointment to any office during their term and for some time thereafter. He wanted legislators ineligible for offices for the same reason he wanted them chosen frequently, able to be recalled, and subject to rotation: to keep them "uncorrupted and virtuous" (XIII, 2.8.170).

B. The Executive and Executive Powers

The executive power was vested in a president, a single person, who was elected by the people indirectly and was eligible for reelection. He possessed a qualified veto as well as the power to nominate officers and judges (with the advice and consent of the Senate) and to make treaties (subject to the assent of two-thirds of the Senate). He was also commander in chief of the armed forces. The Senate therefore, in addition to possessing the legislative power, shared in what was regarded as two executive powers.

In light of Brutus's and The Federal Farmer's distinctive views on republican government, it is surprising that they did not object to the structure of the federal government more than they did. Both Brutus and The Federal Farmer did oppose the Senate's participation in appointment of officers; they would have preferred a separate council of appointment in order to avoid undue influence in the Senate. But Brutus does not say anything about the president, and The Federal Farmer's only objection was to his reeligibility (XIV, 2.8.177). A strict adherence to the public-spirited conception of republican government should have caused The Federal Farmer and Brutus to object to a unitary executive, especially with a qualified veto over legislation. But everyone knew that George Washington would be the first president, and everyone approved of that result.

C. The Judicial Power

Brutus's account of the judicial power (Essays XI–XV) anticipated the full development of judicial review as well as the importance of the judicial branch as a vehicle for the development of the federal government's powers. In a prescient statement anticipating the future Chief Justice John Marshall's court opinion in *McCulloch v. Maryland* (4 Wheaton 316 [1819]), Brutus writes: "The real effect of this system of government, will therefore be brought home to the feelings of the people, through the medium of judicial power" (XI, 2.9.130). This is because, by extending judicial power "to all cases in law and equity, arising under this Constitution," Article III permits the courts "to give the constitution a legal construction." Moreover, Brutus continues, the equity jurisdiction, which referred to the courts of chancery in England, gave the courts power "to explain the constitution according to the reasoning spirit of it, without being confined to the words or letter" (XI, 2.9.136–37).

Brutus does not object to the life tenure for judges, as long as they do not have the power to interpret the Constitution (XV, 2.9.189, 193). In other words, he opposes what came to be known as judicial review. Without that power, the construction of the Constitution would be left to the legislature, and "if they [the lawmakers] exceed their powers, . . . the people from whom they derive their powers could remove them and do themselves right." (XV, 2.9.196). It is interesting that in this context Brutus is willing to trust in the electoral connection between the people and their federal representatives whereas in all other contexts he and The Federal Farmer find this connection inadequate.

Brutus and The Federal Farmer objected to the extensive appellate jurisdiction of the Supreme Court, especially as it affected the right to trial by jury. Article III, section 2 may guarantee a jury trial in criminal cases, but an appellate reconsideration of the facts (as well as the law) would negate that right. In addition, Brutus and The Federal Farmer wanted the right to a trial by jury extended to civil cases and protected against appellate review as well (XIV, 2.9.170–72).

Finally, the Federal Convention, in a compromise between those who favored a full federal court system and those who opposed lower courts, provided that Congress could "ordain and establish" lower courts. Brutus agreed with those who thought that, aside from the Supreme Court's original jurisdiction, the judicial power should have been left to originate in the state courts (XIV, 2.9.183).

III. The Bill of Rights

The Anti-Federalists are best known for advocating a bill of rights. The Constitution would not have been ratified without the promise, first made by Federalists in the Massachusetts Ratification Convention, that Congress would take up proposed amendments if the Constitution was unconditionally ratified. Until that time, the country was faced with the prospect of conditional ratifications by various states, which probably would have necessitated a second convention with little likelihood of agreement on an improved Constitution. But the bill of rights that Madison proposed in the First Congress, most of which then became the first ten amendments, only addressed some of the Anti-Federalist concerns. Because the contested federal legislative powers were not compromised, it can be said that Madison's leadership in framing and getting the Bill of Rights passed in the House, and their subsequent ratification, gained widespread support for the Constitution. Nevertheless, recognition of the importance of a bill of rights reflected the Anti-Federalist emphasis, amply present in Brutus and The Federal Farmer, on securing a people's rights against government. And in at least one respect, the Bill of Rights reflected their interest in republican participation.

Brutus and The Federal Farmer together make two arguments of their own in favor of a bill of rights; they also reply to the Federalist contention that a bill of rights was not necessary in the federal Constitution. I will start with their positive arguments.

Both The Federal Farmer and Brutus support mild and gentle government, which means that they want to make sure that individuals are secure against government oppression. Hence, Brutus expresses greater concern about government misdeeds than inaction (see X, 2.9.98, quoted above). The Federal Farmer makes the case for a bill of rights this way: "If a nation means its systems, religious or social, shall have duration, it ought to recognize the leading principles of them in the front page of every family book" (XVI, 2.8.196).

The Federal Farmer devotes more attention to the jury trial than any other right. His discussion reveals a double interest: that facts should be tried in the "vicinage" (neighborhood) and not be subject to appeals, for the sake of getting it right; and that "common people should have a part and share of influence, in the judicial as well as in the legislative department" (IV, 2.8.53). In this sense, The Federal Farmer's interest in the jury trial reflects his republicanism, and this is why he paired it with representation in an earlier Letter.

The Federal Farmer and Brutus both replied to the Federalist argument, first stated by James Wilson in his State House speech in October 1787, but reiterated by Publius in *The Federalist* no. 85, that a federal bill of rights was not necessary since the legislative branch was limited to the enumerated powers. Brutus quotes Wilson: "'in the former case [state constitutions], every thing which is not reserved is given, but in the latter [the federal constitution] the reverse of the proposition prevails, and every thing which is not given is reserved.'"[14] Brutus immediately presents a twofold response. First, as he demonstrated in the discussion considered above, "the powers, rights, and authority, granted to the general government by this constitution, are as complete, with respect to every object to which they extend, as that of any state government. . . . There is the same reason, therefore, that the exercise of power, in this case, should be restrained within proper limits, as in that of the state governments" (II, 2.9.26). Second, Brutus referred to the specific restrictions on congressional power in Article I, section 9, concerning suspension of the privilege of habeas corpus, bills of attainder, ex post facto laws, and titles of nobility. These constitute prohibitions or severe restrictions on powers that are nowhere expressly given. "The only answer that can be given [to the question, why are these provisions in the Constitution?] is, that these are implied in the general powers granted. With equal truth it may be said, that all the powers, which the bills of right, guard against the abuse of, are contained or implied in the general ones granted by this constitution" (II, 2.9.30).

The Federal Farmer makes the same point about the existence of a "partial bill of rights" in the Constitution, and he then proceeds to discuss other important rights, mainly pertaining to criminal procedure but also including freedom of the press (XVI, 2.8.199–203).

The Anti-Federalists' response to the Federalists' contention that no bill of rights was necessary since the powers given were limited is persuasive. First, the enumerated powers were general, and they included a final "necessary and proper" clause which lends itself to a liberal construction. Second, the existence of some bill of rights provisions, against the federal government in Article I, section 9 and the state governments in Article I, section 10, suggests the need to make sure the list is complete. Otherwise, the enumeration of some might well imply the exclusion of others, especially since there was no statement in the "internal bill of rights" saying that other rights may be implicit. And finally, the state bills of rights could not control the federal government, in light of the supremacy clause (Article VI, section 2).

Conclusion

The Anti-Federalists lost the ratification contest for the very good reason that they could not adequately reply to Publius' challenge not to try to reconcile contradictions: the price of union, in terms of the cost to republicanism, had to be sufficient power in the federal government to provide for the common defense. This, after all, was the main defect of the Articles of Confederation —a defect the Anti-Federalists conceded. Hence, the Anti-Federalists had the weaker argument precisely because they supported union and agreed that an effective government was necessary; they advocated a limitation on key powers—the purse and the sword—that rendered them inadequate given the requirements of national security.

Even the subsequent Bill of Rights did not give the Anti-Federalists victory on the important battles over the power of the purse and the sword. But just as their emphasis on rights over government resonated with Jefferson's aversion to energetic government, so also their wariness about the disproportion between representation of the people and the powers of government resonated with Jefferson's (and Madison's) strict construction of the enumerated powers. Nevertheless, Chief Justice John Marshall's opinion in *McCulloch v. Maryland* laid the foundation for a liberal construction of the powers of Congress. This is the classical source for the view that "necessary" in the clause "necessary and proper" means "convenient" or "useful" in relation to an enumerated power, and not, as Jefferson argued, "without it, an enumerated power becomes nugatory."[15] And Madison's interpretation of the enumeration of powers during the congressional debate on the national bank was much closer to Jefferson's than it was to the Hamilton-Marshall position. Leaving aside the question concerning Madison's consistency, during the ratification debate it was the Anti-Federalists—most notably Brutus and The Federal Farmer—and not the Federalists who emphasized the need to limit the powers of the federal government.

The American Founders created a new form of federalism, as Alexis de Tocqueville noted in *Democracy in America*. "The human mind invents things more easily than words," he wrote. "Here [in America] the central power acts without an intermediary on the governed, administers them and judges them by itself, as national governments do, but it acts this way only in a restricted sphere. Evidently that is no longer a federal government; it is an incomplete national government."[16]

For a time, from 1937 to 1976, it seemed as if American government had become completely national. But ever since our nation's bicentennial, the Supreme Court has reaffirmed its role as umpire of the federal system. It has not returned to the restrictive view of commerce that it held in the days of dual federalism (1880s to 1936), when federal regulation of wages and hours in manufacturing, mining, and agriculture was prohibited. But it takes very seriously the task of protecting the states against broad affirmations of congressional power under the commerce clause, the Fourteenth Amendment's enforcement clause, or congressional taxing and spending powers. The closely divided contemporary Supreme Court decisions on federalism have revived the "strict" versus "loose" construction debate. We have seen that the forerunner of "strict construction" was the Anti-Federalist concern about the breadth of the powers actually granted as well as the potential of the "necessary and proper" clause.

The Anti-Federalist assessment of the Constitution reflected a distinctive form of republicanism, one that emphasized mild government through substantial representation and citizen participation in government via the jury trial. They were more concerned about the ill effects of strong government on the character and inclinations of the people than the ill effects of majority rule or ineffective government. By extension, the Anti-Federalists should have opposed a strong executive more than they did. They opposed eligibility for reelection, but they accepted unity and the qualified veto over legislation. I have suggested that this reflected the immense trust in George Washington, assumed to become the first president. In the ongoing debate over the scope of executive power, however, especially in connection with what can be called the war powers, the Anti-Federalist position, based on their opposition to standing armies, would support Congress and resist presidential power.

Finally, the importance of rights that are secure against government infringement clearly reflects the Anti-Federalist legacy, but the securing of rights by means of the federal judiciary reflects the Federalist legacy. The Supreme Court has interpreted the Fourteenth Amendment to apply most of the original Bill of Rights to the states. This has resulted in the kind of enhanced national power that Brutus predicted and that first took place in *McCulloch v. Maryland*.

Anti-Federalist opposition to a strong national government continues to be reflected in subsequent constitutional controversies. The American people apparently continue to expect the benefits of a strong and secure union and the benefits of republican government. In general, American government has delivered both, but not without liberalizing the meaning of republican government. The Anti-Federalists moved away from the strictest notions of republican government by accepting representation in place of direct participation in government and inequality of wealth (they did not push for sumptuary laws). So Americans today accept equal representation, judicial protection of individual rights, and an even greater inequality of wealth, all of which result in a popular government based more on interest and ambition than on self-denying civic virtue. The most pervasive legacy of Brutus and The Federal Farmer is their emphasis on the popular and public-spirited elements of republican government.

Notes

I would like to thank Samuel Dettmann for reading and constructively commenting on several versions of this chapter.

1. See Herbert J. Storing's discussion of the authorship question in his introductions to each author in *The Complete Anti-Federalist*, 7 vols. (Chicago: University of Chicago Press, 1981), 2:215, 358. This can also be found in the one volume abridgment, *The Anti-Federalist* (Chicago: University of Chicago Press, 1985), 24–25, 103. All references to The Federal Farmer (hereafter *FF*) and Brutus (hereafter *B*) will be from this edition; the citations will be to the number of the Letter or Essay, followed by the three-part number system used in both *The Complete Anti-Federalist* and its abridgment. The abridgment contains all of Brutus and Letters I–VII and XVII of The Federal Farmer. The reader will have to consult *The Complete Anti-Federalist* for the few Federal Farmer references to passages that are not in the abridgment.

2. The Federal Farmer's first set of Letters (I–V) were published from October 8 to 13, 1787, and his Additional Letters (VI–XVIII) from December 25, 1787, to January 25, 1788, in the Poughkeepsie *Country Journal*; they were also published in pamphlet form in New York. Brutus's series of Essays (I–XVI) were published from October 18, 1787, to April 10, 1788, in the *New York Journal*. During this time, the first 77 numbers of *The Federalist Papers* were published in three different New York newspapers. (The final eight numbers were first published in pamphlet form on May 28, 1788.)

3. James Madison, *Notes of Debates in the Federal Convention*, intro. Adrienne Koch (New York: W. W. Norton and Co., 1987), 148 (June 19). The Federal Convention voted by state delegations.

4. Madison, *Notes*, 218 (Mr. Ellsworth said this on June 29).

5. Herbert J. Storing, *What the Anti-Federalists Were For* (Chicago: University of Chicago Press, 1981), 9–10.

6. Madison, *Notes*, 225 (June 30).

7. Storing, *What the Anti-Federalists Were For*, 9–10.

8. *The Spirit of the Laws*, trans. Anne M. Cohler, Basia Carolyn Miller, and Harold Samuel Stone (Cambridge: Cambridge University Press, 1989), 35–36 (bk. IV, chap. 5).

9. *Spirit of the Laws*, bk. VII, chap. 2.

10. Part of this was presented in II, 2.8.15, quoted above; for Brutus's comparable statement, see III, 2.9.42.

11. See *Debates and Proceedings in the Congress of the United States* (*Annals of Congress*) (Washington: Gales and Seaton, 1834), I:761, 767–68, and II:1894–902, 1956–60, 1968.

12. See Mr. Pinckney's speech on June 25, in Madison, *Notes*, 184–85.

13. See Brutus (IV, 2.9.41) for the first point and The Federal Farmer for the second (XII, 2.8.152–54). The Federal Farmer thought that the broad eligibility for office precluded the dividing a state into districts (XII, 2.8.151).

14. II, 2.9.26, quoting Wilson's speech, which can be found in *Pennsylvania and the Constitution, 1787–1788*, ed. John Bach McMaster and Frederick D. Stone (Philadelphia: Historical Society of Pennsylvania, 1888), 143.

15. See his opinion on the constitutionality of the bank in *The Portable Thomas Jefferson*, ed. Merrill D. Peterson (New York: Penguin, 1977), 265.

16. *Democracy in America*, trans. Harvey C. Mansfield and Delba Winthrop (Chicago: University of Chicago Press, 2000), 148–49 (vol. 1, pt. 1, chap. 8).

Chapter 12

The New Constitutionalism of Publius

James R. Stoner, Jr.

Publius is the pen name chosen by Alexander Hamilton for the essays that he, James Madison, and John Jay wrote and published between October 1787 and May 1788 urging ratification of the Constitution. The eighty-five essays appeared in the New York City papers, sometimes at a pace of three or four per week and often in response to essays written to oppose ratification. The first thirty-six essays were published in book form in March 1788 under the title *The Federalist*; a second volume appeared in May containing the remaining forty-nine papers, the last eight of which had not previously been printed.[1] The name Publius is obviously not American or British, but Roman. It refers to Publius Valerius Publicola, who had helped to found the Roman republic and then saved it in its early days from enemies at home and abroad, earning thereby the affection of the people indicated in his name.[2]

America's Publius is an advocate of ratification of the American Constitution of 1787; "he" was invented for this purpose and "authored" a single work. It is tempting to introduce him as *the* authority on the Constitution—but this would be a mistake. He found ready to hand in young America a well-established tradition of constitutionalism—both in the states and at the federal level—which he carefully addressed and skillfully developed. Moreover, his arguments in favor of the Constitution sometimes go beyond what that tradition was willing to bear. For example, in *The Federalist* no. 84, Publius makes the case against including a bill of rights in the Constitution (a point on which he was quickly overruled, albeit with the consent of at least one of his creators), and his views on federalism—that is to say, his ardent nationalism—exceed what the Constitution itself establishes.[3] Lastly, the practical focus of his essays on achieving ratification leaves him little room for rumination on other themes of political thought such as education, which any full account of American constitutionalism ought to address.

Nevertheless, the essays are perhaps more rather than less effective for being works of advocacy rather than pronouncements of authority: even today, one can readily sense the urgency of his cause and feel the pressure of his arguments. Publius understood that constitutionalism requires partisans of its own even as it by definition involves the aim to rise above ordinary partisanship; and he supplies to Americans a political science that, if not expressive of every national ideal, is deeply instructive about the means and even the end of American greatness. That his authors were soon important leaders in the three branches of the new federal government probably helped *The Federalist* achieve such authority as it acquired in the exposition of the Constitution; so too, more poignantly, did the fact that Hamilton and Madison were within a decade of their joint authorship leaders on opposite sides of the first great partisan divide under the new federal government. Aware of the inevitability as well as the danger of partisanship in free government, Publius advocates a form of government that at once permits and restrains partisan sentiments. In the intelligence and candor of his advocacy, and in placing the American Constitution in the perspective of political theory, he helps to give American constitutional discourse its distinctive cast.[4]

A New Federalism

After two centuries of political upheaval that has touched most of the world, the American Constitution today seems a bastion of tradition, and an appeal to the intentions of its Framers is usually thought to be deeply conservative. One can begin to understand Publius as he understood himself only by recognizing that he sees the Constitution as genuinely innovative and its Framers as bold and daring. Indeed, he begins his papers by attributing to his audience something new and splendid: the prospect of proving, as if for the first time and to all mankind, "whether societies of men are really capable or not, of establishing good government from reflection and choice, or whether they are forever destined to depend, for their political constitutions, on accident and force" (1:3).[5] He acknowledges that novelty in itself is not necessarily good by attributing the greater novelty to his opponents, who, he says presciently but against their published statements, aim to divide the American Union into "partial confederacies" (1:4).[6]

As Publius understands and candidly explains, the Constitution would establish a political entity that differed from previous federations or confederations (the words were then synonymous). Confederate republics had been known from antiquity and were celebrated in Montesquieu's *Spirit of the Laws*. The federal government established by the Articles of Confederation was typical of the species; its central authority was constituted by the governments of the member states and made up of delegates that the member states chose.[7] What the new Constitution proposed was a federal government that only conformed in part to this scheme. The new government was to be a republic itself, not a council of republics, and it would cover the whole people who, severally, established the member republics. It would draw its authority from the people and act directly upon them, albeit for limited purposes. Publius describes the form as "partly federal, and partly national," and he carefully sorts the scheme into federal and national components—the former involving the central government in relation to the states and the latter involving it directly in relation to the people (39:257). To lay a national government overtop the member states is the innovation of the Constitution, and Publius explicates its theory. By drawing authority from the people and acting directly upon them, the new "federal" government would avoid the radical vice of the Articles of Confederation (and, he implies, all previous confederate republics): namely, "legislation for states or governments in their corporate or collective capacities," (i.e., for the states as states), which had the consequence that law enforcement was either voluntary or by means of civil war (15:93).

Publius is cautious in defending what he knows to be an innovation, but he has confidence in the innovative spirit of the American people. When the question of the right of the people to form or reform a government is discussed, he quotes or refers to the Declaration of Independence, and he singles out the Americans who wrote the state constitutions for having used the principle of representation to introduce to the world "unmixed and extensive republics" (14:84). He continues:

> But why is the experiment of an extended republic to be rejected merely because it may comprise what is new? Is it not the glory of the people of America, that whilst they have paid a decent respect to the opinions of former times and other nations, they have not suffered a blind veneration for antiquity, for custom, or for names, to overrule the suggestions of their own good sense, the knowledge of their situation, and the lessons of their own experience? To this manly spirit,

posterity will be indebted for the possession, and the world for the example of the numerous innovations displayed on the American theatre, in favor of private rights and public happiness. (14:88)

At the same time that he accepts innovation, however, he repeatedly warns against one kind of innovator: the "theoretic politician," the man "far gone in Utopian speculations" (10:61; 6:28). Not abstract political theory but actual experience is prized, though theory drawn from experience might disclose political necessities that the ordinary eye fails to see. A year before the French Revolution and so before Burke's famous analysis of its misguided trust in theoretical innovation, Publius stakes out a balanced position in which political theory and political experience walk hand in hand. Innovation is not the opposite of experience but its product, for experience shows what does not work and what does.

The center of Publius' defense of the Constitution's innovative substitute for the confederate republic is his argument that the Union must be strengthened not so much by the addition of enumerated powers as by a complete restructuring that will make it effective in achieving its ends. The only really new object given to federal authority is the power to regulate commerce, and for all the controversy this was to generate in subsequent years, in the debate between Publius and the Constitution's detractors it is not at issue, since Congress and most of the states had already endorsed an amendment that would have added the commerce power to the Articles of Confederation (cf. nos. 11, 22, 42, and 45:314). It was not for lack of the commerce power alone that the federal government was failing; rather, it lacked the ability to command respect from foreign powers or even from its member governments. As an example of the former, Publius notes Great Britain's refusal to withdraw its garrisons from the western forts as provided by the Treaty of Paris while it simultaneously asserted that the property claims of its nationals, also protected by the treaty, were being unjustly refused by the state courts (an objection whose justice Publius concedes). Examples of the latter were precisely the inability of the federal government to enforce its own treaty at home as well as the tendency of the states to refuse or at any rate not to pay their requisitions (cf. nos. 3, 15). To be respected abroad and at home—and thus to be able successfully to execute the power of acting on the world stage assigned to it by the Articles—the federal government had to be made, in Publius' phrase, "energetic." It had to be given new powers that were instrumental to the objects already established for it, such as the power to tax, the power to raise troops, and the power to administer justice through its own courts. In other words, it had to be made into a genuine government capable of acting directly on its people and not dependent on intermediaries, thus without the "radical vice" of confederations. Publius presents this as a matter of inexorable logic, following "axioms" or "primary truths" or "first principles" in the science of politics: "that there cannot be an effect without a cause; that the means ought to be proportioned to the end; that every power ought to be commensurate with its object; that there ought to be no limitation of a power destined to effect a purpose, which is incapable of limitation." As he rephrases the point in more political and republican terms, "a government ought to contain in itself every power requisite to the full accomplishment of the objects committed to its care, and to the complete execution of the trusts for which it is responsible; free from every other control, but a regard to the public good and to the sense of the people" (31:193–95; 23:passim).

Having raised the danger of disunion allows Publius not only to declare himself the advocate of a popular cause but also to instruct Americans generally in the national interest. He writes eloquently of the need for unity to prevent the inevitable jealousies and even wars that would accompany multiple sovereign confederations in North America. He draws attention to the peculiar geographical situation of the country: on the one hand, it is more insular than England in comparison to continental Europe; but on the other hand, it is bordered by colonies governed by two of Europe's leading powers, Great Britain and Spain. Though he carefully insists on the distinction between constitutional power and national policy, he clearly recognizes the enterprising spirit of American commerce and the fiscal possibilities carried with it. He explains the need for a power to tax—and not just requisition funds—as essential to establishing the government's credit, which in turn is needed in time of war. In the face of the Anglo-American tradition of distrust of standing armies, he defends the need for a Union army and, as Americans are a commercial people, for a navy as well (see nos. 6–8, 11–12, 24–25, 30). His aim is not exactly to promote particular policies but rather to make them seem important enough to justify the establishment of a federal government able to enact and enforce them. If Americans think seriously about their national interests, they will agree on the need for a strong federal government; and if they agree to that, the "axioms" or "first principles" of political science apply and they must accept the new forms. It is a case not for limiting government but for empowering it. Such, at any rate, is the argument of Publius when he is written by Alexander Hamilton.

From the pen of James Madison, Publius makes a distinct but complementary argument: that a more extensive republic is necessary to protect the national interest and individual rights from the depredations of majority faction and the cabals of narrow-minded politicians in the states. Here the emphasis is not on the need to strengthen the federal government but on the need to limit political power in order to defend individuals against majorities and the officials who flatter them. In the justly celebrated *The Federalist* no. 10, Publius defines a faction as "a number of citizens, whether amounting to a majority or minority of the whole, who are united and actuated by some common impulse of passion, or of interest, adverse to the rights of other citizens, or to the permanent and aggregate interests of the community." Though factions are by definition unjust, Publius' solution is not to eradicate them: "it could not be a less folly to abolish liberty, which is essential to political life, because it nourishes faction, than it would be to wish the annihilation of air, which is essential to animal life, because it imparts to fire its destructive agency." The causes of faction are "sown in the nature of man," and the proper response is not foolishly trying to change this fact but prudently "controlling its effects." Minority factions are controlled by the republican principle, majority rule; therefore, the challenge in a republic is how to harness an unjust majority. The short answer is to expand the republic so that every majority faction in a state becomes a minority faction in the country at large: "Extend the sphere, and you take in a greater variety of parties and interests; you make it less probable that a majority of the whole will have a common motive to invade the rights of other citizens; or if such a common motive exists, it will be more difficult for all who feel it to discover their own strength, and to act in unison with each other." Through a properly ordered federalism, the republican principle of majority rule can obviate the republican problem of majority faction—or in Publius' words, "we behold a Republican remedy for the diseases most incident to Republican Government" (10:57–58, 64–65).

There is much more in *The Federalist* no. 10 than this short summary can capture, but two points should be emphasized. First, Publius notes the advantage of a republic over a "pure" or direct democracy in combating majority faction. He defines a republic here as "a Government in which a scheme of representation takes place," and he hopes that the effect of the people's choosing a few representatives to enact their business will be to "refine and enlarge the public views": in a large republic, there will be, if not a greater proportion, at least more "fit characters, . . . and consequently a greater probability of a fit choice." But Publius also recognizes that the selection in republics of better men than the norm is only a hope, not a necessity, for by election "the effect may be inverted," and "[m]en of factious temper" practicing the "vicious arts, by which elections are too often carried," might come to dominate elected bodies (10:62–63). The large republic that the United States will be under the new Constitution is, after all, "unmixed" or democratic: no aristocratic body is to be established that inherits its position or perpetuates itself—i.e., there will be no "will in the community independent of the majority, that is, of the society itself" (51:351). Good men are certainly needed in government, but a form of government must be chosen that recognizes that "[e]nlightened statesmen will not always be at the helm" (10:60).

Second, though Publius formulates in abstract terms the theory of a greater variety of, and thus a lesser threat from, factions in a large republic, he does not think that all factions are equal. Factions arise from passion or interest, and the factions of passion are further specified to include those that arise from "zeal for different opinions concerning religion, concerning Government and many other points, as well of speculation as of practice" and those that arise from "attachment" to ambitious or charismatic leaders. Passionate factions are said to "inflame" men into "mutual animosities," even without "substantial occasion." Fortunately, such factions, though the most dangerous, are not the most common and durable. This distinction belongs to factions based on "the various and unequal distribution of property," the rights to which originate in "the diversity in the faculties of men." Concerning propertied interests, Publius writes that "[t]he regulation of these various and interfering interests forms the principal task of modern Legislation, and involves the spirit of party and faction in the necessary and ordinary operations of Government." Publius seems to endorse rather than despair at such a situation: although faction is rooted in human nature, if factions can be turned into interests, they can be adjusted, compromised, and assembled into what he later calls "a coalition of a majority of the whole society." One's interest, after all, is an enlightened or at least a calculated judgment about one's own good; and it can or must incorporate the "permanent and aggregate interests of the community" (10: 58–59; 51:353; 10:57). The large, diverse republic will be a commercial republic where peace, prosperity, and justice understood especially in relation to property rights are in the interest of those who stop to think. Thinking about politics in the sober language of interest is integral to the project Publius means to promote.

Publius does not dwell on the legal side of federalism, though he concedes the elements of what was to become the orthodox doctrine on these matters at least until the Civil War: sovereignty is divided between the federal government and the states, with each level responsible for certain objects of government and each sovereign over its sphere. From Publius' point of view, the residual sovereignty of the states is clearly a concession. Even without independent knowledge that both Hamilton and Madison had advocated in the Convention a more powerful and centralized system than the Constitution eventually proposed, it is apparent that Publius' commitment to state sovereignty is contingent—"as far as the sovereignty of the States cannot be reconciled to the happiness of the people, the voice of every good citizen must be, let the former be sacrificed to the latter"—and he defends the equality of states in the Senate as "evidently the result of compromise" and a "lesser evil" than disunion (45:309; 62:416–17).[8] What excites him is not the issue of sovereignty, or the legal right of self-government, but the issue of attachment —the actual public sentiment that underlies political power. In *The Federalist* no. 17, Hamilton attempts to assuage doubts that a Union with direct authority over the people might grow too powerful by noting "the greater degree of influence, which the State governments, if they administer their affairs with uprightness and prudence, will generally possess over the people." The key to their influence is to be found in their objects, especially "the ordinary administration of criminal and civil justice"; as the "immediate and visible guardian of life and property," the states will impress "upon the minds of the people affection, esteem, and reverence, . . . this great cement of society" (17:106–7). Madison's review of the same issue in no. 46 likewise stresses the tendency of most confederations toward dissolution rather than consolidation, since "the first and most natural attachment of the people will be to the governments of their respective States." The states not only watch over people's interests, but their actions are also better known because more immediate; besides, they employ more people, thereby creating webs of loyalty. Only at the beginning of the Revolution, Publius argues, was attachment to the general government strong (46:316).

Despite the states' constitutional advantages—not only in the immediacy of their objects of concern but also in their role in electing parts of the federal government—Publius nevertheless anticipates growing federal influence.[9] The key will be the competition in the provision of good government, a contest Publius is confident the federal government will win. For the reasons developed in no. 10, including the greater likelihood of "fit characters" being elected and the lower likelihood of dominance by a majority faction, there is "a probability that the General Government will be better administered than the particular governments." Moreover, time will be on the side of the center. In an "observation" that Publius says "will not be the less just, because to some it may appear new," he writes that

> the more the operations of the national authority are intermingled in the ordinary exercise of government; the more the citizens are accustomed to meet with it in the common occurrences of their political life; the more it is familiarized to their sight and to their feelings; the further it enters into those objects which touch their most sensible cords, and put in motion the most active springs of the human heart; the greater will be the probability that it will conciliate the respect and attachment of the community. . . . The inference is, that the authority of the Union, and the affection of the citizens towards it, will be strengthened rather than weakened by its extension to what are called matters of internal concern. (27:172, 173–74)[10]

The immediate context of this remark is to deny that the federal government must of necessity work its will through force, but Publius hereby makes the case for functions of the federal government that touch upon ordinary, daily life—things such as the post office, commercial regulation, and the federal courts, that do not exactly displace the functions of the states but do erode their political base. He also foresees what in the twentieth century certainly ensued: that times of war will expand federal authority and by implication patriotic attachment to the whole (45:313). Whether the transfer of affection that Publius anticipates will entail a changed focus of political life—so that the things the more esteemed government can do seem to be the things worth doing—or whether there will simply be an eventual transfer of state responsibilities to the center, Publius does not say.

Publius implies that having several loci of institutional attachment lays the ground for political difference or even faction. In the very first paper (and in every instance where he questions the good faith of his opponents), he draws attention to the distinction between the enlarged views of those who support the Constitution and what he calls "the obvious interest of a certain class of men in every State to resist all changes which may hazard a diminution of the power, emolument, and consequence of the offices they hold under the State-establishments" (1:4). One might infer from this a permanent tendency likely under the new Constitution for parties to divide over the question whether to prefer the federal government or the states. Though it would go beyond what Publius writes to suggest that he means to replace the ancient or natural partisan divide between rich and poor with a division between state and federal men, it conforms to the logic of *The Federalist* no. 10 to observe that the fragmentation of ambitious and popular men into local notables, on the one hand, and a federal class, on the other hand, further obviates the danger to the people of government in the hands of a faction. Publius does not proclaim his new federalism—a "composition" that is "partly federal, and partly national"—to be a substitute for the Aristotelian mixed regime in a world of "unmixed" republics, but the complex and balanced politics that he hopes will result from this new form are not out of harmony with that old ideal.

A New Republicanism

When writing of the need for an energetic government to meet the exigencies of the Union, Publius says that there ought to be "no constitutional shackles" on the government's power to effect its ends (23:147). "No constitutional shackles" does not mean no constitutional limits, however; it means no ordinary interposition by the state governments in the execution of policy and no lists on paper of prohibitions that cripple a conscientious national government in doing its job. The new federal government is not only to be more powerful than its predecessor, the Congress under the Articles of Confederation, but it is also to be a safer depository of power, because it will be better structured. In the first place, it is to be strictly republican; in the second place, it is to respect the principle of the separation of powers. The new engine is not only to be more efficient in furthering national purposes but also less threatening to liberty and so less in need of jealous oversight and interference. Indeed, it will be more efficient in part because it will be more safe.

The republicanism of Publius might seem to some readers a matter of political constraint rather than personal conviction. His emphasis on "good government" and "good administration" seems indifferent to the form of government—indifferent, that is, between republicanism and monarchy—and his call for "energetic government" might seem to invite a concentration of power that would rival if not precisely imitate the British constitution. Hamilton's speech of June 18, 1787, in the Federal Convention, in which he advocated an executive and a senate elected for life, was not publicly known until many years later, but the Anti-Federalist pamphleteers did not hesitate to accuse the Constitution's proponents of seeking to establish a monarchical or aristocratic form of government.[11] Whatever motives operated "in the depository of [Hamilton's] own breast" (1:6), Publius takes seriously the need to vindicate the republican character of the Constitution, not as a political constraint on the Framers that could not be avoided—as he seems to have taken continued state sovereignty—but as an opportunity that ought to be embraced. Of the Constitution's commitment to republicanism, Publius writes:

> The first question that offers itself [concerning the plan of government] is, whether the general form and aspect of the government be strictly republican? It is evident that no other form would be reconcilable with the genius of the people of America; with the fundamental principles of the revolution; or with that honorable determination, which animates every votary of freedom, to rest all our political experiments on the capacity of mankind for self-government. (39:250)

"Reflection and choice" are not to be the attribute only of a founding moment; they are to characterize the form of government chosen as well as the choice.[12]

The challenge of proving the republican character of the Constitution, however, was not a small one. The argument in favor of "extending the sphere" shows that a continental republic would be convenient in preventing majority faction, just as the argument against the "radical vice" of the Articles of Confederation shows that a genuine government is necessary to ensure sovereign respectability; but neither of these arguments proves that a *republican* government of continental scope is possible. On the contrary, the Anti-Federalists made much of Montesquieu's adage that republican government was possible only in a small territory; and though they allowed that representation permits a republic to be more extensive than a single city and its environs, they still thought that representation on a continental level could not possibly reproduce in the national assembly all the different classes, interests, and opinions of the people, thus making the central legislature inevitably an oligarchic clique.[13] This observation was at the heart of their opposition to the Constitution. In their mind, it is not that they opposed strengthening the central government or that they were unduly attached to "state-establishments." Rather, it is that they thought a continental republic was a contradiction in terms: it could never provide sufficient representation of the people in its common bodies, and they refused to sacrifice republicanism or popular rule to the claim of national necessity. Publius' need to prove the new federal government to be republican was thus essential to his vindication of the Constitution. Not only must the government be shown to be republican as well as federal; it also had to be shown to be republican *despite* being federal. Indeed, nothing less was required on Publius' part than a reconceptualization of the meaning of republicanism, especially as it concerns the issue of adequate representation. One might then think that this is where Publius would start his treatment of the new government's structure or form.

Separation of Powers

But Publius does not start with the question of representation. Instead, he introduces his long account of the government's form with a theoretical account of the separation of powers. "The accumulation of all powers legislative, executive and judiciary in the same hands, whether of one, a few or many, and whether hereditary, self appointed, or elective, may justly be pronounced the very definition of tyranny" (47:324). On the one hand, this doctrine clearly has a republican aspect, for it rules out the legitimacy of absolute monarchy in any circumstance, insisting that rule be shared. On the other hand, it anticipates what was to become the typical modern form of republican government—parliamentarism—and rejects that too. Indeed, Publius proceeds to argue that in a republic—that is, in "a government which derives all its powers directly or indirectly from the great body of the people; and is administered by persons holding their offices during pleasure, for a limited period, or during good behavior" (39:251)—the most dangerous branch of government is the legislative, since its members will identify most closely with the people and probably be most trusted by them, and he boldly claims that the experience in every state since independence confirms this danger. Even before discussing the separation of powers according to the function of each branch, Publius insists that the legislative branch be divided and that its two houses be independent of one another in their makeup. Needless to say, the bicameral Congress proposed by the Constitution—with the houses chosen by different rules of apportionment and by different processes of election—perfectly meets the bill. Though Publius will later have much to say about the differences of function and character among the branches, he begins by considering power as a "mass." Those who have it want more, and they are not particular about its kind or purpose: "power is of an encroaching nature," and demarcation of its limits on paper is no more valuable between the branches than it proved under the Articles between the federal government and the states (48:332).

Publius' solution to the problem of encroaching power—or to say what is to his mind the same thing, the problem of ambition—is as theoretically elegant as his solution to the problem of faction. As the problem of faction was solved by the multiplication of factions and their involvement in the federal government, so the problem of ambition is solved by letting "[a]mbition . . . counteract ambition" through institutions carefully designed to mix the kinds of power just a little in order to give each branch the ability to resist encroachment by the others (51:349). To take the example Publius mentions in his discussion of the theory in *The Federalist* no. 51, the presidential veto is a power that is legislative in kind but given to the executive so that he can keep the legislature in check. He later notes impeachment, a power judicial in kind but given to the legislature to allow it to check executive or judicial malfeasance (no. 66). To the objection voiced in Anti-Federalist circles that the powers ought not to be mixed at all, Publius counters first by looking at the mix in the British constitution (cited by Montesquieu as exemplary of proper practice) and then at the various ways in which the powers are mixed in the states. In almost every instance, the new Constitution turns out to demand the stricter separation in practice. Thus, Publius orients the new federal Constitution in relation to both the political theorists' standard of his day, the British constitution, and the American citizens' standard, the constitutions of the particular states. The first is treated with respect, but the new Constitution is shown to be its equal or superior, especially regarding republican forms; the latter are praised for their "many excellent principles" and for providing young Americans with experience in what does *not* work. After all, the state constitutions were made in wartime, without republican experience, and in haste, so no one should take offense at their failings (47:331).

Starting with the separation of powers is typical of Publius' new republicanism because it exemplifies his steadfast insistence that republicanism be considered with analytical clarity rather than partisan zeal. Many have seen in his distrust of what we have come to call "populism" a preference for the aristocratic classes in society, and it is true that he is a staunch defender of property rights, which he thinks the states have infringed and the new government will ensure. But there is nothing in his arguments or his theory that supports a right to rule independent of popular choice or consent. Precisely because the basically popular or republican character of American government is given, Publius feels free to criticize republican practices or platforms; America is mature in its republicanism and so must look with sober resolution upon its faults. He rejects both Jefferson's proposal to refer breaches in the separation of powers to a convention of the people and the Pennsylvania practice of electing a Council of Censors to scrutinize constitutional practice on the grounds that they would only reproduce the partisan action they are meant to correct; besides, such ideas would destroy "that veneration, which time bestows on every thing, and without which perhaps the wisest and freest governments would not possess the requisite stability" (49:340). He demolishes such popular shibboleths as "where annual elections end, tyranny begins" (53:359). When defending the Senate, he writes with more candor than irony that "[t]o a people as little blinded by prejudice, or corrupted by flattery, as those whom I address, I shall not scruple to add, that such an institution may sometimes be necessary, as a defense to the people against their own temporary errors and delusions" (63:424–25). In the same paper, he explains that the difference between ancient republics and American republics "lies *in the total exclusion of the people in their collective capacity* from any share in the *latter* [American republics], and not in the *total exclusion of representatives of the people*, from the administration of the *former* [ancient republics]" (63:428). There is no animus against the people in these remarks, only a rational and realistic recognition of the dynamics of political life. In speaking of the need to cultivate veneration for the Constitution, Publius writes: "[i]n a nation of philosophers, this consideration ought to be disregarded. A reverence for the laws, would be sufficiently inculcated by the voice of an enlightened reason. But a nation of philosophers is as little to be expected as the philosophical race of kings wished for by Plato" (49:340). And then philosophers, too, get their comeuppance in an observation on the sure appearance of passion in "all very numerous assemblies. . . . Had every Athenian citizen been a Socrates; every Athenian assembly would still have been a mob" (55:374). Neither the goodness of the people nor the wisdom of the few can make an unclouded claim to rule; there is among men, writes Publius in his most famous passage, simply no such claim:

If men were angels, no government would be necessary. If angels were to govern men, neither external nor internal controls on government would be necessary. In framing a government which is to be administered by men over men, the great difficulty lies in this: You must first enable the government to control the governed; and in the next place, oblige it to control itself. A dependence on the people is no doubt the primary control on the government; but experience has taught mankind the necessity of auxiliary precautions. (51:349)

The problem of ambition is *the* problem of organizing the government as much as the problem of faction is *the* problem of constituting political society: one way or another, ambitious men will rule, whether they tout the name of the people or the need to hold the people in check. In American politics, the typical conflict will not be between the many and the few but between different men of ambition and talent seeking the good graces of the people—at least on the national level, where the danger of majority faction is reduced. The mechanism of separation of powers appears precisely as the "auxiliary precaution" designed to check ambition; the "auxiliary" comes before the "primary" (i.e., elections) lest Publius' readers mistake his acceptance of republicanism for acquiescence in its traditional forms.

The Legislative

Once the theory of separation of powers has been sketched, Publius turns to a consideration of the particular institutions proposed by the Constitution, and in treating the new Congress, he finally arrives at the question of representation that had figured so large in the Anti-Federalist critique (see nos. 52–58). What is surprising about this discussion to the reader who has been impressed by Publius' attention to mechanism is the traditional and optimistic cast of many of his arguments. To the Anti-Federalist charge that the Constitution intends "an ambitious sacrifice of the many to the aggrandizement of the few," Publius responds:

The aim of every political Constitution is or ought to be first to obtain for rulers, men who possess most wisdom to discern, and most virtue to pursue the common good of the society; and in the next place, to take the most effectual precautions for keeping them virtuous, whilst they continue to hold their public trust. (57:384)

To those who fear the corruption of Congress:

As there is a degree of depravity in mankind which requires a certain degree of circumspection and distrust: So there are other qualities in human nature, which justify a certain portion of esteem and confidence. Republican government presupposes the existence of these qualities in a higher degree than any other form. (55:378)

Of representatives' attachment to their constituents, he writes that "[t]here is in every breast a sensibility to marks of honor, of favor, of esteem, and of confidence, which, apart from all considerations of interest, is some pledge for grateful and benevolent returns" (57:385). Of the constituents' discernment and patriotism, he writes of "the vigilant and manly spirit which actuates the people of America, a spirit which nourishes freedom, and in return is nourished by it" (57:387). To be sure, he needs to say these things to counter the charges leveled against the new legislature that they will be an aristocratic cabal. But he *can* say these things because he has shifted, subtly but decisively, what representation is meant to be: not an organic relation where people choose one of their kind to be their spokesman and mediator but a relationship of agency and choice.

In part, this way of thinking about representation derives from the special character of the federal government. Because its objects are limited, the knowledge required by its representatives is less comprehensive, and so a single representative can know sufficiently the interests of a large district for the few federal purposes. Indeed, though Publius calls the states' sovereignty "residuary," he admits their priority in matters of domestic policy; in formulating tax policy, for example, what the federal representative needs to know and thus convey to Congress is not all the species of property and commerce in his territory but the commercial and tax laws of his state, a knowledge his likely prior service in the state legislature will readily yield. But the federal representative in the House represents not the state but its people, or some district of them, and the agency paradigm is built into the structure of his selection: the written qualifications are minimal in order to maximize the room for electoral choice. The wisely chosen representative is, Publius makes plain, someone who has developed expertise in policy and legislation; longer terms and reeligibility allow those who go to the capital to gain such knowledge about the laws and policies of fellow states and about the national interest in all its detail. The making of national legislation will be a business of negotiation and compromise—the building of coalitions of articulated interests—and not the reiteration of popular sentiment. Nothing shows better Publius' concept of the legislator as agent than the one instance in which he invokes organic principles to explain why all landowners are naturally represented by large proprietors and why manufacturers and mechanics are naturally represented by merchants: the balance in the legislature, he suggests, will be held by members of the learned professions (by implication lawyers), who "truly form no distinct interest in society" and will thus "be likely to prove an impartial arbiter" between the others (35:220–21).

In an assembly of chosen individuals rather than of elevated notables, Publius notices there will be a certain dynamic governed by its size, the terms of office of its members, and other factors that adhere to institutional design rather than social standing. In large assemblies, passion tends to get the better of reason; hence, it is wise to limit their size. Moreover, the larger the assembly, "the fewer will be the men who will in fact direct their proceedings," making particularly foolish the desire in the name of democracy to expand a body's size: "The countenance of the government may become more democratic; but the soul that animates it will be more oligarchic" (58:395–96). Likewise, short terms promote a change of officeholders, and this entails a change of policy and law; again, responsiveness seems democratic, but in fact the frequent change of measures gives an "unreasonable advantage to the sagacious, the enterprising and the moneyed few, over the industrious and uninformed mass of the people. . . . This is a state of things in which it may be said with some truth that laws are made for the *few* not for the *many*" (62:421). Publius' confidence in the ability of political institutions to shape their members' actions given proper institutional design is nowhere more evident than in his account of the Senate (nos. 62–66). The experience of republics everywhere shows the need for a senate to provide stability and character, or rather, the character that comes with stability or steadfastness; and the need for a body with ongoing knowledge of the national interest and an incentive attached to the members' reputations to keep the nation's faith in dealings abroad must be met if the new federal government is to avoid the embarrassments of the old. The happy effect of a Senate where the states are equally represented is a truly bicameral legislature, where the houses are sufficiently distinct in composition and derivation that they will be unlikely to acquiesce in each other's hastiest resolutions or ill-considered plans. To be sure, Publius (especially Jay: see no. 64) supposes that indirect election of senators by the state legislatures will help insure the quality of those with a senatorial chair; but even here, the emphasis is on the length of the term, the knowledge that can be built from experience in office, and the system of never replacing the whole body in a single election—that is, on institutional processes. These processes are meant in the first place to bring the wisest and most virtuous to office; but they are also meant to elicit wisdom and virtue from those in office, whatever their condition when they first arrived in it. Publius does not intend for the Senate to be a pliant instrument in the hands of an individual of outstanding virtue, nor a place where good is done unwittingly by scheming men. Its wisdom and stability depend upon the men who fill it, but these in turn are formed and encouraged in their shared enterprise by institutional parameters wisely chosen and designed.

The Executive

What is said of the Senate is even more true of the president (nos. 67–77): men of extraordinary ambition and political talent are invited to seek an office which is designed in turn to elicit their virtue for the service of the people as a whole.[14] If the Senate is suspect to republicans for appearing aristocratic, the president seems to be a virtual monarch; indeed, Publius is at pains to distinguish presidential power from the prerogatives of the English king, because his opponents have "contrived to pervert the public opinion in relation to the subject" (67:453). Like the Senate, the president is defined as able to resist the momentary pressure of the people in the name of their long-term interest, and like senators, presidents are selected through a process that, though indirect, ultimately begins with no other source than the people themselves. When the president appears too strong, Publius can find plenty in the Constitution that limits his independence, even anticipating restraints on presidential power that did not subsequently develop (e.g., Senate involvement in the dismissal of officials to whose appointments they had given their consent). Publius knew that Washington would be the first to fill the office, but he did not know Jackson, or Lincoln, or the Roosevelts, or Reagan, and so he does not treat the president as the people's tribune or the embodiment of national will. Given his commitment to republicanism—and its elaboration in reference to the principle of the separation of powers, where the authority of any man or institution, even to do good, is always checked—it is hard to imagine that he would see the modern development of the presidency, made possible by the rise of national parties and the democratization of the electoral process in the states, as an unproblematic extension of the office he describes.

And yet, it remains a fair question to imagine what Publius would think of our modern presidency. After all, he describes it as the office that embodies energy in the Constitution, and this from a pen that had written in an early paper that the infusion of energy into the federal government is what that government most needs. "A feeble execution is but another phrase for a bad execution" of the government, and he thinks the Constitution lays the foundation for a presidency that can be strong (70:471–72; cf. 68:461). The key ingredient to energy is unity, which insures secrecy, dispatch, and constancy; and happily this turns out to be the key to republican safety in the monarchical office. A single executive must perforce take responsibility for his actions and their consequences; he can readily be held accountable and blamed if things go bad. To be sure, Publius would give the president a long enough term to prove his policies; and he would leave him reeligible in order to reward and stabilize a good administration and give accountability real meaning against a bad one. Publius recognizes that the federal government can be made strong if it can be made "safe in a republican sense." What is true of the whole is especially true of this part: for all the jealousy he occasions, a republican executive can be made strong by being made responsible to the electorate. In a sense, then, the presidency is the most characteristic institution of Publius' republicanism: it is at once not traditionally republican and yet altogether dependent upon the people for its origin and for the sorts of characters likely to rise to presidential fame.

The Judiciary

The judiciary, by contrast, seems not exactly to fit with the other institutions of Publius' republic (nos. 78–83).[15] In most of his papers on the Constitution, and certainly in those on the president, one hears the voice of Hamilton as the aide-de-camp to Washington in the Revolutionary War; now one hears the voice of Hamilton the lawyer. He was too good a lawyer to twist the law to fit a polemical frame, and his commitment to the rule of law is too great to let the judiciary be described as a matrix of political forces rather than as a legal institution. Publius introduces the judiciary as the branch "least dangerous to the political rights of the Constitution; because it will be least in a capacity to annoy or injure them." He continues:

> The executive not only dispenses the honors, but holds the sword of the community. The legislature not only commands the purse, but prescribes the rules by which the duties and rights of every citizen are to be regulated. The judiciary on the contrary has no influence over either the sword or the purse, no direction either of the strength or the wealth of the society, and can take no active resolution whatsoever. It may truly be said to have neither Force nor Will, but merely Judgment; and must ultimately depend upon the aid of the executive arm even for the efficacy of its judgments. (78:522–23)

But as Publius described the strength of the republican legislature only to divide it up, so he describes the weakness of the judiciary in the system only to justify its reinforcement. The judiciary alone among the major institutions is given permanent tenure on good behavior. This Publius defends with a doctrine as bold as the thing being defended: the judges need the independence that permanent tenure affords in order to vindicate the Constitution against legislation that is contrary to its "manifest tenor"—and this legislation they are to declare null and void. Though the case for what comes later to be called judicial review depends on the existence of a written Constitution, the right or duty of the courts to exercise this prerogative is itself nowhere written in the document. It derives instead, Publius argues, from "the nature and reason of the thing," and he has support for his argument in several cases decided in state courts in the 1780s (though he does not cite them); in the tradition of argument denouncing unconstitutional legislation in the Revolution and the disputes leading up to it; and in some dusty English precedents (long more revered on the American side of the Atlantic than in their land of origin). In implicit response to the suggestion made by the Anti-Federalist Brutus (made a few weeks earlier in the same New York papers where *The Federalist* appeared), Publius insists that the courts will not abuse this power because they will be tied down by "strict rules and precedents"; besides, impeachment "is alone a complete security."[16] "Parchment barriers" are described as inadequate in keeping the branches of government from encroaching on one another and to keep the federal government and the states in accord with their duties; but here an institution is described that will give force to the parchment, while itself being held in check by cords more invisible than even paper words.

Publius can write as confidently as he does about the judiciary because he takes for granted that the judicial power invoked by the Constitution will be formed and governed according to the practices of common law. This becomes clear in his willingness to see judges "mitigating the severity, and confining the operation" of "unjust and partial laws," even without a violated constitutional provision; in his supposition that the bench will be drawn from the bar; and in his assumption that judges will be obliged to study precedents (78:528–29). It is more our ignorance of the common law tradition than his carelessness concerning it that makes his papers on the courts appear naive to the dangers of judicial excess when read from the other side of the twentieth century. Even so, Publius is aware that the common law cannot be assimilated unproblematically into the new frame of government he is defending. In the first place, there are common law judiciaries in the states, and the Constitution is vague about how they will be affected by the new Constitution beyond swearing state judges to acknowledge the supremacy of that Constitution and of federal treaties and laws. Publius guesses that, on the one hand, state judges might sit on federal circuit courts and, on the other hand, that intermediate federal appellate courts will hear appeals from state courts. He rightly suggests that some interweaving of systems will be needed but wrongly anticipates the pattern of separately constituted state and federal court systems with much concurrent jurisdiction and many shared rules that the Judiciary Act of 1789 will devise (81–82:passim; cf. 45:313). In the second place, Publius' own attachment to common law is attenuated by his critique of the jury, especially in civil matters; he interprets the jury "as a valuable safeguard to liberty" (unlike his opponents, who "represent it as the very palladium of free government"), and he would allow the new government latitude to modify and sometimes elude jury trials (83:562). In the third place, he argues in the penultimate paper against the addition to the Constitution of a bill of rights, a kind of document known to common law and indeed usually declarative of many of its protections (no. 84). In short, Publius is happy to invoke common law when it reassures his readers that the new institutions he defends will not innovate against equilibrium, and he is happy to borrow its independent judiciary devoted to the defense of property rights; but he is wary of its ardent traditionalism and its bias toward considering what is ancient to be good.

Conclusion: An Improving Science of Politics

Publius' case for the Constitution taken as a whole is made in the terms of political science, and his political science draws at once on classical ideas and modern developments. As early as *The Federalist* no. 9, after acknowledging the vices of republican government in antiquity, Publius states that "[t]he science of politics, however, like most other sciences has received great improvement" (9:51). None of the developments he catalogues—separation of powers, legislative checks and balances, an independent judiciary, and representation—is specifically republican, but he shows over the course of his papers how they all can be made consistent with republicanism and simultaneously reformed so that the republic is the seedbed of neither despotic faction nor tyrannical ambition. Together with the new form of federalism that is the Americans' own invention, the developments in political science he praises are based on institutional experience, which the American Founders are happy to borrow and assimilate into their new design. The political philosopher closest in spirit to Publius in this regard is probably Montesquieu, whom he often cites; but we have also seen that Publius is not reluctant to correct and develop the master, as he does in relation both to federalism and the separation of powers. There is in this approach a profound respect for traditional learning as well as an openness to the new, and Publius' debt to the tradition appears not only in his account of political institutions but also in his assumptions about human nature. Reason and passion are said to contend in the governance of men; envy and ambition appear as the characteristic vices of the many and the few; prudence is appealed to at every turn; virtue is praised as a matter of course; and the common good is held up as the end of political action. Moreover, in a remarkable discussion of the first principles of science in *The Federalist* no. 37, Publius echoes Aristotle in distinguishing between the level of exactness to be obtained in the precise sciences and what can be expected of politics: in "the works of nature, . . . all the delineations are perfectly accurate, and appear to be otherwise only from the imperfection of the eye which surveys them"; but in "the institutions of man, . . . the obscurity arises as well from the object itself, as from the organ by which it is contemplated." This teaches "the necessity of moderating still farther our expectations and hopes from the efforts of human sagacity"—a lesson in theoretical moderation that nicely complements the "lesson of moderation" in practical politics that emerged from his discussion of partisanship (37:235; cf. 1:4–5 and 85:594).

At the same time, of course, there is much in Publius that hints of the less traditional side of the Enlightenment. When he refers to the Declaration of Independence, he quotes from the early paragraphs on "the transcendent and precious right of the people to 'abolish or alter their governments as to them shall seem most likely to effect their safety and happiness'" (40:265; cf. 43:297); no mention is made of the long middle section with its catalogue of grievances defined in terms of the Anglo-American constitutional tradition, even though nearly every complaint is specifically guarded against in the new Constitution he is defending. As noted before, the protection of property—or more precisely, of the "faculties" from whose diversity "the rights of property originate"—is declared "the first object of government," and men are encouraged to focus on their interests rather than their loves (10:58). One generalization about human nature in an early paper—"men are ambitious, vindictive and rapacious" (6:28)—sounds like something out of Machiavelli's *The Prince*, and the mechanisms for countering ambition with ambition and faction with faction have a clearly modern cast.[17] Though these are called "auxiliary precautions" in the later papers, they are introduced as if primary, since "we well know that neither moral nor religious motives can be relied on as an adequate control" (51:349; 10:61). Indeed, religion rarely appears in *The Federalist*, and then usually as a cause more of faction than of unity. "Christianity" is mentioned only once, merely as a historical demarcation, and even religious freedom is only alluded to in passing rather than discussed thematically, although even the original Constitution included a prohibition against religious tests.[18] In short, there is both a classical and a modern vocabulary in Publius, subtly balanced or mixed. "Justice is the end of government," he writes. "It is the end of civil society. It ever has been, and ever will be pursued, until it be obtained, or until liberty be lost in the pursuit" (51:352).[19] In the first sentence, one hears a classical chord; but in the mention of civil society, and in the quiet hint that justice is destructive of a greater end, liberty, one notes a modern theme.

In one sense, the political science of Publius is encapsulated by the paper that treats slavery at some length in the context of a discussion of the ratio of representation in the House (no. 54). The paper is complex rhetorically because the slaveholding Madison constructs an imaginary colloquy with "one of our southern brethren," of whose reasoning, Publius concludes, "although it may appear to be a little strained in some points, yet on the whole, I must confess, that it fully reconciles me to the scale of representation, which the Convention have established." At issue is whether for the purposes of representation slaves ought to be counted as persons or ignored as property. (On this issue, the North and the South took paradoxical positions in order to secure maximum representation, the former insisting against counting slaves as persons, the latter insisting in favor of it.) Publius' "southern brother" notes the paradox, arguing coolly but not irrationally in favor of the compromise in the Constitution counting three-fifths of the slaves; because the status of slave mixed person and property, slaves were "considered by our laws, in some respects, as persons [he notes the law was supposed to protect them against the violence of others and hold them responsible for their own], and in other respects as property [since compelled to labor, vendible, and subject to be 'restrained in his liberty, and chastised in his body, by the capricious will of another']." Just as coolly and thus unmistakably, Publius' character admits the injustice of slavery: the law of slavery is called a "pretext" that took rights away.[20] Further complicating the question is the compromise on the census: the same number will determine representation and direct taxation, prompting Publius' "southern brother" to expound on the rights of property in relation to representation and to recognize the "imperceptible channel" by which the wealthy influence votes. Through his strange rhetorical device, Publius makes the case for the Constitution's compromise of America's most difficult underlying problem, at once acknowledging abstract justice and bowing to necessity as it was politically understood, and bringing to bear his characteristic analytical insight and his instinct for a workable and meliorative middle way.

Publius' optimism about the imminent ending of the slave trade points to the feature of the Constitution with which he himself ends, and which he foresees will be in no small part responsible for its success: its ability to grow and develop. He quotes Hume to show that time and experience are needed to complete the work of constitutional improvement, and he makes the point as well in his own words: "'Tis time only that can mature and perfect so compound a system, can liquidate the meaning of all the parts, and can adjust them to each other in a harmonious and consistent WHOLE" (82:553; cf. 85:594). This is partly an observation of political theory: about the way tradition can be incorporated into new structures; about growth on a common law pattern as new cases arise and are determined; and about a society's openness to change. But it is also an observation that is specifically about America, for Publius takes note of the push for developing the West and adding new states, arguing that it is a mark of the Constitution's superiority to the Articles of Confederation that it makes specific provision for this. He expects the states to become more closely integrated in their commerce and information and thus in their manners and beliefs. He writes from time to time about an American empire, and he clearly anticipates that the country will be an equal player with the European powers before long. Above all, he believes that the moment of constitutional choice then before the American people is a moment for the display—indeed the foundation—of American greatness, for the American people seem to be marked by Providence to provide for all mankind a model of constitutional governance by providing in the first place an example of constitutional choice.[21] Publius writes to explain that choice and to counsel those Americans who were to make it to see the world beyond their immediate communities and selfish interests; he urges their attention to this great task not only so that they might then return to their ordinary interests without undue interference from hostile forces but also so that they might raise their sights.

In the political science of Publius, the yearning for greatness—ambition—is, like faction, not merely a problem to be solved but an element of human nature that will appear whenever men are free. His America is not designed to crush ambition but instead to guide it—even to nurture it—*as well as* to put it to work for the common good. He praises the American "spirit of enterprise," using the term at first for commercial ventures but in the end applying it to the campaign for the Constitution itself (7:40). He calls "the love of fame, the ruling passion of the noblest minds" (72:488). Ambition, after all, is a faculty or characteristic that is at once rare and common: rare in seeking distinction, common in belonging above all to those who do not start at the top. In that sense, it may be said to reconcile or at least to hold in dynamic balance the humors of the many and the few. Publius is famous for what is often called his pessimistic account of human nature, his distrust of professions of good will on the part of the self-serving and especially on the part of those who flatter the people in order to promote themselves. But this is just the sober side of his confident hope that even the most dangerous passions of man—ambition and avarice—can be allowed to flourish in a modern republic that is properly designed. That America is a field for the cultivation of human faculties (that is, for the realization of human ambitions) in a way that is at once free and restrained (that is, responsible) may not be the only element of our national greatness. But it is surely part of that greatness, and Publius, who praises manly confidence and steady prudence, is surely its friend.

Notes

1. The history of the initial publication of *The Federalist* in book form can be found in *The Documentary History of the Ratification of the Constitution*, vols. 16 and 18, "Commentaries on the Constitution: Public and Private," ed. John P. Kaminski and Gaspare J. Saladino (Madison: State Historical Society of Wisconsin, 1986, 1995), 4:466–71, 6:83–87. See also the editor's introduction to Alexander Hamilton, James Madison, and John Jay, *The Federalist*, ed. Jacob E. Cooke (Middleton, Conn.: Wesleyan University Press, 1961), and the editors' introduction to *The Federalist: The Gideon Edition*, ed. George W. Carey and James McClellan (Indianapolis: Liberty Fund, 2001).

2. See *Plutarch's Lives* (Dryden edition), ed. A. H. Clough (Boston: Little, Brown, 1859), 1:203ff. Plutarch compares the Roman Publius to the Greek Solon and finds him in a way superior, for he succeeded better in devising a popular government that avoided tyranny. See also Martin Diamond, "Publius," in *History of Political Philosophy*, ed. Leo Strauss and Joseph Cropsey, 3rd ed. (Chicago: University of Chicago Press, 1987), 661.

3. On this last point, see Jean Yarbrough, "Rethinking '*The Federalist*'s View of Federalism,'" *Publius: The Journal of Federalism* 15 (1985): 31. As we will see below, Publius even imagines the abolition of the states, has little use for state politicians, and has a keen idea of national greatness.

4. On the centrality of candor to Publius' project, see Albert Furtwangler, *The Authority of Publius: A Reading of The Federalist Papers* (Ithaca, N.Y.: Cornell University Press, 1984).

5. All citations to *The Federalist* are to the edition edited by Jacob Cooke and include the number of the paper followed by the page number.

6. In presenting his own aims as faithful to the spirit of the Revolution, perhaps Publius can justify assuming for himself the name "Federalist," which analytically might be thought better deserved by those he opposed. On the appropriation of the name "Federalist" by supporters of the Constitution, see Herbert Storing, *What the Anti-Federalists Were For* (Chicago: University of Chicago Press, 1981).

7. Montesquieu, *The Spirit of the Laws*, trans. Anne M. Cohler, Basia C. Miller, and Harold S. Stone (Cambridge: Cambridge University Press, 1989), bk. 9.

8. The orthodox account of divided sovereignty, with the federal powers proclaimed only as enumerated and state sovereignty as residual, appears in no. 39. In no. 62, he raises and then dismisses the idea that equal representation in the Senate is a necessary incident of member sovereignty in a federation.

9. The protection afforded the states because they elect parts of the federal government is today alluded to under the phrase: "the political safeguards of federalism." See Herbert Wechsler, "The Political Safeguards of Federalism," *Columbia Law Review* 54 (1954): 543, and more recently, Larry Kramer, "Putting the Politics Back into the Political Safeguards of Federalism," *Columbia Law Review* 100 (2000): 215. It is worth noting that no parts of state government require federal action in order to be constituted.

10. See also Publius' discussion of the gradual assimilation of manners and laws to be expected under the new Constitution in nos. 53, 56, 60.

11. See *Notes of Debates in the Federal Convention of 1787 Reported by James Madison*, ed. Adrienne Koch (Athens: Ohio University Press, 1966), 129–39.

12. For a vigorous defense of Publius' democratic character, see Diamond, "Publius," 665ff. See also David F. Epstein, *The Political Theory of The Federalist* (Chicago: University of Chicago Press, 1984), to which my account is much indebted.

13. Publius notes the Anti-Federalists' recourse to Montesquieu in no. 47. For an example of Anti-Federalist concern over representation, see "Letters from the Federal Farmer," no. VII, in *The Anti-Federalist*, ed. Herbert Storing and Murray Dry (Chicago: University of Chicago Press, 1985), 74ff.

14. The following discussion draws upon Harvey C. Mansfield, Jr., "Republicanizing the Executive," in *Saving the Revolution*, ed. Charles Kesler (New York: The Free Press, 1987), and more generally, Mansfield, *Taming the Prince: The Ambivalence of Modern Executive Power* (New York: The Free Press, 1989).

15. I discuss this matter at greater length in *Common Law and Liberal Theory: Coke, Hobbes, and the Origins of American Constitutionalism* (Lawrence: University Press of Kansas, 1992), chap. 12.

16. The phrases quoted are from *The Federalist* no. 78, except the comment on impeachment, which is from 81:546. The "Essays of Brutus" on the judiciary are XI–XV, in *The Anti-Federalist*, 162–87.

17. Cf. Machiavelli, *The Prince*, trans. Harvey C. Mansfield, Jr. (Chicago: University of Chicago Press, 1985), 66.

18. Compare the treatment of religion in no. 10 and no. 2. For the occurrence of certain words in *The Federalist*, see *The Federalist Concordance*, ed. Thomas S. Engeman, Edward J. Erler, and Thomas B. Hofeller (Middleton, Conn.: Wesleyan University Press, 1980).

19. On the mixed regime in Publius, see Charles Kesler's introduction to *Saving the Revolution.*

20. In an earlier paper, Publius had in his own name called slavery "oppression," denounced the slave trade as "barbarism," and anticipated the eventual abolition of that trade as "a great point gained in favor of humanity" (42:281).

21. On the West, see 38:248–49 and 43:290–91; on the assimilation of the states, see nos. 53, 56, and 60; an "American Empire" is mentioned at 22:146; and the choice of a new Constitution figures prominently in nos. 1, 40, and 85.

Chapter 13

Union, Constitutionalism, and the Judicial Defense of Rights: John Marshall

Matthew J. Franck

It would be pleasant to be able to say that John Marshall's (1755–1835) contribution to American jurisprudence endures, essentially unaltered by subsequent historical developments, in the constitutional law of the United States. But it is not so. Marshall occupies a unique place in the history of the U.S. Supreme Court, bearing contradictory reputations simultaneously. He still earns the appellation "The Great Chief Justice," yet he is widely regarded by "mainstream" scholars in law, history, and political science as the greatest (or worst, depending on the commentator's ideology) of our country's "judicial activists." His contribution to the rule of law is acknowledged far and wide, yet he is routinely described as a preeminently "political" justice—indeed, a "statesman" on the bench. He is justly famous for his opinion in *Marbury v. Madison* (1803), the first case in which the Supreme Court held a provision of federal law invalid under the Constitution; yet, the opinion is frequently characterized as a canny grab for power, and the limited character of the ruling has been conflated with the much later development of judicial supremacy over the law of the Constitution.[1] His great opinions on the scope of national power in our compound system of government, as well as other subjects, are standard fare in every text on constitutional law; yet, the modern Supreme Court pays little heed to many of his most seminal precedents. He is (with Justice Oliver Wendell Holmes, Jr., his only possible rival) the most universally admired justice of the Supreme Court in the nation's history. But he is the least well understood.[2]

Clearly, John Marshall is in need of some rehabilitation. The task for students of Marshall's thought today is to understand him as he understood himself—above all, to resist the temptation to project back onto Marshall the categories of legal and political thought that have overtaken and supplanted his jurisprudential principles in the more than eight score years since his death. His achievements were notable enough without imputing to him accomplishments he would not recognize or commitments he would reject.

What were Marshall's genuine achievements? He transformed the Supreme Court from a collection of individualistic jurists into a collegial institution, speaking as often as possible with one voice through the "opinion of the Court," and thus rejecting the earlier Anglo-American tradition of *seriatim* opinions in which the judges sitting together on appellate courts issued their separate views in every case. He guided his brethren in the establishment of that Court as a truly independent department in the separation of powers, capable of defending itself and its crucial role in interpreting the Constitution and in vindicating those legal rights that fell within its purview. He defended the political science of the Constitution's Framers wherever legal attacks on it were made that came within his reach, preserving the work done at Philadelphia in 1787 in the face of assaults made on it in the name of "states' rights." He brought to legal reasoning, and to opinion-writing, a judicious blend of humility and rigor seldom seen since, penning opinions that were models of lucid logic without a trace of technical affectation. His approach to constitutional questions was unprepossessing, and devoid of any "theory" learned elsewhere and thereafter imposed on the Constitution—other than the traditional methods of common law adjudication befitting a court of law.

The list of "achievements" credited to Marshall that distort the historical truth is longer than this brief account of his genuine accomplishments. The great bulk of scholarly commentary on his career as chief justice would have us believe that he was a "nationalist," a "conservative" defender of property rights, even a reactionary of sorts fighting a rearguard action against the democratic politics of the Jeffersonians and Jacksonians. He is also conventionally held to be the avatar of judicial supremacy, maneuvering his Court aggressively into position as the exclusive or final expositor of the meaning of the Constitution, responsible for policing the boundaries of both federalism and the separation of powers, and dictating to all other political institutions the proper scope and nature of their own powers. In short, Marshall is "known" for vigorously placing the stamp of his own powerful mind on the Constitution.

This conventional account of his career would utterly astonish Marshall (as early variations on such characterizations dismayed him when made by his partisan contemporaries). His "nationalism" was precisely the "nationalism" of the Constitution itself—if such a term may properly be used. His defense of property rights—coming mostly in cases interpreting the contract clause of Article I, section 10—was no more and no less than what a commonsense reading of the Constitution requires. No jurist in our history was more respectful of the right of the people to govern themselves, at the level of the state or at the level of the nation. None was more committed to the proposition that the Constitution makes the coordinate branches of the national government equally authoritative in the exposition of that document, each within its own proper sphere. Could he return to comment on his commentators, Marshall would completely deny—as on one occasion he did deny—that he placed any personal stamp on the constitutional law of his country.[3] By his own lights, which illuminate more than any commentary on his work, American constitutional law unfolded its own logic in the pages of his opinions.

Nor was this mere self-delusion on his part, or a false modesty. This is not the place for a comprehensive review of the many errors made in commentaries on Marshall's work. Suffice it to say that Marshall himself defeats all criticism. Readers who approach his opinions with an open mind will find themselves encountering a legal mind to whom interpretive shortcuts, begged questions, tortured logic, dubious assertions, mere sloganeering, and forced conclusions were quite foreign. There is nothing of the sophist here, making the weaker argument the stronger and carrying all away on a wave of stupefying eloquence. Marshall was the Socrates of American constitutional law, unaffected by interest, class consciousness, or ideology as he sought the truth of things in the cases before him. It is unfashionable to express such frank admiration in this postmodern age, with its unironic pretensions to irony. But there is not a single important opinion of Marshall's that does not surpass every piece of criticism ever written regarding his jurisprudence. It is tempting to say that he stands alone in the history of the Supreme Court as the only justice never to have been wrong about the Constitution. But it may be said without contradiction that no justice is a better instructor for us in how to think about the Constitution.

What sort of man merits such praise? John Marshall was one of those rare creatures, enviable but never envied, who excelled at virtually everything to which he put his hand. A quick study in the scanty experience he had with formal schooling—culminating with a mere summer's course in the study of law—Marshall was also an able soldier and leader of men in the Revolution; a brilliant advocate before the bar; an instinctively natural politician and an accomplished legislator in both the Virginia legislature and the Congress; a sober and careful diplomat abroad and a skillful administrator as secretary of state; a careful historian and biographer of his hero Washington; a convivial and open-handed social companion, devoted friend, and loving husband and father.[4] Had he retired from public life at forty-five rather than taking his seat on the Supreme Court, Marshall would still be a noteworthy if minor figure in the Founding generation. As chief justice for the final thirty-four years of his life, however, he commands our attention with his powerful intellect and his unrivaled contribution to American law.

The Language of American Political Science

The difficulty posed by decades of scholarship on John Marshall is to find something new to say about him. But I believe that something new can be said about Marshall. We can let him, as much as possible, speak for himself, which too few scholars have let him do. This approach is made both easier and harder by the limpid, direct prose in which he expressed himself. While much is made of such famous lines as "[i]t is emphatically the province and duty of the judicial department, to say what the law is" (*Marbury v. Madison* 177), or "we must never forget that it is a *constitution* we are expounding" (*McCulloch v. Maryland* [1819] 407), the penchant for mere phrase-making out of Marshall's opinions, among latter-day justices of the Court as well as scholars, does Marshall the disservice of obscuring the comprehensive character of his constitutional jurisprudence, which can be glimpsed only when we observe patterns within and across all his opinions, seeing these famous phrases in their fullest contexts.

Observing patterns in Marshall's use of language across opinions and over time can prompt fresh thinking as well, and what Marshall, with characteristic precision, did *not* say can spur nearly as much reconsideration of his thought and legacy as what he *did* say. I will begin, therefore, by remarking on expressions in our constitutional vocabulary that Marshall eschews.

"Federalism" is, perhaps surprisingly, a relatively recent description of the American political system—at least where the justices of the Supreme Court are concerned. The word first makes an appearance in the *United States Reports* in an opinion of Justice Felix Frankfurter in 1939.[5] But what about the use of "federal" as an adjective? Marshall uses the word a number of times in his opinions, but nearly always (in sixteen different cases) to modify the noun "courts."[6] On only two occasions did Marshall use the phrase "federal government," and in both instances the phrase was used to refer to the system of government created by the Articles of Confederation.[7] Thus, we find that *never once*, in thirty-four years as chief justice, in the course of writing over 500 opinions, did John Marshall refer—as we so commonly do—to the political system created by the Constitution as the "federal government." For Marshall, plainly, the term "federal" could not be used accurately to describe American constitutional government, though for some reason he accepted the adjective's occasional use to distinguish the courts of the Union from those of the states.

And what of the alternative "national government," so casually used interchangeably today with the term "federal government"? On just *one* occasion in a judicial opinion did he refer to the government created by the Constitution as the "national government," and this occurred in one of the two opinions in which he referred to the Articles of Confederation as having created a "federal government"—thus encapsulating a contrast where we would commonly see an identity.[8]

What are we to make of this pattern? As Tocqueville remarked after visiting the United States near the end of Marshall's life, constitutional government in America "is no longer a federal government; it is an incomplete national government. So one has found a form of government that is neither precisely national nor federal; but one stops there, and the new word that ought to express the new thing still does not exist."[9] In pragmatic fashion, Americans have not yet invented that new word for the new thing established by the Constitution; instead, we use two adjectives alternately that an earlier age would have regarded as contradictions.

But Marshall did not share this latter-day habit of ours, though it had begun to develop in his day. Repeatedly throughout his tenure on the bench he listened to counsel in the cases before him refer to the "federal government" and the "national government," and several of the associate justices who served with Marshall used the terms with equal ease and equal indifference as well. There is something remarkable—something very *studied*—about Marshall's own resistance to the use of these phrases for the American form of government while they became more common all around him. It calls to mind Daniel Webster's comment that Marshall "always wrote with a quill. He never adopted the barbarous invention of steel pens."[10] But in his use of language, even more than in the choice of his pens, Marshall was more studious even than Publius, who can be found using "federal government" and "national government" to mean the same thing on a number of occasions in *The Federalist*.[11]

Marshall's preferred phrases for referring to the central political authority in the United States were "general government," and even more commonly, "government of the Union." Each of these expressions occurs scores of times in his opinions. And they express the fundamental ambiguity, the truly hybrid character, of the Constitution of 1787. The United States government was "general" whereas the states' governments were particular, or, as Marshall often called them, "local."

A final inquiry along these lines concerns Marshall's use of the words "sovereign" and "sovereignty." As Justice James Wilson observed in 1793, "[t]o the constitution of the United States the term *sovereign* is totally unknown. There is but one place where it could have been used with propriety," namely the preamble, where "those who ordained and established that constitution . . . might have announced themselves *sovereign* people of the United States."[12] Certainly, the most strict use of "sovereign" and "sovereignty" would accord with Wilson's remark, for a sovereign power is one that is answerable to no higher human authority. Could such a thing, for instance, be said of the states of the Union?

There are eleven opinions by Marshall over the course of his chief justiceship in which he seems to refer to the several states as "sovereign" or as possessing "sovereignty." In nine of the cases the reference appears in a ruling announced by Marshall, and in one other case, an opinion by Marshall in dissent, *against* the claims of a state claiming some species of sovereign right.[13] In the eleventh case, upholding a state's claim to legislate in the face of a claimed right under the federal Constitution, Marshall's references to the "sovereignty" or "sovereign power" of a state come in a quotation from one of the other ten opinions.[14]

A closer look reveals more. In several of his references to state "sovereignty," Marshall is specifically recalling the situation that existed prior to the adoption of the Constitution, before "these allied sovereigns converted their league into a government."[15] In several more instances, the chief justice denies outright that an alleged state sovereignty exists under the Constitution, as when he avers that "[i]t would be difficult to sustain [the] proposition" that the "powers of the general government . . . are delegated by the states, who alone are truly sovereign."[16] On only one occasion—in the opening line of his great opinion in *McCulloch v. Maryland* (400)—did Marshall use the description "sovereign state" with apparent unself-consciousness to denominate a state whose claims were in controversy before the Court. Considering the thrust of the opinion that followed, we may say that this single unalloyed use of the expression "sovereign state" was a pro forma nod of the head to common usage.

And it *was* common usage. Along with such phrases as "federal government," the expression "sovereign state" seemed to be on everyone's lips but John Marshall's, for it appears countless times in the arguments of counsel and frequently too in the opinions of his colleagues. But Marshall avoided as much as possible the use of "sovereign" to describe the states, taking up such terminology only in cases where claims of sovereignty were advanced on the part of the states, and (but for one instance that may be dismissed as merely a self-quotation) *only in cases where he denied such claims*. When the powers of states were vindicated, Marshall did not refer to the states' "sovereign" powers. For Marshall, the word "sovereign" had a relatively precise *theoretical* meaning, and its application to the *practical* relation between the "general" and "local" governments could only be undertaken with the utmost care.

When required by the arguments in a case to tread with such care over the terrain of the competing "sovereign" claims of nation and states, Marshall emphasized the Union's hybrid political system. "In America, the powers of sovereignty are divided between the government of the Union, and those of the states. They are each sovereign, with respect to the objects committed to it, and neither sovereign, with respect to the objects committed to the other" (*McCulloch* 410). But above all, the plain principle of the Constitution for Marshall was that "the sovereignty of the state . . . is subordinate to, and may be controlled by the constitution of the United States," for "[t]he sovereignty of a state extends to everything which exists by its own authority," but not to things over which the sovereign American people have given control to the general government (*McCulloch* 427–29). That singular people, speaking through the conventions organized in each state, made certain that "the sovereignty of the States is surrendered in many instances where the surrender can only operate to the benefit of the people, and . . . to maintain the principles established in the constitution" (*Cohens v. Virginia* [1821] 382).

In one of his most comprehensive and succinct statements on this subject, it is notable that Marshall reverted to his customary avoidance of the term "sovereignty" in accounting for how political power was apportioned by the Constitution: "America has chosen to be, in many respects, and to many purposes, a nation; and for all these purposes, her government is complete; to all these objects, it is competent. The people have declared, that in the exercise of all powers given for these objects, it is supreme" (*Cohens* 414). A nation for many purposes but not for all: as evidenced by his inclination throughout his career to avoid the term "sovereignty" with its potential for theoretical rigidity, this passage too evinces a recognition by Marshall that theoretical constructs derived from political philosophy were of little help in construing a charter of government so novel, so mixed in its "federal" and "national" character, and so popular in both its basis and its continual functioning.

No man took more seriously than Marshall the admonition of James Madison in *The Federalist* no. 37:

> All new laws, though penned with the greatest technical skill, and passed on the fullest and most mature deliberation, are considered as more or less obscure and equivocal, until their meaning be liquidated and ascertained by a series of particular discussions and adjudications. . . . The use of words is to express ideas. Perspicuity therefore requires not only that the ideas should be distinctly formed, but that they should be expressed by words distinctly and exclusively appropriated to them. But no language is so copious as to supply words and phrases for every complex idea, or so correct as not to include many equivocally denoting different ideas. . . . [An] unavoidable inaccuracy must be greater or less, according to the complexity and novelty of the objects defined.[17]

A review of Marshall's avoidance of certain extraconstitutional expressions as he penned his opinions reveals how exactly his views accorded with Madison's here, and with those of his great colleague on the bench, Joseph Story:

> Constitutions are not designed for metaphysical or logical subtleties, for niceties of expression, for critical propriety, for elaborate shades of meaning, or for the exercise of philosophical acuteness, or juridical research. They are instruments of a practical nature, founded on the common business of human life, adapted to common wants, designed for common use, and fitted for common understandings.[18]

Inasmuch as the Constitution does not speak of the government of the United States as either "federal" or "national" in character, nor say anything explicitly on the subject of "sovereignty," Marshall avoided the use of such words in his opinions as much as possible. They were (and are) not perspicuous words that could be given distinct and exclusive meanings in the American context. Rather would they invite needless "juridical research" with a view to "philosophical acuteness" of a sort that would ossify rather than clarify the practical meaning of the Constitution. Only the "liquidat[ion]" of constitutional meaning by "discussion and adjudication," in discrete circumstances as they arose, could accomplish the adaptation of American government, with its "equivocal" character, to the "common wants" of the Union.

With consistent care in his use of language over many years, Marshall always aimed for the least practicable quantum of "unavoidable inaccuracy" in his opinions. His language was precise where precision was possible, and ambiguous where only ambiguity could convey the truth. He was, in short, astonishingly precise in his oscillation between precision and ambiguity. Whatever it took to avoid being merely "obscure" from a misplaced desire to produce "niceties of expression"—whatever needed to be said to settle an instant case *or unsaid* in order to leave matters open for the future that need not be "liquidated" at the present moment—Marshall met the challenge as no other justice has done. He was, notwithstanding his reputation in certain scholarly circles, the least doctrinaire justice in our history.[19]

The Progress of Marshall's Thought on Judicial Power

Consider again Madison's remark in *The Federalist*, quoted above, that in particular instances, *both* "discussions *and* adjudications" would assist over time in settling the practical meaning of a new law such as the Constitution. This seems to indicate that adjudication alone—the ascertainment of constitutional meaning by the judiciary—would not settle all interpretive questions that would arise under the instrument governing the Union. Did Marshall agree? Or did he view the liquidation of constitutional meaning as exclusively or even primarily the business of the judicial branch of government?

As noted at the outset of this chapter, one of the most famous phrases in all of Marshall's opinions is his observation in *Marbury v. Madison* (177) that "[i]t is emphatically the province and duty of the judicial department, to say what the law is." The full context of that statement has been ably explained by Robert Clinton and others, and will be explored more fully below.[20] Suffice it to say here that nowhere in *Marbury* or elsewhere does Marshall say or imply that "say[ing] what the law is" is exclusively, finally, or authoritatively "the province and duty" of the judiciary in all circumstances. That it is "emphatically" the work of the judiciary is what he does say, and what he means, in the fullness of *Marbury*'s context, is that in cases properly before it, entailing issues about which the judiciary is *capable* of "liquidat[ing] and ascertain-[ing]" the sometimes "obscure and equivocal" meaning of the law, it will undertake to do so. But this must involve, for Marshall, no arrogation of the right of the other coequal branches to place their own stamp on the meaning of the Constitution, often in authoritative ways, as they go about the business of their own functions.[21]

Marshall himself seems to have come to a fuller understanding of the limits of judicial authority, and of the coordinate authority of other institutions to say what the Constitution means, over a period of about a decade prior to his ascension to the bench. At the Virginia Ratifying Convention in 1788, it fell to Marshall, as one of the state's leading lawyers, to defend the design of the judicial branch contemplated by the Constitution. Many have seen his Richmond speech of June 20 as presaging the thought of the chief justice to whom an attachment to judicial supremacy is commonly attributed. Here is what he said on that occasion:

> If [Congress] were to make a law not warranted by any of the powers enumerated, it would be considered by the Judges as an infringement of the Constitution:—They would not consider such a law as coming under their jurisdiction.—They would declare it void. . . . To what quarter will you look for protection from an infringement on the Constitution, if you will not give the power to the Judiciary? There is no other body that can afford such a protection.[22]

Whatever one makes of the first remark above (prior to the ellipses), it is difficult to regard the second remark as anything short of hyperbole uttered in the pressure of a debate where the fate of the Constitution's adoption was still a dicey thing in a critical state. Marshall's agenda on this day was to vindicate the Constitution with all the vigor he could muster, and to reassure wavering members of the convention that the new government would be kept safely within the bounds of its delegated authority. There is no reason to doubt Marshall's sincerity in saying what he says here, but the remark is too facile. To say that "no other body" than the judiciary "can afford . . . protection" from violations of the Constitution is far more than he said in *Marbury* or in any other case in his long judicial career. And lest his words here become a gloss on his subsequent judicial opinions, we should note that in 1788 Marshall had yet to face the very different kind of pressure of living, working, and deliberating *under* the Constitution he defended here. When that opportunity and duty arose twelve years later, he found himself engaged in more "mature deliberations" (in Madison's phrase) in the effort to apply the Constitution to a set of practical circumstances before him.

The occasion was a debate in the House of Representatives over a Republican resolution concerning the fate of "Jonathan Robbins" (actually Thomas Nash), who had been extradited at the president's behest to British authorities and executed for mutiny and murder aboard a Royal Navy vessel. Republicans accused President John Adams of undue interference with the South Carolina court responsible for Nash's detention in the United States—an interference resulting, so they said, in the judicial murder by the British of an American citizen. (Nash was in truth who the British said he was: a British naval deserter, not an American citizen named Robbins.) On February 20, 1800, Edward Livingston of New York introduced resolutions condemning the president's conduct, charging in part that Adams had trespassed on the province of the federal judiciary, which alone, Livingston alleged, could have spoken for the general government on the matter of Nash's extradition.

Marshall rose to respond to the (ultimately defeated) resolutions on March 7, saying that the question of an alien's custody when a foreign sovereign sought his extradition under the terms of such a compact as the Jay Treaty of 1795 "was a case for executive and not judicial decision." He continued:

> [I]t would not be improper to notice a very material mis-statement [of the Constitution] in the resolutions offered by the gentleman from New York. By the constitution, the judicial power of

the United States is extended to all *cases in law and equity* arising under the constitution, laws and treaties of the United States; but the resolutions declare the judicial power to extend to *all questions* arising under the constitution, treaties and laws of the United States. The difference between the constitution and the resolutions was material and apparent. A case in law or equity was a term well understood, and of limited signification. It was a controversy between parties which had taken a shape for judicial decision. If the judicial power extended to every *question* under the constitution it would involve almost every subject proper for legislative discussion and decision; if to every *question* under the laws and treaties of the United States it would involve almost every subject on which the executive could act. The division of power . . . could exist no longer, and the other departments would be swallowed up by the judiciary. . . .

By extending the judicial power to all *cases in law and equity*, the constitution had never been understood, to confer on that department, any political power whatever. To come within this description, a question must assume a legal form, for forensic litigation, and judicial decision. There must be parties to come into court, who can be reached by its process, and bound by its power; whose rights admit of ultimate decision by a tribunal to which they are bound to submit. (*Papers* 4:95–96, emphasis in original)

Later in this lengthy speech, in response to the arguments of other Republican members that "this was a case proper for the decision of the courts, because points of law occurred," Marshall replied:

It is true, sir, these points of law must have occurred, and must have been decided: but it by no means follows that they could only have been decided in court. A variety of legal questions must present themselves in the performance of every part of executive duty, but these questions are not therefore to be decided in court. . . . [The gentleman from Pennsylvania's] observations have the appearance of endeavouring to fit the constitution to his arguments, instead of adapting his argument to the constitution. (*Papers* 4:103)

In these lines from his brief congressional career—just three months before he became the leading figure in the Adams cabinet as secretary of state and a year before he began his tenure on the Court—Marshall displays far more care and sophistication in his account of the scope and limits of the judicial power than he had done in 1788. Based on his March 7 speech, the conclusion is unavoidable that for Marshall it was quite conceivable—indeed, an inevitable consequence of the "division of power" among the three branches of government—that the executive in these circumstances might misconstrue either the treaty governing extradition or the Constitution's own principles governing the president's conduct of his duties (such as his obligation faithfully to execute the laws), and the entire situation would remain beyond the reach of judicial redress. To say otherwise would involve the courts not merely in the "cases in law and equity" allotted to them by the Constitution, but in every question of constitutional meaning, "and the other departments would be swallowed up by the judiciary."[23]

It is interesting to note that Marshall's response to the New York Republican Edward Livingston in 1800 also serves to rebut the views expressed in 1788 by the New York Anti-Federalist "Brutus," who warned his readers that the federal judges would be "authorised to determine *all questions* that may arise upon the meaning of the constitution in law," and that for this reason among others they would be "independent of the people, of the legislature, and of every power under heaven."[24] Brutus, like Livingston, conflated "cases in law and equity" under the Constitution with "all questions" thereunder—the only difference being that Brutus had feared what Livingston appeared to welcome. Marshall answers both of them by pointing out a distinction each had missed, but he recoils, as Brutus had done, from any reading of the Constitution that would aggrandize the power of the judiciary.

Was Marshall himself only "fit[ting] the constitution to his argument" in 1800 to score a partisan debating point in defense of the Adams administration he would soon join? Did the apparently broader view of judicial power to interpret the Constitution with authority, which he expressed in Richmond in 1788, represent his "real" view of the matter, to which he returned once he himself was elevated to the bench in 1801?

This is plausible, but only barely so. Marshall was known as a moderate Federalist in the House, not an "Ultra" or "High Federalist," and he was by no means angling for a position in the Adams administration, though he was a vigorous defender of its policies. Far more likely is that, having actively entered national politics during the Adams years (first on a diplomatic mission to France and then in Congress), Marshall for the first time confronted the practical need to interpret the Constitution in the course of actually exercising its powers. His one earlier brush with the practical application of the Constitution had been as counsel for one of the parties before the Supreme Court in *Ware v. Hylton* (1796), a case he ably argued and deservedly lost.[25] To put the probability most plainly, Marshall was now required to *think harder* about the meaning of the Constitution—to respond to his obligation as a House member, to ponder the relations of the various branches, and to meet the exigencies of the moment under the terms of the nation's new charter. Defending the Constitution's adoption in 1788, before the practical uses of its provisions could be seen in their fullness, was one thing; adapting the solutions of hotly contested policy issues to the terms of the Constitution's structure and language in 1800, while serving in one of its high offices, was quite another.

The conclusion that Marshall went first this way, then that, then back again on the subject of judicial authority requires us to regard him as a politician of a rather low or middling order—at worst, simply seeking partisan advantage wherever it could be found to answer the needs of the moment; at best, displaying exactly that attachment of self-interest to the "rights of the place" that Madison had described as the engine of the separation of powers in *The Federalist* no. 51.[26] Thus, he could have been skeptical, as a congressman, of broad-gauged judicial power to settle all questions of constitutional meaning, simply because he *was* a congressman, and a friend of the current executive administration to boot. And he could then have shed that skepticism and become the judicial supremacist he is often thought to have been as chief justice simply because he *was* chief justice from 1801 onward. Stranger turns have been taken by many American politicians, even by those who have become judges.

The reason for seeing a linear progress in Marshall's constitutional understanding, rather than a seesawing back and forth depending on the office in which he served, is that evidence for an attachment on his part to broad judicial authority while he was chief justice is simply lacking. His views of 1800 appear rather to be his views throughout the long judicial career on which he embarked the following year.

Return for a moment to Marshall's speech during the "Robbins" affair. As he said there, for a legal case to present itself in such a way that the judiciary has authority to act on a constitutional question, questions must take on a legal "shape" involving parties "whose rights admit of ultimate decision by a tribunal to which they are bound to submit." The judicial power exists for the vindication of rights, whether they are grounded in the Constitution, or a statute, or the common law. As he said in the *Marbury* case, "[t]he very essence of civil liberty certainly consists in the right of every individual to claim the protection of the laws whenever he receives an injury. One of the first duties of government is to afford that protection." And the protection of such claims against an injury is peculiarly confided to courts of law, for an injury is, literally, against right (*in jure*): "the laws [must] furnish [a] remedy for the violation of a vested legal right"; and "[t]he question whether a right has vested or not is, in its nature, judicial, and must be tried by the judicial authority" (*Marbury* 163, 167).

Rights, Powers, and the Rule of Law

Injuries, rights, remedies: these are the business of courts. *Law* is the business of all three branches of government, which participate variously in making, executing, and adjudicating the meaning and application of law. When it must "say what the law is," a court does so, in a properly presented case over which it has jurisdiction, in order to settle whether a right has been injured and a remedy is available. If it finds an injury where a right has vested, a judicially applied remedy must in principle be available unless "the peculiar character of the case" dictates otherwise, as was true in *Marbury* itself (163). But when such questions do not present themselves in an adjudicable form at all (a question that goes well beyond simple jurisdictional issues), a court has no more authority—nay, less authority or even none at all—to "say what the law is" than does the legislative or executive branch.

The lawfulness of any particular exercise of political *power* under the Constitution may or may not present an instance in which injuries, vested rights, and remedies are all present in such a way as to make possible (and necessary) a judicial resolution of controversy. Marshall's jurisprudence, in fact, evinces a newly sharp distinction between *power* and *right* in the theory and practice of constitutionalism. Hobbes, Locke, and even *The Federalist* had frequently used the terms "power" and "right" interchangeably.[27] From an abstract point of view, this synonymy makes perfect sense: that which I am free by right to do, I have rightful power to do. But from the point of view of clarity in the practical application of constitutional principles, more is lost than is gained by such an equivocal synonymy. It makes far more sense to speak of the exercise of *power* as a specifically political act—an exercise of authority by some over others in the course of governing a community—and to reserve the word *right* for the individuals so governed, indicating those respects in which persons may expect the fulfillment of legal obligations on the part of other actors, private or public.

It is this distinction between power and right that we can see throughout Marshall's jurisprudence. It will not be surprising, for instance, given the discussion above of his rare use of the word "sovereign" to describe the states, that Marshall was also generally averse to using the term "rights" in connection with the political (especially the legislative) powers of the states, and used it almost exclusively in opinions where he *denied* the pretensions of a state to legislate on some subject or other.[28] Almost equally rarely did he refer to the "right" of Congress to legislate.[29] Marshall's preference was to refer to *power*, not *right*, when he meant political authority, and to speak of *rights* when he meant the civil liberty of individuals, that is, what persons were entitled to under the rule of law as adjudicable in courts.

The clarity of the distinction in Marshall's thought may appear most plainly in his great opinion in *Fletcher v. Peck* (1810). Before ever coming to the question of Georgia's violation of the contract clause of Article I, section 10, Marshall considers from a more abstract point of view whether the Georgia legislature could justly expropriate land it had previously granted (even under the most dubious or corrupt circumstances) by the rescission of the grant:

> If the legislature of Georgia was not bound to submit its pretensions to those tribunals which are established for the security of property, and to decide on *human rights*, if it might claim to itself the *power* of judging in its own case, yet there are certain great principles of justice, whose authority is universally acknowledged, that ought not to be entirely disregarded. (133, emphasis added)

The principle Marshall has chiefly in mind is that the "clearest principles of equity" would compel a court to conclude that subsequent purchasers of land from the original grantees should be "unmolested" by a legislative rescission of the grant, since they purchased it in good faith that a good title would be transferred. But whatever "ought" not to be done, adjudicable legal principles might not be available to redress the defiance of right by power:

> If the Legislature felt itself absolved from those rules of property which are common to all the citizens of the United States, and from those principles of equity which are acknowledged in all our courts, its act is to be supported by its *power* alone, and the same *power* may devest any other individual of his lands if it shall be the will of the Legislature so to exert it. . . .
>
> When, then, a law is in its nature a contract, when absolute *rights* have vested under that contract, a repeal of the law cannot devest those *rights*; and the act of annulling them, if legitimate, is rendered so by a *power* applicable to the case of every individual in the community. . . .
>
> It is the peculiar province of the legislature to prescribe general rules for the government of society; the application of those rules to individuals in society would seem to be the duty of other departments. How far the *power* of giving the law may involve every other *power*, in cases where the constitution is silent, never has been, and perhaps never can be, definitely stated. (134, 135, 136, emphasis added)

And this is precisely the problem: the Georgia *state* constitution is silent on the question whether any court of law can check the legislature's inequitable repossession of property; it is only the contract clause of the federal Constitution (part of that section thereof that "may be deemed a bill of rights for the people of each state" [138]) that comes to the rescue in the succeeding paragraphs of Marshall's opinion.

But let us dwell over these lines for another moment. The power of a legislature is to "prescribe general rules"; the power of courts lies in the "application of those rules to individuals." The former may, within the limits of an applicable constitution, say what are the "human rights" whose vindication may be pressed in courts of law. Should a legislature first grant rights to individuals and later take them away again, however "vested" those rights have become, that may be a raw exercise of unjust power. But no court may undo or reverse such an injustice unless there is, somewhere in an applicable constitution, an adjudicable right that may be set up as a countervailing force against such a use of power. Courts are not authorized to speak generally to issues that arise regarding the contours of political power granted or withheld by constitutions, or regarding the use or abuse of such power. Questions of constitutional power come under the purview of the courts only in relation to the vindication of rights. And, to speak still more precisely, the judicial ambit in such circumstances does not encompass *all* rights—natural, equitable, or derived from the common law—but only those rights that are explicitly identified in a governing legal text whereby (in the words of Representative Marshall in 1800) "parties [can] come into court, who can be reached by its process, and bound by its power; whose rights admit of ultimate decision by a tribunal to which they are bound to submit." Then and only then (in the language of *Marbury*) may a court "say what the law is" with an authority that other institutions are obliged to respect. The trouble in *Fletcher* (133) was that the controversy between the parties was "a question of title," the settlement of which is "usually assigned to a court." But the Georgia legislature's usurpation of the power to settle such a question, or unjustly to leverage its settlement, was unrestrainable by the judiciary in the event that the two constitutions governing its authority—that of the state and that of the Union—were "silent" on the existence of a judicially vindicable right contradicting such a usurpation. Fortunately for the sake of justice, one of those constitutions was not silent.

Were not many of Marshall's rulings concerned explicitly with the allocation of, and limits on, *power* as a matter for judicial decision? Was this not especially so in those cases in which a direct clash presented itself between the nation and the states? This is true, but it does not follow that in such cases the question of *rights* was absent. In *Brown v. Maryland* (1827), for instance, concerning the question whether a state's imposition of a licensing scheme on merchants selling imported goods violated the clause of Article I, section 10 prohibiting the state taxation of imports, Marshall focused not merely on the conflicting claims of state and nation to govern the business of merchants in the import trade. He attended also to the fact that once duties to the United States were paid by the merchant, he acquired "a right to dispose of his merchandise"; not simply "a right . . . to bring the articles into the country, but to mix them with the common mass of property" by subsequent sale (442, 444). Were there no federal duties to pay, such a right would still subsist, thanks to the constitutional prohibition on the states. But there were such federal duties, and in considering the second question in the case—whether the Maryland statute conflicted with the power of Congress to regulate foreign commerce—Marshall again made it clear that a personal right was at stake. "Any penalty inflicted on the importer for selling the article in his character of importer, must be in opposition to the act of Congress which authorizes importation" (448). Conflicting laws attempted to regulate the right of merchants to do their business; the act of Congress created a vested right to do business subject to certain conditions, while the state law in imposing additional conditions violated that right. For Marshall, the case clearly stood at the intersection of powers and rights, as well as at the intersection of conflicting claims of power. That fact bolstered his certainty that a case involving some admittedly murky waters regarding the taxing authority of states nevertheless fell within the judicial authority to "say what the law is."

Consider also *Gibbons v. Ogden* (1824). While the case is commonly understood to represent a clash between the competing *power* claims of New York and the United States to regulate navigation in the waters of the state, the arrival of that contest before the Supreme Court for resolution required a controversy between individuals claiming conflicting *rights* acquired under the two jurisdictions. Aaron Ogden, an assignee of the Fulton-Livingston monopoly on steam navigation sanctioned by the New York legislature, claimed a right to operate his ferry in the state's waters free of competition from Thomas Gibbons, whose boats were "duly enrolled and licensed, according to the act of Congress, to carry on the coasting trade of the United States," and who therefore "insisted on his right, in virtue of that license, to navigate the waters between Elizabethtown [New Jersey] and New York, the acts of the Legislature of New York notwithstanding."[30] Ogden had won an injunction from Chancellor Kent of New York, which was affirmed by the state's highest court. Marshall's Court reversed the decrees of the New York courts, settling the dispute over *rights* between the parties, and *only as a consequence of its performing that duty*, took up the competing claims of *power* by the state and the nation.

Indeed, while Marshall was careful in *Gibbons* to say that only those acts of Congress "made in pursuance of the Constitution" (211) could justly prevail over conflicting acts of state legislatures, and careful as well to state his understanding of the extent of Congress's power over commerce, which "may very properly be restricted to that commerce which concerns more states than one" (194), he took equal care to deny that the exercise of congressional power over commerce was subject to the restraining power of a court concerning itself with whether a particular use of this power was or was not "in pursuance" of the Constitution:

> If, as has always been understood, the sovereignty of Congress, though limited to specified objects, is plenary as to those objects, the power over commerce with foreign nations, and among the several States, is vested in Congress as absolutely as it would be in a single government, having in its Constitution the same restrictions on the exercise of the power as are found in the Constitution of the United States. The wisdom and the discretion of Congress, their identity with the people, and the influence which their constituents possess at elections are, in this, as in many other instances, as that, for example, of declaring war, the sole restraints on which they have

relied, to secure them from its abuse. They are the restraints on which the people must often rely solely, in all representative governments. (197)[31]

In short, while Marshall took the trouble in *Gibbons,* as in many of his other great opinions, to instruct his readers in a proper understanding of the Constitution's division of authority between the nation and the states, the only real issue for the Court, in his view, was whether Gibbons was possessed of a right to ply the coasting trade despite a state law's protection of another's exclusive right. What was *not* truly at issue in the case was whether Congress *could* accord Gibbons such a right. Congress had done so, and its power to do so was "solely" to be restrained or affirmed by the processes of national politics. Presumably, the only "restrictions on the exercise of the power . . . found in the Constitution" that could be enforced authoritatively by a court would be those that state a judicially vindicable right. And no one has a "vested right," adjudicable by a court of law, to the nonabuse of the general grant of power over commerce given to Congress by the Constitution.

Even when the judiciary acted fully within the scope of its admitted authority to adjudicate rights of individuals that took on (in Marshall's words from 1800) "a legal form, for forensic litigation, and judicial decision," Marshall was under no illusions about the possible confrontations that might occur between rights and powers. In the treason trial of Aaron Burr in 1807, over which Marshall presided in the U.S. Circuit Court for Virginia, one of his many opinions during the course of the proceedings concerned a motion for a subpoena *duces tecum* to President Jefferson for the production of documents desired by the defense. When the U.S. attorney opposed the motion, Marshall held for Burr on grounds that the Sixth Amendment right of a criminal defendant to compel witnesses to appear encompassed "the means of rendering it effectual," and that there were no constitutional grounds for distinguishing between the president and any other citizen to whom a subpoena might issue. But he paused briefly and obliquely over the possibility of the president's defiance:

> It cannot be denied, that to issue a subpœna to a person filling the exalted station of the chief magistrate, is a duty which would be dispensed with much more cheerfully than it would be performed; but if it be a duty the court can have no choice in the case.
> If then, . . . a subpœna may issue to the President, the accused is entitled to it of course; and whatever difference may exist with respect to the *power* to compel the same obedience to the process, as if it had been directed to a private citizen, there exists no difference with respect to the *right* to obtain it. (*Papers* 7:42–43, emphasis added)

Here, contemplating the awful prospect of a direct clash between the duty of a court to speak on behalf of rights and the power of a president to disregard such rights, Marshall had to consider not simply the boundaries of authority between one branch of government and another, but power in quite another sense—as simple force. No process of a court could compel a recalcitrant president who was determined not to respect the rule of law, for the judiciary, as Hamilton noted in *The Federalist* no. 78, "must ultimately depend upon the aid of the executive arm even for the efficacy of its judgments," and here the judgment would be directed against the executive itself, which might defeat it by a simple inaction that could not be overborne by any greater force.[32]

In only one of Marshall's opinions does there *appear* to be a case before the Court purely concerning conflicting powers of governments, without any admixture of those rights ordinarily adjudicated by the judiciary. That case is *McCulloch v. Maryland,* which ranks with *Marbury* as among his best-known opinions, but is also, with *Marbury,* one of the least well understood. It will be recalled that *McCulloch* addressed two questions: whether the Congress could create a national bank, and whether a state could tax its operations. As to the first, which took up roughly two-thirds of Marshall's opinion, he described it as a "question . . . in the decision of which the great principles of liberty are not concerned, but the respective powers of those who are equally the representatives of the people, are to be adjusted"—suggesting that the issues raised regarding congressional power were not, strictly speaking, within the competence of a court whose duty was to vindicate vested rights and to defend civil liberty (401). And true to form, at the conclusion of this portion of the opinion, Marshall returned to where he had begun, noting that:

> [T]he degree of [the Bank's] necessity, as has been very justly observed, is to be discussed in another place. Should congress, in the execution of its powers, adopt measures which are prohibited by the constitution, or should congress, under the pretext of executing its powers, pass laws for the accomplishment of objects not intrusted to the government; it would become the painful duty of this tribunal, should a case requiring such a decision come before it, to say that such an act was not the law of the land. But where the law is not prohibited, and is really calculated to effect any of the objects intrusted to the government, to undertake here to inquire into the degree of its necessity, would be to pass the line which circumscribes the judicial department and to tread on legislative ground. This court disclaims all pretensions to such a power. (423)

Marshall has sometimes been criticized for demurring, in *McCulloch*, from a full-blown inquiry into just what made the Bank "necessary and proper" to the accomplishment of any object entrusted to the general government. For after all, judging the "degree of its necessity" *is* a constitutional judgment. But Marshall's answer in the lines above is complete. Such an inquiry is not within the *power* of the judiciary, unless and until "a case requiring such a decision come[s] before it." And the pattern of Marshall's jurisprudence over the course of his whole career informs us of what such a case would look like: it would involve an invasion of a vested *right* possessed by someone capable of pressing its vindication in a court of law competent to vindicate it. No one has a "right" to defeat the creation of a Bank of the United States by the Congress—certainly not the state of Maryland, which under these circumstances possesses no adjudicable rights at all.

Only the second question in *McCulloch* involved in any way an issue regarding such rights. James McCulloch, the cashier of the Baltimore branch of the Bank of the United States, in effect claimed a right not to pay the Maryland stamp tax in the course of circulating U.S. bank notes. Was McCulloch merely a surrogate for the interests of the United States in this respect? Yes, but as Marshall was later to point out in one of his pseudonymous essays defending his opinion, "McCullough, not the United States, is the party on the record; and were it otherwise, that circumstance would bring the case within, not exclude it from, the jurisdiction of the court. The constitution expressly gives jurisdiction to the courts of the union in 'cases to which the United States shall be a party.'"[33] That reminder of the terms of Article III's grant of jurisdiction is a reminder as well that the United States, in some cases, might appear in a court as a holder of rights, even in the absence of a "federal question" giving jurisdiction on other grounds. It is, in substance, the United States—through its officers and agents—that has a right not to be taxed by Maryland. And so, in the final third of his opinion, Marshall turns to the vindication of that right, ruling against the taxing power of the state.

But why, if the first question posed in *McCulloch* did not present any issues regarding adjudicable rights, did Marshall need to devote two-thirds of his opinion to that question? That the question could not be altogether avoided was owing in part to the terms of section 25 of the Judiciary Act of 1789, which provided for Supreme Court review under a writ of error of any ruling of a state's highest court against the validity of a federal law.[34] But could not Marshall have simply referred to Congress's decision to charter the Bank as authoritative, and had done with it? Both in private and in public (albeit under a pseudonym), Marshall provided a somewhat rueful answer to this question. Within a few weeks of the decision, writing to Bushrod Washington, he noted that the "politicians of Virginia . . . have no objection to a decision in favor of the bank, . . . but they required an obsequious, silent opinion without reasons" (*Papers* 8:281). As he again put it some weeks after that to Joseph Story, "[t]hey would have been more merciful had we said simply that it was for the legislature to decide on the necessity & not the court &c." (*Papers* 8:310). This is in essence what the Court *did* say, at least in part, as we have seen above. But it said more: it did not give a "silent opinion without reasons" to support such an exercise of congressional power. It is clear that Marshall was sensitive to the charge that the Court had "travell[ed] out of the case for the purpose of delivering, extrajudicially," its opinion on the validity of the Bank charter.[35] His response to this charge evinces an awareness on Marshall's part of the Court's duty to another, third party in every case of major importance: public opinion. As he said in one of his essays defending the *McCulloch* ruling:

> Suppose the court had said: "Congress has judged of the necessity and propriety of this measure, and having exercised their undoubted functions in so deciding, it is not consistent with judicial modesty to say there is no such necessity, and thus to arrogate to ourselves the right of putting our *veto* upon a law."
> Or suppose the court, after hearing a most elaborate and able argument on the constitutionality of the law, had said: "It is not our intention to bring that subject into discussion. . . ."
> Would this reasoning have satisfied, or ought it to have satisfied the publick?[36]

It would not, says Marshall, because such an opinion, leaving the Bank charter entirely undefended but for a bare assertion of Congress's plenary authority to judge of its necessity, would "insinuate an opinion that Congress had violated the constitution."[37] Far better for public opinion's sake for the Court to do as Marshall did in his *McCulloch* opinion—refute the arguments against the Bank that so fundamentally misconstrued the letter, spirit, and foundations of the Constitution, and in so doing explain the reasons *why* Congress must remain unfettered by the judiciary as it legislates for the nation according to its own ideas of necessity and propriety.

Other cases come to mind in which Marshall was charged with "travelling out of the case" in the course of his opinion—in particular *Gibbons v. Ogden* and *Cohens v. Virginia*. In each instance, it is worth noting that Marshall was prompted to explore principles of the Constitution whose discussion was not necessary to the immediate decision of the case by the arguments of counsel propounding theories inimical to the very foundation of the Union. But only after *McCulloch* did Marshall feel obliged to respond to such complaints in a comprehensive way, and it may have been because he was acutely aware that in deciding the first question in the case, the Court had come closer to "tread[ing] on legislative ground" than at any other time in his career. That the Court had *not* so trodden he was determined to show in his essays afterward. And it should be remembered that the circumstances of the case required the Court to take up the issue of the Bank charter's validity in order to move to the only question in the case that went to the Court's central role in deciding disputes regarding rights: the right of the Bank and its cashier to be free of Maryland's power of taxation.

Judicial Review or Judicial Supremacy?

It is fitting that to conclude our discussion we turn once again to *Marbury v. Madison*. Many are the myths that have grown up around this case, the most prevalent being that it established not just "judicial review" of acts of Congress but "judicial supremacy" over all constitutional questions. It is also said, however, that Marshall had the issues in the case back-to-front: if, as he concluded, the suit of Marbury against Madison had to be dismissed due to a want of jurisdiction on the Supreme Court's part to issue a writ of mandamus, then, it is said, the chief justice should have treated the jurisdictional issue first and dismissed the case without considering any other issues. Marshall identified the issues in this way: "1st. Has the applicant a right to the commission he demands? 2d. If he has a right, and that right has been violated, do the laws of his country afford him a remedy? 3d. If they do afford him a remedy, is it a *mandamus* issuing from this court?" (154). The reason for this order is apparent if we recall that *Marbury* was heard by the Court under its original jurisdiction, and for Marshall the very first thing for a trial court to do is to examine whether the matter pressed by the complaining party poses questions of law that a court may settle. As he had said in Congress in 1800, such questions "must assume a legal form, for forensic litigation, and judicial decision"—they must involve issues of right within the ambit of judicial authority. Marshall's first two questions above address that matter squarely, while his third question—the one giving rise to that part of his opinion that attracts most attention—speaks to a question of *power* as it affects rights.

Another thing to notice is that in considering the first two questions—which took up roughly two-thirds of his opinion—Marshall "did" as much constitutional law as in the final third devoted to his famous holding that in some cases the Court could treat an act of Congress as no law at all. The questions of Marbury's right and of the availability of a remedy prompted a sensitive and careful discussion on Marshall's part of the separation of powers, and of its intersection with the principle of the rule of law.

The critical legal facts regarding Marbury's right, the injury he had received, and his entitlement to any legally available remedy, were these: Congress had created the office of justice of the peace for the District of Columbia with a fixed term of five years, the officer not being subject to removal at the president's (or anyone else's) will. An earlier statute created an implied duty on the part of the secretary of state to deliver such an officer's commission (or a copy thereof) on demand once his appointment was complete. These facts compelled a legal conclusion for Marshall:

> Where an officer is removable at the will of the executive, the circumstance which completes his appointment is of no concern, because the act is at any time revocable, and the commission may be arrested if still in the office. But when the officer is not removable at the will of the executive, the appointment is not revocable, and cannot be annulled. It has conferred legal rights which cannot be resumed. The discretion of the executive is to be exercised until the appointment has been made. But having once made the appointment, his power over the office is terminated in all cases, where by law the officer is not removable by him. The right to the office is then in the person appointed, and he has the absolute, unconditional power of accepting or rejecting it. (162)

The withholding of Marbury's commission, then, was "violative of a vested legal right" (162). But could such a violation be considered as within the power of the executive, so as not to be remediable in courts of law?

> Is the act of delivering or withholding a commission to be considered as a mere political act belonging to the executive department alone, for the performance of which entire confidence is placed by our constitution in the supreme executive, and for any misconduct respecting which the injured individual has no remedy? That there may be such cases is not to be questioned; but that every act of duty to be performed in any of the great departments of government constitutes such a case is not to be admitted. (164)

There "may be such cases," indeed. Marshall proceeded to mark carefully the boundary of constitutional responsibility between the executive and the judiciary:

> [T]he question whether the legality of an act of the head of a department be examinable in a court of justice or not must always depend on the nature of that act. If some acts be examinable and others not, there must be some rule of law to guide the court in the exercise of its jurisdiction. . . .
>
> By the constitution of the United States, the president is invested with certain important political powers, in the exercise of which he is to use his own discretion, and is accountable only to his country in his political character and to his own conscience. . . . In such cases, . . . there exists, and can exist, no power to control that discretion. The subjects are political. They respect the nation, not individual rights, and, being entrusted to the executive, the decision of the executive is conclusive. . . .
>
> But when the legislature proceeds to impose on that officer other duties; when he is directed peremptorily to perform certain acts; when the rights of individuals are dependent on the performance of those acts; he is so far the officer of the law, is amenable to the laws for his conduct, and cannot, at his discretion, sport away the vested rights of others. (165–66)

The reasoning in these passages leads to Marshall's remark, quoted earlier, that "[t]he question whether a right has vested or not, is, in its nature, judicial, and must be tried by the judicial authority" (167). Strictly speaking, it is *only* when the vested rights of other parties are involved that the exercise of executive power becomes amenable to the judicial enforcement of legal (and thus of constitutional) principles. Responding a few pages later to the view some might express that a court would thus "intermeddle with the prerogatives of the executive," Marshall writes:

> It is scarcely necessary for the court to disclaim all pretensions to such a jurisdiction. An extravagance so absurd and excessive could not have been entertained for a moment. The province of the court is *solely to decide on the rights of individuals*, not to inquire how the executive or executive officers perform duties in which they have a discretion. Questions, in their nature political, or which are, by the constitution and laws, submitted to the executive, can never be made in this court. (170, emphasis added)

The core of Marshall's constitutional law could not be plainer than it is in these lines. *Power* questions are *political* questions, not in themselves subject to judicial review—surely not where the coequal branches of the general government are concerned. *Rights* questions, framed properly in a legal shape, are *judicial* questions. Only to the extent that the latter are involved, and incidentally to their decision, may the former even be considered by a court of law. And even then, as the result in *Marbury* itself made painfully clear, the principle that ours is "a government of laws, and not of men" may unfortunately fail to be vindicated, due to "the peculiar character of the case"—due, that is, to the Constitution itself (163).

It is too readily overlooked how heavily the discussion of the first two questions in *Marbury*, including the exploration of the separation of powers, conditions the treatment of the final question. Consider one of the opinion's most famous passages:

> It is emphatically the province and duty of the judicial department to say what the law is. Those who apply the rule to particular cases must, of necessity, expound and interpret that rule. If two laws conflict with each other, the courts must decide on the operation of each. So, if a law be in opposition to the constitution, if both the law and the constitution apply to a particular case, so that the court must either decide that case conformably to the law, disregarding the constitution, or conformably to the constitution, disregarding the law, the court must determine which of these conflicting rules governs the case. This is of the very essence of judicial duty. (177–78)

What exactly are these "particular cases" to which a court must "apply the rule," and in so doing, "decide on the operation" of conflicting statutory and constitutional provisions? If the first two-thirds of the opinion are not to be regarded as a simple mockery, or as a political "cover" for a power grab by Marshall in the final third, the answer must be that "the very essence of judicial duty" is "solely to decide on the rights of individuals," and *only to that extent* to take up questions of the limitations on the powers of other branches of government.

Only a clear view of the vital distinction Marshall always maintained between rights and powers can make sense of his subsequent remark on the Court's purview: "In some cases then, the constitution must be looked into by the judges. And if they can open it at all, what part of it are they forbidden to read or to obey?" (179). The "some cases" are those involving vested legal rights adjudicable by courts. Not all so-called cases will meet such a description. But in those that do (and *only* those that do), once having "opened" the Constitution to "look into" it, judges may have to "read and obey" constitutional provisions ordinarily addressed to other branches—such as the appointment power of presidents—inasmuch as the exercise of legislative and executive powers can give rise to vested rights in myriad ways.

John Marshall's constitutional jurisprudence was guided by this principle for thirty-four years—a principle he stated a year before his appointment to the Court, when he denied that "all questions" under the Constitution are amenable to judicial decision, and affirmed that all "cases in law and equity" requiring a decision on contested rights are so amenable. A proper understanding of *Marbury*, as well as of his other decisions, can recover for us a clear view of the judicial authority so eloquently described by Representative Marshall: a muscular but limited power, modest in scope but robust inside its boundaries. With the same eloquence, and with the same care in choosing some words while avoiding others to characterize the American constitutional order, did Chief Justice Marshall approach the settlement of all those great questions of a Union "neither wholly federal, nor wholly national" that it was possible for his Court to adjudicate.[38] Free men govern themselves by law, and law is language applied to life. Marshall's jurisprudence stands as a striking exemplar of how language properly used can illuminate the relations of the great principles of constitutionalism. Wielding his quill wisely and with surpassing care, the great chief justice instructed us in how to balance and reconcile the rule of law, freedom, and self-government.

Notes

1. *Marbury v. Madison*, 1 Cranch (5 U.S.) 137 (1803). Henceforth in this chapter, page numbers of Marshall's opinions will be cited parenthetically in the text where they are quoted; standard citations for other cases quoted in the text, in chronological order, are as follows: *Fletcher v. Peck*, 6 Cranch (10 U.S.) 187 (1810); *McCulloch v. Maryland*, 4 Wheaton (17 U.S.) 316 (1819); *Cohens v. Virginia*, 6 Wheaton (19 U.S.) 264 (1821); *Gibbons v. Ogden*, 9 Wheaton (22 U.S.) 1 (1824); and *Brown v. Maryland*, 12 Wheaton (25 U.S.) 419 (1827).

2. In an unintentionally hilarious report filed with the Associated Press on February 4, 2001, on an appearance by Justice Antonin Scalia at an event celebrating Marshall in Richmond, Virginia, reporter Anne Gearan had this to say on the difference between the two: "Marshall was a vigorous advocate for judicial power of a scope that modern-day conservatives such as Scalia tend to regard with suspicion. Marshall also favored a strong federal government, while Scalia has voted repeatedly to grant greater power to states at the expense of federal control." The second sentence here, whatever might be said about its characterization of Marshall, can be made intelligible only if it is understood as a contradiction of the first sentence. Justice Scalia's penchant for striking down federal legislation in the name of "greater power to states" makes *him* a "vigorous advocate for judicial power" of a far greater scope than Marshall would ever

have tolerated. It bears recalling that Marshall's Court struck down just one provision of federal law in his nearly thirty-five years on the bench, while it is already becoming difficult to count the number of times Justice Scalia has voted in fifteen years to invalidate federal legislation, frequently in the teeth of precedents of Marshall's that point in the opposite direction.

3. See the essays by Marshall collected in *John Marshall's Defense of McCulloch v. Maryland*, ed. Gerald Gunther (Stanford, Calif.: Stanford University Press, 1969).

4. For details of Marshall's life, readers should turn to Jean Edward Smith, *John Marshall: Definer of a Nation* (New York: Henry Holt, 1996), which deserves to supersede Albert J. Beveridge, *The Life of John Marshall*, 4 vols. (Boston: Houghton Mifflin, 1919), as the standard biography.

5. *Hale v. Bimco Trading, Inc.*, 306 U.S. 375 (1939), at 378.

6. See *Wilson v. Mason*, 1 Cranch (5 U.S.) 45 (1801), at 91; *Dunlop v. Ball*, 2 Cranch (6 U.S.) 180 (1804), at 184; *Strawbridge v. Curtis*, 3 Cranch (7 U.S.) 267 (1806); *Gordon v. Caldcleugh*, 3 Cranch (7 U.S.) 268 (1806), at 270; *Bank of United States v. Deveaux*, 5 Cranch (9 U.S.) 61 (1809), at 85, 86, 91; *United States v. Peters*, 5 Cranch (9 U.S.) 115 (1809), at 136, 139; *Sere v. Pitot*, 6 Cranch (10 U.S.) 332 (1810), at 335, 337; *Slocum v. Mayberry*, 2 Wheaton (15 U.S.) 1 (1817), at 9, 10; *United States v. Wiltberger*, 5 Wheaton (18 U.S.) 76 (1820), at 98; *Cohens v. Virginia*, 6 Wheaton (19 U.S.) 264 (1821), at 383, 390, 396, 398, 399, 402, 403, 415, 419, 420, 421, 422; *Brashier v. Gratz*, 6 Wheaton (19 U.S.) 528 (1821), at 529; *Osborn v. Bank of United States*, 9 Wheaton (22 U.S.) 738 (1824), at 817, 818, 820, 822, 825, 853, 856; *Bank of United States v. Planters' Bank of Georgia*, 9 Wheaton (22 U.S.) 904 (1824), at 907, 908, 909, 910; *Wayman v. Southard*, 10 Wheaton (23 U.S.) 1 (1825), at 21, 28, 38, 49, 50; *Postmaster-General v. Early*, 12 Wheaton (25 U.S.) 136 (1827), at 146, 149; *American Insurance Co. v. Canter*, 1 Peters (26 U.S.) 511 (1828), at 545.

7. See *Cohens v. Virginia*, 6 Wheaton (19 U.S.) 264 (1821), at 417; *Brown v. Maryland*, 12 Wheaton (25 U.S.) 419 (1827), at 446.

8. See *Brown v. Maryland*, 12 Wheaton at 448.

9. Alexis de Tocqueville, *Democracy in America*, trans. and ed. Harvey C. Mansfield and Delba Winthrop (Chicago: University of Chicago Press, 2000), 149. For the classic statement to much the same effect at the time of the Founding, see Alexander Hamilton, James Madison, and John Jay, *The Federalist*, ed. Jacob Cooke (Middletown, Conn.: Wesleyan University Press, 1961), no. 39 (Madison), 257.

10. Webster quoted in Charles Warren, *The Supreme Court in United States History*, rev. ed., 2 vols. (Boston: Little, Brown, 1926), I:603.

11. See, e.g., "federal government" in *The Federalist* no. 31 (Hamilton), 196; no. 45 (Madison), 308; "national government" in *The Federalist* no. 2 (Jay), 8; no. 11 (Hamilton), 69; no. 40 (Madison), 259.

12. *Chisholm v. Georgia*, 2 Dallas (2 U.S.) 419 (1793), at 454 (emphasis in original).

13. See *United States v. Fisher*, 2 Cranch (6 U.S.) 358 (1805), at 396; *Fletcher v. Peck*, 6 Cranch (10 U.S.) 87 (1810), at 136, 137; *Sturges v. Crowninshield*, 4 Wheaton (17 U.S.) 122 (1819), at 192; *McCulloch v. Maryland*, 4 Wheaton (17 U.S.) 316 (1819), at 400, 402, 404, 410, 411, 427, 429, 430, 433; *Cohens v. Virginia*, 6 Wheaton (19 U.S.) 264 (1821), at 380, 382, 406, 414, 417, 418, 434; *Gibbons v. Ogden*, 9 Wheaton (22 U.S.) 1 (1824), at 187, 210; *Osborn v. Bank of United States*, 9 Wheaton (22 U.S.) 738 (1824), at 870; *Bank of United States v. Planters' Bank of Georgia*, 9 Wheaton (22 U.S.) 904 (1824), at 907, 908; *Ogden v. Saunders*, 12 Wheaton (25 U.S.) 213 (1827), at 334, 348 (Marshall, C.J., dissenting); *Weston v. City Council of Charleston*, 2 Peters (27 U.S.) 449 (1829), at 467, 468.

14. *Providence Bank v. Billings*, 4 Peters (29 U.S.) 514 (1830), at 563, quoting *McCulloch*, 4 Wheaton at 429. See also *Weston*, 2 Peters at 466.

15. *Gibbons*, 9 Wheaton at 187. See also *Fletcher*, 6 Cranch at 137; *Sturges*, 4 Wheaton at 192; *Cohens*, 6 Wheaton at 417.

16. *McCulloch*, 4 Wheaton at 403, 402. See also *Fisher*, 2 Cranch at 396; *Fletcher*, 6 Cranch at 136; *Cohens*, 6 Wheaton at 380, 382, 406; *Gibbons*, 9 Wheaton at 210; *Osborn*, 9 Wheaton at 869; *Planters' Bank*, 9 Wheaton at 907; *Weston*, 2 Peters at 468.

17. *The Federalist* no. 37, 236.

18. Joseph Story, *Commentaries on the Constitution of the United States*, abridged by the author (Boston: Hilliard, Gray, and Co., 1833; reprint, Durham, N.C.: Carolina Academic Press, 1987), § 210 (§ 451 in unabridged first edition).

19. Marshall even avoided the use of the word "doctrine" to describe broad patterns or principles in constitutional law, as is customary today. He might speak of a "doctrine" of the common law as developed in adjudicated cases over the course of many years, or of the "doctrine" of a prior case in the narrow sense of its meaning as a precedent. But that judicially enforced "doctrines" could be derived from the Constitution was a notion wholly foreign to his vocabulary.

20. See Robert Lowry Clinton, *Marbury v. Madison and Judicial Review* (Lawrence: University Press of Kansas, 1989), esp. chaps. 1 and 5; Charles F. Hobson, *The Great Chief Justice: John Marshall and the Rule of Law* (Lawrence: University Press of Kansas, 1996), esp. chap. 3; and Matthew J. Franck, *Against the Imperial Judiciary: The Supreme Court vs. the Sovereignty of the People* (Lawrence: University Press of Kansas, 1996), esp. chap. 4. For an admirably succinct statement on this matter, see Clinton, "How the Court Became Supreme," *First Things* 89 (January 1999): 13–19.

21. Unfortunately, this understanding escapes one of Marshall's successors, Chief Justice William Rehnquist, who remarked that for Marshall, "no branch of the federal government—whether it is the Legislative, the Executive, or the Judiciary—is supreme," but that since (again for Marshall, in Rehnquist's view) "the courts have always had the final say in interpreting the provisions of a written agreement," it follows that "the federal courts, and particularly the Supreme Court, [are] the ultimate arbiter[s] of the meaning of the Constitution." The chief justice appears not to notice the self-contradiction in his account of Marshall's views. William H. Rehnquist, "John Marshall," remarks delivered at The College of William and Mary, October 6, 2000, available at: www.supremecourtus.gov/publicinfo/speeches/sp_10-06-00.html.

22. Speech at Virginia Ratifying Convention, June 20, 1788, in *The Papers of John Marshall*, ed. Herbert A. Johnson et al., 10 vols. to date (Chapel Hill: University of North Carolina, 1974–), 1:277. Hereafter, any quotations from this source will be cited parenthetically in the text as *Papers*.

23. For a similar account of the Robbins/Nash affair, see Smith, *John Marshall*, 258–62.

24. "Brutus," no. XI (January 31, 1788) and no. XV (March 20, 1788), in *The Complete Anti-Federalist*, ed. Herbert J. Storing, 7 vols. (Chicago: University of Chicago Press, 1981), 2:419, 438 (emphasis added).

25. 3 Dallas (3 U.S.) 199 (1796). This is the only case in which Marshall appeared before the Supreme Court as counsel. Although he argued numerous cases before the federal circuit court in Virginia before leaving private practice, rarely did those cases require him to argue the meaning of the Constitution.

26. *The Federalist* no. 51, 349.

27. See Thomas Hobbes, *Leviathan*, ed. Michael Oakeshott (New York: Collier, 1962), 134 ("From this institution of a commonwealth are derived all the *rights*" of political authority; emphasis in original); John Locke, *Two Treatises of Government*, ed. Peter Laslett (New York: Mentor, 1965), II: § 3 ("*Political Power* then I take to be *a Right* of making Laws"; emphasis in original); *The Federalist* no. 51, 349 ("The interest of the man must be connected to the constitutional rights of the place"); *The Federalist* no. 78, 522 ("[T]he judiciary, from the nature of its functions, will always be the least dangerous to the political rights of the constitution").

28. See *Fletcher*, 6 Cranch at 136, 138; *Sturges*, 4 Wheaton at 196, 207; *McCulloch*, 4 Wheaton at 428, 429, 430, 432, 433, 435, 436; *Trustees of Dartmouth College v. Woodward*, 4 Wheaton (17 U.S.) 518 (1819), at 629; *Gibbons*, 9 Wheaton at 201, 202, 203, 205, 208; *Osborn*, 9 Wheaton at 859, 863-64, 867; *Brown*, 12 Wheaton at 444, 445; *Weston*, 2 Peters at 466.

29. See *United States v. Palmer*, 2 Wheaton (16 U.S.) 610 (1818), at 630; *Sturges*, 4 Wheaton at 196; *McCulloch*, 4 Wheaton at 411, 412, 416, 417, 419, 424, 430, 435, 436; *Loughborough v. Blake*, 5 Wheaton (18 U.S.) 317, at 318; *Cohens*, 6 Wheaton at 426, 428, 434; *Gibbons*, 9 Wheaton at 202, 207; *Osborn*, 9 Wheaton at 826, 864; *Wayman*, 10 Wheaton at 50; *Brown*, 12 Wheaton at 445, 447; *Jackson ex dem. Anderson v. Clark*, 1 Peters (26 U.S.) 628 (1828), at 635.

30. *Gibbons v. Ogden* (2 March 1824), Marshall's draft opinion, in *Papers* 10:15. The lines quoted here, appearing at the beginning of the opinion, were omitted in Wheaton's report of the case, which begins with Marshall's sixth paragraph; cf. 9 Wheaton (22 U.S.) 1 (1824), at 186. Subsequent quotations of *Gibbons* will be from Wheaton's report.

31. Note here Marshall's rare use of the word "sovereignty," discussed above in this chapter; in the context at hand, he clearly means Congress's plenary authority over a subject accorded to it by the sovereign people of the United States.

32. *The Federalist* no. 78, 523.

33. Marshall, "A Friend of the Constitution" no. IX, *Gazette and Alexandria Daily Advertiser*, July 15, 1819, reprinted in Gunther, *Marshall's Defense*, 214.

34. 1 Stat. 73, at 85–86.

35. Marshall, "A Friend to the Union" no. I, *Philadelphia Union*, April 24, 1819, reprinted in Gunther, *Marshall's Defense*, 84.

36. Marshall, "A Friend to the Union" no. II, *Philadelphia Union*, April 28, 1819, reprinted in Gunther, *Marshall's Defense*, 104–5 (emphasis in original).

37. Gunther, *Marshall's Defense*, 105.

38. *The Federalist* no. 39, 257.

PART THREE:

A DIVIDED NATION
(1820–1865)

》》➤ ◄《《

Chapter 14

John Quincy Adams on Principle and Practice

David Tucker

John Quincy Adams (1767–1848) was born to John Adams, a man who had risen from modest beginnings to become a prominent Massachusetts lawyer, an indispensable revolutionary, and the second president of the United States; and to Abigail Adams, upon whose knee John Quincy watched the Battle of Bunker Hill and whose virtues of head and heart distinguished her in an extraordinary generation. In 1778, when John Quincy was eleven, he accompanied his father on a diplomatic mission to Europe, where the elder Adams was to negotiate a treaty with France critical to the survival of the new Republic. John Quincy returned to the United States, attended Harvard College (graduating second in his class in 1787), and opened a law practice in 1790. Four years later, aged twenty-six, he was appointed minister to the Netherlands. In 1797, he became minister to Prussia. He returned to the United States in 1801 and was elected a U.S. senator from Massachusetts in 1803. Putting the interests of the United States above those of his region and above partisanship, Adams supported President Thomas Jefferson on the issue of the embargo.[1] Having done so, he was in effect recalled in 1807 by the Massachusetts legislature, which was dominated by Federalists. In 1809, he was appointed minister to Russia and then headed the commission that negotiated the Treaty of Ghent, which ended the War of 1812. From 1815 to 1817, Adams served as minister to London.

President James Monroe appointed Adams secretary of state in 1817, a position he held throughout the eight years of Monroe's tenure. As secretary of state, Adams improved the State Department's record keeping and arranged the first training of an American diplomat in Arabic. His diplomatic accomplishments have led many to consider him our greatest secretary of state. He resolved the Florida border question in the Transcontinental Treaty with Spain (a treaty which also established the southern border of the United States through the Rocky Mountains); he defended U.S. territorial claims in the Northwest against British and Russian counterclaims; and he authored the Monroe Doctrine—all of which assured the dominance of the United States across North America.

Secretary Adams was considered a strong candidate for the presidency in 1824, since the third, fourth, and fifth presidents of the United States had ascended to that office from the secretariat. His path was blocked, however, by the formidable figure of Andrew Jackson, military hero and Indian fighter. Although as secretary of state Adams had faced down those in Britain and the United States outraged at Jackson's execution of two British citizens for conspiring with Indians in Florida, Jackson and Adams were now opponents. When the votes were counted, Jackson had more popular and electoral votes than any of the other four candidates. Adams had come in second in both categories. But the election had to be decided by the House of Representatives since Jackson had not received a majority of electoral votes. After an interview between

Adams and the fourth place finisher Henry Clay (in which it appears that Clay was allowed to understand that he would become secretary of state in Adams's administration and thus a leading candidate as the next president), Clay threw his support to Adams, who was elected president. The agreement with Clay became known, through the workings of Jackson's supporters and the newspapers they controlled, as the "corrupt bargain." Opposition to it and to Adams, a man who prided himself on being above faction and beyond partisanship, helped organize the Democratic party. As president, Adams hoped to establish a national program of internal improvements—physical, moral, political, and intellectual—"to which neither the authority nor the resources of any one State can be adequate" (*SW* 367).[2] He was frustrated in this effort by the opposition of Jackson's supporters; and in 1828, he was defeated by Jackson overwhelmingly in the electoral college and soundly in the popular vote.

Following his defeat, Adams retired briefly to private life, devoting his time to repairing his finances and family home in Massachusetts. In 1830, however, Adams accepted candidacy for the House of Representatives. In his customary fashion, he would not campaign. He would not even say that he was willing to serve, since that appeared to him to be too much like asking for a vote. Nevertheless, he won election with nearly three-fourths of the votes cast. Thus began his second career. In a certain sense, Adams had anticipated this career even before he became president. He noted in his diary at the time of the Missouri Compromise that he should begin preparing himself for what he felt sure would be a long struggle over slavery and that a life spent in this struggle "would be nobly spent or sacrificed" (*SW* 302, 303). In the House, Adams became a public champion of the antislavery cause. Opposing the so-called Gag Rule (adopted in 1836, it prevented the House taking up antislavery petitions), Adams endured verbal abuse, a trial for censure, and threats of assassination. He overcame all these, eventually triumphing over the Gag Rule, which was repealed in 1844. Adams died at his desk on the floor of the House while opposing commendations for the generals who had commanded during the war with Mexico—a war he viewed as having no purpose other than the expansion of slavery.

Adams was born and came to maturity with the American republic in a world hostile to its principles. In the first part of his life, therefore, Adams's watchwords were liberty and union, because without union, the liberty of the Republic and its citizens would not be secure. By the time Adams took his seat in the House, America's national liberty was assured, largely through his efforts. A large and still growing republic was on the path to power and greatness. But Adams came to realize, as did others, that as external threats receded, a greater, more profound internal threat (slavery) had taken their place. Adams's watchwords, therefore, became liberty and equality, because without equality, the liberty of the Republic and its citizens would not be secure. As equality came to supercede union in his thinking, Adams came to accept that the Union he had done so much to preserve and fortify had to be risked in order to preserve liberty. This became the great practical issue for Adams and the country, the greatest question of internal improvement.

The foundation of Adams's thinking about politics—indeed, about all aspects of human life—was his understanding of the human condition. Adams accepted the Judeo-Christian tenet that man was a created being who had freely chosen to violate God's law, and who had thus separated himself from God and become fallen, frail, imperfect, and needy. "Evils physical, moral, intellectual beset [man's] path from the cradle to the grave." Man's Creator had compensated him, however, for this otherwise dire condition. Man could improve his condition through improving the arts (or technology, as we would say) and his moral and political condition. Adams believed that it was a command of God that mankind do so. Such improvement was possible above all because man possessed reason, "the peculiar and highest characteristic, which distinguishes man from the rest of the creation." Although formed of clay, man was only a little lower than an angel, as the Psalmist had sung, thanks to this gift of reason. We are aware, argued Adams, "that the thinking part of our nature is not material but spiritual." It is not subject, therefore, to the laws of matter and not perishable with our body. "Hence arises the belief that we possess an immortal soul." Reason, "the immortal part of his nature," elevated man above the merely material and allowed man, as needy as he was, to participate "in the divine nature itself." This participation, however, was intermittent and less than complete. "You and I are competent to *dogmatize*," John Quincy told his father, "that is, *to hold opinions* about 'To Πᾶν' [the whole]. To hold opinions, but not to obtain perfect knowledge." Still, limited as it was, reason elevated man above the merely brute creation; and coupled to a disciplined will, allowed him to improve his condition in this life and prepare for the next, "where the pure in spirit will find that perfection which must be denied to them on earth" (*SW* 401, 292, 278; *LRO* 13–14).

This understanding of human nature and man's place in the whole was not a mere abstraction to Adams but informed his political program. For example, in his First Annual Message, as part of his program of internal improvements, Adams requested public support for the construction of an astronomical observatory—or, as he termed it, "a light-house of the skies." Adams justified the expenditure of public funds on such a project with the obligatory remarks about the advancement of knowledge being useful to the nation. But we should remember that for Adams public utility included notions of morality and intellectual improvement. Astronomy was important for these reasons as well. As he would point out some years after his First Annual Message, the earth and sky, so different in their nature, yet held together "by the mysterious mandate of Almighty power," framed man's world and "indicate to his perception, and foreshow to his reason, the condition of his own existence, compounded of body and soul, of matter and of mind." The earth was open to all the senses, but the heavens revealed themselves only to sight. "So peculiarly adapted to the nature of man is the study of the heavens that of all animated nature his bodily frame is constructed as if the observation of the stars was the special purpose of his creation" (*SW* 402). Astronomical observation was important to Adams because it modeled the ultimate purpose of human life. It was proper, he believed, that government support an activity that had such a lofty moral object.

However related to the ultimate purpose of man's existence, the study of astronomy was far removed from his humble, needy beginning. Adams understood this beginning as the start of a historical process that led through stages toward civilization. The historical process of human development was driven by man's needs—to preserve himself, to cloth and feed himself, and, at a later stage, to understand himself. This process consisted of four distinct socioeconomic stages that developed from man's efforts to satisfy his needs: hunting wild animals, herding domesticated animals, tilling the soil, and living in cities. In each stage, man became better able to meet his needs as he improved technology. Man also became more gentle, more concerned with others. In the first stage, man was capable only of hunting and making war. In the second stage, he learned to care for his flock and, although still nomadic, had some time for the arts, the pleasures of human companionship, and the contemplation of the world around him. In the third stage, private property existed because farmers had to own the land in order to have an incentive to work it and care for it. As men settled down, the relationship between man and wife reached perfection. "Woman, to the hunter, is a slave—to the shepherd she is a possession,—to the husbandman she is the partner and companion of life." Monogamy began to be common at this stage as did monotheism. Families developed strong ties of mutual dependence. Civil society began and patriotism developed. As tillage produced wealth and improvements in technology, the village "thickened," as Adams put it, into a town and cities formed. In time, "the links of mutual interest, and of reciprocal want and supply" between cities and the countryside produced a nation. At this stage, man's needs were met, and civilization—that state in which all the powers of men's minds and bodies could be exercised to their fullest—might exist (*SC* 84, 86).

As Adams suggests, the story of man's development was the story of his moving from the many to the one—from nomadism, polygamy, and polytheism to one home, one wife, and one God (*SC* 83). Three points in this story deserve particular notice: the decisive importance of revelation to Adams (which distinguished him fundamentally from the Founders, including his own father), the ambiguity of the moral progress it makes possible, and the thoroughly social nature of man (*SW* 292).

In keeping with his understanding of the limits of human reason, Adams did not believe that unaided reason was capable of grasping the unity of God. Biblical revelation was necessary for the movement from the many to the one, from barbarism to civilization. Men were capable of moving some way along this path on their own. According to Adams, the transitions from one stage to the next were "as clearly announced in the dispensations of Providence as we have seen them to be in the nature of man." Only revelation, however, allowed mankind to complete its journey. This was so because Adams saw the revelation of a single caring Supreme Being as the necessary foundation for morality and justice. Without the idea of a Supreme Being and the rewards and punishments He dispensed, most men would have no motive to act morally (*SC* 88–89; *SW* 281).

While technological progress was clear at each stage, Adams's discussion of moral progress reveals some ambiguity. When discussing the pastoral stage, the stage when man is a herder of animals, Adams noted that the shepherd was "one of the most impressive images under which the Divine Being himself is presented to the devotion and gratitude of man." This assimilation of the shepherd to the divine suggested to Adams that the pastoral state had some special status among the stages of man's development. Why this might be so appears in the story of Cain and Abel. Cain is a tiller of the soil. According to Adams's historical scheme, he should be at a higher level of development than his brother Abel, who is only a shepherd. Yet it is Cain who is the less generous of the brothers in his offering to God. While the two stages in man's development after the pastoral showed continued moral improvement and progress toward one home, one wife, and one God, they did not possess all the innocence of the pastoral state and certainly possessed greater opportunities to fall away from the moral teachings of Scripture. This perhaps explains why Adams thought that "those in the more advanced stages of society" think of the pastoral stage as one of "tenderness and delight" (*SC* 82).

Whatever may be man's stage of moral and technological development, he is always social as Adams depicts him. That man is needy means that he has to be social. This was clear to Adams in the first instance from considering procreation. Every individual existence depends on the previous union of a woman and a man. Since children are utterly dependent for a long time and require complicated nurturing to survive and prosper, nature indicates that this union should endure. Every individual existence, therefore, presupposes and depends on an enduring social organization: a family. "Man is therefore by the law of nature's God, a *social* being . . . [and] the nuptial union . . . is by the law of nature, the foundation of human society" (*SC* 80; *TSC* 12).

Adams understood the family to be the foundation of society and ultimately of politics in two ways. First, without the procreation and nurturing that took place in the family, there would be no humans to form societies. Second, although social beings, humans had selfish passions. Some of these passions harmonized with social life. For example, a man's desire to improve himself could benefit others. When the selfish passions did not harmonize with social requirements, humans had to learn to control them. The family was the first place that taught this control. By doing so, the family made social life possible. Self-control, of course, was another name for self-government, and thus the family prepared the way for the kind of republican government that the United States enjoyed (*SC* 85–86; *TSC* 11).

Although it prepared men for self-government in a republic, the family itself was not a miniature republic. Children do not originally have self-control; it is learned in the family. Since children lacked control, the family needed a controlling will. "By the law of nature and of God," as Adams saw it, the head of the family was the father and husband. Although the family clearly had a head, what we might call family government was a complicated affair. As the head of the family, the father's will was not unrestrained. The father had greatest authority over the children, but even in this case his will should not be absolute or despotic. Even less so should it be in the case of the husband's authority over the wife (*TSC* 12–13). As at least a somewhat self-controlled individual, the wife was more nearly the husband's equal than were children.

Families, of course, also need help preserving themselves and in meeting their other needs. Just as satisfying these needs is part of what leads to the formation of families, so is it part of the reason that societies form and mankind comes to live in civilized nations. Civilization itself is a web of "mutual interest, and of reciprocal want and supply." All of this confirms that man is social by nature. Man's needs require that he be social and his happiness depends on it; but he can be social only because he is rational. Mankind possesses "the means for rational intercourse with his fellow creatures and of humble communion with his God" (*LRO* 14). This is as true of the most savage hunter as it is of the most civilized city dweller. Man is inherently social, living first in families, then in tribes, then in civil society, and finally in civilized nations—but always living together with others.

Living together, men required some way to organize and direct their common life. They required government, "the exercise of power directing or controlling the will of human beings." If individuals were capable of perfect self-government—"the most important and perhaps the most difficult" kind of government—"no other government would be needed or could exist. But perfect self-government is not allotted to man upon earth." In society at large, as in the family, some way had to be found to control the selfish passions. No individual ever completely mastered them or could be trusted to do so. Therefore, government "of one or more individuals over others" was necessary. "The pursuit of happiness . . . calls for the institution of governments, to regulate and adjust the collisions of interest and of passions incident to the existence of civil society—to secure, as far as the infirmities of human nature will admit, the rights of every one . . . and to harmonize the discordant elements of the social compact" (*TSC* 11; *SW* 400).

The social compact was a way of understanding the nature of government. The body politic is "a voluntary association—a social compact—by which the whole people covenants with each citizen, and each citizen with the whole people." Adams understood, of course, that historically governments had rarely if ever been formed by agreement. He cited the Mayflower Compact as one instance in which "all the individuals of the community" (aboard the *Mayflower*) had given their "unanimous and personal assent" to form a body politic. He remarked of this event, however, that it was "perhaps, the only instance in human history of that positive, original social compact, which speculative philosophers have imagined as the only legitimate source of government." The idea of a social compact was important to Adams not because it was historical but because it explained the nature of government—what it should be. "Voluntary agreement is the only legitimate source of authority among men. . . . [A]ll just government is a compact."[3]

Voluntary agreement was the only legitimate basis of government because power resided in the individuals who formed the government. Power resides in them because these individuals are born equal in their possession of inalienable rights, enumerated in the Declaration of Independence as the rights to life, liberty, and the pursuit of happiness. These rights "can be possessed only upon the condition of respecting the same rights in all other men. The laws of nature and of nature's God therefore are laws of duty, as well as laws of right. . . . The natural equality of mankind is thus the parent of universal freedom" (*SW* 398–99).

In discussing the social compact and the legitimacy of government, Adams wanted to establish two points in order to establish the preeminence of the Declaration. First, Adams insisted that compact or voluntary agreement was necessary to establish legitimate government because the natural equality of men meant that no one had a right by nature to rule over another. Thus, government could only come into existence legitimately when individuals agreed to set one up, and they might legitimately dissolve this government if it no longer secured their rights. Second, he argued that the government thus established could not have absolute power over those who established it because the rights of individuals were inalienable (unless forfeited by wrongdoing). "If the whole compass of human power could be concentrated in one arm, it would be impotent to take away, however it might ravish," the rights of those who form a government. Adams recognized that compacts or voluntary agreements had given rise to governments before the Declaration had established the United States. Governments in England, for example, had been thus established. Yet those involved in the compacts had understood the governments they established to be absolute and unlimited. "It was asserted that by entering into the social compact, man surrendered *all* his rights, and took in return such as ruling power was pleased to bestow upon him." Adams denied that any government could have such power. It could not be granted by those forming a government even if they wanted to because their rights were inalienable. Legitimate government thus required both the agreement of those forming it and the recognition by them that the government established by their mutual compact had only limited power (*SW* 398). According to Adams, the Declaration was the first time that the dual requirements for legitimate government had been met. It was the first time that men had established government according to the laws of nature and of nature's God. "It proved that the social compact was no figment of the imagination; but a real, solid and sacred bond of the social union" (*A* 21).

In discussing the epochal event of the Declaration and its significance throughout his life in a series of July Fourth orations, Adams emphasized equality of rights as the foundation of government rather than political or social or economic equality within the body politic. Despite the ringing declaration that natural equality brought forth universal freedom, Adams was in no sense an egalitarian. On the contrary, he maintained what many today would consider restrictive notions of who should participate in politics and the scope of popular sovereignty. One important restriction on participation followed from Adams's understanding of the role of the family in politics. As the family was the foundation of both society and the body politic, Adams argued that the social compact should be between the whole people and the head of the family—the father and husband—and between the head of the family and the whole people. "The vote, by the law of nature and of God, must be confined to the male sex, because the contract, embracing the whole family, one member of the family must pledge the faith, and stipulate for the rights of the whole." Adams acknowledged that this understanding of the social compact differed from "the theories of modern times," which argued for universal suffrage as the only legitimate expression of sovereign power—the only basis of the social compact and for the operation of government once established. Adams called such ideas "the government merely of numbers." But democracy "is not, never was, never can be, the government merely of numbers" because of the nature of the family and its relation to social and political life. To have its necessary unity, the family must have one head. Therefore, "the laws of nature and of God . . . must limit the law of universal suffrage and cannot be overcome." As the struggle over slavery intensified and the horrors of the French Revolution—"that hideous monster of democracy, begotten by madness upon corruption"—faded in memory, Adams's thinking about the Declaration and American politics shows a growing awareness of and emphasis on the importance of equality; but Adams was never an egalitarian (*SC* 80–81; *TSC* 18–19; *W* 2:457).

Nor did Adams believe that the power or sovereignty of the people was absolute. According to his interpretation of the Declaration, this revolutionary document did not replace the unlimited sovereignty of a king with the absolute power of the people; rather, it limited political power altogether. Prior to the Declaration, all government had been founded upon power. The Declaration founded government upon right—the rights of the people. The argument of the Declaration means that "*all* government is subordinate to the *moral* supremacy of the people." But the people themselves are subordinate to the laws of nature and of nature's God. "The people, who assumed their equal and separate station among the powers of the earth by the laws of nature's God, by that very act acknowledged themselves bound to the observance of those laws, and could neither exercise nor confer any power inconsistent with them." This is the same point Adams made when he argued that rights imply duties: if one is to enjoy his rights, he must respect the rights of others. This duty limits popular sovereignty. Since government can have no more power than those who constitute it, the limits on popular sovereignty constitute limits on government or, as Adams put it, governments have "only the power to do all that may be done of right." Adams expressed this thought another way by saying that "a moral Ruler of the universe, the Governor and Controller of all human power, is the only unlimited sovereign acknowledged by the Declaration of Independence."[4]

The Declaration thus provided a standard by which men could judge the legitimacy of government. But how did this natural standard fit with the historical facts of man's development? By nature man was social. In the earliest state in which Adams describes mankind, however, "hunting and war, the destruction of beasts or the destruction of men are the only" human activities. If mankind was making progress, human history was still largely the story of violence and fraud, of government established through conquest and force. Adams had seen this first hand in Napoleonic Europe. Perhaps it was this experience that led him to believe that monarchy developed because war "requires a leader with absolute and uncontrolled" power. The prevalence of war gave legitimacy to monarchy. War was also the customary origin of slavery: "war gives the right to take the life of our enemy, and . . . this confers a right to make him a slave, on account of having spared his life." Yet as Adams argued before the Supreme Court, the state of nature was not a state of war, and he thus denied any natural right to slavery and, presumably, to monarchy. How did Adams knit together his understanding of legitimate government with man's history? How did he understand the relationship between force in history and right in politics?[5]

As we have seen, human history is a story of human progress. Man rises from the violence and poverty of the hunter to the more peaceful and furnished life of the civilized city dweller. The Declaration expressed the ultimate purpose of this historical process. For Adams, the Declaration was an event of the utmost importance, ranking second perhaps only to the birth of Christ. It was "a leading event in the progress of the gospel dispensation," for it combined the laws of nature and of nature's God. From its perspective, one could look back and see that all previous government was illegitimate, either a matter of force or, if arising from compact, erroneously considered absolute. With this realization came the more important realization that the Declaration provided a political representation of the religious and moral teaching of Jesus that expressed the end toward which men had been working without knowing it as they sought to meet their needs in the long history of human development. The Declaration, we might say, made sense of what to Adams appeared to be the slowly emerging restraint on war and increasing respect for equality that marked human history. It marked an epoch in the movement from the many to the one because in announcing all men equal it announced that human beings, despite their differences, were one. As such, the Declaration provided further impetus toward, if not the Second Coming, then the glorious day when slavery and war would exist no more. Ultimately, then, Adams's understanding of human life and politics was governed not by man's humble beginnings and the rule of force, however much these remained part of human life, but by his glorious end and the rule of right (*O* 5–6, 17, 57–64; *SW* 408; *A* 22).

The lofty end toward which Adams saw man tending explains why he thought government had an expansive purpose. Adams recognized that a government must secure the rights of those who formed it, but he believed that the legitimate purpose of government extended beyond this. Once men had progressed beyond their primitive condition, they could experience in nature what "melts the soul into tenderness and allures it into contemplation." Similarly, once men had a measure of security, they could attend to something more than defending themselves: they could consider the common welfare. In his Inaugural Address, Adams expressed this larger goal by declaring that "the happiness of the people" was "the end of all legitimate government upon the earth." In his First Annual Message, he specified what this meant. "The great object of the institution of civil government is the improvement of the condition of those who are parties to the social compact and no government in whatever form constituted, can accomplish the lawful ends of its institution but in proportion as it improves the condition of those over whom it is established." Adams went on to explain that he meant not just physical improvements but also moral, political, and intellectual ones. Such improvements were "duties assigned by the Author of our existence" (*SC* 81–82; *SW* 356, 360–61).

Adams's expansive view of the objectives of government may have followed from his understanding of the progress toward moral virtue of which mankind was capable; but it seems at odds with his view that governments do not by nature and should not in fact have unlimited power. Given human nature, if governments were to be instruments for ending slavery and war, it would appear that they would need great power—perhaps even totalitarian power, as it came to be called—to change and shape human nature and even perhaps nature as such.[6] But it was precisely such power that Adams argued the Declaration denied to government. Thus, Adams gave to government objectives that he would deny it the power to achieve.

Reverting to Adams's argument about inalienable rights specifying the limits of governmental power does not resolve this mismatch between the ends and means of government. It merely explains one part of it: the limits on the power of government. More than this, referring to the doctrine of inalienable rights makes the contradiction more striking. This doctrine developed as a way of arguing for limits on the supposed absolute power of kings and on the power of government to impose uniformity in religious practice and doctrine. Those who argue that men have inalienable rights that government must respect most often describe government as a vehicle only for securing the free exercise of those rights, subject to the restriction that their exercise not infringe upon the exercise by other people of their rights. In other words, government establishes the conditions in which men may pursue happiness but does not specify what happiness is. It does not do so because happiness is not or cannot be known to be necessarily the same for everyone. In short, there is no common welfare except self-defense and the establishment of the barest conditions permitting the exercise of our inalienable rights. This view does not necessarily mean that government must be entirely neutral with regard to how people act. A government devoted to protecting the exercise of inalienable rights might, for example, make efforts to see that its citizens were the sort of people—rational, industrious, self-controlled—to assert and take advantage of their rights. But this view of the objectives of government is still limited when compared to the account offered by Adams. He distinguished between self-defense and the common welfare as objectives for social and political organization, implying that the common welfare is more than self-defense. Indeed, he virtually identifies the objectives of government with the Second Coming. He does this, again, while maintaining that the powers of government are limited. The tension, then, between the powers of Adams's government and its objectives remains. He denies to government the sovereign unlimited power he claims feudal and monarchist theorists granted to it but attributes to government objectives—moral and intellectual improvement—that these same theorists would have accepted.

One way to defend Adams against the charge of inconsistency would be to note that limited means were sufficient to bring about moral and intellectual improvement because history was tending in that direction. In other words, a government that could help produce rational and industrious citizens but otherwise not restrict the freedom of its citizens would automatically bring about improvement because, thanks to history, the unintended product of rational, industrious activity was such improvement.

For Adams, this argument needs to be made in a different idiom. The limited power Adams was willing to grant government was all that it needed because government was really the handmaiden of God, the only sovereign who should have totalitarian power. Progress toward perpetual peace and universal emancipation was God's plan, and government was at best a weak assistant in its unfolding. Government might therefore proclaim expansive goals commensurate with the Gospel dispensation without demanding power equivalent to the Gospels' Author because the goals it proclaimed were to be achieved on a plane (the providential) different from the one on which government exercised its power. These different planes, like the earth and sky, so different in their nature, were yet held together "by the mysterious mandate of Almighty power." That power—and not the government's—was the primary instrument for carrying out God's plan.

Adams did speak in the idiom of Providence. Almost in the same breath, however, he also spoke of the need for mankind to exert its will to bring about what God intended. Mentioning human will directs us again, if not to the paradoxes of the relationship between God's power and man's will, to the importance of human agency and thus to the role of government in bringing about the glorious end promised to mankind. Directed to the role of government, we are again brought to the paradox that Adams proclaimed lofty ends for government but insisted on limiting the power it had to attain those ends. Ultimately, the best explanation for this paradox is probably Adams's understanding of the human condition. According to the Gospel dispensation, man was fallen. This meant that man could not be trusted with power over his fellows because he was sure to use that power sooner or later not for the common good but for his own selfish ends. "The ferocious spirit of slavery," utterly incompatible with Christianity, and the evil effects of this spirit on American life demonstrated this. In fact, we might say that there was stronger evidence for the selfish nature of man, and thus for the necessity of limiting the power of government, than there was for the glorious end toward which Adams believed mankind tending. Of the whole, even with the Gospel dispensation, men had only opinion or belief. Of the weakness of man and his tendency toward injustice, we have indisputable knowledge. Therefore, the power of the tools, including government, that might fall into the hands of men had to be carefully limited. The paradox of expansive goals, opened by man's reason, and limited means, made necessary by his depravity, highlights the limits of politics and describes, in one sense, the human tragedy, mitigated by the belief in and the hope for the dawn of perpetual peace and universal emancipation (*O* 54–58, 61, 14–15, 50–51, 57).

Accepting this explanation of the tension in Adams's thinking between the lofty objectives of government and its limited power, one might wonder about the prudence of attributing to government such goals, especially in state papers. Was this not simply an incitement for men to strive for what they could not safely achieve? Would not the allure of the goals make men forget the weaknesses of the beings who sought them? Did not Adams's own experience of the French

Revolution show the danger of utopian expectations? Indeed, the United States in the later years of Adams's life experienced a remarkable period of utopian feeling and disrespect for the laws. In the period prior to the Civil War, millennial religions and communal living experiments flourished. People began to imagine that the Second Coming, heaven on earth, could be brought about or at least encouraged, and the fallen nature of man overcome through human exertion. As a result of such sentiments, the Constitution itself was reviled as an unworthy compromise with slavery.

In his emphasis on the efficacy of human will with respect to perpetual peace and universal emancipation, Adams was taking essentially a utopian position. Adams did not support any utopian plans, public or private, presumably because he maintained his belief in the fallen nature of man. Still, his willingness to use the government to foster physical, moral, political, and intellectual improvements went beyond what most Americans accepted and, arguably, encouraged the utopian and even antinomian tendencies at work in the United States. Should we not, therefore, side with those who rejected Adams's espousal of lofty goals and join them in ridiculing, for example, Adams's idea of publicly supported "lighthouses of the skies"?

Perhaps we should. Living at the beginning of the long utopian surge that carried through the twentieth century, Adams was insufficiently aware of how the desire to improve mankind's condition could make things much worse. Perhaps more accurately, we should say that he was insufficiently aware of how thoroughly all restraints on power could be overwhelmed by utopian desires. Yet, in Adams defense, we should remember that to have ignored the lofty goals men could think of for fear of what they might do would have been to betray the best part of human nature. It might even be thought to encourage a reversion to less civilized forms of human association in which men recognized no common good and were only loosely associated with their fellows for narrow purposes such as self-defense and mere material well-being.

Adams saw a tension, then, between principle and practice, and social and selfish passions, running through human affairs. Neither element of this tension could be ignored without risking injustice. Each had to be held in the proper balance. In notes he made for a speech on a motion concerning the purchase of Louisiana, Adams offered one expression of the tension and the balance it necessitated.

> Theoretic principles of government can never be carried into practice to their full extent. They must be modified and accommodated to the situations and circumstances of human events and human concerns. But between those allowances necessary to reconcile the rigor of principle with the resistance of practice, and the total sacrifice of all principle, there is a wide difference. (*W* 3:28)

If we consider Adams's treatment of property and slavery, we can see how he tried to accommodate principle to practice without sacrificing principle. The place to begin considering Adams's treatment of property is his oration commemorating the landing of the first settlers at Plymouth. He noted that these settlers at first adopted "that community of goods and of labor, which fanciful politicians, from the days of Plato to those of Rousseau, have recommended as the fundamental law of a perfect republic." He acknowledged that this arrangement was flattering to human nature and was adopted out of a desire to promote social spirit. But he insisted that "a wiser and more useful philosophy" than Plato's or Rousseau's "directs us to consider man according to the nature in which he was formed." Human selfishness meant that far from promoting justice and harmony, the community of goods and labor produced great injustice by making "the most virtuous and active members of society the slaves and drudges of the worst." As a practical matter, private property encouraged industry. But private property was also just. Adams considered it a law of nature that he "who sows the seed shall reap the harvest." The establishment of private property, like the monogamous family, was a significant step forward in man's journey toward civilization. For this reason, Adams told his listeners that they should cherish "the spirit of harmony" that led to the communal experiment, while recognizing the experiment's failure.[7]

In the oration at Plymouth, Adams accepted both the lofty goals that the settlers sought—thus directing his listeners to the common good—and man as he actually is—thus denying that perfect justice was possible. Its pursuit produced only greater injustice. In his political program and thinking, as well as his speeches, Adams kept in mind the goal of social harmony and the potentially disruptive effect of differences in wealth or property on this harmony. One can see him seeking ways "to reconcile the rigor of principle with the resistance of practice." Although a staunch defender of private property ("We have not succeeded in providing as well for the protection of property as of personal liberty"), in keeping with the republican character of the United States, he was critical of inherited wealth. More important, he understood his program of internal improvements to be in part a means of controlling the divisive effects of economic development and private property. He told a correspondent late in life that he had intended the program to provide "high wages and constant employment to hundreds of thousands of laborers" funded out of the common stock of the public lands. To those accustomed to or accepting of powerful intervention by government in the name of improving man's conditions, the steps that Adams was willing to take to promote social harmony will no doubt seem too timid. These were, however, the steps that Adams felt were both compatible with justice and possible given human nature.[8]

We see a similar interplay of principle and practice in Adams's treatment of the slavery issue. Although opposed to slavery in the early part of his career, Adams did not consider the existence of slavery in the United States a pressing issue. Like the Founders, he accepted the compromises with slavery in the Constitution. Thirty-three years after his remark about principle and practice in the Louisiana Purchase, Adams repeated the same point with regard to the relationship between the principles of our government contained in the Declaration and their practical working out in the Constitution.

> The elements and the principles for the formation of the new government were all contained in the Declaration of Independence; but the adjustment of them to the condition of the parties to the compact was a work of time, of reflection, of experience, of calm deliberation, of moral and intellectual exertion; for those elements were far from being homogeneous, and there were circumstances in the condition of the parties, far from conformable to the principles proclaimed. (*O* 28)

Adams accepted the accommodation of principle to practice in the Constitution because he believed that the compromise with slavery was the price of union. Union was necessary because without it the states would not be secure. They would fear both one another and intervention on the behalf of one state against another by foreign powers, such as Britain, France, and Spain. Lacking security, they would have to invest more in defense; taxes would rise. Standing armies would threaten civil liberties. States would have to submit to the demands of foreign powers in order to have their protection. Soon, the states of North America would be indistinguishable from the weak petty states of Europe, which had no liberty and no peace (*SW* 259, 276–77, 287–88). In short, Adams judged the liberty of the majority to be more important than the liberty of a minority. The harshness of the compromise with slavery was mitigated initially by the belief both that slavery was doomed to extinction and that the preservation of liberty for the majority was the only basis on which one day the liberty of the minority might also be arranged.

Adams's thinking about slavery changed when he came to see, during the agitation over the Missouri Compromise (1820), that slavery was not declining but growing in power and that it therefore threatened to replace liberty as the foundation of the Republic. At that point, continued union became a threat to liberty. "The bargain between freedom and slavery contained in the Constitution of the United States is morally and politically vicious," Adams noted in his diary at the time. Adams thus came to reject the constitutional compromise with slavery. In private, he even expressed the thought that at least a temporary dissolution of the Union, and a war against the slaveholders, might be necessary. The issue then became seeking the right time and terms for this dissolution which would allow the free states ultimately to triumph and reform the Union, including the Southern states, on the basis of liberty. In public, Adams maintained that slavery could only be removed from the Union by constitutional amendment, with compensation to the owners. The federal government could do nothing against slavery in the states where it existed. There, it had the protection of the law. Changing the law of the land meant working to change public opinion, "the queen of the world," so that a constitutional majority would vote against slavery. Building that majority meant pointing out to whites that slavery threatened their liberties, as it did when defenders of slavery and their allies restricted the right of citizens to petition their representatives in Congress on the issue of slavery (the Gag Rule that Adams made infamous). It meant stopping the number of slave states from increasing by preventing the acquisition of territory suitable for a slave economy (for Adams like others believed that the federal government could exclude slavery from the territories of the United States). It meant arguing at length in Congress and in public speech after speech that ideas beloved of slaveholders such as state sovereignty and the right of a state to declare null and void the laws of the United States were untenable in theory and unsubstantiated by history. It meant devising constitutional means other than amendment that could put an end to slavery (as Adams did by arguing that in case of a slave rebellion, the federal government might use the authority of martial law to do away with slavery). By all these means, Adams sought to bring practice into conformity with principle, even as he accommodated principle to practice (*SW* 301–2, 306–7; *O* 52–53).

Given the enormity of slavery, one might well ask why it had to be accommodated at all. Why might those who opposed slavery not act immediately on principle and resort to extra-constitutional means to destroy slavery? Adams once argued that a constitution took precedence over merely legislated law and that every citizen had a right to interpret the constitution and disobey legislated law if in his opinion it contradicted the constitution (*W* 1:127). If such civil disobedience was acceptable in the case of a "law prohibiting theatrical entertainments," why was it not in the case of slavery? To be consistent, should not Adams have argued that natural law was superior to the constitution and that every citizen had a right to interpret the natural law and disobey a constitutional provision that violated his interpretation of this higher law? Was such an appeal to natural law not the basis for the right of revolution found in the Declaration of Independence?

Adams accepted the appeal to higher law and the right of revolution and civil disobedience that that higher law sanctioned. His objection to radical abolitionist attacks on the Constitution and its compromises with slavery was not that the Constitution could not be defied in the name of principle or the higher law. Certainly, everything Adams did and wrote suggests that he believed, as the Declaration had it, that prudence dictated that such appeals should not be made for "light and transient causes." Decent political life required that revolution or disrespect for the laws be the rare exception and never the common practice. Still, Adams believed that appeals to principle could be made and that the abolition of slavery was not a light or transient cause. Yet he urged caution and restraint on abolitionists and others.

Adams took a cautious approach to the abolition of slavery because he believed that the radicalism of the abolitionists—the fact that their program openly threatened war, for example —turned people away from the antislavery cause. Their unwillingness to make the "allowances necessary to reconcile the rigor of principle with the resistance of practice" threatened "the total sacrifice of all principle." If the Union had to be risked, it should be done with the maximum of public support, Adams contended, so that the Union could be reconstituted on the basis of liberty. Extraconstitutional means, acceptable in principle, were likely to produce in practice the opposite of what their advocates and Adams wanted. In fact, Adams's cautious, law-abiding approach to the slavery question won him an influence over popular opinion that he had never had as president and that the abolitionists never attained. With that influence, he was able to lead the country, haltingly and only part way, toward a resolution of the slavery issue compatible with the Declaration and the rule of law. Ultimately, war became unavoidable; but it took place on terms—as Adams had argued it should—that maintained maximum public support for the cause of equality and liberty. With that support, equality and liberty triumphed. By accommodating principle to practice, Adams "avoided the total sacrifice of all principle."

While Adams understood that the tensions that defined human life required flexible mediation, his sense of human depravity led him often to emphasize an almost inflexible regard for the rule of law, lest selfishness make flexibility indistinguishable from villainy. The strength of Adams's respect for the rule of law is evident because he maintained that respect even when it worked against him on issues that were most important to him. For example, in his First Annual Message, while advocating internal improvements, Adams acknowledged that they posed a constitutional issue concerning the power of the government. He urged Congress to "let no consideration induce you to assume the exercise of powers not granted to you by the people." Similarly, Adams opposed legislation implementing the purchase of Louisiana because he believed that Congress had neither the power nor the right to legislate for the people of Louisiana without their consent (*SW* 366; *W* 3:27–30). Whatever good might come from these great initiatives—and Adams thought great good would come from them—was not more important than the harm that might be done by encouraging the exercise of arbitrary power.

In addition to supporting his respect for the rule of law, Adams's sense of man's weakness and tendency to corruption informed his thinking about the structure of government. Here again, his concern was to reconcile the power of the people (principle) with the tendency toward the misuse of power (practice). In his "Life of James Monroe," Adams offered a succinct statement of the problem as he saw it. "All the powers of government, in free countries, emanate from the people: . . . [I]n the delegation of power to the government, the problem to be solved is the most extensive possible grant of power to be exercised for the common good; with the most effective possible guard against its abuse to the injury of anyone" (*SW* 374). Adams was an advocate of bicameralism, for example, because he believed that two legislative houses with checks on each other would help prevent legislative abuses of power. The importance of bicameralism was not a lesson that could be learned through mere theoretical study. Indeed, as Adams pointed out, adherence to the principle that power derives from the people at first led many Americans to insist on unicameral legislatures. Adams would have suspected such an outcome because "to mere theorists . . . there is no idea so seducing as that of simplicity." Experience quickly taught, however, that bicameralism was a more effective guard against the abuse of power than unicameralism.[9]

Adams considered the division of power between the states and the federal government, like the division between branches of government, as a way to guard against the abuse of power; but, he felt that the distribution of power in the Union was not right. The states had too much of it or, at least, public opinion tended to grant them too much. This was a view that Adams held early in his career, when he argued against New Englanders who wished to nullify federal law that conflicted with their interests; and later, when he argued against Southerners, who claimed the same right when federal legislation conflicted with theirs. In 1808, in contention with the Northern nullifiers, he pointed out that if one state could nullify, then all could, and this meant the end of the Union. Therefore, nullification was not a right inherent in the Union but something antithetical to union. As the contest over slavery intensified, Adams added to this argument detailed accounts of the revolutionary period and the development of the Constitution, showing that it was not the states that had formed the Union but the American people. Thus, the states had no standing independent of the Constitution, and the Constitution made them subordinate to the federal government. As such they could not, on their own authority, nullify federal law. In Adams's view, the Constitution created not a confederation but a national government, "complicated with a federation," in which "the national character predominated throughout the system" (*W* 3:192; *SW* 325).

One reason that Adams emphasized the national character of the federal government was his sense that in political disputes a national perspective was more likely to produce a just outcome. Acutely aware of the power of the selfish passions and the weakness of men, Adams continually spoke and acted against the role of interests in politics. He emphasized the national interest over state interests and the common interest over individual interest because in each case this broader interest more closely approximated justice. For the same reason, Adams opposed organized political parties and always stood aloof from them. He believed that they were vehicles only for partial interests, whether individual or regional. He could not see them as necessary in the effort to organize interest in support of principle, as the Republican party proved to be in the fight against slavery. This was one case where Adams proved incapable of accommodating principle and practice.

In foreign affairs, Adams also tried to balance principle and practice, an effort made all the more difficult by the principles upon which Adams tried to act. He believed that one set of principles should govern the conduct of both individuals and nations, for both ultimately had the same purpose. "[T]he truest policy of a nation consists in the performance of its duties. The rights of nations are nothing more that an extension of the rights of individuals . . . and they are all . . . derived from the fundamental position which the author of Christianity has taught us," to do unto others as we would have them do unto us. In a letter to his father, Adams remarked that he could not agree with Stephen Decatur's toast of our country, right or wrong. "My toast would be, may our country always be successful, but whether successful or otherwise always right. I disclaim as unsound all patriotism incompatible with the principles of eternal justice" (*W* 1:139; *SW* 288).

In advocating and trying to arrange free trade among nations, Adams was able to live up to his principles. Free trade was the just policy. The commercial treaties the new nation had negotiated with France and the Netherlands were concluded on the just and magnanimous principles of the Declaration, the first in history to be so concluded (*A* 27). But free trade also served the self-interest of the United States. What about cases in which justice and national interest were at odds?

One case deserves mention. Perhaps Adams's most well-known utterance is a passage in his July Fourth oration of 1821, quoted with approval by liberals during the Cold War and, more in harmony with Adams's meaning, by conservatives since.

> Wherever the standard of freedom and Independence has been or shall be unfurled, there will [America's] heart, her benedictions and her prayers be. But she goes not abroad, in search of monsters to destroy. She is the well-wisher to the freedom and independence of all. She is the champion and vindicator only of her own. She will recommend the general cause by the countenance of her voice, and the benignant sympathy of her example. She well knows that by once

enlisting under other banners than her own . . . [t]he fundamental maxims of her policy would insensibly change from *liberty* to *force*. The frontlet upon her brow would no longer beam with the ineffable splendor of Freedom and Independence; but in its stead would soon be substituted an Imperial Diadem, flashing in false and tarnished luster the murky radiance of dominion and power. She might become the dictatress of the world. She would be no longer the ruler of her own spirit. (*A* 29)

In keeping with the spirit of this passage but against the wishes of many of his fellow citizens, Adams tried to separate the United States from the struggles for human rights and national liberation then raging in Europe and South America. But this passage occurs in Adams's speech after he has asked the question "what has America done for the benefit of mankind?" In answering this question, before the quoted passage, Adams says that the United States has held out the hand of friendship and generous reciprocity to other nations and spoken, "often to heedless and often to disdainful ears," the language of equal justice. The United States, he claims, "without a single exception," has "abstained from interference in the concerns of others" (*A* 28–29). Adams wrote these lines after he had successfully negotiated the Transcontinental Treaty with Spain. In the course of these negotiations, he had ruthlessly exploited Spanish weakness, conspired in before and condoned after the fact Andrew Jackson's illegal invasion of Spanish territory (the Floridas), defended Jackson's judicial murder of two British subjects, one a seventy-year-old man, lied to the Spanish and other foreign governments, and deliberately misled Congress and the American people. At a minimum, we would have to say that in his conduct as secretary of state, particularly in his negotiating of the Transcontinental Treaty, Adams had narrowed as much as one could the difference between "those allowances necessary to reconcile the rigor of principle with the resistance of practice, and the total sacrifice of all principle."

Typically, such fussiness about principle in foreign affairs would be dismissed with a knowing remark about raison d'état, the principle "that the well-being of the state justified whatever means were employed to further it."[10] Moreover, an increase in the security and power of the United States was an increase in the chance that liberty would thrive and conquer the world because the United States was the embodiment of the new order of liberty. Surely, this justified Adams's harsh but necessary conduct—one is tempted to call it Machiavellian—in dealing with the Spanish question. There are two reasons why Adams could not use the ends he sought to justify the actions he took to attain them. First, Adams believed that the American Revolution had intended to establish a new order of the ages. Part of that order was a repudiation of the force and fraud characteristic of European politics. Asserting raison d'état would have obliterated that difference and diminished the Revolution; it would, we might say, have given the Revolution an empire at the cost of its soul. Second, because Adams believed men ignorant, he could not have known that he would achieve the good end he sought. His efforts might have achieved only something evil. If progress is inevitable, we might be justified in the most unscrupulous actions. History will ensure that good comes from evil means. But as we have seen, Adams's faith in moral progress was not that absolute. Nor should it have been. The Transcontinental Treaty opened vast new territories to slavery. Indeed, Adams knew that he was working at least in part for what he would later come to call the slave power, since the agitation over the admission of Missouri as a slave state and the resulting Missouri Compromise occurred as the treaty negotiations concluded and the treaty was ratified.

In defense of Adams and other statesmen, we might recall that those situations which require the sacrifice of principle occur in a world not of their making, a world where "evils physical, moral, intellectual beset [their] path from the cradle to the grave." In such a world, the difference between adherence to principle and its sacrifice may be measured by nothing more than the reluctance to sacrifice principle and the determination to set right what turns out, even unavoidably, wrong. It is in this light that we should understand Adams's return to the House of Representatives and his work there in the antislavery cause, where death took him, in the midst of this work, ever faithful to his duty, his principles, and his country.

Notes

The author wishes to thank Irma Fink and Susan Miller, Interlibrary Loan Department, Knox Library, without whose diligence this chapter could not have been completed.

1. The embargo (1807–1809) forbad virtually all commerce between the United States and other countries. Jefferson proposed this measure, and Congress passed it into law as a means of pressuring Britain and France into respecting American neutral shipping rights. The embargo was particularly injurious to those, including Adams's constituents in Massachusetts, whose living depended on shipping and trade.

2. Quotations from and references to Adams's works are cited in the text using the following abbreviations:

A: *An Address Delivered at the Request of a Committee of the Citizens of Washington, on the Occasion of Reading the Declaration of Independence on the Fourth of July, 1821* (Washington, D.C.: David and Force, 1821).

LRO: *Lectures on Rhetoric and Oratory*, A Facsimile Reproduction with an Introduction by Charlotte Downey (Delmar, N.Y.: Scholar's Facsimiles and Reprints, [1810] 1997).

O: *An Oration Delivered before the Inhabitants of the Town of Newburyport at Their Request on the Sixty-First Anniversary of the Declaration of Independence, July 4, 1837* (Newburyport, Mass.: Charles Whipple, 1837).

SC: "Society and Civilization," *The American Review: A Whig Journal of Politics, Literature, Art and Science*, vol. 2 (New York: George H. Colton, 1845), 80–89.

SW: *The Selected Writings of John and John Quincy Adams*, ed. Adrienne Koch and William Peden (New York: Alfred A. Knopf, 1946).

TSC: *The Social Compact Exemplified in the Constitution of the Commonwealth of Massachusetts* (Providence, R.I.: Knowles and Vose, Printers, 1842).

W: *The Writings of John Quincy Adams*, ed. Worthington Chauncey Ford, 7 vols. (New York: Greenwood Press, [1916] 1968).

3. *TSC* 12; *W* 7:441; and "Oration at Plymouth, December 22, 1802, in Commemoration of the Landing of the Pilgrims," www.worldwideschool.org/library/books/hst/northamerican/OrationatPlymouth/Chap1.html (accessed February 15, 2001), hereafter cited in the notes as "Oration at Plymouth."

4. *O* 26, 27 (emphasis in the original), 24. Adams made the same point about the limits on the power of the people early in his career (*W* 1:70–71).

5. *SC* 81; *O* 58–59; and "Argument of John Quincy Adams Before the Supreme Court of the United States in the case of the United States, Appellants, vs. Cinque, and others, Africans, captured in the schooner Amistad, by Lieut. Gedney, Delivered on the 24th of February and 1st of March 1841," www.multied.com/amistad/amistad.html (accessed June 5, 2001).

6. In his Inaugural Address, when giving a catalogue of advances since the Revolution, Adams remarked that "the dominion of man over physical nature has been extended by the invention of our artists [technologists]" (*SW* 354).

7. "Oration at Plymouth."

8. *W* 6:5–8; *SW* 342; and John Quincy Adams to Charles W. Upham, February 2, 1837, "Ten Unpublished Letters of John Quincy Adams, 1796–1837," *Huntington Library Quarterly* 4 (April 1941): 382.

9. *An Oration Addressed to the Citizens of the Town of Quincy on the Fourth of July, 1831* (Boston: Richardson, Lord and Holbrook, 1831), 27.

10. Henry Kissinger, *Diplomacy* (New York: Simon and Schuster, 1994), 58.

Chapter 15

Union and Liberty:
The Political Thought of Daniel Webster

Sean Mattie

One of the greatest rhetoricians in American history, Daniel Webster (1782–1852) dedicated his public speeches principally to the cause of union. His eloquent defense of the goodness and justice of union was vital to preserving the Republic during the crucial era between the American Founding and the Civil War. Webster, along with Henry Clay and John C. Calhoun, was of the second generation of national statesmen, following Founders like George Washington, Alexander Hamilton, John Adams, and Thomas Jefferson. The demise of these national heroes was not only a profound loss to the country but also raised questions of the character of the Union without them. Webster recognized and responded to these concerns in commemorative addresses that affirmed the Union by casting it as a sacred inheritance from these forefathers, to be faithfully maintained by the next generation and transmitted to posterity.

However, Webster saw that the political events of his era also were crises in the Union. For example, the nullification dispute of the 1830s and the debate over the extension of slavery as the nation expanded westward threatened to substitute an attachment to state or sectional interest for national allegiance to the Constitution and a national sentiment of brotherhood. In response to these crises, Webster used his position in office, particularly as a U.S. senator, to repudiate such threats politically. His addresses on these occasions were of a piece with his oratory and political thought as a whole; they all contended for union against any opinion or action that would lead to dissolution.

Though union was the general theme of Webster's thought and rhetoric, three particular aspects of it stand out. The first is history. Webster argued that America in his own era should have continued as a union because it had already been united as a people since the very colonization of America. The elements of this fundamental tradition were not merely a common language or religion, but, more important, a common politics. Webster argued that free government in the states, the formation of national councils, the common wars for freedom and self-government, and the country's long-standing reverence for George Washington—who symbolized war for republicanism as well as republican government in peace—all constituted a tradition of union in America.

In addition to this historical or tradition-based argument, Webster also defended national union in strictly constitutional terms. His analysis of the Constitution focused on the letter of that law and the fundamental principles that inform the Constitution's text. Literally and by reasonable inference, he argued, the Constitution is the supreme law in American politics; it is the American people's authoritative establishment of national union.

A third aspect of Webster's case for union is the importance of statesmanship. In his rhetoric, he invoked past examples in the American Founders, and Webster was himself an example of statesmanship; in office, he acted decisively to preserve national unity and harmony during periods of crisis. As an implied theme in his thought, statesmanship for union linked the historical case for union with the legal or constitutional argument, and implicitly called for future statesmen to serve the cause of union as the Founders and Webster himself did.

Webster's Historical Case for Union: Republican Tradition

The first great aspect of Webster's argument for union is history or tradition. He took this approach principally and in the most detail in his commemorative orations, such as his addresses on the bicentennial of the Pilgrims' landing in Plymouth and on the passing of John Adams and Thomas Jefferson in 1826. Webster's intention on these occasions was to make clear to Americans the strength of union as a grand tradition and thus to persuade them to revere and to preserve this tradition. His generation of Americans should support union because it had always been integral to their identity. All their ancestors had been essentially united as a people not only since the political Founding in 1787 but also from the very settlement of America. Those settlers were one even before arriving in America. As colonists from England, they brought with them not only the common English language—including its arts, sciences, and literature—but also the "intellectual and moral culture of Europe" (*GS* 147).[1] Though societal American traditions had contributed powerfully to a sense of unity, the most important tradition—because it was the most unifying—in America was a common politics. Through local and national institutions, in common struggle, and embodied in George Washington, America had always been united under republican government.

Equality

Webster noted that the tradition of free government began in the colonial period. When the colonists settled in America, they abandoned the political institution that powerfully formed their own mother country—feudalism. In contrast to England, there were no tenants or landlords in America. To Webster, the crucial first act of the settlers, particularly in New England, was to legislate to affirm the "comparative equality" of wealth that originally existed. The early colonial laws about inheritance and descent were carried over from England, but the American colonists abolished—if they ever even recognized—primogeniture, entail, and any other legal institutions that had tied up inherited property (*WS* 1:210–11). In addition to the rough equality of property that existed from the original settlements, Americans shared adherence to equality under law or to "equal political rights." The colonists brought with them trial by jury, the right of habeas corpus, and the common law to regulate the "social and personal relations" among persons. These legal protections secured Americans against tyranny in the enjoyment of their liberty and property, regulating and enabling "profitable commerce, carried on by men who know that the profits of their hardy enterprise . . . are their own." The common result in America was "diffused wealth" and a great degree of "personal independence"—further conditions favorable to republican government (*GS* 146–47).

Representative Institutions

From the colonial settlement, Americans were united on the principle of local, elective legislatures, another element in the republican tradition. Webster argued that popular representation in assemblies complemented the rights of "person, property, and reputation" enjoyed under law. He recalled to Americans that ancestors in New England insisted on the right of passing local laws and on local administration in their original charters from the Crown. The principle of such self-government was "the acquiescence of the minority in the will of the majority, properly expressed," that is, expressed in accord with fundamental and equal political rights. Webster declared that popular government, as it existed in states, counties, districts, townships, and parishes prepared Americans to observe the same principles when they established national institutions (*GS* 146, 148).

Since the national character of union was at the heart of Webster's political thought, he gave special attention in his narrative to the Continental Congress, which first drew together colonies or states in a body politic. He argued that by 1774, "the affairs of the colonies urgently demanded united counsels throughout the country" in order to address a rupture with Great Britain that seemed inevitable (*WS* 1:298). Thus, the Continental Congress was formed out of delegates from the states and included the most illustrious men in the nation, like John Adams, Thomas Jefferson, and Richard Henry Lee. This elective assembly adopted resolutions on the common rights of the states, on the violations of those rights by England, and on remedies. Most of all, the Continental Congress reinforced and advanced national self-government and union by its 1776 resolution for American independence. Of the importance of the Continental Congress in forming a distinctly national citizenship, Webster asked rhetorically:

> Are there young men ... who wish to learn and to imitate the spirit of their ancestors, who wish to live and breathe in that spirit, who desire that every pulsation of their hearts and every aspiration of their ambition shall be American and nothing but American? Let them master the contents of the immortal papers of the [Continental] Congress, and fully imbue themselves with their sentiments. (*WS* 13:489–90)

War

To Webster, union and American nationality were forged in common struggle as well. He reminded the public that during the first century of their existence in America, the colonies not only had to wrest a living from bare nature but also had to cooperate to defend themselves against human threats. The colonists fought together against both the Indians and the French during the eighteenth century. Of course, the most important struggle shared by Americans was not only for existence but also for independence. Webster declared that the "great and common cause of the Revolution" united the Americans by "new links of brotherhood." In his 1843 dedication of the monument commemorating the Battle of Bunker Hill—the first great battle of the Revolution—he likened the edifice to a national shrine built to symbolize a "glorious ancestry of liberty." The Bunker Hill Monument embodied and invoked in the audience a "nationality of sentiment" and a "patriotic feeling" more powerful than local attachment. The blood shed in the common cause of the Revolution powerfully united Americans across generations and regions, as the dedication drew together Americans from across the nation (*GS* 150).

Washington

The American tradition of self-government—both revolutionary independence and republican rule—was personified in George Washington. Americans had long been united in their reverence for Washington, and Webster described him as the quintessential American—born on American soil of American parents, instructed in the institutions of public education, growing to manhood as the nation grew, and participating in the War of Independence. Webster also celebrated the surpassing excellence of Washington in war and in peace—his military leadership during the Revolutionary War and the "outspread banner of his political and constitutional principles" during the Founding of the Constitution. Union in America would not have been possible without the "uprightness . . . solidity . . . [and] durability" of Washington—the firmness and purity of his public virtues. However, it could not persist without the country's common reverence for Washington and his counsel to uphold the "sacred ties" of national union. Washington symbolized the continuity of the Union: "He is still upholding, by his precepts, his exhortations, and his example, the importance and the value of this Union of the States. In that respect he works now, and will work ever, so long as his memory shall not be effaced from the records of mankind" (*WS* 13:394). In his rhetoric, Webster sought to identify Washington with the Union in order to tie the American people to both. He declared that the "fame and character" of Washington was, like republican union, the common possession of all good persons in America. Although the "colossal grandeur" of Washington towered high, it bound and ennobled Americans as citizens; Americans' veneration for Washington proved them "worthy of such a countryman." The republican virtue of Washington was a standard of human greatness, justice, and happiness that—like republican union—was made available to Americans as their special inheritance:

> To him who denies or doubts whether our fervid liberty can be combined with law, with order, with the security of property; . . . to him who denies that our forms of government are capable of producing exaltation of soul, and the passion of true glory; to him who denies that we have contributed any thing to the stock of great lessons and great examples;—to all these I reply by pointing to Washington! (*GS* 150)

Webster's Constitutional Case for Union: The Letter and Spirit of the Law

The second great aspect of Webster's argument for union was his explication of the Constitution as the authoritative form of American nationality. His defense of the Constitution was so fundamental and systematic that only *The Federalist* exceeds it. Like Publius, Webster was a partisan of the Constitution; he made his theoretical argument not merely for the sake of theory but for the sake of good government during a time of decision. The occasions that prompted Webster's constitutional analysis were the debates in the Senate in the 1830s about the national tariff and the uniform collection of duties in the states. At these times, he faced not only political opposition to the tariff (coming from South Carolina) but also a *doctrine* of nullification, which held that sovereign individual states may constitutionally negate particular acts of the federal government. Webster recognized that nullification not only frustrated particular exercises of federal power; it also profoundly threatened the authority of national government and the existence of the Union. In order to repudiate this doctrine, he addressed the "true principles of the Constitution"—the basis of sovereignty and the extent of federal and of state power (*PDW*

1:326). In this way, he complemented his historical case for political union with an account based on the letter and spirit of the fundamental law of the land.

The Sovereignty of the People

To Webster, the Constitution was founded on the sovereignty of the American people as a whole, that is, as a nation. The rival theory of sovereignty that Webster faced was that expressed by John Calhoun in his 1833 resolution submitted to the Senate: "The *people of the several states* composing these United States are united as parties to a constitutional *compact*, to which the *people of each state* acceded as a *separate sovereign community*, each binding itself by its own particular sovereignty . . . [and] the people of the several states . . . as members thereof, [retain] their sovereignty" (*WS* 6:181–82, emphasis added). Webster's reply was that American nationality and the sovereignty of the united American people were not imaginary or wishful, as Calhoun contended, but instead the only rightful and intelligible basis of American politics. Building on his historical account of American political unity, he declared: "In 1789, and before this Constitution was adopted, the United States had already been in a union, more or less close, for fifteen years." As evidence of political union for national purposes, Webster cited the Continental Congress of 1774 as well as the Articles of Confederation of 1781. Thus, by the time of the establishment of the Constitution, the "people of the United States" were a real political agent, capable of acting with a single will (*WS* 6:187).

To Webster, the adoption of the Constitution by the people as a whole rested equally on an American political axiom as on the historical experience of unity. As he declared: "With us, all power is with the people." They alone are "sovereign" and may "erect what governments they please, and confer on them such powers as they please" (*WS* 6:202). Popular sovereignty entails not only that the Constitution but also the state governments are "made for the people, made by the people, and answerable to the people" (*PDW* 1:330). Webster considered Calhoun's state-oriented doctrine as a proposition of the "sovereignty of government" and declared that it was "an idea belonging to the other side of the Atlantic"—that is, a feudal notion (*WS* 6:202).[2]

As evidence of the sovereignty of the American people as a whole, Webster cited the "direct relations" between the national government and individuals that the Constitution created. One example was the constitutional provision for punishment of individuals for treason and any other crimes committed against the United States. The Constitution also enabled Congress to tax individuals, as by excises. In addition, Congress's power to organize and call forth the militia allowed it to demand military service from individuals. Furthermore, there were direct obligations of the federal government to each citizen of the country; protection was one such duty, and the constitutional power of making war enabled the government to carry it out. Webster asserted that "no closer relations can exist between individuals and any government" than are demonstrated by these clear constitutional powers and obligations (*WS* 6:203).

The right to establish government is of a piece with the right to abolish government—that is, the right to revolution. Reiterating one of the central principles of government in the Declaration of Independence, he held that "civil institutions are established for the public benefit" and that when they cease to answer to this purpose they may be changed. However, the right to revolt or to overthrow government belongs to the people. Webster declares that the "people may, if they choose, throw off any government when it becomes oppressive and intolerable, and erect a better in its stead." Nonetheless, Webster was no revolutionary; his rather abstract support for the people's right to revolt should be viewed in light of his passionate support for the Constitution and union, and in the context of his theoretical defense of it. Webster's rhetorical aim was to defeat a doctrine of state sovereignty—and thereby save union under the Constitution—with an argument about the profound and undeniable sovereignty of the American people (*PDW* 1:329).

The Authority of the Constitution

In Webster's rhetoric, the basic authority of the Constitution follows logically from the sovereignty of the people and from the very words of the Constitution. Referring to the preamble to the Constitution, he argued in emphatic terms that the people of the United States ordained and established a "*constitution*." In its "plain sense and unsophisticated meaning" a constitution is "fundamental law" about "those primary rules" concerning "the very being of the political society, the form of government, and the manner in which power is to be exercised (*WS* 6:185, 186, 199). The political occasion of repudiating the doctrine of state sovereignty prompted Webster to distinguish the Constitution from "a league, compact, or confederacy," to which Senator Calhoun likened it. Webster admitted that under any of these latter alliances, individual sovereigns were bound to each other at will and only temporarily. All were subject to no superior power; each could and had to judge for itself when the terms of the alliance have been violated and thus when the alliance became void.

Webster acknowledged that "the old [Articles of] Confederation [had been] expressly called a *league*," into which "the States, as States, severally entered." He observed, however, that the general government under the Articles had been little more than "a name," as it had been ultimately powerless over matters of revenue and war. Thus, the country sought to quit this "feeble and disgraceful" political condition by deliberately constituting a government with sufficient power for national purposes. Webster underscored this aspect of authority in arguing the difference in principle between a government and a league or compact. The former is distinct as "a body politic," with "powers and faculties to execute its own purposes" (*WS* 6:199, 200).

The American Constitution shared with a league or compact a foundation of consent. But by its nature, the Constitution, once founded, assumed a standing and an authority beyond its temporal origin in consent. As Webster argued: "The Constitution . . . is not a contract, but the result of a contract. . . . When the people agree to erect a government, and actually erect it, the thing is done . . . [t]he compact is executed. . . . Henceforth, the fruit of the agreement exists, but the agreement itself is merged in its own accomplishment." Although our focus here is his ontological argument about the Constitution's *authority*, we observe also that Webster discussed similarly the Constitution's *existence*. The Constitution *is* "perpetual and immortal," and it is fundamentally this way because it "regards itself" so (*WS* 6:200, 211).

Constitutional language as well as political principle declared the Constitution the supreme law of the land. Similarly, the Constitution expressly and in principle grants to the national government incontestable national powers. Webster explained that upon entering the Union, the people of each state surrendered part of their own power to make laws for themselves in order that for "common objects" and through "common government" they should have had a part in making laws for other states. Though the powers of the national government are enumerated and specified, those powers that are listed are supreme and exclusive. Webster argued that the national government's powers of making war and concluding peace, of regulating commerce, and of laying duties represent the decision of a united, sovereign people about the responsibilities of the national government; government's exercise of these powers reinforced the unity that enabled that original decision (*WS* 6:195, 205).

Although there were persons who wished that the states had been left without restraint, the "people of the United States" chose to "impose control" on the power of the states. The Constitution, in text and in principle, places "certain salutary restraints" on the states for national purposes.[3] Webster cited these express prohibitions as a testament against the simple sovereignty of the states. "To make war . . . is an exercise of sovereignty; but the Constitution declares that no state shall make war. To coin money is another exercise of sovereign power, but no state is at liberty to coin money. . . . [T]he Constitution says that no sovereign state shall be so sovereign as to make a treaty" (*PDW* 1:330–31). Furthermore, he argued, the Constitution not only gives Congress power to lay and collect imposts "*without the consent of particular states*" but also expressly prohibits the states from exercising this power (*WS* 6:194, italics in original).

In his career as legal counsel, Webster also invoked the express limitations on state governments in order to argue for the supremacy of the Constitution and the superior power of the national government in national matters. In *Trustees of Dartmouth College v. Woodward* (1819), he persuaded the Supreme Court that the constitutional prohibition on state interference with contracts rendered void a New Hampshire law altering the charter of the college. In *McCulloch v. Maryland* (1819) and *Gibbons v. Ogden* (1824), Webster argued successfully that Congress's constitutional powers over national fiscal operations and over interstate commerce, respectively, are supreme; this supremacy thereby nullified any actions by the state legislatures that impeded these national functions.

Webster acknowledged that though the Constitution limits the powers of the national government by enumerating them, ambiguity and controversy will arise in particular cases concerning the extent of those powers. Indeed, the fundamental theoretical and practical question in the nullification debate was who is to construe finally the Constitution with respect to the power of the national government (*WS* 6:212). Webster replied by arguing that the sovereign people established the national government so as to have this matter decided by "the government itself, in its appropriate branches" (*PDW* 1:340). First, Congress, not the states, must be the judge of the extent of its powers ordinarily and regularly in order for Congress to exercise federal powers at all (*WS* 6:214). Second, the Constitution itself not only contains no particular provision empowering states to pass judgment on national laws, but it particularly declares the states' inability to do so. Webster argued this point by citing Article VI of the Constitution, which holds that "the Constitution, and the laws of the United States which shall be made in pursuance thereof" shall be the "supreme law of the land," anything in the constitution or laws of any state to the contrary notwithstanding (*PDW* 1:341).

Webster argued that the American people and their Constitution grant to the federal judiciary the right and the duty to determine the extent of Congress's enumerated powers—that is, the right and the duty to interpret the Constitution. To support his position, he cited Article III, section 2 of the Constitution, which declares that "the judicial power shall extend to all cases in law or equity arising under the Constitution, laws of the United States, and treaties." Echoing Chief Justice John Marshall's reading of this clause in *Marbury v. Madison* (1803), Webster argued that: "If a case arises under the Constitution, that is, if a case arises depending on the construction of the Constitution, the judicial power of the United States extends to it. . . . No language could provide with more effect and precision . . . for subjecting constitutional decisions to the Supreme Court" (*WS* 6:215). Webster considered the Supreme Court the final arbiter about the limits of congressional power and about restrictions on state governments under the Constitution. The Constitution's supremacy clause and its provision for the national judicial power were powerful evidence that the American people established a "government" competent to exercise power. Had these clauses not been included in the Constitution, or if they were to be ignored by the states, the country would have in effect been a mere "confederation" (*PDW* 1:341).

The Meaning of Nullification

Nullification entailed a regression to confederation and thus a weakening of political union. By its intention, nullification was to begin with each state's "lawfully [deciding] . . . for itself" whether, in a given case, an act of the federal government "transcends" federal authority. If a state were to decide affirmatively, its legislature then would be able to exercise a right "to interfere" with federal laws by arresting the operation of them (*PDW* 1:327). Webster observed that the operation of nullification was intended by its advocates to do no injury to the regular process of the national government. According to them, this "right of resistance" is constitutional—it exists "under the Constitution, and in conformity with its provisions" (*PDW* 1:329; *WS* 6:211). In contrast, Webster argued that nullification was profoundly unconstitutional in principle and would be widely pernicious in practice.

Insofar as nullification, with its supporting doctrine of state sovereignty, was intended to be a principle of government under union, it was incoherent—a principle of "anarchy," not of government. The adoption of the Constitution by the American people proceeded from—and authoritatively reinforced—a basic consensus about national ends and the means for government to attain them. Nullification, a would-be rule for the national government, fundamentally denies this original and ongoing consensus that makes government possible. In one of his several statements on the absurdity of this stance, Webster noted: "[C]ould any thing have been more preposterous, than to make a government for the whole Union, and yet leave its powers subject, not to one interpretation, but to thirteen or twenty-four interpretations? . . . Would any thing, with such a principle in it, or rather with such a destitution of all principle, be fit to be called a government?" Were there to be no consensus among the states about national matters, and no authoritative way to conclude disputes about such matters, then "the whole Union" would be "a rope of sand" (*PDW* 1:332, 342).

By its language and principles, the Constitution is the supreme and fundamental law that commands allegiance. Thus, the Constitution "does not provide for events which must be preceded by its own destruction"; the proposition of a constitutional right to "interrupt the administration of the Constitution itself" is nonsensical (*WS* 6:193; *PDW* 1:329). Webster argued that the right to resist government, for example, by nullification, could not be a right within government but one against government—the right to revolution. This concept had been recognized and invoked in America, as in the Declaration of Independence. There is in man an "inalienable right" to resist oppression, and in "extreme cases" and with "justifiable cause," a people may "relieve themselves from a tyrannical government." The nullification doctrine notwithstanding, there is and could be no middle condition between "submission to the laws, when regularly pronounced constitutional" and "open resistance, which is revolution or rebellion" (*PDW* 1:328–29).

As nullification is in theory revolutionary, so the practice of nullification in the Union would be broadly subversive. Were the legislature of South Carolina, for example, to nullify a federal tariff law, it would defy Congress and the national government in general. Accordingly, the collector of federal duties in that state would be prevented by "the State authorities" from both collecting payment and seizing the goods in lieu of payment. Then the federal marshal with his posse would come on the authority of the national government to aid the collector, while the militia of the state would be called out to sustain the nullification act of the legislature. "Direct collision . . . between force and force" will be the unavoidable result of a state's self-chosen means of redressing laws that it believes to be unconstitutional (*PDW* 1:344). Nullification, built on a premise incompatible with political union, would lead in practice to violent discord.

"Secession" from the Union is a logical extension of the doctrine of nullification; its practical operation would be similarly anarchic and belligerent. To argue this point, Webster supposed that, under the doctrine of secession, one state might hold unconstitutional a law laying duties on imports and respond by withdrawing from the Union; were it to succeed practically, its example might inspire other states. Yet, withdrawal by any state or states would not likely be peaceful for the Union or the seceding parties. For example, a state in its self-styled sovereignty might easily conclude for itself that revenue collected in the past by the national government was "taken out of the pockets of [its] citizens illegally." Accordingly, the state might demand its own form of redress, in the form of "reprisals" and "impositions on the commerce" of other states in the Union; it might resort to "foreign alliances against them" and even to "open war." In such a situation of anarchic hostility, there would arise inevitably a crucial dispute about possession of and responsibility for the national government's concerns. Webster asked, "Whose will be the army? Whose the navy? Who will pay the debts? Who fulfill the public treaties? . . . Who retain the public property?" These problems would be insoluble under disunion, and they illustrate the absurdity of secession in principle and the harm of secession in practice (*WS* 6:191–92).

Webster added that if government under nullification and secession were not to lapse into anarchy, the doctrines would still render the Union oligarchic. Nullification admitted the possibility that what is federal law in one state would not be law in another. Yet, the Constitution was "received as a whole, and for the whole country," and thus if its laws could not be executed "everywhere," they could not for long be executed "anywhere." Therefore, if the resistance of one state to a legislative act were to force a repeal in all the Union, then the political equality of the states—their equal subjection to a national law and their equal participation in governing— would be likewise destroyed. To Webster, the argument for nullification as a right of an individual state was ultimately an argument for rule by an individual state: "Every argument which refers the constitutionality of acts of Congress to State decision appeals from the majority to the minority; it appeals from the common interest to a particular interest; . . . and endeavors to supersede the judgment of the whole by the judgment of a part" (*WS* 6:194, 219). Webster repudiated the nullification doctrine so fundamentally and precisely because he recognized, in an equally fundamental and precise way, the political structure of national union. The Constitution, established by the authority of the unified American people, affirms and guides both that authority and that unity. It renders American national life a matter not of historical drift but of the deliberate action of the American people and their representatives.

Statesmanship in Webster's Case for Union

As we have seen, one aspect of Webster's understanding of union is that history and tradition give strength to union in America. As he declared: "Every year of its duration has teemed with fresh proofs of its utility and its blessings; and although our territory has stretched out wider and wider, and our population spread farther and farther, they have not outrun its protection or its benefits. It has been to us all a copious fountain of national, social, and personal happiness." Webster argued also that the Constitution, by its principles and plain language, embodied the authoritative character of national union. However, even though history and the Constitution supported it, and its advantages had been quite evident, union in America was not self-sufficient, in the sense that it would continue irrespective of particular human opinion or human action (*PDW* 1:347).

In Webster's public speeches, union was the cause of human happiness in America, but politics was the cause of union. He remarked that Americans enjoyed not only a vast bounty of natural resources but also such benefits of civilization as "society," "knowledge," "morals," and "religious culture." But these good things could not have existed except under politics—that is, under "wise institutions and a free government." Such institutions and such government, in turn, required that citizens hold a strong affection for it and resolve to maintain and perpetuate it. The complement and at times the necessary condition for citizens' support of political union was action by statesmen on behalf of union. Thus, the third great aspect of Webster's argument for union was such statesmanship, especially in times of crisis (*WS* 1:323).

The Legacy of Statesmanship

Webster's rhetoric praises the first acts of statesmanship for union, during the era of the Revolutionary War and the Founding of the Constitution. The first action on behalf of political union in America was the assembly of the Continental Congress in 1774, "at which the union of these states commenced." The most important decision taken by the Congress on behalf of the Union was to declare independence from Great Britain. In his eulogy of John Adams and Thomas Jefferson, both delegates to the Congress, Webster imagined the words said by the former to steel the will of that assembly: "Do we mean to submit, and consent that we ourselves shall be ground to powder, and our country and its rights trodden down in the dust? . . . The war, then, must go on. . . . And if the war must go on, why put off any longer the Declaration of Independence?" (*WS* 1:310).

The next great test for union, after the Revolutionary War, was the adoption and the administration of the Constitution. Webster invoked Washington—the embodiment of the Union —as the statesman of this pivotal time, both because Washington presided over the Constitutional Convention in 1787 and because Washington as president inaugurated the first national administration under the Constitution. In 1789, after the ratification of the Constitution but before any attempt to carry it out, "all hearts and all hopes were concentrated" on the political fate of the country. The statesmanship of Washington was to place his immense popular authority in the service of the Constitution: "I see the august form . . . the serene face of Washington, I observe his reverent manner when he rises in the presence of countless multitudes, and, looking up with religious awe to heaven, solemnly swears . . . that he will support the Constitution of his country, so help him God!" From this action, America had a "country," a "union," and a "government able to keep us together" (*WS* 13:487).

Webster himself took up this legacy of statesmanship for union once he began his career in public life. He gave many of his great orations about American history, particularly the history of union in America, on commemorative occasions: the Plymouth Oration (1820) on the bicentennial of the Pilgrims' landing; the eulogy for John Adams and Thomas Jefferson, delivered shortly after their passing on July 4, 1826; and the Bunker Hill Monument Address, issued on its completion in 1843. At these times for public reflection, Webster affirmed and enlightened Americans' patriotism and attachment to political union. However, some of his most eloquent arguments on behalf of union came within political debate, in times of serious national crisis. During two crises—the debate over nullification in the 1830s, and the debate over slavery and the Southwest territories in 1850—Webster's rhetoric was not merely an abstract exposition of the primacy of the Constitution or the perpetuity of national union. On these occasions, his political speech *caused* the primacy of the Constitution and perpetuated national union—that is, Webster's speech was itself statesmanship.

Statesmanship and Nullification

The advocates of nullification presented the doctrine to legitimize and to give a high tone to South Carolina's opposition to the 1828 federal tariff in 1830 and again in 1833. Webster's responses, including his theoretical defense of the Constitution as fundamental law, are contained in his famous Second Reply to Hayne (January 26–27, 1830) and the lesser known but more rigorous speech delivered in reply to Calhoun on February 16, 1833 ("The Constitution Not a Compact between Sovereign States"). Though conceptual brilliance was their greatest merit, the speeches also contain a strong historical case for American union and impassioned words on behalf of national harmony.

In this vein, Webster addressed the policy that seemed to divide the Union—the protective federal tariff, of which the 1828 law was only the latest enactment. He observed that the records of the House of Representatives in the First Congress under the Constitution showed strong support for "so laying the imposts as to encourage manufactures" (*WS* 6:232). Following the War of 1812 and the general peace in Europe as of 1815, the United States undertook more seriously a policy of internal improvements. Central to it was the tariff of 1816, enacted expressly to protect domestic manufactures and to fund national projects abetting internal commerce. Webster declared that the record in Congress showed that "leading and distinguished gentlemen from South Carolina" supported the tariff that year and again in 1824 (*PDW* 1:314).

Although the protective tariff did not have the same standing as the Constitution in Webster's thought, it had been enacted and reenacted under the authority granted to Congress by the Constitution. He added that it had had broad national support and had, as a basic national policy, united the interests of the states in the first decades of the nation's existence. If the operation of the tariff had injured the interest of South Carolina by 1828, this matter could have been dealt with politically, and in a manner consistent with the Constitution's procedures. However, Calhoun's advocacy of nullification had confounded the matter of the tariff by rendering opposition to it a challenge to the Constitution itself. Part of Webster's statesmanship for union was to call attention to that fundamental threat: "[A]fter the passing of the [tariff] law of 1828, despairing then of being able to abolish the system of protection, political men went forth among the people [in South Carolina] and set up the doctrine that the system was unconstitutional. . . . The people did then receive the doctrine . . . [whereas] they had never entertained it before. Nullification influenced the "political sentiments" of the American people and the "opinions" they held to be authoritative. In repudiating nullification, Webster sought to shape those sentiments and opinions in favor of union and to reinforce the basic "affection and harmony" among the parts of the country during a national crisis (*WS* 6:236–37).

In the course of his reply to nullification, Webster argued for the justice of political union. The proponents of nullification believed that they championed the "rights of minorities"—that is, of a state or a few states—as against the oppressive power of "absolute majorities." To these advocates, the enemy was majority tyranny enabled by the national government and, implicitly, by political union itself.[4] The political interest behind nullification challenged the authority of Congress on the grounds that that national power may benefit not the whole nation but only the largest part, that is, constitutional authority would be used for injustice. Webster replied by arguing that the very design for power under the Constitution serves to limit its exercise and to prevent injury to minority interests (*WS* 6:219).

The Constitution provided for government that was authoritative yet safe, that is, nondespotic. In his speeches on nullification, Webster declared that the American people created a limited government, restricting its powers to those specifically granted in the Constitution and reserving "all the rest" to "the State governments" or "the people themselves" (*PDW* 1:330). The national government was also safe by being republican. Republican or popular government rests on two principles or propositions. The first is that there is a "common interest" among those "over whom the government extends." Given this basic community, the government of it may provide for the defense and good of "the whole" without "injustice or oppression" to parts. The second principle or proposition of popular government is that "the representatives of the people," as well as the people themselves, are not corrupt and thus "may be trusted" to exercise power consistently with the common good. On this twin basis of union and security lay the "practicability" of the Constitution as well as of "all free governments" (*WS* 6:222).

Invoking the same fundamental notions to which he appealed in rejecting the proposition of state sovereignty, he declared that the national government ought to be and is limited by its "responsibility to the people" (*PDW* 1:341). In particular, members of Congress are "agents" of the people—"elected by them, answerable to them, and liable to be displaced or superseded at their pleasure." The logical extension of radical distrust of the national government under the Constitution is radical distrust of the people, or of popular government.[5] In contrast, Webster argued that the national government deserved both authority and the "confidence of the people" in that authority, because by the design of the Constitution that government was both republican and responsible to the governed.

Thus, Webster contended, the interest of South Carolina would not have been easily sacrificed to the interest of numerical majority; that is, majority tyranny is impeded by the Constitution. His rhetoric in the nullification dispute attempted to harmonize all interests in the country and to reconcile them to the national government by showing that that government aimed by design at the common good.

Statesmanship and Slavery

By the end of Webster's years in public life, the Union was again brought to a crisis by the matter of slavery. The question of slavery's place in the Union became politically urgent through a dramatic series of events in America's national life: the admission of Texas as a slave state in 1845; the Mexican War of 1846–48; and the United States's acquisition of vast territory in the southwest by the Treaty of Guadalupe Hidalgo. Between 1848 and 1850, Congress was faced with deciding how the territories should be governed, particularly regarding the recognition or prohibition of slavery. In this turbulent period, strong and opposite interests regarding slavery pressed upon Congress for advantage, seriously threatening national unity; there was even talk of secession. Webster's response to this crisis illustrated his own principle of statesmanship for union. In his public speeches, he sought to preserve the moral substance of the Union by denouncing slavery in principle and arguing against its extension to the territories. Yet, greater than even the evil of slavery was the goodness of political union, and Webster sought in his rhetoric to reconcile all interests to the national government and the Constitution.

To assess the status that slavery had or should have had in the Union, Webster argued from both principle and history. He himself had declared slavery—in the form of the African slave trade—to be "odious and abominable," and an offense against "humanity" and "justice" (*WS* 1:221). Webster observed that in the American Founding the people of both North and South also recognized slavery as a "moral and political evil." Though some persons then condemned it as inhuman and cruel and a deprivation of liberty, the more common objection against slavery, according to Webster, was that it caused labor to be viewed as degrading to a free man. Accordingly, the policy around which Americans had been united from the Founding was containment. As Webster declared: "When this Constitution was adopted, nobody looked for any new acquisition of territory to be formed into slave-holding states" (*PDW* 2:522; *WS* 10:41–43). Webster himself publicly stood for containment "from the year 1837" and pledged it "again and again" through 1850 (*PDW* 2:539; *WS* 3:291, 10:44).

Webster's assessment of slavery in the Union was also informed by the Constitution. On the one hand, the Constitution clearly allowed congressional prohibition of the practice of slavery in the territories. Congress had full power over slavery and was able to establish any government and laws that it saw fit. Yet, as Webster noted: "The principles of the Constitution prohibited, and were intended to prohibit, and should be construed to prohibit, all interference of the general government with slavery as it existed in the States." Furthermore, Article IV, section 2 of the Constitution creates, like any other constitutional provision, a national duty in this case; a state must not grant liberty to an escaped slave, but instead must return him to his owner (*WS* 10:43; *PDW* 2:540).

In addition to principle, traditional policy, and the Constitution, recent changes in the political climate had affected the assessment of slavery in the Union. By 1850, the decision about how to govern the new territories had been vexed by sharp action and counteraction on slavery. Beginning around 1835, Northern abolition societies traveled to Southern slave states to agitate for, and in some cases forcibly to effect, the liberation and evacuation of slaves. These actions, along with the reticence in some Northern states to deliver up escaped slaves, aggrieved the South and affected their feelings and opinions about slavery and the Union itself. As Webster noted, slavery had recently come to be defended in the South as not a necessary evil but instead a positive good.[6] In addition, just as a Southern slaveholder came to regard his personal advantage in taking his locally defined property into the new territories, the Southern states had come to see their political interest in the establishment of more slave territories and thus more slave states in the Union. Conversely, the Southern slave interest considered political resistance to its expansion as tantamount to opposition to Southern states themselves. When the great and populous territory of California petitioned for admission to the Union as a free state in 1850, this action also reinforced hard feelings in the South.

The Compromise of 1850, sponsored by Henry Clay in the Senate, sought to diffuse the tensions between the North and South, or between antislavery and slavery interests. California was admitted as a free state, while the Southwest territories would be governed without congressional prohibition on slavery there (and the Texas-Mexico boundary settled). Furthermore, the slave trade was abolished in the District of Columbia, though a tougher fugitive slave statute was also passed. Though deliberately designed to satisfy no party completely, the Compromise of 1850 was intended to keep the peace in the Union in a time of extraordinarily strong divisions. Webster's Senate speech defending these particular measures not only helped them to pass, but also made clear to the public that union was the principle behind the expedient compromises in the legislation.

Webster defended in particular the fugitive slave statute. This seemingly contrasted with his strong stance against the injustice of many Southern positions, including the claims of Southern slaveholders to have chattel slaves recognized as property in jurisdictions outside of their peculiar local laws (*WS* 10:42). However, Webster considered as just the Southern grievance that "individuals" and "legislators" in the North had been disinclined to return "persons bound to service" who had escaped into free states. As he did in the *Dartmouth College* case and in the nullification debate, Webster reminded the states of their subordination to the Constitution and of their obligation not to act against its provisions. He interpreted the fugitive slave clause to be an obligation on "the State itself" that is "binding in honor and conscience." Thus, he supported "proper" federal statutes authorizing federal courts in the states to "do all that is necessary" for the recapture and restoration of fugitive slaves. Although Webster's support for the new fugitive slave statute angered and disappointed prominent antislavery spokesmen in the North, it largely pacified the South.[7] Moreover, his rhetoric adroitly associated the satisfaction of the Southern grievances with the enforcement of the Constitution and with the maintenance—not the disruption—of political union (*PDW* 2:541, 544).

Webster also supported Congress's decision not to legislate slavery out of the southwestern territories. Given his public opposition to the extension of slavery, Webster's approval of Congress's reticence to legislate against the spread of slavery may seem contradictory. However, as his rhetoric shows, his decision was a statesmanlike calculation of the most effective means available at the time to promote the political good of national unity. Webster was confident that the Southwest would be determined to be free by the "natural causes" that "necessarily exclude" slavery there; that is, the legal and practical system of slavery would be "naturally" impossible to establish in the desert and mountains of that region. His speech cast Congress's reluctance to determine politically what would have been determined by geography as a deliberate decision not to "wound the feelings" of the South or antagonize its interests. By Webster's portrayal, Congress's action prudently accomplished two goods that would have been otherwise incompatible —first, the reconciliation of the South to the Constitution and the Union, and second, the containment of slavery (*PDW* 2:539, 563).

In the crisis of 1850, Webster addressed with statesmanlike prudence not only political means but also political ends. His argument for the Compromise of 1850 aimed to cultivate "a better feeling and more fraternal sentiments between the South and the North" and on the "preservation of this Constitution and the harmony and peace of all who are destined to live under it." In a time of national division and bitter sectional rivalry, Webster counseled "forbearance and moderation" to both North and South and attempted to "inculcate principles of brotherly love and affection" among them. As in the crisis of nullification, he sought to preserve the Union not only by addressing the strife at hand but also by recalling to citizens their fundamental consensus on and commitment to "a great, popular, constitutional government" that is guarded by "law and by judicature," defended by the "affections of the whole people," and constructed to "last for ever" (*PDW* 2:546, 550, 551).

To Webster, the cause of freedom and self-government—of majority rule with minority rights—was connected essentially and necessarily to union and the Constitution. That Americans authoritatively assented to this political argument in the crucial era between the American Founding and the 1850s is evidence of the skills of Webster the orator and statesman. By the time of the profound national crisis that was the Civil War, a fellow orator and statesman— Abraham Lincoln—was able to rely on the national sentiment that Webster helped so much to cultivate, a sentiment that supported "Liberty *and* Union, now and for ever, one and inseparable" (*PDW* 1:348).

Notes

1. Quotations from and references to Webster's works are cited in the text using the following abbreviations:

    GS: *The Great Speeches and Orations of Daniel Webster* (Boston: Little, Brown, and Company, 1882).

    PDW: *The Papers of Daniel Webster, Speeches and Formal Writings* (Volume I: 1800–1833, Volume II: 1834–1852), ed. Charles M. Wiltse (Hanover, N.H.: University Press of New England, 1988).

WS: *The Writings and Speeches of Daniel Webster in Eighteen Volumes* (Boston: Little, Brown, and Company, 1903).

2. To Webster, the proposition that government, not the people, is the supreme authority was a hallmark of European politics, with its history of absolute monarchs.

3. Webster refers to the prohibitions on the state governments in Article I, section 10 of the Constitution.

4. Webster implies John Calhoun's political theory of the "concurrent majority," under which minority interests (typically state-based) possess a kind of veto power over acts of the national majority that particularly injure those interests. See, e.g., "Exposition and Protest" and "A Disquisition on Government," in *Union and Liberty: The Political Philosophy of John C. Calhoun*, ed. Ross M. Lence (Indianapolis: Liberty Fund, 1992).

5. In *The Federalist* no. 55, Publius replies similarly to the Anti-Federalist argument that the popular House of Representatives would be unrepresentative and dangerous to liberty: "As there is a degree of depravity in mankind which requires a certain degree of circumspection and distrust, so there are other qualities in human nature which justify a certain portion of esteem and confidence. Republican government presupposes the existence of these qualities in a higher degree than any other form. Were the pictures which have been drawn by the political jealousy of some among us faithful likenesses of the human character, the inference would be, that there is not sufficient virtue among men for self-government; and that nothing less than the chains of despotism can restrain them from destroying and devouring one another." *The Federalist Papers*, ed. Clinton Rossiter (New York: Mentor Books, 1999), 314.

6. See, for example, William Harper, "Memoir on Slavery," in *The Ideology of Slavery*, ed. Drew G. Faust (Baton Rouge: Louisiana State University Press, 1981).

7. *Daniel Webster: "The Completest Man,"* ed. Kenneth E. Shewmaker (Hanover, N.H.: University Press of New England, 1990), xix, xxvi, 4. Ralph Waldo Emerson, who had long admired Webster for his grand style and rhetorical brilliance in public life, condemned him for, as Emerson saw it, turning that natural greatness toward injustice. Webster's decision to support the fugitive slave statute with his reputation and eloquence "was accompanied with everything offensive to freedom and good morals." Emerson added: "There was something like an attempt to debauch the moral sentiment of the clergy and of the youth." *The Selected Writings of Ralph Waldo Emerson*, ed. Brooks Atkinson (New York: The Modern Library, 1968), 867.

Chapter 16

Henry Clay and the Statesmanship of Compromise

Kimberly C. Shankman

> If anyone seeks to know the leading and paramount object of my career, the preservation of this union will furnish him the key.

Henry Clay (1777–1852) seems to be a man of contradiction: the ardent Jeffersonian Republican who devoted most of his career to the championing of the expansive, Hamiltonian plan of economic development that he called the "American System"; the implacable foe of executive power who tried four times to become president; and the "Great Compromiser" who stoked the fires of partisan warfare throughout his career. These manifold apparent contradictions have led most recent commentators on Clay to dismiss him as an essentially unprincipled politician, motivated primarily by ambition and secondarily by envy. From this perspective, the concept of Henry Clay as a political thinker is more or less absurd.

From the perspective of Clay's contemporaries, however, the position looks somewhat different. His most famous follower was Abraham Lincoln, who described Clay as "him whom, during my whole political life, I have loved and revered as a teacher and leader"—hardly the description of a moorless political hack (*AL* 4:184).[1] Furthermore, Clay was widely (although probably apocryphally) attributed with telling a follower that "I would rather be right than be president," and this pronouncement was trumpeted by Whigs as evidence of their leader's commitment to integrity over office. Obviously, this could be no more than meaningless political puffery; but it certainly would be an odd pronouncement to attribute to a man who was held to be unprincipled. In fact, we miss a major dimension of Clay's significance if we do not seek to see his thought as he himself did. Fully appreciating the impact of Clay on American political thought requires a search for the thread of consistency which bound his programs together.

Clay himself does not make this task an easy one. Scanning Clay's speeches for theoretical statements yields only a handful of platitudes. Looking at his actions divorced from his explanation of them reveals only the tired machinations of a singularly inept politician. Neither approach can explain how he came to be understood as a leader of men by his contemporaries, many of them gifted leaders in their own right. It is only by attending carefully to the context in which Clay worked and keeping in mind both his audience and his objectives that Clay begins to make sense.

Clay was born in 1777—stretching the point just slightly, Lincoln said the "infant nation and the infant child began the race of life together" (*AL* 1:121)—and entered politics in his adopted state of Kentucky in 1798. This was the height of the Federalist-Republican warfare. Clay was a staunch Republican and ardent disciple of Thomas Jefferson, and he rose rapidly through the party ranks. By the time he attained national prominence as a rising star in the party, the Federalist party had all but disappeared, and the Republicans enjoyed a virtual monopoly of national power. After attending to the pressing concerns of starting and ending the War of 1812, however, Clay announced his American System of economic development, which proposed policies that seemed to many, including Jefferson himself, closer to those of Jefferson's Federalist arch rival Hamilton than to the Republican orthodoxy.

This economic system, linking a call for a discriminatory protective tariff, internal improvements, a central bank, and control over the distribution of the public lands, was the result of Clay's analysis of both the nation's current economic needs and his assessment of the appropriate social basis for democratic government. As initially formulated, however, Clay neither viewed nor presented his system as an alternative to the dominant Republican ideals of agrarian strict constructionism. Rather, Clay presented his system as a variation, consistent with the basic tenor of the Jeffersonian vision. Knowing that Jefferson held up the ideal of the independent yeoman as the ideal citizen of a republic, producing his own necessities and so not dependent on the caprice of employer or supplier, Clay was careful to emphasize, early in his career, that his system of economic development was not intended to supplant agriculture as the dominant lifestyle in the American economy. It was only when Andrew Jackson (whom Clay both feared and despised as a demagogue) assumed control of the government and the renamed Democratic party that Clay began to emphasize the way in which his system presented an alternative to agrarian orthodoxy. Thus, although the essential concept of the American System remained constant, the elements which Clay emphasized, and in particular the rhetoric by which he justified it, altered considerably.

This rhetorical alteration becomes clear when one compares Clay's major speeches in defense of it. Those delivered prior to 1824, with Jeffersonian hegemony in full swing, differ sharply from his major speech of 1832, which was intended at least in part as a campaign document for the upcoming presidential election, and so designed to clarify the differences between Clay and Jackson.

The early speeches show a strong concern for emphasizing the consistency of the system with Jefferson's praise of agrarian virtue and distrust of luxury and idleness. These speeches present the American System as a method for securing employment for those who would otherwise be unable to labor, and they emphasize the role of the vacant public lands as a safeguard against the oppressive manufacturing conditions which prevailed in Europe and so frightened the Jeffersonians. In 1820, Clay made his clearest articulation of the consistency between his American System and Jeffersonian political economy when he argued that his purpose in developing this system was to transfer to a national scale "the well regulated family of a farmer" which manufactures the necessities of life in its own household. Later, however, Clay dropped the old emphasis on the consistency of the American System with a fundamentally agrarian economy; in fact, Clay clearly indicated that agrarianism is now at odds, in his mind, with economic progress and prosperity. He further revealed a new attitude toward the place of luxury goods in the economy. Whereas in his early speeches he had argued that the American System would inculcate the traditional agrarian virtues of "order, of freedom from debt, of economy," and thus inhibit the growth of a corrupting taste for luxury, in 1832 he asserted that the manufacture and consumption of luxury goods were "innocent gratifications" and that a benefit of the American System was that it allowed the poor as well as the rich some share in them (*P* 9:388).

The shifting emphasis in Clay's presentation of the American System is a reflection of the nature of his thought. As a political actor, Clay always spoke with an immediate purpose and in a particular context; his overriding concern was always to present his thought so that it was politically acceptable both to his fellow citizens and to himself. He always saw himself as a loyal

Jeffersonian Republican, and his particular attachment was to James Madison; his primary political and personal aversion was to Andrew Jackson. His presentation of his programs varied, then, according to his purpose: either to emphasize the consistency with Madisonian principles or the inconsistency with Jacksonian principles. From Clay's point of view, this was not inconsistency on his part, for his understanding of the American System was that it was fundamentally a program designed to support a stable democratic polity; such a polity was sustainable on Madisonian principles but not on Jacksonian ones. Clay's politics were shaped by his thought at the same time as his thought was shaped by his politics.

But why did Clay avoid theoretical statements, burying his principles in his policy proposals? A clue to the answer to this question can be found in his experience. Early in his career, he was an ardent champion of many of the independence movements—from the republics of Latin America to Greece—which swept the world in the wake of the American experiment. Yet he saw the fledgling democracies—many modeled very closely on American principles—succumb to military despotism, anarchic dissolution, or reconquest and resubjugation. He concluded that governing principles alone are not sufficient to safeguard republican forms of government. He became unshakably convinced that prudent statesmanship, focused on adapting and applying general principles to the ever-changing conditions of political life, was the essential key to successful republican government.

In 1820, he articulated his sense of the fragility of republican government, even in the United States: "Our institutions . . . now make us free; but how long shall we continue so if we mould our opinions on those of Europe?" (*P* 1:857–58). Institutions alone could not preserve liberty; it was the moulding of opinion which made successful self-government possible. Because of the importance of opinion, he believed that politics was essentially a prudential, rather than a theoretical, enterprise. Because theories tend to be pushed to the limits of their logic, leading to extremism and inflexibility, a theoretical approach to politics is not only ineffective but actually dangerous to a stable democratic government. Clay's refusal to discuss politics in the abstract was an intrinsic part of his understanding of the requirements of democratic statesmanship; in his approach, the rhetoric by which he presented his programs was an essential part of his politics.

This political treatment of his thought is even more significant when we examine Clay's general approach to constitutional interpretation, and in particular, his understanding of the role of executive power within the Constitution. Clay elaborated a vigorous critique of Jackson's exercise of executive power. Jackson based his actions, however, on a theory of the presidency which had been developed by Thomas Jefferson and his successors in the "Virginia Dynasty." Motives both of political prudence and of personal attachment prevented Clay from making this explicit; in fact, Clay used a Jeffersonian rhetoric of resistance to monarchy as the basis of his critique of Jackson. This only becomes fully consistent and coherent when we look back beyond Jefferson's presidency and see Clay's critique in the context of the constitutional system elaborated by Publius in *The Federalist Papers.*

Even the most casual reading of *The Federalist* nos. 47–51 indicate that separation of powers in the Constitution is directed to solving the problem of legislative usurpation while allowing for a vigorous government. The key was that "the interest of the man must be connected to the constitutional rights of the place." In order to guard against legislative usurpation of executive power, the constitutional system would lead the weaker branch of the legislature (i.e., the Senate) to support the rights of the executive because it would be filled with members—motivated by the "love of fame"—who themselves aspired to fill the executive office, and who therefore wished to preserve for themselves the power to "plan and undertake extensive and arduous enterprises" to secure that fame. Thus, the power of the presidency is the wheel which turns the system of separation of powers: by constructing an office strong enough to attract the ambitious, Publius seeks to use that ambition to counteract the ambition of those who seek to expand the powers of the legislature at the expense of executive power. For this to work, the national government itself must be sufficiently powerful to "attract to its support those passions which have the strongest influence upon the human heart." Here we see the argument, which runs like a thread through *The Federalist*, that governmental power protects, rather than threatens, republican liberty (*FP* 72:437; 16:116).

Jefferson was skeptical, however, regarding this happy coincidence of liberty and power; he also doubted that separation of powers required that degree of blending of the three branches of government that Publius had advocated. Instead, he believed that "the leading principle of our Constitution is the independence of the legislature, executive, and judiciary of each other" (*WTJ* 10:140–43). The system of blended powers was being used, Jefferson maintained, to foster an energetic and overbearing government, rather than a simple and limited one.

Holding that simple and limited government was the key to preserving republican freedom, Jefferson argued that it was essential to maintain a strictly limited interpretation of the powers of the national government. "Our peculiar security is in the possession of a written Constitution. Let us not make it a blank paper by construction" (*WTJ* 8:247–48). The connection between limited federal power and republican freedom in the mind of Jefferson the political thinker is clear; it was grounded in his conception of peculiarly republican political economy. The limitation of federal power was essential to prevent the federal government from embarking on the kind of extensive programs of economic development which would subvert the social basis (agrarianism) of an independent republic. Jefferson the president, however, was faced with the problem of rendering such a limited government adequate to the needs of a young nation. Several times in the course of his presidency, he faced situations in which his conception of the appropriate scope of the constitutional power of the national government (particularly the president) did not provide the power necessary to meet the urgent needs of the nation. To solve this problem, he developed a concept of executive responsibility to substitute for expansive construction of the Constitution.[2]

In other words, Jefferson advocated—as an alternative to expansive constitutional interpretation—the occasional exercise of explicitly extraconstitutional power by the executive. The president was to act, under the press of necessity, outside the confines of the Constitution, and then explain his actions to the people and seek their endorsement of them after the fact. The clearest example of this doctrine is the Louisiana Purchase. In explaining this purchase, Jefferson freely admitted that he had "done an act beyond the Constitution." Yet this was justified, he believed, because it was a "fugitive occurrence which so much advances the good of the country." Therefore, he believed that the members of the government should "throw themselves on their country" for ratification of this admittedly unconstitutional act (*WTJ* 8:244). From Jefferson's point of view, it was better for the executive to explicitly exercise an extraconstitutional power than to sanction an interpretation of the Constitution that would legitimate that exercise. "I had rather ask an enlargement of power from the nation where it is found necessary than to assume it by a construction which would make our powers boundless" (*WTJ* 8:247–48). Accepting such an interpretation would bind the people to the precedent of broad construction, whereas they could disavow the action of an individual acting upon his responsibility without establishing a precedent to bind the future.

Given Jefferson's well-known fears of monarchy, it might seem inconsistent for him to be advocating for essentially uncontrolled executive power. A closer look at his thought, however, reveals that there is no incompatibility. Jefferson's conception of executive power was strongly influenced by the thought of the Viscount Bolingbroke, particularly his *Idea of a Patriot King*.

This work was written in opposition to the ministry of Sir Robert Walpole, often known as the first prime minister of England. The aspect of Walpole's ministry most obnoxious to Bolingbroke was his use of executive branch patronage to reward parliamentary loyalty and to consolidate his legislative power. This was a form of corruption insidiously inimical to free government, and in fact the thrust of the *Idea of a Patriot King* was a call to the king to rally the country in opposition to this ministerial corruption.

Thus, within the body of anti-Walpolean thought that influenced Jefferson was the concept that the executive himself could serve as a means of opposing or preventing monarchical corruption.[3] Indeed, Jefferson's own miserable experience as governor of Virginia would have been enough to demonstrate that mere weakness in the executive was by no means a safeguard of republican liberty. Executive weakness was not the answer to the danger posed by monarchy to republicanism; rather, the answer lay in finding a way to "republicanize" executive power, and his doctrine of executive responsibility was designed to do just that.

Ironically, however, Jefferson's conception of executive responsibility itself became institutionalized in subsequent administrations. So tantalizingly available had the concept of "executive responsibility" become by Monroe's administration that not only the president but even the most junior clerks in the executive branch were invoking the doctrine, making unauthorized purchases not only of great objects such as Louisiana but also of such ordinary things as naval supplies.

Henry Clay's analysis of executive power, then, developed in the context of this Jeffersonian view of the presidency: that executive responsibility could forestall the need for a broad construction of the constitutional powers of the government. His first fully developed critique of executive power, early in the Monroe administration, shows quite clearly that he was particularly concerned with the use of executive discretion as a buttress to a restrictive interpretation of constitutional powers. The substantive issue that drew Clay's concern was the question of internal improvements. While Monroe (and Jefferson and Madison) shared Clay's conviction that the nation desperately needed to improve its system of roads and canals, they did not share his insouciant assurance that the constitutional powers of Congress were sufficient, in the absence of a constitutional amendment, to undertake such projects. In fact, in the waning days of his presidency, Madison had vetoed, on constitutional grounds, an internal improvements bill authored by Clay. Ever the optimist, Clay believed that Monroe would support his legislation. The new president, however, made it clear in his Message to Congress that he shared his predecessor's constitutional scruples, and he insisted that an amendment was necessary to authorize Congress to enact a systematic program of improvement.

While Clay strongly disagreed with Monroe's basic interpretation, what particularly irked him was the fact that on a presidential trip, Monroe had taken it upon himself to order significant improvements be made to certain roads—on his responsibility. In the context of such unilateral executive action on internal improvements, Clay found Monroe's assertion that congressional authorization of such projects would be unconstitutional to be particularly galling. In his response to Monroe's Message, Clay maintained that he "never could admit . . . that the President should take an airing in his barouche . . . and exercise the power of ordering roads, in times of profound peace, whenever [he] pleased, and that the Constitution had denied the power to Congress" (*P* 2:445).

Note that Clay's criticism is not of Monroe's action per se, but of the arrogation of executive power at the expense of an expansive reading of the constitutional powers of Congress. He later made this explicit: "I am so far from condemning the act of the President, to which I have referred, that I think it deserving of high approbation; that it was within the scope of his constitutional authority I have no doubt. . . . But I most solemnly protest against any exercise of powers of this kind, by the President, which are denied to Congress" (*P* 2:485–86).

The roots of Clay's opposition to executive power lay in his reaction to the Jeffersonian conception that executive power could be a substitute for a broad reading of the constitutional powers of Congress. Ironically enough, Clay clung to his antiexecutive stance throughout his life—for unlike Jefferson, Clay had not developed an historically nuanced conception distinguishing executive power from monarchy—as the badge of his (and his party's) legitimacy as heirs of the Jeffersonian tradition. He bitterly resented Andrew Jackson's claim of the mantle of Jeffersonianism, and indeed his opposition to Jackson as both man and president decisively shaped his antiexecutive thought.

There can be no doubt that Clay thought Jackson personally unfit to exercise the office of president. In Clay's estimation, he was "ignorant, passionate, hypocritical, corrupt, and easily swayed by the base men around him"; furthermore, Clay failed to understand how "killing two thousand five hundred Englishmen at New Orleans qualifies him to undertake the various, difficult, and complicated duties of the Chief Magistrate." Not the least of Clay's objections to Jackson was that his popularity was "the result exclusively of admiration and gratitude for military service," which he found a dangerous precedent in a republic (*P* 4:47; 8:4).

The heart of the difference between Clay and Jackson, however, lay in their different understanding of the nature of democracy. Like the Jeffersonian Democrats whose mantle he assumed, Jackson believed in states' rights, agriculture, and limited federal government. His view of democracy presumed a basic conflict between the "humble members of society" against "the rich and powerful." He believed that the rich often had undue influence in the government, making it "the engine for the support of the few at the expense of the many"; thus, it was the president's role, as "direct representative of the American people" to fight such privilege, primarily by reigning in the federal government and leaving "individuals and states as much as possible to themselves." In Jackson's view, the key to maintaining democratic government was to keep the government insofar as possible utterly dependent upon the will of the people: "in all . . . matters of public concern policy requires that as few impediments as possible should exist to the free operation of the public will."

In Clay's understanding, that which most threatened democracy was not corruption but demagoguery. The tyranny he feared most was that imposed by the majority on itself, through its thoughtless accession in the usurpation of power by a favorite who becomes tyrant: "the arts of power and its minions are the same in all countries and in all ages. . . . [I]t avails itself of the prejudice and passions of the people, silently and secretly to forge chains to enslave the people" (*W* 5:627).

This analysis, which put passion at the center of the perils facing republican government, supported Clay's commitment to the American System. The economic development spurred by this system would increase the importance of a wide variety of interests in American politics, and a political focus on interests—capable of being harmonized through the peaceful (and legislatively centered) process of compromise—could supplant the dangerous power of passionate commitment to conflicting principles.

Two great events had impressed upon Clay the limits of the agrarian vision: the War of 1812 and the Missouri Crisis. The war convinced him that national independence required a balanced economy to prevent the "recolonization of these states under the commercial dominion of Great Britain." Thus, his relatively desultory and sporadic defense of American manufacturing was transformed after the war into the grand conception of the American System (*W* 5:451).

The lesson of Missouri was both more profound and more ambiguous, and Clay's reaction to it illustrates the divergence of his thought from that of Jefferson. Jefferson saw the western territories as bulwarks of republican government, providing vacant land to support an agrarian economy. Clay saw the West as a potential hotbed of conflict, drawing people further apart; making it less likely that they would share common cultural and political experiences; and thus weakening the natural ties which reinforced the political bonds of the Union.

Thus, immediately after the resolution of the crisis, Clay wrote to Langdon Cheves that he had come to the "firm conviction" that "there are natural causes, [inherent in expansionism] tending toward disseverance [of the Union], which ought to be counteracted by an enlightened policy." As he later made clear, the American System, which would overcome "every geographical tendency to disunion," was the enlightened policy best suited to overcome those natural causes (*PTJ* 709; *P* 2:58–59; 4:529).

Clay thus rejected the fundamental assumption of Jeffersonian agrarianism of a natural harmony of interest—a "common good" opposed only by those too selfish or greedy to look past their narrow interests—which formed the basis of republican society that both required and enabled republican government to be kept weak. On the contrary, he saw a natural diversity of interest, always freighted with the potential for bitter conflict, yet at the same time also capable of being harmonized through enlightened policy. He saw the statesman's duty as creating the "permanent and aggregate interests of the community" out of the potentially deadly conflict of private interest. That is, in Clay's understanding, the most important task of statesmanship was to demonstrate to those who had conflicting private interests that "we are all . . . bound up and interwoven together, united in fortune and destiny" (*P* 9:77).

Yet for Clay the more important lesson of the Missouri Compromise was not related to the issues that provoked it but rather to the way in which it was resolved. Clay had no hand in formulating the first—and most famous—Missouri Compromise; rather, he formulated the second Missouri Compromise, which was necessary because the constitution which Missouri submitted for approval contained a provision forbidding free blacks from entering the state (which seemed to many clearly to violate the privileges and immunities clause of the Constitution). This provision threatened to undo the first compromise, as the antislavery senators from the North found this just too much to bear.

Clay's solution was as ingenious as it was equivocal—or rather, its genius was its equivocation: he had a committee appointed which recommended an amendment to the act authorizing Missouri's admission to the Union. This amendment stated that a fundamental condition of Missouri's statehood was that nothing in her constitution should be construed to authorize the passage of any law abridging the privileges and immunities of any citizen. Thus, Missouri was allowed to enter with the provision in her constitution, and those who found it obnoxious were allowed to vote that it did not mean what it said.

Almost thirty years later, when introducing his compromise resolutions in 1850, Clay found it useful to reprise the lessons he had drawn from the Missouri Compromise. The nature of this compromise showed Clay that "all this excitement" which had placed the Union in "the most imminent peril and danger" was based primarily upon the fact that the members of Congress "wanted something as a justification . . . of the course they took" (*W* 3:337). Clay thus came to believe that a key element of compromise was ambiguity—that a successful compromise might require significant concessions of interest, but that it must be couched in such a way that it did not require anyone to make an explicit repudiation of principle. He made this point in his admonition to his fellow senators during the debate over the Compromise of 1850: "And how does the honorable Senator expect to arrive at a compromise in which one of these opinions shall be made to triumph over the other? . . . If he wants a compromise, he must take it without asking senators, on the one side or the other, to repudiate their fixed and deliberate opinions" (*W* 6:462).

For Clay, compromise was reached by essentially privatizing the principles that formed the basis for political divisions. In other words, no one is asked to repudiate their fixed and deliberate opinions because everyone's (and therefore no one's) fixed and deliberate opinions are incorporated into law. However, there were limits to the accommodation Clay endorsed through this method of compromise, as is obvious from reflection on the second great compromise with which he was associated—that of the nullification crisis.

This crisis had come about when South Carolina had asserted its power to "nullify" federal laws that the state determined to be unconstitutional. Using fairly ingenious constitutional reasoning to get around the fact that the first power granted to Congress is the power to lay and collect imposts and excises, the political leaders of South Carolina convinced the citizens of the state that United States's tariff policy was unconstitutional, and therefore, the state had the power to refuse to allow it to be enforced within the borders of the state. Of course, the national government could not accept this nullification—which obviously would undermine the tariff policy throughout the nation—and so hostility threatened as Jackson prepared to call out the troops to enforce the collection of the tariff at the port of Charleston. It was in this volatile situation that Clay crafted the Compromise of 1832.

The compromise consisted of two bills: the compromise tariff itself and the so-called force bill, which empowered Jackson to call out the army to enforce the collection of the tariff if South Carolina attempted to enforce her proclamation of nullification. Despite Clay's deep—almost pathological—distrust of Jackson and fear of the consequences of trusting him at the head of an army, he believed the force bill an essential element of the compromise because he believed that the government was "bound by every consideration to maintain the authority of the laws." Nullification lay outside the pale of acceptable opinion because it represented "a pretension at war with the fundamental principle of all representative and free government"—the principle of majority rule. Thus, in the tariff compromise, it was not appropriate to allow the nullifiers to assume that their principles were incorporated in the solution. The Constitution, and the democratic principles it represents, provides the outer limit of acceptable compromise; not even by implication can a doctrine that undermines the authority of the Constitution be incorporated into a legitimate compromise (*W* 5:566).

This points the way to the heart of Clay's understanding of the proper role of statesmanship: compromise is essential because it alone is adaptable to the needs of a diverse nation. The goal of compromise is to deflect attention from the irreconcilable principles that underlie political conflict because they open the door to the intrusion of passion into political discourse. Instead, republican statesmanship most appropriately turns attention to the various interests, which can be reconciled. This intentional obfuscation of principled differences, however, can only work within a framework of basic agreement in principle—agreement to abide by the Constitution.

It is in examining Clay's statesmanship of compromise in relation to the most profound, troubling, and pernicious issue of his time—slavery—that we see the way in which this conception of compromise encompassed his approach to political economy and partisanship. We also see the limits of this approach to republican statecraft, and so see why Clay's approach had to be transcended by his greatest pupil, Abraham Lincoln.

Clay's position on the slavery issue was very similar to that later articulated by Lincoln: Clay clearly and explicitly considered the preservation of the Union as a higher good than the elimination of slavery, and within that basic guiding framework, both men held what could best be described as a radically centrist policy on the slavery issue. They each believed that both slavery and abolitionism were unjust and threatening to the Union; that slavery was a temporary but necessary evil in the existing constitutional system; and that any attempt either to perpetuate slavery by establishing it in the territories or to uproot it by federal action in the states where it existed was both morally wrong and politically pernicious.

And yet there was a significant difference between Clay and Lincoln. Lincoln insisted that the primary focus of statecraft regarding slavery had to be on its intrinsic evil. He insisted that Americans had to acknowledge slavery as inconsistent with the basic principles of liberty, even while they tolerated the existence of the institution in their midst. In fact, it would not really be exaggerating to say that to Lincoln, gaining a consensus regarding the intrinsic incompatibility of slavery with the principle of equality was more significant than any particular policy decision regarding it. Clay, in contrast, worked diligently to keep the question of the morality of slavery off of the political agenda because it was an abstract question, and as such, had no legitimate role in his approach to policy making. For Clay, the goal of forging policy agreement not only over-shadowed, but also absolutely preempted, any concern with establishing a consensus regarding the intrinsic evil of slavery.

This is not to say that Lincoln acknowledged the moral evil of slavery while Clay refused to. In fact, Clay quite consistently acknowledged the moral illegitimacy of slavery. Lincoln often quoted Clay's denunciations of slavery, and Clay probably influenced his own articulation of the moral incompatibility between slavery and democratic government. Lincoln centered much of his antislavery rhetoric around the warning that Americans needed to beware, lest "in our greedy chase to make profit of the Negro, . . . we 'cancel and tear in pieces' even the white man's charter of freedom." This warning was built upon Lincoln's understanding that there was no argument for the enslavement of blacks that could not in turn be used to enslave whites. To emphasize this point during the Lincoln-Douglas debates, Lincoln quoted directly from Clay:

> I know there are those who draw an argument in favor of slavery from the alleged intellectual inferiority of the black race. Whether this argument is founded in fact or not, I will not now stop to inquire, but merely say that if it proves anything at all, it proves too much. It proves that among the white races of the world anyone might properly be enslaved by any other which had made greater advances in civilization. And, if this rule applies to nations there is no reason why it should not apply to individuals; and it might easily be proved that the wisest man in the world could rightfully reduce all other men and women to bondage. (Lincoln, *AL* 2:222, referring to Clay, *P* 10:574–81)

For Clay, the problem was not expressing opposition—even vigorous opposition—to slavery on moral grounds; rather, he objected to the politicization of that opposition. Just as he had opposed the interjection of anti-Masonry or temperance into the political arena, he opposed the interjection of the inherently divisive issue of the morality of slavery on the grounds that it would undermine the possibility of political settlement of the issue. He personally was quite emphatic in maintaining this distinction between private and public opposition; he could go in the same speech from categorically denouncing slavery as "evil" and "wrong" to reassuring his listeners that he would "quarrel with no man for holding contrary opinions" (*LS* 2:609).

Clay's implacable resistance to any attempt to bring the question of the morality of slavery into the public arena is inextricably linked with his overall conception of the role of republican statesmanship. Because compromise was such an essential part of that statesmanship, Clay always wished to avoid discussing any political issue in theoretical terms, for doing so abstracted the issue from the context in which compromise was possible—hence his resistance to articulating any general statement of his political principles. Thus, he always distinguished between the "abstract" question of the intrinsic evil of slavery and the political question regarding dealing with the existing institution:

It may be argued that, in admitting the injustice of slavery, I admit the necessity of an instantaneous reparation of that injustice. Unfortunately, however, it is not always safe, practicable, or possible, in the great movements of states and public affairs of nations to remedy or repair the infliction of previous injustice. In the inception of it, we may oppose and denounce it, by our most strenuous exertions, but, after its consummation, there is often no other alternative left us but to deplore its perpetration and to acquiesce, as the only alternative, in its existence, as a less evil than the frightful consequences which might ensue from the vain endeavor to repair it. Slavery is one of those unfortunate instances. (*W* 3:65)

Of all the "frightful consequences" which Clay enumerated—including race war, the extermination of the African-American people, or the starvation of the suddenly freed but unprepared former slaves— none was as significant to him as the danger to the Union.

For Clay, the ultimate significance of the Union was that it represented an experiment in democratic government, the results of which were by no means assured. It was this dimension of the Union he was referring to when he warned those who spoke of dismembering the Union, either to preserve or to destroy slavery, that "beneath the ruins of the Union would be buried, sooner or later, the liberty of both races" (*P* 9:282).

To understand how Clay could maintain this apparently bizarre position—that in acquiescing to slavery in the present provided the best hope for the ultimate freedom of African Americans —it is necessary to spell out in more detail his conception of the nature of the Union. Clay believed that maintaining the Union required more than a merely political connection; rather, it required "an intimate social and commercial connexion between all parts of the confederacy" (*P* 3:587). This connection, fostered by the economic interdependence created by the American System, both required and maintained a strong sense of shared national purpose. In this Union, Clay believed (and in this case, as in so many of his political calculations, his belief was sustained by his obstinate optimism, which allowed him effectively to blind himself to any amount of contrary evidence) that the radically disparate economic systems of slavery and free labor would come to be seen, by Northerners and Southerners alike, as incompatible. Since Clay believed that the economic superiority of free labor was obvious, he anticipated, in the absence of any outside pressure, a gradual and voluntary movement toward emancipation (see, e.g., *P* 10:574–81).

Thus, Clay attempted to remove the slavery issue from the national agenda because he believed that the attempt to forge political solutions to moral problems provoked a defensive divisiveness that undermined the possibility of widespread commitment to a sense of shared community. In fact, the more slavery was addressed by the abolitionists as a moral issue, the more difficult it became for slaveholders to see or to follow the rational economic incentives that would lead to eventual emancipation. For example, he argued that Kentucky was ripe for emancipation since eliminating slavery would increase both the economic and political power of the state; and he believed that his state might well have adopted a scheme of gradual emancipation at their Constitutional Convention in 1849 but for "the indiscreet and unwise interference, on the subject of slavery, by violent abolitionists in other States" (*P* 10:588).

The abolitionists against whom Clay directed his ire—the "monomaniacs" as opposed to the "rational abolitionists"—were those such as the followers of William Lloyd Garrison, who became increasingly politically active in the 1830s, and who differed considerably from most of those who had previously opposed slavery. The earlier opponents of slavery had accepted the federal consensus that slavery was an issue consigned to the states. The new generation of abolitionists, however, believed that slavery was so immoral that its evil corrupted all who came in contact with it. Therefore, they argued that the citizens of the free states were equally as culpable in the injustice of slavery as the slave masters. They believed that they (and their fellow citizens in the North) bore personal responsibility for the eradication of slavery throughout the Union.

This attitude was reflected in Garrison's slogan "no Union with slave holders," which captured the essentially apolitical nature of this branch of the abolitionist movement. The fundamental concern of the abolitionists was moral purity; the purpose of politics, in their eyes, was to reflect the morality of the citizens. Seen in this light, slavery was a corruption both of the political system and of the morality of the individual citizen. Since the focus of the abolitionist movement was personal, they had two options. They could secure their morality either by achieving the immediate emancipation of the slaves or by disassociating themselves from the slave owners. Thus, Horace Greeley's advice, upon the secession of South Carolina, to "let our erring sisters depart in peace," was not a violation of abolitionist principles. What the abolitionists could not accept was any compromise with the existence of slavery within the Union, for this represented complicity in the continuation of their own corruption.

From Clay's perspective, forcing the issue to the national political agenda was particularly troubling. He believed that the reason that the Constitution had granted "no power whatever to the general government in respect to domestic slavery" was that the Framers saw slavery as a divisive force on the national scene and so left control of it primarily in the states (*LS* 2:366). Yet that decision, Clay believed, represented a compromise not with the justice of slavery but with its existence. Therefore, he found it appropriate to make a sharp distinction between slavery in the states (not amenable to federal control) and slavery in the territories, which Congress could restrict as it saw fit.

Once again, given the similarity between their positions, it is appropriate to compare Clay with Lincoln. Both distinguished between the status of slavery in the states and in the territories, and both thought the latter amenable to federal control while the former was not. Yet there is a significant difference. Lincoln believed that the Constitution must always be interpreted in light of the Declaration of Independence, particularly in light of the great principle of human equality that forms the basis for democratic government. Thus, he believed that it was only possible to compromise with the necessity for protecting slavery as long as there was an explicit condemnation of the justice of slavery. However, Clay distinguished between the principles of the Declaration, which he stated were applicable to "the state of nature," and the Constitution, which as the social contract essentially superseded the Declaration (*LS* 2:596–97). Clay believed that what was essential was not agreement as to the basic principles which informed the Constitution but scrupulous adherence to the terms of the bargain which had been struck in that contract. He was willing to accept—indeed, in many ways he welcomed—a fundamental ambiguity in the meaning of his legislative proposals to deal with slavery. Like the Framers at the time of the Constitutional Convention, Clay apparently believed that the slavery problem could best be dealt with by keeping it submerged so that the attention of the nation could be turned to issues that could unite rather than divide the sections.

An excellent example of this is his action regarding the Compromise of 1850, which dealt with the integration of the Mexican cession (territories obtained as a result of the War with Mexico) into the Union, together with the question of the statehood of California. Clay presented a compromise package, a central feature of which was the admission of New Mexico as a territory with no congressional restriction on slavery during the territorial phase. While this appeared to be a concession to the South, Clay, with many antislavery Northerners, believed that slavery, having been outlawed by Mexico in this territory prior to its being ceded to the United States, did not and could not exist absent a positive legislative enactment. In presenting his compromise resolutions, Clay prefaced them with what he characterized as "two truths": that slavery was unlikely to be introduced in the Southwest territory and that, by virtue of Mexican law, slavery did not currently legally exist there. At the same time, however, he asked the Northern congressmen to agree to forego the legislative enactment of these truths as both unnecessary and inflammatory. The compromise bill that was reported out of the committee chaired by Clay did not contain these provisions, nor did the compromise acts finally accepted by Congress.

In fact, without these truths—especially the second—as part of the bill, there was considerable disagreement as to exactly what the nonintervention aspect of the compromise actually meant. There were two competing views on what would happen if a slaveowner took slaves to New Mexico prior to legislative action establishing slavery (which, of course, was unlikely unless a large number of slave owners moved there). The dominant view, based on the common law maxim that a slave's chains fall off once he touches free soil, was that any slaveholder who took slaves into New Mexico prior to a positive enactment of slavery by law would actually be conferring freedom on his slaves. Many others, however, adhered to the "Calhoun doctrine," and they accordingly believed that slavery was in fact protected by the "instantaneous transmigration" of the Constitution, which in this view carried positive support for slavery. This view thus held that nonintervention secured the rights of slaveholders to implant slavery in these territories.[4]

Not only did Clay not attempt to clarify this situation; he cultivated its ambiguity. For example, the bill reported from his committee contained a clause directing appeals as to the legitimacy of slavery in the New Mexico territory to the Supreme Court. This Clay justified on the grounds that "the question whether the opinions expressed by me and by others, or the opposite ones, be right, can only be decided by the Supreme Court. . . . A question as to whether or not the Mexican law prevails in these territories, or whether the Constitution admits slaves to be taken there, can only be decided by that tribunal" (*W* 6:467). Here we see Clay directly appealing to his fellow legislators to ignore differences in principle for the sake of compromise.

This deliberate cultivation of ambiguity leads one to the central facet of his position on slavery. Clay thought slavery was an evil and inherently unjust. He thought that in the states where it existed, it was a necessary evil, and accommodations had to be reached with it. He thought that introducing slavery where it had not previously existed was on a different moral plane than accommodating slavery where it already flourished. Thus, he could not and would not endorse a measure that explicitly sanctioned the introduction of slavery into territory previously untainted by it. The preservation of the Union, however, was of even higher value than the containment of slavery.

To preserve the Union, Clay believed that the North had to be reassured that slavery would be contained, and at the same time the South had to be reassured that their place as equal partners in the Union was not in jeopardy. The territories would not be used as an instrument of subjugation by excluding Southerners and forging an unbreakable majority to ride roughshod over the rights of citizens of the Southern states. Therefore, the best strategy for saving the Union seemed to him to be getting men to agree to an ambiguous proposition for nonintervention in the territories, even knowing full well that many agreed to it in the belief—directly counter to his own—that this sanctioned the spread of slavery into the territories. Clay preferred to accentuate the ambiguity to secure agreement.

In this he succeeded, perhaps too well, for in 1854 Stephen Douglas (who actually steered the Compromise of 1850 through the Senate in its final form) was to argue that the principle of nonintervention in the New Mexico territory "superseded" the slavery restriction in the Missouri Compromise and so provided the basis for opening the Nebraska territory to popular sovereignty.

There was, however, a significant difference between the popular sovereignty of Douglas and the nonintervention of Clay. In order to justify his stand on popular sovereignty, Douglas found it necessary in public to repress his private feelings about slavery and declare to the world that he "don't care if slavery were voted down or voted up." As Lincoln maintained, for Douglas popular sovereignty was a doctrine of public education. Douglas thought it imperative that the two great sections learn to coexist; he thought this could only be done if the slavery issue were somehow defused; and he thought that the best method of defusing the issue was anesthetizing the moral opposition to the spread of slavery. Thus, popular sovereignty had to be defended on the grounds that slavery itself was not a moral issue.

Like Douglas, Clay wished to remove slavery as a bone of contention from national politics; but he always maintained—even in his major speech against the abolitionists—that he believed slavery itself to be an evil. Clay definitely accepted—even encouraged—ambiguity as to the status of slavery in the compromise proposals, but he explicitly rejected any ambiguity regarding his personal aims and principles: "I owe it to myself . . . to say, that no earthly power could induce me to vote for a specific measure for the introduction of slavery where it had not existed before" (*W* 3:355).

Although it would be unfair to say that this was his intention—for Clay was sanguine by nature, and undoubtedly believed that his interpretation of the constitutional status of slavery would prevail—the effect of what he did was to transform opposition to the spread of slavery from a public to a private position for the sake of compromise. From this it was only a short step to Stephen Douglas's position, articulated in his campaign on behalf of the Kansas-Nebraska Act, that even private opposition should be suppressed for the sake of comity. In the crisis that followed the Kansas-Nebraska bill, both Lincoln and Douglas claimed to be following the path marked by Clay in 1850. It is a measure both of the success and of the limits of his statesmanship that both were right.

Notes

1. Quotations from and references to Clay's works are cited in the text using the following abbreviations:

LS: *The Life and Speeches of the Hon. Henry Clay*, 2 vols., ed. Daniel Mallory (New York: Barnes and Burr, 1860).

P: *The Papers of Henry Clay*, 10 vols., ed. Robert Seager, James F. Hopkins, and Mary Hargreaves (Lexington: University of Kentucky Press, 1959–90).

W: *Works of Henry Clay*, 7 vols., ed. Calvin Colton (New York: Henry Clay Publishing Co., 1897).

Quotations from and references to other authors are cited in the text as follows:

AL: Abraham Lincoln, *The Collected Works of Abraham Lincoln*, ed. Roy Basler (New Brunswick, N.J.: Rutgers University Press, 1953).

FP: Alexander Hamilton, James Madison, and John Jay, *The Federalist Papers*, ed. Clinton Rossiter (New York: New American Library, 1961).

PTJ: Thomas Jefferson, *The Portable Thomas Jefferson*, ed. Merrill Peterson (New York: Penguin, 1975).

WTJ: Thomas Jefferson, *The Works of Thomas Jefferson*, 12 vols., ed. Paul L. Ford (New York: Putnam, 1904).

The opening epigraph of this chapter comes from *W* 4:491.

2. See Robert Scigliano, "The President's Prerogative Power," and Gary Schmitt, "Thomas Jefferson and the Presidency," in *Inventing the American Presidency*, ed. Thomas E. Cronin (Lawrence: University Press of Kansas, 1989), for examples of incidents in which Jefferson felt necessary to exceed his understanding of the limits of federal power.

3. Of course, there are many scholars who would not agree that it is possible to separate Jefferson's reflections on executive power from his fear of monarchy: see, e.g., Morton J. Frisch, "The Hamilton-Madison-Jefferson Triangle," *Ashbrook Essay*, no. 4 (Ashland, Ohio: Ashland University, 1992). See also, however, Ralph Ketcham, *Presidents Above Party: The First American Presidency, 1789–1829* (Chapel Hill: University of North Carolina Press, 1984), for the influence of Bolingbroke on Jefferson. It is interesting to compare Bolinbroke's description of his model of the "patriot King"—Elizabeth I, whom he said "united the great body of the people in her"—and Jefferson's description of his role, as he saw it: "it is the duty of the Chief Magistrate . . . to unite in himself the confidence of the whole people." Bolingbroke, *Idea of a Patriot King*, quoted in Richard Hofstadter, *The Idea of a Party System* (Berkeley: University of California Press, 1969), 20, and Jefferson, *WTJ* 11:133.

4. The common law of slavery is found in Lord Mansfield's decision in the case *Somerset v. Stewart*, Lofft 1, 98 *English Reports*, 499 (Kings Bench 1772). The phrase "instantaneous transmigration of the Constitution" was coined by Thomas Hart Benton to describe Calhoun's territorial theory.

Chapter 17

John C. Calhoun and the Reexamination of American Democracy

John Agresto

John Caldwell Calhoun (1782–1850)—congressman, senator, secretary of war, secretary of state, vice president, and defender of the cause of the American South—has often been regarded both as a major statesman and also as one of the foremost theoreticians of constitutional government. His views of states' rights, liberty, and the nature of the American Union were the theoretical basis of the South's secession and could, with full justification, be regarded as the philosophical cause of the Civil War. Although history might well have shaped his understanding, there is little doubt that his views helped, in turn, to propel history.

Yet, while scholars have often labeled his views as bold and original, within the context of the foundations of liberal democratic government propounded by John Locke and Thomas Jefferson, and within the context of the constitutional regime given to us by James Madison and the Founders, Calhoun's views might best be seen as truly radical and revolutionary. Indeed, Calhoun's philosophy of constitutional government can be fully understood only when seen as a radical overthrow of the philosophy of Locke and a purposeful rejection of the politics of Madison.

Calhoun is, to be sure, best known for his defense of states' rights and his constitutional arguments in favor of the "compact" view of the American Constitution. He regarded the Union as a compact of sovereign and independent states, each of which had the authority to "nullify" the execution of federal law within its borders or, when all else failed, to secede from a union that harmed its perceived interests. Although these are arguments rarely heard these days (whether because they were sufficiently refuted by the constitutional theorists of the Union or because they were made practically moot by the Civil War), the philosophical underpinnings of Calhoun's political and constitutional positions merit better understanding. To do this properly, we need to see Calhoun's teachings in the light of the earliest and best arguments for liberal democratic life.

John Locke, the philosophical father of all modern liberal democracies, begins his inquiry into the basis of legitimate government with the words: "To understand political power right, and derive it from its Original, we must consider what State all Men are naturally in."[1] Calhoun also begins his most systematic inquiry into political life, the *Disquisition on Government* (published posthumously in 1853), in a manner highly reminiscent of Locke: "In order to have a clear and just conception of the nature and object of government, it is indispensable to understand correctly what that constitution or law of our nature is in which government originates."[2] Locke centers his investigation of man's natural condition on an investigation of the state of nature, a state antecedent to political life in which all men are both equal and free. Yet it is exactly this notion of an earlier state to which we might look to discover man's true nature that Calhoun claims utterly to reject. To Calhoun, it is "incontestable" that "man is so constituted as to be a social being" rather than by nature free, equal, and independent (*DG* 3). Indeed, man has never lived in any age or country in any state other than the social and the political (*DG* 3–4).[3] There simply is no prepolitical state of nature as understood by Locke or Hobbes or Jefferson which will help us understand the proper construction of civil society in accord with that nature.

This rejection of the state of nature and the positing of the innate social and political nature of man has at least three major and significant consequences. First, it would seem to argue for the primacy of society and its needs over all other needs. So vital is society that man can neither perfect himself without it nor even live without it (*DG* 5). Second, it undercuts the idea of innate or inalienable rights, since, in theory, rights have their surest foundation in the fact that we possessed them before the organization of society (*DG* 44–45). Third, having argued that government is natural rather than constructed, it removes the rationale for government based on the equal consent of all the governed and thus subverts the strongest of all arguments against slavery. Indeed, Calhoun characterizes what the Declaration of Independence calls the self-evident truths of liberty, equality and consent as "great and dangerous errors," compared to which "nothing can be more unfounded and false" (*DG* 44). To understand these arguments more fully, we must examine Calhoun's view of the nature of society; for it is here, in the needs of society, where government originates.

Although Calhoun insists on seeing man as an associative being who never has nor ever could live in any state of nature, his sociability is of a rather odd and tenuous sort. Only society, Calhoun declares, can satisfy our wants and inclinations, and only society can perfect us morally and intellectually. Only association with others makes "a full development of [our] moral and intellectual faculties" possible; only in association with others can we be raised "much above the level of the brute creation" (*DG* 3). Nonetheless, despite the need for a communal life to make us more than mere animals—despite the overwhelming enrichment it adds to our short lives here on earth—our "individual affections" (that is, our love of self and our own interests) are "stronger than [our] sympathetic or social feelings" (*DG* 4). Despite any innate desire to live in peace with our fellows, our devotion to ourselves and to our own interests is as "all pervading" as the universal law of self-preservation, with which it is essentially connected (*DG* 5). It is our own individual sense of well-being and safety, and not any social sense, which animates our activities. Since man "is so constituted as to feel more intensely what affects him directly than what affects him indirectly through others"; since "our individual are stronger than our social feelings"; and since "the great law of self preservation" is an "all-pervading and essential law of animated existence," conflicts constantly and necessarily arise between individuals (*DG* 4–5). In fact, since every man "has a greater regard for his own safety or happiness than for the safety or happiness of others," what we can observe is a tendency toward a "universal" state of conflict between individual and individual (*DG* 5). Though Calhoun posits the naturalness of the social state, one might think that he sees the true nature of man no differently than Locke or even Hobbes, and therefore is describing something like the state of nature without using those words. But any doctrine of a state of nature antecedent to political life would carry with it notions of human independence and equality, and this, as we will see, Calhoun cannot countenance. Still, this tendency toward self-regard over sociability is so strong in mankind that no other creature in the animal kingdom matches it (*DG* 5). Even such examples as the love of a mother for her infant are "few" and "always regarded as something extraordinary" (*DG* 4).[4]

Although Calhoun talks about the importance of the social state for man to perfect his nature, he actually reserves high praise for man's self-love and self-regard. Calhoun would prefer not to call it "selfishness" since that might lead some to think that it is a "vicious" or "depraved" passion (*DG* 4). Nonetheless, whatever it might be termed, it is wholly natural, virtually all-consuming, God-given, and beneficial for the progress of the race. In fact, while social life helps make us better, it is our innate self-interest by which society itself progresses. In what may well be one of the most full-blown celebrations of human selfishness over sociability, Calhoun declares that the affection that individuals have for themselves is the very ground of all civilization and human greatness. Given our limited understanding regarding what might benefit others, regularized concern for others over oneself would lead to endless confusion and disorder, no less destructive of peace and order than a state of anarchy (*DG* 6). Even if man were naturally benevolent (which he most assuredly is not), his reason is too weak to understand the needs and interests of others. It his own interests and needs that he senses and understands; any attempt to live or work for others in a community of fellow citizens is bound to fail (*DG* 6). For democratic politics, this means that an old solution to the problem of democratic tyranny—namely, the cultivation of "republican virtues" in the hearts of democratic citizens as the basis for democratic government—is here clearly impossible. We are both too weak of mind and too selfish by nature to govern our actions in the light of the needs of others or of the needs of the whole. While this gives Calhoun's analysis an obviously modern, even radically modern, cast, it also is a rejection of Madison's desire to find ways to allow and encourage "enlightened statesmen" to be at the helm of government and to help facilitate the rule by men "of wisdom and virtue."

This desire to pursue our own individual interests and better our condition leads directly to human progress, especially in the area of new inventions and improvements. No organized collective but rather men acting in their own interests harnessed the power of steam, improved armaments, invented the modern uses of gunpowder, and gave mankind the printing press with moveable type. Steam, gunpowder, and modern arms all mean that barbarism will never again be able to overawe civilization, and the invention of printing means that the knowledge mankind has acquired will never again be lost. In such ways does self-interest, which tries so mightily to fracture social life, nonetheless contribute to its progress and perfection (*DG* 47–48).

Despite the naturalness of human self-interest—despite whatever advantages it may ultimately bring to communal and civilized life—there is no doubt that it is also the cause of constant and universal human strife. It is in this state of conflict—in this near war of all against all—that the need for and justification of government arises. It exists not to "secure our rights," as Jefferson would have it, but, contrariwise, to make "society" (into which all are born but in which all have trouble living peacefully) viable. Though man is only fulfilled and satisfied when he lives in society, because of our innate, deep-seated, self-regarding passion, society will disintegrate without government to preserve and protect it. One might think that, having shown the essential self-interest of all mankind with our tendency toward individual aggrandizement and factious warfare, Calhoun might rethink the naturalness of the social state, but he does not. One senses in Calhoun that the need to "prove" that all men at all times are born into already established hierarchies, rules and orders, with some superior and some subordinate, might have other, more urgent, purposes.

"But government, although intended to protect and preserve society, has itself a strong tendency to disorder and abuse of its powers" (*DG* 7). Since all governments are administered by men in whom individual passions and interests are stronger than their social feeling, government's oppression of society, or particular portions of society, is always a strong probability. Rather than preserve and protect society, rulers everywhere have the tendency to run roughshod over the interests of others and work to satisfy their own interests instead.

Obviously, one way to tie the rulers directly to the interests of society is to subject them to frequent elections. But democracy is not a cure for political oppression since it simply allows a self-interested majority to satisfy its interests, through political rule, over the interests of any and all minorities. To put it differently, while government is necessary to prevent one interest from oppressing another, often the greatest source of oppression comes from the government itself. Especially in governments of a more purely democratic sort, there is little to keep a majority faction from invading the interests and suppressing the desires of minorities.

Here, of course, Calhoun starts to sound like James Madison. Indeed, much of the *Disquisition* is a re-presentation of the question Madison raised repeatedly at the Constitutional Convention and in *The Federalist Papers*: How can the tension between democratic rule and individual rights (Calhoun prefers to refer to them simply as "interests") be combined in one political system?[5] Still, while the question may have been similar, the answer Calhoun chose to give is substantially different.

Upon what model shall governments be constructed? To be sure, they cannot be constructed on any model that relies on the cultivation of benevolent rulers devoted to the common good —for, as we have seen, no man or men can know the good of others, much less the good of the whole. Nor should we look for feeble government, and certainly not a government feeble in the face of foreign countries with their own set of interests and designs. The only way, Calhoun argues, is *to invest the ruled with the power to resist the rulers' tendency toward oppression and abuse*. This means, first and foremost, the right of suffrage (*DG* 11). But this solution is problematic in that democracy only transfers the potential abuse of power from the rulers to the majority acting through its representatives. In an analysis highly reminiscent of *The Federalist* no. 10, Calhoun notes that:

> If the whole community had the same interests, so that the interests of each and every portion would be so affected by the action of the government that the laws which oppressed or impoverished one portion would necessarily oppress or impoverish all others—or the reverse—then the right of suffrage, of itself, would be all-sufficient to counteract the tendency of government to oppression and abuse. (*DG* 13)

Since men have varied and not uniform interests and desires, however, democracy all too easily becomes the rule of the greater faction or factions over the less. It was this understanding that led Madison to argue that the first solution to the problem of faction was to be found in an extended, commercial, representative republic that could break the power of faction by the very multiplication of them. But here Calhoun breaks with the Madisonian solution by asserting that "the more extensive and populous the country; the more diversified the conditions and pursuits of its population; and the richer, more luxurious, and dissimilar the people, the more difficult it is to equalize the action of government, and the more easy for one portion of the community to pervert its powers to oppress and plunder the other" (*DG* 13–14).

Unfortunately, the extended republic and the multiplication of factions can become itself the problem through the very activity of compromise and coalition building which the Madisonian solution encouraged. Calhoun saw in this the rise of overbearing and tyrannical majorities.

> If no interest be strong enough . . . a combination will be formed between those whose interests are most alike—each conceding something to the others until a sufficient number is obtained to make a majority. The process may be slow and much time may be required before a compact, organized majority can thus be formed, but formed it will be in time, even without preconcert or design, by the sure workings of that principle or constitution of our nature in which government itself originates. (*DG* 14)[6]

And, in truth, in both the tariff conflict and especially in the crisis over the extension of slavery, the multiplicity of factions that lay at the heart of the Madisonian solution was coming undone, and simple sectional rifts were forming. The Tariff Acts of 1828 and 1832, while greatly favorable to the mercantile interests of the rest of the United States, were extremely damaging to the agricultural interests of the cotton-raising South. And the rise of abolitionist sentiment and the increase in the number of free states threatened, in the South's view, the future existence of its "peculiar institution." It was, it seemed, less difficult than anticipated for the extended and diverse republic to become the house divided.

Madison's solution to the problem of preserving liberty under the form of democratic rule was indeed subtle, complex, and multifaceted. It involved the extension of the size of the nation to be governed; the encouragement of commerce and the multiplication and weakening of faction; a representative system that sought to draw out of the populace representatives possessed of greater wisdom, virtue, and moderation than the people as a whole; a system of governance that might have the beneficial effect of moderating the selfishness of the people themselves and encouraging habits of sympathy, republican patriotism, and virtue—and it all worked through a complex arrangement of federalism, separation of powers, and checks and balances. Madison's constitution was an amazing attempt to make republican government—democratic rule—just, wise, and respectful of human liberty. Yet to Calhoun, all these intertwined institutions and mechanical solutions fell short of preserving the interests of different groups or sections intact. What was called for was something less complicated, something far more direct and simple.

"There is but one certain mode," Calhoun tells us, by which democratic tyranny can be prevented: "[B]y taking the sense of each interest or portion of the community which may be unequally and injuriously affected by the action of the government separately, through its own majority or in some other way by which its voice may be fairly expressed, and to require the consent of each interest either to put or keep the government in action." The system should "give to each division or interest, through its appropriate organ, either a concurrent voice in making and executing the laws or a veto on their execution" (*DG* 20). The establishment of a government composed of these "different and conflicting interests," each with a veto over either the formation or execution of the laws, is what Calhoun calls rule by "constitutional or concurrent majority" (*DG* 23). In simplest terms, while Madison sought to multiply and weaken faction in the pursuit of free government, Calhoun now seeks to coalesce and empower them.

This veto in the hands of certain distinct divisions or interests could legitimately take a number of different forms. It could invest each of the various "classes" of society—for example, king, lords, and commons—with a negative veto over the making or execution of the laws. It might invest each of the major interests in American society—say, commercial, maritime, and agricultural—with a similar veto. It could invest each of the states of the Union with the power to "nullify" unwanted federal laws within their respective borders. It could even take the form, as Calhoun proposes in his *Discourse on the Constitution and Government of the United States* (1853), of a dual presidency, with one president representing the interests of the North and the other representing the interests of the Southern slave states.

In the matter of human equality and liberty, the *Disquisition* was intended to be a refutation of Locke and of Jefferson. Men are not born "free, equal and independent" but members of society. Government is not made to secure our rights but to secure the existence and peace of that society. Government's purpose is to restrain men while protecting certain interests from attack by other interests. But Calhoun's understanding of just government was not only a refutation of Locke and Jefferson; it was also meant to be a rejection of Madison and the scheme of constitutional government he sought to establish.[7] The *Disquisition* questions the intrinsic value or efficacy of a written constitution (*DG* 25), of limited government (*DG* 25–27), and of separation of powers (*DG* 27). Written constitutions are all too easily interpreted by the dominant majority to suit its own preferences; limitations on political power falter when the majority has the ability to read those limitations as they see fit; and separation of powers will not work when a majority finds itself in control of all departments. But, above all, the *Disquisition* calls into question what many regard as the central focus of Madison's constitutionalism—the extended republic and the scheme of representation that follows from it.

We should bear in mind that Madison's idea of the extended republic as the only secure and sensible way of establishing republican rule was, in itself, a rejection of two other possible solutions to the problem of republican instability and injustice. The first was the establishment of popular government on the assumption of a uniformity of interest on the part of the populace or on the expectation of sufficient virtue and patriotism on the part of the people to keep their selfish desires in check. This is not to say that Madison assumed that there was no intrinsic virtue or social sympathy on the part of the people. Indeed, he understands that without some respect for the rights and interests of others and some willingness to act justly even when not coerced, republican government would be an impossibility (cf. *F* 55). Madison hoped that the various modes of representation would call forth into positions of authority "men of wisdom and virtue" and even, perhaps occasionally, "enlightened statesmen." Although Madison never refers to the state of civil society as our natural state, he seems to have a higher regard for man's sociability and fellow-feeling than Calhoun does. *The Federalist* no. 10 explains in detail, however, why these are insufficient foundations for the establishment of democratic regimes.

The second solution was rejected just as forcefully. This is the solution that relies on the idea of a "mixed" constitution or regime—that is, a government which, like Britain, gave each of the great estates or interests the ability to resist encroachments on its powers or interest. In Britain, the estates of king, lords, and commons had come each to be vested with the authority to stop political acts inimical to their desires. It was this model of a "mixed" government that John Adams suggested for the United States in his early *Defense of the American Constitutions*. And it was this model, among others, that Calhoun praises in the *Disquisition* (*DG* 75–81). Calhoun mentions the British constitution along with three other models—that of the Romans, the Poles, and the Iroquois. All four of these had, Calhoun claims, something akin to a concurrent majority constitution. The constitution of Poland went so far as to give total veto power in the election of the king to any one of 200,000 people. Nonetheless, he notes, Poland lasted in this form for over two centuries.

But Madison was trying to do something quite different from simply making certain interests safe and secure. Indeed, there are times when the desires of various interests are simply unjust —"adverse to the rights of other citizens, or to the permanent and aggregate interests of the community" (*F* 10:57). In those circumstances, the will of an interest, no matter how long-standing or extensive, should, in the political arena, lose. To give one example, it might be that the interest of the slave states to expand slavery into the territories is unjust, or against the permanent and aggregate interest of the whole, and it should therefore not be able to have its way or be allowed to hold government hostage until its demands are met.

Directly contrary to Calhoun, the model proposed by Madison sought to call "interest" by its more political name, "faction," and to so extend the orbit of republican rule that all factions would become minority factions and thus, under the workings of majority rule, lose when their various desires and plans failed to convince others of their merit or justice.[8] Whereas "mixed regimes" or "concurrent majorities" sought to solidify and empower a few factions, Madison's genius was to discover ways, within the confines of popular rule, to fracture and weaken them.[9]

Perhaps more to the point, what Madison and the Founders sought to do was to find a way to respect right and protect rightful interests *within the confines of popular rule*. It was *popular government*—government not only *for* the people but also *of* and *by* the people, as Lincoln styled it—which was to be preserved.[10] Of course, majority rule could become oppressive and unjust; this is why the Founders sought, in so many ways, to refine its workings and purify its activity.

But, in the end, it would still be the majority that must rule. To put it differently, while majority rule could be unjust, minority rule was, in its very essence, always unjust. But it is exactly a version of minority rule (and minority rule often at the most crucial junctures of national history) that Calhoun's doctrine of the concurrent majority sought to promote.

Perhaps Madison should here be given his say: The demand that "super-majorities" be required to pass legislation (which, as a retardant on majority rule, is similar to, though milder than, an interest-based negative) is not without its argument.

> That some advantages might have resulted from such a precaution, cannot be denied. It might have been an additional shield to some particular interests, and another obstacle generally to hasty and partial measures. But these considerations are outweighed by the inconveniences in the opposite scale. In all cases where justice or the general good might require new laws to be passed, or active measures to be pursued, the fundamental principle of free government would be reversed. It would be no longer the majority that would rule; the power would be transferred to the minority. Were the defensive privilege limited to particular cases, an interested minority might take advantage of it to screen themselves from equitable sacrifices to the general weal, or in particular emergencies to extort unreasonable indulgences. Lastly, it would facilitate and foster the baneful practice of secessions, . . . a practice subversive of all the principles of order and regular government; a practice which leads more directly to public convulsions, and the ruin of popular governments, than any other which has yet been displayed among us. (*F* 58:396–97)

Aware of the Founders' arguments that a negative in the hands of minority interests would lead to weakness, stalemate, extortion, intrigue, and anarchy, Calhoun responds by saying that the opposite would be the case. Putting forth a somewhat more benign view of man than that with which he began the *Disquisition*, Calhoun predicts that with a free veto in the hands of various interests, each "sees and feels that it can best promote its own prosperity by conciliating the good will and promoting the prosperity of others. . . . [I]nstead of faction, strife, and struggle for party ascendancy, there would be patriotism, nationality, harmony and a struggle only for supremacy in promoting the common good of the whole" (*DG* 38). Since rational men would wish to avoid anarchy at all costs, a defensive power in the hands of minorities would encourage compromise and patriotism, and prompt each interest to select as their representatives only those "whose wisdom, patriotism, and weight of character would command the confidence of the others" (*DG* 38; cf. 36–38, 51–54). As an example, Calhoun points to the fact that trials by jury require unanimity, yet they rarely fail to reach a verdict—indeed, usually a true and just verdict. "Under the influence of this *disposition to harmonize* one [juror] after another falls into the same opinion until unanimity is obtained. . . . Nothing, indeed, can be more favorable to the success of truth and justice than this predisposing influence caused by the necessity of being unanimous" (*DG* 51).[11] Given the picture of human nature painted all along by Calhoun, we would leave it to the careful reader to decide whether or not these conclusions seem strained or contrived. More important, it needs to be asked whether there are not certain issues so central, so vital, to particular factions, yet so inimical to justice or the rights of others, that the faction in question would not prefer to destroy democratic rule rather than compromise.[12]

On the most fundamental level, it is clear that the Founders attempted something far larger than the task before Calhoun. They wished to make, perhaps for the first time in human history, democratic rule become just and intelligent rule. Calhoun had little interest in building up popular government; rather, his clear concern was the protection of particular interests endangered by the progress of democracy. But he had little interest in democratic government as such because he had no belief in the equality and equal liberty of all men. Whereas the Founders struggle mightily to come up with a system of governance that will protect not only rightful minority interests but also the full panoply of minority rights—rights of conscience, of speech, of the press, of personal security, of fair judicial dealing—Calhoun concentrates more simply on defending the interests (that is, primarily the economic interests) of particular minorities. Or, perhaps more correctly, Calhoun rejected the principles of modern natural right because they inexorably led to the principle that no man or men could be governed without consent; that none is the natural servant or slave of another; and that an equal say in political rule is the natural consequence of a society built on equality and liberty. That is, having rejected the idea of the state of nature, one can reject the truth that all men are created equal and endowed with inalienable rights, and reject the idea that no man may use the life, labor, or property of another without his consent. Understanding the intrinsic universality of the idea of natural right, Calhoun, of necessity, had to renounce the principles of Locke and Jefferson and disparage all notions of equality and the rights of man. If it is true, as Calhoun argues, that men will go to extraordinary lengths to preserve themselves and secure their perceived interests, one naturally might then ask if there are not tracts, under the guise of philosophy, that are meant to convince others of the virtue of a position whose singular aim is not the truth but simply the protection and perpetuation of a factional desire.

We have already noted that, where Madison has concern for minority rights, Calhoun speaks more simply of minority "interests." It is their "interests" which must be protected against "oppression"—though it might be hard to fathom why there is a *right* to the protection of their interests without its having some basis in natural rights. Obviously, one might ask the following question: If the interests of the slaveholder is to be protected, or if the interest of the landowner, the merchant, and the yeoman are secured, why not the interests of, for example, the slave? But that would be to assume that all men had some natural right to have their interests protected. There is no such right in Calhoun; there is only the fact that there are interests powerful enough to demand that their desires be respected. How came it to be that the three estates of Britain or the two estates of Rome were vested with a concurrent veto? It was, it would seem, only because they had the strength to demand the "right" but not any intrinsic right to justify its possession.

Nonetheless, insofar as liberty is something esteemed by men, and insofar as the liberty to act on our desires leads to progress and improvements in the material world, liberty cannot be totally disparaged. Yet, rather than the ground and origin of just political regimes, liberty becomes, in Calhoun's hands, "a reward reserved for the intelligent, the patriotic, the virtuous and deserving, and not a boon to be bestowed on a people too ignorant, degraded, and vicious to be capable either appreciating or enjoying it" (*DG* 42–43). Indeed, Calhoun goes so far as to praise even the most extreme forms of human slavery by noting that there could not be "a punishment inflicted on the undeserving more just than to be subject to lawless and despotic rule" (*DG* 43). Having rejected the self-evident truth of human equality and the freedom which flows naturally from that equality, and having rejected the corollary and consequence of equal right, namely, that no man shall be governed without his consent, it was but a short step to this praise of despotism. Despite all attempts by his followers to present his views as an outgrowth or refinement of basic American values, there probably could be no more thoroughgoing rejection of the Founders, their politics, and their principles than Calhoun.

Notes

1. John Locke, *The Second Treatise of Government*, ed. Peter Laslett (Cambridge: Cambridge University Press, 1988), 269 (sec. 4).

2. John C. Calhoun, *A Disquisition on Government* (Indianapolis: Bobbs-Merrill Co., 1953), hereafter cited in the text as *DG*.

3. It should be noted that while the state of nature, to Locke, is prepolitical—indeed, the facts and conditions of that state define the justice and worth of subsequent political rule—it is not necessarily presocial in the sense used by Calhoun. See Locke, *Second Treatise*, 280–81 (sec. 19).

4. Note that it is not even for her children but simply for her "infant" that a mother might suppress her individual interests. Fathers, not to mention other relations or friends, are nowhere in view.

5. In addition to the famous analysis in *The Federalist* no. 10, see also nos. 37, 47–48, 51–53, 55, 57, 63, and 78. Hereafter, *The Federalist*, ed. Jacob E. Cooke (Middletown, Conn.: Wesleyan University Press, 1961), will be cited in the text as *F*, followed by the number of the paper and the page number.

6. Compare Madison in *The Federalist* no. 10: "Extend the sphere, and you take in a greater variety of parties and interests; you make it less probable that a majority of the whole will have a common motive to invade the rights of other citizens; or if such a common motive exists, it will be more difficult for all who feel it to discover their own strength, and to act in unison with each other" (*F* 10:64). And also, "it may well happen that the public voice pronounced by the representatives of the people, will be more consonant to the public good, than if pronounced by the people themselves" (*F* 10:62). But compare Hamilton's notes for June 6, 1787, at the Constitutional Convention: "Maddisons Theory—Two principles upon which republics ought to be constructed—I [,] that they have such extent as to render combinations on the ground of interest difficult—II [,] By a process of election calculated to refine the representation of the People—Answer—There is truth in both these principles but they do not conclude so strongly as he supposes—The Assembly when chosen will meet in one room if they are drawn from half the globe—& will be liable to all the passions of popular assemblies. If more *minute links* are wanting others will supply then [them?]—Distinctions of Eastern middle and Southern states will come into view; between commercial and non commercial states." And finally, "[a]n influential demagogue will give an impulse to the whole—Demagogues are not always *inconsiderable* persons." *The Records of the Federal Convention of 1787*, ed. Max Farrand (New Haven, Conn.: Yale University Press, 1966), 1:146–47. In Madison's defense, it should be noted that he always couches his analysis in terms of "less probable," "more difficult," and "may well happen" rather than in certainties no statesman could give.

7. In the *Disquisition*, Calhoun never refers to any other political theorist or philosopher by name. Although the concurrent majority does have older models—especially Rome and Great Britain—they were models that grew organically and were not "invented" by men thinking philosophically about either nature or natural rights.

8. "In the extended republic of the United States, and among the great variety of interests, parties and sects which it embraces, a coalition of a majority of the whole society could seldom take place on any other principles than those of justice and the general good; and there being thus less danger to a minor from the will of the major party, there must be less pretext also, to provide for the security of the former, by introducing into the government a will not dependent on the latter" (*F* 51:352–53). This speaks both to the rejection of any mixed or concurrent solution as well as to the Founders' more democratic substitution for it.

9. We should not forget that it was the unanimity of all thirteen states required under the Articles of Confederation which led not only to the impossibility of passing certain national legislation, especially in the areas of commerce and taxation, but which also led directly to the calling of the Federal Convention and the superceding of the "concurrent majority" based Articles with the new Constitution.

10. The end would be to preserve both "the spirit and form of popular government," that is, majority rule, and rescue such a government "from the opprobrium under which it has so long labored" (*F* 10:61). Also, it is the "fundamental maxim of republican government," that "the sense of the majority should prevail" (*F* 22:139). In the same paper, Hamilton goes so far as to call all efforts "[t]o give a minority a negative upon a majority" a "poison." *The Federalist* no. 22 is, in fact, a catalogue not only of the theoretical inadequacies but also of the practical impossibility of basing any republican regime on the foundations of concurrent majorities.

11. The only thing that would make this particular analogy of Calhoun's more apt might be if one or both of the parties at trial were also given a decisive veto in the jury's conclusion. But the irrationality of this would, rather awkwardly for Calhoun, underscore Hamilton's and Madison's arguments.

12. In this connection, see Lincoln's Address at Cooper Union and his First Inaugural.

Chapter 18

The Art of the Judge: Justice Joseph Story and the Founders' Constitution

Peter Schotten

With "the possible exception of Coke, Blackstone and Mansfield no English or American jurist exerted an influence on the development of the law greater than that which Story commanded," one prominent historian has concluded, rendering a judgment about Joseph Story's (1779–1845) importance that few authorities would dispute.[1] Today, Story's reputation stems most notably from his efforts as a Supreme Court justice (serving from 1811–1845) and from his authorship of his nation's most influential *Commentaries on the Constitution* (1833).

It is less often recognized just how widespread and robust were the many efforts that Story undertook on behalf of the young Republic. Prior to his appointment to the Supreme Court in 1811 at the age of thirty-two, he had already written one book on law and edited three others, served three terms in the Massachusetts legislature (including a stint as Speaker of the House), and filled an unexpired term in the United States House of Representatives. Later, in addition to his Supreme Court and circuit court duties, there remained much more to do: accepting in 1829 an appointment to the fledgling Harvard Law School (whose success would be largely attributable to him); writing eight major works on American law (not counting numerous revised editions and abridgements); drafting or compiling various laws (including bills extending the jurisdiction of the circuit courts, reforming the U.S. criminal code, revising the national bankruptcy code, and superintending the publication of the massive *Public and General Statutes of the United States*); preparing and presenting numerous essays, encyclopedia entries, and speeches; and making and maintaining influential friendships (most notably with John Marshall and Daniel Webster).

From this description, it might be assumed that Joseph Story's concern was primarily with "the law." But this conclusion would not be sufficiently precise. For almost all of Story's efforts aimed at explicating *American* law as both a foundation for, and reflection of, the American regime (properly understood). Almost every *Commentary*, at least implicitly, aimed at overcoming the influence of local law by advancing the idea of the supremacy of national law as the reflection of a single, unified nation and government.[2] Informing Story's understanding of the United States as a regime was a belief that he shared with the Founders: namely, that the American nation represented a remarkably important, if not watershed, experiment in republican self-government. The Constitution made that experiment possible, both in the sense that it was the nation's fundamental law as well as the product of political wisdom. The Constitution as law, and the Constitution as the result of political wisdom, encompassed Story's constitutional understanding as a thinker and as a judge; both insights directed his jurisprudence as well as his understanding of the responsibilities properly exercised by a Supreme Court justice.

Today, we are moved to ask: although Joseph Story's constitutional understanding proved influential for his time, does it have anything to teach us in our time? Could it be that although Story had some wisdom for his age, he has none for ours? After all, numerous cases have been decided, and many novel constitutional theories advanced, since Story's death; perhaps, we possess today a far superior understanding of the Constitution. Or maybe the American people, or their political and legal leaders, have simply evolved to a more advanced ethical or epistemological state, which allows—or perhaps even requires—them to interpret their "living" Constitution anew. These appear to be the influential, if not the dominant, legal beliefs of our age. Could it be that studying Joseph Story's thought merely allows us to consider old, formerly important canons about the Supreme Court and American self-government? Or, might such a study yield a more substantial result? In order to answer this question and to grasp more fully Story's understanding of the Constitution, we must first disabuse ourselves of contemporary prejudices long enough to consider the possibility that Story could have been both influential and correct. We must, in other words, take seriously that Joseph Story's understanding regarding the importance and meaning of the Constitution was substantially true for his time—and remains true for ours.

Classically educated and well read, Story often reflected upon the specific character of his age. He could do so because he did not believe himself to be merely a product of his age. Nor did Story think that he lived in a time of progress on every front. Rather, he judged his age to be mediocre in literature, history, poetry, philosophy, and metaphysics (*MW* 747–49).[3] Neither was it an era of genius (*MW* 342). But there had been great advances in the law and in politics, and both were notably embodied in the Founding and existence of the United States. The American nation was noteworthy because its government had been consented to, and therefore represented, the will of its people. The product of that consent was most fundamentally manifested at that place where law and politics most profoundly and persistently intersected—within its Constitution, which was the document to whose explication Story devoted much of his life.

Story shared the Founders' belief that the United States represented an extraordinary political accomplishment. It constituted a decisively important, yet nonetheless fragile, experiment in self-government. Other republics had been few and mostly short-lived; furthermore, the challenges facing the young Republic were numerous and severe. Therefore, Story understood his life's work to be that of a political preserver—that is, of a statesman. He sought the nation's preservation by explicating its true constitutional principles (as an enduring source of political wisdom) while he sought to encourage a devotion of those principles (as the foundation of national patriotism). To that end, in his *Commentaries on the Constitution*, he wrote that "[m]y object will be obtained, if I shall have succeeded in bringing before the reader the *true* view of its powers" while "impressing upon Americans a *reverential* attachment to the Constitution, as in the highest sense the palladium of American liberty" (*CC* 1:preface, x–xi, emphasis added).

In Story's opinion, the most persistent threat to the new Union's survival emanated from advocates of state power who posited a states' rights interpretation of the Constitution. It is noteworthy that he wrote his *Commentaries on the Constitution* in the midst of the South Carolina nullification crisis. Story observed that the key evidence relied upon by South Carolina states' rights enthusiasts were miscellaneous writings issued more than thirty years before, during an even greater constitutional crisis. The dispute over the Alien and Sedition Acts had produced the Virginia and Kentucky Resolutions and related documents, reports, and interpretations. In each of these two political disputations, states' rights doctrines such as interposition, nullification, and even secession had been advanced as specific extensions of the first political principle of (state) sovereignty.

Story suspected that many who later advocated such an extraconstitutional states' rights interpretation of the Constitution did so because they had (or would have) opposed the Constitution originally, or because they had not come to terms with its most fundamental principles after its adoption. Now they sought to transform a discredited understanding into a plausible constitutional doctrine. Thus, in the *Commentaries on the Constitution*, Story observed the robust debate that had surrounded the Constitution's adoption produced two parties, one favoring and one opposing that document. Each continued long after the Constitution's adoption; Story noted in the midst of the South Carolina nullification dispute, that "perhaps they have never entirely ceased" (*CC* 1:288, 210). Such a conclusion may seem surprising, perhaps even intolerant, because we are accustomed to viewing early, differing interpretations over the Constitution's meaning as simple, straightforward battles of ideologies (federalist, republican, states' rights, and so on). Story suggested a different alternative: that an understanding of the Constitution can be considered illegitimate if it perpetuated fundamental tenets held by the Anti-Federalists, whose understanding had been decisively defeated when the Constitution was adopted. Thus, against our pervasive understanding which views all politics, including "judicial politics," as mere partisan battles over power and influence, Story sought to remove the Constitution (and its fundamental understanding and authority) from the battleground of regime politics and establish it as the settled object of public veneration.

Story most systematically attempted to insure the Constitution's permanence in his *Commentaries on the Constitution*, where, along with his clause-by-clause analysis of the Constitution, he also offered a remarkably practical adaptation of Lockean political theory presented as a straightforward history of the American people. To that end, Story traced their emergence into a single peoplehood, from their initial settlement of the colonies, to their growing conflict and eventual war with England, to the adoption of the Constitution. By means of this history, he sought to discredit that view which saw the Constitution as having been founded by the states (which retained their sovereignty, or crucial elements of that sovereignty).

The bedrock theoretical principle that informed Story's historical recounting was that the people historically preceded and therefore were superior to the government(s) they created. Story explained that the American people came into being with their opposition to England. The first Congress of delegates, assembled on September 1, 1774, in Philadelphia, constituted the first of several governments and "exercised both *de facto* and *de jure* a sovereign authority" which was wielded, not by "the delegated agents of the governments *de facto* of the colonies, but in virtue of original powers derived from the people" (*CC* 1:201, 145). Although the first Congress was soon superseded, the government it initiated was "terminated only when it was regularly superseded by the confederated government under the articles" (*CC* 1:201, 145). From 1774 onward, every political act embodied the will of the American people. The last, and most estimable, government of the American people was the Constitution, whose adoption was a "still more glorious triumph in the cause of national liberty than even that which separated us from the mother country" (*CC* 1:280, 199).

It was particularly noteworthy that the Constitution's ratification was approved by special state assemblies elected specifically for that task. Story observed that, from the crucial (Lockean) aspect of consent, it represented an important improvement over the Articles of Confederation. The Constitution's authority flowed directly from the consent of the people; its ratification assured that the new government would rest on foundations "deeper than in the mere sanction of delegating authority" (*CC* 1:268, 191, quoting *The Federalist* no. 22). This led Story—referencing Webster—to assert that the Constitution "was made by the people, made for the people, and is responsible to the people" (*CC* 1:397, 304). Webster returned his friend's favor; he advanced Story's history in speeches associating popular sovereignty with the national government. Story's account of history was later propounded by Abraham Lincoln, who, in his First Inaugural Address, adapted Story's theoretical history for identical political ends:

> [W]e find the proposition that, in legal contemplation, the Union is perpetual, confirmed by the history of the Union itself. The Union is much older than the Constitution. It was formed in fact, by the Articles of Association in 1774. It was matured and continued by the Declaration of Independence in 1776. It was further matured and the faith of all the then thirteen States expressly plighted and engaged that it should be perpetual, by the Articles of Confederation in 1778. And finally, in 1787, one of the declared objects for ordaining and establishing the Constitution, was *"to form a more perfect union."*

Story's (and Lincoln's) history aimed at establishing the certain principle that the Constitution was "an act of the people, and not of the States in their political capacities" (*CC* 1:463, 352). From this it followed that in no instance was any state—which necessarily constituted a minority of the whole people—"at liberty to disregard, suspend or annul" the Constitution (*CC* 1:359, 259). Only a popular majority could fundamentally alter such a document—either according to its explicit provisions by "peaceable appeal to the proper tribunals constituted by the government for such purposes"; or extraconstitutionally "by the ultimate appeal to the good sense, and integrity and justice of the majority of the people" (*CC* 1:337, 242–43).[4] Seldom has a doctrine of revolution been so gracefully disguised. And with good reason: Story simultaneously reaffirmed the right of revolution as proclaimed in the Declaration of Independence while discouraging postconstitutional rebellion. To that end, he advocated in his constitutional *Commentaries* the doctrine that ultimate sovereignty resided only in a popular majority; indeed, "according to Mr. Locke, [this] is the true sense of the original compact, by which every individual has surrendered to the majority of the society the right permanently to control and direct the operations of government therein" (*CC* 1:337, 243).

Within the day-to-day workings of the Constitution proper, Story sought to establish the Supreme Court as the final institutional arbiter of the Constitution's meaning. For him, the Supreme Court's undisputed authority was a consequence of clear, constitutional interpretation. In his constitutional *Commentaries*, Story made the following argument in support of his position: (a) The Constitution is the supreme law of the land (Article VI, clause 2); (b) the judicial power extends to all cases in law and equity arising under the Constitution (Article III, section 2); and, therefore, (c) in order to resolve such cases and controversies, as a last resort the Supreme Court is vested with the judicial power to construe laws according the Constitution, a power which necessarily includes an interpretive duty "to declare any unconstitutional law passed by Congress or by a State legislature [or by 'any other department of the national or state governments'] void" (see, for example, *CC* 1:375–79, 275–81, 392, 293–94; and 2:1576, 393–99). With this argument, Story advocated a united or holistic view of the Supreme Court's authority under the Constitution; for the most part, its authority over the states was no different from its authority over the Congress or the executive. Each equally arose from the Constitution. All matters capable of judicial inquiry, "whether in favor or against the constitutionality of the act, by the State or by the national authority, by the legislature or by the executive, being capable, . . . of being brought to the test of the Constitution" were subject to judicial revision by the "final and common arbiter provided by the Constitution itself, to whose decisions all others are subordinate" (*CC* 1:375, 276). By reserving the role as institutional arbiter of the constitutional system to the Supreme Court, Story rejected two important alternate understandings: (1) that each state could serve as a final constitutional umpire, or (2) that the other two branches could, in accordance with their oath to uphold the Constitution, act as both the first and final interpreter of that document.[5] Story spurned both alternatives explicitly, believing that each threatened the coherence and the durability of the Constitution.[6]

Because he believed that the first faulty misinterpretation posed the greatest danger to the permanence of the American nation, Story wrote frequently and passionately in opposition to that constitutional interpretation which postulated each state as final constitutional arbiter. His most enduring refutation of that doctrine could be found in his influential opinion for the Court in the 1816 case of *Martin v. Hunter's Lessee*.[7] The legal dispute reflected a long and troubling history. Three years before, Story had written an opinion for the Court in *Fairfax's Devisee v. Hunter's Lessee* which reversed a Virginia State Court of Appeals decision by holding that Virginia's confiscation of land during the Revolutionary War violated the Treaty of Paris.[8] Not surprisingly, *Fairfax's Devisee* was ill received in that state, where it was widely interpreted as an attack upon both state law and local economic interests. Subsequently, Virginia sought legal redress. Under the leadership of Spencer Roane, Virginia's highest court reviewed Story's opinion in *Fairfax* and found section 25 of the 1789 Judiciary Act conferring Supreme Court appellate jurisdiction of state court decisions to be unconstitutional. Therefore, the Supreme Court had exceeded its legitimate authority when it had decided *Fairfax* and for that reason its opinion was not enforceable.

The consideration of Virginia's legal rebuff of Supreme Court appellate jurisdiction constituted the core of *Martin v. Hunter's Lessee*. At stake was nothing less than the right of a state to determine for itself the constitutionality of its own laws. In rejecting this state "right," Story found support in Article III of the Constitution, particularly in section two. Irrespective of whether cases originated in the states or in lower federal courts, he argued that the Constitution *required* Congress to vest full appellate jurisdiction in the Supreme Court in all cases, in law and equity, arising under this Constitution, the laws of the United States, and treaties made, or which shall be made, under its authority.[9] Therefore, section 25 of the 1789 Judiciary Act was constitutional. Furthermore, Story contended that constitutional powers generally, including the Supreme Court's power over appellate jurisdiction, were to be interpreted broadly, for no construction of a power was to be allowed which plainly defeated or impaired its avowed objects.[10] Specifically, where the judicial power extends to a case, as it did here, Story observed that "it will be in vain to search in the letter of the Constitution for any qualification as to the tribunal where it depends."[11]

Story's broad interpretation of the Supreme Court's Article III appellate power reflected the Founders' Constitution, which simultaneously empowered the national government and restricted the authority of the states. The Constitution intended to deprive the states "altogether of the exercise of some powers of sovereignty, and restrain and regulate them in the exercise of others."[12] Presuming that "state attachments, state prejudices, state jealousies, and state interests, might sometimes obstruct or control, . . . the regular administration of justice," the Constitution sought to remedy this political malady.[13] Specifically, the essential nationwide uniformity of constitutional interpretation necessary for maintaining the political health of the American nation was an intended consequence of the Supreme Court's appellate jurisdiction and the Constitution's supremacy over state laws and constitutions.

Story was also concerned about, but devoted far less attention to, a second misconstruction of the Constitution—the belief that each branch of government was both the first and final interpreter of the Constitution. He attributed this faulty understanding to Jefferson, against whom he waged guerrilla warfare in footnotes throughout his *Commentaries on the Constitution*. Story did not deny that this understanding contained some truth; congressional representatives, as well as the president, were required by their oath of office to uphold, and therefore to interpret and apply, the Constitution when passing legislation and/or acting in accordance with its provisions.

And since almost none of their actions would admit review by the Supreme Court, in virtually every instance each branch of the national government would be the final judge of the constitutionality of its own actions. But this would not be true in every instance. When either branch exceeded its authority, and when the infraction could be cast in appropriate case form, Story offered the remedy that he believed grew out of the Constitution itself: "[t]he main security relied on to check any irregular or unconstitutional measure, either of the executive or the legislative department was, . . . the judiciary" (*CC* 2:1624, 436). Here and elsewhere, Story vigorously asserted that it was the Supreme Court's obligation to invalidate *any* act and action of the other two branches, provided that they were repugnant to the Constitution and that they reached the Court in proper form. Story's interpretation of the Supreme Court's broad constitutional authority was consistent with a generous reading of a case he cited frequently in his *Commentaries on the Constitution*: *Marbury v. Madison* (1803).[14] His language was unequivocal:

> Indeed, wherever, in a judicial proceeding, *any* questions arise touching the validity of a treaty, or statute, or authority, exercised under the United States, or touching the construction of any clause of the Constitution, or *any* statute or treaty of the United States, or touching the validity of any statute or authority exercised under *any* state, on the ground of repugnancy to the Constitution, laws, or treaties of the United States, it has been invariably held to be the case to which the judicial power of the United States extends. (*CC* 2:1647, 452–53, emphasis added; cf. 1:375, 276; 2:1576, 393–99 and 1646, 452–53)

Once the law had been interpreted by the Supreme Court, the Constitution anticipated its uniform application. For that reason, the Supreme Court's interpretation became obligatory and conclusive upon all the departments of the federal government, and upon the whole people, so far as their rights and duties were protected by the Constitution.

Persuasive as Story's explanation of the Supreme Court's authority under Article III seems, a serious problem remains. Story's broad interpretation of the Supreme Court's power would appear to lend legitimacy to an imperial judiciary so often exercised and so often decried in the twentieth century. Yet a runaway judiciary did not concern Story. He frequently repeated the maxim that the judiciary was the weakest of the three branches and his private and public writings reflected the concern that the Court's authority was inadequate to its responsibilities. Additionally, there were interrelated restraints upon the Supreme Court's exercise of judicial power which were obvious to Story but are far less well understood today. They included: (1) that the Supreme Court was bound to follow established rules of interpretation; (2) that the Constitution granted the national government substantial powers which seldom could be reviewed; and (3) that the Supreme Court could only review cases "capable of judicial inquiry and decision." We consider each of these restraints, in turn, below.

First, Story devoted a chapter in his *Commentaries on the Constitution* to explicating rules of constitutional interpretation (see generally *CC* 1:bk. III, chap. 5). He listed nineteen of them. The clear purpose of these rules was to confine justices while, at the same time, pointing them toward a correct interpretation of the document before them. Informing Story's interpretive rules were two fundamental principles. The first was that the Constitution was a legal document. For that reason, Story simply argued that it ought to be interpreted like any other legal document. The key idea was that legal interpretation began with, and concentrated upon, the document itself; this implied that Supreme Court justices should and could avoid bias or prejudice in the process of interpreting the Constitution. To that end, Story supplied various neutral rules of legal interpretation that most often could be traced to Blackstone and were widely accepted at the time. "The first and fundamental rule of the interpretation *of all instruments* is, to construe them according to the sense of the terms and the intention of the parties" (*CC* 1:400, 305, emphasis added). Elaborating upon this "first and fundamental rule," Story suggested that if a provision of the Constitution was in doubt, one looked first to the language; then to the context; then to the structure of the document and the government it created; and, finally, to the intention of its authors.

Story's numerous legal rules of interpretation assumed that the Constitution, as both the highest law of the land and a work of political wisdom, was intelligible; Story noted that it had proceeded upon a theory of its own. Thus, the interpretative rules he advanced assumed not merely that there was a correct interpretative procedure; it assumed that there was an underlying meaning that, in many instances, could be discovered.[15] At the most general level, Story shared with most of the leading American Founders a belief about the meaning and significance of the Constitution's creation of republican government. Most all had agreed that the United States—that first large republic of modernity founded upon the explicit consent of the people—had been a bold political experiment. As James Wilson pointed out in the Pennsylvania Ratifying Convention, the new nation was "almost without precedent or guide, and, consequently without the benefit of that instruction which, in many cases, may be derived from the constitution, and history, and experience, of other nations."[16] Enter the Founders: Story understood them to be "architects of consummate skill and fidelity" who had erected a Constitution whose "arrangements are full of wisdom and order" (*CC* 2:1914, 657). Despite compromises which he appropriately acknowledged, Story believed that the Constitution as a whole presented a coherent and wise understanding of government, and for that reason, its overall, correct construction informed that document's specific provisions.

Both for specific and general constitutional guidance, Story was most dependent upon *The Federalist* and the judicial opinions of John Marshall. He believed that *The Federalist* contained the fullest statement of the Founders' constitutional understanding, while Marshall's opinions contained their clearest application. It was noteworthy that Story published his *Commentaries on the Constitution* some seven years before the release of James Madison's *Journal* of the Constitutional Convention. Therefore, Story found it possible to provide his explicit constitutional guidance absent a detailed, comprehensive history of the Constitutional Convention.

It might seem that Story's reliance upon *The Federalist* and Marshall's legal opinions would prove uncontroversial. But this was not the case. Those who sought to graft an Anti-Federalist, states' rights view to the Constitution instead championed aspects of the language of the Virginia and Kentucky Resolutions (the "principles of '98"), and argued simultaneously that theirs was a true interpretation of the Constitution. To them, *The Federalist* and Marshall's opinions were of dubious constitutional merit (Roane, for instance, labeled *The Federalist* "a mere newspaper publication written in the heat and fury of battle" while Taylor was not above misquoting or attempting to refute it).[17] Their cause found their most respected advocate in Thomas Jefferson, who in 1809 had retired to Monticello and from where (in life and after his death) his words advanced Virginia's political interests by championing the cramped constitutional interpretation of political allies John Taylor and Spencer Roane while attacking the jurisprudence of Marshall (and Story).[18]

It is important to recognize that whatever fundamental constitutional disagreements existed between Story and his constitutional critics, neither side championed a runaway, not to mention, unrestrained Supreme Court. Story's leading critics did not doubt for a moment that Supreme Court justices were bound by rules of constitutional interpretation; nor were most of the rules themselves particularly controversial.[19] To the limited extent that they proved controversial, disputations focused upon the application of these rules. Far more often, critics generally sought to confine the (nationalizing) authority of the Supreme Court. Thus, Virginian Abel Upshur, whose 1840 *Brief Inquiry Into the True Nature and Character of the Federal Government* attempted a refutation of Story's *Commentaries on the Constitution*, argued in favor of limiting the Supreme Court's jurisdiction significantly by severely restricting its ability to reverse state laws and state court decisions. By so doing, Upshur advocated a constitutional understanding which, in this critical respect, restricted the Supreme Court far more than had Story. The Story-Upshur debate demonstrated that while robust constitutional disagreements persisted in the early Republic, neither Story nor his states rights critics advocated anything approaching what we today call judicial activism.

Not only did Story think that the Supreme Court would be confined by the existence of clearly enunciated rules of constitutional interpretation, he additionally identified a second restraining force. He therefore believed that the Constitution created a government whose actions seldom could or would be reviewed by the Supreme Court. Thus, when he interpreted the Constitution consistent with *The Federalist* and the opinions of Chief Justice John Marshall, Story understood it fundamentally to be an empowering document that created a national government capable of acting energetically. *The Federalist* no. 44 (cited by Story) observed that "[n]o axiom is more clearly established in law, or in reason, that wherever the end is required, the means are authorized; wherever a general power to do a thing is given, every particular power necessary for doing it is included." Furthermore, Story emphasized that granting the national government broad authority over a range of subjects intended to prevent political fragmentation by creating great national, unifying interests. Consistent with this end, he advanced generous interpretations, not only of the necessary and proper clause, but other constitutional provisions as well, including the commerce and taxing clauses. And there was more. Throughout the Constitution, the national government implicitly had been assigned tasks (e.g., passing legislation instituting non-self-executing treaties, authorizing writs of habeas corpus exempting congressional representatives from unconstitutional arrest, allowing Congress to suspend habeas corpus, and so on). Story could not have been clearer that the national government was entitled to act in such instances: "the natural, if not the necessary conclusion is, that the national government, in the absence of all positive provisions to the contrary, is bound, through its own proper departments, legislative, judicial, or executive, as the case may require, to carry into effect all the rights and duties imposed upon it by the Constitution."[20] The Founders drafted a Constitution fit to deal with ordinary political problems as well as with future exigencies. In contemporary language, although the Constitution was not a living document (because it often contained a discernable meaning), it did create a living government.

Such an expansive interpretation of national powers gave great leeway to the Congress (and the executive) to act as was thought fit. Story explained that treaties, as well as the national government's "mode of executing" its war, taxing, appropriation, and commerce powers with foreign nations, all could not be reexamined elsewhere. Thus, measures legitimately passed under such a constitutional authority were "exclusively of a political, legislative, or executive character," and "as the supreme authority, as to these questions, belongs to the legislative and executive departments, they cannot be re-examined elsewhere." Even when treaties or taxes were passed upon "motives and grounds wholly beside the intention of the Constitution," Story suggested that a remedy could be effected "solely by an appeal to the people at the elections, or by the salutary powers of amendment provided by the Constitution itself " (*CC* 1:374, 275). In such instances, neither the people nor the states nor the other branches of the national government (including the Supreme Court) possessed any general authority to review tasks the Constitution had assigned elsewhere (and which the officers of the states and the national government were all sworn to uphold).

But, of course, Story hardly believed the Supreme Court impotent. In contrast to questions of a political, executive, and legislative character, there also existed questions that Story characterized as "capable of judicial inquiry and decision" (or, capable "of being made the subject of judicial controversy"). From one vantage point, the existence of this category was empowering. Where such questions existed, the Supreme Court was empowered to act. It was, after all, the final institutional expositor of the Constitution. But in another crucial respect, that the Supreme Court could (only) consider cases capable of judicial inquiry and decision constituted a third, fundamentally important limitation upon the Supreme Court's power. Therefore, while the Constitution authorized the Supreme Court to interpret the Constitution and apply its provisions to contested statutes, it could so act *only* when the contested law or governmental action was capable of judicial inquiry and decision.

So the question is: what did Story mean by questions capable of judicial inquiry and decision? He explained this category when he turned his attention to Article III, section 2's provision that "the judicial power shall extend to cases in law and equity arising under the Constitution, laws, and treaties of the United States." Story asked: what is the meaning of "cases" within this clause? The answer was: a case has two components. It exists when a suit is instituted according to the established legal forms and when it involves a question arising under the Constitution, laws, and treaties of the United States. In Story's words, a case "arises when some subject touching the Constitution, laws, or treaties of the United States is submitted to the courts by a party who asserts his rights in the form prescribed by law" (*CC* 2:1646, 452). Story acknowledged the sense in which the courts, including the Supreme Court, were limited in this regard: "It cannot punish without law. It cannot create controversies to act upon. It can decide only upon rights and cases, as they are brought by others before it. It can do nothing for itself. It must do everything for others. It must obey the laws; and if it corruptly administers them, it is subjected to the power of impeachment" (*CC* 1:534, 399).

Here, it is important to emphasize an important assumption relied upon by Story. He believed that the Supreme Court's power was circumscribed because he understood the rights that could legitimately be asserted in federal courts to be far more limited than is commonly understand today. Specifically, Story—like virtually every leading Founder and legal authority of his age—believed Marshall's opinion in *Barron v. Baltimore* (1833) to be correct.[21] Amendments 1–8 restricted only the national government. And the amendments themselves were understood far more narrowly by Story and his judicial colleagues than they are today.[22]

Thus, by means of distinct arguments, Story simultaneously advanced two distinct positions: he contended both that the Supreme Court exercised legitimate authority as the Constitution's chief institutional arbiter and that it was improbable that it would act irresponsibly or imperially. Undergirding these conclusions was Story's belief that a responsible justice's interpretation of the Constitution was rooted in the document itself; because the Constitution formed a coherent whole that informed its parts, its meaning, with adequate thought and study, could in many instances be discerned. Remarkable as it may seem to legal realists today, Story simply believed that he brought no preconceptions to his judicial capacity as judge.[23] His understanding of constitutional interpretation was vastly at odds with that prevalent contemporary interpretative mode that denies the Constitution any or much intrinsic meaning, choosing rather to "interpret" it in accordance with some sort of preconceived, autonomous, overarching legal or political theory. For Story, it would have been simply illegitimate to approach the Constitution in such a way. For example, how could it be interpreted simply (or even primarily) as a procedural, or a feminist, or an egalitarian charter; or seen only through the lenses of critical legal studies, or economic rights; or understood primarily as a minimalist (common law) document?[24] Behind most all of these and other contemporary "interpretivist" notions is the positivist belief that the law is simply what the judges say it is, and that what *really* matters is that a judge has an autonomous idea, and specifically the *right* idea, of what should be done regarding a preferred legal outcome or social policy. By contrast, when Story said that he intended to propound a true view of the Constitution, he really meant that he brought no new interpretation to his reading of its provisions. To that end, he wrote that "I have nót the ambition to be author of any new plan of interpreting the theory of the Constitution, or of enlarging or narrowing its powers by ingenious subtleties and learned doubts" (*CC* 1:preface, x). In contrast with Story's self-under-standing regarding his constitutional task stood the more creative efforts of states' rights advocate John Taylor: "I once saw a book advertised, entitled 'New Views on the Constitution.' I was startled! What right has a man to state *new* views upon it?" (*LL* 2:506).

The proof that Story was unwilling to inject personal policy preferences (much yet any sort of rigid ideology) into his reading of the Constitution is most easily observed regarding his understanding of natural law. Story's writings as judge and legal commentator clearly demon-strated his belief in the utility, and quite likely the truth, of this idea. Story defined natural law as "that system of principle, which human reason has discovered to regulate the conduct of man in all his various relations" whose obligatory force "upon man is derived from its presumed coincidence with the will of his Creator."[25] He subsequently identified and affirmed specific categories of rights and duties, including Lockean natural rights. Story also identified something like a catalogue of derivative human individual and social virtues which followed from a belief in natural law, specifically noting that each person was "bound to exercise charity in the largest sense; to be just, grateful, kind and benevolent; to promote the general happiness; to speak the truth and to abstain from falsehood; to abstain from oppression anger, revenge, hatred, malice, slander, uncharitableness, persecution, and every other injurious act or passion." He concluded that these duties were incumbent "in respect to all the human race."[26]

The duty on all to avoid oppression, and an oft proclaimed belief in the natural rights of all human beings, implied for Story a clear condemnation of slavery and the slave trade. From time to time, he had occasion to make his concern explicit and his opinions on the matter were well known. In a May 8, 1820, charge to a grand jury, Story described the slave trade in vivid and disconcerting terms in order to support the conclusion that "[t]he existence of slavery, under any shape, is so repugnant to the natural rights of man and the dictates of justice, that it seems difficult to find for it any adequate justification" (*MW* 136). Privately, Story opposed the expansion of slavery into the territories and, later, the admission of slave states to the Union. "The natural rights of men" constituted the standard whose application necessarily condemned the vile institution, a point Story made in his well-known charge:

> And, Gentleman, how can we justify ourselves or apologize for our indifference to this subject? Our constitutions of government declared that all men are born free and equal, and have certain unalienable rights, among which are the right of enjoying their lives, liberties, and property, and of seeking and obtaining their own safety and happiness. May not the miserable African ask: "Am I not a man and a brother?" We boast of our noble struggle against the encroachments of tyranny; but do we forget, that it assumed the mildest form, in which authority ever assailed against the rights of its subjects; and yet that there are men among us, who think it no wrong to condemn the shivering African to perpetual slavery? (*MW* 140)

In a very specific way, Story's jurisprudence reflected his understanding of the relationship between slavery and the slave trade, on the one hand, and natural justice, on the other hand. Thus, Story interpreted legal ambiguities in favor of the slave's natural rights. On this basis, in the 1822 case of *La Jeune Eugenie*, Story found the slave trade to be an offense against "the universal law of society" and therefore a violation of international law.[27] And almost twenty years later, in the case of the *United States v. Amistad* (1841), in the face of other legal ambigu-ities, Story adopted a similar approach.[28] Here he ordered the release of slaves who had revolted against their Spanish crew, only to have been captured by an American man-of-war. At issue was the interpretation of a Spanish-American treaty, whose ambiguities, according to Story, were (again) to be constructed in favor of freedom when human life and liberty were at issue. Thus, he noted that the slaves in revolt were neither murderers nor pirates nor—most important— merchandise. They were freemen who had regained their rights "decided upon the eternal principles of justice and international law."[29]

Yet, in the face of disputes over the Constitution, whose language and intent indisputably encompassed slavery (while at the same time its language never specifically mentioned it), Story's advocacy of natural law principles from the bench was far more restricted. Admittedly, the Founders compromised the slavery question in the Constitution, hoping for its ultimate eradication. Nonetheless, Story understood that the Constitution could no more substitute the Founders' aspirations and expectations for its explicit provisions than it could allow judges to substitute their natural law beliefs for the Constitution's clear meaning. A particularly interesting case in this regard was *Groves v. Slaughter* (1841), where the Supreme Court considered the narrow legal issue of whether Mississippi's constitutional ban restricting the importation of slaves for sale within the state was void without enabling legislation.[30] Story dissented from this holding without opinion, citing precedent and his belief that the state constitutional provision was self-actuating.[31] But there was a substantial constitutional issue lurking behind *Groves*, and it indirectly pointed to the most explosive constitutional question dividing the regime. That question specifically asked whether Mississippi's regulation of the slave trade was a violation of the Congress's (dormant) exclusive commerce power (and more specifically pointed to a related, more fundamental question: did Congress possess *any* power to modify or end slavery and the slave trade?). Justice Thompson for the Court explicitly declined to consider the entire matter, but the commerce clause question evinced specific comments from Justices McLean, Taney, and Baldwin.

Rejecting an argument that had been advanced by Daniel Webster, Story's dissent signaled his belief that Mississippi's constitutional ban on the importation of slaves for sale did not violate the commerce clause. Although elsewhere he had repeatedly advanced a generous interpretation of Congress's commerce power and additionally had often made clear his opposition to slavery and the slave trade, Story now declined to translate either belief into a Supreme Court opinion. In the end, Story could not ignore an important truth: that slavery existed in each state before the Revolutionary War and, absent explicit constitutional restrictions or arguably a specific act of Congress under the commerce clause, a state's authority over slavery and the slave trade within its borders simply was to be presumed constitutional as an exercise of its surviving police powers. But just as states could allow slavery and generally regulate their internal slave trade under the Constitution (subject, of course, to that document's restraints), states could also, under the very same police power, abolish each as well. One lesson was clear: judicial positions taken upon legal issues in cases like *Groves* did not quickly or easily translate into desirable political or social policy. Nonetheless, Story's position in that case has been sometimes viewed as striking a limited antislavery blow; he did vote to invalidate the contracts benefiting slave owners by upholding state constitutional limitations on the slave trade (which admittedly had not been made for humanitarian motives, but rather for the purpose of stabilizing slave prices within Mississippi). But even if these limited antislavery effects can be fairly attributed to Story's *Groves* position, it is crucial to recognize that they appear as the by-product of an important and largely unrecognized, self-imposed restraint. In *Groves*, Story could not bring himself to advocate a novel, expansive interpretation of Congress's power over commerce and slavery, and thus he refused to impose upon the Constitution a natural law interpretation that did violence to its most obvious meaning.

This same attitude held true in Story's opinion for the Court in *Prigg v. Pennsylvania* (1842).[32] The opinion directly addressed the removal of a fugitive slave and her child from Pennsylvania by an attorney working for Maryland employers. The attorney had failed to obtain proper state certification under a Pennsylvania personal liberty statute designed to protect free Negroes from being wrongfully seized as fugitive slaves. The case raised the question directly whether this state statute, and indirectly whether the national Fugitive Slave Act of 1793, were consistent with Article IV, section 2, clause 3's fugitive slave clause mandating the return of escaped slaves (identified in the document as persons "held to service or labor").

Story held that the state law was constitutionally void because it conflicted with the national government's exclusive power to regulate fugitive slaves. Story concluded that the national Fugitive Slave Act of 1793 was a mandatory exercise of national power that was, in almost every provision, clearly constitutional. Despite his profound misgivings regarding slavery, Story recognized that the Constitution's fugitive slave clause was a provision whose meaning was clear and whose adoption was necessary for the Constitution's ratification. The flip-side of Story's insistence that the national government was required to implement the fugitive slave clause was his belief that the states could not legislate on this subject or be compelled to enforce this exclusive national power. He went so far as to suggest that they could prohibit by law participation of their officers in regards to this federal subject matter.

Story's insistence that only federal officers, and not state officials, could be required to enforce the Fugitive Slave Act of 1793 revealed an important antislavery loophole. It opened the door for the passage of personal liberty laws, most notably one passed on the heels of the *Prigg* decision in Story's native Massachusetts. That state's law not only prohibited state judges from recognizing the national act of 1793 and issuing certificates of rendition, but it also prevented state officials from assisting in the arrest of alleged fugitive slaves, and prohibited the use of state jails in the confinement of fugitive slaves. This loophole, no doubt, led Story to declare the *Prigg* decision to be "a triumph of freedom" (*LL* 2:392).

Story's opinion that the national government could not delegate the enforcement of national law to state tribunals or officials can be criticized upon numerous grounds. It seemed: (1) to be in tension with the supremacy clause's injunction that the laws of the United States made pursuant to the Constitution constituted the supreme laws of the land; (2) to be hard to reconcile with Article VI, clause 3's requirement that state officials swear an oath to support the Constitution; and (3) to provide (of all things!) an overly generous interpretation of the states' reserved police powers.[33] In the face of such objections, it is important to emphasize that Story's interpretation in *Prigg* was consistent with his past Supreme Court jurisprudence, with discussions presented earlier in his *Commentaries on the Constitution*, and with his general understanding of federalism interpreted in light of his understanding of legal conflicts.[34] But this would not prove sufficient to answer the most heated criticisms made against Story, advanced less on the ground of his specific interpretation of the Constitution than on the basis of his very attachment to natural justice. Eradicating this vile institution of slavery had become the standard by which abolitionists were willing to judge, not the Constitution's meaning, but its very legitimacy.[35] But Story's political opinions—even his belief in natural law—did not allow him to set aside his obligation as a judge. A judge's duty was explication of the Constitution as law—pure and simple—to the best of one's ability. In Story's words, written shortly after his *Prigg* opinion:

I shall never hesitate to do my duty as a Judge, under the Constitution and laws of the United States, be the consequences be what they may. That Constitution I have sworn to support, and I cannot forget or repudiate my solemn obligations at pleasure. You know full well that I have ever been opposed to slavery. But I take my standard of day, *as a Judge* from the Constitution. (*LL* 2:431)

Story's rejection of natural law in favor of the Constitution's explicit language did not necessarily mean that he rejected a natural law approach altogether. The Constitution's compromise with slavery represented an exception to its instituting of the Lockean principles of the Declaration of Independence, a concession originally made to political necessity and instituted in the hope of securing slavery's ultimate extinction. A far friendlier legal context for natural law jurisprudence existed in cases where state governments sought arbitrarily to alter property rights. Although Story decided several of these cases according to abstract principles of justice, he would also rely upon the contract clause (Article I, section 10, clause 1). Story was an enthusiastic advocate of this clause which simultaneously limited state power while advancing a principle of natural justice (which embodied a Lockean natural right of property). Specifically, natural justice and the contract clause each prohibited states from arbitrarily interfering with the right of property of citizens within their jurisdiction. Story stated the matter clearly: "We know of no case in which a legislative Act to transfer the property of A to B without his consent has ever been held a constitutional exercise of legislative power in any state of the Union." "On the contrary," he added, "it has consistently been resisted as inconsistent with just principles by every judicial tribunal in which it has attempted to be enforced."[36]

Thus, many of Story's most important decisions could be found at the intersection of assuring contract and property rights, on the one hand, and limiting the authority of the states, on the other hand. Justice and law both inclined Story to rule that property, whether privately or corporately held, was legally entitled to protection from arbitrary (state) government action. To that end, he applied the principle broadly. Not only individuals deserved protection. Specifically, in the 1815 case of *Terrett v. Taylor*, Story voided the Virginia legislature's confiscation of land previously granted to the Episcopal Church as a private (religious) corporation.[37] He declared it to be a violation of the fundamental laws of every free government, of the spirit and letter of the Constitution, and of the principles of natural justice. That same year, in *Town of Pawlet v. Clark*,[38] Story again did not refer explicitly to the contract clause, yet he extended to public corporations the same kind of protection he had afforded to private corporations in *Terrett*. In *Green v. Biddle* (1823), Story employed both the contract clause and natural law to extend constitutional protections to interstate compacts.[39] Story's understanding of the broad scope of the contract clause was convincingly advanced in his concurring opinion in the *Dartmouth College* (1819) case.[40] His opinion sought to bolster the weakest elements of Chief Justice Marshall's opinion for the Court, which held invalid a New Hampshire law altering Dartmouth College's charter (as a private eleemosynary corporation granted by the British Crown prior to the Revolution). Specifically, Story undertook to explain the idea of an implied contract, which he believed implicit in the colonial charter founding Dartmouth College, and which therefore made the charter deserving of constitutional protection. In advocating such an understanding of the contract clause, it did not matter to Story if the contract was popular or unpopular. Thus, in 1837, in the well-known dissent in the *Charles River Bridge* case, Story would have extended constitutional protection to an unpopular legislative charter which granted to the Charles River Bridge Company an exclusive right to operate a bridge and collect tolls for an extended number of years.[41] Against the charge that his jurisprudence unfairly stifled competition and economic progress (in this case by condemning the building of the second Warren bridge to be built; in other cases by denying innovation and progress), Story noted that there existed appropriate political remedies. Here, the legislature could have written in reservations, or, if a second bridge was subsequently deemed necessary, then the stockholders in the originally authorized corporation (the Charles River Bridge Corporation) could have been compensated for lost tolls.

As with cases involving slavery, and many of his other opinions, historians have scoured Story's contract clause opinions searching for hidden motives. But here, as elsewhere, Story's constitutional understandings were, for the most part, remarkably straightforward. And despite his consistent advocacy of broad constitutional grants of power to the national government, and despite his condemnation of slavery and the slave trade as well as his sympathetic view of the plight of the American Indian, there remains a proclivity today to understand Story better than he understood himself. The pervasive tendency is to see Story as the prisoner of some sort of ideology, or interest, or sentiment; today he is portrayed, and therefore most often remembered, simply as a conservative.[42]

Perhaps it is too easy to confound Story's sober view of self-government with an opposition to it. But that would be an error. Story's legal and political understandings grew out of study and reflection. Like the Founders and other leading statesmen of his generation, he understood advancements in the law and politics to be a great advance of his age. To that end, he endeavored to conserve a modern-day novelty, the United States's political experiment in self-government, which served as the republican prototype of a remarkably modern regime founded for the purpose of securing natural rights.

Specifically, Story understood the adoption of the Constitution to be the natural and wise fulfillment of the Declaration of Independence. As a Supreme Court justice and as America's foremost legal authority, Story superintended over the Constitution's development and nurturing. As he sought to develop the Constitution's principles, he also attempted to remove it from everyday politics by placing it above politics. This was perhaps the most notable way he pursued a lifelong goal of instilling a reverence for the Constitution as the foundation of the nation's secular political religion.

Story's constitutional understanding defined his actions as a Supreme Court justice. He emphatically championed the Supreme Court as the nation's final institutional arbiter of its foremost constitutional questions. As a justice and as legal authority, he steadfastly refused to substitute the supposed sovereignty of the states for the necessity of a single government. Regarding acts of the national government, he successfully combined his opinion of the essential authority of the Supreme Court with a restrained implementation of its powers. Not even once did he exercise the power of the Supreme Court to reverse any act of the national legislature.[43] All the while, as a judge, Story was guided by the belief that the Constitution intended a coherent interpretation, which he persistently sought to demonstrate. If his constitutional interpretation did not solve, or intend to solve, every legal question, it is hard to deny that it significantly narrowed the scope of important constitutional questions remaining to be resolved. In the end, Joseph Story is best remembered today as an example of an exemplary judge, as an enduring legal authority, and as a thoughtful and sober student of the American regime. Having devoted his life attempting to explicate, to the greatest extent possible, an accurate and (dare we say it?) *true* interpretation and application of the Constitution, we are reminded of a fact that seems odd in an age which simultaneously dismisses the idea of wisdom while elevating that of creativity: we are reminded that Joseph Story's most enduring wisdom was manifested in his persistent efforts to recognize and preserve a wisdom even greater than his own.

Notes

1. Henry Steele Commager, "Joseph Story," in *The Gaspar G. Bacon Lectures on the Constitution of the United States, 1940–1950* (Boston: Boston University Press, 1953), 80.

2. This has been widely acknowledged. See Commager, "Joseph Story," 53; Gerald T. Dunne, *Justice Joseph Story and the Rise of the Supreme Court* (New York: Simon and Schuster, 1970), 310–13; and R. Kent Newmyer, "Justice Joseph Story: A Political and Constitutional Study," Ph.D. diss., University of

Nebraska, Omaha, 1959, 202.

3. Quotations from and references to Story's works are cited in the text using the following abbreviations:

CC: *Commentaries on the Constitution of the United States*, 2 vols. (Boston: Little, Brown, and Company, 1891).

LL: *Life and Letters of Joseph Story*, 2 vols., ed. William W. Story (Boston: C. C. Little and J. Brown, 1851).

MW: *The Miscellaneous Writings of Joseph Story*, ed. William W. Story (Boston: C. C. Little and J. Brown, 1852).

Where applicable, references will be to the volume, section, and page number, respectively.

4. In this section, Story sought simultaneously to reassure and educate by referring to the state constitutions as a model for the U.S. Constitution.

5. The extent to which these two understandings can be made compatible has been insufficiently appreciated. It was not surprising that states rights' advocates, from time to time, favored the authority of Congress at the expense of the Supreme Court, given the fact that the Senate (then chosen directly by the states) was widely understood as the protector of local interests.

6. Since the Supreme Court's authority to strike down unconstitutional laws and acts is implied and not stipulated, much scholarly debate has centered around the question of whether it was intended. A main thrust of that scholarship has been to view the two powers separately. Thus, it is usually conceded that the Supreme Court's power over state courts and legislatures (federal judicial review) was clearly intended, while the Court's broad authority over Congress and the executive (national judicial review) proves more problematical. Story's understanding does not distinguish between the two and therefore raises problems for this entire approach. The clearest and arguably most influential exposition of the contemporary approach can be traced back to Corwin and can be found in the writings of historian Leonard Levy. See Leonard Levy, *Original Intent and the Framers' Constitution* (New York: MacMillan Publishing Company, 1988), chaps. 3–6.

7. 1 Wheaton 304 (1816).

8. 7 Cranch 603 (1813).

9. 1 Wheaton at 329, 332–33, 338–39.

10. This constituted a fundamental rule of constitutional interpretation. See *Martin v. Hunter's Lessee*, 1 Wheaton at 329 and CC 1:428, 327. There Story noted that even the portion of Article III, section 2's exception to powers granted, by declaring that the Supreme Court's appellate jurisdiction shall exist in law and fact "with such exceptions, and under such regulations, as the Congress shall make" reinforced the point that there could be no exception to a power granted if that power had not been granted fully in the first place.

11. 1 Wheaton at 338.

12. 1 Wheaton at 328. See, for example, Article I, section 10.

13. 1 Wheaton at 347.

14. A contrary position, that *Marbury v. Madison* intended only to affirm "that federal courts are entitled to invalidate acts of Congress and the president with finality only when to let such acts stand would violate constitutional restrictions on judicial powers," has been argued most persuasively by Robert Lowry Clinton, *Marbury v. Madison and Judicial Review* (Lawrence: University Press of Kansas, 1989).

15. Today, such an opinion seems naive. Professor Levy states the contemporary view of this matter with characteristic bluntness: "Justices who look to the Constitution for more than a puzzling, if majestic, phrase might just as well turn to the comic strips for all the guidance they will find on how to decide most of the great cases that involve national policy." Leonard Levy, ed., *American Constitutional Law: Historical Essays* (New York: Harper and Row, 1966), 1.

16. *The Debates of the Several State Conventions on the Adoption by the General Convention at Philadelphia in 1787*, ed. Jonathan Elliot (Philadelphia: J. L. Lippincott Company, 1836), bk. 1, vol. II, 421–22.

17. See *Hunter v. Martin*, 4 Mumford (Va.) 1 (1814) at 27 and Paul Zagorski, "John Taylor of Caroline and the Rousseauean Critique of the Constitution," Master's Thesis, Claremont Graduate School, 1973, 62–68.

18. An uproar was caused by the 1829 posthumous release of his private writings, which settled that he had written an extreme draft of the Kentucky Resolutions.

19. An exception were critics who deemphasized the Founders' intentions while emphasizing judgments and opinions expressed at state ratifying conventions.

20. See *Prigg v. Pennsylvania*, 16 Peters 539 (1842) at 616, 618–19. According to Corwin, such "powers have been repeatedly ascribed to the National Government by the Court on grounds which ill accord with the doctrine of enumerated powers." See Edward Corwin, *The Constitution of the United States of America: Analysis and Interpretation*, ed. Norman J. Small and Lester Jayson (Washington, D.C.: U.S. Government Printing Office, 1964), 94.

21. 7 Peters 243 (1833).

22. To see how far removed we are today from Story's understanding, consider how these two factors can combine. For instance, in the case of the First Amendment's establishment clause, Story believed both that it limited only the national government, and that it imposed only religious neutrality (and not complete separation from religion) upon that government. Obviously, such an interpretation of the amendment dramatically limits the claim of deprivation of rights that might be claimed by any person against government. This, of course, is to say nothing about rights not mentioned at all in the Bill of Rights, such as the right to privacy.

23. This conclusion does not deny that Story brought to his task of judging educated conclusions regarding that document's meaning.

24. Referred to, in an admittedly shorthand and incomplete manner, are the writings of a typical section of today's most influential constitutional commentators, including John Hart Ely, Catharine MacKinnon, Ronald Dworkin, Mark Tushnet, Richard Epstein, and Cass Sunstein. Perhaps the most influential has been Charles Beard, who viewed the Constitution primarily as an economic document.

25. Joseph Story, "Natural Law," an unsigned article printed in *Encyclopedia Americana: A Popular Dictionary of Arts, Sciences, Literature, History and Biography*, ed. Francis Lieber (Philadelphia: Desilver, Thomas and Company, 1836), vol. 9, 150.

26. Story, "Natural Law," 152.

27. 26 Fed. Cases 832, 847 (1822). Story's bold formulation was rejected by the Supreme Court three years later in *The Antelope*, 10 Wheaton 66 (1825). Story was not persuaded by Marshall's opinion for the Court. See Story to Bacon, November 19, 1842, *LL* 2:431. Yet he did not dissent, a fact most likely explained by the fact that he generally issued dissents only in cases involving constitutional principles. On this point, see Story to Robert J. Walker, May 22, 1847, in *Papers of Joseph Story: Manuscript Collection*, The New York Historical Society, New York State.

28. 15 Peters 518 (1841). His disposition to interpret legal ambiguities in order to rule against the slave trade constituted a pattern: for example, on the Supreme Court, see *The Plattsburgh*, 10 Wheaton 133 (1825) and *U.S. v. Gooding*, 12 Wheaton 460 (1827).

29. 15 Peters at 595.

30. 15 Peters at 449 (1841).

31. Story to Robert J. Walker, May 22, 1847, *Papers of Joseph Story*, cited in note 27 above. Regarding precedent, Story likely had in mind the Court's opinion in *New York v. Miln*, 11 Peters 102 (1837). Interestingly, Story there dissented from the Court's elevation of state police powers at the expense of the national commerce power.

32. 16 Peters 539 (1842).

33. These factors later led the Supreme Court to reject *Prigg*'s postulate that the states could not be compelled to enforce federal law. See, for example, *Claflin v. Houseman*, 93 U.S. 130 (1876) and *Testa v. Katt*, 330 U.S. 386 (1947).

34. See Story's dissent in *Houston v. Moore*, 5 Wheaton 1, 69 (1820) and *CC* 2:1755–59, 536–39. Story's view of state courts' relative freedom of action regarding federal law received support from Chief Justice Taney in *Kentucky v. Dennison*, 24 Howard 66, 107 (1861). Story's *Commentaries on the Conflict of Laws* had established him as the American expert in this area; for an interpretation of the relevance of his understanding for *Prigg*, see William L. Leslie, "The Influence of Joseph Story's Theory of the Conflict of Laws on Constitutional Nationalism," *Mississippi Valley Historical Review* 35 (September 1948): 212, 220.

35. But as observers from Frederick Douglass to Harry Jaffa have pointed out, abolishing the Constitution would have had the effect of protecting slavery in the South. It is likely that this perception, combined with his hope that slavery's expansion could be confined, bolstered Story's belief (which occasionally wavered) that the Constitution (properly interpreted) could guide the nation through its crisis over slavery.

36. *Wilkinson v. Leeland*, 2 Peters 627, 657–58 (1829). Also see *CC* 2:1399, 273 and John Locke's *Second Treatise of Government*, sec. 138.

37. 9 Cranch 43 (1815).

38. *Town of Pawlet v. Clark*, 9 Cranch 292 (1815).

39. 8 Wheaton 1 (1823).

40. *Trustees of Dartmouth College v. Woodward*, 4 Wheaton 518, 666 (1819).

41. *Charles River Bridge v. Warren Bridge Co.*, 11 Peters 420, 583 (1837).

42. Not surprisingly, each of Story's three biographers emphasize that he was a conservative. See Gerald Dunne, *Justice Joseph Story and the Rise of the Supreme Court* (New York: Simon and Schuster, 1970); James McClellan, *Joseph Story and the American Constitution* (Norman: University of Oklahoma Press, 1971); and R. Kent Newmyer, *Supreme Court Justice Joseph Story: Statesman of the Old Republic* (Chapel Hill: University of North Carolina Press, 1985).

It is perhaps ironic that today Andrew Jackson is regarded as a progressive and Story a conservative. In this respect, consider their divergent opinions regarding the national and state governments' treatment of Indians: note, in particular, that Story joined Justice Thompson's dissent in *Cherokee Nation v. Georgia*, 5 Peters 1, 50 (1831), and his agreement with the Court's opinion in *Worcester v. Georgia*, 6 Peters 515 (1832). Particularly poignant on this subject is a letter written by Story to his wife: "At Philadelphia I was introduced to two of the Chiefs of the Cherokee Nation so sadly dealt with by the State of Georgia. They are both educated men, and conversed with singular force and propriety of language upon their own case, the law of which they perfectly understood and reasoned upon. I never in my whole life was more affected by the consideration that they and all their race are destined to destruction. And I feel, as an American, disgraced by our gross violation of the public faith toward them. I fear, and greatly fear, that in the course of Providence there will be dealt to us a heavy retributive justice" (*LL* 2:79).

43. It is difficult to imagine today that fifty-four years separated the Supreme Court's first invalidation of a congressional act in *Marbury v. Madison*, 1 Cranch 137 (1803), and its second in *Dred Scott v. Sandford*, 19 Howard 393 (1857).

Chapter 19

James Fenimore Cooper:
Nature and Nature's God

John E. Alvis

James Fenimore Cooper (1789–1851) distinguishes himself from most writers of his time by his insistence upon the liabilities he believes to be inseparable from the creditable features of the American regime as he judged it to have become in the early nineteenth century. Popular institutions that among his contemporaries generally met with approval Cooper subjects to an exacting critique. He is unremitting in his strictures against the press, skeptical of popular religion, unenthusiastic in his estimate of the equitableness of municipal and state governments, and doubtful of the benefits of jury trials. One may be inclined to dismiss his criticisms of American democratic manners as the unreflective complaints of a propertied aristocrat who in his personal affairs suffered from some hard dealing at the hands of local demagogues. Yet so to dismiss him would be to overlook his shrewd and generally fair-minded commentary on the national character and on the political habits that support a public life capable at once of sublimity and fatuousness. Cooper can instruct and not infrequently illuminate because he assesses what he considers to be the defects of a democratic republic from a perspective that professes to be, and usually is, thoughtfully democratic and republican.

Cooper insists that he is a democrat in principle, and his account of his political convictions stand scrutiny. He argues furthermore that his principles accord better with the country's Founding Fathers than do those of more unreflectively patriotic democratic partisans. His importance lies in the distinctions he successfully maintains between an advocacy of American institutions answerable to reason and an allegiance partial and impercipient.

Cooper sets himself the task of analyzing American institutions in the light of his distinction between proper and improper understandings of Founding principles. Among these principles liberty and equality are paramount, and of the two ideas the more important to be distinguished in its proper and improper meanings is equality. His concern to correct his countrymen's mistaken notions of the egalitarian premise connects his treatise on democracy with the body of his fiction. Like Tocqueville, Cooper seeks to find room within democracy for souls dissatisfied with the mediocre tendency imparted by popular institutions in their service of passions compounding envy, servility to popular opinion, or worse. He attempts simultaneously to reconcile America to natural aristocrats and gentlemen to America by making appeal to distinctions between democracy as he finds it among his contemporaries and democracy as it ought to be, once was, and could be again.

The American Democrat

The foregoing generalizations position us to understand the title of Cooper's book of reflections upon the national character and its habits of self-government, *The American Democrat* (1838). One comes to appreciate that the title makes an avowal, refers to a description, and adjures its audience to lift its eyes to a standard. Cooper avows his credentials as a partisan of the American species of democracy distinguished from other representatives of the genus popular government. He will take his stand with this improved version of rule by the people because it moderates the excesses he associates with the standard democratic type. He proposes a description that will make clear the distinction on the basis of which this American refinement earns his allegiance. His description, moreover, will lean upon another distinction, one opposing American democracy now debased with American democracy as it was meant to be, and this with the clear implication that his countrymen should relearn the principles that once animated the preceding generation.

The principles that animated the Fathers can be recovered out of the Founding documents. Most authoritatively, they can be drawn out of the Declaration of Independence. Unlike Tocqueville, who devotes a thousand pages to discussing the consequences of equality in America without once mentioning Thomas Jefferson's work, Cooper by contrast ties everything to the foundations Jefferson and the Continental Congress established in 1776.

This is not to say, however, that for Cooper the foundations are self-evident without explanation. The leading proposition of the Declaration—the "self-evident" truth that "all men are created equal"—cannot be grasped without introducing several distinctions requiring an extended discussion of the nature of civil society, human nature, natural and artificial differences among individuals, and the proper limits of the application of the ideal of equality to actual conditions. One cannot properly understand equality, moreover, without understanding its complementary principle, liberty. And to understand equality in the light of liberty one must take into account adjustments to our abstract notions of justice required by making provisions for the security and accumulation of property.

Cooper's discussion of equality seeks to keep in sight the one respect in which the assertion "all men are created equal" is true while noting several misconstructions of the celebrated proposition. The true understanding he takes to be quite confined. It can be expressed only negatively and in opposition to a rival notion of human inequality Cooper identifies with "Jus Divinum."[1] He supposes this survival of medieval thinking to rest upon a combination of the notion of divine right monarchy with a hierarchical class system based upon feudal land tenure. On the basis of this assumption, Cooper can maintain:

> All that the great American proposition, therefore, can mean, is to set up new and juster notions of natural rights than those which existed previously, by asserting, in substance, that God has not instituted political inequalities, as was pretended by the advocates of the Jus Divinum, and that men possessed a full and natural authority to form such social institutions as best suited their necessities. (109)

To see how the Jeffersonian equality principle ushers in a new beginning for political life, Cooper must first dwell upon a distinction between what is natural and what is artificial in civil society. Government itself, taken in abstraction from any of the forms particular governments assume, is a consequence of man's nature. Because human beings are not altogether self-regulating, they require government to coordinate, and especially to place limitations upon, the activities of individuals. Government comes from the hands of nature, ultimately from nature's God. Neither in this political treatise nor in his fiction does Cooper distinguish in the order of first causation an agency of nature from the agency of the Author of nature. By submitting themselves to government, men obey "that consciousness of right which God has bestowed in order that man may judge between good and evil" (75). In *The American Democrat* Cooper does not consider whether men with favorable circumstances might have access to laws of nature and nature's God so as not to require regulation by external human authorities. That consideration will occupy him throughout the five novels that make up the "Leatherstocking" group.

Government is natural, but the forms government takes are the result of human artifice. Cooper's discussion of the various forms of regimes arising over the course of history diverges from that familiar taxonomy canonized by Aristotle which distinguishes among the forms by reference to the ruling power—one, few, many. It also diverges from the Platonic-Ciceronian analysis resurrected in Montesquieu whereby varieties of government are associated with distinct conceptions of the good life. Cooper expresses dissatisfaction with the traditional distinctions because he thinks these blur the one decisive difference: that between despotic governments and republics. Despotic governments invest absolute (understood as unaccountable) power in a single ruler or group. Republics invest "sovereign power in the body of the people" (76). Cooper does not explain at this point how the sovereignty of the people in a republic becomes any less absolute than the unaccountable power of the ruling agency in a despotism. That he thinks popular governments can and sometimes do accommodate despotism is evident from such novels as *The Chainbearer* (1845), *The Redskins* (1846), *Home As Found* (1838), *Wyandotte* (1843), *The Ways of the Hour* (1850), or *The Crater* (1847), all of which portray democratic passions mounting to tyrannical injustice. Cooper's initial distinction between despotisms and republics will be made good only after he has introduced that subspecies in the refinement of republics afforded by the *constitutional* republic.

Before he develops his notion of a constitutional republic, however, Cooper consolidates his claim that only a regime founded upon consent of the governed answers to man's innate liberty. The diversity of the forms of government arises from a single universal right of men to compact for a particular mode of civil association. To deny this, Cooper says, "is to deny to bodies of human beings the right of self-government, a gift of nature" (83). Men taken singly, therefore, have no right to an unconditional liberty. Establishing government is a moral obligation. But men in "bodies" responding to the moral necessity of establishing government must be accorded the liberty of determining to what sort of government they submit themselves. Cooper thus denies that government can be founded in force or conquest while acknowledging that bodies of men exercising their natural right of creating governments may consent to set up despotisms. The great problem, therefore, is how to found nondespotic governments, and, once founded, how to keep them.

America addresses the first part of the problem by expressly dedicating itself in the Declaration to the God-given principle of consent. Acknowledgment of the equality pertaining to men as consenting participants in the founding of civil society is the necessary condition for all nondespotic governments. Yet this condition, necessary though it is, falls short of a sufficient cause for sustaining freedom. In fact, the emphasis upon equality voiced in the Declaration invites misunderstanding, and equality misunderstood is sufficient to produce a despotism which is not the less despotic for having secured a general consent at its origin. Cooper believes that America (or at least the national government) has as yet avoided a bad sequel to promising beginnings because its Constitution has provided institutions adequate to ward off a despotic misunderstanding of equality. But it has not easily or securely avoided such degradation, and bad prospects are at hand threatening a misconstruction of the egalitarian principle prejudicial to property rights.

Equality misunderstood neglects one truth about human nature and another regarding the relation connecting civil society with property. Aside from the one respect just noted—of consent at the origin—human beings are not equal in anything relevant to political organization. They are equal neither in intellectual or moral endowments nor in qualities more obviously dependent upon their bodies. Cooper evidently assumes that even equality of consent ought to pertain only to male adults (106). Unlike Jefferson, moreover, Cooper does not appear to consider slavery an unwarranted restriction of natural equality. At least he observes without condemning the existence of slavery in several of the states (108), and he concludes without regret that the "equality of the United States is no more absolute than that of any other country" (107). In the context of subsequent observations, this statement appears to absolve slaveholding by counting it a consequence of inequalities grounded in nature. Such a position would find confirmation in Cooper's sympathetic treatment of slave owners in the novels. At any rate, Cooper clearly deplores the despotic tendency of improper extension of equality more than objecting to improper restrictions thereupon. We might account for this apparent imbalance by referring it to Cooper's anxiety for dispelling the second of the causes for exaggerated notions of equality—misunderstanding of the importance of property to the total social scheme.

Cooper seeks to confine the operative significance of equality because he is convinced of the overriding necessity of protecting property. "The rights of property," he declares, are "an indispensable condition of civilization" (107). Diversity of the kinds of property and differences in the amounts of property possessed by men ensure that "there can be no equality in their social condition" (107). To the question why can there be no equality in social arrangements with respect to property, Cooper gives an answer that looks not to the origins but to the goal of civil association. He is certainly not unaware that however much inequality of property may be the condition of men prior to government, schemes of government have been undertaken to obliterate or moderate such inequalities. Since he makes no effort to identify unequal possession of property with the natural right of consent in the establishing of civil order, the Cooper of *The American Democrat* leaves somewhat indefinite the connection between property and human nature. By contrast, Cooper the novelist, through portrayals of benign and enterprising landowners in the novels comprising the "Littlepage" series, so personalizes attachments to property as to identify a man's property interests with his essential character.

Yet neither in the novels nor in the political treatise does he leave ambiguous the connection between property and civilization. By "civilization" Cooper understands the proliferation of technical arts and the general rise in material abundance made possible by expansion and improvement of technology accompanied by the distribution of its products through free exchange. By appealing to this progress, Cooper can say: "If we would have civilization and the exertion indispensable to its success, we must have property; if we have property, we must take the consequences of the rights of property which are inseparable from the rights themselves" (110). It is notable that Cooper does not avail himself of the reasoning of John Locke or James Madison, both of whom identify property rights with the most fundamental natural right of liberty. Like the two thinkers mentioned, Cooper believes government ought to protect men in their unequal faculties for acquiring property, but he seems to think the obligation owes to expediency rather than strict moral necessity. At one point, moreover, he appears to conclude that civil society's concern to make men prosper must run counter to its desire to do justice: "the social inequality of America may do violence to our notion of abstract justice, but the compromise of interests under which all civilized society must exist, renders this unavoidable" (109). Cooper presumably would not disagree with Jefferson, Madison, or Abraham Lincoln who all thought inequality of condition a consequence of the equality of rights affirmed by the Declaration. But he sees that consequence to be an adjustment of justice to necessity, or perhaps a mere compromise with desires expedient but dubious, rather than holding inequalities of property to be simply just.

Perhaps for this reason Cooper declines to propose liberty as a principle logically equivalent to equality. Although liberty is not as fundamental, it is more authoritative than equality. As the engine of civilization, it is the more comprehensive of the two Founding ideas, and if Cooper means to confine egalitarian impulses, he hopes to enlarge freedom. Equality properly understood requires nothing other than the repudiation of privileges Cooper deems "factitious," meaning political entitlements vested in a hereditary class. Liberty requires much more. It requires more because unlike equality, which attaches only to a single right inhering in nature at the origin of civil society, liberty comprehends both natural (moral) independence and also that wider sphere of rights produced by the addition of considerations of expediency (i.e., requirements of civilization) to considerations of nature. As one would expect, the addition of expedient considerations embraces rights of property regulated by civil law. But included also is a range of political rights or liberties associated with augmenting property in the community at large.

Like equality, however, liberty is a notion Cooper subjects to a clarification called for by current confusion inasmuch as, again as was the case with equality, liberty in its absolute form is incompatible with the existence of society. Liberty cannot be absolute "in a state of nature even" because without some restraint upon the widest freedom one may conceive the strong would oppress the weak. Accordingly, rational creatures should demand only such latitude of action as consists with other needs of civil society: "We are then to understand by liberty, merely such a state of the social compact as permits the members of a community to lay no more restraints on themselves than are required by their real necessities, and obvious interests" (111). Law determines real necessities and obvious interests while law also makes secure our hold upon a liberty better defined and hence more available than the vague and evanescent freedom we may imagine we could enjoy beyond the bounds of political association. Cooper intends, therefore, to persuade his countrymen to perceive the superiority of liberty under law to natural freedom. If this teaching takes hold, it affords the more than incidental benefit of securing the rights of property, rights the justification of which, as we have just seen, are by no means evident considered in abstraction from their connection with the advantages conferred by civilization.

Liberty is more useful than equality for affording a principle in the light of which one may distinguish the American from other regimes. The novelty of America consists in its having reversed the ordinary relation of rulers to ruled with respect to freedom. In all other regimes that have existed hitherto, rulers have dispensed liberties upon favored portions of a subject population. Notably, this has been the practice of such hereditary monarchies resting upon class differentiated societies as England and France. But the practice has not been confined to countries dominated by kings. The republics previously known to Europe have likewise conceived freedom to be a set of discrete liberties devolving from the rulers to those among the ruled specially blessed by the sovereign. It would be no exaggeration to say that prior to the American Founding only sovereigns had been free and everyone else, whether the subject of a king or the citizen of a republic, attributed whatever liberty he might enjoy to the largesse of the government. America has inverted the traditional order by making the dispensers of liberty a body identical with the recipients and by making that body coextensive with the entire citizenry.

America has devised an operative understanding of liberty "new to the world" (112) by producing state and federal constitutions answerable to a double safeguard for the freedom of its citizens. In the first place, elevating the populace to the position of sovereign enlarges the scope of freedom and removes some "factitious" grounds for confining liberty to a few. Popular sovereignty, however, is not by itself sufficient to effect the kind of liberty America has achieved. Democracies, Cooper once more insists, may be as despotic as any other form of government. America's distinctness resides in the combination of popular sovereignty with other principles that make the regime unique as a nondespotic democracy. These other principles Cooper gathers under the general heading of the "process" whereby the sovereign majority regulates the exercise of its sovereignty. Cooper proceeds to develop his notion of limited government turning from the Founding ideas of the Declaration to the articulation, and limitation, of these ideas in the Constitution.

The evidence that in the eyes of the Framers liberty surpasses equality in importance lies in the text of the Constitution as Cooper reads that document. According to Cooper equality has no place in the Constitution. "Equality is no where laid down as a governing principle of the institutions of the United States, neither the word, nor any inference that can be fairly deduced from its meaning, occurring in the constitution" (110). Even more striking Cooper thinks is a design to provide for liberty against the despotic inclinations of majorities, a design which permeates this statement of the supreme law of the land. Cooper finds restraints upon the majority in the Constitution's enumeration of the objects of national government. Although the majority "elects to office" and "enacts ordinary law," its command over legislation is subject to explicit restrictions, and the enumerated objects confine the exercise even of this restricted competency to "questions that do not usually effect any of the principal interests of life" (113). The latter part of Cooper's statement is rendered somewhat less astonishing if one supposes he thinks wars unusual and if one keeps in mind his assumption that the Bill of Rights confine the national government rather than entrusting it with the responsibility of umpiring the states. Other restrictions on the authority of the majority owe to the incorporation of common law, prohibition of impairment of contracts, and due process stipulations. Moreover, some of the restrictions on majoritarian lawmaking go beyond procedural inhibitions and common law usages to prohibit the national government from enacting certain policies relating to the principal interests of life. Notable among these is the antiegalitarian (or antidebtor) proviso that "nothing shall be made a legal tender but the precious metals" (118).

In view of these several restrictions on the authority of majorities, Cooper feels obliged to reformulate his description of the kind of liberty in pursuit of which the United States distinguishes itself from all previous regimes. At this point in his analysis, Cooper observes that the species distinction "may be defined to be a controlling authority that resides in the body of a nation, but so restrained as only to be exercised on certain general principles that shall do as little violence to natural justice, as is compatible with the peace and security of society" (118). We may pause to take stock of the net effect of those refinements upon democracy Cooper has detected in the American experiment. Popular sovereignty figures for Cooper as a necessary but insufficient condition of liberty properly understood, whereas only after it has been once moderated by such restraints upon majoritarianism as the Constitution provides does popular sovereignty, so civilized, emerge as a condition necessary and almost sufficient for proper liberty. Still, it must be emphasized the improvement is only *almost* sufficient because in Cooper's estimation the design of the Constitution depends in the last resort upon the character of the representatives in Congress, and particularly upon the character of the members of the more democratically responsive House.

We could conclude that Cooper undertakes his comments on the Declaration and Constitution in order to address the classic problem of democratic theory: how to make the many responsible. He addresses that problem at its classic stress point: the vulnerability of property rights to popular mischief. Democratic states ordinarily deserve their bad reputation because the history of democracies has been a record of popularly driven lootings. With or without demagogues to show them the way, regimes dominated by the populace have invariably exploited the law to redistribute the wealth of the comparatively rich among the comparatively poor. In Cooper's view, the Constitution of the United States earns a better name for democracy by solving the classic problem. It has solved the problem by incorporating protections for property into the governing instrument. America's remedy for diseases endemic to democracy is sufficient, however, if—but only if—it also accepts those clarifications in the understanding of equality and liberty which *The American Democrat* proposes. The sovereign people of this democracy must realize, first, that property should be sacrosanct because civilization requires nothing less. The question of the natural justification of private property must be kept out of court. Second, the people must learn, or relearn, the truth that the liberty it seeks can be found nowhere else than in self-imposed limitations upon the popular will, limitations of the sort made operative in the Constitution.

Given this view of the purpose of the Constitution, Cooper's identification of Congress as the most dangerous branch affords no surprises. Congress is the site where the stress point of democracy receives a constant pressure. The Supreme Court owes its authority to no election, and the chief executive, although elected at this time prior to or just at the beginning of the consolidation of party machinery, owes his authority to an indirect election responsive to the propertied interests represented in the state electors. Congress, on the other hand, invites capture by those popular elements that may be tempted to help themselves to the wealth of the people's better situated neighbors. Even under the restraints specified by the Constitution, moreover, Congress retains enough authority to threaten liberty. The threat owes not only to congressional power but to the combination in Congress of power with irresponsibility. Cooper thinks a consideration of numbers suffices to make manifest this danger: there is greater threat to apprehend from Congress than from the executive, as can be seen from the following observations:

> Congress is composed of many, while the executive is one, bodies of men notoriously acting with less personal responsibilities than individuals. . . . [Moreover,] the executive has direct personal responsibilities under the laws of the land, for any abuses of his authority, but the member of congress, unless guilty of open corruption, is almost beyond personal liabilities. (93)

Add to this the considerations that the legislative branch of any government always tends to seize supremacy and that although the citizen may appeal to courts against onerous executive orders, he has no ordinary recourse to appeal against Congress. As for the Supreme Court, although Cooper attributes to it the ultimate authority for deciding upon the constitutionality of laws, he deems that body weak in any contest with Congress on the following grounds. The Court has authority only to interpret, not to make, legislation. It judges only in particular cases. It is exposed to pressures calculated to make successive Courts reverse the judgments of predecessors. Its judgments, even if maintained by successive justices, may be overridden or circumvented by new legislation or, failing new statutes, by constitutional amendment.

The great constitutional problem, therefore, is to keep the branches of government "within their respective spheres" (96). Vigilance in this regard needs stiffening by applying the principle that "the representative who exceeds his trusts, trespasses on the rights of the people" (96). Given the power of Congress, however, and the relative weakness of the other branches, the problem virtually reduces to a matter of contriving any means of cutting Congress down to size. For such an enterprise Cooper can expect little from the Court and not much more from the president. The weakness of the president owes something to the Constitution since his veto is qualified, and unlike the British king he possesses no prerogative of dispensing from duly enacted legislation. But executive feebleness owes more to usage: "the history of the country shows ten instances of presidents' evading responsibility, to one of their abusing power" (104). Although it is not clear that Cooper thinks existing constitutional provisions adequate to impart a weight to the presidency sufficient to counteract a too ponderous Congress, it is certain that Cooper believes a number of presidents have exacerbated the problem by failing to exploit the constitutional resources at their disposal.

If the vital necessity lies in strengthening the president against Congress, one might expect Cooper to look favorably on parties, the means whereby ambitious presidents attain national prominence, concert policy, and influence if not dominate House and Senate. Yet Cooper not only declines to advocate the party system; he deplores it whenever he has occasion to raise the subject. Unavoidable though it may be, party is "an evil" (169). We may find an explanation of the anomaly in Cooper's dread of the threat posed to independent judgment by partisan activity. The section of *The American Democrat* devoted to a discussion of party (225–28) takes the form of an extended malediction itemizing the bad consequences dealt the nation by partisanship. To the influence of party Cooper attributes prejudice, error, "vicious, corrupt, and unprofitable legislation," loss of local independence, displacement of the people by "managers," demagoguery, cant, faction, unreflective passion, personalism, corruption, and mendacity. All but lost in this litany of party evils is the observation that the "effect of party is always to supplant established power" with its corollary "[i]n a monarchy [party] checks the king; in a democracy it controls the people" (227). We would be rash to conclude that Cooper merely overlooks the potential for checking Congress afforded by presidential leadership of a national party. Cooper seems rather to acknowledge that possibility but to discount its value when he weighs the likelihood that executive and legislative branches are more apt to join for despotic projects if they can do so under a party banner. In Cooper's view, political parties produce a tide that first dissolves the separation of powers at the national seat and then washes over the bounds separating local authorities from the general government. Party passion together with party leverage provide the means whereby people good enough taken individually become unworthy of themselves once they have been aggregated. Parties open an avenue to that powerful anonymity by which the people permits itself to become irresponsible. As members of parties, individual citizens allow themselves to think and do what they would be ashamed to think or do in their proper persons without their party masks.

Cooper can draw these conclusions because he perceives beneath the problem of a runaway Congress a more fundamental threat to responsible government at the heart of the regime. The more ominous danger lies in Americans' reverence for public opinion. Cooper's remarks on the undue exaltation of public opinion among his countrymen reveal that his fears attach finally to no merely institutional flaw, and that his hope, such as it is, envisions some alteration yet more fundamental than a tinkering with this or that provision of the Constitution. His fear and hope alike arise out of his estimate of the national character. At stake, he thinks, is nothing less than respect for law.

The most irksome characteristic of Americans is their propensity to substitute public opinion for law. Cooper identifies this tendency with the "besetting vice of democracies," a derangement he believes breeds a brand of tyranny exceeding all others in severity because once established there is no escaping its long reach. Oppressive public opinion, like democratic animus against property, its associated distemper, draws strength from envy (131). It is even more damaging than the yen to expropriate from the wealthy because it draws also upon ignorance and stupidity. Deified public opinion exacts worship, while it prefers flatterers to worthy men who refuse to defer. It tracks down and punishes those few men hardy enough to resist popular sentiment. Yet inasmuch as "the tendency of democracies is in all things to mediocrity" (129), the damage it inflicts would also be middling, an omnipresent but toothless tyranny, were it not that demagogues provide a means of concentrating democratic passions in a single agent. On this head, Cooper invokes the large versus small republic argument but draws conclusions opposed to those on behalf of which *The Federalist Papers* argue the same distinction. Although extensive democracies are less subject to sudden caprice than small states where impulse has less distance to travel, large democracies are more vulnerable to demagogues because the wide electorate is "unable to scrutinize and understand character with the severity and intelligence that are of so much importance in all representative governments" (128). Cooper may be unique among American theorists of the early nineteenth century in that he enlists neither with the proponents of large democracies nor with the champions of small republics. He thinks extent of the sphere of government makes for some difference of effects but these turn out to be merely different kinds of bad effects. To his mind it is a choice insufficiently consequential to make a difference worth troubling over.

In the last resort, humankind needs protection against democratic injuries to truth fully as much as it needs protection of its property. By "truth" we are to understand not merely veracity in the propositions collected to determine policy but, additionally, proper standards for evaluating moral and intellectual virtue. Such standards, because they are not companionable with fondness for the mediocre, run against the grain of the democratic temperament. If there were in the American character nothing other than the democratic grain, sustaining standards of virtue would be simply impossible. But because Americans espouse Christianity and are inheritors of a British liberal tradition, upholding standards of virtue is possible, even if we must infer only just possible. Cooper's fairly skeptical assessment of American possibilities comes into sight once we take account of his ideas on independence of character.

The final sections of *The American Democrat* deal with human excellence under the concept Cooper terms "individuality." He retrieves a phrase from the Declaration to support his contention that individuality is inseparable from "the pursuit of happiness" (229). Individuality proceeds from political liberty and, contrary to what we might have expected from Cooper's earlier identification of liberty with law, he now extols freedom not as liberty to participate in the formation of public policy but as enjoyment of a sphere of action left undetermined by prescriptive legislation. A man is free to the extent he is "left to pursue his means of happiness in his own manner" (228). Not a relativist, Cooper believes there are better and worse ways to pursue contentment and that some distinctions between better and worse are morally binding. *Individuality* is here a term carrying a positive evaluation of character. It is equivalent indeed to "greatness of character" (229) and consists in the ability to locate one's bearings by laws of nature sanctioned by God rather than from public opinion. It enables a man to hold in contempt the "monarch of the country in a social sense" (230), the potentate Cooper nicknames "They say." The man blessed with individuality dissolves distinctions between aristocrat and democrat. In a hereditary aristocracy he will appear a democrat because he rejects factitious privileges in the name of a better founded hierarchy of virtue available to titled and untitled indiscriminately. But in a democracy the individualist will appear an aristocrat because his insistence upon laying claim to justifiable deference for himself and others like him will put him in opposition to the common man intent upon remaining common. Independent manliness is the leading feature of individuality wherever found: "The same principles and manliness that would induce him to dispose a royal despot, would induce him to resist a vulgar tyrant" (153). By the end of Cooper's treatise, we perceive that his title *The American Democrat* could be altered, in the light of clarifications he has provided, to *The American Aristocrat*, provided, of course, one understands his aim is to reinstate respect for those aristocratic by natural endowment. Cooper means to do what he can to make American democracy less inhospitable to moral and intellectual excellence of every sort. Refinement in manners counts as one such excellence, but so too does a decent, manly disregard for the opinions of mankind if it should be that those opinions amount to no more than a matter of "they say."

We have seen how to this end Cooper pleads for a better understanding of equality and liberty. There remains to take account of his similar effort of clarification with respect to religion.

Religion is necessary to produce individuality in the first place and thereafter to sustain personal independence against egalitarian pressures toward servility. A religious outlook enlarges the mind by making one aware of the limitations of politics or of the limitations of life altogether.

> If there is no pure and abstract liberty, no equality of condition, no equal participation in the things of the world that we are accustomed to fancy good, on remembering the speck of time passed in the present state, the possibility that what to us may seem a curse, may in truth be a blessing, the certainty that prosperity is more corrupting than adversity, we shall find the solution to all our difficulties. (232)

An unkind construction of these words might take Cooper to be extolling religion as solution to his difficulty of devising a protection for property. But there is no evidence Cooper pretends to hold religion ultimate while actually holding something other to be so. In any event, if he dissimulates oligarchy here we would have to suppose he dissimulates everywhere since consistently throughout the political as well as his fictional writings Cooper praises pious acceptance of one's lot. Everywhere in the fiction religion braces both wealthy and poor against temptations to impatience in the face of adversities that appear to be about equally distributed among rich and poor. Without religion the rich stand no better prospect of resisting idolatry to public opinion than the poor, and perhaps less. Drawing upon the composure religion encourages, both rich and poor have some chance of manly independence.

But such is true only if they put aside false for true religion. Cooper's religion is Christianity, and to expound its tenets he cites parables recorded in the New Testament. Jesus gives him the type of the manly independent. Yet he remarks that the independence of soul he recommends flourishes more widely in England with its established church than in America which owes its origins to the Puritan movement on behalf of independent congregations. In fact, Cooper traces American servility back to Puritan roots. The church discipline of the early colonies has transmitted to present generations an undue respect for public opinion because under the Puritans' too intimate association of the spiritually and politically elect Americans accustomed themselves to submitting their thoughts and deeds to the scrutiny of church authorities. For Cooper it does not signify that these authorities were more democratic this side of the Atlantic. Indeed, matters stand worse here because, being administered by entire congregations, Puritan church discipline, not to speak of Puritan confusion of jurisdiction properly ecclesiastical with governance properly civil, exacerbates the democratic insistence upon making everything subservient to the popular will. Cooper concludes that America is not Christian but sectarian and perorates with a challenge to recover the essence of Christianity in a doctrine of loving forbearance (234–35). Cooper's refined Christianity appears to reduce to religion by the light of reason alone, a sort of tenderized stoic ethic sparing in espousal of potentially divisive dogma but well adapted to sustaining independent characters. One could say that with religion as with the other aspects of Cooper's political thought he seeks to make the most of what he finds conducive to natural aristocracy in a predominantly democratic polity.

Cooper's Fiction

The same project of reconciling virtue with democratic inclination appears to animate Cooper's best works of fiction. Throughout the novels one observes Cooper suggesting discriminations between proper and improper understandings of equality and liberty similar to the distinctions worked out in *The American Democrat*. Whether the setting be Long Island in the early eighteenth century, as in *Satanstoe* (1845), or the trans-Mississippi plains of the early nineteenth century, as in *The Prairie* (1827), we meet with characters who sort out into two groups: one constituted by those who bring a spirit of aristocratic independence to life in the New World; another numbering those who misuse the greater equality and freedom America has put at their disposal. By reference to this fundamental distinction, Cooper constructs a moral hierarchy ascending from small-minded corrupters of liberty up to a character who embodies his notion of individuality in its most definitive form.

Cooper's characters meet his measure or fall short by displaying their attitude toward property. *Satanstoe* and *The Redskins* forecast the direction American democracy will take by depicting the opposition between landowners and renters in colonial New York. A lesson in legalized predation results from this account of responsible patroons who set their rents low initially to attract settlers only to discover that their renters capture the legislature to prevent rent increases once the land has become productive. By focusing his satire on one of these lease holders, a dogmatic Puritan who combines democratic rapacity with sectarian intolerance, the novel presents a composite image of the two sources of popular despotism endemic to America. Opposed to this rising class of men on the make is a collection of Dutch gentlemen whom Cooper credits with having a responsible understanding of the moral obligations entailed in their property rights.

A somewhat less direct consideration of the problems involved in ownership as well as the social, racial, political, and religious context of property comes to sight over the course of the five novels which make up the Leatherstocking series: *The Pioneers* (1823), *The Last of the Mohicans* (1826), *The Prairie* (1827), *The Pathfinder* (1840), and *The Deerslayer* (1846). These tales span the life of the frontiersman Natty Bumppo from the beginning of his career as a warrior in the 1760s to his death on the western plains in 1806. Under his Dutch family name or under the titles he acquires from Indians ("Deerslayer" from his adopted Delaware tribe, "Hawkeye" from an admiring enemy tribe), Natty embodies those qualities of character in which Cooper finds correctives to the tendencies of his countrymen.

We can best appreciate connections between the political diagnostic arrived at in *The American Democrat* and the remedy portrayed in the Leatherstocking sequence by noting the constancy of Natty's principles from youth to death in old age. His stability carries him through choices respecting occupation and property, marriage, political and ethnic affiliation, religious belief, and the manner of confronting death. The key to grasping his constancy in the midst of a changing world is evident in a remark the young Natty makes to a friend as he prepares to meet death by torture: "Whenever I've done wrong, I've generally found 'twas owing to some blindness of the mind, which hid the right from view, and when sight has returned, then has come sorrow and repentance."[2] Though Bumppo's diction separates his creed from the elegant sophistication of Cooper, the frontiersman's moral formulation resembles Cooper's reliance upon reason rather than sentiment. Like Cooper himself, this illiterate Platonist attributes wrongdoing to intellectual error rather than bad will, an outlook that permits him to regard the failings of others as well as his own with a certain philosophical detachment. He stands out from the feverish people who surround him because he has always available a central intellectual peace which he has cultivated by contemplating divine workmanship in the frame of nature. Natty's illiteracy assists natural piety by insulating Natty's mind from sectarian controversy in religion and from modern scientific curiosity. The representative of the latter he encounters, and dismisses, in *The Prairie* in the person of a biologist who boasts of science's promise to conquer and improve nature for the benefit of man but whose ignorance of first causes Natty exposes, while the scientist, through his selfish, misguided conduct, betrays the shallowness of his own moral understanding.

Cooper leaves his readers in no doubt that his hero's independence proceeds from his having espoused Christianity. Yet the novelist also stresses Natty's is a creed scriptural in derivation but adjusted to a wisdom he has acquired by prudent reflections on life's necessities. Accordingly, as a warrior he rejects pacifist interpretation of charity in the light of his own experience of the necessity of employing force to preserve oneself or to prevent injustice. More generally, Bumppo subscribes to a mode of worship not distinctly addressed to Christ but rather to a divine being who could also be revered under his Indian name of Manitou. His doctrinal interests extend no further than to commit him to a notion of a heavenly judge and dispenser of Providence who sanctions laws discernible through reason, by implication some such God of nature as we see affirmed in the Declaration of Independence. This Creator summons Natty to worship beyond the settlements in temples of His own construction under sun and stars.

To maintain his proximity with nature and nature's God, Natty contrives a life in the world but not of it. He moves between aboriginal Delawares, the English, and various groups of American compatriots maintaining political allegiances as far as these comport with his sense of right—but no further. Cooper's version of Nature's gentleman constantly asserts his white "gifts" among his red tribesmen while also insisting upon certain of his adopted Indian ways against practices of whites he deems opposed to nature. Cooper makes of Natty a sort of roving gauge of natural right reproving deviations he detects from that norm as he moves between the one society to the other. Natty's constancy to bearings he owes to no particular culture defines human freedom in what Cooper considers its true form while the variety of his hero's circumstances permits Cooper to exhibit the elasticity of the standard his natural aristocrat incorporates. A problem arises, however, when one attempts to see how the standard Natty represents can be widely applicable given the extraordinary features of the way of life his choices have fashioned for himself.

Natty is largely immune from the pressures of maintaining property because he owns little and from the passions of acquiring because he desires few possessions. He does not desire much property because there is no moral necessity that he should. There is no moral necessity requiring him to get property because he has no dependents. He has no dependents because in his two opportunities for marriage (with Judith in *The Deerslayer* and with Mabel in *The Pathfinder*) he rejects a spouse in the first, and in the second acquiesces to the beloved woman's rejection of him. Natty enjoys liberty under unusually favorable conditions. In fact, this is a condition of almost complete self-sufficiency that by the reasoning Cooper maintains in *The American Democrat* would go far toward obviating the need for securing property rights. For in that work Cooper had argued that the universal human concern for transmitting property to heirs justifies provisions for protecting property, protections that absent such concerns would be open to question.

This consideration raises the wider issue of whether the implicit teaching of the Leatherstocking novels in regard to civilization can be reconciled with Cooper's explicit views on that subject in the treatise. *The American Democrat* virtually equates civilization with property holding and couples both property and civilization with the advancement of an equality justifiable by reference to human nature. Cooper seems to have Natty endorse this reasoning when he objects to the status of Indian women who he realizes are treated by their husbands as slaves.[3] Throughout the novels white women demonstrate rational and moral capacities at least as estimable as those Cooper assigns to his male characters. There seem to be, therefore, no grounds in nature for treating white women as slaves. There does appear to be a problem, however, in extending this judgment to uncivilized Indian women. The conditions for according women the status toward which their possession of reason points appear to be inseparable from civilization understood as the proliferation of the technical arts applied to society's efforts to develop natural resources. Natty flees the expanding settlements and disdains the technical arts upon the basis of which civilization advances its moral front. But the advantage here seems to rest with civilization rather than with the solitary man's example, an unexpected implication given Natty's status as moral lodestar.

Aside from the problem of reconciling Cooper's teaching on civilization and property in *The American Democrat* with the conduct of Bumppo, there is a problem of squaring the discursive work with the fiction in view of their apparent divergence on the matter of the mutual dependence of civilization and law. In *The American Democrat*, liberty had seemed inseparable from legal provisions regulating its exercise. Given inequality of human faculties, law seems to be necessary to protect the weak and slow witted from the strong and cunning. Yet Natty favors life in a wilderness removed from the reach of law. He approves neither of property, concentrations of population, nor the proliferation of laws necessitated by the first two conditions. We could account for Netty's antinomianism by supposing he does not need positive law since he remains perfectly attuned to natural law. But, if so, what guidance can such a singular figure provide for Americans unlikely to enjoy the frontiersman's uncomplicated accord with a natural environment comparatively pristine as well as unlikely to experience Natty's similarly inviolable solitude? Once we appreciate these paradoxes we may conclude it seems necessary to accommodate the moral standpoint Natty represents to the standard Cooper expounds in his discursive writing. How that accommodation works out, or even in which direction the accommodation operates—toward the explicit argumentation of *The American Democrat* or in the direction of the implied, and apparently opposed, argument of the Leatherstocking tales—might well be the question most challenging for those who seek to learn from Cooper's political thought.

Notes

1. James Fenimore Cooper, *The American Democrat*, ed. George Dekker and Larry Johnston (London: Viking Penguin, 1989), 109. Subsequent references noted parenthetically are to this edition.

2. *The Deerslayer*, ed. Lance Schachterle, Kent P. Ljungquist, and James A. Kilby (New York: Library Classics of the United States, 1985), 938–39.

3. Natty delivers his thoughts on tribal subjugation of women in *Deerslayer*, 935–36.

Chapter 20

Religion, Nature, and Disobedience in the Thought of Ralph Waldo Emerson and Henry David Thoreau

Bryan-Paul Frost

Ralph Waldo Emerson (1803–1882) and Henry David Thoreau (1817–1862) lived their entire adult lives in Concord, Massachusetts. Emerson was one of America's leading essayists, poets, and lecturers, and he was in high demand both in America and Great Britain. Thoreau, while he tried to make a living as a writer and lecturer, was less successful, and he was at various times a teacher, handyman, and ultimately a highly competent surveyor. The two men became fast friends; and although their friendship eventually cooled somewhat, Emerson tried to bring Thoreau's articles and poetry to the attention of others, and it was Emerson who allowed Thoreau to build his famous cabin on the shores of Walden Pond. Thoreau died of tuberculosis near the beginning of the Civil War, and Emerson published a generous but not uncritical eulogy of his life-long friend. Emerson lived some twenty years longer, although his creative capacity diminished markedly in his later years. Ironically, Thoreau's writings have attained an extraordinary posthumous success that rivals, if not eclipses, the success Emerson achieved during his own lifetime.[1]

Notwithstanding the fact that their lives intersected in a number of ways, Emerson and Thoreau merit a place together in American political thought for several reasons. First, while Emerson was the philosophical spokesman for what became known as American transcendentalism, Thoreau most famously attempted to put its principles into practice. Second, both men shared a reverential attitude toward nature; a belief that a divine spirit animated all creation; and that each individual was part of a greater whole or oneness. Third, both men were staunch individualists who saw the individual as the sole source of moral authority and worth, and they encouraged creative self-expression, spontaneous action, and hearkening to one's inner voice or intuition. And finally, fourth, Thoreau is one of the most noted expositors of civil disobedience to unjust government, and many of his views were shared by Emerson. Nevertheless, although both men detested and wrote against slavery, they kept to the sidelines politically and argued that genuine political regeneration could only come about through individual spiritual renewal. We therefore begin this study of their thought by first articulating Emerson's understanding of transcendentalism, religion, and morality; we then turn to Thoreau's description of the life he lived at Walden Pond; and we conclude by discussing the issues of civil disobedience, slavery, and political engagement.

Transcendentalism

Both Emerson and Thoreau are often referred to as belonging to the New England transcendentalist movement, the former as one of its principal architects and advocates, and the latter as one of its most ardent practitioners. In his essay "The Transcendentalist" (1843), however, Emerson denies that transcendentalism is a new or original school of thought: in fact, the roots of transcendentalism (or what he also calls idealism) are as old as thinking itself, and he avers that it is one of only two ways "mankind have ever divided" as "thinkers," the other being materialism (or empiricism). Whereas a materialist (e.g., John Locke) acknowledges the independent existence of an external world accessible through sense impression and confirmed through experience, a transcendentalist or idealist (e.g., Immanuel Kant) privileges his own consciousness and intuition, arguing that the "external world" is mental or spiritual, and is only apprehended or revealed through an individual, self-conscious mind. The transcendentalist does not dispute that objects are perceived by the senses; rather, he questions whether sense perception is an accurate, complete, and final representation of the object in and of itself. "The senses give us representations of things, but what are the things themselves, they cannot tell" (*EWRWE* 81, 86). After arguing that the materialist's confidence in the solidity of facts and figures is ill-founded, Emerson proceeds to make the following comparison:

> In the order of thought, the materialist takes his departure from the external world, and esteems a man as one product of that. The idealist takes his departure from his consciousness, and reckons the world an appearance. The materialist respects sensible masses, Society, Government, social art and luxury, every establishment, every mass, whether majority of numbers, or extent of space, or amount of objects, every social action. The idealist has another measure, which is metaphysical, namely the *rank* which things themselves take in his consciousness; not at all the size or appearance. Mind is the only reality, of which men and all other natures are better or worse reflectors. Nature, literature, history, are only subjective phenomena. . . . His thought—that is the Universe. His experience inclines him to behold the procession of facts you call the world, as flowing perpetually outward from an invisible, unsounded centre in himself, centre alike of him and of them, and necessitating him to regard all things as having a subjective or relative existence, relative to that aforesaid Unknown Centre of him. (*EWRWE* 82–83)

While Emerson's transcendentalist appears at first blush to be wholly sovereign and self-determined, he is also open to influences or forces from without—albeit of a certain sort. The transcendentalist believes in and is receptive to "inspiration," "miracle," "ecstasy," "the perpetual openness of the human mind to new influx of light and power"—in short, to all that is genuinely "spiritual."

> The Transcendentalist adopts the whole connection of spiritual doctrine. . . . He wishes that the spiritual principle should be suffered to demonstrate itself to the end, in all possible applications to the state of man, without the admission of anything unspiritual; that is, anything positive, dogmatic, personal. Thus the spiritual measure of inspiration is the depth of the thought, and never, who said it? And so he resists all attempts to palm other rules and measures on the spirit than its own. (*EWRWE* 84)

Given this brief glimpse into the transcendentalist's rapturous inner life, it is somewhat surprising to read how "solitary" and "lonely" these individuals are.[2] They are solitary because nothing that society can offer appeals to them: popular entertainment, commercial competition, political causes—even the building of empires and the prospect of rule—are all seen as little more than "drudgery" and thoroughly "degrading" in comparison to their talents (*EWRWE* 87).

They are lonely because the human fellowship they seek is so acute and fervent that few persons could satisfy or endure the demands of such a relationship: tolerating neither frivolity nor hypocrisy, they are seen by most persons as rude, shallow, or simply ridiculous (*EWRWE* 88–90). But despite the fact that society treats these individuals as outcasts, and despite the fact they seem to perform no useful occupation, Emerson insists that they are the moral touchstones by which to judge whether "the points of our spiritual compass" are true. Society therefore has a duty and an interest to "behold them with what charity it can" (*EWRWE* 95). In sum, Emerson's transcendentalist is a radically autonomous individual who is nonetheless open to (and perhaps even dependent upon) a certain ecstatic or miraculous spirituality that comes from without and that seems to create and foster an unbreachable gulf between his celestial desires and dreams, and the stale reality that society offers. It is little wonder that Nietzsche found much to admire in Emerson's writings (see *WE* 378, 469–70).

Religion and Religiosity, Christianity and Mysticism

In order to develop more fully this portrait of the transcendentalist, we must attempt to concretize Emerson's elliptical remarks about "spirituality": who or what is this "Universe" which "beckons and calls" the transcendentalist from inactivity "to work"; which issues him the "highest command"; and with which he seeks some resplendent "union" (*EWRWE* 91, 95)? Such a task is made difficult by the fact that Emerson himself doubts whether "profane words" could ever adequately or accurately capture the "transcendent simplicity and energy" of this deity (*EWRWE* 237–38). Ultimately, Emerson's religious understanding might be ineffable or untranslatable because it rests on a wholly individual, and therefore inherently subjective, communion or experience.[3]

Emerson refers to this deity or highest principle in a variety of ways with no discernable difference in meaning: in the essay "The Over-Soul" (1841) alone, he uses the terms "Unity," "Over-Soul," "the eternal ONE," "Highest Law," "Supreme Mind," "Maker," "Divine mind," "Omniscience," and "God" almost interchangeably. All of these terms seem to refer to a transcendent spiritual force or mind or being that permeates and animates all existence—both human and nonhuman nature, organic and inorganic—and that binds and unites everything together in a pure and sublime oneness or wholeness. Every individual is contained within this whole, and each individual contains within himself "the soul of the whole"; moreover, the "beatitude" of the whole of which we are a part is accessible to all, and this whole is both "perfect" and "self-sufficing." Although the ultimate source of both our being and the whole is unknown or hidden, before this "overpowering reality" our soul is laid bare and we are revealed for who we are (*EWRWE* 237).

Our communion with and access to this deity is through our own soul, which Emerson states is neither an "organ," a "function," nor a "faculty": the soul is the unpossessed and unpossessable "background of our being" which transcends time and space. If a man is the "facade of a temple wherein all wisdom and all good abide," the soul would be a light shining from within or behind this facade, illuminating all and giving direction to our will and intellect; and when we allow the soul to "have its way through us," intellect becomes genius, will virtue, and affection becomes love (*EWRWE* 238–39). The perception and disclosure of truth in and through the soul—"an influx of the Divine mind into our mind"—is what Emerson calls "revelation." Although revelation varies in both its intensity and character—from the transfiguring to the tepid, from the prophetic to the prosaic—all persons have the capacity to be so moved and all persons who are so moved belong to the same general class of individuals, whether they be a Socrates or a St.

Paul. One reason for this vast resemblance among "prophets" is that the "nature of these revelations is the same; they are perceptions of the absolute law" (*EWRWE* 243–44). Unfortunately, the precise content of this law is not articulated—indeed, it cannot and should not be articulated. Revelation does not occur through words, and it does not satisfy our "low curiosity" by answering specific "sensual questions."

> Men ask concerning the immortality of the soul, the employments of heaven, the state of the sinner, and so forth. They even dream that Jesus has left replies to precisely these interrogatories. Never a moment did that sublime spirit speak in their *patois*. To truth, justice, love, the attributes of the soul, the idea of immutableness is essentially associated. Jesus, living in these moral sentiments, heedless of sensual fortunes, heeding only the manifestations of these, never made the separation of the idea of duration from the essence of these attributes, nor uttered a syllable concerning the duration of the soul. It was left to his disciples to sever duration from the moral elements, and to teach the immortality of the soul as a doctrine, and maintain it by evidences. The moment the doctrine of the immortality is separately taught, man is already fallen. . . .
>
> These questions which we lust to ask about the future are a confession of sin. God has no answer for them. No answer in words can reply to a question of things. (*EWRWE* 244–45)

We must apparently rest content with Emerson's assurances that if we "forgo all low curiosity" and live in the infinite present of today, these questions will somehow be answered or resolved through the silent workings of the soul (*EWRWE* 245; cf. 173, 249, 398–99). The key to existence is an almost childlike innocence, simplicity, and authenticity with oneself and to others, and thus to the Over-Soul and consequently all creation through it; being insincere, sophistic, or in any way other than oneself signals disharmony in one's soul and thus distances oneself from God (cf. *EWRWE* 85–86, 238, 242, 246, 248–50, 264–67).

These remarks naturally raise the question as to whether Emerson's deity is a caring or providential being: to begin with, in what sense (if any) would one pray to this entity? Certainly, Emerson does not understand prayer in any ordinary or traditional sense. Those who pray or beg to attain some selfish end (material goods or worldly success) falsely assume a "dualism" between themselves and the divine; those who express regret or recite creeds display an "infirmity" of the will or intellect. Properly speaking, prayer is the act of a healthy, self-reliant individual contemplating or celebrating the existence of God within his soul, and prayer can be manifested through the simplest actions, from the farmer weeding his garden to the rower striking the water with his oar (*EWRWE* 147–49). But Emerson's deity is more than a transcendent spirit animating existence, for he also affirms the existence of a "Maker of all things and all persons [who] stands behind us and casts his dread omniscience through us over things" (*EWRWE* 242–43). This supreme creator, however, is much less the God of the Old Testament than the divine mind or soul of Plotinus and the Neoplatonists: the world is an emanation or overflow from the divine mind; all creation is contained within this whole, and all the variety in nature is encompassed within this unity (*EWRWE* 18ff., 118–19, 252ff., 293).[4] Although the divine maker can apparently choose to inspire specific individuals (*EWRWE* 237), and although he sent Jesus into the world (albeit not in the sense of his being the son of God) (*EWRWE* 108), God does not perform miracles in any ordinary or traditional sense of the word. Christianity's moral doctrines and not its miracles are what move Emerson to belief, and the attempt to convert others through miracles is a spiritual abomination: genuine conversion comes through genuine instruction, and this is strictly a matter of free internal acceptance, without any external compulsion whatsoever (*EWRWE* 67–69, 106–8). The greatest miracle of all would seem to be the shattering and transfiguring beauty of the universe as well as the immutable natural laws that govern its operation.[5] At all events, whatever the precise character of this personal and mystic union with the Over-Soul, it seems ecstatic, ineffable, and utterly compelling; it is much more a matter of the heart than the intellect; and it does not rely on traditions, institutions, and rituals.

> Ineffable is the union of man and God in every act of the soul. The simplest person who in his integrity worships God, becomes God; yet for ever and ever the influx of this better and universal self is new and unsearchable. It inspires awe and astonishment. How dear, how soothing to man, arises the idea of God, peopling the lonely place, effacing the scars of our mistakes and disappointments! When we have broken our god of tradition and ceased from our god of rhetoric, then may God fire the heart with his presence. . . .
>   Let man then learn the revelation of all nature and all thought to his heart; this, namely, that the Highest dwells with him; that the sources of nature are in his own mind, if the sentiment of duty is there. But if he would know what the great God speaketh, he must 'go into his closet and shut the door,' as Jesus said. God will not make himself manifest to cowards. He must greatly listen to himself, withdrawing himself from all the accents of other men's devotion. Even their prayers are hurtful to him, until he have made his own. (*EWRWE* 248–49)

One particular aspect of Emerson's religious or moral universe is especially important in this context: the law of "Compensation" (1841). Emerson forthrightly rejects the claim that the wicked prosper and the good suffer in this world. Justice is executed here on earth through a self-enforcing and omnipresent law that it is vain to escape or overpower and that applies as much to individuals as it does to governments and nations: "Every secret is told, every crime is punished, every virtue rewarded, every wrong redressed, in silence and certainty" (*EWRWE* 155, 158–59). He is of course aware that many crimes go unpunished and that many good men are persecuted; the punishment or reward about which he is speaking is an action's inevitable effect upon the soul and whether it strengthens or corrupts it.

> We feel defrauded of the retribution due to evil acts, because the criminal adheres to his vice and contumacy and does not come to a crisis or judgement anywhere in visible nature. There is no stunning confutation of his nonsense before men and angels. Has he therefore outwitted the law? Inasmuch as he carries the malignity and the lie with him he so far deceases from nature. In some manner there will be a demonstration of the wrong to the understanding also; but, should we not see it, this deadly deduction makes square the eternal account. (*EWRWE* 168)

Emerson makes a powerful point: if we really believe that crime is bad for the person who commits it, and if the soul is the most important possession we have, then surely the criminal will suffer spiritually for his criminal action, and over the long run he will come to possess the worst possible thing imaginable—a grotesquely malignant soul. Consequently, no real and lasting spiritual harm can be inflicted upon a genuinely good man by others, and the criminal gains no lasting and real benefit even if he "gets away with" his crime: only the good man can harm himself, and the "successful" criminal has already inflicted untold self-destruction (*EWRWE* 165–69). Emerson's evidence for the law of compensation is twofold. First, he notes that fables, literature, and especially proverbs (which he calls "statements of an absolute truth" and the "sanctuary of the intuitions") abundantly confirm the claim that the soul reaps what it sows (*EWRWE* 161–62). Second, he contends that because nature or God permeates and is represented in every particular object, then the same basic laws govern every part of creation, physical as well as moral: if in the physical world every action generates an equal and opposite reaction, so too in the moral world is every good action rewarded and every evil one punished (*EWRWE* 156–59). It is no wonder, then, that Emerson refers to the law of compensation as a universal law like any other law of nature (cf. *EWRWE* 17ff., 162, 205). And like every other scientific law, Emerson does not hesitate to apply it to the whole of man's actions. He therefore claims that even the greatest calamities—from the death of a loved one to mutilation to financial collapse—will be compensated with unintended positive benefits (*EWRWE* 170–71). In Emerson's moral universe, tragedy makes little sense: there is no unpunished evil and no uncompensated good— nothing which occurs that will not be balanced out in the end. Perhaps this explain why questions such as the afterlife lose their urgency: God has already provided universal justice and compensation for us here on earth to heal any and all wounds we receive (cf. *EWRWE* 172ff., 230, 248–49, 309ff., 318–19, 398–99, 412, 416–18).[6]

Given such a religious understanding, it is hardly surprising to read that Emerson had rather unorthodox views (even as a Unitarian minister) regarding traditional Christianity. For example, in his September 1832 sermon "The Lord's Supper," Emerson argues that a close reading of the Bible indicates that Jesus never intended the Eucharist to become a permanent institutional ritual of the church (*EWRWE* 99–105); and that even if he did so intend, this ritual is actually harmful to the genuine religious sentiment Jesus intended to instill (*EWRWE* 105–9).[7] But as arresting and controversial as Emerson's interpretation of the Bible is, none of these arguments are fundamentally decisive for him. The argument which carries the "greatest weight" and which trumps all others is that Emerson finds this particular ritual "of commemorating Christ" personally unsuitable.

> That is reason enough why I should abandon it. If I believed it was enjoined by Jesus on his disciples, and that he even contemplated making permanent this mode of commemoration, . . . and yet on trial it was disagreeable to my own feelings, I should not adopt it. I should choose other ways which, as more effectual upon me, he would approve more. For I choose that my remembrances of him should be pleasing, affecting, religious. I will love him as a glorified friend, after the free way of friendship, and not pay him a stiff sign of respect, as men do those whom they fear. (*EWRWE* 107)

Because every religious ritual has the potential to impinge upon the autonomy and independence of the soul—upon its freedom to choose the manner and method of worship—no ritual or form can ever be declared inviolate and sacrosanct. "Freedom is the essence of this faith," declares Emerson, and this means that all formal institutions must be "flexible" and judged according to their utility in making men "good and wise." To think otherwise is to betray the very purpose of Christ's crucifixion, for Jesus was sent to deliver mankind from the Jewish religion of "forms" to one of the "heart" (*EWRWE* 108–9). In the final analysis, Emerson himself will judge the worthiness of all traditional ceremonies, conventions, and customs—even those which Jesus might have specifically ordained (cf. *EWRWE* 250–51).

Emerson's departure from the traditional institutions and doctrines of Christianity is even more pronounced in his "Harvard Divinity School Address" (1838). Emerson launches a broadside against two "gross" "errors" in the present administration of the Christian church (*EWRWE* 67). First, the church continues to dwell "with noxious exaggeration about the person of Jesus." Forgetting that all genuine religion is a "doctrine of the soul"—of its "mystery" and "harmony" and "beauty"—the church both distorts and vulgarizes Jesus' teaching by claiming that he was the son of God. Jesus "belonged to the true race of prophets" not because he was divine but because he alone saw the "divinity" and "worth" and "greatness" of all men; and Jesus was sent into the world in order to teach man how to "become like God" and that He "is in me." Jesus understood that "God incarnates himself in man, and evermore goes forth anew to take possession of his World" (*EWRWE* 67–70, 106, 256).[8] Second, by failing to make the soul in all its exalted glory the very foundation of religious instruction, preachers are (unintentionally, to be sure) smothering that joyous and radiant temper in their congregations that characterizes genuine piety, and this, in turn, is corroding the faith of the nation as a whole. Rehearsed rather than inspired; doctrinaire rather than personal; formal rather than uplifting; monotone rather than celebratory—"historical Christianity destroys the power of preaching, by withdrawing it from the exploration of the moral nature of man" (*EWRWE* 73). Emerson offers his auditors a vivid sampling of the sorts of "moral" subjects whose absence in American churches is causing people to think twice about participating in public worship.

> In how many churches, by how many prophets, tell me, is man made sensible that he is an infinite Soul; that the earth and heavens are passing into his mind; that he is drinking forever the soul of God? Where now sounds the persuasion, that by its very melody imparadises my heart, and so affirms its own origin in heaven? Where shall I hear words such as in elder ages drew men to leave all and follow—father and mother, house and land, wife and child? Where shall I hear these august laws of moral being so pronounced as to fill my ear, and I feel ennobled by the offer of my uttermost action and passion? The test of the true faith, certainly, should be its power to charm and command the soul, as the laws of nature control the activity of the hands—so commanding that we find pleasure and honor in obeying. . . . But now the priest's Sabbath has lost the splendor of nature; it is unlovely; we are glad when it is done. (*EWRWE* 71)[9]

As for the solution to the spiritual crisis America faces, Emerson does not advocate the creation of "new rites and forms" but the spiritual reinvigoration of those forms already at hand: "The remedy to their [i.e., rites and forms] deformity is first, soul, and second, soul, and evermore, soul." The current generation of preachers must stride forward in a spirit of fierce independence from all traditional authority (even relying on St. Paul can pervert one's own knowledge or sentiment of God); they must maintain the most rigid personal integrity and virtue (the parrot-like praise from and easy adulation of society are to be spurned); and they must be open to the sublime wonder and limitless potential in man (this is the true gospel of Christ, and it is as alive today as ever) (*EWRWE* 75–78). With injunctions such as these, it is no wonder that after Emerson delivered his Harvard address, many of the faculty publicly disclaimed it. He was not invited back to speak at his alma mater for some thirty years.

Commerce, Politics, and the Individual as Supreme Lawgiver

Given the above description of a mystical union with an omnipresent spiritual force or soul, it is little wonder that Emerson's transcendentalist would see ordinary commercial activity as a waste of time, politics as paltry, and ethics as a matter of self-legislation. Indeed, to respect or trust any authority above and beyond oneself is potentially corrupting in that one would be denying the independence and sovereignty of one's own soul (cf. *EWRWE* 250). Let us examine each of these subjects in turn.

The transcendentalist has no respect for property or labor as such and therefore no interest in the unlimited accumulation of wealth; labor and property are worthy of respect only to the extent that they symbolically represent the multitudinous ways individuals make manifest their particular being. In other words, the artisan or craftsman is respectable to the extent that his unique product expresses or illustrates his own character. Mass production, it would seem, has little dignified about it (*EWRWE* 83, 152–53, 169, 634). But craftsmanship alone is not enough, for the artisan can just as easily fall into a numbing and spiritless routine, without any higher end or purpose to his art and occupation. The transcendentalist craves something noble and worth-while to do, and until that "something" presents itself, he would prefer to remain idle and even to rot with boredom rather than to degrade himself in an unbefitting occupation (*EWRWE* 87, 90–93). Emerson traces the source of this problem to at least two factors: an excessive love of wealth (of which Napoleon is one of the prime examples [*EWRWE* 463–66]) and the division of labor (which makes it difficult for an individual to be a dignified and complete human being [*EWRWE* 43–44]). The best that Emerson does to spell out the corrective to this problem is to once again urge us to hearken to our inner voice. Each person has a unique calling depending upon "the mode in which the general soul incarnates itself in him," and thus every occupation is estimable if done by the right person in the right way (*EWRWE* 177–78).

Emerson moderated his views in later writings such as "Wealth" in *The Conduct of Life* (1860)—but he did so in a uniquely Emersonian fashion. While he still argues that no man can be "whole" until he earns a "blameless livelihood," and while he continues to maintain that each man has a unique "talent" or "career" suited to him alone, Emerson now emphasizes that we all have a duty to be a "producer" as well as a "consumer," that is, to give back "something to the common wealth." Thus, Emerson is not as harsh as one might imagine toward the admittedly "tyrannical" desires and designs of speculators and monopolists—for it is precisely their desire for riches that indirectly benefits the public and makes possible such things as railroads, telegraphs, mills, mines, and the like (*EWRWE* 622–27, 634–35). As for those who would argue that speculators do more harm than good, Emerson contends that there are several "checks and balances" (e.g., competition from other speculators, or the law of supply and demand) which help to insure that property remains in the hands of the "industrious, brave and persevering" (*EWRWE* 626, 631). Even when it comes to regulating the wages of the poor, Emerson contends that things will inevitably work themselves aright only if the state avoids legislating or interfering: continually low wages will increase the number of poor and the rate of crime, and this in turn will require everyone to pay as much in additional taxes as they would have paid increasing the wages of the poor in the first place. "The basis of political economy is non-interference," and England's spirit of "personal" and "pecuniary independence" is the model (*EWRWE* 631–34, 624–25). To the extent that the state has a role, it would be to sponsor and support those institutions that make possible "culture and inspiration for the citizens" as a whole: libraries, public gardens, museums, concert halls, scientific societies, and the like (*EWRWE* 627–28). In sum, one hears Emerson's law of compensation being applied to commercial activity, and this law sits uncomfortably in a socialist or welfare state (cf. *EWRWE* 152–53, 163, 629).[10]

If Emerson's transcendentalist is tepid at best toward the accumulation of riches and wealth, so too is he toward politics in almost all its manifestations: from the great political debates of the day to the building of empires, the transcendentalist finds little in this petty arena to tempt him from his solitude.

> But their solitary and fastidious manners not only withdraw them from the conversation, but from the labors of the world; they are not good citizens, not good members of society; unwillingly they bear their part of the public and private burdens; they do not willingly share in the public charities, in the public religious rites, in the enterprises of education, of missions foreign and domestic, in the abolition of the slave-trade, or in the temperance society. They do not even like to vote. . . .
>
> What you call your fundamental institutions, your great and holy causes, seem to them great abuses, and, when nearly seen, paltry matters. (*EWRWE* 90)

Emerson does not deny that there are "great" and "holy" causes, albeit far fewer than most imagine; but, by the time a potentially worthwhile cause reaches the political arena, it has been prepackaged and predigested for public consumption (*EWRWE* 90–91). Given such a blistering attack on great political issues and institutions—from constitutions to abolition—Emerson rightly concludes that the transcendentalist's un- or a-political outlook is considered a threat to society at large. To say nothing of their not sharing the public burdens that make all decent life possible, their disdainful aloofness from the world is a direct "accusation" of it; and society will not remain indifferent but retaliate at this challenge to what they hold precious and dear. Needless to say, there can be no transcendental political party (*EWRWE* 85, 87).

To the extent that Emerson hopes to improve American society, he directs his appeals for moral reformation at the individual and not the group: there is little or no salvation through political activity unless the individual himself has first been spiritually transformed. In the essay "New England Reformers" (1844), he points out two problems in attempting the former before or without the latter. First, all political reforms tend to be partial. Emerson here disparages piecemeal efforts at social change as futile or misguided given the enormity of the "evil" facing society. By contrast, "a just and heroic soul" will be able to abolish a host of "old" evils through the force of his character and actions in the here and now. Second, reformers overestimate the power of associations or numbers. Groups are no better or worse than the individuals who make them up, and unhealthy individuals make unhealthy groups: indeed, the more united and efficacious a group is politically, the more it will require its members to compromise their unique individuality, forcing out those of superior talent (*EWRWE* 407–10). Thus, Emerson's "revolution" will not be political but private, an attempt to unify our presently disharmonious souls "by the gradual domestication of the idea of Culture . . . [which is] the upbuilding of a man" (*EWRWE* 38, 55–56; cf. 380–81, 386, 642–59). How this "domestication" will occur without radical political changes (e.g., in the education system [cf. *EWRWE* 410–11]) is not clear.

But perhaps the most significant and far-reaching issue of all is Emerson's insistence that the transcendentalist is a self-legislating individual: there is no law or commandment that is unconditionally binding upon him, and there is no institution—no government, no church, no society, and no art—that is worthy of his respect and allegiance unless it "reiterates the law of his mind" (*EWRWE* 83). The transcendentalist's conduct is not governed by prudent deliberation or experiential knowledge but by intuition, spontaneity, and trusting one's instincts—even, it seems, when one can give no rational account of them at the time (*EWRWE* 264–66). Only the spontaneous action—the one which is receptive to the prompting of the divine voice within and which acts upon it—is genuinely obedient to God, and this is why Emerson refers to right actions as submitting to the divine essence rather than as directing or commanding it. By becoming the channel through which the divine makes itself manifest, we at once shed all gross vanity and pretension while simultaneously solidifying and strengthening our own unique character (*EWRWE* 6, 141–42, 237–38, 246, 264–65, 299, 318–21).

> A little consideration of what takes place around us every day would show us that a higher law than that of our will regulates events; that our painful labors are unnecessary and fruitless; that only in our easy, simple, spontaneous action are we strong, and by contenting ourselves with obedience we become divine. . . . O my brothers, God exists. There is a soul at the centre of nature and over the will of every man, so that none of us can wrong the universe. It has so infused its strong enchantment into nature that we prosper when we accept its advice, and when we struggle to wound its creatures our hands are glued to our sides, or they beat our own breasts. We need only obey. There is guidance for each of us, and by lowly listening we shall hear the right word. . . . Place yourself in the middle of the stream of power and wisdom which animates all whom it floats, and you are without effort impelled to truth, to right and a perfect contentment. Then you put all gainsayers in the wrong. Then you are the world, the measure of right, of truth, of beauty. (*EWRWE* 176)

By keeping our soul open to the ebb and flow of the Over-Soul, the truth will be made known to us; we will become genuinely moral by fully and completely listening to the poetry of our own heart, which is itself a reflection of the poetry of the universe as a whole and its animating spirit or mind. Emerson would replace the ancient injunction "Know thyself " with "Trust thyself " because the latter contains or is the means to the former (*EWRWE* 54, 75–76, 133, 150–51, 177, 183, 186, 324, 404ff).

This celebration of individual intuition, integrity, and spontaneity is perhaps nowhere more succinctly and powerfully stated than in Emerson's most famous and inspirational essay, "Self-Reliance" (1841). Like "Moses, Plato and Milton" before, we must learn to heed the flash of genius when it ignites within us, trusting, almost childlike, that God has a purpose in the work that we do and that divinity does not traffic in counterfeit forms. But if God urges us to listen to our heart, society does not, and the more we become accustomed to the ways of the world, the more our native light of genius grows dim (*EWRWE* 132–34). Emerson underlines two problems in particular: conformity and consistency. In respect to conformity, although he censures those who follow the latest fads and fashions, he is also very aware of the "magnanimity and religion" required to resist the "unintelligible brute force" of the majority. The "rage of the cultivated classes" can easily be resisted by a man of culture; but the "growl and mow" of an indignant people takes a near godlike courage to ignore (*EWRWE* 134–38). In respect to consistency, Emerson downplays its import and argues that "genuine actions," over the long run, will exhibit their own logic and integrity (*EWRWE* 138–39). Why Emerson highlights these two problems is that they, more than any others, undermine the self-trust necessary to act spontaneously or instinctively. This is the "source" and "essence" of all "genius," "virtue," and "life"; it is that "deep force . . . behind which analysis cannot go," and all we can do is "affirm" its "presence or its absence" (*EWRWE* 141–42). To those who would argue that Emerson's insistence on individual self-reliance might actually undermine such important institutions as government and the family, as well as (unwittingly) lead one to commit the worst atrocities in the name of "intuition" and "spontaneity," his response (at least in this essay) is: so be it.

> I remember an answer which when quite young I was prompted to make to a valued adviser who was wont to importune me with the dear old doctrines of the church. On my saying, "What have I to do with the sacredness of traditions, if I live wholly from within?" my friend suggested— "But these impulses may be from below, not from above." I replied, "They do not seem to me to be such; but if I am the Devil's child, I will live then from the Devil." No law can be sacred to me but that of my nature. Good and bad are but names very readily transferable to that or this; the only right is what is after my constitution; the only wrong what is against it. A man is to carry himself in the presence of all opposition as if every thing were titular and ephemeral but he. (*EWRWE* 135)

We must give expression to that unique incarnation of the divine within us and avoid being the predictable, herdlike mob of nonentities that we are at present: conformity is the real threat to a vibrant political and civic life and not self-reliance (*EWRWE* 139, 143–45, 153). Indeed, true atheism and impiety is ignoring the divine inspirations in us as they are the sacred source of all life and wisdom (*EWRWE* 141, 255). Self-reliance thus turns out to be God-reliance—albeit the God within as you hear and interpret Him.

Emerson's clarion call for independence is reflected in a number of other important ways in his writings. Just as the individual was the standard to judge the rectitude of an action and the worth of an institution, so the new American nation must do the same and emancipate itself from the tyrannizing effects of a slavish veneration of the "mind of the Past" (especially Europe's) in all its incarnations: history, philosophy, art, architecture, and literature. Although this call for originality can already be seen in the opening paragraph of Emerson's first book *Nature* (1836), perhaps the most stirring expression of this sentiment is his Harvard Phi Beta Kappa address, "The American Scholar" (1837), which Dr. Oliver Wendell Holmes called "our intellectual

Declaration of Independence" (*EWRWE* 3, 846). The moment some form of the past is declared perfect or inviolate, then the present generation will atrophy and cease thinking and creating—it will become a "satellite" of the past rather than its own "[solar] system." The genius of an age is lost when it passively accepts the dogmas of the past and does not actively seize upon and articulate its own creative principles: "The English dramatic poets have Shak[e]spearized now for two hundred years." He thus declares that books "are for the scholar's idle times, . . . when the intervals of darkness come," to be used to guide the scholar back to the light of his own inspirations. Emerson is not rejecting the past outright (his frequent praise of past philosophers and authors and poets demonstrates this); instead, he wants to challenge the "backward" or conservative tendency of all institutions to defend some ancient authority and to use this as an excuse for not progressively moving "forward" (*EWRWE* 46–48, 56). The past must come alive for the present and speak to its concerns and circumstances; and if the past fails to do this, then it need not be studied and certainly not revered. Discard the relics of the past or reanimate them—if Greece or Rome or Constantinople or Paris or London do not speak to us, we need not worry: someone or something else will (*EWRWE* 115–17, 120, 130–31, 140, 150–51, 272–73).

Emerson sees some encouraging signs of intellectual liberation in the growing prevalence of "the near, the low, [and] the common" as a new subject of literature. From the poor to children, from street life to the household, writers are finding these former outcasts as rich thematically as more traditional subjects. Because a universal or divine mind is present in the highest and lowest individual—because "one design unites and animates the farthest pinnacle and the lowest trench"—then even these "suburbs and extremities of nature" are bursting with the same sublime soul, and they can be made the focal point of a literary and spiritual renaissance appropriate for this new era and new nation (*EWRWE* 56–59; cf. 65, 113–14, 130–31, 293, 304). At the end of the day, Emerson applauds the fact that the same egalitarian political movements which both raised the "lowest class in the state" and gave new dignity and respect to the "individual" are now fostering an appropriate egalitarian literature (*EWRWE* 43, 57–58).

Transcendentalism in Practice: Thoreau's *Walden* (1854)

Although Thoreau did not spend some two years at Walden Pond (1845–1847) to prove or disprove Emerson's (or anyone else's) philosophy, his wide-ranging reflections help to unfold that philosophy in a number of significant ways as well as to illustrate Thoreau's own unique focus. Thoreau states that his reason for going to Walden was a simple one: he wanted to live. "I went to the woods because I wished to live deliberately, to front only the essential facts of life, and see if I could not learn what it had to teach, and not, when I came to die, discover that I had not lived" (*WOW* 86). He wanted to whittle life down to its bare essence by discarding all that was superfluous and burdensome. "Simplicity" and "simplify" became his watchwords—not in the sense of trying "to live cheaply" (although he certainly did do this) but in the sense of living with the "fewest obstacles" (*WOW* 19, 84–87). And in good transcendental fashion, he did not recommend his way of life (which he admits is quite "solitary") as a standard for all.

> I would not have any one adopt my mode of living on any account; for, besides that before he has fairly learned it I may have found out another for myself, I desire that there may be as many different persons in the world as possible; but I would have each one be very careful to find out and pursue *his own* way, and not his father's or his mother's or his neighbor's instead. (*WOW* 67)

Each person had to discover their own calling, and they were free to use as little or as much as they chose of Thoreau's experiences (*WOW* 3–4, 11, 15–16, 69, 84–85).

But what precisely does it mean to live life "deliberately"? We can best describe this life in a negative way at first: it is anti-Lockean or anticapitalistic. By and large, Thoreau sees the accumulation of property as a positive burden which enslaves man in a myriad number of ways (*WOW* 6–7). Mounting debt, unending labor, gnawing anxieties, and the incessant desire to impress or keep up with our neighbors, to wear the latest fashion, and to pacify our vanity— everywhere he looks, Thoreau sees men adding unnecessary burdens to their lives, burdens which inevitably crush the spirit of those who attempt to bear them. Thoreau thus catalogues the four essential things which we need to live—"Food, Shelter, Clothing, and Fuel" (*WOW* 12)—and in each case, he shows why he acquired a particular item, what it cost, and the easy, utilitarian spirit in which he acquired it. To those who are "discontented, and idly complaining of the hardness of their lot or of the times," his conclusion is rather shocking (*WOW* 15): "In short, I am convinced, both by faith and experience, that to maintain one's self on this earth is not a hardship but a pastime, if we will live simply and wisely. . . . It is not necessary that a man should earn his living by the sweat of his brow, unless he sweats easier than I do" (*WOW* 67). His was a Spartan existence to be sure—but without any painful repression. In fact, what seems like repression was actually a liberation from a thousand cares, and with this he bought the most precious of all commodities: the independence and leisure to enjoy the present moment. The unleashing of avarice creates desires in us for things we previously did not need or want, and the pursuit to satisfy these desires prevents us from living a noble or elevated existence (*WOW* 13–15, 18, 53, 58, 62–66, 86–87, 156, 303ff).

Thoreau is of course aware of the common rebuttal to his indictment of capitalistic society: we live more secure and comfortable lives. Thoreau is not so sure, and he severely questions whether the mass of civilized human beings is really better off than the savage. In lines that call to mind Locke's *Second Treatise of Government* (sec. 41), Thoreau compares their respective conditions in respect to shelter.

> In the savage state every family owns a shelter as good as the best, and sufficient for its coarser and simpler wants; . . . in modern civilized society not more than one half the families own a shelter. . . . [T]he savage owns his shelter because it costs so little, while the civilized man hires his commonly because he cannot afford to own it. . . . But, answers one, by merely paying this tax the poor civilized man secures an abode which is a palace compared with the savage's. An annual rent of from twenty-five to a hundred dollars (these are the country rates) entitles him to the benefit of the improvements of centuries. . . . But how happens it that he who is said to enjoy these things is so commonly a *poor* civilized man, while the savage, who has them not, is rich as a savage? If it is asserted that civilization is a real advance in the condition of man,—and I think that it is, though only the wise improve their advantages,—it must be shown that it has produced better dwellings without making them more costly. (*WOW* 28–29)

Civilized man purchases a home several times more luxurious than he needs, and it thus takes half a lifetime to own. "Would the savage have been wise to exchange his wigwam for a palace on these terms?" (*WOW* 30). At the end of the day, Thoreau does side with civilization—but not before making it clear how very little civilized man has taken advantage of those material improvements and conveniences civilization has produced (and not before reminding the reader that the comparison he is making is with those of moderate means; the advantage is on the side of the savage in respect to the poor and slaves) (*WOW* 32–33, 38). With a little more ingenuity and a lot more moderation, civilization would be a blessing; as it now stands, the advantages of civilization come at a high price—most important, at the impoverishment of our souls (cf. *WOW* 62ff., 86–87, 109, 163).

What is true for individuals is true for nations: so much of what is claimed to distinguish one civilization above another is little more than frivolity and vanity. Thoreau is especially contemptuous of architecture—of the "insane ambition to perpetuate the memory of themselves by the amount of hammered stone they leave." To say nothing of the human cost involved in erecting such edifices, the desire itself is wrongheaded: nations should "commemorate themselves" with books or better manners or good sense or the spiritual improvement of the people; hammered stone only increases the wealth of princes (*WOW* 54–55; cf. 44–45). Similar remarks are made in respect to America's internal technological improvement (e.g., telegraphs and railroads). Thoreau is not necessarily against such projects, but he does wonder whether they are really necessary, if they genuinely serve any positive purpose, and if the time and money and effort might not have been better spent elsewhere (*WOW* 49–51, 87ff., 104).

It is essential to see that while Thoreau aims to help people in a certain respect—to rustle them out of their spiritual slumber and show them how they could live much simpler and therefore happier lives (*WOW* 15, 47, 80, 305)—Thoreau himself is not an ordinary "do-gooder," and he did not acquire his independence and leisure to squander it in philanthropic endeavors. He offers a twofold reason for his lack of enthusiasm and activity: first, he does not have the altruistic temperament; and second, he wonders whether the more important task is not to improve ourselves first. Similar to Emerson (*EWRWE* 135–36), Thoreau suggests that when we concentrate on our own moral improvement first and foremost, we do more good in the world by our example than through ordinary works of charity. He thus betrays a suspicion of the motives of many (but certainly not all) altruists, and he frankly questions whether the downtrodden are actually being helped by their efforts (and even if the poor want to be helped at all). Philanthropists are prized because of mankind's general selfishness, and it is doubtful whether they are true examples of a great human being (*WOW* 6–7, 69–75, 193–94).

Having articulated what Thoreau rails against, what can we affirm was his positive intention in going to Walden Pond? Without a doubt, the most important reason was to live in as close a proximity to nature as he could, both materially and spiritually, in order to purify and better his soul. Nature is critical for his self-improvement in a number of ways. Perhaps the most obvious, and which constitutes the bulk of his narrative, is the pristine beauty of nature (as compared to the so-called beauty of civilization). One need only read his description of "The Ponds" (*WOW* 164–89), or of winter (*WOW* 266–80) or spring (*WOW* 281–99), to see the restorative—almost medicinal—impact of immersing oneself in such surroundings (cf. *WOW* 36, 283, 655–60). Second, Thoreau sees that one key to education is to have hands-on experience of what one studies and not to fritter away all of one's time in the classroom. By building his own home and growing his own food (among other things), he was able, as he describes it, to "earnestly *live*" life and not merely to "*play*" or "*study*" it (*WOW* 48–49, 290). Third, this manner of living forced him to focus on living in the present, and not in the past or the future. It is not proper to dwell on the mistakes and regrets of the past or to become so preoccupied with future concerns and worries that one forgets to live life in the here and now. Concentrating on the present helps us to live "deliberately"—to cut through the "mud and slush" of so much of "civilized" life—such that our days are no longer regulated by the time-clock or thrown off-track by every new fashion or fad (*WOW* 16, 80, 86–88, 92, 106, 295–96, 306–7, 662). And finally, fourth, embedded within nature is not only the source of life but the source of wisdom itself, and only by sloughing off the cares of civilization can we immerse ourselves in the divine that permeates all nature and discover our own genius (*WOW* 14, 84–85, 90–93, 105–6, 126–27, 196, 204, 290, 298–99, 300ff). There is even a friendship in nature such that no man can really ever be alone in the woods, and this fellowship more than compensates for any material comforts one must forego in order to enjoy it (*WOW* 124–30). In short, Thoreau went to Walden Pond in order to live the good life as he understood it—a life of independence, leisure, and personal self-enlightenment (*WOW* 52–53, 58, 66–67, 79, 158, 181, 300ff).

But Thoreau is not merely the "back-to-nature guru" one might imagine: there are parts of civilization that he finds utterly priceless—namely books, as we see from his paean to the classics in the chapter "Reading." Great literature is "the work of art nearest to life itself," and learning to read well—to genuinely *"understand"* what the author is saying—is a "noble exercise" that requires an enormous amount of "training" and "steady intention" throughout life. In communing with the great minds of the past (and those minds come from the West as well as the East, from Aeschylus to Zoroaster), we transcend time and become "immortal"; by refusing to profit from this "treasured wealth of the world," we are little better than "pygmies and manikins." But even with the emergence of the "modern cheap and fertile press" (which allows editions of the classics to be accessible to a wide audience), most persons prefer to choke down large portions of pulp fiction and romance novels. To correct this lack of culture, Thoreau urges cities to invest their money in what truly matters—not in the building of new city halls but in the creation of a new and "uncommon" educational system, with the liberal arts as the core of the curriculum. Thoreau may have rejected the old and the ancient in every other manifestation (*WOW* 8–9)—but not old books. Every question that concerns us has been addressed by wise men of the past, and their ruminations are as relevant today as ever (*WOW* 94–104).

Notwithstanding his praise of the ancients, reading, and intellectual activity in general, it would be a mistake to think that these constitute on their own the highest way of life for Thoreau: while all of these activities go into making a genuinely noble and enlightened existence, the essential ingredient in that recipe is communing with nature. Immediately after Thoreau offers his wonderful ode to reading, he begins the next chapter "Sounds" with what appears to be a caution or qualification of the theme of the previous chapter.

> But while we are confined to books, though the most select and classic, and read only particular written languages, which are themselves but dialects and provincial, we are in danger of forgetting the language which all things and events speak without metaphor, which alone is copious and standard. . . . No method nor discipline can supersede the necessity of being forever on the alert. What is a course of history or philosophy, or poetry, no matter how well selected, or the best society, or the most admirable routine of life, compared with the discipline of looking always at what is to be seen? Will you be a reader, a student merely, or a seer? . . .
> I did not read books the first summer; I hoed beans. Nay, I often did better than this. There were times when I could not afford to sacrifice the bloom of the present moment to any work, whether of the head or hands. I love a broad margin to my life. Sometimes, in a summer morning, having taken my accustomed bath, I sat in my sunny doorway from sunrise till noon, rapt in a revery, amidst the pines and hickories and sumachs, in undisturbed solitude and stillness. . . . They were not time subtracted from my life, but so much over and above my usual allowance. I realized what the Orientals mean by contemplation and the forsaking of works. (*WOW* 105–6)

The highest life seems to be more aptly described as poetic rather than strictly intellectual, and his philosophic wisdom has a mystic or spiritual quality to it that Thoreau himself seems to situate more properly in the East than the West (e.g., so many of the quotes in *Walden* come from Eastern sources) (*WOW* 58, 84–85, 202, 204–5, 219, 239, 252, 290, 657). His is a sort of inspired life, hearkening to the voice within and without—the voice of his own genius, and the divine or nature. Thoreau is not speaking here about instinct, although he admits the import of sometimes listening to our animal nature (*WOW* 198ff); nor about childlike innocence, as his remarks about the Canadian woodchopper make clear (*WOW* 136–42). Thoreau certainly celebrates the wild more than the intellectual, for the wild or primitive life would seem to have fewer obstacles to an elevated spirituality (cf. *WOW* 198ff., 298, 656–60). Nevertheless, the wild element must be transformed through interaction with the intellect to yield that unique blend which is Thoreau's poetic spirituality—a spirituality that is decidedly ascetic, as sensuality in almost all it forms is the one aspect of nature that must be "overcome" rather than embraced (*WOW* 208).

If *Walden* is Thoreau's personal description of his communion with nature, then the essay "Walking" (1862) is certainly his public-spirited appeal to save it: "in Wildness is the preservation of the World" (*WOW* 644). Explorers "sail" for it; founders draw "nourishment" from it; cities "import" it; and the best art is permeated with it—everything about the wild strengthens the soul and invigorates the senses, and the refinements of civilization look pale and puny in comparison (*WOW* 644–47, 649–51). In order to retain and "cultivate" this untamed element in man, we must set aside the swamps and bogs and deserts and forests from which it rises, allowing them to flourish and decay untouched. But "Walking" is more than a plea to preserve lands for future generations; its principal argument is that civilization's mental and moral health depends upon that preservation. "A town is saved, not more by the righteous men in it than by the woods and swamps that surround it," and the great civilizations and individuals of the past have all been "sustained by the primitive forests" (*WOW* 647–48). Moral excellence thus depends upon keeping large portions of land untouched and open to the public: while Thoreau is not against fences per se, there are clearly limits to what should be consigned as private property (*WOW* 633, 636–37, 656; cf. 163).

From Civil Disobedience to the Brink of Civil War

In the essay "Walking," Thoreau revels in the fact that once one is in the woods, the world of politics is left far behind.

> Man and his affairs, church and state and school, trade and commerce, and manufactures and agriculture, even politics, the most alarming of them all,—I am pleased to see how little space they occupy in the landscape. Politics is but a narrow field, and that still narrower highway yonder leads to it. . . . If you would go to the political world, follow the great road,—follow that market-man, keep his dust in your eyes, and it will lead you straight to it; for it, too, has its place merely, and does not occupy all space. I pass from it as from a bean-field into the forest, and it is forgotten. In one half-hour I can walk off to some portion of the earth's surface where a man does not stand from one year's end to another, and there, consequently, politics are not, for they are but as the cigar-smoke of a man. (*WOW* 633–34)

This statement is emblematic of both Thoreau's and Emerson's philosophy. Although their essays sound political themes, they do not spend time describing the strengths and weaknesses of various types of regimes, constitutional systems, or political policies and practices: indeed, neither thinker spends much time commenting on the events of the day (cf. *WOW* 49–50, 89ff., 690; *EWRWE* 53, 779). But as much as they wished to distance themselves from politics, politics imposed itself upon them, most notably with the issue of slavery and the government that supported it.[11]

Thoreau's essay "Civil Disobedience" (1849) asks how a person ought to "behave" toward the present American government, in particular, and all governments, in general. Thoreau's response is categorical: he can neither respect, recognize, nor associate with a government that holds one-sixth of its population in slavery and that prosecutes an unjust war against Mexico. If

Americans had a right to rebel against England simply because "it taxed certain foreign commodities," then how much more reason do they have to revolt now given the enormity of the evils perpetrated by this government. Thoreau lambasts those who refuse to do justice to the slaves and to Mexico because of the potential economic cost involved, and he holds out little hope for radical change through the political process. The parties offer up but mediocre candidates, and voting itself is little more than a game of chance—a hope that the majority might win and thereafter do right. Voting can hardly be described as actually "*doing*" something for the sake of justice, and a "wise man" will not leave the triumph of right to the luck of the ballot and the force of the majority (*WOW* 670–74).

Given these remarks, one would think that all citizens have a duty, if not to take up arms and revolt, then at the very least to organize, protest, and actively demand change. But Thoreau just as categorically denies this. "It is not a man's duty, as a matter of course, to devote himself to the eradication of any, even the most enormous wrong; he may still properly have other concerns to engage him; but it is his duty, at least, to wash his hands of it, and, if he gives it no thought longer, not to give it practically his support" (*WOW* 674). Since Thoreau claims that he meets the present government "directly, and face-to-face, once a year—no more—in the person of its tax-gatherer," his particular method of "washing his hands" of slavery and war is to refuse to pay his poll tax (*WOW* 678).[12] Rather than seeking to work through the political process in order to abolish or change unjust laws and practices, Thoreau calls on his fellow abolitionists to withdraw their support "in person and property" from the government and to disobey such laws. The political process takes too much time; innocent lives could be lost in the meantime; and Thoreau has no more business petitioning the government to change than the government does him. As for those who would argue that Thoreau's cure to injustice would be worse than the disease, his response is that the government makes it so, and that if everyone would do as he did, the government would quickly chose to eliminate the evil practices (*WOW* 675–80).

It is essential to see that Thoreau's disobedience to unjust law is not meant to strengthen the rule of (just) law per se—on the contrary, the problem is that Americans have an "undue respect for law." By mistaking what is legal for what is right, citizens "resign [their] conscience to the legislator" and thereafter become the dronelike apes of an oppressive and imperialistic government (*WOW* 668–70). An individual must, like Thoreau, obey only those laws that he himself judges are right, regardless of the cost to himself, his family, or even the Union itself (*WOW* 671–72, 680–82). Thoreau clearly has more faith in the efficacy of disobedience to produce positive change than he does in the legal institutions of government; a principled and conscientious lawlessness is the surest way to eliminate egregious instances of injustice (cf. *WOW* 676–78). And it must be stressed that Thoreau is directing his injunctions at egregious instances of injustice such as slavery and war; he is not encouraging people to disobey every law that they consider wrong.

> If the injustice is part of the necessary friction of the machine of government let it go, let it go: perchance it will wear smooth,—certainly the machine will wear out. If the injustice has a spring, or a pulley, or a rope, or a crank, exclusively for itself, then perhaps you may consider whether the remedy will not be worse than the evil; but if it is of such a nature that it requires you to be the agent of injustice to another, then, I say, break the law. Let your life be a counter friction to stop the machine. What I have to do is to see, at any rate, that I do not lend myself to the wrong which I condemn. (*WOW* 677)

In the meantime, however, until more persons are willing to heed his advice, Thoreau simply wants this malignant state to leave him alone; and until it does so, he will continue to reside in

Concord, Massachusetts, taking advantage of the government when he can while refusing to support economically and morally its injustice (*WOW* 687).

Thoreau states that he is not against government—but besides wanting a "better government," it is hard to say precisely what sort of government he is for. He clearly wants government to play a very limited role in people's lives: more often than not, government creates more obstacles than it removes when it attempts to establish or regulate public policy. If governments have a particular obligation, it would seem to be to create the conditions whereby everyone would be allowed to mind their own business (*WOW* 667–68, 693). He is severely critical of majority rule, arguing that the "practical reason" why the majority is allowed to rule is "not because they are most likely to be in the right, nor because this seems fairest to the minority, but because they are physically the strongest" (*WOW* 668). A genuinely "free and enlightened" state must be based on a true "respect" for the individual—from whom "all its own power and authority are derived"—and it is for this reason that democracy is superior to monarchy. Consequently, a "strictly just" state must have the consent of all those over whom it governs—but in order to respect each individual, such a state can have "no pure right over my person and property but what I concede to it." Thoreau holds out the possibility that there may be further improvements in democratic government such that the "rights of man" are better recognized and respected; but unfortunately, he nowhere explains how a state could simultaneously respect the "pure right" of each individual, avoid the tyranny of the majority, and still have a functioning government (*WOW* 693).

In Thoreau's next major essay against slavery, "Slavery in Massachusetts" (1854), he is both more acerbic in tone and more ferocious in his criticisms—but in significant ways his position is clearer and more compelling. He now unequivocally states that slavery is contrary to the eternal law of God, a law that is "written in your being" and that no man or state can long contravene without serious repercussions. No positive law can be considered just which so clearly contravenes the divine law, regardless of whether that positive law has been approved by the majority, upheld by the courts, and declared constitutional. Thoreau's particular target for his scorching indictment is the Fugitive Slave Law, a "law" that he says does not even rise "to the level of the head or the reason; its natural habitat is in the dirt" (*WOW* 702, 708). It is the duty of every citizen not only to refuse compliance with this law but actively to seek to violate it, and thus Thoreau has high praise for the Bostonians who attempted to rescue the fugitive slave Anthony Burns from the city jail (*WOW* 707–8, 710). There are instances of injustice the severity of which require a citizen to "recognize a higher law than the Constitution, or the decision of the majority"; breaking this particular law is now understood as upholding the source of law itself, namely, God, upon which all legitimate laws and constitutions must be based (*WOW* 708–9). "The law will never make men free; it is men who have got to make the law free. They are the lovers of law and order who observe the law when the government breaks it" (*WOW* 703).

Thoreau once again lambasts those who would seek redress through the political process: "These men act as if they believed that they could safely slide down a hill a little way,—or a good way,—and would surely come to a place, by and by, where they could begin to slide up again" (*WOW* 708–9). What each individual, and the state of Massachusetts, must do is immediately put their own moral house in order and dissolve this despicable Union with the slave-holders and slave-holding states (*WOW* 697–98, 709). And Thoreau now reveals for the first time that the recent actions of Massachusetts have so disgusted him that they have irreparably contaminated his private pursuits: he can longer remain immune from the public arena as he suggested in "Civil Disobedience" (*WOW* 674–75, 690).

> I had never respected the government near to which I lived, but I had foolishly thought that I might manage to live here, minding my private affairs, and forget it. For my part, my old and worthiest pursuits have lost I cannot say how much of their attraction, and I feel that my investment in life here is worth many per cent. less since Massachusetts last deliberately sent back an innocent man, Anthony Burns, to slavery. I dwelt before, perhaps, in the illusion that my life passed somewhere only *between* heaven and hell, but now I cannot persuade myself that I do not dwell *wholly within* hell. (*WOW* 711)

Even nature itself loses some of its "beauty" when men are so "base"—although the final image in the essay of the white water-lily confirms that renewal and rejuvenation are possible (*WOW* 712–14).

Thoreau's rhetoric reaches a crescendo in his last major speech against slavery, "A Plea for Captain John Brown" (1859).[13] At the beginning of the essay, Thoreau calls Brown a "transcendentalist above all, a man of ideas and principles"; near the middle, he states that "[n]o man in America has ever stood up so persistently and effectively for the dignity of human nature, knowing himself for a man, and the equal of any and all governments. In that sense, he was the most American of us all"; and by the end of the essay, Thoreau is comparing Brown to Christ Himself: "Some eighteen hundred years ago Christ was crucified; this morning, perchance, Captain Brown was hung. These are two ends of a chain which is not without its links. He is not Old Brown any longer; he is an angel of light" (*WOW* 720, 730, 741–42).[14] Thoreau has moved quite far from counseling nonviolent resistance and the dissolution of the Union: now he is fervently praising a direct assault on that government which supports and condones slavery.

> I know that the mass of my countrymen think that the only righteous use that can be made of Sharps rifles and revolvers is to fight duels with them, when we are insulted by other nations, or to hunt Indians, or shoot fugitive slaves with them, or the like. I think that for once the Sharps rifles and the revolvers were employed in a righteous cause. The tools were in the hands of one who could use them. (*WOW* 738)

But although Brown has assumed a heroic and even mythic status for Thoreau, he once again denies that anyone has a positive duty to eradicate this evil. Near the beginning of the paragraph just quoted above, Thoreau also writes: "At any rate, I do not think it is quite sane for one to spend his whole life in talking or writing about this matter, unless he is continuously inspired, and I have not done so" (*WOW* 737).

In the final analysis, it is hard not to see a tension in Thoreau's position in respect to slavery. On the one hand, he is both horrified at the practice of slavery and increasingly indignant at those who do little or nothing to stop it; on the other hand, he cannot bring himself to admit that one has a positive moral duty to eliminate this evil. He seems caught between his passion to set the world aright and his desire to pursue activities he feels are higher than politics.[15] Unfortunately, it is impossible to know if Thoreau would have altered his position with the conclusion of the Civil War: although he had little good to say about the Republicans, in particular, and the government, in general, by the start of the war he was seriously ill with tuberculosis, and he died the following year (cf. *WOW* 728, 730, 740; *HT* 442ff.).

Emerson shared many of Thoreau's ideas concerning civil disobedience, slavery, and John Brown. In the essay "Politics" (1844), for example, we see an adumbration of many of Thoreau's remarks in "Civil Disobedience." Emerson too argues that "the less government we have the better—the fewer laws, and the less confided power"; that "[g]ood men must not obey the laws too well"; and finally, that the "antidote" to government abuse and force is "the influence of private character, the growth of the Individual" (*EWRWE* 382, 386). Emerson bitterly opposed the Fugitive Slave Law, vowed in his journal that he would never obey it, and roundly criticized Daniel Webster for throwing his support behind it (*EWRWE* 779–92; *WE* 551–58). And lastly, while Emerson's two speeches on John Brown (1859 and 1860) certainly lack Thoreau's fire and passion, Emerson too likens him to a saint and the gallows to the cross.[16] If there is a difference between Thoreau and Emerson it is that the latter, perhaps because he lived through the entirety of the Civil War, had an enormous appreciation and respect for Lincoln and the Emancipation Proclamation (see *EWRWE* 801–6, 829–33). Indeed, although Emerson shared some of Thoreau's antipathy toward government, his homage to the tenth anniversary of the British emancipation of slavery in the West Indies indicates that he was aware of both the possibilities and limitations of politics (*EWRWE* 753–76). Why Emerson did not develop his occasional but lucid remarks about political practice into a more fully developed whole is a mystery. Perhaps Emerson also experienced a tension similar to that of Thoreau: when the political issue's significance was of the magnitude of slavery and civil war, Emerson could not be silent; otherwise, he wrote and spoke with almost unrelenting optimism of the potential greatness of each and every individual soul.

Notes

1. Quotations from and references to Emerson's and Thoreau's works will be cited parenthetically in the text using the following abbreviations:

 EWRWE *The Essential Writings of Ralph Waldo Emerson*, ed. Brooks Atkinson (New York: Modern Library, 2000).

 WOW   *Walden and Other Writings*, ed. Brooks Atkinson (New York: Modern Library, 2000).

(All emphasized words in quotes are contained in the original.) For details on their life and times, readers may consult with profit Gay Wilson Allen, *Waldo Emerson: A Biography* (New York: Viking Press, 1981), and Walter Harding, *The Days of Henry Thoreau: A Biography* (Princeton, N.J.: Princeton University Press, 1992), hereafter cited parenthetically in the text as *WE* and *HT*, respectively. Emerson's eulogy of Thoreau occurs at *EWRWE* 809–25.

2. Indeed, given how old transcendentalism or idealism is, it is also surprising to read that history has never provided a single example of a "pure" transcendentalist (although certain Buddhists seem to have come close). While there have been "prophets and heralds of such a philosophy," it would seem that society quickly and thoroughly crushes those promising youth who are capable of living a completely spiritual existence (*EWRWE* 85, 88–89).

3. In fact, he suggests elsewhere that the very attempt to communicate religion has an inherently corrupting effect. The attempt to communicate Christianity, for example, has exaggerated "the personal, the positive, [and] the ritual" (i.e., the divinity and person of Jesus Christ) at the expense of the soul, the heart, and beauty itself (*EWRWE* 68). Similarly, he also faults "all philosophy" in its attempt to inquire into the divine source of such entities as life, being, justice, and the soul. It would seem that certain subjects are off-limits to philosophical speculation because to communicate one's findings profanes the subject matter and is thus a sacrilege (*EWRWE* 141–42; cf. 320–21).

4. For a representative sample of Emerson's Neoplatonism, see his essay "The Method of Nature" (1841), in *Nature, The Conduct of Life, and Other Essays*, intro. Sherman Paul (New York: Everyman's Library, 1963), 39–56. On the more general influence of Plotinus and the Neoplatonists on Emerson's thought, see *WE* 268–92, 375–87.

5. In other words, natural science only further confirms the existence of God, and Emerson himself welcomed scientific discoveries as greater evidence of His miraculous nature (over and against the immature theories of the Bible) (cf. *EWRWE* 3ff., 68ff., 250–51, 289, 293–95, 318–20, 366ff.).

6. If the law of compensation is as rigid in its application as Emerson claims, one would certainly wonder why anyone would be willing to commit crime or any wrong action. Emerson traces the root of crime to vanity and ignorance—to a futile and blind attempt to enjoy the sensual pleasure of the act without its necessary and concomitant moral pain or sanction. This "disease of the will" is a sign of "rebellion and separation" from God, and God is not indifferent. "'How secret art thou who dwellest in the highest heavens in silence, O thou only great God, sprinkling with an unwearied providence certain penal blindness upon such as have unbridled desires!'" (*EWRWE* 160; but cf. 323, 411ff).

7. Emerson was ordained as the Unitarian pastor of the Second Church of Boston in 1829. In June 1832, his grave reservations concerning the holy sacrament reached a crescendo, and he asked the Church if he might stop administering it in its present form. After considering his petition, the members of the Church were unable to grant it, and they voted to continue administering communion. Because Emerson would "do nothing which I cannot do with my whole heart," he judged it best to resign as pastor, and he stated his reasons for doing so to the congregation in the September sermon (*EWRWE* 109). Although Emerson continued to give sermons to various churches throughout his life, this was his first and last appointment as a permanent pastor. For details of the controversy, see *WE* 186–94.

8. Emerson also suggests the likely reason for how this error originally occurred. It was only natural that a soul as "great and rich" as Jesus', falling among a "simple" people, was bound to overwhelm them. They were thus not able to see that Jesus' true message was that they needed to discover and make manifest the gift of God in their own soul and not that Jesus was the son of God Himself (*EWRWE* 69). Given the simplicity of the "primitive Church," Emerson is very hesitant to adopt any of its doctrines or practices. The early Christians not only refused to shed their "Jewish prejudices" but they were rarely enlightened by the example of Christ Himself. Emerson thus concludes that "[o]n every other subject succeeding times have learned to form a judgment more in accordance with the spirit of Christianity than was the practice of the early ages" (*EWRWE* 105).

9. In perhaps his most telling remark, Emerson states that to the extent people are attending church, it is more for political than for religious reasons: "What was once a mere circumstance, that the best and the worst men in the parish, the poor and the rich, the learned and the ignorant, young and old, should meet one day as fellows in one house, in sign of an equal right in the soul, has come to be a paramount motive for going thither" (*EWRWE* 74).

10. Emerson's remarks about commerce point to perhaps the largest difference between himself and Thoreau, namely that Thoreau is much more critical of England, in particular, and commerce, in general (*WOW* 25, 33, 112ff): even farming, he says, loses its luster when it is pursued for the sake of profit (*WOW* 156, 185–86). Thoreau is most ferocious in his criticisms in the posthumously published essay "Life without Principle" (1863). Thoreau argues that "there is nothing, not even crime, more opposed to poetry, to philosophy, ay, to life itself, than this incessant business." America's single-minded dedication to "work, work, work" has created an "economical and moral tyrant" which few people are able to escape (and perhaps even fewer want to) (*WOW* 748, 765).

11. The other notable issues upon which they commented were the expulsion of the Cherokee Indians from Georgia (Emerson wrote an open letter to President Martin Van Buren in 1838 against their removal across the Mississippi River: see *The Portable Emerson*, ed. Carl Bode [New York: Penguin Books, 1981], 527–31) and the Mexican War (to which both were bitterly opposed).

12. The poll tax was "not a voting tax, but a head tax imposed on every male between the ages of twenty and seventy" (*HT* 200). For the circumstances which led to Thoreau's brief imprisonment, see *HT* 199ff. Thoreau explains these same events at *WOW* 683–87. It should be stressed that Thoreau is not against paying taxes per se ("I have never declined paying the highway tax, because I am as desirous of being a good neighbor as I am of being a bad subject"), nor does he care to withhold only that proportion of his taxes that would go to supporting the war and slavery ("It is for no particular item in the tax-bill that I refuse to pay it. I simply wish to refuse allegiance to the State") (*WOW* 687).

13. See also "The Last Days of John Brown" (1860), in *The Portable Thoreau*, ed. Carl Bode (New York: Penguin Books, 1975), 676–82, a speech which was read for Thoreau at a memorial service for Brown which he declined to attend. Although both Thoreau and Emerson met and helped Brown when he passed through Concord, neither apparently knew all the details of Brown's life nor his plan to raid Harper's Ferry (see *WE* 586–92; *HT* 415–26).

14. If Thoreau has any criticism of Brown it is his belief in the durability and desirability of the Union. "I should say that he [Brown] was an old-fashioned man in his respect for the Constitution, and his faith in the permanence of this Union" (*WOW* 718). Emerson, by contrast, praises Brown on this very point (*EWRWE* 795–96).

15. This tension was noticed and commented upon by the editors of two newspapers which Thoreau had censured in his lecture on John Brown, namely William Lloyd Garrison's *Liberator* and Horace Greeley's *Tribune*. "Garrison's *Liberator*, annoyed that Thoreau had singled it out for particular censure for not defending Brown, dismissed the lecture in three short paragraphs, but acknowledged bitingly that 'this exciting theme seemed to have awakened "the hermit of Concord" from his usual state of philosophic indifference.' The New York *Tribune*, equally annoyed at his chastising, dismissed his ideas as 'foolish and ill-natured' and complained, not without justice, 'Editors like those of The Tribune and The Liberator, . . . while the lecturer was cultivating beans and killing woodchucks on the margin of Walden Pond, made a public opinion strong enough on Anti-Slavery grounds to tolerate a speech from him in defense of insurrection'" (quoted in *HT* 419).

16. See *EWRWE* 795–98 and "John Brown," *The Portable Emerson*, 569–72. Emerson's reference to Brown as a saint was delivered in a Boston lecture entitled "Courage." The remark was expunged when the lecture was printed in *Society and Solitude* (*WE* 591).

Chapter 21

"Proclaim Liberty throughout the Land": Frederick Douglass, William Lloyd Garrison, and the Abolition of Slavery

Richard S. Ruderman

Few today would deny that slavery was the greatest moral evil in the history of the United States. Yet it can be—and has been—debated whether abolitionism is to be praised for having helped to end her greatest moral sin or to be condemned for having provoked her greatest catastrophe. Did abolitionism harden the forces of reaction, making a civil war all but inevitable? Or did it provide the essential impetus for ending slavery? Surely, slavery not only stripped black men and women of their rights to life, liberty, and property, but it also undermined the very principles of liberty and equality on which the country stood. Left undisturbed, it could have been expected eventually to weaken the very foundations of America. As the great black American abolitionist Frederick Douglass argued to the white citizens of America:

> The existence of slavery in this country brands your republicanism as a sham, your humanity as a base pretense, and your Christianity as a lie. It destroys your moral power abroad: it corrupts your politicians at home. It saps the foundation of religion; it makes your name a hissing and a bye-word to a mocking earth. It is the antagonistic force in your government, the only thing that disturbs and endangers your *Union*. It fetters your progress; it is the enemy of improvement; the deadly foe of education; it fosters pride; it breeds insolence; it promotes vice; it shelters crime; it is a curse to the earth that supports it; and yet you cling to it as if it were the sheet anchor of all your hopes.[1]

Yet how could a self-governing democracy justify *enforcing* (even if only through moral suasion) the end of the South's "peculiar institution"?[2] Was political action in this case justified? And was political action of any sort even necessary? Some argued that economic factors would, by themselves, eventually lead to the dissolution of slavery. Others like Democrat Stephen A. Douglas believed (even if he rarely said so publicly, for political reasons) that the general modern spirit of progress would eventually turn slavery into an anachronism that would fade of its own accord.[3] Can the abolitionists' insistence on turning slavery into a moral issue, replete with stigmatizing the beliefs and ways of life of a large body of their fellow citizens, be justified? In order to hazard the beginnings of an answer, this essay will focus on the two most prominent and important abolitionists, William Lloyd Garrison (1805–1879) and his erstwhile protégé, Frederick Douglass (1817?–1895).

To understand the strategy and tactics of these two men, we must first undertake a prior investigation into the general American attitude toward slavery, freedom, and the meaning of self-government. As had been clear at least since the Founding, merely to recognize the evils of slavery neither guaranteed its end nor offered guidance as to what should be done about it. Those Founders who themselves opposed slavery elected to temporize with it rather than lose the chance to forge the Union. They reasoned that absent a successful experiment in free government generally, the cause of freedom for black people would never be won. In addition, they feared for their fate at the hands of freed slaves. As Thomas Jefferson said: "we have the wolf by the ears, and we can neither hold him, nor safely let him go."[4] And while they sought to place slavery in a restricted locale so that the "public mind" could rest in the belief that "it was in the course of ultimate extinction," subsequent developments served to strengthen rather than weaken it.[5] The invention of the cotton gin in 1794 restored the economic viability of slavery. The fact that some Americans desired the continuation of slavery, and that they also expected that their right to self-government would enable them to retain it, led to the development of the notion of "popular sovereignty." This doctrine, championed by Stephen A. Douglas, held that slavery was not a constitutional issue at all but merely a local issue to be decided by the states (or the territories) according to local needs and sentiment.

In response to this festering problem, the political process offered up a series of half-attempts designed to keep slavery from tearing the country apart. Apart from the Constitution's studied refusal to refer to slaves as anything other than "persons" and its denial of protection to the slave trade beyond 1808, little was done to end slavery in the first fifty years of the country's existence. The first major relevant legislative effort was the Missouri Compromise of 1820: while leaving slavery in the South untouched, it made the expansion of slavery illegal north of the 36°30′ line. A subsequent "Great Compromise" was passed in 1850, however, which instituted the Fugitive Slave Act. This act in effect enlisted antislavery Northerners in the cause of slavery by requiring them to return fugitive slaves to their owners. Then came the Kansas-Nebraska Act (1854), which repealed the Missouri Compromise by explicitly allowing slavery in the territories north of the 36°30′ line. Finally, the Supreme Court, in its notorious *Dred Scott* decision (1857), held that a black was not and could never be a citizen of the United States. The years prior to the Civil War, then, saw reasons for a mounting sense of despair on the part of those who sought the end of slavery.[6]

These various obstacles to black emancipation both engendered the abolitionist movement and led to many internal disputes within it. The abolitionists—indeed, all Americans—were confronted with myriad political, moral, practical, and economic questions in contemplating what to do about slavery. In some sense, the questions of how, when, and to where black slaves should be liberated were even thornier ones than the question of whether they should be freed at all. Looking back from the 1870s, Douglass said that "outside the years embraced in the late tremendous war, there had been no period more pregnant with great events, or better suited to call the best mental and moral energies of men" than the years 1848 to 1860.[7] We will now consider how he and Garrison wrestled with these problems.

I

William Lloyd Garrison, the son of a drunkard father who abandoned the family when he was a boy, grew up in poverty. His mother embraced an austere and rigid Baptist sect whose influence would long be felt by Garrison. After a series of random jobs, Garrison discovered his calling—that of newspaper editor. He launched the *Liberator* (on January 1, 1829) as a newspaper devoted to liberty in all its forms but chiefly to the notion of immediate abolition of chattel slavery in the American South. Because Garrison was an ecumenical editor, accepting articles espousing a wide variety of views, it cannot be said that the paper simply reflected his own. Indeed, Garrison's relations with his fellow abolitionists were complex and sometimes heated. While the *Liberator* was, initially, formally associated with the American Anti-Slavery Society (AASS), the society broke ties with the publication in 1838. From then on, the *Liberator* was simply Garrison's own paper, in no way reflecting the society's official positions. Yet such was Garrison's stature by then that this fine distinction was largely lost on the public mind, which continued to view Garrison as abolitionism incarnate. Given Garrison's difficult character, having him as their unofficial spokesman did not always please the abolitionists; for, even as many of his defenders were compelled to admit, Garrison was "self-righteous, dogmatic, lacking in a sense of humor, and prone to think of himself as a martyr to truth in an unbelieving world."[8]

In order to understand Garrison's views—and to see why they were discomfiting to so many abolitionists as well as to slaveholders—we must begin from the fact that, despite his decades-long involvement with the leading political issue of the age, Garrison's was at root an *anti-political* political philosophy.[9] At least at first, his sole motive for action was his belief in God's opposition to slavery. Politics in itself was a fallen activity: it existed only as a result of man's fallen nature and was sinful insofar as it relied on force. Moreover—and here Garrison took a particularly radical, almost antinomian view—it was not a *necessary* evil to which man must somehow accommodate himself. Man was capable of achieving moral perfection. If all Americans could live fully under Christ, they would be free of sin and hence free of all need for coercive government of any kind (see *Liberator*, June 23, 1837). This "perfectionism" lay at the root of Garrison's notorious opposition not only to forming or supporting a third (abolitionist) political party but also to voting altogether—and even, by the 1840s, to continuing the Union. (In 1844, the AASS officially adopted the position that the American Constitution was inherently proslavery and thus that the Union must be dissolved.) Garrison seems to have detected in politics a hidden but powerful tendency to weaken the sense of personal moral freedom and responsibility. Garrison denied that *any* man was ever lacking in moral freedom: "There is no necessity imposed on any man to be a villain, or to sanction villany" (*Liberator*, May 1, 1846). By contrast, politics tempted men to form parties (which diluted personal principles and invited chicanery), to pass laws (which relied on coercion), and to believe that they were, in no small measure, "creatures of circumstance," albeit alterable circumstance. In short, politics rejected the biblical premise that good can come only from good men and (especially in its modern form) elevated the formulation of good policy over the reformation of wicked men.

While Garrison thought that liberal government was no worse than any other, he appears neither to have thought it any better. Many of the basic premises of liberalism—limitations on government's ability to address moral questions, a presumptive deference to majority sentiment, the neutrality of the right of free speech, and so on—were anathema to Garrison. To adopt the generalized indifference to one's fellow's situation that liberalism fosters was little more than giving a free pass to sin. Even the right to free speech, which Garrison enjoyed and exercised as an editor, was not to be seen as absolute: he fiercely denounced an effort to bring some especially obnoxious slaveholders to Boston for a debate (*LWLG* 4:359–65). Freedom of speech must be subordinated to the greater purpose of utilizing speech to praise good and to stigmatize evil.

In advancing the cause of abolitionism, Garrison faced myriad opponents. First, of course, were the slaveholders who simply denied that it was anyone else's business what they did with their private "property." Second, there were those who, whether through concern for freed blacks or through racism, were willing to support abolition only if colonization of blacks (to Liberia) followed. Garrison was a staunch opponent of colonization, believing that it would spare whites from confronting and overcoming their sin of racism. Third, Garrison felt that abolitionism had to be part of a greater whole—namely, the eradication of all forms of oppression and coercion.

He thus found himself at odds with those who opposed women's rights and who supported the notion of government as a positive (and permanent) good. As a result, he found himself in opposition to those who would exercise the power of the ballot box to help bring about the end of slavery. Fourth, Garrison promoted nonresistance, which put him at odds with those who would utilize self-defense as well as governmental power to resist the slave power. Finally, Garrison faced harsh criticism from those abolitionists desirous of starting and supporting a third party (the Liberty party). We will now examine Garrison's position on the most important of these issues.

Garrison claimed a "right" to intervene in slavery not only for the slaves' sake but also for that of the slaveholders. His oft-times scorching rhetoric toward slaveholders must not blind us to the fact that he wished to condemn them only in order to save them from sin. Seemingly untainted by the atomistic "individualism" that Tocqueville feared would reduce the typical American democrat to unconcern with others, Garrison still felt the "pre-Enlightenment" religious impulse to free others as well as himself from sin.[10] In the initial stages of his career, Garrison believed that Jesus and the Bible were squarely against slavery.[11] Any claim, by slaveholder and abolitionist alike, that the Bible in fact lent *support* to slavery was met with mockery, disdain, and rebuke. In addition, he took the antipragmatist view that dedication to principle, even if ineffective or worse, had to be paramount: one must do God's will regardless of the consequences. Yet he also believed that God's support for those doing what was right would in the end ensure their success. Whether these dual beliefs can be sustained, particularly in the absence of the always half-expected success, it is certain that Garrison eventually began to falter in his beliefs. Feeling the weight of a series of articles *by abolitionists* which he had published arguing that the Bible did not in fact condemn slavery, Garrison began to find himself surprisingly open to certain aspects of the Enlightenment's critique of religion. Where he initially insisted on treating the Bible as wholly inspired and—as long as he took it to be antislavery—on following it irrespective of consequences, in 1843 he began to read the Bible "discriminatingly." As though reenacting within himself an earlier America's first brush with Enlightenment principles, Garrison, "who had begun by judging the world by Truth and Right as revealed in the scriptures, ended by judging the scriptures by Truth and Right as revealed by [man's] own Reason" (*Means* 92). By 1845, he had begun to read and admire Thomas Paine. Later that year, Garrison's "conversion" from something resembling fundamentalism to a kind of free-thinking Christianity was complete: "the Bible must stand or fall on its merits, 'by its reasonableness and utility, by the probabilities of the case, by historical confirmation, by human experience and observation, by the facts of science, by the intuition of the spirit. Truth is older than any parchment.'"[12] From this point on, Garrison relied not on the Bible but on his moral sense or "intuition of the spirit" for knowledge of slavery's evil character. That this turn would undermine Garrison's ability to denounce the hypocrisy of slaveholding Christians (who would then be left with the Bible on their side) seems not to have troubled Garrison. Nor did he follow to the end the logical implication of his conversion: slaveholders could no longer be understood as sinners to be avoided but merely as in error, needing enlightenment.

Garrison's accomplishments in undermining the case for colonization are among his most admirable. There were not a few Northerners whose opposition to slavery was accompanied by either racist dislike of blacks or (as in the case of Abraham Lincoln) doubt as to the ultimate ability of the two races to live together in one country. Colonization so stirred in Garrison "the fire of moral indignation" that he was moved to write his only book, *Thoughts on African Colonization* (1832).[13] In it, he denounced the hypocrisy of those of his fellow citizens and Christians who claimed that the Bible and the "laws of nature" bar blacks from effectual equality with whites. And in expressing his "confidence . . . that the demands of justice will be satisfied,"

Garrison asserted that the country should be judged, not by its present practice, but by its ideals as expressed in the Declaration of Independence and the New Testament (*Thoughts* 146–47). As further evidence of the antipolitical character of his political philosophy, we may note here that this "idealism" concerning people was not extended by Garrison to *government*: "It matters not what is the theory of the government, if the practice of the government be unjust and tyrannical" (*Liberator*, May 31, 1844). Individuals can be reformed (indeed "perfected") in the direction of higher principles—governments cannot. The basis for this view becomes apparent in Garrison's later arguments against continuing the Union. Where a government is found wanting in practice (e.g., in failing to end slavery), men, so far from having grounds for hope to reform it, must beware lest its influence corrupt them (see *Means* 210–13). Garrison seems to reject the very possibility of democratic self-government: as soon as men begin to exercise *political* influence over one another, they will be corrupted even by their successes.[14]

The third way in which Garrison alienated himself from many of his abolitionist colleagues concerned his insistence on fighting oppression in all its forms. As suggested above, even many abolitionists who supported such things as equal rights for women or certain forms of religious innovation disapproved of Garrison's efforts to insert them into the abolitionist movement. They argued that any additional cause would alienate as many potential supporters of their sacred and central cause as it might attract. In the words of abolitionist Elizur Wright, Jr.: "It is downright nonsense to suppose that the Anti-Slavery cause can be carried forward with forty incongruous things tacked on to it. You can't drive a three-tinged fork through a hay mow, but turn it around and you can drive in the handle."[15] To be sure, many abolitionists vehemently disagreed with Garrison on the merits of these secondary causes. One might characterize many of them as conservatives in the strict sense: they sought to conserve both Christianity and society itself in recognizable forms, while Garrison sought to introduce striking religious innovations (such as repudiating the institution of the Sabbath and asserting the doctrine of perfectionism), working less to improve society than to dissolve it. After the AASS cut its ties with Garrison's paper, he altered the *Liberator*'s motto to address the vastly expanded concept of "Universal Emancipation." This, he explained in the accompanying article, would entail "the emancipation of our whole [human] race from the dominion of man, from the thralldom of self, from the government of brute force, from the bondage of sin—and bring them under the dominion of God, the control of the inward spirit, the government of the law of love, and into the obedience and liberty of Christ" (*Liberator*, December 15, 1837). One can easily see how those who look to government to establish some degree of separation between religion and the state would be ill at ease with Garrison's views. Moreover, there is something anachronistic (and perhaps ultimately incoherent) about Garrison's animus against "self." The very political philosophy that introduced the rights of life, liberty, and the pursuit of happiness to the world also sought to vindicate the "self" against which Garrison here inveighs. Jefferson's appeal (in the same Declaration to which Garrison would have his fellow citizens recur) to the rights with which men were endowed by their Creator was intended, at least in part, to foster rather than overcome self-assertion. By extending individual rights to all (including, in some hoped-for future, slaves), the Founders sought to destroy the foundation on which any future claim to political superiority might rest. In fact, it was in the desire to rescue *others* from sin that they located the human impulse toward oppression and tyranny. While Garrison repeatedly (and, no doubt, sincerely) insisted that he would abjure the use of force in converting anyone to the true Christianity, liberals might doubt that others would feel so constrained.

Above all, it is hard to see how Garrison can consistently condemn the "self" or the pursuit of one's own good. He himself denied (in the course of rejecting a proposed boycott of slave-produced products) that the slaveholders were in fact motivated by the "love of gain" (*Liberator*,

March 1, 1850). Self-interest in the crudest sense, then, was *not* to blame for the worst evil: that distinction belonged to the longing for "absolute power" or "unlimited sovereignty." But Garrison refused to see how the specific genius of liberalism was to use the former to undermine the latter. Only the desire to have the good for oneself could lead people to reconsider and ultimately reject the glittering but false ways in which the good sometimes presents itself. Garrison may have believed that overcoming one's longing for one's own good was possible, noble, and ultimately productive of perfect justice. But, in every instance known to me, Garrison had to make a surreptitious *appeal* to self-interest every time he proposed overcoming it. One might think, for instance, that in asking Northerners to abandon the Union, Garrison was urging them to sacrifice interest for principle. But as his close friend and colleague Wendell Phillips wrote: "God . . . when He established the right, saw to it that it should always be safest and best. . . . If we do justice, God will ensure that happiness results."[16]

Garrison's uneasy relation with both self-interest and self-sacrifice can perhaps best be grasped in considering his efforts at fostering empathy for the slaves (see *Means* 237–44). Abstract principle (such as love of equality) could not, Garrison feared, move men to action. Not exempting himself, Garrison continuously tried to put himself in the place of the oppressed. The very effectiveness of this procedure, however, entailed blurring the distinction between self-sacrifice and self-interest. If I succeed in identifying with the oppressed, I am relieving myself from that oppressive feeling at least as much as I relieve the oppressed when I oppose slavery. As Jean-Jacques Rousseau explained (*Emile* bk. 4), people who are incorrigibly selfish can feel for others only insofar as they "project" their own selves into the other's place. Unlike Rousseau, however, Garrison seemed unaware that he was reconstructing empathy on a base of selfishness. By contrast, it is worth noting that Lincoln and even Douglass were more apt to try to put themselves in the place of the *oppressors* than the oppressed. They each sought to understand what would from their respective points of view be most unaccountable: Lincoln and Douglass, to see how men no less self-concerned than they might be enticed to give up their slaves; Garrison, to see how slaves (and abolitionists) could pursue freedom without thereby pursuing their own good. Where Lincoln and Douglass sought to understand their wayward fellows by freeing themselves and their audiences as far as possible from moralistic denunciations, Garrison sought to keep the stinger of injustice poked deep inside his bosom.

Garrison's doctrine of nonresistance, which he abandoned only on the eve of the Civil War, was never quite thoroughgoing. While he opposed any violent efforts on the part of slaves or their supporters (such as John Brown), he refused to go as far as his colleague Samuel May, who reproved the Rev. Elijah Lovejoy for resisting the proslavery mob that threatened and finally lynched him for publishing an abolitionist newspaper (*Means* 82–83). For his own part, however, Garrison claimed that he preferred to die at the hands of a mob in Boston (in 1835) than to resist it. When a colleague announced in the midst of the riot that he was abandoning the principle of nonresistance, Garrison replied: "I will perish sooner than raise my hand against any man, even in self-defence. . . . If my life be taken, the cause of emancipation will not suffer" (quoted in *WLG* 42). Whether or not Garrison's death would have impeded the cause of emancipation, it would surely, under these circumstances, have strengthened the forces of mob rule and weakened the rule of law. The politically irresponsible and almost self-indulgent side of Garrison's perfectionism begins to make itself felt here.[17]

In some sense, Garrison's espousal of nonresistance was the inverse of his reliance on moral suasion. In disavowing coercion in all its forms, Garrison appears to take the noblest democratic view—namely, that fellow citizens can be reasoned with on all moral problems. Not unlike contemporary proponents of "democratic dialogue," Garrison insists that a sharp line be drawn between persuasion and compulsion. As a rule, the Garrisonians opposed seeking political measures before constituencies had been built through moral suasion to support them (*Means* 216). But two problems confronted this approach. First, the South erected barriers to the mere distribution of Garrison's paper, and Congress passed the notorious "gag rule" to deny abolitionists a platform. There was, then, little prospect for a dialogue of any sort with the slaveholders. Second, it is not in fact clear that a measure of compulsion is incompatible with genuine persuasion and conversion. Political measures can to some degree precede rather than follow the building of constituencies. Nor must the political measures in question simply have been coercive: inducing the slaveholders to manumit their slaves for some form of payment might well have helped to convince at least some of them to do so.

To comprehend Garrison's brand of moral suasion, we must investigate further the manner in which he conceived converting people to the cause of abolitionism. As befits a newspaper editor, Garrison combined a variety of methods and approaches. In castigating slaveholders, Garrison employed both sarcasm and cold reason (the latter chiefly to reveal the myriad inconsistencies in their arguments). In winning readers to the cause of the slaves, he appealed both to emotion and to principle. But it is crucial to see that all these arrows fit into one large quiver: only a nation brought to its full character as a Christian nation could achieve the moral capacity to end not only slavery but oppression of every kind, including that of coercive government. Of course, Garrison meant by Christianity a very specific type of Protestantism: his writings are rife with casual denunciations of Catholicism.[18] Only a Christian (i.e., Protestant) citizenry will achieve the liberation of both slave and nonslave in a final, utopian, coercion-free society.

To complete our portrait of Garrison's understanding of moral suasion, we must examine his view of the relation between morals and politics. As indicated above, Garrison was highly antipolitical. This view did not, however, entail fatalism. If one stood back from politics (nonvoting, nonresistance, no formation of political parties), one could commandeer the higher moral ground from which a moral revolution could be directed. A politics manned by sinners could not possibly generate anything good, however artfully their institutions sought to channel their self-interest. Politics could not tame or even co-opt sinful passions but would instead always remain their tool. Before one could begin to expect anything worthwhile from politics, one would have to reform the people engaged in it. "The politics of a people," Garrison wrote, "will always be shaped by its morals, as the vane of the steeple is ever indicating in what direction the wind blows" (*Liberator*, March 12, 1847).

Garrison's understanding of "morals" was specifically Christian, above all in its unrelenting hostility toward any form of self-assertion or self-concern. It almost goes without saying that he utterly rejected the classical praise, shared by Tocqueville, of ambition (*DA* 2.3.19). Where Tocqueville saw in ambition the possibility of merging self-concern with a grand and elevated concern for one's community, Garrison saw in it only a petty selfishness that would inevitably detract from one's dedication to a greater cause. It was this view, moreover, that led to Garrison's fierce condemnation of Douglass and a break between the two men. Shortly after rejecting Garrison's anti-Constitution position, Douglass raised the question in 1835 of whether the religious infidelity of some Garrisonians would harm their effectiveness as abolitionists. Garrison responded with an attack both on Douglass personally—for seeking to elevate himself at the expense of the cause—and on blacks generally—for failing to recognize their intellectual inability to understand the meaning of the struggle for freedom. The *Pennsylvania Freeman* (a Garrisonian paper) argued that slavery

> may have penetrated [Douglass's] soul; if he has escaped the bondage of others, he may continue in frightful servitude to self; his change of ownership may be but a transfer of tyrannies from without to within. He may be a representative of . . . the avarice [slavery] engenders, the love of

dominion, the fierce impatience of opposition, the suspicion of motives, the jealousy of superiors, the interpretation of the highest thoughts through the lowest faculties. (quoted in *MFD* 44)

Garrison went on to disparage the abilities of blacks and to assert the general notion that abolitionism could be carried forward only by persons of unusual moral and intellectual ability. Abolitionism, he wrote,

> is not based on complexion, but upon justice; its principles are world-wide, though the victims whom it seeks to deliver are groaning in the southern prison-house; it concerns man as man, not merely as an African, or one of African descent. Unswerving fidelity to it, in this country, requires high moral attainments, the crucifixion of all personal considerations, a paramount regard for principle, absolute faith in the right. It does not follow, therefore, that because a man is identified with a class meted out and trodden underfoot, he will be the truest to the cause of human freedom. Already, that cause, both religiously and politically, has transcended the ability of the sufferers from American slavery and prejudice, as a class, to keep pace with it, or to perceive what are its demands, or to understand the philosophy of its operations. (quoted in *MFD* 45–46)

Let us not allow the insulting character of these remarks to overshadow completely the idiosyncratic and unusual understanding of the moral prerequisites for political action that are stated herein and that bear some analysis. According to Garrison, complete self-sacrifice for the cause is both possible and essential for one who would engage in genuine political or public action. It is almost a correlative that one who acts on his own behalf when combating injustice cannot be presumed ever to attain a "paramount regard for principle." Having misconstrued even the loftiest ambition as petty and self-serving, Garrison undervalues "self" no less than ambition, and he risks elevating the quest for moral purification over the more readily available human motives for loving justice.[19]

Viewing political life as a kind of punishment for men in rebellion against God, Garrison cannot vest any hope in it. The basis of this view would seem to be the following: men rebel against God insofar as they reject His guidance, substituting for it the guidance they attain through unassisted reason. Moreover, in pursuing their own interest and advantage, they are all too likely to seek to manipulate other men, up to and including enslaving them. Government (in the absence of God) is inherently coercive and, given the God-less man's quest for power, politics is an inevitable temptation. Yet, after Garrison's dramatic "conversion" in midcareer into one who does not hesitate to pass reasoned judgment on Jesus and the Bible, one does not find the expected rehabilitation of reason and politics. After rejecting or, at any rate, radically modifying the view that man is a creature of God, what prevented Garrison from adopting the Aristotelian alternative of viewing man as a political animal? The answer is unclear, but it seems to be connected to Garrison's abiding belief in "perfectionism." Moral perfection, perfect freedom from all sin, a life that is "holy" in all its particulars: this, Garrison continued to maintain, was the attainable goal of mankind. Many people, including many fellow Christians, raised doubts about the possibility (and even the desirability) of achieving this goal. In Garrison's own view, however, it was the impoverished and impoverishing outlook of philosophy that made man doubt that the goal could be attained. Garrison was fond of quoting Shakespeare's *Hamlet*: "there are more things in heaven and earth, than are dreampt of in our philosophy" (*LWLG* 1:588).

Garrison's ultimate politicoreligious views constitute a curious amalgam. As befits an autodidactic American of the nineteenth century, they seem to combine aspects of Catholic, Protestant, and Enlightenment thinking. Insofar as they derive from earlier views, his extreme subordination of politics to religion reminds one of the medieval Papalists, a school of thought to which Garrison is otherwise hardly indebted. Yet his insistence that each man be allowed to interpret the Bible by his own lights marks his Protestant rejection of Catholicism. Finally, his insistence on universal natural rights, along with his adoption of certain key features of biblical Higher Criticism, reveal his inheritance from the Enlightenment. If a coherent ground can be discovered for this ecumenicalism, it would appear to be essentially negative: Garrison is tempted by anything that *rejects* the two central premises of classical political philosophy: namely, the naturalness of the political community and the capacity of man to guide himself through reason. Garrison's powerful, life-long, courageous defense of the inherent dignity of enslaved blacks must not blind us to his ultimate rejection of the dignity of man. All men are sinners, and, despite or because of the fact that he stresses their capacity to achieve perfect freedom from sin, their dignity remains for all intents and purposes purely potential. Perhaps this fact accounts for Garrison's pronounced taste for Shakespearean tragedy: one's ultimate hopes are somehow strengthened by continuous exposure to man's sinful, defeated, and failed nature. Garrison may even have preferred to seek punishment for sin rather than freedom from sin. His arguments against colonization, at any rate, differ from Douglass's. Where the latter opposed colonization on the grounds that blacks deserved to stay among and learn from white Americans, the former all but admits that the blacks should remain in America as a punishment for white sinfulness. Not for him, at any rate, is the classical reliance on reason and political life to establish human dignity.

In the end, it may seem that Garrison and his followers cared more about their moral purity than about ending chattel slavery. After all, they insisted on the altogether nonnegotiable nature of their principles, refusing to allow prudential calculations or compromises to undermine them even at the cost of success. This characterization is to some degree an unfair one. The Garrisonians viewed their intransigence, especially on the question of immediatism, as an eminently prudent tactic. Only by presenting an intransigent alternative to the slaveholders' own intransigence could the abolitionists open up a middle ground making eventual reasonable compromise possible.[20] Moreover, Garrison certainly tried to keep his more controversial positions off the official agenda. Few have stated this key principle of political prudence more cogently than he did in chastising fellow abolitionist Charles C. Burleigh for wearing long hair and a beard

> because it is so wide a departure from customary usage as to excite general remark and provoke popular raillery, thus subtracting from his usefulness as a public lecturer. . . . [A]ll things that are lawful are not always expedient. Where there is no moral principle involved, it is sometimes wise to sacrifice what is convenient or agreeable to us, that no unnecessary obstacle be thrown in the way of a great or good cause in which we may be engaged, and which has arrayed against it all that is formidable in universal apostasy, and inveterate in long cherished prejudices. (*Liberator*, May 24, 1850)

Still, Garrison's elevation of intention over results and of morals over politics makes him an excellent example of what Max Weber called the "ethics of conviction." According to this outlook, a man must be concerned more to foster the right moral attitude, both in himself and in others, than to succeed in changing the situation of those he would help. As we have seen, Garrison was never a fully consistent adherent of this ethic. He refused to condemn Rev. Lovejoy for fighting back against the mob that killed him, and—virtually alone among abolitionists—he defended the right of Douglass's supporters to purchase his freedom. As did Weber, Garrison recognized in some small measure that the ethics of conviction had to be supplemented by the "ethics of responsibility," which involves the willingness to strive to have one's principles realized in political action. Now Weber insisted that reason cannot choose either ethic as superior to the other. Frederick Douglass—who moved, as he applied his formidable intellect to the issues, from the former ethic to the latter—appears to have disagreed. We now turn to Douglass in order to test and appreciate the reasons for his development and his ultimate break with Garrison.

II

The inadequacies of Garrison's position were, at first, wholly hidden from Douglass. Inclined, as he confessed, to be a "hero-worshiper," Douglass came utterly under Garrison's spell upon first emerging from slavery into freedom (*LT* 213). At the start and for quite some time thereafter, he fully shared Garrison's "ethic of conviction." Believing that "the purity of the cause is the success of the cause," Douglass went so far as to call upon his supporters to vote Radical Abolitionist in the 1856 Kansas election, even at the risk of throwing the election to the proslavery Democrats. "We deliberately prefer," he said, "the loss of Kansas to the loss of our Anti-Slavery integrity" (*LW* 2:393–94). Conceding Garrison's objectionable character, Douglass stated admiringly that he "made himself unpopular for life in the maintenance of great principles. . . . He has made himself disreputable . . . [by] his uncompromising hostility to slavery, by his bold, scathing denunciation of tyranny."[21] His admiration of Garrison extended at first to the latter's dismissal of the Constitution as a proslavery document. Believing, as Garrison did, that America's principles of government were little better than her nefarious practice, the early Douglass differed from Garrison only when he "out-Garrisoned the Garrisonians" by stating his anti-Americanism baldly: "I have no love for America, as such; I have no patriotism. I have no country. What country have I? . . . I have not, I cannot have, any love for this country, as such, or for its Constitution. I desire to see its overthrow as speedily as possible, and its Constitution shivered in a thousand fragments" (*SSW* 75, 77–78). As late as September 4, 1849, Douglass announced his willingness "at all times to be known as a Garrisonian Abolitionist" (*The Anti-Slavery Bugle*, October 6, 1849).

During the late 1840s, however, Douglass began to consider positions that would eventually lead to a break with Garrison. From the start, they had differed on only one issue: Douglass rejected Garrison's principle of nonresistance. In the 1840s, Douglass began to reconsider two more basic tenets of Garrisonianism: its rejection of political action in favor of moral action, and its rejection of the Constitution as a proslavery document. In May of 1851, Douglass announced, first at a meeting of the AASS and soon after in the pages of his paper *The North Star,* that he had changed his mind and now considered the Constitution to be an antislavery document (*LW* 2:155–56; see also *LT* 260–61).

As a result of this change—which led Garrison to charge "there is roguery somewhere" and to remove Douglass's paper from the AASS's approved list—Douglass did not hesitate to make another. Having determined that slavery was "a system of lawless violence; that it *never was lawful, and never can be made so,*" Douglass went on to conclude "that it is the first duty of every American citizen, whose conscience permits so to do, to use his *political* as well as his *moral* power for its overthrow" (*LW* 2:156, emphasis in original). From this point on, Douglass was able to enjoy the added authority of speaking for, rather than against, the basic principles of the American polity as well as the added power that could be wielded through the political apparatus of the country. In short, Douglass had discovered for himself the spirit of responsible statesmanship.

In considering the complicity of the Constitution with slavery, Douglass eventually confronted the simple yet crucial question: "Where, I ask, could the slave look for release from slavery if the Union were dissolved?" No longer could Douglass accept Garrison's implied answer: "from the wholesale transformation of humanity, chiefly the slaveholders, but also Northerners who, in the final analysis, were morally no better than they." Douglass insisted that, based on his experience, there would be no change within the slaveholders, and so "if the slaves are ever delivered from bondage, the power will emanate from the free States." It followed, then:

> To dissolve the Union would be to withdraw the emancipating power from the field. . . . I am told this is the argument from expediency. I admit it, and am prepared to show that what is expedient in this instance is right. 'Do justice, though the heavens fall.' Yes, that is a good motto, but I deny that it would be doing justice to the slave to dissolve the Union and leave the slave in his chains to get out by the clemency of his master, or the strength of his arms. (*LW* 2:417)

Douglass stated these views in an 1857 speech denouncing the *Dred Scott* decision (which held that blacks could not be citizens), a speech in which he could not bring himself to use his standard salutation "fellow citizens."

In a series of great speeches, beginning with 1852's "The Meaning of July Fourth and the Negro," Douglass explained the reasoning behind his change of mind on the Constitution. He made several key points. First, he asserted that "every American citizen," and not just elected officials or appointed judges, "has a right to form an opinion of the constitution, and to propagate that opinion, and to use all honorable means to make his opinion the prevailing one." There was no reason, then, to feel that Taney's decision, even when supported by the other branches of government, left Americans with the unappealing alternative of glum acceptance or extralegal revolution. Government remained in the hands of its citizens and politics remained a viable option. Second, in explaining how he had come to view the Constitution as a "glorious liberty document," Douglass stated "certain rules of interpretation for the proper understanding of all legal instruments." The chief such rule is that "the written Constitution is [not] to be interpreted in the light of a secret and unwritten understanding of its framers, which understanding is declared to be in favor of slavery." Formal political language, such as that of the Constitution, has an independent status, and it is not to be dismissed as either the rationalizing of preconceived notions or the hypocritical invocations of deceptive notions in which the authors put no credence. Douglass insisted that "the mere text . . . and not any commentaries" written on it must be dispositive of its meaning (*LW* 2:202, 420, 469).

Third, Douglass denied that abolitionism was in any way a historical innovation. "The causes producing it," he claimed, "and the particles composing it . . . have slumbered in the bosom of nature since the world began" (*LW* 2:336). This statement did more than deny that Garrison "originated" abolitionism: it replaced Garrison's view of man's fallen nature with the classical view that man's nature was essentially good, however much that nature could be misled, suppressed, or perverted.[22] This not only spared Douglass from the "fires of moral indignation," but it allowed him to chart a far more effective way of speaking to and dealing with white citizens in need of correction on the slavery issue. For instance, it gave Douglass grounds for feeling the confidence and patience so lacking in Garrison: "My position now is one of reform, not of revolution" (*LW* 2:480). After crediting Garrison with making precisely one innovation in the antislavery movement, namely "immediatism," Douglass was now able to distinguish "what works" from "what would be justified." He noted that "fewer slaves have been emancipated under the influence of this doctrine, in this country, than under the old doctrine of gradual emancipation" (*LW* 2:339).

Fourth, Douglass saw nothing but disaster in the Garrisonian principle of "no union with slaveholders." This notion constituted an "abandonment" of the great idea of abolition. "It started to free the slave. It ends by leaving the slave to free himself " (*LW* 2:350). He goes on to explain the impotence of Garrison's brand of moralism: "As a mere expression of abhorrence of slavery, the sentiment ['no union with slaveholders'] is a good one; but it expresses no intelligible principle of action, and throws no light on the pathway to duty" (*LW* 2:351). And he denies that Garrison retains the moral high ground by refusing to stay in the Union with slaveholders: "To leave the slave in his chains, in the hands of cruel masters who are too strong for him, is not to free ourselves from responsibility" (*LW* 2:416). Unlike Garrison, Douglass was now willing to distinguish the Founders' principles from their (and especially their progeny's) practices and to utilize praise of the former as a powerful means by which to condemn the latter. "With them," Douglass stated of the Founders, "nothing was 'settled' that was not right. With them, justice, liberty, and humanity were 'final': not slavery and oppression" (*LW* 2:186). He then had to explain, however, how those Founders who disapproved of slavery could have so temporized with it. After noting that the Constitution "was purposely so framed as to give no claim, no sanction to the claim, of property in man," Douglass identified the purpose behind the Founders' acceptance of it: "If in its origin slavery had any relation to the government, it was only as the scaffolding to the magnificent structure, to be removed as soon as the building was completed" (*LW* 3:365). If slavery had to be borne as a temporary prop for the construction of the world's first self-governing democracy devoted to freedom and equality, Douglass could accept the need for it. All the remaining principles of the Constitution were inherently antislavery and awaited only their full realization.

III

Beyond the question of abolishing slavery stood the thorny question of what to do with the freed slaves. We begin by noting that "[t]o concede the Negro's right to freedom is not to concede his right to United States citizenship."[23] That is, acceptance of the liberal premise of universal human equality does not yet dispose of the practical question of whether these two races, sharing their particular and horrible history, can live together safely and to their mutual benefit. Pessimism regarding the latter prospect had led many Americans, from Jefferson to Henry Clay to Lincoln, to conclude that separation of the races, via some form of colonization, would have to succeed the abolition of slavery. Because of the mixture of deep-rooted injustices and guilt that would characterize the relationship of whites and freed blacks, observers such as these believed that the two races could never ascend to the relation of trust and confidence in one another that healthy social life required.

Knowing that blacks had the right to be free, Douglass nevertheless stressed more their need for—rather than their right to—American citizenship. Like Garrison, Douglass strongly opposed colonization. But his reasons for doing so differed markedly. Garrison insisted that the policy of colonization represented nothing less than capitulation to white racism. Allowing whites to force the freed blacks to leave the country was tantamount to making the latter pay the price for the continuing sins of the former. Instead, the blacks should stay in America so as to confront whites with their own failings, acting as a prod to self-examination and, ultimately, to repudiation of the sin of racism. In Garrison's view, this was essential because just as blacks had suffered under white hostility and prejudice, so they would prosper only under white caring and indulgence. While eager to accept any lessening of white prejudice that should evolve, Douglass rejected this paternalism and refused to subordinate the needs of his race to "perfecting" the moral character of whites. His reasons were several. While agreeing with Garrison that racism would no doubt constitute a practical barrier to future black accomplishment, he was less concerned than Garrison with the putative psychological effects of racism on blacks. In particular, he doubted that white concern for blacks was what was needed. Instead, he told the whites: "Do nothing with [the blacks]; mind your business, and let them mind theirs. Your *doing* with them is their greatest misfortune" (*LW* 3:188). Even in the case of Garrison himself, the concern for blacks, in general, and for Douglass, in particular, did not preclude racist assumptions. At the height of the furor occasioned by criticism of Douglass's having invited white British abolitionist Julia Griffiths to become his secretary and to live in his home (while he remained married), Garrison's anger at their divergent views allowed him to remark that perhaps "the sufferers'" (Garrison placed this phrase in quotation marks) special circumstances had "transcended their ability as a class to understand all that the cause required" (*AOF* 433). Aside from the personal animosity that followed, this affair taught Douglass that good intentions did not preclude a certain paternalistic attitude toward blacks' abilities. In a letter to Charles Sumner (September 2, 1852), Douglass wrote that the Garrisonian school was "too narrow in its philosophy and too bigoted in spirit to do justice to any who venture to differ from it" (*LW* 2:210).

Moreover, Douglass insisted that the blacks must seek their humanity, their identity, and their successes through their own accomplishments and not through white indulgence, however benign. "No man can be truly free," he stated, "whose liberty is dependent on the thought, feeling, and action of others, and who has himself no means in his own hands for guarding . . . and maintaining that liberty" (quoted in *MFD* 68). In fact, Douglass warned blacks against the temptation of seeking to sustain the posture of victim in order to secure the white man's pity. "Human nature," he wrote, "is so constituted that it cannot honor a helpless man, although it can pity him; and even that it cannot do long, if the signs of power do not arise" (*LT* 143). In order to succeed, blacks must strive to attain strength (moral and intellectual as well as economic and even military). Douglass denied that self-respect was a gift to be granted by others. Other men's prejudices, however obnoxious, remained *their* failings, reflecting badly on them, not on the victims of their prejudice. When he was once made to ride in the baggage car of a train, despite having paid the same fare as the other passengers, some well-meaning white passengers apologized for his being "degraded in this manner." Thereupon "Mr. Douglass straightened himself up on the box upon which he was sitting, and replied: 'They cannot degrade Frederick Douglass. The soul that is within me no man can degrade. I am not the one being degraded on account of this treatment, but those who are inflicting it upon me.'"[24]

Even if the white man were to become the sincere and fully repentant champion of the black, it would not suffice. Neither a change in the moral condition of the whites nor the political condition of the blacks could produce what was needed: a change in the moral and intellectual condition of the blacks, which required that individuals achieve their successes through their own efforts.

> What we, the colored people, want, is *character*, and this nobody can give us. It is a thing we must get for ourselves. We must labor for it. It is gained by toil—hard toil. Neither the sympathy nor the generosity of our friends can give it to us. . . . It is attainable; but we must attain it, and attain it each man for himself. I cannot for you, and you cannot for me. . . . We must get character for ourselves, as a people. A change in our political condition would do very little for us without this. (*The North Star*, July 14, 1848)

Douglass was tempted to go even further. Sensing a lacuna in liberal theory (which was typically directed toward those who were born free and thus needed, in order to be free *and* self-directing, to learn the virtue of reigning in their natural longing for dominion), Douglass was ever alert to the opposing need to educate blacks, trained in servility, to the "manly" virtues. As a result, he tended to stress tougher measures than did most of his fellows. When most black leaders in 1879–81 were encouraging blacks to leave the unreconstructed South for Kansas, Douglass encouraged them to stay. Not only was he prepared to admit that "[n]either the master nor the emancipated slave can at once shake off the habits and manners of a long-established past condition," he even predicted that "suffering and hardships will make the Anglo-African strong."[25] Of course, Douglass insisted that any suffering that blacks should have to bear would exist only in the context of full legal equality, constitutional protections, and reasonable grounds for expecting progress. He vigorously protested against all forms of public discrimination against blacks. But, after emancipation, he consistently supported the notion of government as guarantor of rights, and he rejected the notion of government as provider of any special or preferential help to blacks (see, e.g., *LW* 3:190; 4:164).

Finally, and above all, Douglass opposed colonization on the grounds that blacks had both the right and the need to remain in America among the whites. Having mixed their sweat and blood in the building of the country, it was now as much theirs as anyone's. "We are here," Douglass wrote, "and here we are likely to be. . . . [T]his is our country. . . . We shall neither die out, nor be driven out; but shall go with this people, either as a testimony against them, or as an evidence in their favor throughout their generations." Not only would justice be served by letting the blacks remain in America but both whites and blacks would also profit thereby. Whites would gain the (largely potential) "industry, skill, and invention" of "one sixth part of the energies of the entire nation" (*SSW* 149). Blacks, in turn, would gain something more precious: exposure to the treasures of civilization. Owing not least to their prior disreputable treatment by whites, blacks were largely devoid of cultural developments and attainments. Despite its racism and its scandalous embrace of slavery, white culture had attained the greatest heights in civilization. Through no fault of their own, blacks were in need of staying among whites in America in order to learn from them. "We believe that contact with the white race, even under the many unjust and painful restrictions to which we are subjected, does more toward our elevation and improvement, than the mere circumstance of being separated from them could do." In fact, Douglass went so far as to claim that "the condition of our race has been improved *by their situation as slaves*, since it has brought them into contact with a superior people, and afforded them facilities for acquiring knowledge" (*LW* 2:173, emphasis added).

IV

A brief consideration of Douglass's background will be helpful in understanding his character as well as his difference from Garrison. Douglass was born a slave. He never knew his father (who most likely was a white man) and was separated from his mother while still a boy. Owned by various masters, Douglass partook of a kind of "Grand Tour" of the evils of the slave system. Only once did a small crack appear in the system: the wife of Hugh Auld, one of his masters, sensing his unusual intelligence, taught him how to read. As soon as his master found out about this, he put an immediate end to it, announcing: "give a nigger an inch and he will take an ell. Learning will spoil the best nigger in the world" (*LT* 79). Hearing this outburst, Douglass found himself in complete agreement: an enlarged and questing mind, he realized, cannot and will not tolerate the conditions of servitude. As a result, Douglass not only set out to develop his reading abilities as well as his mind generally on his own, but he also began to calculate ways in which to win his freedom.

The next few years were not without grave setbacks during which, however, Douglass learned not a little about human nature. He was sent by Hugh Auld to live with his son-in-law, Thomas Auld. Master Thomas was a small-minded man who introduced Douglass, after the biblical seven "fat" years with Hugh Auld, to hunger pangs (*LT* 104). When Thomas "got religion," Douglass was induced to hope that "he will emancipate his slaves; or . . . he will at any rate behave towards us more kindly" (108). But Thomas gained only the "*seemings* of piety" and Douglass "saw in him all the cruelty and meanness *after* his conversion which he had exhibited before that time" (109, 112, emphasis in original). Douglass's temerity in assisting at a young white man's Sunday-school—along with his growing refusal to show deference, much less submission, to his master—led to his being sent to Edward Covey, a notorious "Negro-breaker" (113–14). Covey set Douglass to back- and soul-breaking labor, as pointless and brutalizing as it was tedious, and he whipped him weekly for six months. Eventually driven to the brink, Douglass one day refused Covey's orders. After striking Douglass in the head, Covey left him, as he believed, to die. Douglass somehow found the strength to flee back to his master, expecting to find solace there. But his master insisted, to his surprise, that Covey must have been in the right and that Douglass must return to him (128–33). On doing so, Covey immediately chased Douglass into the forest. There, Douglass was befriended by "a genuine African" slave named Sandy who gave him a "root" whose powers would protect him (137). Inclined to dismiss "all pretenders to 'divination,'" Douglass was just then too lacking in confidence in his "book-learning" not to give it a try (138). Covey did indeed show a benign demeanor upon his return, though Douglass suspected that the Sabbath—it being Sunday—and not the root was the real explanation of the change (139). In fact, the next day Covey attacked Douglass. Now, however, Douglass's "hands were no longer tied by [his] religion," and he resisted Covey in a fight reminiscent of Jacob's wrestling with an angel. In the end, Covey failed to whip Douglass at all—and never again did so for the remaining six months of his tenure. But perhaps the chief result of his accomplishment was Douglass's discovery that he "was not afraid to die" (143).

Like Garrison, then, Douglass was that rare man who was willing to die. But unlike Garrison, Douglass refused to submit passively to his fate: if attacked, he would exercise his God-given strength to the fullest, thereby increasing his self-reliance and ensuring that he would never feel that he owed his place in life to the indulgence of any other being. Thus, while both men were feisty and combative, Douglass's toughness outlasted and went deeper than Garrison's. The most important aspect of this greater toughness involves Douglass's more probing and radical cast of mind. Garrison was the kind of man who exploited weaknesses in conventional thinking without always bothering to recognize the degree to which he relied on it. Characteristic was his way of arguing on religious topics. First, he used the Bible to embarrass fellow Christians (e.g., he delighted in demonstrating the lack of biblical texts to support the institution of the Sabbath); then he used reason to embarrass followers of the Bible (e.g., his late recognition that the Bible could not provide an unambiguous ground for abolition): nowhere, to my knowledge, did he raise doubts about the fundamental goodness of his cause, his God, and himself. By contrast, Douglass records how, upon his first escape from Covey, his "mind pass[ed] over the whole scale or circle of belief and unbelief, from faith in the over-ruling Providence of God, to the blackest atheism" (*LT* 131). Prepared by his encounters with Christian slaveholders ("religious slaveholders are the worst"), Douglass's crisis of faith came earlier and went deeper than Garrison's.[26] He had confronted what we might call, with apologies to Kant, the antinomies of religion: both his master's "pious" wife (whose kindness in teaching him to read was instrumental in opening up his entire life) and Covey (with his "religious devotions"), as well as many slaveholders, drew their self-justifications from religion (*LT* 77, 123). Unlike Garrison, whose various American-style adjustments enabled him to remain "religious" all along, Douglass felt the need to engage and interrogate religion. His recognition of the injustice of slavery brought with it doubts about the existence of God. He admits to having been "eager . . . to partake of the tree of knowledge" and, when discovered and chastised by his master for having done so, Douglass, unlike the biblical Adam, betrayed no shame and indicated no regret (*LT* 86). Though he insisted that he was raising doubts only about "slaveholding religion," Douglass remained suspect to many Christians (*N* 71). Following the war, matters came to a head when Douglass announced in a speech that "I want to express my love and gratitude to God by thanking the faithful men and women who have devoted the great energies of their soul to the welfare of mankind. It is *only* through such men and women that I can get a glimpse of God *anywhere*" (*National Anti-Slavery Standard*, May 29, 1869, emphasis added). Over the next year, Douglass found himself denounced by many orthodox black churchmen on the grounds that he had thanked man rather than God for emancipation (*MFD* 179–80).

After one escape attempt was scuttled when Sandy (the "root" man) betrayed his friends to the authorities, Douglass finally escaped for good in 1837. After adopting a trade by which to support himself, Douglass found himself attending meetings of abolitionist societies. Soon enough, he was asked to speak to the attendees of his own experiences. Despite the risk of publicity—he could be recaptured and sent back to slavery—Douglass agreed. He was so effective that doubts immediately were raised about his authenticity: surely, no slave could speak so well. And while his "handlers" never doubted his ability to speak, they doubted his ability to reason out questions of strategy and philosophy. "Give us the facts," one of them told Douglass, "and we will take care of the philosophy" (*LT* 217). Having been introduced to thinking, however, Douglass was not about to stop short now. He engaged in debates of all kinds, carried on spirited and varied correspondences, and perhaps most important, started his own newspaper (*The North Star*, later *Frederick Douglass' Paper*). Garrison himself opposed the latter step. But the responsibilities of running the paper, Douglass said, enforced on him a continued education. As we have seen, that education encompassed both political philosophy and rhetoric. And it was chiefly as a man who thought deeply about both the human condition, in general, and the condition of his own people, in particular, and who then translated his thoughts into bold, thundering, precise, and scathing rhetoric, that Douglass made his indelible mark. As one reporter said of an 1844 Douglass speech: "[It] was not what you could describe as oratory or eloquence. It was sterner, darker, deeper than these. It was the volcanic outbreak of human nature, long pent up in slavery and at last bursting its imprisonment. It was the storm of insurrection" (quoted in *MFD* 24).

V

Both Garrison and Douglass lived beyond the Civil War and continued to fight various battles. But, as Douglass said, none ever quite rose to the level of those fought in the years 1848–60. Though neither man held political office during that period, few influenced events more than they. Between them, they humbled one race and cleared the way for the elevation of another. Comparing the two as we have done, however, enables us to see the difference between agitation and statesmanship. This is not to belittle agitation in any way. It was needed then and will be again in political life. After meeting with Garrison in 1864, Lincoln remarked that he was "only an instrument" in the struggle for emancipation. "The logic and moral power of Garrison and the antislavery people of the country and the army, have done it all" (quoted in *AOF* 568). Douglass himself, when approached by a young black man in later life for advice on what to do with himself as he set out in the 1890s, replied: "Agitate, agitate, agitate" (*LW* 4:149). When, however, agitation is done with patience, with moderation, without self-indulgence, and without ever forgetting the health of the greater whole that cannot be sacrificed to the success of the cause for which one agitates—then one's agitation becomes statesmanship.[27]

Douglass never held a position in which he was responsible for the greater good of the country as a whole. Nor did he generally speak with that responsibility foremost in his mind or on his tongue. While his outlook can be seen as no less "universalist" than Garrison's, his concern was always first and foremost his own race. When emancipation came, it was not altogether surprising that Garrison wished to delay implementing black suffrage (until blacks could be educated to the degree where they would utilize it wisely), while Douglass sought it immediately (as a chief component of that education). Douglass's responsibility, he felt, was the welfare of the blacks; but he learned to appreciate and incorporate the broader concern for the country as a whole, especially as his sometimes testy but always respectful relation with Abraham Lincoln evolved. Lincoln, he said in a remarkable eulogy offered in 1876, often exasperated the blacks. "Lincoln was not," said Douglass, "in the fullest sense of the word, either our man or our model. In his interests, in his associations, in his habits of thought, and in his prejudices, he was a white man." It thus seemed that Lincoln too spoke only for a part, albeit the dominant part, of the whole. Despite the many times that Lincoln's postponements and delays "taxed and strained" the blacks' faith in him, that faith "never failed." Eventually, Douglass was able "to take a comprehensive view of Abraham Lincoln." This entailed interpreting his actions "in the light of the stern logic of great events." When he did so, he came to see that the good of the blacks was in fact enhanced by Lincoln's unshakeable insistence on preferring the good of the country to the good of even its most mistreated part. "Viewed from the genuine abolition ground, Mr. Lincoln seemed tardy, cold, dull, and indifferent; but measuring him by the sentiment of his country, a sentiment he was bound as a statesman to consult, he was swift, zealous, radical, and determined" (*LT* 492, 494, 498).

Garrison became a changed man with the arrival of the Civil War and the election of Lincoln. Jettisoning his pacifism, Garrison supported the war and embraced its aim of rescuing the Union. In December of 1861, he dramatically changed the banner of the *Liberator,* removing the disunionist "covenant with death" slogan and replacing it with the biblical command "Proclaim Liberty throughout the land, to all the inhabitants thereof" (see *AOF* 531). After some initial suspicions, and despite his long-standing objection to involvement in politics, Garrison also came to be a staunch supporter of Lincoln. In the midst of the 1864 election, Garrison stood alone in support of Lincoln's reelection bid at a meeting of the Massachusetts Anti-Slavery Society. He staunchly bore withering attacks from his old friend Wendell Phillips. In language similar to Douglass's, Garrison stated that "we have advanced a quarter of a century in a single year." Having once considered Lincoln a "slow coach," Garrison now had to admit that he had "beaten the Birmingham train."[28]

Both Douglass and Garrison, then, evolved from an "ethic of conviction" to an "ethic of responsibility." Rarely has either ethic enjoyed such impressive champions. While it is unfortunate that Garrison's delay in coming to understand the value of the Union and of politics generally helped lead to a bitter estrangement between the two for almost twenty years, their differences remain instructive to this day. We can see that there are moral outlooks worthy of the name that do not demand a utopian transformation of the human soul. And we find that the defense of a part of a political community can be undertaken in a responsible manner, directed by enlarged and humanizing views. In the end, perhaps their greatest gift to American democracy was to correct what Tocqueville says is its characteristic vice of attributing "almost no influence to the individual over the destiny of the species or to citizens over the fate of the people" (*DA* 2.1.20 [469]). For together and separately, Douglass and Garrison were instrumental in helping to resolve what had been the most intractable and damaging dilemma in American life.

Notes

1. *The Life and Writings of Frederick Douglass*, ed. Philip S. Foner (New York: International Publishers, 1952), 2:201, hereafter referred to as *LW*.

2. As Stephen A. Douglas insisted in a speech that led to the Lincoln-Douglas debates: "I deny [Congress's] right to force a good thing upon a people who are unwilling to receive it." *The Complete Lincoln-Douglas Debates of 1858*, ed. Paul M. Angle (Chicago: University of Chicago Press, 1991), 17.

3. Harry V. Jaffa, *Crisis of the House Divided* (Chicago: University of Chicago Press, 1982), 108–10.

4. Thomas Jefferson to John Holmes, April 22, 1820, in *The Portable Thomas Jefferson*, ed. Merrill D. Peterson (New York: Penguin Books, 1975), 568.

5. Lincoln, "Reply at Ottawa," *Lincoln-Douglas Debates*, 117; see also 205, 269–70.

6. For an eloquent, far earlier statement by Garrison of the desperate situation facing friends of emancipation—especially religious ones—see his "Letter to Thomas Shipley," December 17, 1835, in *The Letters of William Lloyd Garrison*, ed. Walter M. Merrill and Louis Rachames (Cambridge, Mass.: Belknap Press, 1971), 1:582–85, hereafter *LWLG*.

7. *The Life and Times of Frederick Douglass* (New York: Macmillan Publishers, [1892]1962), 265, hereafter *LT*.

8. "Introduction," *William Lloyd Garrison*, ed. George M. Frederickson (Englewood Cliffs, N.J.: Prentice Hall, 1968), 4, hereafter *WLG*. This characterization of Garrison has been contested, to some extent, by Aileen S. Kraditor, *Means and Ends in American Abolitionism: Garrison and His Critics on Strategy and Tactics, 1834–1850* (New York: Pantheon Books, 1967), hereafter *Means*. It has been accepted, more or less, and then defended as appropriate by Henry Mayer, *All on Fire* (New York: St. Martin's Press, 1998), hereafter *AOF*.

9. I use the term "political philosophy" here advisedly, aware that it may be inappropriate to seek "a political philosopher in a Hebrew moralist." V. L. Parrington, *Main Currents in American Thought* (New York: Harcourt, Brace, 1927), 2:344.

10. Alexis de Tocqueville, *Democracy in America*, trans. Harvey C. Mansfield and Delba Winthrop (Chicago: University of Chicago Press, 2000), 2.2.2 (482–84), hereafter *DA*.

11. Garrison was much enamored of the Rev. George Bourne's *The Book and Slavery Irreconcilable* (1816). See, e.g., *LWLG* 2:172n10. The biblical text most cited by slaveholders was Genesis 9:22–27.

12. Garrison, "Thomas Paine," *Liberator*, November 21, 1845. Consider also Garrison's ultimate, Spinozist opinion that the Bible was not "prepared by one mind (and that a divine one)" but was rather "a compilation of Jewish and Christian manuscripts, written in different parts of the world, in ages more or less remote from each other—written nobody knows by whom, beyond what supposition and probability may suggest . . . [able to vindicate almost any] doctrine." R. F. Wallcut, *Selections from the Writings and Speeches of William Lloyd Garrison* (New York: Negro Universities Press, [1852] 1968), 223.

13. William Lloyd Garrison, *Thoughts on African Colonization* (New York: Arno Press, [1832] 1968), 134.

14. Aileen Kraditor, Garrison's most thoughtful academic defender, makes a rare condemnation of Garrison for failing to see the class dimension of problems, treating them instead as individual instances of sinning (*Means* 245–46).

15. Quoted in Kraditor, *Means*, 57. Douglass himself questioned the wisdom of the Garrisonians' willingness to allow John Collins to introduce Fourier's communist ideas into the movement and was chastised by them for his troubles. See Waldo E. Martin, Jr., *The Mind of Frederick Douglass* (Chapel Hill: University of North Carolina Press, 1984), 28, hereafter *MFD*.

16. Quoted in Kraditor, *Means*, 213. Insofar as Garrison and his colleagues relied on this expectation, they were trying to secure their happiness (along with that of others, to be sure) by sacrificing or, at any rate, risking it. Their worthiness for happiness, then, consisted in their indifference to it. And insofar as they continued to harbor a secret longing for happiness, they undermined their worthiness to be awarded it.

17. Even Aileen Kraditor concedes that he may have been an "ultra-individualist" who failed to grasp the importance of political institutions (*Means* 14–15).

18. One gets a flavor of Garrison's reputation, as well as his reasons for questioning Catholicism, in his letter to the editor of *The Boston Transcript* (May 31, 1850): "I am represented to have said, 'There could be no piety in the Romish Church.' This I did not say—this I do not believe. I said of that Church, as such, that inasmuch as it sanctions slaveholding and slave-breeding on the part of its priesthood and lay members, in this country, the slave could not look to it for deliverance from his chains. I said the same thing of the Episcopal, Presbyterian, Baptist and Methodist Churches" (*LWLG* 4:23).

19. Thus, while Garrison's insistence that moral change must precede political change recalls to mind various utterances of Douglass (as well as Lincoln), it is, in fact, quite different. Both Douglass and Lincoln shared the view of Tocqueville (and Aristotle) that morals and politics bear a reciprocal relation to one another (consider Tocqueville's analysis of a "social state": *DA* 1.1.3 [45]). For better or worse, morals are never formed in a vacuum removed from politics. This is not to say that morals are merely the individual manifestation of some political ideology. Rather, they are shaped and colored by the political principles of the regime in which one lives. This is why Aristotle insists that his *Ethics* find its completion in the *Politics*. The subterranean mixture of habits, tastes, and predilections that go into a citizen *prior* to his ever achieving a measure of self-consciousness, let alone self-criticism, suggests that abstract programs of moral education, much less moral perfectionism, are doomed to fail or, at any rate, be perverted. Better, says Aristotle, to set about frankly designing the political regime in which one seeks to have morals flourish.

20. See Kraditor, *Means*, 28. One wonders how treating *oneself* as a means to an end can be considered a moral position by the Garrisonians. It is surely of questionable prudence to expect an increase in intransigence to bring about a strengthening of moderation.

21. Douglass, "Farewell Speech to the British People," in *Frederick Douglass: Selected Speeches and Writings*, ed. Philip S. Foner (Chicago: Lawrence Hill Books, 1999), 64, hereafter *SSW*.

22. Consider also Douglass's extravagant praise of the great men of antiquity for being wholly free of any taint of racism (*SSW* 99–101).

23. Herbert J. Storing, "Slavery and the American Republic," in *Toward a More Perfect Union* (Washington, D.C.: AEI Press, 1995), 146.

24. Booker T. Washington, *Up from Slavery* (New York: Doubleday, Page and Co., 1901), 100.

25. Douglass, *LW* 4:331. Some years later, Douglass suggested that he had been mistaken.

26. Douglass, *Narrative of the Life of Frederick Douglass* (New York: Dover Publications, 1995), 46, hereafter *N*.

27. I hasten to note that Garrison was patient, moderate, and without self-indulgence in his personal life and individual dealings. I speak only of his approach to political problems.

28. Garrison's biographer Henry Mayer notes that "Garrison's political instincts were sound, and his willingness to risk his leadership of the radical abolitionists on Lincoln's behalf would be recognized as an uncommon act of statesmanship" (*AOF* 562–66).

Chapter 22

Abraham Lincoln: The Moderation of a Democratic Statesman

Steven Kautz

> When it was over it seemed to the people that he had all along been thinking their real thoughts for them; but they knew that this was because he had fearlessly thought for himself.—Lord Charnwood

braham Lincoln (1809–1865) is justly praised as "the greatest among those associated with the cause of popular government" (*AL* 326): Lincoln's greatness is the greatness of a *democratic* statesman.[1] His great work was to demonstrate, what many sober men had doubted, "*the capability of a people to govern themselves*" (*CW* 1:113). The tragedy of American slavery and the horrors of the Civil War tested whether this nation or any nation "conceived in Liberty, and dedicated to the proposition that all men are created equal," could long endure. Abraham Lincoln led Americans through these "most perilous hours of the Republic"; and he led us in such a way as to demonstrate, to ourselves and to a skeptical world, that "government of the people, by the people, for the people" is possible. As Frederick Douglass would say to his white fellow citizens in 1876: "Abraham Lincoln saved for you a country." And yet, Lincoln is also justly praised as the Great Emancipator. Douglass continues: "for while Abraham Lincoln saved for you a country, he delivered us from a bondage, according to Jefferson, one hour of which was worse than ages of the oppression your fathers rose in rebellion to oppose" (*OM* 313). Lincoln's great work was thus to restore slavery to a "course of ultimate extinction," upon which (so he often said) the Founders had placed it, and thereby to make our Republic "worthy of the saving" (*CW* 3:18, 2:276). In the end, during the course of a terrible civil war that was forced upon him and upon the North, he was compelled to do more than to restore slavery to a course of ultimate extinction: he would himself free the slaves, in an extraordinary proclamation, as "an act of justice, warranted by the Constitution, upon military necessity" (*CW* 6:30).

What is the relation between the great work of vindicating the capability of a people to govern themselves and the great work, the "act of justice," of emancipating the slaves? The study of Lincoln, and of his nation during an era in which slavery was the principal and sometimes almost the only subject of political controversy, affords an excellent opportunity to think about certain enduring dilemmas of democracy. Injustice and instability (even civil war) are natural vices of democracy (consider *The Federalist* nos. 9–10). Certainly the people shall rule in a democracy; but they will from time to time rule unjustly, as tyrants. In such a case, when the people betray justice, what are the tasks and duties of the democratic statesman? How can a democratic statesman respect *both* the (rightful) claim of the people to rule in a democracy *and* the claims of justice that are denied by that people?

In this chapter, we approach the political thought of Abraham Lincoln through a study of his statesmanship, understanding his speeches in the context of his deeds. Lincoln's virtues enabled him to mediate between the demands of justice and the prejudices of a democratic people that did not love justice well; he thus served both justice and democracy, as far as was then possible. His great achievement was to ennoble a free people by teaching it to recognize the difference between "a wise people's patience with ills they could not cure, and a profligate people's acceptance of evil as their good" (*AL* 97). Lincoln's own wisdom was therefore only the beginning of his statesmanship—or rather, his wisdom was completed by his statesmanship and above all by those virtues that enabled him "to educate and mold public opinion" so that the people he led would learn once again to embrace the truths of the Declaration of Independence (*CW* 2:453).[2]

Perhaps the greatest of the virtues of such a democratic statesman is a certain kind of moderation. Lincoln was no abolitionist; but neither was his moderation that of the trimmer, who seeks only to find the center and who often finds that the political ground is shifting beneath him. The ordinary vice of the trimmer is inconstancy: as the ground shifts beneath him, he shifts with it. That moderation is properly despised; it is a petty vice. But Lincoln's moderation was never a timid pragmatism; his moderation was intransigent rather than inconstant. The moderate Lincoln proved to be a deadlier foe of slavery than the radical abolitionists and a more honorable patriot than the compromise Whigs or the Douglas Democrats. Such moderation is the political virtue that mediates between wisdom and power. It is a love of justice that has a prudent regard for the "weak hands of Justice in this World," but such a regard as does not abandon the cause of justice to its enemies.[3]

I

Moderation is a drab virtue. Why? Why does moderation, when seen in the light of such splendid virtues as justice or courage, seem so vulgar, timorous, ignoble?

A familiar Lincoln jest captures some of our ordinary suspicion of the "moderate" man. Lincoln was one day obliged to face down a delegation of congressional critics of his favorite general, Ulysses Grant. These haughty Republican congressmen included among their complaints this gossip: that Grant was a notorious drunk. Lincoln reportedly disarmed the critics with a joke: find out what brand of whiskey Grant drinks, and if it makes "fighting generals" like Grant, "I should like to get some of it for [my other generals]." There is some doubt whether Lincoln actually said this, above all because he denied saying it. And yet, there is credible testimony that Lincoln remarked, when asked whether the jest was his: "it would have been very good if I had said it"; and, "that is too good for me." Perhaps the story is too good to be true: but the portrait of Lincoln is a fine one.[4]

Hard drinkers can (of course) be great generals. No revelation there. And not much of a joke: it would take a rare moralist to deny *that*. But Lincoln's joke mischievously suggests something more: perhaps there is even some connection between the hard drinking and the other virtues of a "fighting general." That's the play in this joke: Grant is a fighting general not *in spite of* but rather *because of* his hard drinking. Now, is *that* suggestion more than a joke? As it happens, it is possible to inquire further into Lincoln's views on this question; as a young man, he once delivered a remarkable speech—playful yet wise—about drunks and their critics.

Lincoln's 1842 "Temperance Address" is mostly remembered for its condemnation of the tactics of "denunciation" employed by the "old school champions" of temperance. Thus, for example, "the *preacher*, it is said, advocates temperance because he is a fanatic"; and his fanaticism, says Lincoln, leads him to employ "the thundering tones of anathema and denunciation, with which the lordly Judge often groups together all the crimes of the felon's life, and thrusts them in his face just ere he passes sentence of death upon him." Such denunciations are of course ineffective: humanity and "unassuming persuasion," says Lincoln, "addressed by erring man to an erring brother," are better suited to the task of reforming drunkards—and to the tasks of moral reformation more generally (*CW* 1:272–73).

Beyond this, Lincoln also argues that the denunciation of drunkards is also unjust. Lincoln shrewdly notices in this speech that "the demon of intemperance ever seems to have delighted in *sucking the blood of genius* and of generosity"; indeed, the "hearts" and the "heads" of the "habitual drunkards" among us "will bear an advantageous comparison with those of any other class" because "*the brilliant*" and "*the warm-blooded*" are most prone to this and other vices (*CW* 1:278, emphases added). Now Lincoln was himself a moderate man—among his other virtues, he did not drink. And it is worth recalling that, in 1842, he was a member of the party of temperance (the Whig party), which was pledged to the moral reformation of the nation and some part of which was opposed, it was said, not only to slavery but also to "slavery, rum, and Romanism."[5] And yet, Lincoln seems to have known that moderation—even in the evidently petty matter of hard drinking—most often arises not from any "mental or moral superiority" but rather from "the absence of appetite." Lincoln's surprising conclusion is that the so-called vices of immoderation are, often enough, the natural disorders of "brilliant" souls consumed by great and sometimes splendid passions; and the so-called virtue of moderation is, too often, the natural order of the pallid soul who knows no such passions. Immoderation is the path to self-destruction of great souls; moderation is a means of self-preservation of small souls. "What one of us but can call to mind some dear relative," asks Lincoln, "more promising in youth than all his fellows, who has fallen a sacrifice to his rapacity?" (*CW* 1:278). As for virtue: seek out the immoderate youth and tame him, educate and ennoble his immoderate passions; there one will find a true and truly splendid virtue, of which ordinary "moderation" is a pale imitation.

One sees here a small but revealing instance of Lincoln's remarkable *humanity*, an aspect of his moderation. The capaciousness of his "human sympathies" sometimes took the form of a great distaste—occasionally scornful, more often puckish—for moral indignation or self-righteousness or priggery. Often enough, that distaste would be the occasion for a joke—as with the haughty congressmen who were blind to Grant's virtues or the fanatical preachers who were blind to the tragic promise of youths lost to drink. But from time to time, when the stakes were higher, Lincoln's humanity would bring him into profound conflict with those of his partisan friends who were not so immune to the savage pleasures of moral indignation. Thus, as Charnwood reports:

> This most unrelenting enemy to the project of the Confederacy was the one man who had quite purged his heart and mind from hatred or even anger towards his fellow-countrymen of the South. . . . [N]ot many conquerors, and certainly few successful statesman, have escaped the tendency of power to harden or at least to narrow their human sympathies; but in this man a natural wealth of tender compassion became richer and more tender while in the stress of deadly conflict he developed an astounding strength. (*AL* 325–26)[6]

Let us turn, then, from Lincoln's analysis of moderation in the petty matter of hard drinking to his analysis of the greater matter of *political* moderation. In politics, too, moderation most often testifies not to the conquest of a great passion, but to its absence. And here, too, there is also a more splendid moderation that tames and ennobles the great political passions.

II

Patriotism and the love of justice are great passions of republican politics—perhaps *the* great passions of republican politics. But moderation is ugly to *the patriot*. The patriot demands a wholehearted love of the republic—or even, as Montesquieu says, "a renunciation of oneself" —and he suspects that moderation in service to or even in praise of one's community is an apology for selfishness, for the ignoble choice to pursue one's private good at the expense of the common good.[7] And moderation is ugly to the *lover of justice*. The lover of justice demands a wholehearted dedication to its cause, and he suspects that moderation in the pursuit of justice is an apology for an ignoble hardness of heart, or something worse, in the face of wickedness and misery. From the point of view of the patriot or the lover of justice, the moderate in politics—the pragmatist, the trimmer—is one who loves his country or justice halfheartedly.

But Lincoln was a moderate. And so he often seemed, as Charnwood says, "disgustingly well-regulated"—just a bit too calm in the face of the extraordinary injustice of slavery.

> All this provoked in many excellent and clever men dissatisfaction and deep suspicion; they longed for a leader whose heart visibly glowed with a sacred passion; they attributed his patience, the one quality of greatness which after a while everybody must have discerned in him, not to a self-mastery which almost passed belief, but to a tepid disposition and a mediocre if not a low level of desire. We who read of him to-day shall not escape our moments of lively sympathy with these grumblers of the time; we shall wish that this man could ever plunge, that he could ever see red, ever commit some passionate injustice; we shall suspect him of being, in the phrase of a great philosopher, "a disgustingly well-regulated person." (*AL* 115)

Lincoln was no abolitionist. As Frederick Douglass would justly say many years later, "viewed from the genuine abolition ground, Mr. Lincoln seemed tardy, cold, dull, and indifferent" (*OM* 316)—moderate to the point of seeming indifference to the cries of injustice of the slaves and their abolitionist friends. As late as the First Inaugural, Lincoln could write: "'I have no purpose, directly or indirectly, to interfere with the institution of slavery in the States where it exists. I believe I have no lawful right to do so, and I have no inclination to do so'" (*CW* 4:263). Is it quite right to say of such a man that he was a lover of justice, if that love could so easily be tamed? Compare Lincoln's hard-hearted way to the passionate way of a more radical lover of justice, the abolitionist William Lloyd Garrison:

> I am aware, that many object to the severity of my language; but is there not cause for severity? I *will be* as harsh as truth, and as uncompromising as justice. On this subject I do not wish to think, or speak, or write, with moderation. No! no! Tell a man whose house is on fire, to give a moderate alarm; tell him to moderately rescue his wife from the hands of the ravisher; tell the mother to gradually extricate her babe from the fire into which it has fallen;—but urge me not to use moderation in a cause like the present. I am in earnest—I will not equivocate—I will not excuse—I will not retreat a single inch—AND I WILL BE HEARD. The apathy of the people is enough to make every statue leap from its pedestal, and to hasten the resurrection of the dead.[8]

Viewed from genuine abolition ground, by those whose love of justice had not been chastened by political ambition or party politics or popular prejudice, Lincoln's moderation on the slavery question must have seemed an ugly concession to wickedness or base self-interest.

And yet, we know better than this. We learn from as good an authority as Frederick Douglass that there is no ground for doubt about Lincoln's immoderate hatred of slavery; and there is no ground for doubt that his statesmanship was often intransigent. Respecting the latter question, in the sequel to the passage just cited, Douglass continues: "measuring him by the sentiment of his country, a sentiment he was bound as a statesman to consult, he was swift, zealous, radical, and determined" (*OM* 316). Respecting the former question, whether Lincoln truly hated slavery, Douglass concludes:

> [I]t is hardly necessary to say that in his heart of hearts he loathed and hated slavery. . . . The man who could say, "Fondly do we hope, fervently do we pray, that this mighty scourge of war shall soon pass away, yet if God wills it continue till all the wealth piled by two hundred years of bondage shall have been wasted, and each drop of blood drawn by the lash shall have been paid for by one drawn by the sword, the judgments of the Lord are true and righteous altogether," gives all needed proof of his feeling on the subject of slavery. (*OM* 316)

Thus, Lincoln was an immoderate enemy of slavery. And yet, in politics, he was a moderate opponent of slavery, both in the 1850s (when the issue was abolition versus more moderate opposition to slavery *extension*) and at the outset of the Civil War (when the issue was whether emancipation would be a war aim).

Lincoln was also not a wholehearted patriot—or, to speak more precisely, his patriotism was uncommonly moderate and reasonable. Thus, in 1855, Lincoln wrote:

> Our progress in degeneracy appears to me to be pretty rapid. As a nation, we began by declaring that '*all men are created equal.*' We now practically read it 'all men are created equal, *except negroes.*' When the Know-Nothings get control, it will read 'all men are created equal, except negroes, *and foreigners, and Catholics.*' When it comes to this I should prefer emigrating to some country where they make no pretence of loving liberty—to Russia, for instance, where the despotism can be taken pure, and without the base alloy of hypocrasy. (*CW* 2:323)

Lincoln's patriotism was surely not the patriotism of "my country, right or wrong"; his patriotism was conditional—stingy or generous as the times demanded.[9] In the most memorable passage of Lincoln's first great speech, the Peoria speech of 1854, he makes clear the limits of his patriotism:

> Our republican robe is soiled, and trailed in the dust. Let us re-purify it. Let us turn and wash it white, in the spirit, if not the blood, of the Revolution. . . . Let us re-adopt the Declaration of Independence, and with it, the practices, and policy, which harmonize with it. Let north and south—let all Americans—let all lovers of liberty everywhere—join in the great and good work. If we do this, we shall not only have saved the Union; but we shall have so saved it, as to make, and to keep it, forever worthy of the saving. (*CW* 2:276)

Patriotism is a kind of love; but love is blind and love is foolish. The lover is known to imagine virtues where they do not exist, and to be blind to vices that are plain enough; and the lover is prepared to render awful service to his beloved, sacrificing everything, sometimes to no good end. For these reasons, the honorable patriot must learn to measure the community by some standard of political virtue *beyond* the community: this is moderate patriotism. One hears this sort of patriotism praised in Lincoln's eulogy of Henry Clay.

> He loved his country partly because it was his own country, but mostly because it was a free country; and he burned with a zeal for its advancement, prosperity and glory, because he saw in

such, the advancement, prosperity and glory, of human liberty, human right, and human nature. He desired the prosperity of his countrymen partly because they were his countrymen, but chiefly to show the world that freemen could be prosperous. (*CW* 2:126)

In the best case, patriotism is marked by an honorable ambivalence ("partly," "chiefly"), enabling the patriot to know both the duties arising from citizenship and the duties arising from humanity.

Lincoln was a moderate: he had enemies on both the Left and the Right. On the Left, there were those who doubted the quality of his *love of justice*. They understood that his devotion to the Union was more fundamental than his hatred of slavery—or, more precisely, that his hatred of slavery was inextricably bound to his devotion to the Union established by the Constitution and founded on the principles of the Declaration. But Lincoln had enemies on the Right (so to speak) as well—and not only among the Southerners who dared to speak of the "positive good" of slavery. There were those on the Right who doubted his *patriotism*, who understood that Lincoln's devotion to the Union was conditional and that he would, as he playfully said, "prefer emigrating to some country where they make no pretence of loving liberty" rather than to remain devoted to a Union that had abandoned its ancient faith in liberty. Like Clay, Lincoln "loved his country partly because it was his own country, but mostly because it was a free country." And he was prepared to make a civil war to ensure that it would remain a free country. Less moderate patriots were more wholehearted Unionists.

Charnwood captures well Lincoln's moderate soul.

We turn now from John Brown, who saw in slavery a great oppression, and was very angry, and went ahead slaying the nearest oppressor and liberating—for some days at least—the nearest slave, to a patient being, who, long ago in his youth, had boiled with anger against slavery, but whose whole soul now expressed itself in a policy of *deadly moderation* towards it. . . . [W]e shall see him watching and waiting while blood flows, suspending judgment, temporising, making trial of this expedient and of that. . . . Above all, in that point of policy which most interests us, we shall witness the long postponement of the blow that killed negro slavery, the steady subordination of this particular issue to what will not at once appeal to us as a larger and a higher issue. (*AL* 114–15)

Was Lincoln's moderation the moderation of a man whose love of justice and patriotism reflects the absence of those noble passions: was Lincoln "disgustingly well-regulated"? Or was he a moderate of another sort, who resists the temptations of fanaticism (John Brown) or moral radicalism (William Lloyd Garrison) not because he did not experience the "monstrous injustice" of slavery (*CW* 2:255) but because he knew that the available choice for enemies of slavery was between a drunken and self-destructive radicalism and his own "deadly moderation"? Here is Charnwood's conclusion:

As to the man, perhaps the sense will grow upon us that this balanced and calculating person, with his finger on the pulse of the electorate while he cracked his uncensored jests with all comers, did of set purpose drink and refill and drink again as full and fiery a cup of sacrifice as ever was pressed to the lips of hero or of saint. (*AL* 115)

Lincoln himself makes a similar point, in a letter to Joshua Speed:

It is hardly fair for you to assume, that I have no interest in a thing which has, and continually exercises, the power of making me miserable. You ought rather to appreciate how much the great body of the Northern people do crucify their feelings, in order to maintain their loyalty to the Constitution and the Union. (*CW* 2:320)

III

Lincoln had the democratic advantage of actually being, in one sense, a common man. He did not hesitate to cultivate that reputation, and it served him well. He would one day be able to say to a regiment of Northern soldiers: "I happen temporarily to occupy this big White House. I am a living witness that any one of your children may look to come here as my father's child has" (*CW* 7:512). In this respect and others, Lincoln was the first author of the Lincoln myth. But in writing this myth, he had good material to work with. "It is a great folly to attempt to make anything out of me or my early life," Lincoln once said. "It can all be condensed into a single sentence; and that sentence you will find in Gray's 'Elegy':—'The short and simple annals of the poor.'—That's my life, and that's all you or anyone else can make out of it" (*AL* 10). His short autobiography, published for the 1860 campaign, makes for somewhat painful reading, so great is its emphasis on his youthful poverty and commonness—although he does not hesitate to report in that campaign autobiography that he had "studied and nearly mastered the Six-books of Euclid, since he was a member of Congress" (*CW* 4:62). But to all external appearances—that is, if we take no notice of the inner life of this extraordinary youth, who mastered Euclid and imagined himself a Napoleon (*CW* 1:114)—the simple truth is that Lincoln "appeared in every sense of the word like one of the plain people among whom he loved to be counted."

That last remark appears in a fine speech that Joseph Choate (Ambassador to Great Britain under President McKinley and a notable Republican from New York) delivered during his service in England on that "most American of all Americans," Abraham Lincoln. "It is now forty years since I first saw and heard Abraham Lincoln, but the impression which he left on my mind is ineffaceable. After his great successes in the West he came to New York to make a political address." Choate is speaking here of the Cooper Institute address of 1860, the speech that made Lincoln a national political figure.

> He appeared in every sense of the word like one of the plain people among whom he loved to be counted. At first sight there was nothing impressive or imposing about him—except that his great stature singled him out from the crowd; his clothes hung awkwardly on his giant frame, his face was of a dark pallor, without the slightest tinge of color; his seamed and rugged features bore the furrows of hardship and struggle; his deep-set eyes looked sad and anxious; his countenance in repose gave little evidence of that brain power which had raised him from the lowest to the highest station among his countrymen. . . . It was a great audience, including all the noted men—all the learned and cultured—of his party in New York: editors, clergymen, statesmen, lawyers, merchants, critics. They were all very curious to hear him. His fame as a powerful speaker had preceded him, and exaggerated rumor of his wit—the worst forerunner of an orator—had reached the East. . . . A vast sea of eager upturned faces greeted him, full of intense curiosity to see what this rude child of the people was like.

So far we see the Lincoln of myth: the awkward child of a plain and rude people. But "he was equal to the occasion," reports Choate:

> When he spoke he was transformed; his eye kindled, his voice rang, his face shone and seemed to light up the whole assembly. For an hour and a half he held his audience in the hollow of his hand. His style of speech and manner of delivery were severely simple. What Lowell called "The grand simplicities of the Bible," with which he was so familiar, were reflected in his discourse. With no attempt at ornament or rhetoric, without parade or pretence, he spoke straight to the point. If any came expecting the turgid eloquence or the ribaldry of the frontier, they must have been startled at the earnest and sincere purity of his utterances. It was marvellous to see how this

untutored man, by mere self discipline and the chastening of his own spirit, had outgrown all meretricious arts, and found his own way to the grandeur and strength of absolute simplicity.[10]

The appearance (and to some extent the reality) of being (an uncommon) "common man" served Lincoln well. As he once put it:

> [W]hen the conduct of men is designed to be influenced, *persuasion*, kind, unassuming persuasion, should ever be adopted. It is an old and true maxim, that a 'drop of honey catches more flies than a gallon of gall.' So with men. If you would win a man to your cause, *first* convince him that you are his sincere friend. Therein is a drop of honey that catches his heart, which, say what he will, is the great high road to his reason. (*CW* 1:273)

Lincoln would learn to be the "sincere friend" of a democratic people that had begun to lose, or perhaps never quite possessed, the habits and virtues of self-government. The first task of the democratic statesman is to persuade the people, who are powerful but not always reasonable, to listen. Lincoln's commonness, cultivated or not, helped to earn him one of the privileges of "sincere friends": the right to speak harsh truths.

And yet, Lincoln was not only a common man: he also possessed extraordinary virtues and he was driven (as will be seen) by an extraordinary longing for glory. Among his extraordinary virtues, perhaps his writing merits pride of place. Lincoln was, argues Walter Berns, "patriotism's poet"; the Gettysburg Address, says Berns, is "the most beautiful speech in the English language." Lincoln sought, in such poetic speeches as the Gettysburg Address and the Second Inaugural Address, "to cause us to love the Union as he and Henry Clay loved it, because of what it stood for": "What Lincoln did at Gettysburg was to create new mystic chords, stretching from a new battlefield and new graves, to our hearts and hearthstones, *all* over this broad land, South as well as North, reminding us of the cause written in our book, the Declaration of Independence." Speaking of the Second Inaugural, Berns adds: "Lincoln speaks to [Americans] as only a great poet can speak, reminding them of the cause that binds the generations."[11] Beyond this, many of Lincoln's prose speeches are also masterpieces of republican oratory, marrying inspiriting calls for republican virtue to enlightening explications of republican principle. The task of such speeches—for example, the Peoria speech of October 1854, or the July 4, 1861, speech to Congress—is above all to "educate and mold public opinion." What distinguishes Lincoln's oratory is his ability to appeal to both republican passion and republican reason while clearly subordinating the passion to the reason: enlightenment is almost always more fundamental than inspiration in Lincoln's oratory. With the exceptions of the Gettysburg Address and the Second Inaugural, Lincoln's great speeches, including his great war speeches, are remarkably prosaic and reasonable. These speeches are at bottom careful and precise and exacting explications of republican principle, not poetic appeals to republican passion: even the Gettysburg Address almost begins with a "proposition." The two aspects of Lincoln's oratory are complementary: as Berns reminds us, "love and rational judgment are not incompatible or irreconcilable, but they are different."[12]

Lincoln also possessed the more mundane virtues of the skillful politician. Here, I offer just one example, as a representative of many other stories that would illustrate similar virtues. This particular story displays Lincoln's extraordinary mastery of the men around him, not always recognized by those he mastered. The tale of Lincoln's achievement of supremacy over his Cabinet ministers, especially William Seward and Samuel Chase, is well enough known; it has been told with wit and insight by Gore Vidal in his novel *Lincoln*.[13] Another particularly good example of Lincoln's mastery of the great men around him occurred in January 1863, when

Lincoln decided to place the Army of the Potomac under the command of General Joseph Hooker. Here is the letter of appointment:

> General.
> I have placed you at the head of the Army of the Potomac. Of course I have done this upon what appear to me to be sufficient reasons. And yet I think it best for you to know that there are some things in regard to which, I am not quite satisfied with you. I believe you to be a brave and skilful soldier, which, of course, I like. I also believe you do not mix politics with your profession, in which you are right. You have confidence in yourself, which is a valuable, if not an indispensable quality. You are ambitious, which, within reasonable bounds, does good rather than harm. But I think that during Gen. Burnside's command of the Army, you have taken counsel of your ambition, and thwarted him as much as you could, in which you did a great wrong to the country, and to a most meritorious and honorable brother officer. I have heard, in such a way as to believe it, of your recently saying that both the Army and the Government needed a Dictator. Of course it was not *for* this, but in spite of it, that I have given you the command. Only those generals who gain successes, can set up dictators. What I now ask of you is military success, and I will risk the dictatorship. The government will support you to the utmost of its ability, which is neither more nor less than it has done and will do for all commanders. I much fear that the spirit which you have aided to infuse into the Army, of criticising their Commander, and withholding confidence from him, will now turn upon you. I shall assist you as far as I can, to put it down. Neither you, nor Napoleon, if he were alive again, could get any good out of an army, while such a spirit prevails in it.
> And now, beware of rashness. Beware of rashness, but with energy, and sleepless vigilance, go forward, and give us victories. (*CW* 6:78–79)

What an array of virtues must the writer of such a letter possess? Hooker was evidently chastened and humbled by the letter, and he was thereafter a grateful and loyal Lincoln man (*AL* 224–25). (It would be a better story if I could report that Hooker won great glory as a commander; he did not.)

No other statesman of the time possessed Lincoln's combination of political, moral, and intellectual virtues: the incisive and rigorous mind; the capacity to express himself in intransigent argument and in beautiful poetry; the intrepidity of moral judgment tempered by prudence of political judgment; the petty but essential skills of the party boss; the mastery of "great" men; and the ability to gain the confidence and affection of the people.

IV

Lincoln was also an ambitious man, an extraordinary lover of glory. But the love of glory in a statesman will often be a threat to republican institutions. A prince's glory, as Machiavelli argues, can often enough be secured while he otherwise "keep[s] the people occupied with festivals and spectacles"—circuses only, though probably the bread is implicit. The love of glory, then, might lead a statesman to offer the people security and even comfort, and a bit of play, but without real freedom, for the sake of his own glory. But perhaps even this portrait exaggerates the friendship of princes and peoples: "the people love quiet," Machiavelli concedes; and sometimes the love of glory cannot be satisfied quietly. A civil war, for example, might serve a prince's interest in glory, but not the people's interest in quiet and security. Lincoln understood that princely ambition sometimes takes forms unfriendly to republican aspirations: *that princes are often enemies of republics.*[14] Among Lincoln's most important contributions to democratic political thought are his reflections on this problem of political ambition.

We are reliably informed, by Lincoln's law partner William Herndon, that Lincoln's "ambition was a little engine that knew no rest."[15] Thoughtful observers of Lincoln have agreed with Herndon. The most important remark by Lincoln on his own ambition occurred at the end of the campaign in 1858:

> Ambition has been ascribed to me. God knows how sincerely I prayed from the first that this field of ambition might not be opened. I claim no insensibility to political honors; but today could the Missouri restriction be restored, and the whole slavery question replaced on the old ground of 'toleration' by *necessity* where it exists, with unyielding hostility to the spread of it, on principle, I would, in consideration, gladly agree, that Judge Douglas should never be *out*, and I never *in*, an office, so long as we both or either, live. (*CW* 3:334)

This passage suggests that Lincoln is afraid of his own ambition, that he knows he must struggle to crush it so far as there is no coincidence between his good and the public good. But it certainly reveals his awareness that the nation's unhappiness has presented him an opportunity to unleash his ambition—and that too must be troubling to an honorable man.

The question of Lincoln's ambition might not be so troubling but for the presence of a few remarkable sentences in Lincoln's "Address Before the Young Men's Lyceum of Springfield" on "the perpetuation of our political institutions" (*CW* 1:108–15).[16] Lincoln argues that the thirst for fame once sustained, but now threatens, republican institutions in America. Here are the offending sentences:

> Then, all that sought celebrity and fame, and distinction, expected to find them in the success of that experiment. Their *all* was staked upon it:—their destiny was *inseparably* linked with it. Their ambition aspired to display before an admiring world, a practical demonstration of the truth of a proposition, which had hitherto been considered, at best no better, than problematical; namely, *the capability of a people to govern themselves.* . . . The experiment is successful; and thousands have won their deathless names in making it so. But the game is caught; and I believe it is true, that with the catching, end the pleasures of the chase. This field of glory is harvested, and the crop is already appropriated. But new reapers will arise, and *they*, too, will seek a field. It is to deny, what the history of the world tells us is true, to suppose that men of ambition and talents will not continue to spring up amongst us. And, when they do, they will naturally seek the gratification of their ruling passion, as others have *so* done before them. The question then, is, can that gratification be found in supporting and maintaining an edifice that has been erected by others? Most certainly it cannot. (*CW* 1:113–14)

And then follows a stunning passage:

> Many great and good men sufficiently qualified for any task they should undertake, may ever be found, whose ambition would aspire to nothing beyond a seat in Congress, a gubernatorial or a presidential chair; *but such belong not to the family of the lion, or the tribe of the eagle.* What! Think you these places would satisfy an Alexander, a Caesar, or a Napoleon? Never! Towering genius disdains a beaten path. . . . It thirsts and burns for distinction; and, if possible, it will have it, whether at the expense of emancipating slaves, or enslaving free men. (*CW* 1:114)

Perhaps this passage reveals that Lincoln knows the experience of such ambition from the inside. But beyond this, and more certainly, he sees that a field for extraordinary ambition is likely to be open to statesmen of the next generation in America. Lincoln argues that attachment to republican institutions is on the decline among citizens generally (much of the speech concerns the danger of emerging mob rule) and that the presence of slavery in America will inevitably present an opportunity to one of the "loftiest genius" to grasp the glory of a Caesar or a Napoleon, "whether at the expense of emancipating slaves or enslaving freemen." From the point of view of such a man, Lincoln suggests, the fate of slavery counts for next to nothing—the fate of slavery is just an "expense" in a bigger game, even for the imagined Great Emancipator. If this passage anticipates Lincoln's later doctrine that a house divided against itself cannot stand—that the nation must sooner rather than later become all free or all slave—it also suggests that the battle to defeat slavery or to destroy the Republic by extending slavery and thereby abandoning the republican principles of the Declaration of Independence may be fought by men who care little or nothing about slavery: a Caesar from Illinois would be a Lincoln; a Caesar from South Carolina would be a Calhoun.

Can we conclude from this passage that Lincoln conceived of himself, then or later, as such a man? That is much more dubious. Lincoln continues:

> Is it unreasonable then to expect, that some man possessed of the loftiest genius, coupled with ambition sufficient to push it to its utmost stretch, will at some time, spring up among us? And when such a one does, it will require the people to be united with each other, attached to the government and laws, and generally intelligent, to successfully frustrate his designs. (*CW* 1:114)

Lincoln suggests here that a friend of republican institutions who understands the dangers of a new Caesar might undertake to assist the people, to unite them and to attach them to republican principles in anticipation of that danger.[17] Lincoln came to understand his own task to be the task of defending the Republic against the depredations of a new Caesar by "frustrating the designs" of that potential Caesar. But to perform this task required him to recall the people to the good habits of self-government, "to educate and mold public opinion" so that the people would again come "to be united with each other, attached to the government and laws, and generally intelligent."

And yet it is certainly true that Lincoln won enormous glory, a glory eclipsing even that won by the Founders of his country. There is no good reason to interpret Lincoln's democratic statesmanship as a refusal of glory rather than as the choice of the kind of glory that belongs to those who would "acquire it by doing good [rather than] harm" (*CW* 1:114). Lincoln cannot be thought to have in every respect regretted the calamity that nearly destroyed his nation in 1854, because only that calamity could give him the opportunity to exercise his extraordinary powers—and thereby to save his country by restoring it to its republican principles. And if, after taking the field and winning it, Lincoln imagined that his fellow citizens would build a monument like the Lincoln Memorial, perhaps he took some small pleasure in that imagination.

V

Lincoln knew how not to flatter the people: no American statesman was so capable of chastening the people in the spirit of "sincere friendship." The greatest example is the Second Inaugural. Lincoln later remarked that he thought this speech would "wear as well as—perhaps better than—any thing I have produced; but I believe it is not immediately popular. Men are not flattered by being shown that there is a difference of purpose between the Almighty and them" (*CW* 8:356). Here is the most memorable passage in that speech:

> Each looked for an easier triumph, and a result less fundamental and astounding. Both read the same Bible, and pray to the same God; and each invokes His aid against the other. It may seem strange that any men should dare to ask a just God's assistance in wringing their bread from the sweat of other men's faces; but let us judge not that we be not judged. The prayers of both could

not be answered; that of neither has been answered fully. The Almighty has his own purposes. "Woe unto the world because of offences! for it must needs be that offences come; but woe to that man by whom the offence cometh!" If we shall suppose that American Slavery is one of those offences which, in the providence of God, must needs come, but which, having continued through His appointed time, He now wills to remove, and that He gives to both North and South, this terrible war, as the woe due to those by whom the offence came, shall we discern therein any departure from those divine attributes which the believers in a Living God always ascribe to Him? Fondly do we hope—fervently do we pray—that this mighty scourge of war may speedily pass away. Yet, if God wills that it continue, until all the wealth piled by the bond-man's two hundred and fifty years of unrequited toil shall be sunk, and until every drop of blood drawn with the lash, shall be paid by another drawn with the sword, as was said three thousand years ago, so still it must be said "the judgments of the Lord, are true and righteous altogether." (*CW* 8:333)

This passage contains the fullest statement of Lincoln's own theological reflections arising from the question he began to put to himself, apparently, some time in late 1862: how could a just God have made this terrible war (cf. *CW* 5:403–4)? It is March 1865, and the victory of the North is at hand. This is the moment of Lincoln's greatest glory; it is the North's finest hour. Lincoln had achieved the fulfillment (though at an awful price) of his highest hopes: the restoration of the Union together with the emancipation of the slaves. But instead of celebration of a glorious victory, Lincoln offers a theological reflection to *humble and chasten* the victors. Why was this war so terrible? asks Lincoln. A just God, he answers, "gives to *both North and South*, this terrible war, as the woe due to those by whom the offence came." At this moment, Lincoln judges, celebration is best postponed: the people of the North must be warned—with grace and eloquence, to be sure, but the warning is nevertheless unmistakable—against hubris, against triumphalism, against a blindness to our own sins or vices.

Looking to the past, Lincoln reminds his fellow citizens that the offense is "American Slavery" and not only southern slavery (cf. *CW* 2:255). The present task, says Lincoln, is "to finish the work we are in; to bind up the nation's wounds; to care for him who shall have borne the battle, and for his widow, and his orphan"—but to do so in the full knowledge that these wounds were in the most important respects self-inflicted and that the binding and the caring present a suitable occasion for reflection on the failures (as much as the triumphs) of a republican people. For the future, Lincoln counsels restraint and generosity: "With malice toward none; with charity for all." The thought of reunion with the South had long been on Lincoln's mind, at least as far back as the First Inaugural in 1861, where he had said: "I am loth to close. We are not enemies, but friends. We must not be enemies" (*CW* 3:271). The task of reconstruction proved to be unmanageable after Lincoln's death; the enduring difficulties of that task are a vindication of Lincoln's worry and his warning.

VI

Lincoln's great adversary in the 1850s was Stephen Douglas. Douglas's own moderation, very different from Lincoln's, was expressed in the famous maxim, "I care not whether slavery is voted up or voted down." In his 1850s speeches and debates, Lincoln presents a powerful analysis of Douglas's moderation, which he argues is a contemptible fraud. As he put the point in 1854:

This *declared* indifference, but as I must think, covert *real* zeal for the spread of slavery, I can not but hate. I hate it because of the monstrous injustice of slavery itself. I hate it because it deprives our republican example of its just influence in the world—enables the enemies of free institutions, with plausibility, to taunt us as hypocrites—causes the real friends of freedom to doubt our sincerity, and especially because it forces so many really good men amongst ourselves into an open war with the very fundamental principles of civil liberty—criticising the Declaration of Independence, and insisting that there is no right principle of action but *self-interest*. (*CW* 2:255)

Douglas pretends to moderate neutrality between the extremist parties and thus to keep the peace between them; in fact, he is a witting or unwitting tool of the enemies of liberty. Lincoln will later go so far as to argue that Douglas was a participant in a horrible conspiracy, the hidden policy of the Democratic party of the 1850s, whose aim was to nationalize slavery. Such "care not" moderation is as weak as it is contemptible, and so no case for it can be made on grounds of political prudence. One cannot defend Douglas and other such moderates on the ground that their moderation is more likely to bring victory for the cause of justice than the immoderation of (for example) the abolitionists—as some of Douglas's later apologists would argue. Such "care not" moderates will always be defeated, says Lincoln, by those who do care—by those who experience the great political passions that make such moderation intolerable. One need only consider Douglas's own helpless journey in search of an elusive center in the 1850s, a journey that Lincoln foresees, sometimes even finding ways to give Douglas a little push: from the Missouri Compromise to popular sovereignty, to the repeal of the Missouri Compromise, to defense of the Dred Scott decision, to the Freeport Doctrine, to a federal slave code for the territories (though he finally resisted this last step). As the radicals quarrel, the center shifts and such moderates as Douglas find themselves driven before forces beyond their control. "Is it not a false statesmanship," Lincoln asks, "that undertakes to build up a system of policy upon the basis of caring nothing about *the very thing that every body does care the most about?*"—a thing which all experience has shown we care a very great deal about?" (*CW* 3:311). Perhaps moderates are, like Douglas, more often the dupes of the enemies of justice than they are quiet partisans of the lovers of justice, as Lincoln claimed to be.

In the aftermath of the passage of the Kansas-Nebraska Act (which repealed the Missouri Compromise in order to open the Kansas and Nebraska territories to slavery), Lincoln began to express certain doubts about the future of the American republic; indeed, during this period Lincoln's writings sometimes reveal a rather striking pessimism about the likely fate of the American experiment in republican government. Lincoln was fond of saying that "on the question of liberty, as a principle, we are not what we have been" (*CW* 2:318). He speaks of the "pure[,] fresh, free breath of the revolution": "the spirit of seventy-six and the spirit of Nebraska, are utter antagonisms; and the former is being rapidly displaced by the latter" (*CW* 2:249, 275). Or again: "The fourth of July has not quite dwindled away; it is still a great day—*for burning fire-crackers*!!!" (*CW* 2:319). But had not the Founders themselves been authors of an even more terrible compromise with the "monstrous injustice" of slavery, by establishing a Constitution that protected the peculiar institution within those states that might choose to preserve it? Had not the "ancient faith" of the Declaration already been betrayed in 1787? On what grounds does Lincoln argue that the betrayal of the principle of 1776 occurred not in 1787 but in 1854?

The Founders, Lincoln argues, placed slavery on a "course of ultimate extinction." They did so by embracing a principle, a policy, and a hope.[18] The *principle* of the Founding, and of Lincoln's conservative republicanism, was that slavery was wrong, a "monstrous injustice," and contrary to the principles of the American republic. Here is, as Lincoln says, "the sheet anchor of American republicanism": "no man is good enough to govern another man, *without that other's consent*" (*CW* 2:266). It is true that the Founders tolerated slavery, but they did so on grounds of necessity only: "*As those fathers marked it, so let it be again marked, as an evil not to be extended, but to be tolerated and protected only because of and so far as its actual presence among us makes that toleration and protection a necessity*" (*CW* 3:535). Lincoln adduces several pieces of evidence for this claim, beginning with the unwillingness of the Founders even to breathe the name "slavery" in a document that on three occasions directly, and on several more occasions indirectly, treats the institution: "the thing is hid away, in the constitution, just as an afflicted man hides away a wen or a cancer, which he dares not cut out at once, lest he bleed to death" (*CW* 2:274). But the principal evidence for Lincoln's claim that the Founders tolerated slavery only on grounds of necessity is the *policy* toward slavery that the Founders embraced.

The Founding *principle* was that slavery was wrong. The *policy* of the Founders was "the policy of prohibiting slavery in new territory." At the beginning of his first important speech on the slavery question, the Peoria speech of 1854, Lincoln announces: "I wish to MAKE and to KEEP the distinction between the EXISTING institution, and the EXTENSION of it, so broad, and so clear, that no honest man can misunderstand me, and no dishonest man, successfully misrepresent me" (*CW* 2:248). Here we approach one troubling aspect of Lincoln's moderation: he was prepared to maintain (as he says, "not grudgingly, but fully and fairly" [*CW* 3:535]) the existing institution of slavery, which was constitutionally protected. As Frederick Douglass would later say (not quite fairly but close enough to bring a wince): "To protect, defend, and perpetuate slavery in the states where it existed Abraham Lincoln was not less ready than any other President to draw the sword of the nation" (*OM* 312).[19] Lincoln maintains this posture almost to the end. As a result, the hot fights about slavery in the 1840s and 1850s that bring the nation to civil war concerned slavery in the federal territories only—not slavery in the slave states.

Lincoln was surely right about the Founders' policy: the evidence he brings to bear in defense of the claim that the Founders embraced such a policy—in the Peoria speech of 1854 (*CW* 2:247–83) and in the Cooper Institute address of 1860 (*CW* 3:522–50)—is overwhelming. (The Cooper Institute address, for example, presents a meticulous survey of the available historical evidence regarding the attitudes toward slavery expansion of the thirty-nine Founders who signed the original Constitution.) But soon the politics of slavery expansion began to get messy, as Lincoln conceded, first with the Louisiana Purchase and especially with the acquisition of new territory after the Mexican War.

The *principle* of the Founders was that slavery is a "monstrous injustice," incompatible with the principles of American republicanism; the *policy* of the Founders was a prohibition of slavery extension. The *hope* or purpose of the Founders, Lincoln argued, was that the *principle* and the *policy*, consistently maintained, would one day bring the peaceful extinction of slavery. And perhaps the hope was not altogether unreasonable. As long as "the great mass of mankind . . . consider slavery a great moral wrong," says Lincoln, "no statesman can safely disregard it" (*CW* 2:281–82). Those who would perpetuate slavery cannot abide the endurance of the moral opinion that "all men are created equal." On this point, Lincoln cites Henry Clay:

> They must blow out the moral lights around us, and extinguish that greatest torch of all which America presents to a benighted world. . . . They must penetrate the human soul, and eradicate the light of reason, and the love of liberty. Then, and not till then, when universal darkness and despair prevail, can you perpetuate slavery, and repress all sympathy, and all humane, and benevolent efforts among free men, in behalf of the unhappy portion of our race doomed to bondage. (*CW* 2:131)

Or, as Lincoln said, "repeal all past history, you still cannot repeal human nature. It will still be the abundance of man's heart, that slavery extension is wrong; and out of the abundance his heart, his mouth will continue to speak" (CW 2:271). Many, both enemies and friends of slavery, reasonably doubted whether the peculiar institution could long survive in the face of a universal moral opinion condemning it as unjust—and so they might reasonably have hoped for its "ultimate extinction" as long as that opinion was maintained. (And this argument does not yet take into account the very real political and economic consequences for the slave states of the increasing isolation that would have resulted had the policy of refusing slavery extension been consistently maintained.)

The Founders had placed slavery on a "course of ultimate extinction." And yet, Lincoln would write gloomily in 1855 that "experience has demonstrated, I think, that there is no peaceful extinction of slavery in prospect for us" (*CW* 2:318). Or again, from the House Divided speech:

> Either the *opponents* of slavery, will arrest the further spread of it, and place it where the public mind shall rest in the belief that it is in course of ultimate extinction; or its *advocates* will push it forward, till it shall become alike lawful in *all* the States, *old* as well as *new—North* as well as *South.*
> Have we no *tendency* to the latter condition? (*CW* 2:462)

What accounts for this pessimism? We must now examine the series of controversies respecting the status of slavery in those territories acquired after the ratification of the Constitution, principally through the Louisiana Purchase and the treaty concluding the Mexican War.

The Founders' policy of prohibiting expansion of slavery into new territories was gradually defeated; by 1854 or earlier, that policy had been revealed as a fraud (by the Kansas-Nebraska Act if not by the Compromise of 1850). The first great slavery struggle concerned Missouri, a part of the Louisiana acquisition into which slavery had already extended. Missouri sought admission as a slave state, and the North honorably resisted. Here was the first great test of the policy prohibiting slavery extension. The House and the Senate were divided in the way that came to be usual in the years to follow—the House dominated by the North, the Senate by the South—and a stalemate ensued. Missouri was admitted as a slave state in clear contravention of the Founders' policy. In exchange, slavery was prohibited in the territory north of 36° 30′ north latitude (including Iowa and Minnesota, and also, fatefully, Kansas and Nebraska); but it would be permitted in the territory south of that latitude. Here was the first unambiguous defeat of the Founders' policy of prohibiting extension of slavery into new territories.

Looking back from the vantage of the 1850s, Lincoln was prepared to excuse this settlement, brokered by Clay and celebrated more or less universally as a sacred covenant between North and South that forever settled the slavery question between the sections: after all, the concession seemed modest (Missouri) and the reward great (peaceful preservation of the Union). As he puts the point in his Peoria speech: "Much as I hate slavery, I would consent to the extension of it rather than see the Union dissolved, just as I would consent to any GREAT evil, to avoid a GREATER one" (*CW* 2:270). But this is a troubling argument; for Lincoln here expresses a willingness to accept a retreat from the policy of the Founders—on the basis of which slavery had been placed on a course of ultimate extinction—for the sake of preserving the Union. The concession of Missouri, however modest on the ground, was great in principle: at what point do such concessions undermine one's reasonable confidence that slavery will one day be extinguished, since that confidence had been founded on an unwillingness to compromise on precisely this point?

After the admission of Texas and the war with Mexico, culminating in further acquisitions, a question arose concerning the status of slavery in these new territories. Indeed, Lincoln and other Free Soil Whigs had vigorously opposed the war, at least in part because of their fear that this question would tear the Union apart; they had then sought to prohibit slavery in the whole of the newly acquired territory, a measure—the so-called Wilmot Proviso—that repeatedly passed in the House and just as often failed in the Senate. Once again, Clay attempted to broker a "great compromise," with the surprising assistance of Daniel Webster; but this time he failed, and he went home soon to die, and the compromise was saved in the end by the intervention of another moderate champion of Union, the young Stephen Douglas. The Compromise of 1850 once again made possible the extension of slavery into new territories (New Mexico and Utah); from the vantage of those prepared to defend the Founders' policy prohibiting slavery extension, it was a capitulation by the North. But once again, Lincoln approved the compromise, as he does explicitly in his eulogy to Clay, and again on the ground that the great evil of slavery *extension*—and not only the great evil of slavery where its actual presence made its toleration a necessity—would be preferable to the greater evil of dissolution of the Union. It now appears that Lincoln's moderation regarding slavery *cannot* be explained, wholly or in significant part, on the basis of his conviction that the Founders' policy prohibiting the extension of slavery had placed slavery on a "course of ultimate extinction." For that policy had already been abandoned, in deed though not quite in speech, by compromises that Lincoln admired and praised, and that had occurred prior to his firm resolution in 1854 to resist further capitulations to the South. So what, then, *is* the ground of Lincoln's moderation?

Why was Lincoln awakened from his political slumbers only in 1854, and not in 1850, when the South so brazenly resisted the admission of California as a free state in order to extract concessions from the North, including that slavery would be permitted in substantial parts of the Mexican acquisition?[20] The cases cannot be well distinguished on the ground that the Kansas-Nebraska Act opened new territory to slavery and was thus unfaithful to the policy of the Founders prohibiting slavery extension. By now that was old news. We must look elsewhere for an explanation of Lincoln's emerging pessimism regarding the prospects for American republicanism.

Although the *policy* of the Founders had been abandoned, more or less, over time, what about the *principle* that "no man is good enough to govern another man, *without that other's consent*"? Here is the first root of Lincoln's growing intransigence: "an increasing number of men," says Lincoln—including John Calhoun, among others—"for the sake of perpetuating slavery, are beginning to assail and to ridicule the white man's charter of freedom—the declaration that 'all men are created equal'" (*CW* 2:130). When a Southern congressman declared that the Declaration was "a self-evident lie," no one in a crowd of Nebraska men would rebuke him, Lincoln complains (*CW* 2:275). This gradual but fundamental transformation of moral opinion in the nation was not isolated within Southern elites. Douglas himself, Lincoln argues, had practically repudiated the Declaration of Independence. According to Douglas, the Founders did not mean that *all* men were created equal: rather, they "were speaking of British subjects on this continent being equal to British subjects born and residing in Great Britain." Lincoln mocks Douglas's Declaration: "We hold these truths to be self-evident that all British subjects who were on this continent eighty-one years ago, were created equal to all British subjects born and *then* residing in Great Britain" (*CW* 2:406–7). The most dangerous feature of the Kansas-Nebraska Act, then, was not that it opened Kansas and Nebraska to slavery (troubling though that was), but rather that Douglas and his partisan friends defended the act on the basis of principles—the doctrine of popular sovereignty and Douglas's "care not" posture toward slavery—that were incompatible with *the* fundamental principle of American republicanism, that "all men are created equal." According to Lincoln, this is precisely Douglas's role in the program of the Democratic political dynasty ("a conspiracy to make slavery national and perpetual" [*CW* 3:45]): "to *educate* and *mould* public opinion, at least *Northern* public opinion, to not *care* whether slavery is voted *down* or voted *up*" (*CW* 2:465). But this might be achieved only if those in the North were somehow persuaded to abandon their "ancient faith" in the self-evident truths of the Declaration of Independence. Lincoln might have been prepared to accept another slave territory or slave state for the sake of peace with the slave power, as he quietly admitted. But he would not abide this retreat from the *principles* of the Declaration.

The new policy of the Democratic political dynasty had raised the moral stakes in the struggle between the sections. The controversies would no longer concern merely the interest of the Southern states in protecting themselves from the growing strength of the North in the national councils, which might even justify slavery extension against the wishes of the Founders, as in the Missouri and New Mexico cases. Hereafter, the struggles would also concern *the* fundamental moral principle of the Republic. This is the ground of Lincoln's famous suggestion that the house divided against itself could not stand. The nation might endure, half-slave and half-free, so long as that divide did not raise any challenge to the principles of the Republic—so long, that is, as the peculiar institution was protected only as a matter of necessity and not as a matter of right. But once the struggle between the sections became a struggle about political right, nothing short of the victory of one section or the other would finally resolve this quarrel. That is what distinguished 1854 from all previous slavery controversies. It now began to appear that the Union would, one way or another, be destroyed in the ensuing struggle—probably by abandoning its fundamental moral principle, perhaps by dissolution. In the face of this prospect, Lincoln's choice was to advance a program that would open a third possibility: the victory of the *principle* of the North, a victory which could only be achieved by Southern capitulation on the question of political right and so almost certainly by war. As Lincoln said already in 1855, "experience has demonstrated, I think, that there is no peaceful extinction of slavery in prospect for us" (*CW* 2:318).

The fundamental quarrel between Stephen Douglas and Abraham Lincoln, then, concerned their irreconcilable efforts to educate public opinion, and especially public opinion in the North, regarding the fundamental principles of the American regime: either the spirit of '76 or the spirit of Nebraska must prevail.

VII

Moderation is the political virtue that mediates between reason and power. Reason never rules unfettered; perhaps the best practicable regime is therefore, almost everywhere and almost always, a regime whose virtue is not wisdom or justice but moderation, where moderation is the virtue that leaves room for reason, and so for some measure of justice. It is the task of a statesman to grasp the opportunities that will from time to time present themselves in such a place, to teach the stronger to listen to good reasons, to hear the pleas of the friends of justice.

In democracies, it is the task of the democratic statesman to educate the public mind, to teach the people, who are naturally as disposed to wickedness and to folly as are the mighty in other regimes, to love justice, or at least to hear the reasons of the friends of justice. The moderation of such a statesman consists in a prudent regard for the troubles of this task: shouting will not do. The moderate statesman must look now toward justice—toward the principle of the Declaration, that "all men are created equal," for example—and now toward the people, whose passions and prejudices and interests must be consulted—accommodated, tamed, educated—in a democracy. Sometimes those passions and prejudices will be for a time incurable: in such a case, silence or even a deceptive indulgence of prejudice is demanded (see *CW* 3:16). But sometimes the passions and interests of the people might somehow be attached to a nobler end, and the people might thereby be led to listen to the claims of the friends of justice.

What is true of democratic statesmanship in democracy is true above all in a liberal democracy. For that same Declaration which announces the inalienable rights of man also affirms that government derives its just powers from the consent of the governed. Here we have competing principles of justice, and these principles of justice are not always in harmony, as the terrible case of American slavery sufficiently reveals. So Lincoln's task, the task of a democratic statesman in a *liberal* democratic polity, is not only to accommodate the *power* of the people, who are sometimes wicked and sometimes foolish. Lincoln was also obliged to recognize the *justice* of the claim of the people to rule. And he did so wholeheartedly. That is the *principle* of Lincoln's moderation: that the claims of justice made on behalf of the slave ("all men are created equal") had to be harmonized with the lesser, but respectable, claim of the people to rule (both because the people are the stronger and because republican government is somehow just).

Lincoln's democratic instincts were partly grounded on his conviction, only slowly defeated by the unhappy experience of Southern intransigence, that it would be better for the sake of Union and therefore—"paradox though it may seem" (*CW* 1:348)—for the sake of the cause of human liberty in the nation and in the world, for the defeat of slavery to come by *consent* over time (even over a rather long time) than that it be imposed, perhaps by force and in any case in such a way as to destroy the Constitution or the Union. The best evidence for this is an episode from the summer of 1862—when Lincoln vigorously pressed on border state representatives a proposal for voluntary, gradual, and compensated emancipation in those states. When that proposal was finally rejected, in July 1862, Lincoln took the decision within days to issue the Emancipation Proclamation, by which he finally abandoned his long-standing hope to achieve emancipation by consent.[21]

For Lincoln, the democratic principle of justice, the principle of consent, was a secondary (though respectable) principle, and there were moments when it had to be abandoned, but only with great regret. That is why Lincoln could never be persuaded to accept, even on grounds of expediency, Douglas's popular sovereignty principle—that is, Douglas's unqualifiedly democratic policy of letting the people choose slavery or not by consent. This is the error of William Seward and Horace Greeley in 1858, who quietly urged Illinois Republicans to make peace with Douglas, because for a time expediency seemed to counsel the antislavery party to embrace the hope that slavery might be defeated by popular sovereignty. For many years, Lincoln and other prudent men of his time were prepared to bet that slavery could be defeated by consent, but nevertheless in such a way as to preserve the Union and the Constitution understood as founded on the principles of the Declaration. The tragedy of the 1850s and the Civil War is that he lost that bet; his greatness as a statesman consists at least in part in this, that he knew the bet was lost before others did, and that he was prepared to act with what Charnwood called "deadly moderation" once the bet was lost.

VIII

Let us conclude with an account of the principles of justice that were prior for Lincoln to the abolitionists' principle of justice and that guided Lincoln's expedient reluctance to press for abolition as early, as often, and as vigorously as he might have done, even when he had the constitutional power to do so. Lincoln was devoted neither to the Union simply nor to a Union as formed by the Constitution—for if "the *Union,* and the *Constitution,* are the *picture* of *silver,*" the Declaration of Independence is the "apple of gold" around which that picture was framed (*CW* 4:169). Lincoln was devoted to the Union, as formed by the Constitution, and as dedicated to the principles of the Declaration. Dedication to this complex unity of Union, Constitution, and Declaration sometimes required a patient willingness to wait on the people when they were yet unprepared to act decisively against slavery. But this was prudence and not quite a demand of justice. Lincoln was not always so restrained by a concern for consent—not in 1855, when Lincoln said that "the peaceful extinction of slavery is not in prospect for us" and undertook a course of policy that risked civil war; and not in 1862, when Lincoln abandoned his quest for voluntary and compensated emancipation in favor of emancipation imposed by advancing armies.

The move from Union to Constitution to Declaration is an ascent, and when dedication to the Declaration required Lincoln to abandon constitutional form and dedication to the Union for its own sake, he did not hesitate to do so. He busted the Union and made a civil war, and he did not hesitate to fight that war without excessive fastidiousness as to constitutional form. Lincoln was prepared to use nondemocratic means to achieve liberal ends—whether these nondemocratic means were despotic or even unconstitutional is of course another question. Even this picture, of an ascent from Union to Constitution to Declaration, where the priority of the principles of the Declaration might sometimes justify closing one's eyes to threats to the Union or the Constitution, does not quite do justice to Lincoln's extraordinary prudence. There were times when Lincoln was prepared to "hold a veil," as Montesquieu puts the point when discussing a similar question, over the Declaration for the sake of the Constitution—as when the North acquiesced, with Lincoln's approval, in the compromises of 1850 or the admission of Missouri to statehood a generation before, in betrayal of the Founders' Declaration, for the sake of constitutional Union and in the hope that preserving that Union might yet be the best way to remove the veil from the Declaration.[22] And there were times when Lincoln was prepared as well to "hold a veil" over the Constitution or the Union. But in the end, for Lincoln, dedication to Union and to the Constitution could only be justified, in the presence of the monstrous injustice of slavery, so long as the hope endured that the principles of the Declaration would one day thereby be vindicated and that the ultimate extinction of slavery would finally be achieved.

Lincoln embraced several competing principles of justice. First and fundamental, the cries for justice of the slaves demanded an answer. No defensible statesmanship during this period could fail to place at the foundation this injunction: that, sooner rather than later, slavery must die. This was bedrock for Lincoln. Second, the claims of Union deserved respect. This Union established a novel republicanism on the basis of a new science of politics; in 1850 it was not ridiculous to think that the future of republicanism around the world would rise and fall with the fate of this lonely republican experiment. Moreover, preservation of the Union was reasonably thought to be the best means to defeat slavery; the cause of liberty itself, including for the slaves, might depend on preserving the Union that now protected slavery but whose principle of human equality provided the likeliest route to the ultimate destruction of slavery. Third, the just claims of the people to rule in a liberal democratic republic were reflected in Lincoln's aspiration, until the last moment, to secure the destruction of slavery by consent and not by means of the exercise of princely power over a people that would not act for themselves. Fourth, and not least, Lincoln shared the aspiration of prudent statesmen during his time to seek every means of securing the defeat of slavery without civil war, a war which turned out to be more horrible than even the most far-seeing could have imagined. What distinguishes Lincoln's moderate and democratic statesmanship is that he felt the pull of each of these claims of justice. That is the moderation of a democratic statesman: perhaps there is no more splendid virtue than moderation, after all.

Notes

1. Here and throughout, I rely heavily on Lord Charnwood, *Abraham Lincoln* (Lanham, Md.: Madison Books, [1916] 1996), the finest of the Lincoln biographies (hereafter cited in the text as *AL*). The passage that serves as an epigraph appears on *AL* 325. I also rely heavily on another splendid appreciation of Lincoln's democratic statesmanship, Frederick Douglass's "Oration in Memory of Abraham Lincoln," in *The Life and Writings of Frederick Douglass*, ed. Philip S. Foner, 5 vols. (New York: International Publishers, 1955), 4:309–19, hereafter cited as *OM*. For the writings of Abraham Lincoln, I use the *Collected Works of Abraham Lincoln*, ed. Roy P. Basler, 8 vols. (New Brunswick, N.J.: Rutgers University Press, 1953), hereafter *CW* followed by volume and page number.

2. For a more direct approach to Lincoln's political thought in the 1850s, and to the wisdom of Lincoln's understanding of the principles of the Declaration of Independence, see Harry V. Jaffa, *The Crisis of the House Divided: An Interpretation of the Issues in the Lincoln-Douglas Debates* (Chicago: University of Chicago Press, 1982). On the importance for Lincoln of educating public opinion, see Ralph Lerner, *Revolutions Revisited* (Chapel Hill: University of North Carolina Press, 1994), 89–94.

3. John Locke, *Second Treatise of Government*, sec. 176.

4. The story was attributed to Lincoln in a Democratic joke book as early as 1864. For the credibility of the story and Lincoln's plausible denial, see *Recollected Words of Abraham Lincoln*, ed. Don E. Fehrenbacher and Virginia Fehrenbacher (Stanford, Calif.: Stanford University Press, 1996), 92–93, 147, 349, 444.

5. See James M. McPherson, *Battle Cry of Freedom* (New York: Ballantine Books, 1988), 117–44.

6. Here is one further example of the capaciousness of Lincoln's "human sympathies." In 1846, Lincoln was accused of infidelity by a political opponent during a campaign. He refuted that charge in part as follows: "I do not think I could myself, be brought to support a man for office, whom I knew to be an open enemy of, and scoffer at, religion. Leaving the higher matter of eternal consequences, between him and his Maker, I still do not think any man has the right thus to insult the feelings, and injure the morals, of the community in which he may live." This response to the charge of infidelity is the more remarkable for what precedes it—namely, a tolerably clear confession that the charge itself was true, more or less, culminating in this joke: "it is true that in early life I was inclined to believe in what is called the 'Doctrine of Necessity' . . . ; and I have sometimes (with one, two or three, but never publicly) tried to maintain this opinion in argument. The habit of arguing thus however, I have, entirely left off for more than five years" (*CW* 1:382). The handbill is a marvelous example of civility or civic friendship: avoiding as it does *both* the preening moralizing of priest-politicians *and* the more or less open disrespect for religion of some civil libertarians. That is, Lincoln here offered respect as something due to the religious of his community; and he expected respect in turn, from the religious, for his own respectful heterodoxy, which he did little to hide. It seems to have worked, a credit to both Lincoln and his constituents.

7. Montesquieu, *The Spirit of the Laws*, bk. IV, chap. 5.

8. William Lloyd Garrison, in the first issue of *The Liberator*, as reported in Henry Mayer, *All on Fire: William Lloyd Garrison and the Abolition of Slavery* (New York: St. Martin's Press, 1998), 111.

9. On Lincoln's patriotism, see Walter Berns, *Making Patriots* (Chicago: University of Chicago Press, 2001), chaps. 5–6.

10. Joseph H. Choate, *Abraham Lincoln and Other Addresses in England* (New York: The Century Co., 1910), 22–24.

11. Berns, *Making Patriots*, 94, 97–98.

12. Berns, *Making Patriots*, 98.

13. Gore Vidal, *Lincoln: A Novel* (New York: Ballantine Books, 1984).

14. See Machiavelli, *The Prince*, trans. Harvey C. Mansfield, Jr. (Chicago: University of Chicago Press, 1985), chaps. 9, 19, 21.

15. See the discussion in Jaffa, *Crisis of the House Divided*, 189–90.

16. Students of Lincoln have learned from Edmund Wilson and above all from Harry Jaffa that this is a careful and challenging speech and that the reflections in it on political ambition are profoundly disquieting. See the chapter on Lincoln in Edmund Wilson's *Patriotic Gore* (New York: Oxford University Press, 1962) and the chapter on the Lyceum speech in Jaffa's *Crisis* for more thorough analyses of the

argument of this speech. Lincoln was only twenty-nine at the time of the speech.

17. Too many students of Lincoln have, I think, been too readily enthralled by the thought of Lincoln as the Caesar from Illinois. Harry Jaffa (*Crisis*, 23 and 188) raises a crushing objection to this way of thinking about Lincoln. "Was the cause of popular government but the matter from which Lincoln's own fame was to be wrought?" Jaffa asks. If one follows that thought to it conclusion, one is eventually driven, argues Jaffa, to ask this question: "[I]f Douglas had as good a solution to the problem of slavery . . . as Lincoln had, then what justification did Lincoln have to oppose Douglas and to bring on such an angry . . . struggle? The inference is well-nigh inescapable that Lincoln opposed Douglas only to further his own ambitions, [and] that he deliberately accepted the chance of civil war (which Douglas repeatedly accused him of inviting) by his house divided doctrine. . . . If Lincoln forced an illusory alternative upon the country, he must be accused of bringing on the very crisis he predicted, with the end in view not the future freedom of the nation's soil . . . but the political future of A. Lincoln." Few historians have been willing to level that kind of "devastating" charge against Lincoln, however captivated some might be with the imagination of Lincoln as the Caesar from Illinois.

18. This framework is presented in Donald Fehrenbacher, *Prelude to Greatness: Lincoln in the 1850s* (Stanford, Calif.: Stanford University Press, 1962).

19. The (mild) unfairness in Douglass's remark is this: Lincoln argued that the constitutional duty to "protect" and "defend" the institution of slavery in the Southern states would remain binding only so long as the Union established by that Constitution remained dedicated to the principles of the Declaration of Independence, and hence to the "ultimate extinction," not the "perpetuation," of slavery in the Southern states.

20. It is worth noting that Charnwood criticizes Lincoln's judgment regarding the compromises of 1850. "The greatest minds in American politics . . . viewed the question otherwise, but, in the light of what followed, it seems a signal and irreparable error that, when the spirit of aggression rising in the South had taken definite shape in a demand which was manifestly wrongful, it was bought off and not met with a straightforward refusal" (*AL* 77).

21. A further important instance of Lincoln's moderation should be mentioned. The story of Lincoln's conduct of the war should properly have a place in a full account of Lincoln's moderation that is as great as the story of his moderation during the 1850s. Lincoln was reluctant to accede to policies that might transform the Civil War into a "remorseless revolutionary struggle" (as he once named his fear) over the status of slavery in the nation (*CW* 5:49). This reluctance greatly troubled his more radical Republican and abolitionist friends; it was manifested above all in his early understanding of the proper war aim of the North—Union only, not emancipation. According to the ordinary view, some combination of prudence (worry about driving away the border states and Northern Unionist supporters of the war) and constitutional scruple (worry about the limits of presidential or even congressional power to free the slaves) led Lincoln to resist the move toward emancipation. These arguments are true enough. But it is worth emphasizing that Lincoln's reluctance to impose emancipation on an unwilling people is founded in part on his sense of his duties as a *democratic* statesman—and, more generally, on his eager desire that emancipation be achieved by some form of popular consent. That concern is the source of his continuing efforts to induce the border states to accept gradual and compensated emancipation, including as late as the December 1862 Annual Message to Congress, in which he proposed several constitutional amendments encouraging such a policy (*CW*, 5:530). Only after these efforts had been conclusively defeated did Lincoln decide to issue the Emancipation Proclamation, and then only as "an act of justice, warranted by the Constitution, upon military necessity" (*CW* 6:30).

22. Montesquieu, *The Spirit of the Laws*, bk. XII, chap. 20

PART FOUR:

GROWTH OF AN EMPIRE
(1865–1945)

》➤◄《

Chapter 23

Feminism as an American Project:
The Political Thought of Elizabeth Cady Stanton

Melissa S. Williams

W*e hold these truths to be self-evident: that all men and women are created equal.* . . .
So states the Declaration of Sentiments, the manifesto of the women's rights movement
launched by the first Women's Rights Convention in Seneca Falls, New York, in July
of 1848 (*HWS* 1:70–71, emphasis added).[1] Elizabeth Cady Stanton (1815–1902) was the chief
organizer of this convention and was primarily responsible for framing the Declaration that
issued from it. The Declaration of Sentiments followed the form and language of the Declaration
of Independence with great precision, down to enumerating precisely eighteen grievances against
men's rule over women. There was a "long train of abuses" that justified women in throwing off
men's dominion: the denial of the franchise; married women's lack of property rights; and
women's lack of legal personality. Women's right to independence from men—financially,
intellectually, morally, and politically—was the enduring theme of Stanton's political as well as
her more philosophical writing. From the outset, her leadership placed the American movement
for women's rights squarely within the revolutionary tradition of liberal egalitarianism.

As chief founder and leader of the American suffrage movement, Stanton's greatest institutional legacy, realized eighteen years after her death, was the 19th Amendment to the United
States Constitution. Of course, she did not achieve women's electoral enfranchisement alone. She
shares that distinction above all with Susan B. Anthony, her closest friend and collaborator, who
is often remembered more clearly and fondly by textbooks than is Stanton. But if Anthony was
the movement's field marshall, Stanton was its preeminent theoretician. Burdened with the care
of her seven children, Stanton was for many years of the women's movement unable to carry out
the strenuous work of delivering its message on speaking tours. Anthony performed this work
tirelessly, but she relied heavily on Stanton for the ideas and arguments she expressed in those
speeches. In a moment of desperate need for the text of of an important speech, Anthony wrote
to Stanton:

> [F]or the love of me and for the saving of the *reputation of womanhood*, I beg you, with one baby
> on your knee and another at your feet, and four boys whistling, buzzing, hallooing *Ma, Ma*, set
> yourself about the work. It is of but small moment *who writes* the address, but of *vast moment*
> that it be *well done*. . . . Now will you *load my gun*, leaving me only to pull the trigger and let fly
> the powder and ball?[2]

Stanton was doubly constituted as an activist and an intellectual, and each persona blended
with the other in a manner that was simultaneously enriching and limiting. Her conviction that

the principles of the Declaration of Independence were equally applicable to women was what produced her activism. Her activism brought her into contact with women from a broad spectrum of social backgrounds, and this led her to expand her vision of women's equality and social reform. Yet her radicalism on questions of religion—in particular, her rejection of the divine authority of the Bible's teachings—ultimately alienated her from the rest of the movement and rendered her politically powerless. And her anger at the Republican party's failure to support woman suffrage led her to make racist arguments repudiating the 15th Amendment's enfranchisement of black men, arguments that contradicted her own stated principles.

The complex interaction between Stanton's theoretical commitments and her political activities constitutes one challenge in synthesizing her political thought. The fact that she did not write a systematic treatise on politics constitutes another. Stanton left a wide array of writings, and we must cull her political thought from them. These writings include her autobiography, *Eighty Years and More* (1898); her many political speeches; her letters to Anthony and others in the women's movement; her introduction and commentaries on the Bible in her controversial project, *The Woman's Bible* (1895); and her essays, most notably "The Solitude of Self" (1892), written in her later years.

Stanton's political thought begins from the premises of the two Declarations' "self-evident truths": the natural equality of human beings, the existence of basic human rights, and consent as the foundation of legitimate government. A granddaughter of an officer (James Livingston) under George Washington's command during the American Revolution, Stanton believed that the Revolution's republican principles amply provided for justice toward women as well as toward men of all races and classes (*EY* 3–4). Blind custom, class selfishness, and stubborn prejudice were the only real obstacles to women's emancipation as they were to black emancipation; reason was all on the side of full civil and political equality for all American citizens. As she stated in her first speech before the New York state legislature in 1854: "The tyrant, Custom, has been summoned before the bar of Common Sense. . . . Yes, gentlemen, in republican America, in the nineteenth century, we, the daughters of the revolutionary heroes of '76, demand at your hands the redress of our grievances" (*HWS* 1:595).

Stanton conceded that men's achievements in the arts, in letters, and in the sciences surpassed those of women; but men's advantage in these domains was no evidence of superior minds. Rather, it was the inevitable consequence of the obstacles placed in women's paths. "Man's intellectual superiority," she wrote, "cannot be a question until woman has had a fair trial. When we shall have had our freedom to find out our own sphere, when we shall have had our colleges, our professions, our trades, for a century, a comparison then may be justly instituted" (*ECS* 29). Stanton frequently cited a German proverb that "every woman comes into the world with a stone on her head" (*ECS* 115). Yet, she argued, wherever the stone has been lifted—wherever doors have been opened to women—women have had no difficulty holding their own against men. Indeed, she sometimes suggested that women would exceed men's achievements once they had greater opportunity. Where girls have had equal access to education, for example, they have "proven superior to the boys" (*SS* 134).

Neither is there any reason to suppose men to be women's moral superiors, Stanton maintained. If anything, the evidence all runs in the contrary direction. For example, she asked how often women were convicted for public drunkenness or for violent crimes. Thus, Stanton sometimes succumbed to the temptation to present women as morally superior to men (*ECS* 121). This argument was common in the rhetoric of the temperance movement, and perhaps Stanton borrowed it from this sometime-ally of the women's rights movement. On the whole, however, she argued that nature had not made women morally better or worse than men. Those virtues that were touted as women's distinct superiority over men were, she argued, the virtues of self-sacrifice, submissiveness, and docility that made women appealing to men—and kept them in subordination to men (*ECS* 223–24). Far better to relinquish any advantages accruing to women's claim to gentle virtue in favor of full and equal standing as moral agents. If selflessness is a virtue, she argued, let men display it as well as women. "I would have the same code of morals for both" (*ECS* 30).

Even physical differences between men and women give no evidence of men's superiority. In many places in the world, women do physical work more demanding than any refined gentleman in America could hope to sustain. Indeed, one of the forms of woman's oppression is that the burden of physical labor is much more demanding than what men shoulder for themselves. Stanton repeatedly noted other cultures' practice whereby women were yoked with mules or cattle to pull the plow through the field while the men oversaw the work (*ECS* 29 and 210). Women have fought bravely as warriors in many places and times (*ECS* 31). What differences now exist between the sexes' physical capacities are, like intellectual and moral differences, partially if not wholly traceable to the different socialization of the sexes. "We cannot say what the woman might be physically, if the girl were allowed all the freedom of the boy in romping, climbing, swimming, playing whoop and ball" (*ECS* 30).

On Stanton's view, the only significant difference between men and women is that women bear children. But she regarded this as a capacity, not a disability. "There would be more sense in insisting on man's limitations because he can not be a mother, than on woman's because she can be. Surely maternity is an added power and development of some of the most tender sentiments of the human heart and not a 'limitation.'" While child rearing consumes woman's energies and makes it more difficult for her to undertake other pursuits, it also "fits her for much of the world's work; a large share of human legislation would be better done by her because of this deep experience" (*SS* 119). For most moral and practical purposes, then, Stanton is clear that the conditions and abilities of women are the same as those of men:

> We do not find ourselves in human life compelled to spread different tables, to provide apartments at higher or lower degrees of heat for the different sexes. We go to the same churches and lectures, swallow the same theology, go to the same theatres, operas, balls and parties, breathing the same carbonic acid gas. We truck in the same streetcars, railroads, and steamboats and are smashed up and blown up in the same way. . . . Behold! Man eats, drinks, sleeps, and so does woman. He loves, is religious, penitent, prayerful, reverent; and so is woman. He hates, is irritable, impatient, unreasonable, tyrannical; so is woman. (*SS* 132)

Stanton reasoned that the natural equality and essential sameness of men and women logically dictates that they should have the same opportunities, the same responsibilities, and the same rights under law. Yet both society and law treated women as men's subordinates in every respect, and the injustice of this treatment is itself a self-evident truth. Women have reason, but they were barred from colleges and universities and excluded from the professions. Women are spiritual beings, but they were denied the right to act as ministers of the church. Single women had property, and the law recognized them as property owners by taxing them. But they were not permitted to vote for the officers of the state that taxed them, and it is almost needless to add that they could not be elected as political officers themselves. The Revolution's leaders were right to proclaim that "taxation without representation is tyranny," Stanton argued, and there is no simpler demonstration of men's tyranny over women than the fact that women are taxed without having a voice in government.[3]

Single women, at least, had the advantage of a legally recognized right to own property. For married women, circumstances were much worse. Instead of having a right to own property, women were treated as the property of their husbands. Marriage rendered a woman "civilly dead": it subsumed a woman's legal personality under that of her husband. A married woman was not held legally responsible even for her crimes so long as they were committed in the presence of her husband (*HWS* 1:70). If a woman had to work for wages in order to sustain her family, those wages were legally her husband's property to do with as he wished. He could, and often did, take his wife's hard-won earnings to the tavern, drink them away in an evening, and return home to vent his drunken anger on her and their children. Yet the law smiled upon him (*HWS* 1:602). In loveless marriages, men's legal right of sexual access to their wives' bodies made marriage "nothing more or less than legalized prostitution" (*ECS* 129). While a woman had at least an equal interest with her husband in the rearing of their children, she had no legal power to resist his arbitrary authority in dictating their fate. If her husband wished to apprentice his son to supplement his income, rather than educating the child, the wife had no power to resist him (*HWS* 1:602). Reforms such as the Married Woman's Property Bill, which was passed by the New York state legislature in 1848, were the "dawning of civil existence for woman, for now the 'femme covert' must have the right to make contracts" (*HWS* 1:600). Nevertheless, much of married women's subordination to their husbands remained untouched by legal reform.

Of all the legal reforms needed to make women's condition just, none was more urgent or fundamental than the franchise. Stanton's insistence on this point sometimes put her at odds with other advocates for women's rights who believed it so radical a proposal that it would endanger the rest of their agenda for political change. At the Seneca Falls convention, her resolution demanding the franchise passed by a very small margin; and it would not have passed at all had Frederick Douglass not risen to speak eloquently in its defense (*HWS* 1:73). Stanton and Anthony often received a more sympathetic hearing from both men and women when they focused on the reform of marriage laws and the recognition of women's economic rights. Yet both remained firmly committed to the primacy of the vote. "While we would yield to none in the earnestness of our advocacy of these claims, we make a broader demand for the enfranchisement of woman, as the only way in which all her just rights can be permanently secured" (*ECS* 100). To have just marriage laws, for example, "the wife and mother must have a voice in the governing power and must be heard . . . in the halls of legislation" (*EY* 228). "Depend upon it," Stanton wrote, "this is the point to attack, the stronghold of the fortress—*the one* woman will find the most difficult to take, *the one* man will most reluctantly give up" (*HWS* 1:812).

The franchise was the key goal of the woman's rights movement not only as an instrument for bringing about other reforms but also as a symbol of women's social and political standing. The lack of the vote was an ongoing affront to women's dignity as persons and their status as citizens. Stanton's rhetoric on this point often played upon the class and racial prejudices of her white audiences, as in her 1854 address to the New York state legislature:

> We are persons; native, free-born citizens; property-holders, taxpayers; yet we are denied the exercise of our right to the elective franchise. . . . We are moral, virtuous, and intelligent, and in all respects quite equal to the proud white man himself, and yet by your laws we are classed with idiots, lunatics, and negroes; and though we do not feel honored by the place assigned us, yet, in fact, our legal position is lower than that of either; for the negro can be raised to the dignity of a voter if he posssess himself of $250; the lunatic can vote in his moments of sanity, and the idiot, too, if he be a male one. (*HWS* 1:595–96)

Stanton was clear that women's emancipation depended above all on their independence from men both in politics and in other spheres of life. This belief formed the core of her insistence on woman suffrage. Women did not seek men's protection or special recognition for the distinctive virtues of womanhood.

We, as a class, are tired of one kind of protection, that which leaves us everything to do, to dare, and to suffer, and strips us of all means for its accomplishment. We would not tax man to take care of us. No, the Great Father has endowed all his creatures with the necessary powers for self-support, self-defense, and protection. We do not ask man to represent us; it is hard enough in times like these for many to carry backbone enough to represent himself. (*HWS* 1:684)

Women must take on the work of representing themselves because men's experience gives them a poor understanding of women's true interests. "[W]oman alone can understand the height, the depth, the length, and the breadth of her own degradation. Man cannot speak for her, because he has been educated to believe that she differs from him so materially, that he cannot judge of her thoughts, feelings, and opinions by his own" (*ECS* 28). The result is that men face a stark conflict of interests when they legislate for women. It is as impossible for men to legislate in women's interest as it is for the nobleman to legislate in the interest of the serf—or the slave-holder for the slave. "[I]n each case, the one in power fails to apply the immutable principles of right to any grade but his own" (*HWS* 1:597). Men find it impossible to conceive of women as possessing equal capacities to their own, and as long as this remains true, their legislation will be unjustly biased.

Women's independent exercise of the electoral franchise was a necessary condition of their emancipation, but Stanton became increasingly convinced that it was not a sufficient condition. The more she saw of the circumstances of working-class and middle-class women, the more she came to believe in the importance of women's economic independence. Existing laws and social customs constituted an elaborate scheme for women's enforced dependence upon men for their material well-being. Women were reared from childhood to be pleasing to men so that they could hope for the financial security of marriage to a good provider. But at the same time, women were forcibly excluded from the education and from the occupations that could enable them to support themselves without a man's assistance. As a consequence of irresponsible or abusive husbands, or of widowhood, women were too often deprived of the stable support of a male provider and thrown back on their own ill-developed resources. "Fathers, Brothers, Husbands die, banks fail, houses are consumed with fire, friends prove treacherous, creditors grasping and debtors dishonest, and the skill and cunning of a girl's own brains and hands are the only friends that are ever with her, the only source of means of protection and support" (*SS* 114). Women who are secure in their ability to provide for themselves have much greater protection against abusive husbands since they can much more easily leave a household in which they are being ill-treated.

Men have nothing to fear from women's economic independence. Indeed, if we examine their behavior closely, we find that men much prefer women of independent means (*SS* 145). Women's financial independence makes for a healthier marriage—a marriage in which each partner is dedicated to "mutual help and happiness and for the development of all that is noblest in each other" (*EY* 229). A woman with her own means of supporting herself has no need to rush into marriage, and her husband can be confident that she has married him for love rather than out of desperate need.

Women's strong interest in economic independence was one of the keystones in Stanton's arguments for enhancing women's access to education and employment training. Girls should be educated to every useful social pursuit, she argued, and not only the traditional domestic occupations. "I do not wish to undervalue domestic avocations, but the tasks of women vary as much as the tasks of men, and to educate all women for teachers and seamstresses, cooks and chambermaids is to make the supply in the home sphere greater than the demand, thus permanently to keep down wages and degrade all these branches of labor" (*SS* 147). Stanton urged young women to pursue every conceivable occupation, from telegraph operator to homeopathic physician, from theologian to president (*SS* 154). In doing so, they promote not only their gendered interest in pecuniary independence from men but also their human interest in self-development. "It is a great truth to impress on the mind of every girl that she is an independent, creative wildflower, made primarily for her own happiness, making self-development and self-support and the highest good of the race the end of her being" (*SS* 146).

For Stanton, both political and economic independence were intimately connected to something even more fundamental: moral and intellectual independence. The greatest challenge women face is to throw off the weight of irrational custom from their own minds as well as from those of men. Just as custom leads Chinese women to hobble themselves through footbinding and Hindu women to throw themselves on their husbands' funeral pyres, it also leads American women to see themselves only as men's helpmeets and as the ornaments of their husbands' households. The tyranny of custom is often indistinguishable from the tyranny of majority opinion, and neither can offer an adequate response to rational arguments against women's subjugation.

> From our standpoint we would honor any Chinese woman who claimed the right to her feet and powers of locomotion; the Hindu women who refused to ascend the funeral pyre of their husbands; the Turkish women who threw off their masks and veils and left the harem; the Mormon women who abjured their faith and demanded monogamic relations. Why not equally honor the intelligent minority of American women who protest against the artificial disabilities by which their freedom is limited and their development arrested? . . . That a majority of the women of the United States accept, without protest, the disabilities which grow out of their disfranchisement is simply an evidence of their ignorance and cowardice, while the minority who demand a higher political status clearly prove their superior intelligence and wisdom. (*EY* 318)

The conquest of blind custom and prejudice by reason was, in Stanton's view, the defining feature of the American project and of her age. "This nineteenth century" was the century of progress, and Stanton was ever optimistic that the forces of conservatism could not hold it back.[4] Progress depended on the vigilance and activism of individuals with progressive ways of thinking; it was not something that would occur inevitably, without conscious human agency. But Stanton had faith that the American spirit of republicanism, with its celebration of freedom, independence, and equality, was the same spirit that lay behind the nineteenth century's movements for social and political reform. One expression of this confidence was her work with Matilda Joslyn Gage and Susan B. Anthony to begin the project of publishing the *History of Woman Suffrage* in the late 1870s, over forty years before suffrage became a fait accompli whose history could be written. As Anthony famously expressed the sentiment in a speech before the National American Woman Suffrage Association: "Failure is impossible."[5]

In the fields of morals and politics, progress was identical with two goals: the emancipation and enfranchisement of blacks, and the emancipation and enfranchisement of women. Both goals were the logical and necessary extension of American republicanism's defining principle, the natural equality of human beings. Indeed, the two goals were essentially one in Stanton's mind, for the degradation and enslavement of blacks was substantially similar to the status of women. "The mission of [the] Radical Anti-slavery Movement is not to the African slave alone, but to the slaves of custom, creed and sex, as well" (*ECS* 81). As she put it to Republicans during her 1860 address to the New York state legislature:

> Allow me just here to call the attention of that party now so much interested in the slave of the Carolinas, to the similarity in his condition and that of the mothers, wives, and daughters of the Empire State. That negro has no name. He is Cuffy Douglas or Cuffy Brooks, just whose Cuffy he may chance to be. The woman has no name. She is Mrs. Richard Roe or Mrs. John Doe, just

whose Mrs. she may chance to be. Cuffy has no right to his earnings; he can not buy or sell, or lay up anything that he can call his own. Mrs. Roe has no right to her earnings; she can neither buy nor sell, make contracts, nor lay up anything that she can call her own. (*HWS* 1:680–81)

Although Stanton's rhetoric often (as here) analogized the condition of the enslaved black man with the degraded white woman, she did not ignore the burdens of enslaved black women. These women were "doubly damned as . . . beasts of burden in the field, and sad mothers of a most accursed race" (*ECS* 84). Stanton was enraged by the sexual exploitation to which slave women were subjected by their owners and by slavery's consequent violation of the most basic human bonds. "And these are the daughters and sisters of the first men in the Southern states: think of fathers and brothers selling their own flesh on the auction-block!" (*ECS* 84).

In fact, like many other early feminists, Stanton first became involved in the women's rights movement by way of the abolitionist movement. During her childhood in upstate New York, she frequently attended the antislavery meetings of her cousin, Gerrit Smith. Through them she met her future husband, Henry Stanton, an active abolitionist. She attended a great many abolitionist conventions and speeches, including the 1840 World's Antislavery Convention in London. Women delegates were barred from speaking at the convention despite protests from Henry Stanton and others, and this experience helped to forge Elizabeth's determination to fight for women's rights. It was at the London convention that she first met Quaker abolitionist Lucretia Mott, and their experience there was the seed from which the 1848 Women's Rights Convention in Seneca Falls eventually grew.[6] Stanton's abolitionist travels brought her into contact with some of the leading abolitionist and intellectual figures of her day, including Ralph Waldo Emerson, Wendell Phillips, William Lloyd Garrison, and Frederick Douglass.

In the years following the Seneca Falls convention, the two movements were close allies. Frederick Douglass's antislavery newspaper, *The North Star*, published editorials supporting the early women's rights conventions, and other abolitionist newspapers followed suit (while the rest of the press heaped scorn on activist women). Stanton and others came to trust in the support of abolitionist leaders such as Smith, Phillips, and Garrison. Speaking before the American Anti-Slavery Society in 1860, Stanton gratefully acknowledged that "this is the only organization on God's footstool where the humanity of woman is recognized, and these are the only men who have ever echoed back her cries for justice and equality" (*ECS* 81). Throughout the late 1850s and 1860s, Stanton and Anthony made numerous speeches on behalf of the abolition of slavery and of civil and political rights for blacks (and were verbally and physically attacked for their efforts [*ECS* 22]). During the Civil War, they largely put aside their agitation for women's rights and focused their political efforts on slavery.

With the achievement of emancipation and the end of the war, the Radical Republicans' agenda shifted to black enfranchisement. Stanton's expectation was that her abolitionist allies would now press for universal suffrage. "[T]here can be no reconstruction of this government on any basis other than universal suffrage. . . . Every argument for the negro is an argument for woman and no logician can escape it" (*ECS* 122). She was sorely disappointed when Gerrit Smith and others rallied behind the text of the 14th and 15th Amendments to the Constitution, which guaranteed civil and political rights to *male* citizens but did nothing to secure the rights of women. The Radical Republicans argued that to press for both woman suffrage and the enfranchisement of emancipated slaves would produce defeat for both causes and that it was better to pursue them in stages.

Stanton was outraged at what she experienced as a brutal betrayal, and she campaigned heavily against the 15th Amendment. In doing so, she did not shrink from appealing to her white, middle-class audiences with baldly racist and nativist rhetoric. Her speeches of this period frequently invoked the specter of ignorant immigrant and black men ruling over educated, native-born white women. She sometimes stooped lower by appealing to the traditional fear of black men raping white women. In one speech, for example, Stanton recounted the story of a young white woman who killed her infant, the alleged result of such a rape. "With judges and jurors of negroes," Stanton mused, "remembering the generations of wrong their daughters have suffered at the white man's hands, how will Saxon girls fare in their courts for crimes like these?" (*ECS* 123). At these moments, Stanton's advocacy for women's rights was continuous with the darker side of the American egalitarian tradition, a tradition that reconciled itself to (for example) chattel slavery, Native American genocide, and legal discrimination against Chinese workers.[7]

In the years after Reconstruction, Stanton returned to her work promoting women's rights with a renewed energy. As Anthony focused her efforts on consolidating the women's movement around the issue of suffrage, Stanton stressed the importance of creating space within the movement to air the important differences among women. In her address to the founding convention of the National American Woman Suffrage Association, she argued for the universality and inclusiveness of women's cause.

> Wherever and whatever any class of women suffer whether in the home, the church, the courts, in the world of work, in the statute books, a voice in their behalf should be heard in our conventions. We must manifest a broad catholic spirit for all shades of opinion in which we may differ and recognize the equal right of all parties, sects and races, tribes and colors. Colored women, Indian women, Mormon women and women from every corner of the globe have always been heard in these Washington conventions and I trust they always will be. (*ECS* 226)

For Stanton, it was crucial not to lose touch with the idea that women's emancipation was part and parcel of a historical revolution that would ultimately transform all spheres of social and political life. Anthony's leadership of the national woman suffrage associations now became increasingly pragmatic; Stanton, while maintaining a leadership role in the movement, became increasingly radical.

Extending her earlier ideas concerning women's intellectual and economic independence, she identified herself with the causes of free labor and socialism. A fair return of the product of labor to the worker was, she believed, a logical extension of the principle of equality. The extension of educational opportunity to all classes as well as to both sexes was another part of Stanton's reform agenda. Working women's children should be cared for and educated during working hours, she argued, and public scholarships should be extended to the top two hundred high school graduates, male and female, of every congressional district (*ECS* 158–69). Stanton also supported the idea of cooperative housekeeping, a practice she believed would diminish the total sum of women's domestic labor and free them for more educative and enriching pursuits (*ECS* 93).

Stanton's radicalism gradually alienated her from the mainstream of the suffrage movement. But while her views on labor and education were controversial, it was her arguments concerning marriage and religion that most damaged her leadership of the movement. Marriage was properly understood as a contract between equal adults, Stanton maintained, and should be treated within the law as no different from any other contract.

> From a woman's standpoint, I see that marriage as an indissoluble tie is slavery for woman, because law, religion and public sentiment all combine under this idea to hold her true to this relation, whatever it may be and there is no other human slavery that knows such depths of degradations as a wife chained to a man whom she neither loves nor respects, no other slavery

so disastrous in its consequences on the race, or to individual respect, growth, and development. (*ECS* 133)

Liberalized divorce law was the best remedy to women's enslavement in marriage, and unreflective religious belief was the greatest obstacle to this needed reform. Stanton remained committed to the principle she had articulated from the outset of her public life: that marriage should be regarded by the law as a contract like any other (*HWS* 1:598). For the state to involve itself in enforcing marriage vows as sacred was a breach of the principle of separation of church and state.

Stanton grew increasingly bold in her critique of religion, and she was called an agent of Satan for her most ambitious project in this domain, the publication of *The Woman's Bible*. Stanton gathered a number of freethinking women, some of them Hebrew and Greek scholars, to compose a detailed commentary on the Bible's treatment of women. Acknowledging that many intelligent women viewed the project as a pointless exercise, Stanton persisted because of her perception of the growing influence of religion in the suffrage movement and the centrality of religion in sustaining women's subordinate position in marriage and in society. While Stanton did not disavow the existence of a divine power, she did believe that religion did more damage to women's cause than any other source of prejudice. It was essential to challenge it on its own terrain. "The canon and civil law; church and state; priests and legislators; all political parties and religious denominations have alike taught that woman was made after man, of man, and for man, an inferior being, subject to man" (*WB* 7). Stanton proposed to reread the Bible with a rational and critical eye, just as she would read any other book.

Stanton launched this critical review with a careful reading of Genesis 1:26–28, which she interpreted as a clear statement that God is not an exclusively masculine figure:

> If language has any meaning, we have in these texts a plain declaration of the existence of the feminine element in the Godhead, equal in power and glory with the masculine. The Heavenly Mother and Father! "God created man in his *own image, male and female*." Thus Scripture, as well as science and philosophy, declares the eternity and equality of sex. . . . The masculine and feminine elements, exactly equal and balancing each other, are as essential to the maintenance of the equilibrium of the universe as positive and negative electricity, the centripetal and centrifugal forces, the laws of attraction which bind together all we know of this planet whereon we dwell and of the system in which we revolve. (*WB* 14–15)

There is no foundation in Scripture, Stanton argued, for the argument that man's creation was prior to that of woman. She thus blithely dismissed Genesis 2:21–25, the story of God's creation of Eve from Adam's rib, as the deceitful interjection of "a highly imaginative editor" (*WB* 20).

What, then, of the biblical story of the Fall, for which Eve was responsible? This, too, Stanton ascribes to a human source. "It is evident that some wily writer, seeing the perfect equality of man and woman in the first chapter, felt it important for the dignity and dominion of man to effect woman's subordination in some way" (*WB* 21). Even so, Stanton did not find the story of the serpent so damning of woman's character as its male interpreters generally suppose. Indeed, she thinks the story reflects quite well on Eve—and not so badly on the serpent himself:

> The tempter evidently had a profound knowledge of human nature, and saw at a glance the high character of the person he met by chance in his walks in the garden. He did not try to tempt her from the path of duty by brilliant jewels, rich dresses, worldly luxuries or pleasures, but with the promise of knowledge, with the wisdom of the Gods. Like Socrates or Plato, his powers of conversation and asking puzzling questions, were no doubt marvellous, and he roused in the woman that intense thirst for knowledge, that the simple pleasures of picking flowers and talking

with Adam did not satisfy. Compared with Adam she appears to great advantage through the entire drama. (*WB* 24–25)

In this manner, Stanton and her collaborators proceeded to unravel the whole fabric of the biblical justification of man's dominion over woman. Their efforts did not meet with much approval, even within the women's rights movement. Many women in the movement came to the defense of religion; others thought *The Woman's Bible* would weaken public support for important political objectives. In response to those who cautioned that "it is not *politic* to rouse religious opposition," Stanton replied that "[t]his much-lauded policy is but another word for *cowardice*" (*WB* 10–11).

> Let us remember that all reforms are interdependent, and that whatever is done to establish one principle on a solid basis, strengthens all. Reformers who are always compromising, have not yet grasped the idea that truth is the only safe ground to stand upon. The object of an individual life is not to carry one fragmentary measure in human progress, but to utter the highest truth clearly seen in all directions. (*WB* 11)

Stanton's reward was a resolution from the National American Woman Suffrage Association disavowing *The Woman's Bible* and denying any connection to it.

Stanton wrote her most philosophical essay, "The Solitude of Self," at the age of seventy-seven, and she regarded it as the best of all her writings. There she argued that the human condition is ultimately one of radical isolation in which each must answer to her own conscience for the conduct of her life. Like men, women "must make the voyage of life alone" (*ECS* 248). "Nothing strengthens the judgment and quickens the conscience like individual responsibility. Nothing adds such dignity to character as the recognition of one's self-sovereignty; the right to an equal place, everywhere conceded; a place earned by personal merit, not an artificial attainment, by inheritance, wealth, family, and position" (*ECS* 251). This idea of self-sovereignty is the strongest possible ground for women's social and political equality. Developing one's intellectual and moral capacities to the point where one can take full responsibility for one's life is the highest human endeavor, and no individual should be denied the opportunity to achieve that dignity. "To throw obstacles in the way of a complete education is like putting out the eyes; to deny the rights of property, like cutting off the hands. To deny political equality is to rob the ostracized of all self respect" (*ECS* 249). While none of us can take responsibility for the state of another's soul, we share an obligation to create the social and political conditions under which human beings can achieve self-sovereignty. There is no contradiction between individuality, a love of freedom, a belief in equality, and a dedication to the collective cause of social transformation and human emancipation.

For Stanton, then, the pursuit of women's rights was nothing more nor less than an advancement of these very American ideas. Yet her political thought did undergo some changes over the course of her life. In the movement's early years, Stanton's arguments were inspired by the idea of natural rights embedded in the Declaration of Independence; her liberal individualism was deeply shaped by Jeffersonian ideas. Beginning in the 1850s, her thought increasingly emphasized the themes of social progress and individual self-development alongside her earlier emphasis on equality under the law. These are Millian themes, and indeed, like other progressives of her era, she frequently cited the works of John Stuart Mill and Harriet Taylor, especially on the question of women's emancipation. Toward the end of her life, particularly in the essay "The Solitude of Self," Stanton's individualism takes on a more metaphysical aspect than was evident in her earlier writings. Here, her emphasis on "self-sovereignty" evokes a comparison with Ralph Waldo Emerson's essay "Self-Reliance," and Stanton's essay as a whole expresses a view of the human condition that is quite harmonious with transcendentalist philosophy. Yet these changes in Stanton's thought did not render it inconsistent or incoherent. Throughout her life, she was committed to the twin principles of individual equality and individual liberty, and these grounded all her other thoughts about the human condition, in general, and women's condition, in particular. We might say that in her early years she was preoccupied with these principles from a legal perspective; later, from a social perspective; and, finally, from a spiritual perspective. But in moving from the legal to the social to the spiritual she did not leave her earliest commitments behind.

The strong affinities between Stanton's thought and other strands in the American and Anglo-American liberal traditions also raise the question of her originality as a thinker. This is a question that it is more plausible to raise from the distant perspective of the twenty-first century than from that of the nineteenth. We need only to consider how radical her views appeared to her contemporaries to be persuaded that she was an original thinker. Yet she did not seek to be recognized as original; to the contrary, she wished to persuade her co-citizens that women's rights were a logical and necessary consequence of the Founding principles of the American republic. In this, her thought is similar to that of Frederick Douglass and other advocates for abolition, and to that of Martin Luther King, Jr., and other proponents of black enfranchisement and civil rights. The movements for women's rights and for black rights laid claim to the radicalism inherent in the "self-evident truths" proclaimed at the nation's birth. Stanton never faltered in her confidence in the intrinsic connection between the American project to establish a realm of freedom and the project of women's rights. Her clarity and persistence on this point set her apart as a distinctive and important figure in the history of American political thought.

Notes

1. Quotations from and references to Stanton's works are cited in the text using the following abbreviations:

> *ECS*:   *The Elizabeth Cady Stanton-Susan B. Anthony Reader: Correspondence, Writings, Speeches*, ed. Ellen Carol DuBois (New York: Schocken Books, 1981).
>
> *EY*:   *Eighty Years and More: Reminiscences 1815–1897* (Boston: Northeastern University Press, [1898] 1993).
>
> *HWS*:   *History of Woman Suffrage*, ed. Elizabeth Cady Stanton, Susan B. Anthony, and Matilda Joslyn Gage, vol. 1 (Salem, N.H.: Ayer, [1881] 1985).
>
> *SS*:   *The Search for Self-Sovereignty: The Oratory of Elizabeth Cady Stanton*, ed. Beth M. Waggenspack (New York: Greenwood Press, 1989).
>
> *WB*:   *The Woman's Bible*, ed. Elizabeth Cady Stanton (New York: Arno, [1895] 1972).

2. Letter of June 5, 1856, in *The Selected Papers of Elizabeth Cady Stanton and Susan B. Anthony*, ed. Ann Gordon (New Brunswick, N.J: Rutgers University Press, 1997), 1:321–22, emphasis in original.

3. Declaration of Sentiments, in *HWS* 1:70–71. The theme of "taxation without representation" recurs throughout Stanton's writings (see, e.g., *HWS* 1:595 and *EY* 316).

4. Stanton often used the phrase "this nineteenth century" to express the idea that she was living in a progressive era (see, e.g., *ECS* 114).

5. Susan B. Anthony, "Speech at the 1906 Meeting of the National American Woman Suffrage Association," in *Life and Works of Susan B. Anthony*, ed. Ida Husted Harper (Salem, N.H.: Ayer, 1983), 3:1409.

6. The importance of the 1840 convention for the women's rights movement is discussed in *HWS* 1:53–62.

7. For a detailed discussion of the racial and other exclusions endemic to the American political tradition, see Rogers Smith, *Civic Ideals* (New Haven, Conn.: Yale University Press, 1998).

Chapter 24

Mark Twain on the American Character

David Foster

Mark Twain (1835–1910) is usually considered a novelist, an essayist, and a popular humorist rather than a political thinker. But the genres in which he worked do not preclude an interest in political themes, though they may influence how those themes are treated. At the most general level, Twain's political reflections revolve around the character of the political order that emerged in America in the nineteenth century. Three novels in particular stand out for the depth and influence of their treatment of this theme: *The Adventures of Tom Sawyer* (1876), *The Adventures of Huckleberry Finn* (1884), and *A Connecticut Yankee in King Arthur's Court* (1889). The first two depict the adventures of two young boys growing up before the Civil War in the Mississippi River valley, then almost the frontier. One boy seeks to win an honored place in American society; the other, taking advantage of America's expansive geography, seeks to escape it. Through his heroes, Tom and Huck, Twain defends a distinctively American way of life (against implicit claims of European superiority) in part through a searching self-criticism that has itself become part of American lore. A similar mixture of praise and criticism is found in the *Yankee*, where the subject is the modern, industrial society that developed after the Civil War. These novels are not political treatises, but they help us understand the meaning of American politics through their reflections on such themes as Christianity, technology, leadership, slavery, freedom, compassion, law, and aristocracy. Above all, the novels are useful for their extended critical reflections on the character types that flourish in America; for the type of human being a polity tends to foster may be the highest standard by which to evaluate it.[1]

Tom Sawyer and the Quest for Glory

The Adventures of Tom Sawyer is a classic American story of fulfilled ambition. Its hero, a poor young boy without family advantages, is a nobody who becomes a somebody by dint of character and ingenuity. By the end of the story, he is a great hero to the other small boys; he wins a pretty girl's love; and his guardian forgives his past sins as well as any future ones. In the community at large, he is also a hero for braving the vengeance of a dreaded criminal to save an innocent man's life; for saving Becky in McDougal's cave; and for his fabulous wealth. He is profiled and quoted in the newspaper, and there are some who "believed he would be President yet, if he escaped hanging." Judge Thatcher, the story's most impressive man, expects to see Tom a "great lawyer or a great soldier some day," and he believes that one of Tom's lies—a noble, generous, and magnanimous one—deserves a place in history alongside George Washington's celebrated truth about the cherry tree (35). This comparison with Washington just prior to Tom's final act, the founding of "Tom Sawyer's Gang," suggests that Tom is a sort of founder—perhaps a re-founder—of the United States. The novel is a reflection on leadership in the context of American democracy.

Politics are largely absent from *Tom Sawyer*; most of the story occurs in the family, school, and church—the institutions of civil society—or outdoors. These settings reflect the relative insignificance of formal politics in the small towns of the American frontier: Tom's world is characterized by the absence of direct political authority. This absence is also reflected in his personal circumstances. He is an orphan and lives with an aunt and her two children. No allusion whatsoever is made to Tom's father or to Aunt Polly's husband: Tom is growing up without the guidance or discipline of any man. Like American democracy in general, his is a life without patriarchal authority. The closest thing to an authority in Tom's life is his aunt, but she is unfit to deal with the boy's "adventurous, troublesome ways" (1). Tom has no fear of her and is constantly getting into trouble; yet, as she admits, he rarely suffers for his misdeeds. Tom handles Aunt Polly so easily because she is of divided mind about him. On the one hand, Scripture and a strict Calvinist conscience tell her that Tom is full of the "Old Scratch" and that she ought to be whipping him or she is "a-laying up sin and suffering for us both" (1). On the other hand, her conscience struggles with her "heart," which "most breaks" every time she hits him, and she just cannot bear to do it (1). Aunt Polly is unable to reconcile a strict Christian conscience with Christian compassion and so bring unity into her life and Tom's. It is a weakness typical of the town as a whole, and it remains to Tom, who suffers no such division, to devise a coherent unity.

Tom often seems a rebel in home, school, and church; but, unlike his friend Huck Finn, he is not opposed to authority as such. Indeed, he is a leader among the town's smaller boys, especially "in all new enterprises" (11). This leadership has a strong "military" content. His great hero is Robin Hood, and he has organized a weekly "battle" among the boys in which he is the commander of one of the armies. Tom knows he must maintain his position, which he does not hesitate to do with force. Thus, after provoking a fight with the rich new boy whose fine clothes and "citified air" made him feel shabby, Tom tells him: "Now that'll learn you. Better look out who you're fooling with next time" (10). Nor is this resort to force an isolated incident. Later, when Tom is feared drowned, one boy's bid for glory by association with the dead hero fails when he claims to have been licked by Tom: it turns out that almost all the boys could claim the same.

Tom is something of a bully, but his preeminence is not based only on force, as we see vividly in the whitewashing incident.[2] Having convicted Tom of playing hooky from school, Aunt Polly decides to make him work on Saturday. She rightly believes that Tom hates the drudgery and toil of work, but she seems unaware that even more than work Tom hates the ridicule he expects when the other boys find him working while they are free to enjoy themselves. As Tom prepares for a day of drudgery and humiliation, suddenly a "great, magnificent inspiration" came to him (11). He sets tranquilly to work on the fence as an "artist" absorbed in his work. By pretending that whitewashing a fence was a task to satisfy Tom Sawyer—that it was not work but a rare privilege that only a specially skilled few could do—Tom creates in the other boys, who at first try to mock him, a burning desire to whitewash the fence themselves. He succeeds so well that the other boys pay him everything they have to do his work while he lounges in the shade supervising. Like a prototypical capitalist, not only has Tom created a desire that did not exist before, but he also gets others to pay him to satisfy that desire. The capacity for such deceit is Tom's great virtue. Rejecting the aristocratic distinction between noble and base forms of work, he here shows that any labor can be made desirable so long as there is someone with the ability to create a desire for it.

Tom is rewarded for his "honest work" with a choice apple and a lecture by Aunt Polly upon the "added value and flavor a treat took to itself when it came without sin through virtuous effort" (3). What was intended to be a punishment has thus been transformed by Tom's fraud into a means to glory, wealth, and Aunt Polly's affection. Tom, of course, does not explain how this occurred, and he gets the reward both of his own cleverness and of Aunt Polly's belief that he has the virtue she admires. Thus, we see that Tom's virtue is actually a capacity for a certain kind of beneficent deception. The whitewashing of the fence satisfies Aunt Polly because it gives her what she most desires—to see Tom a good Christian worker—and she can now love him with a clear conscience. Tom pursues his ambitions without harming others and while letting people like Aunt Polly think he is a good Christian. Thus does he reconcile Christianity to capitalism.

Tom's capacity for mutually beneficial fraud culminates in a dramatic appearance at his own funeral. Tom, Huck, and Joe Harper had run away and are presumed drowned, and the grieving town has assembled for their funeral service. But just as the whole congregation breaks down in a "chorus of anguished sobs" provoked by the eulogy, the three ragged boys create a sensation by marching up the isle (17). As he looked upon the envying boys about him, the narrator tells us, Tom confessed that this was the "proudest moment of his life" (17). Moreover, the emotions released by his second coming provoke the town to sing "Old Hundred" with a fervor never seen before. The townspeople know they have been tricked but that trick has nevertheless made them feel more genuinely and enthusiastically than before the spirit of the religion to which they usually give lip service. Tom's pursuit of glory is unchristian, but it does not threaten the beliefs of others; indeed, the story suggests that he confirms those beliefs.

As these incidents suggest, Tom's posture toward Christianity is one of the main themes of the work. Especially important in this regard are the scenes that occur in Sunday school and church. Although Tom hated Sunday school with his "whole heart," these gatherings offer fine opportunities for the pursuit of glory. The conventional route to glory for the small children is to memorize enough verses to win a Bible of their own. It is possible, the narrator tells us, that "Tom's mental stomach had never really hungered for one of those prizes, but unquestionably his entire being had for many a day longed for the glory and eclat that came with it" (4). Tom's problem is how to realize this longing. Before services begin, we see him beginning down the conventional path, picking out for memorization the first five Beatitudes—the shortest verses he could find. But even under the diligent tutoring of his stepsister, Tom simply cannot remember them. The problem is not a bad memory—Tom's verbatim reenactments of scenes from Robin Hood testify to an outstanding memory—but the meaning of the verses. The Beatitudes condemn precisely that desire for temporal glory that dominates Tom; his mind, as it were, offers no entry point for the sentiments contained in these verses. The conventional route is plainly unavailable to Tom, who knows besides that a boy "of German parentage" who won as many as five Bibles in this way overstrained his mind and became an idiot. Therefore, rejecting this foreign approach, Tom tries a quintessentially American one: he uses the profits of the whitewashing escapade to buy tickets the other boys had earned by memorizing Bible verses. And when he is rewarded with a Bible and a place alongside the eminent Judge Thatcher on the stage, he pulls off the "most stunning surprise of the decade" (4).

Just as in the earlier incident he had used the boys' labor to impress Aunt Polly with his virtue, so here he uses those same boys' memory work (or mental labor) to win a broader glory in the community at large. By investing his whitewashing profits in this way, he reveals that for him wealth is not an end in itself: glory, which here takes the form of churchly reputation, is even more important.[3] Tom's "mental stomach" may never have hungered for a Bible, but he certainly appreciates the value, in a Christian community, of seeming so to hunger. But there is a problem. Part of Tom's reward is a speech by the judge in praise of his accomplishment. Biblical knowledge, explains the judge earnestly, is what makes "great men and good men," and he therefore expects Tom will be such a man some day. The judge then asks Tom to display some of his valuable knowledge by naming the first two disciples, and Tom expresses his profound ignorance of the Bible by answering, hilariously, "David and Goliath" (4). Tom's reliance on fraud seems finally to have caught up with him; and yet, this humiliation has no lasting consequences. One reason is that, even in failure, Tom demonstrates what really matters—that he is concerned with the good opinion of the community. A second reason is that, contrary to what the judge says, success—at least Tom's success—is not ultimately founded on biblical humility. The judge, who here basks in his own grandeur, will soon be looking up to Tom as an equal to Washington. But it is a lie, rather than any biblical knowledge, that earns Tom this admiration. Either Judge Thatcher misunderstands success or he is as good a pretender as Tom is.

The citizens of St. Petersburg, who believe that Tom may some day be president, fear that he may also be hung. They thereby suggest that there are two paths open to him: the heroic and the criminal. Tom certainly flirts with the latter. When Becky spurns him, for example, he feels no choice but to turn to a "life of crime." Yet, in the end, Tom does become a hero; the criminal of the story is Injun Joe. In fact, it is by defeating Joe that Tom secures his greatest and most enduring glory. What, then, makes the difference between hero and criminal? Both Tom and Injun Joe are fighters, and both love money; but each also loves something more than money. Unlike Tom, the outcast Injun Joe gives no thought to glory: what he seeks in addition to money is revenge for slights to his dignity, which is why he murders Dr. Robinson (11). Injun Joe has not a "speck of compassion," even for women, as his partners in crime are shocked to discover when he plots to mutilate the Widow Douglas to avenge a humiliation inflicted by her deceased husband. Injun Joe simply lacks all feeling for others.

It is no surprise, then, that another thing that preserves Tom from criminality is that he lacks Joe's unfeeling harshness—for Tom has a deep concern for love. This theme is explored in his relations with Aunt Polly and Becky. Although very different, these two relationships have one revealing similarity. It first appears when Aunt Polly punishes Tom for breaking a sugar bowl, too late discovering that Sid was the guilty one. Tom looks to her to correct the injustice with "healing pity"; but, although longing for reconciliation, Aunt Polly cannot admit her fault for fear of diminishing her authority. Tom knows that his aunt is on her knees to him, but instead of initiating a reconciliation he indulges in the first of several bouts of romantic self-pitying. He imagines how Aunt Polly would suffer if he were sick unto death or drowned in the river: then she would pity him and realize his genuine and full value.

Petting and intensifying his sorrow, Tom wallows in an "agony of pleasurable suffering." He is pained that others do not love him as much as he feels he deserves to be loved; but he also feels pleasure because he is dwelling on his own worth and because he is getting revenge by imagining how much others would suffer were he gone. The sorrows of young Tom culminate when he applies this imagination to Becky, the girl with whom he has just fallen in love on account of her yellow hair, blue eyes, and pretty frock. Tom has not yet met Becky and he does not even know her name, but still his love prompts him to agonize over whether she will pity and comfort him or "turn coldly away like all the hollow world" (3). Indeed, as Tom lies on his back in the garden looking up at Becky's window filled with romantic suffering, he adopts an attitude of "worshipful awe" in the "Sacred presence" and enjoys the "holy calm" (3). No doubt the narrator is mocking Tom's excessive romanticism, but this is as close as Tom comes to piety and a sense of the sacred.

Tom gradually wins over both his aunt and the girl. The victory over Aunt Polly comes when Tom produces tangible evidence that he did take thought for her suffering when he was believed dead. Becky, however, is much harder to win over. We cannot here explore Twain's depiction of Tom's turbulent love affair with Becky. Suffice it to say that no sooner has Tom won Becky's love than he loses it by revealing that he had already been—in fact, still was—"engaged" to Amy Lawrence. Becky angrily rejects Tom's explanations for this hypocrisy, and pride and misjudgments on both sides prevent the breach from being healed. Once again "steeped in melancholy," Tom wishes he could die temporarily, but he finally resolves to disappear mysteriously, become a murderous pirate, and fill the world with his name. But this choice for piracy is clearly born of desperation. Even though he believes piracy has potential for universal glory, when Becky falls ill Tom imagines: "What if she should die! . . . He no longer took an interest in war, nor even in piracy. The charm of life was gone; there was nothing but dreariness left." If he must choose, Tom ultimately cares more for love than for war or piracy. Still, all his attempts to heal the breach with Becky fail. And after she grows indifferent to, and even mocks his "showing off," Tom "sneaked off, crushed and crestfallen," a forsaken, friendless boy whom nobody loved. He resolves to "lead a life of crime. There was no choice" (12, 13). Just as love can heal injustice and provide warmth and fullness in a cold, hollow world, so failure in love puts Tom on the path of Injun Joe.

Tom, Huck, and Joe Harper now run away to Jackson's Island, where they play at being pirates. They think they are running away from "civilization," but they remain obsessed with what the town thinks. Still, Tom's break with "civilization" is now as complete as it ever gets; for his actual running away is only one element of his distance from society prompted by the rift with Becky. During this same rift, he also witnesses a cold-blooded murder, sees the murderer tell a lie under oath without being punished by God, and experiences the failure of a superstition after which his "whole structure of faith was shaken to its foundations" (8). When Tom's expectations of his love for Becky are not fulfilled, his attachment to society collapses. Twain thus seems to indicate that it is love that binds Tom to civilization.

Tom, however, does try to live in society without love. When he appears at his own funeral, he becomes such a glittering hero that he decides to be "independent of Becky Thatcher" and live without love: "Glory was sufficient. He would live for glory" (18). Meanwhile, the breach with Becky, Tom's equal in "vicious vanity," grows more bitter. Though she could have prevented it, Becky allows Tom to be whipped for a ruined spelling book. The culminating—and saving—episode occurs after Becky tears the schoolmaster's precious anatomy book. The children are closely questioned by the angry master, and just as Becky is about to be discovered, Tom leaps to his feet proclaiming, "I done it," taking on himself the humiliating public whipping that Becky dreaded. She is so filled with "surprise, gratitude, and adoration" at this unexpected noble act that the breach is entirely healed (20).

It thus appears that Tom finally wins Becky and all the good things her love promises by what seems like a sacrifice. And yet the situation is complicated. Tom's "sacrifice" is in fact another instance of his ability to get what he wants from others with a skillful deception that harms no one. Under the headmaster's ominous questioning, Becky appeared to Tom like a "hunted and helpless rabbit . . . with a gun leveled at its head": her face was "white with terror" (20). This elemental pity for another sentient being who is helplessly vulnerable to sudden death makes him forget the quarrel and cast about for a way to help Becky. Just as Becky is about to be exposed, a "thought shot like lightning through Tom's brain. He sprang to his feet and shouted, 'I done it!'" (20). What can Tom's inspiration have been except the sudden realization that taking Becky's punishment was the way to save her and win the love he was seeking? In other words, Tom did not act from pity alone; pity made him desire to act, but any act also had to be compatible with his own good. Tom accepts the punishment not in a spirit of genuine self-sacrifice but because there is a greater good to be gained.

Tom's sacrifice for Becky is the means by which he reconciles his pursuit of glory with his desire for love. There is no American tragedy in the sense that Tom must choose between glory and love, and having found a way to have both, he is now firmly rooted in society. Tom's fundamental conventionality is revealed when he tells Huck, who thinks he has gone crazy, that he would use a great fortune, if he had one, to get married. If Tom's central problem is now resolved, Injun Joe is still at large and the final episodes of the novel revolve around the problems he poses. These episodes test Tom's attitude toward the fear of death and the law; they consolidate his achievements and we see him becoming a more public man—indeed, a pillar of society. For example, in testifying against Injun Joe in open court, Tom breaks the serious oaths of silence he had made to Huck and risks the terrible vengeance of Joe in order to defend the law and to save the innocent Muff Potter. He thereby wins a more stable glory among the townspeople than he had had hitherto. Similarly, although it was Tom's careless quest for glory that caused Becky and he to get lost deep in the same cave where Injun Joe is hiding, it is also his indefatigable and courageous persistence that saves the two children. Because the search parties had all but given up hope, the reappearance of Tom and Becky is Tom's third return from the dead, and it is "the greatest night the little town had ever seen" (32).

When Tom saw Injun Joe deep in the cave, he discovered the place where Joe hid his loot. After Joe is found dead of hunger and thirst, Tom returns to the cave and recovers the treasure, some $12,000 in gold. This treasure transforms Tom's social position. He already has notoriety and glory, and he has even been several times a hero, but now he is solidly respected. The vast majority are deeply impressed and moved by such wealth, and it more than anything else establishes Tom, in their eyes, as a potentially great man. The wealthy few are also impressed by Tom's wealth, but in their case that wealth helps them to appreciate his nobility. The possession of great wealth is the basis upon which Tom's true value becomes visible.

Tom's last act is to found Tom Sawyer's Gang. It is his final step toward civilization. Earlier in the story, Tom had admired and envied Huck's perfect freedom, but now as a founder or statesman his main task is to persuade Huck to give up that freedom so that he can become "high toned" enough to belong to the gang (6, 35). Tom has discovered an even greater freedom than Huck's: the freedom to found his own society. He has realized the great promise America makes to each individual: to remake it for himself.

Huck Finn: Natural Man against American Conventions

While *Tom Sawyer* is the story of a boy striving to succeed in American society, *The Adventures of Huckleberry Finn* is the story of a boy who wishes to escape from that same society. His dominant impulse is to be free of the restraints and conventions of society and, by implication, thereby to live a more natural life. This impulse receives its severest test as Huck drifts down the Mississippi River on a raft with an escaping Negro slave. In the equality and relative freedom of life on the raft, a friendship develops, and Huck must confront in himself the moral and psychological consequences of race slavery, perhaps the crucial convention of the civilization he is fleeing. Huck is Twain's natural man. His adventures suggest a critique of American society while also indicating the limits of Huck's pursuit of freedom.

Huckleberry Finn has three main parts, the first of which introduces Huck through his dissatisfaction with and escape from St. Petersburg (chaps. 1–11). When the story begins, the town's richest and most respectable citizen, the old Widow Douglas, has decided to adopt Huck and, as he puts it, to "sivilize" him. Just thirteen or fourteen years old, he is poised to enjoy all the advantages of great wealth and high status in America. But Huck is unhappy. The immediate problem is that the widow and her sister, a schoolmarmish spinster, live a life of strict Protestant discipline and decency. Huck, however, has always lived just as he pleases. The son of the town drunk, Huck is almost wholly untutored: he is illiterate, cannot sit still, is ignorant of table manners, and hates shoes and clean clothes—in short, he is a social outcast who is dominated by a passion for freedom.

Huck also suffers because he is unmoved by the Christianity that animates the widow's discipline: he is as unformed by the religion of the "book" as he is by tradition. Yet Huck is not hostile to religion. On the contrary, he has an almost preternaturally active spiritual life, which shows itself in a profound and beautiful sensitivity to all the moods, motions, and sounds of the night, of storms, and of the river. At the root of this sensitivity is an inchoate and bittersweet general dread of death in which the dominant feeling is loneliness rather than terror. Thus, whereas Huck listens carefully to the ladies' homilies, they must contend with a prior religiosity rooted not in providential history but in emotional responses to the immediate natural surroundings. An owl hooting at night makes Huck shiver, not entirely unpleasantly, with awareness of death; but, he can joke about Miss Watson's account of heaven and hell, and he loses interest in Moses because he has been dead so long. Focused on present and immediate circumstances, Huck is incapable of taking a long view, whether it involves the distant past or hope for or fear of the afterlife.

This emotional substratum is combined with a whole set of particular beliefs or superstitions. Huck believes in witches, ghosts, signs, spells, charms, and luck, both good and bad. Almost all these signs concern one's own fate or safety and operate universally and as necessities, independently of one's beliefs and moral character. Belief in such signs would call forth no sacrifices for others, but neither would it lead one to impose on others; and since one can do nothing to bring about good luck or to prevent bad luck (one can only prepare stoically to meet it), Huck's beliefs cannot ground claims to rule. Much of the meaning Huck attaches to signs originates among the slaves, and Jim, his future raft companion, is a particular expert. This paganism seems perfectly suited to two runaways who want above all to be left alone.

The premise of Huck's piety is that there is no personal or providential God to whom one might pray and who renders the past meaningful and the future full of hope or terror. This is especially clear in Huck's reflections on prayer, the most developed theological theme in the book. Huck attends seriously to the ladies' belief that one can get anything for which one prays, but when his own earnest prayers for fishing equipment produce a line but no hooks, he decides that prayer is useless. Nor is he moved by the widow's view that one should pray not for things but for "spiritual gifts," such as the ability to help other people without taking thought for oneself. He sees no "advantage" for himself in this kind of gift because he is concerned primarily with immediate, usually material, benefits to himself. For the same reason, he finds altruism unintelligible: without being harsh or cruel, he is entirely—and innocently—selfish. Later on, when Huck is believed to have drowned, the townspeople set loaves of bread adrift on the river and pray that they will lead to his body. Watching from a concealed place, the very hungry Huck retrieves one of these loaves and reflects that in this case prayer really was efficacious. Characteristically, however, he concludes that while prayer may work for some people, like the widow, it does not work for "low down" types like himself. The Beatitudes teach that it is precisely the low down types who can most expect divine favor, but Huck thinks he is too low even to petition God.[4]

Huck finds the regime imposed upon him by the two well-meaning old ladies tedious and dull. For a time, Tom Sawyer appears to save the day. Huck wants to join Tom's gang, but Tom insists that its members be "respectable" and so Huck stays with the widow rather than running away. But Tom's alternative turns out to be too similar to the widow's to satisfy Huck. Tom's life too revolves around books—not indeed the Bible, but books like *Don Quixote*. Tom is devoted to different goals than is the widow, but he is as much a slave to his books as the strictest fundamentalist is to the Bible, insisting on following them even when he does not understand and cannot explain them. Moreover, Tom invests everyday life with significance rooted in an imagination informed by books, and it is this above all that distinguishes him from Huck. Thus, Tom is satisfied pretending that a Sunday school picnic is a group of Spanish merchants and rich "A-rabs," but the prosaic Huck, who actually expected to see camels and elephants, is disillusioned when there are only picnickers. Tom's story of Arabs and elephants, he concludes, "had all the marks of a Sunday school"—that is, it was purely imaginary and therefore he "couldn't see no profit in it" (3). Accordingly, Huck quits the gang.

Tom's insistence that the members of his gang be respectable implies that the gang is not fundamentally incompatible with civilization. The gang of boys intends to steal, fall in love with beautiful female prisoners, and act nobly. For Tom, society is worthy of support because it provides the opportunity in which to develop the imagination and pursue goals based upon it. Huck, by contrast, always tests the imagination against what he can see, and the rewards of imagination by themselves are not sufficient to justify the sacrifices called for by society. Huck does not explicitly criticize the gang's goals, but it is telling that while he is curious about money and exotic spectacles, he never shows the least interest in love or in noble action. In any case, Tom's strict fidelity to a text of which he is the authoritative interpreter provides a principle of hierarchy that Huck rejects.

Neither the widow's Christianity nor Tom's vision of love and noble action are sufficient to attach Huck to society or to make him submit to its restraints and conventions. Nevertheless, Huck gradually grows accustomed to life with the widow. He would probably have settled in to a fairly ordinary life had not his father Pap reappeared to claim his son's wealth. Pap is as degraded, brutal, and ignorant as the widow is respectable, gentle, and charitable, but he is as essential to antebellum America as she is. For if her gentle Christian charity is one of society's highest virtues, something like Pap's violent racial prejudice is necessary to maintain the slavery from which she also benefits. When Pap's designs on Huck's money are frustrated by legal obstacles, he kidnaps Huck and imprisons him in a secluded cabin. Despite frequent beatings and long periods of lonely confinement, Huck enjoys the easygoing life, and he wonders how he ever got to like the widow's so much. But then one night in a mad frenzy of whiskey and nightmares, Pap tries to kill him. Huck resolves to escape. Bad as life is with his father, however, he cannot stand to return to the widow, so he fakes his own murder and escapes from both at the same time.

Now "dead" to St. Petersburg, Huck plans to find a place in the woods where he can live free of the demands of others. A few days alone on Jackson's Island, however, suffice to revive his loneliness, suggesting that man is by nature a social being. This time his loneliness is ended when he discovers Jim, a slave with whom he was on friendly terms in the widow's household, hiding on the island. And thus, by accident, begins the famous partnership of the white boy and the runaway black slave.

The story of their life on the river is the second part of the novel (chaps. 12–31). In a series of memorable adventures, Twain explores the relation between Huck and Jim, and he contrasts their life on the raft with that in the riverside communities. This contrast is critical of life on shore and raises the question whether the friendship of Huck and Jim suggests a natural standard by which to reject the laws and customs that make the distinction of race a decisive fact. More generally, do the principles that govern life on the raft provide a foundation for a better form of political or social life than that now found on shore?

We cannot here examine all the adventures of the two fugitives, but as an example of how the issues are treated, one can consider the theme of property. Apart from avoiding detection,

Huck and Jim's most urgent problem is food. The river, or nature, partly supplies their needs, but they must also steal from the farms and orchards on shore. Even without women and children to care for, then, Huck and Jim are not self-sufficient but dependent or parasitic on the society they flee. Neither, however, feels "just right . . . [or] comfortable" about stealing (12). Revealing a lingering debt to civilization, Huck wavers between the widow's view that stealing is always wrong and Pap's view that one may always "borrow" something if one intends to pay it back sometime. Neither view is acceptable: the widow's would mean starvation or return while Pap's is only a "soft name for stealing" (12). Jim resolves the impasse by suggesting that they borrow only some kinds of things but not others: they decide to take corn, melons, and chickens, but not to touch persimmons and crabapples. This satisfies Huck because he gets what he needs, because he does not like crabapples, and because the persimmons are not ripe anyway.

Jim's "compromise" makes both of them feel "comfortable"—but why is it "right"? Their taking has no ground except their need, and their action might imply that stealing is justified when and to the extent that self-preservation requires it. But even that is not quite right, for they could have given up melons and still survived. Their view, then, is that stealing is right to the extent that preservation and comfort require. That is to say, by nature there is strictly speaking no property in things as such. And if property is essentially conventional, it is no wonder that Huck, though deeply conflicted in his reasoning, always acts to save Jim from recapture—that is, to prevent Jim from being treated as property.

If all property is conventional, however, why is Jim concerned to distinguish the kinds of things that may be taken from those which may not? One reason is that Huck and Jim thereby get what they need while also respecting (some of) what belongs to others. In other words, they are "moderate" thieves. Certainly the fugitives' needs or desires put them in tension with the surrounding communities; but, they are not rapacious, and those communities need not treat them as mortal enemies. And yet, to consider the crucial distinction, why is it better to take corn and never persimmons than to take some corn and some persimmons? The answer may be that this approach implicitly denies that everything is fair game by nature: some kinds of things, like persimmons—and we may suppose, human beings—are off-limits. Jim can thus survive—even survive comfortably—without introducing a principle that would also justify slavery. Unfortunately, the distinction between melons and persimmons is purely conventional and even arbitrary. Accordingly, we note that while Huck consents to Jim's solution, he does not necessarily accept his principle; he implies that if he did like crabapples or if persimmons were ripe, he might have acted differently. That Huck accepts the limitation suggested by Jim is due apparently to his limited desires, for natural man needs much less than civilized man. But to the very end, Huck accepts that human beings can be owned. His later effort to steal Jim out of slavery is not based on any principle concerning what is and what is not properly owned but on private sentiments. If Huck's thinking (as opposed to his deeds) reveals the natural view, there is no stable natural basis for the protection and regulation of property.

As we have seen, Huck rejects much in American society, but morally and psychologically he is still deeply influenced by slavery. As the raft nears Cairo, where Jim will be free, Huck's "conscience" starts bothering him. He reflects that in helping Jim go free, he is injuring Miss Watson, whose property Jim is. Huck has some respect for law, but his real concern is that Miss Watson has done nothing bad to him. He feels that in helping Jim go free, he would be injuring a woman who has always done good to him—albeit, the good as she saw it. Life under Miss Watson's thumb had made him so lonesome that he "most wished I was dead," but the thought of injuring her now makes him feel so "mean and so miserable I most wished I was dead" (1, 16). What "most froze" Huck, however, was Jim's willingness to steal his children out of slavery; Huck would then be complicit in harming the owner of Jim's children, a man Huck does not even know. One might expect Huck to have some sympathy for Jim, who suffers from the same society he himself is fleeing, but he gives no sign whatsoever of seeing things from Jim's perspective. He has no sense at this point that Jim's feelings for his family might be natural human feelings or that slavery might be wrong. He does not consider slavery an injury to Jim, much less that an injury to Jim is an injury to himself: Huck's conscious reflections reveal no sense of common humanity with Jim. Taking slavery entirely for granted, he is absorbed in trying to avoid injuring anyone who has not injured him. These reflections by a runaway outcast reveal the profound moral effect of slavery and the conventions that support it.

To ease his conscience, Huck resolves to follow conventional morality and help return Jim to his legal owner. A perfect opportunity arises when he is interrogated by two men chasing some runaway slaves, but at the last moment, Huck saves Jim with a masterful lie. The immediate cause of his action is a speech by Jim expressing his satisfaction with Huck, "de bes' fren' Jim's ever had; en . . . de only fren' ole Jim's got now . . . de on'y white genlman dat ever kep' his promise to ole Jim" (16). This speech reminds Huck of Jim's feelings and of Huck's own earlier promise not to betray him. Huck explains that he knew it was wrong to save Jim and he felt bad about it, but he also reflects that had he turned Jim in he would feel bad all the same because then he would have injured Jim, by breaking a promise to a man who treats him as a friend. Huck does not believe in divine reward or in doing right for its own sake, but he does expect morality to pay off in good feelings. He is divided equally between saving Jim and doing the conventionally right thing, but in both cases his standard is to harm no one. Unable to resolve the issue on the conscious level, he blames his inner conflict on his upbringing and resolves in the future not to bother about it any more but to do whatever "come handiest at the time" (16). In the present case, was saving Jim "handiest" because betrayal would have meant enduring Jim's reproaches while Miss Watson is invisible and distant? Or is it that, despite having no account of his action, Huck nevertheless did the right thing by following the prompting of nature? His authentic self—all the more authentic because he does not understand himself—reveals itself in his deed. If this is Twain's suggestion, the episode shows nature (as a sort of instinctual gentleness) triumphing over convention. It also suggests that society, which taught Huck to obey the law, conceals nature from him.

In a dense fog, the raft drifts past the confluence of the Ohio and the Mississippi rivers, thus denying Jim his main chance for freedom. The theme of Huck's relationship to Jim now recedes to the background and the character of the riparian communities becomes a more prominent one. In contrast to the freedom, friendship, and ease of life on the raft, life on shore is full of violence and fraud. In one adventure, Jim hides in a swamp while Huck stays with an aristocratic southern family. The Grangerfords are by far the most attractive family in the book, but their lives are dominated by a senseless blood feud with another family. While Huck is visiting, all the Grangerford boys and men are killed by their rivals. The feud thus reflects a breakdown of the rule of law caused by a strong code of family honor. The character of a society rooted in honor rather than in respect for law is again depicted in all its brutality when Colonel Sherburn coldly guns down an offensive but harmless drunk in broad daylight and yet goes free (in part because the common people are contemptible cowards). After seeing the Grangerfords annihilated, Huck flees back to Jim and the raft. In returning to the raft, which among other things represents life without law, he seems not to appreciate that the violence he has witnessed was rooted in a lack of respect for law.[5] In any case, Huck has no protection from the kinds of people he has just seen, and his gentle natural sentiments provide no basis for establishing the rule of law.

Huck is only marginally more successful at dealing with fraud, the other side of life on shore. This theme is explored in great detail when two nameless con men join the raft and, in a rich satire both of aristocratic European pretensions and of American attitudes toward aristocracy, pretend to be the "Dolphin" of France and the disinherited English duke of Bridgewater. An accomplished liar himself, Huck admires their extraordinary capacity to fake grief and piety and to evoke it in others, though he is sometimes disgusted by the willful gullibility of their victims. He is mostly a passive observer until a scheme to rob three recently orphaned girls of their inheritance seems about to succeed. Huck is moved from his passivity, not by a sense of justice, but by a change in his sentiments. At a certain point, the girls show a sincere and graceful concern to make Huck feel comfortable in their home, and this civility, contrasted with his secret knowledge of the fraud against them, made Huck feel "so ornery and low down and mean" that he decides to help them (26). To this point, the fraud had caused Huck no unease or indignation; but once the girls do him a personal kindness, his attitude is transformed. Huck's efforts prove inefficacious, however; the girls are saved by chance and the suspicions of a doctor and a lawyer.

Huck's experiences in the riparian communities make him appreciate Jim more and call forth the opinion that "there warn't no home like a raft, after all" because there "you feel mighty free and easy and comfortable" (18). But while the contrast between life on the raft and life in those communities favors Huck, it also points to some problems; for that contrast demonstrates that Huck has no way to protect himself against those who love honor and are willing to use force, and he was unable to help the Wilks girls. Both to protect himself and to help those he is inclined to help, Huck needs the assistance of law, but his nature seems incapable of supporting law.

Back on the raft, the aristocrats fall on hard times and sell Jim back into slavery for a few dollars. In a life haunted by loneliness, this is Huck's nadir. Earlier he had wrestled with the morality of helping a runaway slave. He now realizes that if he wants the companionship he has come so to enjoy, he will have to steal Jim out of slavery, and he balks at such a "dirty low-down business" with its direct challenge to the law and conventional opinion (31). This is Huck's great crisis, and the ensuing inner struggle between his "conscience" and his "heart" is distinguished from earlier ones in two ways. For the first time, Huck here considers Jim's good as well as his own. After canvassing the alternatives, he concludes that there is nothing he can do consistent with conventional morality that will not harm both Jim and himself. Second, in this struggle theological questions are paramount. His intense inner pain strikes Huck as proof that there is "One" out there, and that this pain is a "slap in the face" from Providence for his wickedness in stealing Jim from a poor old woman who had never done him any harm. Huck always seeks ease or comfort (rather than pleasure); perhaps that explains why this, his one acknowledgment of a God relevant to him, is based on the pain he feels.

Having had this epiphany, Huck resolves to become a good boy and obey the law. He writes a letter revealing Jim's whereabouts and feels "washed clean of sin for the first time" in his life. Huck is now on the verge of returning to society and accepting its laws and conventions. But then he calls to mind life on the raft and remembers how kind and affectionate Jim has always been to him. He searched but could find "no places to harden me against him." Jim's unbroken record of kindness prompts Huck's famous choice to follow his heart and steal Jim even though, as he believes, this is to break the law and to oppose "Providence": "All right, then," he declares, "I'll go to hell" (31).

Although Huck's authentic natural sentiments (fortified by his experiences with Jim) prevail over the combined pressure of law and religion, he continues denigrating himself as "low down" for not following conventional opinion. Huck never reconciles his sentiments with his opinions, and his sentiments never lead him to examine or change his opinions, even though the Declaration of Independence, a painting of the signing of which he saw at the Grangerford's, suggests a doctrine that would support his sentiments for Jim. In any case, Huck's actions are always determined by sentiments. But Huck does not conclude that laws or political authority more generally ought to be guided by or supportive of natural sentiments or that (natural) sentiments provide the standard by which to distinguish good from bad conventions. Such a conclusion would perhaps be too much to expect from Huck, a mere boy. But if the narrator of the story does not draw this conclusion, does Twain intend his readers so to do?

Even if the example of Huck suggests that slavery is not natural, the story is not very hopeful about the prospect of eliminating slavery where it exists. Huck's decision to disregard the law and save Jim depends not only on Huck being peculiarly out of tune with his society but, even more important, on considerable intimacy with Jim. Very few in a slave-owning society will have experiences of slaves similar to Huck's. Nor is every slave the saint that Jim is, and the routine brutality necessary to maintain slavery keep master and slave too far apart for good feelings to operate. Huck himself, while wishing to free Jim, does not become an abolitionist. Indeed, when Tom later agrees to help steal Jim, Huck feels "bound to say Tom Sawyer fell, considerable, in my estimation" (33).

It is not slavery but society's cruelty to lawbreakers that finally turns Huck against conscience. Jim takes revenge on the aristocrats who had sold him into captivity by informing the local people about their schemes. Huck tries to warn the aristocrats, but too late, and they are tarred and feathered and run out of town on a rail. For Huck, the sight of the suffering aristocrats erases all their perfidy. He has no stomach for the necessary cruelty of punishment. He feels no "hardness" against the aristocrats despite their having made him feel worse than he had ever felt in his life by selling Jim. One can wonder what, if anything, would harden Huck against a man. Huck even feels somehow responsible for the aristocrats' suffering. He lacks all spiritedness. Reflecting on the feelings prompted by the sight of the tarred and feathered men, he declares that "a person's conscience ain't got no sense," and he seems to conclude that a conscience is useless. Huck had earlier rejected conscience in the sense of law-bred opinion; now he also dismisses conscience in the sense of the responsibility one feels, based on one's natural feelings of benevolence, for the suffering of others.

Huck's momentous decision initiates the third and final part of the novel, in which he leaves the river and returns to society to steal Jim out of slavery (chaps. 32–end). Many readers consider this the most problematic part of the novel. The difficulty begins when Huck finds the farm where Jim is being held captive and is there mistaken for Tom Sawyer. "Born again" as Tom, he plays along with the mistake, and when the real Tom arrives, he (Tom) pretends to be Sid. The two boys, each pretending to be someone else, then set out to free Jim. Tom insists on treating Jim as if he were a nobleman in a dungeon and develops an escape plan that involves much unnecessary effort and even some cruelty to Jim. The tasks Tom imposes—and others he can only dream about—drag on for more than one-fifth of the novel and long after they have ceased to be funny. Tom's scheme seems to us to humiliate Jim; it certainly prolongs his captivity at considerable risk to his freedom and even to all their lives. The whole "evasion," as Tom calls it, seems even more absurd because Tom knows (though he keeps this a secret) that Jim is already a free man. In other words, Tom indulges in a juvenile prank that perversely risks the life and dignity of a good man. Why did Twain end the novel in this strange, convoluted way?

One answer could be that the ending vividly demonstrates what the preceding stories of violence and fraud reveal: though a good person, Huck is too gentle to ensure the freedom of his friend. Huck needs help and his acquiescence to Tom's scheme reflects that need. And yet, as the reader (though not Huck) knows, Tom is irrelevant to the freeing of Jim, for Jim has already been freed by Miss Watson's Christian conscience and by the laws that will enforce her will. What, then, if anything, does Tom's reappearance contribute? While Huck provides the desire to free Jim, Tom provides the form in which that desire is realized. He attempts to transform the freeing of Jim from something merely personal into an heroic enterprise. Tom has read all the books on the escapes of famous prisoners, and in managing Jim's escape, he insists on exactly following the "best authorities" on the "custom in Europe" (35). This proves to be impossible and usually absurd because European aristocratic conditions are so different from American democratic ones. The result is a satire on the literature of adventure and on the romantic longings it feeds, a satire that turns us against that literature and those longings when we see the treatment of Jim to which they lead.

The heroic ethic is not, however, entirely rejected. Both Huck and Jim defer to Tom, though not without objections. What they find attractive about Tom is suggested in the two desires that underlie Tom's wish for a proper escape. First, he hopes that the right kind of escape will make for a lot of "talk" and bring "honor"—to himself, but especially to Jim, who has "more gaudier chances than a prisoner ever had in the world to make a name for himself" (38). Second, and more fundamentally, Tom wants to do the right thing in the right way. He adamantly rejects Huck's dull preference for the easy way out. When Huck, who at one point must pretend to be a servant girl, objects to wearing a dress, Tom says: "That ain't got nothing to do with it. The thing for us to do, is just to do our duty, and not to worry about whether anybody sees us do it or not. Hain't you got no principle at all?" (39). As we have seen, Tom is right: Huck is guided by sentiment not principle. Tom, however, seems to have only a noble adherence to principle. He wants to do the right thing because it is the right thing to do. Tom is a gentleman.

When Tom is shot during the escape, Jim must choose between fleeing and staying to help the wounded boy. He stays because he believes that that is what Tom Sawyer would do. This emulation of Tom's nobility is important because it provokes Huck's remark that "I knowed he was white inside." Up to this point, Huck had thought Jim had a good heart and was a good man; but only when he sees Jim's nobility does he recognize a racial affinity with him. Huck's statement may offend the contemporary ear, but in a boy still deeply influenced by racial categories it is an expression of the deepest recognition of Jim's humanity. But Jim's act, and therefore the model that prompted it, is important for another reason. The escape plan fails and Jim is returned to a much harsher captivity than before. In addition, all the things that Tom thought would bring honor backfire: the local people think Jim must have been mad. Their attitude changes only when the doctor describes how devoted Jim was to the wounded Tom. But by Jim's own account, it was the desire to live up to Tom's standards that prompted that devotion. Tom was right after all: it was by doing the right thing that Jim was honored, to the extent that he was honored, among white folks.

During the escape, Huck's goal is merely to get Jim out of the jail. By trying to make Jim a hero, and thus bring him honor, Tom understands as Huck does not that mere freedom is not enough. For Jim to be fully free, the society into which he enters must see him not merely as a former slave, and not merely as a good man, but as an honorable man. This may be Twain's suggestion: at the time of the escape, Jim was already legally free, but now, after evincing his nobility, he is fully free. The third part is thus critical of both Tom and Huck, but it also appears to suggest that some combination of these two is necessary.

Once Jim is free, Huck immediately "light(s) out for the Territory" to foil Aunt Sally, who was going to "adopt me and sivilize me and I can't stand it. I been there before" (43). Huck's return to society was highly qualified and only temporary. *The Adventures of Huckleberry Finn* is, however, narrated by Huck, which implies that he eventually returned to civilization to write his memoir. What was his purpose? The narrative makes clear that Huck is a critical admirer of Tom Sawyer and thus of the adventure books Tom so loves. His own literary effort (which might also be Twain's) seems to be an attempt to give America's Toms an American adventure story to replace the European ones—a story consistent with and supportive of American conditions. This would be an attempt to attach Tom's longing for nobility to Huck's compassion: the former would be moderated and redirected while the later would be made useful to society. Tom's respect for convention would thus be attached to a natural object, which, as we have seen, has little patience with convention and indeed undermines it. That custom can be rooted in nature is a crucial American political belief.

Connecticut Yankee: The Problem of Commercial Progress

When we turn from *Tom Sawyer* and *Huckleberry Finn* to *A Connecticut Yankee in King Arthur's Court*, we move from the frontier to the East Coast and from the antebellum period to the late nineteenth century. The novel tells the story of a man from Connecticut who is "transposed" bodily to the sixth-century England of King Arthur. After a brief period of disorientation and danger, this man uses his knowledge of history and modern science, and a flair for dramatic effects, to save his life and become the second most powerful man in the kingdom. He then initiates a project to bring "civilization"—that is, the late-nineteenth-century enlightenment in science, economics, morals, politics, and religion—to a country ruled by a feudal aristocracy and an established church. The result is a wide-ranging contrast between "civilization" and the political order that is arguably most different from it: medieval chivalry. Because the novel is presented as a "history" written by the Yankee, the novel is a reflection on the character of modern man.

The Yankee introduces himself as "an American. I was born and reared in Hartford, in the State of Connecticut. . . . So I am a Yankee of the Yankees—and practical; yes, and nearly barren of sentiment, I suppose—or poetry, in other words" (A Word of Explanation). This man is the head superintendent of a large arms factory where he excels at inventing and making anything "a body" wanted—"guns, revolvers, cannon, boilers, engines, all sorts of labor-saving machinery" (A Word of Explanation). The Yankee is up-to-date, hard-nosed, technically savvy, energetic, and resourceful. He believes in progress and looks up to no one, unless it is to the great inventors such as Watt and Whitney, in whose footsteps he is walking. Neither an owner nor a mere laborer, the Yankee represents the upwardly rising commercial and industrial classes, the backbone of modern capitalism. He is an archetype of the kind of man who flourishes in the world brought about by the industrial and scientific revolutions.

This man is knocked unconscious in a "misunderstanding" with a subordinate and thereby "transposed" to the sixth century, where he is captured by a knight and taken to Camelot. The Knights of the Round Table are to England what the Yankee is to America—the leading and representative human type. These two human types or alternatives are so opposed that, upon first encountering the attire, speech, and behavior of the knights, the Yankee thinks Camelot must be a circus or a lunatic asylum. He soon entertains other possibilities, but this first impression indicates one of the Yankee's primary qualities: a practical and skeptical scientific rationalism.

The rationalism that pervades everything the Yankee says or does is entirely absent in the knights. The significance of this difference begins to appear when the Yankee is taken by his new master to be exhibited as a prize of war before the other knights. The setting is a great banquet at which the knights tell and listen to stories of heroic martial exploits. When his turn comes, the Yankee is described as a giant, a monster, and a "tusked and taloned man-devouring ogre" whose strange clothes have a special enchantment (4). The scientific Yankee reacts by observing that no one cared about the obvious discrepancies between these statements and the "statistics" or "facts" (4). If the Yankee is almost barren of "poetry," the knights' lives rest on the poetry of martial romance, love, and reverence. The Yankee cannot help but admire the courage of the knights, and he discerns in them "a certain loftiness and sweetness," "a most noble benignity and purity," a "majesty and greatness" (3). And yet, he still debunks the knight's virtues as depending on a boyish love of fighting and "mere animal training" rather than "mental training . . . reasoning": the knights are children or savages rather than mature or rational adults (2). He concludes that "these animals didn't reason" and even "that brains were not needed in a society like that, and, indeed would have marred it . . . [even] perhaps rendered its existence impossible" (3).

The Yankee's rationality is an important strength. When he is sentenced to burn at the stake, he saves himself by pretending to cause a total eclipse of the sun, which he happens to know was about to occur. For him, of course, the eclipse is a merely natural phenomenon that serves to confirm the date; but, for the knights it is an awesome display of magic—indeed, a miracle. Thus, the Yankee not only saves his life and becomes the chief minister of the realm, but he also earns a reputation as a great wizard. The Yankee's power thus rests on fraud or a capacity to take advantage of the ignorance and superstition of the knights. And his success in rising to power seems to confirm his superiority.

While the Yankee could have settled down to enjoy the life of a privileged aristocrat, he conceives the ambition to introduce "civilization" to England. Beginning with what we would call society, he secretly sets in place a patent office, factories of all kinds, schools, a newspaper, an army and naval corps, and even Protestant churches. Once this foundation is firmly established, he plans to found a republic. Brimming with the confidence of a scientific and historical education, he believes this will be an easy task; for he is a "giant among pigmies, a man among children, a master intelligence among intellectual moles."

In initiating this project, one of the Yankee's motives is to alleviate the discomfort of life in Camelot. Even as the second most powerful man in the kingdom, he lacks the little conveniences "that make the real comfort of life" (7). More generally stated, his first goal, after having secured his own life, is bodily comfort—and not just for himself but for the entire nation. He is not, however, altruistic, for he sees a tremendous opportunity here to make money. In addition to seeking comfort and wealth, the Yankee understands the civilizing of England as perhaps the greatest possible test of his capacities and of the modern belief in peaceful progress. He soon notices, however, that despite the great power he now wields, he is not admired or reverenced by the people. He believes that, like an elephant in a circus, he is gawked at for his strength but feared rather than revered because he lacks an hereditary title. It would have been easy to acquire a title, but he wants to be honored for what he values—for his scientific and technological prowess and for benefiting others with them. But these things are not publicly admired in Camelot. To realize his ambition, therefore, the Yankee must first change Camelot's values so that the knights admire the things he is good at. This implies an attack on the protectors of Camelot's values and ultimately a change of regime. Thus, the Yankee's desire for honor or reverence draws him into politics.

The meaning of the change the Yankee contemplates is suggested in what is probably the funniest adventure in the novel: his expedition as a knight to rescue forty-five princesses from three giant one-eyed ogres (11–12). Attired in full armor, the Yankee gives an hilarious account of the many discomforts of this "fashion"; indeed, he is preoccupied with and almost completely discombobulated by them. In contrast, his traveling companion, the titled aristocrat the Demoiselle Alisande la Carteloise (whom the Yankee calls Sandy), is blissfully unconscious of physical deprivation. The Yankee debunks her savage, Indian-like stoicism, but the fact is that physically he is by far the softest person in England. Indeed, the knights quite simply do not give bodily comfort a second thought. Accordingly, they are also totally indifferent to the means by which that comfort is achieved, economics. The Yankee, by contrast, is so preoccupied with comfort and economics that he habitually evaluates almost everything in terms of its economic potential. The most striking example is his treatment of the holiest ascetic in the kingdom. This man has spent the last twenty years on a high platform bowing from the waist—a little more than fifty times a minute by the Yankee's precise count (22). Englishmen see here a man of powerful spirituality; the Yankee sees only wasted energy. He harnesses the hermit to a sewing machine and makes a killing selling holy T-shirts as souvenirs. The Yankee's irreverent and debunking humor suggests a perspective on life that gives the goals of economics primacy over those of politics and religion. By contrast, the knights' unconcern for comfort and economics is the consequence of their valuing something more than comfort: knightly valor or honor and ascetic self-denial, both of which presuppose the ability to master and sacrifice one's body.

Having set in motion his plan, the Yankee embarks on a journey to see the countryside and get to know the people and their ways. He travels first as a knight in armor; then (with the king) disguised as a free peasant; and finally, after being captured and sold, as a slave. He thereby sees England first hand from every angle, except that of the priest.

The Yankee is a critical traveler, and much of his criticism is directed at the knights. As the rulers of England, they embody and defend the martial virtues and way of life that are incompatible with scientific and industrial development. They also form the hereditary aristocracy that is a great obstacle to the Yankee's desire for a republic based on universal male suffrage. The central theme of the Yankee's critique of the knights is that hereditary aristocracy is a slave system that is prone to casual cruelty; that corrupts both the people and the nobles; and that disregards the common good. In particular, he dwells at greatest length on the routine and off-hand cruelty of the aristocracy toward the lower classes. Morgan Le Fay's stabbing of a young page for a minor act of clumsiness; her dungeon of pathetic prisoners; a slave driver who warms his freezing band of slaves by burning a woman at the stake—the Yankee milks such instances of cruelty for all they are worth.

He not only argues that the aristocrats' cruelty causes a lot of suffering but also that it degrades the character of the people. He believes, for example, that all men have by nature a certain element of spiritedness or self-assertion that can lead to demands for dignity and political equality. But when he encounters the docility and humble reverence of the freemen toward the aristocracy, he is troubled and begins to wonder whether long habit, frequent violence, and crushing burdens can destroy even this elemental manhood (20). Bad as hereditary aristocracy is for the people, however, its worst effect is also felt by the aristocrats themselves. A long familiarity with slavery and the habit of superiority ossifies "the superior lobe of human feeling." That is, hereditary aristocracy destroys compassion and with it the sense of a common humanity (21, 25). The exigencies of maintaining a privileged class lead the members of that class to think they can kill, imprison, torture, and enslave the common people almost at will.

In all their political acts, the aristocrats think first about maintaining their class and keeping the people in their place. They think with their titles rather than reasoning about the common good or justice. In a general comment on the partiality that mars the king's judicial decisions, the Yankee observes that it was as if he were a mother holding the "position of milk-distributor to starving children in famine-time; her own children would fare a shade better than the rest" (25). This comment might seem to vindicate Arthur's favoritism for his own class, for it suggests that it is motivated by scarcity: there is not enough to feed everyone, so tough decisions must be made to ensure that at least one class—the one that maintains the realm's political independence—has enough to perform its tasks even if others must do without. If this were true, the Yankee's desire for equal justice would undermine the common good. Yet the Yankee's comment also points to his reply. He would argue that Camelot could overcome scarcity—thereby making equal justice and political freedom possible—by embracing technical progress and free markets rather than protectionist economics. Moreover, the inventor who thinks of a gun as a labor-saving device would argue that new military technology (along with a citizen army) could solve the problem of defense without necessitating a class of knights who need leisure for training in manual weapons. Thus, the class system harms the common good; the Yankee's position is not rooted only in devotion to bodily comfort but is also justified as the means to justice and security.

Although the knights are very powerful, the Yankee identifies the established Church as his biggest problem. Such a church, he says, is "the greatest power imaginable," greater even than the knights and himself combined (8, 16, 18). The Church is the source of the knights' power: it invented the divine right theory of aristocracy; it teaches the people the beauty of self-sacrifice and humility through its interpretation of the Beatitudes; and the kindness of its priests reconciles the people to the system that oppresses them. His fundamental solution—indeed, his only demand in religion—is the elimination of the established Church (16). He argues that each person is an individual who is at his best "morally" when he chooses his own religious garb; but his main argument is that disestablishment is a precondition of political liberty (18).

The Church presents a spiritual obstacle, but the Yankee treats it entirely as a political problem. He makes no attempt to offer an alternative interpretation of the Beatitudes. The reason seems to be that he just does not take religious sentiments seriously. For example, after the Yankee saved the sun, large crowds gathered hoping to witness another miracle. The Yankee is annoyed. He believes that they wish to see a miracle so that they can go home and claim reflected glory: the desire to see a miracle is rooted in vanity and ambition. Perhaps because he knows that his "miracle" was just a trick, he does not even consider the possibility that others might genuinely wish to witness a miracle as evidence of divine presence. So deep is this attitude that it is years before he realizes that Merlin actually believes in magic and is not just a pretender like himself. And even after that, he is surprised when, forced to choose, most of his followers desert to the side of the Church.

Although he does not himself appreciate the religious sentiment of self-sacrifice, the Yankee knows that it is the great obstacle to his plans, and he does muster a variety of weapons against it. He frequently mocks its effects, for example, in his treatment of the bowing hermit and the discomfort of armor. He also points out the hypocrisy of clergymen, who preach self-denial while growing fat themselves. More generally, while admitting that the priests generally care well for their flocks, he also exposes the role of self-sacrifice in supporting the injustices of the aristocracy. Again, he tries to find as many boys like the irreverent "mocking featherhead," Clarence, as possible, and then educate them scientifically. The suggestion is either that there are a certain people who are naturally impervious to the Church's doctrine or that everyone is—if only they are caught early enough and properly educated against it.

Two other weapons complete the Yankee's antiestablishment arsenal. According to the code of chivalry, a knight defeated in combat must do whatever the victor commands. Accordingly, when the Yankee defeats a knight, he sends him out on knightly expeditions dressed in top hats or sandwich boards to promote things like toothpaste and bath soap. Part of the intention is to undermine knighthood by putting its high seriousness in the service of mundane projects, thereby rendering that seriousness ridiculous; but, it is also a furtive way to undermine the Church (16). The connection is suggested when the Yankee performs his greatest miracle, the restoration of water to the well in the Valley of Holiness. The monks who live in this desert valley, England's holiest site, secretly long for a cool, refreshing bath; but, they also believe that bathing is a sin against God. For them, dirtiness is next to godliness. When the well dries up, the monks believe it is a divine punishment for their secret desire. The Yankee, however, restores the water with a spectacular "miracle" and then uses the reverence with which he is subsequently regarded to insist that the monks take a bath with soap (24). His hope that this will undermine the Church rests on the fact that even the monks wish to bathe: the Yankee believes his approach to be superior to that of the monks because it does not oppose but builds upon fundamental human desires. This belief presupposes that the desire for bodily comfort is more deeply rooted in human nature than the desire to overcome or master or rise above the body's demands.

The same incident in the Valley of Holiness reveals another of the Yankee's weapons against the Church. The monks believe that the water has ceased to flow because their sins have angered God. No amount of praying or penance, however, has restored the flow of water. The practical Yankee, by contrast, diagnoses the problem as a leak in the well's wall, which he easily fixes. Thus, the "spiritual" approach fails whereas the Yankee's scientific approach succeeds. The Yankee accommodates himself to his audience and presents his fix as a miracle, but the reader of his history knows the truth: no one of sound mind would prefer the delusion to the truth about nature's forces.

The novel thus makes a strong case for the Yankee, and when he returns to Camelot after his travels, he seems to be on the verge of success. He turns a combat against Sir Sagramour into a defeat of the entire chivalry of England and their champion, Merlin. Soon thereafter, he feels strong enough to reveal his secret system of schools, mines, and factories "to an astonished world" (40). Moreover, King Arthur, having now personally experienced servitude, has abolished slavery, and the Yankee hopes that when the king, who has no heir, dies, the monarchy will be replaced by a republic. At just this moment, however, the Yankee's child falls ill, and he is induced to go abroad in search of a cure. While he is absent, the knights fight a civil war. It is contained when the Church issues an Interdict, which includes the Yankee and causes most of his followers to desert him for the Church.

This collapse of the Yankee's plans culminates in the gruesome battle of the Sand Belt, in which the Yankee, armed with modern technology, destroys 25,000 knights and his own incipient "civilization." The long critique of Camelot thus concludes not in the Yankee's victory but in his tragic self-destruction. Moreover, just as he is about to die amidst the putrefying corpses his weapons had created, the Yankee is put under a spell by Merlin to sleep for thirteen centuries. Merlin, who apparently thinks that to live in the nineteenth century would be a fate worse than death, thereby gets the last laugh. And indeed, the Yankee seems to agree with Merlin. When he awakens from his long slumber, we find him in an old castle among the relics of medieval times, trying to relive his life in Camelot. He speaks and acts as if he belonged in the sixth century. He dreams that he did what he in fact had done—destroy the entire chivalry of England and with it "all that is dear to me, all that could make life worth the living" (Final P. S. by M. T.). When he says this he is thinking above all of his wife and child rather than of his projects or the knights, but they too belong to the destroyed world. The Yankee now misses Camelot more than he had missed America at the beginning. Having experienced both worlds, he judges that medieval England is superior to the modern world.

Were it not for this ending, the novel could be read, as it often has been read, as a celebration of Enlightenment or American progress. But the ending raises a question about the goodness of the Yankee's project—indeed, about the possibility of peaceful progress. Twain seems to suggest that American optimism about technical and social progress is a fatal illusion, and even that, once unleashed, technological power inexorably destroys humanity.

These suggestions would become fully credible only with a critical analysis of the Yankee's idea of progress. The Yankee does not of course offer such an analysis, but a closer look at his history does reveal some problems in his approach. When the Yankee begins his project, he is extraordinarily naive politically. For example, seeing the submissiveness of the common people toward the nobles and priests, he concludes that they are unmanly. He must discover that when one group has an almost absolute power over another, the members of the subordinate group do not reveal their deepest thoughts to every passing stranger. More generally, as he learns more about England, he begins to realize that the transformation of a society does not require a "boss" (i.e., a foreman or businessman) so much as a "statesman." The turning point comes during his visit to Morgan Le Fay. Shocked by her casual murder of a page and the death sentence pronounced on the boy's grieving grandmother, the Yankee (prompted by Sandy) intervenes to save the old woman. He then tours Morgan's ghastly dungeons and is so deeply affected by pity for the inmates that he frees almost all of them, not because they are innocent (though most are) but because he cannot stand even to see or hear their suffering. Compassion is his deepest sentiment. The problem is that, as a principle of statesmanship, compassion cannot distinguish between worthy and unworthy cases.[6] When the Yankee, who has just witnessed the casual murder of the page, perceives that Morgan herself is "really suffering" for fear of him, she becomes the object of his pity (17). "A statesman," he reflects, "gains little by the arbitrary exercise of iron-clad authority upon all occasions that offer. . . . A little concession, now and then, where it can do no harm, is the wiser policy" (17). Thus justified, he mollifies Morgan by unjustly and unnecessarily permitting her to hang a whole band of musicians for playing badly (17). It is therefore not clear that the Yankee's compassionate statesmanship would produce more justice. That compassion is at any rate perfectly consistent with a brutal harshness, as when he regards the peasants who will not rally to his call for a republic as "human muck" (43, 42). The Yankee's pity even threatens his own preservation. After the Battle of the Sand Belt, pity moves him to help the injured knights. In return, he receives a wound that, but for Merlin's spell, would have killed him. The man who boasts that he is nearly barren of sentiment turns out to be dangerously sentimental.

Another problem concerns the Yankee's attitude toward his own project. Once he realizes that he is in the sixth century, he briefly regrets loosing his friends; but he quickly determines that he prefers Camelot to Connecticut. "Look at the opportunities here for a man of knowledge, brains, pluck and enterprise. . . . The grandest field that ever was; and all my own; not a competitor; not a man who wasn't a baby to me in acquirements and capacities" (8). At home, the Yankee is a small fish in a big sea; in Camelot, he is the only whale in a small pond. And he prefers the latter, where he can take credit for inventing soap and mirrors, to the former, where he will just be an ordinary man running a factory. The Yankee prefers Camelot not because he loves its people or because its way of life is superior to that in the nineteenth century—he is in no danger of going native—but as a means to self-development and aggrandizement. The actual achievements of his society are less important to him than his love of progress itself, and he prefers the society that provides the greatest scope for participating in it. In this way, he is fundamentally rootless. No stable goal animates the Yankee's life.

Many of the Yankee's adventures reflect and expand on this aspect of his character, but two are especially revealing. In the story of the king's evil, the Yankee discovers that the people of England really do reverence the king, and he sees that their faith really does heal. Just as we receive this insight into the English soul, a boy passes by selling the first newspaper in history, bringing to fruition one of the Yankee's pet projects. He records that the sound of the newspaper tout "enchanted my soul" (26). He bought a copy and began reading it while the monks, the only literate men in England, looked on in "tranced adoration." Indeed, the Yankee's soul was "steeped in satisfaction, drunk with enjoyment. Yes, this was heaven; I was tasting it once, if I might never taste it more" (26). This is the Yankee's peak experience. Whereas the knights' manliness consists in self-mastery for the sake of noble service to country, the core of the Yankee's being is love of his own productions.

This scene prompts many thoughts, but one of them is surely that the Yankee's satisfaction is not sustainable. The reaction that he finds so satisfying depends on the monks' believing that the newspaper was a miracle, a wonder, "a dark work of enchantment." But in the society the Yankee is trying to create, this experience would vanish, or at least become ever more rare.

People would grow accustomed to constant innovation of all kinds: novelty itself would become routine. To the extent that the Yankee accomplishes his goal, he eliminates the possibility of enjoying the contentment he considers most "divine."

The second point is not based on any one incident but concerns the Yankee's handling of a sphere of life that is not merely "practical." When he woke up from Merlin's curse, it was above all the memory of his wife and child that made him feel he had destroyed everything that "could" make life worth living. Even more than progress and its satisfactions, it seems to be love that attaches the Yankee to the sixth century. But this was something he learned only very late. Prior to being transposed to medieval England, the Yankee, although a fully-grown man, seems to have had no experience of love. In Connecticut, he had been "almost engaged" to one Puss Flannagan. But this romance seems to have been based entirely on telephone calls: Miss Flannagan, a telephone operator, had a sweet voice that the Yankee liked to hear. But the Yankee's problem is not just a lack of experience. When he arrives in England, he is very uncomfortable with anything that hints of sexuality. Quite simply, the Yankee is a prude. Even his marriage to Sandy reflects this. He married her after many years "for no particular reason" except to alleviate his own misplaced fear of compromising her (41). And it is only after the marriage that he becomes aware of her attractions. The Yankee's society seems to have left him almost without eros and entirely unprepared for the erotic side of life.

One problem is that when he finally does stumble upon this part of life, he virtually falls apart, as we see in this gush about his marriage: "People talk about beautiful friendships between two persons of the same sex. What is the best of that sort, as compared with the friendship of man and wife, where the best impulses and highest ideals of both are the same? There is no place for comparison between the two friendships; the one is earthly, the other divine" (41). These sentiments may be true, but the Yankee has just informed us that Sandy strictly honored the custom of chivalry, according to which she was the Yankee's property until another knight won her from him in combat (41, 15). Either Sandy has undergone a miraculous change of character (of which there is no evidence in the novel) or the Yankee is deceiving himself as to their shared ideals. An even greater problem is that when his first child is born, the Yankee loses interest in his public duties. Indeed, it was his preoccupation with his child that made him vulnerable to the Church's tricks. For when the child fell ill, the Church took advantage of that preoccupation to trick the Yankee into taking a long trip abroad for the sake of the child's health. The Yankee's single-minded concern for the "practical" side of life not only leaves him unable to regulate the "practical" things in the light of higher goals (piety or family) but leaves him vulnerable to those who do understand the passions connected with the "poetic" side of life.

The novel's evident sympathy for the Yankee's project, then, is accompanied by a less obvious but still searching criticism of the Yankee's character. The Yankee's flaws do make the final conflagration more understandable, but they do not justify the conclusion that the Yankee's alternative is essentially self-destructive. The devastating end is the consequence not simply of the Yankee's project but of the clash between it and another utterly incompatible system. The clash occurs only because both alternatives are present at once; but, we are reminded in the sections that frame the Yankee's history that the modern world exists, and in that world there is no established Church to oppose the Yankee. While the novel suggests that modern America leaves certain parts of human nature unfulfilled, almost even unrecognized, and that it has nothing in the name of which to limit or guide the quest for bodily comfort, it does not reject modernity as necessarily self-destroying.

Still, the novel is not exactly a wholehearted endorsement of modern America. It suggests various considerations that favor the modern alternative—the relief of poverty and physical suffering, scientific knowledge, political freedom, and so forth. It also suggests certain considerations that favor Camelot such as graceful beauty of character, courage, simple sincerity, and devotion. Similar lists could be compiled of the defects of each. The novel might still speak for modernity if there were a standard by which to rank these considerations, but the novel does not appear to provide such a standard. Twain's purpose seems to have been to lay out the alternatives, not to adjudicate between them. That the conflict between the two alternatives culminates in a mutually destructive war may even suggest that there is no principled way to resolve the issue.

And yet that war is not quite the end of the story. The Yankee's "history" is framed by a brief "Preface," which is attributed to "Mark Twain," and by two sections narrated by one "M. T." The "Preface" is ironically ambiguous about progress and suggests the need for further reflection. The other two parts of the frame suggest still another alternative. M. T. may or may not be an American, but he is modern. In contrast to the Yankee, however, he is not merely practical: he has a literary education, knows and enjoys his Malory, and when we meet him he is using his modern wealth and leisure to tour the relics of the medieval world. This man is neither a rabid progressive like the Yankee is for most of the novel nor the nostalgic that he is after returning to the nineteenth century. The latter option, which is developed in the romances of Sir Walter Scott and Lord Tennyson, suggests that a return to chivalry is the solution to the problems of modernity. Twain is too severe a critic of chivalry to adopt this solution. Yet he is also very critical of the Yankee's progressive modernity. In fact, these seemingly opposite alternatives have something in common; for whereas the progressive Yankee lives for the future, the nostalgic Yankee lives for the past: both seek escape from the present. M. T., however, is a modern man who seeks knowledge of the past, not as a replacement for but as a supplement to the present. Twain's suggestion is that what modern man really needs is knowledge of the past as an aid to sober and frank analysis of the present.[7] By placing the Yankee in Camelot, Twain revealed the problems in the Yankee's progressivism while at the same time discrediting the main alternative to it. He delivers a sobering caution about modern man without lending any support to the idea that we can return to a glorified and nobler past.

Notes

1. I wish to thank the Earhart Foundation for its generous financial support while writing this chapter. References to Twain's writings will be to the number of the chapter in which the quotation appears.

2. My account of this scene relies on Harry V. Jaffa's essay on Tom Sawyer in *The Conditions of Freedom: Essays in Political Philosophy* (Baltimore: Johns Hopkins University Press, 1975), esp. 195–97. I acknowledge here a debt to this remarkable essay, especially to its account of the thematic structure of the novel.

3. Jaffa, *Conditions of Freedom*, 200.

4. It would be difficult to be further removed from the essential meaning of Christianity. Huck seems to hold that there is a God capable of answering prayer but Who is of no consequence for him personally. Huck is not as incoherent as these contradictory views would suggest because he also seems to believe that Christianity is fundamentally a social convention, from which he excludes himself. In any case, Huck's reflections on religion show that his humility, if that is the right word, is not Christian. He is certainly not proud, like Hobbes's natural man. The closest philosophic source of Huck's character is Rousseau.

5. A more complete discussion of Huck's attitude toward law can be found in Catherine H. Zuckert, *Natural Right and the American Imagination* (Savage, Md.: Rowman and Littlefield, 1990), chap. 6.

6. See Catherine and Michael Zuckert, "'And in its Wake we Followed:' The Political Wisdom of Mark Twain," *Interpretation* 3, no. 1 (1972): 85–86.

7. Catherine and Michael Zuckert, "Political Wisdom of Mark Twain," 59–66.

Chapter 25

Pricking the Bubble of Utopian Sentiment:
The Political Thought of William Graham Sumner

Lance Robinson

William Graham Sumner (1840–1910)—Yale graduate, European educated Episcopalian minister, and longtime professor of economics and sociology at Yale University—is routinely characterized as one of America's preeminent and influential social Darwinists. This view of Sumner is typically offered by progressive intellectuals, themselves wedded to evolutionary ideology but prone to anticipate meliorative relief from nature's harshness through expansive government action. Sumner's refusal to pursue the chimera of meliorative government relief in the face of a competitive social order has led writers such as Richard Hofstadter to assert that "it was easy to argue by analogy from natural selection of fitter organisms to social selection of fitter men, from organic forms with superior adaptability to citizens with a greater store of economic virtue."[1] Yet what remains unanswered in these criticisms is how Sumner's argument that superior economic virtue in individuals contributes to the elevation and success of a society is to be considered analogous to the supposed adaptability of an organic form. Virtue and adaptation are not necessarily analogous (an evolutionist might say homologous, meaning things corresponding in structure and evolutionary origin), for virtue is not a natural process as is adaptation. The transmission of virtue requires education of one generation by a preceding generation. Sumner understood the inherent tension between the two concepts and looked to education in the arts and sciences to maintain the inheritance of generations of experience and knowledge. While he may have used the language of evolutionary development to express his ideas in an age suffused with enthusiasm for the latest in scientific theories, it does not necessarily indicate that his explanation of the dynamics of social progress ineluctably follows the harsh and rigid biological prescriptions of Darwinian natural selection.

Indeed, throughout his writings, Sumner maintains a political-economic focus in his consideration of the origins and development of mankind; he argues that "the essential elements of political economy are only corollaries or special cases of sociological principles."[2] The realm of politics remains secondary for Sumner; for it is limited and bounded by the more fundamental rules of society—rules he attempts to define and elucidate through developing the study of sociology.[3] Thus, it is within the constraints of Sumner's social philosophy that we must strive to derive the principles of political order and efficacy. While not primarily a political thinker, Sumner does address a considerable range of political topics of profound importance. The bounded character of politics, informed by his social philosophy, differentiates him from the Progressives of his time, who found nearly limitless potential in politics. The economic emphasis of his political economy informs his rather pessimistic view of the possibilities for human action to ameliorate the effects of the harsh political-economic laws of nature that govern the world and society.

Sumner wrote voluminously on a wide variety of topics, ranging from economics and sociology to education and imperialism. His most commonly recognized work is *What Social Classes Owe to Each Other*, a book-length treatise first published in 1883 as a response to social reformers. This work encapsulates his thought at the time; and in its attempt to define a reasonable foundation for individual obligation, it presages his later move toward a more relativistic sociology. It is, therefore, of particular use as a starting point in any attempt to understand his political thought. Perhaps most noted for his concern for the "Forgotten Man" (the individuals who supply their own needs and upon whom fall the burdens of fulfilling utopian sentiment), the work is also a strong defense of the social and political principles supporting liberty, rights and duties, the state, law, and political institutions. It is this social foundation and political superstructure that creates the conditions under which the forgotten man may for a time be capable of supporting the misguided, costly social equalization and welfare schemes of the sentimental philosophers and politicians that Sumner criticizes so frankly.[4]

Human nature, properly working in conjunction with the inexorable laws of nature and society, may eventually produce the politics of liberty. According to Sumner, nature is harsh and unforgiving, and man must compete with nature to increase the amount of useful goods for his support and comfort. Indeed, it is only through considerable expenditure of effort that such a happy result may occur, for originally "man was just like the brutes." In this condition, "he could wrest nothing from nature"; "his existence was almost entirely controlled by accident"; and he relied on nature for his subsistence because "he possessed no capital" with which to wrest from nature what it would not naturally provide. From this low beginning, man has come to be "an intelligent animal" knowing "something of the laws of Nature," and he can therefore "bring the productive forces of nature into service." It is by some fortuitous accident that humanity emerges with the germ of intelligence necessary to take the first steps out of this primitive condition, "for everything we know about the primitive man shows us that he did not reflect" (*SC* 51–53).

Since this primitive man "could leave no sign of his presence on the earth save his bones," the first record we have is of a "man so far superior to the brutes that he knew how to use fire and had the use of flints." These "first beginnings of capital are lost in the obscurity" of prehistory, but this advance provides mankind its greatest asset: the use of tools to aid him in his existence —or simply put, the acquisition and application of capital. According to Sumner, the use of capital—"force" or "human energy stored or accumulated"—is "the thing which made his civilization possible." He asserts that "[i]f we can come to an understanding of what capital is, and what a place it occupies in civilization, it will clear up our ideas about a great many of these schemes and philosophies which are put forward to criticize social arrangements, or as a basis of proposed reforms" (*SC* 53–54).

The character of man's existence in the primitive state continues after he discovers the use of capital to improve his condition. The "struggle for existence," as Sumner calls it, is one of the inexorable laws of nature that governs mankind's existence on earth, regardless of the state of progress in arts, education, and comfort which he has thus far obtained (*SC* 8, 141, 161, 164; cf. "Sociology" 187, 194). Even in society the struggle for existence continues, requiring that "capital must increase"; for "if the society does not keep up its power, if it lowers its organization or wastes its capital, it falls back toward the natural state of barbarism from which it rose" (*SC* 59). Families, as the original societies, are the foundation of progress in this struggle for existence, for they accumulate capital and pass it on to their heirs, who in turn pass it on ("Sociology" 188). This results in a cascading improvement in the state of human existence under conditions of struggle with nature. By this means, the human race keeps up a constantly advancing contest with Nature. The penalty of ceasing an aggressive behavior toward the hardships of life on the part of mankind is, that we go backward. We cannot stand still. Now, parental affection constitutes the personal motive which drives every man in his place to an aggressive and conquering policy toward the limiting conditions of human life. (*SC* 64)

Regardless of man's political status, he is never free from the limiting constraints of nature around him; his gains against nature are defined in economic terms as the application of an increasing pool of capital and are limited by the economic law of supply and demand. According to Sumner, "[t]he truth is that the social order is fixed by laws of nature precisely analogous to those of the physical order" ("Socialism" 172). In social terms, the law of supply and demand manifests itself in the form of the "law of population and the diminishing return" of land ("Sociology" 189). It is the pressure of rising population in a limited area of land that fosters increased activity in the social forces that are the condition of progress for society as a whole. "Division of labor, exchange, higher social organization, emigration, advance in the arts, spring from the necessity of contending against the harsher conditions of existence which are continually reproduced as the population surpasses the means of existence on any given status" ("Sociology" 188). It follows, then, that the ethics of a particular society will be built upon the foundation of the material conditions affecting that society, specifically the ratio of population to land and the resultant scarcity or abundance of necessary goods in that society.

The law of supply and demand operates through another major principle beyond the struggle for existence. In the struggle for existence, individuals are "wrestling with nature to extort from her the means of subsistence" ("War" 302). There is a second great effect that follows from the struggle for existence: "the competition of man with man in the effort to win a limited supply" ("Sociology" 189). Sumner calls this "the competition of life," which "arises between groups, not between individuals" and is that from which "war arises" from a "collision of interest" between groups competing for the same limited pool of resources ("War" 302). "This competition," according to Sumner, "draws out the highest achievements. It makes the advantages of capital, education, talent, skill, and training tell to the utmost" ("Sociology" 194). Mankind, then, advances from a primitive stage through the effect of some fortuitous accident and thus begins to acquire and apply capital to his condition, thereby improving it. This allows an increase in population, which has the tendency to foster competition for scarce resources; which in turn stimulates the development of improved modes of acquiring and applying capital; and which then improves productivity and allows population to increase even more.

From this competition (which "is a law of nature") we can see the development of ever more complex societal organizations which, as a result of this competition, work to populate the globe and continue to improve the art of capital formation and accumulation ("Socialism" 164). It is

the constant tendency of population to outstrip the means of subsistence [that] is the force which has distributed population over the world, and produced all advance in civilization. To this day the two means of escape for an overpopulated country are emigration and an advance in the arts. The former wins more land for the same people; the latter makes the same land support more persons. ("Socialism" 163)

It is in the attempt to answer questions that arise about how to organize these societies from which spring issues of ethics and morality:

[T]he student of social welfare finds that the limit of social well-being of the society in the progress of time depends on the possibility of increasing the capital faster than the numbers increase. But so soon as he comes to consider the increase of capital, he finds himself face to face with ethical facts and forces. Capital is the fruit of industry, temperance, prudence, frugality, and other industrial virtues. Here then the welfare of society is found to be rooted in moral forces, and the relation between ethical and social phenomena is given in terms of actual facts and not rhetorical abstractions. ("The State as an 'Ethical Person'" 234)

The laws that govern society remain analogous to physical laws and provide the limits within which the politics of a given society operate. The "elementary conditions" of society "are set by the nature of human beings and the nature of the earth" ("Sociology" 187). The nature of mankind, as it really is, consists of "passion, emotion, and instinct," and it is subject to the vices of "cupidity, lust, vindictiveness, ambition, and vanity" (*SC* 65, 27). In order to achieve any advance in his condition, mankind must not only war against nature but his own nature as well. The penalty to mankind for failing to organize in such a way as to keep these natural tendencies in check is to fall "back toward the natural state of barbarism from which it rose" (*SC* 59). It is left to the realm of politics practiced well to recognize the force of these laws of nature and to organize society consistent with them in such a manner that the formation, accumulation, and application of capital is accomplished in as efficient a manner as possible given the material constraints existing at the time. Appropriate political organization will change over time depending upon the shifting trends in material factors: the ratio of population to land and the state of development in the arts and sciences.

Thus, man is essentially a brute undistinguished from any other member of the animal kingdom—except for the beneficial result of a chance accident which introduces him to capital and makes of him a social animal. Unlike in Rousseau's formulation (whose lead Sumner otherwise follows in this description of man's emergence from his primitive form), this brutish existence was neither idyllic nor benign. Rather, man's existence continues as a competitive struggle both against nature and his fellow man; for "only the most meager and inadequate supply for human needs can be obtained directly from nature" ("Socialism" 159). Only his rationality—that fortuitous gift that enabled him to begin to accumulate and use capital—can provide some relief (but not escape) from the brutish laws of nature. Mankind continues to be "subjects of passion, emotion, and instinct" until such progress in the arts and sciences is made as to raise "them to the point where reason and conscience can even curb the lower motive forces"—a benefit enjoyed only by the elite members of society in Sumner's time (*SC* 65). As such, any concept of natural rights is merely conventional, having no grounding in the essentially brutish character of mankind.

Man's reason informs him only in the application of how the arts and sciences can make more comfortable his essentially passionate existence. Reason does not distinguish mankind and the beasts; rather, man is only a particularly gifted beast upon whom chance has smiled in bequeathing the means of accumulating and using capital for his own improvement and comfort. "The motive to all immediate efforts," according to Sumner, "is either self-interest or the desire to gratify one's tastes and natural tendencies" ("Discipline" 71). Passion, then, is the great motive force for the actions of mankind, but this passion is moderated by certain habits (dare we say virtues) necessary to successful fulfillment of desire in the face of an unforgiving nature.[5] Reason acts in the service of the passions to wrest from nature, or other men, that which leads to or is necessary for the comfort and fulfillment of the desires. Far from teaching man the fundamental distinction between man and beast essential to the articulation of classic natural rights, nature merely impels man to succeed, if he will, in the competition for scarce resources with other men and other beasts.

According to Sumner, the concept of natural rights as a fulfillment of human nature providing a basis for politics is nonsensical:[6]

There is a beautiful notion afloat in our literature and in the minds of our people that men are born to certain "natural rights." If that were true, there would be something on earth which was got for nothing, and this world would not be the place it is at all. The fact is, that there is no right whatever inherited by man which has not an equivalent and corresponding duty by the side of it, as the price of it. . . . If there were such a thing as natural rights, the question would arise, Against whom are they good? Who has the corresponding obligation to satisfy these rights? There can be no rights against Nature, except to get out of her whatever we can, which is only the fact of the struggle for existence stated over again. The common assertion is, that the rights are good against society; that is, that society is bound to obtain and secure them for the persons interested. . . . This theory is a very far-reaching one, and of course it is adequate to furnish a foundation for a whole social philosophy. In its widest extension it comes to mean that if any man finds himself uncomfortable in this world, it must be somebody else's fault, and that somebody is bound to come and make him comfortable. (*SC* 116)

Consistent with his brutish understanding of human nature, the only conceivable purpose for natural rights would be for one group to obtain benefits at the expense of another group in their pursuit of comfort. Sumner's conception of man in enmity against nature instead of man as a harmonious part of nature informs his perception regarding the impossibility of natural rights, and hence of no natural-ethical grounding for politics, morality, and law. Each of these is merely conventional, a product of societal invention. Nevertheless, we do know that "competition . . . is a law of nature" ("Socialism" 164). He further asserts that "certain uniform and constant motives, aims, and desires will present themselves as long as human society endures; and that men will, therefore, continue to exert themselves in a certain manner for the satisfaction of their wants. This is what we mean by natural law, and by the field of a science of society" ("Democracy and Plutocracy" 138). Competition is evidenced in the struggle for existence and the competition of life, both of which improves man's condition through the application of capital. Capital, though, "is the fruit of industry, temperance, prudence, frugality, and other industrial virtues" ("The State as an 'Ethical Person'" 234). It is our "reason and conscience" that inform us of the benefit of adhering to these virtues which successfully "curb the lower motive forces" and enable the successful development of civilization (*SC* 65; "Democracy and Plutocracy" 141–42). Despite the fact that rhetorically Sumner decries the notion of natural rights as a foundation for politics, we see that he does in fact provide a natural—if base—foundation for politics. Sumner's critique of utopianism, which he considered to be both impractical and dangerous when applied in a political regime, begins to encroach upon his own understanding of politics. Because he rejects the distinction between man and beast, he shares a conception of human nature with those very utopians, a view of human nature which they use to justify their utopian view of natural rights. Both view man as base and beastly, but Sumner rejects the utopian notion that human nature is infinitely malleable, preferring instead to recognize those forces in nature and society that work to control the excesses of that base nature and direct it toward productive ends. Amidst this confusion it remains to discern what basis exists in nature as a foundation for politics, according to Sumner, despite his protestations against natural rights.

Politics is a conventional creation of society, and unlike society, which is governed by natural laws, it exists in the realm of issues that cannot be scientifically determined.

The evils of society are to a great extent the result of the dogmatism and self-interest of statesmen, philosophers, and ecclesiastics who in past time have done just what the socialists now want to do. Instead of studying the natural laws of the social order, they assumed that they could organize society as they chose, they made up their minds what kind of a society they wanted to make, and they planned their little measures for the ends they had resolved upon. It will take centuries of scientific study of the facts of nature to eliminate from human society the mischie-

vous institutions and traditions which the said statesmen, philosophers, and ecclesiastics have
introduced into it. ("Socialism" 172)

Politicians, statesmen, and other public figures work in a nonscientific arena, and the best that
can be hoped for is that they might be informed by scientific understanding, which would lead
them away from misdirected efforts toward social amelioration. The role of politics is to fashion
an organization fit for the particular social conditions governing a particular society, a society
that itself has resulted from a specific combination of population, amount and fertility of land,
and stage of progress in the development of the arts and sciences. Certain forms of government
will be appropriate to a combination of conditions, and some forms will be inappropriate to the
continued progress of that society.

Insofar as the realms of politics and society coincide, though, those laws which act upon
society also act upon politics, and they therefore provide a foundation in nature for politics.
Sumner, however, discounts the possibility for politics to establish any formal political constitution which would act to shape the character of society outside of the natural laws which dictate
the conditions of existence, calling all such prescriptions visionary or utopian. Society, Sumner
argues, "does not need any care or supervision." It does, however, need to be "freed from these
meddlers—that is, to be let alone" in order that "we may hope to gain some ground slowly
toward the elimination of old errors and the re-establishment of a sound and natural social order"
(*SC* 103–4). Therefore, "[t]he greatest reforms which could now be accomplished would consist
in undoing the work of statesmen in the past, and the greatest difficulty in the way of reform is
to find out how to undo their work without injury to what is natural and sound" (*SC* 102–3).
Constitutional provisions, then, do not have a positive role in creating or shaping society but
rather a negative role in preventing harm from social doctors who would wish to attempt to
design and create a more congenial environment through state action. Left to its own devices
society will, in accordance with the natural laws of competition and advance, preserve itself.
"Institutions and guarantees," however, may contribute to the natural preservation of society as
the tools with which "new foes must be met as the old ones were" (*SC* 95). These guarantees are
not a product of design but rather a "body of laws and institutions which have grown up as
occasion has occurred for adjusting rights. Let the same process go on" (*SC* 104). It remains
unclear in Sumner's thought, however, why those natural laws could not inform statesmen of the
desirability of creating a political order in which just the sort of society Sumner desires would
flourish. Man can reason about the desirability of increasing capital, and improving his capacity
to continue to increase capital, but Sumner denies to him the capacity to foresee and create a
political order capable of promoting that very advance.

The best and most efficient political order, then, is one that inhibits any interruption of the
natural laws of competition. Based upon this economic principle, liberty, equality (of a certain
type), individualism, and private property are crucial to the capability to accumulate capital.
Where capital accumulation is accommodated by these conditions, the most efficient political
order recognizes and promotes these attributes. It is common for statesmen, Sumner argues, to
believe that, like the "chip which floated on the current thought that it made the river go," so
"statesmen and political philosophers think that they make institutions and mould history."
Instead, he claims that: "The thing which makes and breaks institutions is economic forces,
acting on the interests of men, and, through them, on human nature. The statesman who goes
along with these forces, wins great 'triumphs'; but he is like the chip on the current, after all; the
most that he does is to show in which direction it is going" (*SD* 62). The economic forces of
capital accumulation and preservation are the true natural laws that guide human action and are
the source of scientific sociology. The only success politics can hope for is to understand these

phenomena and to act in accordance with them. Politics "is the domain of discretion, judgment, sovereign action" rather than the realm of certainty and science ("Republican Government" 88). Therefore, while politics can act in a way that accords with scientific understanding and that does not inhibit its application, it cannot act directly to interpret and apply the laws of nature as can sociology. Politics exists in the realm of art rather than science—"that is, of the application of scientific laws by human intelligence to the fulfillment of our purposes."

> When we go over to statecraft, we go over to art—to the domain, not of truth but of expediency, not of scientific laws but of maxims. The statesman then may well be guided by maxims drawn from history and experience. No maxim is more than approximately wise, for wisdom cannot be put into absolute statements and injunctions. ("*Laissez-Faire*" 232–33)

Politics reaches its "perfection" only "if political institutions can give security for the pursuit of happiness by each individual, according to his own notion of it, in his own way, and by his own means" (*SD* 103). This is the role of politics and government—to provide "peace, order, and security," while also guaranteeing a continued policy of laissez-faire (which means, according to Sumner, "let us manage for ourselves") (*SD* 107). "Laissez-faire is," for Sumner, "the only maxim which allows of the correct use of history and statistics to secure such knowledge as shall properly guide the statesman in his task," or in other words, to preserve liberty for citizens to pursue their chosen activities ("*Laissez-Faire*" 227, 233).

Consequently, liberty is the most important political principle for Sumner. Liberty, though, is not "a natural endowment, belonging to everybody, a human birthright" ("Liberty" 238). Man is not a political or social animal, as Aristotle would say, but fundamentally a brute who has ascended and in the process discovered the efficiency of social organization. Neither is liberty "doing what one pleases" or "unrestrainedness of action," for "all human and earthly existence is conditioned on physical facts . . . surrounded and limited by the equilibrium of the forces of nature, which man can never disturb" ("Liberty" 237). Therefore, liberty is not a natural right derived from the natural political equality of all humans as humans, for not all humans have achieved the level of civilization—of the application of capital to the relief of their needs—which produces a society capable of recognizing the importance of protecting liberty. For mankind, "the only real liberty which is possible or conceivable on earth, is a matter of law and institutions." Sumner refers to this real liberty as civil liberty because it "must . . . be an affair of positive law, of institutions, and of history" ("Liberty" 240–41). Such a construct is only the product of a relatively mature social and political organization which has developed to the degree wherein it is capable of creating sound laws and institutions: "it does not lie at the beginning of history and of the struggle of the human race on this earth; it lies at the end of it, and is one of the richest and finest fruits of civilization" ("Liberty" 246). This liberty is closely associated with the political principle of laissez-faire because the "notion of civil liberty which we have inherited is that of *a status created for the individual by laws and institutions, the effect of which is that each man is guaranteed the use of all his own powers exclusively for his own welfare*" (*SC* 30). A political structure that promotes liberty also promotes the most efficient aggregation and preservation of capital, for all are equal in the opportunity to provide for themselves; free to pursue the means of doing so and keeping the property or product of that effort; and also responsible for their freedom and beholden to no one as no one is beholden to them.

A laissez-faire system such as Sumner proposes raises the question as to what extent liberty may be realized. Social organization "increases the power of a body of men to extort their living from the earth," but it exacts "the price of mutual concessions and subordination." With greater organization comes greater power but also greater constraint, and "at every step of advancing civilization, while we seem to get nearer this form of liberty, the means of emancipation proves a new bond" ("Liberty" 237). Cooperation is necessary to social advance, but it carries with it the limitation upon liberty consequent to the growth of social organization, which is necessary to achieve higher levels of cooperation. The original and natural level of cooperation existed in the family, for "the relation of parents and children is the only case of sacrifice in Nature" (*SC* 64). Family cooperation, however, is insufficient: "village communities . . . were fit only for a most elementary and organized society" (*SC* 56). Inherent within the natural bonds of affection of the family, however, are the motives for advance beyond the simple village community. "Parental affection constitutes the personal motive which drives every man in his place to an aggressive and conquering policy toward the limiting conditions of human life." Parents pass on to their own children what they have inherited "with increase" from their own efforts. According to Sumner, "it is by this relation that the human race keeps up a constantly advancing contest with Nature" (*SC* 64). This characteristic of parents ultimately leads away from village society to a higher and more complex form of organization—toward a "system of division of functions" (*SC* 56). Dividing functions leads toward greater complexity of organization and an advance in the sciences and arts; but it weakens the family tie as well, which now no longer brings "disgrace for the misdeeds of his relatives . . . but neither does it furnish him with the support which it once would have given" (*SC* 34). A situation arises under this more complex organization in which "the ties by which all are held together are those of free co-operation and contract" (*SC* 56). The natural bonds of family are exchanged for the positive and conventional bonds of society, and he becomes "in a certain sense, an isolated man." Whereas in the old family society man's liberty could be constrained by the actions of his family, "which might pull him down," under the new organization his capital and comfort may increase, but his liberty now is constrained by the social organism itself: he now "cannot escape the deduction that he can call no man to his aid" (*SC* 34). In its struggle with nature, mankind has severed the bonds of family dependence, sacrificing along the way the security that family offers in exchange for the opportunity for "happiness indescribably in excess of what former generations have possessed." The bonds that hold the social organism together now are an "impersonal force—supply and demand" (*SC* 57–58). Liberty is bound by economic relations defined by contract.

The modern industrial society is organized according to the principles of social contract, and the obligations of one toward another are limited to the primarily economic terms of the contract. The result is a "society of free and independent men, who form ties without favor or obligation, and cooperate without cringing or intrigue." Such a society "gives the utmost room and chance for individual development, and for all the reliance and dignity of a free man" (*SC* 24). Contractual relations, however, are "realistic, cold and matter of fact . . . based on a sufficient reason, not on custom and prescription" (*SC* 23). Obligations outside the contract operate "where personal acquaintance and personal estimates may furnish the proper limitations and guarantees" (*SC* 135). Just as in nature and sociology, where "the forces know no pity," so also under contract (*SC* 133). This situation leads Sumner himself to ask the question: "What, now, is the reason why we should help each other?" (*SC* 136). In *What Social Classes Owe to Each Other*, the best response he can come up with is that "[m]en, therefore, owe to men, in the chances and perils of this life, aid and sympathy, on account of the common participation in human frailty and folly." Sumner here relegates "aid and sympathy" to the "field of private and personal behavior." He also argues that the "law of sympathy" indicates that we ought "to do as we would be done by," but he also recognizes that this law is not a "scientific principle" (*SC* 137–38). Mankind ought to help one another because of our common participation in pain and subjection to the vagaries of chance. This is—and Sumner realizes this—no ground for obligation. It is not based upon a common nature in which we all participate and therefore exhibit sympathy for our own, recognizing our common humanity. Rather, we recognize that one day chance may overtake us and limit our own opportunities to act freely to achieve a higher level of comfort; we help others who may be in need in the hope that they may one day reciprocate should we find ourselves in need of help. This ultimately unsatisfying formulation eventually leads Sumner to the reintroduction of custom and prescription in his *Folkways* (1906). In *Folkways*, "[t]he morality of a group at a time is the sum of taboos and prescriptions in the folkways by which right conduct is defined. Therefore morals can never be intuitive. They are historical, institutional, and empirical."[7] Economic relationships alone are not sufficient to the needs of society. Obligations beyond those of a contract are necessary, but these are not to be found by reference to nature, for nature is the harsh mistress of the earth with which mankind must compete for survival. Human nature is malleable, and as such differs at different times and in different societies. The source of obligation beyond contract, then, is to be found in the customs and prescriptions of a given society at a particular time: it is positive and conventional.

In Sumner's time, the United States was the best example of the modern industrial state based upon contract, wherein "status is of the least importance." The contract, he asserts, "is not permanent. It endures only so long as the reason for it endures" (*SC* 23). Two conditions may arise which might threaten the continuance of the contract republic: first, the reintroduction of the "competition of life" under conditions in which the sciences and arts are unable to progress fast enough to keep pace with the growth of population; and second, the threat of plutocracy to democracy and contract in which status is reintroduced as a ruling principle of society in lieu of liberty and independent opportunity. Regarding the first challenge, Sumner argues that regime types are dependent upon the natural conditions of abundance or scarcity at any given time ("Sociology" 194).

> So long as the population is low in proportion to the amount of land, on a given stage of the arts, life is easy and the competition of man with man is weak. When more persons are trying to live on a square mile than it can support, on the existing stage of the arts, life is hard and the competition of man with man is intense. . . . The former society will be democratic; the latter will be aristocratic. ("Socialism" 162–63)

Because of the expanse of its available land, the United States has no immediate need for worry about the threat of regime change dictated by shortage of land to support the existing population.[8] Care must be taken, however, to avoid the problem of attributing the existing conditions to natural causes or to philosophic doctrines. "Men are not aware that they are enjoying conditions which must forever remain most exceptional in human history. They accept the facts as in the external order of nature or they attribute them to philosophical notions or democratic theories" ("On Mores and Progress" 354). Increases in population not offset by equivalent or greater improvements in the sciences and arts will eventually create conditions in which a contract-based republic and democratic government will become untenable. Sumner anticipates the prospect of this development in the remote future, and he warns against sympathetic doctrines which will undermine the efficient laissez-faire system which best supports the necessary continued advance in the arts and sciences.

It is the threat of plutocracy that most captures Sumner's attention—it has a more immediate challenge to the continued operation of the laissez-faire system of social organization. Plutocracy is a "political form in which the real controlling force is wealth" ("Democracy and Plutocracy" 143). Wealth in itself is not a bad thing: "the aggregation of large forces [being] not at all a thing to be regretted," for they are "a necessary condition of many forms of social advance" (*SC* 47). It is the "question of how it will be used" that determines the answer to the "question of its good or ill"; for in itself wealth "is only power, like steam, or electricity, or knowledge" ("The Absurd Effort to Make the World Over" 256). The concentration of wealth is "but one feature of a grand step in societal evolution" ("The Concentration of Wealth" 150). The accumulation of capital is necessary to advance and when used properly produces that desired effect. The difficulty which arises with plutocracy, however, is the disruption of liberty and the truncation of the chances for economic advance by large numbers of society. Sumner argues that:

> In modern times the great phenomenon has been the growth of the middle class out of the mediaeval cities, the accumulation of wealth, and the encroachment of wealth, as a social power, on the ground formerly occupied by rank and birth. The middle class has been obliged to fight for its rights against the feudal class, and it has, during three or four centuries, gradually invented and established institutions to guarantee personal and property rights against the arbitrary will of kings and nobles. (*SC* 89)

Plutocracy threatens the reintroduction of status and privilege in place of the impartial operation of the system of contract. Liberty to pursue and make the most of one's chances is undermined. The United States, Sumner argues, is "deeply afflicted with" jobbery, which is "any scheme which aims to gain, not by the legitimate fruits of industry and enterprise, but by extorting from somebody a part of his product under guise of some pretended industrial undertaking." It is "the vice of plutocracy," and it is the "problem of civil liberty . . . to conquer it" (*SC* 122). This foe, plutocracy, "must be met, as the old ones were met—by institutions and guarantees." Whereas "[t]he old constitutional guarantees were all aimed against kings and nobles," these "new ones must be invented to hold the power of wealth to that responsibility without which no power whatever is consistent with liberty" (*SC* 95). In addition to "constitutional guarantees," there must also be "the independent action of self-governing freemen," men who can bring to bear "fresh reserves of moral force and political virtue from the very foundations of the social body" (*SC* 96, 94). Virtue and laws are necessary to prevent the ascendancy of plutocracy, for plutocracy tends to corrupt, through jobbery, the normal political processes. The threat of plutocracy is its capacity to arrest the advance of society and to put at risk all the progress made thus far in man's quest to dominate (rather than being dominated by) nature.

The state, then, exists within and under the iron laws of nature, and it must have all the power necessary to mobilize the society by any means to ensure the continued advance of that society toward greater prosperity and control over nature. According to Sumner, the state "is like the man clothed and in armor, with tools and weapons in his hand." Tools and weapons themselves are capital, and they are the means to continue to accumulate and use capital in man's quest to liberate himself from the mercy of nature. The state "must act with authority in the line of its determination and must control absolutely the powers at its disposal" ("Republican Government" 82). The character of a regime is unimportant in doctrinal terms, for the important consideration is whether it is appropriate to the current conditions of supply and demand in the relation of population to land. The advantage of republican government is that its "first aim is . . . civil liberty" ("Republican Government" 83). Civil liberty is the most advantageous type of social organization found to date for mobilizing the forces of society in the struggle for existence against the harsh conditions of nature. A regime of civil liberty is best suited to promote opportunity among the citizen body; to give each the chance to demonstrate his capacity to contribute to the advance of society; and thus to prevent any conditions of decline to set in which would lead society back toward barbarism.

Sumner is not immune to feelings of sympathy toward what he calls "the poor man" (*SC* 139). He does, however, very much disagree with the progressives of his age who believed in the capacity of government, through direct action, to achieve an amelioration of the conditions of the poor. Such socialist schemes forget that "a government produces nothing at all"—that "the State cannot get a cent for any man without taking it from some other man, and this latter must be a man who has produced and saved it" (*SC* 107–8). This principle informs Sumner's opposition to two facets of expansive public policy at the time: interest-based welfare schemes and American imperialism.

In the early chapters of *What Social Classes Owe to Each Other*, Sumner identifies the political problem that threatens the future of American constitutional government from two opposing poles: plutocracy and socialism. Sumner argues that: "If anybody is to benefit from the action of the State it must be some of us. If, then, the question is raised, What ought the State to do for labor, for trade, for manufactures, for the poor, for the learned professions? etc., etc.—that is, for a class or an interest—it is really the question, What ought All-of-us to do for Some-of-us?" (*SC* 11). He recognizes the divisive, interest-based character of this formulation. What it really means is "[w]hat ought Some-of-us to do for Others-of-us?" (*SC* 11). Such divisions are based upon a principle of obligation according to which "there are groups of people who have a claim to other people's labor and self-denial." This division creates "classes of the oldest and most vicious type," and for the person obligated, "approaches more or less toward the position of a slave" (*SC* 14, 15). Under any such type of organization, "the State is thus made to become the protector and guardian of certain classes," and the formula that is inevitably used is one in which "A and B decide what C shall do for D" (*SC* 21). The position of C is that of the forgotten man or woman. Sumner argues that the position upon which this obligation is based is nothing more than sentiment, for it conforms neither to reason nor to the fundamental laws which affect all societies (*SC* 108). Therefore, when the state takes the side of one party over another, it commits an injustice and violates those laws of nature, the inexorable operation of which will eventually weaken that state. In the United States, it creates an artificial state of war between opposing groups or classes under conditions where the prevailing proportion of population to land does not require such a competition.

We have seen that Sumner considered plutocracy (and jobbery, its associated vice) to be an untimely threat to liberty in the United States. Sumner perceived a corruption in government that favored the wealthy classes. Such a tilt toward the wealthy would eventually be reasonable as the conditions of the competition of life tightened under increasingly scarce resources; but such conditions did not exist in the United States at the time. The conditions at the time were favorable to the preservation of republican government because resources were abundant, and advances in the arts and sciences were progressing at a faster rate than population pressure. Corruption in government tending toward plutocracy, however, created a progressive response toward socialist welfare schemes that would favor the poor or the working man. Favoritism by the government in either direction put the government in the camp of a favored interest; increased the burden upon the forgotten man; and reduced individual liberty. In either case, government action distorted the free working of the law of supply and demand in order to favor a particular class within society.

Sumner also illuminates a further difficulty for progressive friends of humanity who aim to benefit the downtrodden at the expense of the plutocrats. Just who the downtrodden are that the progressives seek to help remains ill defined.

> Under the names of the poor and the weak, the negligent, shiftless, inefficient, silly, and imprudent are fastened upon the industrious and prudent as a responsibility and a duty. On the one side, the terms are extended to cover the idle, intemperate, and vicious, who, by the combination, gain credit which they do not deserve, and which they could not get if they stood alone. On the other hand, the terms are extended to include wage-receivers of the humblest rank, who are degraded by the combination. (*SC* 20)

This lack of clarity in definition tends to "generalize these classes, and render them impersonal, and so constitute these classes into social pets" (*SC* 108). This proposed beneficence relieves the pressure upon unproductive members of society which under normal circumstances is applied by natural laws in a laissez-faire system.

The lack of a free market for supply and demand is evidenced in a multitude of social and economic disruptions that, in the United States, are moderated by the general affluence of the country and its political institutions, which allow it "to play with all these socialistic and semi-socialistic absurdities" (*SD* 108). The activity of trade unions seeking to raise wages, presented as a fight "between the workmen and their employers," is really instead a burden "upon other persons of the labor class who want to get into the trades" but are prevented from raising their status by this interruption of supply and demand (*SC* 112–13). Unions in this case seek to raise wages not by producing more or by increasing value but rather by creating an artificial shortage of supply to fill existing demand. In reference to social welfare policy, Sumner argues that the expenditure of valuable capital on unproductive members of society takes away from an "industrious laborer" (*SC* 108–9). The effect of "prohibitory, sumptuary, and moral legislation" is to punish the moderate and self-controlled citizen in an effort to control the immoderate citizen (*SC* 115). The seamstress who must buy thread has to work an additional sixteen minutes to pay the tax levied above the market price of thread in order to pay the subsidy for a protected industry whose own laborers do not benefit from the subsidy through an increase in their own wages (*SC* 126–27). Both plutocracy and socialism disrupt the natural mechanism of supply and demand that governs a healthy social organization. When the competition of life heats up due to an increase of population or a growing scarcity of resources, such distortions become intolerable if the society is to survive.

The second facet of Sumner's opposition to government policy activism has to do with American imperialism. Just as government favoritism in the domestic arena tends to distort, if not disrupt, the natural laws that operate upon all societies, imperialism also works to undermine liberty in a republican government. Regarding the situation in Cuba at the time (1896), Sumner argued that "[c]ivilized states are forced to supersede the local jurisdiction of uncivilized or half-civilized states, in order to police the territory and establish the necessary guarantees of industry and commerce" ("The Fallacy of Territorial Extension" 268). "Our system," however, "is unfit for the government of subject provinces" as it is a "confederated state" that was "never planned for indefinite expansion or for an imperial policy" ("Territorial Extension" 269). According to Sumner:

> The fathers of the Republic planned a confederation of free and peaceful industrial common-
> wealths, shielded by their geographical position from the jealousies, rivalries, and traditional
> policies of the Old World and bringing all the resources of civilization to bear for the domestic
> happiness of the population only. They meant to have no grand statecraft or "high politics," no
> "balance of power" or "reasons of state," which had cost the human race so much. ("Territorial
> Extension" 269)

"Colonization and territorial expansion are burdens" which "[g]reat civilized states cannot avoid"; but to undertake such duties requires high "internal vitality"—indeed a "surplus of energy to dispose of" ("Territorial Extension" 270). Reason of state is the homage that great states pay to the principle of plutocracy in the international order, while the sentimental spirit is embodied in the notion of bringing freedom, democracy, and self-government to people not presently enjoying them, regardless of their social conditions. In each of these cases, liberty is sacrificed to the interest of another party, whether it be recognition by other great states through the pursuit of national glory in the world arena or through the uplifting of a less civilized society.

Sumner asks what will be the result should these two interests be combined: "the mixture of sentimental social philosophy and warlike policy." His response is incredibly prescient: "There is only one thing rationally to be expected, and that is a frightful effusion of blood in revolution and war during the century now opening" ("War" 315).

Sumner argued for a policy of political restraint, one which would provide the conditions of continued liberty and national greatness as well as for the poor to achieve greater affluence, not through government charity, but through their own effort. Sumner believed that the welfare issue was an issue of justice, for everything given to the poor by government had come from some other citizen, or group of citizens, who were doing their part to care for themselves. Sumner argued that a country could not indefinitely pursue such a policy in the face of immutable laws of nature, of supply and demand, that would one day exact their toll. Sumner, to cite Winston Churchill's famous phrase, offered the people blood, tears, toil and sweat, but the rewards of those efforts would be rich indeed in achieving "happiness indescribably in excess of what former generations have possessed" (*SC* 57). In the end, Sumner was overwhelmed by those who offered the same rewards without the toil.

Notes

This chapter in no way reflects the opinions, standards, or policy of the U.S. Air Force Academy or the U.S. government.

1. Richard Hofstadter, *Social Darwinism in American Thought* (Boston: Beacon Press, 1992), 57.

2. William Graham Sumner, "Sociology," in *On Liberty, Society, and Politics: The Essential Essays of William Graham Sumner*, ed. Robert C. Bannister (Indianapolis: Liberty Fund, 1992), 193, henceforth cited parenthetically in the text by essay title. All essays cited in the text will come from this handy volume, while essays from other sources will be cited in the notes.

3. Leo Strauss has succinctly articulated the different perspectives of the social and political philosopher. "As regards social philosophy, it has the same subject matter as political philosophy, but it regards it from a different point of view. Political philosophy rests on the premise that the political association —one's country or one's nation—is the most comprehensive or the most authoritative association, whereas social philosophy conceives of the political association as a part of a larger whole which it designates by the term society." Leo Strauss, "What Is Political Philosophy," in *Political Philosophy: Six Essays by Leo Strauss*, ed. Hilail Gildin (Indianapolis: Bobbs-Merrill Company, 1975), 7.

4. William Graham Sumner, *What Social Classes Owe to Each Other* (Caldwell, Idaho: Caxton Printers, Ltd., 1978), 107, henceforth cited parenthetically in the text as *SC*.

5. "That it requires energy, courage, perseverance, and prudence is not to be denied. Any one who believes that any good thing on this earth can be got without those virtues may believe in the philosopher's stone or the fountain of youth" (*SC* 68).

6. Natural rights is merely an historical and conventional mechanism used to promote political liberty as societies emerged from the feudal system of organization. As such, it was useful, but in no way intimately related to human nature. "Some Natural Rights," in *Social Darwinism: Selected Essays of William Graham Sumner*, introduction and notes by Stow Persons (Englewood Cliffs, N.J.: Prentice Hall, 1963), 65–69, henceforth cited parenthetically in the text as *SD*.

7. William Graham Sumner, *Folkways* (Boston: Ginn and Company, 1940), 29.

8. "On the other hand, democracy is rooted in the physical, economic, and social circumstances of the United States. This country cannot be other than democratic for an indefinite period in the future. Its political processes will also be republican" (*SC* 92).

Chapter 26

Booker T. Washington and the "Severe American Crucible"

Peter W. Schramm

The Rise of a Statesman

The same year that Frederick Douglass died, Booker T. Washington (1856–1915) rose to national prominence. In September 1895, he gave a talk at the Atlanta Cotton States and International Exposition. It was a golden opportunity for a man to address a large number of mostly Southern whites and some blacks on a national stage. The talk was well received and was front-page news in the nation's press. Thirty years after the Civil War, the country seemed to have found a voice that spoke for black Southerners in tones of conciliation, economic progress, and hope. A journalist and friend of Washington, Timothy Thomas Fortune, wrote to him from New York a few days after the event: "It looks as if you are our Douglass and I am glad of it" (*P* 4:31).[1] Ten years later, Washington would write a biography of Frederick Douglass and say that his career fell into the period of "revolution and liberation" regarding "the most difficult social problem which any modern people has had to face." The effort to solve this problem "has put to a crucial test the fundamental principles of our political life and the most widely accepted tenets of our Christian faith." Now the period of liberation is closed, and Washington wrote that "[w]e are at present in the period of construction and readjustment" (*FD* 5). It was this period that Booker T. Washington was destined to lead and shape.

Although the Atlanta speech catapulted Washington to national prominence and seemed to make formal his authority as a spokesman for his race, it was Washington's extraordinary life and work that placed him there. As Washington called Frederick Douglass a "self-made man," so it is no overstatement to say that Washington was also a self-made man (*FD* 256). Born into slavery, he hungered for an education and got it. On July 4, 1881, he opened the Tuskegee Normal and Industrial Institute—the first educational institution entirely staffed by blacks—with thirty students enrolled, and the rest of his life revolved around this institution and its educational methods and purpose. He is therefore always identified as an educator. And because of his ceaseless efforts to find a way out of the "great problem, which hangs over our country like a blighting shadow" (*P* 5:37), he is also known as a statesman.[2] It is also worth noting that he has been called "the most powerful black American of his time, and perhaps of all time."[3] For almost a quarter of a century, he had the support of the vast majority of blacks, of Northern white opinion makers, and even of Southern whites. His influence was such that he could make or break careers, and he did.

He saw himself as a Negro and a teacher—an American teacher in the South, a teacher of blacks and of Southern and Northern whites, and a teacher of former slaves and even of former slave owners.[4] He was conscious of speaking in a way that "would gain the interest and sympathy of all three of the classes directly concerned," and in order to do that well he also knew that he had to be able to "enter sympathetically into the three different points of view entertained by those three classes; I have had to consider in detail how the work that I was trying to do was going to affect the interests of all three" (*MLE* 50).

His work was always circumscribed by two massive facts, each of which he had to consider in all his purposes and actions: first, because of slavery, blacks found themselves in a primitive condition and were weak; and second, whites were not only prejudiced against blacks but were also strong. While he insisted that everyone, black and white, live up to "the American standard," he acknowledged that "my race must continue passing through the severe American crucible" (*P* 4:222). The heart of Washington's political thought and statesmanship—its greatness and its possible defect—lay in this twofold approach of emphasizing that the black man in the South must begin at the bottom and of deemphasizing the injustice of being placed there. In his attempt to promote and speak for the black race, he tried to shape public sentiment by tying together the destiny of the two races, always claiming that the prosperity and well-being of one was directly connected to the prosperity and well-being of the other. He attempted to "cement a friendship between the two races that shall be manly, honorable, and permanent." The solution that he proposed was not a political solution as that is ordinarily understood—certainly not a politics that emphasized, at least in public, a demand for civil rights. Rather, it was a solution based on interest and economics. Yet Washington made it clear that "the Negro has always been true to the Stars and Stripes and the best interests of the nation," and that all "the Negro asks is that the door which rewards industry, thrift, intelligence, and character be left as wide open for him as for the foreigner who constantly comes to our country. More than this he has no right to request. Less than this, a republic has no right to vouchsafe" (*P* 7:439–40). Although he started with—and emphasized—necessity and interest, Washington's end or purpose was moral or political: to bring about a free society that did not recognize color as a bar to any achievement.

Yet in attempting to increase the sympathy between the races, he was obliged to consider both the sentiments of Southern whites as well as the harsh political realities in the South after the collapse of Reconstruction, both of which seemed to make the possibility of full citizenship for blacks only a distant goal. And in doing this consistently throughout his life, he was careful to allow those whites who were impressed by his conciliatory language to confuse his means for his ends. Washington was a thoughtful man of action, who, in trying to untie the Gordian knot of race, "effectively masked the ultimate implications of his philosophy."[5] Consequently, whites were pleased and supportive with the pressing projects he was involved in because they did not see that, in the end, Washington would also try to become their teacher. He effectively molded public sentiment on behalf of American blacks by addressing their predicament through stressing their obligations rather than their rights and by arguing that the national race problem will be solved in the South. In doing this, he was willing to acquiesce to the majority's demand that there be racial separation in social life, yet he always argued that blacks are Americans, a part of the great whole, a part of "our complex American civilization" (*P* 10:33). His rhetoric reveals that he was conscious of the ineradicable fact that blacks needed the support of whites and that there was a price for that support. He was willing to pay that price not only because he thought he had to but also because it was good for his people to do so. We suspect that he thought he would be successful because he thought that through his own virtue and the virtues of his own people —manifested in both speech and deed—he would be able, eventually, to persuade all Americans that blacks should be given the opportunity to live up to the American standard and be fully incorporated as citizens. He assumed that merit would count. In the end, perhaps ironically, his authority, political power, and sophisticated rhetoric waned because other blacks, claiming that Washington gave up too much or his way was too difficult, took up the political argument directly and wielded a sword against the knot.

Booker T. Washington was born into slavery, the son of an unknown white man. His mother was a slave cook on a plantation in Franklin County, Virginia. He was around nine years old when emancipation came, and his mother moved her family to Malden, West Virginia, at the end of the Civil War. While working in a coal mine as a boy, he heard a miner talking about a school in Virginia that had been established for Negroes and that poor but worthy students could study there. After an arduous journey at age sixteen, he presented himself at the Hampton Normal and Agricultural Institute, was given a test (to clean a room), and was readily admitted.[6] While there, he worked as a custodian to help defray his expenses.

The Hampton Institute was founded four years earlier by the American Missionary Association and was run by Samuel Chapman Armstrong, a former Union general who had led Negro troops during the war. Its purpose was to educate free Negroes in the practical and industrial arts and to instill within the students all the Christian virtues. It was at Hampton that Washington learned

> what education was expected to do for an individual. Before going there I had a good deal of the then rather prevalent idea among our people that to secure an education meant to have a good, easy time, free from all necessity for manual labour. At Hampton I not only learned that it was not a disgrace to labour, but learned to love labour, not alone for its financial value, but for labour's own sake and for the independence and self-reliance which the ability to do something which the world wants brings. At that institution I got my first taste of what it meant to live a life of unselfishness, my first knowledge of the fact that the happiest individuals are those who do the most to make others useful and happy. (*UFS* 73–74)

After he graduated from Hampton, Washington went home to Malden and taught at a school for Negroes for two years. Then he spent a few months at a Baptist seminary in Washington, D.C., and came to the conclusion that he was not cut out for the life of a minister. He was invited back to Hampton in 1879 to run the night school, and because his performance was exemplary, Armstrong recommended him in 1881—even though the commissioners wanted a white man for the job—to take charge of a new Negro normal school to be established in Tuskegee, Alabama. When Washington arrived in Tuskegee in June, he found no land, no buildings, and no campus. The Alabama legislature—by a deal struck between a former slave owner running for the state legislature and in need of some support from black voters in the county, and a former slave who was willing to get him some votes if he would help blacks establish a school—had appropriated $2,000 for salaries.[7] The only thing that Washington found when he got there were "hundreds of hungry, earnest souls who wanted to secure knowledge" (*UFS* 108). The first classes were held in a shanty so dilapidated that whenever it rained, "one of the older students would very kindly leave his lessons and hold an umbrella over me" (*UFS* 110). Through dogged persistence and determination by the time of Washington's death in 1915 Tuskegee would grow to about 2,000 acres with 100 buildings. It had a faculty of nearly 200, a resident student body of 2,000, and an endowment of nearly $2 million. It was staffed entirely by black men and women. The majority of its graduates became teachers. The unremitting activity that Booker T. Washington launched into upon arriving at Tuskegee on behalf of the school would not cease until his death. The advancement of the Tuskegee Institute became Washington's life work, and the way he and the faculty and the students built it, literally from the ground up, may be said to represent in stone and brick his philosophy of education. It also became the ground of all his influence in the country.

His fame as a leader of his people continued as he gave speeches around the country (which were almost always also fund-raising trips for the Institute), and he was published widely in both the black and white press. He established the annual Tuskegee Negro Conference (seeking to help farmers produce better crops), the National Negro Business League (encouraging black enterprises), and the National Negro Health Week (calling attention to black health issues). He wrote ten books, the most acclaimed being *Up from Slavery,* which was published in 1901 and has not been out of print since. Washington wielded great political power during his life, especially the decade following his Atlanta speech. He had great influence with most wealthy philanthropists of the time, dominated the vibrant Negro press, and had great influence on all federal appointments of blacks. It has also been said that "[d]irectly or through agents, he was the largest employer in the country of black college graduates."[8] Furthermore, it is admitted even by his critics that he was a master of the political art—of the art of the possible. The poet Paul Laurence Dunbar said the secret of Washington's power was "organization, and organization after all is only concentration of force. . . . [H]e is a man of one idea, but that one is a great one and he has merely concentrated all his powers upon it." And, Dunbar continued, "while he is our most astute politician, he has succeeded in convincing both himself and the country that he is not in politics."[9] The breadth of the coalition that he put together for his purpose is proof of this. He used people, black or white, for his own ends by appealing to those particular interests and opinions that most moved each of them. But in accommodating them in the way they demanded, he broadened their interests and opinions in such a way that his always more capacious purposes were well served.

In 1898, President McKinley paid a visit to Tuskegee Institute; Frederick Douglass had already been there. Theodore Roosevelt had a very close relationship with Washington, which began with an invitation to dinner at the White House in 1901. The dinner raised such a political storm, especially in the South, that Roosevelt never again invited any black man to dinner. But he continued to consult Washington on almost all of the minority political appointments he made as president. Wasington's relations with President Taft were never warm, and his influence therefore ebbed. When Roosevelt ran against Taft and Wilson in 1912, Washington, for the first time ever, did not support any candidate. Until then, he had been a loyal Republican at the national level, even though he cultivated good relations with Southern Democrats at the local and state levels.[10] Soon after he took office, Woodrow Wilson—a Southerner and a Democrat— segregated federal employees by executive order and phased out many from civil service.

By this time, rumblings from fellow blacks against Washington's views, policies, and political power had grown into a movement that would eventually move away from Washington's policies and views toward agitation on behalf of civil rights. It was not known at the time that Washington, secretly and through an elaborate game of deception known only to his intimates, had been making extensive efforts against segregation and disenfranchisement in his attempt to undermine the racially restrictive Jim Crow laws that had developed since the end of Reconstruction.[11] The only class of people over whom he had no influence in his life were the racist demagogues Benjamin Tillman, Thomas Dixon, and the others. They always called Washington their insidious enemy.[12] Booker T. Washington died of overwork and arteriosclerosis on November 14, 1915.

Starting from Slavery

The ineluctable fact that Washington began with was that until recently almost all the blacks in the South had been slaves. Although Washington does not want to speak in a "fault-finding spirit" when addressing slavery and its consequences, he does have "a deep feeling of regret for what has been done" (*P* 4:216). Slavery was wrong and unjust and a curse, "a curse to both races," and the effects of the awful institution on blacks (and also whites) was the starting point for his understanding of what should be done for the black man and, more important, what the black man should do for himself.[13] He is addressing nothing less than "the task which American slavery has laid at the doors of the Republic" (*P* 4:216). The "greatest injury that slavery did my people was to deprive them of that sense of self-dependence, habit of economy, and executive power which are the glory and distinction of the Anglo-Saxon race." And we should not expect the effects of two and half centuries of slavery to be "gotten out in 25 or 30 years" (*P* 3:320). Washington's descriptions of the effect of freedom on the slaves are especially moving. Upon hearing that they were now free, the slaves at first wildly rejoiced; but this euphoria was fleeting because "by the time they returned to their cabins there was a change in their feelings. The great responsibility of being free, of having charge of themselves, of having to think and plan for themselves and their children, seemed to take possession of them." It was much like turning a twelve-year-old out into the world to provide for himself. "In a few hours the great questions with which the Anglo-Saxon race had been grappling for centuries had been thrown upon these people to be solved" (*UFS* 21). "That which was three hundred years in doing can hardly be undone in thirty years" (*P* 5:33). Yet, it had to be undone, and Washington's method of education sought to undo it by giving the former slave (and the former master) a method by which he would be able to become free. Besides this, Washington stated that it may be true that "[l]egal slavery is dead, but there is mental, moral, industrial slavery in the South that is not dead, and will not be for years to come" (*P* 3:200–201).

According to Washington, during the period of Reconstruction, "two ideas were constantly agitating" the minds of a large part of the black people. "One was the craze for Greek and Latin learning, and the other was a desire to hold office" (*UFS* 80). Although it was heartening to see that blacks were keenly interested in getting an academic education and being involved in politics, they were making a mistake by starting at the top. In beginning at the top instead of the bottom, too many blacks "grasped for the shadow instead of the substance" (*P* 5:34). They thought that the study of Greek and Latin languages "would make one a very superior human being, something bordering almost on the supernatural." And they thought that once they secured a little of such an education, "they would be free from most of the hardships of the world, and, at any rate, could live without manual labour." It is understandable that a former slave would look on labor as something low and degrading and hold up the "white man before him as the highest type of civilization, but the Negro noted that this highest type of civilization himself did little labour with the hand. Hence he argued that, the less work he did, the more nearly he would be like the white man." So "[w]hen the Negro first became free, his idea of education was that it was something that would soon put him in the same position as regards work that his recent master had occupied" (*FAN* 89; see also *UFS* 128). In part, this explains why so many recently free blacks wanted to become teachers and preachers. While there were many good men among them, "a large proportion of them took up teaching or preaching as an easy way to make a living" (*UFS* 81).

Washington argued that there was a great difference in being worked and working. Being worked as slaves was degrading. But working as free men meant civilization. "The great lesson which we wanted to learn in freedom was to work" (*NS* 49). He stated that the greatest thing that "we have accomplished for the Negro race within the last twenty five years has been to rid his mind of all idea of labor's being degrading. This has been no inconsiderable achievement." He noted that this is not a tangible, physical change, "but a change of the spirit" (*NS* 50–51). At first, the free men only wanted to work long enough to satisfy their immediate wants, "and they could not understand why it was necessary to work any longer." Although Washington admitted that "there is a good deal of human nature in this point of view," he argued that it is good to teach men to become more ambitious: "[w]e should get the family to the point where it will want money to educate its children, to support the minister and the church." When families will have reached this point they will no longer work just a few days a week; they will work six (*NS* 56–57). This is the movement from necessity to civilization, built on the natural connection between labor and property: a person who works is entitled to the fruits of his labor. And as a man moves toward what might be called luxury in his accumulation of property, he will see that the purpose of that work and that property is beyond simply what we would call material accumulation. That purpose is tied to what has always been called civilization, not to say leisure. But Washington reminded his audience that not only were blacks starting at the bottom, they were doing it "in the midst of a pushing, surging, restless, conquering, successful civilization" (*NS* 74). But, of course, blacks will not be confined to the farm or the trades; but if a black man succeeds at such work, Washington was confident that, at the very least, "he could lay the foundations upon which his children and grandchildren could grow to higher and more important things in life" (*UFS* 203). Thus, it was not surprising when Washington stated that "I consider labor one of the greatest boons which our Creator has conferred upon human beings" (*NS* 62).[14]

But Washington also noted that the whole machinery of slavery had a similar effect on the white people. Labor was looked upon by them as "a badge of degradation, of inferiority. Hence labour was something that both races on the slave plantation sought to escape." The slave system, "in large measure, took the spirit of self-reliance and self-help out of the white people" (*UFS* 17). Washington often noted that if people complain of the black man's morals, they should keep in mind that "he has had no standard by which to shape his character" (*P* 2:261). This is a damning remark on those so-called civilized whites with whom the blacks, as slaves and then as free men, came into contact. The whites provided no standard of virtue or morality. They never ruled slaves with the intention of preparing them in any way for freedom because they did not understand freedom. The black man will have to shape his own character, and he will have to make himself free. Washington calls Abraham Lincoln "the Emancipator of America" because he freed not only the black man but also the white man (*P* 5:32). Although the "signing of the Emancipation Proclamation was a great event," it was a symbol of another, still greater and more momentous. "We who celebrate this anniversary should not forget that the same pen that gave freedom to four millions of African slaves at the same time struck the shackles from the souls of twenty seven millions of Americans of another color" (*P* 10:34; see also 4:286).

But Washington argued that although slavery was manifestly unjust, it also became a kind of school for blacks where they were, ironically, given instruction in freedom and the highest form of citizenship.[15] The fact that the black man was brought to the new world against his will and in chains indicates to Washington that he was needed; he helped to make the country, and especially the South, "rich and prosperous" (*P* 5:574). Furthermore, he had not only survived over two centuries of toil, but he had prospered. Not only had his numbers increased, but also "he has made steady gain in acquiring property, skill, habits of industry, education, Christian character" (*P* 7:89). As Washington said, the black man had looked the white man in the face and survived: "I know that almost every other race that tried to look the white man in the face has disappeared." A race that was capable of being thus tested—a race that was capable of being thus transformed—was worth "making a part, in reality as well as in name, of our democratic government" (*P* 4:214).[16]

> With all the conflicting opinions, and with the full knowledge of all our weaknesses, I know that only a few centuries ago in this country we went into slavery pagans: we came out Christians; we went into slavery pieces of property: we came out American citizens; we went into slavery without a language: we came out speaking the proud Anglo-Saxon tongue; we went into slavery with the slave chains clanking about our wrists: we came out with the American ballot in our hands. (*P* 4:214)[17]

Industrial Education

While the federal government gave blacks legal freedom, "it was cruelly wrong in the central government, at the beginning of our freedom, to fail to make some provision for the general education of our people in addition to what the states might do, so that the people would be better prepared for the duties of citizenship" (*UFS* 83). But the past was not something that Washington could change. The question always before him was this: What should the black man do now—given the circumstances that surround him—that would allow him to become more independent, to better prepare himself for citizenship—in short, to become free? Washington's answer began with the fact that the black man had to begin "at the bottom, on a real, solid foundation" (*UFS* 88). Although he always hastened to make clear that he favored any kind of education "that gives strength and culture to the mind," he was most interested in training a student in those occupations that would allow him to become progressively more independent and free. Washington would teach students "some practical knowledge of some industry, together with the spirit of industry, thrift, and economy" (*UFS* 91, 126). He called this education, "education of the hand, head, and heart" (*UFS* 85).

> In our industrial teaching we keep three things in mind: first, that the student shall be so educated that he shall be enabled to meet conditions as they exist *now*, in the part of the South where he lives—in a word, to be able to do the thing which the world wants done; second, that every student who graduates from the school shall have enough skill, coupled with intelligence and moral character, to enable him to make a living for himself and others; third, to send every graduate out feeling and knowing that labour is dignified and beautiful—to make each one love labour instead of trying to escape it. (*UFS* 312)

The purpose of such an education was not merely to learn a trade. It was to acquire a certain kind of discipline that may be called industriousness or moral virtue. Washington called it "character-building" (*UFS* 88). Although it begins with the simple and the necessary, from bathing, to caring for teeth, to how to eat properly, to caring for one's room, in the end it seeks to address the question: What is freedom, and how is it to be obtained (*UFS* 126)? Washington said over and over again that no one gives you true freedom. While it was true that freemen "have equal rights guaranteed by the Constitution," real freedom is the result of "struggle, forbearance, and self-sacrifice" (*P* 7:89, 91). Washington was attempting nothing less than to teach his own race, above all, how to "effectually emancipate itself" (*P* 7:94). Freedom is not to be confused with the apparent freedom of a child at play, or a spendthrift that mistakes parting with his money for freedom, or the man who thinks debauchery is freedom, or the one that mistakes loafing for freedom. The "highest or the most complete freedom," Washington argued, comes slowly,

[a]nd is purchased slowly at a tremendous cost. Freedom comes through seeming restrictions. Those are most truly free today who have passed through great discipline. Those persons in the United States who are most truly free in body, mind, moral, are those who have passed through the most severe training—are those who have exercised the most patience and, at the same time, the most dogged and persistent determination. (*P* 7:92)

That Washington understood that this is difficult is obvious. He stated that both the study of history and everyday observation tells us that there is no other way of doing it. All people who have moved toward civilization have done it the same way. If there were an easier way to do it, he would recommend it: "Standing here today before this audience, when the very soul of my race is aching, is seeking for guidance as perhaps never before, I say deliberately that I know no other road. If I knew how to find more speedy and prompt relief, I should be a coward and a hypocrite if I did not point the way to it" (*P* 7:93).[18]

One of the advantages of slavery is that the black man had a virtual "monopoly of the trades in the South"—the blacksmiths, carpenters, brickmasons, and tinners learned their trades in slavery (*P* 2:260; see also *UFS* 121). But this monopoly did not last long. He cited an example of an ex-slave who had been a skilled mechanic during the days of slavery and used his skills to establish a good business as a house builder and contractor. Then the man died. And in this city of over 30,000 black people, "among them young men who have been well educated in languages and literature, but not a single one could be found who had been trained in architectural and mechanical drawing that could carry on the business which this ex-slave had built up, and so it was soon scattered to the wind." And this was wrong, "when the vast majority of the race is without homes" (*P* 4:215). The young had to be taught such trades in schools because they would not only lose their monopoly on trades but also would no longer be able to be even competitive with whites. Blacks should not only be able to build the homes of other blacks, but they should place themselves in the position of building the homes of whites. As with any other goods, whites will want the best homes built regardless of who builds them. And once there was a commercial relationship established, issues of civil rights would move toward resolution. At first, many whites looked with disfavor on the establishing of Tuskegee Institute. It turned out that there was no brickyard in the county, and people who needed bricks needed to bring them from a distance. So the school started a brickyard, and they used those bricks to build the buildings that Tuskegee needed. And then whites came to buy bricks because the black man made something that the white man wanted. This also had the effect that as they looked at the bricks, "they were led to examine the workings of the school." And thus many of the "old masters" became interested in Negro education (*P* 2:257).

Although Tuskegee did not ignore academic or religious education, it emphasized "industrial, or hand, training as a means of finding the way out of present conditions" (*FAN* 111). Despite the awful and unjust circumstances in which he found himself, the Negro in the United States constantly had to keep in mind his advantages. Washington was not necessarily against redressing grievances, but he thought what needed to be emphasized were the opportunities (no matter how limited) that existed for Negroes.

We have made a mistake, I fear sometimes, in not constantly keeping in sight our advantages. We have had any number of conventions and organizations, whose objects were to redress some grievance. This is right and proper; but with a race as with an individual, it will begin to make progress backward if it is continually dwelling on the dark side; is continually grumbling and finding fault; is continually finding a way *not* to succeed instead of finding a way *to* succeed. It requires a man with no special gift in brain power to find fault with an individual, organization or state of things. After all, what we want—and it is what America honors—is the man who can teach his fellows how to overcome obstacles; how to "find a way or make one." (*P* 3:409)

He claimed that it is industrial education, "in the present condition of our people," that has a "special place in helping us out of our present state." The student ought to have "industrial training in connection with academic training, there go with it a knowledge and a feeling that there is a dignity, a civilizing power, in intelligent labor." Such training in practical things will give him a "certain amount of self reliance or backbone he would not get without such effort on his own part" (*P* 5:577–78). This starting point, this beginning, was both necessary and useful because it would also have an effect on his character. One of the saddest things Washington ever saw was "a young man, who had attended some high school, sitting down in a one room cabin, with grease on his clothing, filth all around him, and weeds in the yard and garden, engaged in studying a French grammar" (*UFS* 122).

Washington never said that this education in practical things was the whole purpose of education; indeed, he had a deep appreciation for a liberal education that frees the mind to pursue the truth, to seek justice, and to appreciate beauty. In fact, he stated that "[e]ducation is meant to change us for the better, to make us more thoughtful, to make us so broad that we will not seek to help one man because he belongs to this race or that race of people, and seek to hinder another man because he does not belong to this race or that race of people." He told his students that all their learning and their books was not an end, "but a means to an end, a means to help us get the highest, the best, the purest and the most beautiful things out of life."[19] Education at Tuskegee, he said to the graduating class of 1891, had given them the "power—that mastery over self—that would enable you to find yourself—that is all any teacher can do for you—that is all education can do, nothing more." Although he and the other teachers could no longer be near them to advise, strengthen, and encourage them, "we have rendered you a greater service if we have made you masters of your own minds, your own appetites, your own bodies" (*P* 3:154). In case there is any doubt about the relationship between education and the American standard, he clarified:

> But you as white people and we as black people must remember that mere material, visible accumulation alone will not solve our problem, and that education of the white people and of the black people will be a failure unless we keep constantly before us the fact that the final aim of all education, whether industrial or academic, must be that influence which softens the heart, and brings to it a spirit of kindness and generosity; that influence which makes us seek the elevation of all men, regardless of race or color. (*P* 5:584)

Washington believed that if the black man was needed by others—if he made things that others would want—he would not only prosper but would go a long way toward securing an honorable and permanent friendship between the races. Washington told the story of a black man at Tuskegee who grew 266 bushels of sweet potatoes on an acre of land. The average production in that area had been but 49 bushels: "You should have seen the white men coming to see how he did that thing. They forgot all about the color of his skin; they did not have any prejudice against those potatoes." They simply knew that there was a black man who could produce more potatoes than they could. "Every white man there was ready to take off his hat to that black man." And Washington's optimism fairly shouted out: "Put such a black man in every community in the South, and you will find that the race problem will begin to disappear" (*P* 5:583; see also *UFS* 202–3). In other words, "[b]rains, property, and character for the Negro will settle the question of civil rights" (*P* 2:257).

All this meant that the black man had to learn to do things as well or better than his white countrymen (*UFS* 40). He had to make "the forces of nature in a large degree work for him" in order to become competitive with the whites. Unfortunately, although blacks had been trained in many useful occupations under slavery, they knew precious little about technology. They had to catch up in this regard as well (as must the whites in the South). A black man in the South planting corn using only a mule cannot compete with the white man in Iowa who used a machine. "Show me a race that is living from day to day on the outer edges of the industrial world; show me a race living on a skimmed milk of other people, and I will show you a race that is a football for political parties. The black man, like the white man, must have this industrial, commercial foundation upon which to rest his higher life" (*P* 5:580).

This kind of education in the habits of industry and commerce would also have an effect on the "moral condition of the colored people throughout the South." And this would have the effect of persuading whites that education was a good thing for black people, and that in turn would affect how they would be seen as citizens. Washington stated that it was already "fast converting the white man to believe in the education of the black man throughout this country. And in proportion as we can convince the white men in every part of the South that education makes black men more useful citizens, in proportion will our problem as a race be solved" (*P* 5:581).

That Washington was optimistic and hopeful does not mean that he was simply uncritical. It is certainly the case that the kind of education he has spoken of, education of the hand, head, and heart, was not necessarily being given the white man. He made very clear, only two weeks after his Atlanta speech, that "[o]ur system of education, or want of education, is responsible" for the prejudice and unjust laws that exist. One powerful example that he used is of a black mother in the North who had always heard criticism that blacks were lazy, shiftless, and would not work. At considerable sacrifice and expense, she had her young son educated in the machinist's trade. He got a job and the happy mother saw him go off to work. "What happened? Had any of the twenty white Americans been so educated that he gave this stranger a welcome into their midst? No, not this. Every one of the twenty white men threw down his tools and deliberately walked out, swearing that he would not give a black man an opportunity to earn an honest living." Other shops were tried with the same result. The ambitious young man became a wreck, a confirmed drunkard with no hope. "I know a good many species of cowardice and prejudice, but I know none equal to this." And it was a system of education, wrongly understood, that was responsible for it. Washington's powerful voice cried out to his countrymen:

> My friends, we are one in this country. The question of the highest citizenship and the complete education of all concerns nearly ten million of my own people and over sixty million of yours. We rise as you rise; when we fall you fall. When you are strong we are strong; when we are weak you are weak. There is no power that can separate our destiny. The Negro can afford to be wronged; the white man cannot afford to wrong him. Unjust laws or customs that exist in many places regarding the races injure the white man and inconvenience the Negro. No race can wrong another race simply because it has the power to do so without being permanently injured in morals. (*P* 4:221)

Washington pitied a man who was "so unfortunate as to get into the habit of holding a race prejudice" (*UFS* 165). For Washington, "a man is a man for 'a that and a' that," and he could "sympathize with the white man as much as I can with the black man"; indeed, "I have grown to the point where I can sympathize with even a southern white man as much as I can with a northern white man." No race could hate another race "without itself being narrowed and drawn down in everything that builds character and manhood and womanhood." And he famously said: "I propose that no race shall drag down and narrow my soul by making me hate it" (*P* 5:583).[20]

Washington praised Abraham Lincoln and said he was worthy of imitation in large part because he was "simple, without bigotry and without ostentation" (*P* 10:36). He was also a self-made man, in every respect. "Lincoln was in the truest sense great because he unfettered himself. He climbed up out of the valley, where his vision was narrowed and weakened by the fog and miasma, onto the mountain top, where in a pure and unclouded atmosphere he could see the truth which enabled him to rate all men at their true worth" (*P* 10:35–36; see also 10:348–50).

Washington's Rhetoric of Hope

Washington was on his way to Atlanta on the morning of September 17, 1895, when a white farmer from rural Macon County confronted him: "Washington, you have spoken with success before Northern white audiences, and before Negroes in the South, but in Atlanta you will have to speak before Northern white people, Southern white people and Negroes altogether. I fear they have got you in a pretty tight place."[21] The farmer was right; the speech at the Atlanta Cotton States Exposition was the perfect test of a speaker's rhetoric. His audience consisted of every category and class of human beings to be found in the United States, all under one roof, all wanting to hear what he had to say, each taking from the speech what seemed to align best with their own view of things. Washington was not yet aware how seriously everyone was taking his appearance. It seemed that every single human being he met along the way knew where he was going and something of the gravity of the event. It was also the largest crowd Washington had ever addressed before.

The talk was a huge success from the very start. At the end of the ten-minute speech, he received the kind of ovation only dreamt of by most speakers. Negroes were crying, white women were throwing flowers unto the stage, and the governor applauded wildly and shook his hand. The editor of the *Atlanta Constitution* stepped forward to announce to the crowd: "That man's speech is the beginning of a moral revolution in America."[22] Both in its effect—on all three classes of people he was speaking to—and its substance, the "Atlanta Exposition Speech" is one of the great speeches by an American. It was universally hailed by one and all to be, in the words of W. E. B. Du Bois (who would, in eight short years, begin to disagree vehemently with Washington's outlook), "a word fitly spoken" (see *P* 4:26).

Washington emphasized that the South could not disregard the massive fact that one-third of its population was of the Negro race. If the South would achieve its highest success, his people could not be ignored. He asked blacks and whites to "'[c]ast down your bucket where you are'—cast it down in making friends in every manly way of the people of all races by whom we are surrounded." He argued that blacks should understand that "whatever other sins the South may be called to bear," when it comes to business and commerce it is in the South where blacks are given "a man's chance." Blacks needed to take advantage of this assumed opportunity and not "permit our grievances to overshadow our opportunities." Likewise, he argued that whites in the South should remember that blacks had been "patient, faithful, law-abiding, and unresentful people" whose fidelity and love had been "tested in days when to have proved treacherous meant the ruin of your firesides." The prosperity of the South did not lie with immigrants (the only group that Washington seemed to be critical of). Rather, blacks and whites in the South need to lace together "our industrial, commercial, civil, and religious life" in a way "that shall make the interests of both races one" (*P* 3:584–85).

Although the two races could become one at this level, he made it clear that he was willing to give the whites something they clearly wanted: "In all things that are purely social we can be as separate as the fingers, yet one as the hand in all things essential to mutual progress." Since

Washington was most interested in the progress of the black race, and since, arguably, the progress of that race did not depend on the kind of social intercourse that whites were unwilling to give, this bow toward a kind of social segregation may not have seemed so important to him as it has to some of his subsequent detractors. Washington knew his audience, and prudence and rhetoric dictated that he should not ask them to give something that they were unwilling to give, at that time. Just to make certain that his meaning was clear, he claimed that "[t]he wisest among my race understand that the agitation of the question of social equality is the extremest folly." And even if this should some day come about, it must come not from "artificial forcing" but must be the result "of severe and constant struggle." He did mention that while it was "important and right" that all privileges of the law be the black man's, "it is vastly more important that we be prepared for the exercise of those privileges." In other words, the "opportunity to earn a dollar in a factory just now is worth infinitely more" than the opportunity to attend the opera (*P* 3:585–86): where the black man might later be allowed to spend the money that he was allowed to earn could be worked out later. Besides, it would seem that if Washington's assumptions about the basis of human nature were correct—and he said that the "Southern people have a good deal of human nature"—it is not difficult to deduce that if it ever became in the white man's interest that the black man spend his money going to the opera, or on anything else, the white man would take it (*P* 2:259).

Despite his emphasis on practical opportunities, Washington was not averse to making what he called "abstract arguments" on behalf of the Negro and his rights (*P* 7:93). It is fair to say that he was more likely to do it when asked to speak in the North or at events that commemorated some historic occasion or person (for example, on the birthdays of Lincoln and George Washington, or the unveiling of the Robert Gould Shaw monument). He explained that "[o]ur republic is the outgrowth of the desire for liberty that is natural in every human breast—freedom of body, mind, and soul, and the most complete guarantee of the safety of life and property" (*P* 7:86). While some of his opponents chastised him for going "too much into the facts" and not saying "enough about the Rights of Man and the Declaration of Independence," he spoke with ease and grace of "that immortal document" and of how the immigrants "laid the foundations for the Nation and established those ideals of justice and equity which found expression in the Declaration of Independence and the Constitution" (*P* 12:260, 13:369; see also 1:426). With the "most profound sympathy," he cited examples of young black men who had gone off to college (even Yale and Harvard) and there have "gained the idea at some point in their career that, because they are Negroes, they are entitled to the special sympathy of the world," and instead of preparing themselves for some definite task in the world, they "started out with the idea of preparing themselves to solve the race problem." They studied a great deal about New England freedom and the history of the antislavery struggle, "and they came out of college with the idea that the only thing necessary to solve at once every problem in the South was to apply the principles of the Declaration of Independence and the Bill of Rights" (*P* 1:428).

But Washington claimed that abstract arguments were not enough; it is not possible to simply apply principles—even if true and universal—to all the particular activities in life because wisdom shows itself in the world in a more complicated manner. The conditions in which his people found themselves—even if it was no fault of their own—dictated to Washington that "we must reinforce arguments with results." He thought that one farm bought, one house built, one school maintained, one successful factory established, one patient cured by a Negro doctor—"these will tell more in our favor than all the abstract eloquence that can be summoned to plead our cause" (*P* 7:93). These results in the end would have the effect of proving to whites that blacks were "freemen, with equal rights guaranteed by the Constitution, and sheltered by the same flag" (*P* 7:89).

The heart of Washington's political thought and statesmanship had two components. One was to emphasize to the black man that he must start at the bottom and work his way up, relying on his own efforts as much as possible, and he must not simply agitate (at least in public) for those natural and civil rights that were his both according to the laws of nature and nature's God as well as the Constitution. The second was to persuade whites—especially Southerners—not only that the black man's efforts to rise to the American standard were noble and dignified but also that this great exertion should be encouraged because it would benefit not just the South but all blacks and whites.

Although Washington exerted great influence for a whole generation, it is arguably the case that he failed in at least one essential respect: to continue to persuade his fellow blacks that their great effort to raise themselves—despite the obstacles of unjust laws and the habits of prejudice manifested ever more publicly by whites—was the necessary condition of both their future prosperity as well as their civil rights. Perhaps Washington was both too demanding and too optimistic in thinking that blacks would continue to respond to his demanding and hopeful exertions. And perhaps his rhetoric was too subtle given the political movement of the South toward legalized segregation and disenfranchisement of blacks. Although Southern whites continued to applaud his encouragement of fellow blacks (as the whites conveniently de-attached that appeal from his larger moral purposes), it was his fellow blacks who decided that the advancement of colored people in America should take a different turn, a turn toward ever increasing political agitation based solely upon the principles at the nation's heart. Increasingly, they became convinced that to do anything else smacked of conciliation and apologizing with injustice.

This attempt to overthrow Washington's authority and influence was eased by his power to dispense patronage, to reward some blacks and punish others, as well as his reputation for being a "Machiavellian prince" willing and eager to wield a "secret stiletto" against his black political enemies.[23] And it may also have been eased by the fact that he kept his secret but direct attacks on Jim Crow legislation more private than he should have. Yet, in order to dethrone Washington, W. E. B. Du Bois and other blacks—mostly from the North with no direct experience in slavery—had to distort Washington's rhetoric and purposes into a form that he himself would eventually be unable to recognize. They made it appear that he did not share their goal of a society that would not recognize color as a bar to any achievement. And so it would seem that Washington's influence lacked permanence. Yet, in the end, even those who think he failed will have to ask themselves whether he merited success.

Despite his constant battles against white racism and black competitors, Washington offered two reasons for the optimism and hope that he had spent his life articulating. First, no member of a race can claim "privileges, or certain badges of distinction" if their own individual worth or attainment is not worthy. Similarly, a mere connection with what is regarded as an inferior race will not in the end hold an individual back—"if he possess intrinsic, individual merit." Washington forcefully stated the basis of this opinion: "Every persecuted individual and race should get much consolation out of the great human law, which is universal and eternal, that merit, no matter under what skin found, is, in the long run, recognized and rewarded" (*UFS* 40–41).

Second, while "[t]he Ten Commandments and the Golden Rule were proclaimed centuries ago," the Anglo-Saxon, with all his growth and strivings, "has not, I think you will agree with me, reached the point where he is living up to them in daily life. And yet, because of this failure, no one has yet been bold enough to propose that we should repeal the Ten Commandments and the Golden Rule." Washington then drew together his point: a government, like every individual, "must have a standard of perfection that is immovable, unchangeable, applicable to all races, rich and poor, black and white, towards which its people must continually strive" (*P* 7:95).

As Washington understood, that striving would be imperfect. But, as he also knew, we must remember that "Man's way is not always God's way" (*P* 7:95).

Notes

1. Quotations from and references to Washington's works are cited in the text using the following abbreviations:

FAN: *The Future of the American Negro* (New York: Negro Universities Press, [1899] 1969).

FD: *Frederick Douglass* (New York: Greenwood Press, [1907] 1969).

MLE: *My Larger Education: Being Chapters from My Experience* (Garden City, N.Y.: Doubleday, Page, and Company, 1911).

NS: Booker T. Washington and W. E. B. Du Bois, *The Negro in the South: His Economic Progress in Relation to His Moral and Religious Development* (New York: Citadel Press, [1907] 1970). This book consists of four chapters, each being a public lecture, two by each man, delivered in 1906 and 1907 in Atlanta.

P: *The Booker T. Washington Papers*, ed. Louis R. Harlan, 14 vols. (Urbana: University of Illinois Press, 1972–1989).

UFS: *Up from Slavery* (New York: Penguin, [1901] 1986).

2. Adam Fairclough, *Better Day Coming: Blacks and Equality, 1890–2000* (New York: Viking, 2001), 41.

3. Louis R. Harlan, "Booker T. Washington and the Politics of Accommodation," in *Black Leaders of the Twentieth Century*, ed. John Hope Franklin and August Meier (Urbana: University of Illinois Press, 1982), 2.

4. "I have never at any time asked or expected that any one, in dealing with me, should overlook or forget that I am a Negro" (*MLE* 49).

5. August Meier, *Negro Thought in America, 1880–1915* (Ann Arbor: University of Michigan Press, 1963), 110.

6. "I was one of the happiest souls on earth. The sweeping of that room was my college examination, and never did any youth pass an examination for entrance into Harvard or Yale that gave him more general satisfaction. I have passed several examinations since then, but I have always felt that this was the best one I ever passed" (*UFS* 53).

7. Emmett J. Scott and Lyman Beecher Stowe, *Booker T. Washington: Builder of a Civilization* (Garden City, N.Y.: Doubleday, Page and Company, 1917), 3, 108, 110. The preface is by Theodore Roosevelt.

8. Harlan, "Booker T. Washington and the Politics of Accommodation," 15.

9. Paul Laurence Dunbar, "Representative American Negroes," in *The Negro Problem: A Series of Articles by Representative American Negroes of Today* (New York: James Pott and Company, 1903), 194.

10. It is interesting to note that the first document that we have by his own hand is "The Minutes of a Republican Rally at Tinkersville," (West Virginia), July 13, 1872 (*P* 2:21). He was then sixteen years old and signed the minutes as secretary, while H. C. Rice, also sixteen, signed as chairman. It is notable that although there were older blacks at the meeting it was probable that only these two young men could read and write. They voted to support the principles of the Republican party and all their candidates for all levels of government and also said that "we will not countenance or support any man who is in any way hostile to the colored people." See also Louis R. Harlan, *Booker T. Washington: The Making of a Black Leader, 1856–1901* (New York: Oxford, 1972), 51.

11. See August Meier, "Toward a Reinterpretation of Booker T. Washington," *The Journal of Southern History*, 23 (May 1957): 220–27, and Louis R. Harlan, "The Secret Life of Booker T. Washington," *The Journal of Southern History*, 37 (August 1971): 393–416.

12. Harlan, "Booker T. Washington and the Politics of Accommodation," 16.

13. Booker T. Washington, "Industrial Education," in *The Negro Problem*, 11.

14. "I emphasize industrial education because I think history teaches that, after all commerce is the great forerunner of peace and civilization" (*P* 4:181).

15. Herbert J. Storing, "The School of Slavery: A Reconsideration of Booker T. Washington," in *100 Years of Emancipation*, ed. Robert A. Goldwin (Chicago: Rand McNally and Company, 1963), 52; see also *UFS* 16.

16. See also Storing, "The School of Slavery," 52.

17. See also *P* 7:88–89. Note as well that he compared the black man's and the American Indian's confrontation of the white man and his refusal "to assimilate the white man's civilization." Either because of war, or white oppression, or "inability to stand the contact with a stronger and more numerous race, the Indian recedes and diminishes" (*P* 7:86–87). But also note his favorable experience in teaching Indians at the Hampton Institute: "I found out that they were about like any other human beings; that they responded to kind treatment and resented ill-treatment" (*UFS* 98).

18. See also Booker T. Washington, *The Story of the Negro*, 2 vols. (New York: Negro Universities Press, [1909] 1969), 2:47–48.

19. Booker T. Washington, *Character Building: Being Addresses Delivered on Sunday Evenings to the Students of Tuskegee Institute* (New York: Doubleday, Page and Company, 1902), 114, 117.

20. In *Up from Slavery* (165), the formulation is even more personal: "I would permit no man, no matter what his color might be, to narrow and degrade my soul by making me hate him."

21. Harlan, *Booker T. Washington*, 213.

22. Harlan, *Booker T. Washington*, 219–20.

23. Harlan, "The Secret Life of Booker T. Washington," 395.

Chapter 27

Co-workers in the Kingdom of Culture:
W. E. B. Du Bois's Vision of Race Synthesis

Jonathan Marks

To his own people—to the sad sweetness of their voices, their inborn sense of music, their broken, half-articulate voices,—he leapt with new enthusiasm. From the fainter shadowings of his own life, he sensed instinctively the vaster tragedy of theirs. His soul yearned to give voice and being to this human thing.

That is how William Edward Burghardt Du Bois (1868–1963) praises his friend, the black-Anglo composer Samuel Coleridge-Taylor. There are perhaps no better words to describe what animates Du Bois's long life and career. In his own life, he sees reflected the life of his whole race. Indeed, as a black and an American acutely aware of the mixed blood flowing through his veins, as a lover of European high art, American democracy, and African music, Du Bois looks into his own soul and sees both the promise of racial harmony and, more immediately and conspicuously, the problem of the color line. "My life had its significance and its only deep significance because it was part of a Problem" (*DD* xxix).[1]

"How does it feel to be a problem" (*S* 3)? Du Bois returns again and again to the question of what it feels like to be black in America. He writes like a man convinced that the salvation of blacks and whites alike depends not only on the revelation of black intelligence and character but also on the revelation of black sensitivity. He seeks to record in all their range and depth the passions of "the souls of black folk," especially the passions stirred by the race problem in America: defiant, dogged hope (*DD* xxix), disappointment (*S* 7), despair (*S* 176), pity (*D* 19), contempt (*S* 4), love (*G* 188), and suffocating anger: "I hate them, Oh! I hate them well. I hate them, Christ! As I hate hell!" (*D* 31).

The thoughts and feelings of blacks are, of course, not uncharted territory before Du Bois comes on the scene. One need only think of Frederick Douglass's great autobiography. Nonetheless, Du Bois takes up as a central theme the way in which the soul of the black American is divided against itself. One is tempted to say that he is the first to offer a rich articulation of the psychological dimension of the race problem. But that formulation is insufficient. Du Bois describes black inner strife not to complete the explanation of a race problem that is already fundamentally well understood but to reveal the nature of the race problem for the first time.

"The problem of the Twentieth Century is the problem of the color-line."

That problem, Du Bois argues, has worldwide significance for people of all races. Sometimes, Du Bois's belief in the greatness of the black soul and his acute sense of the wretchedness of its fate drives his work into a tragic mode. But Du Bois does not offer the inner life of his people primarily to be wondered at, admired, or pitied. A "problem," however difficult, is not yet a tragedy. It may have a solution. Du Bois is not only the poet who reveals the humanity of black people but also the psychologist who investigates the turmoil that afflicts their souls, with a view to understanding and healing it. Nonetheless, when Du Bois describes himself and his people as a "problem," he does not mean to underscore their soul sickness as much as the soul sickness of the entire modern world. Their problem is the problem of the whole century, "for the problem of the Twentieth Century is the problem of the color-line" (*S* 1). Du Bois thinks that black Americans, far from being mere victims, have a heroic part to play in solving that problem.

The problem of the twentieth century has an American and an international aspect. Its American aspect is the legacy of slavery and a host of fresh injustices against blacks, especially in the Jim Crow South. Its international aspect is European and American dominance in Asia, Africa, and South America. Race contact, Du Bois predicts, can only be expected to increase. "The world-old phenomenon of the contact of diverse races of men is to have new exemplification during the new century" (*S* 133). This prospect, he thinks, poses at least two questions, each one so grave as to command the attention of all thinking human beings.

Here is the first question: will Europe and America live up to their democratic and Christian ideals, or will the worship of capital supplant both? Following such predecessors as Douglass and Booker T. Washington, Du Bois assigns black Americans the roles of exemplary democrats and exemplary Christians. As "a concrete test of the underlying principles of the great republic," black Americans call whites to return to their most cherished political beliefs: "there are . . . no truer exponents of the pure human spirit of the Declaration of Independence" (*S* 11–12). And "as the sole oasis of simple faith and reverence in a dusty desert of dollars and smartness," they call whites to return from the worship of money to their most cherished religious beliefs (*S* 11–12). Not only black faith but also black suffering offers to whites a chance, maybe a last chance, for redemption: "Listen, O Isles, to these Voices from within the Veil, for they portray the most human hurt of the Twentieth Cycle of that poor Jesus who was called the Christ" (*D* 144). In the nineteenth century, America, inspired by the "sorrows of these dark children," brought forth Abraham Lincoln, Frederick Douglass, and the abolitionist John Brown, whom Du Bois considered first among a "score of heroic men" who opposed slavery (*JB* 15). In the twentieth century, the "colored world" is "a group whose insistent cry may yet become the warning which awakens the world to its truer self and wider destiny"; "we black folk are the salvation of mankind" (*DD* 172, 141). To be sure, the choice of the controversial, extreme Brown over more sober and effectual figures like Lincoln and Douglass, and the attack on "industrial imperialism" that precedes Du Bois's gesture toward the world's wider destiny, alerts us to the fact that Du Bois, though he appeals to old American ideals, reinterprets them. But we will turn to Du Bois's radicalism later.

American blacks are not merely the keepers of an old American and European faith. As members of "an historic race," they carry their own ideals: "Negro blood has a message for the world" (*S* 12, 5). Here, then, is the second question posed by increasing race contact: will the different races accept the intellectual and spiritual gifts that each has to offer, or will their relations instead be governed by those "to whom the physical differences of race are ridiculous and incomprehensible, to whom mental disagreement is foolishness and [by] those who cannot see that the canons of morality extend beyond their own family, or nation, or color of skin?"[2]

For Du Bois, the great hope implicit in this question, in the American case, is that "some day on American soil two world-races may give each to each those characteristics both so sorely lack" (*S* 11). For the world, Du Bois's heady hope is that every race will be able "to develop for civilization its particular message, its particular ideal, which shall help guide the world nearer and nearer that perfection of human life for which we all long, that 'one far off Divine event.'"[3]

Though Du Bois agitates for equal political rights and economic opportunity, the problem of the color line, at its most profound, is neither political nor economic. Color blindness will not solve it. When Du Bois writes of his people as those who "live within the Veil" (*S* 2), he uses the metaphor advisedly. He could have written, instead, of living in a prison or of being closed in by a wall, as he occasionally but less frequently does. The distinctive characteristic of a veil is not that it impedes progress but that it obscures vision. In a world without the veil, race would be recognized, not discounted, and that recognition would transform humanity. Du Bois's prayer for racial peace in "A Hymn to the Peoples" asks not for an end to the idea that race matters but for the baring of the soul of every race which, he thinks, is the precondition of human perfection.

> Save us, World-Spirit, from our lesser selves!
> Grant us that war and hatred cease,
> Reveal our souls in every race and hue!
> Help us, O Human God, in this Thy Truce,
> To make Humanity divine! (*D* 162)

"A co-worker in the kingdom of culture."

"Double-consciousness" is the curse of the black American, but it is also a "faint revelation of his power" and "his mission" (*S* 5). It is a curse because it means that his soul is divided between a dominant American part, which looks down on his blackness, and a suppressed black part, which peers out through its veil and sees America and its high ideals "stripped,—ugly, human" (*D* 17).

> It is a peculiar sensation, this double-consciousness, this sense of always looking at one's self through the eyes of others, of measuring one's soul by the tape of a world that looks on in amused contempt and pity. One ever feels his two-ness,—an American, a Negro; two warring ideals in one dark body whose dogged strength alone keeps it from being torn asunder. (*S* 5)

It is a revelation of his power and mission because it offers him the possibility and imposes on him the task of merging "his double self into a better and truer self" (*S* 5). It falls to the black American to effect in his own individual soul what must ultimately be effected in the entire world, or in the soul of humanity altogether. He must take on the burden of developing and uniting the race ideals whose conflict threatens to tear him apart.

The heroic mission of the black American, then, is cultural. He must become "a co-worker in the kingdom of culture" (*S* 5). In order to become co-workers in the kingdom of culture, however, blacks must have the appropriate training. Du Bois surpasses all other black American thinkers before and after him in his insistence on the overwhelming importance of higher education in the black college. The black college should serve not only as a tool for economic, social, and political advancement but also and primarily as a haven in which black students can first grapple with the enduring human questions that transcend the veil, and begin to fashion their own distinct contribution to the world's reflection on those questions. It is a "green oasis" in "a wide desert of caste and proscription" not because it is integrated, which it is not, but because it permits black students to enter without race-imposed restraint into the loftiest of human activities (*S* 69). Here is Du Bois's extraordinary description of the students at Atlanta University, where he taught from 1897 to 1910:

> In a half-dozen class-rooms they gather then,—here to follow the love-song of Dido, here to listen to the tale of Troy divine . . . and elsewhere other well-worn ways of knowing this queer world. Nothing new, no time saving devices,—simply old time-glorified methods of delving for Truth, and searching out the hidden beauties of life, and learning the good of living. The riddle of existence is the college curriculum that was laid before the Pharaohs, and that was taught in the groves by Plato . . . and is to-day laid before the freedmen's sons by Atlanta University. (*S* 68–69)

And here is his justly celebrated encomium to the liberating power of great and timeless writers:

> I sit with Shakespeare and he winces not. Across the color line I move arm in arm with Balzac and Dumas, where smiling men and welcoming women glide in gilded halls. From out of the caves of evening that swing between the strong-limbed earth and the tracery of the stars, I summon Aristotle and Aurelius and what soul I will, and they all come graciously with no scorn or condescension. So wed with Truth, I dwell above the Veil. (*S* 90)

This stirring passage is sometimes deployed to defend the "Western canon," the set of books and authors deemed worthy of inclusion in great books programs, against critics who charge it with racial exclusivity. Certainly, Du Bois has little sympathy with the argument that Aristotle and the rest are instruments of Western dominance rather than bearers of vital human truths. Nonetheless, even in the exalted region above the veil, perhaps even especially in this region, the differences between the races do not simply cease to be relevant. It is surely no accident that Du Bois includes Dumas, part of a "great company of mixed-blooded men" in his great company of the best among all literary men and philosophers (*D* 117). The higher education of blacks may produce a kind of spiritual integration, but it will and should not result in spiritual assimilation. On the contrary, the "the rich and bitter depth of their experience, the unknown treasures of their inner life" will "give the world new points of view" (*S* 90). In his insistence that the black people carry a unique and important race ideal, Du Bois anticipates Afrocentrism and the black power movement. He, too, gives race pride a central place in his credo. He, too, attempts to ground that pride in a new and sometimes tendentious history for blacks that begins with ancient Egyptian civilization, extends to the emergence of an independent Africa from under the heel of European oppressors, and points toward a future in which Africa and African Americans can be expected to play a leading role. Nonetheless, Du Bois's emphasis on the significance of race and black race pride is qualified by at least four considerations.

First, Du Bois thinks that the education of blacks must be governed by a "higher individualism," a "loftier respect for the sovereign human soul that seeks to know itself and the world about it; that seeks a freedom for expansion and self-development" (*S* 90). An excessive regard of any kind for race, whether it originates in white discrimination or black pride, cramps the individual soul. When Du Bois tells the story of his own education, he emphasizes the importance for him of overcoming his "narrow racial and provincial outlook" which had taken shape as an equal and opposite reaction to white color prejudice (*A* 159). Crucial to this development was his exposure to Beethoven, Wagner, Rembrandt, and Titian, as well as contact with unprejudiced whites (*A* 156–57). The presence of this observation in the *Autobiography* (1962), which Du Bois composes in his ninetieth year, demonstrates that his dedication to "higher individualism" endured even after his turn to socialism.

Second, Du Bois's emphasis on race is tempered by a "broader sense of humanity" (*A* 157). In the same "Credo" in which he dedicates himself to "Pride of race," he also affirms that however different human beings may be in "form and gift and feature," they differ "in no essential particular" and are "alike in soul" (*D* 1). Du Bois is ever mindful of the need to weave together these two parts of his mission, so that even as he asserts the claims of blacks as the bearers of a unique race ideal, he asks that those claims be judged by standards of justice, humanity, and truth that apply and are recognizable to human beings of every race. And not only Du Bois's demands but also his fondest hopes rest on human, not racial, fellowship. The vision of the best community that emerges from his works is modeled on his experience of political and intellectual friendships which cut across racial lines and are founded not on blood or cultural ties but on "common books, common knowledge, mighty aims," and "delicate reverence for the Thought that led" (*D* 140).

Third, while Du Bois thinks race pride a needed corrective to belief in black racial inferiority, he thinks, nonetheless, that any resolution of the race problem must take into account the shortcomings, whatever their causes, of blacks and other "colored peoples." Certainly, Du Bois thinks that black civilization and its contributions to the world have been unjustly ignored. Certainly, he thinks that Europe and America overestimate their own greatness and underestimate their capacity for and tendency toward barbarity and injustice, which is increasing rather than diminishing in the twentieth century. Certainly, he thinks that it is perverse for whites to build a thesis of natural black inferiority on the black failures for which they themselves bear great responsibility. Nonetheless, he thinks that hard facts must be faced. "Is [European culture] not better than any culture that arose in Africa or Asia? It is. Of this there is no doubt and never has been" (*D* 22). The deplorable state of blacks worldwide, Du Bois thinks, will hardly be improved by pronouncing their cultural condition as not worse than but merely different from that of whites.

> Every colored man living today knows . . . that by practical present measurement Negroes today are inferior to whites. . . . The white folk of the world are richer and more intelligent; they live better; have better government; have better legal systems; have built more impressive cities. . . . The mass of the colored peoples in Asia and Africa, in North America and the West Indies and in South America and in the South Sea islands are in the mass ignorant, diseased and inefficient. (*DD* 174)

While justice demands that black and white people ask how this situation came about and concede the achievements of black people, the interest of blacks demands that, even at great cost in race pride, blacks face this question: "What is the colored world going to do about these current situations?" (*DD* 175).

Fourth, Du Bois's invocation of race pride is softened by his understanding of the mission of the black American which, if it is not "to bleach his Negro soul in a flood of white Americanism," is also not to "Africanize America, for America has too much to teach the world and Africa" (*S* 5). The mission of the black American is, as we have observed already, to "merge his double self into a better and truer self" so that "neither of the old selves [is] lost" (*S* 5). Even later in his career, when Du Bois's anti-Americanism peaks, his vision for the Negro people is still not separate cultural or racial development but "alliance with culture groups in Europe, America, Asia and Africa . . . looking toward a new *world culture*"—presumably a better and truer culture, in which none of the old cultures is to be lost (*TTM* 168, my emphasis).

If Du Bois's emphasis on race pride points to black power and Afrocentrism, and if Du Bois is, in the course of his career, a leader in the pan-African movement, his countervailing emphasis on individualism and humanity points to the civil rights movement, and Du Bois is among the founders of the NAACP. Though the civil rights and black power movements will, of course, be very much at odds with each other later, the ideas and passions at the root of each coexist, not always harmoniously, but in relative peace in Du Bois's thought. That more or less peaceful coexistence owes much to Du Bois's vision of a world culture and of a new self, the offspring of a marriage of white and black race ideals, that suits that vision. By extending the idea of integration from politics and economics to culture, Du Bois offers something to those who demand not only rights but also recognition of a distinct black way of life. At the same time, he reassures those who fear race provincialism, racial disunity, and the thoughtless rejection of those European and American standards to which civil rights leaders wish to be able to appeal. The embrace of a black race ideal, he promises, need not mean the rejection of European and American culture or politics, or the end of all common standards. While this vision has great appeal, much would seem to depend on how Du Bois understands the character and content of different race ideals and what he imagines a marriage of the sort he proposes might look like. It is to this subject that we now turn.

Du Bois's concept of race is notoriously protean. Du Bois wavers on the question of how many races there are. And he wavers, too, on the question of what defines a race and the extent to which blood, climate, and common history play a role in distinguishing races. In *Dusk of Dawn* (1940) and later, Du Bois describes a broad shift in emphasis in his thought from a partly biological to an almost altogether cultural or historical understanding of race. The latter is so broad as to bear almost no relation to race as it is commonly understood and culminates in the suggestion that geography, language, and physical differences matter much less than a heritage of common suffering in defining what it means to be black: "the real essence of this kinship is the social heritage of slavery" which "binds together not simply the children of Africa, but extends through yellow Asia and into the South Seas" (*DD* 117). Nonetheless, Du Bois never abandons the position that blacks have a distinct racial identity and a distinct contribution to make to world culture.

Du Bois thinks that blacks, especially through their connection with Africa, have a great variety of things to teach. Without simply representing primitivism, blacks offer an antidote to the ills of modern life. To temper triumphant individualism, Africa offers "intertwined communal souls" and the idealization of "the family group" and motherhood (*DD* 129; *D* 97). To temper the deadly serious and unremitting modern concern with efficiency and money making, blacks and Africa offer "sensuous receptivity to the beauty of the world," an understanding of "toil as a necessary evil administering to the pleasure of life" to be balanced against "the relative allurements of leisure," and the "divine and African gift of laughter, that echo of a thousand centuries of suns" (*G* 14, 30; *D* 117). To temper modern bigness, Africa offers "village life," "intimate human knowledge that the West misses," and "local self-government" (*DD* 128–29; *D* 40).

If the modern world has something to learn from blacks, blacks need to absorb "modern culture," by which Du Bois means above all modern science. Blacks, especially in Africa, are "vastly ignorant of what the world is doing and thinking, and of what is known of its physical forces"; they suffer "from preventable disease, from unnecessary hunger, from the freaks of the weather" (*DD* 129). While the black race ideal tempers modern civilization, the dominant white race ideal represents the best and worst of modernity—the triumph of a scientific rationality that is both a benevolent healer of mankind's ills and a "Frankenstein monster" that "kills men to make cloth, prostitutes women to rear buildings and eats little children" (*DD* 149). Both Europe and, even more so, America represent the conquest of nature for the sake of humanity as well as the sacrifice of humanity to the gods of efficiency and profit.

Although Europe and America have science in common, Du Bois also frequently treats them as two distinct branches of the white race ideal. Europe's gift is high culture above all, a sense of "the possible beauty and elegance of life" and "manners" (*A* 156). Of these things, Du Bois approves enthusiastically. America, by contrast, is "starved in culture" (*DP* 284). Its gift is democracy, by which Du Bois means the recognition that political power, economic well-being, and some level of educational and cultural attainment can and should be possessed by the majority of citizens. The hero of Du Bois's novel *Dark Princess* (1928) exaggerates the author's position only somewhat when he claims that "America is teaching the world one thing and only one thing of real value, and that is, that ability and capacity for culture is not the hereditary monopoly of a few, but the widespread possibility for the majority of mankind if they only have a decent chance in life" (*DP* 26). America, Du Bois thinks, was the first nation fully to acknowledge the energy, ability, and rights of the people. Though Du Bois grows increasingly bitter toward America and Europe, he never ceases to think that both, however decadent and far from their own ideals, represent something good that the white world has to offer to blacks and to an emerging world culture.

As for how Du Bois imagines a merger between black and white race ideals, his model is a "peculiar spiritual quality which the Negro has injected into American life and civilization," which tells "of the imprint of Africa on Europe in America" (*G* 178). Du Bois points to the example of American religion, especially Methodism and Baptism, in which black and white religion have redressed each other's deficiencies. "Much of superstition . . . for a long time marked Negro religion. . . . But on the other hand it is just as true that the cold formalism of upper class England and New England needed the wilder spiritual emotionalism of the black man to *weld out of both a rational human religion based on kindliness and social uplift*" (*G* 185, my emphasis). He also points to the example of American music. The "Negro folk song" is both "the singular spiritual heritage of the nation and the greatest gift of the Negro people" (*S* 205). This music, rooted in Africa and transformed by the experience of American slaves, has been further developed by "white and colored" composers into "popular songs and into high and fine forms of modern music, until today the influence of the Negro reaches every part of American music [and] of many foreign masters, like Dvorak" (*G* 157).

However compelling and plausible such visions of racial synthesis are, Du Bois may be and has been charged with imagining a black racial ideal, rather than observing it at work in blacks. After all, the characteristics Du Bois attributes to his people, like sensuality, simplicity, wildness, and the rest are the same characteristics that many have professed and occasionally still profess to find in country people and primitives of all races. Though Du Bois undoubtedly fills in his portrayal of blacks with what he knows of their history in Africa and America, the basic outline is not very different from the modern European image of the "noble savage." One must concede the justice of this charge.

"The Negro race, like all races, is going to be saved by its exceptional men."

Du Bois's understanding of the mission of blacks, to become "co-workers in the kingdom of culture," is controversial. Perhaps still more controversial is his understanding of who must lead blacks on this mission. In "The Talented Tenth," an essay published in 1903, the same year as *The Souls of Black Folk*, Du Bois argues in favor of training an elite—a black "saving remnant" to provide the social leadership needed for "an ignorant and unskilled people with a heritage of bad habits": "The Talented Tenth of the Negro race must be made leaders of thought and missionaries of culture among their people. No others can do this work, and the Negro colleges must train men for it. The Negro race, like all races, is going to be saved by its exceptional men" (*TT* 139, 147, 156–57). As in *The Souls of Black Folk*, Du Bois here differs from Booker T. Washington, the most prominent black leader of the time, since Washington stands for industrial training of the many rather than culture training for the few as the best hope for black advancement. Washington deplores the very features of the Negro college that Du Bois celebrates and wishes to build on—that it produces educated blacks who can teach astronomy, Greek, and Latin instead of turning out educated blacks who can teach subjects like agriculture, dairying, and the making of clothing, subjects that poor and unskilled blacks need in order to gain economic independence and to rise. While Washington is today much maligned for demanding too little for blacks, Du Bois has nonetheless never been able altogether to shake the charge that he was an elitist, more concerned with the good of a narrow intelligentsia than with the good of the majority of blacks.

There is no question that Du Bois thinks there is a " rule of inequality" among human beings and even that the rise of the talented tenth will reflect "natural selection and the survival of the fittest" (*S* 70; *TT* 55). Not every black will be suited for higher education any more than every black will be suited for industrial education. Some have "the talent and capacity of university men" while others have "the talent and capacity of blacksmiths" (*S* 70). But far from being inconsistent with Du Bois's understanding of democracy, his acknowledgment of natural inequality and his endorsement of the leadership of a talented tenth are among his most important reasons for praising democracy. In a democracy, artificial distinctions of birth and rank give way and make room for the rise of a natural aristocracy. The heroine of *Dark Princess* exaggerates but does not fundamentally distort Du Bois's position: "We recognized democracy as a method of discovering real aristocracy. We looked frankly forward to raising not all the dead, sluggish, brutalized masses of men, but to discovering among them genius, gift and ability in far larger number than among the privileged and ruling classes" (*DP* 225). The beauty of democracy is not that it allows the people to do without leadership but that it allows an "aristocracy of talent and character" to lead (*TT* 139). No people, especially a people of ex-slaves, can be expected to guide itself; the choice is between the talented tenth and "a hundred half-trained demagogues" (*TT* 150).

Nonetheless, Du Bois does not envision a talented tenth that receives an education and a rabble that does not. The task of the talented tenth is not to keep civilization to itself but to spread it. Du Bois is mindful of the fact that "education is not simply a matter of schools" (*TT* 149). All black children, whether they are destined for the university or not, receive their "life training" from the "group leaders of the Negro people—the physicians and clergymen, the trained mothers and fathers, the influential and forceful men about [them] of all kinds" (*TT* 149). In this way, "the culture of the surrounding world trickles through and is handed on by the graduates of the higher schools" (*TT* 149–50). The culture that filters through is not Greek or Latin or higher mathematics, but rather some "knowledge of life and its wider meaning" which, more than any technical training, makes even a man destined for hard labor more than a beast of burden, "a free workman among serfs" (*TT* 146; *S* 70). Of course, Du Bois concedes, the talented tenth will not drill most black boys and girls in Greek grammar; but they can convey something of the sense of beauty, of morals and manners, and of the heights of human attainment that a genuinely liberal education instills. "It is the trained, living human soul, cultivated and strengthened by long study and thought, that breathes the real breath of life into boys and girls and makes them human" (*TT* 148).

The difference between Washington and Du Bois on the subject of the talented tenth is finally best explained in terms of the latter's unique understanding of the mission of blacks. That difference is not quite as great as the historic quarrel between the two suggests. As Du Bois readily admits, Washington is not opposed to higher education. He simply places much less emphasis on it than Du Bois does. And Du Bois is not opposed to but in fact supports the industrial school as part of his educational strategy, though it occupies far less central a place in his program than it does in Washington's (*A* 236–37). Moreover, Washington does not think blacks are suited only for industrial labor; he also thinks them suited for the professions. He thinks them suited not only for wage work but also and especially for independence and ownership. Finally, he is not unmindful of the fact that blacks require leadership and cannot expect to have it from whites alone. He differs from Du Bois most profoundly on the question of what the mission of blacks in America is. For Washington, that mission is more moral and religious than cultural. The greatness of blacks will be evidenced not by their mastery of and contribution to world culture but above all by their patience before injustice, their steadfastness and success in the midst of obstacles, and their willingness to forgo a spirit of quarrel and complaint in favor of a spirit of generosity and compassion toward their erring white fellow Christians.[4] By contrast, as we have already noticed, Du Bois thinks that the mission of blacks, while moral and religious in part, is cultural above all and requires blacks both to master the ideals of the white world and to preserve and develop their own.[5] Such an enterprise is by its nature more dependent on a black intelligentsia than the one Washington proposes.

Some regard the Du Bois who puts forward the idea of the talented tenth early in his career as a conservative who will soon enough be supplanted by a more radical and democratic Du Bois. But the "Talented Tenth Memorial Address," which Du Bois gives after his decisive turn to socialism and which updates the 1903 essay, demonstrates, if anything, a more urgent elitism. While the function of the talented tenth has indeed changed to encompass "economic reconstruction" and socialist "propaganda," the need for elite group leadership has not diminished (*TTM* 166, 175). In fact, it is only after Du Bois comes to embrace the ideas of Karl Marx that he argues in favor of a kind of voluntary eugenics program to maintain and increase black talent. He proposes "deliberate planning of marriages, with mates selected for heredity, physique, health and brains with less insistence on color, comeliness or romantic sex lure, mis-called love" (*TTM* 175). It is to Du Bois's radicalization that we now turn.

"I believe in Communism."

Du Bois's *Autobiography* contains fulsome praise of the Soviet Union and Communist China. It reads, at times, like Soviet propaganda (*A* 57, 29–43). Recalling a 1959 visit to Russia, Du Bois celebrates the Soviet treatment of intellectuals and writers, lauds the discipline of its people ("few police are in evidence and there is little giving of orders. Secret dread. I sense none."), and blames such restrictions on freedom as he notices on a Western conspiracy that has compelled Soviet leaders to crack down (*A* 34). At a time when Josef Stalin was widely known to be one of the two most ruthless and murderous despots of the twentieth century, Du Bois soft-pedals and excuses Stalin's crimes and dwells instead on his part in Hitler's defeat (*A* 40). He is a member of the American Communist party, which he joined in 1961. How does Du Bois, who appeals so passionately to the ideals of the American Founding in *The Souls of Black Folk*, come to be an unabashed defender of communism?

It is not a sudden conversion. While Du Bois dates his full acceptance of communism to his 1959 visit to the Soviet Union, he also notes that his sympathy with socialism began much earlier, during his time as a doctoral student in Germany (*A* 168).[6] *The Souls of Black Folk*, published in 1903, contains no praises of and even one ambiguous attack on socialism, but it also contains rather ugly attacks on unrestrained capitalism and "industrial exploitation" of laborers by "thrifty and avaricious Yankees" and "shrewd and unscrupulous Jews" (*S* 138). In 1904, Du Bois casts his vote for the socialist candidate and writes that although he would not describe himself as a socialist, he has "many socialistic beliefs."[7] Far from considering socialism inconsistent with the principles of the American Founding, Du Bois continues to appeal to those principles after his explicit embrace of socialism and even after his embrace of communism, by which time he has laid out his argument for such an appeal (*A* 375, 422).

Du Bois interprets the Founding as, above all, a guarantee of equality and democracy. The "Freedom of 18th century philosophy" is no longer sufficient to make good on that promise (*D* 77; cf. *TTM* 167–68). Indeed, "long vested rights and inheritance" are now an obstacle to the "public ownership of capital," which alone will safeguard equality and democracy under the new conditions of the twentieth century (*D* 86). Those conditions are the product of industrialization, which puts "the most important functions of men: work and earning a living and distributing goods and services" into the hands of "modern business enterprise organized for private profit" (*DD* 285, 289). As a result, America has not real democracy but "oligarchy based on monopoly and income" (*DD* 285). Big business leaders, those "tyrants of the industrial age," rule like masters over their dependent workers and America's hapless citizens, who are largely ignorant of the "secret inherent power" that disposes of their fates (*D* 79). Democratic control and public ownership of industry, Du Bois argues, are needed to fulfill the promise of the Founders in the twentieth century.

Du Bois is further radicalized by his increasing estimate of the deep-rootedness of the race problem. His autobiographical work describes three main phases. Early in his career, as a sociologist, Du Bois believes that the race problem can be remedied by the presentation of carefully gathered scientific evidence against theories of black race inferiority. The cause of racism is ignorance, and the remedy is truth revealed by social science. The Negro problem is "a matter of systematic investigation and intelligent understanding" (*DD* 58). This first phase covers, roughly speaking, Du Bois's career as a university professor.

In the second phase, disillusioned by the persistence of racism and even of lynchings, Du Bois concludes that "careful social study of the Negro problems [is] not sufficient to settle them" (*DD* 221). He comes to believe that the cause of the race problem is not only ignorance but also ill will, "the determination of certain people to suppress and mistreat the darker races" (*DD* 221). In response, he turns from the pursuit and dissemination of knowledge to political "agitation and propaganda," especially as the editor of *Crisis*, the official periodical of the NAACP (*DD* 283; *A* 254–62).

Du Bois gradually enters a third and still more radical phase under the influence of Sigmund Freud and Karl Marx. He comes to believe that "not simply knowledge, not simply direct repression of evil, will reform the world" (*DD* 222). From Freud, Du Bois learns that those who would influence human beings must appeal not only to their reason but also to the many irrational forces that govern them: "conditioned reflexes . . . long followed habits, customs and folkways . . . subconscious trains of reasoning and unconscious nervous reflexes" (*A* 228; *DD* 172). Such an appeal requires not only propaganda but also "carefully planned and scientific propaganda" (*DD* 172). From Marx, he learns "that the economic foundation of a nation is widely decisive for its politics, its arts and its culture" and that righting racial injustice is therefore closely connected with socialism, a "revolution in the production and distribution of wealth" (*A* 290–91). The NAACP program, directed toward civil rights and economic opportunity is, consequently, if not wrong, short-sighted. The modest goals the NAACP pursues are not ends in themselves but means to the radical reorganization of the state and of industry (*DD* 289–91). Du Bois, who includes the peace movement among his many causes, denies, with only occasional reservations, that the establishment of socialism or communism will require violence (*A* 57, 291). Nonetheless, one can read the full measure of Du Bois's radicalism in his brief but disturbing description of the requirements of the revolution he has in mind: "human nature can and must and will be changed."[8]

With Du Bois's radicalization comes a modified but not wholly changed conception of the mission of black Americans. Du Bois continues to charge blacks with the development of their own culture (cf. *A* 339). But he begins to emphasize, as a useful foundation for socialism and communism, the communalism that has always been present in his description of the black race ideal. The African tribe, Du Bois argues, was "communistic in its very beginnings" (*A* 403). American blacks in particular may be uniquely prepared for socialism. Because so many obstacles have been put in the way of their economic advancement, they are "not yet divided into capitalists and laborers" to any great extent.[9] Du Bois, at least for a time, believes that the resulting "widespread interclass sympathy" among American blacks make them natural candidates "to guide and lead a distrait economic world" toward a socialist classless society.[10] Even when he observes with anger that the black world is developing a class structure parallel to that of the white world and that successful blacks are aping "the worst of American and Anglo-Saxon chauvinism," he continues to hope that "the Negro's experience in the past" will at least draw the majority of the black intelligentsia to the socialist cause (*A* 393, 371). This intelligentsia can be expected to form a new talented tenth, modified along the lines of Du Bois's new radicalism. It will remain, like the old talented tenth, a preserver and missionary of culture, but its members must also have an "expert knowledge of modern economics" and plan and propagandize for "such economic revolution in industry and just distribution of wealth, as would make the rise of [blacks] possible" (*TTM* 163, 168). In these ways and others, Du Bois fuses his proposed cultural, economic, and political missions for blacks into the ideology of "Pan-African socialism," which attempts simultaneously to recover the African past and to forge the socialist future (*A* 400). This fusion is open to many powerful and perhaps decisive objections, not least of which is that Du Bois seems to vacillate between race and economics as the engine of history. Nonetheless, Du Bois's socialist pan-Africanism, like almost all of his ideas, will prove influential.

"I'm through. I cannot and will not stand America longer. I'm off."

In 1961, Du Bois takes up residence in Ghana at the invitation of Kwame Nkrumah, the president of that country and himself an exponent of pan-African socialism. There, he begins work on an *Encyclopedia Africana*, a project he conceived in 1909. He becomes a citizen of Ghana in 1963 and dies that same year. It is ironic that Du Bois leaves America on the eve of the triumph of the civil rights movement, which he once helped set in motion. He is persuaded that "American blacks can't win."[11] One is tempted to say that Du Bois, in his nineties, is left embittered and behind. It is hard to say that, however, of a man who is in many ways the father not only of the civil rights movement itself but also of the reaction to it. Du Bois's soul, like the souls of black folk he describes, seems to contain and strive to merge warring ideals: not only of cultures or races—European, American, and African—but also of political movements—civil rights and integration, black nationalism and cultural distinctiveness, and black Marxism. It falls to Du Bois to try to effect in his own thought what may later have to be effected in black American political thought altogether.

Notes

1. Quotations from and references to Du Bois's works are cited in the text using the following abbreviations:

> *A*:   *The Autobiography of W. E. B. Du Bois: A Soliloquy on Viewing My Life from the Last Decade of Its First Century* (New York: International Publishers, 1968).
>
> *D*:   *Darkwater: Voices from within the Veil* (Mineola, N.Y.: Dover Publications, [1920] 1999).
>
> *DD*:   *Dusk of Dawn: An Essay toward an Autobiography of a Race Concept* (New Brunswick, N.J.: Transaction Books, [1940] 1984).
>
> *DP*:   *Dark Princess: A Romance* (Jackson, Miss.: Banner Books, [1928] 1995).
>
> *G*:   *The Gift of Black Folk* (New York: Washington Square Press, [1924] 1970).
>
> *JB*:   *John Brown* (New York: International Publishers, 1962). Revision of 1909 edition with new preface and conclusion.
>
> *S*:   *The Souls of Black Folk* (New York: Penguin Books, [1903] 1996).
>
> *TT*:   "The Talented Tenth" (1903), in Henry Louis Gates, Jr., and Cornel West, *The Future of the Race* (New York: Vintage Books, 1997), 133–57.
>
> *TTM*:   "The Talented Tenth Memorial Address" (1948), in *The Future of the Race*, 159–77.

Essays that I have referred to only once or twice are cited in full in these endnotes. The opening epigraph of this chapter comes from *D* 117–18.

2. W. E. B. Du Bois, "The Races in Conference" (1910), in *W. E. B. Du Bois: A Reader*, ed. Meyer Weinberg (New York: Harper and Row, 1970), 408.

3. "The Conservation of Races" (1897), in *W. E. B. Du Bois Speaks: Speeches and Addresses, 1890–1919*, ed. Philip S. Foner (New York: Pathfinder Press, 1970), 78.

4. See especially Washington's 1896 speech on "Democracy and Education," in *African-American Political Thought, 1850–1920*, ed. Howard Brotz (Piscataway, N.J.: Transaction Publishers, 1991), 362–71.

5. That the talented tenth will be charged not only with absorbing Western civilization but also developing the black race ideal is hinted at in *TT* 140, and elaborated in *TTM* 163–66.

6. Du Bois is quoting from comments he made in the 1890s.

7. W. E. B. Du Bois to I. M. Rubinow, November 17, 1904, quoted in David Levering Lewis, *W. E. B. Du Bois: Biography of a Race, 1868–1919* (New York: Henry Holt and Company, 1993), 313.

8. "Socialism and the Negro" (1921), in *W. E. B. Du Bois Speaks*, 346.

9. "The Class Struggle" (1921), in *W. E. B. Du Bois Speaks*, 341.

10. "The Class Struggle," 343.

11. Quoted from *The Future of the Race*, 111. The quote that begins this final section is taken from *DP* 5.

Chapter 28

Henry Adams and Our Ancient Faith

Christopher Flannery

Henry Adams (1838–1918) was born two years after the death of James Madison, when Abraham Lincoln was an obscure young state legislator; he died near the end of World War I, when Ronald Reagan was seven years of age. His American life seemed to connect the eighteenth with the twentieth century even as his thought, which in a sense knew no country, marked the many paths of their mutual divergence. By nature and nurture, Adams was an "American of Americans" (*EHA* 238/938).[1] His great-grandfather, John Adams, was a signer of the Declaration of Independence and the second president of the United States; his grandfather, John Quincy Adams, in whose company he spent his boyhood, was the sixth president and a leader of the antislavery movement in Congress. His father, Charles Francis Adams, was a leader of the Conscience Whigs and was nominated as a vice-presidential candidate by the Free Soil party in 1848. Charles was briefly a member of the U.S. House of Representatives before being appointed by Lincoln as minister to Britain, where he served throughout and beyond the Civil War, with Henry Adams as his personal secretary.

In all the offices they held, each of these Adams ancestors was a faithful champion and guardian of those "revolution-principles" first espoused by John Adams back in 1776.[2] These principles bore an architectonic relation to politics. In the political logic of John Adams and the Massachusetts Constitution, it was because "[a]ll men are born free and equal, and have certain natural, essential, and unalienable rights" that "[t]he body-politic is formed by a voluntary association of individuals: It is a social compact, by which the whole people covenants with each citizen, and each citizen with the whole people, that all shall be governed by certain laws for the common good."[3] Because they understood themselves and their political situation in light of these principles, the American people could "mutually pledge to each other our Lives, our Fortunes, and our sacred Honor" in furtherance of their cause. Through these principles, thoroughly articulated over many years in every medium of public discourse, the "American Mind" (as Jefferson called it) animated and shaped the American body politic and directed it toward its proper end. These revolution-principles were, in John Quincy Adams's words, the principles of "the law of Nature and of Nature's God, which has given to all men the inalienable Right to Liberty."[4] The truth of these ideas transcended historical development and partisan disagreement. These were the principles of Jefferson and Hamilton, Madison and Washington, as they were of "Aristotle and Plato, of Livy and Cicero, and Sydney, Harrington and Lock[e]" —indeed, of "[g]ood and wise men, in all ages."[5] Enshrined in that "old Declaration of Independence," these moral and political principles were understood by Henry Adams's great-grandfather and grandfather, as they were by his older contemporary Abraham Lincoln, to be the "principles of nature and eternal reason."[6] Insofar as the American people could live by and live

491

up to these principles, they would favorably "decide the important question, whether societies of men are really capable or not, of establishing good government from reflection and choice, or whether they are forever destined to depend, for their political constitutions, on accident and force." A nation of such people would be animated by "that honorable determination, which animates every votary of freedom, to rest all our political experiments on the capacity of mankind for self-government." By justifying a decent respect for the capacities of mankind, such a nation could "vindicate the honor of the human race."[7] Fidelity to America's revolution-principles was for all the Adams ancestors the ground of fidelity to the Constitution, the Union, and the American cause; it was the common ground alike of ordinary civic duty and of the highest political ambition; and it joined their lives and their destinies to the life and destiny of their country in its great formative crises, from revolution and Founding to civil war. When Henry Adams was a young man, Abraham Lincoln already spoke of these principles in their authoritative American incarnation as our "ancient faith."[8]

If anyone had a birth right to this American legacy, it would seem to be Henry Adams. With great labor and devotion, those "revolution-principles" were faithfully passed down to him through the generations as the most precious political inheritance. He took them with the utmost seriousness. The bloody civil war fought over them was his first great lesson in politics. He remained attached to the world of these principles his whole life. But his attachment, however deep and even passionate, could ultimately be to him no more than "a matter of taste" or habit: as a matter of conviction, he felt himself "slipping away from" the "fixed principles" of his forefathers as early as his student years at Harvard College (*EHA* 458/1138, 343/1034, 26/743, 63/777). As the years passed, Adams increasingly came to see himself as abiding in a new world, a world in which it was as impossible to believe in the "a priori" truths or "eighteenth century" ideas of his forefathers as it was to believe in the revealed truths of the medieval Church or the incantations of a pagan priest in an ancient temple of Apollo (*EHA* 26/743, 63/777). All such "dogmas" belonged to an old world of which Adams could no longer be a part. Adams refers to these dogmas in different ways in different places, sometimes metaphorically and sometimes conflating views whose differences he elsewhere takes pains to elaborate. "[D]ogma and *a priori* thought," "Puritanism," "fixed principles," "the Church," "Duty," "the eighteenth century," "Unity," "God," "Order," "the moral law," "the Constitution," the "system of 1789," "Quincy," "Plymouth Pilgrims," "the old formulas"—these are a few of the many ways in which Adams refers to part or all of a moral-political world from which he was ineluctably slipping or had irretrievably slipped away, and to which in much of his writing he is bidding heartbroken, if cavalier, farewell (*EHA* 26/743, 63/777, 230–32/930–32, 280–81/976, 343–44/1034–35, 455–56/1136, 472/1151; *Esther* 332). How the "system of 1789" differed from the "Plymouth Pilgrims," or how his forefathers differed from thirteenth-century saints or fifth-century B.C.E. philosophers, was in the end less important for Adams's purposes than how they agreed—in acknowledging the authority of what Thomas Jefferson called simply "[t]he great principles of right and wrong."[9] Adams's famous "education" led him to the point where "he knew no longer the good from the bad."[10] It led him to the point, so characteristic of later generations of educated Americans, where he must place between quotation marks any reference to a nonarbitrary standard of moral judgment independent of human will, whether knowable through reason or revelation, by which an individual and a people could direct their choices and their destinies. His "slipping away" from this ancient faith, both in its broadest terms and in its peculiarly American variety, was momentous for Adams. It constituted the "problem" around which his thought would always revolve: having abandoned the faith of his fathers, he would spend the rest of his life thinking through the necessity for and the consequences of having done so.

All the major writings of Adams's maturity were in one way or another reflections on the historical, political, psychological, and philosophical dimensions of this problem. These extended and imaginative reflections proved to be early explorations of the paths that would be wandered by leading American intellectuals for the rest of the twentieth century, paths which led away from the fixed principles of "nature and eternal reason" toward history and "change"—ultimately, as Adams was fully aware, to "chaos" (*EHA* 230–31/931–32, 451/1132). Adams wrote political journalism, scholarly essays, biography, novels, and a voluminous history of early-nineteenth-century America, in addition to the two books which later generations have found less easy to categorize but more inviting to read: *Mont Saint Michel and Chartres* (1913) and *The Education of Henry Adams* (1918).[11] He also dabbled in poetry and even wrote a history of Tahiti. His extensive life-long correspondence is regarded by some as the most interesting collection of American letters on record.

Adams traveled prodigiously throughout his life and lived many years abroad, paying thoughtful and often studious and systematic attention to what he observed and recording his observations in private and published writings. He was a voracious researcher and reader, who knew as much as any American of his time about American history and world affairs. He tells us that he "passed the best years of his life in pondering over the political philosophy of Jefferson, Gallatin, and Madison," and among the many other serious thinkers to whom he felt obliged to respond in his writings were Augustine, Aquinas, Descartes, Bacon, Spinoza, Pascal, Rousseau, Kant, Hegel, Tocqueville, J. S. Mill, Marx, and Nietzsche (*EHA* 436/1118). His wide-ranging investigations returned again and again to a determined effort to understand science as a necessary method of explaining human—and American—history and as the decisive influence on, and problem of, the contemporary human condition.

Adams was a professor of history at Harvard for several years, served as editor of the influential quarterly the *North American Review*, and was a reluctant president of the American Historical Association. But his official or formal positions were of far less characteristic significance than his informal and personal activities and relations. From earliest childhood to his death, he associated and corresponded with leading figures in politics, letters, and the arts. For decades he maintained a salon in Washington, D.C., where leading politicians, diplomats, and authors regularly socialized. As he said of himself (not as a boast but as a matter of fact), "[n]ever in his life would he have to explain who he was" (*EHA* 64/778). In all his vast array of personal associations—political, social, literary, academic—Adams exerted an active and purposeful informal influence through letters and conversation over the course of several decades.

In his early twenties, Adams expressed to his brother Charles an ambition which, in various ways, he pursued throughout his life: "what we want, my dear boy, is a school. We want a national set of young men like ourselves or better, to start new influences not only in politics, but in literature, in law, in society, and throughout the whole social organism of the country. A national school of our own generation" (*LHA* 1:315). Adams never gave up trying to "start new influences" in the American mind, his own included. For more than half a century, he became a kind of school unto himself—headmaster, faculty, and member of the student body. His early journalism tried to shape American opinion on the great issues of the day—secession, civil war, and political reform. His scholarly essays and books aimed at a different layer of opinion but were as purposeful as his journalism, seeking among other things to establish a new ground for understanding American history. With what he referred to as his "literary art," he wrote novels and such innovative works as *Chartres* and the *Education* in order to influence different audiences through their imaginations (*EHA* [Sam.] 513). With a late if not a last gasp, he wrote a 220-page volume in the form of "A Letter to American Teachers of History" with explicit didactic intentions, and what can be considered his "last work" was a kind of brief, posthumous guide to his writings.[12] His correspondence aimed not only at its contemporary recipients; he was certainly conscious that his letters would be preserved and studied by later generations as well, and this private and personal mode of influence became especially characteristic of him.[13]

The thought of Henry Adams is elusive—sometimes by chance, more often by design. For every measure he takes to reveal it, either he or circumstance seems to take another to conceal it. In his early journalism, first as Washington correspondent for the Boston *Daily Advertiser* (December 1860–March 1861) and then as London correspondent for the *New York Times* (June 1861–January 1862), he wrote anonymously for political reasons. His *Democracy, An American Novel* (1880) was published anonymously. His other novel *Esther* (1884) was published under the name Frances Snow Compton. His history of Tahiti was presented as the memoir of a Tahitian queen.[14] He wrote speeches and policy papers to be delivered or presented by others without attribution. He seemed to think that his massive *History of the United States during the Administrations of Thomas Jefferson and James Madison* (1889–91) would be found unreadable by practically everyone.[15] His most widely read book, the *Education,* aside from its deliberate coyness, was published posthumously, with corrections not anticipated by Adams. An "Editor's Preface" written by Adams was, on his instructions, attributed to the editor, Henry Cabot Lodge; Lodge gave the book a subtitle of his own invention.[16] Adams seems to have regarded the book as the product of "a kind of esoteric literary art": the inner meaning is "sugar-coated" and not likely to be understood by one reader in a thousand (*EHA* [Sam.] 508–14). According to his own private account of his writing habits, he had "never written a chapter less than five times over, unless it were from sheer collapse." Advising his brother Brooks on how to write about John Quincy Adams's role in certain episodes of American history, he wrote that "[m]y own art would consist only in concealing my own art and myself."[17] As Adams says in his *Education,* "[n]o one means all he says, and yet very few say all they mean." Though Adams writes publicly in the *Education* that the purpose of the book is to "fit young men . . . to be men of the world, equipped for any emergency," he confides privately and emphatically that he wrote both *Chartres* and the *Education* not "in order to teach others, but to educate my self": the *Education* "served its only purpose by educating *me,*" and he wrote it merely to "clean my own mind" (*EHA* 451/1132, xxx/722; [Sam.] 507–15). In his extensive private correspondence (destined to be public), he expresses many different and not always reconcilable attitudes and opinions about a wide range of subjects, including the meaning, purpose, and significance of his published writings. His brother Brooks seems only to be respectfully expressing his informed opinion when he writes that "Henry was never, I fear, quite frank with himself or with others. . . . Also he dearly loved paradox" (*DD* 1–2).[18] Adams readily admits that he finds not merely paradox, but contradiction, to be stimulating: "The mind must have a contradiction in order to act at all. My object has always been to supply the contradiction which should compel the mind to fight."[19] He tried to adapt—and sometimes even to distribute —his writings to different audiences, whether young women, young men, teachers, the future, or the rare few of discerning mind or taste. He writes in a number of places that he is constrained to remain silent about the most important things.[20] Conclusions, then, about the thought of Henry Adams must be in a variety of ways cautious or tentative.

Still, however difficult Adams makes it to pronounce ultimate conclusions about his writings, he does mark certain pathways that may be helpful for those seeking an initial acquaintance with his thought. Adams refers to the *Education* privately as "my last Will and Testament," and common opinion seems to have crowned this work as his masterpiece and as the most mature expression of his thought.[21] Some of the things Adams writes in and about the *Education* place that work, and the "problem" of that work, at least tentatively in relation to his other works and to a life-long inquiry.

If we may believe the author of the *Education*, his "literary model" was St. Augustine's *Confessions*.[22] Ostensibly a didactic work for young men framed around the life and times of its nineteenth- and twentieth-century author, the *Education* was written as a "sequel" to, or was meant to "go together" with, *Mont Saint Michel and Chartres*, which was itself ostensibly a didactic work for young women in the form of a study of Gothic architecture and medieval culture (*EHA* xxvii/719; [Sam.] 513). To that "volume on the twelfth century," the *Education* was a "companion study of the twentieth century"; or, it was "a completion and mathematical conclusion from the previous volume about the Thirteenth Century" (*EHA* [Sam.] 509–10, 512). To that "Study of Thirteenth-Century Unity," it was a contrasting study in "Twentieth-Century Multiplicity." *Chartres* was "historically purposeless without its sequel" (*EHA* xxvii–iii/719–20). In particular, the "three concluding chapters" of the *Education* are "only a working out to Q.E.D. of the three concluding chapters" of *Chartres*.[23] Having privately printed *Chartres* in 1904 and the *Education* in 1906, Adams took pains in 1916 to ensure posthumously that future readers of the *Education* would place both works in the context of a single larger inquiry. He does this in the "Editor's Preface" to the *Education*, signed by Henry Cabot Lodge and dated September 1918 (several months after Adams's death).[24] Here, he tells future readers that he was "still pondering over the problem" of the *Education* in 1910, "when he tried to deal with it in another way which might be more intelligible to students," in a "small volume called 'A Letter to American Teachers.'" In fact, he was still unsuccessfully puzzling over the problem as late as 1912.[25]

If "A Letter to American Teachers of History" (dated February 16, 1910) tried to deal with the problem of the *Education* and therefore of *Chartres*, it also explicitly took up the thread of Adams's earlier thought. "[I]n effect," as he says, in the "Letter" he "enlarged [an earlier] paper to the dimensions of a Report," and he privately distributed the "unofficial and personal" report to presidents of American universities among others. The earlier "paper" was a "short address" (dated December 12, 1894) submitted in absentia to the American Historical Association by its departing president, Henry Adams.[26] In that short valedictory address, Adams reflected upon anxieties that had cast their shadow upon him over "the last ten years" (*DD* 132–33). Thus, in his "last work," written in 1916 and delivered by proxy from the grave, Adams leads his readers back more than thirty years to 1884 to trace his anxious thoughts about an old problem.[27] But his anxiety and the problem that was the source of his anxiety did not go back only to 1884; they were of older vintage.

The problem casting a shadow over Adams was a certain "tendency of history." In the first instance, this was a tendency of history as a discipline; but this turns out to have profound implications for the tendency of history itself. Adams was anxious about the irresistible tendency of historians, following "the violent impulse which Darwin [and others] gave to the study of natural laws," to try to "create a science of history." Adams identifies himself as one who, since 1857 or 1859, "never doubted" the inexorability of this tendency. It was a tendency of history that

> cannot be other than what it is. That the effort to make history a science may fail is possible, and perhaps probable; but that it should cease, unless for reasons that would cause all science to cease, is not within the range of human experience.... Science itself would admit its own failure if it admitted that man, the most important of its subjects, could not be brought within its range. (*DD* 126)

The tendency of history to become scientific was necessary and irresistible not only to the extent that "Science" as a method of explaining "man" was necessary and irresistible but also to the extent that "man" and "history" must become subject to the forces unleashed by "Science." From 1857 to 1918 (with signposts in 1884, 1894, and 1910) Adams thus traces his concern with this "tendency of history," which received its latest thrust by a violent impulse given by science to the study of the natural laws. Anxiety over various aspects of this "problem" is a leitmotif of Adams's writings from the time he was barely out of college until his death. As epistolarian, journalist, novelist, historian, teacher, and "literary artist," Adams explores innumerable dimensions of this inexhaustible theme, and he lets the world know that he had not concluded his exploration when he was gathered to his fathers, from whose ancient faith this tendency of history had carried him away.

The scientific study of history sought to discover the "necessary sequence of cause and effect, a force resulting in motion which cannot be other than what it is. Any science of history must be absolute, like other sciences, and must fix with mathematical certainty the path which human society has got to follow" (*DD* 129). Adams's mature professional interest in American history was a "scientific interest" in these terms. Any history that would be a "true science" would "establish its laws" for its subject. Such a history, he well understood, would amount to studying the choices of human beings and the destinies of nations as one "studied the formation of a crystal" (*HUS* 1332–34). As he wrote to fellow historian, Francis Parkman, in 1884: "I am satisfied that the purely mechanical development of the human mind in society must appear in a great democracy so clearly . . . that in another generation psychology, physiology and history will join in proving man to have as fixed and necessary a development as that of a tree; and almost as unconscious."[28] In the eye of Adams the scientific historian, his great subjects Jefferson, Madison, and Monroe

> appear like mere grass-hoppers, kicking and gesticulating, on the middle of the Mississippi River. There is no possibility of reconciling their theories with their acts. . . . They were carried along on a stream which floated them after a fashion without much regard for themselves. . . . My own conclusion is that history is simply social development along the lines of weakest resistance, and that in most cases the line of weakest resistance is found as unconsciously by society as by water. (*LHA* 2:490–91)

Adams was aware that the American people "were not disposed to make of their history" such "a mechanical evolution" as his science would make it. They seemed conscious that "of all the misfortunes that could befall the national character, the greatest would be the loss of the established ideals which alone ennobled human weakness," and that these "ideals" were invisible to the mechanical scrutiny of the scientific eye.[29] Adams saw clearly that his science of history decided in the negative "the important question, whether societies of men are really capable or not, of establishing good government from reflection and choice." In the world according to Adams the scientific historian, all is diminished to accident and force. An America understood in these terms could not, of course, be a nation that in any way might "vindicate the honor of the human race." The greatest of men are, from this vantage point, helpless insects at best. There can be no ordering of action by "theories." Politics and statesmanship disappear. They are replaced by mechanical efforts to accommodate the predominant forces of one's time or to anticipate the direction of blind fate. In such an America, there are no more grounds for "honorable determination" than there is capacity of mankind to govern itself.

Adams sincerely sympathized with his countrymen in their misfortune. He was fond of the "established ideals" of the earlier America to which he devoted many years of study and thousands of carefully written pages. He found these ideals (or "dreams" or "illusions" as he also called them) expressed in the "theories" of Jefferson, whose opinions he thought were shared by the majority of Americans in the period with which his *History* is concerned (1801–1817). But already by the end of this period, he thought that the grounds for believing in these ideals had eroded. Jefferson himself had asked: "And can the liberties of a nation be thought secure when we have removed their only firm basis, a conviction in the minds of the people that these liberties are of the gift of God? That they are not to be violated but with his wrath?"[30] But Adams the scientific historian found that the wrath of God no longer sustained the liberties of America. "God was no longer terrible" to the American of 1817, whose character was better expressed by Jefferson's other famous pronouncement: "it does me no injury for my neighbor to say there are twenty gods or no God."[31] This was an epochal change. "For the first time in history, great bodies of men turned away from their old religion, giving no better reason than that it required them to believe in a cruel Deity, and rejected necessary conclusions of theology because they were inconsistent with human self-esteem." And having turned away from God, the Americans of 1817 must relinquish the political "ideals" that depended on Him. Carried on the current of history, Americans had necessarily moved in politics as far from "the temper of mind . . . in which the Constitution had been framed" as they had moved in religion from God (*HUS* 1344).

Adams the scientific historian thus thought he saw that as early as 1817 the "established ideals" of 1789, which alone ennobled the American people, had been left in the wake of the currents of history.[32] He was deeply conscious of the moral-political significance of his scientific conclusions. As a scientist, he was fully convinced that these "ideals" could only do their necessary work in the world—they could only ennoble the American people—so long as they were understood to be true. For Adams the literary artist, political society was in this way like the Gothic arch about the heavenly aspirations of which he rhapsodized in *Chartres* (695): "never let us forget that Faith alone supports it, and that, if Faith fails, Heaven is lost." At the end of writing his *History*, Adams was left asking, as a scientific historian, "[w]hat ideals were to ennoble" future American society—"what object . . . must . . .[it] aspire to attain?" (*HUS* 1345). He had no answer then or ever. His science could not vouchsafe one, though it did not stop him from recognizing that for America—as for "mankind"—the central question must always be "what its object is, or whether it has an object." Without an answer to this question, life appeared to Adams as chaos or anarchy. But as a scientific historian, he understood that "[m]ankind could not admit an anarchical . . . universe" (*Chartres* 660, 611, 684).

Adams's science revealed in this way that science and society had irreconcilable interests. The conclusions of science could be death and dishonor to society. But science—the tendency of history—will not be denied. Speaking on behalf of scientific historians, Adams writes:

> A science cannot be played with. If an hypothesis is advanced that obviously brings into a direct sequence of cause and effect all the phenomena of human history, we must accept it, and if we accept it we must teach it. The mere fact that it overthrows social organizations cannot affect our attitude. . . . [W]e must follow the new light no matter where it leads. (*DD* 131)

Adams imagines the coming generation of necessarily scientific historians standing in the same relation to society as did Galileo two hundred and fifty years before. Their scientific conclusions, like those Adams was already reaching, may undermine the faith on which the good of their country depends. They may even be obliged by prudent political authority to "recant or repudiate [their] science." But they must still, as Galileo allegedly did, say "in secret if not in public, 'E pur si muove [And yet it moves].'" The seriousness of this problem leads directly to the characteristic reticence of Adams's writing. As he writes in 1894 to his fellow historians: "the shadow of this coming event has cast itself upon me, . . .[and] in the last ten years, it has often kept me silent where I should once have spoken with confidence, or has caused me to think long and anxiously before expressing in public any opinion at all" (*DD* 132–33). Adams's conclusions about the tendency of history, to the extent that he was willing or determined to write responsibly, must be expressed—if at all—in a private, personal, informal, unofficial, or cryptic manner. The most important things to be said are too important or too delicate to be uttered publicly or formally. They must be withdrawn by art even as they are being uttered, like a legendary last word muttered sotto voce while leaving a room where an historic episode has just concluded—a word which, despite or rather because of its near privacy or silence, is remembered as defining the moment for the rest of time. The conclusion to Adams's 1894 valedictory address, to which he directs future readers in his more final valediction of 1918, expresses with burlesque gravity a considered disposition informing all of Adams's writing on serious questions: "Beyond doubt silence is best. In these remarks, which are only casual and offered in the paradoxical spirit of private conversation, I have not ventured to express any opinion of my own; or if I have expressed it, pray consider it as withdrawn" (*DD* 133). As private secretary to his father when minister to England in the 1860s; as unofficial consultant to his friend Secretary of State John Hay thirty years later; as an anonymous journalist; as a scholar who writes impenetrably; as a private correspondent unwilling to offer official or professional opinion to his fellow teachers and historians; as an "artist" whose "esoteric literary art" is the art of concealment—in all these characteristic roles, Adams with increasing self-consciousness bowed to what he regarded as the necessity to "be civil towards the idols of the forum" (*Chartres* 611). As he writes in a 1909 letter about his *Education*: "[I]t is private . . . . Especially its privacy is vital to it." Adams's need for privacy was perhaps even greater than Galileo's, for the "tendency of history" had carried Adams beyond Galileo in a decisive respect. Unlike Galileo, he did not care "whether the earth moves or not" (*EHA* [Sam.] 515–16, 517).

It did not matter to Adams the scientist—it was an irrelevant question—whether a given scientific theory was true or false. Indeed, science required more credulity of its devotees than did the mysteries of medieval faith (*Esther* 281–84, 319, 330). Science, as such, had nothing to teach about the "nature" or the "reality" of things. Galileo's theories or Darwin's theories, like Jefferson's "theories" or belief in the divine power of the Virgin, were merely different ways of looking at things—different "formulas." Neither as a scientist nor as a historian did Adams concern himself with the truth of such formulas. As he says in the *Education* (231–32/932), "he really did not care whether truth was, or was not, true." Nor did he expect the sophisticated student of his own argument to "be concerned with the question whether it is true, which has no meaning for him." He expected his readers to be concerned only with whether his arguments proved "convenient," which meant "useful" to "their own purposes" (*EHA* [Sam.] 518). In fact, in a world that must submit to be commanded—as it must submit to be explained—by mechanistic modern science, "[c]onvenience was truth" (*EHA* 457/1138). If the theory was convenient— and so long as it proved convenient—it would prove irresistible (*DD* 190, 226–27, 260–61). And it would prove convenient so long as it continued to explain or predict events. As J. S. Mill wrote in 1865, in a work familiar to the young Adams: "Foresight of phenomena and power over them depend on knowledge of their sequences, and not upon any notion we may have formed respecting their . . . inmost nature."[33] In Adams's science, as in the science of Francis Bacon of which he was a life-long student, "knowledge and human power are synonymous."[34]

In 1826, just a few days before his death, Thomas Jefferson could write with his characteristic optimism about a science that revealed the "palpable truth" about the "inmost nature" of its subject and about the harmony between the progress of this science and the rights of man: "All eyes are opened, or opening, to the rights of man. The general spread of the light of science has already laid open to every view the palpable truth, that the mass of mankind has not been born with saddles on their backs, nor a favored few booted and spurred, ready to ride them legitimately, by the grace of God."[35] This is a world apart from the science of Henry Adams. Just a few decades after Jefferson's letter, Adams wrote to his brother, Charles Francis Adams, Jr., in a remarkably similar metaphor but with a very different point: "Man has mounted science, and is now run away with. I firmly believe that before many centuries more, science will be the master of man. The engines he will have invented will be beyond his strength to control" (*LHA* 1:290). From the irresistible point of view of Adams's science, man and his "rights" can only be understood mechanically as the product of a "social organism" (*DD* 260). Insofar as such a science is to instruct man, it can teach him nothing about his "inmost nature." It can teach only one lesson: how to "enlarge the power and empire of mankind in general over the universe."[36] It has nothing to say about the objects for the sake of which such power should be used, even or especially when this power is to be exercised in scientific empire over man himself. In full and anxious recognition of this, Adams felt compelled, not by the truth but by the sheer brute force of science as the tendency of history, to seek out and subject himself to some "necessary sequence of cause and effect"; he was abjectly determined that "the current of his time was to be his current, lead where it might" (*EHA* 232/932). In the end, he found that current bearing him to mystifying and repugnant depths. Indeed, "nihilism had no bottom" (*EHA* 430/1113, 457–58/1137–38).

It was true that Darwin had given a violent impulse to the study of natural laws; he had started or exposed a tendency of history that undermined an ancient faith, which was founded on the "law of nature and of nature's God." But to some Darwinians—not to Adams or to Darwin—Darwin's theories seemed to take the place of the old formulas or the old faith. To such optimistic or progressive people, "Natural Selection seemed a dogma to be put in the place of the Athanasian creed; it was a form of religious hope." Adams "warmly sympathized" with this view, as he warmly sympathized with the hopeless ancient faith of earlier Americans; "but when he came to ask himself what he truly thought, he felt he had no Faith," whether in the laws of evolution or the laws of nature and nature's God. He felt, as he says, "that the idea of one Form, Law, Order, or Sequence had no more value for him than the idea of none; that what he valued most was Motion, and that what attracted his mind was Change" (*EHA* 231–32/932). The education of Henry Adams finally taught him to regard "motion" or "change" as the fundamental phenomenon. His work records the wanderings of a mind that has become unmoored from all "fixed principles" and has set sail rudderless on a sea of change. For Adams, the scientific student of the human condition, "Chaos was the law of nature" (*EHA* 451/1132).

But chaos would not do. It may be that "[t]he old formulas had failed," that "[t]he moral law had expired—like the Constitution" (*EHA* 472/1151, 280/976). It may be that there was nothing fixed in the universe in which a man could believe and that nihilism knew no bottom. Nonetheless, philosophers knew that "since they could find no bottom, they must assume it" (*EHA* 430/1113)—or rather create it. "The Church was gone, and Duty was dim, but Will should take its place" (*EHA* 232/933; *DD* 193ff.). Apparently, philosophers could no more bear anarchy than could mankind. Every self-respecting man had to "invent a formula of his own for his universe, if the standard formulas failed." And they had failed in spades. The new formula to be invented need not concern itself with its "absolute truth"—presumably, convenience would suffice (*EHA* 472/1151). But convenience is not much of a port in the kind of storm unleashed upon Adams, and Adams's mind, adrift on a sea of aimless change, is forever drawn by hopeless longing to some port of permanence. Adams felt this longing "to the last fibre of his being" (*EHA* 469/1148–49). Once he had given up the fixed principles of his forefathers, it drew him helplessly toward mystical faith, on the one hand, and material determinism, on the other hand—to the Virgin and the Dynamo, as recorded in his two most well-known books, *Chartres* and the *Education*. But his hopelessness—not because he saw it to be founded on any truth, but purely because of its blind compelling force —would no more let him consummate his longing than his Esther could allow herself to marry the clergyman she loved or the scientist who loved her (*Esther* 355).[37] His thought is forever fecklessly suspended between the one thing needful and the self-consciously willful insistence that it does not exist.

However much his education rendered Adams rudderless and taught him that change was at the root of all things; that the world had left behind in ringing quotation marks the "truths" of 1776 and 1789; that faith and reason must be replaced by will; and that man must invent a formula for his meaningless universe —still, Adams professes, and we may believe him, that his moral universe had one fixed point that did not vanish, that seems to have persevered through his "education." That was, mirabile dictu, George Washington: not an idea but a real man, or the idea of a real man. "George Washington was a primary . . . , an ultimate relation, like the Pole Star, and amid the endless restless motion of every other visible point in space, he alone remained steady, in the mind of Henry Adams, to the end." As Brooks Adams put it, Washington remained for Adams as he had been for John Quincy Adams and John Adams before him, "the model and the standard" (*EHA* 47–48/762–63; *DD* 104–5). What Adams's reasoning could not confirm for him—the existence, one might say, of genuine good—was practically confirmed somehow beyond question by experience, if vicarious experience. But example yearns for precept. Washington's nobility is diminished immeasurably when his cause is abandoned. In the world of Henry Adams, Washington—however desperately Adams would have it otherwise— must also drift away with the jetsam of history on the sea of aimless change.

In July 1858, when twenty-year-old Henry Adams was seeking education in Germany, Abraham Lincoln invited fellow citizens to reflect on what it is that unites Americans as Americans.[38] He ran his memory back "about eighty-two years" and saw that what was then a "very small people" had in the course of those years become "a mighty nation," vastly greater in "everything we deem desirable among men." He fixed upon "something that happened away back" that was "in some way or other . . . connected with this rise of prosperity." In particular, he fixed upon those "fathers and grandfathers [who] fought for the principle they were contending for" and from whose deeds "the degree of prosperity we now enjoy [had] come to us." Here was a bond. Those Americans who are "descended by blood from our ancestors" can remind themselves of "all the good done in this process of time[,] of how it was done and who did it, and how we are historically connected with it." When we do this, "we feel more attached the one to the other and more firmly bound to the country we inhabit." But this would not suffice. "[P]erhaps half our people" are not descendants of these ancestors. They have come or their ancestors have come more recently from other parts of the world to settle here. What will attach them "the one to the other" as Americans? What will bind them to the country they have chosen to inhabit? Lincoln offers the answer that is characteristic of his thought.

> If they look back through this history to trace their connection with those days by blood, they find they have none, they cannot carry themselves back into that glorious epoch and make themselves feel that they are part of us, but when they look through that old Declaration of Independence they find that those old men say that "We hold these truths to be self-evident, that all men are created equal," and then they feel that that moral sentiment taught in that day evidences their relation to those men, that it is the father of all moral principle in them, and that they have a right to claim it as though they were blood of the blood, and flesh of the flesh of the men who wrote that Declaration, and so they are. That is the electric cord in that Declaration that links the hearts of patriotic and liberty-loving men together, that will link those patriotic hearts as long as the love of freedom exists in the minds of men throughout the world.

Nearly a century after Lincoln's reflections and a generation after Adams's death, when America was vastly greater still in everything deemed desirable among men, a recent German immigrant returned to Lincoln's theme. He quoted the same passage of the Declaration of Independence, to whose weight and elevation Lincoln had added immeasurably: "We hold these truths to be self evident, that all men are created equal." He followed Lincoln in acknowledging America's dedication to this proposition as a cause of its power and prosperity, which now had no rival among "the nations of the earth." And he raised a question: "Does this nation in its maturity still cherish the faith in which it was conceived and raised?"[39] The answer, at least so far as it concerned the most learned and privileged Americans, was no different than the answer that would be given by the most highly educated Americans of the early twenty-first century: "no." Even those learned Americans who did still "adhere to the principles of the Declaration of Independence" had come for the most part—largely under the influence of German thought—to view these principles as "ideals" or "ideology" or "myth." Adams had anticipated these intellectuals and their heirs—our contemporaries—by half a century and more, in part because, as his biographer suggests, he looked for his understanding of these principles "beyond the laws of nature and of God to the primeval forests of Germany."[40]

Henry Adams was, indeed, "blood of the blood, and flesh of the flesh, of the men who wrote that Declaration." By birth and history, Adams was more connected with the American Revolution and Founding than it is possible to be today. This was a man who in 1898, in his sixtieth year, while sojourning in London, could see and did see the American victory in the Spanish-American War as part of a personal, American, and historic drama extending over one hundred and fifty years. An unbroken line of Adamses, beginning with his great-grandfather John Adams and including (modestly) himself, had played a part in the drama of building the American empire or, as Adams put it, "of bringing England into an American system." We can believe Adams when he writes of this global and transgenerational drama that "[h]e carried every scene of it, in a century and a half since the Stamp Act, quite alive in his mind" (*EHA* 362–63/1051–52). Adams was American in a way in which few if any of his contemporaries could be, and which has after him become impossible. And yet, he found it impossible to be an American in the most decisive sense, in a way that was understandable to "good and wise men, in all ages," and available in principle to all men of all times.

Notes

1. Quotations from and references to Adams's works are cited in the text using the following abbreviations:

DD: Henry Adams with Brooks Adams, *The Degradation of the Democratic Dogma* (New York: Macmillan Company, 1919).

EHA: *The Education of Henry Adams*, ed. Ernest Samuels (Boston: Houghton Miflin, 1974), and *The Education of Henry Adams*, in *Novels/Mont Saint Michel/The Education* (New York: Library of America, 1983). When citing the *Education* hereafter, I will cite both editions, the Samuels edition first, as follows: *EHA* 238/938. The Samuels edition has useful notes and appendices; the Library of America edition is more commonly available. When citing something exclusive to the Samuels edition, I will use the abbreviation Sam., e.g., *EHA* (Sam.) 238.

HUS: *History of the United States during the Administrations of Thomas Jefferson and James Madison* (New York: Library of America, 1983).

LHA: *The Letters of Henry Adams*, ed. J. C. Levenson, Ernest Samuels, Charles Vandersee, and Viola Hopkins Winner, 6 vols. (Cambridge, Mass.: Belknap Press of Harvard University Press, 1982).

When citing Adams's novels as well as *Mont Saint Michel and Chartres*, I will cite the Library of American edition above and use a short abbreviation (e.g., *Chartres*). Adams was also, among other things, one of the "new Americans" (*EHA* 239/939) and an "American in search of a father" (*EHA* 229/930).

2. John Adams, "Novanglus," in *Papers of John Adams*, ed. Robert J. Taylor (Cambridge, Mass.: Belknap Press of Harvard University Press, 1977), 2:230.

3. Massachusetts Constitution, March 2, 1780, in *The Founders' Constitution*, ed. Philip B. Kurland and Ralph Lerner (Chicago: University of Chicago Press, 1987), 1:11ff.

4. Quoted in Ernest Samuels, *The Young Henry Adams* (Cambridge, Mass.: Harvard University Press, 1948), 79.

5. John Adams, "Novanglus," and Alexander Hamilton, "The Farmer Refuted," in *The Founders' Constitution*, 1:91.

6. Lincoln's speech at Chicago, July 10, 1858, in *The Collected Works of Abraham Lincoln*, ed. Roy P. Basler (New Brunswick, N.J.: Rutgers University Press, 1953), 2:499, and John Adams, "Novanglus."

7. Alexander Hamilton, James Madison, and John Jay, *The Federalist Papers* (New York: New American Library, 1999), 1, 208, 59.

8. *The Collected Works of Abraham Lincoln*, 2:266.

9. Thomas Jefferson, "A Summary View of the Rights of British America," in *The Founders' Constitution*, 1:441.

10. *EHA* 89/801. Compare Mrs. Madeleine Lightfoot Lee, the heroine of Adams's *Democracy, An American Novel*, whose political education reached the point where she could say, with Adams's self-mockery, "I have got so far as to lose the distinction between right and wrong" (99).

11. Each of these books was printed and distributed privately several years before these dates of publication. See "Notes on the Texts," in *Novels/Mont Saint Michel/The Education*, 1217–25.

12. Edward Chalfant, *Improvement of the World, A Biography of Henry Adams: His Last Life, 1891–1918* (North Haven, Conn.: Archon Books, 2001), 361ff., 502.

13. As anecdotal evidence of the immediate and lasting success of his efforts, his *Education* won the Pulitzer Prize (1919) just a year after his death, and as the twentieth century was coming to a close, Modern Library selected the *Education* as the best nonfiction book in English in the century. Whatever the ultimate merits of these honors, as measures of his influence they are to some extent confirmed by the publication of a new edition of his letters in the 1980s, the republishing of his major works by The Library of America in the same decade, and by the continuing scholarly interest in his work—more in literature departments than in history departments as it turns out. Helping Adams in an informal, private way to start new influences in yet another century, the president of Adams's alma mater, Neil L. Rudenstine, encouraged the Harvard incoming class of 2004 to consider the "immense value" of reading Adams's *Education*.

14. Chalfant, *Improvement*, 56.

15. Chalfant, *Improvement*, 273; see also *Improvement*, 13, where Chalfant asserts that Adams deliberately made his *History* impenetrable; for argument purporting to support this contention, see Chalfant, *Better in Darkness, A Biography of Henry Adams: His Second Life, 1862–1891* (Hamden, Conn.: Archon Books, 1994), 556, 862–63, 865, 870–71, 873.

16. *EHA* (Sam.) xxi–xxv, 541n13; see also Chalfant, *Improvement*, 501ff.

17. Chalfant, *Improvement*, 322 and 340.

18. The title of the book, *The Degradation of the Democratic Dogma*, was chosen by Brooks Adams for his compilation of a few related essays by Henry published after Henry's death.

19. Adams to Edward H. Davis, February 3, 1911, cited in Chalfant, *Improvement*, 640n12.

20. *DD* 133; *Chartres* 611. In *EHA* 148/855, Adams quotes an "economist of morals" to the effect that "[t]he world can absorb only doses of truth."

21. *EHA* (Sam.) 508. As usual, Adams expresses other views as well.

22. See *EHA* (Sam.) 512 and 514. Adams also compares his *Education* with autobiographical works by Benjamin Franklin, Rousseau, Gibbon, and Benvenuto Cellini.

23. *EHA* (Sam.) 512–13. As Adams writes to William James, the concluding chapters of *Chartres* were meant to "hide . . . a sort of anchor in history. . . . I knew that not a hundred people in America would understand what I meant." In the *Education*, he meant to "hide—in a stack of rubbish meant only to feed the foolish—a hundred more pages [the concluding chapters] meant to complete" the last hundred pages of *Chartres* (*EHA* [Sam.] 509–10).

24. The "Editor's Preface" was written by Adams and sent to Lodge in March 1916, with a copy of the *Education* to be "printed as I leave it," which it was not (*EHA* [Sam.] 541n13, xxi–xxv).

25. *EHA* xxviii/720; (Sam.) 541n13. See also *EHA* (Sam.) 540n7 and the letter referred to there on 515–18, where Adams elaborates on his intention and "the problem" with which he was concerned in the *Education*.

26. Both of these writings are included in *DD* 125 and 137.

27. In 1884, Adams also privately circulated the first section of his *History of the United States during the Administrations of Thomas Jefferson and James Madison* and pseudonymously published *Esther: A Novel*.

28. *LHA* 2:562–63. See *Chartres* 688: "The only difference between Man and a Vegetable was the Reflex Action of the . . . Mind. . . . The apparent freedom was an illusion."

29. *HUS* 1334. Also see *DD* 229. Adams's language demonstrates that the effects of the tendency of science have fully taken hold in his own mind: all moral principles necessarily dissolve into mere "ideals."

30. Thomas Jefferson, *Notes on the State of Virginia* (New York: Harper and Row Publishers, 1964), 156.

31. *HUS* 1344, 123; Jefferson, *Notes*, 152.

32. Adams the literary artist records other dramatic moments when "the moral law" or "his Constitution of 1789" become no longer tenable (*EHA* 343–44/1034–35, 280/976).

33. Samuels, *The Young Henry Adams*, 134.

34. Francis Bacon, *Novum Organum*, I.3 and I.129, in *Advancement of Learning and Novum Organum* (New York: Willey Book Co., 1900), 315, 366.

35. To Roger C. Weightman, June 24, 1826, in *The Portable Thomas Jefferson*, ed. Merrill D. Peterson (New York: Penguin Books, 1975), 585.

36. Bacon, *Advancement of Learning*, 315, 366.

37. "There is no science which does not begin by requiring you to believe the incredible" (*Esther* 284). In both of Adams's novels, the main character is a woman looking for meaning in life—whether in politics, religion, or science—some ground of permanence in a world of flux. Neither finds it. It is nowhere to be found. But Adams the "literary artist" makes it clear that the most attractive characters will long for it, nonetheless.

38. One of the first things readers learn about Madeleine Lightfoot Lee, in Adams's *Democracy* (3) is that "tortured by *ennui*," she had turned to the reading of "philosophy in the original German, and the more she read, the more she was disheartened that so much culture should lead to nothing—nothing." See *EHA* 369/1057 for how Adams, "hunted by ennui," "entered the practice of his final profession."

39. Leo Strauss, *Natural Right and History* (Chicago: University of Chicago Press, 1953), 1.

40. Samuels, *The Young Henry Adams*, 256–57. Adams also anticipated Leo Strauss, *Natural Right and History*, 8, in his conclusion that "the fundamental dilemma, in whose grip we are, is caused by the victory of modern natural science."

Chapter 29

Jane Addams as Civic Theorist: Struggling to Reconcile Competing Claims

Jean Bethke Elshtain

Jane Addams (1860–1935) is remembered as a great American social reformer. She is often called the "first social worker," a characterization that radically understates her efforts and distorts her understanding of what her pioneer social settlement, Hull-House, situated in Chicago's 19th ward, was all about.[1] For Addams, the settlement aimed at creating citizens, not serving clients, and it provided a site for the mutual interpretation of the social classes. She insisted that the settlement should be a place for dialogue, debate, experimentation—a communal location for the life of the mind capaciously understood. Her view of the settlement and her own efforts to be of use in a civic sense were hard-won. Much of the importance of Jane Addams as a social and political thinker is the way in which she ties together public and private imperatives, demonstrating that human beings live complex social lives that cannot be sealed off into compartments that have little to do with one another. This posed special difficulties for women. Addams's earliest contributions to political thought dealt with this conflict.

The Family Claim and the Social Claim

Hull-House opened its doors on September 18, 1889, and it had been up and running for three years when Jane Addams delivered a paper that was destined to become one of her most famous essays: "The Subjective Necessity for Social Settlements." This paper and its twin, "The Objective Value of a Social Settlement," provide a strong sense of Addams's passionate commitment, her ability to analyze social conditions critically, and her recognition that in hard, constructive work lay not only her salvation but that of many other educated young women. She—and they—were not traditional charity workers: far from it. Instead, the gospel of Hull-House begins with "the theory that the dependence of classes on each other is reciprocal" (*JAR* 14).[2] This "subjective necessity" derives from motives that are based on reasoned conviction and passion. What young people seek and require is an "outlet for that sentiment of universal brotherhood which the best spirit of our times is forcing from an emotion into a motive" (*JAR* 14).

There are three lines of "subjective pressure" that point toward the social settlement idea: (1) the desire to make the social organism democratic; (2) the desire to share "the race life"—the reference point is the human race—and to bring as much social energy as possible to the task; and (3) the desire to enact a "certain *renaissance* of Christianity, a movement toward its early humanitarian aspects." Building a democratic culture is the heart of the matter. Americans now have democracy in a political sense, Addams argues, for the "gift of the ballot" has been given to "the negro." But black Americans and many others live in "social ostracism" even as women languish outside the franchise altogether. We offer the franchise to the immigrant man once he is naturalized, she tells her listeners, but then we "dub him with epithets deriding his past life or present occupation, and feel no duty to invite him to our houses" (*JAR* 15). Our democracy has not yet realized its full social possibilities.

Addams does not have socialism in mind when she speaks of socializing democracy here and elsewhere; rather, she references the breaking down of barriers between people in order to make it possible for human beings to realize their full sociality. "Our consciences are becoming tender in regard to the lack of democracy in social affairs," and this suggests that America is entering a "second phase of democracy" in which we find common places in which to meet and to offer hospitality to one another: clubhouses, libraries, galleries, public conveyances, playgrounds, and the settlement itself (*JAR* 16). These should be—or now are—available to all. Addams was convinced that human beings yearn for knowledge; that each one of us can be set afire mentally and ethically; and that learning must not be confined to schools but must go on in villages and extension movements, among dock-laborers in New York harbor and in little villages in New England and the Midwest. Education can deliver us—by which she means vouchsafe to us transformed bodies and minds.

Indeed, the settlement is itself "a protest against a restricted view of education" and part of the effort to "socialize democracy." This means that a settlement must "never lose its flexibility, its power of quick adaptation, its readiness to change its methods as the environment may demand." The settlement speaks to broad and generous yearnings for a fuller life and use of the faculties. The "great mother breasts of our common humanity" must not be withheld from any of our children. Starving the faculties kills as well.

The "zest for discussion" is in full throttle, she writes exuberantly. "Chicago is full of social theorists," and these social theorists hawk their wares regularly at Hull-House. Even though one may not find some of the wares appealing, to suppress and to bottle them up is unwise, for then "there is danger of explosion. . . . Nothing so disconcerts a social agitator as to find among his auditors men who have been through all that, and who are quite as radical as he in another direction." Thus far, however, Hull-House has not succeeded in getting the "capitalist and the working-man" to "meet as individuals beneath a friendly roof," but hope springs eternal (*JAR* 43–44). All of Hull-House's many activities point to a shared end: the building up of a culture of democracy in the social sense.

Addams's democratic faith was nurtured in the bosom of the Protestant Social Gospel. She finds the direct application of Christianity in the movement toward this higher virtue. Politics is necessarily an ethical enterprise, ethics being "but another word for 'righteousness,' that for which many men and women of every generation have hungered and thirsted, and without which life becomes meaningless" (*JAR* 14).[3] This is a complex task which requires preserving much that has gone before but at the same time experimenting and creating new social forms to deal with transformed conditions. Unfortunately, if the "instinct to conserve" is "combined with a distrust of the new standard," a "constant difficulty in the way of those experiments and advances" is created—especially where women are concerned. This is so because women are keenly attuned to what she calls "the family claim." Their training tends to make them content with responding to this claim alone. But by Addams's day, the "social claim"—to participate in civil society and the building up of a democratic culture—has become more exigent. The frustration is that when a woman responds to this wider social claim, she is often pitched into a destructive moral conflict (as was the case with Addams herself, who spent eight years "all at sea" about her purposes and was felled with a late-nineteenth-century malaise called "neurasthenia," which we would probably call depression today). Her perplexed parents likely saw only a "foolish enthusiasm" in her determination to "undertake work lying quite outside of traditional and family interests" (*JAR* 77). In a sense, Addams puts a query to her society: Why press forward with higher education for women if the social avenues in which that education might be realized are blocked?

Always a mediator and a moderate, Addams seeks the adjustment of the familial and the social in such a way that no legitimate claim is abandoned. There is a difference between the temporary violation of a legitimate claim in the service of some other vital claim, but the repudiation of a legitimate claim is destructive. What happens when there is a "collision of interests, each of which has a real moral basis and a right to its own place"? What should be done with "the struggle between two claims, the destruction of either of which would bring ruin to the ethical life" (*JAR* 78)?

According to Addams, society has at least begun to recognize the possibility of tragic conflict, but it seems not to have found a way to place these claims together and to give each its due. From the beginning of recorded history, the "claim of the state in time of war has long been recognized, so that in its name the family has given up sons and husbands and even the fathers of little children" (*JAR* 78). To a life-risking purpose based on a claim widely regarded as legitimate, society sends some of its children forth to die and, even worse, to kill. Why not send children forth to sustain life? If men can, and have, acted conscientiously in behalf of the social claim, why not women?

Grown-up sons are also citizens: they are familial and civic beings. But what of the grown-up daughters? America sends a few to college, and then it confines them to unhappiness because the family cannot let the daughter go. Addams goes on to muse about the nature of the moral claims involved and, as with all her work, a theory of moral development is imbedded in her argument. She avoided abstract, systematic tracts, insisting that the best way to develop an argument was through a strong narrative.

Perhaps the family claim triumphs because it is concrete and exigently represented and felt. But would the family claim be dissipated were it extended beyond the domestic hearth? Is the social claim really that abstract? Certainly it is often presented in that light by certain sorts of political theorists and philosophers. But Addams always brings things back to earth. When physicians are advising rest to young women and families are advising European tours (it is middle-class young women she has in mind), what she really needs is "simple, health-giving activity, which, involving the use of all her faculties," will help her to forge forth because she has found a way to think communally rather than just individualistically (*JAR* 82).

To this end, young women must be brought into contact with the harsh realities that are now hidden from them because they are considered too strenuous for woman's delicate constitution. As a result, she does not see "the feebleness of childhood, the pathos of suffering, or the needs of old age." But, like a young man, she dreams of "self-sacrifice, of succor to the helpless and of tenderness to the unfortunate" (*JAR* 83). Why must these dreams be distrusted unless they fall within the well-worn grooves of a traditional family claim? Why not have some confidence that human beings are too closely bound up with one another to rest content for very long with merely individualistic anthems and purposes?

For Addams, women lived lives that stressed responsibility, care, and obligation. These were, in a sense, thrust on them. She made it clear that this should not be taken as evidence of women's moral superiority but should be seen instead as evidence of a form of moral necessity that can—and that often has—served as a source of female power and authority. The imperatives of this realm must be extended more generally. That is the rock-bottom ground of her civic philosophy and her social feminism.

The King Lear of Chicago

Over and over again, Addams revisited the theme of collision between authentic claims—each of which is genuine and exerts a legitimate tug on our moral faculties as well as personal and political commitments. This occurred perhaps nowhere more famously than in her analysis of the Pullman Strike that roiled Chicago in the summer of 1894. She interpreted the strike through the lens of Shakespeare's *King Lear*. Lear's tragedy derives from his absorption in "his own indignation" and his subsequent failure to "apprehend his child's thought." In his anger, he loses "the faculty by which he might perceive himself in the wrong." So it was with the famous Mr. Pullman, for whom "domination and indulgence" went together as they did for poor King Lear (*JAR* 167).

According to Addams, the Pullman Strike confronted the citizens of Chicago with a drama that epitomized and, at the same time, challenged the code of social ethics under which Americans then lived. "It sometimes seems as if the barbaric instinct to kill, roused on both sides, the sharp division into class lines, with the resultant distrust and bitterness, can only be endured if we learn from it all a great ethical lesson" (*JAR* 163).[4] Addams assumes Mr. Pullman's philanthropic intent as one motive—certainly not the only one—in creating a town within which those he paternalistically called his workers and their families could live, shop, go to church, and educate their children. The town was part of the Hyde Park area, but George Pullman exercised direct—nigh absolute—control over his village. Everything in the town was "responsible to the Pullman corporation." According to one historian, Pullman "refused to brook any sort of political opposition" in his town. Labor organizers and those considered too radical were "barred from the town by the simple expedient of denying them the right to rent or use public halls."[5] Shakespeare's great drama brings Addams closer to a sympathetic understanding of Pullman and of his striking workers.

The events surrounding and flowing from the strike serve to remind us that the social claim and its modes of expression are as unsettled as the family claim appears settled. But this family claim has changed, demonstrating that societies can adjust to new exigencies. When we reflect on Lear, Addams claims, we find his relations to his children archaic. We know that our morality around family ties has moved beyond parental domination based on a dreadful power to give and to take away the means of livelihood. In Lear's case, this power extends to bestowing land or sending a child into exile. Lear illustrates the playing out of "mal-adjustment between individuals" in a "personal and passionate" way. Our modern tragedy is trickier because it involves "two large bodies of men, an employing company and a mass of employes [*sic*]" (*JAR* 165). But there are significant parallels.

Lear and Pullman both feel the sting of what they interpret as ingratitude. Lear is cut to the quick by Cordelia's inarticulateness and lack of effusiveness in stating, when Lear demands it, her affection for him, her father. Addams faults Cordelia's "lack of tenderness" and the cold way she ignores her old father's plea for indulgence. But he is the one who brings on the tragedy. He goes overboard in his anger and sinks into a pit of self-pity and recrimination that leads to madness and to a slow reawakening of his senses—but by then it is too late. Pullman, a man "dined and feted throughout Europe as the creator of a model town, as the friend and benefactor of workingmen," finds himself inexplicably "execrated by workingmen throughout the country." His refusal to give the representatives of his workers even ten minutes of his time shows the selfish motives hidden beneath the industrial relations, especially in a town organized the way Pullman had organized his. The latent dictatorial possibilities in Pullman's position rise to the surface just as they did for Lear, and everything falls apart. Pullman speaks the language of an individualist ethic. By contrast, the workers had learned to say "the injury of one is the concern of all," with "brotherhood, sacrifice, the subordination of individual and trade interests to the good of the working class" being their by-words (*JAR* 170).

There is little doubt which side Addams is on, but she takes that side with a heavy heart because the individual virtues that enabled Pullman to rise in life—especially hard work—are real virtues; but they are insufficient to this new day. Being good to people in a paternalistic way is not the same as trying to understand them, to listen to them, and to be fair to them. To be sure, the interests of labor and capital are not identical; but must they be openly hostile, the political equivalent of war with unconditional surrender of one side the only alternative? Here, as elsewhere, Addams warns against class hatred and the rhetoric of war and martial fervor as a method of social change.

A narrow definition of emancipation plagues the workingman as well, especially if what he seeks is what the employer has. In this case, the upshot of a successful social conflict would be a new boss just like the old boss. An astute moral psychologist, Addams is attuned to resentment as a degraded motive for social change, for this leads to turning the tables rather than transforming a situation so that no one has authoritarian power over the lives of others. Many workers are captured by a false doctrine of emancipation, but on the question of Pullman's despotic control over his town, it is the workers who are right. Over the long run, however, the claims made by, and in behalf of, workers and all who toil must be governed by the democratic ideals of consent and dedicated to "slow but sane and strenuous progress" (*JAR* 174). Otherwise, failure is certain.

In another essay mapping familial and social conflict, "Filial Relations," Addams associates her views with two of her revered civic heros: Abraham Lincoln and Guiseppi Mazzini (the Italian political theorist and leader of the *risorgimento*). She draws upon Mazzini's best-known text, *The Duties of Man*. Mazzini placed duty before rights. Rights, he argues, "cannot exist except as a consequence of duties fulfilled, and . . . one must begin with the latter in order to arrive at the former."[6] In her essay, Addams also places "duties to humanity," vague as that or these may be, as a primary duty. One rises to this duty on the back of other duties, including those of son, husband, father—Mazzini's examples, to which Addams would add daughter, wife, and mother. Being a citizen of one's own country also helps one to aspire to an even wider citizenship. The issues posed by the Pullman Strike pitted a narrow understanding of a paternalistic familial ethic (for Pullman thought of himself as a benevolent, if controlling, father) against a wider understanding of the nascent social morality imbedded within the new industrial relations. This new ethic will take years to crystallize. The civic settlement is one vital embodiment of the new claim and offers creative, nondestructive ways to mediate those legitimate claims that tug on us and either pull us apart or help us to achieve a wider, more balanced, and more capacious life.

The Development of Individual and Social Morality

Addams's understanding of such a capacious life rests on an embedded theory of moral development. That theory holds that we are all creatures born with blind, unformed appetites. These appetites yield to moral motives slowly, through a process of education that touches the heart. The heart—her nontechnical term for complex human sensibilities and beliefs—is touched through the senses at first, but gradually the appetites yield to psychic impulses. These, in turn, are mingled with reason as the child grows up and are transformed into moral motives. If children suffer from violence and neglect—if their spirits are crushed and their inventive eyes and hands and bodies are stymied—they might well be doomed to an impoverished existence even should external impediments disappear.

Such a child may well be impervious to what Jane Addams called the gentler aspects of life. To the extent possible, parents, teachers, and an entire culture should not magnify and deepen the fears of childhood through social neglect, abuse, and unreasonable expectation. If adults could but remember the terrifying fears of each and every child—of being lost, of abandonment, of death—and if cultures could find ways to allay the sadness and tragedy over which human beings do have a measure of culpable control, then we should have made gentler the aspects of our shared world and have blighted many fewer vulnerable, growing human minds and bodies.

To do this, Jane Addams begins by asking: What *is* the concrete situation? Addams and her Hull-House associates always assessed the empirical reality in which parents and children found themselves. They saw that parents under terrible economic and cultural stress often compelled their children to labor without surcease at horrible tasks under unhealthy and even dangerous conditions. The child is pressed to the breaking point; and if the pressure persists, that child may grow to an adult victimized by his or her habits of resentful obedience. There is such a thing as normal growth for a child. For an adult to compel an immature child to take on tasks beyond that child's strength is disastrous. Addams describes such situations in dire and dismal terms. By contrast, appeals to the child's senses, particularly the sense of adventure and the longing for beauty that all children share, help to mold those moral motives into solid habits that enable the child, as adult, to live out such motives in his or her own raising of children, participating in democratic citizenship, determined labor and work, and service to a church or a community. We can be saved for fellowship, but we are also saved *through* fellowship—from birth to death.

That Jane Addams drew general significance from norms derived from her upbringing in Cedarville, Illinois (population 750)—norms that she insisted were not particular to Cedarville—puts her on a collision course with many nineteenth-century giants of political and social theory. For example, her contemporary, Karl Marx, held that rural life was one of idiocy. Marx was convinced that rural life, or small-town life, could not serve as the staging ground for the full socialization of life through labor that would at one point implode, giving way eventually to the ultimate revolution and all the putative glories of classless society. In this process, all useless persons, societies, and cultures, as Marx excoriated them, would be swept away into the dustbin of history. Addams was never much interested in apocalyptic theories that did violence to lived life and belied the concreteness of particular places and ways of being. Grand theories wiped out stories and reduced the human race to faceless, anonymous nonbeings. She never trafficked in such categories as "proletariat" or "bourgeois"; she never talked about "mass society"; and she never wanted to lose any face in the crowd. She had learned her small-town lessons well.

In an April 10, 1899, interview with the *Chicago News*, Addams extolled the bicycle as a form of exercise. When asked if this was particularly beneficial to the poorer and middle classes, she said: "There [*sic*] is where I wish to make an exception. I object to that word class. It is un-American. There are no classes in this country. The people are all Americans with no dividing line drawn. But I think the bicycle is a good thing for the workingman. . . . It gives him recreation and exercise and while riding to and from his work he enjoys the open air." Whatever one thinks of Addams's hope that tired workingmen might find their health improved by bicycling, the most interesting moment is her truculent dismissal of the word "class." Of course, there were dividing lines in America. But it was one thing to acknowledge an empirical reality that separated people; it was another to use a collective category to classify hundreds of thousands of people and, in so doing, to obliterate their distinctiveness. Americans should think of one another as neighbors and fellow citizens who have had vastly different experiences. We are obliged to interpret ourselves one to the other and to do all we can to ease the situation for those who are hard pressed. Jane Addams practiced what she preached when it came to attunement to the uniqueness of each and every person, however insignificant he or she might seem to be.

If the Addams way resists Marxian grandiosity, it also resists mid-twentieth-century absurdity. For Jane Addams, human beings are not poised in terrible oppositions to one another. We do not live in that bleak universe limned by twentieth-century existentialists, like Jean-Paul Sartre, to whom every man is an enemy to every other ("Hell is other people") and in which every moment is a struggle for existence and for appropriation of that which is not one's own.[7] The routine and seemingly spontaneous cooperation Addams saw around her growing up—and later found in the poor helping one another in their "teeming quarters"—convinced her of that. If much of her own childhood had lent itself to imaginative play in a forest and unhurried time in which to enact dramas of "obscure significance," it also gave her a secure foundation of rough and ready social egalitarianism.

City Life and the Snare of Vice

Jane Addams emphasized what she called revelation. She used the word not so much in a theological sense as in an anthropological one: the importance of revealing that which is human in general and adding thereby to the storehouse of human knowledge. In the process of so doing, one treats what it means for each person to reveal herself through some medium or another. One of the most severe effects of poverty was the way in which it stymied or hid the unique and irreducible features of a living human being by affording no way those features could be revealed. Part of the pathos of immigration lay in the way that much about immigrant parents and grandparents was hidden from view—their Old World dress, music, poetry, craft—as they attempted to adjust to life in overcrowded, ugly tenements and dreadful work at low pay. As their children "Americanized," they often grew embarrassed at their parents' accents, habits, and appearance. Interpretation was needed once again.

Jane Addams worked very hard to interpret youth to frightened and angered elders. She understood the young person's search for excitement as a protest—one that often goes awry but is a protest nonetheless—against a life that is dull, gray, and deadening, the life the working young faced each and every day. Sympathetic knowledge is on full display in Addams's 1909 text, *The Spirit of Youth and the City Streets*, said to be her favorite among her books. It captures youth's ebullience and the need for that vivacity to be held within capacious, life-sustaining forms if it is to enhance life over time rather than to sputter out in a flurry like a moth's wings just before the moth dives into the vortex of the destroying flame. There may be great romance in the notion of youthful ardor snuffed out in a spasm of creativity, or orgiastic love, or political activity that will brook no compromise, or the terrible beauties of the most terrible of activities —war.[8] But this is romance that destroys rather than builds, and its undoubted allure is not for Jane Addams. More important, it is ardor of a sort ill-suited to the building of a democratic political culture that is *not* a warrior culture. From time to time, there may be a need for heroes; but, when a culture is forming citizens with a sense of responsibility and duty, heroes will rise up when they are needed—or so Addams believed.

What does turn-of-the-century Chicago offer to the spirit of immigrant youth? In *A New Conscience and an Ancient Evil* (1912), it was a dispiriting picture. The city was formless—out of control—and thus incapable of carrying the burden of civic formation and the creation of selves. There were no clear channels through which civic life and aesthetic life and adventure might flow. There were no safe places for children to play. There was no regulation of low-paid jobs: work "days" sometimes lasted sixteen hours. There were no limits to how old or young a worker might be, and even children as young as four were taxed beyond limit and destroyed in the process. There were no sanitation standards, and sweat shops were often carriers of smallpox and tuberculosis, diseases that spread from worker to worker, and carried in the garments and blankets and towels produced to the population at large. Even something as basic as water was filled with pollutants and bacteria that could be deadly, especially to the very young, the old, and the ill.

A kind of corrupt order, to be sure, pertained in city administration; but, because it was corrupt it was also capricious. Often those judges, policemen, and aldermen who tried to be honest got disgraced through set-up scams in order to get them out of the way so that profitable avenues of graft might remain open. Worse, argued Addams, there was the terrible confusion and anomie of peasants, thrust from the fields of Calabria to the garbage-packed streets and refuse-strewn alleyways of Chicago. Their young men drifted, courting disaster or crime. Their young girls were duped into believing that in America girls got married by just moving in with someone. In this way, they are drawn into the pit of vice and disease, often trailing home only to die in disgrace from syphilis or gonorrhea.

Given her emphasis on form, Jane Addams defied the age-old myth of the woman as one who is always threatening to disrupt order (e.g., Nemesis or Fortuna); who is given to outbursts and nonsensical cravings; who cannot handle the ordered complexities of law and citizenship (e.g., a Fury rather than an Athena); or who finds serious responsibility too much altogether. She reversed the equations: it is the men who run Chicago who are the antic princes presiding over a veritable riot of disorder in the name of order; it is those industrialists who desire to keep labor as cheap as possible and workers as disorganized as possible; they are the ones who tax human beings—especially women and children—to their very limits and force women into the kinds of jobs they say women are not really suited to, even as they separate women from the tasks they insist women are suited to—namely, nurturing those children. Organizing schools and play-grounds means fighting for social forms—for institutions—against the denizens of formlessness. For Addams, the city should be a thing of beauty for all its citizens—in the construction of its buildings, including its schools, in the provision of free public libraries, and in the generous dotting of the city with theaters (for theater was a major Hull-House undertaking). Addams joined like-minded persons in sparing the wandering shore of Lake Michigan from private speculative development in order to protect a natural wonder that was provided freely for all to enjoy—shoring it up (literally) and enhancing it for generations to come.

In *A New Conscience and an Ancient Evil*, Addams delivers up lay sermons intended for the civic church of her city and her country. Should people not look at the situation before them? If they refused to avert their eyes, they would see cheap gin palaces that overstimulate youth, poison a few of them with bad stuff, but mostly just empty their pockets, forcing desperate boys and girls alike into debt. To pay off that debt, the purveyors of cheap pleasure offer the boys good money as procurers or decoys to lure the girls into vice. To the girls they offer the temporary stopgap of a chance to meet a few men, to get paid for it, and to get out of debt quickly. The die is cast and some young lives may well be doomed.

The modern city also degrades that which should be exalted (*NCAE* 16–17). There is, first, the "wrecked foundations of domesticity" as families implode from the pressures that come from all directions. Generations are driven apart. Men feel helpless and useless and desert their families. Women and young children are driven into soul-killing and body-weakening labor. The surroundings in which they find themselves is rodent and bug infested, dark, dirty, an aesthetic and health catastrophe, a firetrap. Imaginations run wild in what Addams frankly calls degenerate directions given the horrible overcrowding, the absolute lack of privacy for intimacy, the overagitation of young minds who cannot really comprehend what they see and hear but are vaguely excited by it all.

The path to freedom open to all in America cannot be denied to the young. But it is "made safe only through their own self-control" (*NCAE* 53). Addams here is relying on the Protestant code of inner-directed conscience and the forming of such a strong sense of ethics that one need not be guarded or chased around to be certain one is in compliance. Addams sees no other way for America. The youth's quest for adventure should be neither crushed nor permitted to degenerate into vice. It should be recognized, as societies have long done, by sustaining complex rites of initiation into the adult community, often accompanied by communal affirmation and celebration. The spirit of adventure was once the purview of "the hunt, of warfare, and of discovery"—at least for young men (*SYCS* 53). Camaraderie, danger, adventure, beauty—how could a young person not be attracted to such? But the city provides little channels for the realization of adventure. Youth are educated and then driven to distraction because what is expected from them is often so dull: the world's dour restraint clashes with their high hopes and their ardent desire to make something of themselves.

Some of Jane Addams's critics assaulted the lay sermonizing of *A New Conscience and an Ancient Evil*, portraying it as hysterical and puritanical. But Addams makes it clear that she's no puritan in the derogatory sense. After all, it was the "soldiers of Cromwell" who "shut up the people's playhouses and destroyed their pleasure fields." Ever since that time, "the Anglo-Saxon city has turned over the provision for public recreation to the most unscrupulous members of the community" (*NCAE* 7). The result is that joy is confused with lust and gaiety with debauchery. This confusion invites the debauched to sell debauchery, and sell it they will and do: even in Jane Addams's day the traffic in vice was a multimillion dollar affair. Addams understood that absolute interdiction of vice was a utopian fantasy. Her worry was that too many young people, yearning for their house of dreams and with their young selves in the throes of often tumultuous development, got dragged down into an orb of vice from which they did not have the power and strength to emerge.

Addams associates her civic sermons with a Social Gospel message. After all, the good news of Scripture is a source of "inexpressible joy." Why do so many Americans forget this and permit the lambs to be "caught upon the brambles," entrapped in joylessness where joy instead should be? Addams makes a pitch for joy that affirms life and permits it to perdure—in contrast to those outbursts of pleasure that are intense momentarily but coarsen the spirit over time.

For Addams, the search for righteousness and the quest for beauty are linked. She was convinced that all human beings have deep within them an unformed desire to share in a common life and to protect and cherish weaker things. We would never have survived as a species were this not the case. These impulses can be driven out of us or go into hiding. But it is the task of adults to nurture these tendencies in the young. City youth must share in the "common inheritance of life's best goods," so moral authority should speak "with no uncertain sound if only to be heard above the din of machinery and the roar of industrialism." Then and only then can it exert "itself as never before to convince the youth of the reality of the spiritual life"—a reality that should be charming, beautiful and, in its own way, seductive (*SYCS* 155–57).

City Housekeeping as Experimentation

The term municipal or civic housekeeping associated with social or civic feminism is easy enough to mock. It seems to imply that politics can be replaced by housekeeping on a grand scale, and no doubt some social reformers had such in mind. Addams was not so naive. Indeed, she taxed the doctrinaire socialists of her day for the ideological naivete they exhibited about the glories of the socialist future, noting that one ardent socialist (during the course of the weekly

Hull-House drawing-room discussions held under the auspices of "The Working People's Social Science Club") had declared that "socialism will cure the toothache." A second interlocutor, not to be outdone, upped the ante, insisting "that when every child's teeth were systematically cared for from the beginning, toothaches would disappear from the face of the earth" (*TYHH* 179–80).

Even as she deplored fanaticism and the notion that nothing is more important than the right theory, she opposed politics as violence and resolutely refused to glamorize social unrest. Episodes like citywide strikes may be exciting, but they turn a town into "two cheering sides" as if one were a spectator at a sporting event. Fair-mindedness goes down the drain. Her quest for balance and for a politics that best fits the quotidian norm a social democracy should embody takes expression frequently as a determination to *mitigate*: she and Hull-House and settlements in general would mitigate a situation. We rarely use the term nowadays in this way, but she has in mind to make milder and more gentle; to render anger and hatred less fierce and violent; to relax the violence of one's action; to alleviate physical or mental pain; to lighten the burden of an evil of any kind; to reduce severity; to moderate to a bearable degree. The politics of a socialized democracy was about mitigation in precisely the same ways.

In *Twenty Years at Hull-House* (1910), Addams had written that a settlement is "an experimental effort to aid in the solution of the social and industrial problems which are engendered by the modern conditions of life in a great city" (*TYHH* 125). Municipal housekeeping is such an experiment. One cannot help but observe that most of the departments in a modern city "can be traced to woman's traditional activity."[9] This was a central motif of Addams's argument for the municipal ballot for women. Two points can be made. First, it makes no sense to disallow women to vote on matters that so directly concern them; second, in light of women's traditional activities, she possesses the insights and expert (if informal) knowledge needed by cities in order to deal with the manifold problems that have emerged in the overcrowded immigrant city—unsanitary housing, poisonous sewage, contaminated water, infant mortality at alarming rates, the spread of contagion, adulterated food, impure milk, smoke-laden air, ill-ventilated factories, dangerous occupations, juvenile crime, unwholesome crowding, prostitution, and drunkenness. When the city was a citadel, it may have made sense that "those who bore arms" were the only group "fully enfranchised." As Addams writes: "There was a certain logic in giving the franchise only to grown men when the existence and stability of the city depended upon their defense, and when the ultimate value of the elector could be reduced to his ability to perform military duty."

But cities no longer settle their claims by force of arms. Instead, the city depends upon "enlarged housekeeping." No "predatory instinct" serves us here, nor does "brute strength," not when one is dealing with "delicate matters of human growth and welfare." Is it not possible that tending to the city has failed "partly because women, the traditional housekeepers, have not been consulted as to its multiform activities"? Addams stresses that "ability to carry arms has nothing to do with the health department maintained by the city which provides that children are vaccinated, that contagious diseases are isolated and placarded, that the spread of tuberculosis is curbed, that the water is free from typhoid infection." A new era of civic humanitarianism may be upon us, or so Addams devoutly hopes. Women must participate.

In a 1915 pamphlet entitled "Why Women Should Vote," Addams charges contemporary women with failing to "discharge their duties to their households properly simply because they do not perceive that as society grows more complicated it is necessary that woman shall extend her sense of responsibility to many things outside of her own home if she would continue to preserve the home in its entirety."[10] Life in a crowded city quarter affords no sanctum sanctorum to the meticulous housekeeper. She may scrub day and night, dust round the clock, close the blinds and shutters (assuming she has windows and can occasionally see sunlight)—but the meat she puts on the table may nonetheless be tainted, the drinking water surging with bacteria, and the winter overcoats and cloaks sent from infected sweatshops. Addams educates women who represent many languages and traditions but share concern for the well-being of their children to understand in what that well-being now consists.

The Moral Balance Sheet

When one studies what Jane Addams liked to call "the moral balance sheet," one all too often sees that a small group's interest goes one direction while the public interest and the good of the commonweal goes another. Addams embraced an *ecological* perspective before the term was in widespread use: hers was a *social ecology*. She was insistent that environmental impact (as we call it nowadays) must include the effects upon real men, women, and children in a community or in all the communities that will either derive the putative benefits or suffer the drawbacks of some proposed change. She set her sights on ethical change because she recognized that human beings cannot separate politics from ethics.

Necessary to the realization of this vision is sloughing off the last vestiges of "militarism in city government," the theme of chapter two in *Newer Ideals of Peace* (1907). This means diminishing the use of "penalties, coercion, compulsion, remnants of military codes, to hold the community together" (*NIP* 34). Since the city is a form of housekeeping writ large (where one must tend to food, garbage, child-care, misbehavior, breakdown of social relationships, a budget, and so on), relying on force of arms makes no sense here. Instead, we must invite all into political fellowship. It is political fellowship she has in mind when she talks about social democracy. She does not want government to nationalize everything or to dominate and take over; she favors cooperative alliances between government on all levels. But what really animates her is the possibility of fellowship, on the one hand, and the repudiation of an attitude of contempt or patronage, on the other hand. Necessary to fellowship is activating social intercourse, creating channels for creative social cooperation, and ending onerous and demeaning tests for voting or for office.

As we move to end the demeaning and cruel exploitation of people, we must reject the "Anglo-Saxon temptation of governing all peoples by one standard." We are one people, but Americanization does not mean putting everyone on a procrustean bed and trimming until we are all one size. In the standardization approach, there lurks a survival of militarism: namely, the spirit of the conqueror toward an inferior people, an ethos that has "many manifestations, but none so harmful as when it becomes absorbed and imitated and is finally evinced by the children of the foreigners toward their own parents." There is every reason to hope that a cosmopolitan bond will be forged that will substitute for the frayed old bonds of militaristic atavisms. Her ideal of the modern city is one in which solidarity does not depend upon sanctions nor a "consciousness of homogeneity but upon a respect for variation, not upon inherited memory but upon trained imagination" (*FYHH* 367).

In *The Second Twenty Years at Hull-House* (1930), her treatment of "Immigrants under the Quota, 1919–1921" bemoans the exaggerated acceptance of standardization. What happened in this era violated all that was best in the American method, understood by her as one in which citizens reach their own ends "through voluntary action with fair play to all interests involved," which in turn tends toward "wider justice" (*FYHH* 289, 295, 305). The Quota Act of 1921 (the National Origins Quota System)—passed in the aftermath of wartime repression—told in "no uncertain terms" that some immigrants were considered undesirable, the immigrants in question being Latins and Slavs. The Quota Act separated families without warning because family members who had not yet emigrated, including husbands and wives, could not unite with those already here.

The Immigrants Protective League compiled one heartbreaking file after another filled with desperate letters asking how one could get to Chicago or bring one's husband or wife or child to Chicago. Letters detailed just how hard the person was working to become fluent in the English language. But the Quota Act took no pains over individual cases, leading Addams to bemoan "this callous land of ours." We are determined, it seems, to discriminate against Southern and Eastern Europeans because they are swarthy or Catholic or for some other illegitimate reason. Addams observes another sadness flowing from America's long-standing problem of racial separation and prejudice. She observes that when Mexican immigrants first arrived in America, they "mingled freely with the negroes from the south" and, given their own relatively darker skins, they soon became victims of the same prejudice meted out against the "dark-skinned man. So we witnessed the phenomenon of Italians picking up native-born white attitudes towards Negroes and applying them to Mexicans as well." Friction and hatred followed. In the summer of 1921, a "colored man had been lynched in an Italian neighborhood about half a mile from Hull-House." One friend of Addams observed ruefully: "Of course this would never have happened in Italy; they are becoming Americanized." A horrific commentary: that a lynching is a sign of Americanization.

This was especially tragic according to Addams because the newcomers to our shores might have helped America face its racial past and present "with courage and intelligence," especially Mediterranean immigrants. This was so because "they are less conscious than the Anglo-Saxon of color distinctions. . . . They listened with respect and enthusiasm to a scholarly address delivered by Professor [W. E. B.] DuBois at Hull-House on a Lincoln's birthday, with apparently no consciousness of that race difference which color seems to accentuate so absurdly." We—we proud Americans—have a lot to learn and even more to live up to.[11] We can learn from so many who have come here and disturbed the best of the old foundations as little as possible. This is an unshakeable Jane Addams's credo, and it runs spiritedly against that current that is so much of the American story of striving, overturning the old, shaking up the received, shunning the past, racing into the future for it is bound to be better—bound to be—than whatever was, or even is.

The First World War and Addams's Fall from Grace

Jane Addams's fall from public grace as a result of her pacifist stance during World War I and her defense of immigrants, including those under suspicion of disloyalty, seems startling. Perhaps, however, the real surprise is that it took the war to congeal discontent about her views into a rousing chorus of disapproval that continued unabated for most of the 1920s. For Jane Addams had long been at odds with her countrymen and women in the matter of war and peace and the relation between the two; it took America's entrance into the war in 1917 to make these differences manifest. From 1914 on, Jane Addams's political thought is dominated by the themes of internationalism and pacifism.

Unlike such great progressives as the philosopher John Dewey, Jane Addams never made her peace with war. She certainly did not trumpet the war's social possibilities as industry, educational curricula, and so much else got nationalized and centralized through the machinery of the national government in order to mount a unified war effort. That a nation-state at war more closely resembles what Randolph Bourne (who, along with Addams, was a progressive dissenter and hold-out against the war effort) called a cold-eyed snake, was painfully manifest to her. Jane Addams was not given to animal metaphors but she certainly encountered a pitiless yet agitated entity poised against her as her prewar argument for newer ideals of peace went through the crucible of testing in wartime.

For Jane Addams, the state—at least that state known as the American polity—should embody and represent (in Lincoln's words) the "better angels of our nature": it should express the "commonality" of a nation's "compassion." Prior to the outbreak of World War I, Addams, together with most of her contemporaries, rode the waves of a heady optimism that carried with it the articulation of a positive state that promotes a common good. This state has a nurturing as well as a coercive side. It takes seriously its role as civic educator. Addams believed that the more the state moved in the direction of the compassionate tending of its citizens, the more it would move away from war.

Her systematic reflections on what she called a "new and dynamic understanding of peace" call for the strengthening of international law. Surely, she argues in *Newer Ideals of Peace*, international codes will one day mandate relations between nations analogous to those that now pertain between citizens and their government in a democratic society. She was convinced that the nations of the world are displacing warfare (with the West making the move first as it is the most highly developed region). Even as humankind evolved out of tribal life, so our social morality will move steadily forward in a manner that enables us to generate "social affections" of a cosmopolitan nature. The only way to do this is to tie together domestic and international law. What stands in the way of such a venture, she asks rhetorically? Does not enlightened opinion everywhere recognize a new humanitarianism afoot? Do we not see it operating every day "in the immigrant quarters of a cosmopolitan city," where people speaking a bewildering mix of languages and dialects and coming from nations and regions that were enemies historically find themselves nose to nose and learn to work and to play together.

The immigrant city paves the way for a new internationalism: from city to cosmos. Jane Addams has seen this internationalism in operation. She gives the example of a South Italian Catholic being "forced by the very exigencies of the situation to make friends with an Austrian Jew representing another nationality and another religion, both of which cut into all his most cherished prejudices." But he finds it harder to sustain these prejudices in his new situation, and he thus "modifies his provincialism for if an old enemy working by his side has turned into a friend, almost anything may happen" (*TYHH* 307–8). In the cosmopolitan city people "are forced to found their community of interests upon the basic and essential likenesses of their common human nature; for after all, the things that make men alike are stronger and more primitive than the things that separate them."

She is daily amazed by the "manifestations of altruism" in the congested quarter of Chicago she inhabits. She sees how people respond to the "demands of social justice." To be sure, for many years to come the majority will believe "that war is noble and necessary both to engender and cherish patriotism." But even as they trumpet such notions they daily live in "the kingdom of human kindness." Sooner or later they will weigh these two claims against one another and one—the nobility of war claim—will fade: this is Jane Addams's confident prewar hope. The human race is at long last building a social cathedral out of diverse materials but to a shared end. Industry and commerce have pushed America into internationalism. New modes of communication mean no country is, or can remain, isolated. The "progressive goodness of the race" lies near at hand. Each nation "quite as a natural process will reach the moment when the virile good-will will be substituted for the spirit of warfare," she had argued in *Newer Ideals of Peace*.

This is Jane Addams at her most optimistic and, arguably, her least persuasive. The horror of the slaughter of the western front made all prewar optimism seem both naive and forlorn. The certain conviction of evolutionary stages—from militarism to a nonmilitant internationalism—was no longer persuasive. We also sense in Addams's argument an abandonment of her quest for balance, the need to maintain a careful tension between claims that compete but neither of which should be abandoned. This is what she searched for in her discussions of the family claim and the social claim. But when it comes to what she persistently represents as the "military party" or claim, she finds only a negative, something that the human race can and should abandon altogether. How does this square with her intuition that any perduring tradition bears within it a potent truth that must not be jettisoned? The answer is that it does not. Because she elides national defense and security to militarism and authoritarianism, she glosses over tough questions of whether there are ways to provide for the common defense that do not incite contempt and cruelty. Instead, she extols the blessings of a new dispensation: civic communion brought about through pacific means.

One marker of this new fellowship is generosity in welcoming immigrants to their new civic homes, wherever these may be. It includes the beguiling prospect of more women taking their place alongside men in civic life; it includes protecting and educating children in a consistent, fair, and compassionate way; it requires the creation of a new morality that does not worship at the altar of material success achieved by any means necessary; it eschews warlike method and rhetoric and rejects "blind adherence" to "my country right or wrong"; and it brings forbearance and toleration to a new level. We cannot do without patriotism, she insists, but we must cease founding that patriotism on war. Contrasting industrialism to militarism, she defines industrialism as a force that is liberating and reconciling newfound human energies in and through the socialization of industry—in contrast to the old militarism, which suppresses as a way of governing.

Addams's evolutionary optimism is tied to her conviction that human beings are more similar than they are different. It follows that what unites us is stronger than what divides us. She rejects what she calls static notions of human nature like those of the eighteenth century (including America's Founding Fathers), citing what she calls empty talk of "inborn rights." Instead, evolutionary thinking demonstrates that rights are by no means inalienable but, instead, are "hard-won in the tragic process of experience." Human equality is not given prima facie but instead emerges through a dynamic process: the engagement of human beings with a social surrounding that permits—indeed, even requires of them—that they recognize their commonalities.

By minimizing the ways in which the operation of power at all levels of government helps to create and to secure the context Addams celebrates—the multinational city in which everyone is a candidate for civic membership—she evades the distinction between a great city within a nation-state and the individual sovereign state in its relation to an international arena absent an overarching authority. If every state is analogized to Chicago and its internal context, then what political body plays the role of the United States government or its equivalent? Her answer was some form of international law or international organization that did not yet exist but must be promoted and eventually secured. This effort dominated the last twenty years of her life.

Jane Addams's commitment to democratic teaching prompts her to question her own judgement. In *Peace and Bread in Time of War* (1922), she asks: In a democratic society with institutions and structures available to register and to evaluate the popular will, can one stand apart in a time of national crisis?

> In the hours of self-doubt and self-distrust the question again and again arises, has the individual or a very small group, the right to stand out against millions of his fellow countrymen? Is there not a great value in mass judgment and in instinctive mass enthusiasm, and even if one were right a thousand times over in conviction, was he not absolutely wrong in abstaining from this communion with his fellows? (*JAR* 320)

She confesses that she desperately missed the comradeship felt by the millions of supporters of the war.

While a war is going on, pacifism is gutted. Her problem was that she could not find a way to embody pacifism in concrete practice during the war. It must have riled Addams that her advocacy was denounced for the very thing she had struggled throughout her life to avoid—namely, a well-meaning but ineffectual sentimentalism that fails to grapple with the complexities of the world.

The Long Road of Woman's Memory Revisited

In her writings both during and after the war, Addams struggled to find in women's memories and actual experiences, including the horrific realities of the war itself, at least the nascent beginning of a culture of peace. Perhaps pacifists had been overoptimistic in their belief that such a culture was already *there* in some sense and could be enhanced to break the hold of war. In *The Long Road of Woman's Memory* (1916), Addams gives a platform to the many women she spoke with "during the great European war who had sent their sons to the front in unquestioning obedience to the demands of the State, but who, owing to their own experiences, had found themselves in the midst of that ever-recurring struggle, often tragic and bitter between two conceptions of duty, one of which is antagonistic to the other" (*LRWM* 115). In *The Long Road*, she created two composite women designed to embody the women she encountered everywhere during her trips to Europe in the war years. Addams begins with a woman whose son was an accomplished professor. This women had learned to regard "the government as an agency for nurturing human life." Then her son was shot down; his body thrown overboard "into a lonely swamp." She received a last letter from him in which he observed that science itself had been enlisted for the war effort and that he, an industrial chemistry professor, had been consulted about asphyxiating gases. The woman comments bitterly: "I know how hard it must have been for him to put knowledge acquired in his long efforts to protect normal living, to the brutal use of killing men." Mind you, the mother continues, her son was a "red-blooded, devoted patriot" like other scientists; but they were developing an international mind, as men of science are wont to do, given the fact that scientific developments proceed through a collaboration that knows not national boundaries.

If such an international community of scientists exists, why not some sort of international government? If scientists can hone such contacts and develop them—into what some international relations thinkers now call epistemic communities—why cannot women get together? To fail to do so is to disregard an "imperative instinct." And here is a famous quote, attributed to one of these prototypical interlocutors, although it clearly has Jane Addams's stamp on it:

> Certainly the women in every country who are under a profound imperative to preserve human life, have a right to regard this maternal impulse as important now as was the compelling instinct evinced by primitive women long ago, when they made the first crude beginnings of society by refusing to share the vagrant life of man because they insisted upon a fixed abode in which they might cherish their children. Undoubtedly women were then told that the interests of the tribe, the diminishing food suppply, the honor of the chieftain, demanded that they leave their particular caves and go out in the wind and weather without regard to the survival of their children. But at the present moment the very names of the tribes and of the honors and glories which they sought are forgotten, while the basic fact that the mothers held the lives of their children above all else, insisted upon staying where the chldren had a chance to live, and cultivated the earth for their food, laid the foundations of an ordered society. (*LRWM* 126–27)

Feminism is then counterposed to militarism as two stark opposites ("an unalterable cleavage"). Militarists believe "government finally rests upon a basis of physical force"; but feminists must, if feminism is to mean anything at all, "necessarily assert the ultimate supremacy of moral agencies. Inevitably the two are in eternal opposition." This sets up the sort of stark duality Addams generally rejects, but she makes it clear in *The Long Road* that the opposition is not between men and women as such but between two contrasting attitudes.

Addams's second respondent contrasts with the sophisticated mother who could articulate so artfully her opposition to the war (and who sounds so much like Addams herself). This next woman is simple; her internationalism is humble and is founded not "upon theories, but upon the widespread immigration of the last fifty years, interlacing nation to nation with a thousand kindly deeds." It turns out the woman has a brother in California and she—an Italian peasant woman—had "visualized America as a land in which all nationalities understood each another with a resulting friendliness which was not possible in Europe." She has a hard time wrapping her mind around the fact that the shrapnel which killed her son came with a "Made in the USA" label. The old woman's eyes are troubled and anguished, but she remains faithful to an understanding of moral unity.

Addams says that she

> caught a glimpse of an inner struggle, as if two of the most fundamental instincts, the two responsible for our very development as human beings, were at strife with each other. The first is tribal loyalty, such unquestioning acceptance of the tribe's morals and standards that the individual automatically fights when the word comes; the second is woman's deepest instinct, that the child of her body must be made to live. (*LRWM* 136–37)[12]

As Addams had recognized from the beginning of her public life and had stated clearly so many times—most notably in analyzing the family claim and the social claim—both of these are legitimate, not illegitimate, claims. If you assume you can toss one out because the two may come into conflict, you radically oversimplify the moral life; you violate our deepest moral intuitions.

Unsurprisingly, she concludes the chapter by holding up the "eternal Antigone" who "makes no distinction between her suffering brothers who make war on each other." She surely recognized, however, that the key term in the Antigone reference is to brothers. It is the texture, density, and intimacy of that relationship that makes all the difference. It is much harder by far to generalize that personal tie of affection to "all young men who might be my brothers" or "all young men who might be my son." But that is what her vision of peace requires.

Jane Addams was not only a great public citizen, but she was a civic thinker of the first rank. Given contemporary concerns with the health of American civil society, it is surely appropriate to turn to a premier theorist of civil society, Jane Addams of Hull-House, and to renew one's acquaintance—or perhaps to encounter for the first time—a supple, capacious thinker and a gifted writer who throughout her life held out the promise of American democracy. The promise of American democracy sounds alien, at best, to our jaded ears. But for Addams, democracy was about making possible the doing of simple tasks in peace: the daily tasks of tending to bodies and bellies, of making a home and a family, of sustaining friendships, of trying to be a decent citizen of a good community. It was this affirmation of everyday life Addams reflected and refracted in her life's work and in her very being. She had sturdy sources to draw upon: the experiences of a small town, a fine public education, a strong moral center in her upbringing, and the great texts in Western politics, religion, law, and literature to populate her mind and to join her on her pilgrim's progress. If to this we add her capacity for friendship, we find the raw materials that went into the making of an extraordinary American life.

Notes

1. Addams became acquainted with the settlement house movement that began in mid-nineteenth-century England in 1887–1888 during one of her extended trips to Europe. Inspired by the writings of social theorists and reformers like John Ruskin and Thomas Hill Green, settlement beginnings were humble enough. In 1875, an Oxford tutor, Arnold Toynbee, moved to Whitechapel, a derelict part of London, in order to witness terrible social conditions firsthand. Ten years later, the first social settlement, named Toynbee Hall, was founded. At the height of the settlement house movement in the United States, there were hundreds of social settlements all over the country, concentrated primarily (but not exclusively) in urban areas. Residents of Hull-House were those who lived and worked there, some for short stays (six weeks to six months) and others for years or their entire life. Hundreds of nonresidents flowed in and out of the settlement. Hull-House was Addams's permanent address from 1889 until her death in 1935.

2. Quotations from and references to Addams's works are cited in the text using the following abbreviations:

> *FYHH*:   *Forty Years at Hull-House* (New York: MacMillan, 1935).
> *JAR*:   *The Jane Addams Reader*, ed. Jean Bethke Elshtain (New York: Basic Books, 2002).
> *LRWM*: *The Long Road of Woman's Memory* (New York: MacMillan, 1916).
> *NCAE*:   *A New Conscience and an Ancient Evil* (New York: MacMillan, 1912).
> *NIP*:   *Newer Ideals of Peace* (New York: MacMillan, 1907).
> *SYCS*:   *The Spirit of Youth and the City Streets* (New York: MacMillan, 1909).
> *TYHH*:   *Twenty Years at Hull-House* (New York: MacMillan, 1910).

3. As Addams sets forth her understanding of ethics, she also insists that to attain "individual morality" no longer suffices—one must come to grips with new realities and meet the demands of a "social morality."

4. Addams typically uses an event or series of events as a heuristic device in order to make more explicit the lessons she finds imbedded in the event or events. This in turn (or so she stalwartly and devoutly hoped) would contribute over time to the building of a "higher social morality" which for her meant a more democratic culture.

5. Almont Lindsay, *The Pullman Strike* (Chicago: University of Chicago Press Phoenix Books, 1942), 62, 64.

6. See Guiseppi Mazzini, *The Duties of Man* (London: J. M. Dent, 1894), 16, and Addams, "Filial Relations" (*JAR* 76–87).

7. The quotation is from Jean-Paul Sartre's play, *No Exit*, trans. Stuart Gilbert (New York: Knopf, 1947).

8. On the beauty and spectacle of war and its deep attraction, see my *Women and War* (Chicago: University of Chicago Press, 1992).

9. This quote and the ones that follow, unless otherwise noted, appear in a newspaper column, "Jane Addams Declares Ballot for Woman Made Necessary by Changed Conditions," *Chicago Record Herald*, April 1, 1906, 3.

10. Jane Addams, "Why Women Should Vote." The text is available at http://www.douglass.speech. nwu.edu. The National Woman Suffrage Association pamphlet original is in the Swarthmore College Peace Collection. A version of the piece also appeared in *Ladies Home Journal* 27 (January 1910): 21.

11. Addams is not without her own cultural short-sightedness, of course, especially in the matter of an anticlericalism that at least some Catholic prelates construed as tantamount to anti-Catholicism. Hull-House was openly celebratory of Italians like Garibaldi, and Addams thinks that anticlericalism, being a tradition, is rightly recognized. Addams got on well, by all accounts, with her Italian neighbors. She had allies among some in the Catholic hierarchy in Chicago; others found her suspect, worrying that Hull-House initiatives aimed to supplant Catholicism's network of schools and charitable organizations. Still, they existed side by side through the years. A full account of Addams's views of Catholicism and the relationship with the Chicago church would make a book unto itself—a book that, to my knowledge, has not been written.

12. This commitment to nurturance is part of what Addams considered "Woman's Special Training for Peacemaking," *Proceedings of the American Peace Congress*, II (1909): 253–54.

Chapter 30

Herbert Croly's Progressive "Liberalism"

Thomas S. Engeman

Herbert Croly's (1869–1930) *The Promise of American Life* (1909) is now considered the keystone or center piece for any new American public philosophy. Richard Rorty, for example, looks to *The Promise*'s patriotic nationalism as an antidote to the antidemocratic extremism of the post-1960s Left.[1] E. J. Dionne, another Progressive revivalist, calls Croly "the Progressive Era's master thinker," and finds him mainly responsible for the healthy moderation of Progressive liberalism. For Dionne, the Progressives sought only moderate reforms: "The Progressive's goal is not to strengthen government for government's sake, but to use government where possible to strengthen the institutions of civil society."[2] Agreeing with both Dionne and Rorty, Irving Kristol suggests that Croly "was a liberal reformer with essentially conservative goals."[3]

Unfortunately for the Progressive revivalists, if a politically moderate and patriotic Herbert Croly ever existed, he lived only within the now yellowing pages of his first and best-known book, *The Promise of American Life*. While these contemporary myth-makers are free to consider *The Promise* "authoritative" and ripe for appropriation, Croly did not. He argued his thought continued to progress in response to a rapidly changing "political landscape" and advancing climate of opinion. The catastrophe of the Great War, the new dawn of the Bolshevik Revolution, and America's self-satisfied return to "normalcy," all served to alienate Croly from any serious patriotic vision of "the promise of American life." Already in his next book, *Progressive Democracy* (1914), written before the catastrophe of World War I, Charles Beard and J. Allen Smith's radical historiography were cited approvingly by Croly (*PD* 47–50).[4] Because Croly's utopianism progressed toward ever more radical means and ends, the following study seeks to understand Herbert Croly as he understood himself (cf. George Soule, *NR* July 16, 1930). In particular, I take seriously his obvious desire to be the principal intellectual architect of a new Progressive Era in American politics. When Croly argued that the Soviet republic was a noteworthy experiment in Progressive democracy, he revealed that at the heart of the Progressive movement was the same antidemocratic pathology Richard Rorty condemns on the contemporary American Left. For this reason, Herbert Croly wanted ideals with political teeth. Since he believed he knew the political good, Croly sought praxis—the radical transformation of the existing political world. Mere theoretical ideals, or public philosophies, were important but less significant than the hard-boiled politics necessary to implement them. The democratic public philosophy of *The Promise of American Life* was quickly replaced with the more militant ideals of the International Workers of the World, the Peoples' Power League, and Leninist Russia.

While many use the term "Progressive" to refer to the Progressive party, the Progressive Era marked a distinct period in American thought and history. By and large, the Progressives were in favor of an administrative state, the creation of a new American society or new republic based on social science, and, most of all, on socialism or communism. Socialism and communism seemed the only alternative to the ravages of capitalism. Further, Progressives believed that the Constitution and natural rights had been designed to defend the economic elites of the Founding. Radical Progressives like Croly wanted to overthrow capitalism and the liberalism of the American Constitution through peaceful means if possible, and through violent means if necessary. While there were moderates who rejected the communism of the radicals and accepted more moderate forms of state socialism, they remained in the shadow cast by the radicals. Socialism's unpopularity with American voters, however, guaranteed that progressivism remained politically impotent.[5]

Croly, like the Progressives generally, fervently taught a "new science of politics for a new age." Where the scientific revolution in industry promised a new economic utopia, similar advances in the social sciences promised equally revolutionary progress in society and politics. Herbert Croly was one of the Progressive visionaries most confident of the possibility of a new utopian republic through the perfection of the social sciences. After writing *The Promise of American Life* and *Progressive Democracy*, and after advising the progressive presidents Theodore Roosevelt and Woodrow Wilson, Croly advanced the Progressive revolution as founder and editor-in-chief of *The New Republic* from 1914 until his stroke in 1928. By almost any standard, Croly's *The New Republic* became the leading American journal of liberal political opinion and remained faithful to its founder's vision throughout most of the century. Edward Stettner refers to *The New Republic* as "perhaps Croly's most important achievement. Under his editorship, it was a distinguished 'journal of opinion' that provided its readers with superb commentary on a wide range of political and cultural issues. I doubt that any American journal since has matched the intellectual level of *The New Republic* under Herbert Croly."[6]

A scientific revolution in politics is a familiar conceit to students of the American Founding. In *The Federalist*, Alexander Hamilton, James Madison, and John Jay (speaking as Publius), defended the new Constitution as an "experiment of an extended republic" made possible by the new political science. On these new scientific principles, the Founders "reared the fabrics of governments which have no model on the face of the globe." Publius argues:

> The science of politics, however, like most other sciences has received great improvement. The efficacy of various principles is now well understood, which were either not known at all, or imperfectly known to the ancients. . . . [These are] wholly new discoveries or have made their principal progress towards perfection in modern times.[7]

Later, Publius even more enthusiastically embraced the new science of politics:

> But why is the experiment of an extended republic to be rejected merely because it may comprise what is new? . . . Happily for America, happily we trust for the whole human race, they pursued a new and more noble course. They accomplished a revolution which has no parallel in the annals of human society: They reared the fabrics of governments which have no model on the face of globe. They formed the design of a great confederacy, which it is incumbent on their successors to improve and perpetuate.[8]

By seeking to overturn the existing constitution, the Articles of Confederation, Publius certainly appeared to its defenders, the Anti-Federalists, to be a dangerous innovator and projector in American politics. For Publius, as for Herbert Croly, a new experimental politics issued from a new science of politics.

But instead of Publius' heroes, David Hume and Baron de Montesquieu, Croly was enthralled by the new positivist, behavioral sciences of the American Political, Psychological, and Sociological Associations. The essence of the new social science was the development of new research methodologies to "understand, predict, and control human behavior." As editor of *The New Republic,* Croly saw himself as the leading Progressive intellectual drawing the lessons of the behavioral sciences for reform (Soule, *NR* July 16, 1930).

With the other Progressives, Croly argued that the behavioral sciences made the theory and practice of the Founders obsolete. The Founders' claim to have discovered an eternal knowledge of nature and human nature acquired without the new methodology of the social sciences was naive and absurd. Their arguments in favor of individualism, liberty, and rationality were the opposite of the Progressive view of social learning. Moreover, the Founders' understanding of human nature fostered human selfishness and weak liberty-loving political institutions. The later permitted the rich and powerful to defend their interests—through their right to private property—against the poor. Thus, the new behavioral view of human nature required a new political science. Croly believed modern psychology would discover the truths of human nature with the same exactness with which modern medical science was curing diseases. With the exact knowledge of social scientists, politicians could create public policies based on verifiable scientific truth in all areas of society. Perfect planned communities were possible. Progressive societies could safely subordinate individual liberty in order to attain scientific social policies truly beneficial to human welfare. If utopian public policies were possible, all restraints on public power were harmful to progress. Therefore, natural rights, separation of powers, and congressional representation of political and regional interests were all features of the Founders' Constitution destined for abolition. Croly spoke positively of popular dictatorships like Lenin's which, he believed, were carrying progress to the people forcefully and effectively. Free political institutions were nothing; Progressive social policies (medicine, education, housing) were everything. In Croly's view, these policies were so intrinsically perfect that they would be popular by necessity. Therefore, every revolution fought for the Progressive scientific goals was by necessity democratic.

Croly sought to replace the Founders' extended commercial republic with an administrative state based on the new social sciences. Originally, Croly believed the Founders' political thought and constitutional practice could be transformed through the Progressive practice of political officeholders: "Hamiltonian means for Jeffersonian ends." *The Promise of American Life* looks for progressive presidents to substitute the administration of social scientists for that of constitutional officeholders. Freeing administrators from legal restraint and oversight enables them to create a new society, transforming American life without necessitating a formal change in the political or constitutional regime. Almost immediately after writing *The Promise,* Croly came to see that the contradiction between the old and the new political science was too great to be remedied by presidential practice alone. Croly turned from patriotic reform to the overthrow of the existing political system in the name of a new peoples' democracy. He argued that under the current constitutional system the popular will was continually subverted by an antidemocratic Constitution, highjacked by the influence of money and a reactionary society. The recalcitrance of the propertied classes fueled the increasing radicalism of Croly's major books and of *The New Republic.* Let us look more closely at what George Soule called Croly's "hard-boiled radicalism."

A New Nationalism for a New Society

The Promise of American Life argues that the economic crisis resulting from the new industrialization can be remedied by a renewed constitutionalism. Indeed, *The Promise* suggests Theodore Roosevelt's presidency had begun to realize a new democracy by uniting the strong presidency of Alexander Hamilton with the egalitarian social and political ends sought by Thomas Jefferson. A nearly century-old tradition of increasingly strong presidential leadership was consummated in Theodore Roosevelt's administration:

> [Roosevelt] was the first political leader of the American people to identify the national principle [Hamilton] with an ideal of reform [Jefferson]. He was the first to realize that an American statesman could no longer represent the national interest without becoming a reformer. . . . Theodore Roosevelt is Hamiltonian with a difference. Hamilton's fatal error consisted in his attempt to make the Federal organization not merely the effective engine of the national interest, but also a bulwark against the rising tide of democracy. . . . The whole tendency of [Roosevelt's] programme is to give a democratic meaning and purpose to the Hamiltonian tradition and method. He proposes to use the power and resources of the Federal government for the purpose of making his country-men a more complete democracy in organization and practice. (*PAL* 168–69)

Strong executives like Theodore Roosevelt combine presidential leadership with egalitarian, progressive goals. *The Promise* thus argues for a new patriotism based on a new nationalism. To create the progressive republic America has only to return to its best political traditions to realize the new promise of social science righteousness. Progressivism, then, is the legitimate heir of a great American political and constitutional tradition.

When he wrote *Progressive Democracy* a few years later, Croly recognized the "new republic" demanded a more radical repudiation of the Founders' "philosophical" political science and Constitution than was offered in *The Promise*. As a result, *Progressive Democracy* begins with a wholesale rejection of the Founders' oligarchic politics and "pedantic rationalism":

> In framing the traditional political system the Fathers believed they could guarantee the righteous expression of the popular will by a permanent definition of the fundamental principles of right, by incorporating these specific principles in the fundamental law and by imposing obedience to these principles on the organs of government whereby the popular will is expressed. Considering the prevailing conceptions of the nature of political sovereignty and the function and powers of the human reason, they could have hardly adopted any other method. But another method did exist. It is bound to be tried by the political enterprise of an age which possesses a different conception of the nature of political sovereignty, which has abandoned the innocent yet pedantic rationalism of the eighteenth century. (*PD* 210)

To overcome the Founders' legalistic constitutionalism necessitates a "new national [political] ideal" dedicated to "social righteousness." Conversion to this new ideal proves an arduous task.

To demonstrate its difficulty, Croly invokes the greatest metaphor of American political history, the errand of the Pilgrims into the wilderness: "The journey which humanity is undertaking towards a completer fulfillment of individual and social life may be helpfully compared to the journey of a company of pilgrims in the dark over a rough and dangerous country towards a goal which is as remote as its desirable" (*PD* 184). Unfortunately, our new American pilgrims have sinned through selfishness and "class division." "Because they persist in quarreling about the route," they "may never reach the holy city." The "Bill of Rights" is the false deity of the old liberal faith promoting selfishness and dissension. "Instead of conceiving it [the Bill of Rights] as a torch, they conceived it to be a radiant sun . . . protecting the abundance of those who had grown fat in the valley" (*PD* 218). Like a ferocious Moses, Croly condemns individual rights as the American "golden calf," a false faith and stumbling block to progress and social righteousness. Only Croly's new faith in social righteousness can unite the warring pilgrims in their holy pilgrimage: "This new common faith sanctifies those who share it. All the brethren become objects of mutual solicitude. A fellow-feeling is born, which helps and prompts the pilgrims to reach a better mutual understanding. Thus faith in the unique value of the pilgrimage becomes a profoundly socializing influence" (*PD* 191). Social science creates the social solidarity which permits the new pilgrims to pursue the endlessly rewarding journey of social salvation. In sum, the ideal of Progressive democracy proves not to be an end, like the constitutional, legal system of the Founders, but a continual process or pilgrimage finally embodied in a progressive social/ political system advancing steadily with the advance of social science.

Croly's ultimate goal is the creation of a potent national administrative government. For Croly, administration must replace the politics of the Constitution because only advanced administrative governments can create new societies capable of infinite progress and perfection. Every existing political institution and practice demands radical reform to realize the utopia of social righteousness. In particular, scientific administrators must replace partisan politicians:

It is a mischievous idea that the expert is merely a specialist. The ability to deal with men, to meet practical emergencies, to adapt a rule to a situation, to cooperate with non-office holders rather than merely to order them about, to envisage a program or a law in its actual operation among men and women—abilities of this kind are more necessary to an administrator than to any one else. (*PD* 375)

Every aspect of American politics, including the common law and separation of powers, will be reformed in a Progressive administrative state. Even the seemingly bedrock democratic principle of the consent of the governed in open popular elections is rejected. In the new administrative republic, "the administrator must manage to be representative without being elective. . . . An administration which is to be representative without being elective must be kept articulate with the democracy, not by voting expedients, but by its own essential nature" (*PD* 372–73). The creation of new social programs will inevitably create broad public support, thereby eliminating the need for contentious debate and "politicized" electoral contests.

The new republic, established by the new administrative state, will finally realize in practice the long pilgrimage to social science righteousness. For Croly, psychology is the key social science—only psychology is capable of emancipating the "mass of the people" from superstition and repression. If traditional humanistic or religious education liberated the few while enslaving the many, Croly's social scientific education socializes and liberates everyone:

Modern psychology affords no sufficient excuse for a morality of repression (as is practiced by Catholic Christianity). It conceives both individual and social life as fundamentally active, and it is able to translate both emotion and thought into the results or forms of activity. . . . More and more are social psychologists seeking to discover social outlets for the expression of human instincts. (*PD* 421)

Sexuality is key to the new education. Croly seeks to have "sexual attraction made the excuse for candid, mutual curiosity rather than reciprocal illusion" (*PD* 429). But to abandon traditional religious morality, and the classical education in human nature, "calls for faith" and confidence in the progressive future. "Faith is the primary virtue demanded by the social education of a democracy."

Ultimately, the new education will realize Christian ideals. "Thus the progressive democratic faith, like the faith of St. Paul, finds its consummation in a love which is partly expressed in sympathetic feeling, but which is at bottom a spiritual expression of the mystical unity of human nature." Where traditional means of providing Christian charity have failed, the progressive faith will succeed: "Philanthropy is manifestly only a means of temporary alleviation, which brings with it the serious danger of fastening on individuals responsibilities which should be recognized as collective. The amount of permanent good which can be accomplished merely by giving is pathetically small" (*PD* 427).

In place of the religious philanthropist, local administrative officials—the ministers of Croly's faith—will prove highly effective:

> The administrator is more a counselor and instructor than a [moral] probation officer. He is the agent not of a merely disciplinary policy, but one of social enlightenment and upbuilding. He must seek, above all, to use the authority of the state and its material and scientific resources for the encouragement of voluntary socializing tendencies and purposes. (*PD* 354)

In the same vein, he suggests:

> The kind of administrator that I am describing must obtain the standing of an expert, he must also be something more than an expert. He is the custodian not merely of a particular law, but of a social purpose of which the law is only fragmentary expression. As the custodian of a certain part of the social program, he must share the faith upon which the program depends for its impulse; and he must accept the scientific method upon which the faith depends for its realization. Thus with all his independence he is a promoter and propagandist. . . . He qualifies for his work as an administrator quite as much by his general good faith as by his social competence. (*PD* 361–62)

In particular, the new administrator transforms the isolated and impoverished peasantry into the middle class of a modern egalitarian society.

The full realization of Croly's new social justice requires a massive paternalism which must gain popular support:

> The amount of assistance which a people can wholesomely receive from the government depends upon the amount of public interest and public spirit which the governmental mechanism and policy demands of them. A government does not become unbearably paternal merely as a consequence of the scope of its social program. The policy or the impolicy of its fatherly interest in the welfare of its citizens depends less upon the extent of its active solicitude for them than upon the extent to which this active solicitude is the result of a free and real choice of the popular will. (*PD* 214–15)

In spite of his protestations about the sanctity of popular consent, Croly was more interested in output or results than the technicality of formal elections. Convinced that the palpable rewards of social science and the administrative state would *always* rally the people, he encouraged radical experiments designed to create new republics.

As we have seen, Croly sought to ennoble his speculative vision of social science righteousness by comparing it to the pilgrimage of believers. This comparison, of course, argues the opposite of his intention. While the simile illustrates the aspiration for justice and perfection shared by Christians and modern, secular reformers, it reveals why Progressive idealism lacks any depth or height. Unlike biblical faith—grounded in the greatest philosophy and theology, and expressed in a high culture—the new social righteousness has only its scientific theories, and the peculiar solace of modern art, to define and ennoble it. Implausibly, Croly argued there was nothing lost to humanity in the substitution of this vague, ideological vision of social science righteousness for the millennia of Christian and classical life, thought, and art.

From Patriotic Nationalism to Hard-Boiled Radicalism

If America's cup was overflowing with promise in 1909, by 1914 it lacked righteousness. In this brief period, Croly reversed his ground. *Progressive Democracy* abandoned *The Promise*'s patriotic Founding for a broadside against it. The second book announced a new "inquisition . . . to challenge the old system, root and branch." His new inquisition is fueled by the radical historiography of Charles Beard and J. Allen Smith:

> The recent investigations of Professor Charles Beard indicate that the Constitution was framed chiefly by owners of personal property and their representatives, who lived in and around the larger cities of the Atlantic seaboard. . . . The American democracy rallied to an undemocratic Constitution, and have until recently remained loyal to it, because of the nature of their own economic interests. (*PD* 48, 51)

Until this new enlightenment, America's democrats blindly accepted the Founders' oligarchy from ignorance of the new political science. "The deification of an undemocratic Constitution was the work of a democracy which wholly failed to understand the proper relation between political power and popular economic and social policy" (*PD* 51). Since it is virtually impossible to amend or otherwise legally reform the Constitution, Croly argues that Progressives must enlighten public opinion against it. Progressive leaders and radical reform movements can educate the people in the new righteousness.

In the pilgrimage to the new republic, the states offer the best laboratories for policy experimentation. Unlike the federal Constitution, the state constitutions are generally easy to reform, "[offering] to the American people a unique and priceless opportunity for collective experimentation, which seeks to accomplish social purposes by means of democratic political agencies" (*PD* 245–46). Despite significant constitutional reforms in Oregon, California, Wisconsin, Colorado, and Kansas, Croly expressed discontent with the states' too great pragmatism (*PD* 284–98). The reforms of the "Peoples' Power League" offered a promising radical model for change, particularly in their reduction of legislative independence. Under their proposal the legislature was no longer "to represent districts or organized parties or the public reason or the leadership of any one class." It will now represent the "salient and significant phases of public opinion," leaving traditional interests without effective power (*PD* 301). The regional and economic "interests" lose their central place because traditional legislatures have been redoubts of privilege. In any case, under the League's newly proposed state constitutions, a powerful executive molds public opinion and easily directs the weak, reformed legislatures. Informed by Progressive social science and guided by a strong executive, democracy will finally be perfected.

While social science can "modernize" American life, radical political parties and social organizations like the International Workers of the World (IWW) and the Peoples' Power League must force reform by galvanizing public opinion. They dramatize oppression, promoting crises in the public mind about the justice (and future) of existing society. In Croly's view, industrial oppression and violence demands a "social war" to end the one-sided conflict. The outcome of this "social warfare" should be "a much more general and intense feeling of class consciousness," resulting in universal unionization. Croly's unionization is best exemplified by the syndicalism of the violent IWW:

[This] newer unionism instead of seeking gradually to force employers to grant better terms to wage-earners, roundly declares that business belongs by right to the people whose work contributes to its success; and they propose to capture and take away the industries of the country from their present owners by essentially violent and revolutionary means. Whenever this newer unionism shows its head, it is ruthlessly and often violently suppressed. A man who repudiates with abhorrence the proposed revolutionary methods of syndicalism may still believe that it is infusing into unionism a necessary ferment and into modern economic civilization a *necessary ideal.* (*PD* 388, emphasis added)

As we will discuss below, Croly endorsed the "ideals" of the Peoples' Power League, the IWW, and the Soviet republic, while still professing attachment to democratic government. In his support for anticonstitutional and antidemocratic movements and regimes, the radical Croly proved more committed to the revolutionary policies necessary for social righteousness than to the institutions and procedures guaranteeing popular self-government.

Political and economic radicalism was required to counter the violence inherent in industrial societies. The authoritarianism and violence of modern economies results from the discipline necessitated by scientific methods of production and management: "scientific management is an exacting master. The workers are required to submit to an amount and degree of regimentation not dissimilar to that required by an army" (*PD* 402). This demand for disciplined labor cannot be realized through wages and terminations. Only in a workplace democracy can workers be justly bound to their loss of liberty:

Such severe discipline [as is required by industrial society] cannot be imposed upon free men by a merely external authority or for any exclusively self-regulating purpose. . . . They must be free to accept or reject it. Scientific management must bring with it as a condition of its acceptance the self-governing work-shop. (*PD* 402)

Workplace democracy only legitimates the authoritarian character of modern industry:

The morale of the scientifically managed industries, which are self-governing communities, will be superior to that of the business autocracies, just as the morale of an army of patriots, who are fighting on behalf of a genuinely national cause, is superior to that of an army of merely mercenary or drafted soldiers. The severer the discipline which men are required to undergo, the more they need the inspiration of disinterested personal motive and complete acquiescence in the purpose for the benefit of which the discipline has been contrived. . . . Just because science is coming to exercise so much authority and be capable of such considerable achievements, a completer measure of industrial and political democracy becomes not merely natural, but necessary. . . . All along the line science is going to demand of faithful and enlightened men an amount of self-subordination which would be intolerable and tyrannical in any but a self-governing community. (*PD* 403–5)

The discipline demanded by scientific industry dictates a new science of administration. Discussing the "new administration," Croly employs only military metaphors:

Thus the administration . . . must provide a general staff for a modern progressive democratic state. It is created for action. It is the instrument of a clear, conscious, resolute and inclusive purpose. . . . The planning department of a progressive democratic state will have much more to do than the general staff of an army. It will always be fighting chiefly to convert its enemies, but it will be planning not for the sake of fighting, but for the sake of learning and building. (*PD* 370–71)

The success of modern democracy rests on the planning of the administrative general staff.[9]

One can instructively compare Croly's social science radicalism with the more democratic positivism of John Dewey. Croly was more authoritarian than Dewey because he was convinced that neither individuals nor societies were capable of becoming truly rational. Men live by faith in symbols or ideals to which they are always irrationally attached. Confidence in scientific enlightenment and democratic procedure is insufficient without a living faith in its perfection or end. The Pilgrims undertook their errand and experiment in the American wilderness in response to the militant demands of sainthood and eternal life, not pragmatic self-government. Revolution is the contemporary equivalent to the earlier Puritan rebellion.

The "Progressivism" of the Soviet Republic

The post-Christian, positivistic Croly searched for sufficiently powerful new ideals and movements to propel the modern pilgrimage to social science righteousness. As we have seen, his first great ideal or vision was the renewal of American patriotism in the new nationalism of *The Promise of American Life*. His subsequent rejection of this "conservative" ideal resulted from his conviction that the national government was not as amenable to progressive change as he once thought. Capitalism and social conservatism were such powerful enemies of progress that they would trump any credible political reform. As a result, *Progressive Democracy* argues for the new radicalism seen in the Peoples' Power League, the IWW, and the various progressive parties. Even these radical movements, however, proved in the end insufficiently powerful to break capitalism's satanic spell. America would always be a fallen angel, and so Croly came to believe that Karl Marx, and not Auguste Comte or the American Political, Psychological, or Social Science Associations, was the true Columbus of social righteousness. This new "conviction" seemingly guaranteed that Croly's last radical vision would be the "hyper" progressive Soviet republic. In Croly's third incarnation as the apostle of Progressive reform, his *The New Republic* became one of the Soviets most pious and stalwart defenders.

Croly embraced the Russian Revolution from the first. In early 1917, he extolled the first "February revolution" led by Aleksandr Kerensky and welcomed the prospect of future revolutions to come:

> The Russian revolution is magnificent, but it is portentous. Sooner or later analogous causes will provoke analogous effects, not only in the pseudo-despotisms where they are expected but in the pseudo-democracies where they are not expected. Such a colossal error as the present war demands an equally colossal expiation. During the next twenty-five years the heart of western civilization will be searched, its shams exposed, and its final integrity tested. If there has been a real need, as so many patriots have proclaimed, of the purification by war, there will be no less a need of purification by revolution. (*NR* March 24, 1917)

By 1919, *The New Republic* had become a staunch witness for the Soviet republic and bulwark against the anticommunist critics of the revolution's second, grotesque issue:

> The Soviet Republic . . . is an experimental state which has used confiscation in order to do away with capitalism, which has proposed to live by substituting labor for property as the source of individual independence and social cohesion. The rulers of [the imperialist powers] France, Great Britain, Italy and probably of this country are not reconciled to the licensing of such a drastic experiment. (*NR* January 25, 1919)[10]

Croly savagely condemned the military intervention of the Western powers resulting from their "selfish" desire to suppress the Soviets' heretically "drastic experiment" in social righteousness. Such intervention, he argued, merely provoked Soviet militancy, preventing the "inevitable development" of the Soviet republic into a peaceful regime promoting social welfare. Peaceful economic competition, not the violent overthrow of the capitalist powers, would be the Soviets' true test, the one Croly believed they wished to pursue. "Their test is coping with the practical problems of producing and exchanging goods in competition and association with the business organizations of other nations" (*NR* February 15, 1919).

The peace-loving Soviets were attacked by the imperialist powers because of their opposition to private property. Since they are not economically self-sufficient and are attacked on all sides by the major powers, Lenin and his associates have been *forced* to work "for the Bolshevizing of Germany. They believed that if a proletarian dictatorship were established in Germany the combined states could be made economially self-sufficient." Thus *The New Republic* justified the Soviet's budding imperialism.[11] Nevertheless, ever optimistic, Croly piously predicted that "Lenin is enough of a statesman fully to realize the inexorable nature of this condition of survival," and so will pursue economic reform and not further revolution or violence (*NR* February 15, 1919).

Believing in Lenin's idealism and practicality, Croly accepted his claim that if the capitalist states stopped their aggression, peace would be answered with peace. As the keepers of social righteousness, the Soviet leadership are scientifically pledged to abandon revolutionary class warfare to secure the blessings of peaceful progress:

> Those who have prophesied rightly as to the tragic mistake of intervention have all along prophesied also that the restoration of peace would bring either the fall of the Bolsheviks with the advent of more moderate parties, or the gradual penetration of the whole Soviet system with men and ideas who would modify the extremist tendencies of the present regime. . . . We believe [this prophecy] will be fulfilled because we believe that the Bolsheviks have secured the loyalty of non-Bolshevist Russians who are defending the first revolution and the fatherland against counter-revolutionists and invaders. We believe that peace will relax the discipline of Red Russia as it had the discipline of every other belligerent, that party interests will reassert themselves, that the opposition will compel the granting of civil liberty, and the process of compromise will set in with the revival of industry. (*NR* December 3, 1919)

Because the Soviet republic embodied the true principles of progressive democracy, *The New Republic* endlessly justified its actions. Lenin was the peaceful and progressive Russian statesman; his opponents were dictators, terrorists, and enemies of democracy:

> According to information recently published in the British press the Soviet government has since the signing of the armistice steadily increased in strength. Better order now prevails in revolutionary Russia than at any time since the fall of the Romanoffs. Food distribution is more throughly organized than at any time during the whole war. Factories, managed not by committees of employees or employers but by the Soviet government in consultation with such committees, are starting to work wherever raw materials are obtainable. The terror, which was always grossly exaggerated in American press reports, has ceased. . . . According to the usually accurate New-Statesman, if the election for a constituent assembly were held at the present time, more Bolshevist candidates would be seated than those of any other party. . . . Such is the result up to date of French, English, and American policy in Russia. By its persistent misunderstanding of the Soviets and its enmity to them, it has slowly but steadily enabled the extreme advocates of a class dictatorship to capture the Russian revolutionary government and to win the support of a considerable minority or an actual majority of the Russian people. (*NR* January 25, 1919)

In this rhetorical exercise, the Soviet government is portrayed as the best of the revolutionary governments which replaced the Romanoffs, while the latter are demonized as "the most corrupt government, the most detestable despotism which has survived among the nations of the modern world" (*NR* March 24, 1917).

While Croly often dismissed Western claims of Soviet violence as exaggerated, and occasionally condemned the Marxist theory of *violent* class warfare, shortly before his death *The New Republic* defended the regime's most violent practice. Because the rapid collectivization of agriculture was necessary to fulfill the new Five-Year Plan, it argued that the liquidation of the obstructionist kulaks should be understood as a pragmatic use of administrative discipline:

> The success of large-scale collective farming depends in the last analysis on the cooperation of the peasant masses, on their conscious interest in the fate of Communism in Russia. The kulaks, in the opinion of the government, contribute an obstacle to the establishment of the famous "link" between peasants and workmen. They hamper "collectivization" at a moment when the country is straining every nerve to carry out the Five Year Plan. Opposition, or even indifference, is now nothing short of treason. The kulaks as a class must be "liquidated." In Communist terminology "liquidation" can mean only one of two things: exile or death.

But the capitalist kulaks have proven tenacious:

> In essence, the kulak is a "capitalist in embryo." He is afflicted with capitalist psychology. His interest in private gain for private ends outweighs his loyalty to society. Not only does he constitute an obstacle to the development of the economic policies of the Soviet government: he is a political danger as well. Deprived of the franchise since 1928, the kulak still exerts such influence on elections to the village soviets as to threaten the dictatorship of the proletariat at its source.... As a group, the kulaks are more numerous and more difficult to exterminate than the bourgeoisie. Unlike the bourgeoisie, they are not concentrated in definite and easily accessible localities, nor are their "class" characteristics as clearly marked. Scattered throughout the length and breadth of the land, enjoying in many regions a degree of influence over the poor and middle peasants, they can be eliminated only in the course of long and arduous guerilla warfare, and *not without grave economic loss to the state*. ... To paraphrase Lenin, it may be said without exaggeration that within the boundaries of Russia, Communism is now engaged in fighting a last and decisive battle against capitalism.[12]

And so *The New Republic* justified mass murder in the name of social justice.

For Croly, the revolutionary Bolshevik republic, having overthrown a corrupt, feudal despot, appeared a new shining city on the hill bringing a righteous new enlightenment out of tsarist darkness. Believing all existing societies reactionary, it was inevitable that Croly would be attracted to the purest experiment in the new practice of the science of politics. If Lenin's Russia violently defended her revolution, she was forced to do so in order to counter the aggression of the reactionary regimes. Croly thus saw the Bolsheviks as they wished to be seen, as the keepers of the true progressive flame—the vanguard of the budding new republics promised by the developing natural and social sciences. They were not, in his opinion, a totalitarian terrorist regime fighting a permanent war to maintain their absolute power—which was the view of Winston Churchill and George Orwell, among others. Unhappily, the latter view ultimately proved to be the true or really "hard-boiled" case.

Aware of the class warfare central to Bolshevik ideology, Croly's *The New Republic* continued to view the Soviet Union and her satellites and clones throughout the world as blueprints of a true militant democracy, the fortress of social righteousness. Arguably, Croly's most significant and blameworthy contribution to the twentieth century was to postpone for the first thirty years of Soviet existence the beginning of the true liberation undertaken by the Cold War. During this deadly interim, Soviet Russia waxed in economic and military power, and Lenin and Joseph Stalin perfected the terrorism of the GPD, the killing machinery of the gulag, financed a myriad of guerrilla wars, and suckled fraternal totalitarian regimes everywhere. Africa has seemingly most fully reaped the fruits of this policy, progressing relentlessly into the nightmare of total revolution. Almost needless to say, *The New Republic* was in the forefront demanding rapid Western decolonization. Decolonization created a unique opportunity for Soviet "aid" and influence to work their magic by destabilizing an entire continent, launching the new imperialist African wars onto a totally new level of mass violence and genocide. Ethiopia, Angola, and Mozambique most faithfully followed the overall party model of the Soviet republic.[13] As a consequence of Soviet style progressivism, the sociologist R. J. Rummel estimates the Soviet Union and Communist China together killed slightly over ninety-seven millions of their own civilian populations.[14] Finally, because of the belated decision to contain the Soviet experiment in democratic social righteousness, a position still opposed by *The New Republic* in the 1940s, the Western nations eventually paid trillions of dollars and 85,000 American lives on the snow capped ridges of Korea and the steaming rice patties of Vietnam.[15]

In conclusion, Croly believed that the productive economic and behavioral sciences were the climax of the revolutionary reforms of the modern world beginning with the Protestant Reformation. His Progressives were the new pilgrims seeking the overthrow of the Old World and the creation of a new city of (social science) righteousness. For Croly, the administrative state was the church of his new, effective faith.[16] If his new faith promised a new equality and liberty, it also demanded sacrifices of body and spirit. Ultimately, the new faith transcended the vestigial vessel of the old liberal faith, constitutional democracy, and the civil institutional devices guaranteeing political liberty and popular consent. Therefore, the experimental, progressive Soviet republic, militantly public spirited like Jean-Jacques Rousseau's Sparta and Geneva, but imbued with the new science castigated by the same author, offered the best model and means to correct the fatal errors of the Founders' commercial republic. Croly apparently believed that the success of the Soviet Union would prove "as momentous in history as was the discovery of America at the end of the Middle Ages. Not only shall we know that capitalism as we have experienced it is undesirable, but that a different and better order is actually possible."[17]

The pro-Soviet policy of Croly's *The New Republic,* both in the early years of the Bolshevik Revolution and again in the early years of the depression, is more reflective of his radicalism than the patriotic nationalism briefly on display in *The Promise of American Life.* Therefore, Richard Rorty and E. J. Dionne wrongly "appropriate" Herbert Croly for their new patriotic public philosophy. As we have seen, if these authors truly entered the great editor's house of horrors, they would commune not with a modern, egalitarian Alexander Hamilton, but the dark shades of V. I. Lenin and Joseph Stalin, Croly's new "Legislators," and with their creation, progressivism Soviet style.[18] A patriotic—much less a "conservative"—public philosophy for modern liberalism was not any serious part of Herbert Croly's radical pilgrimage to social righteousness. Croly's true contribution to American political thought was to link the development of the social sciences to a doctrine of radical social progress in direct opposition to the existing Constitution and society. Like the Marxists who professed to love Catholics and hate Catholicism, Croly loved American populism and technological prowess while hating American capitalism and constitutionalism.

The most moderate (and ultimately incorrect) interpretation of Croly's thought is therefore the doctrine of the "living Constitution." The "living Constitution" suggests that officeholders should slowly and secretly transform the Constitution, or the "political and judicial process," in order to move seamlessly to a "postconstitutional" administrative state. They should clandestinely reform and subvert, while denying their intentions. In this view, Croly's new public men will occupy the moral high ground, proclaiming themselves to be the true patriots—defenders of the Constitution and the American way—while re-creating both the Constitution and society in their image.

A utopian theorist, Croly sought to realize a new republic through the leadership of intellectuals and the media, employing the new knowledge of social science. The birth of this "new republic" will necessitate, as the case demands, either the peaceful or violent destruction of the existing Constitution. But can any regime be destroyed or created without an extended period of dictatorship? Croly knew the answer. But, as arguably the twentieth century's most influential public intellectual, Croly knew enough to know that proclaiming oneself a patriot and democrat enabled one to be as radical and authoritarian as one wished. "When on the cage of an elephant [or tiger] you see the inscription 'buffalo,' don't believe your eyes."[19]

Notes

1. Richard Rorty, *Achieving Our Country: Leftist Thought in Twentieth-Century America* (Cambridge, Mass.: Harvard University Press, 1998), 10, 15, 46–49.

2. E. J. Dionne, *They Only Look Dead: Why Progressives Will Dominate the Next Political Era* (New York: Simon and Schuster, 1996), 188, 297, 300.

3. Irving Kristol, "When Virtue Loses All Her Loveliness," in *The Neo-Conservative Reader*, ed. Mark Gerson (Reading, Mass.: Addison-Wesley, 1996), 114.

4. Quotations from and references to Croly's works are cited in the text using the following abbreviations:

> NR:	*The New Republic*, cited according to the journal's date.
> PAL:	*The Promise of American Life* (Boston: Northeastern University Press, 1989).
> PD:	*Progressive Democracy* (New Brunswick, N.J.: Transaction Publishers, 1998).

5. The Great Depression changed the terms of the economic debate from the nationalization of industry to that of economic regulation. John Maynard Keynes came to argue that government could successfully manage the economy without the need of public ownership. Private ownership and public control could be effectively combined in a mixed economy. This advance exorcized the specter of state socialism from political attack, freeing the New Deal from the opprobrium visited on the Progressives' economic radicalism. Not wishing to exclude the radicals, however, the New Dealers redefined the term liberalism to combine the two wings of the political Left, with progressive socialism becoming the crazy cousin, and junior partner, in a managed capitalism under the guidance of an activist state. What Croly had called the older liberalism now became known as conservatism.

6. Edward Stettner, *Shaping Modern Liberalism: Herbert Croly and Progressive Thought* (Lawrence: University Press of Kansas, 1993), 171.

7. Alexander Hamilton, James Madison, John Jay, *The Federalist Papers* (Middletown, Conn.: Wesleyan University Press, 1961), no. 9, 51.

8. *The Federalist* no. 14, 88–89.

9. Croly accepted the social Darwinist view of the inherent warfare present in both nature and society. His new republic would embrace the necessity of violence. William Dean Howells was one of the few major intellectual figures who consistently condemned the violent, military metaphors of radical reformers like Croly. In *Their Silver Wedding Journey* (New York: Harper, 1899), Howells has his characters travel to Germany to condemn militant Hegelianism at its source.

10. One must ask if it is fair to conflate the strongly pro-Soviet outlook of *The New Republic* with Croly's personal opinion. In fact, there is *every* reason to do so. According to Walter Lippman: "All the editors were to be free and equal, although in fact Croly was the editor-in-chief" (*NR* July 16, 1930). Moreover, Croly's proclaimed expertise was in foreign policy. I agree with the tenor of Edward A.

Stettner's interpretation that anything published in unsigned editorials (and in signed editorials and articles for that matter) were approved by Croly himself. As we will see more fully below, George Soule and Edmund Wilson, both called back to *The New Republic* in the twenties by Croly to bolster the editorial board, were also serious admirers of the Soviet experiment. While *The New Republic*'s support of the Soviet republic waned in the twenties, it waxed again in the depression. See Stettner, *Shaping Modern Liberalism*, 155, 161, 169.

11. *The New Republic* published a special supplement on August 4, 1920, blasting the anti-Bolshevik tenor of American newspaper coverage of the Russian civil war. The broadside was especially critical of the *New York Times*. The *Times* shortly changed course, dispatching the infamous Walter Duranty to Moscow. On Duranty, see Robert Conquest, *Reflections on a Ravaged Century* (New York: W. W. Norton, 2000), 123ff.

12. Vera Micheles Dean, "The Struggle in Russia," *NR* March 5, 1930.

13. Stéphane Courtois et al., *The Black Book of Communism* (Cambridge, Mass.: Harvard University Press, 1999), 33ff., 683–704.

14. R. J. Rummel, *Death by Government* (New Brunswick, N.J.: Transaction Press, 1994), 4. See also, Courtois, *The Black Book*, 4.

15. Why did *The New Republic* so consistently pursue Croly's vision after his death? A major reason was Bruce Bliven. Croly hired the radical Bliven in 1923. "Gradually Bliven and Croly came to divide the journal's political writing and Bliven took over the affairs of the magazine whenever Croly was away from the office." Bliven assumed the editorship of *The New Republic* on Croly's death in 1930 and continued in this post until 1955. See David W. Levy, *Herbert Croly of The New Republic: The Life and Thought of an American Progressive* (Princeton, N.J.: Princeton University Press, 1985), 279, 300.

16. In his final, unpublished manuscript, *The Breach of Civilization,* Croly experimented with the recovery of "the moral and religious vision, the 'authoritative knowledge' that Catholicism had once symbolized." The "evils that plagued modern life . . . stemmed from the introduction of Protestant subjectivism, materialism, and individualism at the expense of a unified and authoritative moral system." But Croly could never find the "new method" which would allow Christianity to be safely taught, and he continued in his true devotion to Progressive politics. Even here the radical Croly averred: "'The way to render a capitalist society immune from revolutionary socialism . . . is to treat revolutionary agitation not as itself the removable cause of social insecurity, but as a natural effect of social irresponsibility, helplessness, and impiety.'" See Levy, *Herbert Croly*, 291–92.

17. "It seems to me that we shall not be equipped to discuss the subject [of American liberalism] intelligently unless we know to what extent Croly went on to develop his position [beyond *The Promise of American Life*]. . . . Certainly *The New Republic* has never stood for historic liberalism in public affairs, but for something radically different. . . . Croly understood . . . that a revolutionary crisis might eventually arise in the course of the struggle to bring desirable changes, but, in the absence of such a crisis, he favored a progressive policy which would make use of existing institutions to approach the true national ideal. After the War he certainly did not count on a 'benevolent and intelligent capitalism' to reform itself. He wanted, rather, more and stronger dissenting economic groups, such as labor organizations, and a radically progressive party, based on the interests of the economically disinherited—particularly the industrial workers and farmers—which would put pressure on the owners and arrivists. . . . Whether the ultimate result would be a new [social] order achieved through evolutionary process, or a breakdown resulting from a too immobile business leadership, he did not venture to predict. It appears to me, therefore, that an accurate statement of the primary issue, . . . as far as those who have understood and agreed with Croly are concerned, is not whether we should abandon political liberalism [i.e., support for the Declaration of Independence and the Constitution]—which we have not been espousing. . . . More important than anything else in its potential effect is, of course, the Russian experiment. . . . If it goes on in the course of time to produce at least as high a standard of living as ours without our insecurity, to demonstrate the possibility of planning and control over a complex industrial system and to offer a full measure of the more intangible satisfactions, the effect will be as momentous in history as was the discovery of America at the end of the Middle Ages." George Soule, "[Herbert Croly's] Hard-Boiled Radicalism," *NR* January 21, 1931.

Soule's article reflects the "outcome of conversations among the editors of *The New Republic*" concerning "the position of the contemporary progressive" following the death of Herbert Croly. The other article commissioned by the editors was written by Edmund Wilson (*NR* January 14, 1931). Like Soule, Wilson follows Croly, and the editorial position of *The New Republic*, in arguing that the Soviet experiment, like the International Workers of the World and the Peoples' Power League, is positive because it stimulates a more radical public opinion and politics. "The apparent success of the [Soviet] Five Year Plan has affected the morale of all the rest of the world—and of the Americans surely not least. In the course of this winter of our capitalist quandary, the Soviets have emerged from the back pages of the newspapers . . . [and even in] the reactionary papers one feels as much admiration as resentment. After all, the Communist project has almost all the qualities that Americans glorify—the extreme of efficiency and economy combined with the ideal of a herculean feat to be accomplished by common action in an atmosphere of enthusiastic boosting. . . . I believe that if the American radicals and progressives who repudiate the Marxian dogma and the strategy of the Communist party hope to accomplish anything valuable, they must take Communism away from the Communists, and take it away without ambiguity or reservations, asserting emphatically that their ultimate goal is the ownership of the means of production by the government and an industrial rather than a regional representation. What we need in this country is a genuine opposition, and it is a long time since the liberals have had one. A genuine opposition must, it seems to me, openly confess that the Declaration of Independence and the Constitution are due to be supplanted by some new manifesto and some new bill of rights."

18. A completely typical review in *The New Republic* of three books on Lenin begins in this way: "Lenin died on January 21, 1924. He has ever since been universally regarded as one of the greatest revolutionary leaders of all time and as a political genius who left his indelible imprint upon a whole epoch. His gigantic stature was recognized not only by the workers, peasants and party comrades who mourned his loss, but also by his enemies among the bourgeoisie and privileged classes of Russia and of the world who welcomed his passing in the vain hope that the proletarian state which he had built would crumble without his hand to sustain. Seven years after his death, the time has still not come to measure the length of the shadow which his figure casts down the vista of history. Subsequent developments have merely made it clear that his role as the destroyer of one social order has been eclipsed by his role as the builder of another, and that a final estimate of his statesmanship must wait until the Red revolution which he led has achieved, or has failed to achieve, the goals he set for it." Frederick L. Schuman, *NR* May 13, 1931.

19. Kouzma Proutkov, quoted in Alexandre Kojève, "The Emperor Julian and His Art of Writing," in *Ancients and Moderns*, ed. Joseph Cropsey (New York: Basic Books, 1964), 95–113.

Chapter 31

Theodore Roosevelt and the
Stewardship of the American Presidency

Jean M. Yarbrough

Theodore Roosevelt (1858–1919) was the 26th president of the United States, the youngest and arguably most energetic man ever to fill that office. Too sickly a youth to be sent away to school, he was educated at home until he matriculated at Harvard in 1876. By that time, he had largely overcome the debilitating asthma of his childhood through sheer physical effort and launched himself into his studies with characteristic vigor. Charles W. Eliot was then the president of Harvard—the first scientist to serve in that post. Under his leadership, Harvard made far-reaching changes that would transform it from a sleepy New England college, led by Protestant divines, into a modern university. Following the German model, Eliot greatly eased undergraduate course requirements and encouraged students to pursue their individual bents. Roosevelt's was toward the natural sciences, though he chaffed at the time required in the laboratory (another German innovation) when he wanted to be out in the field. Uncertain what to do with his life, he was apparently persuaded by Professor J. Laurence Laughlin of the economics department that his talents were more needed in politics than in science. The young Roosevelt telegraphed his future interests in a commencement address on the "Practicability of Giving Men and Women Equal Rights," in which he argued for greater equality of rights for women, except for voting. In Roosevelt's mind, the sheer physical ability to fight for one's rights was a vital component of suffrage. After being graduated Phi Beta Kappa, he enrolled in the newly established School of Political Science at Columbia. There he studied for a brief time with John W. Burgess, a Germanophile who believed in the superiority of the Teutonic race. Burgess introduced his students to the latest political science import from Germany, the historical-comparative method of analysis, which applied the methods of the physical sciences to demonstrate that history was the unfolding of a rational plan for human beings. Thus, by the time he completed his formal schooling and entered into political life, he had already had considerable exposure to the great intellectual movements of the day—evolutionary biology and historicism—that would shape his political thinking.

This was not, however, how Roosevelt understood his education. Reflecting on his Harvard years in his *Autobiography* (1913), written after his failed attempt to win the presidency on the Progressive ticket, Roosevelt maintained that "very little in my actual studies helped me in after life." His principal objection was that nowhere in college did he learn about the need for collective action and collective responsibility. His early education both at home and at Harvard had taught him only about individual responsibility, and although Roosevelt continued to insist that this was a "prime necessity," he later came to believe that it was not enough. It was part of a man's duty not merely to take care of himself but also "to join with others in trying to make things better for the many by curbing the abnormal and excessive development of individualism in a few."[1] In no small measure, he learned this by rolling up his sleeves and doing; but he also credited the writings of Walter Weyl and Herbert Croly in helping him to see the light. (Roosevelt had read Croly's *The Promise of American Life* soon after it was published in 1909 and was greatly impressed with it.) In a larger sense, however, these thinkers did not change his intellectual horizon as much as reinforce the more progressive elements already present within it and give them a sharper theoretical edge. Roosevelt started out as a Republican reformer, uneasily combining admiration for the Constitution with the evolutionary biology and historicism that dominated his age. But after he had read Croly and spoken with him, he became increasingly persuaded that the political science of the Framers was largely obsolete and that the movement of history pointed to an ever more expansive national government, aimed not at the protection of individual rights but at the material and spiritual well-being of the whole. Evolutionary biology, properly understood, might serve as a useful ally in this political task. Yet even as he grew more critical of their handiwork, Roosevelt continued to praise the character and lives of his American heroes.

Two years out of Harvard, Roosevelt published his first work, a study of the Naval War of 1812, which laid out many of the themes of his political career. The book made an argument for a strong navy and criticized the "criminal folly" of Presidents Thomas Jefferson and James Madison for their inadequate preparations prior to the outbreak of war. From the start, Roosevelt was a strong nationalist who regarded Jefferson as an incompetent, conniving demagogue. (Not until his Bull Moose run for the presidency would he have anything good to say about Jefferson.) His study of American history—and given the number of volumes he published, it is remarkable that he never formally studied history—had convinced him that those who supported an energetic national government were right. Among the Founders, George Washington and Alexander Hamilton were his heroes. He wrote a largely admiring biography of fellow New Yorker Gouverneur Morris. As a rising Republican politician and public intellectual, he thought highly of *The Federalist Papers*, and in several early essays, he recommended it to other aspiring reformers for its judicious blend of theory and practice.

Nevertheless, his praise of Hamilton and other early nationalists was not unqualified. Roosevelt seems rather to have accepted Jefferson's (and also Croly's) argument that the Federalists who supported a strong central government were no friends of the common man. In his view, Abraham Lincoln was the first president to show how a strong people might have a strong government and yet remain the freest on earth.[2] Moreover, where Hamilton labored to bring forth the commercial republic and admired the entrepreneurial character it tended to promote, Roosevelt took a far more critical view. Like Hamilton, Roosevelt was a New Yorker, but, growing up in the Gilded Age, he saw the East in very different terms. In numerous essays written during the 1880s and 1890s, the young Roosevelt made the East the symbol of everything decadent and effeminate in American life. "Purely commercial ideals" were "mean and sordid," producing weak and fearful men, "incapable of the thrill of generous emotion" and lacking in the capacity for nobility and greatness (*W* 13:3–12). Although Roosevelt acknowledged that material prosperity was a precondition for national happiness, he insisted that wealth alone could never lead to national greatness.

Surprisingly, the South (home of Roosevelt's maternal ancestors) fared somewhat better in his estimation. Although it had betrayed the democratic principle by continuing to maintain slavery, it had fought with honor and courage in the Civil War. Unlike the commercial North, the South still cultivated the martial virtues and continued to hold out for something higher than "mere material prosperity" (*W* 7:26, 16:26–35).

But it was the West that synthesized—to use the Hegelian concept so much in vogue after the Civil War—the virtues of the free North and the spirited fighting South to create what was best in the American character. The West could train the effeminate Easterner in the "manly virtues," while it taught the proud Southerner valuable lessons in democratic equality (*W* 13:27–35). Moreover, the West stood for the right mix of individualism and social cooperation. It was, therefore, to the West that Roosevelt looked to "shape the destinies of this nation" (*W* 13:355–68). Roosevelt was not disappointed; it was in fact the West that first and most fully embraced the Progressive cause.

Roosevelt not only insisted on tempering the softer metal of commercial society with the "iron" virtues of the West, but he also vigorously defended westward expansion. Whereas Hamilton was skeptical about how far republican government could be extended, Roosevelt in his early biography, *Thomas Hart Benton* (1886), outdid even the Missouri senator in his enthusiasm for "manifest destiny." What made it possible for the United States to expand across the continent was the Framers' decision, contained in Article IV of the Constitution, to permit new states to enter the Union on terms of equality. In his biography of Gouverneur Morris, Roosevelt criticized his fellow New Yorker for opposing this provision and trying to keep these new states in permanent subjection to the East.

In *Thomas Hart Benton* and *The Winning of the West* (1889), as well as the essays that make up *The Strenuous Life* (1899), Roosevelt not only defended manifest destiny, but he did so in unapologetic Darwinian terms. It was both inevitable and desirable that these raw, pushing, brawling westerners should seek to swallow up the lands occupied by nations or races too weak to resist. Such expansion was "part of the order of nature" (*W* 13:450–59). In Texas, the Mexicans proved no match for the virtues of that "barbaric race" of frontiersmen, who, "careless of the rights of others," looked on the possessions of the weaker races as their "natural prey" (*W* 7:114).

Roosevelt's treatment of the pioneer's encounter with the Native Americans was equally unsentimental. In his view, it was "maudlin nonsense" to defend the Indians' claims to the West (*W* 7:38). The tribes currently occupying these lands had no moral claims; they were there simply because they had succeeded in butchering earlier tribes. Although Roosevelt conceded that the Americans had not always dealt fairly and honestly with the Indians, he insisted the United States had acted with more "generosity" than other conquering nations (*W* 9:56).

Roosevelt's enthusiasm for manifest destiny was not limited to the American encounter with weaker, more backward, nations. Where American territorial ambitions were concerned, Roosevelt yielded to no one—not even the "civilized" British. Thus, he approved of Benton's refusal to compromise with Britain over Oregon on the grounds that "we were the people that could use it best and we should have taken it all" (*W* 7:173). Roosevelt could scarcely hide his disappointment that national policy at that time was largely shaped by the "more cautious and timid" wealthy classes of the Northeast, who "have never felt much of the spirit which made the West stretch out impatiently for new lands" (*W* 9:172–73).

The contrast with Roosevelt's hero, Lincoln, could not be more striking. Not only did Lincoln support the Whig policy of conciliation with Great Britain, but he warned that the annexation of Texas would further complicate the problem of slavery. Roosevelt, by contrast, insisted that manifest destiny had little, if anything, to do with slavery. It had rather to do with the insatiable "greed" of all westerners, slaveholder and free alike, to lay claim to whatever land they could wrest from weaker, inferior races (*W* 7:112). Analyzing the decades before the Civil War, Roosevelt's sympathies lay with the Democrats rather than with his hero Lincoln. Writing about this period with the advantage of hindsight, and in thrall to the vaguely Hegelian view of history as the progress of freedom, he seemed to take it for granted that manifest destiny could only further that end. Roosevelt's celebration of manifest destiny, with its odd blend of social Darwinism and Hegel, flies in the face of America's Founding principles in still another respect: for what kind of freedom is it that celebrates the right of the stronger to conquer the weaker and treat their land as its prey? This is not the language of Roosevelt's heroes—Washington, Hamilton, and Lincoln—all of whom accepted the self-evident truths of the Declaration.

Roosevelt's tendency to view nations in racial terms and to see social progress in terms of the survival of the fittest tended during this period to spill over into public policy matters as well. As a rising Republican reformer in the 1880s and 1890s, Roosevelt had also acquired a reputation as a public intellectual. In a book review of Charles Pearson's *National Life and Character* written in 1894, the same year that he was considering a run for mayor of New York City, Roosevelt noted approvingly that democratic nations have instinctively practiced a healthy "race selfishness" by preserving the most temperate parts of the globe for themselves. In contrast to aristocratic societies which admitted alien races to work for them, democratic societies recognized the "race foe" and took steps to keep out the "dangerous alien" (*W* 13:200–22). (Negro slavery he considered a throwback to aristocratic times.) Although Roosevelt favored measures that would foster the rapid and complete assimilation of immigrants, this only applied to whites. He favored tight immigration policies for nonwhites, and he maintained that unrestricted Asian immigration on the Pacific Coast would be a "calamity" (*W* 7:103). Roosevelt believed that the races that formed these different civilizations should remain apart to preserve their distinctive character (*A* 392–98).

During this same period, Roosevelt also began to speak out on behalf of "race virtue" and to warn against the dangers of "race suicide" or "race decadence." Initially begun as a campaign against "old stock" Easterners, whose birth rates had declined both absolutely and relative to the newly arrived immigrant populations, Roosevelt would in time broaden his message to include all Americans, then members of the English-speaking race, and finally, in 1910, citizens of Republican France, whose birthrate was declining even more precipitously (*W* 13:506–29).

In this respect, "race virtue" functioned as part of Roosevelt's larger critique of modern commercial society and its tendency to produce timid, self-indulgent, and even cowardly citizens. Roosevelt used the bully pulpit to criticize the "coldness," the "selfishness," and the "shrinking from risk" that suffocated the sense of duty or perverted it into "improper" channels. He deplored the "twisted eugenics" that emphasized quality over quantity. What was needed in America was a "deep moral awakening," a radical shift in public opinion that would "shame" those "small souls" who neglected their fundamental duty to preserve their race. No nation, he warned, could become great or remain great unless it consisted of "good breeders" (*W* 12:184–207).

Sometime during the 1890s, Roosevelt began to back away from the bleak social Darwinism that ran through his earlier histories. In both *Thomas Hart Benton* and *The Winning of the West*, he had seen the triumph of the English-speaking race in terms of natural selection or survival of the fittest. But reviewing several recent works on evolution, Roosevelt began to give greater weight to the Lamarckian theory of adaptation to explain evolution and progress. What matters, he now stressed, is not so much who the fittest are as how well the unfit can adapt and pass on to their progeny the character traits of the fittest. Individuals, he thought, could pass on both selfish and altruistic traits: "love of order, ability to fight and breed well, [and a] capacity to subordinate the interests of the individual to the community." Without specifically mentioning here the plight of the blacks in America, the implications for racial progress seemed clear. Although Roosevelt regarded the black race as intellectually and morally inferior to the white race at this particular historical moment, he was confident that blacks could make progress by "adapting" themselves to the more advanced white race and passing these traits on genetically to their children (*W* 13:223–41).

As science, of course, the theory of adaptation was mistaken, as Roosevelt was finally forced to concede at the end of his life. But the larger difficulty was that Roosevelt the natural scientist assumed that evolutionary biology provided the key to understanding how society works and how social progress occurs. Science would now supply the answers to questions that had formerly belonged to the province of religion and philosophy. Progress was guaranteed as long as societies acted in conformity with these newly discovered laws of nature, which viewed persons in terms of distinct racial categories rather than as individuals. Nor did these theories place much stock in natural rights. The view of nature that informed these evolutionary theories was a far different thing than "the laws of nature and of nature's God" to which the Declaration appealed.

Unlike many of the leading intellectuals of his day, Roosevelt was not, however, a thoroughgoing racialist. His "scientific" racialism mixed uneasily with the democratic individualism he had learned from his heroes, in time bending the former in a humane and liberal direction—though ultimately the two could never be reconciled. On the one hand, he sought to keep out alien races; on the other hand, he insisted that those members who were living in America be treated as individuals and accorded the same rights as whites. This was true not only for the Asians but also for blacks. (Roosevelt deplored the hyphenated-American.) As a public official, he appointed blacks to political office, and he was the first American president to invite a black man, Booker T. Washington, to dinner at the White House. In a Lincoln Day speech to the Republican Club of New York City in 1905, Roosevelt urged both North and South to act in good faith on the principle of giving to every individual—black or white—his due, recognizing his worth as a man and granting him the same opportunities to develop himself to the best of his abilities. Thus did Roosevelt's Americanism do battle with his racialism.

The closing of the frontier, which Roosevelt anticipated in his histories, presented a different dilemma. How would Americans continue to develop the old "iron" virtues their pioneer forefathers had cultivated so naturally? Coming of age in the decades following the Civil War and in times of unprecedented prosperity, there was no necessity for wealthy Americans to cultivate these virtues. And they did not. In an essay extolling "The Manly Virtues" (1894), Roosevelt opined that American men must "be vigorous in mind and body, able to hold our own in rough conflict with our fellows, able to suffer punishment without flinching, and, at need, be able to repay it in kind with full interest." Such virile traits were precisely what a "peaceful and commercial civilization," rendered "cautious and timid," was all too inclined to dismiss. If America was "ever to amount to anything," every citizen must be willing to stand up and fight for his rights (*W* 13:27–35)—and he meant this literally. The task before Roosevelt's "softer" age was to find some way to keep these virtues alive. As Roosevelt saw it, they were not simply a part of the pioneer past but part of "true manhood."

Although Roosevelt offered a number of ways to turn effete Easterners into manly men, including stints in the Wild West and participation in competitive team sports, the Spanish-American War provided him with the opportunity to speak out in defense of American empire. Here, too, the contrasts with his early historical studies are instructive. Whereas Roosevelt the historian relied on a crude and racially tinged social Darwinism to justify American expansion in the West, Roosevelt the warrior switched course to defend American rule over Cuba, Puerto Rico, and the Philippines after the Spanish-American War. He now insisted that rule over these former Spanish colonies was justified only if it served the native peoples in their struggle toward civilization. "It is our duty," he announced at the Minnesota State Fair in 1901, "toward the people living in barbarism to see that they are freed from their chains" (*W* 13:469–80).

But empire turns out to be good not only for the ruled; it benefits the rulers as well. It enables men once again to embrace "The Strenuous Life" by building up American military power and taking on new responsibilities in the world. Timid, lazy, and overcivilized men, "who have lost the great fighting masterful virtues," may shrink from the strenuous life, but this, Roosevelt insists, "is the only national life which is really worth leading." And it is the only way that a nation can achieve greatness. Accordingly, Roosevelt dismisses as "cant" the arguments of critics who complain that rule over these colonies contradicts the American commitment to "liberty" and "the consent of the governed" (*W* 13:319–31). But do these critics not raise a serious question? What happens to republican self-government when the manly virtues necessary to defend freedom are divorced from the Founders' vision of limited government and, following Darwin, placed in the service of continual expansion and growth? Is it true, as Roosevelt supposes, that nations must expand or decline (*W* 13:430–41)? To put the question somewhat differently: Does Roosevelt's effort to revive the manly fighting virtues, however admirable the desire to rekindle patriotism and courage in a generation turned soft and weak, lead inevitably to imperialism and war? And if so, is there—as many of those who opposed the Spanish-American War at the time argued—something about Roosevelt's embrace of the strenuous life and national greatness that is fundamentally at odds with republican self-government?

Roosevelt's fame in leading the Rough Riders (the volunteer cavalry regiment he assembled to fight in the Spanish-American War) established him as a national hero, and it won him in short order the governorship of New York (1899–1900) and then a spot on the Republican party ticket as candidate for vice president in the election of 1900. After the assassination of President William McKinley, Roosevelt was sworn in as president in 1901. He was forty-two. As a Republican reformer out of the Progressive wing of the party, Roosevelt set to work to infuse the national government, and especially the executive, with energy and efficiency. Drawing on the presidencies of Andrew Jackson and Abraham Lincoln, both of whom had exercised their considerable presidential powers, Roosevelt developed his own, still more expansive, theory of executive power. Roosevelt saw the president as "the steward of the people," with the right and the duty to do whatever the needs of the nation required unless such action was specifically prohibited by the Constitution or the laws. No longer would the president have to cite some specific grant of power to justify his actions. Stewardship was the perfect expression of Roosevelt's moral energy: unlike previous executives, he would not, as he explained in his *Autobiography,* suffer his talents to be hidden in a napkin, or content himself with the negative virtue of not doing harm when he was convinced that there was so much good he could accomplish (*A* 372–84). This was a novel reading of executive power, far exceeding Hamilton's arguments in *The Federalist*, where energy depended upon a limited scope for governmental power. It paved the way for the gradual transfer of the source of presidential authority from the Constitution directly to the people, which under the Progressive impulse is still going on today. In this vein, he was the first president to characterize his policies with a slogan designed to appeal to the people: the "Square Deal."

As "steward of the people," Roosevelt argued that the national government must have the power to curb monopolies and, in the landmark *Northern Securities* case (1903), persuaded a divided Supreme Court to reverse its earlier ruling and uphold this interpretation. But how should this power be used? Populists and democrats insisted that the trusts should all be broken up. Their goal was to restore competition and revive nineteenth-century notions of individualism. But Roosevelt believed these large-scale trusts and corporations offered considerable economies, and was generally unwilling to see them broken up—unless, like the Sugar, Tobacco, and Oil Trusts, they were engaged in criminal conspiracies or fraudulent activities. The more efficient approach—and efficiency was *the* Progressive virtue—was to establish independent federal regulatory commissions comprised of disinterested experts who would compel the trusts to serve the public interest. He tended to regard competition as a historical relic, and he looked on new cooperative relations between business and government as the wave of the future.

During his first term, Roosevelt believed himself honor-bound to retain McKinley's cabinet and pursue his policies. But after winning reelection in his own right, he felt free to press his more expansive reading of the Constitution and of executive powers. In so doing, he cast himself as the heir to Lincoln's method of constitutional interpretation, which, Roosevelt stressed, elevated human rights over property rights whenever the two conflicted (*A* 400). His Annual Message of 1905, the first of his second term, unleashed a flurry of legislative proposals, including pure food and drug and meat inspection laws, government supervision of insurance companies, government investigation of child labor, employer liability laws for Washington, D.C., and, of highest priority, a law giving the Interstate Commerce Commission power to regulate railroad shipping rates. This last proposal, which Roosevelt signed into law as the Hepburn Act in 1906, arguably laid the foundation for the modern regulatory state. By the end of his second term, Roosevelt was using his "bully pulpit" to call for graduated income and inheritance taxes, and criticizing the judiciary for being too subservient to corporate interests. He established numerous unpaid civilian commissions, the best known of which was the Commission on Country Life, to gather information which would help the national government develop new programs and extend its sphere of action to improve the lives of ordinary people. At the same time, Roosevelt continued to insist that the duty of the government is to secure the rights of the individual to life, liberty, and the pursuit of happiness. But he reinterpreted these rights in light of the changed economic and social conditions of the day: "the right of the worker to a living wage, to reasonable hours of labor, to decent working and living conditions, to freedom of thought and speech and industrial representation" (*A* 487). Where government in the past had played only a "negative" role, it must now take on an active role in securing these rights.

In what became one of the hallmarks of the Roosevelt administration, he also invoked the "stewardship" theory to justify for the first time the use of federal power to conserve America's natural resources. During his presidency, the federal government acted to establish the national park system, along with wildlife refuges and national monuments. Yet, in contrast to today's environmentalists, Roosevelt's conservation efforts were not so much directed at barring private corporations from developing public lands as insuring that these resources were developed in such a way as to increase their usefulness in the future and making sure that the public received fair compensation for these valuable rights (*W* 15:443).

Roosevelt also believed that stewardship carried with it an aesthetic dimension that would reflect the greatness of America in its public buildings, sculptures, and monuments. Among the artists he commissioned was the sculptor Augustus St.-Gaudens, who designed a system of coins for the national mint, which Roosevelt judged "more beautiful than any coins since the days of the Greeks," as well as sculptures of Admiral Farragut, General Sherman, and Abraham Lincoln (*W* 11:282–87). Similarly, Roosevelt commissioned other artists to design national medals and public buildings in Washington. He also appointed a Fine Arts Council, consisting of "the best architects, painters and sculptors in the country, to advise the Government on the erection and decoration of all new buildings." Roosevelt justified taking action on these matters because "they add to the beauty of living and therefore to the joy of life" (*A* 434).

Finally, stewardship found its expression in Roosevelt's muscular foreign policy, though there was more of a constitutional warrant for the vigorous exercise of executive power in this area. Although Roosevelt detested boasting, he made it clear to other nations that the United States was always willing to back up its words with actions: "Speak softly, and carry a big stick" (*W* 13:469–80). As president, he reaffirmed and expanded the Monroe Doctrine to bar not only European meddling in the Western Hemisphere but also to justify precisely such intervention by the United States. In what became known as the Roosevelt Corollary, he dispatched American troops to Santo Domingo and the Isthmus of Panama, then under the control of Colombia. After securing Panama her independence, the United States entered into a treaty to construct and administer the Panama Canal. As a further recognition of America's growing power, Roosevelt was asked to mediate the end of the Russo-Japanese War and, for his efforts, was the first American to win the Nobel Peace Prize. To crown his foreign policy achievements, he dispatched the Great White Fleet in a worldwide cruise to build popular support for the administration's ambitious naval buildup and to demonstrate the power of American naval forces to the world.

The opposite side of Roosevelt's stewardship theory of executive power was his growing disdain for the separation of powers—which first developed while he served as president of the Police Commission in New York City (1895–97) and later as governor of New York (1899–1900). In contrast to the *The Federalist*—which argued that the constitutional distribution of powers not only limited government but also, paradoxically, generated power and promoted those qualities of good government not usually found in popular rule—Roosevelt dismissed this "old school" doctrine simply as a brake on what public officials could accomplish (*W* 17:306–14). Much better, he thought, was to concentrate political power in the hands of one or a few (most likely in the executive branch) and then devise ways of holding them to account. What he sought above all were efficiency and results, and he regarded the separation of powers as inimical to these ends. As president, he seems to have regarded Congress and the courts as subsidiary institutions that kept government from achieving any positive good. He charged that the courts in particular had "been twisted into an exaltation of property rights over human rights," and he invoked the example of Lincoln to combat this (*A* 400). In a remark that echoes Oliver Wendell Holmes, whom Roosevelt appointed to the Supreme Court in 1902, he observed that the judges "knew legalism, but not life" (*A* 83). Yet after the courts began ruling in his favor, he defended them against charges that they had violated their proper role and were now making the law rather than judging it. If the legislature refused to act, the blame lay with the no-account lawmakers rather than the courts. Roosevelt did not care which branch of government made policy; the critical point was that, if there was a pressing social need, some institution did. As he observed in a different context (involving his cooperation with Democratic senator Ben Tillman to secure passage of the Hepburn Act), "I did not care a rap for the mere form or show of power; I cared immensely for the use that could be made of the substance" (*A* 372).

For similar reasons, Roosevelt had little appreciation of federalism. As the successor to the Federalist and Whig parties, the Republican party was the national party. The Democrats were the party of "states' rights." To be sure, there was a branch of progressivism that saw the states as "laboratories of democracy," but Roosevelt, like Croly, was too much of a nationalist to associate himself with this view. The social and economic problems of his day could be solved only by the vigorous exercise of national power. His first important speech after reading Croly's *The Promise of American Life* was appropriately called "The New Nationalism," apparently to distinguish it from the older Hamiltonian version which sought to apply energetic national power to a few limited ends.

Finally, Roosevelt took on the Republican party "machine" of his day, which he viewed as corrupt and uninspired. As Roosevelt frequently observed, the Republican party was first formed out of moral opposition to the extension of slavery in the territories. Back in the glory days of Lincoln, the party stood for something more than mere economic interests; it was, to use Tocqueville's phrase, a "great party," animated by a high moral cause. But during the postbellum period, the Republican party had lost its way and returned to the more mundane (and Whiggish) task of promoting the economic interests of the business classes. Roosevelt tried to revive the moral idealism of the Republican party by hitching it to the cause of reform. Invoking Lincoln, Roosevelt argued that the Republican party should once again place human rights over the rights of capital (*W* 17:359–78). When he failed to win the party's endorsement in 1912 (as a result of careful parliamentary maneuvering by his old friend Elihu Root, who feared that the ever more radicalized Roosevelt was undermining the Constitution), he broke with the Republicans and formed his own Progressive, or Bull Moose, party. One of the principles of the new party was to find a way to overcome the obstacles placed in the way of the popular will by the Constitution.

As a political reformer and as president of the United States, Roosevelt's experience was largely confined to America. But after he stepped down from the presidency, Roosevelt agreed to a speaking tour of the European capitals. Among the speeches he delivered in the spring of 1910, two are noteworthy for giving a sense of the direction of his thought. In England, Roosevelt delivered the prestigious Romanes Lecture, reserved for distinguished men of science, at Oxford University on the topic "Biological Analogies in History." What is remarkable about this speech is that Roosevelt here used his understanding of biology and evolution explicitly to blunt the significance of race in society. Although he now acknowledged that scientific opinion was divided over the role of natural selection, mutation, and his own favorite, inheritance of acquired characteristics, Roosevelt himself continued to stress the ability of different races to adapt to their environment and pass these changes on to their offspring. As a result, racial lines become more blurred, undermining the claims to racial superiority. Roosevelt could be speaking for himself and his teachers when he observed that, whereas only a half century ago writers took pride in claiming membership in the Aryan or Teutonic race, we now know that these are linguistic and not racial categories after all. There is no "pure" Aryan or Teutonic race. Indeed, Roosevelt went so far as to doubt that race had played much of a determining role in the development of civilized societies. Retreating from the argument of his histories, he now maintained, "a great nation rarely belongs to any one race" (*W* 12:25–60). What matters more than race in the pursuit of national greatness is the character of a people, and character is something that persons of any race can acquire and pass on to their children. Thus, by the time Roosevelt embarked on his Progressive campaign, he had largely toned down the racialism and social Darwinism that supplied the intellectual framework for his early work. (He did, however, continue to back tough immigration policies for nonwhites and to warn against "race suicide" in friendly nations.)

On the whole, Roosevelt followed the general "evolution" of Progressive thought, shifting from science to history to explain the course of social progress. In turning to history, Roosevelt was not embarking on an entirely new course. His early studies of American history had largely been informed by a belief in progress, albeit progress cast principally in the Darwinian discourse that dominated the 1880s. But by 1910, history, understood in the vaguely Hegelian sense as a movement from the plane of low, selfish interests to the higher plane of ethical, self-sacrificing ideals became the organizing principle of his thought and action.

Roosevelt first elaborated on this theme in his lecture at the University of Berlin entitled "The World Movement." Where the guiding spirit of the English lecture was clearly Darwin, Roosevelt turned sharply Hegelian at Berlin. Surveying the movement of history from one stage of civilization to another, until finally a truly world-historical civilization had emerged, Roosevelt concluded that progress to "a higher and more permanent plane of well-being than was ever attained by any preceding civilization" was still possible if nations would nurture in their citizens the qualities that would make this dream come true. Roosevelt's "dream" is worth quoting in full, because it shows the extent to which he was no longer interested in reforming the liberal republicanism of the Founders but now sought to transcend it. What he envisioned "for the present stage" of world progress was the emergence of states in which morality, ethical development, and a true feeling of brotherhood shall all alike be divorced from false sentimentality, and from the *rancorous and evil passions* which, curiously enough, so often accompany professions of *sentimental attachment to the rights of man*; in which high material development in the things of the body shall be achieved without *subordination of the things of the soul*; in which there shall be a genuine desire for peace and justice without loss of those virile qualities without which no love of peace or justice shall avail any race; in which the fullest development of scientific research, the great distinguishing feature of our present civilization, shall yet not imply a belief that intellect can ever take the place of character—for, from the standpoint of the nation as of the individual, it is character that is the one vital possession. (*W* 12:61–84, emphasis added)

After a whirlwind tour of the European capitals, the former president returned to America to do battle for the soul of the Republican party. Over the next two years, as he unsuccessfully sought the Republican nomination and then ran for president on the Progressive party ticket, Roosevelt tried in a series of speeches to explain what the Progressive movement might mean for America. To begin with, it meant a rejection of American exceptionalism. Where once republican America had prided herself on her superiority to the monarchies of Europe, the United States was now lagging behind the governments of western Europe, and especially Germany, in her commitment to social welfare. (Roosevelt in his campaign speeches frequently singled out Germany for praise.) Having only recently emerged as a united nation after the Civil War, it was now time for America belatedly to join in the movement of world history.

The Progressive movement also meant the end of the old "shopworn" notion of individual rights, and especially property rights. Because these rights were grounded on a permanent view of human nature as essentially self-interested, Roosevelt regarded the whole idea of natural rights as scientifically wrong and morally obsolete. Darwin had shown that human beings were constantly evolving, and Roosevelt could see that Americans of his day were different from what they were even one hundred years before. They could progress beyond the selfish passions that underlay what in these vastly different times was nothing more than a "sentimental" attachment to natural rights. From a moral standpoint, the doctrine of natural and inalienable rights fared no better. It encouraged excessive individualism in a few while failing to satisfy the spiritual, and often even the material, needs of the great majority. At best, it attained a purely "legal" justice in which the inalienable rights of the individual were protected without regard for the well-being of the majority. If America was to progress to "ethical" justice, citizens would have to learn to think less about their individual rights and more about rights "developed in duty" (*W* 17:74–99, 13:593–95).

In his "New Nationalism" speech (1910), Roosevelt explained what this meant for property rights. The test of whether a man had a right to his fortune was no longer whether it was honorably obtained. It was not enough that it should have been made without harming the community. Because the value of property is socially determined, the new test of whether one may enjoy the fortune one has made is social utility. Those who enjoy "special privileges" must show that their wealth, power, and position actually "benefit" the community. The Progressive state is frankly redistributionist: "the central condition of progress" must be to "take from some men or class of men the right to enjoy power, or wealth, or position, or immunity, which has not been earned by service to their fellows" and distribute these goods to "men who have earned more than they possess" (*W* 17:5–22).

As a result, the Progressive movement placed a heavy emphasis on character-building, or what Herbert Croly called "reconstruction"; for Americans could not learn to think differently about the relationship between rights and duties without first acquiring new moral and civic virtues. The "new republic" would require a superior kind of citizen, one capable of mastering his passions and appetites and following the dictates of conscience rather than interest. As Roosevelt never tired of saying, in this ascent to a higher moral plane the average man and woman would need "many virtues" (*W* 17:100–7). Roosevelt was absolutely correct when he observed that progressivism, though it sought certain economic reforms, was essentially "an ethical movement" aimed at nothing less than the reconstruction of the American character.

Roosevelt's attack on individual rights arguably meant an attack on the very idea of constitutional government (both Elihu Root and Henry Cabot Lodge thought so), though Roosevelt himself denied this. This was because Roosevelt (in contrast to what he had argued in *Thomas Hart Benton*) now believed that the purpose of the Constitution was to secure the happiness and well-being of the many, not to protect the rights of the individual at their expense. Majority tyranny may once have been a danger, but no longer. Roosevelt agreed with "that keen and profound thinker" James Bryce, who argued that this "once dreaded" danger had now disappeared (*W* 17:190–203). Now, it is the wealthy minority that rides rough shod over the majority. At the present time, the majority is too demoralized to tyrannize over anyone. The task of the Progressive statesman was to remoralize the individual by wresting control of the government from the special interests who use the Constitution to defeat the popular will. The people must become their own masters. Nothing must limit their will, not even the Constitution. Roosevelt supported Progressive reforms that enabled the people to legislate directly through the initiative and referendum, hold their representatives accountable through direct elections and recall, and even to reverse state court decisions when after due deliberation the people determined that these rulings run contrary to the collective good. Surprisingly, in view of the large number of constitutional amendments that passed during the Progressive Era, Roosevelt favored the more direct, plebiscitary methods of asserting popular control because they were more efficient. The amendment process took too long, was too cumbersome, and could be misinterpreted by a too powerful and out of touch judiciary. Roosevelt would teach the people to appreciate the Progressive virtue of efficiency. By circumventing the forms, he would get results.

These reforms do not, as their critics contend, spell the end of representative government with its constitutional safeguards. They simply make representatives more responsive, hold the representatives accountable to the will of the people, and help the people achieve genuine self-mastery. Accordingly, Roosevelt can declare himself both a supporter of the "absolute right" of the people to govern themselves and an "emphatic believer in constitutionalism" (*W* 17:119–50).

In asserting the absolute right of the people to govern themselves, Roosevelt claimed to be following in the footsteps of Lincoln, whom he cites in nearly every important speech during the Progressive campaign. In these years, Roosevelt focused on two of Lincoln's greatest accomplishments. First, he had helped to realign the party system and create a new party organized around high moral principle, which is what Roosevelt himself hoped to achieve in 1912. Second, he had strenuously opposed the Supreme Court in *Dred Scott* (1857), just as Roosevelt objected to the string of state and federal court decisions that in his view (and here again he invoked Lincoln) elevated the rights of capital or property over the rights of people. But try as he might to associate himself with Lincoln's cause, and in turn to appropriate Lincoln's principles for the Progressive cause, the two were fundamentally irreconcilable—and for largely the same reasons that Roosevelt's Americanism and his Darwinism-racialism could not be squared.

One look at the Republican platform of 1854 makes clear the difference between the two parties. That platform begins by paraphrasing the Declaration to the effect that whenever parties become subversive of the ends for which they are established or are "incapable of restoring the government to the true principles of the Constitution," the people have a right and a duty to organize new parties upon such principles and with such views as the circumstances and exigencies of the nation may demand. The Republican party originated in the wish to restore the government to the true principles of the Constitution. By contrast, the Progressive party assumed that these principles—understood as the protection of individual rights, along with the separation of powers, limited government, and federalism designed to secure this end—have been rendered obsolete by changing social and economic conditions. Accordingly, in his restatement of the Republican platform, Roosevelt omitted this crucial phrase (*W* 17:360–78). The political party he wished to form does not take the Constitution as its polestar; it looked only to the future.

When Lincoln announced in his First Inaugural that the people and not the Court are ultimately sovereign, he was not calling on the people to overthrow the constitutional procedures set in place to overrule misguided court decisions. Instead, he sought to work within the constitutional system to change the rule of law the decision announced. As chief executive, sworn to uphold the Constitution, he vowed to enforce the decision, but he would enforce it narrowly and would refuse to recognize it as a precedent for future action. In the meantime, he would work to arouse public opinion to elect Republicans so he might alter the composition of the Court and, by changing the Court, reverse the decision. As president, Roosevelt did follow this approach in opposing the *E. C. Knight* case (1895), which dealt a blow to Congress's efforts to regulate interstate commerce by drawing a sharp line between manufacturing and commerce, and holding that Congress had no power under the Sherman Antitrust Act to regulate manufacturing. The *Northern Securities* case, decided during Roosevelt's first term, did not revisit the distinction between manufacturing and commerce, but it did broaden Congress's power to regulate the trusts.

But once out of office, Roosevelt adopted a far more radical course. Whether mistakenly or by design, Roosevelt the Progressive now read Lincoln's First Inaugural as an affirmation of his own emerging view that the majority of the moment are, and should be, sovereign even over their Constitution. During the Progressive campaign of 1912, he interpreted Lincoln's opposition to *Dred Scott* to mean that Lincoln favored a "recall" by the people of that decision rather than a rallying cry to work through their elected representatives in accordance with the procedures laid down by the Constitution. And he ignored completely that the decision was overturned, not by "recall," but by the Thirteenth and Fourteenth Amendments (*W* 17:360–78). In short, the difference between Lincoln and the Roosevelt of 1912 is that, by Roosevelt's own definition, Lincoln was not a Progressive but a "reactionary." In organizing a new political party to oppose slavery, Lincoln looked back to "the old policy of the Fathers" and sought to lead a wayward nation back to its Founding principles—within the limits laid down by the Constitution. He did not, as Roosevelt did, regard those principles, or the country's fundamental charter, as obsolete.

While it is arguable whether Progressive reforms undermine or reinforce constitutional government, there is no doubt that progressivism spells the end of limited government. Roosevelt explicitly said so, and with some relish. In a campaign speech in 1912, Roosevelt criticized his Democratic opponent Woodrow Wilson precisely for his defense of limited government. In keeping with his historicist premises, Roosevelt declares the idea of limited government "a bit of outworn academic doctrine. . . . It can be applied with profit, if anywhere at all, only in a primitive community such as the United States at the end of the eighteenth century." At this historical moment, limited government fosters a "chaotic scramble of selfish interests," and selfish interests are by their very nature corrupt (*W* 17:306–14).

In his definition of corruption, as well as in his remedy, Roosevelt the Progressive crusader has moved well beyond where he began. As a Republican reformer, Roosevelt had first established himself on the political scene by taking on specific forms of corruption, such as bribery and extortion. He then judged it unrealistic, and even demagogic, to try to ban campaign contributions by corporations. Such proposals were "merely intended to deceive during the campaign the voters least capable of thought." Instead, he argued for full disclosure of all contributions and urged the people to select men of good character who would pursue impartial justice. As late as 1900, he believed that there were two dangers—corruption and demagoguery—and the task of the public official was to steer a course between them.

By the time of his Progressive campaign, only one evil was still standing. The line between statesmanship and demagoguery became ever more blurred, as the Framers feared it would if public officials regularly—and not just at election time—took their case directly to the people. Roosevelt himself had once recognized this when he dismissed as "mischievous and untrue" the doctrine that the will of the people should prevail even over that of the Constitution, and he heaped scorn on those politicians—all Democrats—who proclaimed the moral perfection of the average voter (*W* 7:79–80). But now, dazzled by his own Progressive rhetoric—which placed a premium on reason and conscience, while denigrating interest as low and sordid—Roosevelt came to regard any interest that did not actively benefit the public as a "special interest." There was no place in ethical government for special interests. In almost biblical language, Roosevelt declared that "special interests must be driven out of politics." To this end, he reiterated his call for a law to prohibit the use of corporate funds "directly or indirectly for political purposes" (*W* 17:5–22). The new Republic must rise above the interest-group politics and sectional rivalries of the old Republic; it must consider politics from the higher standpoint of morality. What is at stake in ethical government is nothing less than the soul of the nation—for nations like individuals have souls. The task of ethical government, as Roosevelt already signaled in his Berlin speech, was to foster a high level of bodily goods and satisfactions without subordinating the goods of the soul. From 1910 on, he would drive this point home in ever more prophetic language.

In the short run, Roosevelt's crusade for righteousness was electrifying. One can only imagine what it was like to stand in that Chicago auditorium and listen to Roosevelt's "Confession of Faith," which ended with him proclaiming, "we stand at Armageddon and we battle for the Lord," while the faithful chanted "The Battle Hymn of the Republic." But seen from the vantage point of a new century, progressivism seems like nothing so much as a desiccated form of liberal Protestantism, a displacement onto the secular world of whatever remained of religious belief for educated Protestants after Darwin. As such, it was destined in the early decades of the twentieth century to be relegated increasingly to the sidelines, as new waves of Catholic and Jewish immigrants sought the good old material benefits that America had always offered its newcomers, rather than a thin, but still identifiably, Protestant moral revival. But as these later generations were, without even knowing it, schooled in Progressive principles and in turn grew disenchanted with "mere" material goods, it was inevitable that the spirit of the old Bull Moose would rise again.

Notes

1. *Theodore Roosevelt: An Autobiography* (New York: DaCapo Press, 1985), 27–28, hereafter cited in the text as *A*.

2. *Gouverneur Morris*, in *The Works of Theodore Roosevelt*, national edition, 20 vols. (New York: Charles Scribner's Sons, 1926), 7:327, hereafter cited in the text as *W*.

Chapter 32

Woodrow Wilson, the Organic State, and American Republicanism

Ronald J. Pestritto

The only professional political scientist ever to become president of the United States, Woodrow Wilson (1856–1924) was a prolific scholar long before his entry into public life as governor of New Jersey in 1910.[1] And while his presidency certainly offers fertile ground for study, it is Wilson's corpus of work as an academic that makes him such an important figure in the tradition of American political thought. Wilson's academic work serves as one of the primary intellectual foundations of progressivism in the United States, a movement the impact of which is nearly impossible to overstate in terms of understanding our political life in the twentieth century.

Before winning the governorship of New Jersey, Wilson held academic posts at Bryn Mawr, Wesleyan, and his alma mater Princeton, becoming the president of Princeton in 1902. After departing from the University of Virginia Law School and running a private law practice for a short time, Wilson did his graduate work at Johns Hopkins. Johns Hopkins University was explicitly established to mirror the European model of the university, and Wilson was among the first generation of political scientists educated there by a faculty at least partly trained in Europe and steeped in the tradition of German philosophy and state theory. Wilson's major political writings, on which he began work even before entering Johns Hopkins, reflect the German philosophy of history and conception of the state, and consequently strike a sharp contrast with many of the fundamental principles of American constitutionalism. Understanding Wilson's scholarship, therefore, is integral to comprehending the transformation in American political principles that the progressive movement ushered in around the turn of the twentieth century.

In his commentary on the constitutionalism of the American Founders, Wilson is perhaps most critical of its principle of limited government. For the Founders, the essential task of government was the protection of the life, liberty, and property rights of individual citizens. They took great care, as explicated in *The Federalist*, to distinguish American republicanism from older forms of self-government. While the so-called "petty republics" of ancient history had allowed the majority to control and wield the powers of government in a largely unfettered manner, Publius explained that the United States would distinguish itself by allowing the "cool and deliberate sense of the community" to govern while simultaneously guarding the rights of individuals from the threats of factious majorities. It was the very idea that majority faction poses the greatest danger to self-government which led the Founders to circumscribe carefully the scope of political authority. The scope of the federal government was limited not only by a written enumeration of its powers, but even more importantly by several institutional "improvement[s]" like the separation of powers and representation, which were designed to filter out the passionate impulses of the majority "adverse to the rights of other citizens, or to the permanent and aggregate interests of the community." For the Founders, the government's duty to protect rights from the threat of majority faction was grounded in the "laws of nature and of nature's God," and the role of government was therefore permanent. It was this transhistorical understanding of the regime's principles to which Wilson most clearly objected.

The purpose and role of government, Wilson contended, must be understood most fundamentally in terms of the particular historical age of which that government is a part and from which it draws its spirit. In providing an overview of Wilson's thought, this chapter will focus primarily on Wilson's historicism and organic concept of the state, which he lays out for the most part in his book *The State* (1898) as well as in an important early essay entitled "The Modern Democratic State." Wilson's critique of both modern social contract theory and the classical cycle of regimes merits particular attention and lays the groundwork for his explication of modern democracy and its principles. This understanding of the foundations of politics leads Wilson to propose significant changes to the American separation of powers arrangement. Accordingly, the latter part of the chapter will take up three primary elements of Wilson's institutional argument: (1) his call for a parliamentary form of government and criticism of Congress in *Congressional Government* (1885); (2) his subsequent emphasis on popular leadership in *Constitutional Government in the United States* (1908) as well as the earlier foundations of this leadership argument in essays like "Leaders of Men"; and (3) Wilson's call for an independent class of bureaucratic experts to administer progress in the modern state in writings such as "The Study of Administration" as well as in the lectures he delivered annually on public administration at Johns Hopkins University.

Wilson's Historicism and Organic Concept of the State

Perhaps the most obvious influence on Wilson, especially if one pays particular attention to his early writings, is Burke. On one level, much of Wilson's basic approach to political questions seems a Burkean reaction against social contract theory and the importation of such transhistorical theory into politics. Upon examination of the corpus of his work, Wilson can be seen to take this general Burkean inclination in several important directions. Institutionally, Wilson has a strong admiration for the British parliamentary model of government, whose gradual development out of a long historical tradition has a significant influence on his view of American constitutionalism. A second important direction is Wilson's Darwinism. While Darwin was probably even more influential on several of Wilson's contemporaries, Wilson certainly does sound Darwinian themes in his call for a constant adaptation of politics to the changing historical environment and an interpretation of the American Constitution according to the "Darwinian principle."[2] Yet the third and by far most important direction in which Wilson's thought develops is in its Hegelianism. Wilson's graduate education at Johns Hopkins seems to have been a decisive influence in this regard, although one can certainly see historicist themes in his earliest writings as well, especially those on religion. Even more than Burke or Darwin, Wilson's thought owes a substantial intellectual debt to Hegel, especially when one considers the historicism and organic state theory that serve as the backbone for Wilson's political arguments.

Wilson cites Hegel directly in his discussion of the role of philosophy or abstract thought in politics. Politics, Wilson contends, is not grounded in anything that transcends the particulars of any given historical epoch. The political principles of any age are instead reflections of its corresponding historical spirit. Wilson explains that "the philosophy of any time is, as Hegel says, 'nothing but the spirit of that time expressed in abstract thought.'"[3] This reference is taken from the preface to Hegel's *Philosophy of Right*, where Hegel argues that philosophy, properly understood, does not suggest what "ought" to be, but rather reflects historical reality. So in discussing the philosophy of the state, Hegel contends, one does not attempt to derive some transhistorical principle and use it as a guide or standard (i.e., to distinguish between nature and convention); rather, the philosophy of the state is simply a clear understanding of the actual state that history has bequeathed. As Hegel explains, his work is

> poles apart from an attempt to construct a state as it ought to be. The instruction which it may contain cannot consist in teaching the state what it ought to be; it can only show how the state, the ethical universe, is to be understood. . . . To comprehend what is, this is the task of philosophy, because what is, is reason. Whatever happens, every individual is a child of his time; so philosophy too is its own time apprehended in thoughts. It is just as absurd to fancy that a philosophy can transcend its contemporary world as it is to fancy that an individual can overleap his own age.[4]

In his textbook on government—entitled *The State*—Wilson works this reasoning out into a comprehensive argument on fundamental political principles. Wilson himself remarked that he found his research for *The State* "tedious," because he had to gain so much command of German that he "wore out a German dictionary while writing it."[5]

Wilson begins his discussion of the role of government by contending that government cannot be discussed properly by asking what its functions "ought" to be. Such a question would ground government on mere opinion, whereas "sound reasoning concerning government . . . is at all points based upon experience rather than upon theory. . . . What government does must arise from what government is: and what government is must determine what government ought to do."[6] So all thought, Wilson explains, is contingent on its historical environment. This contingency means that one cannot talk about different societies in terms of "just vs. unjust," which would require some abstract principle that can serve as the standard for such a judgment. Rather, Wilson discusses various societies in terms of their being more or less historically advanced. In commenting on our progress from the earliest forms of government, Wilson explains that the difference between societies is that some have remained mired at a primitive stage, while others have escaped from such "tutelage of inexorable custom" to adopt the more historically advanced principles of modern times. In fact, modern practices are usually more advanced than modern political ideas; our principles of government, therefore, need to catch up with historical reality —or our political "oughts" need to take their bearing from what actually "is" (*The State* 16–17).

In order to understand modern government, Wilson rejects looking to some abstract notion of justice, instead examining in detail what government actually has been and how it has evolved. Mirroring Hegel's method in *The Philosophy of History*, Wilson seeks to explicate the principles of modern politics by looking to what history has actually given us in the modern state and how such a state came to be. The state is an organic entity, Wilson asserts; it can grow and it can travel. The earliest form of the state was the primitive family or tribe, which was nomadic. This early society traveled and grew, adapting to new environments and making whatever adjustments were necessary in order to survive. The various major races of the world were "progressive" in this way, and government had its historical foundation in the progress of these races (*The State* 8, 13).

The manner in which Wilson believes progress was achieved in human history also mirrors Hegel's argument, insofar as advances were made through a dialectical process. Historical progress came through clashes of opposing customs. Tribes or peoples might develop attachments to different opinions or customs, and the antagonism and ultimate conflict between the competitors gave rise to something more advanced. In order to move history forward, major conflicts were necessary; since custom was normally a matter of religious faith, fighting between competing customs or faiths was frequently severe. Only progress came out of this dialectical process, because history only goes in one direction. "Of course," Wilson explains, "in such a competition the better custom would prevail over the worse." This argument leads to the inevitable conclusion that history advances via historically superior races or peoples defeating inferior ones, or that history favors some races over others. Indeed, Wilson comments that there are various "stagnated nationalities" who, through isolation, have not had the opportunity of coming into conflict with their superiors and who are, therefore, mired well back in the historical journey. Progress in such cases can come only when the customs and faith of such stagnated nationalities are overcome by those nationalities for whom the time is ripe—whose spirit is favored by history. Wilson's racism, which is subtly acknowledged in some of the better histories of him although rarely discussed, seems clearly connected to his adoption of this dialectical theme of German historicism. In addition to racial conflict, Wilson also reasons that progress probably had something to do with the migration of peoples. As peoples moved, the conditions of their environments changed, and so their ideas and conventions necessarily adapted and advanced accordingly (*The State* 19–21).

In several of Wilson's earliest writings, historical progress is characterized in explicitly religious language, and progress itself becomes something of a divine mission to be pursued with religious fervor. In the essay "Christian Progress," Wilson explains that the divine mission is for individuals to engage in "soul-progress." This "soul-progress" is a journey, one which we do not really control ourselves, but in which we are instead moved by God. The journey of "soul-progress" travels in only one direction; there is no going backwards. As Wilson writes of the individual's soul-progress: "there is no armor for his back, . . . to retreat is death" (*PWW* 1:234–35). The theme of progress as a religious battle, as God gradually triumphing on earth through the works of men fighting for progress, is emphasized in another of Wilson's early essays, "Christ's Army." Wilson depicts the fight for progress as a battle between the forces of righteousness and the devil's army of darkness, which is "marshaled by fiends under the dark banners of iniquity." Wilson explains that "there is no middle course" in this battle, "no neutrality"—one is either for righteousness or against it. In the early stages of the battle, the dark army scores many successes over the forces of good, but over time the righteous army becomes increasingly triumphant. "Thus," Wilson writes, "the battle of life progresses and the army of Saints ever gains ground under divine generalship" (*PWW* 1:180–81). As Hegel argues, the process of historical progress represents the gradual actualization of God's divine plan on earth, and so Wilson's battle culminates in the final victory of good over evil.

Wilson's assertion that human progress came at least partly out of a conflict between antagonistic customs also helps us to understand an important problem in politics. Given the origin of government in the family or tribe, and the strong religious attachment to the conventions of one's own tribe, it ought to be no surprise that we tend to have undue attachments to principles that are outdated or historically inferior. This observation is integral to Wilson's argument on the principles of the American Founding. While our undue reverence for the past is not as severe as many more ancient societies, Wilson contends that "we have ourselves in a measure canonized our own forefathers of the revolutionary era, worshiping them around fourth of July altars" (*The State* 15). Such faith-based attachment to the principles of our past presents a problem insofar as it makes it more difficult for us to modify those principles in accord with the present age.

The Social Contract

Wilson contends that the American attachment to the historically inferior principles of social contract theory has presented a serious obstacle to progress. His historical view of American principles is a "destructive solvent" to the social contract theory of thinkers such as Hooker and Locke which was so influential on the early Americans (*The State* 9). While social contract theorists like Locke looked to an abstract account of human nature in order to frame the purpose and scope of civil government, Wilson counters that the foundation of government can be uncovered only by looking to the actual history of its development, not to conjecture or theory. He admits that our historical knowledge of society's actual beginnings may be limited, but even limited historical knowledge is far superior to engaging in "a priori speculations" about the origin of government. Social contract theory rests upon a universal account of human nature, one that can be brought into any particular historical environment as a standard for just government. Yet Wilson reasons that looking at our contemporary human nature tells us nothing about human nature in past ages, which is why he contends that any theory of government "founded upon our acquaintance with our modern selves" cannot be universal (*The State* 1). Social contract theory is best understood as a product of the particular age in which the social contract philosophers promulgated it. The mistake of the social contract theorists—much like the mistake of the American Founders—was not in establishing certain principles of government for their own age, but in thinking that such historically contingent principles could in fact transcend history and define just government for all ages.

It is this mistaken, ahistorical notion of the social contract that Wilson puts at the center of the French Revolution, and he joins the conservative critics of the revolution by focusing on the pernicious influence of abstract theory. Government, Wilson reasons, cannot be properly founded on revolution, which attempts to overturn the historical order; it must instead develop out of the gradual, organic process of historical evolution. Europe had suffered from a failure to recognize this distinction. "Democracy in Europe, outside of Switzerland, has acted always in rebellion, as a destructive force: it can scarcely be said to have had, even yet, any period of organic development." Only through a gradual process of evolution can government be founded on a unified common will, which Wilson contrasts to the passions of "Parisian mobs" (*PWW* 5:67, 75).

The basic problem with democratic revolutions is in their characterization of democracy as a universal principle; in fact, no government can be founded on the notion of principle. The fathers of democracy put it forth as "the single principle and crown of government," while the truth is that government develops out of the reality of history, not the spontaneous proposing of principles or theories. "The construction of government," Wilson writes, "is not a matter of inspiration; reform is not a matter of invention." Historical contingency must be recognized: "Never a doctrine arrogated to itself absolute truth and perfect nutritiousness for all men alike but was eventually convicted of being only relatively true, and nutritious only under certain conditions and for certain persons." Even democracy itself, Wilson reasons, "has proved only a relative, not an absolute, good." This is why Americans still do not have an accurate conception of democracy. Their understanding, based upon the rhetoric of the Founding, conceives of democracy from the perspective of "abstract principles." So Wilson seeks to correct this misunderstanding by showing how democracy grew out of a long history of political development, from an evolutionary "order in which democracy may be seen to be but a single term" (*PWW* 5:61–63). Wilson employs the British model of democracy to correct the mistaken early American view precisely because British democracy evolved gradually from historical tradition.

Wilson contrasts the "slow and steady stages of deliberate and peaceful development" of democracy in England to the notion of democratic "revolution." A nation cannot simply adopt a government by choice, Wilson explains, which is why England is different from other nations. "The English alone have approached popular institutions *through habit*. All other races have rushed prematurely into them through mere impatience with habit: have adopted democracy instead of cultivating it." Wilson cites Burke as a champion of his organic understanding of the democratic state and uses Burke to attack the "theoretical democrats" who rely on principle divorced from history. Democracy must be seen as "the result of history, not of theory" (*PWW* 5:63–65). Wilson elaborates: "The historical view of government is in any case the only fully instructive view; in the case we are considering—the case of history's latest political fruit, democracy—it is the only view not utterly barren. Only history can explain modern democracy either to itself or to those who would imitate it" (*PWW* 5:65). The historical view of democracy has an important meaning for American institutions. If we cease to understand our democracy as one founded on timeless principles, and instead adopt the evolutionary conception of democracy, we free ourselves to make fundamental institutional alterations. If we "extend those lines of development" of which American democracy has been a part, Wilson argues, we will realize that we "can make further permanent advances. We have not broken with the past: we have, rather, understood and obeyed it." One does not break with the past, in other words, when one understands that the past represents constant change and development. The only way one breaks with the past, ironically, is by maintaining a misguided faith in the timelessness of its principles. Wilson notes that the written constitution, which distinguishes America from England, has exacerbated this problem. Written constitutions are misleading in that they appear to endorse the social contract concept of government. Given its social contract understanding of constitutionalism, Wilson explains that it was only natural for the Founding generation to see its forms of government as "definite creations." Unfortunately, such a view has proved an impediment to growth in later generations of Americans. The difficulty of the amendment process adds to the problem by reinforcing the idea that change and adaptation is generally to be avoided. "We have been too much dominated," Wilson concludes, "by the theory that our government was an artificial structure resting upon contract only," and insufficiently cognizant of the true historical foundation for the state (*PWW* 5:65, 67–68).

The contention that the true principles of government come from history leads Wilson to launch into a long discussion of the origin and history of the major tribes and peoples of the world—a discussion which occupies the bulk of Wilson's energy in *The State*. In looking to the actual history of human development, Wilson finds that social organization originated in the history of "kinship." The family was the first state, which is why Wilson investigates the characteristics of the primitive family and concludes that the modern state grew gradually out of the patriarchal family. The state's actual historical origins in the family disprove the notion of a voluntary contract as the basis for government or for any relations among individuals in society. Historically speaking, individuals in the families and tribes that constituted early societies were not radically autonomous and were not free to contract agreements. They were born into relations with and obligations to others over which they had no control. Hence, the "law of status"—not contract—governed the early conceptions of social order (*The State* 2–5, 8–9).

The argument against social contract theory also requires Wilson to discuss the role of natural law and the theorists who promoted it, whom Wilson identifies as Hobbes, Hooker, and Locke. Social contract theory, according to Wilson, comes from the state of nature argument that the original or natural condition of human life was individual autonomy, from which, "as a result of deliberate choice, in the presence of the possible alternative of continuing in this state of nature, . . . commonwealths came into being." Political society, under such an account, is a human construct that is circumscribed by the more fundamental and ahistorical law of nature. Such a view of government, Wilson asserts, gives far too much credit to human choice. The social contract theorists "bring the conception of conscious choice into the history of institutions. They look upon systems as *made*, rather than as developed." Here Wilson's criticism of social contract theory reflects Rousseau, who argued that the early contractarians had erred in their conception of government by ascribing many things to the state of nature that were, in fact, the product of man's historical development. Wilson seems to have been conscious of the Rousseau-ian nature of his argument, since the conclusion to the section of *The State* in which Wilson discusses social contract theory is made up entirely of a long citation from John Morley's book on Rousseau (*The State* 10–11, 13).

So Wilson turns away from conjecture about a state of nature and looks instead to history for his understanding of government. *The State* consequently begins with a discussion of the patriarchal family, which Wilson identifies as the true original condition of man. In such a condition, there is no concept of individualism. "All that [the individual family members] possessed, their lives even and the lives of those dependent upon them, were at the disposal of [the] absolute father-sovereign." Wilson contrasts this factual beginning of society with the radical autonomy posited by social contract theory, and concludes that the state of nature concept has led to an unfounded emphasis on the individual. The modern state originated in the historical structure of the family, Wilson argues, and is, therefore, a cohesive and fundamental political unit in its own right. The historical reality of the state's origins undermines the claim of "Locke and Locke's co-theorists" and shows how the individual was really an indistinguishable part of a larger community. Even as society developed in history, Wilson claims, "it grew without any change of this idea" (*The State* 5–6, 13–14).

Democracy Ancient and Modern

Wilson's rejection of social contract theory and the state of nature concept on which it is based does not mean that he embraces a return to the ancient political theory that the social contract theorists sought to replace. Even though Wilson's grounding of society in the family or tribe sounds certain Aristotelian themes, Wilson is just as critical of ancient thought as he is early modern thought. Of the latter, he remarks that the "theory simply has no historical foundation"; and the former, according to Wilson, "exaggerates the part played by human choice" (*The State* 11–12). Here Wilson refers to the ancient account of the origin of regimes that emphasizes the statesmanship of the lawgiver as fundamental. He explains that the ancient idea of social organization relies too heavily on the exercise of prudence by certain great individuals, or on the ability of human choice to affect historical events. Human thought and action is conditioned by its historical environment, and the ancient notion of statesmanship makes the mistake of assuming that great individuals can transcend that environment. Contrary to the ancient notion of prudence, a statesman does not take some abstract principle of justice and apply it as best he can in a particular historical situation; rather, the historical situation itself gives rise to its own principles.

Wilson is also critical of the Aristotelian cycle of regimes, and he wishes "to contrast the later facts of political development with this ancient exposition." While the Aristotelian cycle had suggested a continuous model of regime change based both upon chance events and the prudent (or imprudent) choices made by individuals, Wilson argues that history, in fact, leads to the *permanent* victory of modern democratic government. "Democracy seems about to universally prevail," Wilson contends, because the democratic form of government is the most consistent with the spirit of modern times. The idea of democracy has triumphed, which is why, unlike earlier forms of democracy, modern democracy is permanent. Wilson writes that "the cardinal difference between all the ancient forms of government and all the modern" is that "the *democratic idea* has penetrated more or less deeply all the advanced systems of government" (*The State* 32, 35–36). This is where the earlier, American Founding-era liberalism had an important role to play. While Founding-era liberalism was imperfect because it emphasized the permanent status of the individual, its victory was an essential step in the eventual triumph of modern democracy. Modern democracy came to fruition through a dialectical process: earlier, more primitive forms of self-government had to rise up and subsequently be overcome in order for history to bear its final fruit. Such reasoning also leads Wilson to praise feudalism—not because there was anything inherently good about it, but because of its historical utility: "Such a system was fatal to peace and good government, but it cleared the way for the rise of the modern State by utterly destroying the old conceptions." The Founding-era notion of the primacy of individual rights—where the state exists for the individual—was, in turn, an "inevitable" reaction against feudalism and earlier forms of statism. That modern democracy has triumphed over its earlier forms "is thus no accident, but the outcome of great permanent causes" (*The State* 38–39).

As Wilson explains in "The Modern Democratic State," the history of the state's development culminates in modern democracy—there is no more advanced form of government. "Democracy is the fullest form of state life: it is the completest possible realization of corporate, cooperate state life for a whole people" (*PWW* 5:92). This is where Wilson's Hegelianism seems to win out over his Darwinism. Instead of an endless adaptation to essentially random changes in environment, Wilson consistently refers to democracy as the intended result of history, the final stage of historical progress. Democracy "is poison to the infant," Wilson writes, "but tonic to the man." It "is a form of state life which is possible for a nation only in the adult age of its political development." The idea that democracy is the permanent end of history is an important component of Wilson's rejection of the Aristotelian cycle. When history brings about conditions whereby people act as a whole, with a unified will, true democracy has arrived for good. "The cycle of Aristotle," Wilson concludes, "is impossible. For this democracy—this modern democracy—is not the rule of the many, but the rule of the *whole*." The unity of will in modern democracy shows that society has put behind it the Aristotelian problem of the many ruling only for their own interest at the expense of the few. In modern democracy, Wilson explains, "childish fears have been outgrown." The Aristotelian cycle—like all theories of government—was a reflection of and therefore contingent upon the historical realities of its own epoch. Aristotle had erected a "philosophy of politics upon generalizations rooted in the changeful fortunes of Hellenic states the old world over." But modern democracy is different; many political thinkers fail to grasp the distinction because they fail to take into account the different historical spirit of contemporary self-government. So while the history of the twentieth century subsequent to Wilson might be cause for reevaluation, Wilson contends that modern democracy will not degenerate into tyranny, even though "many theoretical politicians the world over confidently expect modern democracies to throw themselves at the feet of some Caesar" (*PWW* 5:71–74, 76, 80–81).

Unity and the Modern State

The unity of the modern democratic state is what makes it permanent. Wilson argues that the dialectical process of the state's development, having gotten beyond the "disintegration of feudalism," has led to a unity of will that underlies modern democracy. Wilson characterizes modern society as "the whole" which "has become self-conscious, and by becoming self-directive has set out upon a new course of development" (*The State* 40). The "common will" underlying modern democratic government is what distinguishes it from ancient democracy, where the spirit of the times was not ripe for genuine democratic institutions. The real authority behind any government, Wilson explains, is the common will or spirit of the society. Even the despotic governments of past ages were based upon the common will of society, insofar as one understands the common will as an implicit expression of the spirit of the age. Wilson applies this notion of implicit will to the American Founding. The Founding generation was under the impression that it made a conscious choice of the form of government, when in fact the choice was the consequence of the spirit of the Founding era. Wilson concedes that there may have been some genuine choice exercised over minor issues—"modifications" on questions of detail—but in general the Founders' "choice" was a reflection of the spirit of the Founding epoch (*The State* 28–29).

Wilson contends that the absence of the proper condition—a unified democratic will—helps to explain the failure of the French Revolution. The French did not enjoy national unity, so the historical conditions were unripe for true democracy. Wilson comments that "Paris rioted away the liberties of France at the Revolution because it was only in Paris that there was any life. The rest of the country, never having had imperative thoughts of its own as to the way in which it should be governed, could not have them now" (*PWW* 5:82). The *revolutionary* character of the French attempt at democracy, its failure to wait for it to evolve out of the proper historical conditions, doomed the effort from the start. A necessary condition for lasting democracy, Wilson argues, is "homogeneity of race and community of thought and purpose among the people." Wilson's historicism leads him to a form of corporatism—a democracy grounded in races or groups as the fundamental political entities. Wilson explains that "there is no amalgam in democracy which can harmoniously unite races of diverse habits and instincts or unequal acquirements in thought and action." Racial purity is important because democracy requires a "habit of concerted purpose and cooperate action," or a group that is "accustomed to act as an organic body" (*PWW* 5:74–75). History moves forward not on the basis of individual action but instead by the organic development of groups or races in their corporate capacity. The contrast with Publius' argument in *The Federalist* no. 10 is important to note. For Publius, modern democracy can only succeed in a territory with many diverse interests, so that individual rights can be protected from majority faction. For Wilson, the focus is not on individual rights but on the unity of national will.

Wilson explains that government is merely the instrument of society's common will. The will of society evolves in accord with history, and government serves as the means by which society implements its organic will in a given era. It is improper to characterize government, therefore, as a necessary evil which poses a potential threat to society. Wilson asserts that government "is no more an evil than is society itself. It is the organic body of society: without it society would be hardly more than a mere abstraction." Government represents the implicit will of society, and it ties the individual to society by using its power to bring individual self-development in line with societal self-development. Government is the "means" by which "individual self-development may be made at once to serve and to supplement social development." Wilson even concedes his admiration for certain aspects of socialist government, which aims "to bring the individual with his special interests, personal to himself, into complete harmony with society with its general interests." Expressing both Rousseauian and Hegelian themes, Wilson explains that such a harmony between the subjective and the general represents a "revolt from selfish, misguided individualism." The socialists are right, Wilson contends, to criticize the modern industrial organization which has "magnified that self-interest which is grasping selfishness." The distinction that Wilson makes between the socialists and himself is that the socialists attack all competition as leading to a magnification of selfishness, whereas he merely attacks "unfair competition." Wilson's goal is to maintain individual self-development, but also to remedy the situation whereby individual self-development is encouraged at the expense of social development. History culminates in the unified will of modern society. Government, therefore, must protect society "against the competition that kills" and must reduce "the antagonism between self-development and social development to a minimum" (*The State* 60–62).

The unified will of modern society calls for development, while government makes it happen. "Government is merely the executive organ of society," Wilson explains, "the organ through which its will becomes operative." The will of society evolves historically; "society can be changed only by evolution," not revolution, which "is the antipode of evolution." As society evolves organically through the stages of history, its will informs and empowers different forms of government. Wilson admits that the form of government during any given historical epoch is not of great importance, as long as the government is grounded in the spirit of that epoch; the forms of government "exhibit the stages of political development." Wilson again cites Morley's account of Rousseau on this point, asserting that the force employed by the government is always designed to harmonize the subjective interest of the individual with the will of society. Every form of government has such an aim: "The forms of government do not affect the essence of government: the bayonets of the tyrant, the quick concert and superior force of an organized minority, the latent force of a self-governed majority—all these depend upon the character and development of the community" (*The State* 30–31).

In particular, Wilson writes that government implements the will of society through "adaptation of regulation." The government, through regulation, enables the society to stay current with the historical development of its own will. Therefore, Wilson explains, "there must be constant adjustment of governmental assistance to the needs of a changing social and industrial organization." As Wilson makes clear in his proposals for American institutions, the time had arrived for administration; the will of society was essentially unified in its understanding of the aims of government, so the most important task of government was to employ the necessary regulatory means to achieve the basic ends on which society was implicitly agreed. Wilson also reminds us that adaptive regulation implements the will of the *whole* society; we do not each individually choose our own way to evolve. We all face the same circumstances, and our common will must govern: "The circumstances of the case," Wilson contends, "are not, so far as government is concerned, the circumstances of any individual case, but the circumstances of society's case, the general conditions of social organization" (*The State* 62). No individual can self-develop through excessive economic self-interest. We all must develop together, which means that society sets the parameters for development:

> One of the most indispensable conditions of opportunity for self-development government alone, society's controlling organ, can supply. All combinations which necessarily create monopoly, which necessarily put and keep indispensable means of industrial or social development in the hands of a few, not the few selected by society itself, but the few selected by arbitrary fortune, must be under either the direct or indirect control of society. To society alone can the power of dominating by combination belong. It cannot suffer any of its members to enjoy such a power for their own private gain independently of its own strict regulation and oversight. (*The State* 62–63)

Because the state is simply the instrument of society's will for development, Wilson writes that it is both "beneficent" and "indispensable." Its regulatory power is not a potential threat to individual freedom, because that power is the organ of our own will. "If society itself be not an evil, neither surely is government an evil, for government is the indispensable organ of society" (*The State* 60).

As an indispensable and beneficent organ of society, Wilson contends that the state ought to enjoy a wide scope of power. Contrary to the Founders' constitutionalism, Wilson's state does not operate under any permanent limits to its authority. Rather, the state is both empowered and limited by the common will of society. The extent to which this common will endorses state power is contingent upon the particular stage of society's historical development. The Founding generation's strict limits on state power were proper expressions of the spirit of the Founding era. But contemporary state power, according to Wilson, needs to reflect the fact that the common will of society has evolved and that the country is operating within a more advanced historical spirit. The mistake of the Founders was to assume that their principles of limited government, which were appropriate for their own age, ought instead to serve as permanent limits to state authority in all ages. This mistake comes from the Founders' reliance on ahistorical social contract theory for establishing the aims of government, which fails to ground state power in the actual history of its development. Consequently, Wilson reasons, "government does not stop with the protection of life, liberty, and property, as some have supposed." There is no permanent principle which mandates the protection of private property; it may be regulated by the state to varying degrees depending upon the particular historical stage of development in which society finds itself. In principle, government is given broad power over an array of issues—Wilson names trade, labor, corporations, public works, sanitation, education, and sumptuary laws as examples. The extent to which government actually does exercise power over such issues is determined by society's historically conditioned will. Even political liberties and privileges, Wilson asserts, are not immune from the exercise of state power if the will of the people in a particular age endorses state action. The fundamental point is that the scope of state power is not limited by abstract or transhistorical principle. In this way, Wilson explains, there is no essential difference between modern liberal societies and ancient despotisms: in each, government exercises the power that the spirit of the times allows. As had been the case in ancient societies, "government does now whatever experience permits or the times demand; and though it does not do exactly the same things it still does substantially the same kind of things that the ancient state did" (*The State* 50–56).

The limits that America's written constitution places on the power and flexibility of the state merely reflect the principles of government particular to the Founding epoch. In his later political writings, where he deals more directly with American constitutional politics, Wilson employs his historical approach and places the American Constitution within a long pattern of historical development. "There was a time when America was blithe with self-confidence," he explains, but now "there are forces at work which she did not dream of in her hopeful youth" (*NF* 28). The problem was that America had not changed its old forms, or "processes of popular government," and so the old constitutional order was standing in the way of progress. In *Constitutional Government*, Wilson urges that the U.S. Constitution must not be interpreted as a rigid set of rules and mechanical limitations on government. Rather, a genuine "constitutional government," Wilson argues, is one "whose powers have been adapted to the interests of its people."[7] The interests of the people, as Wilson explained in *The State*, change and evolve as history moves forward, so genuine constitutional government, which is merely the organ of society's will, must adapt accordingly.

Wilson made his constitutional views part of his campaign rhetoric in 1912. In *The New Freedom*—an edited collection of his 1912 addresses on the campaign trail—an important theme is the contrast Wilson makes between a Newtonian and Darwinian understanding of the Constitution. He characterizes the constitutionalism of the Founders as Newtonian, because they had understood a written constitution mechanically—one that put strict, formulaic limits on the exercise of state power. The Founders had constructed the government "with true scientific enthusiasm"; they were "scientists in their way," which was the "best way for their age"—not the best way for the modern age. As Wilson had argued in his earlier writings, a constitution is properly understood organically, not mechanically. The Founders failed to perceive that "government is not a machine, but a living thing." It falls under the "theory of organic life. It is accountable to Darwin, not to Newton." Government, like any organism, is "modified by its environment." The old, rigid constitutional structure of limited government, therefore, must be discarded, because "no living thing can have its organs offset against each other, as checks, and live." Wilson claims that all progressives wanted was to "interpret the Constitution according to the Darwinian principle" (*NF* 46–48).

Wilson emphasizes in *Constitutional Government* an important point that he had previously developed in *The State*: a significant obstacle to a progressive constitutionalism was the Founding-era notion that the ends of government are permanent—namely, the protection of individual rights which are derived from the transhistorical "laws of nature and of nature's God." The various institutional means that the Founders had devised in order to achieve these permanent ends—what Publius called the "great improvement" to the "science of politics"—were also obstacles to progress, especially the separation of powers, bicameralism, and federalism. Whereas the Founders had considered these institutional mechanisms to be improved *means* to retaining the timeless *ends*, or "excellencies of republican government," Wilson's objection is to the very notion of permanent goals for government.[8] This distinction comes across perhaps most clearly in Wilson's interpretation of the Declaration of Independence. Its meaning, he contends, is that the idea of liberty is timeless but that the ends of government may be changed. Of the Declaration, he writes:

> We think of it as a highly theoretical document, but except for its assertion that all men are created equal it is not. It is intensely practical, even on the question of liberty. . . . It expressly leaves to each generation of men the determination of what they will do with their lives, *what they will prefer as the form and object of their liberty*, in what they will seek their happiness. . . . In brief, political liberty is the right of those who are governed to adjust the government to their own needs and interests. (*Const. Gov.* 4, emphasis added)

The "form" of liberty is left to the discretion of each generation. Consistent with his argument in *The State*, Wilson understands government as a mere instrument for the common will of society; and since that common will evolves as history progresses, so too must the very nature and role of government.

The Separation of Politics and Administration

What does Wilson's historicism and organic theory of the state mean for American political institutions?[9] Wilson had argued in *The State* that the actual forms of government are not really that important, or that "the forms of government do not affect the essence of government." This is because the point of government is to adapt its form and purpose to the evolving common will of society. As history brings society to a point where its will is increasingly unified, which is the essential historical condition for the advent of the modern democratic state, the primary task of government becomes its ability to find the specific means necessary to achieve the goals on which the will of society is implicitly agreed. Consequently, Wilson explains, the most important feature of government in the modern democratic state is administration. Regulation is the means by which government implements the implicit will of society. This regulation must be adaptive —it must enable society to stay current with the evolution of its own will (*The State* 30, 62). Politics is the arena in which society expresses its will; administration is the arena in which government carries out that will. Since history brings society to a point where its will, at least at the implicit level, is unified, the role of politics decreases in importance while that of administration increases. The essential task ceases to be figuring out what it is that society wants done, and becomes instead figuring out how to do it. As Wilson puts it in "The Art of Governing": "The period of constitution-making is past now. We have reached new territory in which we need new guides, the vast territory of *administration*" (*PWW* 5:52).

Wilson makes a very clear distinction, therefore, between politics and administration. In fact, Wilson substitutes this separation of politics and administration for the traditional separation of powers constitutionalism, which he believes to lie at the heart of the limited notion of government that must be overcome. The general key to Wilson's separation of politics and administration is to keep the former out of the way of the latter. Administration, after all, is properly the province of scientific experts in the bureaucracy, whose competence in the specific technological means required to accomplish those ends on which we are all agreed gives them the authority to administer or regulate progress unhindered by the realm of politics. Politics can claim no such expertise.

In order to understand how Wilson's fundamental thought manifests itself in his institutional proposals, one must examine both halves of the politics-administration dichotomy. First, Wilson's plan for the political arena is developed in two stages: the early Wilson emphasizes the importance of Congress and a cabinet form of government responsible to a legislative majority; the more mature Wilson becomes disillusioned with Congress and looks instead to the popular leadership of a strong and charismatic president as the key to transforming American political institutions. Second, Wilson's vision for the realm of administration relies on a highly educated bureaucratic class that can rise above politics and employ scientific, or "value free," methods of operating through regulation the increasingly complex apparatus of the modern state. While Wilson's writings on politics—Congress and the presidency in particular—have a strong popular flavor and call for a much more direct connection between public opinion and political institutions than the Founders had thought prudent, the true nature of both sides of the politics-administration divide is government by political elites. Public opinion is given much greater emphasis in Wilson's rhetoric, yet it really becomes less authoritative in his new institutional scheme. In order to explain how this is so, each half of the politics-administration dichotomy will now be briefly considered.

Popular Leadership and the Political Institutions

It is clear in *The State* that Wilson is a great admirer of the British parliamentary system. There his argument focuses on the gradual development of British democracy and, based upon Burke, his strong preference for it over the revolutionary and abstract character of the French Revolution. But Wilson also admires the particular manner in which the British Parliament conducts its business and the role that it plays in the overall British constitutional order. His analysis of the character of Parliament as an institution, and the many things that he believes American institutions could learn from it, is influenced not only by Burke but also by the long study Wilson made of Walter Bagehot's writings. What Wilson learned from Bagehot was that Parliament is an institution ideally suited for separating politics and administration. Under the parliamentary model, the legislature closely reflects public opinion, while a separate, permanent, apolitical bureaucracy manages the business of day-to-day governing. Wilson's vision for Congress—expressed most famously in his book *Congressional Government* (which served as his doctoral dissertation)—wants the legislature to be much more closely tied to public opinion, on the one hand, yet wants most of the real decision-making power shifted away from legislators and into the realm of bureaucracy, on the other hand. The energy of this increasingly democratized Congress needs to be channeled into its "informing function," which Wilson contends is to "be preferred even to its legislative function."[10] Through debate that needs to be more open to the public eye, Congress is urged to become more dependent on the will of the people; yet, that public will is really to have no more say over actual governing, since Congress itself is urged to cede such responsibility to the professional, unelected administrators.

Wilson also looks for Congress to provide leadership. Under the separation of powers scheme, there is no coordination between the different branches of government—no one branch or official is responsible for moving the whole of government in a particular direction. In his early writings, Wilson seeks to overcome this lack of cohesion with an accountable Congress that will serve as a superintending embodiment of the public will. Consequently, he calls for a breakdown in the separation between the legislative and executive branches along the lines of a parliamentary system. At one point, Wilson even suggests allowing congressional leaders to serve as cabinet officials (*PWW* 2:627–28). This way, state action would cease being checked by antagonisms between the president and Congress, and instead the government could exercise its power in a more efficient, coordinated manner. Yet without real leadership in Congress, Wilson laments that there can be no real leadership in national politics. The Congress that Wilson observed in the latter part of the nineteenth century was so disorganized internally, with its secretive debates and a committee system where power was dispersed among a variety of chairmen each with his own personal fiefdom, that it could not fulfill the leadership role Wilson has in mind. Wilson believes that perhaps a stronger, accountable party system can help to achieve a closer connection between public will and public policy. Parties in the legislature should be clearly organized, under leaders who are easily recognized. In this way, voters can—through their electoral support or rejection of these prominent party leaders and their parties—make known their will and bring it to bear in the lawmaking process (*Cong. Gov.* 57–61, 79–80).

As Wilson's thought on American institutions matured, he became more convinced that Congress would never be able to fulfill the new institutional role that he was contemplating for it. The impediments to national leadership that Wilson had seen in Congress in his early writings convinced the later Wilson that Congress would never sufficiently embody the unity of national will needed to lead the "politics" side of the politics-administration dichotomy. This realization led Wilson to turn to the popular leadership of the president. He writes that "the House seems to have missed . . . the right to be [the nation's] principal spokesman in affairs." Because the House had "greatly weakened itself as an organ of public opinion," the president's popular leadership needed to be developed and strengthened (*Const. Gov.* 109).

Wilson looks to the president for the same reason that he had initially focused on Congress: he seeks leadership that can coordinate all the disparate parts of government and overcome the tedious separation of powers system in favor of an efficient vehicle for the exercise of state power. Wilson realizes that the president is the public official most directly connected to the public will, and as such it is the president who can rise above the separation of powers and lead the whole of government on the basis of the public's unified will. This is why Wilson emphasizes the personal leadership traits of the president, not his office or his constitutional duties. The president comes to embody the public will through his personality and connection to the people, not through his connection to the Constitution. The constitutional president is merely one of three parts of government, whereas the person of the president can lead the whole of government through his direct connection to the whole will of society (*Const. Gov.* 65–67). If the president is to provide the kind of coordination and leadership that Wilson envisions—if he is to overcome the rigid separation of powers structure that seeks to confine public officials to their respective branches—then the president will need some extraconstitutional tools in order to accomplish his mission. For Wilson, these tools consist of a reinvigorated party system and an aggressive style of direct popular rhetoric. The party system is a way for the president to exercise leadership over fellow party members in the other branches and levels of government and to coordinate their efforts in a way that circumvents the formal separation of powers. The party is an "exterior organization . . . whose object it shall be to bind [the branches] together in some sort of harmony and cooperation" (*Const. Gov.* 207). Popular rhetoric is to be employed not only to put the president into more direct contact with public opinion but also as a means for the president to use public opinion as a way of moving both the government and the people themselves in the direction that the president believes history to be traveling. It is in this way that the democratic nature of Wilson's rhetoric can also facilitate an elite form of political leadership.

Even though many of Wilson's political writings complain that the institutional scheme of the Founders puts governing at too great a distance from public opinion, and even though Wilson's proposals for Congress and especially the presidency call for those institutions to come into much more direct contact with the public will, Wilson's actual argument on presidential power and rhetoric does not allow for as much popular control of governing as might first be believed. While the political institutions become democratized in a certain way, this democratization tends to put power in the hands of governing elites who have advanced knowledge of the spirit of the age and the course of history. It is certainly the case that Wilson's famous chapter on the presidency in *Constitutional Government* emphasizes the president's connection to the people. Yet Wilson's president seems to serve not merely (or even primarily) as a follower of the public's will, but as its potential shaper and leader.

The ideal leader is someone who can take his own vision of society's direction and use popular rhetoric to draw the people to it and move them accordingly. It is for this very purpose that the democratic nature of Wilson's presidency is essential. A more democratized presidency is one that is more amenable to the tools of popular rhetoric; it is one where the leader can use his mastery of popular rhetoric to mold public opinion. Wilson writes that "a president whom [the country] trusts can not only lead it, but form it to his own views." Such a president leads by "giving direction to opinion" (*Const. Gov.* 66, 68). As Wilson had explained in *The State*, government is the means by which society keeps up with evolution of its own implicit will; government must adapt to the changes in public will brought about by the force of history. In his essay "Leaders of Men," Wilson suggests that a good leader is not so much concerned with simply figuring out what the public will is and using government to implement it. Rather, the leader seems to be a particularly keen interpreter of the spirit of the times, and may therefore know the direction in which history is pulling the public will better than the public itself (*PWW* 6:659). The purpose of the leader's skillful popular rhetoric, at least partly, is to convince the public that he in fact has the most advanced vision of history's course and that his vision represents the future course of their own will. For Wilson, the presidency must be made more democratic precisely so that the president's rhetorical skill can be employed to move the masses more efficiently in the direction that the leaders believe history is traveling (*PWW* 6:649–50).

Wilson's argument on elite leadership is also evident in his discussion of the proper historical conditions for genuine democracy. In "The Modern Democratic State," Wilson writes that the improved education of modern times has effected an essential condition for the advent of democracy. This is an education where the elites are better equipped to lead, and the people are better equipped to follow that elite leadership: "Where all minds are awake some minds will be wide awake. And such are the conditions of common counsel: a few minds to originate and suggest, many minds to weigh and appreciate; some to draw up resolutions, many to consider them. . . . Not everybody can lead: but everybody can have a voice in deciding results" (*PWW* 5:91). Universal education helps to make the people capable of considering leadership suggestions. But modern education not only aids in facilitating political leadership; it also is essential to developing an elite class of scientific experts who will serve as the nation's administrators. While political leaders are responsible for moving the public will in the direction of history, the educated administrative apparatus must manage the daily details of progress.

Apolitical Administration

Even in his earliest writings, Wilson sounds the call for a class of educated experts who can rise above the corruption and narrowness of politics. Wilson saw a political system mired in special interest conflict, and he concluded that a young, apolitical class was what the country needed in order to right itself. Much in the same manner that today's culture eschews partisanship of any kind, especially among the young, Wilson writes that "it would not be the part either of wisdom or of good will to encourage young men to do service in the partisan contentions of politics" (*PWW* 2:33). Instead, Wilson contends that this young, educated, apolitical class must focus its energies on "national administration." He elaborates:

> The greatest issue of the time seems an issue of life and death. If the national administration can be reformed it can endure; if it cannot be, it must end. Robust as its constitution has proved to be, the federal government cannot long continue to live in the poisonous atmosphere of fraud and malfeasance. If the civil service cannot by gentle means be purged of the vicious diseases which fifty years of the partisan spoils system have fixed upon it, heroic remedies must be resorted to.

The focus of the newly educated nonpartisan class must be to bring "a new spirit"—"not a new party"—to "the present treatment and future settlement of this and others of the pressing questions of public administration." Wilson again expresses the theme that modern education is integral to training this new class of apolitical experts. In particular, the elite universities should take it as their primary mission to train those who will objectively administer the state. "An intelligent nation cannot be led or ruled save by thoroughly-trained and completely-educated men," Wilson explains. "Only comprehensive information and entire mastery of principles and details can qualify for command." Wilson trumpets the power of expertise—of "special knowledge, and its importance to those who would lead" (*PWW* 2:34–36).

Expertise is necessary for national administration because, as Wilson argues in "The Study of Administration," the "business" of governing has become increasingly complex. The politics-administration distinction allows this complex business of the modern state to be handled by a professional class of experts, instead of by a multiplicity of politicians with narrow, competing, and subjective interests. Wilson praises the civil service movement because it sought to professionalize government—making it more efficient in terms of both personnel and organization. The new personnel would be more efficient administrators because they would be divorced from the realm of politics (*PWW* 5:370). It is for this purpose of reducing political control over administration that Wilson attacks the practice of senatorial courtesy in executive appointments. It is a "very sorry, unseemly thing," Wilson writes, to give individual senators the power to reward political supporters through the de facto appointment power that senatorial courtesy provides them. In particular, the practice is anathema to the idea of civil service reform, and Wilson recognizes that, if civil service reform is to advance, the constitutional prerogative of the Senate to confirm appointments must recede in significance. "By common consent," he reasons, "civil-service reform must grow, and stretch its branches far and wide, even though its roots do spread themselves in such a way as inconveniently to encroach upon and cramp certain constitutional principles" (*PWW* 5:44–45). Wilson's solution to the conflict between civil service reform and the "advice and consent" power of the Senate is to place the appointment power exclusively in the hands of a single executive. In this way, corruption cannot be hidden among a group of relatively obscure individuals in the legislature, and it will be more difficult for politics to taint the vital mission of administration (*PWW* 5:48).[11]

The important point for Wilson is the idea that administrative principles and constitutional or political principles are quite distinct. Wilson refers to "the patriotism" and "the disinterested ambition" of the new professional class that will enable it objectively to adjust government to the modern spirit. The attempt to bring administration within the constitutional order—to look for administrative authority to rest on more fundamental constitutional authority—had created a significant obstacle to efficient adaptation. If we understand the clear distinction between politics and administration, or between constitutional law and regulation, it "might deliver us from the too great detail of legislative enactment; give us administrative elasticity and discretion; free us from the idea that checks and balances are to be carried down through all stages of organization" (*PWW* 7:122). Wilson relies heavily on European sources for his study of administration. His sources were foreign precisely because his approach to administration was a novelty to American constitutionalism: namely, the notion that there are legitimate state powers beyond those granted by the Constitution to the political branches of government. As he explains:

> The functions of government are in a very real sense independent of legislation, and even constitutions, because as old as government and inherent in its very nature. The bulk and complex minuteness of our positive law, which covers almost every case that can arise in Administration, obscures for us the fact that Administration cannot wait upon legislation, but must be given leave, or take it, to proceed without specific warrant in giving effect to the characteristic life of the State. (*PWW* 7:121)

Wilson suggests that the question of how far the law circumscribes the scope of administrative discretion is an unsettled question in America, and he urges that administration be properly understood and given as wide a sphere as possible. This wide sphere for administration means that it would have to cross over the traditional separation of powers boundaries; indeed, Wilson contrasts the theory of separation of powers to what he calls the "actual division of powers," where there are many "legislative and judicial acts of the administration" (*PWW* 7:134–38).

The wide berth that Wilson wants to give to administrative decision making helps to answer the question of who it is that actually governs under Wilson's system. While Wilson is an advocate of making politics much more directly connected with public opinion, his writings show that the public is not to be brought more directly into the realm of administrative decision making. "The problem," Wilson explains, "is to make public opinion efficient without suffering it to be meddlesome." Public opinion is a "clumsy nuisance" when it comes to the "oversight of the daily details and in the choice of the daily means of government." So while public opinion ought to be brought more directly into politics, politics must confine itself to general superintendence—to the role of expressing the unified will of the nation. "Let administrative study," Wilson writes, "find the best means for giving public criticism this control and for shutting it out from all other interference" (*PWW* 5:374–75).

Wilson places administrative power on an entirely different plane from constitutional power, and it is this sharp distinction between constitutional politics and administrative discretion that differentiates Wilson from those earlier American thinkers who had also placed great importance on national administration—particularly Alexander Hamilton. While it is common for scholars to refer to Wilson and Hamilton in the same breath on matters of administration, and while Wilson himself occasionally found it convenient to claim the label of "Hamiltonian," it is essential to remember that Wilson saw his argument on administration as something almost completely foreign precisely because the American tradition had failed to perceive the sharp contrast between constitutional and administrative power. Wilson explains that administration "stands apart even from the debatable ground for constitutional study. . . . Administrative questions are not political questions." This is why Wilson has to admit that it is difficult to conceive how one might place administrative discretion of the sort he had in mind within the traditional constitutional order: "One cannot easily make clear to every one just where administration resides in the various departments" (*PWW* 5:371). The key feature of Hamilton's argument for national administration, by contrast, was its placing of administrative authority (as broad as Hamilton surely envisioned it) in a subordinate position within the constitutional order. While Hamilton advocated an energetic national administration, his vision was different from Wilson's insofar as administrative power was always understood to be an instrument of an energetic executive and therefore accountable to the constitutional authority granted to the executive by the people. In *The Federalist* no. 68, Hamilton does, after all, call it a "heresy" to say that "For forms of government let fools contest—that which is best administered is best."[12] Here he essentially calls Wilson a heretic, since it is Wilson's argument that the form of government is not nearly as important as its ability to implement the common will through administration. For Hamilton, unlike Wilson, one could not conceive of administrative powers somehow bestowed upon the state outside of the formal grant of power by the Constitution to the political branches.

The other, even more fundamental, difference between Hamilton and Wilson, which helps to demonstrate the sharp contrast between Wilson and the Founders' constitutionalism in general, is their understanding of the ends of government. For Hamilton, an increasingly energetic national administration was important as an improved *means* to the permanent and limited ends of government. In other words, Hamilton saw the increased administrative power of the national government as a way to better secure the natural rights of individuals—the timeless goals of any just government. From the perspective of Hamilton and many of the Founders, the practice of government in most states during the 1780s constituted a grave failure to fulfill the fundamental obligation of government to secure rights (the paper money rage is a primary example), and a newly energized national government was seen as a potential solution to that problem. In this respect, while Hamilton differed markedly with Thomas Jefferson on the question of means, they were agreed on the essential purpose and role of government, with which the historicist state theory of Wilson is directly at odds.

The use of the labels "Hamiltonian" and "Jeffersonian"—both by the Progressives themselves and by those who have written about the Progressive Era—to distinguish between various elements of the movement is, therefore, misleading. While Hamilton and Jefferson disagreed passionately about the means of government, they were far more akin to each other on the fundamental principles of government than either of them is to Wilson. In the literature on the American political tradition, some historians and political scientists prefer to use the "Hamiltonian vs. Jeffersonian" dichotomy to characterize the differences between progressive figures like Wilson, on the one hand, and Herbert Croly or Theodore Roosevelt, on the other. As useful as such a distinction might be in analyzing the diversity of the Progressive movement, it also poses the danger of hiding the far more fundamental principled difference between progressive liberalism, which is grounded in historicism, and Founding-era liberalism, which is grounded in transhistorical natural rights theory and to which Hamilton and Jefferson were both primary adherents.

Such a contrast between Wilson's and the Founders' constitutionalism will strike some as creating a tension with those of Wilson's writings that adopt the mantle of Jefferson, Hamilton, or the Founders generally. It is certainly the case that Wilson does, at times, place his own thought within the constitutional tradition of the Founding generation. But in this regard, there is an important distinction between Wilson's substantial academic writings and his political writings. In his scholarly writings and lectures, Wilson is quite clear that the nature of his thought does not derive out of the American tradition. He emphasizes in his arguments on administration that a great difference between the American tradition and the state theory that he wishes to import is that the Americans do not consider administration to be a discipline distinct from constitutional study. Wilson makes it a point to highlight this departure from the American tradition in his lectures on administration, which he gave annually at Johns Hopkins from 1888 to 1897. If one looks to the section on "the literature of the science" from Wilson's published notes for the Johns Hopkins lectures, one will find listed under modern sources sixteen German titles, twelve French, and one English. Wilson explains that the single English-language source—Frank J. Goodnow's *Comparative Administrative Law*—is "the only systematic work in English devoted distinctively to Administration as a separate 'discipline'" (*PWW* 7:118–20). It is here in his scholarly work that Wilson is at his most intellectually honest. It was not as if no Americans had written about national administration or that they considered it unimportant— Hamilton is but one prominent example. Rather, the American administrative argument did not conceive of administrative power as something separate from constitutional power, and this was a conception that had to be corrected by German state theory. In defense of his admiration for "the administrative systems of France and Germany," Wilson writes famously in "The Study of Administration": "If I see a murderous fellow sharpening a knife cleverly, I can borrow his way of sharpening the knife without borrowing his probable intention to commit murder with it" (*PWW* 5:379). As for his political writings and speeches, where Wilson tends to claim the tradition of the Founders as a foundation for his own arguments, it is clear that Wilson understands the difference between an academic and a popular audience. In American politics, a prudent politician knows that he will get much further claiming the authority of Jefferson, Hamilton, and the rest of the Founders than he will by trumpeting Hegel and Herbert Spencer. Any thorough study of Wilson's actual thought, however, including that aspect of it expressed in his political writings, reveals a stark contrast indeed with the constitutional tradition on which the country was founded.

Notes

1. The author wishes to thank the Earhart Foundation for a fellowship research grant that supported the research for this chapter.

2. Woodrow Wilson, *The New Freedom* (New York: Doubleday, Page and Company, 1913), 48, hereafter cited in the text as *NF*.

3. Wilson, "The Study of Administration," in *The Papers of Woodrow Wilson*, 69 vols., ed. Arthur S. Link (Princeton, N.J.: Princeton University Press, 1966–1993), 5:361, hereafter cited in the text as *PWW*.

4. G. W. F. Hegel, *Philosophy of Right*, trans. T. M. Knox (London: Oxford University Press, 1967), 11.

5. Henry Wilkinson Bragdon, *Woodrow Wilson: The Academic Years* (Cambridge, Mass.: Belknap Press, 1967), 173. Wilson's comments were made to Charles H. McIlwain, whom Bragdon interviewed.

6. Wilson, *The State*, revised special edition by Edward Elliott (Boston: D. C. Heath and Co., Publishers, 1918), 41–42, hereafter cited in the text.

7. Wilson, *Constitutional Government in the United States* (New York: Columbia University Press, 1911), 2, hereafter cited in the text as *Const. Gov.*

8. Publius, *The Federalist Papers*, ed. Charles R. Kesler and Clinton Rossiter (New York: Mentor, 1999), no. 9, 40–41.

9. An overview of Wilson's thought can emphasize several different themes. This chapter focuses most of its energy on Wilson's fundamental political principles—his historicism and organic state theory. Considerations of space prevent us from commenting extensively on Wilson's plan for transforming American institutions other than the brief arguments here on his separation of politics and administration, and his popular leadership model.

10. Wilson, *Congressional Government* (Gloucester, Mass.: Peter Smith, 1973), 198, hereafter cited in the text as *Cong. Gov.*

11. Wilson also connects this problem to the municipal appointment power of mayors and the corruption that comes from the involvement of city council members.

12. *The Federalist Papers* no. 68, 382.

Chapter 33

The Making of the Modern Supreme Court: Oliver Wendell Holmes, Jr., and Louis D. Brandeis

David F. Forte

Oliver Wendell Holmes, Jr., (1841–1935) and Louis D. Brandeis (1856–1941) are the progenitors of the modern Supreme Court and, through the Court, of much of modern America. Holmes and Brandeis were as disparate as two men could be: one the Yankee Brahmin, self-conscious heir to America's natural aristocracy; the other a German Jew seeking a new America. Holmes was the pessimistic skeptic and was outspokenly honest about his skepticism; Brandeis was the optimistic progressive who was sometimes dissimulative in his methods. One despaired of social betterment; the other made it his life's work. One focused on the process of the law and rejected any larger good; the other dedicated his life to a change in social relations and used the law as one means to that end. Despite his philosophy, Holmes became an icon of the Progressives. He craved the adulation and left to the Progressives to make of his skepticism what they would.

Together, the seemingly incongruent philosophies of Holmes and Brandeis became the philosophy of generations of legal academics, law students, law clerks, and judges. The modern Supreme Court justice came to define his persona and his office in their image. From Holmes, the modern judge learned to reject the moral hold of precedent and of the constitutional structure that had previously cabined the judicial craft; from Brandeis, he learned how to construct a social program while clothing it in judicial form. Strangely, Holmes believed that the Supreme Court should be a restrained actor in the government, and Brandeis believed in small government. Both were far more restrained than their followers turned out to be. Yet from their legacy, the modern Supreme Court became a chief catalyst in the social redefinition of America and a partner in the expansion of governmental power. In the process, the Court redefined the Constitution of 1787.

Social Darwinism and the Common Law in Holmes's Jurisprudence

Every man is his own agent in life. Yet every person comes to accept or to reject proffered models and ideas. Beyond his innate brilliance and extraordinary ambition, there were three particular influences that shaped the life of Oliver Wendell Holmes, Jr.: his father, his experience in the Civil War, and the new philosophies that came to dominate American intellectual life immediately following the Civil War. Although Holmes's relationship with his father, Dr. Oliver Wendell Holmes, was not without friction, the elder Holmes profoundly influenced his son. Dr. Holmes had turned from a short but eminent life in academic medicine to that of an essayist. He eschewed the care of individuals and sought instead their admiration. He was remarkably successful in the endeavor, crafting literary and discursive gems that were popular among the middle class and the literati. He counted among his friends Ralph Waldo Emerson and Henry Wadsworth Longfellow. From his father, Holmes, Jr., absorbed a standard of what constituted social success. Surrounded by luminaries, the younger Holmes set himself the goal to become one. He carried into life Puritan culture without Puritan belief. He had no faith, but he did have style, duty, and craft. Along with his father, Holmes also understood the power of the well-crafted phrase, the structured argument, and the mastery of language. Like his father, Holmes sought the role of the influential observer, the trenchant essayist; but, unlike his father, Holmes did not turn away from the practice of his profession, in his case as lawyer and judge.

Dr. Holmes's most famous collection of essays, *The Autocrat of the Breakfast Table*, appeared in 1859. In topics ranging from class reunions to the nature of literary criticism, the senior Holmes affected an attitude of the casual but witty and confident critic, skewering the pretensions of philosophies and opinions he found wanting. His freethinking philosophy was garbed in an avuncular style, in contrast to the more elegant manner of his friend Emerson and the New England Transcendentalists. The younger Holmes replicated the same observational stance when he later set about to dismantle the received structures and traditions of American law but with far more rigor and depth. In fact, what most irked Holmes was his father's diffidence, particularly before the Civil War when Holmes, Jr., was a committed abolitionist and his father something of a lukewarm unionist. Even later, when Holmes gave up on virtually all ideals, he retained in his character a passionate embrace of the world of ideas. After he retired from the Supreme Court when he was nearly ninety-one years old, Holmes continued his rigorous regimen of reading "for improvement." Moreover, he worked at his craft of judging in a way his father had never done to medicine. His later admirers gave him an Olympian status, but Holmes's own kind of diffidence never became distance. His Civil War diary is filled with a gritty realism, and his judicial opinions have a fresh directness.

The two Holmeses did share a committed freethinking philosophy—a felt manly and intellectual disdain for religion and its perceived superstitions. After receiving a serious and possibly mortal chest wound at the Battle of Ball's Bluff, Holmes recalled:

> Of course when I thought I was dying the reflection that the majority vote of the civilized world declared that with my opinions I was *en route* to Hell came up with painful distinctness—Perhaps the first impulse was tremulous—but then I said—by Jove, I die like a soldier anyhow—I was shot in the breast doing my duty up to the hub—afraid? No, I am proud—then I thought I couldn't be guilty of a deathbed recantation—father and I had talked of that and we were agreed that it generally meant nothing but a cowardly giving way to fear.[1]

Holmes's experience in the Civil War pushed the freethinking philosophy of his father into a harder-edged skepticism, sometimes darkened with hues of cynicism. He later told a young admirer that "[a]fter the Civil War the world never seemed quite right again," and to his parents he confessed that he was not the same man.[2] At the beginning of the Civil War, Holmes was an enthusiastic abolitionist. He had been a bodyguard to Wendell Phillips against gangs of unionists. He precipitously left Harvard College to enlist, but he was called back to finish his exams and to graduate. By the war's end, he cared little for the situation of the freedman, and in his years on the bench, he did little to ameliorate the plight of the Negro.

Wounded three times in the war, Holmes was witness to its carnage and human waste. He was no longer inclined to see a higher purpose in the effort and turned aside an offer to accept a commission as major in the newly organized 54th Massachusetts, the black regiment organized under Robert Gould Shaw. His own regiment, the 20th Massachusetts, was dubbed the "Copperhead regiment" because of the anti-Negro opinions of many of its officers. After he was wounded at Antietam, Holmes lost hope. The Union effort, he believed, was directed only at "the subjugation . . . of a great civilized nation." "Believe me," he wrote, "[w]e shall never lick 'em."[3] Holmes later came to see the value of war as in the struggle itself—not in what it accomplished. What one fights for was illusory, but that one fights allows one "to come down to truth" (*LWV* 47).

Wounded a third time at Chancellorsville, Holmes's deepest cut of all was likely the death of his closest friend, Major Henry L. Abbott. Completely out of sympathy to the Union cause, Abbott nonetheless fulfilled his duty, conducting himself in battle with coolness and grace. He carried himself with perfect composure during the terrible battle of Fredericksburg, Holmes later declared, "in obedience to superior command to certain and useless death, when the order he was obeying was countermanded" (*LWV* 223n47). At his death, the commanding general had said of Abbott that "[m]y brigade lost in him its best soldier" (*HJ* 83). For his part, Holmes declared: "In action he was sublime. . . . [F]or us, who not only admired, but loved, his death seemed to end a portion of our life also" (*HJ* 23). Abbot became an icon for the skeptical Holmes. He had fought for no cause. But he fought to fight—to engage in the struggle. And this became, for Holmes, the meaning of life. "[L]ife is war, and the part of man in it is to be strong" (*LWV* 47). He later said, "I rejoice at every dangerous sport which I see pursued. The students at Heidelberg with their sword slashed faces, inspire me with sincere respect" (*LWV* 22).

When his term of service was up, Holmes had had enough of the war and did not reenlist. He returned to Cambridge and entered Harvard Law School. He began his practice in 1867. Holmes was remarkably well placed among the young intellectuals of his day. For example, he counted as intimates William and Henry James and Henry Adams. His friends John Gray and Henry Ropes began the *North American Law Review*, and Holmes began his scholarly career writing frequent articles for it and reviewing many books. He plunged into reading American and English legal digests in order to write commentaries on recent cases. James Bradley Thayer, a member of the law firm in which Holmes worked and later a renowned member of the faculty of Harvard Law School, hired Holmes to produce a new edition of *Kent's Commentaries*. Holmes also began lecturing at Harvard Law School, counting among his students Brooks Adams and Henry Cabot Lodge.

Although he also read avidly in philosophical works, Holmes had already found his touchstone. While he was recovering from his wounds after Chancellorsville and undoubtedly deep in despair about the war's outcome, he read Herbert Spencer's *Social Statics and First Principles*.[4] Its theory (later called "social Darwinism") gave Holmes an organizing principle for a life that had lost its luster—that had become a struggle without ideals—a modern echo of his inherited, attenuated Puritanism. He remarked of Spencer, "I doubt if any writer of English except Darwin has done so much to affect our whole way of thinking about the universe" (*LWV* 49). Social Darwinism provided for Holmes something that made a larger sense of a world otherwise without meaning. When confronted with the optimism of Brandeis, Holmes confessed that he thought Thomas Malthus had the better view of things. It was Holmes's belief in the mechanism of social Darwinism, not morality and certainly not "Providence," that led him to say sincerely that "everything that happens, happens for the best." Holmes's view of struggle would be the principle that would later help him to inform his understanding of the deeper forces of the law. In this regard, it is important to note that Holmes did not accept the natural rights element of Spencer's philosophy. Even later in life when he began to defend the right of free expression, it was not as an element of human rights but of social necessity.

In 1872, Holmes and a coterie of rising new intellectuals met frequently to discuss new ideas. Such groupings were not an innovation; they had been part of New England intellectual life for some time. This group included lights like Henry James, Charles Pierce, and Chauncey Wright, who would be among those who would help to usher in an age of the allied philosophies of pragmatism, scientism, positivism, and historicism (see generally *MC*). Holmes was in his medium; for he had decided to make his mark upon the world as a man of ideas, and those ideas would be in the law.

James Bradley Thayer had not only given Holmes the opportunity for scholarly fame in editing *Kent's Commentaries*, but he was also the instrument that obtained for Holmes positions of great social prominence. Working with Holmes's admirer and recent Harvard Law School graduate Louis Brandeis, Thayer obtained an anonymous grant to fund a chair for Holmes at the law school in 1882. The same year, Thayer lobbied to have Holmes appointed to a seat on the Massachusetts Supreme Judicial Court, the bench on which Holmes's maternal grandfather had been chief justice. The appointment came through, and after only a few months on the faculty of Harvard Law School, Holmes's judicial career had begun.

His intellectual stature, however, had already been earned. In 1881, he published his seminal work, *The Common Law*. In its opening paragraph, he penned a phrase that has likely been the most oft-quoted aphorism in American legal language: "The life of the law has not been logic: it has been experience." He furthered developed his thesis: "The felt necessities of the time, the prevalent moral and political theories, institutions of public policy, avowed or unconscious, even the prejudices which judges share with their fellow-men, have had a good deal more to do than the syllogism in determining the rules by which men should be governed."[5] As stated, Holmes's thesis might be seen as simply an elegant defense of pragmatism. Various scholars have not only attributed pragmatism to Holmes, but he has also been placed in the schools of analytical utilitarianism, scientific materialism, historicism, and even a proto-existentialism.[6] But Holmes detested pragmatism as a philosophy and denied he was a utilitarian. He had little patience with philosophies that pretended to solve everything. Of course, being the irascible skeptic he may have simply been following the stylistic lead of his father by skewering any of the contemporary intellectual fads. In fact, there are strong undercurrents of all those philosophies in Holmes. For example, he does reflect the historicist tradition to explain the development of the law. Sir Henry Maine's writings had opened up a method of explication that Holmes adapted to his uses.[7]

But Oliver Wendell Holmes, Jr., had his own philosophy. The "felt necessities of the time" that drive the law turn out to have a particular content for him: a social Darwinist mechanism by which one social group seeks to dominate others.[8] Self-preservation and dominance were the twin impulses that at bottom drove the law, though older legal forms may live on providing a salutary sense of historical continuity. In *The Common Law*, for example, Holmes opines that vengeance lay at the base of theories of liability, whether the offending agent be a person or an inanimate object. Vengeance and retaliation, of course, are the instinctive reactions of a being that seeks to preserve itself. Holmes explains that as civilization developed, rectification requires the pursuit of the offender through to its owner or master, and later, in particular and refined instances, to the owner who is at fault. Many of the original forms of the law that lay in simple vengeance remain but with a rationale that now includes notions of fault-based liability. "The truth is, that the law is always approaching, and never reaching, consistency. It is forever adopting new principles from life at one end, and it always retains old ones from history at the other, which have not yet been absorbed or sloughed off. It will become entirely consistent only when it ceases to grow" (*CL* 36). That the historicist understanding of law's development described merely the form of the working out of the social Darwinist drive is seen more particularly in his treatment of the criminal law. There, Holmes took pains to divorce the criminal law from any moral basis whatsoever. Although he states that the criminal law also had its source in the instinct for vengeance, once society is organized, the rationale is solely to prevent harms that society regards as unacceptable. He develops an "external" theory of the criminal law, defining offenses not by the moral guilt of the actor but by whether the action is unacceptable to the dominant forces of society.

In his discussion of murder, for example, malice is without moral content. Holmes defines malice solely as intent, and then, in his famous exegesis, defines intent as foresight, and foresight as what a man of ordinary prudence (not the actual man committing the act) should know of the peril of the circumstances he is in at the moment he chooses to act. A man who chooses to fire a gun at another man is presumed to know that the action of the gun, its aim, and the trajectory of the bullet will likely cause the death of the object of his action. The reasons for the action (save self-defense, which the community regards not as a danger but as a necessary protection) are irrelevant. When Holmes gets to more difficult questions, such as the punishment for felony murder and other crimes that seem at odds with his neat notion of intent, he is untroubled. Some circumstances are seen by the community as so dangerous that even the reasonably prudent man will be held to account if he acts in that way. This becomes a form of strict liability. "No society has ever admitted that it could not sacrifice individual welfare to its own existence," he writes (*CL* 43). "The reason for punishing any act must generally be to prevent some harm which is foreseen as likely to follow that act under the circumstances in which it is done" (*CL* 67). Holmes admits that the rules of the criminal law fall harder on the weakest. "For it is precisely to those who are most likely to err by temperament, ignorance, or folly, that the threats of the law are the most dangerous" (*CL* 51). But, as Holmes avowed elsewhere, that was the cost of how the struggle of history worked itself out.

Many have said that Holmes destroyed the legal formalism that had typified American legal thought, particularly since the days of Joseph Story. Holmes, it is said, opened the door for judges to mold the common law in light of the realities of modern day industrial life. Others have claimed that Holmes had set up a straw man—that the law was not nearly so rigid or formal as he had claimed and that the hallmark of American political and legal culture was its optimistic grounding in the realm of experience. Many modern legal commentators have subjected *The Common Law* to withering criticism. Whether or not the critics are correct, what Holmes had accomplished in fact was a fundamental normative change in the manner in which judges saw their role.

Previously, judges had been restrained by a sense of their own illimitable power. Over centuries, judges had developed a normative set of self-imposed limits within which they should exercise their office. In the words of Michael Polanyi: "The freedom of this subjective person to do as he pleases is overruled by the freedom of the responsible person to act as he must."[9] It was this tradition that led the Framers to devise so few checks upon the judicial branch. They did not think them necessary. It was this tradition that had led Alexander Hamilton to opine optimistically that the courts are the least dangerous branch, asserting that they use judgment not will (*The Federalist* no. 78). Until Holmes, even though they repaired to experience, judges nonetheless still saw law as a "given," and they believed that they were interpreting it within a larger tradition of natural law. True, natural law as a discipline had been in long decline, but its inheritance provided judges with a sense that they were operating within a preexisting context. They were not at sea to make law what they wished it to be. In contrast, Holmes disdained the natural law. In 1915, he wrote an essay that constituted a frontal attack on the tradition from the avowed perspective of skepticism. For Holmes, one's preferences were the only touchstone of reality. Natural lawyers, he argued, were "in that naïve state of mind that accepts which has been familiar and accepted by them and their neighbors as something that must be accepted by all men everywhere."[10]

Since at least the time of John Marshall, judges also saw themselves as part of a larger structure in the constitutional separation of powers. Holmes was respectful of the legislative process in the states and in the Congress—much more so, in fact, than many of his colleagues. But he did so not so much because of some sense of a structural obligation of the place of judges, but rather because he thought that political battles in a social Darwinist fashion should be played out in the combat zone of the legislature, and to the victor in that theater belonged the political spoils. Dissenting in the famous case of *Meyer v. Nebraska* (1923), in which the Supreme Court had struck down a state law forbidding the teaching of German in the public and private schools of the state, Holmes said that "it appears to me to present a question upon which men reasonably might differ and therefore I am unable to say that the Constitution of the United States prevents the experiment being tried."[11]

The last constraint on judges was the common law itself. The common law respects the positive law: the positive law of statutes, understood through rules of statutory interpretation; the positive law of the court, understood by recourse to precedent; and the positive law of the case, constrained by *res judicata*. The judge is called outside of himself to find the law from particular authoritative sources. It was this sense of the common law that Holmes's legal theory eventually undid, although in a great irony, Holmes's very mastery of the forms of the common law operated to keep him in practice as a restrained judge. Justice Edward White, a close friend of Holmes on the Supreme Court, told Holmes that "[y]ou profess skepticism, but act on dogma," by which he meant the principles of the common law (*HJ* 266). But Holmes gave to future judges the normative permission to let loose of the positive law constraints of the common law and make law according to what they believed was "the felt needs of the time."

Had Holmes not become a judge or a famous professor, *The Common Law* would have assured his place in American legal theory. It provided a new kind of theory by which to understand the common law that was almost Blackstonian in its reach but with an entirely different view of the values that underlay the law. It changed the basis upon which much of the common law had been understood and substantively displaced Blackstone. It was a paradigmatic work in an era when intellectual life hungered for and championed major paradigm shifts nearly everywhere. It evinced a high level of scholarship and a mastery of historical and case materials. Although many of the doctrines it espoused were never fully accepted by later courts, it nonetheless provided relatively uncomplicated touchstones by which whole areas of law seemed to be made more comprehensible: the external theory of criminal law, foreseeability as the source of liability, the reasonable man test, and, most significantly, a recasting of the role of the common law judge. "In a deeper sense," Holmes wrote

> [w]hat the courts declare to have always been the law is in fact new. It is legislative in its grounds. The very considerations which judges most rarely mention, and always with an apology, are the secret root from which the law draws all the juices of life. I mean, of course, considerations of what is expedient for the community concerned. (*CL* 35)

Strictly speaking, what the judges have done does not constitute the law. Rather, as he famously said in his later seminal essay, *The Path of the Law* (1896), "[t]he prophecies of what the courts will do in fact, and nothing more pretentious, are what I mean by the law" (*CW* 3:393). Thus, Holmes focuses political power ultimately on the judge. The judge decides cases on the basis of expediency, and society seeks to divine from what judges have done in the past what they may do in the future. We all wind up dependent on the not-entirely-predictable judge. And society becomes more dependent on the lawyer to provide some guidance on what actions a judge may or may not approve. It is little wonder, therefore, that later judges, imbued with the Holmesian ethos, presumed a right to rule over society that would have been foreign to the earlier common law judge as well as the earlier Supreme Court justice.

Virtually all observers agree that Holmes's theory led to the school of legal realism, which had its heyday at least in the academy beginning in the 1930s. But Holmes found legal realist thinker, Jerome Frank, who had been one of his clerks, to have a crabbed and distorted view of the law. Holmes himself hardly ever acted in an arbitrary or dictatorial manner from the bench. For his fifty years as a judge, he was on the whole careful, restrained, and a craftsman of the law. It was his very craftsmanship, even more than his ideas, that drew scores of brilliant legal minds to revere him. It was also his personal tolerance, a beneficent side to his skepticism. Holmes welcomed the company of Jews and Catholics, who found many other opportunities in the law closed to them. As Holmes himself understood, artistry in any endeavor, whether it be war or the law, reflects a deep human value. "Life is painting a picture, not doing a sum" (*HJ* 304). The very mastery of the common law both restrained him and made for his reputation.

Another element that restrained Holmes in his judging was his positivism—his life-long campaign to separate morals from the law. It was the source of his well-known dictum: "If you want to know the law and nothing else, you must look at it as a bad man, who cares only for the material consequences which such knowledge enables him to predict, not as a good one, who finds his reasons for conduct, whether inside the law or outside of it, in the vaguer actions of conscience" (*HJ* 392). Even though Holmes held that one's values were solely a matter of personal preference, the fact that he vehemently held morals to be outside the law operated to prevent him from imposing his own moral preferences through the Court. "It has given me great pleasure to sustain the Constitutionality of laws that I believe to be as bad as possible," he wrote to a relative (*MC* 67). In interpreting statutes (as well as contracts), Holmes was a textualist. He eschewed looking for the intent of the parties, or of the Framers, or of the social policy that lay behind the enactment.

He had no trouble enforcing the episodic and often irrational preferences of the public. The preferences he applied were those arrived at in the political process. Not only did Holmes's theory of law make placing his own substantive values in the law illegitimate, his consistent social Darwinism gave legitimacy for the political process, within which groups vied for dominance, to make the decision as to what was expedient for society. Perhaps the most salient example was his dissent in *Lochner v. New York* (1905). In that case, the majority of the Supreme Court struck down, as a violation of substantive due process, a New York law that limited the weekly hours that a baker could work. The majority, Holmes believed, was permitting the social Darwinist conflict to take place in the market. That was the wrong arena, thought Holmes. The arena of determinative conflict was the political, not the economic. In a famous phrase, he intoned that "[t]he Constitution does not enact Mr. Herbert Spencer's Social Statics."[12] The Progressives cheered, but Holmes was not making a progressivist point. In a turn of irony that would have delighted his father, Holmes was making Herbert Spencer subject to Herbert Spencer. Herbert Spencer's own ideas would be tested by the engine of political social Darwinism. If they were accepted, then they would triumph. If not, then Herbert Spencer would die by his own sword. Even the theory of social Darwinism must win or lose in the Darwinian struggle of the political process.

From 1882 until 1902, Holmes sat on the Supreme Judicial Court of Massachusetts, rising in 1899 to be chief justice. During those years, Holmes became known for further developing certain doctrines of the common law, such as the elements of the law of criminal attempts. After Theodore Roosevelt had read one of Holmes's addresses extolling the virtues of wartime combat, he was appointed to a seat on the United States Supreme Court in 1902, where he sat for another thirty years. There, when he came to interpret the Constitution, he did so through the lens of the common law. He found little legitimacy in the idea of original intent, for what had moved the Framers might not be what was needed in modern society. Rather, he looked to common law and Supreme Court precedents to determine what the meaning of certain phrases were, although, true to his version of the common law, he was always ready to adjust them to meet society's evolving needs as determined by the political branches. Even in the way he drafted his opinions, he followed what he thought was the common law tradition. "I think to state the case shortly and the ground of decision as concisely and delicately as you can is the real way. That is the English fashion and I think it civilized" (*HJ* 256). For Holmes, the Supreme Court was a common law court and the Constitution a common law document. In his celebrated opinions on free speech, where he first coined the phrase "clear and present danger," Holmes actually decided the early cases on the basis of the common law theory of criminal attempt, a topic in which he believed himself to be an expert.[13]

As justice, he continued to apply his theory that the dominant opinion arising out of the political process should be given deference. If it meant that blacks in the South remained in an inferior position, so be it; if it meant that business in the North had to knuckle under to progressivist legislation, so be it; and if it meant that the mentally retarded could be forcibly sterilized, so be that too.

In *Giles v. Harris* (1903), for example, the Court had to decide whether the overt attempt by the Alabama legislature to disenfranchise blacks should be allowed. Holmes wrote the opinion upholding the state. "[R]elief from a great political wrong," he lectured, "if done as alleged, by the people of a State and the State itself must be given by them or by the legislative and political departments of the government of the United States."[14]

The same principle obtained in economic matters. Holmes believed that monopoly was the natural outcome of economic competition. He thought the congressional attempt, supported as a substantive matter by some members of the Court, to prevent this natural outcome was misguided. But he believed more strongly that it was in politics, not economics, that the outcome of competition should have its natural outcome, regardless of the economic or social effects. Dissenting when the Court struck down the federal law restricting child labor, Holmes said, "I thought that . . . this Court had always disavowed the right to intrude its judgment upon questions of policy or morals."[15] In virtually every case in which the government sought to regulate the economy, Holmes was on the side of the government, no matter how foolish he thought the government's efforts were. Even when the government sought to regulate morals on the basis of the commerce clause (in this case forbidding the transportation of lottery tickets), Holmes cast the deciding vote in favor of Congress.[16] In one prominent instance when Holmes did oppose the government's attempts to stifle a contractual agreement among the nation's largest railroads, he based his view primarily on a narrow reading of the antitrust statute and not on a belief that business should be free of governmental regulation.[17] Similarly, Holmes upheld a Fifth Amendment (takings clause) claim of the Pennsylvania Coal Company against a statute prohibiting mining that would cause the subsidence of overhead houses or streets, stating that the regulation had "gone too far." But part of the reason why Holmes sided with the coal company was his belief that the government had already contracted away its rights earlier with the coal company.[18] The common law force of contract law weighed in on Holmes's evaluation of the facts.

Holmes was generally true to his word. He did not often opine on the substance of the legislation before him. When it came to the mentally handicapped, however, all the impulses of his social Darwinism came to the surface. In the famous case of *Buck v. Bell* (1927), in which a Virginia law compelling the sterilization of "mental defectives" was at stake, Holmes wrote the majority opinion upholding the statute. "It is better for all the world, if instead of waiting to execute degenerate offspring for crime, or to let them starve for their imbecility, society can prevent those who are manifestly unfit from continuing their kind. . . . Three generations of imbeciles are enough."[19] It was not a new view for Holmes. He had long spoken of the day when the "inadequate" would be eliminated. After *Buck v. Bell*, he wrote to friends of the real pleasure the decision had given him (*LWV* 27, 67).

The Progressives believed Oliver Wendell Holmes, Jr., was their ally when he upheld regulatory legislation designed to help workers, regulate business, enforce morals and health, and restrict child labor. He was, of course, generally unsympathetic to their social goals (although some Progressives favored eugenics). But the Progressives were certain that he had become one of them when it came to the free speech cases that flowed into the Court after World War I. Harold Laski and Felix Frankfurter did much to burnish his image among Progressive opinion in the country. In the first three speech cases to come before the Court in 1919, Holmes wrote the majority opinion. Although he used the phrase "clear and present danger" that seemingly would have protected speech that was merely controversial, the Court did uphold all three convictions.[20] In *Abrams v. the United States* (1919), decided the same year, there seemed to be a significant change. His dissenting opinion was taken to champion individual expression even over the needs of the state.

In *Abrams*, a group of Russian immigrants to the United States called for a general strike to protest American troops being sent to Russia to oppose the new Bolshevik regime. They were convicted under a law that forbade interfering with the production of arms for the war. The Supreme Court upheld the conviction. In opposition, Holmes first acted as the common law judge. The statute, as he read it, required proof of specific intent to curtail the production of arms for the war against Germany. Such specific intent had not been proven. Then Holmes acted as the social Darwinist. "[T]he ultimate good desired is better reached by free trade in ideas—that the best test of truth is the power of the thought to get itself accepted in the competition of the market." Holmes expanded the political venue for the struggle for dominance from the legislative forum to the larger discursive forum. Finally, Holmes gave the "clear and present danger" some real bite. "It is only the present danger of immediate evil or an intent to bring it about that warrants Congress in setting a limit to the expression of opinion where private rights are not concerned."[21] In *Gitlow v. New York* (1925), he repeated the clear and present danger formula but returned to his social Darwinist defense of free speech: "If in the long run the beliefs expressed in proletarian dictatorship are destined to be accepted by the dominant forces of the community, the only meaning of free speech is that they should be given their chance and have their way."[22]

Taking his deference to the legislature on economic matters with his now eloquent defense of free expression, Holmes became "the great dissenter" and hero of the Progressive elements in American politics. Some believed that his change in later life on free expression had come from the influence of his friend and colleague on the Court, Louis Brandeis. But Holmes remained Holmes. Speech was protected because of its connection to the political struggle—not because it was the birthright of an American and certainly not because it was the way to reach objective truth.

Brandeis and the Social Reform of the Constitution

Louis Brandeis's life was not the law. It was social reform, and he bent every effort, every skill, and every means available to him to that cause. He was born in Louisville, Kentucky, of cultured German Jewish parents who had escaped the chaos of the 1848 revolutionary fervor that swept Germany and Europe. His parents were intensely concerned with social issues in the United

States, including, of course, slavery and abolitionism. He remembered his mother carrying provisions to the Union troops. His heroes were Abraham Lincoln and his uncle, Lewis Dembitz, an abolitionist lawyer who was a delegate to the Republican convention of 1860. In fact, Brandeis changed his middle name from David to Dembitz in an act of admiration. He was very well read as a child and his family had him educated in Germany when he was an adolescent. He credited his German education with teaching him how to think, but he found the social and political atmosphere there stifling and longed to return to the United States to study law.

Meanwhile, his father, who had been initially successful in business, fell upon hard times. Watching the economic struggle of his father affected Brandeis deeply, and he committed himself to make enough money not to be in financial want. Returning to the United States, Brandeis determined to go to Harvard Law School. He entered in 1875 and immediately adopted the Puritan ethos around him of frugality, public service, a work ethic, and noblesse oblige. It became his leitmotif for the rest of his days. His German intellectual training served him well in the new system of learning the law at Harvard established by Dean Christopher Columbus Langdell. He graduated with the highest grades, and after a brief stint practicing in St. Louis, he returned to Boston to begin practice there in 1879. He was extraordinarily successful in his practice and eventually became a multimillionaire.

He partnered with Samuel Dennis Warren and through him was introduced to Holmes, with whom he began a cordial friendship. Brandeis kept up his connections with Harvard; he published an article on trusts and estates, clerked for Chief Justice Gray of the Massachusetts Supreme Judicial Court, and was asked to lecture at Harvard when James Bradley Thayer went on leave. He was so successful that Dean Langdell offered him a position as assistant professor. He declined from nagging fears about his health but mainly because he wanted more experience in litigation. It was in the activity of facts, conflicts, and disputes that he thrived, and despite his academic brilliance, he would have been out of place to have been permanently in the classroom.

He mixed very well with the Yankees of Boston, was physically active, and, like Holmes, was a prodigious reader. In everything he did, there was high energy. He soon became immersed in social and Progressive causes. He was one of the first people to organize an all-fronts attack for his causes, including letter-writing campaigns, editorials, gaining prominent supporters, meetings with adversaries, constant lecturing, and coordinating with groups who had overlapping interests. Among those interests that he fought against were the well-connected private trolley lines of Boston, corrupt legislators, gas companies, and life insurance companies. He engineered many major reforms of these industries through the Massachusetts state legislature. He vigorously fought for unionization, though he wanted them to be incorporated so they would not abuse their own workers. He argued for both jobs for the poor and leisure for the worker. As the years passed, he grew more active in Jewish affairs, eventually becoming a prominent Zionist. He gained national notoriety in 1910 by leading the exposure of land management corruption in the Taft administration, and he deftly handled a hostile congressional committee in hearings that lasted nearly four months. He was an incessant preacher to those who would listen (his clerks nicknamed him "Isaiah"), and Holmes once remarked that Brandeis's nagging got on his nerves a bit.

Brandeis's brilliant sense of political argumentation in a legal context came to the fore in the brief he submitted to the Supreme Court in the case of *Muller v. Oregon* (1908). Hired to defend a state law limiting hours women could work in certain industries, he somehow had to overcome the recent precedent of *Lochner v. New York* that seemingly decided the same point against the state just three years before. His brief marshaled the same kinds of evidence and argumentation he would use before state legislative committees. He put forward facts and social research from around the world to show that women were a class in special need of protection by the state and therefore an exception to the rule enunciated in *Lochner*. There had been briefs before with social facts included, but none with the thoroughness and tightness of argument that Brandeis put forward. This innovation, later called the "Brandeis brief," was designed to convince the Court that the legislature had what would later be called a compelling interest in the health of women. It was a means to allow the state legislature to have more discretion in solving social and economic problems. The Brandeis brief was not, as it later was claimed to be, an invitation to the Court to legislate on social matters. Rather, it was designed, as Holmes had long argued, to remove the courts from deciding social issues.

In words that would be ridiculed later in the century, Brandeis argued that in "structure and function women are differentiated from men. Besides these anatomical and physiological differences, physicians are agreed that women are fundamentally weaker than men in all that makes for endurance: in muscular strength, in nervous energy, in the powers of persistent attention and application."[23] He also included a eugenic argument that would appeal not only to Holmes but also to a broad spectrum of intellectual opinion. Overwork will tax the health of women, which will injure her offspring and result in children who will be impaired in some fashion, thereby harming the community in the long term.

Brandeis's political and legal values were thoroughly within the contemporary Progressive tradition. His theory of the polity was centered on the individual. He sought to undo large concentrations of power, particular in business and finance. Like a modern Anti-Federalist (an ideological ancestor of Progressivism), he trusted the local democracies of the states to accomplish the people's will. Reform would come through the states. His model was of small competitive business, though with necessary regulations from the center. At the invitation of Robert La Follette, Brandeis joined the National Progressive Republican League in 1910, and he worked hard in Congress to toughen the antitrust laws. When La Follette later ran for president as a Progressive in 1924, he asked Brandeis to resign from the Supreme Court and run as the party's vice-presidential candidate. Brandeis refused. But in 1912, he publicly supported and worked for Woodrow Wilson, whom he had not known previously.

Following the election, Brandeis quickly became one of Wilson's closest advisers, putting into concrete form programs that reflected Wilson's academic progressivism. With Brandeis's advice, Wilson backed the creation of the Federal Reserve System. Two years later, Brandeis had a close hand in the passage of the Clayton Act, which strengthened the antitrust laws. He also pressed Wilson to create the Federal Trade Commission to regulate business. Although Wilson wanted him in the administration, he and Brandeis could not find a suitable post until a Supreme Court vacancy occurred. Brandeis lobbied to gain the seat, and Wilson nominated him in 1916. There was a controversial confirmation process, partly because of Brandeis's prominence as a Jew, but also because his opponents saw him as a political actor with insufficient judicial temperament. It turns out that their diagnosis was based on more than prejudice, for Brandeis never stopped his political lobbying for the rest of his career.

Once on the Court, Brandeis pursued a Progressive agenda on two levels. Judicially, he was nearly as restrained as was Holmes. To Brandeis, the states were the engines of Progressive reform. Most legislation that was contested before the Court was state legislation. To free the states from the constraints of judicial supervision was therefore a primary aim of Brandeis. Dissenting in a case in which the Court struck down a state tax as discriminatory, Brandeis sought to return more taxing discretion to the states.[24] In *New State Ice Company v. Liebmann* (1932), the Court held that the licensing of an ice business by the state of Oklahoma was an unfair imposition on the right to carry on a lawful business. Dissenting again, Brandeis justified his vision of an active, reforming federated polity.

The discoveries in physical science, the triumphs in invention, attest the value of the process of trial and error. In large measure, these advances have been due to experimentation. In those fields experimentation has, for two centuries, been not only free but encouraged. Some people assert that our present plight is due, in part, to the limitations set by courts upon experimentation in the fields of social and economic science; and to the discouragement to which proposals for betterment there have been subjected otherwise. There must be power in the States and the Nation to remould, through experimentation, our economic practices and institutions to meet changing social and economic needs.[25]

From his skeptical and social Darwinist perspective, Holmes had argued that state law which could be found "reasonable" should be upheld. That could only be done on a case-by-case basis. Brandeis went further. He tried to press his views into the text of the Constitution and thereby lock in his perspective. In the *New State Ice Company* case, for example, he wrote: "I cannot believe that the framers of the Fourteenth Amendment, or the States which ratified it, intended to deprive us of the power to correct the evils of technological unemployment and excess productive capacity which have attended progress in the useful arts."[26] But he left it as a matter of belief. He made no attempt to try to find out what was the actual understanding of the Framers. Similarly, in his famous opinion in *Erie Railroad Company v. Tompkins* (1938), speaking for the Court, he did away with federal common law, holding that federal common law jurisdiction was not just based on an improper application of federal law. Rather, he said, it was contrary to the Constitution itself. From now on, in diversity jurisdiction cases, the Court must apply the appropriate state law.[27]

As justice, Brandeis usually allied with Holmes in voting to uphold state and federal regulatory legislation, although, of course, for different reasons. Holmes believed that the dominant opinion in the political process should have its way, whereas Brandeis supported the cause of Progressive reform by keeping the Court out of the picture. He became known on the Court for his insistence that every jurisdiction element of a case be shown before the Court would hear it. "Considerations of propriety, as well as long-established practice, demand that we refrain from passing upon the constitutionality of an act of Congress unless obliged to do so in the proper performance of our judicial function, when the question is raised by a party whose interests entitle him to raise it."[28]

Brandeis's opinions, however, were not as restrained as his votes. In *Erie Railroad Company v. Tompkins*, for example, he reached out to overrule a long-established precedent even though that issue had not been argued before the Court and the case could have been decided on statutory grounds. Despite his insistence that the Court's duty was not to pass on the wisdom of state legislation, he often engaged in parading facts to demonstrate the wisdom of the state's choice. He once said that the "Brandeis brief" should have been called "What Every Fool Knows." Differing from Holmes, he said that "nobody can form a judgment that is worth having without a fairly detailed and intimate knowledge of the facts."[29] His opinions tended to be much longer and fact-filled than Holmes's, who usually showed little faith, one way or the other, in the value of the particular state regulatory scheme before the Court.

Brandeis asserted that the expertise to understand modern industrial life lay with state legislatures and administrative agencies. Nonetheless, the very fact that he engaged in detailed social justification of legislation in his opinions gave later judges an example by which they felt themselves competent to induce social change on their own through their decisions. Brandeis's decisions were restrained, but his opinions portended a new and even more intrusive judicial activism than what he himself confronted.

In free speech cases, Brandeis was much more vigorous in defending free expression. Where Holmes saw speech as necessary to the working out of combat among groups in the political sphere, Brandeis went further. He believed speech was protected because of the need of the individual for self-expression.

> Those who won our independence believed that the final end of the State was to make men free to develop their faculties; and that in its government the deliberative forces should prevail over the arbitrary. . . .They believed that free to think as you will and to speak as you think are means indispensable to the discovery and spread of political truth.[30]

In fact, Brandeis's political values were strongly centered on the individual where Holmes's were centered on the group. As early as 1890, he and Warren had published a groundbreaking article on the individual right to privacy in which they stated that the "common law secures to each individual the right of determining, ordinarily, to what extent his thoughts, sentiments, and emotions shall be communicated to others."[31] Thirty-eight years later, Brandeis vehemently protested the "invasions of individual security" in his dissent in *Olmstead v. United States* (1928), when the Supreme Court upheld the right of the government to wiretap without the need of a warrant. In a nearly direct quote from his 1890 article on privacy, Brandeis asserted, again without a look at actual history, that "[t]he makers of the Constitution undertook . . . to protect Americans in their beliefs, their thoughts, their emotions, and their sensations."[32] Here was a radical form of individualism being moved from the common law into the Constitution.

Holmes viewed the Constitution through the lens of the common law; Brandeis viewed the Constitution through the lens of social reform: neither spent much time investigating the Constitution as the Framers saw it. Holmes ignored the intent of the Framers because he believed that the law changed over time to meet new needs as defined by the dominant political party, though the form of the law may remain; Brandeis ignored the Framers because, being part of the Progressive tradition, much of what they had done was irrelevant to modern conditions. The Progressive party's platform of 1912 demanded "such restrictions of the power of the courts as shall leave to the people the ultimate authority to determine fundamental questions of social welfare and public policy."[33] The platform also called for the people to have a right to reenact social legislation over its invalidation by the courts. Brandeis was not in favor of such an awkward solution. He preferred to direct reform at the Constitution itself. The Constitution was an "experiment—itself perhaps the greatest of human experiments," and so modern legislative experiments have the same moral basis in being allowed to stand. "Since the adoption of the Federal Constitution, and notably within the last fifty years, we have passed through an economic and social revolution which affected the life of the people more fundamentally than any political revolution known to history."[34]

To the extent that the Constitution was undemocratic, it was an obstacle; to the extent it protected property rights, it was an obstacle. The courts, he said, "applied complacently eighteenth-century conceptions of the liberty of the individual and of the sacredness of private property" (*BD* 61). The Constitution must be made mutable according to modern needs. "Has not the recent dissatisfaction with our law as administered been due, in large measure, to the fact that it had not kept pace with the rapid development of our political, economic, and social ideals? In other words, is not the challenge of legal justice due to its failure to conform to contemporary conceptions of social justice?" (*BD* 61). The only practical options were: (1) to have the Court stand out of the way when it came to legislative reform; and (2) to emplace modern (that is progressivist) notions of liberty and governmental power into the constitutional structure. On the one hand, "rights of property and the liberty of the individual must be remolded from time to time to meet the needs of society."[35] On the other hand, "general limitations on the powers of government, like those embodied in the due process clauses of the Fifth and Fourteenth Amendments, do not forbid the United States or the states from meeting modern conditions by regulations which 'a century ago, or even half a century ago, probably would have been rejected as arbitrary and oppressive.'"[36] Ultimately, Brandeis regarded his campaign to have the Court pay attention to social facts to have been successful. The public's "fury against the courts has abated" because of "a better appreciation by the courts of existing social needs" (*BD* 61).

Although Brandeis wanted to adapt the very meaning of the Constitution to the values of progressivism, he seems not to have wanted to "legislate" from the bench in the sense of imposing substantive social policy. In that sense, he retained the progressivist orthodoxy that unelected judges were an illegitimate source of policy making and that legislatures would fulfill the need for reform. Yet Brandeis remained a social activist to his dying day. Beginning in 1916, Brandeis secretly began paying Felix Frankfurter to engage in political activities that Brandeis thought were wise. The payments were ostensibly for expenses, but in fact Brandeis had hired Frankfurter as his agent and Frankfurter thought the relationship in those terms. Throughout the next twenty-five years, Brandeis through Frankfurter was unceasing in his efforts to gain reforms through Congress and the executive. It included commenting on drafts of legislation, developing connections among people who were well placed politically, and becoming something of an éminence gris to the progressivist journal, *The New Republic*. Dozens of prominent political personalities came to visit Brandeis at his home to discuss political reforms and to receive the justice's lobbying. Brandeis's and Frankfurter's hopes raised when Franklin Delano Roosevelt assumed office. They worked hard to place young lawyers—their protégés—in federal departments and agencies. Brandeis also sought to have Roosevelt adopt his own program, including vast public works spending, a progressive income tax, and a general raising of taxes, but he was only partially successful. To the end, he continued to want talent and power to remain with the states. Nonetheless, his lobbying through Frankfurter, and his placing of so many protégés in key positions, did in fact move much of the locus of reform to the federal government.

Conclusion

Oliver Wendell Holmes, Jr., and Louis D. Brandeis made the modern Supreme Court. These two brilliant and seminal justices, known in their day for their restraint, nonetheless gave the weapons and the impulse to justices who would not share their judicial temperaments. Perhaps each of them would have been chagrinned at the extent to which judges today ignore the traditional constraints on their jurisdiction, impose social values directly upon the people, and increase the power of the central government over the states.

Holmes and Brandeis operated within the structure that had been established over centuries by judges and the judicial system. It was a normative structure that looked to the judge's role as a servant of the law. That tradition helped to inform the craft of these two individuals and to bequeath to them a sense of judicial restraint. But Holmes's theories destroyed the normative basis for restraint. His restraint became his style, his subjective preference. Modern judges, freed from the formal and natural law constraints of judging, would bring a different preference and a different style.

Holmes provided the form for modern judicial activism and Brandeis the substance. The particular political values of individualism and governmental power over the economy lay at the bottom of the expansion of rights under the Bill of Rights and the rejection of structural restraints on Congress in modern times. Brandeis's attempt to read back into the Constitution his values has been taken to heart in many areas of constitutional jurisprudence. Finally, his conception that law was merely instrumental to furthering political goals has had an enormous effect on what judges have come to see as a legitimate role. Brandeis worked behind the scenes for decades to pursue his political objectives. Modern judges are not permitted to play that double game. Instead, they sometimes pursue their political objectives from the bench. And when this occurs, the Court becomes a source of extraordinary social readjustments, unchecked by Congress, and often contrary to what the states may believe is a better policy.

Notes

1. Quoted in Sheldon M. Novick, *Honorable Justice: The Life of Oliver Wendell Holmes* (Boston: Little, Brown, 1989), 50, hereafter cited in the text as *HJ*.

2. Louis Menand, *The Metaphysical Club* (New York: Farrar, Straus, and Giroux, 2001), 69, hereafter cited in the text as *MC*.

3. Albert W. Alschuler, *Law without Values: The Life, Work, and Legacy of Justice Holmes* (Chicago: University of Chicago Press, 2000), 44, hereafter cited in the text as *LWV*.

4. Mark De Wolfe Howe, *Justice Oliver Wendell Holmes* (Cambridge, Mass.: Belknap Press of Harvard University Press, 1957), 1:156.

5. Holmes, *The Common Law* (Boston: Little, Brown, and Co., 1881), 1, hereafter cited in the text as *CL*.

6. On pragmatism, see Thomas C. Grey, "Holmes and Legal Pragmatism," *Stanford Law Review* 41 (1989): 787, and Catharine Wells Hantzsis, "Legal Innovation within the Wider Intellectual Tradition: The Pragmatism of Oliver Wendell Holmes, Jr.," *Northwestern University Law Review* 82 (1988): 541; on analytical utilitarianism, H. L. Pohlman, *Justice Oliver Wendell Holmes & Utilitarian Jurisprudence* (Cambridge, Mass.: Harvard University Press, 1984); on scientific materialism and historicism, David H. Burton, *Political Ideas of Justice Holmes* (Rutherford, N.J.: Fairleigh Dickinson University Press, 1992), 22 and 36; and on proto-existentialism, see *LWV* 19.

7. In law school, Holmes had read Maine's influential *Ancient Law: Its Connection with the Early History of Society and Its Relation to Modern Ideas* (1861).

8. That point is made particularly by Albert W. Alschuler. Although his argument is not without flaws, Alschuler's evidence that Holmes, as a man of his times, was a social Darwinist is strong.

9. Michael Polanyi, *Personal Knowledge: Towards a Post-critical Philosophy* (Chicago: University of Chicago Press, 1958), 309.

10. Holmes, *The Collected Works of Justice Holmes*, ed. Sheldon M. Novick (Chicago: University of Chicago Press, 1995), 3:446, hereafter cited in the text as *CW*.

11. *Meyer v. Nebraska*, 262 U.S. 390 (1923). Holmes's dissent was in the companion case of *Bartels v. Iowa*, 262 U.S. 404 (1923), at 412.

12. *Lochner v. New York*, 198 U.S. 45 (1905), at 92.

13. See *Schenck v. United States*, 249 U.S. 47 (1919); *Frohwerk v. United States*, 249 U.S. 204 (1919); and *Debs v. United States*, 249 U.S. 211 (1919).

14. *Giles v. Harris*, 189 U.S. 475 (1903), at 488.

15. *Hammer v. Dagenhart*, 247 U.S. 251 (1918), at 280, Holmes dissenting.

16. *Champion v. Ames*, 188 U.S. 231 (1903).

17. *Northern Securities Co. v. United States*, 193 U.S. 197 (1918), at 404–8, Holmes dissenting.

18. *Pennsylvania Coal Co. v. Mahon*, 260 U.S. 393 (1922), at 414.

19. *Buck v. Bell*, 274 U.S. 200 (1927), at 207.

20. See note 13 above.

21. *Abrams v. United States*, 250 U.S. 616 (1919), at 630 and 628, Holmes dissenting.

22. *Gitlow v. New York*, 268 U.S. 652 (1925), at 673, Holmes dissenting.

23. Quoted in Philippa Strum, *Louis D. Brandeis: Justice for the People* (Cambridge, Mass.: Harvard University Press, 1984), 114.

24. *Liggett Company v. Lee*, 288 U.S. 517 (1933), at 541, Brandeis dissenting.

25. *New State Ice Company v. Liebmann*, 285 U.S. 262 (1932), at 310–11, Brandeis dissenting.

26. *New State Ice Company v. Liebmann*, at 311.

27. *Erie v. Tompkins*, 304 U.S. 64 (1938). On this decision, see also Edward A. Purcell, Jr., *Brandeis and the Progressive Constitution: Erie, the Judicial Power, and the Politics of the Federal Courts in Twentieth-Century America* (New Haven, Conn.: Yale University Press, 2000).

28. *Ashwander v. T.V.A.*, 297 U.S. 288 (1936), at 341. He summarized the jurisdictional rules as follows:

> 1. The Court will not pass upon the constitutionality of legislation in a friendly, nonadversary, proceeding.
>
> 2. The Court will not "anticipate a question of constitutional law in advance of the necessity of deciding it."
>
> 3. The Court will not "formulate a rule of constitutional law broader than is required by the precise facts to which it is to be applied."
>
> 4. The Court will not pass upon a constitutional question although properly presented by the record, if there is also present some other ground upon which the case may be disposed of.
>
> 5. The Court will not pass upon the validity of a statute upon complaint of one who fails to show that he is injured by its operation.
>
> 6. The Court will not pass upon the constitutionality of a statute at the instance of one who has availed himself of its benefits.
>
> 7. "When the validity of an act of the Congress is drawn in question, and even if a serious doubt of constitutionality is raised, it is a cardinal principle that this Court will first ascertain whether a construction of the statute is fairly possible by which the question may be avoided" (346–48).

29. Nelson Dawson, *Louis D. Bandeis, Felix Frankfurter, and the New Deal* (Hamden, Conn.: Archon Books, 1980), 13.

30. *Whitney v. California*, 274 U.S. 357 (1927), at 375, Brandeis concurring.

31. Louis D. Brandeis and Samuel D. Warren, "The Right to Privacy," *Harvard Law Review* 4 (1890–91): 193, reprinted in Ervin H. Pollack, *The Brandeis Reader* (New York: Oceana Publications, 1956), 90.

32. *Olmstead v. United States*, 277 U.S. 438 (1928), at 478, Brandeis dissenting.

33. Richard Hofstadter, *The Progressive Movement, 1900–1915* (Englewood Cliffs, N.J.: Prentice Hall, 1963), 129–30.

34. Oral argument in *Settler v. O'Hara*, 243 U.S. 629 (1914), in *Brandeis on Democracy*, ed. Philippa Strum (Lawrence: University Press of Kansas, 1995), 73, hereafter cited in the text as *BD*.

35. *Truax v. Corrigan*, 257 U.S. 312 (1921), at 376.

36. *Olmstead v. United States*, at 472.

Chapter 34

John Dewey's Alternative Liberalism

David Fott

ohn Dewey (1859–1952) was born in Burlington, Vermont. After his graduation from the University of Vermont, he taught high school for three years in Oil City, Pennsylvania, and in Vermont. He received his Ph.D. in philosophy from Johns Hopkins University in 1884, and for the next several years he taught at the University of Michigan and the University of Minnesota. In 1894, he moved to the University of Chicago, where he founded the University Elementary School (later called the Laboratory School) to put into practice his educational views. In 1904, Dewey was offered a professorship at Columbia University, with appointments in the Department of Philosophy and the Teachers College; he remained there for the rest of his career.

Dewey's published books and articles, as well as his speeches, fill thirty-six volumes, so it is impossible to do more than list the most important ones here. His early work was characterized by a neo-Hegelian idealism; the textbook *Psychology* (1887) was from that period. His abandonment of a metaphysical Absolute and move toward naturalism and pragmatism were manifested in "The Reflex Arc Concept in Psychology" (1896) and *Studies in Logical Theory* (1903). His major works in psychology and education were *How We Think* (1910, revised 1933), *Democracy and Education* (1916), *Human Nature and Conduct* (1922), and *Experience and Education* (1938). He criticized the directions taken by earlier philosophers in *Reconstruction in Philosophy* (1920) and *The Quest for Certainty* (1929). In the field of political thought, he wrote *The Public and Its Problems* (1927), *Individualism, Old and New* (1930), *Liberalism and Social Action* (1935), and *Freedom and Culture* (1939). *Experience and Nature* (1925) was an attempt to develop a naturalistic metaphysics. *Logic: The Theory of Inquiry* (1938) adapted logic to pragmatist thinking. Dewey delved into aesthetics with *Art as Experience* (1934).

We may begin to understand Dewey's political thought in its relation to previous American political thought by drawing contrasts between it and the Declaration of Independence. We cannot go far in this direction, however, without also exploring the main lines of his work in psychology and education. Only then can we come to grips with the alternative liberalism that he would substitute for that of the Declaration.

Democracy and Science:
Dewey's Critique of the Declaration of Independence

Dewey was a leading figure in the school of thought known as pragmatism, which is the only philosophical school of thought native to the United States. A highly respected critical history of pragmatism defines it as follows:

[It is] a theory of knowledge, experience, and reality maintaining . . . that thought and knowledge are biologically and socially evolved modes of adaptation to and control over experience and reality; . . . that all knowledge is evaluative of future experience and that thinking functions experimentally in anticipations of future experiences and consequences of actions—thus in organizing conditions of future observations and experience. Thought is a behavioral process manifested in controlled actualizations of selected, anticipated, and planned possibilities of future experience. . . . [T]heorizing over experience is, as a whole and in detail, fundamentally motivated and justified by conditions of efficacy and utility in serving our various aims and needs. . . . [A]side from esthetic and intrinsic interests, all theorizing is subject to the critical objective of maximum usefulness in serving our needs.[1]

With this in mind, we can now turn to Dewey's critique of the Declaration of Independence.

The Declaration announces that "We hold these truths to be self-evident, . . ." According to Dewey, no truth is self-evident. Pragmatism holds that *truth* is a term referring to "verified beliefs, propositions that have emerged from a certain procedure of inquiry and testing." That procedure is the modern scientific method of observation, hypothesis, and experimentation (*M* 6:28).[2] Science is the only means to truth, and that fact implies the tentativeness of all truth, because every proposition could at some point be disproved.

The Declaration proclaims that men "are endowed by their Creator with certain unalienable Rights," rights that inhere in us as individual human beings. Moreover, it suggests that the grounds for that and the other self-evident truths are "the Laws of Nature and of Nature's God." Dewey rejects both of those claims. In his view, "nature is not an unchangeable order, unwinding itself majestically from the reel of law under the control of deified forces. It is an indefinite congeries of changes" (*M* 4:47). The view of nature as unchangeable lies at the root of the liberal individualism of Thomas Hobbes and John Locke, with their notion of a prepolitical state of nature. Dewey rejects that notion on more than one ground: "The idea of a natural individual in his isolation possessed of full-fledged wants, of energies to be expended according to his own volition, and of a ready-made faculty of foresight and prudent calculation is as much a fiction in psychology as the doctrine of the individual in possession of antecedent political rights is one in politics" (*L* 2:299). One cannot define an individual solely in terms of separateness; points of contiguity with others must also be recognized. Dewey does appear to be ambivalent on that point. In the same book, *The Public and Its Problems*, he also writes that "I would not say" that individuals "have no point nor sense except in some combination" (*L* 2:278); in a later work, he remarks that the individual "is a value in potential humanity and not as something separate and atomic" (*L* 14:277). The conclusion he draws is not that individuals should have no rights but that "actual, that is, effective, rights and demands are products of interactions" among human beings in society (*L* 3:100).

According to the Declaration, our inalienable rights include "Life, Liberty and the pursuit of Happiness." Dewey's notion of liberty differs considerably from what has been the dominant American understanding of the term. "The real fallacy," he writes, "lies in the notion that individuals have such a native or original endowment of rights, powers and wants that all that is required on the side of institutions and laws is to eliminate the obstructions they offer to the 'free' play of the natural equipment of individuals" (*L* 3:100). The negative conception of liberty —liberty as freedom from external restraint—is incomplete. In contrast to the individualistic tradition, Dewey defines liberty as "that secure release and fulfillment of personal potentialities which take place only in rich and manifold association with others" (*L* 2:329). In his day, Dewey sees the main threat to liberty as coming not from the government but from societal forces, especially entrenched economic interests and the development of large, impersonal organizations arising from the increased use of machines. In that case, government must be seen as a means toward the securing of liberty. Liberty, in turn, exists in order to make people more adaptable to a variety of situations that may arise as a result of their choosing. Such adaptability is crucial if people are to be capable of "growth" (a concept to be explained below).

The Declaration also states that "all men are created equal." Neither Thomas Jefferson nor the other Framers ever definitively spelled out the meaning of equality there; the safest claim that can be made is that the phrase refers to an equality of inalienable rights. While preferring to ignore the word "created," Dewey has a much more expansive reading of equality:

> It means that every existence deserving the name of existence has something unique and irreplaceable about it. . . . As philosophy it denies the basic principle of atomistic individualism as truly as that of rigid feudalism. For the individualism traditionally associated with democracy makes equality quantitative, and hence individuality something external and mechanical rather than qualitative and unique. In social and moral matters, equality does not mean mathematical equivalence. It means rather the inapplicability of considerations of greater and less, superior and inferior. . . . It implies, so to speak, a metaphysical mathematics of the incommensurable in which each speaks for itself and demands consideration on its own behalf. (*M* 11:52–53)

But if Dewey might find the Framers' conception of equality insufficiently exalted, he clearly considers their general perspective too much so. "The fundamental defect" of early liberalism, he says, "was its lack of perception of historic relativity" (*L* 11:290). It did not understand that the notion of the individual in the state of nature could be used to stifle political liberty as well as to promote it, which happened when advocates of laissez-faire economics attacked governmental intervention for the sake of the poor. "Ideas that at one time are means of producing social change have not the same meaning when they are used as means of preventing social change. This fact is itself an illustration of historic relativity" (*L* 11:291). Science has taught us that the meaning and validity of ideas and principles vary with the purposes to which they are put. Thus, Dewey claims that "the connection between historic relativity and experimental method is intrinsic" (*L* 11:292).

God is invoked in one way or another at a number of places in the Declaration, and not just in the passages already cited. Dewey's calls for human independence—at least those made after he began to develop his pragmatism in the 1890s—make clear his view that humans cannot be independent if they rely on a supernatural God for ultimate judgment and execution of natural laws. Prior to the first decade of the twentieth century, Dewey's writings could at least be interpreted in a theistic way; they include such articles as "The Obligation to Knowledge of God" (1884). Yet from around 1900 on, Dewey's published work deals very little with the existence of God. Even *A Common Faith* (1934), his major work on religion, does not ask and consider whether the God of the Bible exists. Dewey would later remark that that book was addressed specifically to those who have already rejected supernatural religion (*L* 14:79–80).

In *A Common Faith,* Dewey draws a distinction between religions, which science has shown to be untenable, and religious experience, which has validity. We must see religions as relative to cultures, and hence their aspiration to represent eternal truth as misguided, and we must instead seek "the ways in which reverence and obedience would be manifested, if whatever is basically religious in experience had the opportunity to express itself free from all historic encumbrances"—that is, institutional encumbrances such as the church (*L* 9:6). Religious experience occurs within—and cannot occur apart from—aesthetic, scientific, moral, or political experience. An experience has religious quality when there is "the unification of the self through allegiance to inclusive ideal ends, which imagination presents to us and to which the human will responds as worthy of controlling our desires and choices" (*L* 9:23). Religious experience refers to "the attitudes that lend deep and enduring support to the processes of living"; such experience is where reverence may properly be shown (*L* 9:12). A religious attitude is comprehensive, recognizing the dependence of man upon nature.

> Natural piety is not of necessity either a fatalistic acquiescence in natural happenings or a romantic idealization of the world. It may rest upon a just sense of nature as the whole of which we are parts, while it also recognizes that we are parts that are marked by intelligence and purpose, having the capacity to strive by their aid to bring conditions into greater consonance with what is humanly desirable. Such piety is an inherent constituent of a just perspective in life. (*L* 9:18)

According to Dewey, faith in obtaining truth through continual inquiry into man's natural situations is more religious than faith in obtaining truth through revelation: the fact of competing, alleged revelations demands empirical investigation, he suggests, and empirical inquiries into the supernatural divert attention from realizing our ideals. Dewey's belief in the religiosity of scientific inquiry is seen in his willingness to use the term "God" for "the unity of all ideal ends arousing us to desire and actions" or for the "*active* relation between ideal and actual" (although he says that the term is only for the benefit of those who would otherwise despair or feel isolated) (*L* 9:29, 34, 36). This God was not a personal Being but rather a process—a striving for an ideal. To use the term in that way was to remove the distinction between the religious and the secular, to bring religious experience into "every aspect of human experience that is concerned with estimate of possibilities, with emotional stir by possibilities as yet unrealized, and with all action in behalf of their realization. All that is significant in human experience falls within this frame" (*L* 9:39).

Although Dewey's rejection of "the Laws of Nature and of Nature's God" seems to be his most important rejection of the Founding, that rejection must be studied more closely. It may be less of a rejection than one would originally think; for in that phrase, Jefferson seems to say that belief in God is not necessary for understanding the fundamental political truths of inalienable rights and government by the consent of the governed. God is presented not as legislator of moral laws but rather as creator of nature, the laws of which are obeyed by humans. If the laws consist at least in part of self-evident truths, then human reason is capable of comprehending them without recourse to divine revelation. To be sure, this does not fully capture the essence of Jefferson's view of the importance of religion for politics. We need only remind ourselves that the author of the Declaration also asked: "And can the liberties of a nation be thought secure when we have removed their only firm basis, a conviction in the minds of the people that these liberties are of the gift of God?"[3] Jefferson clearly believed that religious conviction on the part of the populace is a crucial underpinning of democracy.

An initial impression may be that Dewey takes the opposite view on that matter, but his treatment of democracy suggests otherwise. "The foundation of democracy," he writes, "is faith in the capacities of human nature; faith in human intelligence, and in the power of pooled and cooperative experience. It is not belief that these things are complete but that if given a show they will grow and be able to generate progressively the knowledge and wisdom needed to guide collective action" (*L* 11:219). Similarly, in *Freedom and Culture,* Dewey stresses the need "to face the issue of the moral ground of political institutions" (*L* 13:179). The need is particularly great, he asserts, since belief in natural law or natural rights is no longer credible. It must be replaced with "a faith based on ideas that are now intellectually credible and that are consonant with present economic conditions." What is required is "an adequate theory of human nature in its relations to democracy" (*L* 13:150). Dewey calls for "faith in the potentialities of human nature," where "the word *faith* is intentionally used" to substitute for a supposedly discredited Christianity, formerly thought to be a grounding for natural law, which was itself the grounding for democracy (*L* 13:151, 152). Thus, he sees a need to invoke a religious term—albeit atheologically and even antitheologically—in order to support his advocacy of democracy.

For Dewey, the justification of democracy is found not only in a faith in human nature but also in the close similarity of democracy to scientific method.

> It is of the nature of science not so much to tolerate as to welcome diversity of opinion, while it insists that inquiry brings the evidence of observed facts to bear to effect a consensus of conclusions. . . . [F]reedom of inquiry, toleration of diverse views, freedom of communication, the distribution of what is found out to every individual as the ultimate intellectual consumer, are involved in the democratic as in the scientific method. (*L* 13:135)

As we have seen, that method alone can arrive at the truth of a problematic situation.

Dewey's commitment to science approaches the status of an absolute. The experimental philosophy of life "is itself a theory to be tested by experience" (*M* 8:201). But by what sort of experience or standards can we tell the worth of science, which is then to be applied toward the making of all other moral judgments, including those concerning political institutions? Elsewhere, he writes that the experimental attitude toward life "is clearly a faith, not a demonstration. It too can be demonstrated only in *its* works, its fruits." But again, by what standards can this be demonstrated? Dewey then hedges. "Perhaps the task is too hard for human nature. The faith may demonstrate its own falsity by failure. . . . But an honest soul will also admit that the failure is not due to inherent defects in the faith, but to the fact that its demands are too high for human power; . . . and that the experiment must be passed on to another place and time" (*M* 13:308–9). Apparently, the connection between historical relativism and science is not so straightforward as Dewey seems to think; he shows himself to be an inconsistent historical relativist when faced with the prospect of applying that doctrine to the validity of scientific method.

Dewey's commitment to democracy is at least equally fundamental. From early in his career, he maintains that democracy is "an ethical conception, and upon its ethical significance is based its significance as governmental." (*E* 1:240). Democratic government is merely "the effective embodiment of the moral ideal of a good which consists in the development of all the social capacities of every individual member of society" (*M* 5:424). The sort of society required for this development is one

> where there is a wide and varied distribution of opportunities; where there is social mobility or scope for change of position and station; where there is free circulation of experiences and ideas, making for a wide recognition of common interests and purposes, and where utility of social and political organization to its members is so obvious as to enlist their warm and constant support in its behalf. (*M* 10:138)

This "free circulation" cannot be limited to certain spheres of life if democracy is to be fully realized. "To be realized it must affect all modes of human association, the family, the school, industry, religion" (*L* 2:325).

Education and Growth

Closely tied to Dewey's faith in democracy and science is his concept of growth. Dewey writes in *Democracy and Education* that education is a means toward the "social continuity of life" (*M* 9:5). It is a part of every social group because the preservation of the group is not merely a physical matter; knowledge, customs, and ways of life must also be preserved. The fact that humans are capable of indefinite "growth" increases the importance of education over time: "With the growth of civilization, the gap between the original capacities of the immature and the standards and customs of the elders increases" (*M* 9:6). Schools are one means of conducting education, which should simplify and purify the student's environment. Purification aims at creating not a problem-free situation but one in which the "trivial," "dead," and "perverse" aspects of the environment are eliminated from children's activities (*M* 9:24). Schools, however, are "a relatively superficial" means of education (*M* 9:7). Education is present wherever there is communication, the goal of which is the formation and maintenance of the shared beliefs and practices that make community possible. All institutions have a role to play, and all are to be judged according to their "effect in enlarging and improving experience" (*M* 9:9). What Dewey means by enlarged and improved experience is not immediately clear, but the distinction surely depends on a separation of education from mere training in a skill. Education involves acquiring the means to take the initiative in shaping the common activities of society, which are crucial in the process of forming meanings (*M* 9:20).

Although Dewey's educational thought has been lambasted as laissez-faire, the charge is unjust: he understands that such acquisition requires significant direction of the activities of the student by the teacher. His general advice is that control be exercised in those cases that "are so instinctive or impulsive that the one performing them has no means of foreseeing their outcome" (*M* 9:32). Wherever direction is exercised, it must be with regard to the harmonization of individual and society. Insofar as learning is not directed toward the student's ability to participate in social activities, "ordinary vital experience fails to gain in meaning" (*M* 9:12). But education also provides distance from society's expectations, which will usually determine a person's intellectual activity unless he can critically examine those expectations. "The way our group or class does things tends to determine the proper objects of attention, and thus to prescribe the directions and limits of observation and memory" (*M* 9:21).

To understand Dewey's discussion of education as direction and growth of mental powers, we must understand something of his psychological theory. He writes that "[c]haracter and mind are attitudes of participative response in social affairs" (*M* 9:326). Elsewhere, he elaborates: "The natural unaided mind means precisely the habits of belief, thought and desire which have been accidentally generated and confirmed by social institutions or customs" (*M* 14:225). Not only does this passage suggest Dewey's belief that there is very little we can say about human nature apart from social conditions; it also identifies mind itself with a set of habits that are social functions (*L* 13:286–87). Mind is "power to understand things in terms of the use made of them"; and meaning itself therefore comes from the social use made of things and not from the simple association of sensory images (*M* 9:38). Of course, the meanings of things are limited by the things in human experience. Dewey is convinced that people in modern times have a decisive advantage over those of ancient times: our superior control of natural forces, through the method of modern science, provides superior stimuli. "A body of knowledge is transmitted, the legitimacy of which is guaranteed by the fact that the physical equipment in which it is incarnated leads to results that square with the other facts of nature" (*M* 9:42). It is the application of science in machines, and technology in general, that assures Dewey that an enhanced way of life is available to us that was not possible for the Greeks.

But Dewey does not assume the inevitability of progress with the rise of modern science and technology. Regress is possible as well as progress, and human beings have a responsibility for the promotion of the latter, or "growth." Whence do we take our bearings? Dewey insists that nature does not provide a fixed standard. He does not deny that education requires a degree of adjustment or adaptation to the environment; but, he refuses to characterize human behavior in terms of the evolutionary model of adaptation: "Adaptation, in fine, is quite as much adaptation *of* the environment to our own activities as of our activities *to* the environment" (*M* 9:52). Viewed merely in terms of conformity to the environment, adaptation does not leave enough room for human creativity.

"Growth" is one of Dewey's most controversial concepts because it has no absolute content for him. "Not perfection as a final goal, but the ever-enduring process of perfecting, maturing, refining is the aim in living" (*M* 12:181). Growth itself is "the only moral 'end.'" This implies "that the educational process has no end beyond itself" (*M* 9:54). Given the supposed failure of all absolutist philosophies to justify their ends, Dewey sees no alternative to that conclusion. Education is not preparation for a completed state to be arrived at in the future. Indeed, the result of a view of education as preparation is that students will be lethargic—they will have no urgency in their daily lives. Moreover, education is not an unfolding from within of the student's potentiality toward a certain end. That was the educational theory of Friedrich Wilhelm August Froebel, and Dewey criticizes it for relying on an a priori conception of development as grasping mainly mathematical symbols that lead the way to an Absolute. It was also the teaching of Georg W. F. Hegel; and despite Dewey's great and acknowledged debt to Hegel throughout his philosophical career, by 1916 he was long past the point of relying on anything like a Hegelian *Geist*. Growth must be the end of education because modern science has destroyed the ancient view of the universe as purposive and tending toward rest and finality (*M* 13:404–5). But he is also prepared to say that education in general has no aims (*M* 9:114). Dewey here shows his dissatisfaction with the abstractness of modern morality, especially as seen in the writings of Immanuel Kant. For Kant, morality consists of maxims of action that can be universalized so as to apply to all rational beings in a way that treats such beings as ends in themselves; the particular consequences that would follow from the action are irrelevant to the decision, as is the historical context. For Dewey, by contrast, context and consequences are always relevant to deciding the direction that intellectual and moral education should take.

Does Dewey's opposition to traditional views of education result in a clear notion of what he means by education and living as "growth"? He is well aware of one standard objection: it is possible to grow in morally objectionable ways as well as upright ones (*L* 13:19–20). Moreover, he does give at least one criterion for education and growth: growth requires freedom, both in the negative sense of absence of restraint and in the positive sense of ability to do (*L* 2:329). It also means for Dewey, to use Karl Marx's and Friedrich Engels's phrase from the *Manifesto of the Communist Party,* that "the free development of each is the condition for the free development of all." The growth of the society depends on the growth of each of its members. Such development requires the full participation of all in social life.

Throughout his career and particularly in his works on education, Dewey insists that there is no conflict between the good of a fully developed individual and the good of society. The child naturally wants "to serve" his fellows in society, and educators must understand that the "law" in intellectual and spiritual affairs is "co-operation and participation" (*E* 5:64, 65). "What one is as a person is what one is as associated with others, in a free give and take of intercourse." That the activities of life are bound up with emotions appears to indicate that there is no separate inner world for an individual apart from his relations with others (*M* 9:129, 132).

Central to Dewey's educational approach is the linkage of thinking and acting, or theory and practice. On his view, students should learn facts of mathematics or history in the context of performing some practical activity. Conversely, no training in a particular skill should be without a theoretical component that would enable the student to understand the skill in its larger context. Dewey thus stands doubly opposed to education as it has traditionally been conceived in America: both the classical education that emphasizes the reading of great books and the vocational training that usually has no room for the liberal arts and sciences.

Undergirding Dewey's educational views is a thoroughly modern understanding of the relation between philosophy and science. Traditionally, philosophy "claimed that it was in possession of a higher organ of knowledge than is employed by positive science and ordinary practical experience, and that it is marked by a superior dignity and importance" (*M* 12:92). Socrates and Plato sought to reconcile the imaginative beliefs that governed Athens with the more mundane knowledge of the artisans by finding a sound basis for morals in metaphysics —namely, the theory of the Forms—as opposed to custom. According to Dewey, this project of replacing custom with metaphysics is "the leading theme of the classic philosophy of Europe, as evolved by Plato and Aristotle" (*M* 12:89). This metaphysics held that what is truly real is ideal, nonmaterial, atemporal, changeless; the inferior kind of being is the opposite of those qualities, accessible to observation by the senses. It follows that knowledge at its highest level is contemplative and not practical; hence, we arrive at the dichotomy of theory and practice. The task of philosophy became the disclosure of the truly real and the attainment of certainty through the building of a system, and this building of a system was to be accomplished by the use of reason freed from passion. Disclosure of the truly real would provide guidance in practical affairs. But ancient philosophy failed to convince that it had arrived at the desired certainty. It could not have succeeded because its project was misconceived.

According to Dewey, philosophy must instead: (1) renounce belief in antecedent Being; (2) make clear what revisions are needed in traditional judgments about values; and (3) project "ideas about values which might be the basis of a new integration of human conduct"— integration, that is, of conduct stemming from scientific beliefs with conduct stemming from beliefs about values (*L* 4:37). Philosophy should have a part in a reconciliation of facts and values, but it must first humble itself and recognize its limitations. A proper "reconstruction" of philosophy "will regard intelligence not as the original shaper and final cause of things, but as the purposeful energetic re-shaper of those phases of nature and life that obstruct social well-being" (*M* 12:108). Such a reconstruction will leave aside speculation about an original shaper and a final cause because scientific method cannot answer those questions.

In Dewey's eyes, philosophy and science are not synonymous:

> Philosophy as itself science is a humbug and played out. But take all the science there is, and there is a question: What is its bearing on the conduct of life—not in detail, but with reference to general lines of policy forming—using the word policy to apply to the relatively more comprehensive ends by means of which activities hang together over a period of time and a fairly wide human area.[4]

Thus, he believes that philosophy and science are not so closely related today as they should be: we must respect the findings of science not only in a certain sphere but also in the spheres of religion, morals, and politics; and philosophy must search for values, for the uses to which science and technology should be put.

Perhaps it could go without saying that much of Dewey's overall project hinges on whether he has an optimal understanding of philosophy and science. If Socratic philosophizing is, contrary to the founders of modern science, the highest form of the pursuit of wisdom, contemplation may be a worthy end in itself rather than merely instrumental in the search for values. If science has sometimes advanced without completely open communication among all people—for example, if science has ever advanced through the efforts of those who did not fully share their results for fear of persecution—then the link between science and democracy is weaker than Dewey supposes. Dewey himself is well aware that the results of scientific experimentation may be used for undemocratic ends.

An Alternative Liberalism

The Public and Its Problems is Dewey's most thorough attempt to return to first political principles and his fullest treatment of political theory. He begins the book by remarking on the importance of discerning what the state is rather than what it should be. He finds "the key to the nature and office of the state" in the distinction between private and public (*L* 2:245). Some actions have consequences that affect only "the persons directly engaged in a transaction," while the consequences of other actions "affect others beyond those immediately concerned" (*L* 2:243–44). The former sort of action is properly considered private; the latter, public.

Those who are indirectly affected by the actions of others need someone to look after their interests. Dewey assumes that they will be too numerous to make regulatory decisions completely by themselves. Representatives and other public officials constitute the government; but, they do not by themselves form the state, for the state includes the public as well as the government. Thus, Dewey defines the state as "the organization of the public effected through officials for the protection of the interests shared by its members" (*L* 2:256).

How far does the state extend? Dewey claims that "the line between private and public is to be drawn on the basis of the extent and scope of the consequences of acts which are so important as to need control, whether by inhibition or by promotion" (*L* 2:245). He insists that the limits of the state cannot be specified in advance; rather, they must be determined experimentally. As further guidance, he adds that public actions can be known by "the far-reaching character of consequences, whether in space or time; their settled, uniform and recurrent nature, and their irreparableness" (*L* 2:275). Yet Dewey refuses to call any particular association private. In principle, the state may "fix conditions under which *any* form of association operates" (*L* 2:280).

Dewey's lack of a fixed attachment to any set of democratic institutions shows his experimentalism. "There is no sanctity in universal suffrage, frequent elections, majority rule, congressional and cabinet government" (*L* 2:326). They are to be modified to suit the needs of the state to perform its regulatory function. The key precondition for the attainment of this end is awareness on the part of the members of the public that they constitute a public—an awareness that they have an interest in common with one another. This key precondition is also the central problem, for the "democratic public is still largely inchoate and unorganized" (*L* 2:303). The large scale of modern society has extended the area over which consequences of actions have effect, and in an impersonal way, so that a public does not know that it exists. Indeed, it is more accurate to say "a public" than "the public," for a distinctive body of citizens is formed every time a transaction has indirect consequences. In modern times, there are "too many publics and too much of public concern for our existing resources to cope with" (*L* 2:314).

Thus, the central political problem for Dewey is to facilitate the self-identification of publics. Accomplishing this goal requires "improvement of the methods and conditions of debate, discussion and persuasion," which in turn depends upon "freeing and perfecting the processes of inquiry and of dissemination of their conclusions" (*L* 2:365). On the one hand, Dewey recognizes that much of this inquiry will be performed by experts and not by the majority of people; on the other hand, he concludes *The Public and Its Problems* by stressing the importance of local communities through which the results of inquiry must work in the formation of public opinion. Public opinion must be prepared to judge the work of experts in terms of the public interest or interests.

The purpose of that inquiry—the purpose of the state itself—is not aggrandizement of the state but promotion of the peaceful and fruitful functioning of the associations that make up local communities.

When a state is a good state, when the officers of the public genuinely serve the public interests, this reflex effect [i.e., of the state on private associations] is of great importance. It renders the desirable associations solider and more coherent; indirectly it clarifies their aims and purges their activities.... In performing these services, it gives the individual members of valued associations greater liberty and security. (*L* 2:279–80)[5]

Dewey's notion of a public or publics has the role in his thought that civil or political society has in earlier liberal thought, especially that of Locke. For Locke, the unanimous act of individuals leaving the state of nature establishes a civil society: the first and only independent act of that civil society is to decide by majority rule where to place the legislative power, which Locke describes—following Hobbes—as *"the Soul that gives Form, Life, and Unity* to the Commonwealth."[6] For Dewey, in contrast to both Hobbes and Locke, it is at least one "public" that is created—theoretically—before the government and hence the state, and the state "comes into existence" in order to regulate the indirect consequences of actions (*L* 2:244). "Society" as a unity is not meaningful for Dewey; he says that "there is no one *thing* which may be called society, except" the "indefinite overlapping" of private associations (*L* 2:279).

Along with other social contract thinkers, Hobbes and Locke agree on the basic point that civil society is an association of independent human beings. The creation of a public marks a coming together on the part of a group of individuals who were previously separate (functionally, not metaphysically, speaking). It also signifies the recognition of a commonality by those people, who until then might have seen themselves as having only the barest minimum of shared purposes. How does Dewey's public differ from the traditional liberal notion of civil society? One main difference lies in the degree of unity available. Civil society for Locke can never be more than a qualified solidarity: the qualification resides in the right that each individual retains to act for his self-preservation. The individual surrenders the power to do what he thinks fit for his self-preservation only "so far forth" as his preservation permits, because people "will always have a right to preserve what they have not a Power to part with."[7] It is simply not in accordance with human nature for harmony among the members of a civil society to be guaranteed. The individual is properly concerned primarily with himself and his own preservation; but, as Locke says, "the preservation of the Society" is its "first and fundamental natural Law," the rule by which it must govern itself.[8]

By contrast, Dewey holds out the hope of complete unity or integration between individual and society. Dewey does not expect a problem-free society, one in which individuals never encounter difficulties or find themselves at odds with one another or with society. In fact, he expects new problems to arise as old ones are solved. But he does envision and hope for an absence of hostility among people, an absence of a state of affairs in which people see no possibility of harmonization of their goals and thus the need to contest one another. So little is human nature fixed in its needs or the manifestations of those needs according to Dewey that, while he is willing to grant a general, natural need for combat or striving against something, he does not admit that such combat must take the form of individuals opposing one another; it could instead manifest itself in fighting disease or another social ill (*L* 13:286–87).

Dewey's opposition to traditional liberal individualism is not a rejection of liberalism per se. Indeed, Dewey remains a liberal in three major respects. First, he advocates government by deliberate decision making. Decisions about the regulation of indirect consequences of actions in the public interest are to be made either by citizens themselves or by their representatives: *representative democracy*, therefore, is not an oxymoron for him. Particular representative institutions have nothing venerable about them in themselves, but Dewey clearly believes in the need for some sort of institution in which officers of the citizenry will gather to make judgments in the public interest (*L* 2:283, 287).

Second, Dewey favors limited government. Although his experimentalism will not allow a specification of any definite limits to the scope of government, he teaches that the purpose of government is to facilitate and enhance the activities of associations, not to envelop them in a larger entity called the state (*L* 2:279–81). The state is "a distinctive and secondary form of association, having a specifiable work to do and specified organs of operation" (*L* 2:279). He writes that "only the voluntary initiative and voluntary cooperation of individuals can produce social institutions that will protect the liberties necessary for achieving development of genuine individuality" (*L* 14:91, 92).

Third, Dewey wants to preserve a wide range of individual rights. In the 1930s, he was accused of encouraging a dangerous collectivism; and he did not always stress the need for the protection of the rights of individuals, such as those in the Bill of Rights. By 1939, however, in light of the development of fascist and communist regimes, he concedes that:

> I should now wish to emphasize more than I formerly did that individuals are the finally decisive factors of the nature and movement of associated life. . . . [I]ndividuals who prize their own liberties and who prize the liberties of other individuals, individuals who are democratic in thought and action, are the sole final warrant for the existence and endurance of democratic institutions. (*L* 14:91, 92).

Those accusations against Dewey in the 1930s were the result of his advocacy of industrial democracy and socialism. He called for workers to have "direct participation in control" over their work, and by the 1910s he had come to believe that such a condition was impossible when the "animating motive is desire for private profit or personal power" (*M* 9:269, 327–28). Fundamental social and economic change would be required—of a more radical sort than the New Deal provided—in order for society to produce other than stunted individuals. Having flirted for a while with the notion of state capitalism (i.e., joint regulation of the economy by public officials, heads of industry, and representatives of labor) as a transitional phase to socialism, in the 1930s he proposed direct enactment of a huge program of public works; redistribution of wealth via taxation; and nationalization of public utilities, natural resources, banking, transportation, and communication.

Yet those measures were to be steps toward a goal that Dewey could not comfortably characterize as state socialism. His initially favorable impression of the Soviet Union quickly soured as Stalin carried out his plans. Ultimately, Dewey rejected Marxism on the ground that it was virtually impossible to arrive at democratic ends through the use of nondemocratic means, as the Soviet Union was ostensibly committed to do. If socialism were to become other than oppressive, it would have to involve decentralization of power and the securing of institutions that would allow for dissent. Even guild socialism, he came to believe, would probably involve a too-powerful state. Perhaps Dewey can be excused for not being more specific about what sort of system would embody his triple goals of democracy, socialism, and liberalism.

Conclusion

Does Dewey's democratic thought represent an improvement on the liberalism of the Declaration of Independence? In order to answer that question we must accept Dewey's judgment of 1939 concerning the "decisive" importance of the powers and rights of individuals. How well would a Deweyan liberalism protect those powers and rights? A full answer to that question cannot be attempted in this chapter; but we may move toward the heart of the matter by asking whether Dewey is prudent in his hope for a complete integration between the individual and society. Does the evidence exist to support the claim that tensions among human goods are removable? Or does not history point toward ineradicable tensions among the various human goods?

Also problematic, then, is Dewey's insistence that everything in education be done with a view toward social good. One might well ask: would his educational principles, if followed to the letter, produce a John Dewey? Dewey understands that he needed space free from direct public or social involvement to think, but he does not make allowance for that solitude in others.

That neglect, in turn, casts some doubt on Dewey's psychological theory. Dewey dislikes the word "reason" to describe the human ability to think because it indicates too much a separate faculty that must be located somewhere in the mind. He much prefers the term "intelligence," which "has something to do" (*M* 12:134–35). But intelligence, according to Dewey, turns out to be nothing other than a collection of social habits: "Concrete habits do all the perceiving, recognizing, imagining, recalling, judging, conceiving and reasoning that is done" (*M* 14:124). On this view, it seems impossible that a human being could possess a unique (not to mention divinely inspired) spark that makes him or her a unique person. Rather, the uniqueness of intelligence must be *wholly* accounted for by a different grouping of habits. How can this theory explain the master strokes of genius that produced many of the literary, artistic, philosophical, scientific, or technological breakthroughs in human history? It is highly doubtful that reason is the simple equivalent of social intelligence.

Dewey does not go so far as to say that it is impossible to distinguish between the mental powers of two people. But he does emphasize the impossibility of understanding the mental powers of one person apart from the social context in which that person lives. The individuality of any one person develops through a process of give-and-take with his fellows (*E* 5:413). As we have seen, the experimentation that characterizes a well-ordered life involves a partial reliance on the view of others. The testing of details of one's own plan of life requires approval, or potential approval, of a significant number of one's fellows—what we have seen Dewey call "a consensus of conclusions."

Dewey apparently considers the danger posed by what Alexis de Tocqueville calls "tyranny of the majority" to be slight—despite America's all-too-obvious problems with racial relations. He suggests that widespread scientific education and the cooperation it fosters will do more to prevent tyranny—in its various forms—than will the cultivation of originality in people such as himself. Dewey suggests that the terms "genius" and "originality" are usually applied to an individual deviation from custom that cannot be explained in any other way (*L* 1:169–70).

What we must decide is whether Dewey is correct, whether widespread scientific education is more valuable than the originality of a few in forestalling tyranny of the majority. That is a difficult question. A critical spirit among a citizenry will keep that citizenry ready to test a dominant opinion when the circumstances present themselves. But if the desired result is a "consensus of conclusions," if the result of the test must be widely shared, how likely is it that the test would eradicate an unfounded or dangerous dominant opinion? Would a minority likely be able to convince a majority to abandon that opinion?

In contrast, if we depend on the originality of a few, how much influence can so few iconoclastic individuals have over the thoughts and actions of a majority? They may be adept at avoiding the informal pressures to conform to the majority, but how can they hope to counteract the formal pressure, expressed through law and government?

We may thus conclude that Dewey's solution is more effective in preventing laws from being passed that tyrannize over a minority, while an effort to promote genius and originality will do more to ward off social pressure. Therefore, in a liberal society that trumpets individual rights, where both sorts of tyranny must be prevented, we must judge Dewey's attempt to reformulate American independence as at best incomplete.

Notes

1. H. S. Thayer, *Meaning and Action: A Critical History of Pragmatism*, 2nd ed. (Indianapolis: Hackett, 1981), 431.

2. Parenthetical references to Dewey's writings are to the set of volumes published by Southern Illinois University Press in Carbondale and edited by Jo Ann Boydston. The volumes are divided into three series: *The Early Works, 1882–1898* (5 vols.), *The Middle Works, 1899–1924* (15 vols.), and *The Later Works, 1925–1953* (17 vols.). References in the text to this series will consist of *E* for *Early Works, M* for *Middle Works*, and *L* for *Later Works*, followed by the volume and page number.

3. Thomas Jefferson, *Notes on the State of Virginia,* Query XVIII, in *The Portable Thomas Jefferson*, ed. Merrill D. Peterson (Harmondsworth: Penguin, 1975), 215.

4. John Dewey and Arthur F. Bentley, *John Dewey and Arthur F. Bentley: A Philosophical Correspondence, 1932–1951*, ed. Sidney Ratner and Jules Altman (New Brunswick, N.J.: Rutgers University Press, 1964), 629.

5. If the distinction between private and public is the key to understanding the state, Dewey says relatively little about that distinction. He observes that the terms "individual" and "social" are not correspondingly equivalent to "private" and "public" because private acts may have social consequences and yet not be deemed public (*L* 2:244). For example, a philanthropist's donations may have widespread effects, but those donations are not publicly required. We could, however, hope for more examples than the few Dewey gives.

6. John Locke, *Second Treatise of Government*, secs. 96, 134, 212 (quotation from 212; italics in original). Compare Thomas Hobbes, *Leviathan*, chap. 29.

7. Locke, *Second Treatise*, secs. 129, 149.

8. Locke, *Second Treatise*, sec. 134 (both phrases italicized in original).

Chapter 35

Franklin Delano Roosevelt
and the Second Bill of Rights

Donald R. Brand

Franklin Delano Roosevelt (1882–1945) changed the character of the American regime by changing its ends. He believed that the regime established by the American Framers was incomplete because the ends of government that they had identified were too limited to secure the happiness of the people. The original ends were first announced in the Declaration of Independence and then translated into a more specific list of civil liberties in the Constitution and the Bill of Rights. Our government was created to secure the *natural* rights to life, liberty, and the pursuit of happiness, the latter being closely associated with the right of property. Our Constitution authorized and empowered institutions that could both prevent others from depriving us of those rights and minimize the probability that government itself would become oppressive.

In contrast, Roosevelt spoke of a new and expansive agenda for government under the rubric of *human* rights. In his Eighth Annual Message to Congress in 1941, popularly referred to as his Four Freedoms Address, Roosevelt described the New Deal in terms of four essential freedoms. The first two freedoms he identified, "freedom of speech and expression" and the "freedom of every person to worship God in his own way," closely approximate conceptions of the American Framers. Indeed, the general logic of the Four Freedoms Address was to embrace implicitly all of the rights identified in the Bill of Rights through the endorsement of freedom of speech and freedom of worship. The third freedom on Roosevelt's list, "freedom from want," defined the distinctive character of the New Deal and represented a departure from our constitutional tradition. To secure this freedom or right the federal government would have to expand dramatically its regulatory and welfare responsibilities. The fourth freedom, "freedom from fear," defined as a foreign policy objective the creation of an international order that would prevent aggressor nations from threatening the security and rights of other nations.[1]

Roosevelt's new concept of freedom was central to his understanding of the New Deal. His first systematic articulation of New Deal principles, the 1932 Commonwealth Club Address, was a call for an "economic declaration of rights, an economic constitutional order" (*PPA* 1928–32: 752). Roosevelt was ambivalent, however, about the expansion of the power of the federal government that his new rights agenda would entail. While he committed the federal government to new regulatory and welfare responsibilities, he also sought to reinvigorate civil society; to encourage private associations and groups to regulate themselves; and to foster self-control through moral renewal and a rededication to the communities in which we live.

These two reform strategies, one focusing on the state and the other on civil society, proved largely incompatible. As the federal government expanded to guarantee freedom from want, it usurped the role of civil society and undermined some of the communities the New Deal tried to foster. Alternatively, when the New Deal did succeed in encouraging new and more vigorous forms of community, they often proved an impediment to the realization of the expansive rights agenda. Roosevelt's ambitious attempt to found a new economic order precluded a division of labor between the federal government and private sector groups that would have allowed them to reinforce one another. Measured by its own standards, then, the New Deal fell short of its goals.

The Critique of Traditional Liberalism

Roosevelt introduced the concept of an "economic declaration of rights" to address a problem he perceived in the changing character of American society. In the nineteenth century, Jeffersonian Democrats could safeguard democracy by preserving the sanctity of property rights and limiting the scope of the state. Roosevelt characterized this era as "the day of the individual against the system, the day in which individualism was made the great watchword of American life." The Western frontier made land substantially free to all, and "no one, who did not shirk the task of earning a living, was entirely without opportunity to do so." When the economy collapsed in this era, the federal government did not have to intervene because "most of the people lived partly by selling their labor and partly by extracting their livelihood from the soil, so that starvation and dislocation were practically impossible" (*PPA* 1928–32:746).

Roosevelt argued that by the beginning of the twentieth century, the closing of the Western frontier and the Industrial Revolution had transformed our situation. A nation of farmers had become a nation of increasingly urbanized employees, often working for large and powerful corporations. Depressions and unemployment became far more serious threats because working men did not have the resources to survive adverse circumstances. In addition, "industrial combinations had become great uncontrolled and irresponsible units of power within the state." While the financial titans who had built America's industrial base had performed a valuable social function in the latter half of the nineteenth century, now "our industrial plant is built," if not "overbuilt," and these financial titans could, if not controlled, become "the despots of the twentieth century" (*PPA* 1928–32:749–50).

Controlling the incipient oligarchy called first and foremost for an ethical revolution. Roosevelt repeatedly hurled invectives at America's financial elite, describing them as morally corrupt. They were "unscrupulous money changers" who "know only the rules of a generation of self-seekers" (*PPA* 1933:12). Their "irresponsibility and greed" threatened to reduce the working man to "starvation and penury" (*PPA* 1928–32:749). The confidence needed to facilitate economic transactions and promote economic growth "thrives only on honesty, on honor, on the sacredness of obligations, on faithful protection, on unselfish performance"; but the oligarchs were capable only of "callous and selfish wrongdoing." Roosevelt called for a new generation of business leaders who were "willing to sacrifice for the good of a common discipline" (*PPA* 1933:12, 14).

Roosevelt's reference to financial titans is revealing. He directed his harshest attack against bankers who use "other people's money" (a phrase he took from Louis Brandeis) for reckless speculative investments (*PPA* 1933:13). Although Roosevelt repeatedly clashed with America's business elite, he always retained some respect for entrepreneurs like Henry Ford who had built factories and offered employment to many. Building America's industrial plant had been a substantial contribution; but with its completion, the age of the entrepreneur was over. What Roosevelt could not abide were speculators who had become wealthy by financial chicanery, exploiting the working man without contributing to genuine economic prosperity. Samuel Insull's Power Trust personified this evil. Roosevelt believed that Insull had built a business empire by manipulating investors with deceptive corporate structures that maximized his profits while depleting power companies of essential investments.[2]

The building of our industrial base had not delivered, in Roosevelt's views, on the promise of material prosperity for many working Americans, and the poverty that remained widespread had more to do with the maldistribution of wealth than it had to do with ineradicable scarcity. To replace the harsh inequalities of the old economic order, Roosevelt called for greater equality in the distribution of wealth and even for the establishment of an "economic democracy." He championed a highly progressive income tax structure that would soak the rich and dampen income inequalities. He presented economic democracy as a logical corollary of political democracy and therefore consistent with traditional political ideals. Government acceptance of the "responsibility to save business" was to be understood as the responsibility to "save the American system of private enterprise *and economic democracy*" (emphasis added). According to Roosevelt, the New Deal was simply heeding "the warning of Thomas Jefferson that 'widespread poverty and concentrated wealth cannot long endure side by side in a democracy.'" Proclaiming his fidelity to the American political tradition, Roosevelt described his reforms as an effort to "preserve the American ideal of economic as well as political democracy, against the abuse of concentration of economic power" (*PPA* 1936:482, 486). Extending the concept of democracy to encompass economic life, however, entailed a fundamental transformation in the character of American government.

Roosevelt's Transformation of Liberalism

Roosevelt called for "the development of an economic declaration of rights, an economic constitutional order," in his 1932 Commonwealth Club Address. The modest elaboration of the concept "an economic constitutional order" that he provided implied new responsibilities for the federal government. The right to life, reinterpreted as the "right to make a comfortable living," implied that government must assure individuals the opportunity to work for decent wages. "Our government . . . owes to every one an avenue to possess himself of a portion of that plenty sufficient for his needs, through his own work" (*PPA* 1928–32:752, 754). As president, while Roosevelt looked first and foremost to the private sector to generate work opportunities for individuals, he instituted programs like the Works Progress Administration, the Civilian Conservation Corps, and the Public Works Administration to provide government jobs for those who could not find private employment. These programs not only addressed the immediate problems posed by the Great Depression, but they also exemplified the new economic order that would arise out of the ashes of economic catastrophe.[3]

Roosevelt's first concern was providing jobs for the unemployed, but he did not suggest that the able-bodied were entitled to a minimal level of support even if they refused to work. In the Commonwealth Club Address, he noted that even though a man had a right to a comfortable living, "[h]e may by sloth or crime decline to exercise that right" (*PPA* 1928–32:754). Roosevelt recognized that direct government relief, the "dole," could be morally corrupting by encouraging sloth.

> The lessons of history, confirmed by the evidence immediately before me, show conclusively that continued dependence upon relief induces a spiritual and moral disintegration fundamentally

destructive to the national fiber. To dole out relief in this way is to administer a narcotic, a subtle destroyer of the human spirit. . . .

The federal government must and shall quit this business of relief. (*PPA* 1935:19–20)

Nevertheless, Roosevelt's admonition against subverting the work ethic of the able-bodied was complemented by a concern for those who could not work. Anticipating the Social Security program, Roosevelt alluded to "the burdens of those parts of life which in the nature of things, afford no chance of labor; childhood, sickness, old age." Society could afford to succor those who could not work because "our industrial and agricultural mechanism can produce enough and to spare" (*PPA* 1928–32:754).

In his Eleventh Annual Message to Congress in 1944, Roosevelt provided his fullest elaboration of his new conception of the ends of the American polity. As in the Four Freedoms Address, Roosevelt did not repudiate the ends established in the American Founding; rather, he sought to add additional "economic rights" to the list of "political rights" guaranteed by the Bill of Rights. Here his itemization of political rights was more fulsome: they included not only the rights of speech and press and to freedom to worship, but also such due process rights against arbitrary punishment as the right to trial by jury and the freedom from unreasonable searches and seizures. (Notably absent is any reference to the right to property, an omission perhaps foreshadowed in Roosevelt's description of all of the rights in the Bill of Rights as political rights.) As important as these rights were, they "proved inadequate to assure us equality in the pursuit of happiness." With the superior insight of those who come later in history, the New Dealers "have come to a clear realization that true individual freedom cannot exist without economic security and independence." Quoting an unnamed source, Roosevelt asserts: "Necessitous men are not free men" (*PPA* 1944–45:41; cf. 1936:233).

Roosevelt's Second Bill of Rights elaborated the promise to provide freedom from want. It included in a slightly abbreviated form "the right to a useful and remunerative job"; "the right to earn enough to provide adequate food and clothing and recreation"; the right of every farmer to a "return which will give him and his family a decent living"; the right of every businessman to "trade in an atmosphere of freedom from unfair competition and domination by monopolies at home or abroad"; "the right of every family to a decent home"; "the right to adequate medical care"; "protection from the economic fears of old age, sickness, accident and unemployment"; and "the right to a good education." This list was not meant to be exhaustive, but it did articulate the premises of the New Deal and define the agenda of the progressives who would follow in Roosevelt's footsteps (*PPA* 1944–45:41).[4]

Government and the Rights Agenda

Roosevelt understood that additional rights entailed new powers to protect those rights. The era of big government was dawning as the federal bureaucracy expanded and assumed new regulatory powers to supervise banking, the stock market, transportation, and the power industry. New Dealers pledged to eliminate unfair competition throughout the business world. In some cases, new regulatory agencies were created; in other cases, older agencies acquired new regulatory powers.

Even the traditional structure of American political parties would have to be reformed to accommodate them to the new political economy. The decentralized parties inherited from the nineteenth century were amalgams of diverse interests loosely associated around broad and vague political principles. They were ill suited to serve as the vanguard of liberalism because they did not provide the disciplined congressional majorities that Roosevelt needed in order to enact new reforms. After the extraordinary legislative successes of the first "Hundred Days" in 1933 and the second "Hundred Days" in 1935, Roosevelt had been stymied by conservatives in his own party who joined ranks with his Republican opponents to defeat court and administrative reform as well as wages and hours legislation. In a radical departure from accepted political practice, Roosevelt intervened in five primaries in 1938 in an attempt to defeat conservative Democrats and replace them with loyal New Dealers. Roosevelt admonished voters to go to the polls and "consider the fundamental principles for which his party is on the record." Roosevelt wanted to align the contest between the two political parties with "clashes between the two schools of thought, generally classified as liberal and conservative." Then the liberal party, the party of reform and progress, could enlist partisan zeal in the service of "new remedies," and it could "use government as an instrument of cooperation to provide these remedies" (*PPA* 1938:398). Roosevelt's commitment to economic rights transformed liberalism into an ideology of the state.

Roosevelt's state-building, however, was tinged with ambivalence. The primary means utilized by the state for securing rights is law. The expansive rights agenda embraced by Roosevelt entailed an exponential increase in legal duties and a vast new centralized apparatus of federal law enforcement—a bureaucratized regulatory state. The federal bureaucracy did in fact grow significantly in the New Deal, but Roosevelt resisted the development of a legal ethos in the administrative apparatus of the New Deal. Roosevelt therefore opposed the 1940 Walter-Logan bill, which sought to reduce administrative discretion by legalizing administrative procedures. Roosevelt's veto message was a classic expression of legal realist skepticism of legal formalism:

> A large part of the legal profession has never reconciled itself to the existence of the administrative tribunal. Many of them prefer the stately ritual of the courts, in which lawyers play all the speaking parts, to the simple procedure of administrative hearings which a client can understand and even participate in. Many of the lawyers prefer that decision be influenced by a shrewd play upon technical rules of evidence in which the lawyers are the only experts, although they always disagree. Many of the lawyers still prefer to distinguish precedent and to juggle leading cases rather than to get down to the merits of the efforts in which their clients are engaged. For years, such lawyers have led a persistent fight against the administrative tribunal.[5]

Roosevelt succeeded in replacing the Walter-Logan bill with a watered-down Administrative Procedures Act that preserved great scope for discretionary administration.

Roosevelt's opposition to the legalization of bureaucracy is in part explained by the historical origins of the New Deal. A conservative judiciary had defended property rights and declared unconstitutional such important New Deal innovations as the Agricultural Adjustment Act and the National Industrial Recovery Act. Roosevelt lamented what he referred to as the "horse and buggy" constitutional interpretation of the conservative majority, and in contrast to their restrictive interpretation of federal powers to regulate commerce, he called for a broader understanding more consistent with the intent of the Framers. Sounding conservative by later standards, Roosevelt deplored activist judges who read their policy predilections into the Constitution, specifically accusing the Court of "acting not as a judicial body, but as a policy-making body." He wanted judges who would find the law—"enforce the Constitution as written"—not make the law (*PPA* 1937:125–26).[6]

Roosevelt despaired when none of the conservative judges on the Court retired in his first term and he could not reshape the Court in a more liberal direction. Then, flush with a resounding electoral victory in 1936, Roosevelt began his second term boldly proposing a plan to expand the size of the Supreme Court, hoping thereby to provide new seats that could be filled by justices sympathetic to the New Deal. Critics of the Court-packing scheme claimed that Roosevelt's plan would undermine the independence of the judiciary, and many would have preferred that Roosevelt propose constitutional amendments to provide the legal authority for New Deal regulatory measures. Roosevelt dismissed the amendment route as impracticable in this case, but, more fundamentally, he criticized the Article V amendment procedures. "No amendment which any powerful economic interests or the leaders of any powerful political party have had reason to oppose has ever been ratified within anything like a reasonable time" (*PPA* 1937:131).

Roosevelt's progressivism—his confidence that the future held improvements and that the task of political reform was to keep abreast of the times—made him skeptical of obstacles to change. The Framers of the American Constitution, however, did not assume that change was synonymous with improvement, and they deliberately made it difficult to amend the Constitution so that it could protect rights from the whims and passions of factious majorities.[7] For the same reason, the Framers had sought to assure the independence of the judiciary from potentially factious majorities by provisions such as the appointment of judges for life terms, removable only by impeachment for "Treason, Bribery, or other high Crimes and Misdemeanors."

Roosevelt ignored the problem of factious majorities, and he criticized his opponents for their attempt "to block the mandate of the people" as expressed in elections. Roosevelt compared the three branches of American government to a team of three horses with the American people in the driver's seat. Ignoring the logic of checks and balances, Roosevelt stressed the need for the horses to work together, and he lamented that "two of the horses are pulling in unison today; the third is not." He insisted that the courts should not put property and contract rights above "the need to meet the unanswered challenge of one-third of a Nation ill-nourished, ill-clad, ill-housed." Roosevelt was confident that economic rights would supplement rather than detract from political rights. He tried to reassure the American people that his Court-packing scheme would reorient the Court without infringing "in the slightest upon the civil or religious liberties so dear to every American" (*PPA* 1937:123–24, 131–32).

Tempering Hyper-Liberalism

Roosevelt did not embrace the logic of his economic bill of rights without reservations. It is not clear whether he fully understood the statist implications of this vision, but he was notably reluctant at endorsing the creation of a sovereign power requisite to the task posed by the proclamation of a Second Bill of Rights. Roosevelt's belief that he could found a new economic order that did not entail a leviathan state rested upon his hope that the New Deal could spark a movement of moral reform—a reconstructed civil society and a new ethic of community and cooperation. The selfish individualism of the old order would be replaced by a "new individualism" whereby the individual saw himself as a member of the community and was willing to sacrifice self-interest for the sake of the common good. Roosevelt realized that "changes in ethics alone" would not suffice and that government regulation of business would be required so that the new moral code would be fortified with the coercive powers of government (*PPA* 1933:12). Nevertheless, the New Deal could not succeed without "a re-appraisal of values" that elevated the community above the individual (*PPA* 1928–32:751).

Roosevelt's hopes for a moral renewal focusing on community were a source of his ambivalence concerning the individualism inherent in a rights-based economic constitutional order. This ambivalence was visible in his commitment to rural resettlement. Roosevelt's Second Bill of Rights presupposes an industrial order and an economy of abundance. The productivity associated with the Industrial Revolution fueled the aspiration to overcome economic necessity—to provide freedom from want. The symbol of the new economic order is the factory, not the family farm. Nevertheless, Roosevelt could not repudiate his attachment to a simpler and, as he believed, a more wholesome age. The farmer's vulnerability to the whims of climate and other natural forces and his struggles to maintain a modest standard of living could not shake Roosevelt's attachment to farming as a lifestyle. Whereas Karl Marx lamented "the idiocy of rural life," and Lenin and Stalin brutally relocated peasants to industrial settings, Roosevelt saw in rural *communities* a healthy antidote to the ruthless and self-interested individualism of the modern age and a salutary proximity to nature.

Roosevelt resisted a choice between promoting community and his agenda of (implicitly individualist) economic rights. He insisted that rural communities were compatible with his new economic order. The New Deal contained many programs of assistance for farmers that were intended to provide freedom from want. The Agricultural Adjustment Act (AAA) created agricultural cartels under government supervision to restrict the supply of agricultural commodities to markets, thereby (it was hoped) raising the income of farmers. Rural electrification brought one of the greatest benefits of industrial civilization to rural communities. The New Deal provided new legal obstacles to the repossession of bankrupt farms, and other agencies provided credit for farmers to sustain them through hard times.

Improving life in the country would encourage rural resettlement. Roosevelt was convinced that even a return to prosperity would leave residual unemployment, and he therefore promoted rural-urban communities practicing "subsistence farming" in proximity to factories and centers of handicraft production that would provide part-time employment to supplement farm income. Twenty-five million dollars were appropriated for subsistence homesteads in the National Industrial Recovery Act (NIRA), and a Subsistence Homestead Division was established in the Department of Interior. By 1935, there were twenty operational homestead communities, the most famous of which was named Arthurdale; and Roosevelt had consolidated the administration of the program into a new Resettlement Administration. The resettlement communities, however, never became economically self-sufficient and therefore never offered a viable communitarian alternative to the traditional individualism of the American farmer.[8]

Moreover, programs like the AAA provided benefits for farmers at a cost. Farmers were no longer free to grow whatever they wanted and bring it to market. Failure to abide by crop restrictions would entail penalties, even if the excess were grown for domestic consumption. The self-reliance of farmers was undercut by their dependence upon subsidies to survive. Moreover, the character of agricultural groups changed as government regulation and subsidies redefined farming. Organizations that facilitated collective self-help endeavors became lobbyists intent on maintaining a positive cash flow of government benefits. Whether these lobbying organizations schooled citizens in the art of associating in the manner Tocqueville envisioned in *Democracy in America* is an open question. For Tocqueville, citizens took responsibility for the well-being of the polity; they did not just instrumentally use government to further their narrowly defined self-interest.

Just as Roosevelt's commitment to rural resettlement demonstrated his belief that small, territorially based communities could overcome the corrosive individualism of modern society, so his commitment to the National Recovery Act (NRA) demonstrated his belief that functionally based communities like trade associations and trade unions could perform the same role in an industrial context. Roosevelt's commitment to the regulatory state notwithstanding, his most ambitious program for addressing the depression attempted to relegate the state to a supporting role. In his 1932 Commonwealth Club Address, Roosevelt anticipated the division of labor between the state and private associations that the NRA sought to institutionalize: government "should assume the function of economic regulation only as a last resort," because businessmen were acknowledging their responsibility and were seeking "a form of organization which will bring the scheme of things into balance, even though it may in some measure qualify the freedom of action of individual units within the business" (*PPA* 1928–32:752–55).

Roosevelt attributed the depression to "unfair methods of competition" which led to "cut-throat prices." The collapse in the prices of goods had in turn compelled wage reductions that reduced the purchasing power of workers, exacerbated the downturn in industrial production, and increased unemployment. Competition itself became suspect in the New Deal economic order that stressed cooperation as its dominant value.[9]

Roosevelt was confident that the vast majority of businessmen shared his analysis of the causes of our economic problems and supported his call for a new ethic of cooperation and community to moderate competitive individualism.

> You and I agree that this condition must be rectified and that order must be restored. The attainment of that objective depends upon your willingness to cooperate with one another to this end and also your willingness to cooperate with your Government.
>
> In almost every industry an overwhelming majority of the units of the industry are wholly willing to work together to prevent overproduction, to prevent unfair wages, to eliminate improper working conditions. In the past success in attaining these objective has been prevented by a small minority of units in many industries. I can assure you that you will have the cooperation of your Government in bringing these minorities to understand that their unfair practices are contrary to a sound policy. (*PPA* 1933:156–57)

Trade associations could draft codes of fair trade competition to counteract the competitive pressures to slash wages; but, without government powers to enforce these codes, such efforts would be futile because of "cut-throat underselling by selfish competitors unwilling to join in such a public-spirited endeavor" (*PPA* 1933:202). Under the NRA, government supervision of the code-drafting process was provided to assure that industry carried through on its pledge to increase wages and reduce working hours for labor, thereby increasing reemployment and purchasing power. In addition, consumers would be protected from any attempt by industries to use the code-drafting process to raise prices unduly through cartels.

The hybrid structure of the NRA, with its projected division of labor between trade associations and government, proved unworkable and unstable. As cartels developed and noncompliance with code provisions became epidemic, government became more heavy-handed in its scrutiny and supervision of code provisions and more aggressive in its enforcement activities. Industries began to complain of government regimentation, and opposition to the NRA became widespread. Mistakes had been made in the implementation of the program; but the problems with the NRA can be traced to the very conception of the program, and they could not have been remedied by administrative reforms. Roosevelt had underestimated the extent to which government enforcement guarantees would necessitate government control over industry. As the state co-opted trade associations as agents of its endeavors, the dynamism of civil society was depleted. Driven by its commitments to secure economic rights and provide labor with a living wage, government regulation of business gradually usurped the functions the NIRA had reserved for voluntary trade associations. The logic of rights had trumped the ethic of cooperation.

The New Deal commitment to securing the economic rights of working men and women led to a complex relationship with labor unions. Roosevelt was sympathetic to labor unions, and he recognized that unionization would enhance the bargaining power of workers and provide higher wages and better working conditions. Section 7a of the NIRA therefore compelled industries to include in their codes of fair trade competition a provision guaranteeing labor the right to organize and bargain collectively. This new right simultaneously appeared to further the realization of an economic constitutional order and to be consistent with Roosevelt's repudiation of traditional individualism and his emphasis on community. It encouraged workers to cooperate for the sake of securing common interests. By legitimating unions, government had ratified union ethics according to which workers who would not act in solidarity with their fellow workers were derided as selfish scabs.

Under the auspices of the NRA, labor union membership increased dramatically, and strikes for recognition of labor unions multiplied. Nevertheless, the NRA and union leaders were soon embroiled in a bitter dispute over administrative interpretations of Section 7a. With Roosevelt's support, NRA administrators insisted that unions could gain rights of representation only for those workers who voted for them in free labor elections. In these elections, more than one union could compete for recognition, including company unions that largely served management's interests. Labor unions would be represented at the bargaining table in numbers proportionate to their voting strength among workers.

Opposing the NRA interpretation of Section 7a, union leaders insisted that company unions were a vehicle for management co-optation of labor and that the independent union that won a majority of labor support in an election should be entitled to represent all of the workers in that industry. From a union perspective, multiple unions fragmented labor solidarity, providing opportunities for business to play one union off against another and weakening labor in its negotiations with business. Labor's preferred interpretation of Section 7a ultimately triumphed when it was included in the Wagner Act of 1935, but Roosevelt resisted the Wagner Act until the NRA was declared unconstitutional by the courts. When the Wagner Act became the only alternative protecting labor's right to organize and bargain collectively, Roosevelt finally endorsed it.

Roosevelt's reluctance to embrace the Wagner Act and its encouragement of union solidarity is rooted in the rights orientation of his new economic order. The individualism implicit in the rights orientation made Roosevelt skeptical of claims of solidarity that empowered the majority but ignored minorities within the workforce. His democratic commitments made him skeptical of labor bosses whose ability to win a majority in a labor election did not guarantee their accountability to the rank and file. His liberal ideology impeded him from adopting a realistic approach to furthering the interests of labor. Labor's interests ultimately prevailed, but only because the Supreme Court forced Roosevelt's hand.

Roosevelt's most notable successes in promoting community were associated with his challenge to the social and political dominance of white, Anglo-Saxon Protestants. Despite his membership in this elite, Roosevelt worked consistently throughout his career to broaden the ethnic foundations of American society and to provide social standing and political opportunities for excluded groups.

Catholics and Jews were the most notable beneficiaries. In 1924 and again in 1928, Roosevelt supported Al Smith as a presidential candidate. In the campaigns, Roosevelt tried to overcome the bias against Al Smith's Catholicism, recognizing that Smith's ascent to the highest office in the land would symbolize the full inclusions of Catholics within the American polity. One of Roosevelt first actions as president was to promote the repeal of Prohibition, a moral venture that had always drawn its support from Protestant reformers and had been strongly opposed in Catholic constituencies. Taking Prohibition off the political agenda removed a stigma from Catholics and created new political opportunities for Catholic politicians. Likewise, the inclusion of Jews in Roosevelt's top political and judicial appointments was similarly an important step in bringing them within the political mainstream.

Roosevelt's actions in these matters demonstrates the role that government can play in breaking down prejudices. Even African Americans, the victims of the most intense prejudices, received modest recognition. Roosevelt's support for Marian Anderson's Lincoln Memorial concert after the Daughters of the American Revolution had denied her access to Washington D.C.'s Constitution Hall sent an inspiring message to African Americans and opened at least a crack in the wall of segregation that excluded them from full American citizenship.

The politics of inclusion practiced by Roosevelt strengthened ethnic ties and provided a rich additional source of community for individuals. Before Roosevelt's overtures to ethnic voters helped to raise their social standing, ambitious individuals from these groups had been torn between repudiating their ethnic roots for the sake of advancement or foregoing opportunities for the sake of solidarity. After the New Deal, the necessity for making such unpalatable choices would be reduced. Ethnic identity became a political and economic strength rather than a liability.

Roosevelt's success in lowering the barriers of prejudice in American politics is one of his most notable achievements, but this accomplishment was achieved because the tensions between state and community that subverted his efforts to build community on territorial and functional identify did not emerge in the case of ethnicity. Roosevelt never proposed a cultural bill of rights to correspond to the economic bill of rights; he never suggested a cultural entitlement, enforceable by government, to live in a society free from prejudice. This did not imply that government should do nothing to create a culture of tolerance or that government was powerless to influence opinions. It did imply that prudence should guide the use of government power and that punishment of prejudice was not obligatory per se. Roosevelt recognized limitations in the use of state power to overcome social and cultural prejudice that he did not recognize in combating economic inequality.

Roosevelt's approach to civil rights clearly demonstrates the triumph of pragmatism over ideology. Without denying the injustices of segregation, Roosevelt nevertheless subordinated progress in race relations to the more pressing task of economic recovery. Cultivating Southern Democrats whose votes he needed for recovery measures, he refused to support even the most elemental demands for racial justice embodied in antilynching laws. In response to a New Dealer's plea to him to endorse a bill to abolish the racially discriminatory poll tax, Roosevelt responded that "politics is the art of the possible."[10] No such pragmatic calculus had been at work in his call for a new economic order in the 1932 campaign.

The New International Liberal Order

Just as the aspiration to achieve freedom from want legitimated a vastly expanded agenda of domestic policies by the federal government, so the aspiration to achieve freedom from fear legitimated a dramatic expansion in international commitments. Once American involvement in World War II became inevitable, Roosevelt devoted his efforts to overcoming isolationism and laying the groundwork for the integration of the United States into a new international order when the war was over. In urging Americans to accept new international responsibilities, Roosevelt was following in the footsteps of his political mentor Woodrow Wilson; and he remained mindful of Wilson's failure to secure ratification of the Versailles Treaty and membership in the League of Nations. His ambition, however, was not simply to succeed where Wilson had failed. Roosevelt's foreign policy differed from Wilson's international idealism primarily in the emphasis that it accorded to economic development as a corollary to the spread of democratic political institutions. Roosevelt's new international order was a cosmopolitan version of the New Deal.

The affinities linking Roosevelt's foreign policy to Wilson's were evident in his drafting of the Atlantic Charter. On August 4, 1941, Roosevelt met with Winston Churchill for four days on the American battleship *Augusta* off the coast of Newfoundland. He pledged to Churchill that the U.S. Navy would take on a more aggressive role in protecting convoys in the Atlantic, and he agreed to a joint statement of war aims even though the United States was formally still a neutral nation. These joint war aims, the Atlantic Charter, were a reaffirmation of the Wilsonian ideal of self-determination. Just as Wilson had incorporated this ideal into his Fourteen Point Proclamation of War Aims in 1918 (e.g., urging that specified boundaries be redrawn in accord with "recognizable lines of nationality" and encouraging respect "for every peace-loving nation which, like our own, wishes to live its own life, determine its own institutions"), so Roosevelt and Churchill renounced aims of "aggrandizement, territorial or other," and rejected "territorial changes that do not accord with the freely expressed wishes of the people concerned." Furthermore, both statesmen committed themselves to "respect the right of all peoples to choose the form of government under which they will live; and they wish to see sovereign rights and self government restored to those who have been forcibly deprived of them."[11]

The Fourteen Points and the Atlantic Charter also resemble one another on the issue of free trade. Wilson's program entailed "absolute freedom of navigation upon the seas" and the "removal, so far as possible, of all economic barriers and the establishment of an equality of trade conditions among all the nations consenting to the peace." In the Atlantic Charter, Roosevelt and Churchill seek a peace that "should enable all men to traverse the high seas and oceans without hindrance," and they endeavor "to further the enjoyment by all states . . . of access, on equal terms, to the trade and to the raw materials of the world which are needed for their economic prosperity" (*PPA* 1941:314–15).

Finally, the Fourteen Points implicitly identifies the arms race that preceded World War I as one of its major causes, and it therefore urges that "adequate guarantees be given and taken that national armaments will be reduced to the lowest point consistent with domestic safety." The Atlantic Charter does not immediately call for universal disarmament; but it does call upon all the nations of the world to abandon "the use of force," and it stresses that peace is unattainable "if land, sea, or air armaments continue to be employed by nations which threaten, or may threaten, aggression outside of their frontiers." Aggressive and potentially aggressive nations must be disarmed "pending the establishment of a wider and permanent system of general security." A system of general security in conjunction with "other practical measures" will "lighten for peace-loving peoples the crushing burdens of armaments." While the Fourteen Points explicitly anticipated the League of Nations in its call for a "general association of nations" to afford "mutual guarantees of political independence and territorial integrity to great and small states alike," the Atlantic Charter implicitly anticipated the United Nations in its call for a system of general security.

Where the Fourteen Points and the Atlantic Charter differ is in the latter's internationalization of the New Deal. The Atlantic Charter calls for international collaboration "with the object of securing, for all, improved labor standards, economic advancement, and social security." It looks forward to a world where "men in all lands may live out their lives in freedom from fear and want." These latter words clearly echo Roosevelt's 1941 Annual Address to Congress and its reference to the Four Freedoms. Indeed, when Roosevelt presented the Atlantic Charter to Congress, he embellished the charter's reference to freedom from want and fear with a reminder that "the declaration of principles includes of necessity the world need for freedom of religion and freedom of information." This elaboration linked the Atlantic Charter to the first two freedoms described in the Four Freedoms Address.

After the United States had entered World War II and had begun to plan for a new postwar international order, it sometimes appeared as if Roosevelt was moving away from Wilsonian idealism. Wilson's League of Nations supplemented by a World Court would have been based on the legal equality of all nations as recognized by international law. Seemingly more realistic, Roosevelt acknowledged that an effective international agency would have to recognize inequalities among nations, and he placed his hopes for world peace on cooperation between the four nations that he believed would dominate the postwar world: the United States, the Soviet Union, Britain, and China. "Britain, Russia, China, and the United States and their allies represent more than three-quarters of the total population of the earth. As long as these four Nations with great military power stick together in determination to keep the peace there will be no possibility of an aggressor Nation arising to start another world war" (*PPA* 1943:558). Roosevelt referred to these nations as the Four Policemen, and he expected each to secure order within the sphere of its influence. This scheme for cooperation among the great powers (seemingly reminiscent of the Holy Alliance after the Napoleonic Wars) eventually found expression in a modified form with the creation of the U.N. Security Council.

Nevertheless, Roosevelt's departures from Wilsonian idealism were modest. As the name Four Policemen suggests, the role of the great powers in Roosevelt's postwar vision was to enforce international law. "The rights of every Nation, large or small, must be respected and guarded as jealously as are the rights of every individual within our own Republic" (*PPA* 1943:558). The policing nations were not to be rivals pursuing distinctive national interests but collaborators jointly securing universal interests. As Roosevelt made clear in an address to Congress on the Yalta Conference, his references to the spheres of influence of the Four Policemen had nothing to do with a realistic construction of a balance of power.

> The Crimea Conference was a successful effort by the three leading nations to find a common ground for peace. It ought to spell the end of the system of unilateral action, the exclusive alliances, the spheres of influence, the balances of power, and all the other expedients that have been tried for centuries—and have always failed.
>
> We propose to substitute for all these a universal organization in which all peace-loving nations will finally have a chance to join. (*PPA* 1944–45:586)

Although Roosevelt's concept of the Four Policemen was an enforcement mechanism for international law and morality (and therefore linked to Wilsonian idealism), his application of Wilsonianism is nevertheless paradoxical. For Wilson, lawful and peaceable relations among nations presuppose the establishment of republican governments. Wilson insisted that "just government rests always upon the consent of the governed," and when ambitious tyrants subverted democratic government, "there can be no lasting or stable peace in such circumstances."[12] In this regard, Wilson follows his philosophic mentor Immanuel Kant, who called for a federation or league of republican states to promote international law and morality.

Why would Roosevelt have believed that a brutal Communist dictator like Joseph Stalin would play a constructive role in promoting international peace, law, and morality?[13] Roosevelt did not dispute Wilson's claim that domestic political order and international conduct were intimately intertwined. Roosevelt described democracy as "a covenant among free men to respect the rights and liberties of their fellows," and respect for the rights of fellow citizens became the foundation for respect for the rights of citizens of other nations. "International good faith" is described as "a sister of democracy" (*PPA* 1939:1). Additionally, religion (a belief that God created man and bestowed upon him a fundamental dignity of spirit) was a foundation of respect for rights. Therefore, Roosevelt concluded that "religion, democracy, and international good faith—complement and support each other."

> Where freedom of religion has been attacked, the attack has come from sources opposed to democracy. . . . And where religion and democracy have vanished, good faith and reason in international affairs have given way to strident ambition and brute force. . . .
>   We have learned that God-fearing democracies of this world which observe the sanctity of treaties and good faith in their dealings with other nations cannot be indifferent to international lawlessness. (*PPA* 1939:1–3)

Given the publicly proclaimed atheism of the Soviet Union, Roosevelt's political thought would seemingly have prepared him to be as suspicious of communism as he was of Nazism.

Roosevelt never assumed that Hitler could be tamed and transformed into a civilized participant in a new world order by forceful opposition or even military defeat. The very character of the Nazi regime was a threat to international peace, and it was for that reason that nothing less than the unconditional surrender of Germany could terminate hostilities. Germany had to be reconstructed from the ground up—rebuilt as a democratic nation.

Nevertheless, Roosevelt implicitly rejected any conception of totalitarian regimes that would have linked Nazism to communism. Roosevelt did not identify Stalin with Hitler; indeed, he looked forward to friendship with the Soviet Union. In a fireside chat on the Teheran and Cairo Conferences, Roosevelt reported: "I may say that I 'got along fine' with Marshal Stalin. He is a man who combines a tremendous, relentless determination with a stalwart good humor. I believe he is truly representative of the heart and soul of Russia; and I believe that we are going to get along very well with him and the Russian people—very well indeed" (*PPA* 1943:558). Roosevelt's confidence that he could manage Stalin and convince him to cooperate in the establishment of a new and just international order in part not only reflects a naive faith in the power of his own charm and the potential for personal diplomacy to overcome conflicting interests; it also sheds fundamental light on his understanding of the Soviet Union. Stalin was "truly representative" of the Russian people because his forced industrialization of the Soviet Union laid the groundwork for achieving freedom from want; and with the achievement of this fundamental right progress in the achievement of other political rights could be anticipated, including the formal mechanism associated with representative democracy which the Soviet Union lacked.

Roosevelt's hopes for the Soviet regime dated to the very beginning of his political career, and they could not be completely erased even at the nadir of U.S.-Soviet relations (i.e., after the Soviets signed the Nonaggression Pact with Germany in 1939 and then invaded Poland and Finland). In 1940, Roosevelt spoke to an American Youth Congress on the south lawn of the White House.

> More than twenty years ago, while most of you were very young children, I had the utmost sympathy for the Russian people. In the early days of Communism, I recognized that many leaders in Russia were bringing education and better health and, above all, better opportunity to millions who had been kept in ignorance and serfdom under the imperial regime. I disliked the regimentation under communism. I abhorred the indiscriminate killings of thousands of innocent victims. I heartily deprecated the banishment of religion—though I knew that some day Russia would return to religion for the simple reason that four or five thousand years of recorded history have proven that mankind has always believed in God in spite of many abortive attempts to exile God.

I, with many of you, hoped that Russia would work out its own problems, and that its government would eventually become a peace-loving popular government with a free ballot, which would not interfere with the integrity of its neighbors.

That hope is today either shattered *or put away in storage against some better day.*[14]

Roosevelt proceeded to characterize the Soviet Union at that time as "a dictatorship as absolute as any other dictatorship in the world," and he condemned its aggression against Finland; but he resisted the conclusion that these facts revealed something fundamental about the character of the Soviet regime.[15]

Roosevelt's desire to expand the sphere of human liberty notwithstanding, the natural tendency of his expansive understanding of human rights, particularly with its inclusion of economic rights, was to blur the distinction between freedom and tyranny. While Roosevelt recognized that the Soviet Union denied its citizens the basic freedoms guaranteed by our Bill of Rights, he also believed that communism promoted forms of economic redistribution that benefited the common man and therefore secured his economic rights. For example, when Roosevelt addressed Congress after the Yalta Conference, he described the changes in the use of the palaces and villas of Yalta after communism was introduced. "Before the last war, it [Yalta] had been a resort for people like the Czars and princes and for the aristocracy of Russia—and the hangers-on. However, after the red Revolution, and until the attack on the Soviet Union by Hitler, the palaces and the villas of Yalta had been used as a rest and recreation center by the Russian people" (*PPA* 1944–45:576). As dubious as this claim is empirically, it is revealing the Roosevelt would introduce it in an assessment of the character of the Soviet regime. If the right to a paid vacation is a fundamental right, as the U.N. Declaration on Human Rights subsequently asserted in its itemization of economic rights (an itemization that took its inspiration from Roosevelt's Second Bill of Rights), then the purported democratization of vacation opportunities in the Soviet Union might tend to mitigate the criticism that it denied its citizens the right to speak or the right to practice their religion. Such calculations obfuscated the despotic character of the Soviet regime.

Roosevelt repeatedly demonstrated a propensity for finding redeeming characteristics in the Soviet system. He suggested to his secretary of labor, Frances Perkins, that communism provided a secular outlet for the intensely religious spirit of the Russian people. He then favorably contrasted Russians, including Russians under communism, who "want to do what is good for their society," with Americans: "We take care of ourselves and think about the welfare of society afterwards."[16] Roosevelt's hope was that Americans could be awakened to their social responsibilities without sacrificing their political liberties. Indeed, the New Deal had already begun a shift from a laissez-faire economy to a mixed economy, where government assumed new responsibilities guaranteeing freedom from want in addition to traditional liberties. At the other extreme, the Soviet Union would democratize and liberalize. Focusing on religious freedom, Roosevelt told Averell Harriman that "the atheistic Communist system would not be able to suppress permanently the deeply religious tradition of the Russian people. In time . . . greater freedom was bound to evolve."[17] The American and Soviet systems would thereby converge.

Roosevelt's inability to understand that the threat posed by the Soviet Union was analogous to the threat posed by Nazi Germany was the most significant foreign policy failure of his presidency, and this failure was associated with his expansive conception of economic rights. His focus on economic rights blurred the distinction between liberal and tyrannical regimes by diverting the attention of citizens and statesmen from traditional liberal concerns with political institutions and practices to questions of economic development. According to Roosevelt, any regime that promoted modernization and industrialization was, knowingly or unknowingly, laying the groundwork for liberalization and democratization. Promoting economic development could thus become the dominant goal of American foreign policy in the confidence that this sufficed to build a world hospitable to liberal democracies. The history of communism should disabuse us of any such illusions.

Conclusion

Woodrow Wilson's progressivism called for disinterested citizens and leaders with an aptitude for eliciting a moral majority to counter the baneful influence of powerful special interests. The struggle that defined progressivism was the struggle against urban machines, where governance seemed synonymous with trading in particularistic benefits. In the moralistic horizon of progressivism, the pursuit of economic self-interest in politics was corrupt. Wilsonian progressivism was also committed to an international order of republican regimes federated through a League of Nations and regulating their behavior in accordance with the norms of international law. The moral aspirations of progressivism had widespread appeal to middle-class Americans who longed for righteous causes and ennobling themes, but this enthusiasm could also wane if the demands for sacrifice were excessive. World War I overtaxed the moral energies of many Americans, and progressivism collapsed in its wake.

It is against this backdrop of Wilsonian idealism that we can situate the New Deal in the American political tradition. Franklin Roosevelt had been a protégé of Wilson, and there are powerful affinities between progressive reformers and New Deal reformers. What is distinctive about the New Deal, however, is the formulation of a second, economic Bill of Rights supplementing the original political and civil rights of the original Bill of Rights. The Second Bill of Rights vulgarized the high-minded idealism of progressive reformers. Demands for sacrifice and service were displaced by self-righteous and self-interested demands for economic entitlement. Linking the moral dignity of rights to the powerful motive of self-interest proved politically irresistible. The New Deal succeeded in expanding progressivism's core middle-class political constituency to include workers, farmers, Catholics, ethnic urbanites, and African Americans. The New Deal coalition was also more enduring and less subject to the vagaries of moral enthusiasm. Nevertheless, the New Deal exacerbated problems of liberal governance.

Governance becomes more difficult first and foremost because civil society is weaker where economic demands are conceptualized as rights. To compromise a demand grounded in rights is morally suspect; and the state, not civil society, is the guarantor of rights. Since a vibrant civil society is an indispensable nexus for participation in community in a liberal society, the weakening of civil society leaves individuals increasing isolated from one another. Individualism is a problem in democratic polities, as Tocqueville noted in *Democracy in America*, because individuals who are no longer tied to one another in voluntary associations cannot develop the sense of political efficacy that will provide a foundation for democratic citizenship. Adding rights to those already identified in the Bill of Rights, as Roosevelt did in developing his list of economic rights, jeopardizes the security of all rights.

Notes

1. *Public Papers and Addresses of Franklin D. Roosevelt*, 13 vols., ed. Samuel I. Rosenman (New York: MacMillan Company, 1938–1950), 1940 Volume, 663–72. Henceforth, this work will be cited in the text as *PPA* followed by year of the volume and page number (e.g., *PPA* 1940:663–72).

2. Samuel Insull of Chicago built a vast network of power companies held together by a pyramid structure of holding companies. The collapse of Insull's power empire in 1932 hurt many small investors and created a propitious political environment for regulatory reform targeted at the elimination of holding company oligopolies in the power industry.

3. For a good description of the character of New Deal relief policy, see Edwin Amenta, *Bold Relief* (Princeton, N.J.: Princeton University Press, 1998).

4. Premising economic rights upon the assertion that "necessitous men are not free men" poses conceptual and practical dilemmas that plagued the New Deal regime. Can human necessities be determined with precision? How are we to distinguish claims rooted in necessity or need from claims that express desires, which are illimitable? Men driven by necessity may not be free, but Roosevelt pledged that the New Deal would more expansively provide "freedom from want." Taken literally, this would imply a repudiation of any conception of limited government. New Deal rhetoric could be enlisted to justify the development of an expansive nanny state that smothers individual responsibility through the soft despotism of its solicitude for economic well-being. (The reference to soft despotism is an allusion to Alexis de Tocqueville's discussion of the form of despotism to which a modern democratic society is particularly prone. See Tocqueville, *Democracy in America*, vol. II, pt. IV, chaps. 6 and 7.)

5. Cited in Paul Verkuil, "The Emerging Concept of Administrative Procedure," *Columbia Law Review* 78 (1978): 273.

6. Roosevelt also wanted to promote his new rights agenda without dramatically expanding the role of the judiciary within the framework of American government. Thus, the New Deal is historically associated with an emphasis on judicial restraint and deference by courts to legislative decisions, a judicial approach personified in the jurisprudence of Felix Frankfurter. Only later, when the next generation of progressive reformers sought to fortify Roosevelt's economic rights agenda and to add to it a host of additional rights, did progressives embrace the legalization of the administrative state. For these progressives, Roosevelt's call for judges to "enforce the Constitution as written" would prove an unacceptable straightjacket, and they embraced the idea of a living constitution that would adapt to the realties of a modern industrial economy.

7. See Alexander Hamilton, James Madison, and John Jay, *The Federalist*, ed. Jacob Cooke (Hanover, N.H.: Wesleyan University Press, 1961), no. 49, 338–43.

8. Arthur Schlesinger, *The Coming of the New Deal* (Boston: Houghton Mifflin Company, 1959), 361–73.

9. See Donald R. Brand, "Competition and the New Deal Regulatory State," in *The New Deal and the Triumph of Liberalism*, ed. Sidney Milkis and Jerome Mileur (Amherst: University of Massachusetts Press, 2002).

10. Harvard Sitkoff, *A New Deal for Blacks* (New York: Oxford University Press, 1978), 45.

11. *PPA* 1941:314–15. Woodrow Wilson's Fourteen Points Address can be found in *The Papers of Woodrow Wilson*, 69 vols., ed. Arthur S. Link (Princeton, N.J.: Princeton University Press, 1966–1994), 45:534–39.

12. *Papers of Woodrow Wilson*, 27:172–73.

13. The Four Policemen vision also attributed a great power role to China that was unrealistic: China was torn by strife between the forces of Mao Zedong and Chiang Kai-shek, and it would not have been capable of imposing stability in an Asian sphere of influence.

14. Robert E. Sherwood, *Roosevelt and Hopkins* (New York: Harper and Brothers, 1948), 138, emphasis added.

15. Roosevelt's views were carried to their logical extreme by Henry Wallace, Roosevelt's vice president from 1940 to 1944. In his 1942 "Free World" speech, Wallace contrasted American political democracy with Russian economic democracy: "Some [i.e., Wallace and like-minded progressives] in the United States believe that we have overemphasized what might be called political or bill-of-rights democracy. Carried to its extreme form, it leads to rugged individualism, exploitation, impractical emphasis on states' rights and even to anarchy. Russia, perceiving some of the abuses of excessive political democracy, has placed strong emphasis on economic democracy. This, carried to an extreme, demands that all power be centered in one man and his bureaucratic helpers. Somewhere there is a practical balance between economic and political democracy." See Henry A. Wallace, *Democracy Reborn* (New York:

Reynal and Hitchcock, 1944), 198. Wallace's sympathies with the Soviet experiment were more overt than Roosevelt's, but Roosevelt saw in Wallace a like-minded progressive who shared his commitment to economic democracy. In 1940, Roosevelt chose Wallace as his vice president over the objections of party leaders because he was a "true liberal." Roosevelt's selection of Wallace was a sequel to his 1938 party purge debacle, an attempt to identify the Democratic party with ideological liberalism. Roosevelt was so adamant in his choice of Wallace that he threatened not to run in 1940 unless the party convention ratified his choice. See James MacGregor Burns, *Roosevelt: The Lion and the Fox* (New York: Harcourt, Brace and World, 1956), 428–29.

16. Frances Perkins, *The Roosevelt I Knew* (New York: Harper and Row, 1946), 87.

17. Kenneth S. Davis, *FDR: The War President: 1940–1943* (New York: Random House, 2000), 605–6.

PART FIVE:

NEW CHALLENGES AT HOME
AND ABROAD
(1945–present)

》》➤ ◄《《

Chapter 36

Ayn Rand: Radical for Capitalism

William Thomas

I. Rand's Significance

The late twentieth century saw a resurgence in America of a strain of thought variously called "libertarianism," "classical liberalism," and "market liberalism." Like the liberalism of the nineteenth century, libertarianism envisions a government of limited scope and strictly defined powers, consistently upholding rights to freedom of speech, freedom of contract, and the right to own and use property. It critiques the welfare state and economic regulation as both unjust and inefficient, and endorses laissez-faire capitalism as the economic system that maximizes justice, human well-being, and individual liberty.

Libertarianism per se is not a dominant political movement in America, but its themes have been sounded on both the Left and Right in such causes as economic deregulation, concern for privacy rights, and opposition to state-sponsored racism. Although this renaissance is due to the work of several major and many minor intellectuals, perhaps no single figure has been more influential in promoting this view of human liberty than Ayn Rand (1905–1982).[1] Since the publication of her novel *The Fountainhead* in 1943, Rand's works have enjoyed perennially high sales and are widely cited by readers as a source of personal inspiration, appearing ubiquitously on lists of favorite novels or books that the public rates most influential. In 1991, a survey by the Library of Congress and the Book of the Month Club found that Rand's *Atlas Shrugged* was the second most common response from their sample of readers to the question: "What book has most influenced your life?" (As might be expected, in first place, by far, was the Bible.) A popular memoir of the 1970s libertarian movement was aptly entitled *It Usually Begins with Ayn Rand*.[2] Beyond the arena of strictly libertarian thought, Rand has been a significant contributor to the turn in American culture toward placing individual self-fulfillment and self-esteem at the center of personal and policy concerns.

Rand's influence on American political thought comes not only from her dramatic advocacy of liberty and opposition to collectivism in her novels, but also from the distinctive arguments she brought to bear on the issues. Those arguments called for and sketched out a new ethical approach to political issues and gave a fresh cast to ideas such as natural rights and limited government. Her viewpoint put her in conflict with both the Left and the Right in twentieth-century America, and, true to her individualism, she did not back down from the challenge of forging and advertising an alternative perspective of her own.

II. Rand's Life and Work

Ayn Rand was born Alissa Rosenbaum in St. Petersburg, Russia, on February 2, 1905.[3] She grew up in a middle-class Jewish family and was deeply affected by the Russian Revolution, which drove her family to live in the Crimea for a time and during which her father's pharmacy was expropriated. She narrowly escaped being purged from college, graduating from the University of Leningrad just ahead of a wave of expulsions that removed all students of bourgeois background.[4] She recalled later in life that she had determined at a very young age to become a writer, and that as far back as she could remember she had seen herself standing in opposition to the basic ideas that permeated Russian politics on both the Right and Left. These included collectivism, authoritarianism, and dogmatism (and, more generally, antirational epistemological doctrines—from the Christian appeal to faith to Leninist "dialectical materialism"). She became a student of film and studied screenwriting, and it was through the cinema that she encountered America, which seemed a promised land of opportunity, achievement, and liberty. She determined to escape the Soviet Union to seek her fortune in that free, prosperous society.

Rosenbaum arrived in the United States in 1926 and took the name Ayn Rand. She applied herself to her chosen goal with a steadfast will, seeking work in Hollywood as soon as she could get there and rising over time through a string of odd jobs to screenwriting. During the 1930s, she published her first novel, *We the Living* (1936), and a novelette, *Anthem* (1938).[5] Her first major popular breakthrough came when she scored a Broadway hit with her play *Night of January 16th* (1936).[6] She made her reputation with her novel *The Fountainhead* (1943), which became a surprise, word-of-mouth bestseller in the mid-1940s.[7] Her magnum opus, *Atlas Shrugged*, came out in 1957 and, while received poorly by the critics, it too was a great popular success.[8] In the 1960s, Rand collaborated with psychologist Nathaniel Branden in publishing a magazine and offering courses based on her philosophy, which she came to call "Objectivism."[9] By the mid-1960s, their magazine, *The Objectivist*, had more than 20,000 subscribers. Their courses and book service were exposing a new generation to the writings of "old Right" figures such as Isabel Patterson and free-market economists such as Henry Hazlitt and Ludwig von Mises. Branden and Rand's relationship suffered a personal and professional rupture in 1968, and Rand's following diminished as a consequence; but, she continued writing philosophy and political and cultural commentary, as she had since the early 1960s in speeches and essays. Most of Rand's nonfiction works have been compiled in volumes such as *The Virtue of Selfishness*, *Capitalism: The Unknown Ideal*, and *The New Left: The Anti-Industrial Revolution*.[10] Rand died in 1982, and many of her papers have been published posthumously by her estate.

Although political and philosophical themes permeate all of Rand's fiction, three novels stand out especially for their political content: *We the Living*, *Anthem*, and *Atlas Shrugged*. Based to some degree on Rand's own experiences living in the Soviet Union, *We the Living* tells a tragic story of the death of love and of idealism under the totalitarian oppression of the Communist party. Death is not merely metaphorical under such a system, and even the capable, creative heroine is unable to escape, dying near the border in an attempt to flee the country. In Rand's account, communism is both an economic and humanistic disaster, a system that raises mediocrity and incompetence to power and destroys the conditions required for human beings to live and flourish.

The novelette *Anthem* projects the long-term effects of Marxism into a distant future. Collectivism and irrationality have triumphed in a dystopia that has no concept of the first-person singular pronoun. Since the very existence of individuals is denied, social custom rigidly circumscribes individual choices. Under such repression, society has regressed to a medieval level of technology amidst the ruins of industrial civilization. *Anthem* does not focus on the precise form of the political system that has emerged, although its general characteristics can be discerned. Instead, Rand highlights the profoundly detrimental effects on the human mind and spirit of consistently pursuing a collectivist ethos. Rand shows us that only the individual who identifies himself as such, and who recognizes his entitlement to his own life and choices, can begin the rebuilding process.

Atlas Shrugged is set in a version of America fast on its way to total collectivism and economic collapse. The novel centers on the people who provide the "motor of the world," that is, those who produce the goods and ideas that keep society going, be they industrialists, engineers, artists, scientists, or philosophers. As the brightest minds and best workers mysteriously disappear, the novel's heroine, Dagny Taggart, struggles to keep her family's railroad running in the face of ever-increasing government regulation. The novel's primary concern is the underpinning that liberty requires. Rand's conception of liberty is encapsulated in the basic political dictum that "Congress shall make no law abridging the freedom of production and trade" (*AS* 1168). People permit, and even demand, the suppression of freedom because they do not value it—because they hate the fact that liberty allows some to achieve things others cannot. Ultimately, freedom depends on a respect for the power of the individual human mind: the power to make its own personal and moral decisions; the power to shape a person's character; the power to know the world; and (last but not least) the power to create new products, processes, industries, and wealth. The novel attacks philosophical views such as skepticism, altruism, and the dichotomy—deriving notably from Augustine and Descartes—between mind and body. In lengthy speeches by the principal characters, Rand sketches the philosophical system that she would erect in place of the received tradition, with her politics as its outcome. In an afterword to the novel, Rand offered a brief summary of that system, Objectivism: "My philosophy, in essence, is the concept of man as a heroic being, with his own happiness as the moral purpose of his life, with productive achievement as his noblest activity, and reason as his only absolute."

III. Rand's Political Theory

Rand's political theory has three main elements, all of which draw upon the classical liberal political tradition. First, the foundation of the political system should be respect for the fundamental right to live free from physical force.[11] Second, government has the strictly limited function of protecting rights. Third, government power should be exercised in accordance with objective laws. As Rand explained, these elements amount to the advocacy of a system of laissez-faire capitalism:

> *Capitalism is a social system based on the recognition of individual rights, including property rights, in which all property is privately owned.* The recognition of individual rights entails the banishment of physical force from human relationships: basically, rights can be violated only by means of force. In a capitalist society, no man or group many *initiate* the use of physical force against others. The only function of the government, in such a society, is the task of protecting man's rights, *i.e.*, the task of protecting him from physical force; the government acts as the agent of man's right of self-defense, and may use force only in retaliation and only against those who initiate its use; thus the government is the means of placing the retaliatory use of force under *objective control*. (*CUI* 19)

A. Rights and Force

For Rand, human rights are essentially negative and unitary. What one has a right to is one's own life. Because life is "a process of self-generated and self-sustaining action," to have a right to life is ultimately to have the right to act in support of one's life, i.e., to have liberty of action (*VOS* 15). And because to support life one must use and consume resources, a right to life and liberty must entail a right to property. Thus, the rights of life, liberty, and property enshrined in many eighteenth-century documents are not disparate, but whole. Furthermore, in this conception it is very clear that a right to the "pursuit of happiness," as declared in the U.S. Declaration of Independence, is another way of expressing this same right: not an entitlement to happiness or well-being, but the freedom to seek it.

Rand offered a solution to a basic dilemma in political theory. On the one hand, there were those thinkers, exemplified by John Locke, who held that rights were *natural*, inherent in the makeup of human beings and usually placed there by the Creator and recognized by the light of reason. On the other hand, there were those, such as Jeremy Bentham and J. S. Mill, who noted that no such essence was evident, and could discern no sign of political entitlements deriving from any deity. Rights therefore were *human principles*, and as such were determined by the utilitarian principle of conducing to whatever would benefit the collective happiness of mankind. The trouble with the utilitarian account, however, is that the very need for concepts of rights seems to fall away, since ethical principles and laws are replaced by the pragmatic pursuit of social utility. This pragmatism, however, leaves the door open for a wide variety of political regimes, even oppressive ones, to try out their policies so as to observe the effect on social utility. Finally, since this utility is collective, it has been difficult for this tradition to uphold the sanctity of the individual as a political principle, although this is precisely the basic function of rights on the classical liberal account.

Rand accepts the basic critique of traditional natural rights doctrine. For Rand, rights are not mysterious traits, somehow part but not part of normal human nature; rather, they are simply principles concerning human action. Like all knowledge, rights have had to be discovered by human beings, and so it is understandable that the political implementation of rights has had a historical development that has reflected the social and cultural conventions of the places and times in which it has taken place. But this does not mean that in the end our basic conceptions of rights should be heterogeneous, any more than the laws of physics should be heterogeneous. According to Rand, rights principles are objective because they are justified by fundamental facts about humanity. Thus, Randian rights are indeed "natural," in the sense that they derive from human nature, even though they are not inherent in human beings nor endowed by any higher authority.[12] Because Rand clarifies how it is that reason can discern rights from human nature, her theory may in a sense be seen as revising or completing the theory of Locke. In Rand, it is human nature—that is, the needs of an individual human life and the means individual humans must employ to fulfill those needs—that provides the grounding for rights, just as human nature grounds Rand's entire ethical system. The key is that advancing one's own life and happiness is the greatest ethical good one can achieve, and one's right to life, liberty, and property secures the freedom to pursue this highest good for all individuals equivalently in their social interactions.

In defining rights as principles enshrining an individual's need for freedom from the initiation of force, Rand urges her readers to draw a sharp distinction between phenomena such as social pressure or market forces that have often been called "coercive," and real or threatened physical coercion. Faced with physical force, one is literally at risk of one's life. In the form of theft, physical force can deprive one of one's goods (which are, generally, the means that enhance one's enjoyment of life, and, more fundamentally, the means by which one secures oneself from inclement weather, malnutrition, and ill health). In the form of physical attack, force confronts its victim with injury and death.

No other putatively "coercive" interaction threatens one's life and well-being in so wholly destructive a manner. In an economic context, for example, both parties interact voluntarily. Should one party withdraw his cooperation (as when a factory owner fires a worker, or when a worker quits his job), neither party loses any benefits except those that were voluntarily conferred in the interaction itself. The loss of a chance to trade denies a person a positive-sum interaction, but leaves him in possession of his faculties, his life, and his goods; the loss of health or wealth through force takes place in the context of a zero or negative-sum interaction, in which at least one party is a net loser.

Fraud, in Rand's view, is another instance of physical force. In effect, a fraud is equivalent to a theft. Since the victim of a fraud has not agreed to the actual content of the fraudulent transaction, his goods are, in effect, alienated from him without his consent. Essentially, Rand asks us to notice that it is the physical aspect that distinguishes fraud from mere dishonesty: a fraud requires that some property be taken from the victim.

This is very different from the disappointment one might experience in not being offered a job in the open market, where, although one does not gain a positive benefit, neither has one's self or property been injured. It is interesting that we do not usually view the loss of a romantic partner as a case of "coercion." Here we understand that two lovers *choose* to expose themselves to the risk of heartache, and are better off for doing so. Yet economic interaction is much the same in Rand's view: much may be at stake in either case, but one may always walk away with one's fundamental faculties and one's wealth intact. One remains free in this fundamental and vital sense as long as one is free from force: "The precondition of a civilized society is the barring of physical force from social relationships—thus establishing the principle that if men wish to deal with one another, they may do so only by means of *reason:* by discussion, persuasion and voluntary, uncoerced agreement" (*VOS* 108).

Rand argues that in general, physical force faces the individual with a profound contradiction: to act either as his reason dictates to be in his interest—and thus incur injury from those who would coerce him—or abandon his judgment and act as others demand—and thereby avoid injury. On the one hand, a person drafted into a wartime army against his will faces death or imprisonment for "desertion" (i.e., going back to the course of life he would choose by his own judgment); on the other hand, he would face injury or death on the battlefield. Rand argues that in view of this, it was profoundly immoral and improper for anyone, and especially a government, to employ force for paternalistic reasons. "An attempt to achieve the good by physical force is a monstrous contradiction which negates morality at its root by destroying man's capacity to recognize the good, i.e. his capacity to value. Force invalidates and paralyzes a man's judgment, demanding that he act against it, thus rendering him morally impotent" (*CUI* 23). It may seem odd for Rand to argue that physical force attacks the mind and morality, but Rand does not view mental activity as possible apart from action in the world. Rand's view of the role of practical reasoning and action in the creation of a full life is similar to the Aristotelian doctrine that human flourishing is actualized through the free actions of the individual.[13] Just as one cannot learn a skill without doing it—as one cannot conduct research or acquire a profession without undertaking the many minute choices and actions that each requires—Rand argues generally that a disembodied contemplation is not possible apart from practical action to bring one's conclusions into effect. An artist denied access to his tools finds that his skills atrophy, and this principle applies to mundane activities as well: a person forcibly denied the ability to choose among lines of work or styles of clothes, for instance, is closed off from thinking meaningfully about these aspects of his life.

B. Government and Law

Rand defined government as "an institution that holds the exclusive power to *enforce* certain rules of social conduct in a given geographical area" (*VOS* 107). It is coercive power that distinguishes government from all other social institutions, and Rand focuses on this fact. Such an institution is justified solely for the purpose of securing the freedom of individuals in society from the initiation of physical force against them. Thus, the protection of the right to life, liberty, and property is the purpose of government and strictly circumscribes its proper arena of activity. In its functions, Rand's basic conception of government is similar to what Robert Nozick calls "the night-watchman state of classical liberal theory," a conception widely held in the eighteenth and nineteenth centuries.[14]

> The proper functions of a government fall into three broad categories, all of them involving the issues of physical force and the protection of men's rights: *the police*, to protect men from criminals—*the armed services*, to protect men from foreign invaders—*the law courts*, to settle disputes among men according to objective laws. (*VOS* 112)[15]

Rand argues that the provision of civil law (primarily contracts and torts) is the main positive service that government provides. Police and the armed services, by contrast, serve in a negative role: they protect citizens from threats. Civil law provides objective, just, and peaceful means of resolving disagreements and disputes, and it provides the context needed for reliable long-term planning and contracting (*VOS* 110–11). In turn, the ability to plan and contract is a necessary condition for the prodigies of global capitalist production and the wonders and conveniences of modern life. Without these legal institutions, society collapses into warring camps; each interaction invites violent dispute; and life at best becomes inconvenient, less productive, and more brutal.

As noted, paternalism is not compatible with Rand's conception of government. Rand strongly held that basing a political system on a moral view did not reduce the law to the principles of morality. The freedom she advocated in the political sphere did not entail a moral endorsement of whatever it might be that people would choose to do with that freedom. Her view of the proper functions of government results in a political vision with a deeply liberal cast. Rand's radically limited government provides each individual with freedom of expression and of lifestyle as much as it provides for freedom of commerce and industry. For example, laws on sexual conduct or for censoring published material would not be consistent with her rights-based system.

Rand advocated objectivity in the law, and she was deeply concerned at the tendency of lawmakers to produce vaguely worded laws and regulations, and to leave officials open-ended discretion. For Rand, law is "objective" when it is expressed in clear language and does not leave wide scope to individual officials, who may act in an arbitrary or power-seeking manner. The standards behind the law must be intelligible and the law's requirements must be capable of being known in advance. These points are the basic elements of the rule of law, and Rand is far from alone in promoting this idea. Rand's distinctive contribution to this familiar point is her emphasis on the epistemological bases of the law and the vital importance of conceptual precision there. For this reason, Rand criticized the widespread usage of indefinable terms such as "the public interest" in American political discourse.[16]

Rand rejected the very idea of associating government actions with the "public interest" or the "general will," arguing that there is no interest nor will apart from that of individuals. Consequently, she held that treating a group of people, or a sum of their attributes, as a whole—without regard for the differences among the individuals concerned—is simply a gross error of logic, an instance of reifying an abstraction. There is no "public interest" in Rand's view; rather, there are only the interests of the members of the public. Thus, the government is in no position to hold lands in trust for the public or to attempt to fine-tune the economy in the name of the commonweal.

Nevertheless, there is a sense in Rand's thought in which the members of the public do share basic concerns. Humanity is not a random assortment of entities, but a species whose members' attributes fall within a range. In the political sphere, the creation of objective, rights-protecting law—focused on the life and freedom of the individual—requires the identification of the basic interests that all have in common. Unlike more expansive conceptions of public interest, rights-protecting law in the public's interest is an idea that can be defined and validated.

The idea of a public interest, or a "general will," is often used as a justification for democratic government. The democratic process, in this view, expresses the will of society. After a vote, "the people have spoken." Rand's view of government, by contrast, is fundamentally republican, concerned primarily with the freedoms of individuals and the structure of government. She seems to regard democracy as a secondary consideration. For Rand, a democratic society need not be a just one. In *Atlas Shrugged*, for example, she portrays the politicians as villains not due to the manner of their election, but because of the irrational, unconstrained, oppressive policies they put into practice. And, in fact, every vote has winners and losers; the people do not speak with a unitary voice. This is why for Rand the ideal society is not "democratic"; rather, it is a "free society," where the meaning of freedom is correctly defined and implemented in the laws. Representative democracy is the best available means of naming officials, but it is a form of government that threatens the minority unless rigorously constrained.[17]

It was a commonplace of twentieth-century political and legal thought to presume that wide ranges of human interaction were of a public character, with the participants undertaking significant obligations to the public at large. Rand, however, presumes that virtually all action is private in character, with the particular obligations involved restricted to the parties explicitly taking part. Just as what a family does in a home is private, so any interaction on one's own property that consists in voluntary trade among consenting individuals is also private. Opening a store on private property is a private action with no meaningful "public" character because the store is made available to customers on whatever basis the owner chooses, and each customer is present (or not) by choice, acting freely and individually.

In Rand's view, private actions in this expansive sense are presumed to be within the prerogative of the individuals who take part in them, unless the actions violate someone's rights or the law (which is only to uphold those rights). By contrast, all government action is presumed to violate rights and the law unless it is an instance of an enumerated power undertaken in an authorized manner (again, in keeping with a system of law based on rights): "A private individual may do anything except that which is legally *forbidden*; a government official may do nothing except that which is legally *permitted* " (*VOS* 109–10).

Rand's political vision rejects many of the features of the twentieth-century American political order. She held that antitrust law—and indeed any law to restrict freedom of contract or commerce—should be repealed.[18] Many labor laws, including collective bargaining statutes, violate the rights of individual workers and employers. A military draft is illegitimate; military service should be voluntary (*CUI* 226). All governmental entitlement programs violate the rights of the individuals who must support them, and no person has a fundamental right to the produce of another.[19] Rand demanded an end to the governmental subsidization of education and regarded most child-rearing decisions (short of abuse) to be the proper province of a child's parents or legal guardian.

Rand argued that the government should own no property except that necessary for the performance of its proper functions. Thus, federal lands should be privatized, and even nature parks should be a matter for private organization and provision. (The Nature Conservancy's method of purchasing areas and setting them aside for protection is a model of the kind of wilderness protection methods that might exist under Rand's system.) A limited government has no business promulgating economic regulations; thus, she opposed environmental regulation except in resolving emergencies. On this principle, she opposed the existence of the U.S. Food and Drug Administration, holding that threats to health can be adjudicated in the courts if they are genuine, and that otherwise market competition will be no worse than the government's efforts—and likely far better. It is crucial to note that while Rand rejected most critiques of the effects of laissez-faire as inaccurate, she did not guarantee that the market will efficiently provide any particular good or service. Rather, she emphasized the inherent injustice and inefficiency of restricting the individual's responsibility for his own choices and of imposing bureaucratic or legislative decisions by force.

Rand was in favor of the extension of private property to as many areas as possible; rights being human principles, they could be legitimately extended on objective grounds. Thus, she offered arguments in favor of patent and copyright law (*CUI* 130–34). She was similarly an early advocate of the privatization of the electromagnetic spectrum, and she also opposed the Federal Communication Commission's activities regulating the content of broadcast speech (*CUI* 122–29). She favored the geographic as well as the conceptual extension of private property, and saw privatization, rather than regulation, as the answer to environmental problems that arise in tragedy-of-the-commons cases. At the end of the twentieth century in the United States, this last point was receiving recognition in widespread attempts to implement property schemes for allocating access to oceanic fishing grounds and efficiently limiting the emission of atmospheric pollutants.

Rand opposed the income tax—and indeed all taxes—holding that government in a free society would subsist on some form of voluntary financing (*VOS* 116–20). Her critics within the libertarian tradition have questioned whether such a strictly circumscribed state is possible, and have doubted that, given Rand's doctrine of rights, any state can function in the manner she envisions. These critiques usually adopt a libertarian-anarchist point of view, in which the functions of government are to be provided by private "defense agencies" and competing law courts.[20] Agreeing with Rand that government finance can only be voluntary in a rights-based system, the anarchists argue that people should be at full liberty to choose which system of law to work under or which policing force to hire to enforce their claims. Rand's response to the anarchists was that no such liberty was possible: anarchy would be a state of oppression, not freedom. She held that voluntary action is only possible when one is free from force, and that therefore it is impossible to have market competition (or even a proper market) for the provision of protection from force. Anarchism, in practice, would amount to civil warfare (*VOS* 112–13). Freedom can only be sustained, Rand held, in the proper institutional context, and the purpose of government is to secure that context.

It was vital to Rand that government be constitutionally limited, but she held that at root no constitutional structure would sustain limited government unless it was supported by a culture dominated by individuals who properly understood its requirements and valued its basic principles.[21] She therefore regarded cultural change as the key to improvement in political life, and focused her energies on cultural criticism and philosophy.

IV. Rand's Moral Revolution

At the time Rand was writing her novels, the intellectual consensus held laissez-faire capitalism, and the classical liberal political system it presupposes, in very low regard. A widespread interpretation of nineteenth-century economic history associated the capitalism of that period with exploitation, corruption, and suffering. The great industrialists of the past were denounced as "robber barons," and the free-market economy was seen as violent and chaotic.[22] Various forms of collectivism, from fascism to the democratic socialism of the New Deal, were the most fashionable forms of thought. Laissez-faire's defenders were few, and their views were not regarded as a legitimate social critique. It was in this atmosphere that Rand's magnum opus, *Atlas Shrugged*, arrived in 1957. It attracted a following of millions and drew tens of thousands to the literature of classical liberal economists and political thinkers, providing the spark that energized and revived the moribund movement to advance and develop those ideas.[23]

Rand was familiar with the "old Right" and was dismayed by what she saw of the "free-market" movement in the 1940s. She campaigned for Wendel Willkie in 1940 but was disappointed by his move toward the center as the campaign advanced. In later years, she was appalled by conservatives' failure to identify and advocate the principle of laissez-faire. She thought ill of the resulting state of affairs in which Americans typically call their existing system "free-market capitalism," despite the fact that government expenditure accounted for over a third of the U.S. economy by the last quarter of the twentieth century and economic activity was subject to a wide range of regulations, restrictions, and licensing requirements. In the face of this default among capitalism's self-avowed defenders, Rand strove to articulate a defense of a free-market system that was not subject to the weaknesses of the conservative position. In particular, she was aware that a political position could not be adequately defended except in the context of a consistent philosophy, and she had a very clear idea what the central ideas of such a philosophy would have to be. In the "Introduction" to *Capitalism: The Unknown Ideal*, she explained the relationship between her political views and her philosophy of Objectivism as a whole:

> Objectivism is a philosophical movement; since politics is a branch of philosophy, Objectivism advocates certain political principles—specifically, those of laissez-faire capitalism—as the consequence and the ultimate practical application of its fundamental philosophical principles. It does not regard politics as a separate or primary goal, that is: as a goal that can be achieved without a wider ideological context. . . .
>
> Objectivists are *not* 'conservatives.' We are *radicals for capitalism*; we are fighting for that philosophical base which capitalism did not have and without which it was doomed to perish. (*CUI* vii)

And in "For the New Intellectual" (1961), she laid out the issue starkly: "The world crisis of today is a *moral* crisis—and nothing less than a moral revolution can resolve it: a moral revolution to sanction and complete the political achievement of the American Revolution."[24]

The contradiction Rand sensed was that capitalism had only defenders, not advocates; the conservatives most associated with free-market positions were advocates of a moral view and a traditionalism that were at odds with their economic ideals:

So long as the "conservatives" ignore the issue of what destroyed capitalism, and merely plead with men to "go back," they cannot escape the question of: back to *what*? And none of their evasions can camouflage the fact that the implicit answer is: back to an earlier stage of the cancer which is devouring us today and which has almost reached its terminal stage. That cancer is the morality of altruism. (*CUI* 200)

In much of contemporary ethics, there is a distinction between those acts that are exclusively to one's own benefit and those which, to some degree, are to the benefit of others. The former are sometimes called "selfish" or "egoistic," and the latter are called "altruistic" ends or even simply "moral ends."[25] In the latter usage, any generous or benevolent act lies in the province of altruism. But this is not how Rand analyzes the issue.

Rand attacks altruism in its nineteenth-century sense (the sense in which Auguste Comte employed the term) as a doctrine that equates moral worth with the subordination of the self to society. "The basic principle of altruism," states Rand, "is that man has no right to exist for his own sake, that service to others is the only justification of his existence, and that self-sacrifice is his highest moral duty, virtue and value."[26] "By this definition," comments Objectivist philosopher David Kelley, "the paradigm of altruism is complete self-immolation, as in the story of Jesus, who died to atone for the sins of mankind; or the martyrdom of the Christian saints; or the demands of totalitarian leaders in [the twentieth] century that their citizens sacrifice their freedom, prosperity, and even their lives for the good of the nation."[27] According to Rand, altruism is the premise that unites the Communist and the Christian, the socialist and the fascist. In American history, it is a moral view that is the thread of continuity from the Protestant reformers of the Great Awakening to the nonreligious New Left.

"The world is perishing from an orgy of self-sacrificing," wrote Rand at the height of the Second World War (*TF* 684). She meant that civilization itself was in danger not just from the war, but from the altruism upheld by all sides in the war. Altruism was the guiding moral principle in both American and European politics before the war, and it would continue in that role afterwards. Capitalism is a system that makes each person ultimately responsible for his own choice of actions and allows each person the freedom to make the most of his life; it is incompatible with a moral doctrine that belittles that life. Capitalism rests on a set of legal principles that are themselves derived from the principles of individual rights. But rights to individual liberty are not compatible with a moral view that urges the sacrifice of all one's principles and goals to the needs of the nation, the party, the church, the race, the majority, or the needy. This was Rand's distinctive moral insight.

From her start, America was torn by the clash of her political system with the altruist morality. Capitalism and altruism are incompatible; they are philosophical opposites; they cannot co-exist in the same man or in the same society. Today, the conflict has reached its ultimate climax; the choice is clear-cut: either a new morality of rational self-interest, with its consequences of freedom, justice, progress and man's happiness on earth—or the primordial morality of altruism, with its consequences of slavery, brute force, stagnant terror, and sacrificial furnaces. (*FNI* 54)

Rand's solution to this contradiction in the Western moral tradition was to propose a fundamental revision of morality, with each individual's own life and happiness as the unequivocal base of his moral code. The facts of one's biological nature, and the general principles applicable to the needs of human life in general, then provide an objective basis for one's virtues and values, without reference to tradition or the supernatural, nor, at least in its fundamentals, to society at large.[28] Rand's ethic of "rational selfishness" envisions "three cardinal values . . . which, together, are the means to and realization of one's ultimate value, one's own life. . . : Reason,

Purpose, Self-Esteem, with their three corresponding virtues: Rationality, Productiveness, Pride" (*VOS* 25).[29] The key to Rand's ethical vision was her view of the role of reason and production in human life. "Man cannot survive except through his mind," Rand wrote. "From the simplest necessity to the highest religious abstraction, from the wheel to the skyscraper, everything we are and everything we have comes from a single attribute of man—the function of his reasoning mind" (*TF* 679).

Rand's conception of reason placed importance on logical thinking, but it was more than a mechanical view of the mind. Human consciousness is distinctively conceptual. We gain great practical power from our ability to assimilate vast amounts of information in abstract concepts, principles, and theories. The application of this knowledge to practical problems allows us to engage in open-ended processes of production, the potential of which has been epitomized by the economic growth since the Industrial Revolution. Rand's view that all people could live as proud, productive, and rational individualists provided the basis for her view of the proper stance toward society. Her politics of individual rights derived both moral legitimacy and practical support from a social ethic of justice toward others and interaction through trade. Rand characterized trade not merely as economic exchange, but as any voluntary exchange to mutual benefit. In this expansive sense, she saw trade as a basic principle of social interaction, one that required neither the sacrifice of one's self to the ends of others nor the sacrifice of others to one's own ends.[30]

Her rejection of altruism and the Judeo-Christian ethical tradition put Rand firmly at odds with the nascent neoconservative movement. In 1957, William Buckley's *National Review* greeted *Atlas Shrugged* with a blast of condemnation, and Rand returned the favor with incendiary talks like her 1960 Princeton University speech "Conservatism: An Obituary."[31] That same year, she came out with "Faith and Force: Destroyers of the Modern World." Rand shared with the conservatives a sense that America suffered from a moral sickness, but the diagnoses were largely incompatible. Rand's philosophy is an atheistic outlook that exalts the potential quality of human life. She refused to accept either late-twentieth-century neoconservatism's equation of individualism with licentiousness or its reduction of the nonreligious pursuit of happiness to a crude materialism. In fact, Rand saw irrationality (including religious appeals to faith), a lack of psychological independence, and hatred of material achievement as primary symptoms of the moral disease. While neoconservative political thought leaned toward economic liberalization (and in that respect shared some common ground with Objectivism), it also tended to advance governmental paternalism in support of moral and religious causes. Against this, Rand endorsed personal liberty in sexual matters, advocated abortion rights, and stood in total opposition to any connection between the state and religion.

Rand attacked the Left with as much force as she attacked the Right, reserving especial contempt for the neoprimitivism of the New Left (her 1971 essay collection was aptly entitled *The New Left: The Anti-Industrial Revolution*). Her diagnosis of this nominally "progressive" movement noted it not for innovation but for its recycling of the same ethical premises that were undermining the Right: altruism, irrationalism, and statism.[32]

It is something of an irony that Rand's idiosyncratic views and her intransigent independence also put her at odds with the libertarian movement that grew up in the 1960s and 1970s. Although the movement drew both inspiration and intellectual ammunition from Rand's work, its character as an unsystematic political creed created a conflict with Rand's comprehensive project for philosophy. Rand was concerned that libertarians who did not properly tend to the philosophic basis of their political ideas would fail to uphold consistently the principle of liberty. She took the widespread advocacy of anarchism among libertarians to be evidence of this, and she refused to be called a libertarian herself.[33]

Rand's "moral revolution" aimed at erecting a moral culture and political order based firmly on a new and consistent conception of rational egoism. But critics were quick to argue that Rand was merely rehearsing a familiar kind of argument, putting forward a "simple material system," or advocating a pop-Nietzschean philosophy that glorified the strong and powerful at the expense of the rest in society.[34]

It is a commonplace in philosophy that egoism is necessarily the opposite of morality, because the egoist will act for his self-interest in each situation, and thus may not do what is moral, or even what is conducive to social harmony.[35] A standard example of this is to imagine an egoist who comes upon a valuable item in a situation where he can take it and escape detection. Suppose the item is a painting: does the egoist steal the painting, violating the strictures of common-sense morality? If one's self-interest simply consists in having wealth or owning beautiful and rare objects, then it seems straightforward that an egoist will be happy to take the painting. Indeed, if he is a "rational egoist" and realizes the fact that he can get away with the theft, his very morality tells him to do it. This demonstrates the inherent amorality of egoism, holds the critique, since common sense tells us that stealing the painting is morally abhorrent. Egoism thus cannot provide a foundation for morality and liberty because it in fact allows for nothing but unbridled selfishness and pragmatic, prudential reasoning. Rand's egoism, in this view, is necessarily rapacious.

Critics have argued on similar grounds that, far from putting political liberty on a firm foundation, Rand denies the understanding of morality and rights that the law requires. These critics hold that because egoism necessarily is a prudential and practical ethic, it can have no respect for rights as such.[36] This argument is based on the premise that rights are inherently deontological—that is, that rights are unwavering, universal moral duties that derive from the requirements of moral reasoning or from a higher authority. But how can such absolute obligations be squared with the rational pursuit of self-interest? In Rand's view, rights are practical moral principles: they are potentially subject to modification on prudential grounds. It is supposed that when the imaginary egoist of our example chooses whether or not to steal the painting, he may consider *practical* consequences such as how the owner will react to the loss of his painting or what the police might do. But the owner's *rights* do not matter for such a calculation. In this critique, then, Rand's moral argument cannot provide rights with the moral force they require, because in effect her ethic is one of pragmatic action and not of deontological principle.

Inasmuch as these critiques presuppose a blinkered concept of self-interest, they misrepresent Rand's view of social relations and impose a false dichotomy between principle and prudence. Rand argued that a proper egoism—one consistent with human nature and actual human interests—was neither rapacious nor unprincipled. While she regarded the pursuit of wealth as an essential human activity, she did not reduce rational self-interest to nothing but that pursuit. A full life also contains friendships, creative work, and a host of other values.

Furthermore, she held that there is a fundamental harmony of interests "among rational men," one that derives from the productive power of the individual mind (*VOS* 50–56). Because human beings can live by reason, they can all flourish without being in fundamental conflict with each other over resources or values. Production is the proper mode of human existence, and as producers, humans are capable of creating the material goods they require if they are allowed the freedom to do so and the ability to use the fruits of their labors. Physical resources may be scarce, in some sense, and there may be competition to use them; but the human mind is, as the economist Julian Simon has argued, "the ultimate resource."[37] Rand argued that in fact what we regard as "resources" depends on human abilities to produce and human needs for products. For example, the deserts of Arabia today are regarded as a vast natural resource because human beings have invented the means to extract and use petroleum; how much petroleum is available for use depends crucially on the means people invent for extracting and refining it.

In Rand's view, human reason makes voluntary cooperation and mutual understanding possible. She envisions a society of traders, exchanging economic and nonmarket values with each other voluntarily and to mutual benefit. She holds that as rational beings we are competent to be responsible for ourselves; disagreements among people employing reason can be resolved through appeals to evidence. Rand is well aware that even reasonable people will in the course of their affairs often disagree. This is an inevitable result because we are not all aware of the same facts: we do not all share the same context of knowledge. But our reason makes it possible to resolve such disputes peacefully, and this is why it is to everyone's advantage to have a legal order that ensures an objective process of sorting through the facts to adjudicate disagreements.

Finally, because our moral principles can have the same objective status as scientific principles, they are as absolute in their proper context as the rules by which engineers construct a bridge or fire a rocket. Rand's moral principles are prudential, but they are supposed to be practical because they are objective principles applying, in their most general formulations, to the full range of situations normal to human life. Faced with the possibility of stealing a painting, rights are the first principles an egoist should reflect upon, because rights principles summarize and unify complex arguments and multitudinous facts that make respecting the property and lives of others a prudent course of action. Rand would be quick to point out that neither paintings nor any other significant values are easily attained by theft or fraud in real life.

Rand argued that morality should be formulated only for practical employment on earth as we know it.[38] She called Objectivism "a philosophy for living on earth."[39] She saw no use in considering hypothetical situations that were unlikely to be part of normal life, and she considered it irrational to demand that a moral code be held to any standard other than its practical consequences on earth. Thus, in response to any hypothetical case of a rational egoist attempting to succeed in furthering his own well-being (holistically considered) by theft, fraud, or murder, Rand's unvarying reply was that, were one to trace the consequences of acting in such a manner, taking care that the setting be realistic, by far the most likely outcome would be failure accompanied by arrest, death, or some similar harm.[40] Objective moral principles should properly reflect this fact.

It should also be noted that Rand's harmony of interests thesis is not a claim that there is no competition in society. Rather, it is the thesis that a society that secures freedom to produce and trade (and in which each individual regards his interests as the furtherance of his life and happiness) makes it possible for all to flourish. Two people waiting for a taxi cab may compete to get the first one, but in a broader sense neither's well-being comes at the expense of the other. It is in both their interests that cabs be readily available; it is inevitable, but trivial, that no two people can take the same cab to different locations at the same time. Their interests coincide profoundly in securing a social system that allows them to jockey peacefully on a street corner for a taxi (*VOS* 53).

Rand advocated rights as principles to be observed at all times in society if individuals sought to advance their own well-being over the long term. Rand held that it was not practical to expect that one's own rights be protected without upholding the rights of others.[41] One therefore has multiple prudential reasons for regarding rights as vital and true principles worthy of scrupulous respect. Rights in Rand's conception can thus apply with the strength required for the basis of law, without any need for a deontological interpretation of moral obligation.[42]

V. Conclusion

Critiques of Rand that denounce her for a cold materialism are simply off-point. Rand looked out on the world and saw endless vistas of possibility for human beings. Hers was not the despairing, postreligious nihilism that characterized so many twentieth-century philosophers. Rand's works endow the essential activities of modern human life—including productive work, the use of human reason, and exchange through the marketplace—with the spiritual stature of moral greatness. That her works have this inspirational value is clearly evident in their enduring popularity. Rand projected a sense of nobility appropriate to modern scientific and industrial civilization, embracing business life and technology with a wholehearted appreciation of their potential. This is one basic aspect of the vision she projected in her novels, and it is this exalted view of industry, individualism, and the free market that had the strongest effect on American culture of all her ideas.

But Rand was also distinctive for giving her readers a sense of coming at social and political problems with a clean slate. She was a "radical for capitalism" not only in her indifference to public opinion and her willingness to champion ideas that the mainstream widely abhorred, but also in her method of analysis. As the philosopher Lester Hunt has noted: "the cardinal value of all [Rand's] work . . . [is] her 'radicalism' . . . in the very literal sense of a tendency to approach an issue in terms of its root (*radix*) in the issues that underlie it."[43] She stands out among classical liberals for the clarity with which she declared her political ideal and her indifference to tradition, and especially in her ruthless quest for the fundamental issues embedded in any question. Rand set down standards and definitions: freedom as freedom from force, rights as principles sanctioning that freedom, and rights as unified by a right to life and expressed in an objective code of law. These ideas shaped the terms in which a new movement of free-market advocates would debate political theory. When Rand spoke of liberty, her wide following knew exactly what she was arguing for. Her legacy has been to point classical liberalism in a fresh direction, inspiring two generations of free-market thinkers and offering a distinctive and thoroughly integrated moral defense of the political order that laissez-faire requires.

Notes

1. For an account that combines scholarship with a firsthand perspective, see Roy A. Childs, Jr., "Ayn Rand and the Libertarian Movement," in *Liberty against Power: Essays by Roy A. Childs, Jr.*, ed. Joan Kennedy Taylor (San Francisco: Fox and Wilkes, 1994), 265–81.

2. Jerome Tuccille, *It Usually Begins with Ayn Rand* (New York: Stein and Day, 1972).

3. See Chris Matthew Sciabarra, *Ayn Rand: Life and Thought* (Poughkeepsie, N.Y.: Atlas Society, 1999) and *Ayn Rand: The Russian Radical* (University Park: Pennsylvania State University Press, 1995) for more on Rand's childhood. Barbara Branden, *The Passion of Ayn Rand* (New York: Doubleday, 1986) is the only book-length biography of Rand published to date.

4. Sciabarra, *Ayn Rand: The Russian Radical*, 77.

5. Ayn Rand, *Anthem* (London: Cassell and Company, 1938); rev. ed. (Los Angeles: Pamphleteers, Inc.,1946); and *We the Living* (New York: Macmillan Company, 1936).

6. Ayn Rand, *Night of January 16th* (New York: Longmans, Green, 1936).

7. Ayn Rand, *The Fountainhead* (New York: Bobbs-Merrill Company, 1943); 25th anniversary edition (New York: Signet, 1993). Future references are to the 25th anniversary edition, hereafter cited in the text as *TF*.

8. Ayn Rand, *Atlas Shrugged* (New York: Random House, 1957), hereafter cited *AS*. For the critical reception of *Atlas Shrugged*, see Mimi Reisel Gladstein, *Atlas Shrugged: Manifesto of Mind* (New York: Twayne Publishers, 2000), 19–25.

9. *The Objectivist Newsletter* (1962–1965) and *The Objectivist* (1966–1971), edited by Nathaniel Branden and Ayn Rand until 1968; thereafter, edited by Rand alone. Rand also edited *The Ayn Rand Letter* (1971–1976).

10. Ayn Rand, *The Virtue of Selfishness* (New York: New American Library, 1964), hereafter *VOS*; Ayn Rand, *Capitalism: The Unknown Ideal* (New York: New American Library, 1967), hereafter *CUI*; and Ayn Rand, *The New Left: The Anti-Industrial Revolution*, 2nd rev. ed. (New York: Signet, 1975).

11. See Tara Smith, *Moral Rights and Political Freedom* (Lanham, Md.: Rowman and Littlefield, 1995), for a book-length treatment of individual rights based on Rand's account.

12. For a recent similar account of natural rights, see Randy Barnett, *The Structure of Liberty* (Oxford: Oxford University Press, 1998), 4–12.

13. See, e.g., Douglas B. Rasmussen and Douglas J. Den Uyl, *Liberty and Nature* (LaSalle, Ill.: Open Court, 1991), 72–75.

14. Robert Nozick, *Anarchy, State, and Utopia* (New York: Basic Books, 1974), 25.

15. Note that Rand here uses "men" in a generic sense.

16. See Ayn Rand, "Vast Quicksands," *The Objectivist Newsletter* II, 7 (July 1963): 25, 28.

17. For an example of Rand's view of unrestricted "mixed economy" democratic government, see "The New Fascism: Rule by Consensus" and "The Wreckage of the Consensus" (*CUI* 202–35). For Rand on democracy, see "How to Read (and Not to Write)," *The Ayn Rand Letter* I, 26.

18. Alan Greenspan, "Antitrust" (*CUI* 63–71), is an essay on the subject that Rand endorsed.

19. For a detailed Objectivist exposition of the history of and argument against entitlements and the welfare state, see David Kelley, *A Life of One's Own: Individual Rights and the Welfare State* (Washington, D.C.: Cato Institute, 1998).

20. The classic libertarian-anarchist text is David Friedman, *The Machinery of Freedom* (New York: Harper and Row, 1973). Nozick, *Anarchy, State, and Utopia*, presents a detailed discussion of the anarchist position. For an anarchist critique focused on Rand, see Roy Childs, Jr., "Objectivism and the State: An Open Letter to Ayn Rand," in *Liberty against Power*, 145–56.

21. Leonard Peikoff, *The Ominous Parallels: The End of Freedom in America* (Briarcliff Manor, N.Y.: Stein and Day, 1982), makes a comparison, endorsed by Rand, between the culture of Weimar Germany with that of late-twentieth-century America, arguing that the political implications are equivalent.

22. Matthew Josephson, *The Robber Barons* (New York: Harcourt, Brace and Co., [1934] 1995), is the source of this characterization.

23. For an exposition of the moral view of *Atlas Shrugged* in relation to its intellectual context, see Nathaniel Branden, *The Moral Revolution in "Atlas Shrugged"* (Poughkeepsie, N.Y.: Atlas Society, 2000).

24. Ayn Rand, "For the New Intellectual," in *For the New Intellectual* (New York: Random House, 1961), 54, hereafter cited in the text as *FNI*.

25. See, for example, Kurt Baier, *The Moral Point of View* (Ithaca, N.Y.: Cornell University Press, 1958). Baier writes that the moral point of view "cannot (logically) be identical with self-interest" (190).

26. Rand, "Faith and Force: The Destroyers of the Modern World," in *Philosophy: Who Needs It* (New York: Signet, 1984), 61.

27. David Kelley, *Unrugged Individualism: The Selfish Basis of Benevolence* (Poughkeepsie, N.Y.: Institute for Objectivist Studies, 1996), 6. For a further discussion of the historical usage of altruism, see Kelley, *A Life of One's Own*, 52–54.

28. Tara Smith, *Viable Values: A Study of Life as the Root and Reward of Morality* (Lanham, Md.: Rowman and Littlefield, 2000), is an extensive scholarly exposition of Rand's approach to ethics.

29. For a summary of Rand's ethical theory, see "The Objectivist Ethics" (*VOS* 13–35).

30. See *AS* 1022 for a summary of Rand's view of trade.

31. Branden, *The Passion of Ayn Rand*, 296–97.

32. Rand's reasons for opposing the New Left are detailed in the essays collected in *The New Left*.

33. See, e.g., Rand, "What Can One Do?" in *Philosophy: Who Needs It*, 202. For a Rand-inspired attack on libertarianism, see Peter Schwartz, "Libetarianism: The Perversion of Liberty," in *The Voice of Reason*, ed. Leonard Peikoff (New York: Meridian, 1990), 311–33. A contrary view, also Rand-inspired, is to be found in David Kelley, *The Contested Legacy of Ayn Rand* (New Brunswick, N.J.: Transaction, 2000), 36–38.

34. Whittaker Chambers, "Big Sister Is Watching You," *National Review* (December 28, 1957): 594–96, cited in Branden, *The Passion of Ayn Rand*, 297.

35. See, for example, Louis Pojman, "Egoism, Self-Interest, and Altruism," in *The Moral Life* (New York: Oxford University Press, 2000), 557–64.

36. See, for example, Eric Mack, "On the Fit between Egoism and Rights," *Reason Papers* 23 (Fall 1998): 3–21.

37. Julian Simon, *The Ultimate Resource* (Princeton, N.J.: Princeton University Press, 1981).

38. On the context of ethics, see Rand, "The Ethics of Emergencies," in *VOS* 47–48.

39. *Journals of Ayn Rand*, ed. David Harriman (New York: Plume, 1999), 697.

40. Leonard Peikoff, "My Thirty Years with Ayn Rand: An Intellectual Memoir," in *The Voice of Reason* (New York: Meridian, 1990), 340–41, gives an example of Rand analyzing a "con-man" scheme.

41. Rand, "Textbook of Americanism" (pamphlet), 7, cited in *The Ayn Rand Lexicon*, ed. Harry Binswanger (New York: New American Library, 1986), 215.

42. Smith, *Moral Rights*, 101–19, contrasts a Randian view of rights with both the deontological conception and the consequentialist conception, arguing that Rand's rights are more properly characterized as "teleological."

43. Lester Hunt, "What Is Living in the Philosophy of Ayn Rand," *Reason Papers* 23 (Fall 1998): 79–82.

Chapter 37

Walker Percy's American Thomism

Peter Augustine Lawler

Walker Percy (1916–1990) was both a novelist and a philosopher. He was also a Catholic convert, and he wrote, in part, to lead us to the truth of his faith. He published six novels, two collections of his philosophical essays, and *Lost in the Cosmos: The Last Self-Help Book* (1983), a strange and funny mixture of fiction and philosophical prose. During his most productive years, he wrote fiction in the morning and philosophical essays in the afternoon. He was, despite great acclaim and a National Book Award, unsure he was a great novelist. He thought his theoretical work on the natural and distinctive foundation of human language, and therefore of human consciousness, was more important and would be his chief claim to fame.

The importance of Percy for this book is as the most able and penetrating representative of the final moment of a dissident tradition in American thought. The Southern Agrarians opposed, from an aristocratic view, the technological mediocrity of industrial America.[1] At the end of that Agrarian movement, thought turned away from the virtues of the South in particular to a revival of the thought of St. Thomas Aquinas in an American context. The racism and regional narrowness of even the best Southern thought disappeared. It was replaced by a more balanced and rational criticism of the dominant tradition in American political thought in the literary art and essays of Percy, Flannery O'Connor, and a very few others.

Percy understood himself, above all, as a twentieth-century Thomist. He defended the "Scholastic view" that human beings "share certain characteristics with other creatures" but also "are capable of certain perfections peculiar to themselves." For the Thomist, the human being is "distinguished from the beast in being endowed with soul, intellect, free will, reason, and the gift of language." Language is the fundamental natural human capability, the one responsible for the development of the others. With that gift, human beings can name things, think about them, convey thoughts with words that can be understood by others, come to much of the truth about nature and something about themselves, and exercise their freedom well or badly (*SSL* 257, 117).[2]

Man becomes man, Percy observes, by "breaking into the daylight of language" (*MB* 45). Humans became human in the sense of our species becoming qualitatively distinct at some recent point in the evolutionary process. But in the natural development of the particular human creature, humans become human, or children acquire language, all the time. This "transformation of the responding organism into the languaged human . . . is undoubtedly the most extraordinary natural phenomenon in all of biological behavior, if not the entire cosmos, and yet the most commonplace of events, one that occurs every day under our noses." Percy wonders why we do not wonder more about what is genuinely extraordinary, the commonplace mystery of becoming or being human (*SSL* 282).

Aliens Are Us

Because the capacity for language and so consciousness is natural, its emergence introduces fundamental discontinuity into nature that cannot be accounted for by the species' adaptation to its environment. "Neo-Darwinian theory," Percy observes in *Lost in the Cosmos*, "has trouble accounting for the strange, sudden, and belated appearance of man, the conscious self who speaks, lies, deceives himself, and also tells the truth" (*LC* 161). That does not mean that evolution did not occur, but it does mean that at some relatively recent point something happened that could not have been expected and cannot be explained according to the general principles of Darwinian theory. Percy imagines a conversation between two scientists stalled in an elevator in the Rockefeller Foundation building. The one who challenges the Darwinian position asks "how do you account for the fact that with the appearance of man . . . almost immediately thereafter [follows] a train of disasters and triumphs which seem to have very little to do with adaptation to an environment," from suicide to heroism to "child abuse and loving care for the genetically malformed" (*LC* 197)? The dogma of modern scientists is the inability to acknowledge this natural discontinuity.

Our species obviously exists for more than self-preservation. We are, in fact, the only animals capable of consciously and perversely acting against self-preservation. We can commit suicide and murder, not to mention heroically risk our lives, for no reason the evolutionist can explain. Language is a natural human capacity, and so is consciousness (as well as wondering and wandering, which will be discussed later). But they cannot be explained in terms of the homogeneous and generally correct theory of evolution. For Percy, homogeneous natural science is, more than anything else, a barrier to self-understanding. Percy presents a *"thought experiment"* to show why this is the case:

> Imagine you are the scientist who has at last succeeded in puncturing the last of man's inflated claims to uniqueness in the Cosmos. Now man is proved beyond doubt to be an organism among other organisms, a species in continuity with other species, a creature existing in interaction with an immanent Cosmos like all other creatures. . . . Now, having placed a man as an object of study in the Cosmos in however an insignificant place, how do *you*, the scientist, the self which hit upon this theory, how do you propose to reenter this very Cosmos where you have so firmly placed the species to which you belong? Who are you who has explained the Cosmos and how do you fit into the Cosmos you have explained? (*LC* 170)

This description applies to modern scientists in general—to all those Cartesians who have divided reality into minds and bodies, into two rational and separate systems. Such scientists do not acknowledge the existence of a third reality: the human self or soul. But in *Lost in the Cosmos,* Percy's particular target is the great popularizing physicist Carl Sagan. His book means to be a response to Sagan's *Cosmos,* the best-selling book of science of all time, which was also the basis of an equally successful television series.

Carl Sagan cannot locate Carl Sagan in the Cosmos he otherwise so elegantly and perhaps completely describes. Percy understands and admits that he sometimes shared the scientist's motivation to transcend the dreariness of ordinary life. He also knows that the experience of the scientist or philosopher is the activity most pleasurable for human beings, so much so that all other human activities "are spoiled by contrast" (*LC* 143). But the trouble is that transcendence cannot define a whole human life. Sagan cannot, in fact, become more than human by reducing, scientifically, all other human beings to beings just like the other animals. He cannot turn himself into a God-like mind thinking about subhuman bodies. Sagan remains a self, a soul, born to trouble. His science cannot tell how to do what he must do: reenter the world of his own kind. As a merely natural being with the capacity for language, the scientist must be part of the world he describes. So he is living proof that his attempt to reduce human nature to an indistinguishable part of nature as a whole must fail. There are no chimp scientists; no other animal wonders about the truth and attempts to account for the Cosmos. No other animal, for that matter, is miserable in the absence of God.

Percy sees Sagan searching the Cosmos for other intelligent beings and asks: "Why is Carl Sagan so lonely?" Part of the answer, of course, is that he mistakenly reduced his fellow human beings to beings unworthy of love or even wonder. To put the matter differently, why does Sagan search the Cosmos for aliens when no extraterrestrials imaginable are as strange and wonderful as those right here on earth? Human beings, according to Percy, are alienated or aliens by the very nature of their being here. Another part of the answer to Percy's question is that Sagan's search is a diversion from what he really knows or does not know. Sagan is diverting himself from the inexplicable mystery of the alien Sagan, which includes Sagan's rather singular loneliness (*LC* 127–74). "Carl Sagan," Percy observes, "explains everything without God, from the most distant galaxies to our own individual nastiness, which is caused by our reptilian brains" (*SSL* 261). But the truth is that he never made a serious attempt to explain his own activity as wonderer and wanderer (of the galaxies and cosmos) in a way that rules God out.

The discovery of extraterrestrial intelligence, Percy explains, cannot give Sagan the help he really needs. If the extraterrestrials, having found some help beyond scientific explanation, are both highly intelligent and benignly untroubled, they will stay away from us, knowing that we are "born to trouble." Or what is more likely, being self-conscious and mortal, with longings beyond that for self-preservation, they will be as screwed-up as we are. They will be curious and murderous, loving and hateful, truth-tellers and liars. They will possess most, if not all, of the qualities that connect us to, and alienate us from, each other and the Cosmos (*LC* 214–20).

Sagan's naive view of extraterrestrials (expressed most poetically in his book and film *Contact*)—that their great intelligence will somehow make them benign and untroubled—is connected to his naive view of the moral evolution of our species. Percy mocks the scientist's belief that human aggressiveness fades away as science progresses, and that human aggressiveness is rooted in the reptilian origins of our brain and not in human self-consciousness (*LC* 217). Sagan, in truth, cannot begin to explain why human beings are either sentimental or cruel, or cruel because they are sentimental.

The truth is that modern scientists, from Descartes to Marx to Sagan, become incurable romantics when thinking about experiences of self or soul, and so when thinking about the historical or scientific future of our species. They cannot resist abandoning the discipline of reason because the truth is that such experiences are leftovers from their science. Sagan becomes most unscientific when he diverts himself from the most interesting or curious human question: What is an alien? He and we know from personal experience that he is neither pure intelligence nor untroubled tranquility.

The truth is also that aliens from other galaxies are not likely to be able to tell us anything that we cannot discover for ourselves through the old-fashioned Socratic search for self-knowledge. They will not make our biblical religion more or less credible than it is now. They will need help as much as we do, and they will have longings, particularly for love, that only a personal God can satisfy completely. And they will be unable to tell us for sure whether or not such a God exists.

Percy says that he finds reading Sagan more "diverting" than anything else. Sagan's "unmalicious, even ignorant, scientism" gets Percy's mind off what he really knows about the greatness and misery of being human (*LC* 201–2). Scientism is the ideology based on the premise that all that exists can be explained in the same reductionistic way. A diversion, according to Pascal, is what human beings employ to get their minds off themselves. For both Sagan and Percy, Sagan's scientism is a diversion. Percy knows that but Sagan does not.

Percy is amazed that Sagan can account for the whole history of science, from the ancient Ionians to the present, with no contribution at all from the Christians (*LC* 201–2). But the Christians, such as Pascal, understand better than their Greek predecessors why it is that human beings wander, and the relationship between wandering and wondering. Human beings wander—or experience themselves as aliens at home nowhere in particular—because they wonder—or desire to know the truth about all things. Percy uses a quote from a great admirer of Pascal, Friedrich Nietzsche, to open *Lost in the Cosmos*: "We are unknown, we knowers, to ourselves. Of necessity, we remain strangers to ourselves . . . as far as ourselves are concerned we are not knowers." The being that knows the Cosmos is necessarily a leftover from the Cosmos he knows. As a knower, he finds himself elusive; he cannot know himself the way he can a rock, a frog, or a galaxy. Because he cannot locate himself anywhere in particular in the Cosmos, he experiences himself as a wanderer.

But Percy's understanding of the human being as a wonderer and wanderer is not, in fact, wholly Pascalian or Nietzschean. He is no existentialist, although he accepts the existentialist criticism of the impersonality of scientism. "The existentialists have their flaws," Percy explains, and "[o]ne of them is their contempt for science" (*CWP* 12). We *are* knowers because of our natural capability for language, and our existence is not merely accidental or absurd or without natural purpose. Nature is heterogeneous. Our mode of being, what we have been given by nature, cannot be integrated into nonhuman being. We alone among the animals are knowers by nature, and so we cannot help but be displaced or alienated or lonely by nature. Our selves, our souls—we can know only because we are more than mind—cannot be located in the Cosmos we can describe, and so insofar as we wonder, we wander. Percy views himself as a Thomist because he claims to do justice to both Greek or philosophic wondering and Christian wandering.

Pop Cartesianism

Percy's *Lost in the Cosmos* is the last self-help book. It was written to replace the thousands of self-help books found in our larger bookstores. Those books, Percy explain, are pop Cartesian. They are popularized versions of modern or Cartesian philosophy. Percy learned from Alexis de Tocqueville that the Americans are Cartesians without ever having read a word of Descartes. Sagan's *Cosmos* was a failed attempt at a self-help book. It was an attempt to free people of their troubles and obsessions by convincing them that they are fundamentally no different from the other animals. They are just bodies with really big brains. Not only did the book not work for Sagan's huge audience; it did not work for Sagan himself.

Percy's analysis of American life today is mainly oriented around a particularly perplexing paradox. People feel more homeless than ever in the world Cartesian scientists have made with the intention of making them feel completely at home. People today are particularly ready to hear that their homesickness is a misperception, that they have no reason not to enjoy themselves in the unconstrained and prosperous environment that has been created to meet all their needs as consumers. The pop Cartesians tell them, in effect, that the world is divided into scientists and consumers—or angels and pigs—and that human experience not connected with either the pleasure of knowing or material enjoyment is an illusion.

The pop Cartesian experts—Carl Sagan, the talk show host Phil Donahue (the most hilarious part of *Lost in the Cosmos* is a fictional last Donahue show), therapists, educators, and so forth—say that human beings should not be anxious in the midst of their good fortune. The experts' intention is therapeutic. They aim to correct through redescription any experience that produces an uncomfortable and unproductive mood. Their theory is that language and mood do not correspond to reality, and so that language should be used to change moods to make people comfortable. As our leading professor of philosophy Richard Rorty says, we should privilege comfort over truth, or call true whatever makes us comfortable.[3]

Percy observes that what Americans believe—or are told to believe by the experts whom they hope will provide answers for all the troubles and mysteries of human life—remains persistently contradicted by what they actually experience. They become pop Cartesians—or mouth therapeutic platitudes—only by denying what they really know about themselves. And their real problem is that they become increasingly more dislocated because complete self-denial is impossible. As science explains more and more about nonhuman reality, they actually know less and less about themselves. The American, as the Pascalian Tocqueville first described, is restlessly dissatisfied in the midst of "affluence," experiencing "some sense of loss that he cannot understand" (*MCWP* 82, 232–33). The result is "that people are, by and large, probably lonelier than ever." Despite all the expert emphasis on human relations or getting along with others, loneliness remains "the twentieth-century disease." The pop Cartesian is "a lonesome ghost in an abused machine." So "despite an embarrassment of riches," he "is in fact impoverished and deprived, like Lazarus at the feast" (*SSL* 210; *CWP* 308; *MB* 44; *LC* 74).

From the Pursuit of Happiness to the Pursuit of Diversion

The disorienting impoverishment of the thought of contemporary Americans—their inability to reflect on the true source of human joys and troubles—is present, in a more muted form, in American thought from the beginning. The Jeffersonian defines the self "as an individual entity created by God and endowed with certain inalienable rights and the freedom to pursue happiness and fulfill his potential." Thomas Jefferson defines man, officially, as a creature, but he holds that the creature was endowed with the purpose of pursuing this-worldly, rational, self-won happiness. This definition is an untenable mixture of a small dose of Christianity with a large dose of Cartesianism, lacking the integrity of either of its parts. Its nominally Christian defense of the individual is undercut by its "scientific" view that man is a "higher" or particularly clever organism and nothing more. But if this understanding of the human being is true, "[i]t follows that in a free and affluent society the self should succeed more often than not in fulfilling itself. Happiness can be pursued and to a degree caught" (*LC* 12). But this description is clearly not true, and in Percy's view the standard American self-understanding retains some force because of the influence of a mixture of scientific expertise and patriotic prejudice.

For Percy, the standard, American, Jeffersonian self is not so different from the one described by Phil Donahue. It is an early form of the soft utopianism characteristic of Cartesian progressivism. The American pursuit aims at creating a future where "scientists know like angels, and laymen prosper in good environments, and ethical democracies progress through good education." Scientific progress would be accompanied by moral progress "through education and the application of the ethical principles of Christianity." And the result is that "man [is] made to feel more and more at home" (*MB* 25). Percy's description captures nicely

Jefferson's faith in the goodness of the right mixture of education, science, and Jesus. But it is also a description that is far from a true account of the distinctive predicament of the human self.

The modern world is replaced by the postmodern one for anyone who can come to see the naive untruth of the progressivism of Jefferson, Donahue, and Sagan. Our century has not been the coming of universal peace and brotherhood, but a time of ideological war, angry self-destruction, deranged and violent eroticism, and other forms of self-denial and self-hatred. Percy's self-help book means, in part, to be a scientific explanation of the misery of Americans in the midst of prosperity. He explains why "Mother Teresa of Calcutta" is right to say that affluent Westerners are more impoverished, in the crucial respect, than the poor of Calcutta. Percy shows that "the impoverishments and enrichments of a *self* in a *world* are not necessarily the same as the impoverishments and enrichments of an *organism* in an *environment*" (*LC* 122).

Human beings, people with selves, are miserable when they experience themselves as lost or displaced in the Cosmos for no reason or explanation. When their fundamental experience is of nothing, they will do whatever they can to divert themselves from what they really know. They will defer to the impersonal lies of experts, or they will make unrealistic claims for autonomy. Percy sees that the miserable foolishness of what Pascal calls diversion is what the philosopher "Heidegger calls fall[ing] prey to everydayness" (*SSL* 158). But Percy, in his realism, is not a Heideggerian: he does not identify nothingness with the truth; he explains that there is a natural foundation for fundamental human experiences of alienation; and he is no atheist. The difference between Percy and the classical realism of Plato and Aristotle has to do with their "Ionian" connection with Sagan: their official teaching is that man is at home in the Cosmos because the human mind is at home there. Percy agrees that there is truth to that view, but the problem is that human beings are more than minds and bodies. All human beings, even scientists or philosophers, are something other than mind. As Pascal, the Christian, says, there is an element of diversion in all science and philosophy. The "ancient" diversion is that human beings are already at home through the mind, and that diversion is in large measure shared by modern physics. The "modern" diversion is that the world can be transformed to make human beings completely at home through science.

Percy observes that for Americans the Jeffersonian pursuit of happiness has become "the pursuit of diversion" (*LC* 186). That pursuit is why they are, as Tocqueville first said, restless in the midst of affluence. They work not for material comfort but to purchase diversions. The life of the diverted self is unreasonable and unhappy, and it cannot be explained by the pop Cartesian expert. But because the frenzied self-avoidance of the diverted self is really a close encounter with the reality of self-ignorance, the diverted self is closer to the truth than the Jeffersonian self.

The pursuit of diversion becomes more insistent as it becomes more unsuccessful. The diverted self is gradually replaced by the bored self and the disappointed self. The success of the Jeffersonian project means the possibility of "increased leisure." But that leisure is accompanied with "an ever heightening self-consciousness." So leisure, perversely enough, comes to be experienced not as a human good but misery to be avoided (*LC* 185, 70).

Even sex, often celebrated as the most successful diversion, has become disappointing. Contemporary theorists are obsessed with genital sexuality, as seemingly the only way for the theorist or transcendent ghost to reenter the real world of bodies. But the scientific or expert attempt to liberate the erotic from the Christian tradition of repression and familial responsibility has really produced a "trivialization" or "demotion" of eros "to yet another technique for need-satisfaction of the organism" (*LC* 192). The ever so serious attempt to free sex from distinctively human longings has produced not the mechanical contentment of animal rutting, but more disorienting dissatisfaction. The sexual relationships of human beings are humanly fulfilling only when understood as part of the communication between man and woman, two selves, in the social context of sharing a home, family, and life (*LC* 9).

The angry disorientation Percy describes is responsible for much of the ideological violence and misanthropic projects to bring human distinctiveness to an end that marked the twentieth century and will continue in the twenty-first. The nihilistic revelation of the emptiness of modern science or "humanism," when wholly detached from Christian premises, is the main cause of the angry, ideological slaughter of our century, beginning with Verdun, continuing through Nazism and communism, and now through our apparently compassionate affirmation of euthanasia, abortion, and other forms of the so-called right to die. Death, the thinking goes, is better than the low quality of life we now live, despite our health, wealth, and freedom. Actual death is better than what Percy calls "death in life" (*SSL* 162).[4] He disagrees with Allan Bloom and Richard Rorty that the whole story about Americans today is increasingly sophistication and niceness. He does not think they are characterized by flatness of soul—that they have become clever animals and nothing more. They mouth therapeutic platitudes, but they do not really believe them. They are angry, deranged, and dislocated because they do not know what to think or do. Percy's self-help is to show them why they are alienated by nature as beings with language, as beings who wonder because they wander. And he gives that self-help not only in *Lost in the Cosmos*, but perhaps even more memorably in his novels.

Will Barrett's Wondering and Wandering

Percy's most memorable characters, Binx Bolling of *The Moviegoer* (1961) and Will Barrett of *The Last Gentleman* (1966), are detached, disoriented inhabitants of our therapeutic democracy. They are wanderers, because they are searchers or wonderers. Only when Binx and Will become able to wonder about themselves as wonderers and wanderers, when they are no longer diverted in one way or another by the impersonality of modern science, do they become somewhat at home with ineradicable homelessness or alienation. Until then, they fall prey to the aimless relativism of democracy. Unable to believe the therapeutic lie that they can live as well-adjusted animals in good environments, they have no idea what to think or do. For now, I will only say more about Will.

Will Barrett is an isolated, highly self-conscious individual. He spends his time thinking by himself, mainly about himself. His recurring question is "What to do?" He had been abandoned by his father, who had committed suicide, and by his family's clearly obsolete aristocratic way of life, and he lives in freedom, abundance, and with considerable leisure. As the abandoned "last of the line," he is free "to see things afresh." In fact, he is too free. His life appears to him as "pure possibility"; an indefinitely large number of choices or lifeplans are open to him. But he lacks the resources from tradition or religion or family or political life to think clearly about himself, connect with others, and really focus on his past or future. Freed up from authority or personal dependence on others or God, he believes he must not only think but know with scientific or Cartesian certainty before he can act. He is paralyzed by the fact that what he wants—perfect self-knowledge—is not available to a human being, the being who thinks (*LG* 3–5).

Will attempts to, but finds he cannot, "engineer" his identity through the expert principles of popularized science and the self-knowledge they claim to provide (*LG* 41). He thinks for a while that he will achieve self-knowledge through rational self-creation. But the self-conscious effort "to adapt myself to my environment and score on interpersonal relationships" proves futile and just too hard (*LG* 284). The abstract or fuzzy principles of that science (such as personal growth and creativity) never really account for or name his distinctively human longings. He has enough irony, partly a residue of his father's aristocratic distance and partly by nature, to know enough never really to become a pop Cartesian. Although "he made the highest possible score on psychological aptitude tests, especially in the areas of problem-solving and goal-seeking," he "still could not think what to do between tests" (*LG* 9).

Will appreciates that "the American revolution had succeeded beyond the wildest dreams . . . so that practically everyone in the United States is free to sit around a cozy fire in ski pants," and that he was somehow unfortunate not to be able to be happy doing that (*LG* 22). "An immense melancholy overtook him" on occasion for no reason experts could explain, and he noticed that his experience, not often acknowledged, is not uncommon among free and prosperous Americans, when they are, for example, trying to be entertained or diverted by paintings in Manhattan's Metropolitan Museum of Art (*LG* 46, 26–28). The hateful experience of something like pure possibility or the pure democracy described by Socrates (Book 8 of *The Republic*) was becoming common.

Will does know that the democratic utopia of pure possibility, of life unconstrained by necessity, is hell. As the novel's narrator says: "Lucky is the man who does not secretly believe that every possibility is open to him" (*LG* 4). He knows he is miserable in good environments, and he also knows that he feels better when confronted unexpectedly by necessity, such as the natural necessity of a hurricane or the honorable challenge of fighting off redneck racists (*LG* 325). But opportunities to deal with natural catastrophes or engage in honorable combat are rare in our democratic world.

Will's detachment from the past, from others, and from reality itself is even the cause of psychological and physiological disorders. He suffers from intermittent amnesia and déjà vus. He is often confused about time. He is unsure what has really happened, and unsure whether all he has seen and done has not happened before. The being who is stuck with pure possibility cannot be sure he is anywhere in particular. Time and place are, in human experience, intertwined. To uproot human beings too radically from their connections with the past, with particular persons and places, deprives them of the precondition of all human identity or genuine self-consciousness. It is true that most human beings live most of the time in the past or the future and so rarely live well as human beings in the present. But being deprived of the past and the future does not really give us the present, as it does for Rousseau's natural man. The experience of pure possibility places us nowhere in particular, not even in the present. Will thinks that "the locus of pure possibility" is that "[w]hat a man can be the next minute bears no relation to what he is or what he was the minute before" (*LG* 356).

Percy describes Will's uprooted or homeless condition as postmodern. The postmodern world emerges when modern language—modern words—is exposed as empty and exhausted. The expert language repeated by Will with little conviction about having "much to learn about the psychological insights of the World's great religions" and "rewarding interpersonal relations" seem to us to be no more than silly platitudes, although we hear them all the time. But we seem not to have an alternative language—better words—to express the way things really are.

Percy's own view of the future of human beings is far from despair or even radical pessimism. He opens *The Last Gentleman* with a quote from the German Catholic philosopher and theologian Romano Guardini:

> We now know that the modern world is coming to an end. . .; at the same time, the unbeliever will emerge from the fogs of secularism. He will cease to reap benefit from the values and forces developed by the very revelation he denies. . . . Loneliness in faith will be terrible. . . . Love will disappear from the public world, but the more precious will be the love which flows from one

lonely person to another. . . . [T]he world will be filled with animosity and danger, but it will be a world open and clean.

The modern world was a mixture of Christianity and modern science. It avoids nihilism only insofar as the values derived from revelation retained some dignity and credibility. The modern world ends when "the fogs of secularism," which obscured the vision of even Mr. Jefferson, are replaced by the clarity of the unbeliever. But Percy does not accept the apocalyptic view of relatively clear-sighted unbelievers. If they saw everything, they would see the persistence of human longing, of love. Love, in fact, remains possible in the ruins of the modern world, whether those ruins are merely intellectual or the actual destruction of the great cities and suburbs we built to be at home. Percy often writes of the inevitable return of social, political, and spiritual life in the ruins. And Will Barrett's experience of postmodern loneliness turned out to be the prelude to his own love, the love of one lonely, disoriented self for another.

Will ends up joyfully connected with a solitary, despairing genius-scientist who believed that suicide is the only reasonable response to postmodern emptiness, to being "doomed to the transcendence of abstraction" (*LG* 354). Will's new friendship with Sutter Vaught is the culmination of Will's journey, the story of the novel, one in which he gradually comes to think less abstractly, to see the reality of nature and human nature more clearly, and finally to locate himself to some extent in the world of human beings, especially those who know best that they are wonderers and wanderers by nature.

The very possibility of being conscious or knowing with another is a refutation of the dogma of unbelief or the primacy of solitude. At the novel's end, Will and Sutter are finally ready to talk with each other about the true cause of human homelessness, and the real possibility of human and divine love. Freed from various diversions, they are now able to think about love and death—and so the corresponding human responsibilities—as the natural limitations to human possibility. Because they have found some real definition to human liberty or identity, to the self or soul, they are no longer in a position to rule God out.

Recent experiences such as the revolution of 1989 (which may have ended a period of revolution beginning in 1789) have confirmed what Percy argues: neither political revolution nor linguistic therapy can eradicate the human self or soul, making human beings totally at home in the world. Human nature has triumphed over various efforts at scientific transformation. But if human beings can actually change human nature—the effort at the heart of the biotechnological project that may well characterize the twenty-first century—then perhaps experience, even recent experience, cannot be our guide. Technology, which has transformed nonhuman nature and actually made us less at home, is being employed to transform human nature, eradicating the parts of our nature which are at the sources of our experiences of homelessness or alienation. Percy explains that the dominant tendency in psychotherapy is to use drugs and chemicals to alter moods, whereas the older goal of psychoanalysis was to understand them. The greatest danger to human liberty today might be called chemotherapy (*MCWP* 187).

The War against Drugs: Chemotherapy versus Psyche-iatry

In this final novel, *The Thanatos Syndrome* (1987), Percy considers the philosophical foundation of the biotechnological project, the reasons for its likely failure, and the necessity of political resistance to it. This novel's "only message," Percy says, is that it is "better to be a dislocated human than a happy chimp" (*MCWP* 202). Beginning perhaps with Descartes and certainly Rousseau, modern thinkers have tended to choose the chimp. Their political project gradually became reducing a "stressful human existence to a peaceable human existence" (*TS* 202). The chemotherapeutic scientist agrees with the pop Cartesian expert that anxiety and depression are treatable symptoms of a disease that can and should be cured to produce an orderly, stress-free, nice, reasonable life. Why should human beings be unnecessarily miserable, especially when the misery is the source of so much socially undesirable behavior? The old-fashioned answer is that such experiences of self or soul point the person in the direction of the truth and are integral to human nature or the human condition. But the scientist's seemingly reasonable response is that whenever the experience is eliminated, by whatever means, the alleged reality to which it points—the self or soul—also disappears.

The Thanatos Syndrome presents an ambitious, illegal experiment—a pilot project with national potential. A group of government-funded physicians and scientists treat the water supply of a large section of Louisiana with a self-suppressing chemical, heavy sodium. Their scientific hypothesis "is that at least a segment of the human neocortex and of consciousness itself is not only an aberration of evolution but is also the scourge of life on earth, the source of wars, insanities, and perversions—in short, those very pathologies which are peculiar to *Homo sapiens*" (*TS* 195). It is Rousseau's famous hypothesis in his *Discourse on Inequality*, but with one difference: Rousseau distinguished between animal nature and human history. Natural man, considered precisely, is an oxymoron. The chemotherapists observe that human beings really are naturally different from the other animals. That natural difference is the source of all the pathologies peculiar to human history. Human distinctiveness is a natural aberration to be corrected on behalf of evolution's general intention.

Chemotherapy or biotechnology promises to *make* modern science wholly true. So far, that science, when examining human beings, has become progressively less empirical. It abstracts from the truth about the self or soul. By so doing, it becomes less a scientific description and more an ideal for human transformation. The idea is to perfect human beings by freeing them from their flaws, their malformation. Why can science not change human nature with the modern, chimp ideal in mind?

I can only mention here some parts of Percy's answer to that question. The scientists who administer the treatment exempt themselves from it. They really do not imagine a future full of beings who are docile animals and nothing more, because they themselves would become miserably superfluous. Only someone as coldly rational as the philosopher Alexandre Kojève could really contemplate the self-destruction of himself and his kind in the name of reason and contentment. The scientists in the novel imagine, with Marx, perfect *human* beings, an impossibility. And they end up killing *real* human beings—through abortion, euthanasia, and so forth—on this mission impossible. The only way to eliminate the suffering and defects of children, finally, is to kill them all.

These scientists also use the project to satisfy their own human obsessions or perversions. They dangerously operate outside the law designed to restrain us all, aiming to deprive others of their rights by depriving them of the capacity to exercise them. The only thing more dangerous than the rule of experts who claim to rule impersonally is those same despots armed with biotechnology. Our biotechnological future will not be as members of our species living indefinitely long lives in egalitarian contentment—content because we are no longer moved by love and death. It could well be the deranged few exploiting the zoned out many, hiding their human, tyrannical impulses with the compassionate rhetoric of expertise.

The chemotherapists' view of compassion, whether they understand it or not, leads to the killing not only of deformed children and the terminally ill but eventually to eradication of all human reality. Self-conscious mortals are the only beings in the Cosmos who deserve our pity. But it turns out that the scientists have little real concern for those whom they treat. They manipulate others to alleviate their own anxiety. Their pity is really self-pity. Our theorists, such as Richard Rorty, are wrong when they say that the antidote to human cruelty is tenderness or pity. The self-pity that envelopes our science or theory—the false perception that the self or soul itself is a cruel deformity—has been the main cause of the ideological terror and killing of the twentieth century, the spectacular century of death.

But Percy does more than illuminate the character of contemporary and future tyranny. He also shows that it is better to be a dislocated human than a contented chimp. Human beings can really live well with the truth about their distinctively human experiences, and the joys that accompany them are more than adequate compensation for their misery. The protagonist of the novel, Dr. Tome More, is a "psyche-iatrist," or an old-fashioned dialogic Socratic doctor of the soul (*TS* 16). He discovers, through careful attention to what his patients say, that ordinary human life is flawed and often rather feckless, but it is not completely irresponsible, uncourageous, and self-deceived. People are stranger and more courageous than our theorists say; they really do not want to be freed from the truth about death. The psyche-iatric view is that most human beings experience terror and anxiety, or failures of self-deception or diversion. They have the capacity to live fairly well with those experiences and to find some human compensation through love and dialectical self-exploration of their misery.

More knows that the beginning of our consciousness of language and speech is also a social experience of communication with other alienated selves. Anxious experiences are painful in themselves, but even that pain can be accompanied by pleasure when we begin to speak and write of them with and for others. Percy himself takes pleasure in "naming" human alienation as "the Judeo-Christian view of man in trouble" and "the way man is" by nature. The psyche-iatrist assists his patient in experiencing the pleasure of such naming (*CWP* 217–18). More's view, finally, is the same as Will Barrett's at the end of *The Last Gentleman*; but in More's case he affirms it without reservation only because he was compelled to think about and act against the challenge of the chemotherapists.

Percy versus Prozac

Percy's view is that the depressed or melancholic, if they reflect with others on their miserable dislocation, can see through the platitudes of scientific humanism to the truth about our being and even to the possibility that the Thomistic version of Christian anthropology and Christian revelation might be true. This view has aroused great controversy over the last decade. Peter Kramer, for example, devotes a chapter of his best-selling and very thoughtful *Listening to Prozac* to doubting that Percy's celebration of depression and melancholy is much more than delusion. Prozac can so improve such a person's life that he experiences a transformation in his very being. He is freed from his miserable experiences in a way that enhances memory and self-understanding and contributes to optimism and personal productivity without any unpleasant side effects. Kramer comes close, at least, to agreeing with *The Thanatos Syndrome*'s chemotherapists.

The Prozac-taker is not some zoned out "last man" but an intelligent, reflective, outgoing, risk-taking person in a good mood. Kramer admits that Prozac or a similar drug could have deprived us of the novels of Percy and Dostoevsky. But it now seems that their self-understandings are untrue anyway. We no longer see any profundity, Kramer contends, in their brushes with suicide and searches for God. Depression and melancholy are merely biological disorders with a biological remedy; they are not some gateway to the truth about being. A person feels more at home, because he really is more at home, after taking the Prozac capsule.[5] Kramer recommends a new aesthetic of optimism and sanguinity for this new world.[6] Knowing that mood is a function of a chemical balance keeps us from privileging bad moods because they are more truthful. We are free to choose the ones that make us productive and happy.

What is now possible through mood-enhancing drugs (the effects of which we can expect will become progressively more safe and predictable) may soon be achieved even more effectively through gene therapy and other forms of biotechnology. We may well eradicate those aspects of our natures that cause us not to feel at home. Perhaps we will no longer be religious, metaphysical, political, or even polymorphously erotic beings. As Francis Fukuyama argues in *The Great Disruption*, we may remain social beings, but the circle of sociality will shrink and simplify. The most pressing reason to read Percy today is to discover why it is better to be a dislocated human being than a contented chimp, and why when we surrender part of our nature in the name of happiness we are actually subjecting ourselves to tyrants. More important, we might learn that part of the strangeness and goodness of man is what Percy calls his "incurable God-directedness" (*SSL* 261).

It is worth emphasizing that we Americans now seem to lack the moral standpoint to resist such biotechnological alteration. Communism, in fact, was much easier to resist. It was clearly rooted in terror and tyranny, and the standpoint of resistance was most clearly human nature. But now not only human nature but nature itself seem ambiguous and imprecise terms. One meaning of nature is what we have been given and cannot change, an ineradicable limit to human effort. But now almost everything natural seems technologically alterable. Even our dependence on this planet and any particular fixed span of life may no longer be necessary. All living beings will still have to die sometime, but we may be able to choose how much we are moved or determined by that fact.

Most uses of biotechnology, including, of course, Prozac capsules, seem beneficial to us all. They cure mental and physical illness, prolong life, and alleviate suffering. And the distinction between preserving human life and enhancing it through natural transformation is hard to maintain in particular cases. Even if there were American moral restrictions, which are unlikely in our progressively more libertarian society, it would still be easy to find the technology we desire in the Internet-connected world. Technology apparently has made the moral defense of national borders impossible.

Why should not biotechnology free us to be fully at home to enjoy the good things of the world? According to Percy, the best human life is to be at home with one's homelessness or alienation, and so to be free to enjoy the good things of the world while being conscious of their limitations. All the enjoyment that has been given to human beings in particular depends on us knowing the truth about our alienation. Here, to begin with, Percy does agree with Allan Bloom: Love does depend upon death. The good things of the world would vanish if we ever became as free as the chemotherapists want to make us.

Notes

1. See Donald Davidson et al., *I'll Take My Stand: The South and the Agrarian Tradition* (New York: Harper, 1930).

2. Quotations from and references to Percy's works are cited in the text using the following abbreviations:

> *CWP:*   *Conversations with Walker Percy*, ed. Lewis A. Lawson and Victor A. Kramer (Jackson: University Press of Mississippi, 1985).

LC: *Lost in the Cosmos: The Last Self-Help Book* (New York: Farrar, Straus, and Giroux, 1983).

LG: *The Last Gentleman* (New York: Picador USA/Farrar, [1966] 1999).

MB: *The Message in the Bottle* (New York: Farrar, Straus, and Giroux, 1975).

MCWP: *More Conversations with Walker Percy*, ed. Lewis A. Lawson and Victor A. Kramer (Jackson: University Press of Mississippi, 1993).

SSL: *Signposts in a Strange Land* (New York: Farrar, Straus, and Giroux, 1991).

TS: *The Thanatos Syndrome* (New York: Farrar, Straus, and Giroux, 1987).

This overview borrows here and there from my various publications on Percy over the years. The most important of these is *Postmodernism Rightly Understood: The Return to Realism in American Thought* (Lanham, Md.: Rowman and Littlefield, 1999), especially chaps. 3–4.

3. See *Postmodernism Rightly Understood*, chap. 2.

4. On the issues raised in this paragraph, see Percy's *The Thanatos Syndrome*.

5. Peter D. Kramer, *Listening to Prozac* (New York: Penguin, 1997), chap. 9: "The Message in the Capsule." The title, of course, is a correction of Percy's philosophic *The Message in the Bottle*.

6. Peter D. Kramer, "The Valorization of Sadness," *The Hastings Center Report* 30 (March/April, 2000).

Chapter 38

Russell Kirk's Anglo-American Conservatism

James McClellan

ussell Kirk (1918–1994) is widely regarded as "the principal intellectual founder of the American conservative movement in the post World War II era."[1] An independent scholar, he taught briefly at Michigan State University but resigned in 1953 over a dispute concerning the school's academic standards and never again held a regular teaching post. Kirk later quoted his mentor, Edmund Burke, to explain his disdain for an academic career: "He that lives in a college after his mind is sufficiently stocked with learning," said Burke, "is like a man who, having built and rigged and victualled a ship, should lock her up in drydock" (*EPT* 198).[2] Determined to become a professional "man of letters," Kirk returned to his ancestral home in the remote village of Mecosta, Michigan, where for the next half-century he worked out of an old wood-working factory that he had converted into a library.

Here he produced an astounding array of publications. He was the author of twenty-eight books, including his magnum opus, *The Conservative Mind* (1953), and the editor of thirteen others. He founded and edited two journals, *Modern Age* and *The University Bookman*, and published hundreds of articles and reviews in magazines, journals, and newspapers. He also wrote forewords or introductions to scores of books by other scholars, contributed essays to some twenty-five anthologies, and wrote a column on education, "From the Academy," for *National Review* from 1955 to 1980, as well as a weekly newspaper column, "To the Point," for thirteen years. This is not to mention his public appearances and lectures, which brought him every year to hundreds of college campuses, learned societies, and political groups across the land.[3]

No less impressive is the wide range of academic subjects addressed by Kirk in these multifaceted writings. They include history, literature, politics, philosophy, religion, education, economics—even fiction. Our task, however, is not to measure the enormous influence that Russell Kirk exerted as a prominent figure in the conservative movement, but to determine the nature and substance of his political theory and to assess his contribution to American political thought. This necessarily limits the scope of our inquiry to a small selection of his writings rather than a single work. Kirk did not produce a philosophic treatise as such; nor did he speculate on ideal forms of government. "There exists no single best form of government for the happiness of all mankind," he asserted. "The most suitable form of government necessarily depends upon the historic experience, the customs, the beliefs, the state of culture, the ancient laws, and the material circumstances of a people" (*POP* 275). Indeed, Kirk was not a political philosopher in the strict sense but an intellectual historian who reflected deeply and critically on the origin and development of the Anglo-American conservative political tradition.

The Conservative Mind

The Conservative Mind, illuminating a neglected but important element of the American political tradition, lifted Kirk from obscurity in 1953 into the national limelight. Unprecedented in American intellectual history, this erudite compendium of learning, based on an extended analysis of conservative literature since the French Revolution, presents the main principles of Russell Kirk's political thought. It is also the seedbed for most of his other works in intellectual history, including, inter alia, his biographical study of *Edmund Burke* (1967), *Prospects for Conservatives* (an abridgement of *Program for Conservatives* [1954], now out of print), *Enemies of the Permanent Things* (1969), *The Roots of American Order* (1974), and *The Politics of Prudence* (1993).[4] Most of these writings, it should be noted, went through two or more editions. Kirk continued to revise and perfect his thinking over the years, and his ability to deepen and expand his initial inquiry resulted in important modifications and improvements to his original theses. Particularly noteworthy in this respect is *The Conservative Mind*, which was expanded in 1960 to include T. S. Eliot and went through seven editions.

Kirk explains at the outset of *The Conservative Mind* that the book is both "a prolonged essay in definition" and "a historical analysis of a mode of regarding the civil social order." It is thus "not a manual for partisan action" but an attempt to determine the meaning of conservatism and to apprehend its basic principles of moral and social order. This is accomplished through an analysis of the views and careers of certain Anglo-American writers and public figures, beginning with Edmund Burke. Conservative thinkers from the continent of Europe are beyond the scope of Kirk's study, partly because their efforts were invariably tied up with different issues pertaining to the Catholic Church and the restoration of monarchy. "Only Britain and America among the great nations," observes Kirk, "have escaped revolution since 1790," and this attests to the durability and singularity of their deeply rooted conservatism (*CM* 3, 5).

Persuaded that Burke represents "the true school of conservative principle," Kirk further limits his field to an analysis of thinkers who are in line with Burke. Among the Americans selected, John Adams and John C. Calhoun, says Kirk, are the most important. Others include John Randolph of Roanoke, Fisher Ames, John Marshall, James Fenimore Cooper, Orestes Brownson, Nathaniel Hawthorne, James Russell Lowell, Henry Adams, Brooks Adams, Irving Babbitt, Paul Elmer More, and George Santayana. Burke and Benjamin Disraeli are the two most significant figures among the British. Others include Thomas Babington Macaulay, Sir Walter Scott, Samuel Taylor Coleridge, Robert Southey, William Wordsworth, George Canning, John Henry Newman, Walter Bagehot, James Fitzjames Stephen, Sir Henry Maine, William Hartpole Lecky, Arthur Balfour, W. H. Mallock, and T. S. Eliot. The single exception to Kirk's exclusion of continental thinkers is the addition of Alexis de Tocqueville—"chiefly because of his enduring influence upon Americans and Englishmen" (*CM* 5).

The conservative tradition established by these thinkers dates back to 1790, when Edmund Burke published his *Reflections on the Revolution in France*. This was the year that "the prophetic powers of Burke fixed in the public consciousness, for the first time, the opposing poles of conservatism and innovation." Modern conservatism, in other words, is a body of thought that began with Burke's opposition to the doctrines of the French Revolution. The historic struggle between conservatism and liberalism may thus be seen as a continuing debate on the revolutionary ideas and objectives that gave rise to the French Revolution. At a more fundamental level, conservatism, on the one hand, is a repudiation of the French Enlightenment and the doctrines of progress, rationalism, secularism, and egalitarianism; and, on the other hand, an affirmation of traditional political theory rooted in the teachings of the ancient philosophers and church fathers.

This word "conservative" did not become a political term until the early nineteenth century, appearing first in France to describe those politicians who were influenced by Burke and wanted to reconcile the best of the old order with the necessities of the new age. The term then passed to England and the Tory party subsequently changed its name to the Conservative party, signifying that the party represented a fusion of the so-called Portland Whigs, who were followers of Burke, with the Tories in office. The term then passed to America, where it was first employed in the 1840s by such figures as John C. Calhoun, Daniel Webster, and Orestes Brownson. In the nineteenth century, conservatism in Europe came to mean hostility toward Jacobinism and the "armed doctrine" of the French Revolution. Leading conservatives on the continent, such as Friedrich Gentz, Joseph de Maistre, François Guizot, Louis Bonald, and Alexis de Tocqueville, were all disciples of Burke or were influenced by his writings. As the century wore on, conservatism came into opposition against other forms of radicalism, including utilitarianism, socialism, and Marxism; and "liberalism" came to signify sympathy with the revolutionary ideals of *liberté, egalité, et fraternité.*

Kirk concedes that the words "conservative" and "conservatism" are not easily defined. Conservatism, of course, is not a political system or ideology that purports, like positivism or Marxism or Nazism, to rest on a scientific basis. Indeed, it has been said that "conservatism is the negation of ideology." Although it embraces certain values, their application often differs from age to age and from country to country. Conservatism in Argentina, for example, differs markedly from conservatism in Austria. As Kirk notes, "conservatism offers no universal pattern of politics for adoption everywhere. On the contrary, conservatives reason that social institutions always must differ considerably from nation to nation, since any land's politics must be the product of that country's dominant religion, ancient customs, and historic experience."[5]

Despite the vagaries and varieties of the conservative tradition, it is nevertheless possible to identify some of the basic principles of conservative thought that most conservatives have shared during the past two centuries. In *The Conservative Mind*, Kirk listed certain canons of conservatism, the list differing somewhat from edition to edition as a result of Kirk's continued study of the subject; and in his anthology, *The Portable Conservative Reader* (1982), he offered yet another version consisting of six major premises.[6] Upon further reflection, Kirk expanded the list to ten principles in *The Politics of Prudence*, one of his last publications (*POP* 15–26). The following canons, he concludes, tend to form a common thread of belief among Anglo-American conservatives, particularly in the twentieth century.

Principles of Conservatism

First, "the conservative believes that there exists an enduring moral order." Such a conviction often reflects a belief in natural law. There are two types of order: the inner order of the soul and the outer order of the commonwealth. Man is part of that order. Hence, the nature of man cannot be changed; it is a constant. Likewise, moral truths are fixed and permanent; and all social questions are questions of private morality. Political problems, argues Kirk, are at bottom religious and moral problems. A society in which individuals are governed by a "belief in an enduring moral order, by a strong sense of right and wrong, by personal conviction about justice and honor, will be a good society—whatever political machinery it may utilize; while a society in which men and women are morally adrift, ignorant of norms, and intent chiefly upon gratification of appetites, will be a bad society."

Second, "the conservative adheres to custom, convention, and continuity." They are checks upon man's anarchic impulse and upon the innovator's lust for power. Old customs help to create a sense of community, enabling people to live together peaceably. Ancient law passed on from generation to generation is at base a body of conventions, and it is through conventions that society avoids perpetual disputes about rights and duties. Continuity is the means of linking generation to generation. "Conservatives are champions of custom, convention , and continuity because they prefer the devil they know to the devil they don't know." Not all change is reform, said Burke; and when change is necessary, it should be slow and gradual so as not to uproot old interests abruptly or arbitrarily.

Third, "conservatives believe in what may be called the principle of prescription." In politics, it behooves us to abide by precedent and precept, for the human race has acquired habits, customs, and conventions of remote origin that are woven into the fabric of our social being. Prescription generally refers to rights and duties established by immemorial possession or usage; their chief sanction is their antiquity. The prescriptive rights of property, not to be confused with abstract natural rights excogitated by philosophers, are especially important safeguards against majority tyranny and redistributive schemes of despotic governments. Burke also used the word "prescription," it should be noted, as signifying the hallowed character a political institution acquires over many generations.

Fourth, "conservatives are guided by their principle of prudence." In the statesman, said Burke (and Plato before him), prudence is a major virtue. Public measures should be judged by their probable long-run consequences and not simply by temporary advantage or popularity. The problem with radicals is that they rush at their objectives without being mindful that they are running the risk of creating new abuses worse than the evils they hope to abolish. "The conservative declares that he acts only after sufficient reflection, having weighed the consequences."

Fifth, "conservatives pay attention to the principle of variety. They feel affection for the proliferating intricacy of long-established social institutions and modes of life, as distinguished from the narrowing uniformity and deadening egalitarianism of radical systems." If a society is to maintain a healthy diversity, there must be orders and classes, differences in material condition, and many forms of inequality. The only true forms of equality are equality at the Last Judgment and equality before the law; all other attempts at leveling lead inevitably to coercion, injustice, and social stagnation. Ultimately, if natural and institutional differences are destroyed, presently a tyrant will establish new and artificial forms of inequality.

Sixth, "conservatives are chastened by their principle of imperfectibility." The religious doctrine of original sin warrants our attention since human nature suffers from certain grave faults. "Man being imperfect, no perfect order ever can be created." Utopia is an impossibility, an illusion of secular rationalism that is incompatible with the true nature of man. Even a free, just, and orderly society can expect some evils to be lurking in the shadows. "The ideologues who promise the perfection of man and society have converted a great part of the twentieth-century into a terrestrial hell."

Seventh, "conservatives are persuaded that freedom and property are closely linked." All great civilizations have been built upon the foundation of private property; and the more widespread it is, the more stable and productive is the commonwealth. Economic leveling through redistributive tax schemes, confiscation of property, and suppression of competition is not conducive to liberty or economic progress. The institution of private property has been a powerful instrument for teaching individual responsibility, for supporting general culture, for raising mankind above the level of mere drudgery, and for providing leisure to think and freedom to act. "To be able to retain the fruits of one's labor; to be able to see one's work made permanent; to be able to bequeath one's property to one's posterity; to be able to rise from the natural condition of grinding poverty to the security of enduring accomplishment; to have something that is really one's own—these are advantages difficult to deny."

Eighth, "conservatives uphold voluntary community, quite as they oppose involuntary collectivism." Historically, the spirit of community has been a hallmark of American civilization, despite its decline in recent times. In a genuine community, decisions most directly affecting the lives of citizens are made locally and voluntarily; but when they pass by default or usurpation to a central authority, then community and self-government suffer. "A central administration, or a corps of select managers and civil servants, however well intentioned and well trained, cannot confer justice and prosperity and tranquility upon a mass of men and women deprived of their old responsibilities. That experiment has been made before; and it has been disastrous."

Ninth, "the conservative perceives the need for prudent restraints upon power and upon human passions." Power is the ability to dominate others against their wills. A government that allows an individual or small elite to dominate the wills of their fellows without restraint is a despotism, whether monarchical, aristocratic, or democratic. The conservative endeavors to limit and balance political power so that both tyranny and anarchy may be avoided. "Constitutional restrictions, political checks and balances, adequate enforcement of the laws, the old intricate web of restraints upon will and appetite—these the conservative approves as instruments of freedom and order."

Tenth, "the thinking conservative understands that permanence and change must be recognized and reconciled in a vigorous society" (*POP* 15–26). Change is inevitable; we must all obey the great law of change. But slow and gradual change is often the most likely to take root and bring about the desired improvement; for "hasty innovation may be a devouring conflagration, rather than a torrent of progress" (*CM* 9). Prudent change, then, is the means of social preservation. Just how much change is needed in a society, and what kind it should be, depend upon the circumstances of an age and a nation.

Such, then, are the ten basic principles of conservative thought that have evolved since Burke first warned his countrymen that the French Revolution would end in despotism. In applying these conservative principles, Kirk has also given added meaning to them by developing a number of key concepts, most of them taken directly from Edmund Burke's writings.

First is the concept of the "moral imagination," which recurs throughout Kirk's writings. The range and power of the conservative imagination contrasts sharply, argues Kirk, with the liberal's lack of imagination. In particular, it is what Burke called "the moral imagination" that gives the conservatives greater insight and wisdom. By the term "moral imagination," Kirk explains, "Burke meant that power of ethical perception which strides beyond the barriers of private experience and events of the moment."[7] It is at odds with the "idyllic imagination" of Jean-Jacques Rousseau and the "diabolic" imagination of a decadent society. Moreover, it "is the principal possession that man does not share with the beasts. It is man's power to perceive ethical truth, abiding law, in the seeming chaos of many events. Without the moral imagination, man would live merely from day to day, or rather moment to moment, as dogs do. It is the strange faculty—inexplicable if men are assumed to have an animal nature only—of discerning greatness, justice, and order, beyond the bars of appetite and self-interest" (*EPT* 119). The "moral imagination," in other words, "shows us what we ought to be." It is a combination of intuition, instinct, imagination, and long experience; and it "is the key to the recovery of order and harmony in the individual soul and ultimately in the whole of society."[8]

Another defining word used frequently by both Burke and Kirk that differs from ordinary usage is the word "prejudice." As indicated by *Webster's Dictionary*, "prejudice" is a pejorative term: an adverse opinion without just grounds or before sufficient knowledge; an irrational attitude of hostility directed against an individual or group. But Burke had a different view and looked favorably on "prejudice." As Burke put it in his *Reflections on the Revolution in France*: "Prejudice is of ready application in the emergency; it previously engages the mind in a steady course of wisdom and virtue, and does not leave the man hesitating in the moment of decision, skeptical, puzzled, and unresolved. Prejudice renders a man's virtue his habit" (*CM* 17). By the word "prejudice" Burke thus meant, as Kirk puts it, "the half intuitive knowledge that enables men to meet the problems of life without logic-chopping" (*CM* 42). Prejudice, then, is not bigotry or superstition, but prejudgment—which intuition and ancestral consensus of opinion supply when a man lacks either the time or knowledge to make a decision predicated upon pure reason.

A final illustration of Kirk's creative rhetoric is his frequent reference to the "permanent things"—a term borrowed from T. S. Eliot. "A conservative," Kirk observes, "is a person who is a guardian of the permanent things." These include the established institutions of society—the church, the family, and "inherited political institutions that insure a measure of order and justice and freedom, a life of diversity and independence, a life marked by widespread possession of private property."[9] The "permanent things" are thus the normative goals of a healthy society, "those principles of morals and politics and taste which abide from age to age, which create the truly human person, and which cement the civil social order."[10] But the most enduring contributions to the "permanent things," Kirk concludes, are made by religion and Christianity.

The Contribution of Edmund Burke

To comprehend fully the creative source of Kirk's political thought, we must ultimately examine his treatment of Burke's ideas; for Burke serves, as we have previously noted, as the foundation for his rendition of the Anglo-American conservative tradition. Kirk freely acknowledges his debt to Burke and makes no claims of originality. This is not to say that Kirk is simply a popularizer of Burke. Russell Kirk is an original thinker, to be sure, but his originality stems not from devising new systems of government but from his ingenious and exhaustive utilization of historical materials, many of them obscure or forgotten, and from his ability to discern common threads of thought scattered throughout a multitude of diverse writings spanning hundreds of years.

Kirk's analysis of Burke's political theory, appearing as chapter two of *The Conservative Mind*, is an extended essay that serves as the main reference point for his rendition of the Anglo-American conservative tradition. Parenthetically, the essay also redresses misconceptions about Burke's thought that had gone unchallenged earlier, including the putative notion that Burke subscribed to a utilitarian ethic and the doctrine of natural rights. As a result, *The Conservative Mind* not only laid the groundwork for the conservative intellectual movement that was to follow, but it also revived interest in Burke (owing largely to Kirk's revisionist interpretation of his thought) and stimulated further study in Burke's ideas.

Burke's political activities encompassed four distinct political struggles: (1) restraining royal authority; (2) the American Revolution; (3) the trial of Warren Hastings; and (4) the French Revolution. The latter, engaging Burke in the twilight of his brilliant parliamentary career, elicited the main tenets of the conservative philosophy that he developed. Like Russell Kirk, he made little effort to form his ideas into a systematic treatise or organized compendium of political doctrines; for his writings on the French Revolution were largely a response to political events as they unfolded. They include his *Reflections on the Revolution in France*, published in 1790 after Burke broke with Fox's Whigs; *A Letter to a Member of the National Assembly* (1791); *An Appeal from the New to the Old Whigs* (1791); *A Letter to a Noble Lord* (1796); and *Thoughts on a Regicide Peace* (1796–1797). These writings had a powerful, almost immediate, impact on England and the history of Europe. Many who at first welcomed the French Revolution, such as James Mackintosh, William Wordsworth, Samuel Taylor Coleridge, and Robert Southey, were soon converted by Burke over to the opposition. Burke's writings, asserts Kirk, "first checked in Britain an enthusiasm for French innovation; presently made possible Pitt's rallying of British patriotism against France; and then inspired a reaction against leveling principles which kept the English Constitution almost unaltered during four decades. His influence is still strong in the world" (*CM* 24).

In general, observes Kirk, Burke's conservative rejoinder was a reply to the rationalism of the philosophes and the romantic sentimentalism of Rousseau—"the insane Socrates." But Burke's assault did not end with the French Enlightenment; his animadversions also extended eventually to Jeremy Bentham's nascent utilitarianism. Likewise, contends Kirk, Burke disavowed many of the principles of John Locke, the official philosopher of Whiggism whose theories had influenced Rousseau and Bentham. Here, then, are the tenets of eighteenth-century radicalism repudiated by Burke, according to Russell Kirk:

> (1) If there is a divine authority in the universe, it differs sharply in its nature from the Christian idea of God: for some radicals, it is the remote and impassive Being of the deists; for others, the misty and new-modelled God of Rousseau.
>
> (2) Abstract reason or (alternatively) idyllic imagination may be employed not merely to study, but to direct, the course of social destiny.
>
> (3) Man naturally is benevolent, generous, healthy-souled, but in this age is corrupted by institutions.
>
> (4) The traditions of mankind, for the most part, are tangled and delusory myth, from which we learn little.
>
> (5) Mankind, capable of infinite improvement, is struggling toward Elysium, and should fix its gaze always upon the future.
>
> (6) The aim of the reformer, moral and political, is emancipation—liberation from old creeds, old oaths, old establishments; the man of the future is to rejoice in pure liberty, unlimited democracy, self-governing, self-satisfying. Political power is the most efficacious instrument of reform—or, from another point of view, the demolition of existing political power. (*CM* 27–28)

Burke's response to these radical doctrines formed the basis of his conservative philosophy. At the core of his thinking was Christian orthodoxy. He believed that revelation and reason, and an assurance beyond the senses, tell us that the Author of our being exists, and that He is omniscient. Burke's position, as summarized by Kirk, holds that "God's purpose among men is revealed through the unrolling of history. How are we to know God's mind and will? Through the prejudices and traditions which millennia of human experience with divine means and judgments have implanted in the mind of the species. And what is our purpose in this world? Not to indulge our appetites, but to render obedience to divine ordinance" (*CM* 29). The so-called Age of Reason, protested Burke, was an Age of Ignorance, ignorance based on abstract doctrines of rationalism divorced from history and reality. Above all, the rationalists had an overweening confidence in human rationality; they misunderstood and distorted the true nature of man and ascribed to the human species intellectual and moral attributes that had no basis in reason, revelation, or history.

In particular, Burke denounced the state of nature theory devised by Rousseau and other philosophers, as well as its correlative doctrines of the social contract and natural rights. Even before the French Revolution erupted, Burke had inveighed against the idyllic fantasy of a free, happy, lawless, and propertyless state of nature. Standing squarely in the tradition of classical natural law philosophy (which he helped to restore), Burke denied that man ever lived in a state of nature. With Aristotle, St. Thomas Aquinas, and Richard Hooker, he insisted that man, by nature, was a social and political animal. His natural state, as demonstrated in history, was the family and community; someone living the life of a hermit, wandering alone in the forests, was either a beast or a god. Rousseau's noble savage, the supreme individualist, was surely a mythical being. No less fanciful was the notion that man consciously and voluntarily left these austere environs by means of a social contract in order to protect so-called rights he had possessed in the state of nature.

"I may assume," said Burke,

> that the awful Author of our being is the author of our place in the order of existence; and that having disposed and marshalled us by a divine tactic, not according to our will, but according to His, He has, in and by that disposition, virtually subjected us to act the part which belongs to the part assigned to us. We have obligations to mankind at large, which are not in consequence of any special voluntary pact. They arise from the relation of man to man, and the relation of man to God, which relations are not a matter of choice. . . . The instincts which give rise to this mysterious process of nature are not of our making. But out of physical causes, unknown to us, perhaps unknowable, arise moral duties, which, as we are able perfectly to comprehend, we are bound indispensably to perform. (*CM* 31)

The whole state of nature concept, then, was ultimately incompatible with the Christian religion. "He who gave us our nature, to be perfected by our virtue," wrote Burke in the *Reflections*, "willed also the necessary means of its perfection. He willed therefore the state. He willed its connection with the source and original archetype of all perfection" (*CM* 33).

If man never lived in a state of nature, and the social contract is also a fallacy, then what becomes of the natural rights doctrine that is constructed upon these suppositions? In a word, it collapses. The idea that the state is morally or contractually obliged to protect all of the individual "rights" that prehistoric man is thought to have enjoyed in some anarchic, primordial state is simply illogical and unhistorical. This is not to say, however, that individuals do not have rights. In an oft-quoted passage deemed by Kirk to be Burke's "most important contribution to political thought," Burke offered this description of the true rights of man:

> Far am I from denying in theory, full as far is my heart from withholding in practice, (if I were of power to give or to withhold,) the *real* rights of men. In denying their false claims of right, I do not mean to injure those which are real, and are such as their pretended rights would thoroughly destroy. If civil society be made for the advantage of man, all the advantages for which it is made become his right. It is an institution of beneficence; and law itself is only beneficence acting by rule. Men have a right to live by that rule; they have a right to do justice, as between their fellows, whether their fellows are in public functions or in ordinary occupation. They have a right to the fruits of their industry, and to the means of making their industry fruitful. They have a right to the acquisitions of their parents; to the nourishment and improvement of their offspring; to instruction in life, and to consolation in death. Whatever each man can separately do, without trespassing upon others, he has a right to do for himself; and he has a right to all which society, with all its combinations of skill and force, can do in his favor. In this partnership all men have equal rights; but not to equal things. He that has but five shillings in the partnership, has as good a right to it, as he that has five hundred pounds has to his larger proportion. But he has not a right to an equal dividend in the product of the joint stock; and as to the share of power, authority, and direction which each individual ought to have in the management of the state, that I deny to be amongst the direct original rights of man in civil society; for I have in my contemplation the civil social man, and no other. It is a thing to be settled by convention. (*CM* 54–55)

And what is the status of these natural rights, queried Burke on another occasion, if they are constitutionalized and "further affirmed and declared by express covenants, if they are clearly defined and secured against chicane, against power, and authority, by written instruments and positive engagements"? The answer, he said, is that "they are in a still better condition: they partake not only of the sanctity of the object so secured, but in the solemn public faith itself, which secures an object of such importance." Accordingly, Burke continued, "the things secured by these instruments may, without any deceitful ambiguity, be very fitly called the chartered rights of men" (*CM* 49).

On the basis of these considerations, Kirk contends that "the true natural rights of men . . . are equal justice, security of labor and property, the amenities of civilized institutions, and the benefits of orderly society. For these purposes God ordained the state, and history demonstrates that they are the rights desired by the *true* natural man" (*CM* 56). It seems obvious, indeed, that "absolute liberty" and "absolute equality" are conspicuously unnatural conditions. The idea that all men are equal, said Burke, is a "monstrous fiction." Men are unequal in most respects—in mind, in body, in strength, in every imaginable circumstance save one: "the true moral equality of mankind" (*CM* 58). A society stripped of its diversity and individuality would soon sink into a barren state of tedium and despair, only to be succeeded by new forms of inequality, artificial and tyrannical.

Likewise, argued Burke, the claim of the natural rights philosophers that all men have a natural right to exercise political power, and that the majority has the right to govern, is a doctrine without any historical or moral foundation. Citing Montesquieu, Burke contended that pure democracy is an artificial political device that is inconsistent with the natural order of things. "Out of civil society nature knows nothing of it; nor are men, even when arranged according to civil order, otherwise than by very long training, brought at all to submit to it" (*CM* 59). Democracy, it may thus be seen, may be wholly good or bad, or admissible in part, according to the country, the age, and the particular circumstances under which it is adopted. In Kirk's words: "Possessing the franchise, holding office, and entrusting power to the people—these are questions to be settled upon practical considerations, varying with time, circumstance, and the temper of a nation" (*CM* 59).

It would be erroneous to assume, however, that Burke rejected every form of majority rule or government by consent; for he believed that the principle of majority rule would be quite acceptable if it were limited primarily to a class of men qualified to rule by virtue of their tradition, station, education, property, and moral character. Burke estimated that in Britain, this body included some four hundred thousand men. "It is said," he observed, "that twenty-four million ought to prevail over two hundred thousand. True, if the constitution of a kingdom be a problem of arithmetic. . . . The will of the many, and their interest, must very often differ; and great will be the difference when they make an evil choice" (*CM* 61). Insisting that he was no friend of unchecked aristocracy, he insisted nevertheless that rule of a natural aristocracy offers the best prospect of good government.

In a memorable passage, so widely disseminated that it has, in Kirk's opinion, probably contributed to the preservation of constitutional government in Britain and America, Burke described this aristocracy he so greatly admired:

> To be bred in a place of estimation; to see nothing low and sordid from one's infancy; to be taught to respect one's self; to be habituated to the censorial inspection of the public eye; to look early to public opinion; to stand upon such elevated ground as to be enabled to take a large view of the wide-spread and infinitely diversified combinations of men and affairs in a large society; to have leisure to read, to reflect, to converse; to be enabled to draw the court and attention of the wise and learned wherever they are to be found; to be habituated in the pursuit of honor and duty; to be formed to the greatest degree of vigilance, foresight, and circumspection, in a state of things in which no fault is committed with impunity, and the slightest mistakes draw on the most ruinous consequences; to be led to a guarded and regulated conduct, from a sense that you are considered as an instructor of your fellow-citizens in their highest concerns, and that you act as

a reconciler between God and man; to be employed as an administrator of law and justice, and to be thereby amongst the first benefactors of mankind; to be a professor of high science, or of liberal and ingenuous art; to be amongst rich traders, who from their success are presumed to have sharp and vigorous understandings, and to possess the virtues of diligence, order, constancy, and regularity, and to have cultivated an habitual regard to commutative justice—these are the circumstances of men, that form what I should call a *natural* aristocracy, without which there is no nation. (*CM* 62–63)

What is truly natural, contended Burke, is the ascendancy of the natural aristocracy, not domination by men of mediocre talents. And it is the duty of a statesman to make use of the abilities of this class in the affairs of state; for leadership by men of birth, intellect, and property is surely one of the greatest gifts of advanced civilization.

These references to Burke's writings provide more than an intimation of the Burkean foundation of Russell Kirk's conservative philosophy. To be sure, Kirk's rejection of the doctrine of natural rights—the formative mainstay of political radicalism since the eighteenth century —and his opposition to its concomitant "ideology of Democratism" may be traced directly to the teachings of Edmund Burke. Training his guns on American democracy, Kirk asserts that the "democratic despotism" anticipated by Alexis de Tocqueville has become a clear and present danger, and that the old "territorial democracy" extolled by Orestes Brownson before the Civil War, now "much decayed," has degenerated into plebiscitary democracy. Echoing his mentor, Kirk avers that "the modern mind has fallen into the heresy of democracy—that is, the ruinous error of *vox populi, vox dei.*" Nowadays, he concludes, democracy has come to mean simply "one man, one vote." This is the absolutist democracy of the philosophes, a system of government based upon the "presumption that one person's judgment is as good as any other person's (aside, perhaps, from the accumulation of university degrees); a hankering after perfect equality of condition, although that may not be obtainable immediately; and a confidence that the American pattern of democratic institutions could and should be imposed upon all the world" (*POP* 274, 279).

The Roots of American Order

The Roots of American Order stands out as one of Russell Kirk's most important achievements since the publication of *The Conservative Mind*. Originally published in 1974, it is nevertheless prefatory to his *Conservative Mind* in that it seeks to identify and explain the political, historical, philosophical, religious, and constitutional precedents that led to the creation of the American republic. The American conservative tradition, that is to say, is the culmination and refinement, in Kirk's judgment, of certain intellectual and cultural forces that date back to ancient civilization. These are the "roots" of order that define the meaning and character of American life: "the roots of moral order, of order in the soul; and the roots of the civil social order, of order in the republic." Kirk's exegesis of the evolution of the "civil order" will necessarily be our chief concern, bearing in mind, however, that, "[a]ll the aspects of any civilization arise out of a people's religion: its politics, its economics, its arts, its sciences . . . are the by-products of religious insights and a religious cult. . . . Thus all order . . . could not have come into existence, had it not grown out of general belief in truths that are perceived by the moral imagination" (*RAO* 5, 14).

In the main, writes Kirk, "American *political* institutions owe little, directly, to the example and the experience of the Israelites or the Jews." The political writings of John Adams illustrate the point: Adams relied heavily upon Greek and Roman political experience in developing his philosophy of government and offered no account of the states of Israel and Judah. This is because he understood that "it is the prophets of Israel and Judah, not the kings, who teach us the meaning of order." The major contribution of Israel to modern social order, Kirk surmises, is in laying the foundation for the natural law philosophy or the idea of a Higher Law, and in establishing "the understanding that all true law comes from God, and that God is the source of order and justice" (*RAO* 17).

The Hebraic roots of American order, concludes Kirk, stem from the Law of Moses, principally the Decalogue, and from the teachings of the prophets. From the Ten Commandments came the idea of man's sinfulness, that man is by nature capable of both good and evil. Laws are therefore necessary to restrain every man's will and appetite. This view, says Kirk, influenced the Constitution-makers to reject the dogma of the French Enlightenment that all men are by nature good. As Thomas Jefferson declared, despite his rationalistic bent, we must not put our trust in the alleged goodness of man but "bind him down with the chains of the Constitution." Likewise, adds Kirk, the Hebraic understanding of Covenant, which spread throughout Western civilization, had a significant impact on American political thought in the formative era. "The idea of an enduring covenant, or compact, whether between God and people or merely between man and man, took various styles in various lands and ages; it passed into medieval society through Christian teaching, and became essential to the social order of Britain, from which society most settlers of North America came" (*RAO* 28). In sum:

> A principal difference between the American Revolution and the French Revolution was this: the American revolutionaries in general held a biblical view of man and his bent toward sin, while the French Revolutionaries in general attempted to substitute for the biblical understanding an optimistic doctrine of human goodness advanced by the philosophes of the rationalistic Enlightenment. The American view led to the Constitution of 1787; the French view, to the Terror and to a new autocracy. The American Constitution is a practical secular Covenant, drawn up by men who (with few exceptions) believed in a sacred Covenant, designed to restrain the human tendencies toward violence and fraud; the American Constitution is a fundamental law deliberately meant to place checks upon will and appetite. The French innovators would endure no such checks upon popular impulses. (*RAO* 29)

The Legacy of Greece and Rome

The ancient Greek commonwealths, according to Kirk, provided the Framers of the American Constitution with few precedents worth following—except in the sense that they had a negative influence. For the Greek political experience was a history of blunders marked by class conflict, disunity, internecine war, and the arrogance of power, all of which the Framers wished to avoid. No Greek commonwealth, not even Athens or Sparta, succeeded in establishing a sound and lasting constitutional order. This is not to slight the salutary influence of Greek culture, however, for "[n]o other race has produced, within a brief period, so many brilliant individuals. . . . The Hellenes were the cleverest people of antiquity, and the best soldiers; yet they spent their energies in destroying one another" (*RAO* 52).

Certain Greek thinkers nevertheless had an influence on the American mind in the early Republic. Foremost among these was Solon, the towering lawgiver of Athens whom members of the Founding generation came to know through Plutarch's *Lives of the Noble Grecians and Romans*. Kirk suggests that the American Constitution "has in it some tincture of Solon's prudence." More specifically, Kirk ventures to assert that had Solon never lived, the document "might have been less strongly marked by the concepts of 'checks and balances,' of compromise among interests and classes, and of 'mixed government' that Solon expressed and in considerable degree established in rising Athens." This is not to overlook the fact that, "[l]ong after Solon, these principles would be reexpressed by Plato, Aristotle, Polybius, Cicero, and other classical writers on politics; they would enter into the theory and the fabric of constitutional government throughout western Europe and (in a diversity of forms) throughout the New World" (*RAO* 60, 61).

Because the American Founders were looking for practical models of government, applicable to their circumstances, they found little direction in the pages of Plato or Aristotle's treatise on politics. Rather, contends Kirk, "it is Plato's and Aristotle's analyses of the human condition . . . and their theories of justice, that have been incorporated into American concepts of order." Plato affirmed that God is the measure of all things and proclaimed the immortality of the individual soul. He taught that "the cleansing liberation of that soul ought to be our chief object here on earth; we must free ourselves from false loves and degrading appetites, that we may conform to the nomos, the law, of a transcendent God. The soul, separable from the body, endures forever." Though Plato's *Republic* suggests certain political reforms, it is actually an inquiry, asserts Kirk, into the real nature of spiritual and social harmony; it is not a model constitution. Similarly, Aristotle distinguished three forms of government—monarchy, aristocracy, and the commonwealth—and favored a mixed government that incorporated the virtues of all three forms. "Thus, the Greek idea of political and social balance, as the Americans found it expressed by Aristotle and Polybius and Plutarch, was incorporated directly into the American Constitution" (*RAO* 74, 81, 82, 94).

In contrast with the Greeks, who were so well endowed with imagination and artistic genius, the Romans were a more practical people—grand engineers, tireless political administrators, masters of military organization and strategy. Above all, they had strong social institutions and a genius for the law that gave the world *Pax romana*, the Roman peace. They conquered the world in a little more than half a century. Their best critic was Polybius, a Greek historian who resided in Rome and counseled many Roman leaders. His historical analysis of Roman character, the Roman constitution, and the Greek city-states was of special interest to the Framers of the American Constitution. For Rome was a republic at first, and the Roman constitution described by Polybius during the Punic Wars incorporated both checks and balances and a separation of political functions; it was partly monarchical, partly aristocratic, and partly democratic. By the time of the second war with Carthage, the Roman constitution "stood at the height of its success. It was the 'mixed government' praised by Aristotle, but which Aristotle had thought almost impossible to maintain on a grand scale." It united all of the citizens and allowed men of ability and good character to reach positions of authority, especially in the Senate, where men of humble origin were enrolled for life. From this, Kirk determines that the Framers "imitated" the Roman institutions of checks and balances "as best they could," created an executive office that resembled somewhat the Roman consular imperium, and established a Senate that "was intended to function, in part, as had the Senate of Rome" (*RAO* 100, 101, 102).

Of the Roman leaders who prepared the way for ordered liberty in the early American republic, none contributed more, says Kirk, than the great Roman lawyer, Cicero. A model of republican virtue, he struggled to restore the constitution after Caesar was assassinated, only to be murdered himself by Mark Anthony's soldiers. Many American leaders read Cicero's *Republic*, his book on *The Laws*, and his *Duties* or *Offices*, not to mention his letters and orations. His writings are especially important, in Kirk's estimation, because they contain the most detailed of early discussions of the idea of natural law and advanced *jus naturale* as a jurisprudential principle. "True law is right reason in agreement with Nature," Cicero wrote in *The Republic*.

It is of universal application, unchanging and everlasting; it summons to duty by its commands, and averts from wrongdoing by its prohibitions. . . . We cannot be freed from its obligations by Senate or People, and we need not look outside ourselves for an expounder or interpreter of it. And there will not be different laws at Rome and at Athens, or different laws now and in the future, but one eternal and unchangeable law will be valid for all nations and for all times, and there will be one master and one rule, that is, God, over us all, for He is the author of this law, its promulgator, and its enforcing judge. (*RAO* 108)

This oft-quoted passage, made famous over the centuries by jurists, including English and American, expressed in elementary terms the natural law philosophy that was later developed throughout Western civilization. Even after Rome fell, natural law principles exerted a powerful force in the compilation of law published by the Emperor Justinian at Constantinople. Through the Church and the medieval schoolmen, and especially through the work of the jurisconsults of Bologna and St. Thomas Aquinas, Ciceronian natural law dominated political and legal theory down to the seventeenth century. "More than a hundred and thirty years after Alaric took Rome," notes Kirk, "the Emperor Justinian published in the East the *corpus juris civilis*, his elaborate consolidation of Roman law, incorporating the natural law doctrines of such famous Roman jurisconsults as Gaius and Ulpian. That monumental work still is the foundation of modern law in Western Europe, and has influenced, if less directly, the laws of England and the United States" (*RAO* 135).

The Medieval and Modern Periods

At bottom, the natural law concept established the idea that there is a higher law governing the universe to which the ordinary laws of mankind should conform. Through the writings of St. Thomas Aquinas and the medieval schoolmen, the natural law philosophy was adapted to Christianity, thereby affirming that: (1) God was the author of this law; (2) natural law provided ethical and moral standards to determine the legitimacy of man-made law; and (3) the natural law was knowable through reason and revelation. The American idea of a fixed constitution, superior to ordinary law, sprang from this notion of a hierarchy of laws. Canon law, much of it derived from Roman law, was initially applied in England only by ecclesiastical courts, but over time principles of canon law—and hence Roman—were gradually absorbed by the English common law and equity courts. This may be explained by the fact that some English judges in the Middle Ages were also members of the clergy, trained in canon law. In this way, Christian or traditional natural law became a part of English law. Citing Sir Henry Maine, the eminent English legal historian, Kirk further observes "that Henry de Bracton (often called the father of English law) in the reign of Henry III, borrowed from the Roman Corpus Juris the whole form of his own book on the common law, *De Legibus Angliae* (1260)." No man was above the law. "The king himself," Bracton wrote, "ought not to be under man but under God, and under the Law, because the Law makes the king. Therefore let the king render back to the Law what the Law gives to him, namely, dominion and power; for there is no king where will, and not Law, wields dominion" (*RAO* 189, 190).

Being judge-made law, the common law nevertheless had a popular element. Much of it incorporated the social customs and mores of the people, including their Christian values, and the common law courts generally enjoyed popular acceptance down through the ages. The English people were, in fact, jealous of their common law rights. It was their law, the product of their historical experience. "And if the common law was the foundation of order," states Kirk, "also it was the foundation of freedom" (*RAO* 190). To be sure, no monarch dared to defy it after the thirteenth century, so deeply was it entrenched; and by the eighteenth century it would be exalted even higher, culminating in Sir William Blackstone's great classic, *Commentaries on the Laws of England* (1765). More copies of this multivolume work were sold in America than in England, so popular was Blackstone among American lawyers. Many of the Framers were familiar with Blackstone. Despite the widespread opposition to everything English immediately after the Revolution, Americans continued after 1787 to rely upon Blackstone and the common law system of law they had inherited from the mother country and adapted to American circumstances. Jeremy Bentham, the utilitarian foe of Blackstone and Burke, offered to codify all of the laws of the new Republic, but President James Madison politely rejected his offer, affirming the common law foundation of American jurisprudence that extends down to the present.

In the history of political thought, however, the seventeenth and eighteenth centuries proved to be a turning point and a challenge to the primacy of the natural law tradition that Cicero and the ancients had bequeathed to Western civilization. This was the time of the Enlightenment and the natural rights doctrines of Thomas Hobbes, John Locke, and Jean-Jacques Rousseau. Together, these thinkers revolutionized political philosophy by offering radically new theories of government respecting the nature of man, the origin of political society, political obligation and consent, and the rights of man. Rejecting the Aristotelian view that man is, by nature, a political and social animal who is instinctively inclined to live in family and civic groups, from the small village to the city-state, the natural rights philosophers insisted that man's natural condition is the state of nature. Here, man once lived a solitary existence as a rugged individualist enjoying absolute freedom. For different reasons, depending on the philosopher in question, man ultimately left the state of nature. This he accomplished by means of a social contract, whereby those living in a state of nature agreed among themselves to establish society. In other words, society was an artificial construct, consciously created. The main purpose of this social contract was to gain better protection for the rights that every man enjoyed in the state of nature. Depending again on the particular philosopher, these rights included self-preservation or life, liberty, property, equality, and the right to revolt against authority if those rights were not adequately protected. In exchange for the state's promise to protect these "natural" rights, the individual agreed to obey political authority. This imaginary agreement thus purported to provide an ethical justification for obedience to government based on the consent of the people. This, in greatly simplified form, is the general thrust of the new natural rights philosophy that emerged in the Enlightenment. Individual rights being the ultimate criterion for judging the legitimacy of government action, the doctrine of natural rights is not to be confused with the traditional natural law, which served as a moral basis for judging positive law and focused on man's Christian duties rather than his secular "rights."

Hobbes, who has been called the founder of modern political philosophy, "divorced politics from religion," notes Kirk, and "converted the classical and Christian theory of natural law, as expounded by Aquinas and [Richard] Hooker, into a mere statement of the general rules by which men have found it convenient to live together. He . . . replaced the idea of society as a providentially-ordained covenant, governed by love, with the idea of society as a collection of selfish individuals, kept from one another's throats by the sword of an absolute monarch" (*RAO* 271). Locke, on the other hand, opposed royal absolutism and defended the Revolution of 1688. His *Second Treatise of Government*, one of the major works of English political theory, sought to establish the proposition that government is based on free contract, that political authorities hold power only as a trust from the people, and that the people may use their strength rightfully when this trust is violated and overthrow the government. Kirk contends, however, that "[i]n most matters, Locke was not an original thinker, but rather a synthesizer or populizer." His emphasis upon "primitive freedom" endangers the well-being and spiritual continuity of society;

for he has "nothing to say about the Christian view of society as a bond between God and man," and "there is no warmth in Locke, and no sense of consecration." Individual self-interest, "utility not love, is the motive of Locke's individualism." Kirk concludes that, "what he really was after, at the heart of the matter, was not metaphysical apprehension, but rather a passable symbolic explanation—perhaps we may call it a myth—to account for the existence of Englishmen's rights" (*RAO* 285, 286, 287).

Rousseau presented very different ideas about the state of nature, the social contract, and natural rights, but Kirk treats Rousseau's ideas summarily, principally because Rousseau and his followers had little or no impact on the roots of American order. Nor, for that matter, did Hobbes enjoy much of a following in the American colonies, despite his impact in Europe as a metaphysician. Locke's influence on the American mind was considerable, however, and although Kirk concedes as much, he insists nevertheless that some American scholars have overstated the case for Locke. To what extent did Locke's political theories affect American political leaders during the latter half of the eighteenth century? Kirk's reply to this question minimizes the role that Locke played in the American Revolution. "From studies of Americans' reading during that period," he writes, "the answer seems to be that educated Americans often mentioned Locke on the eve of the Revolution, but seldom read his books at first hand" (*RAO* 291). Looking beyond the Revolution to the Federal Convention of 1787 and the essays in *The Federalist* supporting the Constitution, we find even less evidence of Locke's influence at this time, as he is virtually ignored in these debates. Indeed, it is Montesquieu who seems to have made the greatest impression on those who participated in the creation of the Constitution, judging from the frequency of quotations from his *Spirit of the Laws* and the references to his doctrine of separation of powers.

"The Americans would make use of Locke," concludes Kirk, "but they would not worship him." This was true even of Jefferson, who allegedly plagiarized Locke in writing the Declaration of Independence. Quoting Jefferson's biographer, Gilbert Chinard, Kirk writes: "The Jeffersonian philosophy was born under the sign of Hengist and Horsa, not of the Goddess Reason." By this, explains Kirk, Chinard meant that

> Jefferson was more influenced by his understanding of English history (especially of the Anglo-Saxon period, beginning with the landing in Britain of the Teutonic chieftans Hengist and Horsa) than he was influenced by the rationalism of the Enlightenment. Jefferson knew his Locke, and praised him highly; but in his Commonplace Book and his public papers, Jefferson cited more frequently such juridical authorities as Coke and Kames. And Jefferson denied that he had copied the Declaration of Independence from Locke's *Second Treatise*.

Similarly, John Adams, the most learned of the Federalists, praised Locke on a few occasions in his ten volumes of writing, but treated Locke "merely as one of several commendable English friends of liberty—'Sidney, Harrington, Locke, Milton, Neville, Burnet, Hoadly . . .'." In brief, Kirk's thesis is simply that "the thinking Americans of that day found their principles of order in no single political philosopher, but rather in what has been called the 'Great Tradition,' drawn from Hebrew and classical and Christian teaching, and tested by the personal and natural experience of their British ancestors and their own colonial life" (*RAO* 292–93).

Edmund Burke and the Counterrevolution:
"To restore what once was, and so may be again"

Against this backdrop loom four thinkers from the late eighteenth century who took issue with Hobbes and Locke, with the doctrine of natural rights, and, in some cases, with the French Enlightenment itself. Moreover, argues Kirk, these thinkers had a much greater impact on American thinking:

> The eighteenth century men of ideas whose direct influence upon Americans was strongest stood in partial or total opposition to the philosophes generally and the Encyclopedists particularly. Montesquieu, with his devotion to the hard lessons of historical knowledge; Hume, with his good-natured contempt for the cult of Reason; Blackstone, governed by legal precedent and prescription; Burke, appealing to the great traditions of medieval and Christian and classical belief—these were American teachers in the latter half of the eighteenth century. (*RAO* 349)

Montesquieu, rejecting the social contract theories of both Hobbes and Locke, argued that the best government of his age was the constitutional monarchy of England, where the citizens enjoyed liberty under law—a system of ordered liberty based on historical experience and produced in part by a separation of powers and checks and balances. Likewise, Blackstone championed ancient precedent, long-standing usage, and common law rights, helping to preserve the legacy of English law in the new Republic. "The natural law described by Blackstone," writes Kirk, "was rooted in Christian ethics"; and the rights of Englishmen, said Blackstone, consisted of "the right of personal security, the right of personal liberty, and the right of private property," not the abstract rights derived from Locke's social contract theory (*RAO* 371).

The inclusion of David Hume here in *Roots of American Order* is somewhat inconsistent with Kirk's offhanded dismissal of Hume in *The Conservative Mind*. Quoting Samuel Johnson, Kirk originally found Hume to be "a Tory by chance," whose skepticism was deemed anathema to the Burkean tradition. But in the twenty year span between the publication of *Conservative Mind* and *Roots*, Kirk had an opportunity to delve more deeply into the Scottish Enlightenment, and in particular Hume's writings, prompted in part by the realization that the Framers, especially Madison and Hamilton, were greatly influenced by Hume. Kirk concluded that beyond his seeming impiety, Hume had a profound understanding and appreciation of prescriptive order. In addition, Kirk disclosed in a 1981 article that many of John Adams's ideas that Kirk had initially considered original were actually those of Adam Smith, ideas Adams had "borrowed" from Smith's *Theory of Moral Sentiments*.[11] The addition of Hume and Smith as "pillars of order," argues Forrest McDonald, has served to strengthen the conservative tradition:

> To bring the Scots into the pantheon was to give conservatism an even broader and firmer intellectual foundation than Kirk had provided before. Hume and Smith shared Kirk's (and Burke's) belief in a transcendent moral order, in social continuity, in the principles of prescription, in prudential and natural change as opposed to forced change on the basis of abstract theoretical systems, in variety and inequality, and in the imperfectibility of man.[12]

Hume contended in his philosophical treatises, writes Kirk, that "our impressions, morals, and tastes are the products of Nature, rather than Reason," and he "stood for the old cause against whiggery, for faith against Reason, for Nature against the Rights of Man." Hume thus "demolished Rationalism by rational argument . . . and the theory of the social contract upon which Montesquieu had cast strong doubts by his commonsensical powers" (*RAO* 360).

Kirk, it is important to note, is not alone in his revisionist interpretation of Hume's place in the intellectual history of the West. Recent studies by Hume scholars posit that Hume's six-volume classic, *The History of England*, should share some of the spotlight with Burke's *Reflections* in laying the foundation for a counterrevolution against the ideology of the French Revolution. The final segment of Hume's *History* elucidates the reign of the Stuarts, including the trial and execution of Charles I, the English Civil War, and the establishment of a Puritan republic under Cromwell. The bold assertion that the people had a legal right to put on trial and execute their king astounded seventeenth-century Europe, and Hume's account of these events served as a memorable forewarning in the eighteenth century that monarchical government was in jeopardy and that history might repeat itself.

But Hume's influence was not limited to the English-speaking world. During events leading up to the French Revolution, and for many years thereafter, Hume's account of the English Civil War was used by the French to gain an understanding of their own predicament. As a noted authority on Hume has observed,

> Hume had interpreted the revolution in England that led to the execution of Charles I and a Puritan republic under the military government of Cromwell as an intellectual and spiritual pathology mixed with ambition. What the Puritans eventually sought was not reform but a total transformation of the social and political order in accord with a religious ideology. Hume's narrative seemed isomorphic to what was happening in France. The goal of the French Revolution was not reform but a root and branch transformation of society. The Jacobins stood for the Puritans, and the Jacobins' self-evident truths of the rights of man stood for the self-certifying enthusiasms and revelations of the Puritans; Louis XVI was Charles I, and Napoleon was Cromwell.[13]

Notwithstanding these considerations, Kirk welcomes Hume to the struggle against Jacobin ideology, but he does not entertain the notion that Hume's *History* rivals Burke's *Reflections* as the founding document of the Anglo-American conservative tradition in modern thought.

Less than a third of *Roots* is devoted to life on this side of the Atlantic. The American component of Kirk's study is limited essentially to the decade surrounding the drafting of the Declaration of Independence and the framing of the Constitution, and it concludes with a brief survey of "American disorder" in the early nineteenth century. This book is therefore not a discourse on American history but a prolegomenon to the origin and meaning of the conservative principles that have shaped American government and society since the Founding. As M. E. Bradford aptly puts it, *Roots of American Order* is basically a "Burkean preface" to a study of the American past.[14] Simply stated, *Roots* shows what has been preserved since the dawn of civilization, and *The Conservative Mind* shows who in the English-speaking world has endeavored to preserve it since the French Revolution. Kirk incisively encapsulates the patrimony he has traced in these words:

> The roots of order twist back to the Hebrew perceptions of a purposeful moral existence under God. They extend to the philosophical and political self-awareness of the old Greeks. They are nurtured by the Roman experience of law and social organization. They are entwined with the Christian understanding of human duties and human hopes, of men redeemed. They are quickened by medieval custom, learning, and valor. They grip the religious ferment of the seventeenth century. They come from the ground of English liberty under law, so painfully achieved. They are secured by a century and a half of community in colonial America. They benefit from the debates of the eighteenth century. They approach the surface through the Declaration of Independence and Constitution. They emerge full of life from the ordeal of the Civil War. (*RAO* 472)

It cannot be overemphasized, however, that in Kirk's mind the dominant influence is British; for the American heritage is, a fortiori, largely a part of the British experience. The filter through which Western values came to American shores was British, and when Americans decided to pursue their own destiny, they retained that love of liberty, justice, and order they had inherited from the mother country. "Our political tradition," concludes Kirk, "is rooted in two bodies of belief and custom: first, the Christian religion; second, the English and colonial historic experience in politics, with the fruits of representative institutions, local government, private rights, and the supremacy of law" (*EPT* 177).

In the final analysis, Kirk leaves us with the impression that the critical juncture in the political evolution of Western man is the Enlightenment, or, more specifically, the intrusion of natural rights doctrines; and that the whole school of natural rights is basically in opposition to Christianity and the natural law tradition, if only because the natural rights thinkers looked upon a secularized nature rather than Christian morality and historical experience as the source of man's rights, ignoring entirely the obvious precept that such rights necessarily require duties for their implementation. In the words of T. S. Eliot, as quoted by Kirk: "As philosophy derives its sanction from ethics, and ethics from the truth of religion, it is only by returning to the eternal source of truth that we can hope for any social organization which will not, to its ultimate destruction, ignore some essential aspect of reality" (*POP* 273). It is difficult to escape the conclusion that, in Kirk's opinion, the debate on the French Revolution is an ongoing affair, and that modern man, despite the corruption of his "inner" and "outer" order, may yet find the home of his fathers. The conservative tradition, which seeks to preserve and perpetuate the Christian civilization endowed by his ancestors, points the way.

Epilogue

As we have seen, it is often necessary to extract the political thought of Russell Kirk from the many volumes of his writings, where it is usually framed and embellished by the ideas of Burke and other great conservative thinkers. An exception to this general pattern is Kirk's essay on "Authority, Just Government, and Ordered Freedom" in the concluding section of his *Enemies of the Permanent Things*. Written fairly early in his career, this essay succinctly expresses the warp and woof of Kirk's political thought in terms of his own mature reflections. Albeit this essay is entirely consistent with his Burkean interpretations of men and ideas of the past, it nevertheless stands out as an attempt by Kirk to speak for himself and not simply as a disciple of Burke:

> Civilized man lives by authority; without some reference to authority, indeed, no form of truly human existence is possible. Also, man lives by prescription—that is, by ancient custom and usage, and the rights which usage and custom have established. Without just authority and respected prescription, the pillars of any tolerable social order, genuine freedom is not conceivable. . . . Genuinely ordered freedom is the only sort of liberty worth having: freedom made possible by order within the soul and order within the state. Anarchic freedom, liberty defiant of authority and prescription, is merely the subhuman state of the wolf and the shark. (*EPT* 282)

From this it follows that good government is instituted to secure justice, order, and freedom through respect for legitimate authority. Good government, simply put, is "government which seems consonant with the general welfare." This may be achieved, Kirk asserts, through adherence to two norms or principles. First, for a government to be good, it must allow "the more energetic natures among a people to fulfill their promise, while ensuring that these persons shall not tyrannize over the mass of men." The tendency during the past century and a half toward egalitarianism has served to undermine this principle; for "equality in political power has tended to lead toward equality of condition." Men are not equal, and "a government which ignores this law becomes an unjust dominion, for it sacrifices talents to mediocrity." The resulting degradation "frustrates the natural longing of talented men to realize their abilities" and "impedes any improvement, qualitatively, of the moral, intellectual and material condition of mankind." In the long run, it also harms the well-being of the general population, which is deprived of responsible leadership. A prudent politician striving to promote the common good will endeavor to seek a "balance between the claims of the uncommon man and the common man" (*EPT* 288, 289, 290).

The second principle of good government, reasons Kirk, is that the form of government adopted should be in keeping "with the traditions and prescriptive ways of its people." As Kirk sees it, "a prudent government is no artificial contrivance, no invention of coffeehouse intellectuals, got up abstractly to suit the intellectual whim of the hour. Governments hastily designed upon theories of pure reason ordinarily are wretched and short-lived dominations." What he has in mind is the revolutionary France of the Parisian philosophers, which hardly compares favorably to "the success of the American and British governments." Their praiseworthy constitutional systems resulted from "preference for growth, experience, tradition and prescription . . . over any closet-metaphysician's grand design" (*EPT* 288, 292, 293).

Beyond these two basic principles, which have universal applicability, Kirk is not prepared to venture. These two norms, he concludes, are the only principles of government that are essential in the pursuit of good government. There are no other invariable rules of politics "which may be applied, uniformly, universally, and without qualification, to all societies in all ages." The American Constitution, he boasts, is a conservative constitution; but he agrees with Daniel Boorstin that it is "not for export." Nor is the utopian regime of the Jacobins. There is no such thing as a constitution that is "calculated to work wonders everywhere." Both the British and American Constitutions have worked rather well; "but they cannot be transplanted with much more success than one experiences when trying to transplant a . . . flowering plant that prefers its native soil to the tidy garden." A fatal mistake of the French revolutionaries was "their endeavor to remake France upon the model of what they took English politics to be" (*EPT* 293).

In fine, the everlasting and unrelenting task of the conservative movement, strictly from the standpoint of political theory, is to preserve and protect Anglo-American political and legal institutions, including the traditional rights and duties they have generated, and to isolate and destroy alien ideologies spawned by the French Enlightenment, ideologies and natural rights doctrines that have already infected the body politic and now threaten the very existence of Great Britain and America, if not all of Western civilization.

Notes

1. John P. East, *The American Conservative Movement: The Philosophical Founders* (Chicago: Regnery Books, 1986), 17. "It is customary—and correct—to point to Kirk," notes George H. Nash, "as the principal disciple of Edmund Burke in the post war era; less often noted is his recovery of an American conservative tradition." *The Conservative Intellectual Movement in America since 1945* (New York: Basic Books, 1976), 67.

2. Quotations from and references to Kirk's works (in which many quotes from Edmund Burke appear) are cited in the text using the following abbreviations:

    CM: *The Conservative Mind: From Burke to Eliot,* 7th ed. (Washington, D.C.: Regnery Publishing, 1986).

EPT: *Enemies of the Permanent Things* (New Rochelle, N.Y.: Arlington House, 1969).
POP: *Politics of Prudence* (Bryn Mawr, Pa.: Intercollegiate Studies Institute, 1993).
RAO: *The Roots of American Order* (Washington, D.C.: Regnery Gateway, 1991).

3. See Charles Brown, ed., *Russell Kirk: A Bibliography* (Mount Pleasant, Mich.: Clarke Historical Library, 1980). Brown's complete and updated bibliography is available in electronic form at the Russell Kirk Center for Cultural Renewal, Mecosta, Michigan. A useful, selected bibliography covering the entirety of Kirk's career is provided in James E. Person's *Russell Kirk: A Critical Biography of a Conservative Mind* (Lanham, Md.: Madison Books, 1999), 221–27.

4. *Edmund Burke: A Genius Reconsidered* (Wilmington, Del.: Intercollegiate Studies Institute, 1997) and *Prospects for Conservatives* (Washington, D.C.: Regnery Publishing, 1989). Other works by Kirk on political thought include his *Randolph of Roanoke: A Study in Conservative Thought* (Indianapolis: Liberty Fund, 1997); *Redeeming the Time* (Wilmington, Del.: Intercollegiate Studies Institute, 1996); *The Conservative Constitution* (Washington, D.C.: Regnery Publishing, 1990); and *The Political Principles of Robert A. Taft*, coauthored with James McClellan (New York: Fleet Press, 1967).

5. *The Portable Conservative Reader*, ed. Russell Kirk (New York: Viking Press, 1982), xiv–xv.

6. *Portable Conservative*, xv–xviii.

7. Russell Kirk, *Eliot and His Age: T. S. Eliot's Moral Imagination in the Twentieth Century* (LaSalle, Ill.: Sherwood, Sugden, and Co., 1984), 7.

8. *CM* 285; East, *American Conservative Movement*, 27.

9. "Interview with Russell Kirk," *Continuity*, no. 18 (Spring/Fall 1994): 8.

10. Russell Kirk, *Confessions of a Bohemian Tory* (New York: Fleet Publishing Corp., 1963), 230.

11. Russell Kirk, "Three Pillars of Order: Edmund Burke, John Adams, and Adam Smith," *Modern Age* 25 (Summer 1981): 226–33, reprinted in Kirk, *Redeeming the Time*, ed. Jeffrey O. Nelson (Wilmington, Del.: Intercollegiate Studies Institute, 1998), 254–70.

12. Forrest McDonald, "Russell Kirk: The American Cicero," in *The Unbought Grace of Life: Essays in Honor of Russell Kirk*, ed. James E. Person, Jr. (Peru, Ill.: Sherwood, Sugden, and Co., 1994), 17.

13. Donald Livingston, "Forward," in Laurence L. Bongie, *David Hume: Prophet of the Counter-Revolution* (Indianapolis: Liberty Fund, 2000), vii–viii.

14. M. E. Bradford, "A Proper Patrimony: Russell Kirk and America's Moral Genealogy," in *Unbought Grace of Life*, 74.

Chapter 39

The Two Revolutions of Martin Luther King, Jr.

Peter C. Myers

Widely revered as the spiritual leader and the most powerful spokesman of the civil rights movement in twentieth-century America, Martin Luther King, Jr., (1929–1968) dedicated his brief, remarkable life to the abolition of a regime of pervasive racial segregation and to its replacement with a regime of comprehensive integration in American social, economic, and political life. King was born into a middle-class family in Atlanta. The son and grandson of prominent Baptist ministers, he was ordained a minister while an undergraduate at Morehouse College. He received a bachelor's degree in sociology from Morehouse in 1948, a B.A. in divinity from Crozer Theological Seminary in 1951, and a Ph.D. in systematic theology from Boston University in 1955.[1] As a pastor in Montgomery, Alabama, he became active in the civil rights cause by helping to organize in 1955 a successful boycott of the local bus company. In 1957, he was elected the first president of the Southern Christian Leadership Conference (SCLC), an umbrella organization of church-based affiliates established to coordinate nonviolent civil rights activism throughout the South. In the late 1950s and early 1960s, he led nonviolent protests against racial segregation and disfranchisement in numerous Southern cities. His 1963 Birmingham campaign and March on Washington were particularly successful in gaining national publicity for his movement and in building support for the passage of the Civil Rights Act of 1964. In 1964, King was awarded the Nobel Peace Prize.

After the passage of the Voting Rights Act of 1965, King endeavored to broaden the movement both in its geographic reach and its objectives, turning his attention to conditions of poverty and "de facto" racial segregation in Northern cities. Confronting more formidable difficulties in the attempts to change socioeconomic conditions rather than laws and to preserve the discipline of nonviolence in demonstrations involving the urban poor, he achieved less impressive success in his Northern campaigns. He aroused still greater controversy as an increasingly outspoken critic of the Vietnam War, insisting on the close interrelatedness of his civil rights, antipoverty, and antiwar sympathies. With the assistance of close advisers and others, he wrote five books. Particularly helpful in explaining the principles governing his earlier and later campaigns are *Strength to Love* (1963), *Why We Can't Wait* (1964), and *Where Do We Go from Here?* (1967). King was assassinated in Memphis on April 4, 1968.

This chapter presents an exposition and assessment of King's moral and political thought. It begins with a discussion of King's first principles, in which he finds the direction and the ultimate justification for the revolution that he means to lead. Sections two and three present King's account of the proper means and ends of the civil rights movement. The chapter concludes with an appreciation of King's achievements and some critical reflections on his distinctive contributions to the tradition of American political thought.

I. First Principles

Like the abolitionist movement of the preceding century, the civil rights movement that arose in the mid-twentieth century was in large part theologically inspired. This does not mean that it was inspired by faith in opposition to reason. As the movement's leader, King often appeals to followers and potential followers in the rationalist, natural rights language of the Declaration of Independence. The Declaration, he observes, contains "the most eloquent and unequivocal expression of the dignity of man ever set forth in a sociopolitical document." Its principles, in their "amazing universalism," provide strong justification for the cause of equal civil rights and racial integration (*SL* 68; *TH* 98, 208; *STF* 190).[2] The Declaration and the Bible share common moral ground, as both affirm "the sacredness of human personality" (*TH* 119; also *SL* 3). Nonetheless, King makes clear that his moral principles derive their deepest inspiration and justification from his Christian faith rather than liberal moral philosophy. "The end of life is not to be happy. The end of life is not to achieve pleasure and avoid pain. The end of life is to do the will of God, come what may" (*TH* 36, 10; cf. *SL* 54–56, 133–34). The teachings of Jesus Christ, not those of John Locke or Thomas Jefferson, provide King's primary inspiration (*STF* 84).

Three elements of King's Christian theology are particularly important in shaping his moral and political vision: (1) the doctrine of "personalism"; (2) the concept of universal love or agape; and (3) the dictates of the "social gospel."

The doctrine of personalism constitutes much of the moral framework of King's Christian theology. As King summarizes it, personalism holds that "the clue to the meaning of ultimate reality is found in personality"—even that "only personality . . . is ultimately real." King identifies this doctrine as his "basic philosophical position." It supplies him with "metaphysical and philosophical grounding for the idea of a personal God, and . . . for the dignity and worth of all human personality" (*STF* 100). Personality, as King understands it, "means simply self-consciousness and self-direction." These attributes are limited in human beings and unlimited in God. "To say that this God is personal . . . is to take what is finest or noblest in our consciousness and affirm its perfect existence in him." Therefore, in God "there is feeling and will, responsive to the deepest yearnings of the human heart" (*SL* 141–42). This belief in a conscious, willing, feeling, loving God supports King's frequently stated conviction that "the universe is on the side of justice" (*STF* 106; *TH* 9, 141; *SL* 141). Against purportedly scientific materialism, which reduces man to "a transient accident of protons and electrons traveling blind" (*SL* 54–55; *TC* 72), King maintains that the universe manifests a moral order and purpose. The moral order of the universe centers on the relation of divine and human personality. As "human worth lies in relatedness to God," so "the essence of man is found in freedom," or in the powers of self-consciousness and self-direction by virtue of which human beings resemble their Creator. Justice begins with an affirmation of the God-given freedom and dignity of the human person (*TH* 118–22).

The real heart of King's Christian ethic is not, however, the principle of interpersonal respect but rather the sentiment of love. In a sermon in which he affects to summon the voice of the Apostle Paul, he declares that "I have discovered that the highest good is love. . . . It is the great unifying force of life. God is love. . . . Here we find the true meaning of the Christian faith and of the cross" (*SL* 133–34; also *WWGFH* 190–91). Christian love requires the love of God, then the love of one's neighbor, and finally of one's enemies as oneself. Lest this neighbor-love seem a requirement beyond the capacities of human beings in their sinfulness and partiality, King distinguishes various forms of love. What is required is not eros, as expressed in romance or in the soul's yearning for the divine; nor is it philia, the reciprocal love of personal friends. What is required instead is agape, which King describes as "understanding, redeeming good will for all men." Agape is "disinterested love," springing "from the *need* of the other . . . for belonging to the best in the human family." More specifically, agape supplies others' need for community by dissolving the sentiments of mistrust and hatred that disable them from loving their fellow human beings. It "makes no distinction between friend and enemy," and it ultimately involves "a recognition of the fact that all life is interrelated . . . and all men are brothers" (*STF* 104–6; also *SL* 36–37, *TC* 72–74).

Lending further substance to King's personalism and to his concept of agape is his strong affirmation of the dictates of the "social gospel." Against the "Greek" (neo-Platonic) belief that the body is inherently evil, King explains that "the body is both sacred and significant in Christian thought." Therefore, "the gospel at its best deals with the whole man, not only his soul but also his body, not only his spiritual well-being but also his material well-being." While he is troubled by the tendency of the social gospel's leading theologian, Walter Rauschenbusch, toward "identifying the Kingdom of God with a particular social and economic system," King strongly approves of Rauschenbusch's insistence on the social responsibilities of the church (*SL* 89, 138). The church must avoid excessive spiritualism as well as excessive materialism. King rejects in particular any religion "that professes to be concerned with the souls of men and is not concerned with the slums that damn them, the economic conditions that strangle them, and the social conditions that cripple them" (*STF* 36; also *SL* 122).

From these theological fundamentals, King derives the justification for his program of political and moral reform. His personalism and his concept of agape provide justification for his campaigns against racial segregation and discrimination. Both principles support his moral universalism. So far as human dignity is grounded in our common classification as divinely created, self-conscious, self-directing, free, loving beings, it does not derive from the accident of racial identification (*SL* 17, 130; *TH* 92–93; *WWGFH* 190). Segregation or discrimination based on such accidental qualities is an affront to the dignity of human personality, signifying a denial either of our common personhood or of the moral primacy of personhood. It is also a violation of the command of neighbor-love. Further, in conjunction with his embrace of the social gospel, this concept of agape underlies King's insistence that desegregation is only "negative" or "eliminative" in character; it is a necessary but not sufficient aim of social reform. Although it is a clear moral imperative, it represents only the first step of a movement whose ultimate aim is full integration. More broadly, the elevation of agape over mere interpersonal respect means that communitarianism ultimately supersedes liberalism in King's moral vision. Agape seeks to bind together—to restore or to create—a "beloved community" (*SL* 23, 40; *STF* 105; *TH* 118, 123). And as the fracturing of the American community appears also in class-based divisions, the achievement of genuine community requires socioeconomic as well as racial integration (*WWCW* 23).

This discussion suggests that with respect to its major objectives, King's movement divides into two phases. The changes in objectives represented by the movement's transition from its Southern to its Northern phase are considered below. But as King's characteristic choice of means constitutes as important a part of his legacy as the ends he employs them to achieve, it is necessary first to consider his understanding of the proper means for achieving the objectives of desegregation and full integration.

II. The Method of Nonviolent Direct Action

Although both his main objectives and his chosen means undergo a significant evolution or even transformation as the movement proceeds, King's fundamental commitment to the method of nonviolent direct action remains constant. This commitment reflects, first and foremost, an insistence on the morality of means as well as of ends. King emphatically rejects the Machiavellian and Marxist-Leninist doctrine that "the end justifies the means" and the accompanying enthusiasm for purportedly constructive violence. He therefore affirms that "the first principle in the movement is the idea that means must be as pure as the end" (*TH* 45; also 102; *TC* 70–71). Seeking to dismantle a regime of legally and socially enforced segregation in a manner that helps to foster true integration and harmony, King finds a happy marriage of morality and efficacy in the practice of nonviolent direct action. It offers "the most practically sound and morally excellent way for the Negro to achieve freedom" (*WWGFH* 63). For present purposes, three aspects of this method merit particular attention: (1) the emphasis it places on direct action or activist protest; (2) the insistently nonviolent character of its activism; and (3) its affirmation of the legitimacy, under certain circumstances, of violating positive laws.

In view of its revolutionary heritage, King maintains that America is a natural home for the practice of nonviolent direct action (*WWCW* 25; *TH* 349). Approvingly quoting Frederick Douglass on the unparalleled revolutionary significance of the Emancipation Proclamation of 1863 (*SL* 62; also *WWGFH* 78–79), King proclaims that the year 1963 marks a third American revolution. So far as he assumes leadership of this third, culminating American revolution, King implicitly presents himself as the twentieth-century successor of Thomas Jefferson and Abraham Lincoln. Whereas the first declared the birth of a nation and the second gave it a new birth of freedom, King means to guide the nation into its maturity, moving it finally to realize its promise of equal freedom for all. And in at least one important respect, King holds "the Negro Revolution" to be the greatest of all American revolutions.

King's frequent employment of revolutionary rhetoric to describe the civil rights movement is of manifold significance. He means to draw attention not only to the depth and profundity of the change that he seeks but also to the movement's relatively sudden, popular, and activist character. Its characteristic methods are sometimes described as "passive," but King rejects that description. "It is not passive nonresistance to evil, it is active nonviolent resistance to evil" (*STF* 102). To adopt a posture of passivity is to cooperate with injustice or, at best, to trust in the benign agency of time to overcome it (*STF* 212). But "time itself is neutral. . . . Now is the time to make real the promise of democracy." Painful experience teaches that "freedom is never voluntarily given by the oppressor; it must be demanded by the oppressed" (*WWCW* 86, 80; cf. *AMLK* 303). It is necessary for the aggrieved to demand that justice be done and that it be done immediately. "The hundreds of thousands who marched in Washington . . . summed up everything in a word—NOW" (*TH* 167; also 217–18; *WWGFH* 191).

This emphasis on revolutionary activism marks King's most significant point of divergence from what had been, prior to his movement, the mainstream approach to racial reform. In particular, King's revolutionary activism sets him apart from the most influential of such groups, the National Association for the Advancement of Colored People (NAACP). Skeptical of the direct-action approach, the NAACP preferred to pursue reform through strictly legal channels, mainly by the careful selection of test cases for litigation in federal courts. While acknowledging that this "legal approach" had secured many important victories in the twentieth century, King judges the NAACP's strategy insufficiently activist. However impressive its successes in securing favorable judicial mandates, unsatisfactory progress in the implementation of those mandates revealed "the doctrine of legal change" as a "doctrine of slow token change"(*WWCW* 33–34, 42). Moreover, King judges the prevailing approach insufficiently democratic. Just as he objects to the reliance on the race's "talented tenth" advocated by W. E. B. Du Bois (the most prominent of the NAACP's founding fathers) as "a tactic for an aristocratic elite," he finds similarly objectionable the NAACP's implicit placement of the rights of ordinary blacks in the hands of a small elite of lawyers and judges. In contrast to this educated elite as well as to hierarchical "armies of violence," King's nonviolent army displays "an amazing universal quality," embracing equally the lame and the able, lawyers and laundresses, "Ph.D.'s and no-D's" (*WWCW* 33, 38–39; also *WWGFH* 17). The "Negro Revolution" represents the greatest American revolution in that it represents "the greatest mass action crusade for freedom that has ever occurred in American history" (*WWCW* 25; also 116; *TH* 349).

A related and still more significant advantage of King's approach lies in its pedagogical power. A true revolution changes institutions and people (*WWCW* 117). The salutary pedagogical effect of revolutionary activism lies in a transformation of black Americans' self-understanding. King laments the submissiveness that he initially found in Montgomery's black community (*STF* 36–37). A major benefit of the direct-action movement lies in its power to dispel this attitude of frightened, hopeless dependence. Providing a creative new answer to Douglass's insistent question, "What are the colored people doing for themselves?" (*WWCW* 22), the direct-action movement awakens in blacks "a new self-respect and new determination." Discovering that he "can take direct action against injustice without waiting for the government to act or a majority to agree with him or a court to rule in his favor," the black protester under King's leadership experiences a self-revelation. He learns that "he [is] *somebody*"—a genuine agent, a person capable and worthy of freedom (*TH* 44; *STF* 211; *WWCW* 30; *WWGFH* 43–44).

Whereas this third American revolution differs from the second in its character as a mass action undertaken and led by blacks themselves, it differs from the first in its insistently nonviolent character. While he enthusiastically employs the rhetoric of revolution to stimulate a spirit of righteous activism, King firmly rejects the association of revolutionary activism with violence. In this respect, he differs both from his contemporary rival Malcolm X and from his great predecessor Douglass, who famously declares himself fully a man as a result of his violent resistance to a brutal slavebreaker: "I had reached the point at which I was *not afraid to die*."[3] For King, too, the will to resist oppression requires that the demand for a free life overcome the desire for mere life or physical safety. But whereas Douglass found this courage in his own self-overcoming act of violent resistance, King finds it in his faith in a providential God who commands his children to make peace.[4] Thus, the task is to sustain a spirited militancy akin to that of Douglass while avoiding the dangers and evils of violence. King insists that to be militant "merely means to be demanding and to be persistent. . . . It is possible to be militantly nonviolent" (*TH* 661). In composing his first major speech, King frames a question that would remain central to his leadership of the direct-action movement. In a characteristic attempt to reconcile seeming opposites, he asks: "How could I make a speech that would be militant enough to keep my people aroused to positive action and yet moderate enough to keep this fervor within controllable and Christian bounds?" (*STF* 59–60). Nonviolent action represents a golden mean, a synthesis that incorporates the virtues of militancy and moderation and avoids the faults inherent in the extremes of submission to injustice and violent resistance (*STF* 212–13).

The basis and substance of this insistence upon nonviolence require some clarification. One must first observe that as his career progresses, King's pacifism becomes, in important respects, more pronounced and unyielding. Affirming throughout his career the principle of nonviolence in domestic protests, he applies that principle in his later years to international conflicts as well. The most prominent example is his outspoken opposition to U.S. involvement in the Vietnam War, in which he not only denies the wisdom and justice of prosecuting that particular war but also declares his categorical judgment that "war is obsolete." Implicitly rejecting the Augustinian conception of just war, King maintains that in the nuclear age, war can no longer produce even negative goods, such as checking the spread of evil regimes (*TC* 67; *SL* 29, 140).

King's increasingly categorical rejection of violence does not reflect a quasi-Kantian spirit of indifference to the practical consequences of his position. His pacifism does not represent a demand that violence be renounced, though the world may perish.[5] In large measure, violent warfare is immoral and nonviolence is moral *because of*, not *despite* or *irrespective of*, their practical consequences. As he rejects violent warfare in view of both its inherent and its consequent evils, so he embraces nonviolent direct action as good both in itself and in its consequences. King is particularly concerned to emphasize the beneficial effects of nonviolence as a means of protesting injustice. In the light of this concern, he sees a moral distinction between the use of violence and the use of certain other forms of force. Because, as a rule, unjust rulers do not voluntarily surrender their power, an effective protest must be somehow both moral and forceful. By distinguishing violent from nonviolent forms of force, King is able to renounce violence even as he applies moral, spiritual, and economic forms of force to pressure his adversaries.

With the deepening of his study of the method of nonviolent action, King gains confidence in the power of this method to achieve needed social and political change while avoiding the evils attendant upon other forms of protest. As a student, he found troubling and challenging Nietzsche's glorification of power and his accompanying contempt for Christian morality as a morality of weakness. In later years, he finds similarly troubling the objection to his movement's methods by advocates of "black power." In response to both challenges, he endeavors to find within Christian morality the resources necessary for the exercise of real social power. Ironically, he finds in the thought and practice of a non-Christian an inspiring reminder of the potential within Christian morality for supporting effective social protest. While the fundamental spirit and motivation of the protest movement derive from Christianity, King observes, "Gandhi furnished the method."[6] As "I delved deeper into the philosophy of Gandhi," he explains, "I came to see for the first time that the Christian doctrine of love, operating through the Gandhian method of nonviolence, is one of the most potent weapons available to an oppressed people in their struggle for freedom" (*STF* 96–97, 84–85; *SL* 138). Whereas violent rebellion would surely be suicidal for black Americans (*WWGFH* 27, 56–57), creative nonviolence can supply effective arms against injustice. "Love is the most durable power in the world" (*SL* 40, 134). The nonviolent protests of Gandhi and his followers "freed more than three hundred and fifty million people from colonialism." The "nonviolent resistance of the early Christians . . . shook the Roman Empire." Even in American history, King (more problematically) maintains, nonviolent "boycotts and protests . . . laid the basis for freeing the colonies from unjust domination" (*WWCW* 37; cf. *TH* 149).

A brief review of the procedures typical of the movement's nonviolent protests can clarify the nature of their power. These protests commonly involved mass marches, demonstrations, and "sit-ins" at segregated facilities. Their immediate purpose, King explains, is "to create such a crisis and foster such a tension" that a segregationist community is forced to negotiate with the protesters (*WWCW* 79). The efficacy of such protests in producing the desired tension depends upon their power to arouse sufficiently dramatic resistance by the defenders of the existing order. And as King makes clear, the most dramatic form of such resistance involves the use of violence, whether by angry citizens or by local or state law-enforcement officials, against resolutely nonviolent protestors. The nonviolence of King's protests consists only in protesters' refusal either to initiate or to respond in kind to acts of violence. "'Rivers of blood may have to flow before we gain our freedom,'" he approvingly quotes Gandhi, "'but it must be our blood'" (*STF* 103). A proper protest is designed not to provoke violence or injustice but rather to expose that which already exists. Originating in response to the daily reality of (often violent) injustice, the nonviolent protest is designed to relocate that injustice to a context more favorable to its victim.

It is designed to "force [the] oppressor to commit his brutality openly—in the light of day—with the rest of the world looking on" (*WWCW* 37). The successful protest pressures a community into negotiations by exposing to public view the most vivid demonstrations of the community's injustice, as well as the hatred and fear that lie at its root, and relying on the hitherto latent decency of the majority of the community's members to move it to public action.

As with the activist approach, the moral efficacy of nonviolent protest also lies in its power to transform individuals. For protesters, the key lies in the experience of suffering. "Unearned suffering is redemptive," King maintains. "Suffering . . . has tremendous educational and transforming possibilities" (*STF* 103, 220; *SL* 141; *AMLK* 119). The present struggles present an opportunity to contribute profoundly to the nation's moral health. King sees "in this generation's ordeals the opportunity to transfigure both ourselves and American society" (*SL* 83; also *STF* 214; *WWCW* 151). Again in contrast to spurious appeals to "black power"—in which flamboyant assertions of manhood betray a psychology of despairing, nihilistic self-indulgence (*WWGFH* 44–48)—nonviolent protest at its best bespeaks not the weakness but the great moral and spiritual strength of its practitioners (*TH* 148). It demands of them enormous courage, discipline, and self-sacrifice. It requires a resilient faith in themselves, in the justice of their cause, in the ultimate justice of their nation, and even in the unfolding moral design of nature itself. It raises in them a proper sense of pride, as they gain from their sufferings a deeper knowledge of the worth of freedom and demonstrate anew their worthiness of it. As they overcome their oppression by others, nonviolent protesters master their own lower passions of fear, self-pity, and vengeful anger. They demonstrate a profound capacity for self-government by at once asserting their rights and forgiving and loving those who have denied them those rights (*SL* 25–40; *STF* 103–4). With all this in mind, King emphasizes the dignifying power of suffering in nonviolent protest: "By recognizing the necessity of suffering in a righteous cause, we may possibly achieve our humanity's full stature" (*SL* 83; *STF* 220; *WWCW* 40).

Nonviolent protest appeals likewise to the best in the erstwhile perpetrators and supporters of injustice. Its immediate purpose is to arouse the conscience, to awaken "a sense of moral shame in the opponent, and thereby bring about a transformation" (*STF* 99; also 102, 217; *TH* 336). To stimulate a sense of shame in this way is to employ a refined mixture of persuasion and compulsion to move one's adversaries to reform. To appeal thus to others' sense of shame is to bring to bear a certain form of force, but it is a form of force designed to persuade rather than to conquer. King maintains that nonviolence "does not seek to defeat or humiliate the opponent, but rather to win his friendship and understanding" (*STF* 102; 213, 221). Renouncing the pleasure of triumph even in a worthy cause, the nonviolent protester brings the guilty to confront dramatically the conflict between their unjust practices and the imperatives of conscience that those practices can rarely entirely suppress. He allows his opponents to triumph over themselves.

Triumph over others is unnecessary and ultimate reconciliation in friendship is possible by virtue of the ultimate decency of the American majority. In contrast to the more militant advocates of black nationalism, King denies that white America, in general, is irredeemably racist. Rather, the problem is that in their relations with black Americans, too many white Americans allow their consciences to be overcome by sentiments of pride and fear, both born of an overwhelming sense of guilt (*TH* 148–49; *STF* 215). For this reason, too, to attempt to reform race relations by violent means is a grave mistake. Violence by blacks works "to intensify the fears of the white majority while relieving its guilt"; it thus supplies a justification for greater repression (*TH* 68). To love and forgive whites is therefore an imperative of black self-interest as well as moral charity. Once again, agape "springs from the *need* of the other person. . . . The Negro must love the white man, because the white man needs his love to remove his tensions, insecurities, and fears" (*STF* 105; cf. 215; *WWGFH* 59–61). Violence destroys community; it can be a proper means of resistance, if ever, only to a movement seeking national independence, not to one that seeks integration (*SL* 6, 132; *STF* 216; *WWGFH* 61–62). Nonviolence, by contrast, creates the conditions for "the beloved community"; it destroys enemies only by making friends of them (*SL* 38–41; *STF* 219–21). By perfecting this exemplary mixture of righteous assertiveness, forgiveness, and charity toward all, King hopes that black Americans can make a special contribution to the moral reformation of the American soul and even of Western civilization as a whole (*STF* 224; *TH* 317–18).

It is necessary to add, however, that this somewhat idealized account corresponds to King's design better in the earlier than in the later phase of his movement. Encountering firm resistance to his later socioeconomic demands, King ascribes that resistance to a broader, deeper racism among whites than he had previously estimated. Accordingly, he alters his conception of direct action. While he insists to the last on nonviolence, his later activism is meant to coerce rather than to persuade. "Nonviolent protest must now mature," he declares in late 1967, "to correspond to heightened black impatience and stiffened white resistance. . . . There must be more than a statement to the larger society; there must be a force that interrupts its functioning at some key point" (*TC* 15; also *TC* 53–56, *WWGFH* 1–22, 67–101). King does not apply to this proposal the concern that he raises about the likely effects of violent protests. Either he does not believe that a program of escalated, disruptive, coercive disobedience is similarly likely to intensify white resistance, or, more probably, he simply reasons that desperate times require desperate measures. Judging the condition and temper of blacks and the poor a matter of revolutionary urgency, he seems to conceive of coercive protest as a risk necessitated by the circumstances.

The third and most controversial element of King's direct-action method is the practice of "civil disobedience." The NAACP's strictly legal, litigation-centered strategy is not only insufficiently democratic and activist, it is also based upon an excessively positivist or conventionalist understanding of law. Invoking as authorities such diverse exponents of the idea of a higher, suprapositive law as Socrates, St. Augustine, Gandhi, and Henry David Thoreau, King holds that an unjust law is no true law and affirms a moral obligation of noncooperation with evil or injustice (*STF* 51, 91; *TC* 74). He therefore affirms that at least in certain circumstances, extralegal protest is morally right and even obligatory.

King provides his most concentrated discussion and defense of civil disobedience in his single most famous writing, his 1963 "Letter from a Birmingham Jail" (*WWCW* 76–95). In this letter, he acknowledges a legitimate question concerning the coherence of this position. "Since we so diligently urge people to obey the Supreme Court's decision of 1954 outlawing segregation in the public schools . . . , [o]ne may well ask: 'How can you advocate breaking some laws and obeying others?'" (*WWCW* 82). In response, he points primarily to the distinction between just and unjust laws. Although he nowhere attempts a fully developed treatment of this extraordinarily difficult question, King sketches his understanding of the distinction as follows. At the center of the idea of justice lies an affirmation of the moral equality and dignity of human persons. In general, "any law that uplifts human personality is just. Any law that degrades human personality is unjust." More specifically, "an unjust law is a code that a numerical or power majority group compels a minority group to obey but does not make binding on itself. This is *difference* made legal." Likewise, a facially just law may be made unjust by its arbitrary application. Further, "a law is unjust if it is inflicted on a minority that, as a result of being denied the right to vote, had no part in enacting or devising the law" (*WWCW* 82–83).

Although this brief discussion in the "Letter from a Birmingham Jail" does not comprehend all important aspects of King's understanding of justice and injustice, it suffices to indicate his estimate of the breadth of the ground for legitimate disobedience. The potentially very large breadth of that ground appears most clearly upon consideration of King's third specified criterion of injustice, the denial of the right to vote. Applied literally, this criterion would render illegitimate, in most if not all states, all state and federal laws passed before 1965, including state and federal constitutions. The breadth of King's criteria of illegitimacy points to the need for prudence in their application. But King leaves mostly for readers and observers the task of inferring how his prudence, or his synthesis of militancy and moderation, guides his judgments as to which unjust laws to disobey. For the moment, it suffices to say that King apparently regards as a sufficient defense of extralegal protest his general insistence on conscientious action in pursuance of his egalitarian understanding of justice. But to understand more fully King's conception of the movement's proper means or methods, it is necessary to consider them in the light of the ends that he designs them to achieve.

III. Ends: King's Dream

King's most memorable summary of the goals of his movement appears in his most famous speech, "I Have a Dream," delivered in 1963 at the March on Washington for Jobs and Freedom.

> So I say to you, my friends, that even though we must face the difficulties of today and tomorrow, I still have a dream. It is a dream deeply rooted in the American dream that one day this nation will rise up and live out the true meaning of its creed—we hold these truths to be self evident, that all men are created equal. . . .
> I have a dream that my four little children will one day live in a nation where they will not be judged by the color of their skin but by the content of their character. (*TH* 219)

At first sight, King's vision of a just nation may appear to be a straightforward extension of the logic of the Declaration of Independence. Because racial differences are irrelevant to moral personhood, they cannot justify differences among human beings in the possession of natural, civil, or political rights. Moreover, the principle of equality in personhood also yields a strong presumption in favor of social integration among persons of different racial or ethnic groups. Granted, the Declaration's principle of fundamental jural equality does not imply the immediate necessity or possibility of a universally inclusive political community. To affirm that all persons possess certain natural, unalienable rights is not to imply that all persons, irrespective of cultural heritage and group identification, are immediately capable of living harmoniously together under a common set of laws. But the Declaration's principle does imply that, so far as particular, local circumstances do not permit such inclusiveness, such circumstances are to be judged retrograde and prudent measures are to be devised to reform them. Whatever the doubts of notable American Founders and statesmen concerning the possibility of a racially integrated American nation, King can justly claim that his vision of a "color-blind" nation—securing racially and ethnically neutral citizenship and association—is fully consonant with the spirit of the Declaration. So far as he aspires to teach the nation to judge persons by character rather than color, King, along with the Declaration, propagates an understanding of equality that incorporates the best of both democratic and aristocratic (or meritocratic) principles, mandating respect both for persons' sameness in the possession of fundamental rights and for their differences in various measures of merit. For the same reason (again like his nineteenth-century predecessor Douglass), King hopefully envisions a fully integrated, racially amalgamated community in which black identity does not simply disappear but instead contributes to the shaping or reshaping of a composite, synthetic American nationality (*WWGFH* 52–54; *TH* 318, 665–66).

Notwithstanding the eloquent simplicity of this formulation, the meaning and concrete requirements of this vision of a just America remain controversial. Viewed in the context of his more detailed elaborations of it in other writings and speeches, King's "Dream" is more expansive and bears a more complicated relation to the Declaration's principles than this brief statement indicates. To see this more clearly, it is helpful first to follow King's suggestions of a division of his movement into two phases. King variously describes these two phases as earlier and later, regional and national, negative and positive, destructive and constitutive, race- and class-oriented, desegregative and integrative, and reformist and revolutionary phases (e.g., *TH* 118, 189, 403–4; *WWCW* 23; *WWGFH* 3–4). But these distinctions do not quite adequately clarify the movement's change in focus. In both phases, the movement endeavors to do both the negative, destructive work of desegregation and the positive, constitutive work of building an integrated community. King's most revealing characterization rests instead on distinctions between two conceptions of equality and two classes of rights that the two phases of the movement aim, respectively, to secure. Whereas the first phase represents a struggle to secure formal rights and equality, the second seeks the "realization of equality" or to secure "real and substantial freedom" (*WWGFH* 4; also 130; *WWCW* 135). The essential evolution is from a movement seeking to secure equal protection under law for the exercise of civil and political rights to one seeking to secure a distribution of economic and social resources sufficient to equip all persons to reap substantial benefits from the exercise of their rights.

Within the mainstream of American political opinion, King is remembered and celebrated mainly for the objectives and achievements of the first phase. In concrete terms, the first of these objectives is the dismantling of the regime of legally enforced racial segregation, in commercial public accommodations as well as in public schools, concentrated in the states of the Old Confederacy. This aspect of desegregation is the general aim of most of King's major campaigns through 1964, including those staged in Montgomery and Birmingham and the "Freedom Rides" in Mississippi, as well as less successful efforts elsewhere. These campaigns can be understood as demands for the securing of individual rights and freedoms, so far as segregation restricts access to certain public accommodations and thus infringes on rights of association and travel. King understands his continuing campaigns for open-housing laws in a similar light.

Segregation is not only wrong in principle; it also inflicts deep wounds on its specific victims and on the nation as a whole (*STF* 190, *TH* 92–93). The "ultimate tragedy of segregation" is that it "not only harms one physically but injures one spiritually. It scars the soul and degrades the personality" (*STF* 37). In keeping with the arguments of such distinguished observers as Jefferson, Lincoln, Douglass, and Booker T. Washington (among others), King affirms that a regime of racial supremacy damages the souls of the dominant class along with those of the subordinate class. Much more than those earlier black leaders, however, he calls attention to the emotional and psychic damage sustained by blacks. "The central quality in a Negro's life is pain" (*WWGFH* 102). Echoing the argument that played a prominent role in *Brown v. Board of Education* (1954), King holds that segregation induces in blacks a false sense of inferiority relative to whites, imposing upon them a sense of invisibility or a "fatiguing, wearisome hopelessness" (*WWGFH* 110; also 119–20; *STF* 37; *TH* 121). He acknowledges that he, too, experiences segregation as an obscuring of selfhood (*STF* 19, 21). Only after overturning once and for all the regime of racial segregation, therefore, can the mass of black Americans recover or develop the sense of agency proper to fully free, rights-bearing citizens.

The other major objective of the movement's first phase, gaining prominence especially with the famous 1965 march from Selma to Montgomery, is the securing of voting rights. Like Douglass and Du Bois, and in contrast to the public position of Washington, King holds voting rights indispensable to black freedom and equality. The right to vote is "the most fundamental of all the privileges of democracy." Without it, one can make no meaningful claim of self-possession (*TH* 188, 197). The denial of this right has rendered blacks' persons and properties insecure in the South, forcing many to migrate north only to find themselves isolated in urban ghettoes. At a minimum, King argues in a 1957 speech, the voting right will enable blacks to defend themselves against Southern oppression, thus freeing them from dependence upon the federal government (*TH* 197–98). In later years, however, he conceives alternatively of the voting right as the crucial means for securing remedial assistance for blacks and for enacting a progressive agenda for the nation as a whole. "It is now obvious that the basic elements so vital to Negro advancement can only be achieved by seeking redress from the government at local, state, and federal levels. . . . Our vote would place in Congress true representatives of the people who would legislate for the Medicare, housing, schools and jobs required by all men of any color" (*TH* 183). King reflects in 1967 that "with Selma and the Voting Rights Act"—following closely upon the passage of the Civil Rights Act of 1964—"one phase of development in the civil rights revolution came to an end" (*WWGFH* 3).

Yet the very securing of these legal guarantees illustrates to King the limited efficacy of merely legal reforms. Without denying the importance of the *Brown* ruling and the subsequent legislative victories, he insists nonetheless that those victories "did very little to penetrate the lower depths of Negro deprivation" (*TH* 403–4). They effectively combated one form of segregation; but in fact "Negroes . . . live within two concentric circles of segregation. One imprisons them on the basis of color, while the other confines them within a separate culture of poverty" (*WWCW* 23). To overcome segregation completely, the liberal revolution effected in phase one requires completion by a more comprehensive revolution in phase two.

As noted above, at the bottom of King's insistence on the interrelatedness of racial segregation and economic disadvantage is his deep commitment to the theology of the social gospel. In the "revolutionary gospel of Jesus Christ," King hears a call to transform economic conditions that cripple human souls (*SL* 100, 96), and he finds the source of his sympathy for essential elements of the socialist or social-democratic critique of classical political liberalism. He repeatedly rejects communism, especially for its atheism and materialism (*STF* 92–93; *SL* 93–100, 139; *WWGFH* 186–87). But he does not maintain that communist theory contains no important truths. Rather, he affirms that communism and capitalism both represent partial truths; and as he focuses his attention on the shortcomings of his own society, he finds in communist theory a useful source of critical insights. Whereas communism neglects the individualist, personal aspect of human life, capitalism fails correspondingly to appreciate the social aspect of life and the value of collective endeavor. The "good and just society," King concludes, "is . . . a socially conscious democracy which reconciles the truths of individualism and collectivism" (*WWGFH* 187; also *SL* 99–100; *TH* 250). As the drift of this argument (along with other, more private evidence) makes clear, this reference to a "socially conscious democracy" signifies his ultimate allegiance to some form of democratic socialism.[7]

On the basis of this social theology, King rejects the classical Hobbesian-Lockean account of the foundation of political society. "From time immemorial men have lived by the principle that 'self-preservation is the first law of life.' But this is a false assumption. I would say that other-preservation is the first law of life" (*WWGFH* 180). In King's view, not jural independence but instead "mutuality" or interdependence epitomizes the natural human condition and constitutes the basis of the natural or divine law (*SL* 71–72; *WWGFH* 52–54, 101, 180–81; *TH* 122, 254). This argument lends perspective to King's frequent appeals to the Declaration, from which he derives a conception of fundamental natural or human rights that differs significantly from those held by the document's principal author, Jefferson, and its philosophic progenitor, Locke.

Troubled by what he regards as the deficiencies of the classical liberal account of rights, King insists that socioeconomic or welfare rights must be acknowledged among the unalienable rights affirmed in the Declaration. To guarantee rights in form but not in substance is to render that guarantee meaningless for the large numbers of people who lack the means to benefit from the exercise of their rights. The right to own property or to dispose of one's labor to acquire it is of little benefit to one without the training required to secure gainful employment. The right of access to a public accommodation or to a prosperous neighborhood is of little benefit to one who cannot afford to dine at a restaurant, much less to buy a home (*WWCW* 135–36). The withholding of communal assistance from such persons constitutes a real breach of the Declaration's promise. If "a man doesn't have a job or an income, he has neither life nor liberty nor the possibility for the pursuit of happiness. He merely exists" (*TH* 274; also 409). King's language is quite dramatic on this point. For the millions of poor people in America, "there is a kind of strangulation in the air. In our society it is murder, psychologically, to deprive a man of a job or an income. . . . You are in a real way depriving him of life, liberty, and the pursuit of happiness, denying in his case the very creed of his society" (*TC* 55). Poverty and unemployment constitute "an economic holocaust" whose main victims are blacks (*WWCW* 146).

This concern for socioeconomic as well as racial inequality manifests itself in King's advocacy of various remedial policy programs. In principle, King approves of race-specific compensatory measures. He argues that because "our society has been doing something special *against* the Negro for hundreds of years," it must "do something special *for* him now, in order to balance the equation." He declares, "*All* of America's wealth today could not adequately compensate its Negroes for his [*sic*] centuries of exploitation and humiliation" (*WWCW* 134; *TH* 367). In considering Indian policies of preferential treatment for members of the untouchable caste, he sees an analogy between Indian untouchables and American blacks, although he does not clearly indicate whether he envisions such preferences as race- or class-based (*TH* 158–59; cf. *TH* 367–68, *WWCW* 134–37). Yet, however strongly he approves of race-specific compensation, he believes it both just and prudent to advocate more broadly targeted remedial programs: "economic aid . . . should benefit the disadvantaged of *all* races" (*TH* 367).

The remedies that King proposes are relatively modest in scope in his early years and grow progressively more radical and ambitious as his career proceeds. In his first book, *Stride toward Freedom* (1958), he appeals for federal assistance only in the form of antidiscrimination laws and focuses on labor unions as the main institutional agents of black economic progress. Along similar lines, he insists that as they work to overturn the regime of racial segregation, blacks must also work independently to improve their own economic status by developing their own financial institutions and saving and investing wisely. The "Negro . . . must not wait for the end of the segregation that lies at the basis of his economic deprivation; he must act now to lift himself up by his own bootstraps" (*STF* 202–5, 222). A few years later, however, in *Why We Can't Wait* (1964), King takes a significantly expanded view of societal, hence governmental, responsibility to provide assistance to those who have little or no ability or opportunity to acquire on their own. "I am proposing, therefore, that, just as we granted a G. I. Bill of Rights to war veterans, America launch a broad-based and gigantic Bill of Rights for the Disadvantaged, our veterans of the long siege of denial" (*WWCW* 137; also *TH* 366–69). As the analogy with the G. I. Bill suggests, King conceives of this program as a series of coordinated measures indirectly addressing specific aspects of the problem of poverty, such as education, job training, and access to credit for housing and entrepreneurial ventures. Still later, he endorses a simpler yet even more ambitious approach. Declaring that the "time has come for us to civilize ourselves by the total, direct, and immediate abolition of poverty," King alters the emphasis of his proposals from stimulating productivity and thrift to facilitating broader consumption. "We . . . must make the nonproducer a consumer. . . . We have so energetically mastered production that we must now give attention to distribution." The "solution to poverty is to abolish it directly by a now widely discussed measure: the guaranteed income" (*WWGFH* 166, 163, 162; cf. *TC* 14, *TH* 247). Although he never simply renounces his call for economic self-help among blacks, in this latest period King expresses notably greater skepticism concerning such exhortations. "It's all right to tell a man to lift himself by his own bootstraps, but it is a cruel jest to say to a bootless man that he ought to lift himself by his own bootstraps" (*TH* 271).

Characteristically, King defends these proposals both on grounds of right, or compensatory justice, and with a view toward their salutary prospective effects. He contends that prolonged racial discrimination, poverty, and unemployment—all sustained by pernicious social policies—operate as root causes of many social ills, including criminal and rebellious activity, among blacks. "It is incontestable and deplorable that Negroes have committed crimes, but they are derivative crimes. They are born of the greater crimes of the white society" (*TC* 8). But if such ills are largely the results of malicious and poorly conceived policies, King reasons, then they can be largely remedied by benevolent and well-conceived policies. Notwithstanding his critique of political and theoretical materialism, he expresses remarkable optimism in anticipating the near-term effects of his remedial program.

> A Bill of Rights for the Disadvantaged would immediately transform the conditions of Negro life. The most profound alteration would not reside so much in the specific grants as in the basic psychological and motivational transformation of the Negro. . . . I contend that the decline in school dropouts, family breakups, crime rates, illegitimacy, swollen relief rolls and other social evils would stagger the imagination. (*WWCW* 137–38; cf. *WWGFH* 164; *TH* 366)

Especially during his final few years, this domestic reform program becomes increasingly interrelated with King's powerful concern to promote justice beyond national boundaries. The focal point of this concern is his vigorous opposition to U.S. involvement in the Vietnam War, which he announced publicly in early 1967. Blaming the war effort for diverting expenditures from antipoverty efforts, King admonishes his government and fellow citizens: "A nation that continues year after year to spend more money on military defense than on programs of social uplift is approaching spiritual doom" (*TC* 33; cf. *TC* 22–23; *TH* 232). The war poses grave difficulties also for his attempts to persuade the "angry young men" of Northern ghettos to seek domestic reforms only through nonviolent means. "But they asked, and rightly so, what about Vietnam? . . . Their questions hit home, and I knew that I could never again raise my voice against the violence of the oppressed in the ghettos without having first spoken clearly to the greatest purveyor of violence in the world today: my own government" (*TC* 23–24). He declares the Vietnam War "one of the most unjust wars that has ever been fought in the history of the world" (*TH* 275).

Ultimately, the domestic concerns that inspire King's opposition to the war merge into the most profound humanitarian concerns. Honored as the recipient of the 1964 Nobel Peace Prize, King receives the award as "a commission to work harder than I had ever worked before for 'the brotherhood of man.' This is a calling which takes me beyond national allegiances" (*TC* 25). Increasingly viewing his ministry from this transnational, humanitarian perspective, he places greater emphasis on the relations of the black American struggle as well as the conflict in Vietnam to a worldwide struggle for justice and peace. King warns that America has reached a crisis in the late 1960s amid its struggles over civil rights and the Vietnam War. This American crisis is a particularly important instance of a broader crisis confronting modern Western civilization and even all humankind. "It is midnight" in the social and moral order of America and the West (*SL* 58–59). The crisis cannot be resolved by piecemeal reforms. "These are revolutionary times," he declares in late 1967; "all over the globe men are revolting against old systems of exploitation and oppression" (*TC* 33; cf. *WWGFH* 189–90).

As he comes to view the American civil rights revolution as one theater in a global revolutionary conflict, King's ambivalence with respect to his American heritage deepens significantly. Throughout much of his career, King conceives of his revolution as an *American* revolution—a revolution of American ideals against much American practice. Viewed in this light, the Declaration and the Constitution represent "great wells of democracy which were dug deep by the founding fathers," and King's aim is to make their health-giving waters available to all Americans (*WWCW* 94). But in his final years, notwithstanding his continuing statements of admiration for the Founding documents (*WWGFH* 70–71, 130, 199–200), King seems to call for a revolution of more radical ideals against American ideals and practice alike. The revolution that he ultimately envisions represents "the widest liberation movement in history." It is a revolution of the non-West against the West. It is a revolution of underdeveloped nations of color against the developed, industrialized, colonialist nations of the world. "The storm is rising against the privileged minority of the earth, from which there is no shelter in isolation and armament" (*WWGFH* 169–70; *TC* 17). At a still deeper level, it is "a radical revolution of values," a battle against "the giant triplets of racism, materialism, and militarism" (*TH* 240; also *TC* 32; *WWGFH* 133, 186). King conceives of the crisis in American values as symptomatic of a profound malady in the very heart of modern Western civilization. The proud desire of America and other liberal-capitalist nations to be superior—their "drum-major instinct" (*TH* 264)—along with their ethic of competitive acquisitiveness betrays a deeply rooted, modern, Western will to achieve human self-sufficiency or mastery over nature. In terms recalling Rousseau, King contends that although this deep form of pride has produced in Western societies an enormous material abundance, it has done so at the cost of social and spiritual impoverishment. Western societies suffer from a deep, alienating confusion of means and ends, such that power and possession are given priority over the enrichment of human personality and community (*SL* 74–76; *WWGFH* 171–72).

Even as his second-phase movement encounters resistance in his final years, not only from black nationalists and white supremacists but also from traditional liberals and conservatives, King presses on with intensifying revolutionary fervor. He conceives of the ultimate aim of his movement in truly apocalyptic terms. "The American Negro of 1967, like Crispus Attucks, may be the vanguard in a prolonged struggle that may change the shape of the world" (*TC* 17). This revolution against the disordered values of the modern West means also a revolution against age-old ills, seemingly inherent in the human condition itself. Ultimately, King's protest against black poverty in America becomes a call for "an all-out world war against poverty" (*WWGFH* 178; *AMLK* 261). His protest against white racism in America becomes a call for the elimination or radical devaluation of national divisions (*TC* 68; *TH* 234, 253). His protest against American involvement in Vietnam becomes a call for the total, final elimination of violent warfare among or within human societies (*WWGFH* 183–86; *TC* 67–68, 77; *TH* 253).

On the other side of this revolutionary struggle lies King's famous dream, more fully elaborated as an apocalyptic vision of a new America and a new world—a thoroughly, finally integrated world community bound by ecumenical, humanitarian love (*WWGFH* 190; *TC* 18; *TH* 151, 242). He provides no blueprint of the institutional details of this "beloved community," but he makes clear that he considers the achievement of this new world order an immanent possibility. And he makes equally clear that he identifies this new order with the embrace of a fully universalized Christianity and, at times, even with the immanent establishment of the Kingdom of God itself. "We need to make a supreme effort . . . to enter into the new world which is now possible, 'the city which hath foundation, whose builder and maker is God'" (*WWGFH* 185). King's vision of a fully just, fully integrated society is based on the radical Christian doctrine of the unity of humankind. "We are all one in Jesus Christ" (*TC* 72; also *SL* 102). His call "for a world-wide fellowship that lifts neighborly concern beyond one's tribe, race, class and nation is in reality a call for an all-embracing and unconditional love for all men." This humanitarian love transcends racial, national, socioeconomic, and even historical religious divisions. The universal spirit of Christian love reaches fulfillment in a truly ecumenical "Hindu-Moslem-Christian-Jewish-Buddhist belief about ultimate reality" (*WWGFH* 190; also *TH* 242–43). King affirms that with the establishment of this new order, at once thoroughly cosmopolitan and radically communitarian, in which "human justice, brotherhood, secure peace, and abundance for all" have become effective realities, "the Christian era will truly begin" (*TH* 328).

IV. Critical Reflections

Due to the circumstances of his death and to the persistently controversial character of his major concerns, to achieve a clear-sighted, fair-minded critical appraisal of the thought, work, and legacy of Martin Luther King, Jr., is no easy task. But if such circumstances make critical scrutiny especially difficult, they also make it especially necessary. King urged his fellow citizens to extend and to transform principles that constitute the very foundation of American liberal republicanism. Given the enormous, enduring importance and power of King's appeal, it is imperative for American citizens and all students of political thought to subject this appeal to sympathetic, careful, critical examination. Challenging questions arise in particular through a critical reconsideration of two of King's most prominent themes: (1) the practice of "civil disobedience," and (2) the nature of a fully just, integrated community.

The clearest instance of King's attempt to maintain a moderated militancy and the focal point of his understanding of political obligation is his practice of civil disobedience. The notion of legitimate protest outside the boundaries of positive law holds a place in the American political tradition not only through the writing of Thoreau but also, more fundamentally, as an implication of Locke's account of the social compact. According to Locke, the individual members of political society hold an unalienable right to judge the legitimacy of their government and to act on their judgment as their prudence dictates. As Locke himself and his thoughtful disciples acknowledge, however, this doctrine is both indispensable and dangerous to the cause of legitimate government, and so it must be applied in practice only with great circumspection.

In the American political tradition, the most powerful statement of the dangers appears in Abraham Lincoln's 1838 Springfield Lyceum speech, "On the Perpetuation of Our Political Institutions." In this speech, commenting on recent eruptions of mob violence, Lincoln warns generally of the mortal dangers that lawlessness poses to republican government—irrespective of whether it purports to serve righteous or corrupt ends. As examples of unpunished lawbreaking multiply, the effects are, first, to embolden those already criminally inclined and, second, to alienate the normally lawful from their government. The remedy for this characteristically republican or democratic malady is to make "reverence for the laws . . . the *political religion* of the nation." Although bad laws may exist and deserve quick repeal, "still while they continue in force, for the sake of example, they should be religiously observed."[8] In insisting on fidelity to positive law, Lincoln does not reject Locke's teaching of a natural right to resist governmental illegitimacy. But in view of the great dangers of the state of nature, Locke and Lincoln agree, extralegal action is to be contemplated only when the evil is deliberate and of great magnitude, only as a last resort, and, above all, only when prudence dictates that such action is more likely to strengthen than to weaken the cause of legitimate government.

Notwithstanding his admiration of Thoreau, King's defense of civil disobedience differs significantly from that of his nineteenth-century predecessor on the specific point that concerns Lincoln. Whereas Thoreau proclaims defiantly that positive law represents nothing more than the rule of force and "never made men a whit more just," King holds that by changing behavior and forming habits, laws contribute importantly to the formation of moral sentiments (*STF* 33, 199; *WWGFH* 100–101; *TH* 100–101, 123–24).[9] King takes more seriously than Thoreau the concern that civil disobedience may prevent the achievement of a just community by undermining the rule of law that is indispensable to it. Yet he insists, contrary to Lincoln, that the person who conscientiously disobeys a law "is in reality expressing the highest respect for law" (*WWCW* 83–84; *STF* 62). King offers several arguments in support of this remarkable claim.

In part, King's strategy of civil disobedience is designed to reveal protesters' deeper lawfulness and thus to differentiate them from criminals and anarchists. Even as they disobey positive laws, King's disciplined protesters obey a higher law that commands nonviolence, and they do so often at personal and physical risk and against their own emotional inclinations. Further, they show respect for positive laws as well as for higher laws by voluntarily submitting to the positive-law punishments for their disobedience.

More fundamentally, King's claim of high respect for law derives from the premise that an unjust positive law is not a true law. According to this reasoning, to violate an unjust statute or ordinance to the end of bringing the positive law into conformity with justice, thereby qualifying it as law proper, is to honor the true idea of law. As he is deeply and increasingly impressed by the lawless character of the American political society in general, King sees his practice of civil disobedience less as a significant cause of anarchy than as a corrective response to it. In this context, it bears repeating that King's program of nonviolent direct action is widely credited for substantial legislative achievements. Although significant legislative reform might well have occurred absent King's activism, it is surely true that King's activism at least accelerated the passage of the Civil Rights Act of 1964 and the Voting Rights Act of 1965, laws that have done much to secure blacks' equal rights as members of civil society and as citizens. Further, it seems exaggerated to argue that the years since King have witnessed increases in the incidences of civil disobedience, general lawlessness, and popular alienation from constitutional, republican government to levels dangerous to the stability of the American political system. And even if one believes that those incidences have risen to dangerous levels, it would be difficult to ascribe primary or substantial responsibility for them to King's activism. So it appears unlikely that King's activism has produced the generally corrosive effects of which Lincoln warns, and it is possible that it has served to increase respect for the law by making the law more respectable.

Yet concerns akin to Lincoln's persist. In considering the near-term consequences of King's activism, one must notice not only his legislative successes but also the fact that during the period of King's greatest prominence, protests against racial injustice in the United States—including some that King helped organize—assumed an increasingly violent character, and large-scale riots erupted in many cities in the mid-1960s.[10] In response, King persistently urges nonviolence and repeatedly denounces rioting as an immoral, irrationally destructive expression of anger. But these denunciations are not unequivocal. Alongside them, King expresses sympathy for rioters' underlying motivations and charges that the ultimate causes of riots are historical criminality, oppression, and resistance to reform on the part of whites (see *TC* 7–16, 55–58, 76; *WWGFH* 12, 21–22, 56–60, 112–13; *TH* 322–24, 359–62, 383, 412).

The relation of King's movement to eruptions of civil disorder marks a significant point of division between King's defenders and his critics. On the one hand, one could argue that it is not reasonable to expect so sweeping a social reform to be accomplished in a perfectly peaceful, orderly manner and that in fact, as King contends, the riots were relatively mild in the damages they inflicted. From this perspective, one might favorably compare King's response to the riots with Jefferson's response to Shays's Rebellion.[11] On the other hand, taking a more critical view, one might contend that King's equivocation confers a measure of moral legitimacy on the rioters, rendering it more difficult for his fellow citizens to identify and resist assertions of mob rule and weakening his message of respect for law (lower or higher), peace, and orderliness. Moreover, whatever the adequacy of his response to the riots, the facts remain that King employs his extraordinary rhetorical powers to activate and intensify (mainly) blacks' anger and enlist it in the service of a revolutionary social movement; that he ascribes to that movement a unique moral power by virtue of its nonviolent, higher-law discipline; and that as events unfold, he fails to maintain this crucial discipline among all whom his movement arouses.

At one level, this failing reflects the fact that King implicitly rejects Locke's insistence on the enduring dangerousness of the state of nature and therefore takes less seriously than do Locke and Lincoln the vital importance of prudence in the conduct of extralegal protest or resistance. At a deeper level, it appears to reflect King's excessive faiths in the redemptive power of revolutionary speech and action and in his own prophetic power to govern his revolutionaries' anger. Both of these faiths appear ultimately rooted in his faith in the providential, irresistible, imminent occurrence of revolution in some form. But from either a religious or a secular, rationalist perspective, one may question the wisdom of this faith and its effect on King's moral-political prudence. This question derives its importance not merely from the riots of the 1960s, nor from any direct effects of King's specific acts of extralegal protest. Rather, its main importance concerns the potentially broader, more enduring effects on black and white Americans' morale and on the prospects for national integration that may result from an imprudent, excessively enthusiastic cultivation of the revolutionary spirit on King's part.

By virtue of his vision of an integrated community, especially as it concerns race relations, King appears foremost as a representative of the higher moral tradition of American political thought. His conception of agape as the bond of a just political community identifies him, here again, as a moral-political descendent of Jefferson and Lincoln, who both appeal, at critical moments in the nation's history, to a friendship in the sharing of transpartisan, humanitarian ideals as the substance of a proper American patriotism.[12] But King's agape differs importantly, in both its nature and its practical implications, from the moral-political friendship that Jefferson and Lincoln envision. The deeper questions inhering in those differences concern whether King's arguments are consistently well designed to elevate rather than to debase, to unite rather than to divide—to nourish rather than to impair the development of the moral sentiments that bind a healthy community.

Contrary to some segregationist and neoabolitionist views, King's famous aspiration to teach the nation to judge by character, not color, clearly accords with any coherent, historically faithful understanding of the original meaning and promise of the Declaration of Independence. Further, he agrees with the wiser representatives of the liberal tradition in acknowledging the limited efficacy of purely formal guarantees of rights for securing rights and civic health in a liberal republic. Like Locke, Montesquieu, Jefferson, and Tocqueville, in their varying ways, King affirms the need to attend to the moral, social, and cultural conditions that best promote the proper exercise and defense of rights. The conjunction of these principles might permit, given the historical circumstances, a limited scheme of race-specific remedial measures. As we have seen, however, King elects to conform more strictly with the principle of race-neutrality in advocating measures targeting assistance to the poor or disadvantaged irrespective of race. Yet, despite their inclusiveness, his proposed socioeconomic remedies confront difficulties of their own. The difficulties arise from the design of King's specific remedial proposals and, ultimately, from the expanded conceptions of segregation and integration that engender them.

To date, experience does not seem to support King's optimistic prediction that his proposed remedial program would rapidly effect dramatic declines in the incidences of numerous social ills from which blacks suffer disproportionately. Decades after the replacement of segregation laws with federal laws securing equal civil rights for all Americans, and after the spending of huge sums on Great Society-inspired social programs, the incidences of the ills King mentions have not diminished. To the contrary, in important respects (including crime and illegitimacy), they have significantly intensified.[13] In King's defense, one must add that, alongside many critics of federal welfare policies initiated or expanded in the 1960s, he objects emphatically to programs that yield perverse, destructive incentives for family breakup or paternal abandonment (e.g., *TH* 191). Nonetheless, one must question whether educational assistance, job-training, guaranteed employment, or guaranteed income programs could effect the needed changes in morale—in the internalized sense of agency or responsibility—to cure the ills with which King is concerned. More pointedly, one must question whether King's centralized, social-democratic, redistributive antipoverty program is adequately designed to effect the uplift of human personality that characterizes truly just laws.

This question points in turn to more fundamental questions concerning the aptness of King's analogy between racial and socioeconomic inequalities and the affirmation of welfare rights that proceeds from it. King views material poverty as more than a social ill; it is a genuine injustice, a violation of the fundamental rights of the poor. Not only the direct or proximate victims of slavery and racial segregation but indeed all those who qualify as materially impoverished hold rights to compensatory assistance. The rights of the victimized to compensation expand into rights claimed by the poor upon the labor of the nonpoor. What, then, is the basis, in evidence and argument, of the claim that adult persons hold fundamental rights to material assistance from others or, depending on their relative circumstances, fundamental obligations to assist others to produce or even to consume?

King's answer recurs ultimately to his doctrine of interdependence. Material wealth is the product of a "vast treasury of ideas and labor to which both the living and the dead had contributed." It "always comes as a result of the commonwealth" (*SL* 71). As it is socially produced, so it is socially owned and should be distributed to the benefit of all members of society. King presents this argument in part as a useful corrective of dogmatic individualism. Yet one may question whether King has adequately thought through the implications of his prescribed remedy for the concept of individual personhood as the basis of natural human rights. So far as our material wealth is the product of many others' ideas and labor, must not our labor itself likewise be the product of external ideas and labor? If King's doctrine of interdependence requires us to deny the individual's right to the product of his labor, must it not also require us to deny the individual's ownership of his labor itself—that is, of his thoughts and actions? If its implication is to reject the classical liberal, Lockean account of independent, personal self-ownership that underlies the affirmation of natural human rights and government by popular consent in the Declaration of Independence, then on what alternative basis does King affirm these principles in the Declaration? How does King's doctrine of interdependence or "mutuality" cohere with his own earnest affirmations of the freedom and dignity of individual persons—of their individual responsibility for virtue and vice?

A further consideration is relevant in this context. King's later shift in strategy (supporting redistributive measures designed to facilitate consumption rather than developmental measures designed to stimulate productive industry) proceeds in significant part from his characteristic inclination to demand immediate results. But one must question whether King's insistence on the "fierce urgency of *now*" (*WWGFH* 191), so effective in its application to the campaign to end legally enforced racial segregation, is properly applied to the large scale socioeconomic problems with which he is also concerned. What is the likely effect, especially on the motivations and morale of the poor, of policies that implicitly sever the right of consumption from the duty of productive industry? Mindful of King's insistence that just ends can be secured only through just means, one must question whether the desired end of broadly distributed prosperity can be dependably secured absent the widespread cultivation of the virtues and competencies supportive of productive industry. The endeavor to cultivate the requisite virtues and competencies may make the achievement of this desired end a frustratingly slow, laborious process, just as conformity with the procedural requirements of fair trials may slow the administration of justice to criminals and their victims. But in both cases, to employ the proper, deliberate means is to maximize one's assurance of the ultimate achievement of the desired end. It is surely necessary to take cognizance of the limits of purely formal guarantees of rights and to endeavor, accordingly, to secure the conditions for the fruitful exercise of those rights. But it is possible to do so without thereby losing sight of the vital importance of employing proper, deliberate procedural means—of formality—for the achievement of justice and happiness in civil society. In important respects, King is admirably scrupulous in insisting on respect for the proper forms or means. But in demanding an immediate solution to the problem of poverty, as the previous century's radical abolitionists had demanded an immediate solution to the problem of slavery, King supplies an example of the hostility to formality that Tocqueville ranks among the deepest maladies to which modern democracies are susceptible.[14]

The urgency with which King demands socioeconomic integration reflects his own deeply rooted revolutionary enthusiasm. King labors to escalate blacks' and other Americans' revolutionary anger because he believes that the Christian gospel is socially revolutionary and that an apocalyptic revolution may be at hand. The deepest difficulties in King's thought and practice appear rooted in this revolutionary enthusiasm. From it derive both his greatest achievements and his most serious failings.

Excessive, imprudently conceived calls for revolution endanger the cause of integration in general, so far as they tend to effect a dramatic sharpening of partisan divisions. Given that serious revolutionary appeals necessarily involve charges of the illegitimacy of the existing order, those who defend the existing order or resist its sudden, radical alteration inevitably come to appear, in the eyes of the revolutionary, as morally obtuse, weak, or vicious defenders of tyranny. It is instructive that King himself, widely and justly admired for his teachings of redemptive love and understanding for one's adversaries, does not refrain from likening his partisan adversaries to dangerous criminals—even, in some cases, to followers of the most notorious tyranny in the twentieth century. Justice and prudence alike may warrant employment of the rhetoric of tyranny and revolution in controversies involving truly fundamental differences in moral principle. But do they likewise recommend King's references to the incidence of poverty as an "economic holocaust," to opponents of a federally guaranteed annual income as, in effect, murderers, and to American prosecutors of the Vietnam War as Nazis (*WWCW* 146; *TC* 55; *TH* 236; *WWGFH* 182)? At minimum, it would require much more argument than King provides to show that the serious but relatively common socioeconomic divisions that concern him, and even the partisan divisions over the war, represent controversies over fundamental moral and constitutional principles, resolvable only through revolutionary measures. Absent such an argument, King's calls for total revolution appear gratuitous and more apt to divide than to unite.

King's powerful revolutionary enthusiasm poses dangers not only to partisan comity but also, in the course of time, to the morale of Americans, in general, and black Americans, in particular. The more radical or millenarian King's vision of integration becomes, the more it comes to represent a standard of justice so elevated that in its light all existing and realistically conceivable human societies must appear unjust. The dangerous general effect of adopting such a standard would be to impair citizens' capacities to make reasonable distinctions between legitimate and illegitimate governance. One likely manifestation of this impairment would be a heightened, debilitating mistrust among many Americans with respect to their government's capacity to do justice at home and abroad, and especially in its relations with nonwhites. Among black Americans in particular, another likely manifestation of this impairment would be a perpetuated consciousness of oppression and grievance, with destructive political and psychological consequences. Whatever their effect in the short term, their chronic effect is likely to be enervating, as that consciousness becomes perpetual and the revolutionary vision proves unachievable. Over time, the consciousness of oppression breeds a culture of self-consuming anger and reflexive opposition. In such a culture, human agency appears increasingly in only truncated forms; political activity narrows, appearing increasingly in demands for assistance or in reflexive gestures of theatrical protest. Beneath such gestures lie, increasingly, sentiments of anger and despair at the presumed futility or disloyalty of striving for achievement through mainstream channels.

In his sympathetic yet critical discussion of "black-power" and black-nationalist ideologies, King shows a clear awareness of these dangers (e.g., *WWGFH* 44–47, 121–22). Yet his own revolutionary enthusiasm leads him implicitly to affirm the black-nationalist view of black Americans as a colonized people—even as a vanguard in a worldwide anticolonial, anticapitalist revolution. In his intensifying millenarian zeal for a comprehensive, integrative revolution, King proclaims the deepening illegitimacy of the American regime at the very moment of its greatest promise of genuine liberation for black Americans. In this way, he risks propagating the same perpetuated sentiment of aggrieved, despairing opposition that he decries as both cause and consequence of black-nationalist perspectives. It would represent a tragic irony of King's final years if he pursued his longing for humanitarian integration to such extremes that it became itself a renewed source of division. At least in those final years, the fate of King's attempt to preserve a moderate militancy would then illustrate the wisdom in Tocqueville's observation concerning the nature of the revolutionary spirit: "One should not also forget that the same energy which makes a man break through a common error almost always drives him on beyond what is reasonable. . . . That . . . is the reason why, even in the case of the most necessary and hallowed revolutions, one seldom finds revolutionaries who are moderate."[15]

In conclusion, without ignoring or denigrating those qualities that he draws from the distinctive experience of black Americans, one may observe that Martin Luther King, Jr., represents a quintessential American, exemplifying the most elevating as well as some of the more problematic qualities of American democracy. In the more problematic elements of his thought and practice, King arouses concerns akin to those of Tocqueville and Burke, who worry about modern democrats' frequent impatience with formal or procedural justice; their proneness to millenarian zealotry; their inclination to demand or accept the excessive expansion and centralization of governmental power; and their sympathy for a debased, leveling understanding of human equality. Nonetheless, in his belief in the possibility of revolutionary change and in the power of heroic individuals in collaboration with ordinary people to effect it; in his faith in the moral governance of the universe, informed by a universal moral law to which all may appeal to expose unjust positive laws and practices; in his devotion to the causes of human equality, liberty, individual rights, democratic government, and progress toward an ever-more inclusive and just human community, King exemplifies the highest ideals of American democracy.

Notes

1. The reader should be aware of a now solid consensus among King scholars that King plagiarized his doctoral dissertation as well as some of his graduate school papers at Boston University. In addition, the issue of plagiarism in some of his published works is raised by the historian David Garrow in his

history of King's leadership of the civil rights movement, *Bearing the Cross: Martin Luther King, Jr., and the Southern Christian Leadership Conference* (New York: Vintage Books, 1986), 112. Without denying their importance, I leave aside, for the purposes of the present chapter, the difficulties that this issue poses for the task of forming a comprehensive judgment of King's character. For a recent discussion both critical and sympathetic to King that points to the essential evidence, see Michael Eric Dyson, *I May Not Get There with You* (New York: Free Press, 2000), 137–54.

2. Citations of King's works appear in the text, abbreviated as follows. *Stride toward Freedom: The Montgomery Story* (New York: Harper and Brothers, 1958) is cited as *STF*; *Strength to Love* (Philadelphia: Fortress Press, [1963] 1981) as *SL*; *Why We Can't Wait* (New York: New American Library, 1964) as *WWCW*; *Where Do We Go from Here: Chaos or Community?* (Boston: Beacon Press, 1967) as *WWGFH*; *The Trumpet of Conscience* (New York: Harper and Row, 1968) as *TC*; *A Testament of Hope: The Essential Writings and Speeches of Martin Luther King*, ed. James M. Washington (New York: Harper-Collins, 1991) as *TH*; and *The Autobiography of Martin Luther King*, ed. Clayborne Carson (New York: Warner Books, 1998) as *AMLK*. All italicizing appears in the original quoted text unless otherwise noted.

3. Frederick Douglass, *The Life and Times of Frederick Douglass* (New York: MacMillan, 1962), 143, emphasis in the original.

4. King gives this account of his own transformative experience at a moment in early 1956 at which, harassed by repeated death threats and feeling frightened and exhausted, he uttered a midnight prayer in his kitchen. "At that moment I experienced the presence of the Divine as I had never experienced Him before. It seemed as though I could hear the quiet assurance of an inner voice saying: 'Stand up for righteousness, stand up for truth; and God will be at your side forever.' Almost at once my fears began to go. . . . I was ready to face anything" (*STF* 134–35).

5. Cf. Immanuel Kant, "Perpetual Peace: Appendix I," in *Kant's Political Writings*, ed. Hans Reiss (Cambridge: Cambridge University Press, 1977), 123–25.

6. In response to a criticism published in *Christian Century*, King suggests that in a larger sense, Gandhi does belong to the Christian tradition. "I believe that in some marvelous way, God worked through Gandhi, and the spirit of Jesus Christ saturated his life. It is ironic, yet inescapably true, that the greatest Christian of the modern world was a man who never embraced Christianity." Quoted in Garrow, *Bearing the Cross*, 200.

7. See also King's early acknowledgment of his socialist sympathies to Coretta (*AMLK* 36) and the evidence presented in Stephen Oates, *Let The Trumpet Sound: The Life of Martin Luther King, Jr.* (New York: Harper and Row, 1982), 492; Garrow, *Bearing the Cross*, 140, 364, 382, 562, 591–92; and Dyson, *I May Not Get There with You*, 88–89.

8. Lincoln, "Speech to the Young Men's Lyceum of Springfield, January 27, 1838," in *Abraham Lincoln: A Documentary Portrait through His Speeches and Writings*, ed. Don E. Fehrenbacher (Stanford, Calif.: Stanford University Press, 1977), 36–40.

9. See Henry David Thoreau, "Civil Disobedience," in *American Political Thought*, ed. Kenneth M. Dolbeare (Chatham, N.J.: Chatham House Publishers, 1989), 232.

10. Stephan and Abigail Thernstrom report that during the years 1964 through 1968, 329 riots erupted in 257 U.S. cities. Following King's murder in 1968, violent upheavals occurred in at least 125 cities. See *America in Black and White* (New York: Simon and Schuster, 1999), 159, 175.

11. In a letter to James Madison written shortly after the rebellion, for instance, Jefferson remarks that "a little rebellion, now and then, is a good thing, and as necessary in the political world as storms are in the physical." In *The Life and Selected Writings of Thomas Jefferson*, ed. Adrienne Koch and William Peden (New York: Modern Library, 1944), 413.

12. For an elaborate discussion of this theme with reference to Jefferson and Lincoln, see Harry V. Jaffa, *A New Birth of Freedom* (Lanham, Md.: Rowman and Littlefield, 2000), 1–72.

13. For a thorough compilation of the relevant empirical evidence, see Stephan and Abigail Thernstrom, *America in Black and White*.

14. Alexis de Tocqueville, *Democracy in America*, ed. J. P. Mayer (Garden City, N.Y.: Doubleday, 1969), 698–99 (vol. 2, pt. 4, chap. 7).

15. *Democracy in America*, 597 (vol. 2, pt. 3, chap. 11).

Chapter 40

Malcolm X: From Apolitical Acolyte to Political Preacher

Lucas E. Morel

Born Malcolm Little in Omaha, Nebraska, Malcolm X (1925–1965) was the son of a West Indian mother and black Baptist preacher. His father was a local organizer for Marcus Garvey's United Negro Improvement Association, which promoted black separatism and pan-Africanism. After moving to Lansing, Michigan, Malcolm suffered the death of his father (under suspicious circumstances) and several years later saw his mother committed to a mental institution. A top student in elementary school (who was elected the seventh-grade class president), Malcolm told his English teacher he wanted to be a lawyer; he was told, "[t]hat's no realistic goal for a Nigger," and he soon asked to go live with his half-sister Ella in Boston. He took a job as a shoe-shine boy, later became a street hustler in New York, and eventually was imprisoned for burglary before his twenty-first birthday. Malcolm read voraciously in prison and was introduced to the teachings of Elijah Muhammad and the Nation of Islam (NOI) by his siblings and inmates. Paroled in August 1952, he went to live in Detroit with his eldest brother Wilfred. After meeting Elijah Muhammad, he began recruiting converts for the local NOI temple and officially adopted "X" for his surname (to represent his lost African family name). He quickly rose through the ranks of temple ministers in the Nation. Malcolm married Betty X (née Sanders) in January 1958, who bore him four daughters while he was alive and twins after his death. In 1959, Malcolm X and the Nation of Islam gained national prominence with the airing of "The Hate That Hate Produced," a documentary by Mike Wallace and Louis Lomax, and subsequent articles in *U.S. News & World Report* and *Time* magazine. By 1960, Malcolm X had started or helped start over a hundred temples with thousands of converts, founded the Nation's newspaper *Muhammad Speaks*, wrote a syndicated column entitled "God's Angry Men" for major black newspapers, and became Elijah Muhammad's chief spokesman.

His popularity soon distanced him from rival ministers at the Chicago headquarters and at a time when rumors of Elijah Muhammad's infidelity became too pronounced to ignore. In 1963, Malcolm X began working on his autobiography with Alex Haley. After calling John F. Kennedy's assassination in November 1963 a case of "the chickens coming home to roost," he was silenced for ninety days by Elijah Muhammad. Convinced that jealous rivals were undermining his reputation with the ailing Elijah Muhammad, Malcolm X left the Nation of Islam in March 1964 and announced the formation of the Muslim Mosque, Inc. After a pilgrimage to Mecca in April, where he became a Sunni Muslim, he returned to America as El-Hajj Malik El-Shabazz and formed the Organization of Afro-American Unity. No longer asserting that whites were "devils," but still skeptical of American institutions to secure the civil rights of black Americans, Malcolm argued that the civil rights movement needed to be taken to a more receptive forum like the United Nations and World Court. Denounced by his protégé Louis X (Farrakhan) in *Muham-*

mad Speaks as "worthy of death" and suspecting he was poisoned during a tour of Africa, Malcolm X saw his death as imminent. On February 14, 1965, his home was firebombed, and on February 21, Malcolm X was shot to death as he began a speech at the Audubon Ballroom in Harlem.[1]

African, not American: The Repudiation of White Hegemony

The first thing to be said about Malcolm X as a political thinker is that during his seventeen-year association with the Nation of Islam, he did not consider politics a legitimate activity for black Americans. He believed that the U.S. governments (both state and federal) represented the interests of whites exclusively, which made political participation by black Americans a waste of time at best, and complicity in their own oppression at worst. The "so-called Negro," as black Americans were called by the leader of the Nation of Islam, Elijah Muhammad, needed to stay as far away as possible from the white institutions of power.[2] These institutions included not only political parties, offices, and elections but also schools, workplaces, and social venues. According to the Nation of Islam's religious dogma, the one true God, Allah, destined whites for imminent annihilation. Therefore, the less entwined blacks were with white society, the better. "Separation of the so-called Negroes from their slave-masters' children is a MUST. It is the only solution to our problem. . . . I am for the separation of my people from their enemies; that they share not in the enemies' destruction" (*MBA* 36 and 110). Or as Malcolm X put it: "You don't integrate with a sinking ship" (*SU* 107).

But if black Muslims were forbidden from participating in the American political system, that did not prevent Malcolm X from commenting on the political implications of the Nation of Islam's teachings. A quick study under Elijah Muhammad, Malcolm X became the national spokesman for a rapidly growing religious sect that was both anti-Christian and anti-American.

Founded by W. D. Fard in 1930, the Nation of Islam drew primarily from two sources: Marcus Garvey, and Noble Drew Ali's Moorish Science Temple.[3] Marcus Garvey came to the United States in 1916 from Jamaica and formed the United Negro Improvement Association. His "Back to Africa" movement extolled the virtues of racial purity and black pride while denigrating white philanthropy as inimical to black self-improvement. To prepare for a liberation of "Africa for the Africans," Garvey promoted pan-Africanism in the United States by encouraging racial self-determination: for example, economic cooperatives, including grocery stores, laundries, restaurants, and hotels, were to be set up by blacks and for blacks. Timothy "Noble" Drew Ali founded his Moorish Science Temple in 1913. More religious than political, the Moors practiced a bowdlerized form of Islam and identified their black, American members as Asiatics or Moors, not Negroes. They sought a nation for themselves as essential to the true practice of their religion, and they believed in a race-based religious pluralism. The Moors also preached a strict personal morality and believed that because whites (or "Europeans") had robbed the Moors of their rightful possession of the earth, God's judgment upon whites would soon restore blacks to global prominence.[4]

As a member of the Nation of Islam, Malcolm X believed that the only way to be free from the cultural hegemony of white America was through the reeducation of the so-called Negro. Central to that reeducation was the rejection of the traditional Christianity of black America. "This is white man's Christian religion," Malcolm X wrote, "to brainwash us black people! . . . [T]his blue-eyed devil has *twisted* his Christianity, to keep his *foot* on our backs . . . to keep our eyes fixed on the pie in the sky and heaven in the hereafter . . . while *he* enjoys *his* heaven right *here* . . . on *this* earth . . . in *this life*" (*AMX* 205). Elijah Muhammad concurred: "There is no hope for us in Christianity; it is a religion organized by the enemies [the white race] of the Black Nation to enslave us to the white race's rule" (*MBA* 221). The United States was "the Good-Ship Jesus," intent on carrying blacks away from their true selves and heritage to be exploited under a white man's religion. As Elijah Muhammad wrote: "The slave-master has robbed my people of their God, religion, name, language, and culture" (*MBA* 37). A new religion was needed for a new (i.e., reeducated) people, and that religion was Islam, "the true religion for the black man" (*AMX* 212). Elijah Muhammad called Islam "the natural religion of the Black Nation" (*MBA* 80).

Malcolm X therefore read current events in light of Nation of Islam eschatology. With "the race problem" in the U.S. as *the* problem in modern-day America, Malcolm X believed only God's "Messenger," Elijah Muhammad, knew the true nature of the problem and how it could be solved. America's leaders should therefore talk to him to receive "God's analysis" (*SU* 108). What was the solution? "Get this powder keg out of your house—let the black people in this country separate from you, while there's still time" (*SU* 111). In short, he appealed to the white man's self-interest—not his conscience, justice, or charity—for the attainment of a separate black state for Elijah Muhammad and his followers, which could well include all 22 million black Americans then residing in the United States. "We want nothing short of a home on this earth that we can call our own—not to be servants and slaves for other free nations" (*MBA* 222). Self-understanding for black Americans could only come through their becoming a nation unto themselves. Regarding the constitutional model for this new black nation, the Nation of Islam was less specific: "We do not expect to build, nor do we desire to build a government patterned after the order of the white race" (*MBA* 226). But whatever sort of government was eventually to be created, it would have to be based upon a genuine and exclusive self-introspection by blacks. "If we want freedom, justice and equality, we must look for it among ourselves and our kind, not among the people who have destroyed and robbed us of even the knowledge of ourselves, themselves, our God and our religion" (*MBA* 233).

Malcolm X summed up the collective history of black Americans as slavery in one form or another. The contemporary life of a black American was life as an "ex-slave," a term the Nation of Islam used to suggest not their liberation from bondage but their continued enslavement under other forms. Indeed, the "X" in Malcolm X represents the unknown surname of Malcolm and all black people who had been robbed of their heritage by white oppressors.

> The Muslim's "X" symbolized the true African family name that he never could know. For me, my "X" replaced the white slavemaster name of "Little" which some blue-eyed devil named Little had imposed upon my paternal forebears. . . . Mr. Muhammad taught us that we would keep this "X" until God Himself returned and gave us a Holy Name from His own mouth. (*AMX* 203)

As Muhammad himself wrote: "I warn you, my people, discard your former slave-master's names and be willing and ready to accept one of Allah's Pure and Righteous Names that He Alone will give our people from His Own Mouth!" (*MBA* 55). Thus, the Nation of Islam does "not teach them to disregard their family names—they do NOT KNOW them" (*MBA* 178).

The failure of American society to incorporate blacks on an equal basis, especially prior to the 1964 Civil Rights Act and the 1965 Voting Rights Act, meant that separation was necessary for true freedom to occur. In this light, integration was an elaborate act of self-loathing. As Elijah Muhammad wrote, "[i]ntegration means self-destruction" (*MBA* 223). The integration offered by white America amounted to mere tokenism. "What gains? All you have gotten is tokenism—one or two Negroes in a job or at a lunch counter so the rest of you can be quiet" (*SU* 103–4). Thus, Malcolm X believed blacks should not yearn for what whites did not intend to grant in full.

Moreover, white society was destined for destruction for its corrupt ways—a destruction presaged by sufficient black self-awareness of the extent of white indoctrination. The coming "racial explosion" would follow when blacks become dissatisfied not only with white society but also with the established civil rights organizations and prominent blacks "posing as leaders" (*SU* 110). In addition to Martin Luther King, Jr., director of the Southern Christian Leadership Conference (SCLC), these included the heads of the National Association for the Advancement of Colored People (NAACP), the Congress of Racial Equality (CORE), and the Student Nonviolent Coordinating Committee (SNCC). What united these leaders and their organizations was the belief that the white man was capable of changing his ways. "Our aim is not to defeat the white community," King explained, "not to humiliate the white community, but to win the friendship of all of the persons who had perpetrated this system in the past." As King famously put it in his "I Have a Dream" speech: "The marvelous new militancy which has engulfed the Negro community must not lead us to a distrust of all white people, for many of our white brothers, as evidenced by their presence here today, have come to realize that their destiny is tied up with our destiny, and they have come to realize that their freedom is inextricably bound to our freedom."[5]

In contrast, Malcolm X saw the white man as "a devil" and thus incapable of reform. "Don't change the white man's mind—you can't change his mind, and that whole thing about appealing to the moral conscience of America—America's conscience is bankrupt. She lost all conscience a long time ago" (*MXS* 40). As he said in a 1963 interview: "We contend that the white man is a devil. If he is not a devil, let him prove it!" (*SU* 104).

Although Malcolm X saw black citizens as "the victims of Americanism" and not its beneficiaries, this did not prevent him from speaking the language of "God-given rights," "natural rights," and "human rights" (*MXS* 26). Here, Malcolm X drew selectively from the American Founding. In particular, he used the language of "rights" and "revolution" to highlight the injustices committed against black Americans and the need for a separate, independent black nation. For example, he countered claims that the Nation of Islam was "anti-white" by drawing upon the quintessential American principle of equality: "We want only an equal chance on this earth, but to have an equal chance we must have the same thing the white man himself needed before he could get this nation started. . . . WE MUST HAVE SOME LAND OF OUR OWN!" (*EMP* 419).

Malcolm X even borrowed from Lincoln's Gettysburg Address when, speaking at a 1960 rally in Harlem, he declared the rally "of Black people, by Black People, and for the benefit of Black people" (*EMP* 413). In this same speech, he argued that as "a collective mass of Black people we have been deprived, not only of civil rights, but even our human rights, the right to human dignity . . . the right to be a human being!" (*EMP* 414). For a minister who prefaced many of his remarks with "Mr. Muhammad says," he was not averse to employing the more secularist "rights talk" of the Enlightenment as found in the Declaration of Independence.[6]

But Malcolm X interpreted previous attempts at securing rights for black Americans—like the Emancipation Proclamation, the 13th, 14th, and 15th Amendments, and the *Brown v. Board of Education* (1954) school desegregation decision—as covering up and further complicating the problem of racial discrimination. "All of this is hypocrisy that has been practiced by the so-called white so-called liberal for the past four hundred years that compounds the problem, makes it more complicated, instead of eliminating the problem" (*SU* 111).[7] At bottom, the logic of Malcolm X's political—as opposed to theological—rhetoric evinced an affinity for the principles of the United States but a conviction of the white man's inability to practice what he preaches. This is not to say he believed in human equality categorically, for he professed that blacks deserve to rule the world insofar as they are the "Original Owners" of "the whole earth" (*EMP* 420).

Malcolm X's "Message to the Grassroots" (1963), delivered two weeks before the assassination of President John F. Kennedy, presented as strident and political a speech as Malcolm X allowed himself as a minister and spokesman for the Nation of Islam. He emphasized that race trumped all other differences among human beings, especially in the United States. Speaking to a predominantly black and non-Muslim audience in Detroit, he stated: "You don't catch hell because you're a Methodist or Baptist, you don't catch hell because you're a Democrat or Republican, you don't catch hell because you're a Mason or an Elk. . . . You catch hell because you're a black man" (*MXS* 4). He highlighted religion, politics, and even fraternal orders to illustrate how pervasive racial prejudice was in America. Malcolm X suggested that the depth of American racism made even the profound importance of religion and politics to human happiness take a back seat to the more fundamental determinant of race. By virtue of their common ethnicity, black Americans have "a common oppressor, a common exploiter, and a common discriminator" in white Americans. With Marxist overtones, he argued that once blacks "realize we have a common enemy," then blacks would be able to put aside lesser differences and unite against their common oppressor.

Malcolm X then turned to that most political of subjects—revolution—to counter Martin Luther King, Jr.'s, message of nonviolence and brotherly love. In 1963, at the height of his popularity as the chief spokesman for the modern civil rights movement, King combined biblical and republican principles to protest segregation of blacks in the South. His "Letter from a Birmingham Jail," written while in solitary confinement for defying a federal judge's injunction not to march, offered a Christian defense of civil disobedience—a literary marvel matched only by his mesmerizing "I Have a Dream" speech before the Lincoln Memorial in August 1963.[8] (The following year would see passage of the landmark Civil Rights Act of 1964 and King awarded the Nobel Peace Prize.)

In contrast to King's conservative appeal to the Declaration of Independence and U.S. Constitution, Malcolm X preached the need for a revolution that leads to a new black homeland. In particular, he distinguished between "Negro" and "black" revolutions: the former denotes the peaceful attempts of King and the mainstream civil rights movement to protest injustice, which Malcolm X derided as a "turn-the-other-cheek" revolution (*MXS* 9). As Elijah Muhammad wrote, "I will most certainly not teach you to love the devil" (*MBA* 236). Desegregation of public accommodations, for example, does not constitute a revolution. For Malcolm X, the desire of black Americans to integrate with white society was like "trying to crawl back on the plantation" (*MXS* 10). Instead, a truly "black" revolution must produce what revolutions throughout history have always produced—land. Endorsing Muhammad's view that there "can be no freedom without a people having their own land. . . . We need land wherein we can build our own society free from the tension, hatred and violence that have accompanied our race relationship with the white race of America" (*MBA* 56 and 129), Malcolm X stated: "Land is the basis of all independence. Land is the basis of freedom, justice, and equality" (*MXS* 9).

Establishing a new homeland through revolution was no polite affair, for true revolutions are "bloody," "hostile," admitting of "no compromise," and something that "overturns and destroys everything that gets in its way." In a stinging rebuke to King's nonviolent, Christian overtures to his oppressor, Malcolm X proclaimed: "Who ever heard of a revolution where they lock arms, . . . singing 'We Shall Overcome'? You don't do that in a revolution. You don't do any singing, you're too busy swinging." He boasted that the Koran does not teach its adherents to suffer peacefully. "Our religion," he observed, "teaches us to be intelligent. Be peaceful, be courteous, obey the law, respect everyone; but if someone puts his hand on you, send him to the cemetery" (*MXS* 9, 12).

During the early 1960s, Malcolm X made so many appearances at American universities that he claimed his campus popularity was second only to Republican presidential aspirant, Barry Goldwater.[9] Notwithstanding his growing popularity, as late as November 1963 he described his relationship to Elijah Muhammad in the most submissive terms: "I am his slave, his servant, his son. He is the leader, the only spokesman for the Black Muslims" (*SU* 107). But one month later, he would fill in for Elijah Muhammad in New York City, which proved to be his swan song as the lead spokesman for the Nation.

After the Nation of Islam: Malcolm X and the Meaning of Mecca

On December 1, 1963, Malcolm X gave a speech entitled "God's Judgment of White America," which closed with sharp criticisms of the now dead president, John F. Kennedy. Assassinated only a week earlier, Kennedy was revered by most black Americans. Therefore, Elijah Muhammad directed his ministers not to comment on the president's death. After his speech, Malcolm X was asked about the assassination and replied that it was a case of "the chickens coming home to roost."[10] Elijah Muhammad silenced Malcolm X for ninety days, ostensibly to disassociate the Nation of Islam from his remarks. Several months earlier, however, Malcolm X had shared with Elijah Muhammad that he knew of the rumors about Muhammad's infidelities but, if necessary, could cite verses from the Koran and the Bible to present Muhammad's liaisons as fulfillment of prophecy. Given Malcolm X's popularity both in and out of the Nation of Islam, and his abstemious obedience to their moral code (in contrast with Muhammad's own sexual indiscretions, which led to his siring several children by his secretaries), Muhammad made an example of Malcolm X to bolster his control of the Nation of Islam. When the ninety-day suspension became "indefinite," Malcolm X realized he was "being set up" (*AMX* 309). On March 8, 1964, he announced that he was leaving the Nation of Islam to form his own mosque: Muslim Mosque, Incorporated. Its aims would be primarily religious, to help "rid our people of the vices that destroy the moral fiber of our community" (*MXS* 21). Malcolm X held fast to black nationalism, however, emphasizing that its economic, political, and cultural principles and programs would derive from racial solidarity.

Malcolm X left the Nation of Islam at the climax of Martin Luther King, Jr.'s, fame as leader of the civil rights movement. During 1963 and 1964, King was chosen *Time* magazine's "Man of the Year"; drew national attention to "Bull" Connor's barbaric law enforcement; penned his "Letter from a Birmingham Jail"; delivered his most famous speech ("I Have a Dream") at the March on Washington; saw passage of the 1964 Civil Rights Act; and received the Nobel Peace Prize. To justify an alternative message for black liberation in America, Malcolm X painted a stark contrast between his philosophy and that of the most popular civil rights spokesman of his day.

He said that he could only afford to be nonviolent with those who were nonviolent with him. Malcolm X became more vocal about not being "handcuffed by the disarming philosophy of nonviolence," calling King a "Modern Uncle Tom" who was subsidized by "so-called liberal" whites to "keep Negroes defenseless" (*SU* 106, 111). Malcolm X affirmed the right of blacks to self-defense from lawless aggression in what would become his signature statement on the matter—"by any means necessary" (*MXS* 24, 116, 201, 203, 212).

In April 1964, Malcolm X traveled to Mecca and returned five weeks later a Sunni Muslim, taking the name El-Hajj Malik El-Shabazz to signify the completion of the *hajj* or "pilgrimage" to Mecca, the holiest city of orthodox Islam. The trip also helped forge his commitment to fighting racism at home by appealing to the court of world opinion. He formed a nonreligious group to promote social, educational, and political reform: the Organization of Afro-American Unity (OAAU). The OAAU stressed Afro-American and African unity, an international approach to fighting "colonialism and imperialism." Malcolm X wanted to build on the unease that former colonial powers had about the African revolution underway in the 1960s. He took their anxiety as a sign of the strength that blacks in America could have if they unite with their brothers in Africa (*TFS* 79–80). He remarked that "the only thing power respects is power" (*TFS* 81).

As an orthodox Muslim, however, Malcolm X dropped his separationist rhetoric. He now extolled the common humanity of people, but he was quick to add that one could not force integration. "I'm not a racist, I don't believe in any form of segregation or anything like that. I'm for the brotherhood of everybody, but I don't believe in forcing brotherhood upon people who don't want it" (*TFS* 105). In contrast to the Black Muslims and in striking affinity with the message of Martin Luther King, Jr.'s, "I Have a Dream" speech, Malcolm X said that "the real religion of Islam doesn't teach anyone to judge another human being by the color of his skin" but by "the man's deeds. . . . White, black, brown, red, yellow, doesn't make any difference what color you are" (*TFS* 84–85).

Nevertheless, because the United States was controlled by "racists and segregationists" who carried their oppression worldwide, race was not an irrelevant factor in forging coalitions to fight the American power structure. Malcolm X believed that black Americans were more African than American, a tie to an ancestral land and heritage that he credited the Nation of Islam for sparking in the post-World War II era. "Just because you're in this country doesn't make you an American. . . . You've got to enjoy the fruits of Americanism. You haven't enjoyed those fruits. You've enjoyed the thorns" (*TFS* 97). This also moved him to push for an international fight for the rights of blacks in America. "And one of our first programs is to take our problem out of the civil rights context and place it at the international level, of human rights, so that the entire world can have a voice in our struggle" (*TFS* 104). Domestically, Malcolm X advocated a mass voter registration drive. But he hastened to add that "we don't believe in voter registration without voter education." In this, he was willing to work with other civil rights organizations that were working to increase black registration and voting in the South (*TFS* 104–5).

He no longer saw whites as devils, but he still insisted that they should be judged by what they did and not what they said they would do to secure the rights of blacks. "He can't stop being white. We've got to give the man a chance. He probably won't take it, the snake. But we've got to give him a chance."[11] With an international perspective gained from his travels abroad and conversion to an orthodox Islam comprising many races, he sought enforcement in the World Court of the rights of black Americans.

In language curiously reminiscent of the Declaration of Independence, he argued for hauling the United States into the United Nations on human rights violations. "Human rights are something you were born with. Human rights are your God-given rights. Human rights are the rights that are recognized by all nations of this earth" (*MXS* 35). In this 1964 speech, entitled "The Ballot or the Bullet," he continued: "When you expand the civil-rights struggle to the level of human rights, you can then take the case of the black man in this country before the nations in the U.N."[12] This reflected a belief that the corruption of the American regime was so bad that no remedy should be sought under existing state or federal constitutions. "Civil rights keeps you under his restrictions, under his jurisdiction. Civil rights keeps you in his pocket. Civil rights means you're asking Uncle Sam to treat you right" (*MXS* 35). Moreover, with race still looming as the overriding determinant of one's rights, Malcolm X followed Marcus Garvey's logic in concluding that black Americans would have a better chance of a fair hearing in a forum where blacks would not find themselves so outnumbered as they did in the United States.[13] In the United Nations, Malcolm X believed that black Americans would be joined by many others: "our African brothers, . . . our Asian brothers, . . . [and] our Latin-American brothers can throw their weight on our side." With a not-so veiled threat of violence to secure the "human rights" of black Americans, Malcolm X said of Uncle Sam: "Let the world know how bloody his hands are. Let the world know the hypocrisy that's practiced over here. Let it be the ballot or the bullet."[14]

By disavowing any allegiance to Elijah Muhammad, Malcolm X freed himself of the religious restraints that had previously kept his social activism focused on gaining converts to the Nation of Islam rather than political reform. From now on, he would preach a message of racial uplift that included a political element. He said of his involvement with the Nation of Islam, "I was a zombie then—like all [black] Muslims—I was hypnotized, pointed in a certain direction and told to march" (*TFS* 231). Looking back on the Nation of Islam's policy of nonengagement, he wrote that "privately I was convinced that our nation of Islam could be an even greater force in the American black man's overall struggle—if we engaged in more *action*" (*AMX* 295).

He gave a simple definition of his program of black nationalism: "The political philosophy of black nationalism means that the black man should control the politics and the politicians in his own community; no more" (*MXS* 38). Economically, he called for black ownership of the stores and businesses—in general, of entire black communities. In short, he sought wholesale independence from white employers. Finally, Malcolm X's black nationalism called for black unity to "remove the evils, the vices, alcoholism, drug addiction, and other evils that are destroying the moral fiber of our community" as well as community beautification "so that we will be satisfied in our own social circles" instead of continued drives to integrate "where we're not wanted" (*MXS* 39). In this pre-Mecca speech, the racial element of Malcolm's nationalism is still prevalent—something he would gradually jettison after hearing complaints from white Muslims with whom he sought brotherhood as spiritual brothers and sisters.

Malcolm X never wrote a book or tract presenting a political program or philosophy. He emphasized action over thought, which shaped the content of his political beliefs. This held true especially in the last few months of his life. In an interview published in the *Young Socialist*, Malcolm X shared that his definition of black nationalism was undergoing a change; he had met Muslims in northern Africa who shared his militancy and revolutionary goals but who were white. In his last formal speech before he died, Malcolm X made this shift explicit: "The Negro revolution is not a racial revolt" (*MXS* 217). He confessed he would be "hard pressed to give a specific definition of the overall philosophy which I think is necessary for the liberation of black people in this country" (*MXS* 212–13). Malcolm X's assassination on February 21, 1965, brought to a premature end his nascent philosophy of international black liberation and nationalism.

The Legacy of Malcolm X

The year Malcolm X died, Stokely Carmichael took up the banner of Black Power most visibly. Ironically, that year found Carmichael wresting control of the Southern Nonviolent Coordinating Committee from John Lewis, its erstwhile president and devotee of Martin Luther King, Jr. In 1966, Carmichael (a.k.a. Kwame Turé) joined up with Bobby Seale and Huey P. Newton, who had formed the Black Panther Party for Self-Defense in Oakland, California.

The original Black Panther Party bore little resemblance to its Oakland, California, manifestation. The former started as a SNCC-inspired voter registration drive in the summer of 1966 to give blacks in Lowndes County, Alabama, an alternative to the lily-white primary of the Democratic Party (signified by a white rooster). Despite a population that was 80 percent black, there were no black officials. The Lowndes County Freedom Organization arranged the primary, the first involving blacks since Reconstruction, and placed a sign with a black panther (the mascot of a local high school) to indicate its partisan affiliation.

The Black Panther Party for Self-Defense, which arose in response to the 1965 riots in Watts, California, applied Marxist-Leninist philosophy, Frantz Fanon's anticolonialism, and Mao Tse-tung's *Red Books* to the racial crisis in America. Their emphasis on gun ownership derived from Malcolm X's teaching as well as a concern for police brutality toward black Americans. The Black Panthers used "self-defense" in their name as a tribute to the Deacons for Defense of Justice, a Louisiana-based group of former World War II and Korean War veterans who protected meetings of the nonviolent Congress of Racial Equality and patrolled black neighborhoods at night to counter threats from the Ku Klux Klan.[15] In 1967, Stokely Carmichael published his philosophy and program as *Black Power: The Politics of Liberation in America*, a manifesto coauthored with Charles V. Hamilton.[16] Eldridge Cleaver, author of *Soul on Ice* (1968), joined the Nation of Islam because of Malcolm X and followed him when he left the Nation to form his own Muslim mosque. Cleaver later joined the Black Panthers as their minister of information. The Black Arts movement of the late 1960s, led by Amiri Baraka (a.k.a. Leroi Jones) with Don Lee and Larry Neal, along with black studies courses, programs, and centers at American colleges and universities, also found their muse in Malcolm X's black power rhetoric.

Malcolm X influenced not only liberal and left-wing figures but also conservative standard-bearers like Associate Justice Clarence Thomas, who owns an extensive collection of audio recordings of Malcolm X's speeches.[17] Even the *Wall Street Journal* issued a paean entitled "Malcolm X, Conservative Hero."[18] With Spike Lee's screen adaptation of *The Autobiography of Malcolm X* in 1992, the apotheosis of Malcolm X was complete, as his name, words, and image became part of the warp and woof of American popular culture.

Notes

1. Quotations from and references to Malcolm X's works are cited in the text using the following abbreviations:

AMX: *The Autobiography of Malcolm X*, Malcolm X with Alex Haley (New York: Random House, 1964).

EMP: "Minister Malcolm X Enunciates the Muslim Program," in *Black Nationalism in America*, ed. John H. Bracey, Jr., August Meier, and Elliott Rudwick (Indianapolis: Bobbs-Merrill Co., 1970).

MXS: *Malcolm X Speaks: Selected Speeches and Statements*, ed. George Breitman (New York: Grove Weidenfeld, 1965).

SU: "A Summing Up: Louis Lomax Interviews Malcolm X," in *A Malcolm X Reader: Perspectives on the Man and the Myths*, ed. David Gallen (New York: Carroll and Graf Publishers, 1994).

TFS: *February 1965: The Final Speeches* (New York: Pathfinder, 1992).

2. Regarding the term "Negro," Elijah Muhammad said that "I say *'so-called'* because you are *not* a *'Negro.'* There is no such thing as a race of *'Negroes.'* You are members of the Asiatic nation, from the tribe of *Shabazz!* 'Negro' is a false label forced on by your slavemaster" (cited by Malcolm X in *AMX* 258–59). See also Muhammad's *Message to the Blackman in America* (Newport News, Va.: United Brothers Communications Systems, [1965] 1992), 34, hereafter cited in the text as *MBA*: "We are not Negroes, because God, whose proper name is Allah, has taught me who we are." On Elijah Muhammad generally, see Karl Evanzz, *The Messenger: The Rise and Fall of Elijah Muhammad* (New York: Pantheon Books, 1999), and Claude Andrew Clegg III, *An Original Man: The Life and Times of Elijah Muhammad* (New York: St. Martin's Press, 1997).

3. For the theology of the Nation of Islam, see Mattias Gardell, *In the Name of Elijah Muhammad: Louis Farrakhan and the Nation of Islam* (Durham, N.C.: Duke University Press, 1996), chap. 7, "A Nation of Gods: The Creed of Black Islam," 144–86.

4. See C. Eric Lincoln, *The Black Muslims in America*, 3rd ed. (Grand Rapids, Mich.: William B. Eerdmans Publishing Company, [1961] 1994), chap. 3, "Black Nationalism: The Minor Leagues," 47–62.

5. Martin Luther King, Jr., *I Have a Dream: Writings and Speeches That Changed the World*, ed. James M. Washington (New York: HarperCollins Publishers, 1992), "The Power of Nonviolence," 30, and "I Have A Dream," 103.

6. The Declaration of Independence affirms that human beings are "endowed by their Creator with certain inalienable rights." Moreover, the purpose of government is not to grant these rights, for they are already possessed by each human being, but "to secure these rights," that is, to enable individuals to be free to exercise the rights they already possessed by virtue of their humanity. In addition, Malcolm X defended the right of black Americans to form rifle clubs to defend their lives and property whenever "the government seems unable or unwilling to protect them." He added: "If the government thinks I am wrong for saying this, then let the government start doing its job" (*MXS* 22).

7. According to Elijah Muhammad, "[y]ou are not American citizens or members of the white man's world" (*MBA* 130). "Remember, if you are black or a member of the Black Nation you are un-American" (*MBA* 186).

8. For an examination of the conception and writing of King's "Letter from a Birmingham Jail," see S. Jonathan Bass, *Blessed Are the Peacemakers: Martin Luther King, Jr., Eight White Religious Leaders, and the "Letter from Birmingham Jail"* (Baton Rouge: Louisiana State University Press, 2001). King wrote his "letter" in response to the public criticism voiced by eight Alabama ministers of the Roman Catholic, Protestant, and Jewish faiths. See "A Group of Clergymen: Letter to Martin Luther King," in *Basic Issues of American Democracy: A Book of Readings*, ed. Hillman M. Bishop and Samuel Hendel, 6th ed. (New York: Meredith Corporation, 1970), 282–83, for the contents of their public letter to King, which was published in the *Birmingham News* and *Birmingham Post-Herald* on April 13, 1963, as well as the *New York Times* on April 14, 1963.

9. On December 5, 1964, Malcolm X debated at Oxford Union, London, in favor of the motion that "extremism in defense of liberty is no vice, moderation in pursuit of justice is no virtue." Barry Goldwater first uttered this statement on July 16, 1964, in his acceptance speech for the presidential nomination at the 1964 Republican National Convention.

10. See *AMX* 307, and Louis A. DeCaro, Jr., *On the Side of My People: A Religious Life of Malcolm X* (New York: New York University Press, 1996), 191–92.

11. Marlene Nadle, "Malcolm X: The Complexity of a Man in the Jungle," *Village Voice* (February 25, 1965), cited in *TFS* 242.

12. Elijah Muhammad also distinguished human rights and universal rights from civil rights (*MBA* 240).

13. See Marcus Garvey, "The True Solution of the Negro Problem" (1922), in *African-American Social and Political Thought, 1850–1920*, ed. Howard Brotz (New Brunswick, N.J.: Transaction Publishers, [1966] 1999), 554–55.

14. Cf. Abraham Lincoln, "Message to Congress in Special Session" (July 4, 1861), in *The Collected Works of Abraham Lincoln*, ed. Roy P. Basler, 9 vols. (New Brunswick, N.J.: Rutgers University Press, 1955), 4:439: "It is now for them to demonstrate to the world, that those who can fairly carry an election, can also suppress a rebellion—that ballots are the rightful, and peaceful, successors of bullets; and that when ballots have fairly, and constitutionally, decided, there can be no successful appeal, back to bullets."

15. See *The Black Panthers Speak*, ed. Philip S. Foner (New York: Da Capo Press, 1995), and Adam Fairclough, *Race and Democracy: The Civil Rights Struggle in Louisiana 1915–1972* (Baton Rouge: Louisiana State University Press, 1995).

16. Stokely Carmichael and Charles V. Hamilton, *Black Power: The Politics of Liberation in America* (New York: Random House, 1967).

17. See Andrew Peyton Thomas, *Clarence Thomas: A Biography* (San Francisco: Encounter Books, 2001), 128, and Juan Williams, "A Question of Fairness," *Atlantic Monthly* (February 1987): 70–82.

18. Kevin Pritchett, "Malcolm X, Conservative Hero," *Wall Street Journal* (November 10, 1992). See also Gerald Early, "Their Malcolm, My Problem: On the Abuses of Afrocentrism and Black Anger," *Harpers* (December 1992): 62–74.

Chapter 41

Betty Friedan and Gloria Steinem: The Popular Transformation of American Feminism in the Late Twentieth Century

Natalie Taylor and Daryl McGowan Tress

This chapter explores the political thought and influence of two of the most prominent feminist leaders of the latter half of the twentieth century: Betty Friedan (1921–) and Gloria Steinem (1934–). Addressing issues of women's status, rights, and quality of life, their publications, notably Friedan's *The Feminine Mystique* (1963) and Steinem's *Ms.* magazine (founded in 1972), spoke to a wide audience of Americans and powerfully shaped public attitudes about women. Friedan and Steinem advocated political and public activism to change laws and customs that discriminated against women (in educational and employment opportunities, for example). Yet, despite their common cause, Friedan and Steinem had different visions of feminism and its goals, and these differences soon emerged as conflicts between the directions each one recommended for the women's movement. Friedan's feminism sought to expose the formal and informal constraints keeping women strictly within the domestic sphere; she urged not that women abandon family life but that they enhance or supplement it, chiefly with paid work outside the home. Steinem's feminism, more in keeping with the radical temper of the times, expanded to emphasize many "gender issues" such as rape, pornography, and lesbian rights. This chapter examines Friedan's and Steinem's considerable success in moving feminism into the mainstream of American life. At the same time, we consider the different feminist ideas they promoted, which reflect fundamental disputes within the women's movement.

I

As the author of *The Feminine Mystique*, Betty Friedan gave voice to thousands of American women who were dissatisfied with their traditional roles as wives and mothers. As the founder of the National Organization of Women (NOW), arguably the most important group promoting the equality of women, Friedan is credited with starting the women's movement in the United States during the 1960s. Friedan's contributions have brought immense change to the lives of American women—and men. In retrospect, Friedan claims that she did not set out to bring about such far-reaching social change. Instead, she believes the success of *The Feminine Mystique* and the effectiveness of the women's movement was "a miracle of convergence of my life and history . . . one thing leading to another" (*MLSF* 13).[1]

697

Betty Friedan was born in 1921 in Peoria, Illinois, to Harry and Miriam Goldstein. Friedan's father immigrated from Russia and her mother was born in the United States, herself the daughter of Jewish immigrants from Hungary. Friedan's early childhood memories were of her mother's unhappiness, which infected everyone around her. Friedan also recalls her parents fighting over money. During the depression, Mrs. Goldstein would buy things and ask her children to keep her purchases a secret from their father. This created the sense that Friedan's father was the enemy. From her earliest recollections, Friedan was convinced that her mother would have been happier, and consequently a better wife and mother, if she would have had "work to do." Throughout her writings, Friedan attributes her commitment to women's equality and independence to her mother's discontent.

Mrs. Goldstein encouraged her daughter to pursue a life different from her own and to attend Smith College, like many of Peoria's privileged young women. Friedan thrived at Smith, making many friends, rising to intellectual challenges, and editing the school's newspaper. Looking back, she describes herself and her friends as "college liberals trying to become radicals, with romantic visions of communism." Friedan thought of herself as a revolutionary (*MLSF* 57). Upon graduation from college, she knew that she did not want to share her mother's lifestyle, but there were few alternatives for women in the early 1940s. Any job she might take was assumed to be temporary—until she married. As an indication of the monumental change in women's lives and their outlooks, Friedan reports that it did not even occur to her that she could pursue her interest in journalism and seek employment at a large newspaper, such as the *New York Times*, like her male contemporaries. She briefly attended graduate school in psychology, but left the academy when graduate study began to threaten her more traditional expectations of marriage.

In the years following college and graduate study, Friedan earned her living as a writer for the *Federated Press* and the *UE News*, the publication of the United Electrical Workers, one of the period's most progressive labor unions.[2] Although she had some sympathy for communist ideas, she gradually became disappointed with them. She began to recognize the discrepancy between communism as an abstract theory and the reality of the lives of those around her: "I began to feel an aversion to any and all political dogma that didn't seem to come from real life" (*MLSF* 73). Friedan also notes the influence of Hannah Arendt's 1959 essay, *On Revolution*, which considers the significance of revolutions in the modern age. Arendt notices that change alone is insufficient to explain revolution. Instead, a desire "to liberate and to build a new house where freedom can dwell" characterizes revolution. In addition, Arendt associates "irresistibility" to revolution: in other words, it is an historical force beyond the control of particular human actors.[3] In particular, Friedan was struck by the distinctive status Arendt assigns to the American Revolution. Unlike the French or the Russian Revolutions, the American Revolution resulted in a constitution that embodies a democratic process of continued questioning and rebirth. Friedan would return to Arendt's understanding of American democracy when considering the work and goals of the women's movement.

Friedan's work on the labor movement's publications came to an end when she became pregnant with her second child in 1952. She had been lucky that she had been able to continue working after the birth of her first child, but her employer was unwilling to allow her maternity leave following the second. Friedan admits that at the time being fired was something of a relief. Her study of Freudian psychology informed her that she would find her greatest fulfillment as a wife and mother. Yet Friedan found herself in the very circumstances that had made her mother unhappy. Because she was not working, her husband had to "carry the whole burden" of the family. She was not satisfied by volunteer work and wished she were earning money. Balancing the care of her children and home with writing, Friedan began to publish articles in popular women's magazines.

It was during this period that *Modern Women: The Lost Sex* was published.[4] The authors, Mariani Farnham and Ferdinand Lundberg, were Freudian psychoanalysts. Farnham and Lundberg pointed to a growing discontent among suburban housewives and attributed it to their high levels of education. They held that too much education prevents women from adjusting to their roles as wives and mothers. Suspecting that it was not education that was keeping women from enjoying marriage and motherhood, but a narrow definition of woman, Friedan prepared a response to *Modern Women*. She wrote a comprehensive questionnaire for Smith alumnae, the responses to which indicated that women who had interests outside of the home enjoyed their families more. Friedan wrote about these results in an article that she submitted to many of the popular women's magazines. It was rejected everywhere. Yet the dissatisfaction of the women in Friedan's circles assured her that she was identifying a widespread problem among American women. It was from this article that the idea for *The Feminine Mystique* grew. Published in 1963, *The Feminine Mystique* would be Friedan's most influential book, and arguably the impetus to the modern women's movement. In the wake of its publication, women across the country insisted that "it changed my life."

The Feminine Mystique is a refutation of the conventional wisdom about women's happiness. Instead of relying on the works of psychologists and social scientists who had considered the role of women in society, *The Feminine Mystique* drew on Friedan's "personal truth" as well as the experiences of her Smith classmates, her neighbors, and her friends. As one who both experienced and observed the feminine mystique, Friedan renounced the "so-called accepted truth" in order to report a "new, larger truth about women" (*MLSF* 106).

Friedan begins *The Feminine Mystique* by identifying "The Problem That Has No Name." Due to the combined influences of tradition and the popularization of Freudian psychology, women believe their greatest fulfillment will come from their femininity. A truly feminine woman is not supposed to be interested in higher education, career, or even political participation. She simply devotes herself to husband and children. "Millions of women lived their lives in the image of those pretty pictures of the American suburban housewife, kissing their husbands goodbye in front of the picture window, depositing their stationwagonsful of children at school, and smiling as they ran the new electric waxer over the spotless kitchen floor" (*FM* 18). Despite her seemingly ideal life, the suburban housewife feels discontented but cannot identify the cause. The "problem" could not be explained by women's material circumstances. Indeed, the more money and comforts they had, the greater the dissatisfaction the women felt.

In order to determine the cause of "the problem that has no name," Friedan looks to women's magazines and the image of woman presented in them. The woman who is portrayed is "fluffy and feminine." Judging from the magazine pictures and articles, the readers are interested only in subjects pertinent to happy marriages and well-maintained homes (*FM* 36). Friedan is stunned to find that women's interests are supposedly limited to kitchen, nursery, and bedroom, even in the year that Castro led a revolution in Cuba and the civil rights movement began in the United States.

Through these widespread images of woman, the "feminine mystique" is perpetuated.

The feminine mystique says that the highest value and the only commitment for women is the fulfilment of their own femininity. . . . This femininity is so mysterious and intuitive and close to the creation and origin of life that man-made science may never be able to understand it. . . . The mistake, says the mystique, the root of women's troubles in the past is that women envied men, tried to be like men, instead of accepting their own nature, which can find fulfilment only in sexual passivity, male domination, and nurturing maternal love. (*FM* 43)

Despite the "sophisticated trappings" of the feminine mystique, the women in America were beginning to sense that the feminine mystique left them in a mindless routine of domestic drudgery. The "problem that has no name" is a vague desire for "something more." Friedan does not dismiss the joy that comes with children: she simply rejects the notion that motherhood and the femininity associated with it must come at the expense of women's humanity. Friedan tells the readers of *The Feminine Mystique* that the imagination is what distinguishes human beings from animals and from the "stuffed dolls" that women are made to resemble. The human mind has an idea and the individual shapes a future to realize that vision—that is, the ability to create characterizes human beings. The American woman's nagging, undefined wish for "something more" is simply the human desire to imagine and create one's own future.

True to her understanding of the American political system, Friedan suggests that "the problem that has no name" is evidence of our ever-changing democracy. She considers the pioneers. Of course, the burdens of caring for the physical needs of men and children fell to women, but those women shared the pioneering spirit. In the latter half of the twentieth century, we have a greater degree of freedom from the constant work of physical necessity than women had a century and a half ago. "The American frontiers are of the mind, and of the spirit" (*FM* 67). The democratic institutions of America do not disappoint Friedan. She appreciates that in the early 1960s, more than at any previous time in history, women enjoy greater access to higher education. The paradox, however, is that young women in the 1950s and 1960s do not take advantage of their opportunities to develop their human potential.

Friedan holds Freudian psychology responsible for the feminine mystique. In the 1940s, the traditional roles of women were promulgated by educators and social scientists. Ironically, the more educated a woman became, the more she encountered these "sophisticated" prejudices about femininity. Friedan's own experience stands as an example. She rejects, however, the Freudian explanation of woman. After all, Freud's studies were based on middle-class, Viennese women in the Victorian era. Friedan charges that Freud and his followers in the United States made a universal human pattern out of attitudes that reflected the decaying Austrian empire at the turn of the nineteenth century. Freud's psychology simply could not be used to understand the experience of American women in the middle of the twentieth century.

In America, girls grow up feeling free and equal to boys. Many go off to college and find jobs after graduation. The crisis in women's identity comes, Friedan writes, when they leave college or their jobs for their strictly feminine roles as adults. The development of women is arrested. In a comparison that Friedan later came to regret, she likens the suburban home to a comfortable concentration camp. Women, like prisoners, are forced to give up their individuality and blend into a mass. Their uniquely human capacity to imagine their future and prepare for it is sacrificed to misguided conceptions of femininity.

The Feminine Mystique proposes "A New Life Plan for Women." In a radical claim for her time, Friedan informs women that they simply do not have to choose between a career and marriage. Women must dispel their illusions about homemaking and marriage. Housework is a practical matter and should be done quickly and efficiently. Furthermore, women must give up their romantic expectations of marriage and acknowledge that the family will not be the only means to their fulfilment. In addition to more realistic expectations of homemaking and the family, women must pursue and sustain their own interests, which requires a serious commitment to education and training. Friedan also advises women that they must be paid for their work. Regrettably, paid employment is the only work our society values. Women may pursue their new interests while their children are in school or by creating communal child care arrangements.

Today, many people recognize women as full human beings and believe they should be able to seek higher education and to pursue careers outside of the home. Friedan's solution to "the problem that has no name" may seem obvious and rather insignificant. In 1963, however, Friedan's description of the "problem that has no name" resonated powerfully with women all across America, many reporting that they each felt alone in their unhappiness. By lifting the veil of the feminine mystique, Friedan gave housewives a sense of relief and empowerment.

In the 1960s, Friedan's advocacy of the humanity of women moved from the theoretical to the practical level. As a result of President Kennedy's Commission on the Status of Women in 1961, state commissions were established to follow up on the issues listed in the original report. Representatives from these state commissions, who themselves were active in their local arenas, in turn met annually in Washington, D.C., where networking and further organizing took place. The politically active women battled for the inclusion of sex discrimination as one of the prohibited categories in the Civil Rights Act of 1964, along with discrimination based on race, creed, and nationality. They won this important fight. The Equal Employment Opportunity Commission, however, did not take seriously women's discrimination complaints. This failure provoked a number of influential women at the 1966 meeting of the annual conference on the status of women, Betty Friedan among them, to form a women's rights organization that could lobby on behalf of women in Washington. Friedan named the new group the National Organization for Women (NOW). NOW elected Friedan as its first president, and quickly positioned itself in the public eye with sophisticated public relations strategies.[5] Its new membership was wide-ranging: professional women, traditional housewives, women from labor unions, and women from some radical political organizations.

In its statement of purpose, NOW commits itself to true equality for all women and a fully equal partnership between the sexes. With the prospect of a longer life-span by the second half of the twentieth century, it is no longer necessary (or even possible) for women to devote their entire lives to childbearing and child-rearing. In addition to that change, the NOW statement of purpose holds that newer technology eliminates the demand for muscular strength in most jobs. The physical qualities that once kept women out of the workplace no longer seem relevant. NOW's statement of purpose reflects once again the influence of Hannah Arendt's *On Revolution* on Friedan. Friedan sees this as a revolutionary era, when American men and women confront laws and customs which have prevented women from enjoying full rights and equality of opportunity. In the United States, the individual—and not the husband and wife or the family—is the fundamental political entity. Understanding women simply as part of a larger social unit, even if that unit is one as meaningful as the family, compromises a woman's individual rights and freedom. The protection guaranteed to individuals by the American Constitution must be extended in order to end sex discrimination. For Friedan, "there's no question, however, that the women's movement was and *is* the second chapter of the American Revolution" (*MLSF* 180). Friedan's belief in the democratic process, initiated in the American Revolution and institutionalized by the Constitution, gives the United States the capacity for great social innovations—certainly innovations which would allow for women's equality of opportunity.

Though NOW was and is dedicated to the belief that women are individual human beings, the statement of purpose is mindful of women's relationship to men. The equality of opportunity that women seek need not come at the expense of the family. NOW simply does not accept the notion that women must choose between the family and a profession. Indeed, NOW's statement of purpose rejects the premise that a man must carry the sole burden of supporting himself and his family. It rejects the belief that a woman is entitled to lifelong financial support from her husband. The liberated woman differs greatly from the woman veiled by the feminine mystique. This woman neither expects special privileges nor harbors enmity toward man. Again, we see Arendt's influence on Friedan. The American Revolution was unique in that the "oppressed" did not become the "oppressor," assuming authoritarian control over the governed. Friedan anticipated that the revolution brought about by the women's movement would also establish a new and different relationship between the "oppressed" and the "oppressor." Indeed, given the complicated relationship between women and men, it would be wrong to understand their relationship in such simplistic terms. In certain respects, men are victims of the feminine mystique as well, and cannot be understood as the enemy. The true equality of women would bring about a new, more fulfilling relationship between men and women.

Understanding the women's movement in the context of the American political system, Friedan identified two priorities for the women's rights movement in her report to NOW following its first year. The true equality of women in the United States would not be realized without enacting the Equal Rights Amendment and establishing abortion rights.[6] The ERA would give legal protection to women's equal opportunity and to the accomplishments that would surely follow. Instituting a legal safeguard was imperative for Friedan. In her autobiography (*My Life So Far* [2000]), written more than thirty years after the founding of NOW, Friedan continues to regret the ERA's demise in 1982. In addition to explicit constitutional protection, Friedan also believes that women's equality can be assured only if women have control over their bodies. Women must decide whether or not they will bear children, and so women must have access to legal abortion. Only by making the choice to bear children can motherhood be a happy occasion for women.

Though Friedan is often considered the founder of the women's movement, the intellectual and social tumult of the 1960s saw other women (and men) challenge the traditional roles of women. Foremost among these younger, bolder feminists was Gloria Steinem.

II

Neither an elected politician nor a political theorist in the strictest sense, Gloria Steinem has been a formidable social leader on women's behalf in the second half of the twentieth century. Steinem is perhaps best known as the cofounder and editor of *Ms.* magazine, launched in 1972 as the first glossy, mass-circulation publication to define and spread the feminist message beyond its prior, relatively limited circles. She is a journalist who has written four books and dozens of articles documenting and defining the cultural transitions of the day. Like Friedan, Steinem was active in the formation of politically significant organizations, such as the National Women's Political Caucus and Women against Pornography. And she served as the most publicly visible spokesperson for the women's cause in the United States in the 1970s and 1980s, engaging the media effectively to popularize the feminist message and its political demands. In short, Steinem was the most prominent women's leader in the century's later decades. This was a time of competing versions of feminism and, as we shall see, her vision for women's liberation matched neither Friedan's liberal ideas about women's equality nor the radical feminism that opposed conventional political and social arrangements. Steinem created a new and widely appealing feminism drawn from a range of feminist perspectives.

Gloria Steinem was born in Toledo, Ohio, in 1934. Journalism and feminism were both part of her family background. Her parents, Ruth and Leo Steinem, met at the University of Toledo where they worked on the school newspaper that Leo founded, writing columns, editing, and selling copies around campus.[7] Her paternal grandmother, Pauline Perlmutter Steinem, was an active suffragist early in the century; she argued for women's rights in a 1914 newspaper essay and chaired the Education Committee of the National American Woman's Suffrage Association, where she urged the inclusion of women's contributions to American history.[8] Steinem's girlhood was erratic. Her father's business ventures involved the family in an unconventional lifestyle and frequent travel that kept Steinem from attending school regularly. Her parents later divorced after a long-troubled marriage, and at age eleven Steinem became the primary caretaker for her mother, who by then had serious mental illness.[9] This difficult period of her life ended when she was seventeen. She moved to Washington, D.C., to live with her older sister for a year before starting college. In 1952, ten years after Friedan graduated from Smith College, Steinem enrolled at the prestigious women's college. Steinem excelled academically, and in 1956 she graduated magna cum laude, having majored in government. After Smith, she spent two years in India on a fellowship. She eventually returned to the United States, settling first in Cambridge, Massachusetts, and soon thereafter in New York City, in 1960, to begin her career in journalism.[10]

One of Steinem's most celebrated early articles was "I Was a Playboy Bunny" (1963). For this assignment for *Show* magazine, Steinem went undercover at the Playboy Club in midtown Manhattan, reporting on the realities of the business from the point of view of the women who worked as cocktail waitresses, or "Bunnies," at the club. The article predates her affiliation with feminism, and Steinem had misgivings about it after it was published, fearing that it might be misused and that her own public image would remain linked with the Playboy Club. But she came to recognize its virtues, and it is plain that "I Was a Playboy Bunny" displays some of the best features of Steinem's later, successful feminist writing and rallying. Central to the power of this article, and of Steinem's feminism at its best, is that it derives from her own experiences and firsthand observations of women's condition. In the article, she candidly reports with humor and without cant on the unglamorous treatment of female employees by the management and customers at the glamorous Playboy Club. In this passage, Steinem describes the scene around her in the dressing room as she is fitted for the skimpy Bunny costume:

> A girl rushed in with her costume in her hand, calling for the wardrobe mistress as a wounded soldier might yell, "Medic!" "I've broken my zipper," she wailed, "I sneezed!"
> "That's the third time this week," said the wardrobe mistress sternly. "It's a regular epidemic." The girl apologized, found another costume, and left.
> I asked if a sneeze could really break a costume.
> "Sure," she said. "Girls with colds usually have to be replaced." (*OAER* 35)

As a young reporter, Steinem was a sharp and witty observer, and she combined these talents with a developing sensibility about women's mistreatment. Her commitment to observing "on the ground"—from women's own perspective—stood in contrast to a more theory-driven feminism that was taking root in some progressive political organizations at the time, as well as in some areas of the academy (e.g., Shulamith Firestone's transformation of Marxist political and economic theory in the service of feminism). Steinem's reporting built around her developing sense that taking up women's own point of view reveals both serious and subtle injustices. She modeled and made legitimate precisely this personal, as opposed to "expert," approach to the social and political world for a generation of American women. One need only compare "I Was a Playboy Bunny" with the typical magazine fare of the day to recognize the extraordinary shift of outlook Steinem introduced to a mass audience. That she made this new outlook seem so natural, comprehensible, and appealing was characteristic of Steinem's feminist contributions.

Another dimension of Steinem's public role emerged in "I Was a Playboy Bunny," namely, her striking good looks. Her beauty gained her entrée for the exposé of the Playboy Club, allowing her to pose as a Bunny. Later, when she was formally involved in feminist activities, the cameras were drawn to her photogenic face more and more frequently. But her appearance became something of a debated topic: for women generally, it was sometimes a flash point for a new awareness of the social power accorded to feminine appearance; and for the feminist leadership in particular, it easily polarized opinion about how feminism should represent itself and just what it stood for.[11]

In the early 1960s, Steinem was not yet involved with organized feminism, but she was friendly with other visible leftist causes of the day, carrying food and cigarettes, for example, to Puerto Rican radicals protesting in Harlem. She recalls that her sympathies with such causes led her more and more to feel dissatisfied with mainstream journalism. As a woman, her assignments were generally to report on such topics as vacations and holiday foods. Steinem published many pieces in popular magazines during the 1960s, did some script-writing for the TV political satire show *That Was the Week That Was*, and was herself a rising young celebrity in the cultural capital of the country, gathering a circle of very highly placed friends in publishing, politics, and the arts. A sign of her growing status was the weekly column she garnered in 1968 in the new *New York* magazine. Entitled "The City Politic," it offered her a platform for reporting on the issues she took seriously and the causes she endorsed, even while she continued to write about the "beautiful people." The late 1960s was a period of radical chic, and the issues Steinem took seriously were often those of the New Left, such as fundraising for Cesar Chavez's efforts to unionize migrant farm workers. Among her many activities, she was personally involved in George McGovern's presidential candidacy and supported his antiwar stance in her articles.

After some initial reluctance, Steinem came into feminism in 1968. An acquaintance and leader of NOW, Jean Faust, invited Steinem to participate in a demonstration at the elite Plaza Hotel in New York, which banned women from lunch in its Oak Room.[12] Although Steinem declined to participate (telling Faust she preferred to be a humanist rather than a feminist), she went to observe, and watching the protest had an important impact on her: seeing women stand up for themselves allowed her to do the same for herself. Her own feminist turning point occurred a month later. Steinem was covering an event entitled "Abortion: Women Tell It Like It Is," sponsored by a radical women's group, the Redstockings, in a Methodist church in New York's Greenwich Village. The event included a short drama followed by a "speak-out" in which women panelists told of their personal experiences with pregnancy and abortion. The evening resonated powerfully with Steinem, whose feminist contribution characteristically would center on validating women's own social, political, and emotional perspectives. She understood the importance of the abortion issue from firsthand experience; she had had an unwanted pregnancy shortly after graduating from college and procured an illegal abortion, alone. Moreover, Steinem, whose general political outlook kept her keenly sensitive to exclusion in a democratic society, recognized the injustice of women's virtually complete exclusion from the abortion discussion that directly impacted their lives. At the time, the New York state legislature had been holding hearings about modifying the state's abortion law. The Redstockings were denied a role in the testimony on the grounds that the lawmakers wished to hear only from the fourteen experts it selected: thirteen male physicians, lawyers, and other professionals along with one nun. In these important public deliberations, as in the public image of the Playboy Club, women's perspectives were virtually absent, and women's experiences were made invisible.[13] That night at the Redstockings event, Steinem had a powerful insight about women's subordination in society, and a strong emotional response accompanied the insight (*OAER* 17–18). It was the beginning of her feminist life—that is, the beginning of her commitment to ending the injustices, public and private, that women suffered. For Steinem, the first step in ending injustice involved raising awareness among both the agents and the victims of injustice. Better than Friedan, Steinem understood women's alienation from each other and how it impeded social and political change. In addition to forging social and political bonds among women, she saw that it would be necessary to move women into public decision-making roles.[14]

As a journalist, Steinem immediately set about researching and writing about feminism and the women's liberation movement. She wrote the article she considers to be her first fully feminist piece in the spring of 1969: entitled "After Black Power, Women's Liberation," it appeared in her "City Politic" column in *New York* magazine. Two important themes emerged in Steinem's thinking. In the first place, she astutely saw that the new women's liberation movement drew on two different sources or constituencies. On the one hand, there were liberal, middle class, mostly white women affiliated with the National Organization for Women with reformist goals. On the other hand, there were radical-intellectual activists, for the most part also white and middle class, who were coming into their feminist groups from participation in other social movements and who had more far-reaching political agendas. The fundamental tension, not to say conflict, between the views of these two groups was to become a major factor in the subsequent history of the women's movement in the United States. It was at a relatively early date that Steinem identified the two sources of "second wave feminism" and their differences.[15] In the second place, Steinem realized the importance of the civil rights movement as a call to feminists for greater inclusion of women of color into the movement, and the achievements of the civil rights movement as a model for feminism.

Steinem was undoubtedly a pioneer, but not a trailblazer, in the new consciousness that developed during this decade. Her personal feminist turn occurred five years after the 1963 publication of Friedan's *The Feminine Mystique*, and at a time when several federal and state initiatives already were underway to study and improve "the status of women." In other words, the climate had been readied for Steinem's engagement with feminism by a number of factors: the popularity of Friedan's book; the social realities of greater numbers of women in the workplace; the increased availability of contraceptives; and the visible social activism and spirit of defiance in the culture at large.[16] And not only had women's liberation been growing in numbers during the 1960s, it was becoming stronger, more organized, and dedicated.

Although not yet involved with NOW, Steinem quickly became intensively active and highly visible in the women's movement. As an enthusiastic and charismatic feminist speaker, she was much in demand on the lecture circuit throughout the country. She spoke tirelessly at small grassroots meetings, on college campuses, and in influential settings such as the Women's National Democratic Club in Washington, where she was celebrated by socialites and politicians such as Henry Kissinger and George McGovern.[17] When *Time* magazine ran a cover story about the women's liberation movement that year, Steinem's picture was featured and she was invited to contribute an essay.[18] She also appeared on television talk shows. In short, she became feminism's "star."

By 1970, the American women's movement had gained great momentum. A "Women's Strike for Equality" was planned for August 26, 1970, the fiftieth anniversary of the women's vote. Women were to refuse to do their menial jobs. Steinem and Friedan were both leaders at this important event. On the day of the strike, Friedan, along with an eighty-year-old suffragette and a young radical woman wearing blue jeans, led a march down Fifth Avenue in New York City. Behind these women, who spanned the generations, were an estimated 30,000 women who represented all social and economic backgrounds. Housewives wore aprons and carried signs with slogans such as "Don't Iron While the Strike Is Hot." The march ended in a rally with speeches by prominent feminists including Bella Abzug and Kate Millet, along with Steinem and Friedan. In addition to the march in New York, there were organized and spontaneous demonstrations in ninety cities and small towns across the United States. For Friedan, the Women's Strike for Equality signified the strength and unity of the movement.

The apparent unity of the women's movement would be short lived. Just a few months later, Kate Millet told a *Time* magazine reporter that she was bisexual. This announcement created a new furor directed against the women's movement. It was at this time that the Women's Strike Coalition organized a protest. Friedan assumed that the purpose of the gathering was to protest the New York state legislature's restrictions on abortion and child care. In light of the new controversy over Millet's sexuality, however, other leaders of the women's movement felt it was important to demonstrate their solidarity with Millet. The protesters were encouraged to wear lavender arm bands and to distribute leaflets that stated: "It is not woman's sexual experience that is under attack—it's the freedom of all women to openly state values that fundamentally challenge the patriarchy."[19] For Friedan, this was a turning point in the women's movement. She felt that engaging in "sexual politics" was a mistake because it would be divisive and distract women (and men) from serious political action. Steinem, on the other hand, would see such issues as a natural component of feminism.

By 1971, Steinem's popularity was growing rapidly. The magazine articles were not simply about the women's movement but were more and more about Steinem herself: in *Vogue* and *McCall's* she was portrayed as a role model; by contrast, in a critical article in *Esquire* reflecting a broad cultural animus toward women's liberation, she was called "the intellectual's pinup."[20] Even the positive public characterization brought problems, however. Creating a "star" or "leader" hierarchy within the women's movement was decried by the radical membership, who saw its elitism as an expression of male social organization. And not only radicals denounced Steinem's celebrity. Betty Freidan, too, seemed to question Steinem's leadership abilities. Later, Friedan grudgingly acknowledged Steinem's role in the women's movement, admitting that "certainly Gloria helped give it glamor, and that was a good contribution" (*MLSF* 189).

At this time, Steinem was more than a spokesperson for and symbol of feminism; she had become increasingly involved in political organizing as well. Together with Brenda Feigen Fasteau, she founded the Women's Action Alliance in 1970; and with Bella Abzug, Shirley Chisholm, and Betty Friedan, she was one of the leaders of the National Women's Political Caucus (NWPC) in 1971. The group intended to address in particular the underrepresentation of women in the U.S. Congress, the Supreme Court, and other major political arenas. At the beginning of the decade, no women were seated on the Supreme Court; there were no female state governors; and few women were elected to Congress. This new group recognized the need to promote women in politics, but the question of *how* to do that soon arose. From the start, there was a battle in the NWPC. Should the group support any woman who was a serious political candidate (Friedan's position); or should it support only those candidates, women and possibly men as well, who endorsed a particular agenda for women's liberation (Abzug's position)? Steinem aligned herself with Abzug and her more restricted, "correct" approach. The compromise that NWPC finally adopted was to list a number of issues, ranging from specifics like abortion rights and repeal of contraceptive laws to big, progressive ideals such as income redistribution, and to identify them as "guidelines" for local chapters rather than as firm criteria for endorsements.[21] This compromise, an unhappy one from Freidan's perspective, drove a further wedge between Friedan's politically broad-based feminism and the narrower version Steinem espoused. And the more publicity Steinem's media-friendly feminism received, the more Freidan spoke out against its radical intentions, making especially evident the rift between NOW's moderate aims and the more extensive goals of Abzug's supporters. Though still active in many of these organizations, Friedan was excluded from their leadership as the women's movement aligned itself squarely with radical social ideas.

Although the tension between the liberal and radical camps of the women's movement existed almost from the start, the movement was still small enough so that considerable interaction and mobility among representatives of both outlooks took place, and young enough that partisans of either camp might modify their points of view. In 1971, Brenda Feigen Fasteau, legislative vice president for NOW, had the idea that she and Steinem should form an organization to provide women with needed information for starting local action projects, especially ones pertaining to education. Together that year, Fasteau and Steinem founded the Women's Action Alliance (WAA), and they set about to find funding for the WAA. The story goes that when they realized that a newsletter was unlikely to yield the funding they needed, Fasteau suggested that Steinem should start a magazine as a way of raising money. The idea of a glossy magazine that addressed women from a feminist point of view had floated around, both within the magazine publishing world and within some feminist groups; but, for different reasons, the idea had been abandoned.[22] After some initial reluctance, Steinem agreed to pursue the venture. The first magazine of its kind, *Ms.* would powerfully shape public opinion about women both nationally and internationally. The far-reaching feminist message was neither simply *moderate*, if to radical feminists that meant mild-mannered and docile, nor was it aggressively and unacceptably *radical* to the NOW membership. Rather, *Ms.* forged something new—a synthesis and transformation of sometimes startling feminist ideas that nonetheless could be absorbed rapidly and widely into American life.

Although Steinem would publish several successful books in the 1980s and 1990s (documenting changes in the cultural contours with respect to bringing the feminist ideas to a wider public), it was her editorial direction of *Ms.* magazine that was to have the greatest impact.[23] The extraordinary inaugural issue of *Ms.* reveals her talent as editor.[24] It is a snapshot of the women's movement at the time. Steinem mixed ideas from the moderate center and extreme end of the movement, and made the mix coherent and winning both to advertisers and ordinary readers. Thus, she included articles reflecting Freidan's liberal feminism (although Friedan's name is absent from the masthead and the "Contents" page) along with others presenting a radical perspective. For example, Vivian Gornick offers an extended interview with the psychologist Matina Horner (soon to be named president of Radcliffe College) who was researching women's "fear of success." Horner discusses the common assumption equating femininity and domesticity that leads to conflicts for women as they face possible success in the public world. Horner's findings concur with Friedan's claim in *The Feminine Mystique* that learned social attitudes about femininity keep adult women house-bound and unable to pursue serious public activities. A practical article about setting up child-care centers by Linda Francke and Dorothy Pitman Hughes addresses an issue women face in taking a full role in the public sphere and develops a liberal remedy for it. But the radical political approach, one that links feminism with more insidious causes and broader social issues such as racism, poverty, and homophobia, is also present in *Ms.* from the start. Johnnie Tillmon writes eloquently from her firsthand struggles with poverty in "Welfare Is a Women's Issue." Her article suggests that an extensive network of causes constrains women—namely, an oppressive power structure (later routinely referred to as "the partriarchy") that systematically dictates the lives of women and other subordinated groups of people.

Steinem, however, did more in *Ms.* than present ideas from both the liberal middle and the radical end of the women's movement; she also synthesized the two and created a new kind of feminism. Her own writing, along with her sure eye for selecting writers who themselves were moving in this new direction, allowed her to create a vibrant version of feminism for the public in the 1970s and 1980s.[25] Steinem's own written contribution to the inaugural issue, the lead article entitled "Sisterhood," amalgamates liberal and more radical views and points optimistically to the future. "Sisterhood" makes the analogy between sexual, racial, and class subordination, stating that members of all these groups are treated like servants and/or children: "It will take a coalition of such ["out"] groups to achieve a society in which, at a minimum, no one is born into a second-class role because of visible difference, because of race or sex" (49). At the same time, she is attuned to the subjective and psychological effects of oppressive structures. Steinem speaks with feeling about her own growing sense of personal liberation; and speaking directly about one's personal experience was integral to the early phase of the women's movement for both liberals and radicals. But although Steinem's writing, here and elsewhere, begins with the personal, her manner transcends the merely subjective. Her readers are meant to recognize the patterns of their own experience in her descriptions. She claims hopefully that the shared features of women's lives allow women of very different circumstances (i.e., of different races, classes, ages, and so forth) to connect in sisterhood across these boundaries.

Other articles in the first issue of *Ms.* demonstrate the pervasiveness of women's mistreatment. Consistent with Steinem's approach, they stay true to the particularities of the writers' circumstances while they signal the depth and extent of the attitudes that subordinate women everywhere. Jane O'Reilly's classic "The Housewife's Moment of Truth" tells of the "click" women experience on recognizing, often in seemingly insignificant events or remarks, their servile role. O'Reilly offers an example. She and a friend are finishing the clean-up after serving a big breakfast to house guests, when a male guest straggles into the kitchen, sits down at the table, and says to the two women, "How about something to eat." The women look at each other: click, click. O'Reilly concludes: "We are all housewives, the natural people to turn to when there is something unpleasant, inconvenient or inconclusive to be done" (55–57). Judy Syfers echoes O'Reilly in her contribution, "I Want a Wife"—a phrase one still hears, thirty years later, even from women who do not call themselves feminists. In this short article that brilliantly captures the asymmetry of women's and men's lives, Syfers imagines what her life might be like if she had someone to care for her children throughout the day, run an organized home for her, and put her needs first everyday.

These three pieces by Steinem, O'Reilly, and Syfers represent the new, public feminism and its three leading ideas: (1) *sisterhood*, unifying women across their social differences, even as sisterhood draws attention to the significance of those social factors; (2) women's *knowing*, validated by other women, and based on women's experiences and stories; and (3) the blunt *unfairness* that women experience throughout their lives as their sex is continually linked with inferiority. Adding to its political outlook, *Ms.* published new work by distinguished or soon-to-be distinguished fiction writers and poets—for example, Sylvia Plath's poem "Three Women: A Play for Three Voices" appeared in the first issue. In the United States and around the world, women read *Ms.* and immediately connected with its feminist message.

There were, of course, numerous contradictions Steinem faced in creating the *Ms.* combination of feminist ideas and popular appeal. Examination of *Ms.* magazine's contents, including its articles, illustrations, and advertising, would give a fuller picture of the tensions confronting the women's movement in the early 1970s. For instance, Susan Edmiston's "How to Write Your Own Marriage Contract" explicitly favors the equality of the sexes. Edmiston approvingly cites Mary Wollstonecraft, the great eighteenth-century liberal defender of equal rights for women, and NOW's efforts to change unfair marriage laws. But her article is illustrated with a full-page photograph of a man and woman tied together with heavy ropes; here and in the magazine's other graphics showing women bound or somehow imprisoned, the nonverbal suggestion seems less about equality and more about the coercion and captivity of marriage or motherhood as such. These radical messages, even if subliminal, were odd when juxtaposed with status quo advertisements portraying women eager to attract men and win their favor.

Furthermore, from its inception *Ms.* expressed the radical potential of feminism, even when it is based on liberal ideals of equality and autonomy. Thus, the inaugural issue featured an interview conducted by Annie Loedt, founder of the New York Radical Feminists, entitled "Can Women Love Women?" in which her unnamed interviewee discusses her first lesbian relationship. She tells Loedt: "Because it's a natural question, if you want to remove sexual roles and if you say that men and women are equal human beings, well the next question is: why should you only love men?" (121). Friedan was highly wary of this brand of sexual politics, maintaining that it threatened to tar the women's movement as a whole as "man-hating" and make feminists appear to be antimarriage and antimotherhood. Steinem either disagreed about the risk, or was bold—or rash—enough to forge ahead nonetheless as a matter of principle. Finally, a close look at *Ms.* reveals what is missing: in the context of *Ms.* and the feminism of the time, the feminism was encompassed by the debate between progressive liberals and radicals, largely excluding maverick or alternative visions, such as a conservative feminism. Moral opposition to abortion, for example, was perceived as antiwoman and antifeminist. Despite the movement's best aspirations to sisterhood, not all women's views were tolerated.

Steinem's inclusion of articles that reflected both moderately liberal and radical perspectives in *Ms.*, along with her own creative synthesis of those perspectives, was not sufficient to quell the tensions within the movement, and between the movement and the nonfeminist world at large. The disputes within feminism, and the risks *Ms.* took of alienating some of its readers and advertisers, left *Ms.* losing money by the late 1970s and Steinem with the constant task of promoting and propping up the magazine.[26] Steinem often found herself in the thankless middle, much as Friedan had been. On the one hand, she was under attack from the radical feminists for abandoning radicalism in exchange for commercial or bourgeois success; and on the other hand, from conservative groups for the magazine's allegedly pornographic content.[27] Steinem weathered these and other storms, and in the 1980s and 1990s she continued to play a role at *Ms.* She personally furthered the feminist cause in many ways—for example, by means of charitable foundations, like her *Ms.* Foundation, as well as through an extensive public speaking schedule and her several published books.

Somewhat estranged from the women's movement, Friedan's distance gave her a new point of view from which she measured its achievements. Her observations about the past and future of the movement comprised her second book, *The Second Stage* (1981). Although the ERA had not been ratified, women enjoyed greater opportunity outside the home than ever before. From Friedan's perspective, the women's movement had moved through the first stage: it had overcome the feminine mystique. The women's movement was entering the second stage and its challenge was to dissolve the "*feminist* mystique." Just as the feminine mystique had led women to believe their greatest fulfillment would be found in the home, the feminist mystique led women to believe they would only find satisfaction outside the home. In *The Second Stage*, Friedan presents a frank reconsideration of her own claims about the lives of women. In particular, and most significantly to many women, Friedan returns to her assertion that "it is not as difficult as the feminine mystique implies, to combine marriage and motherhood and even the kind of lifelong personal purpose that once was called 'career'" (*FM* 342). Friedan acknowledges the practical difficulties that women face in balancing their work and their families. Writing in a time of economic uncertainty, Friedan underlines the feminist demand for equality in the work place. It was and remains a matter of survival for many women. Although women were enjoying greater achievements in the work place, Friedan appreciates that the traditional family (i.e., the role of wife and mother) continued to be important to most women. The failure of the women's movement "was our blind spot about the family. It was our own extreme reaction against that wife-mother role: that devotional dependence on men and nurture of children and housewife service which has been and still is the source of power and status and identity, purpose and self worth and economic security for so many women."[28] If the women's movement had not been diverted by sexual politics, it would have been able to address the pressing economic concerns of women and to prevent the alienation felt by many women because the movement seemed to ignore their personal concerns.

Friedan expects that the family will be the new feminist frontier. It is necessary to the women's movement, and to American democracy, to transcend the polarization between equality and family. Extremists on both the Right and the Left had taken advantage of this dichotomy in order to further their own political agendas. Friedan suggests, instead, that women's new experiences should inform new standards at home and at work, such as "flextime." To be sure, greater flexibility in both the home and the office promised to make women's participation in the workplace easier. It would also allow men to spend more time at home and to enjoy their families more than they had in the past. Friedan argues that for the women's movement to be successful in the second stage, both men and women must transcend their traditional gender roles and foster both masculine and feminine qualities.

The Second Stage was criticized from both the political Right and the Left. Given the direction that feminism had taken, Friedan's efforts to restore the importance and the dignity of the family were not well received within feminist circles. Neither were her efforts applauded in conservative circles. Though Friedan advocates the family, she does so with the expectation that traditional masculine and feminine roles need to be transformed. Just as Steinem had weathered these storms, Friedan rose to new challenges. In her third major work, *The Fountain of Age* (1993), Friedan again draws on her own experiences of aging and celebrates the new possibilities in growing older.[29]

Friedan and Steinem dramatically changed the lives and attitudes of Americans with respect to the role of women. Their leadership helped to bring women into American politics and to move women ahead in education and the workplace. By writing and speaking publicly on behalf of women, they increased the awareness of women's status and changed the definition of femininity. They vastly improved women's condition, both public and private. They accomplished these changes by giving serious attention to women's personal experiences. Eschewing the experts, both Friedan and Steinem reported not only on the dissatisfactions in their own lives resulting from the narrow definition of woman but also the lives of the women they met while working for women's equality. In doing so, they gave voice to thousands of American women who had been unheard. Although both placed a great deal of importance on the experience of women, they developed different political interpretations of those experiences. Friedan articulated a more classically liberal position, while Steinem's views moved well to the political Left. Over time, however, the rift between their approaches has closed appreciably. First, it has become plain that both were correct in certain respects. Friedan was right to predict that the increasingly radical face of feminism would engender a backlash; today, many young women espouse—or take for granted—feminist principles such as equal professional opportunities, yet few identify themselves as "feminists." Steinem was correct that women's status is a complex social matter involving multiple forms of subordination. Ending that subordination requires the concerted and diverse political efforts of women in addition to the changes and choices women make in their personal lives. Second, they both have come to see that feminism would have to adapt, even if its new expression departs from their original visions. Friedan has come to a greater appreciation of the economic and social challenges that women's equality involves. Steinem has come to accept the pace of change in a democracy, and indeed, to respect the different goals and different sense of "liberation" held by a new generation of women. Together, Friedan's and Steinem's contributions continue to provide the background for today's discussion about women's full equality and the direction of feminism.

Notes

1. Quotations from and references to Friedan's works are cited in the text using the following abbreviations:

    FM: *The Feminine Mystique* (New York: Bantam Doubleday Dell, 1983).

    MLSF: *My Life So Far* (New York: Simon and Schuster, 2000).

Quotations from and references to Steinem's works are cited in the text using the following abbreviation:

    OAER: *Outrageous Acts and Everyday Rebellions* (New York: Holt, Rinehart, and Wilson, 1983).

2. In *Betty Friedan and the Making of the Feminine Mystique: The American Left, the Cold War, and Modern Feminism* (Amherst: University of Massachusetts Press, 1998), Daniel Horowitz argues that Friedan's participation in the labor movement and the Communist party informs her feminism. According to Horowitz, Friedan was discouraged from greater association with communism by McCarthy-era politics. Friedan maintains that her feminism grew out of her relationship to her mother and her own experiences. Horowitz explains her continued denial of a connection between communism and feminism as a persisting fear of neoconservatives' eagerness to discredit her, in particular, and feminism, more generally.

3. Hannah Arendt, *On Revolution* (New York: Viking Press, 1963), 28 and 45.

4. Mariani Farnham and Ferdinand Lundberg, *Modern Women: The Lost Sex* (New York: Harper and Brothers, 1947).

5. Sydney Ladensohn Stern, *Gloria Steinem: Her Passions, Politics and Mystique* (Secaucus, N.J.: Birch Lane Press, 1997), 196–97.

6. The proposed Equal Rights Amendment reads as follows in its entirety: "1. Equality of rights under the law shall not be denied or abridged by the United States or by any State on account of sex. 2. Congress shall have the power to enforce by appropriate legislation the provisions of this article. 3. This amendment shall take effect two years after the date of ratification." For a discussion of the ERA in the context of the Constitution, see Dorothy McBride Stetson, *Women's Rights in the U.S.A.: Policy Debates and Gender* (Pacific Grove, Calif.: Brooks/Cole Publishing Company, 1991).

7. Stern, *Gloria Steinem*, 11–12.

8. Stern, *Gloria Steinem*, 8–9.

9. After her mother's death, Steinem movingly described this ordeal in "Ruth's Song (Because She Could Not Sing It)" (*OAER* 129–46).

10. *Current Biography Yearbook* (New York: H. W. Wilson Co., 1988), 543.

11. See Stern, *Gloria Steinem*, 209ff., for discussion of Steinem's good looks in relation to the movement.

12. Stern, *Gloria Steinem*, 186–87.

13. Stern, *Gloria Steinem*, 188.

14. We must ask, too, what her feminist insight was. Stern, *Gloria Steinem*, 191–92, writes that "[i]n a sense, seeing gender used as a caste system is exactly what the feminist realization was" and that "[f]eminism provided Gloria with an ideology that so comprehensively explained her life to her that it would not be an exaggeration to say she became a feminist fundamentalist. Everything could be explained and judged with that belief system." While Stern is correct that the early feminist framework Steinem adopted was both very comprehensive and simple, allowing for quick explanations and denunciations, Stern also notes that Steinem "never lost her visceral reaction. She responded instinctively to women in need." Steinem's feminism was not simply ideological.

15. As feminism in the second half of the twentieth century was called, to distinguish it from "first wave" American feminism and its fight for suffrage.

16. Stern, *Gloria Steinem*, 193–94.

17. Stern, *Gloria Steinem*, 210–11.

18. *Time*, August 26, 1970.

19. *It Changed My Life: Writings on the Women's Movement* (New York: Random House, 1976), 158.

20. For Steinem as a role model, see Stern, *Gloria Steinem*, 226; for Steinem as the "intellectual's pinup," see Leonard Levitt, "SHE," *Esquire* (October 1971), cited in Stern, *Gloria Steinem*, 230.

21. Stern, *Gloria Steinem*, 241.

22. Stern, *Gloria Steinem*, 262–63.

23. These books include *Outrageous Acts and Everyday Rebellions* (1983); *Marilyn* (New York: H. P. Holt, 1986); *Revolution from Within: A Book of Self-Esteem* (Boston: Little, Brown, and Co., 1992); and *Moving Beyond Words* (New York: Simon and Schuster, 1994).

24. The magazine was initially published as an inset of *New York* magazine in December 1971 and then launched independently in the spring of 1972. Page references in the text are to the inaugural issue.

25. It could be argued that Steinem not only changed feminism, but that she, and feminism, helped change the shape of liberalism in the United States. She infused radical or progressive elements into the message of women's liberation which originally claimed the liberal principles of equality and self-determination for women. Her synthesis of the liberal and radical outlooks in journalism brought several key ideas from radical politics to popular attention; Steinem's presentation, in writing and in her public speaking engagements, made them seem sensible and acceptable. Indeed, many of these ideas, such as systematic subordination of women and minorities, are now a regular dimension of liberal politics.

26. See Stern, *Gloria Steinem*, chap. 25, on the difficulties *Ms.*'s advertising policies generated with potential advertisers.

27. See Stern, *Gloria Steinem*, chap. 26, on the radical feminist attack, including Betty Friedan's making common cause with some radicals against Steinem's supposed early CIA involvement, as well as 285–86 on efforts to ban the magazine made by some right-wing groups in the late 1970s.

28. Betty Friedan, *The Second Stage* (Cambridge, Mass.: Harvard University Press, 1998).

29. Betty Friedan, *The Fountain of Age* (New York: Simon and Schuster, 1993).

Chapter 42

John Rawls's "Democratic" Theory of Justice

David Lewis Schaefer

I

John Rawls (1921–2002) was one of the most influential American democratic theorists of the twentieth century. His work, in comparison with that of most prominent political thinkers, has a peculiarly academic character. As signified by the title of his major book, *A Theory of Justice* (1971), Rawls approaches political issues from the standpoint of "theory," aiming to enunciate a set of principles that will promote greater agreement among people's judgments of justice. His practical goal is to bring about a "well-ordered" society that is "effectively regulated by a public conception of justice" that "everyone accepts," so that even "among individuals with disparate aims and purposes," the "general desire for justice limits the pursuit of other ends" (4–5).[1]

The "main idea" of Rawls's theory is to employ the social contract device adopted by such modern philosophers as Locke, Rousseau, and Kant, but raise it "to a higher level of abstraction." Whereas those thinkers used the social contract to explain how and why human beings who are naturally free and equal could be understood to have imposed a particular sort of government on themselves so as better to secure their particular interests, Rawls employs it to determine the "principles of justice for the basic structure of society" that would be agreed on by "free and rational persons concerned to further their own interests . . . in an initial position of equality." He calls this approach "justice as fairness" (11).

The "original position of equality" is Rawls's substitute for what previous contract theorists termed the state of nature. Unlike his predecessors, Rawls does not represent the original position as reflecting human nature, much less any actual historical condition. Rather, it is designed "*so as* to lead to a certain conception of justice" (11, emphasis added).[2]

What then underlies the particular conception of justice that the original position is designed to produce? On the one hand, Rawls "assume[s] . . . a broad measure of agreement that principles of justice should be chosen under certain conditions," notably that "no one should be advantaged or disadvantaged by natural fortune or social circumstances" in the choice, and that it should not be influenced by people's particular "conceptions of the good." On the other hand, any proposed set of principles can be tested by whether they "match our considered convictions of justice," in that they "would lead us to make the same judgments about the basic structure of society which we now make intuitively and in which we have the greatest confidence" or in doubtful cases "offer a resolution which we can affirm on reflection" (16–17). This latter mode of testing and validation seems modeled on the practice of legal reasoning, in which judges faced with a series of precedents attempt to articulate principles that would explain the courts' previous decisions,

713

while generating an intuitively satisfying decision in the case before them. (But as we shall note, there are important differences from the common law approach.)

Rawls argues for the superiority of his account of justice to three rival theories that he labels perfectionism, utilitarianism, and intuitionism. Both perfectionism and utilitarianism are "teleological" theories, which define what is right or just "as that which maximizes the good" (20–22). While perfectionism conceives the good as "the realization of human excellence in the various forms of culture" (a doctrine that Rawls attributes to Aristotle and Nietzsche), utilitarianism defines it as "the satisfaction of rational desire" (22–23). According to Rawls, the central defect of utilitarianism (and perhaps of perfectionism as well) is that it is unconcerned with how the sum of satisfactions in a society is distributed among individuals, opening the possibility that some people would be required to sacrifice their own good, including their freedom, for the sake of the greater good enjoyed by others. Thus, it "does not take seriously the distinction between persons" (23–24).

In contrast to teleological theories of justice, Rawls's theory is a "deontological" one which makes justice "prior" to the good: it allows the pursuit of the good only insofar as is compatible with the primacy of justice, and restricts the satisfaction of people's "propensities and inclinations" accordingly (26–27). But justice as fairness is also distinct from another deontological theory, intuitionism, which holds "that there is an irreducible family of first principles which have to be weighed against one another" to identify a just policy in particular situations, without providing "priority rules" for determining the balance (30). In contrast, justice as fairness limits the role of intuition by establishing priority rules among the principles of justice and by specifying a particular standpoint from which a social system is to be judged (37, 39).

Rawls proposes a set of two principles of justice that he maintains would be chosen in the original position. As stated in the revised edition of *A Theory of Justice* (slightly condensed), they are as follows:

> First: each person is to have an equal right to the most extensive total system of equal basic liberties compatible with a similar liberty for all.
> Second: social and economic inequalities are to be arranged so that they are both (a) to the greatest benefit of the least advantaged . . . and (b) attached to offices and positions open to all under conditions of fair equality of opportunity. (266)[3]

According to a priority rule Rawls attaches to the principles, they are ideally "to be ranked in lexical order," meaning that the first principle must be satisfied before recourse is made to the second; thus, "liberty can be restricted only for the sake of liberty," not for the sake of social and economic goods (266).[4] The basic liberties secured by the first principle include "political liberty (the right to vote and to be eligible for public office) and freedom of speech and assembly; liberty of conscience and freedom of thought; freedom of the person, . . . the right to hold (personal) property, and freedom from arbitrary arrest and seizure as defined by the concept of the rule of law" (53).

Rawls attributes the priority of liberty to a common sense conviction of the "inviolability" of each individual that may not be overridden for the sake of society's aggregate welfare (24–25). The second principle is intended "to mitigate the influence of social contingencies and natural fortune" on people's "distributive shares." Rawls believes that the last part of this principle, mandating fair equality of opportunity, reflects a widely shared recognition of the need to prevent "excessive accumulations of property and wealth" and to maintain "equal opportunities of education for all." But even this "liberal" principle "intuitively . . . seems defective" by itself, since it permits economic gains "to be determined by the natural distribution of abilities and talents" among the populace, an outcome that "is arbitrary from a moral perspective" (63–64).

Hence arises the most novel aspect of Rawls's theory: the rule that social and economic inequalities are legitimate only if they improve "the expectations of the least advantaged members of society," which he calls the "difference principle" (65). The ground of this principle is that since "inequalities of birth and natural endowment are undeserved," they "call for redress." It presupposes a willingness "to regard the distribution of natural talents" among human beings as "a common asset," so that "those who have been favored by nature . . . gain from their good fortune only on terms that improve the situation of those who have lost out" (86–87).[5] And it promotes the spirit of fraternity, making fellow citizens like members of a family who, Rawls maintains, "commonly do not wish to gain" except "in ways that further the interests of the rest" (90).

Having outlined the intuitive grounds for his principles, Rawls attempts to demonstrate that they would be chosen in the original position. He designs this situation to include "conditions that are widely thought reasonable to impose on the choice of principles," while "lead[ing] to a conception that characterizes our considered judgments in reflective equilibrium" (105). He first summarizes "the circumstances of justice" in which principles are to be chosen: human beings are viewed as sufficiently "similar in physical and mental powers" that "no one among them can dominate the rest," as "vulnerable to attack," and as existing in a condition of "moderate scarcity" of resources. They have "roughly similar" or complementary "needs and interests," but also hold distinct conceptions of the good entailing "different ends and purposes" and hence a "diversity of philosophical and religious belief, and of political and social doctrines" (109–10). But to prevent the parties in the original position from biasing the selection of principles to favor themselves or their particular conception of the good, Rawls supposes that their choice is made under a "veil of ignorance." No one knows "his class position or social status," his "natural assets and abilities," "his conception of the good . . . or even the special features of his psychology such as his aversion to risk." Moreover, "the parties do not know the particular circumstances of their own society," such as "its economic or political situation" or "level of civilization and culture," or even "to which generation they belong." They know only "the general facts about human society," including "political affairs and the principles of economic theory . . . and the laws of human psychology" (118–19).

The final step in preparing the original position is to adopt an index of primary social goods in terms of which the choosing parties assess rival theories of justice. Even though they are ignorant of their particular views of the good, Rawls judges it rational for the parties to suppose that they each want the largest possible share of primary goods, which include "rights, liberties, and opportunities, and income and wealth" and "a sense of one's own worth," which is "perhaps the most important" such good (79, 123, 386).[6] (Although it may turn out that the conception of the good that some people hold once the veil of ignorance is removed does not entail a desire to maximize these primary goods, such maximization cannot hurt them in Rawls's estimation since "they are not compelled to accept more if they do not wish to" [123].)

Given the foregoing assumptions, Rawls argues that his two principles would be adopted in the original position because they represent "the maximin solution to the problem of social justice." The maximin rule ranks alternatives "by their worst possible outcomes," favoring the policy that guarantees the least well-off person a satisfactory minimum rather than aiming at higher gains at the risk of greater losses (132–34). From this perspective the two principles, which guarantee equal liberties to all and maximize the social and economic well-being of the least advantaged, seem a far safer bet than utilitarianism, which might be interpreted to justify oppressing or enslaving some individuals for the sake of the greater happiness of others (145–47).[7]

Having spelled out the reasoning that would lead persons in the original position to agree on the two principles, Rawls endeavors in Part II of *A Theory of Justice* to demonstrate that the principles "define a workable political conception, and are a reasonable approximation to and extension of our considered judgments" (171). He describes the application of the two principles successively at the level of constitutional design, for which the principle of equal liberty is the primary standard; the legislative stage, where the second principle is operative, subject to the priority of the first; and the "application of rules to particular cases by judges and administrators" along with the decision by individual citizens of whether to obey those rules as applied (174–75). As was true of the original position, Rawls's account of these stages is intended not as an empirical description of political decision making but as a theoretical construct for illustrating a just political order (173n2).

In applying the first principle, Rawls aims "to bypass the dispute about the meaning of liberty" between "proponents of negative and positive liberty," for instance, since this debate is really concerned with "the relative values of the several liberties when they come into conflict" (176). He suggests rather formalistically that such conflicts be resolved simply by increasing one liberty to the point where the marginal gain balances out the loss from limiting another one (202). To illustrate how his principles of justice "guarantee a secure protection for the equal liberties," however, Rawls discusses the grounds for freedom of conscience. He argues that "equal liberty of conscience is the only principle that the persons in the original position can acknowledge." Being ignorant of their particular religious or moral convictions, they "cannot take chances with their liberty" by adopting a principle that would allow "the dominant religious or moral doctrine to suppress others." Rawls finds it "unnecessary . . . to argue against" the contention that people's religious duties supersede the principle of equal liberty, since "an understanding of religious obligations and of philosophical and moral first principles shows that we cannot expect others to acquiesce in an inferior liberty" (180–82).

Thus a just constitution must guarantee equal liberty of conscience for all citizens, and government is prohibited from favoring any particular religion, or from favoring religion as such over atheism. Rawls rejects the arguments of Locke and Rousseau for limiting religious tolera-tion for the sake of public order as based on insufficient "historical experience" (186, 189–90). And he suggests that the principles of justice can likewise "adjudicate between opposing moralities" by promoting an attitude of toleration (194).

Turning to political justice, the principle of equal liberty dictates that all citizens have an equal right to participate in and determine the outcome of the lawmaking process. Though the constitution may limit an elected legislature's powers, "in due course a firm majority of the electorate" must be able to achieve its aims (194–95). To "preserve the fair value" of the equal political liberties in a society that allows private ownership of the means of production, "property and wealth must be kept widely distributed and government monies provided . . . to encourage free public discussion." "Historically," Rawls observes, "one of the main defects of constitutional government" has been the toleration of "disparities in the distribution of property and wealth that far exceed what is compatible with political equality" (198–99).

At the legislative stage, Rawls stresses that since the two principles derive from an "ideal of the person" and of a just society, they settle "the long range aim of society . . . irrespective of the particular desires and needs of its present members" and set "limits on the conception of the good" they may pursue (230–31). While emphasizing that economic inequalities must conform to the difference principle, he adds that justice does not inherently favor a market economy over "a liberal socialist regime" (239–42, 246). Indeed, Rawls does not reject outright the arguments of Burke and Hegel on behalf of hereditary aristocracy; he comments only that to be persuasive, their claim "that the whole of society including the least favored benefit from certain restrictions on equality of opportunity" must be supplemented by demonstrating that to eliminate these inequalities would specifically hamper the long-term opportunities of the disadvantaged (264–65). Even though, as he acknowledges, "it is a political convention of a democratic society to appeal to the common interest," Rawls holds that it is most consistent with the democratic "ethos" to focus policies on benefitting the least advantaged (280–81). Finally, he explains why the perfectionist principle dictating that society be organized "to maximize the achievement of human excellence in art, science, and culture" must be rejected: since persons in the original position lack "an agreed criterion of perfection," they cannot define justice in terms of its achievement. (It is acceptable to expend public funds to promote artistic and scientific excellence only through an "exchange branch" to which each contributing taxpayer has specifically authorized this use of his funds. But Rawls adds, somewhat obscurely, that "the principles of justice do not permit subsidizing universities and institutes, or opera and the theater" unless such activities help "secure the equal liberties" and assist "the least advantaged") (286–87, 291–92).

At the stage of individual compliance with the law, Rawls enunciates a doctrine of "civil disobedience and conscientious refusal" (309). When citizens agreed to be bound by a constitution embodying the majority principle, he holds, they can have done so only on the assumption that "in the long run the burden of injustice should be evenly distributed over different groups in society, and the hardship of unjust policies should not weigh too heavily in any particular case" (312). And they retain a right to civil disobedience, understood "as a public, nonviolent, conscientious" violation of law aimed at bringing about a change in the government's policies (320), and to the conscientious refusal to comply with a legal injunction or administrative order (323). While acknowledging a possible "limit on the extent to which civil disobedience can be engaged in without leading to a breakdown in the respect for law and the constitution," Rawls observes that "if justified civil disobedience seems to threaten civic concord, the responsibility falls . . . upon those whose abuse of authority and power justifies such opposition" (328, 342). He does not address the problem of *un*justified civil disobedience.

The last part of *A Theory of Justice* elaborates the "theory of the good" that was used to characterize "the interests of the persons in the original position," argues that justice and goodness are "congruent" in a well-ordered society, and shows "how the theory of justice connects up with . . . the good of community" (347). Whereas in formulating the principles of justice Rawls relied on a "thin theory" of the good which assumed the utility of primary goods for all plans of life, he now employs those principles to develop a "full theory" of the human good (348). This will enable him to show that acting in accordance with the principles of justice "is a good thing" for the agent (349).

Fundamental to Rawls's understanding of the good is the notion that happiness consists in the "successful execution . . . of a rational plan of life." But rationality has only an instrumental sense, that is, the selection of apt means to achieving one's ends. Since "different individuals find their happiness in doing different things," reason cannot judge the relative value of those ends, and all citizens should be "left free to determine their good" (359, 393). For instance, for a person "whose only pleasure is to count blades of grass," the good "is indeed counting blades of grass" (379). Whatever one's ends, however, Rawls is confident that justice as fairness best meets the requirement that a rational person "always . . . act so that he need never blame himself no matter how his plans finally work out," since the standpoint of the original position guarantees that even the least advantaged person is better off than he could have been under any other scheme (371). And since Rawlsian justice precludes publicly assessing the relative value of different people's ways of life, it engenders a "democracy in judging each other's aims" that "is the foundation of self-respect" for all individuals, whose happiness depends on knowing that others appreciate their endeavors (388). Even though existing societies may be tarnished, for instance, by the majority's prohibiting "certain religious or sexual practices" that it finds abhorrent, justice as fairness requires that we move as speedily as possible toward just institutions that will protect the right of individuals to engage in whatever such practices they wish (so long as they do not violate others' equal liberty) (291, 395).

Rawls next proceeds to demonstrate the "stability" of a well-ordered society based on the principles of justice (397). He explains that since such a society will eliminate "arbitrary authority," its members should "suffer much less from the burdens of oppressive conscience" and hence find it easier to regulate their behavior by their sense of justice (429). Knowing that a just society reflects "the unconditional concern of other persons and institutions for our good . . . must strengthen our self-esteem." It engenders "a closer affiliation" with them as well as a "love of humankind" (437–38).

At this point, Rawls elaborates "the basis of equality," that is, "the features of human beings in virtue of which they are to be treated in accordance with the principles of justice." The two chief such features are their presumed capacities to have a conception of their good and "a sense of justice, a normally effective desire to apply and to act upon the principles of justice, at least to a minimum degree." But even if some people lack the latter capacity, "it would be unwise in practice to withhold justice [from them] on this ground," since "[t]he risk to just institutions would be too great." And granted the prudent assumption that all persons have "a certain minimum" moral capacity, all are entitled to equal liberty; a greater such capacity is simply "a natural asset like any other ability" and hence calls for no special reward (441–43).

The final obstacle to the full realization of fair equality of opportunity is the family, since some individuals (we note) inevitably profit from the morally arbitrary advantage of having parents who are wealthier, better educated, or more loving (265, 448). But "within the context of the theory of justice as a whole," "there is much less urgency" about working to abolish the family, since the difference principle "redefines the grounds for social inequalities": those who receive lesser genetic or familial endowments are psychologically compensated by knowing that the differences "are made to work to [their] advantage" (448).

In his last chapter, Rawls undertakes to demonstrate "the good of justice" by showing that justice as fairness harmonizes with "goodness as rationality" (450). He first explains how the moral instruction that shapes citizens of the well-ordered society, far from violating their freedom, conforms to principles that "best express their nature as free and equal rational beings" (452). Constraining each individual to act in accordance with those principles rather than the dictates of his "erring conscience" exhibits our respect for him "as a person" (455).

Besides the respect thus given to human freedom, the two principles help perfect "the social nature of mankind" as well as man's character as a "historical being" (458–60). The well-ordered society "is a social union of social unions" in which all members "realize their own and another's nature" through joint activities that the principles of justice permit. (The historical aspect reflects the dependence of their achievements on those of prior generations.) In accordance with the principle of "democracy in the assessment of one another's excellences," the activities of various particular associations are not "rank[ed] in value." But as a consequence of knowing that all citizens "act from principles to which all would agree in an initial situation of equality," it can be said (as Socrates maintains in describing the "best city" in Plato's *Republic* [462c–d]) that "all find satisfaction in the very same thing" (461).

One obstacle to this totalization of community—since Rawls's well-ordered society, unlike Socrates', still permits the ownership of private property (as well as, provisionally, the existence of private families)—might be the passion of envy. But even though "in theory the difference principle permits indefinitely large inequalities in return for small gains to the less favored," Rawls is confident that "the spread of income and wealth should not be excessive." Moreover, since "we tend to compare our circumstances with others in the same or in a similar group as ourselves," and in a well-ordered society "the more advantaged do not make an ostentatious display of their higher estate," Rawls anticipates that the members of such a society will "take little interest in their relative position as such." Above all, "the need for status is met by the public recognition of just institutions" which assure all citizens of their own worth (470, 477).

As Rawls's demonstration of "the good of justice" approaches its culmination, the radically communal character of his claims is combined in a remarkable manner with a quasi-Nietzschean, though also neo-Kantian, doctrine of the "self." "The self," Rawls explains, "is prior to the ends which are affirmed by it" (491). Each person in a just society is understood to "fashion his own unity" rather than act in accordance with a preexistent natural unity that he finds in himself. But he does so only *within* the "essential unity of the self [that] is already provided by the conception of right" (493). Taken together, these remarks suggest that the doctrine of right or justice is itself a human construction, by which mankind imposes meaning on an otherwise arbitrary universe or, as Rawls puts it, gives "the self free reign" over "the contingencies and accidents of the world" (503).[8] As a result, the priority of the self proves in a well-ordered society to be identical with the unity of the species:

> [I]n a well-ordered society this unity [of the self] is the same for all; everyone's conception of the good as given by his rational plan is a subplan of the larger comprehensive plan that regulates the community as a social union of social unions. The many associations . . . being adjusted to one another by the public conception of justice, simplify decision by offering definite ideals and forms of life that have been developed and tested by innumerable individuals, sometimes for generations. Thus in drawing up our plan of life we do not start de novo; we are not required to choose from countless possibilities without given structure or fixed contours. (493–94)

Because "the priority of right and justice securely constrains" people's deliberations about their good, we need not fear that they will aim at a good that violates justice. Rather, as we "participate in one another's nature" through cooperation in a just society, "the self is realized in the activities of many selves" (494–95). As Rawls conceives the just social order, it is apparently impossible for human beings to form associations ("factions" in the language of *The Federalist* no. 10) whose goals are antithetical to one another, or to the common good. The just society, it appears, is effectively beyond politics.[9]

At last, in a manner that formally parallels Socrates' endeavor in Book IX of the *Republic*, Rawls addresses the question of whether being "guided by the standpoint of justice accords with the individual's good" (497). The case against injustice includes the "psychological costs" of having to deceive others; the difficulty of avoiding doing harm to those dear to oneself in a well-ordered society where people's "ties of affection and fellow feeling . . . extend rather widely"; and being deprived of the "great good" that comes from "participating in the life" of such a society. Positively, "acting justly is something we want to do as free and equal rational beings" so as "to express our nature as free moral persons" (499–501).

Any persons who nonetheless find that "the affirmation of their sense of justice is not a good" for them may justly be threatened with penalties to make them comply with the rules of justice, Rawls holds, since they benefit from other people's observance of those rules. Should just arrangements "not fully answer to their nature," Rawls responds, "their nature is their misfortune." (In other words, we are tempted to say, if you're the kind of person for whom justice as fairness is good, then justice as fairness is good for you.) But Rawls is confident that "granted a reasonable interpretation of human sociability," it will seldom be necessary to invoke "constraining arrangements to insure compliance" (503–5). It is hard to know what this confidence rests on.

II

Considering Rawls's aim and his findings, the acclaim that *A Theory of Justice* has won in the academic world is not surprising. Not only does Rawls appear to supply concrete political content to an Anglo-American school of philosophizing that had often been judged merely abstract and "irrelevant" to actual human life but his specific political program also appeals to beliefs that are widely held in the contemporary academic community. (Even academics who dissent from Rawls's redistributionist economic program often share the libertarianism he espouses in other spheres of life, denying government the authority to favor religion over irreligion or to regulate people's sexual "life styles" in the name of a particular vision of the good.)[10] But to assess his teaching we need to look beyond the academic horizon and ask how far his account of justice genuinely advances our understanding, and promises to promote the well-being of a citizenry governed by it.

To this end, we must reconsider the difference between the "original position," from which Rawls professes to derive the principles of justice, and the state of nature, as described in somewhat varying terms by such philosophers as Hobbes, Locke, and Rousseau, on which the original position is loosely modeled. As noted, what most obviously sets the original position apart from previous accounts of the state of nature is that Rawls does not base his description on an empirical analysis of the most powerful tendencies in human nature. That only Rousseau, of the philosophers just named, represented his description of the state of nature as historical is beside the point in this regard: as Hobbes remarks, even though the entirety of mankind may never have lived in a nonpolitical condition, his account (as Locke also argues) represents a recurrent real possibility, as seen in the relation among nations, and, more important, among individuals in times of civic chaos. Moreover, the reader can readily test Hobbes's account of what life would be like without government by extrapolating from his own everyday conduct and the judgments it implies about how other human beings would behave in the absence of government.[11] For each of these philosophers (as well as for Kant, whom Rawls cites as a model), consideration of the state of nature is essential to assessing the legitimacy of any particular political order, because it enables us to test the conformity of such an order to our natural needs.

Rawls, of course, claims that even though the original position has no foundation in human nature, determining the principles of justice that would be chosen in such a condition has moral relevance, inasmuch as it embodies conditions that are "fair." And he maintains that one "can at any time . . . simulate the deliberations of this hypothetical situation, simply by reasoning in accordance with the appropriate restrictions" (138). But both these claims embody serious difficulties.

To begin with, it is not at all evident that any actual human being can simulate what it would be like to reason under the veil of ignorance. To *imagine* that one has suspended awareness of one's "place in society," his "natural assets," his "conception of the good," and "the special features of his psychology," so as to issue judgments from "the perspective of eternity" (514), is quite different from succeeding in doing so. How can Rawls or anyone else know what judgments he would make under conditions that remove all substantive character from his "self"?[12] What ground can anyone have for believing that his judgments of justice can somehow be made independent of his psychology or his view of what is good? Beyond this, what can it mean to know "the general facts about human society" while somehow forgetting the actual facts of one's own society? Does not our "general" knowledge of human things originate in, and require constant testing against, our particular, everyday experience?

These epistemological problems aside, it is not apparent why anyone should regard the parties to the original position as "representing" himself or any human being. What would a being be like who lacked awareness of his specific character, capacities, or beliefs? Why should any actual human being be influenced in his moral judgment by what he thinks such beings would choose?

A vast literature has noted difficulties in the reasoning by which Rawls purports to derive his principles from the original position—for instance, his recommending them as "those a person would choose for the design of a society in which his enemy is to assign him his place," even though persons in the original position are *not* supposed to "assume that their initial place in society is decided by a malevolent opponent" (133).[13] Another major problem in this derivation is the index of primary goods that Rawls invents as a substitute for people's actual but unknown conceptions of the good. Rawls's claim that it is rational to maximize one's share of such goods, regardless of whether one ultimately cares for them, since no one is forced to accept them, passes over the problem that from the standpoint, say, of a believer in biblical religion, not all forms of liberty are beneficial to society as a whole, and a surfeit of wealth can have the harmful effect of diverting people from the things that really matter. (The same is true from a "communitarian" perspective like Rousseau's, or that of the civic republicans of early modernity.) What ground can Rawls have for dismissing such concerns?[14]

Of course, it is of the essence of liberalism, as seen in the Declaration of Independence and other Founding documents, to emphasize securing people's rights to life, liberty, and property rather than imposing a particular religious doctrine or conception of the good on the citizenry. But nothing in the Declaration or Constitution mandates that government adopt an official position of neutrality between religion and irreligion, let alone avoid encouraging certain substantively moral or admirable ways of life over others.[15]

In other respects, Rawls's doctrine passes well beyond American constitutional liberalism in an antiliberal direction. To prohibit the more talented or industrious from gaining except on terms that serve not merely the common good but the particular benefit of the least advantaged has no ground in the Constitution, and directly violates the natural right of all individuals to the pursuit of happiness that is specified in the Declaration. The same can be said of Rawls's mandate for "democracy in judging one another's aims," an outgrowth of contemporary relativism rather than of any provision of the Declaration or Constitution. Granted that self-respect is an essential component of happiness, Rawls's contention that it is chiefly or entirely dependent on how one is regarded by others would seem to undermine instead of encourage the spirit of self-reliance that a free society presupposes.[16] Who could possibly feel pride, we must ask, because his activities are publicly valued at the same level as those of someone who devoted his life to counting blades of grass? Indeed, how far is self-respect something that government or society can "distribute" to human beings at all?

Beyond these difficulties, the reasoning by which Rawls derives specific political consequences from his principles of justice is critically flawed in two respects. First, if one can imagine persons reasoning about how religious beliefs and practices should be treated while under a veil of ignorance, it seems far more plausible to suppose they would conclude that government should support and encourage whatever religion seems (once the veil is lifted) most likely to be *true* rather than that it should treat all religious beliefs with strict impartiality. (This goes as well for judgments of people's moral well-being, which Rawls arbitrarily excludes on account of the absence of a criterion of perfection, only to substitute his own unsupported view of the human good in Part III.) Surely a far better case for broad religious toleration can be found in such substantive writings as Locke's *Letter Concerning Toleration* and the Virginia Statute on Religious Freedom drafted by Thomas Jefferson, neither of which depends on any veil of ignorance. (Such writings also take account of the possible pragmatic reasons for limiting toleration that Rawls dismisses without argument.)[17]

The second critical flaw relates to the ground of the difference principle. If no one can be said to "deserve" his natural assets, why should anyone (including the least advantaged) be said to deserve their fruits? Moreover, if, as the difference principle supposes, the natural assets of different individuals are to be regarded as commonly owned, even while their possessors retain them, why should it not follow that the gains people make as a consequence of their talents (or of other causes) are enjoyed no less in common, even as their acquirers most directly profit? (In other words, why bother to redistribute them?)[18] Does not the ground of the difference principle embody the very fault Rawls found in utilitarianism of failing to "take seriously the distinction between persons"?

For the foregoing reasons, Rawls's claim to derive his interpretation of justice from an original position of equality is dubious. In addition, consideration must be given to the substantive difficulties that those principles embody.

With respect to the first principle, Rawls's avoidance of trying to determine how the various forms of protected liberty should be balanced against one another—notably, the relative weight of political and individual liberty—makes it doubtful that the asserted priority of liberty offers much help in resolving the fundamental controversies that arise in a liberal political order. (Especially troubling in this connection is Rawls's curious doctrine of the "fair value" of political liberty, which devalues such liberty to the extent it fails to secure the unlikely goal of equalizing all individuals' political influence [197–98, 246].)[19] Beyond this, Rawls's notion that a proper understanding of liberty prohibits government from banning sexual relationships that are thought to be "degrading and shameful" (prostitution? incest? polygamy? bestiality?) goes well beyond even the most libertarian Supreme Court decisions.[20] Particularly striking (although reminiscent of Kant) is Rawls's attempt to combine a morally libertarian program with the language of moral duty. Surely we must wonder how far a people raised and governed in accordance with that program could possibly acquire the fortitude of character necessary to maintain and defend a system of liberty, however understood.

Rawls's consignment of *economic* rights and freedoms to a lower priority than noneconomic forms of liberty similarly departs from the American Founders' understanding, although it has a relatively recent jurisprudential counterpart in the "preferred position" doctrine first enunciated by the Court in the 1930s. That doctrine is open to question because it disregards the interdependence *between* economic freedom and other forms of liberty.[21] Nor does Rawls seem adequately to have worked out the relation between his principle of fair equality of opportunity and other aspects of liberty: how far is the mandate that one's class position not affect his educational opportunities compatible with the freedom of parents to raise their children as they wish (63)? Would not that mandate, for instance, require the outlawing of private schools?[22]

Most obvious are the difficulties entailed by the difference principle. Practically speaking, Rawls gives little evidence of having thought through his notion of the "least advantaged" when he ordains that all social and economic inequalities be organized to improve their lot. How do we determine which class is the least advantaged—the poorest? the physically or mentally handicapped? the friendless? victims of massacres abroad? Should we focus our energies only on serving the one percent of the population who are least advantaged, or should they have to share their gains with, say, the next four percent? Finally, what is meant by "social" inequalities, and how far is it within government's capacity to remedy them?[23] And if the good of self-respect is most important yet chiefly dependent on how one is regarded by others, should not this social good have been given priority along with the rights and liberties covered by the first principle?[24]

There is a marked contrast between the rather conventional welfare-statist practices that Rawls himself generally infers from the difference principle and the Nietzschean rhetoric in which it is sometimes couched.[25] (The very use of that rhetoric is remarkable in view of the fact that the entirely socialized vision of the human species that Rawls enunciates in Part III appears reflective of the outlook most despised by Nietzsche, that of the "last man.")[26] One wonders how far Rawls has considered the implications of his project of compensating for the arbitrariness of nature or fortune: could even the fullest effort to alleviate the lot of the least advantaged (however defined) seriously mitigate the seeming arbitrariness of the fate of individuals? Despite the relative mildness of his specific political proposals, does not Rawls's endeavor to remake the world so as to overcome its arbitrariness reflect the same dangerously utopian spirit, arising in the wake of the "death" of God, that characterized the totalitarian ideologies that generated so much evil during the twentieth century?[27]

But what then of Rawls's claim that his approach is a necessary safeguard against theories like utilitarianism and perfectionism, which threaten to sacrifice the rights of some or the good of many, respectively, to the satisfaction of many and the perfection of the few? The short answer is that there is no evidence that either of these theories, in the sense given them by Rawls, ever has had or is likely to have significant influence on public policy; but, to the extent that serious objections can be raised to the principles of liberty and equality on grounds of human excellence or the common good, Rawls really has no response to them. With respect to utilitarianism in particular, who (outside the groves of academe) would argue that a certain policy should be adopted because it would raise the average utility or "net balance of satisfaction" in a society, though at the cost of inflicting great suffering on a few individuals?[28]

Within the history of political philosophy, cogent arguments have indeed been made against the liberal principles of universal liberty and equality. But the force of these arguments is hardly to be defeated by saying that they violate principles that "we" find intuitively appealing. In fact, as we have seen, Rawls himself does not maintain that the arguments put forth by such thinkers as Burke and Hegel to the effect that the common good is best served by a relatively open hereditary aristocracy are incompatible with his difference principle, but merely adds the requirement that they *also* show that such inequalities particularly benefit the least advantaged. (It is hard to see how even the least advantaged could benefit in the long run from policies that *detracted* from the overall good of the society of which they are members.) Contrariwise, although Rawls criticizes John Stuart Mill's arguments for liberty based on its substantive benefits to human beings because those arguments will not necessarily "justify an equal liberty for all," and claims that by contrast "justice as fairness provides strong arguments for equal liberty" (184), Rawls, unlike Mill, does not actually provide an argument for liberty, but merely asserts its intuitive appeal.

The contrast between the substantive arguments made by thinkers such as Burke, Hegel, and Mill about the nature of the good society and Rawls's formalism is enormous. It is evident that grounding political society in a particular religious faith, in the collective pursuit of military glory, or in the cultivation of literary and artistic excellence instead of maximizing Rawlsian primary goods would run contrary to the "intuitive" judgments of representative inhabitants of liberal societies. But is it not the fundamental task of philosophy to question rather than presuppose the dominant assumptions of one's time? Should not a philosophic defender of liberalism offer substantive reasons that may persuade those not already committed to his cause? And even for partisans of liberalism, is there not much merit to Aristotle's observation that one best preserves a particular regime not by pushing its defining principle to an extreme, but rather by moderating it with institutions and practices based on plausible alternative principles?[29] This, at any rate, appears to have been the perspective of the American Founders.[30]

Rather than represent an improvement on the constitutional liberalism of the Founders, Rawls's theory constitutes a decayed variant of liberalism, obviously parasitic on the teachings of Locke and Rousseau (which explains why Rawls's "intuitions" favor liberty and equality), yet shorn of the solidity of the Lockean doctrine of natural rights as a security for liberty, the practical realism of Locke's and the Founders' outlooks, and Rousseau's hardheaded treatment of the requisites of community and civic virtue. None of these thinkers tried to make justice prior to the good, because they recognized, as Aristotle had observed long before, that all human beings by nature seek what they believe is good for themselves, and that anyone who *professes* to put justice ahead of goodness is liable to self-deception, and to providing truly unjust men with a mask to cover their intentions.[31] Justice can endure only if it is given a real foundation in human nature and in institutions that take account of that nature—not an abstract, constructed "nature" of hypothetical beings who lack the defining attributes of humanity. "Moral theory" as Rawls conceives it appears a poor substitute for substantive political philosophy.

III

We can look only briefly at Rawls's refinement of his theory in a later book, *Political Liberalism* (1993).[32] While the more recent volume retains Rawls's two principles of justice as well as his vision of the good society as a "social union of social unions" essentially unchanged, its major innovation is a rhetorical one.[33] Rawls now represents the principles as "a strictly political conception of justice" rather than "a moral doctrine of justice general in scope." The change in terminology reflects Rawls's conclusion that the idea of a well-ordered society presented in *A Theory of Justice,* according to which "all its citizens endorse this conception on the basis of . . . a comprehensive philosophical doctrine," is "unrealistic," since "a modern democratic society is characterized . . . by a pluralism of incompatible yet reasonable comprehensive doctrines." Political liberalism as Rawls conceives it aims to develop "a conception of political justice for a constitutional democratic regime that the plurality of reasonable doctrines . . . might endorse" on the basis of an "overlapping consensus" among them (*PL* xv–xvi).[34]

The fundamental problem that concerns Rawls in *Political Liberalism* is the same as that which inspired *A Theory of Justice*: the current lack of "agreement on the way the basic institutions of a constitutional democracy should be arranged" so as "to satisfy the fair terms of cooperation between citizens regarded as free and equal." This problem is manifested, Rawls believes, in "the deeply contested ideas about how . . . the claims of both liberty and equality" are to be adjusted (*PL* 4, 300). The aim of justice as fairness, he now explains, is to provide "a publicly recognized point of view from which all citizens can examine . . . whether their political and social institutions are just," on a basis "independent of the opposing and conflicting philosophical and religious doctrines" they hold (*PL* 9). Hence he represents the doctrine as a form of "political constructivism," according to which "once reflective equilibrium is attained, the principles of political justice (content) may be represented as the outcome of a certain procedure of construction (structure)" (*PL* 89–90). For the sake of accommodating different people's notions of truth, it "does without the concept of truth" (*PL* 94). To illustrate: rather than "look for something for the reasonableness of the statement that slavery is unjust to consist in, as if the reasonableness of it needed some kind of grounding . . . constructivism thinks it illuminating to say about slavery that it violates principles that would be agreed to in the original position by the representatives of persons as free and equal" (*PL* 124). While citizens are free to buttress such a notion by reference to their own criteria of truth, in agreeing to be governed by "the political conception [of justice] as the basis of public reason on fundamental political questions," they recognize that "one another's comprehensive views are reasonable, even when they think them mistaken," and hence avoid insisting that others accept their own comprehensive view of truth. Thus, "a liberal view removes from the political agenda the most divisive issues, serious contention about which must undermine . . . social cooperation" (*PL* 127–29, 157). "The political philosophy of a constitutional regime" as Rawls conceives it is "autonomous" from any "natural basis" (such as the doctrine of natural rights); it suffices that "we can learn this normative scheme and use it to express ourselves in it in our moral and political thought and action," since it draws on the "shared fund of implicitly recognized basic ideas and principles" in our "public culture" (*PL* 8–9, 87–88).

Central to Rawls's revision of his theory is the distinction between rationality and reasonableness. As in *A Theory of Justice*, Rawls conceives rationality as a purely instrumental or calculating faculty, used to determine the most efficient means to a person's ends or to balance his "final ends by their significance for [his] plan of life as a whole." Reasonableness, by contrast, disposes people "to propose . . . fair terms of cooperation and to abide by them willingly, given the assurance that others will likewise do so" (*PL* 48–52). In an apparent retreat from his claim in *Theory* that justice as fairness represented the rational choice of purely self-interested parties in the original position, Rawls now argues that those parties must be conceived as being concerned to promote a just society *as well* as to advance their respective conceptions of the good. While still maintaining that being just in his sense is conducive to each person's good, Rawls denies that the moral skeptic who challenges this claim can or must be answered by reason (*PL* 52, 106, 180).

It is doubtful that Rawls's attempt to sever his theory from a grounding claim to truth will render it any more persuasive to those whose intuitions did not incline them to agree with his version of liberalism from the outset. (Can one imagine the constructivist case against slavery inspiring the cause of emancipation as the "comprehensive doctrine" of natural rights once did?) Equally dubious is Rawls's claim that his doctrine will remove the most divisive issues of contemporary democratic politics from the realm of dispute, especially considering the manifestly partisan inferences that he purports to draw from it, such as a guaranteed right to abortion during the first trimester (*PL* 243n32), full constitutional protection for "the advocacy of revolutionary and subversive doctrines" (*PL* 342), and the necessity of restrictions on campaign expenditures so as "to establish the fair value of the political liberties" (*PL* 360).[35]

Above all, we wonder why Rawls continues to regard the fact of peaceful disputation about justice as a blemish to be cured by inducing everyone to accept a particular theory, rather than as a healthy characteristic of republican self-government. In this regard, his enterprise is reminiscent of the recent Supreme Court's troubled endeavor to "settle" various controversial issues like abortion by removing them from the sphere of permissible political debate. In contrast not only with the great tradition of liberal political philosophy but also with that of common law jurisprudence, Rawls severely constrains the scope of empirical political and legal reasoning whereby the principles of individual liberty are harmonized with the requirement of democratic political consent and with the varying necessities of statesmanship.[36]

IV

In his last programmatic treatise, *The Law of Peoples* (1999), Rawls enunciates a "political conception of right and justice" for "international law and practice" (*LP* 3).[37] The "basic charter" of the law of peoples incorporates eight "familiar and traditional principles of justice among free and democratic peoples," including respect for the freedom and equality of all peoples and for human rights, the "duty of nonintervention" and a prohibition on war other than for reasons of self-defense, and the "duty to assist other peoples living under unfavorable conditions that prevent their having a just or decent political and social regime" (*LP* 37). Rawls represents the adoption of these principles as the outcome of a second original position among parties who choose under a veil of ignorance that prevents their knowing the size, population, or relative strength of the peoples whose interests they represent (*LP* 32–33). But unlike the parties to the domestic original position, the representatives in the second-level position "are not given a menu of alternative principles and ideals from which to select," but "simply reflect on the advantages of these principles . . . and see no reason to depart from them or to propose alternatives." They debate only the many possible interpretations of the eight principles (*LP* 41–42).

Rawls represents the Law of Peoples as a "realistically utopian idea" that will generate "stability for the right reasons," as distinguished from "stability as a balance of forces" (*PL* 44). In response to the "realist" view that international relations inevitably remain "an ongoing struggle for wealth and power," Rawls cites both the modern movement toward democratic reform and Montesquieu's argument that commerce tends to generate peace and such virtues as industry and probity (*PL* 46). Additionally, however, a secure democratic peace presupposes that member nations assure to their own citizens equality of opportunity, "a decent distribution of income and wealth," "society as employer of last resort," basic health care, and public financing of elections (*PL* 50). While citing the absence of wars among constitutionally secure liberal states, Rawls attributes the tendency of "allegedly constitutional democratic regimes" like the United States to "intervene in weaker countries" and overthrow "democracies" like Allende's Chile to "monopolistic and oligarchic interests" in the former (*LP* 51–53).[38]

The second part of "ideal theory" regarding international relations governs the relations between liberal and nonliberal peoples. It dictates recognizing the latter "as equal participating members in good standing of the Society of Peoples" so long as they "meet certain specified conditions of political right and justice" and thus are "decent" (*LP* 59–60). A "decent hierarchical people" must satisfy two criteria. First, it must renounce aggressive aims. Second, it must guarantee to its members such human rights as life, liberty, property, and "formal equality" before the law; impose "*bona fide* moral duties and obligations" on all its citizens; and have laws that are "guided by a common good conception of justice" incorporating a "decent consultation hierarchy" and the right of political protest (*LP* 64–66, 71–72). Since human rights do not depend on any particular comprehensive religious or philosophical doctrine, Rawls is confident that they will be acceptable to decent hierarchical peoples (although this seems tautological, since he has defined such peoples partly by their acceptance of such rights). Hence he infers that they will be willing to adopt the eight principles of international justice (*LP* 68–69).

Whereas forceful interference in the affairs of liberal and decent nonliberal societies is forbidden, "outlaw states," which violate human rights, merit condemnation and "in grave cases" forceful sanctions or even intervention. It is a "consequence of liberalism and decency" not to "tolerate outlaw states" (*LP* 80–81). ("Outlaw states" include not only notoriously evil regimes like Nazi Germany, but expansionist autocracies like Spain, France, and the Hapsburg Empire in the early modern period [*LP* 105–6].) Only societies that honor human rights—that is, liberal and decent societies—along with "benevolent absolutisms," have the "right to war in self-defense" (*LP* 92). Even in fighting just, defensive wars, these societies are bound by "principles regarding the conduct of war" dictating that they distinguish carefully among the outlaw state's leaders, its soldiers, and its civilian population (who by definition, in an outlaw state, "cannot be those who organized and brought on the war"). Hence such attacks on the civilian population of outlaw states as the atomic bombing of Hiroshima and Nagasaki were "very grave wrongs." More generally, "well-ordered peoples must respect, so far as possible, the human rights of members of the other side" so as to set a good example for them (*LP* 94–96).

The immunity of civilians to military attack may be violated only during a "supreme emergency," such as Britain may have faced during the first years of World War II. It is a "duty of statesmanship" to prevent people's wartime passions from influencing the course of policy (just as, in *Theory*, Rawls argued that "the long range aim of society" must be fixed without regard to the particular desires of its present members). The effectiveness of America's armed forces during World War II would not have been affected, in Rawls's judgment, by abstaining from attacking civilians (*LP* 98, 101–2). (He does not address the issue of bombing factories used for military production.)

Beyond their duty to protect human rights against violation by outlaw states, well-ordered societies are obliged to assist "burdened societies," which "lack the political and cultural traditions, the human capital and know-how, and, often, the material and technological resources needed to be well-ordered." "Merely dispensing funds will not suffice to rectify basic political and social injustices" unless the burdened society's political culture is improved. In fact, since political culture is a greater determinant of a society's economic well-being than its natural resources are, Rawls refrains from holding that wealthier countries are obliged to redistribute their wealth internationally in accordance with the difference principle (*LP* 106, 108–9, 116–17).[39]

While aiming at a worldwide "just and well-ordered society of peoples," all of whom accept and abide by the Law of Peoples, Rawls does not favor world government, fearing (with Kant) that it would become a global despotism (*LP* 36). He also defends the right of countries to limit immigration so as to prevent their cultures from being overwhelmed by "global capitalism" (*LP* 39n48). (We note the apparent tension between this concern and Rawls's reliance on Montesquieu's spirit of *doux commerce* to pacify international relations.) But *The Law of Peoples* ends on a remarkably apocalyptic note: if a "reasonably just Society of Peoples" cannot be attained, "one might ask, with Kant, whether it is worthwhile for human beings to live on the earth" (*LP* 128).

Its conclusion aside, *The Law of Peoples* differs from Rawls's previous writings in its greater reliance on a few informed works of political history and fact-based political theory in place of purely abstract reasoning and unfettered appeals to "intuition." To be sure, *The Law of Peoples* still exhibits Rawls's unfortunate habit of issuing ex cathedra judgments on debatable issues of public policy (including, this time, not only military strategy in World War II and U.S. foreign policy toward Latin America, but also unemployment benefits, without which he asserts "there would be massive starvation in every Western democracy" [*LP* 109]). In some respects Rawls's historical judgments seem to have been frozen in the academic world of the 1970s: he rightly condemns Hitler and Nazism but avoids mentioning Stalin or criticizing communism; he treats the former USSR as an actual republican "federation" akin to the European Community (*LP* 70); and he goes so far as to attribute Hitler's demonic evil to the influence of Christianity (*LP* 20–21), without of course addressing his professed socialism. We may doubt, moreover, that advocates of (for instance) traditional but by historical standards "decent" Islamic rule will find that Rawls's criteria of decency, such as the requirement that "any group representing women's fundamental interests must include a majority of women," allow "significant room for . . . a people's self-determination," as he claims (*LP* 61, 110). Nonetheless, Rawls's late move in the direction of grounding justice in a sensitivity to the facts of political life rather than entirely in personal intuitions was a promising one. The relative sobriety that this sort of evidence induces might, we judge, have had a salutary influence had Rawls applied it to the original formulation of his theory of justice.

Notes

1. Unless otherwise noted, parenthetical page references are to the revised edition of *A Theory of Justice* (Cambridge, Mass.: Belknap Press of Harvard University Press, 1999). This text was actually completed in 1975. The first edition was published in 1971.

2. In Rawls's bluntest formulation, his theory specifies the dictates of justice "apart from all historical conditions. What counts is the workings of social institutions now, and a benchmark of the state of nature . . . plays no role. It is a historical surd, unknowable, but even if it could be known, of no significance." *Justice as Fairness: A Restatement* (Cambridge, Mass.: Harvard University Press, 2001), 55. Future references to this work will be identified by the abbreviation *JF*. Rawls further stresses the artificiality of the original position at *JF* 81, 87.

3. In a later formulation (cited as "better" at xii of the revised edition of *Theory*), the first principle guarantees "an equal right to a fully adequate scheme of equal basic liberties which is compatible with a similar scheme of liberties for all," while the order of the (a) and (b) clauses of the second principle is reversed. See Rawls, *Political Liberalism* (New York: Columbia University Press, 1993), 291, hereafter cited as *PL*. Rawls made the first change to emphasize "that the scheme of basic liberties is not drawn up so as to maximize anything," but only to secure the conditions necessary for individuals to actualize their two moral powers of having a capacity for a sense of justice and pursuing their particular conception of the good (*PL* 19, 331–33). But neither change seems to affect the fundamental substance or ground of the principles. Of greater significance, though undeveloped by Rawls, is his concession in response to a Marxist critique that "the first principle covering the equal basic rights and liberties may easily be preceded by a lexically prior principle requiring that citizens' basic needs be met" (*PL* 7). See the following note.

4. The qualification "ideally" refers to the fact that the lexical ordering can be applied only in circumstances where social and economic conditions permit it; if they do not, "the basic liberties can sometimes be restricted" (476; cf. 55, 132, 216–18). However, Rawls focuses his analysis almost entirely on the ideal case.

5. In a later and somewhat starker formulation, Rawls explains that under the difference principle, "however willing people are to work to earn . . . greater shares of output, existing inequalities must contribute effectively to the benefit of the least advantaged. Otherwise the inequalities are not permissible" (*JF* 64).

6. A slightly more specific, five-part list of primary goods is provided in *JF* 58–59.

7. In a subsequent account, Rawls describes the maximin rule as "decisive" only in supporting the first principle, not the second one (*JF* 43n3, 96–97).

8. In *PL* 89–129, Rawls expressly describes his doctrine as a form of "constructivism." A constructivist view was already implied in *Theory* by Rawls's notion that we "choose" rather than discover the principles of justice.

9. Rawls distinguishes his well-ordered society from Marx's communist society, governed by the precept "From each according to his abilities, to each according to his needs," only in presupposing that "the limitations of moderate scarcity" of resources still exist: *Collected Papers*, ed. Samuel Freeman (Cambridge, Mass.: Harvard University Press, 1999), 252. But given Rawls's (Marxian) assumption that we each participate in one another's natures in the well-ordered society, it appears that disagreements over the distribution of goods will be so mild as hardly to resemble politics in any meaningful sense.

10. This is true, for instance, of Rawls's Harvard colleague Robert Nozick, who criticized Rawls's economic program from a libertarian perspective in his *Anarchy, State, and Utopia* (New York: Basic Books, 1974). The "utopia" sketched in the last chapter of Nozick's book markedly resembles Rawls's "social union of social unions."

11. See Thomas Hobbes, *Leviathan*, ed. Edwin Curley (Indianapolis: Hackett Publishing Co., 1994), chap. 13, 77–78, as well as the last paragraph of Hobbes's "Introduction."

12. See, on this score, Michael Sandel, *Liberalism and the Limits of Justice* (Cambridge: Cambridge University Press, 1982), especially 177–80. In *Political Liberalism* Rawls acknowledges that there is "no practicable way actually to carry out this deliberative process" but proceeds on the following page, rather confusingly, to repeat his claim that we can enter the original position "at any moment simply by conducting our moral reasoning about first principles in accordance with the stipulated procedural constraints"

(273–74). He also acknowledges the impossibility of "know[ing] what we would have been like had we not belonged to" a particular society (276), but does not appear to have considered the implications of this concession for the possibility of reasoning under the veil of ignorance.

13. Another ad hoc assumption Rawls adds to determine the choice in the original position is that "the person choosing has a conception of the good such that he cares very little, if anything, for what he might gain above the minimum stipend" (134).

14. In *Political Liberalism* Rawls responds simply, "I hold that justice as fairness is fair to conceptions of the good . . . even though some conceptions are judged not permissible and all conceptions do not have the same chance to flourish" under it, consoling those who lose out by explaining that "[n]o society can include within itself all forms of life" (184–85, 197). The curious notion of being "fair" to a conception of the good, as if it had a disembodied existence of its own, contributes to the abstractness of Rawls's approach. The question remains whether this abstract notion of fairness can possibly justify the elevation of Rawls's preferred vision of the good society over others, without any substantive assessment and comparison of their merits and grounds.

In *Justice as Fairness* Rawls denies that his account of justice requires "continual economic growth over generations to maximize . . . the expectations of the least advantaged," citing "Mill's idea of a society in a just stationary state where (real) capital accumulation may cease" (63–64). But to the extent he retreats from the aim of maximizing primary goods, Rawls undermines the supposition that the choice of principles in the original position is based on a "rational" calculation of one's own good made under a veil of ignorance—rather than on a predetermined notion of the good society that Rawls has imposed independently. If the absolute sum of wealth possessed by the least advantaged does not matter so much after all, why should they care so greatly about the relative shares they enjoy?

15. Consider George Washington's account of the dependence of popular morality on religion in his Farewell Address, the key role played by religion and *moeurs* in Tocqueville's account of the causes of American prosperity and liberty, and Justice Douglas's dictum in *Zorach v. Clauson* (1952) that "we are a religious people whose institutions presuppose a Supreme Being." On the virtues that liberalism presupposes but which neutralist liberalism like Rawls's fails to support, see William Galston, *Liberal Virtues* (Cambridge: Cambridge University Press, 1991).

16. Susan Shell points out that this account of self-respect directly contradicts the teaching of Rawls's putative model Kant: "'Kantianism' and Constitutional Rights," in *Old Rights and New*, ed. Robert A. Licht (Washington, D.C.: AEI Press, 1993), 158.

17. The "historical experience" that Rawls claims belies the need for any limits to toleration seems to be narrowly confined, we note, to that of modern liberal democracies. The intolerance previously displayed by proselytizing sects and feared by Montesquieu, Locke, and Rousseau was overcome in those regimes thanks (among other causes) to the softening influence of commerce advocated by the first two thinkers, and the consequent weakening of the influence of religion as such on political life. By contrast, Rawls's mandate of strict governmental neutrality between religion and atheism, and between sexual restraint and libertinism, threatens to fan the flames of religious controversy in the public sphere, and heighten political tensions between fundamentalists and liberals, as can already be seen in the response to judicial decrees regarding such issues as church-state relations, abortion rights, and "gay marriage" in recent years; cf. Galston, *Liberal Virtues*, 258, 269–73. At the same time the civic tranquility fostered by commerce would seem to be further threatened by Rawls's difference principle, with its implied appeal to class envy.

18. See Michael P. Zuckert, "Justice Deserted, Or, What Is Really Wrong with Rawls," *Polity* 13 (1981): 466–83. In *Justice as Fairness* Rawls is emphatic in distinguishing the sort of deservingness entailed by his "political conception" of justice from "moral desert," an idea that must be avoided in public life since judgments about it reflect people's "conflicting conceptions of the good" (*JF* 73). One might wonder why he should regard the conception of desert manifested in the difference principle as any less controversial. Rawls's answer is that the dictum that no one deserves his place in the distribution of native endowments is a "moral truism" that nobody would deny and all reasonable doctrines would endorse; that it is impossible for free and equal persons "not to view it a misfortune . . . that some are by nature better endowed than others"; and that the difference principle is consequently the only one through which the more and less advantaged can be reconciled on the basis of "democratic equality" (*JF* 74–76). Yet he also

concedes that "the difference principle is not often expressly endorsed" and "may prove to have little support in our public political culture at the present time" (*JF* 132–33).

19. See also the reference in note 3 above to Rawls's subsequent acceptance of the subordination of the basic rights and liberties to the proviso that citizens' "basic needs" first be met, thus legitimizing the rationale typically offered by Communist regimes for the denial of civil liberties.

20. Curiously, Rawls devotes some four pages to an account of "natural shame," "moral shame," and "guilt," but defines them in utterly formal or relativistic terms: "It is our plan of life that determines what we feel ashamed of" (388–92).

21. See, e.g., Thomas S. Schrock, "The Liberal Court, the Conservative Court, and Constitutional Jurisprudence," in *Left, Right, and Center*, ed. Robert Goldwin (Chicago: Rand McNally, 1965), 87–120, and Milton Friedman, *Capitalism and Freedom* (Chicago: University of Chicago Press, 1962), chap. 1. By contrast, note Rawls's studied agnosticism on the relative compatibility of socialism and free enterprise with political liberty and justice: *Theory*, xv–xvi, 239–42, 246; cf. *PL* 7–8n, 298, 338–39; *JF* 114, 138–39. Going beyond agnosticism, he finally concedes the possibility that Marx's view "that no regime with private property in the means of production" can be just may be "in good part true," although "the question is not yet settled" (*JF* 178).

22. Note also Rawls's subsequent reference to the need for unspecified "qualifications" to the right of emigration from liberal societies (perhaps to prevent the more talented or industrious from escaping the effects of the difference principle?): *PL* 222, 277; *The Law of Peoples* (Cambridge, Mass.: Harvard University Press, 1999), 74n15. In *Justice as Fairness* (94n14), Rawls provides a noncontroversial illustration of such qualifications: "those properly convicted of certain sufficiently serious crimes may not be allowed to emigrate pending serving their sentence." But he appears to leave room for further restrictions on emigration by saying simply, "I shall not discuss these qualifications."

23. In *Theory* (84), Rawls himself judges it "impossible to avoid a certain arbitrariness in identifying the least favored group," and more or less leaves matters there. In *Justice as Fairness* (59), he unqualifiedly identifies the least advantaged as "those belonging to the income class with the lowest expectations." He offers no justification for focusing on poverty as the only sort of disadvantage that is relevant to justice or the enhancement of self-respect. Presumably, he does so because it is the only one that he conceives to be directly remediable by governmental policies; but, without reflection on the relative significance of economic causes of unhappiness as distinguished from other ones, we cannot know how far the pursuit of political justice as Rawls conceives it is worth the sacrifices he calls for on its behalf. As a corrective, see the penultimate scene of Aristophanes' *Assemblywomen* for the working out of a scheme to compensate for a serious sort of disadvantage (physical age and ugliness) that Rawls does not seem to have considered, and a certain "queuing" problem that results.

In *Political Liberalism* (181–82), Rawls does suggest expanding the list of primary goods used for "interpersonal comparisons" to include such goods as "leisure time, and even certain mental states such as freedom from physical pain." It is disturbing to imagine how a government might undertake to "redistribute" such goods, as this suggestion seems to encourage; regarding the former, see note 25 below.

24. At *Theory* 478–79, Rawls raises the possibility "theoretically" of including self-respect in the index of primary goods in response to the problem of "excusable envy," but describes the problem as an "unwelcome complication" in view of the simplicity that is desirable in a public conception of justice.

25. In speaking of Rawls's recommended policies as typically conventional, I leave aside his occasional speculations about the possible abolition of the family and the use of eugenic policies to mitigate natural inequalities (92), since Rawls himself does not seem inclined to pursue them. Note, however, Rawls's openness in principle to R. A. Musgrave's proposal of "a lump sum tax on natural abilities" to compel the more talented to work harder so as to generate more income to be redistributed to the less advantaged; the proposal "is not an interference with liberty until it infringes upon the basic liberties," and Rawls is uncertain "when this happens": *Collected Papers*, 252–53. Passages like these (along with his references to limiting the right of emigration and his sanctioning of "regulations of freedom of speech and of the press" to ensure their "fair value" [*JF* 149–50]) should give pause to those who persist in regarding Rawls as a partisan of liberty. (See, however, *JF* 157–58 for sensible second thoughts on Musgrave's proposal.)

26. As noted by Allan Bloom, "Justice: John Rawls Vs. the Tradition of Political Philosophy," *American Political Science Review* 69 (1975): 648–62, at 662; cf. 655.

27. Cf. Irving Kristol, "About Equality," *Commentary* 54 (November, 1972): 41–47, and the novelist André Malraux's remark that he ceased being a socialist once he realized that socialism would never cure broken hearts or traffic accidents. Rawls's remarks about the unacceptable arbitrariness of the world bear comparison with Genesis 1:31. For the apocalyptic element in his outlook, consider the closing line of *The Law of Peoples*, cited below. For the curious or perverse sort of practical judgment which that outlook may generate, consider note 38 below (citing Rawls's suggestion that contemporary America may be no more democratic than "Germany between 1870 and 1945," i.e., even including the Nazi period).

28. Within the domain of academic philosophy, indeed, the most notorious contemporary utilitarian, Peter Singer, has made headlines with his use of the felicific calculus to elevate lower animals to a higher status than human infants or disabled persons. Public response to Singer's arguments, however, so far seems to confirm the impression that they are (fortunately) unlikely to have significant direct influence outside the academy.

29. Aristotle, *Politics*, 1309b18–1310a11, 1320a1–16. The central concern of Tocqueville's deservedly acclaimed *Democracy in America* can be described as the reconciliation of the democratic principle of equality with elements of the aristocratic principle of excellence.

30. Cf., in this regard, James R. Stoner, Jr., *Common Law and Liberal Theory: Coke, Hobbes, and the Origins of American Constitutionalism* (Lawrence: University Press of Kansas, 1992), 4–5 et passim.

31. If Kant may indeed be regarded as a model for Rawls's elevation of the just over the good, it suffices to contrast the stern impartiality commanded by the Kantian categorical imperative with the manifest partisanship of Rawls's difference principle to highlight the gap between them. See also note 16 above.

32. For a fuller treatment see my "Rawls Redux," *Political Science Reviewer* 25 (1996): 151–209.

33. The chief innovation in the initial formulation of the two principles is the inclusion in the first principle of the requirement that the "fair value" of "the equal political liberties . . . be guaranteed" (5). That requirement is omitted from another formulation in the same volume (291), cited in note 3 above.

34. As in the notes, parenthetic page references to *Political Liberalism* in the text are prefaced by the acronym *PL*.

35. In "The Idea of Public Reason Revisited," appended to *The Law of Peoples*, Rawls explains that the abortion mandate was only his "opinion . . . not an argument" (169); but in the same essay he extends the scope of justice to dictate such policies as a demand, "on behalf of children," to remedy women's "unjust share of the task of raising, nurturing, and caring for their children." "[T]he principles of justice," he remarks, "put essential restrictions on the family and all other associations. . . . If the so-called private sphere is alleged to be a space exempt from justice, then there is no such thing" (161–62).

36. See, on the use of Rawls's "political conception of justice" and his notion of "overlapping consensus" by defenders of the Court's continued adherence to its abortion rights doctrine, as well as the influence on the Court of his notion of "personhood," Paul O. Carrese, "Judicial Statesmanship, the Jurisprudence of Individualism, and Tocqueville's Common Law Spirit," *Review of Politics* 60 (1998): 465–95, at 470n, 477. The influence of Rawls's doctrine of overlapping consensus derived from the "public political culture" that removes controversial issues from the political agenda may also underlie Chief Justice Rehnquist's opinion in *Dickerson v. United States* (2000) denying Congress's power to overturn the Court's previous *Miranda* decision on the ground that so-called Miranda warnings to criminal suspects, regardless of their constitutional foundation or lack thereof, "have become part of our national culture." On Tocqueville's endeavor to defend democratic politics *against* the influence of abstract, general theories like Rawls's, see Carrese, and also James W. Ceaser, *Liberal Democracy and Political Science* (Baltimore: Johns Hopkins University Press, 1990), chap. 7.

37. References to *The Law of Peoples* will be prefaced with the abbreviation *LP*. Separately published in 1999 were Rawls's *Collected Papers*; but most of the material in that volume had been incorporated, in one form or another, into the three monographs that I treat in this chapter. In 2000, an edited version of Rawls's notes for his course on the history of ethics, *Lectures on the History of Moral Philosophy*, was published by Harvard University Press; but these lectures, dealing with Hume, Leibniz, Kant, and Hegel, do not elaborate or alter the account of justice presented in his other books. The subsidiary role to which

Rawls consigns the history of philosophy is signified by his remark in the introduction to the *Lectures* that the various philosophical questions addressed by different authors are "shaped by the system of thought from within which they are asked," leaving it to "us to consider by contrast our own scheme of thought ... from within which we now ask our questions" (17–18; cf. 329 and Rawls's explicit agreement with the historicist view of R. G. Collingwood at xvi). The one element of the *Lectures* of direct interest with respect to Rawls's own doctrine is his account of how his theory of justice ostensibly responds to Hegel's criticisms of liberalism (365–69).

Besides the aforementioned volumes, in 2001 Harvard University Press published *Justice as Fairness: A Restatement*, based on a lecture course on political philosophy that Rawls taught in the 1980s. The book modifies Rawls's account of his theory only in minor respects beyond those stated in *Political Liberalism*; I have indicated the key modifications and clarifications in these notes.

38. In *Justice as Fairness* (101n23), Rawls further questions the democratic character of the United States, suggesting that "one might" judge "our constitutional regime" to be "largely democratic in form only," owing to the same sort of lack of "political will for a democratic regime" from which "Germany between 1870 and 1945" suffered.

39. We wonder why Rawls does not consider the implications of the primacy of culture for the problem of *domestic* poverty. If the primary cause of poverty in America, as numerous perceptive social scientists have observed, is a cultural one, that is, a "cycle of dependency," would not the redistribution of economic goods and the relativism in judging alternative "life styles" that Rawls espouses only exacerbate the problem? (See, e.g., Myron Magnet, *The Dream and the Nightmare: The Sixties' Legacy to the Underclass* [New York: William Morrow, 1993].) Rawls himself, however, in a 1982 essay specifies that "the least advantaged are, by definition, those who are born into and who remain in that group throughout their life," so that the prospect of social mobility offered by the principle of equal opportunity "is irrelevant" to the application of the difference principle ("Social Unity and Primary Goods," *Collected Papers*, 364). This seems a terribly pessimistic, not to say demeaning, view for a liberal society to adopt.

Chapter 43

Henry Kissinger: The Challenge of Statesmanship in Liberal Democracy

Peter Josephson

Though he is best known as a practitioner of balance of power politics, Henry Kissinger (1923–) situates his practical politics in a theoretical framework. He explains that his work approaches American foreign policy "from a philosophical perspective," one concerned not only with security but also with "the national purpose" (*YOR* 13).[1] Indeed, the interaction between practice and theory, and the possibility of joining the two through acts of statesmanship, is the chief concern of his work. Yet the relationship of the statesman to his community is often difficult, perhaps especially when the regime is a liberal and democratic one. If prudent foreign policy requires a statesman, then liberal and democratic political societies may be placed at a disadvantage. In Kissinger's account (and as philosophers have long observed), democracy is not congenial to the development of the most elevated qualities. Moreover, it may be difficult for a statesman to persuade a popular government to adopt a policy built on foresight and understanding. Robert Stewart Castlereagh was British foreign secretary in the early part of the nineteenth century and, with Prince von Metternich of Austria-Hungary, was one of the heroes of Kissinger's political history of European diplomacy. Castlereagh represented an isolationist and liberal nation at a delicate time. With Metternich, Castlereagh created a system of conferences to address security concerns in Europe. Though Kissinger reserves higher praise for Metternich, Castlereagh's situation may tell us most about the relation between the statesman and the liberal democratic regime.[2] The defense of liberal democracy requires the work of aristocratic statesmen; yet, the realism of such men and women runs against the grain of liberal idealism, though in the end it serves the cause of freedom.

Kissinger's work raises three interrelated concerns. First, for Kissinger the "statesman" represents a special, highest type. He partakes of both philosophy and politics (and in some sense is superior to both philosophers and politicians), and in his work he demonstrates special creativity, freedom, and will. Second, Kissinger addresses the special problem of providing prudent leadership—leadership bent on shaping history—in a liberal and egalitarian society. When all are free, how does a leader assert authority? When all are equal, how does one opinion claim superiority over others? What Kissinger presents to us in very clear terms is the problem between politics—the "salesmanship" necessary to move interest groups or agencies—and what he calls "substance"—the creative development of "right" and realistic programs for the nation (*AFP* 20–23, 30–34; *WHY* 4–7). Finally, there is Kissinger's subtle and complex recognition of the importance of moral concerns as legitimating and therefore persuasive political principles and also as the ends or goals of policy. In Kissinger's words, American foreign policy "must fulfill the best in America" (*AFP* 190). Kissinger is famous for his realism and for his critique of American idealism. Still, his realism has a strong, though perhaps not entirely American, moral compass. We must explore Kissinger's conception of the purpose or meaning of America if we are to understand his philosophic approach to foreign policy, and we must wonder about a philosophy that appears to disdain American idealism.

The Heroic Statesman

More than any other actor, the statesman must combine theory and practice. He finds himself situated, uncomfortably, between the philosopher and the politician. For Kissinger, the "statesman" is a special sort of person. The statesman transcends the work of intellectuals, both in the difficulty of what he attempts to accomplish and in the morality of his work. He combines intellectual and moral virtues in a way that neither academics nor politicians alone may do (*WHY* 4). Intellectuals analyze, but statesmen "build." The analyst studies what he chooses; the statesman must address problems that are imposed on him. The analyst studies at leisure; the statesman always faces pressures of time. The analyst runs no risk, for his exercise is academic. The statesman runs enormous risk, and not only to himself (*D* 27–28; *YOU* 615). Where the philosopher may enjoy contemplating paradoxes, the statesman must resolve them; where the philosopher pursues moral absolutes, the statesman confronts the limits of possibility (*AWR* 22–23, 82; *D* 113). Kissinger observes that a statesman is not "a philosopher or dreamer. At some point he must translate his intuition into reality" (*YOU* 648, 459–60; *AWR* 326). He describes his own "moment of responsibility," when he was forced to leave mere academics and make real policies. "Problems were no longer theoretical. . . . The philosopher's test is the reasoning behind his maxims; the statesman's test is not only the exaltation of his goals but the catastrophe he averts. . . . The dialogue between the academic and the statesman is therefore always likely to be inconclusive" (*WHY* 54–55). The statesman must put intellect to work in the real world and combine his intellectual virtue with practical virtues. Therefore, the statesman actually has a greater intellectual virtue than academics because the statesman must simultaneously see both the short- and long-term effects of his policies (*YOR* 357; *WHY* 704–5). Such a "great man" has special capacities of insight and a special courage. He "understands the essence of a problem," "focuses on the relationship of events to each other," and "has a vision of the future." Statesmanship "requires above all . . . nuance and proportion," "intuition," and "the ability to perceive the essential" (*YOU* 647; *WHY* 39). The statesman makes policy for the future, not the present. At some level he must make the future, but he has few signposts to follow. The work of international relations in particular is the most thoughtful and most conceptual area of politics. It requires the greatest foresight and subtlety, and it is through this work that our understandings of justice face the severest tests. It is therefore most difficult and most noble (*D* 189; *WHY* 130).

While the statesman attends to realities that the philosopher might ignore, he is no mere politician. His work is circumscribed by historical and cultural circumstances. Because he must join theory and practice, "any statesman is in part the prisoner of necessity." This "solitary individual" recognizes these limits and works within them to create a "moral act." Because realism makes morality effective, the statesman's work is not only most intellectual but also most noble (*WHY* 54–55; *AWR* 324–25). For the statesman, foreign policy is not merely "a theory but . . . a series of realities." Virtue without power is impotent. Politics requires persuasion, but "the feeble can seldom persuade" (*YOR* 94, 235, 532, 706). Americans in particular do not understand the necessity of power. In part, the difficulty in liberal democracies is that the skills that make a politician successful are not the same as the skills of the statesman. Statesmanship thus requires foresight that the public naturally lacks, and so men of substance must rise almost against the grain of democratic politics. They work "beyond partisanship" with "selflessness and integrity" to form an "aristocracy" that preserves democratic freedom. At stake in the work of the statesman is not only the nation's power but its domestic cohesion. Free societies cannot remain united and free simply by managing the present and hoping for the best. A leader may "strive" to "create" and "shape the destiny of his people," but in doing so he acts apart from the democratic ethos. In a democracy, these leaders must pursue a course that the public may not understand. For this reason, the statesman is usually unappreciated in his own time. The "incentive of most states-men" is "the accolade of history" (*WHY* 17–20, 22–23, 55, 1139).

Politicians, perhaps especially politicians in Castlereagh's England or Kissinger's America, are characterized by pragmatism more than maturity and foresight. In the nineteenth century, British policy was typically pragmatic but therefore also reactive. It responded to events, in Kissinger's account, more often than it foresaw or shaped them. That Britain succeeded in that time was due in part to its "splendid isolation," the fact that it could remove itself from many of the European crises which did not seem to affect the nation's immediate interests. Put another way, attention to interest is dependable, and it produced marked consistency in British policy (*D* 96–97, 100). In America, too, "problems are dealt with as they arise. . . . This often involves the risk of slighting long-term issues which may not have assumed crisis proportions" (*AFP* 32–33). The pragmatist has the advantage (at least over the philosopher) of addressing problems in the real world. But the pragmatist's vision is limited; he does not foresee nor shape long-range events. The difficulty with pragmatism is that "[c]reativity, innovation, sacrifice pale before tactical considerations of dealing with day-to-day concerns" (*NFC* 6). As a result, a pragmatic nation may defend its immediate interests quite well, but it must expend enormous resources in violent efforts to protect those interests. "All too frequently a problem evaded is a crisis invited." History and necessity shape our possibilities, but history is not inevitable. Oftentimes crises may be averted entirely through prudence and foresight, but these are not the qualities of the pragma-tist. The pragmatic nation veers between isolationism and complete commitment. It is alternately "defensive" and "crusad[ing]" (*AWR* 107). One of the great advantages of the partnership be-tween Kissinger and President Richard Nixon was that the two men could combine theory and practice; they "complemented each other's qualities." Kissinger brought theory to the policy; Nixon brought a pragmatic or political perspective. Nixon's "single most important quality was the ability to make bold decisions" and to "impos[e] his will on circumstances" (*YOR* 44–45, 47). He lacked either "nuance[d]" understanding or Kissinger's capacity for "theoretical analysis" (*WHY* 126, 163, 299, 303–4, 308). Nixon was interested in strategy but not in diplomacy. Kissinger brought a knowledge of history and theory and an ability to pursue long-range strategies; Nixon brought "insight" (*YOR* 47). In some way, together they produced a statesman. According to Kissinger, this combination is critical because the future must be shaped or it will impose itself as catastrophe. As a result, shaping the future remains "the key test of democratic statesmanship" (*YOU* 746).

Domestic politics often intrudes on the ability of statesmen to pursue policies of substance (*WHY* 4–6, 399–401, 415). The clearest example of the problem from Kissinger's perspective is Congress's assertion of authority over American foreign policy in the wake of Watergate. Kissinger witnessed the rise of congressional authority not only in Indochina but also in America's relations with Greece and Turkey during the Cyprus crisis, and especially in Senator Henry Jackson's "ideological crusade" against the Soviets over issues of trade and emigration (*YOR* 192, 306–7). In Kissinger's view, the failure of America's post-Vietnam policy in Indo-china was the result of congressional restrictions on our ability to defend our allies, keep our commitments, and enforce the Paris Accords that ended the Vietnam conflict. America's "self-indulgence" manifested itself as withdrawal and endangered freedom "everywhere" (*WHY* 1461; *YOU* 37, 327, 355, 357, 369). These legislative indulgences were possible because the public is fickle. In 1974, voters chose a Congress that vehemently opposed Nixon administration policy— the very policy the electorate had overwhelmingly endorsed just two years earlier. Kissinger understands that voters were disenchanted with the man, but the result was a reversal of policy in Indochina, Africa, and in the relations of the United States with the Soviet Union. After Watergate, the executive increasingly faced the problem of justifying its policy to the public. Attention to domestic politics, and especially to the idealism of the American tradition, became a prerequisite for the conduct of any foreign policy (*YOR* 835, 873, 878). A relatively subtle policy like détente—which required a balance between the pursuit of peace and the defense of freedom, or between cooperation and confrontation—therefore failed as a domestic political issue but not as a strategy. By the fall of 1975, President Ford's ability to steer America's foreign relations became subject to the necessities of electoral politics. Serious policy making became increasingly difficult, and in 1976 Kissinger recommended that Ford not seek a new SALT agreement "because it was too divisive to conclude an agreement while conducting a primary and then a presidential campaign." "[W]ith the presidential nominations approaching, reasoned debate was at an end" (*YOR* 860–61, 866, 895, 836).

The problem of the relation between substance and politics does not arise only for liberal regimes, or only for the United States—it is inherent in all regimes. In the late nineteenth century, the "Eastern Courts . . . in a way proved even more susceptible to nationalistic public opinion than the representative governments." Leaders in "autocratic" Germany were "extremely sensitive to public opinion" (*D* 163, 184). Even a totalitarian state like the Soviet Union faced such difficulties. There, internal bureaucratic and leadership struggles in the late 1960s and early 1970s made formulating and pursuing a strategic diplomatic program quite difficult until Brezhnev consolidated his power (*WHY* 526–27; *YOR* 264–65). Later, Mikhail Gorbachev struggled to balance his foreign and domestic political concerns.[3] Communism fell in eastern Europe in part because the leadership was pressed to respond to public pressures for democratization and economic development (*D* 787, 793). Kissinger observes a similar dynamic at work in China (*DAN* 136).

Similarly, the difficulty of constructing a lasting policy is not confined to democratic regimes: this is increasingly the political reality for all countries. In imperial Austria, Metternich's system depended on his personality and his labor, and it was not sustained after he left the scene (*AWR* 322). Bismarck's system required flexibility and nuance, but attention to public opinion reduces flexibility, and nuance may be incompatible with the age of "mass public opinion" (*D* 105, 160–61, 166). The systems of Metternich and Bismarck were too complex and relied too heavily on the success of one man. "A foreign policy achievement to be truly significant must at some point be institutionalized; it must therefore be embedded in permanent machinery." The Nixon practice of centering foreign policy making in the White House was temporarily expedient; but if the policy is to survive the policy maker, it must become custom (*YOU* 434). For this reason, Kissinger's move out of the White House to the State Department offered the opportunity to overcome the problem that Metternich and Bismarck could never fully address.[4] Ironically, Nixon's policy has proven more lasting than Bismarck's. Both Presidents Carter and Reagan, liberal critics of Nixon's foreign policy, ultimately agreed with the outlines of Nixon's diplomacy (*YOR* 880, 897; *DAN* 141). "Probably the most abiding tribute to Nixon's legacy is that most of the relationships and strategies launched during his presidency have sustained the foreign policy of all of his successors to this writing [i.e., to 1999]" (*YOR* 92, 151).

Yet the problem of the statesman "is especially characteristic of the United States," in some measure because democracy embraces equality and not individual excellence. "In such an environment little opportunity exists for real creativity." But the preservation of democracy "requires leaders willing to stand alone" (*NFC* 3, 341). Americans are reluctant to do this; we are happiest when we know what the majority wants. The difficulty is that the majority is not an especially rational actor. The rational actor, the statesman, must do his work without the majority but in the context of majority rule. From the perspective of the regime, his work appears undemocratic, though it aims at preserving the nation's liberty. The statesman must act on an "intuition" of the future; he is like a "prophet," or one of the visionary "heroes" of ancient dramas (*AWR* 329). Kissinger emphasizes the statesman's heroism (for example, overcoming democratic "illusions" will require "heroic effort"), though on at least one occasion Kissinger observes that there is a connection between heroism and "monomaniacal determination" (*NFC* 8; *WHY* 442). Kissinger the statesman becomes the heroic and creative figure who reshapes the world according to his perception of its realities and its moral possibilities.

Given the virtues necessary for statesmanship, the education of the statesman must be of a particular sort. Kissinger writes for the young, for a generation "born after 1960" that lacks training for foreign policy and doubts whether we need one at all (*DAN* 30). He worries that the "scholarship of scientific determinism" leads us to believe that individuals are impotent (*AWR* 324–25). The great statesmen of the past "saw themselves as heroes who took on the burden of their societies' painful journey from the familiar to the as yet unknown." Today, politicians would rather be "stars" than "heroes." This is in part the result of our training in mass media. Statesmen historically learned from books and were taught thereby to analyze and to think conceptually. One problem in the new world is that the "visual image" replaced "the written word," and as a result "the process of learning was transformed from an active to a passive mode." Instead of "concepts," we get only "impressions" (*YOR* 28–29, 1077; *D* 834). This is a genuine difficulty because the world is difficult to read. In short, statesmen confront problems of epistemology as well as policy.

The difficulty is further exacerbated by the tendency since the Kennedy administration for presidents to consult academics and analysts to help make policy. The result is that academics now aspire to join the "political struggle." This practice was designed to produce more statesmanlike programs, but it had the perverse effect of narrowing the perspective of academics (who now had a concern and interest in attending to short-range goals) at the expense of long-range analysis. "[I]t foreshortened the perspective of intellectuals on the outside but ambitious to participate by focusing them on the immediate and the tactical." Faced with Vietnam, the foreign policy establishment lost its self-assurance and sense of direction, and it abandoned its duty "to contribute balanced judgment, long-term perspective, and thoughtful analysis" to the public debate. In short, the practice resulted in the decline of the analytical class and the rise of the political or ideological class. The sort of statesmen Kissinger considers most sober-minded and prudent become, in his analysis, something of an endangered species. Crusaders and enthusiasts take their place, or they become crusaders themselves (*YOR* 86, 1070–71, 1074). Years before he entered the Nixon administration, Kissinger warned that in a "pragmatic society" intellectuals come to feel a sense of "guilt" over their "pursuit of knowledge for its own sake." "There are many who believe that their ultimate contribution as intellectuals depends on the degree of their participation in what is considered the 'active' life." Because of the nature of bureaucracy, the intellectual who contributes to policy making risks losing his "independence" and his capacity for "creativity" (*NFC* 349, 353). Presumably, Kissinger himself was prey to the difficulty he foresaw. In fact, the Nixon administration's own policies and actions may have contributed to this turn toward ideology. As academics and the foreign policy agencies increasingly turned to politics and away from "substance," Nixon sought to establish a new center of foreign policy expertise or statesmanship in the White House itself. As Kissinger explains (without reference to the particular concerns of his president), the changing culture of the bureaucracy "drives the executive in the direction of extra-bureaucratic means of decision" (*AFP* 22–23).[5] Nixon's move in that direction resulted in new political restraints on the executive. Besides the reassertion of congressional power in international affairs, Presidents Carter and Reagan were elected as representatives of an "anti-Nixonian" shift toward placing moral concerns at the center of American foreign policy. Kissinger seeks to combine theory with practice, but today's politicians are too idealistic and today's academics are too pragmatic. There are no more aristocrats.

The Problems of Peace

Peace is highly desired, difficult to achieve, and even harder to preserve. Kissinger understands that this is especially true for liberal democracies like the United States, in part as a result of our idealism and in part because of our disinclination to accept the lessons of history. In this context, it is helpful to return to the example of Lord Castlereagh. Castlereagh began his career as part of the British tradition of pragmatic foreign policy. Kissinger describes Castlereagh's rapid education in the realities of the construction of peace: Castlereagh's tutor was Metternich. Castlereagh left England with instructions from the British cabinet to work for the overthrow of Napoleon. He came to understand that peace in Europe would require self-restraint. "Castlereagh had come to accept the Austrian interpretation"—Metternich's interpretation—"of the goal of the war." That goal was to maintain the continental equilibrium by means of a coalition or "Congress" of European states and to establish and preserve a shared, conservative conception of legitimacy in the face of the revolutionary example in Napoleonic France. In this, Castlereagh separated himself from British public opinion. When he introduces us to Castlereagh, Kissinger reports that he had a reputation as "an ogre to liberalism." The foresight of the "statesman" even led Castlereagh on occasion "to *violate* his instructions" (*AWR* 29–30, 108, 122, 168). Negotiating with the Russian tsar Alexander—who tried to use British public opinion against Castlereagh —the foreign secretary replied: "I must be guided by the dictates of my own judgment and not suffer myself to be biased by any supposed wishes formed in England in ignorance of the real circumstances." Castlereagh felt a sense of "responsibility"; he was not moved by mere "popular will" but by "the evaluation of interests not apparent to the multitude." But he also failed politically, therefore, to move public sentiment to support this new and far-reaching policy. "Castlereagh was out of tune not only with his contemporaries but with the entire thrust of modern British foreign policy. He left no legacy" (*D* 91). Castlereagh lived "the tragic isolation of the hero, who, because he cannot communicate, must walk in solitude." He was able to end British isolationism, but only for a time, and only by first addressing Britain's immediate interests and objectives. He accomplished the creation of the conference system, which was "beyond the comprehension of the Cabinet or the British people," only through "a succession of ambiguities." From a certain perspective, he dealt with foreign powers in "good faith" and with his own country through a presentation of appearances or illusions. In his last foreign policy speech to the House of Commons, Castlereagh presented a policy which, in Kissinger's view, was "doomed to failure, because it remained forever incomprehensible to the British public" (*AWR* 124, 221, 276). His statesmanship failed because of his inadequacies as a politician: he could not persuade the British. For Kissinger, the lesson is that "any public official" engaged in diplomacy must practice "hypocrisy" (*YOU* 431).

Castlereagh's goal was peace in Europe, and surely this is the goal of liberal regimes. In his paper on "Universal Peace," James Madison argues that republican governments will be most peaceable because the people who decide whether to go to war are also the ones who will bear the cost of the conflict.[6] Immanuel Kant makes an early suggestion that the growing commercial interdependence of nations will also encourage the development of peaceful and liberal governments.[7] We require, therefore, an explanation as to how or in what circumstances the goal of peace might prove "incomprehensible" to a liberal regime. An energetic and liberal nation may be very good at waging war, but such a regime is not especially well-prepared to maintain peace. War "has no inherent limit," and therefore the nation which can marshal the greatest enthusiasm or which can most readily think itself engaged in a moral crusade can best wage war, at least in the short term. While war requires unlimited commitment and fervor, the "logic of peace is proportion, and proportion implies limitation" (*AWR* 138, 69, 107, 112–13).

From the perspective of the statesman, therefore, times of peace and plenty are actually much more difficult than times of crisis. In a time of crisis it is fairly simple to galvanize public opinion and activity in the interest of national preservation; but, peace does not obviously require action or engagement. In the absence of immediate danger, nations lack the foresight to prepare for (and forestall) future threats. Castlereagh failed "to bring his country into a system of collective security because [Britain] did not feel threatened by foreseeable dangers and thought that they could deal with them alone or, if need be, find allies at the last moment" (*D* 91). Peace can undermine both domestic unity and alliances with foreign powers because the threat which brought unity to the coalition seems absent. "Centrifugal elements" become "increasingly evident." Peace "tend[s] to disintegrate a wartime alliance if nothing holds it together save the memory of common danger" (*AWR* 39, 105; *YOU* 55; *D* 809). Kissinger observes the same dynamic at work among NATO nations through the 1990s (*DAN* 45). The difficulty is that the accomplishment of peace undermines the maintenance of the instruments or the "will" necessary to ensure peace (*WHY* 1256).

Liberals most stake a claim to be peaceable, but they are least inclined to do the work necessary to maintain the peace. While Kissinger acknowledges that détente might "beguile" the West, he insists that the failure of this policy should be attributed to our post-Vietnam "isolationism," to the rise of congressional authority and the concomitant breakdown of the traditional patterns of congressional leadership, and perhaps most especially to the collapse of executive authority in the wake of Watergate (*WHY* 1143; *YOU* 330). Détente proved too difficult a concept for a democratic society that was accustomed to "looking at international relations as a morality play." For such a nation, it is difficult to think about cooperation and confrontation with the same power at the same time (*YOR* 845; *WHY* 1254). "[H]abits" of isolation reassert themselves, and it is difficult for a statesman to explain to politicians and the public why a complex and costly policy is of benefit when there is no obvious enemy. Castlereagh never solved this problem. His system of European conferences was "precautionary," but the British idea of foreign policy was "defensive." The British were prepared to wage war against France, but they could not foresee that the defeat of France would only enhance the relative power of Russia. The great irony is that to maintain a political commitment to peace, one must gin up a threat, and even an occasional war (*AWR* 228, 221–22, 52).

An effective policy of peace is especially challenging to liberal democracies for two reasons. First, the pursuit of peace requires uniting power in the executive. The "essence of foreign policy" is the accumulation of "nuances in pursuit of long-range goals," and for this reason, the executive is the only possible actor who can effectively chart foreign policy. The president ought to be "the symbol of national unity" (*D* 741; *YOR* 50, 74). But our liberal democracy abhors the concentration of power: we either separate powers or add checks and balances in order to avoid the dangers of concentrated power.[8] The centralization of authority reminds us of the requirements for solitary and creative statesmanship that Kissinger has outlined. It was to avoid or minimize political intrusions on statesmanship that Nixon centered his foreign policy team in the

White House (*WHY* 26–29).[9] In the American context, the president's national security advisor is best situated "to take the 'big view'" because he has no responsibility to any agency, and even his responsibility to other branches of government is limited (*YOU* 433). On occasion, and in spite of his subsequent protests that such was not the case, Kissinger would act without consulting Nixon and sometimes even contrary to the president's instructions. Sometimes Kissinger justifies this by the fact that Nixon could and did change his instructions; questionable orders might be overturned, and so it was better to wait to see if they were repeated. Kissinger therefore did not follow Nixon's instructions to arrange a 1970 summit with the Soviets because he thought it was a bad idea; he waited for better instructions. In April 1972, Kissinger disobeyed Nixon's express orders to cut off talks preparatory to the Moscow summit. Nixon eventually changed his mind; in the interim, Kissinger conducted his own policy. On other occasions, Kissinger justifies his actions (as Castlereagh did) by his greater understanding of the particulars of the moment. For example, during his shuttle diplomacy in the Middle East, he was ordered back to Washington, but he stayed to complete the agreement (*YOU* 833, 608; *WHY* 305, 446–47, 495, 566, 1157, 1168, 1351, 1424, 1420; *AWR* 124, 168). In each instance, an unelected, creative statesman acted with a degree of autonomy from elected representatives.

One element of this centralization of power is the enhanced capacity it offers for secret action. Kissinger argues that secrecy is a necessary part of diplomacy because it preserves a capacity for flexibility and allows limited action. Secrecy is vital especially in the early stages of negotiations in order to permit discussions to unfold free of political pressures. A policy that is developed in public almost necessarily lacks nuance and makes compromise more difficult. Kissinger conducted secret negotiations routinely, with the Vietnamese, the Soviets, the Chinese, and in the Middle East. By acting secretly in initial approaches to China, both sides maintained control of the process and of the costs had the approach failed, and they kept bureaucratic infighting to a minimum (*WHY* 453, 704–5, 762–63, 803). As an example of the benefit of conducting diplomacy secretly, Kissinger offers the negotiations in the Middle East. Egypt and Israel each had political reasons not to accept proposals offered by the other side; for example, accepting an Israeli proposal would make Anwar Sadat appear weak. Proposals that appeared to result from American influence were more politically acceptable. But when diplomacy is conducted in public, no such masking is possible. Public negotiations make compromise more difficult for both sides. It is because secrecy is an important tool when developing a flexible and nuanced policy that Kissinger treated the publication of the Pentagon Papers (which offered public revelations of Johnson administration policy making) so seriously (*WHY* 729–30; *YOU* 116, 803).[10]

Kissinger believes this practice of secrecy was necessary given the difficulty of what Nixon was trying to accomplish, but he understands that it carried a cost. The trouble is not that the practice produces poor substance but that it is bad politics. The system of conducting foreign policy from the White House to the exclusion of the departments "ought never to be emulated," especially because it creates problems of implementation and execution (*WHY* 448, 805–6). Nixon might have accomplished more had he sought and won congressional approval for his policy, at least in broad outline. For example, congressional approval of the Paris Peace Accords might have committed Congress to the enforcement provisions of the Vietnam settlement (*YOU* 304–5). Liberal democracy requires greater openness. This means that the requirements of liberal democratic politics impose considerable constraints on the development of a subtle and rational foreign policy. But when the political environment presents great obstacles, the accomplishment of the statesman is most noble or praiseworthy.

The second reason that a policy of peace is a special challenge for liberal democracy is that the liberal approach to peace is not very realistic. American idealism is founded on two opinions:

first, that the system of government in the United States is the best in the world; and, second, that everyone else would be better off if they adopted it (*D* 18). The regime has a tendency toward unilateralism and moral absolutism. Indeed, liberal moralism may itself contribute to policies which in practice undermine the pursuit of peace. A policy shaped fundamentally by ideals is by its nature immoderate and virtually unlimited in its applications. Such a policy leads either to isolationism or to empire (*YOR* 34). Prime Minister William Gladstone embarked on a moral crusade in foreign policy, a crusade that made action impossible and that led to the withdrawal of Britain from the global stage; the unbalanced system that resulted contributed to the outbreak of World War I (*D* 163). America's liberal pragmatism makes it unwilling to confront challenges early. Our moralism prevents us from pursuing realistic opportunities that may carry a short-term moral cost; we choose to remain aloof and pure for as long as possible (*WHY* 1158; *DAN* 239). In contrast to the Chinese, who conduct their affairs "in the great classical tradition of European statesmanship," the United States lacks the "conceptual" and "historical" basis to develop a diplomacy of foresight. That Americans conceive of conflict as "unnatural" is a further problem in the modern world, where our adversaries are patient enough to take incremental bites of our security. The challenges to national security seem ambiguous, almost until it is too late. Our tendency is to react to them hesitantly when in fact we might better deflect a challenge—and with less cost—at its inception (*YOU* 50, 980–81).

The alternative to the morality of isolation is that we become zealots of democracy and in doing so even act contrary to our democratic principles. Democracies that are motivated by moral concerns may have difficulty restraining their crusades. Democracies cannot claim that they are less likely to go to war because of their popular political institutions (or because of the ties of the global marketplace), as Wilson and Madison had argued. Kissinger reminds us that at the outset of World War I, there was considerable popular enthusiasm for the conflict (*D* 161, 221; *DAN* 77). To be sure, Wilson held that because democracies are peaceable, it is in America's interest to make the world safe for democracy. Yet if taken seriously, Wilson's moral policy ("to remake the world in its own [democratic] image") would require "the overthrow of German and Austrian domestic institutions." Kissinger reminds us of G. K. Chesterton's phrase: "virtue runs amok" (*D* 219; *DAN* 243–44, 264, 273).

In short, when moralism draws America into international politics, it may lead us toward empire. Historically, balance of power systems have been rare; empire has been more common. It is for this reason that the Congress of Vienna is so critical: it is an example of an orderly world without empire, and therefore a model for a United States that has rhetorically opposed empire even while it became an empire (*D* 21). American idealism must be moderated with a sense of the national interest. Attention to interest can act as a restraint on our missionary zeal because our interests are more limited than our ideals (*YOR* 1074–75; *DAN* 158). Without such restraint we overreach, as we did in Vietnam, and the public withdraws into isolationism. American policy in such circumstances expands and contracts; it is inconstant and undependable. And such a policy is felt as American dominance, not leadership, in much of the world. This was the root of Kissinger's concern for an apparently honorable end to the war in Vietnam. Without an honorable peace, the isolationist element in America would reassert control over policy. Kissinger seeks to combine pragmatism and idealism—to moderate the moralist and to give moral direction to our security concerns (*YOU* 60; *YOR* 1076).

One way a statesman might address the intrusion of domestic politics on his larger project is to deliberately court domestic political support. The "central dilemma of the statesman" and "the core question of leadership in a democracy" is to what extent a leader must follow his own "judgment" and to what extent he must "submit" to the "public mood." He must accomplish his substantial purposes in the context of the restraints imposed by the domestic culture and politics.

The statesman "must be a visionary and educator," but he should not attempt "to play God" (*YOU* 309, 1208). "Domestic support" is the "acid test" of a policy. There are two aspects to this test. It must be supported by the bureaucracy, a bureaucracy which tends toward conservative programs. It must also harmonize with history and national experience (*AWR* 326). A policy that does not fit in the context of a culture has little chance for political support, no matter how prudent it may be. The purpose of education is to understand the limits of our idealism, or to learn respect for the art of the possible. The great lesson of the Ford administration, a lesson that really began during the Nixon years, was that "American foreign policy had to come to terms with its limits." Ironically, if America could learn to live within the limits of power politics, it could accomplish more (*YOR* 1068; *D* 707, 756, 810, 835). As long as idealistic public opinion has not been educated for the real world, "no serious national policy" is possible. Kissinger acknowledges that his skills "were strategic analysis and diplomacy" and not the political skill of "mobilizing popular constituencies." Political skills prove necessary to diplomacy in order to implement and execute the policy (*WHY* 516; *YOR* 1074). Central to Kissinger's project, therefore, is an account of the relation between the statesman and the political community. Without such education, we face again the "gulf" between the perceptions of statesmen and the sentiments expressed in public debate, the same gulf that Castlereagh faced and that was manifested again during the later part of the Vietnam War (*WHY* 482; *DAN* 256).

Kissinger therefore recognizes the critical importance of the statesman's duty to educate the public. Nations learn by accumulated experience, but learning by experience teaches us about what has happened. If the world changes, experience is a poor guide. To accomplish his work, the statesman must build on the "experience" of his people in order to shape "its future." This returns the statesman to the problem of "permanence," of establishing a policy which survives his own implementation of it (*AWR* 329–30). Because the challenges in the modern world are so complex and so ambiguous, the "most important task of the second Nixon administration was therefore psychological: to educate the American public in the complexity of the world we would have to manage." The public had to learn how to be vigilant against "ambiguous and seemingly marginal assaults" at the same time that we pursued "coexistence" with our adversary. Nixon failed miserably in his role as educator, a role Kissinger describes as a "moral challenge." Kissinger observes that much of this failure was the result of Watergate and the public's loss of confidence in Nixon. After Vietnam and Watergate, and the secretive practices of the Nixon White House, the "domestic climate" was "ill suited for any thoughtful discussion" (*YOU* 981, 983, 1029, 1209; *D* 731, 741). But even before Watergate Nixon indicated that he was not inclined to do the most difficult work of reshaping opinions to produce a public and a bureaucracy that is prepared to maintain a policy after the statesman is gone. Given the choice of imposing "discipline" on the bureaucracy, Nixon decided instead to "circumvent" it. The backchannel system of negotiations had the effect of "imposing coherence" on the foreign policy process by centralizing that process in the executive. But instead of producing a sentiment favorable to his policy, Nixon's tactics only encouraged opposition (*WHY* 841; *YOR* 79).

Nixon's political failure is just a small part of the larger "moral collapse" of the foreign policy aristocracy. Yet the disparity between public opinion and prudence is not a necessary one. The American public, or the silent majority, supported the policies of Nixon and Kissinger in Vietnam (*WHY* 292–93). And on occasion Kissinger claims greater "faith in democracy" than his critics demonstrate (*YOU* 243). For all the demands for an idealist policy, Kissinger believes that over the long term, moral concerns cannot sustain public support. The reality of our interests is strong enough to sway even ardent idealists in times of crisis. Watergate eroded the authority of the executive, and Kissinger feared that such erosion would cripple the capacity of the United States to conduct a coherent foreign policy. In the wake of Watergate, American foreign policy was sustained through a kind of "bluff" (*YOR* 18). In the end, even Kissinger's critics tacitly acknowledged that diplomacy requires a central authority for its conduct, though they continued to condemn such authority. A "national instinct for self-preservation" trumped partisan political concerns and impelled the public and Congress to create in Kissinger "a surrogate center around which the national purpose could rally" (*YOU* xx, 76, 122, 125–26, 416, 446; *YOR* 189). International action "can be sustained only if the public is convinced that the interests at stake justify the cost" (*DAN* 258). Perhaps the best example of a popular failure to understand a policy is the case of détente and the linkage that helped shape it. The idea that events in one part of the world may be linked together, either naturally or through negotiations, is a fundamental element in a realistic approach to the world. The complex amalgam of cooperation and confrontation that marked détente was too difficult to explain to society at large. The linkage that produced it seemed to compromise America's moral standards too much (*YOR* 845). In an "interdependent" world, events are linked by "reality, not policy." "One of the principal tasks of statesmanship" is to recognize linkages and use them to "create a network of incentives and penalites to produce the most favorable outcome" (*D* 717; *WHY* 129). But the statesman must also educate the public, in terms the public can accept, of the rightness of such a strategy.

The National Soul

One of the surprising aspects of Kissinger's thought is the degree to which he claims that a moral concern shapes his realpolitik. In an appearance before the Senate Foreign Relations Committee in September 1973, Kissinger expressed the view that the conduct of American foreign policy is not merely a problem of practical or technical concern. Our policy "expresses our ideals, our purposes and our hopes for the world. It must fulfill the best in America." The challenges of politics "closely reflect our view of ourselves. They require a sense of identity and purpose as much as a sense of policy. Throughout our history we have thought of what we did as growing out of deeper moral values. America was not true to itself unless it had a meaning beyond itself" (*AFP* 190). As he explains in the first volume of his memoirs, America's pursuit of peace must also reflect our concern for what we call "justice." Much earlier, in *A World Restored* (1957), Kissinger remarked more broadly that "any international settlement represents a stage in a process by which a nation reconciles its vision of itself with the vision of it by other powers." The nation believes it stands for a particular conception of justice, and this is especially true of democratic nations, "for government functions effectively only when most citizens obey voluntarily and they will obey only to the extent that they consider the demands of their rulers just" (*AWR* 144; *WHY* 841, 1245). We should observe that in this passage Kissinger does not yet explore the question of whether the rulers must actually behave justly, or only seem to; if the ruler's purpose is to win obedience, then perhaps the rhetoric of justice is sufficient. Given his critique of American idealism, the good that Kissinger envisions as representative of America may not be a particularly American good. It is fine to say that a moral concern is at the center of our politics—but which moral concern?

Kissinger acknowledges that the "subtlest critique of our policy held that our emphasis on the national interest ran counter to American idealism and national character." The policy and approach of the Nixon administration was "un-American" in that it placed "national interest" ahead of America's "historical perception" of itself as a nation fundamentally guided by disinterested attention to principles and values. Kissinger believes this critique "reflects a lack of faith in democracy" (and implicitly democracy is capable of a realistic policy), but it is a lack of faith he shares (*YOU* 242–43; *WHY* 1089). Kissinger is therefore eager to show that his style of diplomacy is not at all "un-American," that it fits into the American political tradition. In *Diplomacy* (1994), that tradition is represented largely by Theodore Roosevelt. Elsewhere, Kissinger indicates that Founders like Alexander Hamilton also had a nuanced understanding of international diplomacy (*DAN* 248, 240). Though George Washington spoke of avoiding entangling alliances, Kissinger treats this as rhetoric with a subtle diplomatic purpose. The policy actually employs European conflicts to balance European powers in the new world in the service of American interests (*WHY* 58–59). In a similar vein, he treats the American Revolution in a way that verifies the importance of a history and culture of liberty, and diminishes adherence to the ideal of liberty. For the most part, revolutions for liberty end in "new tools of authority," as the French and Russian Revolutions ended. True liberty must develop out of history, customs, and social unity. Toleration is only possible in societies that face no "irreconcilable schisms." From Kissinger's perspective, therefore, the American Revolution is really a restoration of historic free institutions and not so much a rebellion. It does not reflect a philosophical devotion to "a single standard of virtue"; indeed, adherence to such a standard too easily collapses into tyranny (*WHY* 1063; *DAN* 264, 273). Where an idealist embraces the "truths" of the Declaration of Independence, Kissinger emphasizes that "we hold" these things to be true. Our ideology is a servant of our culture. Western democracy is thus the result of an unfolding historical process, "an evolution extending over centuries" (*YOR* 1072–73; *WHY* 1088). Kissinger employs our culture of freedom to turn us toward a consideration of history—the world as it works—and away from idealism.

The fundamental difficulty with mere idealism is its approach to history. Our idealism suggests that our institutions and experiences are universally applicable. We believe in the myth of the self-made man, that we may be free of the past and that the future offers limitless possibilities. Kissinger recognizes that this refusal to be bound by history "confer[s] a great dignity, even beauty, on the American way of life." At the same time, American idealism lacks "a complex understanding of new realities." The American idealist tradition "emphasizes universal truths rather than national characteristics" (*D* 833; *YOU* 88). During the Cold War, the ultimate test of our idealism was the crusade to save and transform Vietnam. In Vietnam, we found that our tradition of universal truths is not readily applicable in other contexts. If Vietnam offers any lesson at all, it is a lesson in the limits of American power and interests, and the necessity of establishing an intellectual framework that makes those limits palpable and acceptable. The lesson of Vietnam is that we must be realists (*YOR* 1071–72; *YOU* 85; *DAN* 247, 257, 267, 272).

Kissinger's view of the development of American democracy indicates something of his separation from the philosophic understanding of other American thinkers. His account is historical, reminiscent of the work of Friedrich Hayek. Hayek held that society develops through history and not according to a rational or philosophic plan. As a result, the world is considerably more chaotic, and more free, than many other liberals contend.[11] Similarly, Kissinger concludes that "democracy did not result from a single decision but rather from an evolution extending over centuries." Our knowledge and understanding are essentially limited. Recognizing these limits is part of a mature policy; only by recognizing limits may we transcend them. From the perspective of the historian, this is probably correct; but, from the perspective of political philosophy, it raises doubts about the foundations of our liberal idealism. If our beliefs and our character are the result of social evolution, then they may not finally be true: there may finally be no morality but only constructions, interpretations, uses. "[S]acrifices" are "meaningful" when we make them so. To be sure, he also declares that "violations of human rights cannot be condoned by invoking stages of historical evolution" (*YOR* 1072–73; *WHY* 55). And yet he has, so to speak, let the cat out of the bag. The fundamental virtue of the statesman is not wisdom or piety or justice (though moderation makes a strong claim). The greatest virtue is a courageous creativity, and this is necessarily the work of one man alone. In this sense, Kissinger objects to democracy more than he does to liberalism. When "all advice tends to become equivalent," as it does in egalitarian societies, then it is increasingly difficult to "choos[e]" an "interpretation" of history. The United States, "to be true to itself," must stand for human rights because this is our conception of justice; but it is not justice simply or purely. By this interpretation, extreme idealism is of course folly, and not even especially moral. For Kissinger, the United States has demonstrated its moral "worthiness to survive" when it faces a serious test of survival and emerges victorious (*NFC* 7, 9, 343, 349–53; *WHY* 55).

The American tradition of idealism is best understood as a tradition—an historical development—and not as a true claim to a superior philosophic understanding of justice (*DAN* 237–51). Any American claim to a superior philosophic understanding of justice is suspect because our history is unique and therefore not likely to produce a concept that might be translated easily to others. Our idealist tradition is a result of our unique geographic situation through the nineteenth century. Americans "traditionally" see foreign relations as a series of episodes, "discreet self-contained problems" that are unrelated to one another. The American image of international relations is of "an essentially benign world whose harmony was interrupted occasionally by crises that were aberrations from the norm." We conceive of conflict as "unnatural" and of peace as normal (*YOU* 980; *WHY* 61). We segment foreign policy into episodes and absolutes rather than a "continuum requiring constant attention and adjustment" and "the shaping of reality by means of nuances." America came to believe that it could make straightforward choices in foreign policy between good and evil (choices that proved elusive in its domestic politics)—that it would face no moral compromises in its foreign policy but instead could expect "perfection" (*YOR* 33, 97). The Wilsonian tradition of diplomacy identifies the quest for peace with a crusade or mission of spreading its ideals and disdains calculations of equilibrium. To some degree, this tradition depends on the idea that America does not act from a sense of interest at all but from an unselfish devotion to justice (*D* 45). Wilsonian America "rebel[s]" against the simple truth that "great goals" and "the noblest ends" in foreign policy are accomplished only in "imperfect stages." We must learn to moderate our "idealism" with our "interest" (*YOR* 48, 107; *YOU* 989). "To be truly American, any concept of national interest must flow from the country's democratic tradition and concern with the vitality of democracy around the world" (*DAN* 31). Interest is a moderate guide to policy because it is limited. It invites us to engage with the world, and it does not permit us to dominate it. What we must learn most of all is the practical limits of our power, and therefore especially the limits of our idealism.

Kissinger looks to history and culture for guidance in a way that is realistic, though it is not entirely comfortable in the context of the American ethos. This approach raises anew the question about the place of our idealism in the real world. Kissinger explored a Kantian approach to the "Meaning of History" in his undergraduate thesis.[12] Kissinger objected to Kant's "teleological history" because it did not permit enough room for individual action. He returns—very briefly—to Kant's essay on *Perpetual Peace* in the first volume of his memoirs. In the new nuclear age, he writes, "peace has become a moral imperative." The difficulty is that if we make peace "the *sole* objective" of policy, then we risk capitulation to "the most ruthless" in an effort to avoid war. The pursuit of peace, without real power behind it, leads to events like the appeasement of Hitler at Munich in 1938. The Kantian end is best served by Machiavellian means. In Kissinger's hands, the "moral imperative" of peace is sometimes cast as a moral imperative simply and sometimes as a means to some other end. "Every new President" must face "the moral necessity of avoiding nuclear war," because "[i]f he is perceived otherwise" he will lose domestic support for his policy. Before he can act as a practical guide, "the President must establish his moral leadership" (*WHY* 67–68, 70). But this treatment is different from the Kantian one or puts a new light on Kissinger's Kantian claim. A show of the Kantian concern has become a means to Machiavellian power. The lesson of Wilson is that America cannot sustain international action without a justification from "moral faith." The public's perception of a leader's moral compass matters because it is a useful instrument for shaping popular opinion. The "faith" of the people in their leaders is "a precious asset" (*D* 50; *YOU* 979, 1031). Morality is reduced to an element of realism, and a pragmatic element at that.

All politics implies some conception of the good. What is the good at which Kissinger's policies aim? There is something of the Machiavellian in Kissinger's treatment of morality. To win the power to do good, one must appear good but not necessarily be good. But like Machiavelli, Kissinger describes layers of moral action. Realist policy does not simply employ a mask of virtue to hide its viciousness. Viciousness is sometimes a necessary instrument for accomplishing a moral end. Kissinger aims to combine theory and practice, idealism and pragmatism, in a way that moderates both of these extremes. To overcome this tension, Kissinger claims that securing the nation is the most moral act possible. This realist morality is justified by the Hamiltonian understanding that national leaders have special duties and therefore special moral concerns. Kissinger and Hamilton presume that there is a national or common interest to defend, that the United States is something other than a pluralist or individualist agglomeration of private interests. Kissinger writes that leaders and statesmen have a special moral obligation "to our own people" (*WHY* 1349). Alexander Hamilton argues that once leaders take on the duty of national defense, then "as a necessary consequence . . . there can be no limitation of that authority." Our desire for limited liberal democratic government must, Hamilton reminds us, bow to the "necessity" of national security (*The Federalist* no. 23). Leaders and statesmen who defend the liberal nation must employ an authority that is at least potentially illiberal; at some level, this is a moral burden to them. At the same time, the exercise of such authority to preserve the free nation is itself a moral act. Both Hamilton and Kissinger conclude that the liberal idea is necessarily limited by the reality of international relations. The question then is not whether Kissinger used moral claims as an instrument of policy; he tells us that a statesman does that. The issue is the morality of using morality as an instrument. The moral purpose requires amoral or immoral means that are justified through a moral facade. This formula makes international affairs especially contentious and difficult because it raises questions about the very idea of justice that the nation embraces.

The ultimate questions of international relations are questions of justice. "The whole domestic effort of a people exhibits an effort to transform force into obligation by means of a consensus on the nature of justice." Politics is about claims to the good, and as such can provide meaning to life. This experience—this development of a common conception of justice—collides with the international experience. Different nations define legitimacy, and therefore justice, in different ways. Getting along in the world requires reconciling different understandings of justice or compromising the nation's ideal. In this context, two problems arise. First, it is difficult for statesmen to resolve problems because they often lack a shared conception of legitimacy. Second, and "perhaps more importantly," even if statesmen may agree among themselves, "they will not be able to legitimize the attainable international consensus domestically." Domestically, a shared conception of justice implies "unity of will and execution" (*AWR* 328–29; *DAN* 20). At the level of international politics that domestic consensus is applied contingently, which is to say that the national ideal is compromised. For example, in 1813 the growing strength of Britain and Prussia, and the decline of a French power that could balance them, left Austria profoundly weakened. For Metternich, that meant that the defense of his nation and its conception of justice must be achieved "with gentler means." Kissinger points out that such a tactic of "collaboration" places a strain on the moral principles of the nation. Collaboration might damage "the national substance," and this is so because it requires a leadership which dissembles, which appears sincere but is not. "In such periods the knave and the hero, the traitor and the statesman are distinguished, not by their acts, but by their motives." For this reason, "many nations" (and not only liberal democracies) exhibit a "rebellion against foreign policy" (*AWR* 20, 328–29).

America's conception of justice confronted the reality of compromised ideals during the Vietnam War. Vietnam, a policy born out of unlimited American idealism, ultimately proved most divisive. "The real debate" over America's policy on Vietnam came to be "over the definition of national honor." Kissinger hoped that ending the war on "honorable" terms would end America's internal divisions (*YOR* 466, 1071).[13] National unity itself became an important value because "internal divisions" could be "exploited" by the Soviets "to undermine government credibility and perhaps the cohesion of our society" (*WHY* 226–27, 523, 801; *YOR* 99). Furthermore, the domestic turmoil the war produced undermined the nation's capacity for genuinely moral action abroad. An honorable peace could satisfy idealists on the Left and the Right, members of the peace movement as well as those who insisted on a commitment to defend the independence of South Vietnam. Kissinger hoped that the Paris Peace Accord might make possible "reconciliation" in America as well as give "meaning" to the sacrifices of the war (*YOR* 466; *WHY* 1349). At the end of his memoirs, Kissinger claims that the Nixon-Ford foreign policy was designed to pursue moral aims incrementally, within the limits of real power. "Traditional American values . . . provide the inner strength" for the nation to pursue its interests in an ambiguous world as it strives toward goals that are by their nature provisional. Yet Nixon's emphasis on American interests is not in the American tradition and cannot be conducted as a moral crusade; the defense of interests requires "staying power." In the case of Vietnam, this meant that the executive had to defend American interests but in a way that appealed to American morality. Americans, like the British of Castlereagh's time, are not comfortable with ambiguity and gradualism. "Our message of balance ran up against the Wilsonian sense of American mission" (*D* 742; *YOR* 1070).

Were the United States to "overthrow an allied government," it would commit the ultimate "act of dishonor." Such dishonor is both a moral problem and, more realistically, would "mortgage America's international position for a long time to come." Kissinger describes the relationship between our moral commitment and our prudential concern in this way: "It would be inhumane, ignoble, and destructive of larger interests elsewhere to withdraw while fighting continued against those who had relied on us" (*WHY* 282, 1307; *YOU* 83). Concomitant with his concern for honor is a concern for America's credibility. For Nixon, too, ending the war was necessary to maintain "America's standing in the world" (*D* 703). For Kissinger and Nixon, morality and prudence intersected in Vietnam. Once the nation had committed itself to defend South Vietnam, it became essential—as a matter of morality and prudence—that we not abandon an ally. The problem in Vietnam is how to leave, and yet honor our commitments and demonstrate (to our allies and to the Soviets) that we will continue to honor our commitments in the future (*WHY* 227–28, 510, 515; *YOR* 94, 469). The concern for honor is therefore instrumental to the realist's concern for security. But security is not quite an end in itself. The statesman seeks to make secure the nation and therefore to preserve the nation's conception of justice. Kissinger defends the Nixon administration's policy in Vietnam partly on moral grounds, noting that both Nixon and Ford insisted that we had a "moral obligation"—one we had taken on voluntarily—to defend the South Vietnamese (*YOR* 471, 526, 542). The aim of the policy in Vietnam was to end the war without undermining United States power to build and maintain a security system that preserves free nations. The moral end—preserving freedom—requires means that many Americans felt were immoral. The work of a statesman to accomplish his moral end therefore faces a political problem. A popular opinion about national honor is necessary to support the power that is required to accomplish the moral end.

In Kissinger's view, those on the Left who opposed the war were really trying, and failing, to address a metaphysical question. They looked for "meaning" in their lives but found themselves in a "spiritual desert" (*WHY* 299–300). They failed to locate meaning because they did not understand that meaning must be found in a political-historical context. The question of meaning is related to the question of identity, and the answer to the question of identity is in part a political answer. Political relations define one state against others or apart from others. Where philosophy aims to comprehend universal nature, politics is necessarily particular. Politics requires patriotism. Patriotic attachment to the political regime suggests a claim about which state—or which life—is highest or best. To demand an end to patriotism or honor is to ask for an end to politics understood as a declaration of justice or the good, or to demand ideological imperialism. What gives America its unity—unity necessary for the maintenance of a strong nation—is its insistence on the "universal applicability of the idea of liberty." Though many on the Left are critical of our nation's historical failings, they take seriously the "truths" Jefferson describes in the Declaration. This unity with respect to our ideals is a vital part of our security posture. It "provide[s] the faith to sustain America through all the ambiguities of choice in an imperfect world" (*D* 811, 836). It also does not prepare us for those ambiguities. American liberalism teaches that we are naturally free, bound only to those relationships we choose. If we are perfectly free—if all choices are open to us—then how can we know what to choose? The protesters confront an existential crisis. The crisis is not of their making. Idealism led us to Vietnam, but when our ideals failed we were left adrift.

As Bismarck noted, politics is the art of the possible, not the ideal. But politics must be guided by an ideal. Statesmen look to idealism in part to know what it is they should create. Morality guides the ultimate purposes of our policy. No nation can "define its choices" without a "moral compass" that gives meaning to "sacrifices" (*WHY* 55). Without a "moral element," pragmatism leads to "brutality" and "stagnation." But "moral conviction" without "a sense of reality" leads to "fanaticism." "We cannot abandon national security in pursuit of virtue. But beyond this bedrock of all policy, our challenge is to advance our principles in a way that does not isolate us in the long run." Kissinger seeks to "blend morality and power," or to pursue moral ends within the realistic limits of power (*YOR* 1070, 1076). The limit on our pursuit of principle is our preservation. At the same time, the rhetoric of morality may serve as a useful instrument of realism. Metternich's task was to preserve Austria's "integrity" in the face of the revolutionary period in Europe, but Kissinger adds that adherence to Austrian principles "in the course of time was bound to bring Austria powerful allies." Honor, in this treatment, is an instrument of power (*AWR* 17, 22). In America, this means that "no serious American maker of foreign policy can be oblivious to the traditions of exceptionalism by which American democracy has defined itself" (*DAN* 20). Foreign policy requires an appreciation of the "reality" of psychology and therefore of "public opinion." That psychological component is related to popular perceptions of morality: a moral argument wins American public opinion. "[V]alues and principles would inspire our efforts and set our direction," but the actual strategy would reflect the fact that the world requires compromise, "imperfect choices, partial fulfillment" of our moral goals. The democratic ideal is essential for "domestic cohesion," but it cannot serve as a "mechanical blueprint" for foreign policy. Leaders must therefore "endow" their objectives "with a meaning compatible with the values of their society." Moral values and ideology thus serve a political purpose; in reality, a strategy for peace and freedom must proceed incrementally. This is a subtlety hard to communicate to the American people (*YOU* 98, 706, 979; *WHY* 1089). Kissinger acknowledges his failure to pursue a realist policy within the rhetoric of the American tradition.

The great example of a successful mixing was the presidency of Ronald Reagan. Kissinger bestows particular credit on Reagan, but he also qualifies that credit considerably. Reagan's view of foreign policy was "strictly American-utopian." Reagan believed that "communist intransigence" was based on "ignorance"; if Gorbachev could be educated, the Soviet Union's policy would change. His attitude reflects "the irrepressible American conviction that understanding between peoples is normal, that tension is an aberration, and that trust can be generated by the strenuous demonstration of goodwill." Reagan was "bored" by the "details" of foreign policy: "Analysis of substantive issues was not his forte." Yet his foreign policy was consistent and relevant, and his doctrine had "considerable intellectual power." Kissinger concludes that "a sense of direction and having the strength of one's convictions are the key ingredients of leadership" (*D* 765, 769, 770–71). Kissinger's problem is to explain the success of the liberal Reagan, a man who lacked a sense of nuance and limits. Reagan understood less but accomplished more because he was able to tap into the idealistic strands of the national soul as he crafted a fairly hardheaded policy. He was the first president to take both ideological and geostrategical offensives, to offer a "synthesis" of Wilsonian rhetoric and inspiration and "geopolitical perspicacity" (*YOR* 109–11; *DAN* 250). Reagan's success was due to his ability to employ realistic means and idealistic rhetoric, and to use his rhetoric for strategic advantage. Reagan and his advisers used the issue of human rights "as a tool for overthrowing communism." Most important, Reagan's foreign policy was marked in the end by "an almost Machiavellian realism." Reagan aided democrats, Islamic fundamentalists, rightists, and warlords. They "shared a common enemy, and in the world of national interest, that made them allies." The difference between Reagan and Nixon was therefore not in their approach to Soviet aggression but in the tactics and rhetoric they employed. Reagan followed Wilson in describing our opposition to the Soviets in terms of American exceptionalism. Nixon "took American idealism seriously" but also felt obliged to relate American ideals to "the way the world actually worked." Nixon followed Theodore Roosevelt in placing American interests at the center of his conduct of policy. Nixon understood the world, but Reagan understood "the American soul." As a result, Reagan was capable of "uniting" the American people in a way Nixon never could. He was, moreover, extraordinarily fortunate. "The phenomenon of Reagan sprang from a fortuitous convergence of personality and opportunity." A sign of Reagan's good fortune is the extraordinarily bad fortune of his counterpart, Mikhail Gorbachev. "[F]ortune simply would not smile on Mikhail Gorbachev" (*D* 706, 766–67, 772–75, 792, 802). Kissinger is aware that fortune is not the same as luck. A nation's fortune can be made good. Like Reagan, Nixon aimed at the destruction or transformation of the Soviet Union, but as a long-term strategy (*YOR* 884; *YOU* 989). What in 1968 is a long-term strategy bears fruit in 1988 as an immediate possibility. In the long run, Reagan's policy would have threatened the cohesion of the Atlantic alliance, but he "transformed what had been a marathon race into a sprint" (*D* 784). The Cold War ended before the disunity in the alliance could be felt. Reagan appeared at the right time, as the statesmanship and policies of the early 1970s (many of which were continued into the Reagan administration) bore their fruit.

Creating the Future

One of Kissinger's most recent works is for the generation "born after 1960" (*DAN* 30). His concern is for a future that will be managed without him, and he hopes to shape the new statesman. Neither isolationism nor empire are possible in the twenty-first century. "What *is* new" in the new world order "is that, for the first time, the United States can neither withdraw from the world nor dominate it" (*D* 19). We must learn to live within the limits of what is possible. Typically, Americans do not understand that our power has real limits, limits that are political in nature and so cannot easily be overcome by advances in technology or weaponry (*YOR* 1069). For the first time, the new order distributes power-centers "around the entire globe," and it does so in an environment in which leaders and "their publics" experience events "instantaneously and simultaneously" (*D* 808). The work of analysis is now much more difficult because the enhanced role of the public exacerbates the pressures of time. The public lacks the patience and fortitude to see a difficult policy to fruition. The "dilemma of the modern democratic leader" is that it takes longer "for a policy to bear fruit," while "the down side" of a policy shows itself "immediately." In this world, we require "a permanent American participation" that depends "on the ability to accumulate nuances" (*YOU* 193; *YOR* 107). We now need "far more subtle applications" of diplomacy. Absent an overriding ideological concern, nations will increasingly pursue policies that reflect their national interest (*D* 803, 805).[14] Yet in an interdependent world no nation can act alone; each must adjust its policies and moderate its behavior. It is increasingly unrealistic for America to expect to dominate or direct international affairs; we must rather lead. Nixon saw this first, and such leadership is not entirely in accord with the attitude of Wilsonian idealism (*YOU* 621; *YOR* 93). History is an imperfect guide to our future, but Kissinger finds that Wilsonian idealism is becoming even "less relevant" and "less practicable." He therefore advises that we return to a study of the periods prior to Wilson's presidency for clues to the world we can shape now. The new international order "bears many similarities to the European state system of the eighteenth and nineteenth centuries, and to practices which American statesmen and thinkers have consistently questioned." Metternich and Bismarck become the models—in some ways positive and in some ways negative—for future American policy (*D* 805, 810; *DAN* 41).

The great lesson of Metternich and Bismarck is that neither values nor power are enough in themselves to preserve peace. Metternich succeeded in establishing an international order because the heads of state in Europe also shared a conviction regarding what constituted legitimacy. This shared conviction provided a sense of "unity." He succeeded in providing stability during a time of revolutionary change. But Metternich's system depended on him, on his work alone; because the statesman is a "solitary figure," he inevitably faces a problem in his attempts to establish a lasting system. Metternich never set a task for himself that carried the real possibility of failure; he never had to "contemplate an abyss . . . as a challenge to overcome." In the end, Metternich's detachment prevented him from accomplishing something genuinely creative (*AWR* 319–20, 322). He was not sufficiently heroic. Metternich's balance of power required a system of shared beliefs, an almost Wilsonian concern for law and legitimacy, and a relatively large number of actors who would be able to shift and thus maintain the balance of power. The Cold War world was an especially difficult time for a policy of "nuance" and "balance." Because the Cold War world was bipolar, unity among allies was essential and departures from that unity especially dangerous. The opening of relations with China edged the Cold War world from one like Bismarck's toward one like Metternich's. Metternich was the model for Kissinger's triangular diplomacy, a diplomacy that aims at "equilibrium" and that permits greater nuance and flexibility in policy making (*WHY* 67–69, 178, 192, 1049). The result is a policy that Kissinger hopes has committed the United States to permanent engagement in international affairs at the same time that it makes domination less desirable and less possible.

Bismarck's realpolitik, however, diminished the importance of a shared understanding of legitimacy and proceeded instead from an understanding of the central fact of power. Bismarck did not deny the "efficacy of moral consensus," but he treated it as only one element of power. Bismarck rested Prussia's claim "on its strength rather than on universal values." Clashing interests, especially the "geopolitical rivalry" between Austria and Russia, transcended the unity established by shared moral values (*D* 128, 146–47, 158, 169). What Kissinger finds remarkable about Bismarck is his "moderation after victory" (*WHY* 110). His aim was to achieve secure borders; that accomplished, he exercised a restrained, "prudent," and "stabilizing foreign policy." His "magnificent grasp of the nuances of power" enabled him to replace "philosophical constraints" with self-interested "self-restraint." Bismarck understood that as the "strongest" state in Europe, Germany proved "disquieting to its neighbors," and therefore that the strongest state must exercise the greatest moderation. Still, Bismarck's intricate realpolitik served "the preservation of peace." This is a policy that works when the number of major actors is relatively few; it is also inherently unstable (*D* 126–28, 133–34, 166, 169; *WHY* 110). Having based his policy on the balance of power and the defense of interests, Bismarck found that he could make no claim to moral legitimacy, nor could he use arguments from moral legitimacy to tie the nations of Europe together. Those who followed him could not integrate the teaching of self-restraint into their policy making because Germany possessed no "integrating philosophical framework" but only a reliance on power. Over time, Bismarck's successors "relied more and more on sheer strength." The "spirits of power" could not be restrained or managed. The more Germany relied on military strength, the more it encouraged its neighbors to build their armaments (*D* 131, 134, 169–70, 172).

Obviously, Metternich's reliance on a shared conception of legitimacy appeals to Wilsonian idealists. Yet Kissinger finds that Bismarck's style of unilateralism may be most in keeping with the American tradition (*D* 835). We are not good at accepting limits or at acting in cooperation with others. Our unilateralism is related to our idealism. Kissinger is critical of contemporary human rights advocates who pursue justice even at the expense of peace. They "trust jurists more than they do statesmen." This trust not only threatens sovereignty and the practice of self-government, but it also "risk[s] substituting the tyranny of judges for that of governments; historically, the dictatorship of the virtuous has often led to inquisitions and even witch hunts" (*DAN* 237, 273). Bismarck's system descended into the politics of raw power and then to the world wars. With Bismarck's passing, as with Metternich's in the previous generation, the system of peace itself collapsed. Kissinger fears the same will happen to the equilibrium he and Nixon established unless we can construct a system along the lines of the one Metternich maintained in the first half of the nineteenth century. In our case, this means constructing a system of shared democratic values combined with balance of power realism. Faced with crusaders, on the one hand, and isolationists, on the other hand (each aiming at an impossible purity), a moderate policy is most appealing. A balance of power system cannot be established once and for all; it "requires constant tending" (*D* 119, 810, 834).

Kissinger has two messages to impart to America. The first of these is directed to democrats. The statesman is not a democratic character, and the regime distrusts him. If his work is necessary to the regime, if individuals of special insight, creativity, and courage are important for shaping the future, then such aristocratic characters must rise quietly, almost in opposition to the character of the regime. Their schooling, their acculturation for aristocratic work in the service of democracy, is a special problem. They must endure in the face of what is likely to be some degree of censure from the nation they serve. The second lesson is for liberals (of the Left and the Right) who insist that idealism must be the centerpiece of American policy. Kissinger makes the obvious argument that we cannot make our ideals into reality without getting our hands dirty. Our idealism requires that someone be impure; it is the statesmen who bear that burden. More subtly, Kissinger points to a particular understanding of the liberal claim to be uniquely moral among regimes. The liberal regime, pressed to its limit, is not essentially different from others. As Hamilton pointed out centuries ago, in the real world liberal idealism encounters the same requirements of security as any other regime. It is better at persuading people that it is different.

Liberalism best masks the troubling reality of politics. A statesman must then accomplish the work of realism while demonstrating respect for the liberal soul he defends. Democracy and liberalism thus impose special obstacles to the work of the statesman. The defense of liberal democracy is therefore most difficult and in that sense most noble. We need beasts to democracy and ogres to liberalism if we are to defend democracy and liberalism.

Notes

1. Quotations from and references to Kissinger's works are cited in the text using the following abbreviations:

AFP: *American Foreign Policy: Expanded Edition* (New York: W. W. Norton, 1974).

AWR: *A World Restored: Metternich, Castlereagh and the Problems of Peace 1812–1822* (Boston: Houghton Mifflin Company, 1973).

D: *Diplomacy* (New York: Simon and Schuster Touchstone, 1994).

DAN: *Does America Need a Foreign Policy? Toward a Diplomacy for the 21st Century* (New York: Simon and Schuster, 2001).

NFC: *The Necessity For Choice: Prospects of America Foreign Policy* (New York: Harper and Brothers, 1960 and 1961).

WHY: *White House Years* (New York: Little, Brown, and Co., 1979).

YOR: *Years of Renewal* (New York: Simon and Schuster, 1999).

YOU: *Years of Upheaval* (New York: Little, Brown, and Co., 1982).

2. When Castlereagh failed to persuade the British to engage in continental politics, he committed suicide (*AWR* 310–11; *D* 91). In Kissinger's account, statesmen in other regimes encounter similar political constraints, if not as obviously. See, for example, his analysis of Metternich's relations with Emperor Francis I of Austria (*AWR* 72–74, 76, 79–82, 212). Kissinger finds a similar problem in "other countries in the free world." He calls this a "spiritual malaise" (*NFC* 352). Kissinger explicitly compares Castlereagh's relation to Britain with Woodrow Wilson's relation to the United States (*D* 96, 80).

3. On the other hand, Sadat, representing an authoritarian system, has the power to make "sweeping gestures" that democracies find difficult to understand (*YOU* 829).

4. The U.S. Foreign Service approaches foreign policy in a way that "reflect[s] much of American attitudes and historical experience." The State Department is very good at producing people with expertise in particular areas, but not at providing "leadership grounded in a philosophy of the world and guided by a sense of purpose" (*YOU* 444–45). It treats problems as they arise, and because it segments the world by regions, it lacks a comprehensive strategic picture of the whole (*WHY* 589–91).

5. For an account of a similar process, but specific to the character of Nixon himself, see *WHY* 11ff.

6. *The Mind of the Founder: Sources of the Political Thought of James Madison*, ed. Marvin Meyers (Hanover, N.H.: Brandeis University Press, 1981), 192. In contrast, see Hamilton's *The Federalist* no. 6.

7. Kant makes these suggestions, which of course do not define the entirety of his theory, in "Perpetual Peace" and in "Idea for a Universal History with a Cosmopolitan Purpose." Both pieces are in *Political Writings*, ed. Hans Reiss, trans. H. B. Nisbett (New York: Cambridge University Press, 1970), 51, 114.

8. In the wake of Watergate, the American executive was weakened, but Kissinger extends his observations in this regard to describe in general the "dilemma of the modern democratic leader" who lacks both the time and sometimes the authority to develop a nuanced policy (*YOU* 193).

9. The chief problem with the culture of bureaucracy is that it stifles the "creativity" of which statesmen are capable (*WHY* 39). The decline of executive authority after Watergate meant that actors in agencies were free to pursue their own tactics (*YOR* 487, 559). Kissinger's move to the State Department at that time enabled him to move with the shift in power.

10. At the same time, it is important for Kissinger to show, not quite persuasively, that the most criticized decisions (the bombing of Cambodia, for example) were not secret (*WHY* 502). The Cambodia action illustrates the essential problem of statesmanship. United States action against the North Vietnamese

sanctuaries in Cambodia was militarily and diplomatically successful but a failure on the stage of domestic politics (*WHY* 508–9).

11. In *The Constitution of Liberty* (Chicago: University of Chicago Press, 1960), 29, Hayek calls this the "main contention" of his chapter on freedom.

12. There is a good, brief account of Kissinger's undergraduate thesis in Michael Joseph Smith's *Realist Thought from Weber to Kissinger* (Baton Rouge: Louisiana State University Press, 1986), 194–99.

13. Kissinger's much-derided quest for peace with honor is often treated cynically, but for a man who prides himself on his realism Kissinger is quite free of cynicism when speaking of the importance of America's honor in Vietnam. Kissinger takes such moral commitments personally. The foreign born may have a special feeling for America that the native born lack. They are better able to appreciate the historical forces that shape the nation and its role in the world. For a Jewish boy in Nazi Germany, America "was a dream, an incredible place where tolerance was natural and personal freedom unchallenged." Ending the war in Vietnam on positive terms seemed to Kissinger an essential component in maintaining America's capacity to act as a moral beacon. "I believed in the moral significance of my adopted country." America, "alone of the free countries, was strong enough to assure global security against the forces of tyranny" (*WHY* 229).

14. Kissinger believes that the "new world order" will be typified by "continental-type states," and not by a world government developed out of the United Nations or the World Trade Organization. As Aristotle pointed out long ago, politics is different from economics. India, China, and the European Union are examples of the type (*D* 807–8; *DAN* 217).

Chapter 44

Irving Kristol and the Reinvigoration of Bourgeois Republicanism

Laurence D. Cooper

We have all been instructed in the inadequacies of political labels. Labels simplify; they obfuscate; they distort and deceive. Nevertheless, labels matter; for they embody perceptions which, irrespective of their accuracy and fairness, constitute an important reality in politics. And they matter all the more when their accuracy and fairness are not at issue. When this is the case—when, for example, a thinker embraces the label himself and chooses to be known by it, making it the centerpiece of two book titles—it offers itself as the natural gateway to his thought.

Since the early 1970s, Irving Kristol (1920–) has been known and happy to identify himself as a neoconservative, in some ways as *the* neoconservative.[1] Friends, critics, and observers have recognized Kristol as the leading and even the defining figure of neoconservatism, both intellectually and strategically. In accepting this compound and neologistic label, Kristol reminds us both of his (and his intellectual companions') distinctiveness among American conservatives and of the evolution of his political thought. Not only was his a new kind of conservatism; conservatism was a new position for him at the time that the label was first affixed. To take up the second point first, Kristol's intellectual odyssey began on the Left and took him across the Center before finally ending, it seems safe to say, on the (democratic) Right, where he has resided for more than thirty years now.[2] Or so it seems when we judge him by the persons and policies he has supported. Yet when judged from a deeper perspective that looks at his philosophical premises and the character of his political reasoning, an underlying consistency comes into view, a consistency ironically mirrored in the fact that, wherever he has resided on the ideological spectrum, Kristol has always needed recourse to that same prefix: before he became a neoconservative, he has said, he was (briefly, in his youth) a neo-Trotskyist and neosocialist and then a neoliberal. And for all the differences between the positions to which this "neo" has been affixed, the prefix itself has appealed in each instance to a remarkably consistent set of principles and reservations, principles and reservations that might be characterized as classical rather than modern, realistic rather than utopian, skeptical rather than dogmatic, prudent and reformist rather than revolutionary—in a word, conservative, so long as that word is understood in the way that will be developed in this chapter. Thus, it is only a slight exaggeration to say that Kristol has always been a kind of (a "neo") conservative.[3]

Although a current in the broader waters of American conservatism, neoconservatism was something new when it appeared and something distinctive for better than two decades thereafter. (By the mid-1990s it seemed clear, to Kristol and to most other observers, that neoconservatism had been "pretty much absorbed into a larger, more comprehensive conservatism" [*A* 40].) What neoconservatism *is*, or was, is in some way the theme of this entire chapter: seldom has an "ism" not named for an individual been so closely, almost synonymously, associated with one. But before proceeding to an exploration of Kristol's thought on its own terms, let us briefly examine the historical context and significance of that thought by taking up three more limited questions. What *kind* of a thing is neoconservatism; how is it distinct from the conservatism that preceded it (and that, in fact, frequently looked askance at it); and what, in outline at least, has been Kristol's part in it?

Lacking a unified practical program, neoconservatism can hardly be said to have constituted a "movement," notwithstanding many loose (or deliberate) claims to the contrary. Nor, being composed of a group of independent intellectuals who frequently disagreed on matters of policy, did neoconservatism ever want to be a movement. Rather than a movement, Kristol argues, neoconservatism might more accurately be thought of as an "impulse" or "persuasion" (*A* ix; cf. *R* 75). That the leading lights of neoconservatism began their careers to the left of any kind of conservatism has much to do with the cast of their eventual "persuasion." Thinking of themselves at the beginning as dissident (and then disillusioned) liberals, in the popular sense of that term, they never shared, either at the beginning or subsequently, traditional conservatism's principled objection to the development of an American welfare state. Rather, they criticized many of the particulars of the welfare state as these were developed and implemented in the 1960s, and they brought to the task the sophisticated tools of the social sciences in which many (though not Kristol) had been trained. Whereas traditional conservatism had understood itself to be engaged in battle against advancing statism or socialism, neoconservatism took as the target of its critique contemporary liberalism—that is, liberalism as it developed during and after the years of the "Great Society" (*A* 379). Neoconservative analysts argued that liberal social policies were bound to have or were already having unintended ill effects, and they offered diagnoses of such effects and alternative policies. On the whole, this stance was consistent throughout the years of the neoconservative episode; certainly it remained Kristol's position. Long after he had begun to call himself a neoconservative and had altogether ceased to think of himself as any kind of liberal in the popular sense—Kristol readily admits that his changed position on the political spectrum was as much a result of his own (rightward) movement as of liberalism's (leftward) movement—he continued to call, not for an end to the welfare state, but for a conservative one—one that promotes (or at least does not discourage) the "bourgeois virtues" and does not create dependency or weaken family ties (*TC* 126–27; *A* 346).

Social welfare policy was only one area in which neoconservatism broke with liberalism and went on to stake out positions of its own. Other areas of difference have included political economy, crime policy, foreign policy, and what one might call "cultural politics"; within the latter are included such matters as education and the arts, pornography and obscenity, and the place of religion in American public life. The breadth of this list suggests a certain depth as well. And indeed, much of Kristol's writing has been devoted to analysis and critique of what he has come to call "liberal metaphysics, the view of human nature and of social and economic realities, on which [liberal] programs were based" (*A* x). This "metaphysics," more than any particular policy stance, has been the focus of what he has called his own Cold War. This focus, in turn, points to two further features of neoconservatism, in general, and Kristol, in particular. First, neoconservatives believe in the power—indeed the primacy—of ideas in politics. Second, in criticizing one kind of "metaphysics," Kristol necessarily engages in and promotes a "metaphysics" of his own.

In both of these respects, neoconservatism differs from traditional conservatism—from conservative politicians in particular but also from most earlier conservative thinkers, whose disdain of ideology and speculative reason and whose preference for tradition and prescription have tended (in Kristol's view) to leave them effectively disarmed in a modern world governed, for better or worse, by ideology.[4] The philosophical roots of neoconservatism are neither in the self-described conservative tradition nor in Burke or any other modern conservative, but in classical political philosophy—above all in Plato and Aristotle. This is something about which Kristol has been quite explicit (*R* 76).[5] Perhaps in the spirit of classical political philosophy, however, he has not been very expansive on the matter. Nevertheless, a number of common elements can be discerned in Kristol's thought and classical political philosophy. Kristol, like the classical thinkers, insists on the need for virtue in a self-governing citizenry; holds that beliefs concerning the good and the just are crucial determinants of the legitimacy of a regime; respects religion as a vital source of meaning, and hence of happiness and stability; mistrusts and warns against utopian politics (while appreciating the uses of utopia *in thought*); eschews the notion that all societies everywhere and always ought to be governed by the same kind of regime; and embraces prudence and political moderation as keys to successful statesmanship. Each of these themes is a major strand of classical thought and each, in ways to be seen below, is vital to the thought of Irving Kristol.

The "major contribution" of neoconservatism, according to Kristol, has been to enlarge "the conservative vision to include moral philosophy, political philosophy, and even religious thought, [thereby making] it more politically sensible as well as politically appealing" (*A* 37). Most of this newly imported thought—including religious thought—draws its spirit and sometimes its substance from the wells of classical political philosophy.[6] Indeed, it is their classical provenance and the resulting cast of mind that perhaps most distinguish Kristol and neoconservatives from *all* other twentieth-century currents in American political thought. Here, though, it is perhaps necessary to offer the following proviso. To ground one's political thought in classical—which is to say, premodern—philosophy need not, and in Kristol's and neoconservatism's case does not, indicate any longing for a return to premodern politics or even any belief in the superiority of premodern politics. (Indeed, Kristol has repeatedly stressed that neoconservatism differs from—and has invigorated—traditional conservatism by being forward-looking.) Properly understood, classical political philosophy would counsel *against* any such longing or intent. Classical political philosophy, at least when it speaks to practical politics, takes its bearing from a respect for the given and eschews the notion that all societies ought to try to adopt a single, best form. Kristol does the same, and criticizes much modern ideology for an unrealistic and hence brutally coercive universalism.

As a social thinker, Irving Kristol has generally inhabited the ground between political philosophy and public policy. That ground is important, because influential, but exposed, because unprotected by the fortresses of specialists' credentials.[7] Kristol's political essays—always essays, though of varying length—consistently evince a practical intent, though that intent is sometimes as broad as framing a grand civilizational question (e.g., how to reconcile a vigorous religious impulse with secular institutions and prejudices) in the interest of arriving, eventually, at a more adequate understanding of our society and its ills. (At other times, particularly in shorter writings for wider circulation, the practical intent has been relatively narrow and concrete, though this more transient journalism has not been reprinted in his books.) Kristol's practical intentions, by the account of friends and critics alike, have borne fruit. As noted above, his thought and neoconservatism more generally have had significant influence on the larger body of the conservatism by which they have been absorbed. In light of the political successes of this "more comprehensive" conservatism, it seems fair to say that this influence on conservatism has amounted to influence on public discourse and public policy.[8] Neoconservatism can hardly be said to have conquered America or even a major political party, but it has scored its share of victories, among which perhaps the greatest has been to force policy debate back to first principles.

Liberalism, Capitalism, and Bourgeois Society

The overarching theme of Irving Kristol's political writings is the question of liberal-capitalist society: its nature and history, its virtues and failings, its requirements and its prospects.[9] Alternatives to liberal capitalism are not ignored, but neither are they much explored as options worth pursuing. For liberal capitalism at its best Kristol offers only two cheers; for any known, currently viable alternative, however, he offers no cheers at all.

We had best begin with a brief discussion of terms. "Liberal," "capitalist," "bourgeois"— each of these words is used by Kristol, sometimes alone and sometimes in combination, to describe the American regime. If the terms seem to be used interchangeably, it is because, in Kristol's view, they are for all practical purposes organically linked with one another. The organic link between liberalism and capitalism is strongly suggested by the fact that "history does not provide us with any instance of a society that repressed the economic liberties of the individual while being solicitous of his other liberties" (*TC* xi).[10] Capitalism, Kristol argues, "may not be a sufficient condition for a liberal society [but] it does seem to be a necessary condition of it," for capitalism produces a diffusion of wealth and status and therewith power. Indeed, this diffusion makes a fair degree of political and religious liberty practically inevitable. If it does not guarantee a fully liberal society, it poses considerable obstacles to autocratic government (*R* 165–66; *A* 287–88). This is something the Founding Fathers understood very well. The political system they built protected property rights, encouraged the operation of a domestic free market, and applied the principle of diffusion to the institutions of government. They "*intended* this nation to be capitalist and regarded it as the *only* set of economic arrangements consistent with the liberal democracy they had established" (*TC* 3; *R* 202; *A* 211, emphasis in original).[11] The Founders assumed what Adam Smith assumed about human nature and encouraged what he encouraged: they viewed self-interest as amenable to rational and moral governance, mainly *self*-governance, and, as such, something to be endorsed rather than condemned (*R* 167; *A* 288–89).

It is in its embrace of commerce and material self-enrichment—or rather, in the character of this embrace—that liberal-capitalist society qualifies as "bourgeois" society, when it *does* qualify as bourgeois. A bourgeois society is a liberal society whose energies are largely devoted to the orderly pursuit of private gain on the understanding that gain is connected to certain virtues and dependent upon certain noneconomic foundations. The "bourgeois virtues" are private virtues, the sort of qualities that once would have been referred to as domestic virtues: industry, thrift, sobriety, self-discipline, and the like. The noneconomic foundations on which bourgeois society understands itself to rest include communal institutions (including but not limited to political institutions) and the commitment to these institutions by a citizenry whose self-interest is either enlightened or tempered enough to generate it. A bourgeois citizen—and citizen *is* the word, for he is more than a consumer and his bourgeois virtues are supplemented by republican ones— believes in self-government in both the personal and the civic sense. Kristol considers the United States to have been bourgeois in its origins and for most of its history—though at least once he has referred to contemporary America as "post-bourgeois," owing to the triumph of anti-bourgeois cultural currents.[12] He views these recent currents with alarm. In his view, it is not capitalism simply but bourgeois capitalism—capitalism which carries a particular self-understanding and self-justification—that is organically linked to liberalism and that can sustain a prosperous, stable, and free society. Hence, it his professed goal, speaking on behalf of neo-conservatism, "to infuse American bourgeois orthodoxy with a new self-conscious intellectual vigor" (*R* xiv).

The appeal of capitalism at its inception was threefold.

> First of all, it promised continued improvement in the material conditions of all its citizens, a promise without precedent in human history. Second, it promised an equally unprecedented measure of individual freedom for all of these same citizens. And lastly, it held out the promise that, amidst this prosperity and liberty, the individual could satisfy his instinct for self-perfection—for leading a virtuous life that satisfied the demands of his spirit (or, as one used to say, his soul)—and that the free exercise of such individual virtue would aggregate into a just society. (*DI* 92; *TC* 257)

Looked at from one point of view, these promises were modest: they neither required not promoted resplendent or heroic virtue; they were within reach of ordinary men and women. Yet precisely because the goods it promised were within the reach of ordinary people, capitalism was in another sense extraordinarily ambitious. How well has capitalism fulfilled these promises? With respect to the first two promises, the answer is: quite well overall, notwithstanding periodic economic downturns. And it is largely because of this performance that capitalism has survived and that it deserves to survive. With respect to the third promise, though, the answer is less cheering. At some point, the promise of a virtuous life and a just society was subverted "*by the dynamics of capitalism itself*, as it strove to fulfill the other two—affluence and liberty" (*DI* 94; *TC* 259, emphasis added).[13] And if its performance on the first two promises has been the source of its survival and success, its failure to deliver on the third promise has been the proximate source of its—and thus many of America's—spiritual or cultural (and hence political) ills. But the failure to fulfill the third promise has not been coeval with capitalism, even if the roots of the failure were present in capitalism from the start. Thus, we need to consider first the history of American capitalism and then its nature.

Liberal Capitalism's Troubled History

In Kristol's analysis of the history of American capitalism, three "stories" or transformations stand out. Liberal capitalist society has seen: (1) major institutional and demographic changes; (2) major changes in the way it understands and justifies itself; and (3) the development of a culture antagonistic to liberal capitalism. In each of these areas, Kristol finds that liberal capitalism has departed radically from the vision of its early theorists and founders in ways they would have found troubling, and in ways he too finds troubling. For reasons of space, we will examine only the second and third categories. The first story is not unimportant—its chief elements are (a) the rise to economic predominance of the large corporation and (b) the urbanization of the American populace—but its most important effects are cultural and political and some of these, at least, can be addressed in the context of the second and third categories.[14]

The characterizations and arguments made on behalf of liberal capitalism by its defenders and propagators have changed significantly over the course of its existence. The original understanding and defense of capitalism were bourgeois in the sense explained above. Not only did its proponents believe in its ability to deliver on the three promises already discussed (affluence, liberty, and virtue), but they also argued that the specific distribution of goods in a free-market economy was just—indeed, more just than any other distribution—because goods came proportionately to those who had earned them. And to have earned them meant not simply to have achieved a certain level of ability; it meant to have demonstrated merit as a person, which is to say moral merit. A link was presupposed between the value of one's economic *doing* and the virtue of one's moral *being*. As of the time of the Civil War, in the North at least, the United States

> was still in good measure a bourgeois society in which the capitalist mode of existence involved moral self-discipline and had a visible aura of spiritual grace.... It was a society in which it was agreed that there was a strong correlation between certain personal virtues—frugality, industry, sobriety, reliability, piety—and the way in which power, privilege, and property were distributed. And this correlation was taken to be the sign of a just society, not merely of a free one. (*DI* 96–97; *TC* 261)

In our own time, however, "the most intelligent" defenders of capitalism have preferred to eschew moral considerations, holding instead that capitalism's goodness consists in its being a free social order; indeed, they have tended to *oppose* a free society to a just one (or else have defined "justice" as whatever result the free market has rendered), arguing that apportioning goods according to merit necessarily presupposes a moral arbiter, which by its nature would be an unfree institution.[15]

"But can men live in a free society if they have no reason to believe it is also a just society? I do not think so." Here we encounter a key tenet of Kristol's "metaphysics": "in the same way as men cannot for long tolerate a sense of spiritual meaninglessness in their individual lives, so they cannot for long accept a society in which power, privilege, and property are not distributed according to some morally meaningful criteria" (*DI* 97; *TC* 262). And so, leaving nonmoral defenses to the scholastics who purvey them, the majority of citizens persist in subscribing to one or another more morally grounded arguments. None of these, however, carries the force that the bourgeois defense once did. Many people continue to believe in the old bourgeois understanding, now more familiarly known as the Protestant Ethic (or some ecumenical variant thereof), but this is now believed to apply, and in fact does apply, only at the lower socioeconomic levels: "no one seriously claims that [the traditional bourgeois] virtues will open the corridors of corporate power to anyone, or that those who now occupy the executive suites are—or even aspire to be—models of bourgeois virtue" (*DI* 98–99; *TC* 263). Others hold either with a neo-Darwinian defense, according to which those who succeed have thereby shown themselves most deserving, or with a technocratic defense, which claims that wealth and power are distributed according to performance or services rendered. But neither of these defenses succeeds any better than the first. On the contrary, the Darwinian argument offends our nature as political and moral beings; and the technocratic case both overstates the social good that attaches to material prosperity and in any case is vulnerable to the vicissitudes of economic life: legitimacy tied exclusively to performance will be a short-lived legitimacy, if it is any kind of legitimacy at all. The result of this situation is that the American social order suffers from a continuing crisis of legitimacy. Justification is wanted, justifications are offered, but a compelling consensual justification is not to be seen.[16]

The third story of liberal capitalism's transformation concerns the appearance and development of an antibourgeois counterculture, a culture that criticizes less our society's failure to realize its ideal than the very ideal itself (*R* 28; *A* 107). This story too bears on liberal capitalism's crisis of legitimacy, which may make it appear to be an extension of the second story. But it is not. The second story is a tale of liberal capitalism's (ailing) defense. It ends (in the 1970s, when Kristol related it) with a populace whose majority wants to be able to affirm the liberal capitalist social order more than it is able to. The third story, by contrast, is a story of repudiation and attack. As such, it is the more radical phenomenon.

Modernity, and especially liberal modernity, were themselves born as countercultures. For millennia, people had taken for granted that it was possible to have—and that at least some people, some "elite," did have—an a priori knowledge of what constitutes happiness for all people. Thus, humankind acquiesced in a variety of social orders which accorded wide-ranging authority to an elite. This, of course, was an illiberal state of affairs, or, as liberalism might have it, a *pre*-liberal state of affairs. It was also a noncapitalist state of affairs, very much on principle: the idea was that "a free market, not being guided by the wisdom of the elite, was bound to be ultimately frustrating, since the common people could not possibly know what they *really* wanted or what would really yield them 'true' happiness" (*TC* 58–59; *A* 95). The rejection of this philosophical presupposition was one of liberal modernity's distinctive features.

> Modern, liberal, secular society is based on the revolutionary premise that there is no superior, authoritative information available about the good life or the true nature of human happiness, that this information is implicit only in individual preferences, and that therefore the individual has to be free to develop and express these preferences. (*TC* 60; *A* 96)

Perhaps the first thing to say about the counterculture of recent years, at least insofar as it has propounded or adumbrated a political agenda, is that it repudiates this "revolutionary premise": its rejection of the free market in the name of higher spiritual goods is a rejection of liberal modernity's (and liberal capitalism's) presupposition concerning the nonexistence of authoritative information about the good. Or, to put it positively, the counterculture effectively asserts that it is in possession of authoritative information regarding the good life and that this information deserves political expression. Thus, "what we are witnessing in Western society today are the beginnings of a counterrevolution against [the liberal capitalist] conception of man and society." The revolutionaries, however, have not owned up to the character of their enterprise, that is, to their reassertion of a premodern premise: "It is a shamefaced counterrevolution, full of bad faith and paltry sophistry, because it feels compelled to define itself as some kind of progressive extension of modernity instead of, what it so clearly is, a reactionary revulsion against modernity" (*TC* 60; *A* 96). So Kristol writes in 1973, before the idea of the "postmodern" has gained wide currency. In subsequent years, the idea of the postmodern would make it possible to repudiate the presuppositions of modernity without seeming to represent any kind of return to premodernity—which may be just as well, for if the antibourgeois counterculture has resurrected a key premodern tenet, it has done so only in the most formal way. The *content* of its information regarding the good life partakes of no major premodern orthodoxy. That content, while including a fair degree of economic collectivism, embraces a degree and kind of personal freedom that most premodern thinkers and peoples would have found licentious in nature and anarchic in its results. Kristol, himself in various ways an heir to premodern thought (i.e., classical political philosophy), makes a similar judgment, though he expresses his verdict in a modern word: nihilism.

"*The enemy of liberal capitalism today is not so much socialism as nihilism*" (*TC* 66; *A* 101, italics in the original). The weakness of the socialist threat to capitalism is easier to see today than it was when this line was written in 1973. But whence the threat from nihilism? The story is a long one and its roots are to be found both in the nature of liberal capitalism and in the philosophical foundations of modernity. Liberal capitalism has sparked hostility from its inception. By 1865 or so, contempt for bourgeois society among highly cultured people was widespread: artists and intellectuals had begun routinely to reject the politics and culture of the majority and to constitute, quite self-consciously, a dissenting or adversary culture. Self-descriptive words like "highbrow" and "avant-garde" nicely capture, respectively, this group's sense of superiority and its determined opposition to the political and cultural mainstream. (It is important to note that no single political position was implied by membership in this dissenting culture: until 1914, its members were as likely to oppose liberal capitalism from the Right as from the Left.) This peculiar, indeed, unprecedented situation, in which the leading cultural lights stood at odds with the values and ideals of their civilization, lasted for about a century, until it gave rise to a new state of affairs: namely, the broadening of the dissenting culture into a much more popular counterculture. Undoubtedly this occurred for myriad reasons, but three reasons stand out. First, there was a dramatic increase in the number of people receiving higher education, which meant an increase in the number of people being introduced to the antibourgeois views that had already dominated high culture for quite some time. (It is striking to note that those regarded as the greatest philosophers of the late nineteenth and twentieth centuries and the vast majority of great literary artists of the same period have been as one in their contempt for bourgeois society.) This, of course, was a function of affluence and leisure, that is, of capitalism's very success, and thus stands as an example of capitalism's "dangerous dialectic" (*TC* xi). Second, the increasing numbers of people receiving higher education meant increasing numbers among whom religious faith was in decline, as the correlation between education and skepticism, dating at least to the nineteenth-century "crisis of faith," continued to hold true. Finally, the faith that had substituted for traditional religion as a source of morality among nineteenth-century intellectuals—that is, secular humanism, or the faith in reason and progress—itself began to collapse. (Secular humanism, according to Kristol, most decidedly *is* a faith. Its teachings, which "can be summed up in one phrase: 'Man makes himself,'" are based on "all kinds of inferences about the human condition and human possibilities that are not, in any authentic sense, scientific. Those inferences are metaphysical, and in the end theological.")[17] The decline of traditional religion is something Kristol seems to regard as accidental in an important sense: decline may well have been inevitable given the nature of liberal capitalism as it was originally conceived, but this religion was (and is) not itself fatally flawed; hence, a revival is not precluded, especially if political adjustments were made. The collapse of secular humanism, however, Kristol does attribute to internal fatal flaws. As a practical matter, most people require a religious basis for morality.[18] Precisely because it does not appeal to tradition or the divine, "[s]ecular rationalism has been unable to produce a compelling, self-justifying moral code. . . . And with this failure, the whole enterprise of secular humanism—the idea that man can define his humanity and shape the human future by reason and will alone—begins to lose its legitimacy" (*A* 133). A second flaw is even more fundamental. "If there is one indisputable fact about the human condition it is that no community can survive if it is persuaded—or if it even suspects—that its members are leading meaningless lives in a meaningless universe." Secular humanism recognizes this challenge and responds by supplanting divine Providence and prerogative with human autonomy and creativity—but to no avail, as reflected in the fact that the dominant thinkers of the past century and "the main currents of thought in American universities today [the early 1990s]—postmodernism, deconstruction, varieties of structuralism—are all contemptuous of the universities' humanist heritage. . . . Secular humanism is brain dead even as its heart continues to pump energy into all of our institutions" (*A* 451–52).

The consequence of the decline of secular humanism coupled with the decline of traditional religion is nihilism. And given the number of people for whom this situation obtains (nothing close to a majority, but a powerful and, *because powerful*, a growing group), one may speak of them as constituting a "nihilistic anticulture." This anticulture, according to Kristol, embraces and belligerently espouses not only the death of God but also the moral consequence of God's death, which secular humanism had nobly but vainly sought to refute: "if God is dead, everything is now permitted" (*A* 131–32). The ethos of this anticulture—"cynical, nihilistic, and exploitative"; "candidly sensationalistic and materialistic"; "the ethos of a carnival"—shows signs of proving tiresome: "The original excitement of the counterculture is certainly gone; there is already a sense of tedium about the whole business—too many 'lifestyles,' too many transient, 'protean' selves" (*A* 146).[19] It is unclear whether it can last. But even if it expires, there is no guarantee that it will be succeeded by anything more congenial to liberalism or even by anything less nihilistic. The revelation of secular humanism's inadequacies, to which the counterculture has been a response, threatens to discredit more than just secular humanism:

> A spiritual rebellion against the constrictions of secular humanism could end up—in some way, it has already ended up—in a celebration of irrationalism and a derogation, not simply of an overweening rationalism, but of reason itself. In these circumstances, the idea of an ordered liberty could collapse under pressure from a new spiritual and ideological conformity that rushes in where liberals fear to tread. (*A* 146)

Liberal Capitalism's Nature and Problematics

Such are the "highlights" of a troubled and changeful history. What is it about the nature of liberal capitalism that has left it open to such turbulence and even crisis? There are many parts to the answer, beginning with the dynamism of the system and the progressive nature of technology, two factors which militate against stability. Then, too, there is the phenomenon of capitalism's "dangerous dialectic." Somehow, against all modern-rationalist expectations, increased affluence has brought an increase in such social pathologies as crime, delinquency, alcoholism and drug addiction, and, as a result of increased cynicism, a *decrease* in civic-mindedness and public-spiritedness. And "a similar kind of debasement" has occurred in the political realm: "The purpose of politics becomes the maximum gratification of desires and appetites, and the successful politician is one who panders most skillfully to this 'revolution of rising expectations,' a revolution which affluent capitalism itself generates and before which the politics of bourgeois democracy prostrates itself" (*R* 175–76; *A* 297–98). This politics is not only debased; it inevitably disappoints, with potentially dangerous results. The democratic state becomes ever more powerful, yet it still cannot meet the demands made upon it; the growth of those demands outstrips that of the state, leaving many to wonder whether a nondemocratic state might do better (*R* 175–76; *A* 297–98).

And there are other problematics besides, some of which have more to do with the vagaries of capitalist economics, others with democracy itself.[20] But the chief source of liberal capitalism's present ills—the locus of its most consequential inadequacies—is to be found precisely where the countercultural critique directs its fire, namely, in the realm of psychic or spiritual aspiration. The gravest ills of liberal capitalism or bourgeois society arise from two related facts: that it is by nature prosaic and that it is by design strictly secular.[21]

"Bourgeois society is without a doubt the most prosaic of all possible societies" (*R* 28; *A* 107). Other societies—none perhaps today, but those from the past which continue to lay claim to our respect and admiration—have been

> formally and officially committed to transcendent ideals of excellence—ideals that could be realized only by those few of exceptional nobility of character—or to transcendent visions of the universe wherein human existence on earth is accorded only a provisional significance. But bourgeois society is uninterested in such transcendence, which at best it tolerates as a private affair, a matter for individual taste and individual consumption, as it were. . . . It is a society organized for the convenience and comfort of common men and common women, not for the

production of heroic, memorable figures. It is a society interested in making the best of this world, not in any kind of transfiguration, whether through tragedy or piety. (*R* 28–29; *A* 107–8)

Because it has been devoted to satisfying the ordinary desires of ordinary people, bourgeois society has always enjoyed considerable popularity among common people, even if that is somewhat less true today than once was the case. But for precisely the same reason it has always been *un*popular with artists and intellectuals. From the point of view of these *un*common people, bourgeois society suffers from "three great flaws." First, it is a boring society and one whose primary activity, commerce, coarsens and trivializes the human spirit. Second, although it offers its writers and artists freedom of expression and even the opportunity for fame and affluence, it deprives them of something they crave even more, namely, the status that comes with being "taken seriously." And third, "a commercial society, a society whose civilization is shaped by market transactions, is always likely to reflect the appetites and preferences of common men and women"—which is to say, by "vulgar" appetites and preferences. (Although their professed democratic faith makes it difficult for them to recognize this, artists and intellectuals are "by their very nature 'elitists'"; "they believe that a civilization should be shaped by an *aristoi* to which they will be organically attached, no matter how perilously" [*R* 32–33; *A* 111–12].) Most people, of course, neither are nor aspire to be artists or intellectuals. Many, however, especially with widened access to higher education, are influenced by them. And even apart from whatever influence it may have exercised, the artists' and intellectuals' dissatisfaction has served as a sort of paradigm. Almost from the start, their active contempt for bourgeois society was echoed by a more moderate but nevertheless "pervasive disquiet among those who, more successful than others in having bettered their condition, had the leisure to wonder if life did not, perhaps, have more interesting and remote possibilities to offer" (*R* 30; *A* 109). The uneasiness of many of its most accomplished citizens, combined with the contempt of its most articulate ones, indicated from the start that bourgeois society suffers politically for its prosaic character.

Bourgeois society is saved from the consequences of its prosaic character to the extent that its citizens are able to transcend their lives as economic actors and find spiritual or existential nourishment. For if bourgeois society does not promote or officially dedicate itself to transcendent ideals, neither does it preclude them. Here, though, we are brought to the second great inadequacy or problematic of liberal capitalism mentioned above. Historically, most people, most of the time, have found in religion the chief or even the only source of existential meaning, consolation, and moral encouragement. It is religion, therefore, that might have been counted on to limit the disillusionment and consequent instability brought about by bourgeois society's prosaic character. But what might have been did not materialize, at least not indefinitely or to a sufficient extent; for traditional religious faith has declined considerably since the dawn of the liberal capitalist epoch. The most significant aspect of this decline is not the number of people professing belief of some kind—indeed, it is not clear that this number has declined in America —but rather the intensity of their professed belief, as manifest in their sense of religious obligation and their trust in the promise of after-worldly consolation. And this decline has occurred, argues Kristol, in significant part because liberal society conceives of religion "as an essentially 'private affair' neither needing nor meriting public sanction" (*R* 122; *A* 309).[22]

But the political significance of religion—and of secularism—goes far beyond their (in)ability to stem the effects of liberalism's prosaic character. For one thing, morality, as a general practical matter, requires religious grounding. Hence, a decline in religious faith is apt to mean a decline in moral rectitude as well. Kristol praises the American Founders (and Adam Smith) for understanding the necessity of morality to the regime's success. But he faults them for failing to realize that the morality they championed requires a publicly sanctioned religious foundation: "The bourgeois capitalist revolution of the eighteenth century was successful precisely because it did incorporate the older Judeo-Christian moral tradition into its basically secular, rationalist outlook. But it erred in cutting this moral tradition away from the religious context that nourished it" (*A* 133). Beyond the consequences for morality are other consequences, stemming particularly from declining faith in the consolations of life after death. The significance of this decline would be difficult to overstate: "I think it possible to suggest that the decline in the belief in personal immortality has been the most important *political* fact of the last hundred years; nothing else has so profoundly affected the way in which the masses of people experience their worldly condition" (*TC* 175; *A* 168). One consequence of this decline is that "the demands placed upon liberal society, in the name of temporal 'happiness,' have become ever more urgent and ever more unreasonable" (*TC* 63; *A* 99). Just as religion is the major source of morality for most people, so it is the major source of the sort of stoical resignation—the ability to tolerate frustration—that every society requires. Yet by disestablishing and thereby diminishing religious faith, "liberal civilization finds itself having spiritually expropriated the masses of its citizenry, whose demands for material compensation gradually become as infinite as the infinity they have lost" (*TC* 63; *A* 99).

The decline of religious faith has also diminished the force of law. "Another, and related, consequence of the disestablishment of religion as a publicly sanctioned mythos has been the inability of liberal society ever to come up with a convincing and generally accepted theory of political obligation" (*TC* 63; *A* 99). Every society requires a measure of public-spiritedness among its citizens, including, necessarily, the willingness by at least some of its citizens to die for it. This has always been an awkward fact for liberal philosophy, which, in its embrace of worldly self-interest as the source of all obligation, has had to resort to unconvincing utilitarian theories. In practice, liberal societies *have* managed to inspire self-sacrifice. Yet they have done so by appealing to "the secular myth of nationalism," a myth which "is not intrinsically or necessarily bourgeois" and which could easily prove subversive of the bourgeois order (*TC* 64; *A* 100).

Finally, the decline of religion contributes to the "problem of publicly establishing an acceptable set of rules of distributive justice" (*TC* 64; *A* 100). As noted above, most people demand a morally grounded or "metaphysical" justification of society's inevitably uneven distribution of goods. Such a justification becomes more difficult with the dissolution of traditional religious faith. The problem of establishing consensual rules of distributive justice "does not arise so long as the bourgeois ethos is closely linked to what we call the Puritan or Protestant ethos, which prescribes a connection between personal merit—as represented by such bourgeois virtues as honesty, sobriety, diligence, and thrift—and worldly success" (*TC* 64; *A* 100). With the weakening or demise of that ethos—a result of the weakening or demise of the faith for which it is named—the problem does arise, leading in many cases to "simpleminded egalitarianism" as the only plausibly moral principle of distribution.

Kristol acknowledges that the decline in religious faith has roots in the philosophical presuppositions of modernity itself, irrespective of the distinctive features of bourgeois society. But in his analysis, these original philosophical influences are given less weight than more proximate political-sociological ones. Clearly, in his view, the decline of religion in the Western democracies is *primarily* rooted in the design of liberal capitalist society, which is to say that primary responsibility lies with the designers of that society and their heirs—the re-designers, as it were—in subsequent generations. Indeed, the error of the Founders was compounded by those subsequent generations. The Founders were aware of the necessary moral foundations of a free society and even, in most cases, of the needed religious basis of morality; their error was in taking it for granted that these religious (and hence moral) foundations would remain solid without much public sanction. Their heirs in subsequent generations extended this error by further restricting the place of religion in public life, replacing a secular governing philosophy with a secular*ist* one. A secular regime is one which remains neutral as between particular religious sects; a secularist regime is neutral as between religion and irreligion (*A* 372).

> The educated classes of liberal-bourgeois society simply could not bring themselves to believe that religion or philosophy was that important to a polity. *They* could live with religion or morality as a purely private affair, and they could not see why everyone else—after a proper secular education, of course—could not do likewise. (*TC* 66; *A* 101, emphasis in original)

By the late twentieth century, however, this secularist faith had worn thin. The political significance of religion and a moral philosophy associated with religion has begun to be evident, and "even those who thought they were content with a religion that was a private affair are themselves discovering that such a religion is existentially unsatisfactory" (*TC* 66; *A* 101).

Utopianism and Its Antidote

In his pronouncements concerning religion, we have encountered some of the key tenets of Kristol's "metaphysics" and therewith much of the basis of his critiques of eighteenth-century and contemporary liberalism.[23] As one who specializes in uncovering what he deems to be the hidden metaphysics of other social systems and thinkers, Kristol is accordingly frank about his own. Perhaps his most basic metaphysical statement is this: "All people, everywhere, at all times, are 'theotropic' beings, who cannot long abide the absence of a transcendental dimension to their lives" (*A* 143). But it is not only with respect to man's religious needs and nature that Kristol's metaphysics are consistent with the prevailing metaphysics of the Judeo-Christian tradition. Notwithstanding the differences between the two faiths, and leaving aside various "gnostic" or "prophetic" heterodoxies, Judaism and Christianity have traditionally subscribed to a "mixed" view of human nature. Through work, dedication, and God's grace, human beings are capable of goodness, and in fact they have natural inclinations in that direction. But they also are fundamentally flawed and limited in their goodness, and this too is a fact of their nature. A similar view obtains in the Socratic-Aristotelian tradition of classical political philosophy. Classical philosophy does not speak of "original sin"—neither, for that matter, does Judaism—but both classical philosophy and traditional Judaism subscribe to something comparable, according to Kristol: like traditional Christianity, they do not believe in the unadulterated goodness of human nature, and they regard as utopian the notion that humanity has it within its unaided power to redeem itself from all its ills, especially through politics.[24] Kristol shares this skepticism and sees the notion of redemptive politics and utopianism generally as increasingly pervasive features of the modern world and the source of many of our ills. This is one of his long-standing and characteristic themes.

"The modern world, in its modes of thinking, has become so utopian that we do not even know when we are utopian or to what degree we are utopian" (*R* 320; *A* 434). The utopian mode of thought emerged strongly in the sixteenth and seventeenth centuries for reasons that are not wholly understood but which surely included the confluence of post-Reformation millenarianism (which accustomed people to the idea that history was moving toward wholesale redemption); the new scientific rationalism (which posited that reality could be fully comprehended by man's abstract reason); and the advent of modern technology (which seemed to bear out the claims of scientific rationalism and engendered hopes not only of understanding but of mastering nature and human destiny) (*TC* 160–62; *A* 190–92). For a long time, the utopian temper was held at least somewhat in check by the doctrine of original sin. (The effects of the utopian temper have also been mitigated by the diffusion of power, which has been the source of liberal society's otherwise inexplicable stability.) As that doctrine has lost its hold on the Western mind, however, the utopian temper has become increasingly predominant. It can be discerned at the heart of all of modernity's radical political ideologies, and it has infused—and reshaped—much liberal thought and practice as well. Indeed, that which goes by the name "liberal" in today's popular discourse is *essentially* utopian.[25] And even those who do not call themselves liberal have been influenced by the utopian temper. This is easily seen in the character of our political rhetoric—in the character of what we say and, perhaps even more revealing, in what we do *not* say: "We utter clichés in politics as if they really were clichés—for example, 'a world without war'" (*R* 320; *A* 434–35). It is today unimaginable, Kristol writes, that a president of the United States would say on television that there will never be a world without war, that human beings as we know them will always fight—despite the fact that such a speech would be true. Much of the burden of Kristol's public policy analysis, particularly with respect to social welfare and foreign policy, has consisted in identifying and rebutting what he takes to be their utopian presuppositions.[26] But it is not only with respect to this or that policy that utopian thinking is harmful. Our habit of judging an actual social order by utopian standards has pernicious general effects: "It encourages a moral self-righteousness about one's 'ideals' combined with a moral affectlessness about the means by which these ideals are to be 'realized,' and this combination is as explosive as it is self-destructive" (*TC* ix–x).

Fortunately, not all modern thought and practice is utopian. Even more fortunately, the American polity does not rest on a utopian philosophical foundation, for it grew out of the rationalism of the Anglo-Scottish Enlightenment, which Kristol contrasts sharply with its more dramatic—more utopian—French counterpart. "The Anglo-Scottish Enlightenment was no less rationalist than the French, but it found its appropriate expression in a calm historical sociology rather than in a fervent political messianism" (*R* 151; *A* 271). This same contrast applies to the revolutionary fruit of the two Enlightenments. Unlike *their* French counterparts, the makers of the American Revolution for the most part held a sober view of human nature and human possibilities. They were self-conscious, and their enterprise was

> infused by *mind.* . . . By mind, not by dogma. The most fascinating aspect of the American Revolution is the severe way it kept questioning itself about the meaning of what it was doing. Enthusiasm there certainly was—a revolution is impossible without enthusiasm—but this enthusiasm was tempered by doubt, introspection, anxiety, skepticism. (*R* 81; *A* 238, emphasis in original)

This doubt and skepticism arose precisely from the revolutionaries' keen awareness of the insuperable frailties of human nature. On balance, the Founders concluded that a combination of republican virtue and sound institutions could overcome the effects of what Madison, "in his matter-of-fact way," called "a degree of depravity in mankind." Their confidence outweighed their anxiety. It never extinguished it, however, which testifies to the Founders' nonutopian cast of mind.

Such a cast of mind would be available to us, if only we could come to see our present utopianism for what it is. "For the real antidote to utopianism is a self-conscious understanding of utopianism. A utopianism which knows itself to be utopian is already on the way to denying itself, because it has already made that first, crucial distinction between dream and reality" (*TC* 169; *A* 198). To administer this antidote has certainly been one of Kristol's goals. Another goal has been to lay out the principles of nonutopian alternatives in various areas of public policy.

Here, for example, would be included the following: his advocacy of a conservative welfare state; his promotion of social policy that is friendly (within the bounds that liberal governance will allow) to virtue, religion, family, and cultural health (here falls Kristol's proposal that we return to a liberal regime of censoring pornography and obscenity); and his call for a more realistic and nationalist foreign policy.[27] Such policies, he suggests, would align contemporary governance with the republican philosophy of the American Founding, which he deems far more wise than the utopian democratic "faith" that has supplanted it.

Defending Bourgeois Society: Prospects and Tasks

That the antidote to utopianism is a self-conscious understanding of utopianism reflects the primacy of ideas in politics, one of the core tenets of Kristol's "metaphysics" and an indicator of the task that he sees ahead. If the root of our ills are intellectual, then so, of necessity, must be the cure:

> The modern world, and the crisis of modernity we are now experiencing, was created by ideas and by the passions which these ideas unleashed. To surmount this crisis, without destroying the modern world itself, will require new ideas—or new versions of old ideas—that will regulate these passions and bring them into a more fruitful and harmonious relation with reality. (*TC* 169; *A* 198)

However philosophically basic the task, though, the practical goal of Kristol's work, at least for as long as he has understood himself to be a neoconservative, has been confidently fixed. To surmount "the crisis of modernity" has meant to save bourgeois society by defeating its utopian and its nihilistic enemies.

> To put it in somewhat grandiose terms: Neoconservatism aims to infuse American bourgeois orthodoxy with a new self-conscious intellectual vigor, while dispelling the feverish mélange of gnostic humors that, for more than a century now [in 1983], has suffused our political beliefs and has tended to convert them into political religions. (*R* 14)

The first requirement of this invigoration is that bourgeois society be made to overcome its traditional underestimation of ideas, for the defense of bourgeois society, while begun in intellectual precincts, must ultimately be secured by political leaders and their followers.[28] Salvation through such means might also be an enrichment, and an ennobling, of the thing saved.

But *can* bourgeois society be saved? The chief reason for optimism may be that, for all its demoralization and the inability of its leaders to defend it where it most needs defending, liberal capitalism continues to survive—and, materially at least, it more than survives. Its opponents have either already fallen or are on their way to doing so. Fascism and communism are gone. Socialism, a species of utopian rationalism, has been forced to resort to coercion and repression against insufficiently responsive populations and has therefore been discredited as an idea. (Kristol calls the demise of the socialist idea "tragic," for it was "the one alternative to capitalism that was rooted in the Judeo-Christian tradition and the Western civilization which emerged from that tradition." With the death of socialism, "anticapitalism is becoming synonymous with one form or another of barbarism and tyranny" [*R* 114; *A* 300].) And the utopian romanticism that has been the source first of modernism in the arts and then of postmodernism is similarly fated to collapse, for its attempt to achieve transcendence within the secular self is mired in self-contradiction. But if liberal capitalism survives, it does so joylessly, because it lacks the religious foundation that once supplied a moral code and the possibility of finding a transcendental meaning in life (*R* 40–41; *A* 120–21). And even this modest triumph is endangered in the long run (or even in the short run if there should be a major economic crisis) by the "nihilistic anticulture" discussed above. The destructive capacity of nihilism, it seems, is not hampered by nihilism's inability to deliver on its own promise of joy through liberation.

In the end, the survival and enrichment of bourgeois society will require the restoration of its spiritual health through a reinvigoration of its cultural, largely religious, foundations. "Restoration," of course, implies some sort of return to what once was, and would therefore seem to be impossible. But in fact this sense of impossibility, the idea that the clock cannot be turned back, derives from a dubious "romantic-rationalist" conception of history. According to Kristol, "human history, read in a certain way, can be seen as full of critical moments when human beings deliberately turned the clock back" (*R* 40–41; *A* 120–21). Two major examples are the Reformation in Christianity and the codification of the Talmud in Judaism. "So the possibility is open to us—but, for better or worse, it is not the only possibility." And as the examples just cited suggest, the processes by which such a restoration would occur, if it *were* to occur, are beyond anyone's ability to plan or even to know—as, for that matter, is the final shape of the "restored" bourgeois culture (*A* 146–47). No cultural reformation, however successful, *simply* turns back the clock. The only sure bet would seem to be that, in one form or another, religion is likely to play a more central role in American life (*A* 452–53).[29]

Conclusion

Irving Kristol defends bourgeois society because he considers it the best available regime in the modern (or postmodern) age. By the rough standards of politics and history, it has delivered on its promises of affluence and freedom, and it might well be reconstituted so as to satisfy once more the moral and spiritual aspirations of its citizens. And if it does not, and by its nature *cannot*, devote itself to transcendent or resplendent virtue (such devotion being incompatible with liberalism's commitment to personal freedom), it can at least permit and to an extent even encourage them. Because he defends an existing order that he sees as besieged and ailing; because he seeks to restore it to a health it once enjoyed; and because that health consisted in popular adherence to a religious orthodoxy and belief in republican virtues, Kristol is properly thought of as a conservative, more properly a reformist conservative, notwithstanding that the regime he defends is liberal and that the religious foundation he advocates is also liberal. Such is the paradox of most American conservatism. Kristol frankly concedes that there is nothing about liberal capitalism that makes it intrinsically superior to all other regimes, and he does not shrink from specifying the unavoidable costs of bourgeois life even in its best possible condition. As we have seen, he offers two, not three, cheers for the society he defends. In this he departs from most popular conservatism and reflects the sober influence of classical political philosophy. Yet neither this sobriety about the goal he seeks nor the admitted uncertainty of its being achieved (another legacy of classical philosophy, with its emphatically nonprogressive view of history) has diminished his much remarked-upon cheerfulness. Here I would offer the following suggestion: the classical legacy, far from being an obstacle to cheerfulness, may be a *source* of it, in two ways. First, just as political utopianism inevitably leads to disillusionment, political realism liberates one to appreciate a reasonably good regime for the great good fortune that it is. And second, the belief in the political primacy of culture makes of the battle of ideas a battle for the future direction of civilization: it invests political thought with an import that could not fail to exhilarate, even as it sobers, a spirited thinker.

Notes

1. See, for example, "Confessions of a True, Self-Confessed—Perhaps the Only—'Neoconservative,'" in *Reflections of a Neoconservative: Looking Back, Looking Ahead* (New York: Basic Books, 1983) as well as *Neoconservatism: The Autobiography of an Idea* (New York: Basic Books, 1995). The label Kristol adopted was first affixed, with pejorative intent, by a socialist critic.

Henceforth, quotations from and references to Kristol's works are cited in the text using the following abbreviations:

A: *Neoconservatism: The Autobiography of an Idea* (New York: Basic Books, 1995).
DI: *On the Democratic Idea in America* (New York: Harper and Row, 1972).
R: *Reflections of a Neoconservative: Looking Back, Looking Ahead* (New York: Basic Books, 1983).
TC: *Two Cheers for Capitalism* (New York: Basic Books, 1978).

Since each of Kristol's books comprises separate essays which have usually appeared elsewhere as well, citations will include each of the books in which the essay appears.

2. A label inevitably ratifies a reality that has preceded it. Certainly by the late 1960s and probably by the middle of that decade (with the cofounding in 1965 of the quarterly journal, *The Public Interest*), Kristol's writings were already recognizable, in retrospect, as neoconservative, despite the fact that he still considered himself a dissident liberal.

3. And thus an essay on his political thought need not concern itself too stringently with the distinctions between earlier and later periods. Reflecting on a half century's published work in 1995, Kristol notes (with some surprise) his "homogeneity of approach, the consistency of a certain cast of mind. . . . I think it is fair to say that what might be called a 'neoconservative imagination' is something that I have always possessed, long before the very term itself was invented, and long before there was any kind of neoconservative 'movement'" (*A* ix–x).

4. "The world would doubtless be a nicer and healthier place if large ideas were kept at a distant remove from political power. The close conjunction is a dangerous one. But the world is what it is. It is a world of media, a world where habit and custom are weak before the forces of communication. It is, therefore, a world where ideas and their articulation are indispensable to effective conservative government" (*TC* 134–35; *A* 353). The modern world, being a world of scientific-technological innovation and economic growth, responds only to future-oriented politics, which is to say ideological politics (cf. *R* x).

5. Kristol's classical roots developed only after he had become skeptical of various liberal and democratic tenets. "I had to discover for myself, uneasily and fumblingly, many things which a serious student of political philosophy—someone soundly versed in Aristotle's *Politics*, for example—might have known early on" (*DI* viii).

6. "All political philosophers prior to the twentieth century, regardless of their personal piety or lack thereof, understood the importance of religion in the life of the political community. Neoconservatives, because of their interest in and attachment to classical (as distinct from contemporary) political philosophy, share this understanding" (*A* 381).

7. The following self-description from 1970 bears out the latter point explicitly and the former point implicitly, I think, with its invocation of Voltaire: "I am a journalist, at best a man of letters, and I am keenly aware that, as Voltaire observed, a man of letters resembles a flying fish: 'If he raises himself up a little, the birds devour him; if he dives, the fish eat him up.' I take this to mean that insofar as I refer to general ideas, I shall be devoured by the scholarly eagles, and that insofar as I refer to particular details, I shall be eaten alive by the scholarly sharks. On the other hand it is in the nature of a flying fish that he cannot for too long skim nervously along the surface. That suits neither his instincts nor his appetite" (*DI* 48; *R* 95; *A* 313).

8. Consider, for example, that most conservatism has made its peace, albeit in some cases a colder peace than Kristol has advocated, with the idea of a welfare state. That a conservative president in the 1980s and Speaker of the House of Representative in the 1990s would publicly praise Franklin Roosevelt perhaps reflects this influence.

9. In a broad sense all of Kristol's writings speak to politics, though some do so quite indirectly—for example, studies of Freud and Einstein in which the cultural and political implications of various kinds of rationalism are explored.

10. It should be noted that both the liberalism and the capitalism endorsed by Kristol are not "pure" versions. The individual freedom entailed by the kind of liberalism he supports stops short of license: a crucial and in Kristol's view an oft-forgotten distinction. And the capitalism he endorses entails an economy based largely, but not exclusively, on private ownership and free markets: political considerations, in his view, speak against laissez-faire economics.

11. Although the word "capitalism" had not yet been invented, Kristol believes it represents well enough what the Founders, and Adam Smith, for that matter, had in mind.

12. Interestingly, the full phrase was "the post-bourgeois bourgeois world," leaving unclear the extent of the antibourgeois triumph in America (*TC* 169; *A* 197).

13. Also see *TC* xi, where Kristol refers to this situation as "a dangerous dialectic."

14. On the rise of the corporation, see Parts One and Two of *TC* and Part Four of *R* (especially "Corporate Capitalism in America," which appears in both books and is reprinted in *A*). On urbanization, see "Urban Civilization and Its Discontents" in *DI*, *R*, and *A*. In the latter essay, Kristol stresses the magnitude of urbanization and our ignorance as to its long-term political implications, an ignorance cum complacency which gives no thought to the deep concerns of the Founders and, for that matter, nearly the whole Western philosophical tradition regarding the effects of urban life on republican virtue.

15. Kristol cites Friedrich von Hayek as "the most intelligent defender of capitalism today [1970]." The view of justice as whatever the market has rendered, which is an ex post facto theory of justice, was articulated by Mandeville and Hume and is discernible in the work of such twentieth-century defenders of capitalism as Milton Friedman. See "Capitalism, Socialism, and Nihilism" in *TC* 64–65 and *A* 100–101.

16. Another part of capitalism's changing self-understanding is seen in the history of economic theory. In the nineteenth century, Adam Smith's optimism regarding the near-universal distribution of benefits in a capitalist society was succeeded by a series of more pessimistic orthodoxies, beginning with the teachings of Malthus. By the mid-twentieth century, economic theory, finally responding to the facts, had returned to something like Smith's more hopeful vision, but not before damage had been done to capitalism's standing; and even this more hopeful vision is a vulgarized and reductionist version of Smithian theory. See "Adam Smith and the Spirit of Capitalism" in *R* 169–74 and *A* 291–96.

17. "'Man makes himself.' That is to say, the universe is bereft of transcendental meaning, it has no inherent teleology, and it is within the power of humanity to comprehend natural phenomena and to control and manipulate them so as to improve the human estate" (*A* 446–47).

18. Kristol pointedly does not preclude the possibility of finding in philosophy the substitute for religion in this regard—and in other regards—but the possibility is so rare as to be without political significance.

19. The "counterculture" of these quotes seems to be synonymous with the "anticulture" cited above.

20. Space constraints permit no more than a nod to a few of these problematics. A market economy, Kristol writes, has by its nature three major weaknesses. "The first is the self-interested nature of commercial activity." Although most persons accept the legitimacy of self-interest in general, they mistrust *other persons*' self-interest. "The second is the occasional . . . malfunctioning of the system. The third [and most important] is the growing tendency . . . to frustrate the system's working by imposing ever-heavier burdens [collectivist, redistributionist, and regulatory] upon it" (*A* 124). And American democracy itself has problematics, beginning with its tendency to convert its original democratic *philosophy* into a religious *faith* in democracy. See "American Historians and the Democratic Idea" in *DI*, *R*, and *A*. Another "crucial weakness" of American democracy is that its emphasis on individualism makes it very difficult, perhaps impossible, to "satisfy the natural desire for community among human beings" (*R* 321; *A* 436).

21. That these two facts are more significant than others is my interpretation; Kristol nowhere, to my knowledge, explicitly ranks them in this way.

22. See also *TC* 63 and *A* 99, where he claims that the disestablishment of religion had "unquestionably" led to "a diminution of religious faith and a growing skepticism about the traditional consolations of religion—especially the consolations offered by a life after death."

23. It is important to remember that, in Kristol's usage, "metaphysics" refers to one's "view of human nature and of social and economic realities"; it does not refer to anything like Aristotle's "first philosophy" (*A* x).

24. Regarding Christianity and Judaism, see "Christianity, Judaism, and Socialism" in *R* 320–21 and *A* 434–35. Regarding classical political philosophy, see "Utopianism, Ancient and Modern" in *TC* 157–60 and *A* 187–90. It is necessary to speak of *traditional* Christianity and Judaism because some contemporary versions, in Kristol's view, have absorbed some of the utopian features of secular humanism.

25. "What is wrong with liberalism is liberalism—a metaphysics and a mythology that is woefully blind to human and political reality" (*A* 486).

26. Regarding social welfare policy, see especially Section Two of *A* ("Race, Sex, and Family") and Part Three of *TC* ("What is 'Social Justice?'"); regarding foreign policy, see *R*, V ("Neoconservatism and Foreign Policy").

27. It should be noted that Kristol has promoted these policy goals as much through his editorial and publishing work—especially as coeditor and publisher, respectively, of *The Public Interest* and *The National Interest*—as through his own writing. As noted above, he cofounded *The Public Interest*, a journal of domestic public policy, in 1965. He founded *The National Interest*, a journal of foreign policy and world politics, in 1985. For his written policy advocacy, apart from the issue of censorship (which is treated in "Pornography, Obscenity, and the Case for Censorship" in *DI* and *R*), see the texts cited in the preceding note.

28. Regarding bourgeois society's traditional underestimation of ideas, see, for example, *TC* 169 and *A* 198; see also *A* 128, where Kristol attributes this indifference to Adam Smith, calling it a "stupendous error" whose influence has haunted Western civilization for two centuries.

29. Notwithstanding the recent appearance of "neopagan impulses bubbling up from below," it is "reasonable to anticipate that the overwhelming majority of Americans, as they turn to religion, will turn to some version (perhaps in modified form) of Christianity." So Kristol wrote in 1991. By 2000, he had noted the appearance of a new religious sensibility in America, which he called "Transcendental Individualism," and speculated that it will have a profound impact on politics. "Terms like Left and Right, along with liberalism and conservatism, are already beginning to seem anachronistic." "Faith à la carte: Religion and politics in an era of good feeling," *Times Literary Supplement*, May 26, 2000.

Chapter 45

The Jurisprudence of William Joseph Brennan, Jr., and Thurgood Marshall

Bradley C. S. Watson

We seek here to examine the jurisprudence of William Brennan (1906–1998) and Thurgood Marshall (1908–1993) with the intent of examining their place in the history of American political thought. The best access to a jurist's thinking is undoubtedly to be had through a close reading of his most authoritative pronouncements—i.e., the decisions the jurist has written during his tenure on the highest court of which he has been a member. To the extent we are interested in the political thought of the jurist, such decisions that bear directly on the Constitution will be of most concern. We will therefore concentrate our analysis on the most important of such decisions of Brennan and Marshall.

It is worth noting two important caveats at the outset. First, the reader should recognize that legal adjudication—even constitutional adjudication—is not philosophy, and jurists are constrained in their effort to get to the truth of the political things in a way that philosophers are not. Court decisions, as will become apparent, often reflect a search for consensus: within the court itself, within a larger legal community, or within society as a whole. In addition, jurists often participate in, but do not write, judgments. It is much harder to claim that such judgments are fully reflective of the jurist's final thoughts on the matter before the court, as compared to judgments he himself writes. Second, our analysis will, inevitably, criticize both Brennan and Marshall. In so doing, our aim is neither to deny the importance of the civil rights they attempted to vindicate nor to doubt the sincerity of their passionate commitment to them. Rather, we seek to make clear the nature of their political thinking and the principles put at stake in vindicating those rights in the manner that Brennan and Marshall chose.

Schools of Constitutional Interpretation

We should first note that there are five prominent schools of thought that supply or suggest principles of constitutional interpretation to America's courts. Understanding, in brief compass, the nature of these schools helps us limn the precise place of Brennan and Marshall in the American political tradition.

The first school might be called original or Founders' intent; the second, textualism; the third, natural standards; the fourth, organic; and the fifth, liberal principles.[1] We do not mean to imply that these categories are mutually exclusive or fully self-contained. Of necessity or preference, individual legal theorists or jurists may adopt more than one stance, or set of theoretical orientations, even in the context of a single constitutional controversy or adjudication. Likewise, the individuals or movements we associate with each of these schools are for illustrative purposes only; they are by no means exhaustive or even paradigmatic. Nevertheless, these categories do serve to highlight important sources of division in constitutional thinking.

The original or Founders' intent school of jurisprudence implies that the paramount concern of a judge in interpreting the Constitution is to ascertain the intent of its authors and/or ratifiers. Adherents tend to the view that courts must not themselves legislate or be beholden to popular opinion, and that the best way to avoid each of these failings is through fidelity to the intentions of the Founders insofar as those intentions have not themselves been formally amended. The original intent school attempts to fix constitutional interpretation to something less fleeting than judges' preferences or the perceived demands of the times, but in so doing it raises its own set of potential problems. Some are evidentiary and historical in nature: how can we know with reasonable certainty what was generally intended, and who must share this intent before it becomes dispositive? Some are hermeneutic: what if the text and the Founding intentions appear in some way to be at odds with one another?[2] And, perhaps most fundamentally, some betray what we will here call a historical consciousness: why ought we be bound by the intent of those who lived and died long before contemporary problems arose?

Textualism, like original intent, is a kind of originalism. It is, practically speaking, so closely allied with original intent that the two modes of interpretation seem almost to merge in many applications. It is, however, theoretically distinct. The doctrine is best understood as an attempt to deal with the evidentiary and hermeneutic problems raised by original intent. Textualism emphasizes fidelity to the actual words of the laws and the Constitution, and the plausible constructions that can be put on those words using certain reasonable canons of construction. The meaning of the Constitution is not to be found in the subjective intent of its Framers or ratifiers, but in how it was originally *understood*, based on its text. The Founders' writings are useful not because they reveal their *intent*, but because they may shed light on this understanding.[3] Textualism does not deal with the problem of historical consciousness—as it might be asked why we should be bound by the intent of another era, it might equally be asked why we should be bound by the text of another era.

The natural standards approach to jurisprudence attempts to answer the evidentiary, hermeneutic, *and* historical consciousness critiques of originalism. In this sense, it is the most comprehensive approach to constitutional interpretation.[4] A jurisprudence of natural standards would not necessarily be hostile either to Founders' intent or textualism, as long as each of these is grounded in principles that transcend historical contingency. Exponents of what we are here calling natural standards maintain that in order to know what American constitutional originalism *was* and *is* (whether we are speaking of an originalism of Founders' intent or objectified meaning), we must have recourse to the understanding of natural rights which permeated the American Founding. In this understanding, put forth most forcefully by Harry V. Jaffa, overarching principles based on the nature of human beings and their place in the cosmos informed the Founders' understanding and must still ground the textual provisions of the Constitution.[5] The will of the people is indeed expressed in the Constitution, but *why* the will of the people ought to be taken as authoritative is in turn grounded in the natural equality of human beings. No man is so naturally superior to another to have the right to rule over another without that person's consent. In this view, textualism (in the form of the Declaration's claim that all men are created equal), Lockean natural rights (rooted in the nature of the human things), and Founders' intent (which reflects an appreciation for a version of Locke's theoretical doctrine) merge and are in complete harmony with one another. Furthermore, we may say that we *ought* to obey the text and objectified intent (which was also the subjective intent) of the Founders because these things are rooted in a natural order which transcends historical contingency, and which reflects both what is naturally right and what is positively required by the natural law. If we accept the notion of natural standards we could say, for example, that Chief Justice Taney clearly erred in *Dred Scott v. Sandford* (1857) insofar as he held slaves not to be full rights-bearing citizens under the Constitution. He erred not only because he misinterpreted the intention of the Founders and the meaning of their text, that is, he was not being the originalist he thought he was, but because his understanding of the nature of law was in error. Even assuming that Taney's flawed originalism had in fact been correct, he could still have concluded that a human law that violates the natural law is not the highest law of the land; it is merely command.[6] And to violate the natural rights of human beings is to violate the natural law.[7]

In sharp contrast to each of the schools of thought we have considered to this point, the organic school grows out of early-twentieth-century Progressive thought. Progressivism tended to see state and society as organisms that could live or die, flourish or decay, depending on their ability to respond to the dictates of changing times and circumstances. Progressivism borrowed the notion of continuous historical movement from Hegelianism, and the notion of all organisms' never-ending struggle for survival from Darwinism. The end result was a philosophy of history that demanded responses to unique historical circumstances, but denied that any fixed principles—particularly constitutional or natural principles—could provide those responses. For the Progressives, a constitution represents only the time-bound preferences of men who could not have anticipated the demands of the future; and nature represents only a process—the ceaseless struggle for survival—but not an end.

Progressivism engendered what came to be known in the early twentieth century as sociological jurisprudence, that is, judicial decisions based on empirical analyses of pressing social problems rather than legal principles as traditionally understood. This type of jurisprudence was exemplified by the "Brandeis brief," a term still used to describe a submission to a court that is long on social analysis and short on any form of originalism or discussion of common law principles. But while the alleviation of the human condition may have been the raison d'être of sociological jurisprudence, for many of the early Progressive jurists the demands of history and the evolutionary process could not be discounted. In their view, strong ideas, institutions, and individuals are the ones that survive and prosper; weaker ones fall by the wayside, and indeed ought to do so. So Oliver Wendell Holmes, in supporting a program of compulsory sterilization, argued that "three generations of imbeciles are enough," the risk being that such individuals would "sap" the strength and impede the development of society.[8]

Another movement—legal realism—was an offshoot of this organic understanding of constitutional interpretation and the sociological jurisprudence that grew from it. Moving far beyond the notion that courts ought to take social facts and conditions into account, the realists, commencing in the 1920s, argued explicitly that judges made the law rather than applied it. This lawmaking arose from a number of economic, social, and psychological stimuli. Further, judges must make law in order keep the system current with changing times. As each of the schools we are examining, save for natural standards, is a variation of legal positivism, so the organic and liberal principles schools can, additionally, be rightly understood as kinds of legal realism. Legal positivism and legal realism are still commonly, and sometimes dominantly, employed in law schools in discussions of jurisprudence, although, as we have seen, they are far from comprehensive.

This leads us to the liberal principles school of constitutional interpretation, which emphasizes the triumph of one historical contingency in particular: the liberal universalism of rights as mediated through a contemporary understanding of egalitarian individualism. This school of thought may be understood as an essentially ossified version of the organic revolution. By way of preface to William Brennan's thought, let us note here that he exemplifies this view in parts of a 1985 address on constitutional interpretation.[9] He claims, on the one hand, that constitutional interpretation is time bound: it has no "static meaning." A twentieth-century judge must interpret the Constitution in light of considerations fundamentally different, he claims, from those that entered the minds of the Framers. Many or most of their views are bound to be "anachronistic." Despite this pronounced historicism (so characteristic of the organic school), Brennan also reminds readers that he views capital punishment as unconstitutional "under all circumstances." This is because such punishment is contrary to the "very essence of human dignity," which in turn is bound up with the notion that such punishment irrevocably strips all rights from those who—potentially at least—have human dignity and are capable of exercising rights. (This potentiality for the exercise of rights—dispositive with reference to capital punishment—retreats in significance for Brennan when he considers the question of abortion.) Brennan claims that this view of the human individual embodies a community striving—but insofar as it transcends historical contingency, it appears to reflect what communities strive for at the end of history.

Human dignity and other asserted principles of this school tend to be linked by an egalitarianism that is stringent insofar as it precludes distinctions among human beings on grounds that, historically and philosophically, many have claimed to be rationally justifiable. These principles may then be asserted to interfere, in the name of the Constitution, with certain governmental practices that are seen adversely to affect certain classes of citizens that have intentionally been marked by law for differential treatment. There is a concomitant species of liberal principles reasoning that seeks to limit governmental restrictions on the conduct of individuals. The liberal principles school often elevates, morally and legally, certain human practices above others in order to justify wide-ranging prohibitions on governmental regulation of them.[10]

Brennan's Organic Individualism

William Brennan served on the High Court from 1956 to 1990 and was undoubtedly one of the most influential justices in its history. At the heart of Brennan's thinking is an organic understanding of the tightly braided liberal principles of freedom and equality. His was an egalitarian individualism, emphasizing the need for a relatively unfettered liberation of human individuality supported by a judicial apparatus dedicated to securing the conditions for such liberation.[11] This individuality is directed not so much toward material aggrandizement as toward a variety of forms of self-expression.[12] For Brennan, as for the Progressives, liberation and personal growth are linked, as are liberation and centralization. Brennan's nationalism, however, is not the nationalism of rhetorical leadership, as it was for the Progressives. It is rather the nationalism of a federal court system taking on the role of schoolmaster to the nation.

The evolution of Brennan's thinking, and the essential constancy at its core, can be seen through a survey of his decisions. Early in his career on the High Court, he was a participant in many of the key civil and voting rights decisions of the late 1950s and early 1960s. Concurring in *Cooper v. Aaron* (1958), Brennan wrote separately to reassert federal courts' control over the desegregation process, and the notion of federal judicial supremacy generally.[13] He forcefully reiterated the basic principle, first enunciated in *Marbury v. Madison* (1803), that "the federal judiciary is supreme in the exposition of the law of the Constitution" and that state institutions—legislative, executive, or judicial—were not authorized to nullify this supremacy. Such a position, in itself, might be considered unexceptional, but it must be understood in conjunction with the other facets of Brennan's thought.

Writing the majority decision in *Baker v. Carr* (1962), Brennan unleashed the "reapportion-ment revolution" in America.[14] *Baker* held that state electoral apportionment controversies—traditionally understood as among the most inevitably political of problems—were justiciable in the federal courts.[15] Brennan enunciated a loose "political questions" doctrine for future judicial involvement in such matters. The case involved numerically unequal districting in Tennessee and the alleged failure, as a consequence of that districting, of the Tennessee state legislature to *represent equally* each individual voter in the state. Brennan held that a justiciable issue existed under the Fourteenth Amendment's equal protection clause. He would later concur with majority opinions authorizing the now commonplace (but constitutionally unmentioned) requirement that districting must accord with the "one man, one vote" principle.[16]

In dissent in *Baker*, Justice Felix Frankfurter noted the paradox of such a finding (which also happened to be inconsistent with the High Court's decision just sixteen years earlier):[17]

> One cannot speak of "debasement" or "dilution" of the value of a vote until there is first defined a standard of reference as to what a vote should be worth. What is actually asked of the Court in this case is to choose among competing bases of representation—ultimately, really among competing theories of political philosophy—in order to establish an appropriate frame of government for the State of Tennessee and thereby for all states of the Union. What Tennessee illustrates is an old and still widespread method of representation—representation by local geographical division. . . . [Appellants] would make the Equal Protection Clause the character of adjudication, asserting that the equality which it guarantees comports, if not the assurance of equal weight to every voter's vote, at least the basic conception that representation ought to be proportionate to the population. . . . To find such a political conception legally enforceable in the broad and unspecific guarantee of equal protection is to rewrite the Constitution.[18]

Brennan's First Amendment jurisprudence had from the outset been notable for its emphasis on the liberation of the individual from traditional or politically imposed standards. In *New York Times v. Sullivan* (1964), the common law of libel took a uniquely American turn.[19] For the majority, Brennan wrote a decision that had the effect of protecting libelous speech directed against public officials in the absence of a showing of "actual malice," that is, that the speech was uttered with actual knowledge of its falsehood or reckless disregard thereof. Brennan's role as conciliator and seeker of consensus became apparent in this case when he diverged from the views of some allies to argue against an unqualified immunity from libel suits in the case of an individual who criticizes official conduct. Nonetheless, his decision continues to this day to have the effect of making it more difficult to succeed in such suits in the United States than in most other common law nations.

On the separate but related questions of obscenity and flag burning, Brennan betrays a similar concern for individual self-expression at the expense of state regulation thereof. In his dissent in *Paris Adult Theater I v. Slaton* (1973), Brennan claims that "in the absence of distri-bution to juveniles or obtrusive exposure to non-consenting adults, the First and Fourteenth Amendments prohibit the state and federal governments from attempting wholly to suppress sexually oriented materials on the basis of their allegedly 'obscene' contents."[20] Of course, the First Amendment neither explicitly protects expression, as opposed to speech, nor explicitly guarantees that juveniles be protected from exposure to whatever it does protect. (The absence of concern as to what children might be exposed to seems natural enough if what is constitution-ally protected is limited to political speech.)

Brennan's understanding therefore seems, under the surface, to contain some theory either as to what is appropriate for man qua man; or for Americans at this particular stage in their nation's development; or for Americans at the end of constitutional history. Discounting the first of these three alternatives, we are left with the second or third, and possibly some combination of each. At the very least, Brennan is of the view that certain rights of consenting adults are inviolable, whatever the grounding for these rights and this inviolability.

Writing for the majority in *Texas v. Johnson* (1989), Brennan likewise holds that an individual's interest in burning an American flag outweighs any asserted state interest in preventing breaches of the peace or preserving the flag as a national symbol.[21] Placing such emphasis on free speech—even in the form of conduct that is primarily expressive—is arguably the most noticeable characteristic of contemporary American constitutional jurisprudence. Under such a jurisprudence, expression routinely trumps any asserted interests to the contrary, even when, as in the present case, the restriction on expression still leaves open myriad other means and media to convey exactly the same message. So powerful is this bias one oftentimes finds it shared even by more conservative justices (as, for example, Justice Antonin Scalia, who concurred with Brennan in the present case).

Also under the aegis of protected First Amendment freedoms—especially freedom of belief and association—Brennan in *Elrod v. Burns* (1976) and *Rutan v. Republican Party* (1990) interjected federal judicial management into the personnel decisions of public officials.[22] In *Elrod*, Brennan held for the majority that patronage dismissals of public employees in non-policy-making positions was an unconstitutional infringement on their rights under the First Amendment. He held that asserted governmental interests in democratic accountability—furthered by patronage—did not outweigh such First Amendment claims. Under this weighted balancing, only a "paramount" interest of "vital" import could justify a state infringement. In *Rutan* (authored by Brennan just before his retirement from the Court), this line of reasoning was picked up and applied to promotions, transfers, hirings, and recalls of laid-off state workers, even when political party building was cited as a reason for partisan control of the process. Brennan's reasoning in *Rutan* stands in sharp contrast to the biting dissent of Justice Scalia, who in this instance remarked that "when a practice not expressly prohibited by the text of the Bill of Rights bears the endorsement of a long tradition of open, widespread, and unchallenged use that dates back to the beginning of the Republic, we have no proper basis for striking it down."

We should note in passing that the apparently broad right of freedom of association vindicated in *Elrod* and *Rutan* is arguably in some degree of tension with the curtailment of this right in the name of racial or gender equality. The right is subject to significant curtailment—judicially and legislatively—when asserted by employers or other legally recognized entities if it is seen to come into conflict with preferred versions of equality. Brennan's—and the modern Court's—concern tends to be for the individual or legally constructed groups of individuals rather than the spontaneous associations generated by a civil, commercial society.

Brennan is hardly consistent on this point, however. As a defender of affirmative action, Brennan would allow private employers to retain one area of wide latitude in personnel matters, relatively free from judicial scrutiny. Writing for the majority in *United Steelworkers v. Weber* (1979), Brennan held that private employers may discriminate *in favor* of minority employees when they are acting to undo racial imbalance in the workforce.[23] His reasoning in *Weber* in many ways parallels his earlier reasoning in *Katzenbach v. Morgan* (1966), where he held Congress had a near plenary power, under section 5 of the Fourteenth Amendment, to extend voting rights guarantees beyond the bounds set in judicial decisions, including even those of the Supreme Court itself.[24] In an otherwise uncharacteristic deference to legislative authority, Brennan in effect held that Congress can expand the substantive content of constitutional rights as defined by the Supreme Court, but not contract the same. Of course, even the definition of expansion or contraction in this context might be subject to dispute—a dispute to be resolved no doubt, were Brennan to have his druthers, in line with liberal principles.

Perhaps paradoxically in light of *Weber* and other decisions, Brennan is often remembered as one of the foremost defenders of the doctrine of equal protection under the Fourteenth Amendment. In *Craig v. Boren* (1976), Brennan established a heightened category of judicial scrutiny for governmental gender classifications.[25] Rather than requiring that such classifications merely have a rational basis, Brennan required that they must serve "important" state purposes and must be "substantially related" to such purposes. Such a test is less rigorous than the Court's "strict scrutiny" test for racial classifications. Nonetheless, under heightened scrutiny government actions or programs that seek to respond to what many would claim are important natural or socially constructed differences between men and women are much less likely to pass constitutional muster.

Brennan's thought has been influential too in the broad right to privacy that, in various applications, has been protected by the Court since the mid-1960s. In *Eisenstadt v. Baird* (1972), Brennan helped lay the foundation for the pivotal majority decision of Justice Harry Blackmun in *Roe v. Wade* (1973).[26] Brennan wrote for the majority that the constitutional right to privacy enunciated in *Griswold v. Connecticut* (1965) must be interpreted broadly to include a notion of inviolable individual rights:

> If under *Griswold* the distribution of contraceptives to married persons cannot be prohibited, a ban on distribution to unmarried person would be equally impermissible. It is true that in *Griswold* the right of privacy in question inhered in the marital relationship. Yet the marital couple is not an independent entity with a mind and heart of its own, but an association of two individuals each with a separate intellectual and emotional makeup. If the right of privacy means anything, it is the right of the *individual*, married or single, to be free from unwarranted governmental intrusion into matters so fundamentally affecting a person as the decision whether to bear or beget a child.[27]

Thus, while *Griswold* guaranteed that the use of contraceptive devices by married couples could not be legally infringed, *Eisenstadt* essentially obliterated any distinction between married and unmarried couples with respect to access to contraceptives. This case therefore presaged legal developments—at the state as well as federal level—that have slowly but surely, in the name of individuality, eroded marriage as an institution rooted in nature or salutary tradition and deserving of special legal protections and entitlements.

Quite apart from the high-profile controversies that still swirl around the purported constitutional privacy right and its emanations and penumbras, Brennan's protection of individual claims against society's deliberative choices has, as we have already noted, manifested itself in numerous ways. Indeed, preventing legislative discretion in areas that impinge on individualistic claims has been a hallmark of Brennan's jurisprudence. To the areas already discussed, we should add Brennan's support for a relatively unrestricted individual right to the benefit of government programs. For example, in *Shapiro v. Thompson* (1969) Brennan found the right to travel to be fundamental—implying that the strictest judicial scrutiny be applied to any law that impinges on it.[28] Under this strict standard, states were prohibited from imposing a durational residency requirement as a condition of eligibility for welfare benefits. In *Goldberg v. Kelly* (1970), Brennan for the Court created in effect an entitlement to welfare pursuant to the due process clause of the Fourteenth Amendment.[29] Such a finding places on a state the requirement of a full evidentiary hearing before an impartial adjudicator before the state can terminate welfare benefits.

But once again Brennan's thinking is hardly a model of consistency. When it comes to the individual's right to property—as protected by the takings clause of the Fifth Amendment—Brennan would allow state actors to exercise far more discretionary power than in other areas.

Writing the dissent (joined by Marshall) in *Nollan v. California Coastal Commission* (1987), Brennan criticized the majority's imposition of "a standard of precision for the exercise of a State's police power."[30] The police power in question was California's insistence that property owners convey an uncompensated public easement on their land in return for a building permit. The purpose of such a requirement was allegedly to protect ocean views. Such a conveyance, in the view of the majority, clearly amounted to a taking of property for public use, requiring compensation, while for Brennan and Marshall it was merely a "restriction" on the use of property. Thus, in the case of takings which infringe individual rights, Brennan appears, paradoxically, concerned by what he takes to be an overly solicitous, "cramped standard" that would unduly limit the "flexibility" of state actors. Brennan's relative lack of concern with the right to property as traditionally understood also stands in some contrast to his creation, in *Goldberg*, of "new" property rights in welfare cases.

In a miscellany of other decisions—all in accord with his basic theoretical orientation—Brennan insisted on strict separation of church and state, voted to further limit governmental control of obscenity, restrict loyalty oaths, and expand habeas corpus and other rights of the accused in criminal matters.[31] Perhaps the most telling encapsulation of Brennan's thought can be found in his death penalty jurisprudence. In dissent in *Gregg v. Georgia* (1976), Brennan held capital punishment to be cruel and unusual, and therefore contrary to the Eighth Amendment (as applied to the states through the incorporation doctrine).[32] The basis for this finding was that capital punishment allegedly treats human beings as less than human, violating a general guarantee of civilized treatment implied by the amendment—this despite the fact that capital punishment was widely if not universally accepted at the time of the Founding and is specifically averred to as a possible criminal sanction in the Fifth and Fourteenth Amendments to the Constitution. We should pause here to note that Brennan's philosophical position on capital punishment seems rooted in late-twentieth-century liberal principles: it implies a vaguely worked out theory of individual dignity that trumps all else—even *explicit* constitutional text. To the extent it is coherent, Brennan's position can be said to be at substantial odds with major theories and theorists of punishment not just in the United States but in the Western tradition as a whole. Philosophers as diverse as Plato, Hobbes, and Hegel have each, for his own highly developed reasons, thought capital punishment to be both just and necessary. Indeed, Brennan's liberal humanitarianism seems to be almost the polar opposite of Hegel's idealism on this score. For Hegel, it is not capital punishment that is dehumanizing, but the denial to a human being of any punishment that is precisely commensurate with the crime he has committed. Guilty individuals, to claim their humanity and thereby separate themselves from mere irrational beasts, have a *right* to punishment as a signal to the social order as a whole that they *are* in fact human and can be held fully accountable for their actions.

Thus, Brennan can be seen as a key player among the Court's liberal justices, who together argued for, and created, an ever-expanding catalog of protected individual rights and expanded federal powers. Strong national institutions, constantly evolving to dedicate themselves ever more squarely and comprehensively to securing equality of access to moral and political liberation, are essential elements of Brennan's thought as they were for earlier Progressive thought. Late in his career, Brennan came to emphasize the importance of state courts interpreting their state constitutions more liberally than the federal Constitution was construed by an increasingly conservative Supreme Court. In short, the state courts were to be vigorous and independent, but only insofar as they stepped into the breach to pursue Brennan's national, egalitarian, individualist vision. Brennan thus sits at the intersection of the organic and liberal principles schools of constitutional thought, the former generally being used as a vehicle for pursuing the objectives of the latter.

Marshall's Evolving Constitution

As the first black member of the U.S. Supreme Court, Thurgood Marshall's tenure from 1967 to 1991 was of unique symbolic importance. His contributions as a jurist were significant, although not as comprehensive or momentous as Brennan's. This is at least partly because his emphasis on a constantly evolving constitutional framework seemed to lack, in principle if not in practice, the relative refinement and tendentiousness of Brennan's philosophical vision. Before examining Thurgood Marshall's thought in detail, we should note that he affirms his allegiance to the organic understanding of the Constitution in an essay commenting on that document's bicentennial.[33] He commences by denying that the meaning of the Constitution was fixed at the Philadelphia Convention, and indeed denying that the Founders were politically or morally wise men. The Constitution, in Marshall's view, is an evolving document, forged through amendment, civil war, and most especially, changed understandings of its terms. In Marshall's mind, especially on the question of slavery, the compromises of the Constitution are identical with the principles of the Constitution. He takes the "original intent" of the Constitution to be the intent as interpreted by Taney in *Dred Scott*. In Marshall's view, Taney's judgment, far from being a contradiction of the Founders' views, was an accurate reaffirmation of them. The Founding understandings of liberty, justice, and equality were flawed, and the road to constitutional progress has been paved by those who strove to improve or overcome them. The Constitution is a living document not because its original meaning lives, but rather because this meaning has died and allowed new growth to spurt.

While Marshall emphasizes an organic model of constitutionalism, we can see his preference for certain post-Founding developments over others. Although he favors a living Constitution, he wants its branches to grow in one direction—toward an egalitarian sun. He also appears to have some confidence that they will so grow—the apparent contingency of the historical process has, in fact, at least some objective component. We should note, however, that progressivism as a political doctrine—particularly as exemplified by Woodrow Wilson—betrays this tone of Hegelian objectivity more than progressivism in its legal incarnations, which tends toward Darwinism in Oliver Wendell Holmes and a kind of unphilosophic optimism about the future, and skepticism of the past, in Marshall.

It is worth noting too that Marshall's career prior to joining the High Court was in many ways as notable as his career on it. From 1939 to 1961 (when he was first appointed to the bench), Marshall headed the Legal Defense Fund, which began as the litigation arm of the National Association for the Advancement of Colored People (NAACP). As counsel in *Smith v. Allwright* (1944), *Shelley v. Kraemer* (1948), and *Brown v. Board of Education* (1954), Marshall was at the forefront of civil rights litigation designed to ensure equal opportunities for blacks to participate in and benefit from public institutions.[34] *Allwright* was a case sponsored by the NAACP, for whom Marshall acted. The case sought to challenge so-called white primaries in Texas, which were designed to keep blacks from participating in Democratic party nominating conventions, and therefore, because of the dominance of the Democratic party in the state, from full participation in the general election. The Court held, by an 8 to 1 margin, that such primaries were unconstitutional. Parties, though private organizations not within the contemplation of the Founders, were held to be part of the overall election machinery in the state and therefore governed by the protections of the Fifteenth Amendment. *Allwright* can be seen as a leading case in the development of the constitutional doctrine associated with "public function." Private actors can, in effect, be deemed to be performing a public function—and therefore be bound by the Constitution in the way that those performing purely private functions cannot. The elasticity of this notion is such that it has been applied to shrink progressively the private sphere in relation to the public in the realm of civil rights.

In *Shelley*, the Court held that courts—as state actors—were forbidden under the equal protection clause of the Fourteenth Amendment and the due process clause of the Fifth Amendment from enforcing racially restrictive covenants in the title to real property. Although the covenants themselves were the product of private actors acting in a private capacity, they could not rely on state action for their enforcement. This interpretation, although not attacking such covenants directly, effectively killed them by making them unenforceable at law. The interpretation thus further blurs the distinction between public and private and effectively changes the nature of courts in contract matters from neutral arbiters to agents of the public good.[35]

It should be remembered that the landmark *Brown* case held the "separate but equal" doctrine in public education to be an unconstitutional violation of the equal protection clause. The most notable feature of *Brown*'s reasoning, following the arguments of plaintiff's counsel, was its acceptance of various sociological and psychological theories as to the *effects* of segregation on blacks. The case contained almost nothing by way of examination of Founders' intent, textual interpretation, or natural standards. It was at once a throwback to the heyday of sociological jurisprudence and an assertion of the primacy of social impact analysis in modern civil rights controversies.

When Marshall was appointed by Lyndon Johnson to the Supreme Court in 1965, the times were propitious for development of his own version of an organic constitutionalism mindful of the alleged effects of various types of public and quasi-public activity. But he also displayed a willingness to assert the primacy of liberal principles in the form of abstract and controversial constitutional doctrine. His First Amendment jurisprudence is particularly instructive in this regard. In *Stanley v. Georgia* (1969), Marshall wrote for a unanimous Court that possession in one's home of legally obscene materials cannot be punished.[36] Although the First Amendment is implicated in his decision, so is the Fourth Amendment's search and seizure provisions, and the still developing constitutional doctrine of "privacy." The lack of clarity in the majority's reasoning (relying as it does on a smorgasbord of constitutional provisions and doctrines, much like other cases that more squarely deal with asserted "privacy" rights) has led—if not to an abandonment—then at least to an avoidance of the implications of *Stanley*.[37] In *Police Department of Chicago v. Mosley* (1972), Marshall delivered the majority opinion of the Court that struck down a Chicago ordinance that allowed peaceful labor picketing outside a school, but prohibited other forms of picketing.[38] The Court thereby established the principle that the state may not favor certain types of speech over others, even in an area as (arguably) sensitive as a school zone.

The extent to which Marshall was committed to the notion of an organic Constitution, with courts nurturing and directing the growth of the organism, is made clear in two of his most notable dissents. In both *Dandridge v. Williams* (1970) (in which he was joined in dissent by Brennan) and in *San Antonio School District v. Rodriguez* (1973), Marshall articulated the notion that courts should use a flexible sliding scale when deciding whether equal protection violations have occurred.[39] Under the traditional analysis (to which we referred earlier in our discussion of *Craig v. Boren*), the Court would subject "suspect" governmental categories, such as race—or alleged governmental infringement of "fundamental" rights—to the strictest standard of judicial scrutiny. This involves the state proving that the governmental classification or infringement of rights—and the governmental actions that are taken pursuant to them—are directly and immediately related to a compelling governmental interest. All other classifications, categories, or infringements enshrined in law could be justified merely on the basis of their being "rational" and reasonably related to a state interest, and they are presumed to be so unless those challenging them can demonstrate otherwise.[40]

Marshall's proposal for a flexible sliding scale—never accepted by a majority of the Court—would almost certainly have been a recipe for unprecedented judicial construction. Considerations the Court should take into account, according to Marshall (and Brennan) in *Dandridge*, would include "the character of the classification in question, the relative importance to the individuals in the class discriminated against . . . and the asserted state interests in support of the classification." As Marshall notes in *Rodriguez*, a "spectrum of standards"—far from demonstrating incoherence—is actually to be preferred over a finite, rationally cognizable set of judicial tests.

Finally, it is illustrative to note that Marshall and Brennan each wrote separate dissents in the death penalty case of *Gregg v. Georgia*, which was decided by a margin of 7 to 2. (Indeed, Marshall made a principle of dissenting in every case supporting the death penalty subsequent to *Gregg*.) With Brennan, Marshall reiterated his opposition to the death penalty on the basis that it is "excessive"—because it is irremediably violative of human dignity. He also reiterated his view, first expressed in *Furman v. Georgia* (1972), that the death penalty is unconstitutional because a "fully informed" American people would, he claimed, reject it—this even though *constitutional* majorities of those same people, in the majority of states, had accepted it.[41] Under Marshall's new test of what an informed citizenry would demand, it becomes the Court's role to determine when the American people are in fact informed, and to prevent them from acting when they are not.[42] Marshall explicitly claims that the "prediction of the views of an informed citizenry" might be the basis for a constitutional decision. That is, once the Court comes to a determination that ill-informed political choices were made, this determination apparently takes on constitutional status sufficient to overturn choices *actually* made by the popular branches.

In sum, we may say the constitutional understanding presented by Marshall in his bicentennial address was mirrored by his jurisprudence, which emphasized not the birth or fixed structure of the Constitution but its life and organic mutability. This aligns his thinking closely with that of Brennan. Together, they were the modern justices operating most explicitly within the parameters of the Progressive, organic model of constitutional interpretation.

Conclusion: Organic Individualism

In the end, it is difficult to claim that the thought of Brennan and Marshall discloses fully coherent principles of legal interpretation. They share the early Progressive tendency—of Brandeis and Holmes, among others—to show great deference to legislative judgments (especially national judgments expressed through Congress) in the economic realm. In the realm of civil rights, however, they are judicial activists to the core. Their informalism—linked to their organic understanding of the Constitution—thus betrays neither a consistent hostility toward legislative power nor a consistent support for it. In their hostility to originalism, however, they show a willingness to step outside the bounds of Madisonian constitutionalism to secure the triumph of an administrative state dedicated to leveling, and of the individual passions dedicated to unfettered expression. Their Hegelianism is thus modified by their romantic—almost Rousseauian—individualism, which is itself linked to a more Darwinian conception that the truth, in combat with falsehood, will win out. As Rousseau thus blends seamlessly with Darwin in their thought, we see their vision of a constantly evolving society and constitutional order that eschews stasis in favor of growth toward a confidently asserted, greater future. This future is in turn guided and limited by the superintending hand of governmental rationality in the form of certain fixed liberal principles. The protection of expression secures the competitive ground from which the general will emerges, strengthened, to move forward to the next level of social advancement.

We would be remiss if we did not note in conclusion that nationalism and individualism are linked in a way that Brennan and Marshall do not contemplate. As Tocqueville argues in *Democracy in America*, a mass of atomized individuals is relatively defenseless against a centralized administration. Without intermediate institutions to stand between them and government, individuals become powerless pawns or sycophants of the sovereign. Nowhere do the conditions for this danger seem more ripe than in the growth, on the one hand, of centralized administration in the name of equality, and on the other hand, in radical individuality in the name of the First Amendment and the right to privacy. Whether Brennan and Marshall can be seen as defenders of civil rights or fathers of soft despotism thus remains an open question.

Notes

1. The first two schools are each types of constitutional originalism; the last two explicitly eschew such originalism. The third—natural standards—might be compatible with constitutional originalism, but this depends on the nature of the original constitution.

2. The most infamous utilization of the doctrine of original intent—mingled with textualism—was Chief Justice Roger Taney's in the *Dred Scott* case (1857). Writing the 7-2 majority opinion, Taney purported to discover that the Founders did not intend slaves to be counted as citizens, or individuals with full rights. His reasoning relies largely on an examination of an alleged historical record which elucidated, in Taney's view, what the Founders must have *meant* by constitutional provisions—including the Declaration's assertion of natural equality—that *on their face* either do not exclude blacks from citizenship or appear positively to include them. Taney certainly understood himself to be an "originalist," interpreting text in light of what he claimed to be the Founders' intent. It is not our aim here to demonstrate that Taney's reading of the historical record was in error, although the documentary evidence to this effect is overwhelming. See, for example, Thomas G. West, *Vindicating the Founders: Race, Sex, and Class in the Origins of America* (Lanham, Md.: Rowman and Littlefield, 1999) for a concise summary and explication of this evidence. Rather, our interest is in demonstrating that subscribing to the doctrine of Founders' intent (or, more broadly, originalism) is in itself hardly dispositive on the critical question of what this intent or original meaning actually *is*.

3. Textualism's primary and most consistent contemporary expositor and practitioner is Justice Antonin Scalia. Both at the level of the Constitution and of subconstitutional statutory interpretation, Scalia maintains that the judge's role is to have reference to the "objectified intent" of the lawgiver as expressed through the text of the law. The lawgiver must be interpreted to *mean* what the lawgiver *promulgates*. To have reference to the subjective intent of the lawgiver is contrary to the very notion of a rule of law because it is tantamount to the legendary Neronian trick of posting edicts so high that no one can read them. See Antonin Scalia, *A Matter of Interpretation: Federal Courts and the Law* (Princeton, N.J.: Princeton University Press, 1997). Scalia maintains that his approach to interpretation is one of original or objective meaning rather than "strict constructionism." Alternatively, it is a constructionism that allows a text to bear all the meaning it may reasonably bear—no more, but no less. Neither literalism nor nihilism is appropriate when interpreting texts. For example, in *Oregon v. Smith*, 494 U.S. 872 (1990), Scalia held that the text of the free exercise clause in no way compels the government to exempt individuals from generally applicable laws not directed at religious practice, even though such laws may have the incidental effect of proscribing the religious practices of some. To interpret the clause otherwise would be to create, without a textual basis in the Constitution, an anomalous private right to ignore generally applicable laws.

A view widely held by the educated public and certain constitutional scholars alike is that "conservative" jurists of our own day adhere to the doctrine of original intent. However, any such unqualified association is problematic; confusion in this area seems to abound. See, for example, David Lyons, "Constitutional Interpretation and Original Meaning," *Social Philosophy and Policy* 4 (1986), who suggests Chief Justice William Rehnquist and Judge Robert H. Bork are originalists of one sort or another —intentionalist or textualist. But he does not say which sort. Many such jurists, in addition to Scalia, in fact cleave to a textualism of one form or another. Rehnquist and Bork are perhaps most commonly understood as originalists who would decide constitutional controversies based on the intent of the Founders. However, neither man subscribes to the doctrine of original intent in any straightforward way. For example, Rehnquist, dissenting in *Wallace v. Jaffree*, 472 U.S. 28 (1985), in which the majority held a moment of silence in public schools to be unconstitutional, seems on one level to rely largely on the intent of the Founders, but it is an intent confirmed by the understandings and actions of their political contemporaries and contemporaneous interpreters. For Rehnquist, the arguments of James Madison and others in the First Congress—to the effect that Congress should not establish a religion—are not conclusive on the meaning of the establishment clause. They are useful because they represent the best available evidence of the intentions and the *understandings* of those who drafted, introduced, or ratified the relevant clause. (This, of course, does not rule out the possibility that other, contrary evidence of a similar sort might be introduced.) The meaning of their words is in turn reinforced by the actions of the First Congress in enacting the Northwest Ordinance, which clearly provided for the governmentally sponsored enhancement of "religion, morality, and knowledge." In short, the historical/constitutional interpretations of the American people and their institutions, and the traditions and practices that grow out of them, help define, with tolerable precision, the meaning of constitutional text, and this meaning ought to be fixed until the text is formally amended. On the basis of a lengthy review of such historical understandings, Rehnquist concludes that the establishment clause cannot, in light of its limited and apparently widely understood purpose, be interpreted to demand absolute governmental neutrality as between religion and irreligion. Rehnquist would therefore overturn a line of cases that have the effect of establishing this (constitutionally spurious) "high wall of separation" between church and state. (This constitutional doctrine was explicated by the High Court in *Everson v. Board of Education*, 330 U.S. 1 [1947].)

Robert Bork argues that if we are to have judges bound by the law, they must be "bound by the only thing that can be called law, the principles of the text, whether Constitution or statute, as generally understood at the enactment. . . . [T]he judge is bound to apply the law as those who made the law wanted him to." See Bork, *The Tempting of America: The Political Seduction of the Law* (New York: The Free Press, 1990), 5. This understanding seems to require specific reference to the intent of the key constitutional Founders (for Bork, these are the ratifiers) or authors of legislation, whom we take to be authoritative. However, Bork also insists that in speaking of the intent or understanding of the ratifiers, he is using a shorthand formulation for a common public understanding, not a search for idiosyncratic personal intentions. See Bork, *Tempting*, 144. This qualification is important because of the weaknesses of original intent as described. Indeed, one is hard pressed to find compelling examples or exemplars of original intent in "pure" form.

4. Although, because of its comprehensiveness, it must exist at a level of abstraction that makes its application to many real-world cases and controversies difficult at best.

5. See, for example, Harry V. Jaffa, with Bruce Ledewitz, Robert L. Stone, George Anastaplo, *Original Intent and the Framers of the Constitution: A Disputed Question* (Washington, D.C.: Regnery Gateway, 1994). "Natural standards" jurisprudence invariably involves some version of natural right, natural law, or natural rights jurisprudence. The distinctions between these concepts—all of them hostile to a historicist approach—need not detain us here.

6. This indeed is precisely the position maintained by Justice Curtis in his *Dred Scott* dissent.

7. Only a legal positivist could assert otherwise, and we should note that all the schools of constitutional interpretation we are examining, save for the present one, are varieties of legal positivism, or law as the unadulterated product of sovereign command. Does a natural standards approach, practically speaking, inform American jurisprudence? Generally the answer is no. This is somewhat surprising in light of the twin facts that originalism has its adherents, and that the Founders' language and arguably their objectified and subjective intent were assertions of the existence and practical force of the laws of nature and nature's god. Nonetheless, the idea that the American constitutional order might be grounded in such laws is for the most part alien to constitutional interpretation. One notable exception may be found in the jurisprudence of Justice Clarence Thomas. For example, in a 1995 case on the constitutionality of certain federal affirmative action programs, Justice Thomas held such programs to violate the Declaration's holding that

all men are created equal. See *Adarand v. Pena*, 515 U.S. 200 (1995). The extent to which Thomas will develop this jurisprudence remains to be seen.

8. *Buck v. Bell*, 274 U.S. 200 (1927).

9. William Brennan, "The Constitution of the United States: Contemporary Ratification," in *Judges on Judging: Views from the Bench*, ed. David M. O'Brien (Chatham, N.J.: Chatham House Publishers, 1997).

10. In this regard, it is instructive to consider the abortion argument posited by leading legal theorist Ronald Dworkin in *Life's Dominion: An Argument about Abortion, Euthanasia, and Freedom* (New York: Alfred A. Knopf, 1993). Dworkin concedes that government can enforce a variety of protective and preservative laws with respect to everything from endangered species to historic architecture. So to claim government may not place substantial restrictions on abortion requires an argument that procreative issues fall into a different class. He begins his argument by asserting that we cannot infer that there is no constitutionally protected right to abortion merely because there is no textual provision or discernible intent to this effect. Rather, he claims that it is the abstractness of the Constitution that gives theorists of liberal principles (as opposed, seemingly, to theorists of natural law or rights) their entrée into a necessary, and therefore legitimate, interpretive enterprise. The abortion controversy should be considered as an aspect of a legitimate state interest in encouraging responsibility, rather than prohibiting the taking of life or potential life. The state may encourage, through various regulations, the individual decision-making processes of autonomous individuals, but it may not preempt such decision-making processes by enforcing a (majoritarian) conformity. (We should not forget the possibility, if we take the natural standards approach at all seriously, that there may in fact be kinds of conformity that are demanded regardless of the majority will, and oftentimes contrary to it.) Considering abortion in this light is in turn justified by the asserted notions that governmental preemption of individual decision making affects particular individuals to a far greater extent in the case of abortion than other cases, and that views of human life are far more intrinsically related to our sense of self than are views of the environment or the historical worthiness of certain buildings.

Let us make plain what Dworkin's reasoning leaves implicit. That is this: it is characteristic of the liberal principles school that its foundational principles, linked almost invariably to a notion of human dignity and its concomitants—human agency and authenticity—seem themselves contingent. Who, for example, is to say that conceptions of human life are more vital to one's sense of self (or some other "highest" principle) than conceptions of the environment, particularly for a committed environmentalist who may well see the nonhuman environment as higher in dignity than the human? In an effort to claim that interpretive principles based on originalism and natural standards are destined to be anachronistic and out of keeping with the times, and to imply that a purely organic set of interpretive principles might not protect critical individual rights, the liberal principles school ends up unmoored in text, intent, nature, or a historical process which might (in principle at least) have some objective component. We must be permitted to borrow Hegelian phraseology: the wills of those wedded to liberal principles appear hopelessly confined to the realm of pure subjectivity.

11. For a fuller explication of the philosophical origins and significance of egalitarian individualism, see Bradley C. S. Watson, *Civil Rights and the Paradox of Liberal Democracy* (Lanham, Md.: Lexington Books, 1999).

12. This stands in contradistinction to the "possessive individualism" aptly described by C. B. Macpherson in *The Political Theory of Possessive Individualism: Hobbes to Locke* (Oxford: Oxford University Press, 1962).

13. *Cooper v. Aaron*, 358 U.S. 1 (1958).

14. *Baker v. Carr*, 369 U.S. 186 (1962).

15. The traditional understanding was enunciated by the Court in *Colegrove v. Green*, 328 U.S. 549 (1946).

16. *Wesberry v. Sanders*, 376 U.S. 1 (1964); *Reynolds v. Sims*, 377 U.S. 533 (1964).

17. *Colegrove v. Green*, 328 U.S. 549 (1946).

18. *Baker v. Carr*, 300. It is worth noting that contemporary proponents of "campaign finance reform" inevitably base their arguments on a premise similar to that criticized by Frankfurter: it is wrong, and perhaps even deleterious to the Constitution, for some participants in the political process to exercise

influence disproportionate to others. That this appears to be an inevitability—based on levels of commitment, experience, and intelligence as well as financial resources (not to mention the effectiveness of one's elected member of Congress)—and that the Constitution already takes account of this inevitability in the form of Madison's argument for an extended sphere—seems lost on those committed to change. Further, there is no more a constitutional answer to the question of the "right" level of effectiveness of one's voice in the representative institutions of government than there is to Frankfurter's question of the "value" of a vote.

19. *New York Times v. Sullivan*, 376 U.S. 254 (1964).

20. *Paris Adult Theater I v. Slaton*, 413 U.S. 49 (1973).

21. *Texas v. Johnson*, 491 U.S. 397 (1989).

22. *Elrod v. Burns*, 427 U.S. 347 (1976); *Rutan v. Republican Party of Illinois*, 110 S.Ct. 2729 (1990).

23. *United Steelworkers of America v. Weber*, 443 U.S. 193 (1979).

24. *Katzenbach v. Morgan*, 384 U.S. 641 (1966).

25. *Craig v. Boren*, 429 U.S. 190 (1976).

26. *Eisenstadt v. Baird*, 405 U.S. 438 (1972); *Roe v. Wade*, 410 U.S. 113 (1973).

27. *Griswold v. Connecticut*, 381 U.S. 479 (1965).

28. *Shapiro v. Thompson*, 394 U.S. 618 (1969).

29. *Goldberg v. Kelly*, 397 U.S. 254 (1970).

30. *Nollan v. California Coastal Commission*, 483 U.S. 825 (1987).

31. In his concurrence in *Abington v. Schempp*, 374 U.S. 203 (1963), which declared Bible readings in public schools to be unconstitutional, Brennan explicitly eschewed reference to Founding intent and/or textual understanding. Given changed circumstances, "any views of the eighteenth century" are bound to be inadequate (even, we must infer, if those views have not in any way been subject to formal amendment).

32. *Gregg v. Georgia*, 428 U.S. 153 (1976).

33. Thurgood Marshall, "The Constitution: A Living Document," in O'Brien, ed., *Judges on Judging*.

34. *Smith v. Allwright*, 311 U.S. 649 (1944); *Shelley v. Kraemer*, 334 U.S. 1 (1948); *Brown v. Board of Education*, 347 U.S. 483 (1954).

35. One could also argue that this merely reemphasizes a role that common law courts have long played in certain "private" matters that seem to demand solutions contrary to public policy.

36. *Stanley v. Georgia*, 394 U.S. 557 (1969).

37. See, for example, *Bowers v. Hardwick*, 478 U.S. 186 (1986), where a 5-4 majority of the Court refused to extend the right to privacy to homosexual conduct, even in the privacy of one's home. See also *Osborne v. Ohio*, 495 U.S. 103 (1990), where a 6-3 majority (Marshall among the dissenters) refused to strike down a state statute criminalizing the possession of child pornography.

38. *Police Department of Chicago v. Mosley*, 408 U.S. 92 (1972).

39. *Dandridge v. Williams*, 397 U.S. 471 (1970); *San Antonio School District v. Rodriguez*, 411 U.S. 1 (1973).

40. Although, as we have mentioned, a third, intermediate tier of scrutiny was later established in *Craig v. Boren* (1976), with Brennan writing for the 7-2 majority.

41. *Furman v. Georgia*, 408 U.S. 238 (1972).

42. Such a determination, we might add, would be a tall order for even the most skilled political scientist. The Founders believed that the only way to approximate popular political choice based on full information was through establishing the people's "cool and deliberate sense" via the deliberative, popularly elected, constitutional branches of government. Most informed specialists would argue that there is little in the public opinion literature to suggest that we can somehow do better today by relying on the judgment of the least popular branch.

Chapter 46

The Textualist Jurisprudence of Antonin Scalia

Ralph A. Rossum

On June 24, 1986, Antonin Scalia (1936–), at the time a judge on the U.S. Court of Appeals for the District of Columbia Circuit, was nominated by President Ronald Reagan to serve as an associate justice of the United States Supreme Court. On September 17 (Constitution Day), he was confirmed by the Senate by a vote of 98–0.[1]

Scalia's Textualist Jurisprudence

Since ascending the High Bench, Justice Scalia has assiduously and consistently pursued a textualist jurisprudence. He argues that primacy must be accorded to the text, structure, and history of the document being interpreted and that the job of the judge is to apply the clear textual language of the Constitution or statute,[2] or the critical structural principle necessarily implicit in the text (*O* 852).[3] If the text is ambiguous, yielding several conflicting interpretations, Scalia turns to the specific legal tradition[4] flowing from that text—to "what it meant to the society that adopted it" (*H* 108).[5] "Text and tradition" is a phrase that fills Justice Scalia's opinions.[6] Judges are to be governed only by the "text and tradition of the Constitution," not by their "intellectual, moral, and personal perceptions." As he remarked in his concurring opinion in *Schad v. Arizona* (1991): "[W]hen judges test their individual notions of 'fairness' against an American tradition that is deep and broad and continuing, it is not the tradition that is on trial, but the judges" (650).

For Scalia, reliance on text and tradition is a means of constraining judicial discretion. Scalia believes that "the main danger in judicial interpretation of the Constitution—or, for that matter, in judicial interpretation of any law—is that the judges will mistake their own predilections for the law" (*O* 863).[7] Faithful adherence to the text of a constitutional or statutory provision, or, if that is ambiguous, to the traditional understanding of those who originally adopted it, reduces the danger that judges will substitute their beliefs for society's. Scalia's textualism was on full display in his dissent in *Troxel v. Granville* (2000). In that case, the Court struck down a Washington state law—permitting "[a]ny person" to petition for visitation rights for a child "at any time" and authorizing state superior courts to grant such rights whenever visitation may serve a child's best interest—on the ground that it unconstitutionally infringed on the fundamental right of parents to rear their children. "In my view," Scalia argued, "a right of parents to direct the upbringing of their children is among the . . . 'other rights retained by the people' which the Ninth Amendment says the Constitution's enumeration of rights 'shall not be construed to deny or disparage.'" However, he continued that the Constitution's refusal to "deny or disparage" other rights is far removed from affirming any one of them, and even farther removed from authorizing judges to identify what they might be, and to enforce the judges' list against laws duly enacted by the people. Consequently, while I would think it entirely compatible with the commitment to representative democracy set forth in the founding documents to argue, in legislative chambers or in electoral campaigns, that the state has no power to interfere with parents' authority over the rearing of their children, I do not believe that the power which the Constitution confers upon me as a judge entitles me to deny legal effect to laws that (in my view) infringe upon what is (in my view) that unenumerated right. (91–92)[8]

For Scalia, the Court's opinions in the companion cases of *Board of County Commissioners, Wabaunsee County v. Umbehr* (1996) and *O'Hare Truck Service v. Northlake* (1996) fully demonstrate the justices' willingness to substitute their beliefs for the traditional beliefs of society. In his combined dissent in these cases, Scalia ridiculed the "Court's Constitution-making process" that prompted his colleagues to declare that the freedom of speech clause of the First Amendment protects private contractors from government retaliation for their exercise of political speech (*Umbehr* 686). (In the former case, a trash hauler alleged that he had lost a county contract after he criticized the board in a letter to the editor of a local newspaper; in the latter, a towing firm alleged that it was barred from getting towing referrals after the owner refused to contribute to the mayor's reelection.) Scalia noted that "rewarding one's allies" and "refusing to reward one's opponents" is "an American political tradition as old as the Republic." Zeroing in on this old tradition, he asked:

If that long and unbroken tradition of our people does not decide these cases, then what does? The constitutional text is assuredly as susceptible of one meaning as of the other; in that circumstance, what constitutes a "law abridging the freedom of speech" is either a matter of history or else it is a matter of opinion. Why are not libel laws such an "abridgment"? The only satisfactory answer is that they never were.

Scalia's anger was palpable:

What secret knowledge, one must wonder, is breathed into lawyers when they become Justices of this Court, that enables them to discern that a practice which the text of the Constitution does not clearly proscribe, and which our people have regarded as constitutional for 200 years, is in fact unconstitutional? (688)

Scalia understands that the Constitution creates two conflicting systems of rights: one is democratic—the right of the majority to rule individuals; the other is antidemocratic—the right of individuals to have certain interests protected from majority rule. Scalia relies on the Constitution's text to define the respective spheres of majority and minority freedom, and when that fails to provide definitive guidance, he turns to tradition to tell the Court when the majoritarian process is to be overruled in favor of individual rights. He believes that by identifying those areas of life traditionally protected from majority rule, the Court can objectively determine which individual freedoms the Constitution protects.[9] As he argued in his combined dissent in *Umbehr* and *O'Hare Truck Service*, "I would separate the permissible from the impermissible on the basis of our Nation's traditions, which is what I believe sound constitutional adjudication requires" (695).

Scalia therefore would overrule the majority only when it has infringed upon an individual right explicitly protected by the text of the Constitution or by specific legal traditions flowing from that text.[10] In his dissent in *United States v. Virginia* (1996), in which the Court declared that the exclusively male admission policy of the Virginia Military Institute violated the equal protection clause of the Fourteenth Amendment, he declared that the function of the Court is to "preserve our society's values, not to revise them; to prevent backsliding from the degree of restriction the Constitution imposed upon democratic government, not to prescribe, on our own authority, progressively higher degrees." The Court is not to "supersede" but rather is to "reflect" those "constant and unbroken national traditions that embody the people's understanding of ambiguous constitutional texts" (568). As he eloquently argued in his dissent in *Rutan v. Republican Party* (1990), in which the Court held that political patronage violates the free speech rights of public employees:

> The provisions of the Bill of Rights were designed to restrain transient majorities from impairing long-recognized personal liberties. They did not create by implication novel individual rights overturning accepted political norms. Thus, when a practice not expressly prohibited by the text of the Bill of Rights bears the endorsement of a long tradition of open, widespread, and unchallenged use that dates back to the beginning of the Republic, we have no proper basis for striking it down. Such a venerable and accepted tradition is not to be laid on the examining table and scrutinized for its conformity to some abstract principle of First Amendment adjudication devised by this Court. . . . When it appears that the latest "rule," or "three-part test," or "balancing test" devised by the Court has placed us on a collision course with such a landmark practice, it is the former that must be recalculated by us, and not the latter that must be abandoned by our citizens. (95–96)

In *Harmelin v. Michigan* (1991), Scalia's text-and-tradition approach was again on display. In it, he held that the "cruel and unusual punishments" clause of the Eighth Amendment does not prohibit the imposition of a mandatory term of life in prison without possibility of parole for possessing more than 650 grams of cocaine. Announcing the judgment of the Court, he rejected the plaintiff's contention that his sentence was unconstitutional because it was "significantly disproportionate" to the crime he had committed. Scalia noted that "this claim has no support in the text and history of the Eighth Amendment." Concerning the text, he observed that "to use the phrase 'cruel and unusual punishment' to describe a requirement of proportionality would have been an exceedingly vague and oblique way of saying what Americans were well accustomed to saying more directly" (994, 977). Concerning history, he surveyed English constitutional history since the promulgation of the English Declaration of Rights as well as eighteenth- and nineteenth-century American constitutional and legal history to show that the "cruel and unusual punishments" clause was understood only "to outlaw particular modes of punishment" (e.g., drawing and quartering, breaking on the wheel, flaying alive, and so on), not to require that "all punishments be proportioned to the offense" (981). Therefore, he was led to argue that *Solem v. Helms* (463 U.S. 277 [1983]), in which the Court had held that the Eighth Amendment does contain a proportionality guarantee, was "wrong" and should be overturned.

While his textualist approach led Scalia in *Harmelin* to reject a criminal defendant's claim, it does not always. Thus, in *Coy v. Iowa* (1988), it led him to uphold the right of a defendant (in this case, a man convicted of two counts of engaging in lascivious acts with a child) literally to "be confronted with the witnesses against him" and to overturn his conviction because Iowa law allowed the two thirteen-year-old girls he was charged with sexually assaulting to testify behind a large screen that shielded them from the defendant. For Scalia, the text was unequivocal and governing:

> Simply as a matter of English, it confers at least "a right to meet face to face all those who appear and give evidence at trial." Simply as a matter of Latin as well, since the word "confront"

ultimately derives from the prefix "con-" (from "contra" meaning "against" or "opposed") and the noun "frons" (forehead). Shakespeare was thus describing the root meaning of confrontation when he had Richard the Second say: "Then call them to our presence—face to face, and frowning brow to brow, ourselves will hear the accuser and the accused freely speak." (1016)

Scalia does not restrict his text-and-tradition approach to criminal procedural matters; he applies it across the constitutional board, as he did in *Pacific Mutual Life Insurance Co. v. Haslip* (1991), when he denied that the due process clause places limits on the size of punitive damage awards. He cited Sir Edward Coke, William Blackstone, James Kent, and Joseph Story, all of whom argued that due process means simply the "law of the land," and he concluded that the due process clause is met if the trial is conducted according to the settled course of judicial proceedings.[11] "[I]f the government chooses to follow a historically approved procedure, it necessarily provides due process" (31).[12]

He has also applied his text-and-tradition approach to the establishment clause. In his dissent in *Lee v. Weisman* (1992), Scalia argued that the establishment clause "was adopted to prohibit such an establishment of religion at the federal level [as the Church of England constituted in England] and to protect state establishments of religion from federal interference" and that it did not bar nonsectarian prayers at public school graduation ceremonies (641). Likewise, it led him to complain in *Board of Education of Kiryas Joel v. Grumet* (1994) that:

> The Founding Fathers would be astonished to find that the Establishment Clause—which they designed "to ensure that no one powerful sect or combination of sects would use political or governmental power to punish dissenters"—has been employed to prohibit characteristically and admirably American accommodation of the religious practices (or more precisely, cultural peculiarities) of a tiny minority sect. I, however, am not surprised. Once this Court has abandoned text and history as guides, nothing prevents it from calling religious tolerance the establishment of religion. (732)

The judge's duty, as he described it in his dissent in *Planned Parenthood v. Casey* (1992), is to "read the text and discern our society's traditional understanding of that text" (1000). Discerning the original meaning is "the starting point and the beginning of wisdom" (*H* 108). Nevertheless, Scalia occasionally drifts from his "text-and-tradition" moorings. *Texas v. Johnson* (1989), the Texas flag-burning case in which he joined in Justice Brennan's majority opinion striking down Texas's ban on burning the American flag, is a glaring example. It is true that during his Senate confirmation hearings, Scalia defined speech as "any communicative activity" (*H* 51), and, by that definition, flag burning was communicative activity and thereby speech protected by the First Amendment. What is problematic, however, is not the logic of Scalia's conclusion but rather his premise: there is absolutely no textual or historical evidence to support the contention that the society that adopted the First Amendment understood it to cover all communicative activity. Another glaring case in point is Scalia's unquestioned acceptance of the incorporation doctrine—the argument that the Fourteenth Amendment incorporates the provisions of the Bill of Rights and thereby makes them applicable to the states. This is possibly explained by his reluctance to be perceived as a Don Quixote tilting at windmills. As he observed in *Albright v. Oliver* (1994): "[O]ur decisions have included within the Fourteenth Amendment certain explicit substantive protections of the Bill of Rights—*an extension I accept because it is both long established and narrowly limited*" (275, emphasis added).

Scalia believes that "the rule of law is the law of rules"—this is the title of his Oliver Wendell Holmes, Jr., Lecture delivered at Harvard Law School in 1989.[13] He argues that where the text embodies a rule, judges are simply to apply that rule as the law. Where text and tradition fail to supply a rule, there is no rule; hence, there is no law for judges to apply to contradict the actions of the popular branches and therefore no warrant for judicial intervention. This was his argument in *Romer v. Evans* (1996), in which he unleashed a powerful attack on the Court for "tak[ing] sides in the culture war" and invalidating Colorado's Amendment 2 denying preferential treatment to homosexuals.

> Since the Constitution of the United States says nothing about this subject, it is left to be resolved by normal democratic means, including the democratic adoption of provisions in state constitutions. This Court has no business imposing upon all Americans the resolution favored by the elite class from which the Members of this institution are selected, pronouncing that "animosity" toward homosexuality is evil. (651, 636)

This was also his argument in his concurring opinion in *Cruzan v. Director, Missouri Department of Health* (1990), in which the Court rejected the petitioner's contention that she had a "right to die." Scalia wrote:

> While I agree with the Court's analysis today, and therefore join in its opinion, I would have preferred that we announce, clearly and promptly, that the federal courts have no business in this field; that American law has always accorded the State the power to prevent, by force if necessary, suicide—including suicide by refusing to take appropriate measures necessary to preserve one's life; that the point at which life becomes "worthless," and the point at which the means necessary to preserve it become "extraordinary" or "inappropriate," are neither set forth in the Constitution nor known to the nine Justices of this Court any better than they are known to nine people picked at random from the Kansas City telephone directory; and hence, that even when it is demonstrated by clear and convincing evidence that a patient no longer wishes certain measures to be taken to preserve her life, it is up to the citizens of Missouri to decide, through their elected representatives, whether that wish will be honored. It is quite impossible that those citizens will decide upon a line less lawful than the one we would choose; and it is unlikely (because we know no more about "life-and-death" than they do) that they will decide upon a line less reasonable. (293)

In *A Matter of Interpretation* (1997), Justice Scalia succinctly spelled out both the origins of judicial policy making and his reasons for rejecting it. Judicial policy making arose in the old common law system in England where judges, unconstrained by statutes or a written constitution, exercised the "exhilarating" function of making law. From there, it eventually spread to modern American law schools, where impressionable "law students, having drunk at this intoxicating well," come away thinking that the highest function of the judge is "devising, out of the brilliance of one's own mind, those laws that ought to govern mankind. How exciting!" He noted a key problem with this approach: "democracy." As Scalia insisted: "It is simply not compatible with democratic theory that laws mean whatever they ought to be mean, and that unelected judges decide what that is" (*MI* 7, 9, 22).

Scalia has castigated the Court for its contemptuous disregard of the democratic principle in several powerful dissents. In *Umbehr* and *O'Hare Truck Service*, he accused his colleagues of "living in another world. Day by day, case by case, it is busy designing a Constitution for a country I do not recognize." He warned the public that "[w]hile the present Court sits, a major, undemocratic restructuring of our national institutions and mores is constantly in progress" (711). Likewise, in *United States v. Virginia*, he acerbically noted that much of the Court's opinion concerning Virginia Military Institute and its all-male student body was "devoted to deprecating the closed-mindedness of our forebears with regard to women's education." He therefore felt obliged to "counterbalance" the Court's criticism of our ancestors and to say a word in their praise: "[T]hey left us free to change." The virtue of the democratic system with its First Amendment "that we inherited from our forebears" is that "it readily enables the people, over time, to be persuaded that what they took for granted is not so, and to change their laws accordingly." That system, he continued, "is destroyed if the smug assurances of each age are removed from the democratic process and written into the Constitution." But that is exactly what "this most illiberal Court" has been doing: it has "embarked on a course of inscribing one after another of the current preferences of the society (and in some cases only the counter-majoritarian preferences of the society's law-trained elite) into our Basic Law" (567).[14]

Scalia's Understanding of the "Whole Theory of Democracy"

Scalia is criticized for a "vulgar majoritarian" understanding of democracy.[15] This criticism is based in large part on a lecture he gave in May of 1996 at the Gregorian University in Rome (where his son was a student). During the question-and-answer period that followed, he declared that:

> [I]t just seems to me incompatible with democratic theory that it's good and right for the state to do something that the majority of the people do not want done. Once you adopt democratic theory, it seems to me, you accept that proposition. If the people, for example, want abortion the state should permit abortion. If the people do not want it, the state should be able to prohibit it.

He went on to declare that "the whole theory of democracy . . . is that the majority rules; that is the whole theory of it. You protect minorities only because the majority determines that there are certain minority positions that deserve protection."[16] This criticism is also based on statements he made in his reply to Laurence Tribe's commentary on his essay in *A Matter of Interpretation*. In dismissing Tribe's "aspirational" theory of constitutional interpretation, Scalia wrote: "If you want aspirations, you can read the Declaration of Independence, with its pronouncements that 'all men are created equal' with 'unalienable Rights' that include 'Life, Liberty, and the Pursuit of Happiness.' Or you can read the French Declaration of the Rights of Man." But, he continued, "[t]here is no such philosophizing in our Constitution, which, unlike the Declaration of Independence and the Declaration of the Rights of Man, is a practical and pragmatic charter of government" (*MI* 134).

Scalia's critics point out that his theory of democracy bears no relation to the nation's traditional understanding of the limits of the principle of majority rule, so perfectly captured by Thomas Jefferson in his First Inaugural Address: "All, too, will bear in mind this sacred principle, that though the will of the majority is in all cases to prevail, that will to be rightful must be reasonable; that the minority possess their equal rights, which equal laws must protect, and to violate would be oppression."[17] According to Jefferson and the traditional American understanding, "the minority possess their equal rights" independently of the majority; their equal rights are antecedent to majority rule, and majority rule is circumscribed by them. As Harry V. Jaffa has written, the traditional American understanding was that: "[T]he foundation of all our free institutions is the doctrine that, under the laws of nature and nature's God, all human being are endowed with certain unalienable rights, and that it is for the sake of these rights that governments are instituted. As these rights belong *a priori* to every person, they are of necessity the rights of every minority."[18] Scalia's critics also wonder how someone who argues, as he does, that "[i]n textual interpretation, context is everything," could fail to consider the Declaration of Independence and its theory of democracy in constitutional context (*MI* 134).

Scalia is vulnerable to the first criticism. He simply has not developed a well-thought-out understanding of the principles of democracy and, perhaps as a consequence, appears to assume that democracy everywhere operates as it does in the United States at the beginning of the new millennium: where the Constitution, as amended, protects the rights of minorities; where the Constitution itself and its subsequent amendments were ratified by extraordinary majorities; and where the principal threat to democracy is not majority rule trampling on the rights of minorities but the Court itself threatening the right of the majority to rule itself. Concerning the second criticism, however (that he has rejected an aspirational theory of constitutional interpretation), Scalia is on firmer ground. He has defended himself by observing that, at least with respect to the Bill of Rights:

> The context suggests that the abstract and general terms, like the concrete and particular ones, are meant to nail down current rights, rather than aspire after future ones—that they are abstract and general references to *extant* rights and freedoms possessed under the then-current regime. The same conclusion follows from the evident purpose of the provisions. To guarantee that freedom of speech will be no less than it is today is to guarantee something permanent; to guarantee that it will be no less than the aspirations of the future is to guarantee nothing in particular at all. (*MI* 135, emphasis in original)

Scalia's Rejection of Legislative History

As a textualist, Justice Scalia totally rejects reliance on legislative history or legislative intent. He made it very clear during his Senate confirmation hearings that he was not "enamored" with the use of legislative history and reliance on committee reports. As he told Senator Charles Mathias (R–Md.):

> Once it was clear that the courts were going to use them [committee reports] all the time, they certainly became a device not to inform the rest of the body as to what the intent of the bill was, but rather they became avowedly a device to make some legislative history and tell the courts how to hold this way or that. Once that happens, they become less reliable as a real indicator of what the whole body thought it was voting on. (*H* 106)

He invariably criticizes his colleagues for turning to committee reports, or even floor debates, to ascertain what a law means. His extensive "inside the beltway" experience has made him savvy to how often congressmen will withdraw actual amendments to bills under consideration in the House because they are told by the floor leaders of the bill that they will take care of the congressmen's concerns through the drafting of the legislative history. In *U.S. v. Taylor* (1988), he perspicaciously drew out the consequences:

> By perpetuating the view that legislative history *can* alter the meaning of even a clear statutory provision, we produce a legal culture in which the following statement could be made—taken from a portion of the floor debate alluded to in the Court's opinion:
>
>> Mr. DENNIS: "I have an amendment here in my hand which could be offered, but if we can make up some legislative history which would do the same thing, I am willing to do it."
>
> We should not make the equivalency between making legislative history and making an amendment so plausible. It should not be possible, or at least should not be easy, to be sure of obtaining

a particular result in this Court without making that result apparent on the face of the bill which both Houses consider and vote upon, which the President approves, and which, if it becomes a law, the people must obey. I think we have an obligation to conduct our exegesis in a fashion which fosters that democratic process. (345)[19]

Scalia argues that the Court is to interpret the text alone and nothing else.[20] The law should be understood to mean what it says, and say what it means. Otherwise, as Scalia noted in his Court of Appeals dissent in *Illinois Commerce Commission v. Interstate Commerce Commission* (1994), compromise, so essential to the legislative process, "becomes impossible." "[W]hen there is no assurance that the statutory words in which [the compromise] is contained will be honored," both sides to a compromise "have every reason to fear that any ambiguity will be interpreted against their interests" in subsequent litigation.[21] Likewise, if the law does not mean what it says and does not say what it means, citizens are left at a loss concerning how they should conduct themselves. As he said in *U.S. v. R.L.C.* (1992): "It may well be true that in most cases the proposition that the words of the United States Code or the Statutes At Large give adequate notice to the citizen is something of a fiction, albeit one required in any system of law; but necessary fiction descends to needless farce when the public is charged even with knowledge of Committee Reports" (309).

Scalia insists that the Court should focus its attention on the text alone. As he argued in *Wisconsin Public Intervenor v. Mortier* (1991): "We should try to give the text its fair meaning, whatever various committees might have had to say—thereby affirming the proposition that we are a Government of laws, not committee reports." He took some satisfaction in the fact that:

> Today's decision reveals that, in their judicial application, committee reports are a forensic rather than an interpretive device, to be invoked when they support the decision and ignored when they do not. To my mind that is infinitely better than honestly giving them dispositive effect. But it would be better still to stop confusing [lower courts] and not to use committee reports at all. (621)[22]

Scalia's contempt for the use of legislative history leads him to some interesting exchanges with his colleagues. In *Chisom v. Roemer* (1991), he was provoked to declare that there is a mistaken

> notion that Congress cannot be credited with having achieved anything of major importance by simply saying it, in ordinary language, in the text of a statute, "without comment" in the legislative history. As the Court colorfully puts it, if the dog of legislative history has not barked, nothing of great significance can have transpired. . . . We have forcefully and explicitly rejected the Conan Doyle approach to statutory construction in the past. . . . We are here to apply the statute, not legislative history, and certainly not the absence of legislative history. Statutes are the law though sleeping dogs lie. (406)[23]

In *United States v. Thompson/Center Arms Co.* (1992), he ridiculed Justice David Souter for resorting "to that last hope of lost interpretive causes, that St. Jude of the hagiography of statutory construction, legislative history" (521).

Scalia's textualist critique of legislative history has produced dramatic results. Judge Patricia Wald of the U.S. Court of Appeals for the District of Columbia noted that in its 1981–1982 term, the Supreme Court looked at legislative history in virtually every statutory case, regardless of whether it thought that the statute had a clear meaning on its face.[24] In 1995, Gregory Maggs observed that by the early 1990s, legislative history was being cited in only about 40 percent of statutory cases. He offered a reason:

With Justice Scalia breathing down the necks of anyone who peeks into the *Congressional Record* or Senate reports, the other members of the Court may have concluded that the benefit of citing legislative history does not outweigh its costs. It is likely for this reason that the percentage of cases citing it has decreased dramatically. No one likes an unnecessary fight, especially not one with as formidable an opponent as Justice Scalia.[25]

Scalia has influenced members of Congress no less than his colleagues on the High Bench. When the House Judiciary Committee was drafting a 1991 anticrime bill, *Congressional Quarterly* reported that "some members suggested resolving a dispute by putting compromise language into a committee report, which accompanies a bill to the floor. But Barney Frank (D–Mass.) warned off his colleagues with just two words, 'Justice Scalia.'"[26]

Scalia's Originalism

Although Justice Scalia emphatically rejects legislative history and intent, he is described, and describes himself, as an originalist. On the surface, this suggests another tension: if it is a mistake to consult extrinsic evidence of Congress's intentions as found in a law's legislative history, why is it appropriate for him to consult extrinsic evidence of the Framers' intentions as found, say, in *The Federalist*? The tension is heightened further as a result of Scalia's assertion in *Tome v. United States* (1995) that "the views of Alexander Hamilton (a draftsman) bear [no] more authority than the views of Thomas Jefferson (not a draftsman) with regard to the meaning of the Constitution" (167).

The answer to that question is that Scalia is a particular kind of originalist. What he means by originalism is revealed by illustration in his Holmes Lecture, "The Rule of Law as the Law of Rules": "If a barn was not considered the curtilage of a house in 1791, . . . and the Fourth Amendment did not cover it then, unlawful entry into a barn today may be a trespass, but not an unconstitutional search and seizure."[27] For Scalia, originalism is synonymous with the doctrine of original meaning. Scalia seeks the original meaning from the text of the document itself and from what its words meant to the society that adopted it; at the same time, he ignores altogether the subjective preferences or intentions of those who wrote it (*H* 48, 108).[28]

Scalia contrasts his originalism with nonoriginalism, which he defines as a method of interpreting the Constitution "not on the basis of what the Constitution originally meant, but on the basis of what judges currently [think] it desirable for it to mean" (*O* 852). According to Scalia, the principal defect of nonoriginalism is "the impossibility of achieving any consensus on what, precisely, is to replace original meaning, once that is abandoned." He notes that nonoriginalists invoke "fundamental values as the touchstone of constitutionality," but he observes that "it is very difficult for a person to discern a difference between those political values that he personally thinks important, and those political values that are 'fundamental to our society.' Thus, by the adoption of such a criterion judicial personalization of the law is enormously facilitated" (*O* 862–63). He also observes that those values that are "fundamental to our society" can both expand and contract. Describing nonoriginalism as "a two-way street that handles traffic both to and from individual rights," he contrasts it with his originalism as displayed in *Coy v. Iowa*, in which he secured the confrontation rights of a criminal defendant against legislation passed by a state less concerned with the text and tradition of the Sixth Amendment than with the "emotional frailty of children and the sensitivity of young women regarding sexual abuse" (*O* 856).

Scalia acknowledges that originalism "is also not without its warts." "Its greatest defect," he argues, "is the difficulty of applying it correctly."

[I]t is often exceedingly difficult to plumb the original understanding of an ancient text. Properly done, the task requires the consideration of an enormous amount of material—in the case of the Constitution and its Amendments, for example, to mention only one element, the records of the ratifying debates in all the states. Even beyond that, it requires an evaluation of the reliability of that material—many of the reports of the ratifying debates, for example, are thought to be quite unreliable. And further still, it requires immersing oneself in the political and intellectual atmosphere of the time—somehow placing out of mind knowledge that we have which an earlier age did not, and putting on beliefs, attitudes, philosophies, prejudices and loyalties that are not those of our day. It is, in short, a task sometimes better suited to the historian than the lawyer. (*O* 856–57)[29]

That very defect, however, is for Scalia a virtue. Because "historical research is always difficult and sometimes inconclusive," originalism will lead to "a more moderate rather than a more extreme result." Scalia argues that since judges inevitably think that "the law is what they would like it to be," their errors in "judicial historiography" will be "in the direction of projecting" upon the past "current, modern values." Originalism ends up as "something of a compromise, . . . not a bad characteristic for a constitutional theory" (*O* 864). Yet a better argument for him—one consistent with his criticisms of the "Court's Constitution-making"—would have been to say that, since historical research is often inconclusive and the original understanding is unclear, there is no warrant for the Court to invalidate an act of the popular branches on the grounds that it is inconsistent with the Constitution's original meaning. After all, as Scalia continues, originalism is far more compatible than nonoriginalism with "the nature and purpose of a Constitution in a democratic system."

A democratic society does not, by and large, need constitutional guarantees to insure that its laws will reflect "current values." Elections take care of that quite well. The purpose of constitutional guarantees . . . is precisely to prevent the law from reflecting certain changes in original values that the society adopting the Constitution thinks fundamentally undesirable. Or, more precisely, to require the society to devote to the subject the long and hard consideration required for a constitutional amendment before those particular values can be cast aside. (*O* 862)[30]

Thus, Scalia the originalist cites and quotes from *The Federalist* to reveal constitutional history—to show how those who drafted and ratified the Constitution saw its various structural provisions and principles as means for achieving the ends the Constitution was drafted to secure. He studies the Framers and especially *The Federalist* not to find out what the Framers, either individually or collectively, would have done if faced with a specific contemporary constitutional issue, but rather to understand (given the words they used) how they designed the Constitution to work and, on that basis, to ascertain how, institutionally, they intended for that issue to be addressed. What he finds from his study is that seldom, if ever, was the judiciary intended to be the branch that would resolve these issues. Just how limited Scalia regards the judicial role is apparent in his criticism of Justice Holmes's famous reply to Chief Justice Marshall's dictum in *McCulloch v. Maryland* (17 U.S. 316, 431 [1819]) that "the power to tax [is] the power to destroy." Holmes qualified Marshall's statement by asserting: "The power to tax is not the power to destroy while this Court sits."[31] While acknowledging that "the notion that predicted evils cannot occur 'while this Court sits' is comforting," Scalia sees no need for the Court to save anyone. Constitutional structure, not an activist Court, will ensure that the power to tax does not result in the destruction of the federal government. "I would have thought it a better response to Marshall's dictum that the power to tax the activities of the federal government cannot constitute the power to destroy the federal government so long as the tax is generally applicable and nondiscriminatory—because it is implausible that the state would destroy its own citizens as well."[32]

In his dissent in *Hoffmann-La Roche v. Sperling* (1989), Scalia admonished his colleagues not to "abandon" their "'passive' role in determining which claims come before them, . . . which I regard as one of the natural components of a system in which courts are not inquisitors of justice but arbiters of adversarial claims" (181). According to Scalia, the role of the Court is not to articulate a theory of justice and discover new rights based on that theory but to ensure that the majority does not contract the sphere of rights traditionally protected. If new theories of justice are to be articulated and if the sphere of protected rights is to be expanded, such expansion should be done by the will of the majority—not the Court.

Scalia's Reliance on Constitutional Structure

What Scalia also finds from his originalist, text-and-tradition approach is that the Framers generally, and *The Federalist* in particular, placed great emphasis on constitutional structure. During his confirmation hearings, Justice Scalia was asked by Senator Strom Thurmond (R–S.C.) why he thought the Constitution had endured for so long—why he thought it had come to be "the oldest existing Constitution in the world today." Scalia responded as follows:

> I think most of the questions today will probably be about that portion of the Constitution that is called the Bill of Rights, which is a very important part of it, of course. But if you had to put your finger on what has made our Constitution so enduring, I think it is the original document before the amendments were added. Because the amendments, by themselves, do not do anything. The Russian constitution probably has better, or at least as good guarantees of personal freedom as our document does. What makes it work, what assures that those words [in the Bill of Rights] are not just hollow promises, is the structure of government that the original Constitution established, the checks and balances among the three branches, in particular, so that no one of them is able to "run roughshod" over the liberties of the people as those liberties are described in the Bill of Rights. (*H* 32)

Scalia's response is most instructive. First, he says that our "liberties" are "described" (but not created or secured) by the Bill of Rights. Second and more important, Scalia identifies "the structure of government that the original Constitution established, the checks and balances among the three branches, in particular," as the reason for the Constitution's protection of liberties, and hence its longevity. His answer to Senator Thurmond is reminiscent of James Madison's argument that the Bill of Rights he was proposing did no more than "expressly declare the great rights of mankind secured under this Constitution."[33] Madison believed that rights are secured not by "parchment barriers" (i.e., by prohibitions written into the Constitution) but rather by governmental structure (i.e., that "double security" that arises when power "is first divided between two distinct governments, and then the portion allotted to each, subdivided among distinct and separate institutions").[34] Scalia clearly agrees—at least with regard to separation of powers. As he argued in *James B. Beam Distilling Company v. Georgia* (1991), "the division of federal powers [is] central to the constitutional scheme." Moreover, he continued, "it seems to me that the fundamental nature of those powers must be preserved as that nature was understood when the Constitution was enacted" (549).

This need to preserve the structure of the Constitution—and especially separation of powers—was central to Justice Scalia's dissent in *Morrison v. Olson* (1988), in which the Court upheld the constitutionality of the statute that authorized the appointment of an independent counsel to investigate a high-ranking member of the executive branch. Scalia's textualist jurisprudence generally demands deference to the popular branches but not in separation of powers cases. As he pointed out in *Morrison*, in such cases, the "caution that we owe great deference to Congress's view that what it has done is constitutional . . . does not apply."

> Where a private citizen challenges action of the Government on grounds unrelated to separation of powers, harmonious functioning of the system demands that we ordinarily give some deference, or a presumption of validity, to the actions of the political branches in what is agreed, between themselves at least, to be within their respective spheres. But where the issue pertains to separation of powers, and the political branches are (as here) in disagreement, neither can be presumed correct. The reason is stated concisely by Madison: "The several departments being perfectly co-ordinate by the terms of their common commission, neither of them, it is evident, can pretend to an exclusive or superior right to settling the boundaries between their respective powers. . . ." *Federalist* No. 49. The playing field for the present case, in other words, is a level one. As one of the interested and coordinate parties to the underlying constitutional dispute, Congress, no more than the President, is entitled to the benefit of the doubt. (704–5)

Feeling no obligation to presume the constitutionality of the independent counsel statute, he complained that the Congress had "effectively compelled a criminal investigation of a high-level appointee of the President in connection with his actions arising out of a bitter power dispute between the President and the Legislative Branch"; he further objected that the Congress also removed "the decisions regarding the scope of [any] further investigation, its duration, and finally whether or not prosecution should ensue" from "the control of the President and his subordinates" and placed them instead in the hands of a "mini-Executive that is the independent counsel." Quoting the language of Article II, sec. 1, cl. 1 of the Constitution providing that "[t]he executive Power shall be vested in the President of the United States," he declared that "this does not mean some of the executive power, but all of the executive power" (703, 732, 705).[35] He then proclaimed that the independent counsel statute must be invalidated on "fundamental separation of powers principles" because "governmental investigation and prosecution of crimes is a quintessentially executive function," and "the statute before us deprives the President of exclusive control over that quintessentially executive activity" (705, 706).

The Court majority's response conceded that the statute reduced the president's control but insisted that he preserved "sufficient control" to "perform his constitutionally assigned duties" and that the statute did not "interfere impermissibly with his constitutional obligation to ensure the faithful execution of the laws" (702, 692). Scalia's rejoinder was direct: "It is not for us to determine, and we have never presumed to determine, how much of the purely executive powers of government must be within the full control of the President. The Constitution prescribes that they all are." He accused the Court majority of replacing "the clear constitutional prescription that the executive power belongs to the President with a 'balancing test,'" and of abandoning the "text of the Constitution" as the "governing standard" in favor of "what might be called the unfettered wisdom of a majority of this Court, revealed to an obedient people on a case-by-case basis." Waxing indignant, Scalia proclaimed: "This is not only not the government of laws that the Constitution established, it is not a government of laws at all" (709, 711, 712). He chided the Court for adopting an "*ad hoc* approach to constitutional adjudication" whose "real attraction, even apart from its work-saving potential," is that "it is guaranteed to produce a result, in every case, that will make a majority of the Court happy with the law. The law is, by definition, precisely what the majority thinks, taking all things into account, it ought to be." For his part, however, Scalia preferred "to rely upon the judgment of the wise men who constructed our system, and of the people who approved it, and of the two centuries of history that have shown it to be sound" (734).

Declaring that "if to describe this case is not to decide it, the concept of a government of separate and coordinate powers no longer has meaning," Scalia bitterly attacked his colleagues for their failure to abide by what "the text of the Constitution seems to require, . . . the Founders seemed to expect, and . . . our past cases have uniformly assumed." He sought to preserve separation of powers, because, as he noted, "without a secure structure of separated powers, our Bill of Rights would be worthless, as are the bills of rights of many nations of the world that have adopted, or even improved upon, the mere words of ours" (703, 734, 697). Scalia's argument is clear: by refusing in this case to defer to Congress and by steadfastly protecting constitutional structure, he can be restrained and deferential elsewhere—that is, he is spared the need in other cases to protect constitutional rights that are better secured by structure than by judges.

During a 1988 panel discussion on separation of powers, Justice Scalia assessed his legal career and commented that "if there is anyone who, over the years, [has] had a greater interest in the subject of separation of powers [than I], he does not come readily to mind."[36] His dissent in *Morrison* certainly supports his contention; so, too, does his opinion for the Court in *Plaut v. Spendthrift Farms* (1995).

In *Plaut*, Scalia declared for a seven-member majority that Congress violated separation of powers by "requiring the federal courts to exercise 'the Judicial Power of the United States' in a manner repugnant to the text, structure, and traditions of Article III." It did so when it passed a law requiring federal courts to reopen final judgments in private civil actions under the Securities Exchange Act for those plaintiffs whose suits for fraud and deceit in the sale of stock had been dismissed as time-barred because of an earlier Court decision that had the effect of reducing the length of time in which such suits could be filed. Scalia recognized that Congress was motivated by good intentions—the desire to assist defrauded shareholders hurt by the Court's earlier ruling. Nevertheless, he insisted:

> Not favoritism, not even corruption, but power is the object of the separation-of-powers prohibition. The prohibition is violated when an individual final judgment is legislatively rescinded for even the very best of reasons, such as the legislature's genuine conviction (supported by all the law professors in the land) that the judgment was wrong.

The doctrine of separation of powers, he continued,

> is a structural safeguard rather than a remedy to be applied only when specific harm, or the risk of specific harm, can be identified. In its major features, it is a prophylactic device, establishing high walls and clear distinctions because low walls and vague distinctions will not be judicially defensible in the heat of interbranch conflict. (228, 239)

He likened what Congress had done in *Plaut* to its widespread use of legislative vetoes declared unconstitutional in *Immigration and Naturalization Service v. Chadha* (462 U.S. 919 [1983]) and asserted that "legislated invalidation of judicial judgments deserves the same categorical treatment accorded by *Chadha* to congressional invalidation of executive action." He concluded: "Separation of powers, a distinctively American political doctrine, profits from the advice authored by a distinctively American poet: Good fences make good neighbors" (240).

Scalia's invocation of Robert Frost prompted Justice Stephen Breyer, who concurred only in the judgment of the Court and not in Scalia's opinion, to respond in kind: "As the majority invokes the advice of an American poet, one might consider as well that poet's caution, for he not only notes that 'Something there is that doesn't love a wall,' but also writes, 'Before I built a wall I'd ask to know/What I was walling in or walling out'" (245). Breyer's selection of these particular passages from Frost highlights the chasm that exists between Breyer and Scalia—and more generally between the Court and Scalia—concerning separation of powers. Unlike Breyer and most of Scalia's colleagues, Scalia loves the wall of separation of powers. He loves it because, as he said in his *Morrison* dissent, "without a secure structure of separated powers, our Bill of Rights would be worthless." He loves this wall and wants it kept high and strong because, as he noted in *Plaut*, "low walls . . . will not be judicially defensible in the heat of interbranch conflict." He also loves the wall of separation of powers, because, as he said in *Morrison*, it was built by and reflects the "judgment of the wise men who constructed our system, and of the people who approved it, and of the two centuries that have shown it to be sound." Additionally, unlike Breyer and those others, Scalia would never quote a passage that implies that it is his job to build the wall and to decide what to wall in or wall out. True to his text and tradition jurisprudence, Scalia would argue that the justices are to secure the wall of separation of powers built by the Framers, not wonder whether it is worthy of their love—and certainly not replace it with one of their own design. The decisions of the Framers concerning constitutional structure are for the justices to secure, not alter or second-guess.

Interestingly, Scalia's interest in preserving separation of powers has not been matched by his interest in preserving federalism.[37] While he argued in *James B. Beam Distilling Company* that "the division of federal powers" is central to the Constitution and that "those powers must be preserved" as they were understood "when the Constitution was enacted," Scalia has written no important federalism opinions,[38] preferring instead to join the opinions especially of Chief Justice William Rehnquist[39] and Justices Sandra Day O'Connor[40] and William Kennedy.[41] He has offered two explanations for his lack of interest in preserving federalism. During his confirmation hearings, he argued that the "primary defender of the constitutional balance" between the federal government and the states

> is the Congress. It is a principle of the Constitution that there are certain responsibilities that belong to the State and some that belong to the federal government, but it is essentially the function of the Congress—the Congress, which takes the same oath to uphold and defend the Constitution that I do as a judge—to have that constitutional prescription in mind when it enacts the laws. (*H* 81)

His other explanation is, to put it bluntly, that federalism is dead and that he is not interested in expending judicial resources attempting to resuscitate a corpse. As he wrote in *Regulation* magazine in 1979: "[C]onstitutional provisions subsist only as long as they remain not merely imprinted on paper, but also embedded in the thinking of the people. When our people ceased to believe in a federal government of narrowly limited powers, Congress's constitutional interpretation disregarded such limitations, and the courts soon followed."[42]

Conclusion

In *A Matter of Interpretation*, Justice Scalia acknowledged that his textualist jurisprudence is regarded in "some sophisticated circles" of the legal profession as "simpleminded—'wooden,' 'unimaginative,' 'pedestrian.'" He rejected this characterization and denied that he was "too dull to perceive the broader social purposes that a statute is designed, or could be designed to serve, or too hidebound to realize that new times require new laws"; he simply insisted that judges "have no authority to pursue those broader purposes or to write those new laws" (*MI* 23). During his distinguished career on the Supreme Court, Scalia has remained faithful to the "text and tradition" of our written Constitution and has rejected the intellectual fads and novel theories of interpretation that have the invariable effect of transferring power from the popular branches to the judges. In so doing, Scalia reminds his colleagues of the most important right of the people in a democracy—the right to govern themselves as they see fit and to be overruled in their governance only when the clear text or traditional understanding of the Constitution they have adopted demands it.

Notes

1. Quotations from and references to Scalia's works are cited in the text using the following abbreviations:

> *H:*   *Hearings before the Committee on the Judiciary on the Nomination of Judge Antonin Scalia to be Associate Justice of the Supreme Court of the United States*, Committee on the Judiciary, United States Senate, Ninety-Ninth Congress, Second Session, J-99-119 (Washington, D.C.: U.S. Government Printing Office, 1987).
>
> *MI:*   *A Matter of Interpretation: Federal Courts and the Law*, ed. Amy Gutmann (Princeton, N.J.: Princeton University Press, 1997).
>
> *O:*   "Originalism: The Lesser Evil," *University of Cincinnati Law Review* 57 (1989): 849–65.

Page numbers of Scalia's opinions will be cited parenthetically in the text where they are quoted; standard citations for cases quoted in the text, in chronological order, are as follows: *U.S. v. Taylor*, 487 U.S. 326 (1988); *Morrison v. Olson*, 487 U.S. 654 (1988); *Coy v. Iowa*, 487 U.S. 1012 (1988); *Texas v. Johnson*, 491 U.S. 397 (1989); *Hoffmann-La Roche v. Sperling*, 493 U.S. 165 (1989); *Rutan v. Republican Party of Illinois*, 497 U.S. 62 (1990); *Cruzan v. Director, Missouri Department of Health*, 497 U.S. 261 (1990); *Pacific Mutual Life Insurance Co. v. Haslip*, 499 U.S. 1 (1991); *Chisom v. Roemer*, 501 U.S. 380 (1991); *James B. Beam Distilling Company v. Georgia*, 501 U.S. 529 (1991); *Wisconsin Public Intervenor v. Mortier*, 501 U.S. 597 (1991); *Schad v. Arizona*, 501 U.S. 624 (1991); *Harmelin v. Michigan*, 501 U.S. 957 (1991); *U.S. v. R.L.C.*, 503 U.S. 291 (1992); *U.S. v. Thompson/Center Arms Co.*, 504 U.S. 505 (1992); *Lee v. Weisman*, 505 U.S. 577 (1992); *Planned Parenthood of Southeastern Pennsylvania v. Casey*, 505 U.S. 833 (1992); *Albright v. Oliver*, 510 U.S. 266 (1994); *Board of Education of Kiryas Joel v. Grumet*, 512 U.S. 687 (1994); *Tome v. U.S.*, 513 U.S. 150 (1995); *Plaut v. Spendthrift Farms*, 514 U.S. 211 (1995); *Romer v. Evans*, 517 U.S. 620 (1996); *United States v. Virginia*, 518 U.S. 515 (1996); *Board of County Commissioners, Wabaunsee County v. Umbehr*, 518 U.S. 668 (1996); *O'Hare Truck Service v. Northlake*, 518 U.S. 712 (1996); *Troxel v. Granville*, 530 U.S. 57 (2000).

2. Scalia searches out the ordinary meaning of the words used when the provision was adopted, frequently consulting dictionaries of the era. In fact, Scalia consults dictionaries more often than any of his colleagues. See Note, "Looking It Up: Dictionaries and Statutory Interpretation," *Harvard Law Review* 107 (1994): 1437, 1439.

3. For Scalia, separation of powers represents such a critical structural principle. "Indeed, with an economy of expression that many would urge as a model for modern judicial opinions, the principle of separation of powers is found only in the structure of the [Constitution,] which successively describes where the legislative, executive, and judicial powers shall reside. One should not think, however, that the principle was less important to the federal framers. Madison said of it, in *Federalist* No. 47, that 'no political truth is certainly of greater intrinsic value, or is stamped with the authority of more enlightened patrons of liberty.' And no less than five of the *Federalist Papers* were devoted to the demonstration that the principle was adequately observed in the proposed Constitution." Scalia, "The Doctrine of Standing as an Essential Element of the Separation of Powers," *Suffolk University Law Review* 17 (1983): 881.

4. In *Michael H. v. Gerald D.*, 491 U.S. 110, 127n5 (1989), Justice Scalia refers to this as "the most specific level at which a relevant tradition protecting, or denying protection to, the asserted right can be identified."

5. Scalia uses tradition to interpret only ambiguous constitutional texts; as he said in *Rutan v. Republican Party* (96n1), "no tradition can supersede the Constitution."

6. See, for example, *Stenberg v. Carhart*, 530 U.S. 914 (2000); *Department of Commerce v. Clinton*, 525 U.S. 316, 349 (1999); *Minnesota v. Carter*, 525 U.S. 83, 92 (1998); *Lewis v. Casey*, 518 U.S. 343, 368 (1996); *Witte v. United States*, 515 U.S. 389, 407 (1995); *Plaut v. Spendthrift Farms*, 514 US. 211, 217 (1995); *Waters v. Churchill*, 511 US. 661, 684 (1994); *Callins v. Collins*, 510 U.S. 1141 (1994); *Herrera v. Collins*, 506 U.S. 390, 427 (1993); *Richmond v. Lewis*, 506 U.S. 40, 54 (1992); *Planned Parenthood of Southeastern Pennsylvania v. Casey*, 505 U.S. 833, 980, 983, 998, 999, 1000, 1001 (1992); *Morgan v. Illinois*, 504 U.S. 719, 751 (1992); *California v. Acevedo*, 500 U.S. 565, 581 (1991); *Cruzan v. Director, Missouri Department of Health*, 497 U.S. 261, 300 (1990); *Rutan v. Republican Party of Illinois*, 497 U.S. 62, 97 (1990); and *McKoy v. North Carolina*, 494 U.S. 433, 466 (1990).

7. See Gregory E. Maggs, "Reconciling Textualism and the *Chevron* Doctrine: In Defense of Justice Scalia," *Connecticut Law Review* 28 (1996): 393, and Bradley C. Karkkainen, "Plain Meaning: Justice Scalia's Jurisprudence of Strict Statutory Construction," *Harvard Journal of Law and Public Policy* 17 (1994): 401.

8. See also Scalia's response to a question by Senator Howard Metzenbaum (D–Ohio) during his Senate confirmation hearings: "[A] constitution has to have ultimately majoritarian underpinnings. To be sure a constitution is a document that protects against future democratic excesses. But when it is adopted, it is adopted by democratic process. That is what legitimates it. . . . [I]f the majority that adopted it did not believe this unspecified right, which is not reflected clearly in the language, if their laws at the time do not reflect that that right existed, nor do the laws at the present date reflect that the society believes that right exists, I worry about my deciding that it exists. I worry that I am not reflecting the most fundamental, deeply felt beliefs of our society, which is what a constitution means, but rather, I am reflecting the most deeply felt beliefs of Scalia, which is not what I want to impose on the society" (*H* 89).

9. The meanings of those constitutional provisions that are ambiguous are not fixed in time; tradition can evolve, and, for Scalia, the appropriate way for such evolution to take place is through the people via their elected state legislatures and Congress. As he said in *Burnham v. Superior Court*, 495 U.S. 604, 627 (1990): "The difference between [me] and Justice Brennan has nothing to do with whether 'further progress [is] to be made' in the 'evolution of our legal system.' It has to do with whether changes are to be adopted as progressive by the American people or decreed as progressive by the Justices of this Court."

10. Timothy Raschke Shattuck, "Justice Scalia's Due Process Methodology: Examining Specific Traditions," *Southern California Law Review* 65 (1992): 2743, 2776–78.

11. See also his rejection of substantive due process in *TXO Production Corp. v. Alliance Resources Corp.* 509 U.S. 443, 471 (1993), when he declared: "It is particularly difficult to imagine that 'due process' contains the substantive right not to be subjected to excessive punitive damages, since if it contains *that* it would surely also contain the substantive right not to be subjected to excessive fines, which would make the Excessive Fines Clause of the Eighth Amendment superfluous in light of the Due Process Clause of the Fifth Amendment" (emphasis in the original).

12. Scalia's discussion of "historically approved procedures" needs one important qualification: broad contemporary societal consensus can purge an "historically approved practice." As he said in *Haslip* (39): "State legislatures and courts have the power to restrict or abolish the common-law practice of punitive damages, and in recent years have increasingly done so. . . . It is through those means—State by State, and, at the federal level, by Congress—that the legal procedures affecting our citizens are improved. Perhaps, when the operation of that process has purged a historically approved practice from our national life, the Due Process Clause would permit this Court to announce that it is no longer in accord with the law of the land."

13. "The Rule of Law as the Law of Rules," *University of Chicago Law Review* 56 (1989): 1175.

14. See "The Doctrine of Standing," 881 and 896, wherein Scalia described federal judges as individuals who are "selected from the aristocracy of the highly educated, instructed to be governed by a body of knowledge that values abstract principle above concrete result, and (just in case any connection with the man in the street might subsist) removed from all accountability to the electorate. . . . Where the courts, in the supposed interest of all the people, do enforce . . . policies that the political process itself would not enforce, they are likely (despite the best of intentions) to be enforcing the political prejudices

of their own class."

15. See Larry P. Arnn and Ken Masugi, "The Smoke of a Burning White Flag: Law without a Regime, Form without Purpose," *Perspectives on Political Science* 28 (Winter 1999): 16.

16. Antonin Scalia, "Rome Address," *Origins, CNS Documentary Service* 26, no. 6 (June 27, 1996).

17. *Thomas Jefferson: Writings*, ed. Merrill D. Peterson (New York: The Library of America, 1984), 492–93.

18. Harry V. Jaffa, *Storm over the Constitution* (Lanham, Md.: Lexington Books, 1999), 117.

19. See also his Court of Appeals opinion in *Hirschey v. F.E.R.C.,* 777 F.2d 1, 7, n. 1 (1985).

20. As one critic of Scalia's rejection of legislative history complains, individual members of Congress "can no longer express their intentions effectively in any way other than incorporating them in the legislation itself." Note, "Justice Scalia's Use of Sources in Statutory and Constitutional Interpretation: How Congress Always Loses," *Duke Law Journal* (1990): 160, 188.

21. 749 F.2d 875, 893 (1984). This Court of Appeals opinion provides further evidence of Scalia's keen appreciation for the workings of the legislative process.

22. In his concurring opinion in *Thunder Basin Coal Co. v. Reich,* 510 U.S. 200, 219 (1994), Scalia declared that he found "unnecessary" the majority's discussion of the legislative history of the statute under consideration. "It serves to maintain the illusion that legislative history is an important factor in this Court's deciding of cases, as opposed to an omnipresent makeweight for decisions arrived at on other grounds."

23. In Conan Doyle's *Silver Blaze*, Sherlock Holmes solves the mystery on the basis of the dog that did not bark. On the issues raised in this paragraph, see also Ralph A. Rossum, "Applying the Voting Rights Act to Judicial Elections: The Supreme Court's Misconstruction of Section 2 and Misconception of the Judicial Role," in *Affirmative Action and Representation: Shaw v. Reno and the Future of Voting Rights*, ed. Anthony A. Peacock (Durham, N.C.: Carolina Academic Press, 1997).

24. Patricia M. Wald, "Some Observations on the Use of Legislative History in the 1981 Supreme Court Term," *Iowa Law Review* 68 (1983): 195.

25. Gregory E. Maggs, "The Secret Decline of Legislative History: Has Someone Heard a Voice Crying in the Wilderness?" in *The Public Interest Law Review 1994*, ed. Roger Clegg and Leonard A. Leo (Washington, D.C.: National Legal Center for the Public Interest, 1994), 72.

26. "Congress Keeps Eye on Justices as Court Watches Hill's Words," *Congressional Quarterly Weekly Report* 49 (1991): 2863.

27. Scalia, "The Rule of Law as the Law of Rules," 1184.

28. See also Scalia's concurring opinion in *Minnesota v. Dickerson*, 508 U.S. 366, 379 (1993): "I take it to be a fundamental principle of constitutional adjudication that the terms in the Constitution must be given the meaning ascribed to them at the time of their ratification. Thus, when the Fourth Amendment provides that '[t]he right of the people to be secure in their persons, houses, papers, and effects, against unreasonable searches and seizures, shall not be violated,' it 'is to be construed in the light of what was deemed an unreasonable search and seizure when it was adopted.' The purpose of the provision, in other words, is to preserve the degree of respect for the privacy of persons and the inviolability of their property that existed when the provision was adopted—even if a later, less virtuous age should become accustomed to considering all sorts of intrusion 'reasonable.'"

29. Scalia also identifies a second "serious objection to originalism: In its undiluted form, at least, it is medicine that seems too strong to swallow" (*O* 861). He confesses that "in a crunch I may prove a faint-hearted originalist. I cannot imagine myself, any more than any other federal judge, upholding a statute that imposes the punishment of flogging. But then I cannot imagine such a case arising either" (*O* 864). See also his testimony during his Senate confirmation hearing (*H* 49). In truth, however, Scalia has proven to be anything but a "faint-hearted originalist," as his opinion in *Harmelin v. Michigan* (above) attests.

30. See also Antonin Scalia, "Assorted Canards of Contemporary Legal Analysis," *Case Western Reserve Law Review* 40 (1990): 581: "To keep government up-to-date with modern notions of what good government ought to be, we do not need a constitution but only a ballot-box and a legislature" (595). "[C]hanges in the Constitution, when thought necessary, are to be proposed by Congress or conventions and ratified by the States. The Founders gave no such amending power to this Court. Our duty is simply to interpret the Constitution, and in doing so the test of constitutionality is not whether a law is offensive to our conscience or to the 'good old common law,' but whether it is offensive to the Constitution" (596).

31. *Panhandle Oil Co. v. Mississippi ex rel. Knox*, 277 U.S. 218, 223 (1928).

32. Scalia, "Assorted Canards of Contemporary Legal Analysis," 590.

33. Helen E. Veit et al., *Creating the Bill of Rights: The Documentary Record from the First Congress* (Baltimore: Johns Hopkins University Press, 1991), 78. For a detailed analysis of Madison's argument that the Bill of Rights does not create or secure rights but only declares those rights that are secured by constitutional structure, see Ralph A. Rossum, "*The Federalist*'s Understanding of the Constitution as a Bill of Rights," in *Saving the Revolution: The Federalist Papers and the American Founding*, ed. Charles R. Kesler (New York: Free Press, 1987), 219–33.

34. Alexander Hamilton, James Madison, and John Jay, *The Federalist*, ed. Jacob E. Cooke (New York: Meridian Books, 1961), no. 51, 351.

35. See Scalia's similar formulation of the judicial power in *Freytag v. Commission of Internal Revenue*, 501 U.S. 868, 908 (1991): "Article III begins '*The* judicial Power of the United States'—not '*Some of* the judicial Power of the United States,' or even '*Most of* the judicial Power of the United States'—'shall be vested in one supreme Court, and in such inferior Courts as the Congress may from time to time ordain and establish'" (emphasis in the original).

36. Quoted in Christopher E. Smith, *Justice Antonin Scalia and the Supreme Court's Conservative Moment* (Westport, Conn.: Praeger Publishers, 1993), 39.

37. M. David Gelfand and Keith Werhan, "Federalism and Separation of Powers on a 'Conservative' Court: Currents and Cross-Currents from Justices O'Connor and Scalia," *Tulane Law Review* 64 (1990): 1443. "Justice Scalia has been especially vocal and aggressive in advocating a formalist approach to separation of powers, while showing much less concern for the protection of federalism values."

38. Scalia's opinion for the Court in *Printz v. United States*, 521 U.S. 898 (1997), would seem to contradict this assertion. In *Printz*, the Court considered the constitutionality of those provisions of the Brady Handgun Violence Prevention Act that commanded the "chief law enforcement officer" (CLEO) of each local jurisdiction to conduct background checks on prospective handgun purchasers on an interim basis until a national instant background check system became operational in late 1998. Scalia held for a five-member majority that this congressional command was "fundamentally incompatible with our constitutional system of dual sovereignty" (935). A careful reading of his opinion, however, makes clear that Scalia's reference to federalism was merely a part of his coalition-building strategy. Ultimately, Scalia found federal commandeering of state officials to be unconstitutional not so much because it violated the principle of federalism but because it violated separation of powers. He noted that "[t]he Constitution does not leave to speculation who is to administer the laws enacted by Congress; the President, it says, 'shall take Care that the Laws be faithfully executed,' personally and through officers whom he appoints." The Brady Act, however, effectively transferred this responsibility to thousands of state and local law-enforcement officers in the fifty states, who, as Scalia pointed out, "are left to implement the program without meaningful Presidential control (if indeed meaningful Presidential control is possible without the power to appoint and remove). The insistence of the Framers upon unity in the Federal Executive—to insure both vigor and accountability—is well known. That unity," Scalia concluded, "would be shattered, and the power of the President would be subject to reduction, if Congress could act as effectively without the President as with him, by simply requiring state officers to execute its laws" (922–23). This argument comes, of course, directly from his dissent in *Morrison v. Olson*. In *Morrison*, Scalia wrote for himself alone; in *Printz*, by sugarcoating his separation-of-powers argument with a defense of federalism, he was able to write for a five-member majority.

39. See, for example, *United States v. Lopez*, 514 U.S. 549 (1995), *Seminole Tribe of Florida v. Florida*, 517 U.S. 44 (1996), *Florida Prepaid Postsecondary Education Expense Board v. College Savings Bank*, 527 U.S. 627 (1999), and *United States v. Morrison*, 529 U.S. 598 (2000).

40. See, for example, *New York v. United States*, 505 U.S. 144 (1992), and *Kimel v. Florida Board of Regents*, 528 U.S. 62 (2000).

41. See, for example, *City of Boerne v. Flores*, 521 U.S. 507 (1997), and *Alden v. Maine*, 527 U.S. 706 (1999).

42. Antonin Scalia, "The Legislative Veto: A False Remedy for System Overload," *Regulation* (November/December 1979): 20.

INDEX

Abbott, Henry L., 571
Abraham, 32
Abrams v. United States, 577
Abzug, Bella, 705, 706
Achaean League, 173
Act of Succession, 48
Adam and Eve, 29, 142
Adams, Abigail, 83, 271
Adams, Brooks, 494, 500, 571, 647
Adams, Charles Francis, 491
Adams, Jr., Charles Francis, 493, 499
Adams, Henry, 491–503, 571, 647; and
    Abraham Lincoln, 500–501; *Democ-*
    racy, An American Novel, 494; *The*
    Education of Henry Adams, 493–95,
    498–99; *Esther*, 494, 500; on George
    Washington, 500; and history of Ta-
    hiti, 493–94; *History of the United*
    States during the Administrations of
    Thomas Jefferson and James Madison,
    494, 497, 499; "A Letter to American
    Teachers of History," 493–95; literary
    art of, 493–94, 498; *Mont Saint Michel*
    and Chartres, 493–95, 497, 499; on
    "revolution-principles," 491–92; on
    the science of history, 495–500; on
    statesmanship 496–97
Adams, John, 60, 83, 88, 114–31, 134,
    142, 167, 168, 186, 187, 188, 189,
    196, 254, 256, 271, 287, 288, 289,
    296, 321, 491, 500–501, 647, 655,
    660–61; on checks and balances, 121;
    Defense, 126, 129; "A Government of
    Laws and Not of Men," 114–15; on
    human nature, 124; "Novanglus," 195;
    on religious liberty, 121; on rule of
    law, 114; and Thomas Nash, 254;
    "Thoughts on Government," 114
Adams, John Quincy, 2, 271–85, 491, 494,
    500; the corrupt bargain, 271–72; on
    Declaration of Independence, 275–77;
    First Annual Message, 273, 277, 283;
    and House of Representatives, 272;
    Inaugural Address, 277; "July Fourth
    Oration of 1821," 284; "Life of James

Monroe," 283; on private property,
    280; on revelation, 274; as secretary of
    state, 271; on slavery, 277, 279, 281–
    82; on social nature of man, 275;
    Transcontinental Treaty, 284–85
Addams, Jane, 504–20; on Americaniza-
    tion, 510, 514–15; on civic housekeep-
    ing, 512–14; on the family claim and
    social claim, 504–6, 517, 519; "Filial
    Relations," 508; and Hull-House, 504–
    5, 509, 511, 513, 515, 519; *The Long*
    Road of Woman's Memory, 518–19; on
    the "moral balance sheet" and stan-
    dardization, 514–15; on moral devel-
    opment, 508–10; *A New Conscience*
    and an Ancient Evil, 510–12; *Newer*
    Ideals of Peace, 514, 516; on pacifism,
    515–19; *Peace and Bread in Time of*
    War, 517; on the Pullman Strike, 507–
    8; *The Second Twenty Years at Hull-*
    House, 514–15; *The Spirit of Youth*
    and the City Streets, 510; "The Subjec-
    tive Necessity for Social Settlements,"
    504–5; *Twenty Years at Hull-House*,
    513; on urban life and vice, 510–12;
    "Why Women Should Vote," 513–14
Administrative Procedures Act, 602
Aeschylus, 368
Africa, 480, 482, 485, 489, 532, 688, 693,
    694, 736
Agricultural Adjustment Act, 602, 604
Albright v. Oliver, 790
Alexander, Tsar, 738
Alexandria Conference, 103
Ali, Timothy "Noble" Drew, 688
Alien and Sedition Acts, 106, 186, 188,
    326
American Anti-Slavery Society, 378, 380,
    425
American Communist party, 487
American Historical Association, 493, 495
American Missionary Association, 466
American Philosophical Society, 92
American Political Science Association,
    149

About the Editors and Contributors

Bryan-Paul Frost received his B.A. from St. John's College in Santa Fe, New Mexico, and his Ph.D. in political science from the University of Toronto. He is currently the James A. and Kaye L. Crocker Endowed Professor of Political Science as well as adjunct professor in the Department of Philosophy at the University of Louisiana at Lafayette. He is editor and cotranslator (with Professor Robert Howse) of Alexandre Kojève's *Outline of a Phenomenology of Right* (Rowman and Littlefield, 2000). He has published articles on Kojève, Raymond Aron, and Cato the Younger. He is currently working on a manuscript on Aristotle's *Rhetoric* and civic education, a collection of essays celebrating the one hundredth anniversary of Raymond Aron's birth, and he is completing a manuscript on Kojève's political philosophy as a whole.

Jeffrey Sikkenga is assistant professor of political science at Ashland University in Ashland, Ohio. He is also an adjunct fellow at the John M. Ashbrook Center for Public Affairs. He received his B.A. in government and foreign affairs from the University of Virginia and his Ph.D. in Political Science from the University of Toronto. His areas of scholarly interest and publication include the history of political thought, the American Founding, and the U.S. Constitution. He is editor of *Transforming American Welfare* (Acton Press, 1999) and coauthor of *The Free Person and the Free Economy* (Lexington Books, 2001).

John Agresto is president of John Agresto & Associates, an educational consulting firm, and senior scholar in the liberal arts at Wabash College. He recently retired as the fourth president of St. John's College in Santa Fe. Prior to that, he held a number of senior positions at the National Endowment for the Humanities, including acting chairman. He began his teaching career at the University of Toronto in 1971. In 1972, he joined the faculty of Kenyon College where he taught until 1978, when he was awarded a fellowship to the National Humanities Center in North Carolina. He subsequently joined the staff of the center and served as its projects director for three years prior to going to Washington. He is a graduate of Boston College with an A.B. in political science and holds a Ph.D. in government from Cornell. In 1989, he was awarded an Honorary Doctor of Letters from Kenyon College. He is the author of *The Supreme Court and Constitutional Democracy*, editor and contributor to two other books, and author of numerous articles in both liberal education and politics. Mr. Agresto is a former member of the Independent Commission on the Arts and former commissioner of the Columbian Quincentenary Commission. He was recently named the George Washington Distinguished Professor of the Society of the Cincinnati.

John E. Alvis is a professor of English at the University of Dallas where he also teaches in a doctoral program, the Institute for Philosophic Studies. He has taught at that university for thirty years and has been associated with Liberty Fund since 1981. He was one of two visiting scholars at Liberty Fund in the first year of that program (1993), and he has been at various times an

Earhart Fellow. Since 1996, he has served as director of the M.A. Program in American Studies at the University of Dallas. He is coeditor with Thomas G. West of *Shakespeare as Political Thinker*, editor of *Areopagitica and Selected Political Writings of John Milton*, and author of *Shakespeare's Understanding of Honor* (1990) and a book on Homer and Virgil, *Divine Initiative and Heroic Response* (1995). He has also published essays on Milton, Melville, and O'Neill. A play on the Hamilton-Aaron Burr duel was published in 1987 in *The College* (St. John's, Annapolis). He is currently finishing a book on liberty in American literature and has recently completed a full-length drama on Woodrow Wilson.

Donald R. Brand is an associate professor of political science at College of the Holy Cross where he teaches courses in American national institutions and American politics. He received his Ph.D. from the University of Chicago in 1982. Brand is the author of *Corporatism and the Rule of Law: A Study of the National Recovery Administration* (Cornell University Press, 1988). In addition, he has published articles in several edited books and in *Political Science Quarterly*, *Political Science Reviewer*, and *Polity*. He is currently working on a book entitled "The Decline of Sovereignty in American Government."

Paul O. Carrese is associate professor of political science at the U.S. Air Force Academy. He holds masters degrees in politics and philosophy and in theology from Oxford University and a doctorate in political science from Boston College. He has been a Rhodes Scholar, a Beinecke Scholar, and a postdoctoral fellow in the Program on Constitutional Government, Harvard University, and he has taught at Boston College and Middlebury College. He coedited, with Robert Faulkner, a new edition of John Marshall's one-volume biography of Washington, *The Life of George Washington: Special Edition for Schools* (Liberty Fund, 2001), and is the author of *The Cloaking of Power: Montesquieu, Blackstone, and the Rise of Judicial Activism* (University of Chicago Press, 2003). He has published articles and lectured on Montesquieu, Tocqueville, Machiavelli, constitutionalism, modern republicanism, American constitutional law, the American Founding, and the just war tradition, and has directed conferences on ancient and modern statesmanship, Plutarch, and Washington.

Laurence D. Cooper is assistant professor of political science at Carleton College. Author of *Rousseau, Nature, and the Problem of the Good Life* (Pennsylvania State University Press, 1999) as well as articles on Rousseau and Plato, he is currently working on a series of studies on Platonic and post-Platonic understandings of eros and thymos (spiritedness).

Murray Dry is Charles A. Dana Professor of Political Science at Middlebury College, where he teaches courses in American political thought, constitutional law, and political philosophy. He saw Herbert J. Storing's *The Complete Anti-Federalist* through the press, made the selections for Storing's *The Anti-Federalist*, and has published several articles and book chapters on the American Founding. He has also published several essays on the First Amendment (*Supreme Court Review*, *Constitutional Commentary*, and *Journal of Supreme Court History*), and he is currently completing a book on the subject ("Civil Peace and the Quest for Truth: The First Amendment Freedoms in Political Philosophy and American Constitutionalism"). His most recent publication was "Tolerance and the Constitution: The Case of Gay Rights," in *Courts and the Culture Wars*, ed. Bradley Watson (Lexington Books, 2002).

Jean Bethke Elshtain is the Laura Spelman Rockefeller Professor of Social and Political Ethics at the University of Chicago. She is the author, coauthor, or editor of some fifteen books, as well as author of over 400 essays in scholarly journals and journals of civic opinion, and some 175 book reviews. She recently published an intellectual biography of Jane Addams entitled *Jane Addams and the Dream of American Democracy* (Basic Books, 2001).

Thomas S. Engeman is associate professor of political science at Loyola University Chicago. He is the author (with Raymond Tatalovich) of *The Presidency and Political Science: Two Hundred Years of Constitutional Debate* (Johns Hopkins University Press, forthcoming), editor of *Thomas Jefferson and the Politics of Nature* (University of Notre Dame Press, 2000), *The Federalist Concordance* (University of Chicago Press, 1988), and (with George C. S. Benson) *Amoral American: Sources of Morality in a Liberal Society* (Hoover Institution Press, 1975), as well as numerous articles and book chapters in political philosophy and American political thought. He has received grants from the Haynes, E. B. Earhart, and Woodrow Wilson Foundations as well as the National Endowment of the Humanities.

Christopher Flannery is professor of political science and chairman of the Department of History and Political Science at Azusa Pacific University, where he has taught since 1987. Before coming to Azusa Pacific University, he was vice president of the Claremont Institute for the Study of Statesmanship and Political Philosophy. He received a Ph.D. in government from the Claremont Graduate School and a M.A. in international history from the London School of Economics and Political Science.

Steven Forde received his Ph.D. from the University of Toronto and is currently professor of political science at the University of North Texas. His work covers the history of political philosophy and includes a book on Thucydides, *The Ambition to Rule: Alcibiades and the Politics of Imperialism in Thucydides*. He is currently working on several articles on Franklin, and early modern political thought.

David F. Forte is professor of constitutional law at Cleveland State University. He holds degrees from Harvard College; Manchester University, England; the University of Toronto; and Columbia University. During the Reagan administration, Professor Forte served as chief counsel to the U.S. delegation to the United Nations and alternative delegate to the Security Council under the title of counselor for legal affairs. He has authored a number of briefs before the U.S. Supreme Court, and has frequently testified before the U.S. Congress on human rights and international affairs issues. His advice was specifically sought on the approval of the Genocide Convention and on worldwide religious persecution. He has also been called to testify before the state legislatures of Ohio and Idaho as well as the New York City Council. He has assisted in drafting a number of pieces of legislation for the Ohio General Assembly dealing with abortion, international trade, and federalism. He has sat as acting judge on the municipal court of Lakewood, Ohio, and he was chairman of the Professional Ethics Committee of the Cleveland Bar Association. He has received a number of awards for his public service. His Holiness, John Paul II, appointed Dr. Forte as consultor to the Pontifical Council for the Family. The State Department sent Professor Forte to Jordan for a series of speeches and discussions with prominent groups and leaders. Professor Forte was a Bradley Scholar at the Heritage Foundation, and visiting scholar at the Liberty Fund. He has been president of the Ohio Association of Scholars, and is also adjunct scholar at the Ashbrook Center, as well as being on the Board of Academic Advisers to the Buckeye Institute. He writes and speaks locally and nationally on topics such as constitutional law, religious liberty, the rights of families, Islamic law, and international affairs. His recent books include *Natural Law and Contemporary Public Policy*, published by Georgetown

University Press, and *Studies in Islamic Law: Classical and Contemporary Applications*, published by Austin and Winfield. He is currently writing a book on the political history of the early Supreme Court.

David Foster is an associate professor and chairman in the Department of History and Political Science at Ashland University. He has published articles on John Locke's understanding of the Bible, natural freedom, and the family, and on liberal and civic education.

David Fott is associate professor of political science at the University of Nevada, Las Vegas. Born in Clarksville, Tennessee, he received his B.A. summa cum laude from Vanderbilt University and his A.M. and Ph.D. from Harvard University. He has taught political theory and American political thought at UNLV since 1992. Fott is author of *John Dewey: America's Philosopher of Democracy* (Rowman and Littlefield, 1998), as well as articles on Dewey, U.S. presidential power, and Jane Austen. For the journal *Political Theory* he has translated, and written an essay on, Montesquieu's "Discourse on Cicero." He is currently translating Cicero's *On the Republic* and *On the Laws* (Focus Publishing, forthcoming).

Matthew J. Franck is professor and chairman of political science at Radford University, where he has taught political philosophy, American politics, and constitutional law since 1989. He earned his B.A. in political science at Virginia Wesleyan College, and his M.A. and Ph.D. in political science at Northern Illinois University, and has previously taught at Marquette University and Southern Illinois University. He is author of *Against the Imperial Judiciary: The Supreme Court vs. the Sovereignty of the People* (Kansas, 1996), and coeditor and coauthor (with Richard G. Stevens) of *Sober as a Judge: The Supreme Court and Republican Liberty* (Lexington Books, 1999). He has published essays and reviews in *Review of Politics, Interpretation, Journal of Politics, Texas Review of Law and Politics, Perspectives on Political Science, Claremont Review of Books*, and the *Catholic Social Science Review*. In 1998, Franck was Fulbright Professor of American Studies in the Graduate School of International Studies at Yonsei University in Seoul, South Korea. He is currently at work on a book entitled "Strict Scrutiny: A Critical Lexicon of Supreme Court Sense and Nonsense."

Peter Josephson is assistant professor of politics at Saint Anselm College in Manchester, New Hampshire, where he helped to design the major track in international relations. He also taught political theory and international relations for four years at the University of New Hampshire. He was born and raised in Anchorage, Alaska. Josephson received his B.A. from Oberlin College in Russian and Soviet studies, an M.A. from the University of New Hampshire (his thesis on "Poetry and the Ends of Philosophy" examined Socrates' treatment of the poets), and holds a Ph.D. in political science from Boston College (1998). He is the recipient of grants and fellowships from the Earhart Foundation and the Lynde and Harry Bradley Foundation. Josephson is the author of *The Great Art of Government: Locke's Use of Consent* (University Press of Kansas, 2002).

Steven Kautz is associate professor in the Department of Political Science at Michigan State University. He is the author of *Liberalism and Community* and is currently working on a book on the political thought of Abraham Lincoln. Kautz received his Ph.D. from the Committee on Social Thought at the University of Chicago in 1988.

John Koritansky received his A.B. from Cornell University and his Ph.D. from the University of Chicago. His teaching career has been entirely at Hiram College, where he is professor of political science. He is the author of *Alexis de Tocqueville and the New Science of Politics* (Carolina Academic Press, 1986) as well as numerous articles and book chapters in political philosophy and American politics. He has recently edited and published *Public Administration in the United States* (Focus Press, 1999). He is currently working toward a book concerning thoughts on religion among several major political philosophers.

Peter Augustine Lawler is Dana Professor of Government at Berry College in Georgia. Author or editor of eight books and over a hundred scholarly articles and chapters, he has been chair of the politics and literature section of the American Political Science Association. He is executive editor of *Perspectives on Political Science* and an advisory editor of *Modern Age*. His book, *Postmodernism Rightly Understood: The Return to Realism in American Thought*, includes two chapters on Percy. His latest book is entitled *Aliens in America: The Strange Truth about Our Souls* (ISI Books, 2002).

Howard L. Lubert is assistant professor of political science at James Madison University, where he teaches courses in American political thought, constitutional law, and American politics. He received his B.A. from Rutgers University and his Ph.D. from Duke University. Prior to accepting his position at James Madison, he taught at Alma College and Rutgers. His dissertation examined the creation of federalism in the American Founding from the Stamp Act crisis to the ratification debates. He recently wrote an essay on John Dickinson for the *Encyclopedia of the Enlightenment* (Oxford University Press, forthcoming). He is currently writing an essay on Benjamin Franklin for a forthcoming collection of articles on religion in the American Founding.

Harvey C. Mansfield is William R. Kenan, Jr., Professor of Government at Harvard University; **Delba Winthrop** is lecturer on politics at Harvard University. Together they have recently published a translation of Tocqueville's *Democracy in America*. Mansfield has also translated three works by Machiavelli and is the author of books on Edmund Burke, on executive power, on Machiavelli's politics, and on Machiavelli's *Discourses on Livy*. Winthrop has published articles on Aristotle, Tocqueville, and Solzhenitsyn.

Jonathan Marks is assistant professor of political science and philosophy at Carthage College. He received his Ph.D. from the Committee on Social Thought at the University of Chicago in 1997.

Sean Mattie is visiting professor in the Department of History and Political Science at Hillsdale College. He received his B.A. from Middlebury College, his M.A. from Boston College, and his Ph.D. from the University of Dallas in 1999. His dissertation was entitled "Substantive Due Process: A Controversy of Justice and Legitimacy." He has written for the Acton Institute for Religion and Liberty and the Ashbrook Center for Public Affairs at Ashland University.

James McClellan is the James Bryce Visiting Fellow in American Studies at the Institute of U.S. Studies, University of London. He holds a Ph.D. in political science from the University of Virginia and a J.D. from the University of Virginia School of Law. Dr. McClellan has taught American government, political theory, and constitutional law at the University of Alabama, Emory University, Hampden-Sydney College, and Claremont McKenna College. He has also been a professional staff member of the U.S. Senate, and from 1981 to 1983 was chief counsel and staff director of the Subcommittee on Separation of Powers of the Senate Committee on the Judiciary. From 1983 to 1993 he was president of the Center for Judicial Studies and editor of *Benchmark*, and from 1993 to 1998 served as the director of publications of Liberty Fund. His publications include *The Political Principles of Robert A. Taft* (coauthor with Russell Kirk, 1967); *Joseph Story and the American Constitution* (1971, 1990); *The Federalist: The Gideon Edition* (coeditor with George Carey, 2000); James Madison's *Notes of the Debates in the Federal Convention of 1787* (coeditor with M. E. Bradford); *John Taylor of Caroline, New Views of the Constitution* (editor, 2000); and *Liberty, Order and Justice: An Introduction to the Constitutional Principles of American Government*, 3rd ed. (1989, 1991, 2000).

Lucas E. Morel is assistant professor of politics at Washington and Lee University. He is author of *Lincoln's Sacred Effort: Defining Religion's Role in American Self-Government* (Lexington Books, 2000) and editor of the forthcoming book, *Raft of Hope: Ralph Ellison's "Invisible Man" and the Politics of the American Novel*. Dr. Morel holds a Ph.D. in political science from the Claremont Graduate School.

Peter C. Myers is professor of political science at the University of Wisconsin-Eau Claire. He teaches courses in the history of political philosophy, American political thought, and American politics. He received his Ph.D. in political science at Loyola University Chicago in 1992. In 1992, he was awarded the American Political Science Association's Leo Strauss Award for the best doctoral dissertation in the field of political philosophy. He is the author of *Our Only Star and Compass: Locke and the Struggle for Political Rationality* (Rowman and Littlefield, 1998) and has published scholarly articles on the political thought of John Locke and on Mark Twain's *The Adventures of Huckleberry Finn*. He is currently working on a study of the political thought of Frederick Douglass.

Ronald J. Pestritto is associate professor of politics at the University of Dallas. He also serves as an adjunct fellow at the Claremont Institute for the Study of Statesmanship and Political Philosophy and at the John M. Ashbrook Center for Public Affairs at Ashland University. He is author of *Founding the Criminal Law: Punishment and Political Thought in the Origins of America* (Northern Illinois University Press, 2000) and of a forthcoming book on the political thought of Woodrow Wilson. A recipient of fellowships from the John M. Olin Foundation and the Earhart Foundation, he holds a Ph.D. from Claremont Graduate University.

Lance Robinson is an associate professor of political science at the U.S. Air Force Academy. He received his Ph.D. from the Claremont Graduate School in 1997. His dissertation, entitled "The Stewardship Theory of the Presidency: Theodore Roosevelt's Political Theory of Republican Progressive Statesmanship and the Foundation of the Modern Presidency," is an examination of the formative elements of President Theodore Roosevelt's understanding of politics and progressive ideology.

Michael J. Rosano is an assistant professor of political science at the University of Michigan-Dearborn. He specializes in political theory with emphasis on American political thought and classical political philosophy. He received his B.A. in political science from Rutgers University and his M.A. and Ph.D. in political science from the University of Toronto. He has published scholarly articles on Platonic political philosophy and the problem of political obligation, and is preparing a manuscript on the relation between classical nobility, Christian charity, and modern liberty in the political thought of Alexander Hamilton. He won the University of Michigan-Dearborn's Distinguished Teaching Award in 1998.

Ralph A. Rossum is the Henry Salvatori Professor of American Constitutionalism and director of the Rose Institute of State and Local Government at Claremont McKenna College. He earned his M.A. and Ph.D. from the University of Chicago and is the author of seven books, including *Federalism, the Supreme Court, and the Seventeenth Amendment: The Irony of Constitutional Democracy*; *American Constitutional Law* (with G. Alan Tarr, sixth edition); *Reverse Discrimination: The Constitutional Debate*; *The Politics of the Criminal Justice System: An Organizational Analysis*; and *The American Founding: Politics, Statesmanship, and the Constitution* (with Gary L. McDowell), and over sixty book chapters or articles in law reviews and professional journals.

Richard S. Ruderman is associate professor of political science at the University of North Texas. He has published essays on statesmanship, political judgment in Aristotle, Homer, and parental choice in education in various scholarly journals, and a chapter on Homer in *Political Philosophy and the Human Soul: Essays in Memory of Allan Bloom* (Rowman and Littlefield, 1995). He received his Ph.D. from the Committee on Social Thought at the University of Chicago in 1990. He is currently working on a study of statesmanship in liberal democracies.

Richard Samuelson received his M.A. and Ph.D. in American history from the University of Virginia and his B.A. from Bates College. He currently holds a Government of Ireland Fellowship at the National University of Ireland, Galway, where he is writing a book on "The Imperial Crisis, 1763–1776." He wrote the essay included in this volume while he was a visiting postgraduate scholar at Liberty Fund in Indianapolis, Indiana, where he also completed his book on "The Adams Family and the American Experiment." He has published articles or reviews in the *William and Mary Quarterly*, *New England Quarterly*, *Review of Politics*, *Commentary*, *The Pubic Interest*, and other publications.

David Lewis Schaefer is professor of political science at Holy Cross College. His books include *Justice or Tyranny? A Critique of John Rawls's "A Theory of Justice"* (1979); *The Political Philosophy of Montaigne* (1990); *Sir Henry Taylor's "The Statesman"* (coeditor, 1992); *Freedom over Servitude: Montaigne, La Boétie, and "Of Voluntary Servitude,"* (editor and contributor, 1998); and *Active Duty: Public Administration as Democratic Statesmanship* (coeditor and contributor, 1998). He is currently writing a book titled "John Rawls and the American Political Tradition."

Peter Schotten received a B.A. from the University of Washington in political science (1969), and earned a M.A. (1972) and Ph.D. (1974) in government from Claremont Graduate School. Since then, he has taught at Augustana College, Sioux Falls, South Dakota, where he is professor of government and international relations. He is the coauthor of *Religion, Politics and the Law: Commentaries and Controversies* as well as of a college textbook, *Understanding Politics: Ideas, Institutions and Issues*. In addition, he has written a number of scholarly articles, focusing upon the Constitution, the Supreme Court, and upon selected issues in American constitutional law.

Peter W. Schramm is professor of political science at Ashland University and executive director of the John M. Ashbrook Center for Public Affairs. He has taught at Claremont McKenna College and California State University, and he was director of international education, U.S.

Department of Education. His Ph.D. is from Claremont, and he also holds an M.A. from the London School of Economics and Political Science, University of London. He is a former Earhart Fellow and has edited, coedited, and contributed to a number of books, including *Natural Right and Political Right*, *The 1984 Election and the Future of American Politics*, *American Political Parties and Constitutional Politics*, *Separation of Powers and Good Government*, *Statecraft and Power*, and wrote the "Introduction" to Lord Charnwood's *Abraham Lincoln: A Biography* (Madison Books, 1996).

Kimberly C. Shankman is currently dean of the College at Benedictine College. Prior to that, she was professor and chair of the Department of Politics and Government at Ripon College, where she had been since 1985. Her book *Compromise and the Constitution: The Political Thought of Henry Clay* was published by Lexington Books in September 1999. Her other recent scholarship includes the article (coauthored with Roger Pilon) "Reviving the Privileges or Immunities Clause to Redress the Balance among States, Individuals, and the Federal Government," which was published in the fall 1998 issue of the *Texas Review of Law and Politics*. She received her B.A., M.A., and Ph.D. from Northern Illinois University. Her major fields of research are American political thought and constitutional law, and she also teaches in the broad area of American government.

James R. Stoner, Jr., is associate professor of political science at Louisiana State University. He is the author of *Common Law and Liberal Theory: Coke, Hobbes, and Origins of American Constitutionalism* (Kansas, 1992), and of a forthcoming study, also with Kansas, of the common law dimension of American constitutional law. He was recently appointed by President George W. Bush to the National Council on the Humanities. In 2002–2003, he was Visiting Fellow at the James Madison Program in American Ideals and Institutions at Princeton University.

Natalie Taylor completed her dissertation on Mary Wollstonecraft in the Department of Political Science at Fordham University. Her essay on Henry Adams, "The Landscape of Democracy," appears as part of a symposium on politics and literature in *The Legal Studies Forum*. She currently teaches at Skidmore College.

Aristide Tessitore is professor of political science at Furman University. He is the author of *Reading Aristotle's "Ethics": Virtue, Rhetoric, and Political Philosophy* (SUNY Press, 1996), and editor of *Aristotle and Modern Politics: The Persistence of Political Philosophy* (Notre Dame University Press, 2002). Professor Tessitore has published widely in the area of classical political philosophy and is currently working on the political thought of Alexis de Tocqueville.

William Thomas is manager of research and training at The Objectivist Center (formerly: Institute for Objectivist Studies) in Poughkeepsie, New York. He has a M.A. in economics from the University of Michigan, where he is a Ph.D. candidate and where he taught the economic history of the United States and China. He has been a lecturer at Gadjah Mada University in Indonesia and conducted research under the auspices of the People's University of China. He is a graduate of Oberlin College, where he was elected to Phi Beta Kappa. Thomas is the coauthor of the forthcoming survey *The Logical Structure of Objectivism*. He has published essays on topics in politics, ethics, and epistemology. He has spoken internationally on the theory of individual rights and Ayn Rand's philosophy of objectivism.

Daryl McGowan Tress is associate professor of philosophy and director of the Office of Prestigious Fellowships in the Graduate School of Arts and Sciences at Fordham University. Her areas of specialization are ancient philosophy and feminism. In 2000–2001, she was awarded a fellowship at the Radcliffe Institute for Advanced Study at Harvard University for her work on ancient ideas pertaining to the origin of human life. Her articles on feminism and philosophy appear in *Signs*, *Public Affairs Quarterly*, and *Interpretation*. Her recent chapter on values in the natural world appears in *Thinking about the Environment: Our Debt to the Ancient and Medieval Past* (Lexington Books, 2003).

David Tucker is an associate professor in the Department of Defense Analysis at the Naval Postgraduate School. Before coming to the Postgraduate School, he served in the Office of the Secretary of Defense for Special Operations and Low-Intensity Conflict and as a foreign service officer in Africa and Europe. He has taught at the University of Chicago and Harvey Mudd College. He holds the Ph.D. in history from the Claremont Graduate School. His publications include *Skirmishes at the Edge of Empire, the United States and International Terrorism* (Praeger, 1997); "What Is New about the New Terrorism and How Dangerous Is It?" *Terrorism and Political Violence* (Autumn 2001); "Responding to Terrorism," *Washington Quarterly* (Winter 1998); "'Hope to the World for all Future Time,' America and the World after the Cold War" (Ashbrook Center, February 1992); "Jefferson and the Practice of Empire," in *Natural Right and Political Right* (Carolina Academic Press, 1984); "Wealth and Commonwealth," *Reviews in American History* (September 1981); and "The Political Thought of Jefferson's *Notes on the State of Virginia*," in *The American Founding: Politics, Statesmanship, and the Constitution* (Kennikat Press, 1981).

Eduardo A. Velásquez received his B.A. from the University of California at Santa Barbara (1986), and his M.A. and Ph.D. in political science from the University of Chicago (1988 and 1994). He is presently associate professor of politics at Washington and Lee University. His research and teaching focus on the relationship between political philosophy and contemporary literature, film, and music. He is currently writing on political myth making in the works of J. K. Rowling. Velásquez is contributing editor to *Nature, Woman, and the Art of Politics* (Rowman and Littlefield Publishers, 2000) and *Love and Friendship: Rethinking Politics and Affection in Modern Times* (Lexington Books, 2002).

Karl-Friedrich Walling enlisted in Army Intelligence in 1976. Upon release from active duty, he studied at St. John's College in Annapolis, Maryland, earning his B.A. in liberal arts in 1984. He did his graduate work at the University of Chicago, where he completed a joint Ph.D. in social thought and political science in 1992. He has been a research fellow at Harvard University, a visiting scholar at Colorado College, and a fellow at the Liberty Fund. He has taught Great Books and most fields of political science at Michigan State University, the University of Chicago, Carleton College, the U.S. Air Force Academy, and Ashland University. He published a much revised version of his dissertation, *Republican Empire: Alexander Hamilton on War and Free Government* in 1999 and *Strategy and Policy* in 2002. He is currently a professor of strategy at the Naval War College in Newport, Rhode Island, where he is working on a book on strategy and politics in Thucydides' *Peloponnesian War*.

Bradley C. S. Watson is associate professor of political science and fellow in politics and culture at the Center for Economic and Policy Education, Saint Vincent College, Latrobe, Pennsylvania. His books include *Civil Rights and the Paradox of Liberal Democracy* and *Courts* *and the Culture Wars*. He has written in a wide variety of professional and general interest forums, including *Armed Forces and Society, Claremont Review of Books, Encarta Encyclopedia, Modern Age,* and *Perspectives on Political Science.* He is a contributor to *Rethinking the Constitution* (Oxford, 1996). Watson is an adjunct fellow of the Claremont Institute for the Study of Statesmanship and Political Philosophy, and the John M. Ashbrook Center for Public Affairs at Ashland University. He has taught at Claremont McKenna College in California and Norwich University in Vermont, and he has practiced as a civil litigation lawyer in Vancouver, Canada. In addition to institutional awards, Watson has received fellowships from numerous national and international organizations, including the Heritage Foundation, the John M. Olin Foundation, the John Templeton Foundation, and the Social Sciences and Humanities Research Council of Canada. He was educated in Canada at the University of British Columbia, where he received a B.A. in economics and political science, and at the Queen's University Faculty of Law, where he received an LL.B. (J.D.); in Belgium at the Institute of Philosophy of the Catholic University of Louvain, where he received an M.Phil.; and in the United States at the Claremont Graduate University, where he received an M.A. and a Ph.D. with concentrations in political philosophy and American government.

Melissa S. Williams is associate professor of political science at the University of Toronto. She is the author of *Voice, Trust, and Memory: Marginalized Groups and the Failings of Liberal Representation* (Princeton, 1998), which received the 1999 Foundations of Political Theory best first book prize in political philosophy. She has published and spoken widely on such issues as affirmative action, feminism, group rights, and American political thought.

Jean M. Yarbrough is Gary M. Pendy, Sr., Professor of Social Sciences and professor of government at Bowdoin College. She is the author of *Thomas Jefferson on the Character of a Free People* (University Press of Kansas, 1998) as well as numerous articles, book chapters, and review essays on the Founders, federalism, and the Constitution.

Michael P. Zuckert is Nancy Dreux Professor of Political Science at the University of Notre Dame. He received his Ph.D. from the University of Chicago and his B.A. from Cornell University. He has published extensively in the fields of modern political philosophy, American political thought, and American constitutional history and theory. His books include *Natural Rights and the New Republicanism* and *The Natural Rights Republic.* He has published a number of essays directly relevant to Madison, including "Federalism and the Founding." He is currently completing a book on the American Founding called *A System without Precedent,* in which Madison is a central figure.